Gypsy and Traveller Law

Available as an ebook at www.lag.org.uk/bookshop/ebooks

LAG eBook

The purpose of Legal Action Group is to promote equal access to justice for all members of society who are socially, economically or otherwise disadvantaged. To this end, it seeks to improve law and practice, the administration of justice and legal services.

Gypsy and Traveller Law

THIRD EDITION

Edited by Marc Willers QC and
Chris Johnson

the access to justice charity

Legal Action Group
2020

This edition published in Great Britain 2020
by LAG Education and Service Trust Limited
National Pro Bono Centre, 48 Chancery Lane, London WC2A 1JF
www.lag.org.uk

Second edition 2007
First edition 2004

British Library Cataloguing in Publication Data
a CIP catalogue record for this book is available from the British Library.

FSC
www.fsc.org
MIX
Paper | Supporting responsible forestry
FSC® C020438

This book has been produced using Forest Stewardship Council (FSC) certified paper. The wood used to produce FSC certified products with a 'Mixed Sources' label comes from FSC certified well-managed forests, controlled sources and/or recycled material.

print ISBN 978 1 908407 48 1
eBook ISBN 978 1 908407 51 1
bundle (print and eBook) ISBN 978 1 912273 96 6

Typeset by Refinecatch Ltd, Bungay, Suffolk
Printed in Great Britain by Hobbs the Printers, Totton, Hampshire

Foreword

Dr Siobhan Spencer MBE

It was a surprise and a pleasure to be asked to contribute this foreword for the latest edition of *Gypsy and Traveller Law* and what an honour to follow in Lord Avebury's footsteps who wrote the foreword for the second edition in 2007.

I was excited when the first edition came out, as it was a specialist book on an area of law that was long overdue. Being interested in equal rights not just for my own people but for other native peoples I had followed the great, great niece of Louis Riel who first produced a handbook of law for the Métis people in 1999. I remembered thinking, 'what if we the Romany people could have a handbook like that'? and, in 2004, along came the first edition. In 2012 I received my law degree so that I could advocate for my community, often referring to this book.

I know how busy all the authors are daily, working on their cases, in the courts and at planning inquiries and it is a credit to them that they have found time to update us all in this area of law. This book will be a useful resource for law firms, advocates, support groups and Citizens Advice Bureaux. It may also be useful for politicians, whether local or national, to refer to, because it is important to know about the history and why we are at the point we are.

The Highways Act 1959 and the Caravan Site Control and Development Act 1960 caused hardship to many Gypsy and Traveller families, as they returned to winter quarters to find them now gone. According to the history of my own family, many farmers and landowners were frightened of court fines because they had no facilities on their land for caravan dwellers.

There has always been a misconception that Gypsy and Traveller families travelled all the year through. In reality, there was always a winter yard and for many the travelling period would not be until

March to late October. This base from which to travel is not a new notion. Families that were uprooted from these traditional sites swelled the numbers who were now on the road all year round. When I look back, I can remember my aunt telling my mother about three little girls who had been killed in an eviction in Brownhills. In the 1960s times were hard.

The statutory duty to provide sites for Gypsies and Travellers finally came through the Caravan Sites Act 1968, thanks to the tireless work of Lord Avebury. So, there was some respite, but not enough sites were built and many people had great difficulty in obtaining the provision that was needed. The Cripps Report in 1977 identified that obtaining sites was extremely problematic. Indeed, only 38 per cent of local and district authorities had identified and provided at least some sites by the time the duty was repealed by the Criminal Justice and Public Order Act 1994.

Sometimes people say there has been absolutely no improvement since 1994 but that would be to do the authors of this book and people like Lord Avebury a disservice. Gypsies and Travellers are now using the law for themselves. When the statutory duty to provide sites was repealed, support groups came together to try and influence the future. These groups persuaded the government to issue planning guidance that required local authorities to carry out a quantitative assessment of need for sites and identify land to meet that need. However, local authorities failed to assess the need and would then try and get around any provision by producing lists of criteria-based policies which ensured a Gypsy or Traveller site would not be able to be established anywhere. Cases were fought by support groups and, in 2006, the groups persuaded the government to issue more positive planning advice on site provision. With that advice in place a considerable number of sites were granted planning permission between 2006 and 2015 (albeit many of these were temporary permissions).

However, in 2015, life looked rather bleak for Gypsy and Traveller people when the government changed the definition of what it means in planning terms to be a Gypsy or Traveller and we found ourselves in the situation where many of us are no longer considered Gypsies or Travellers under planning law. There is something perverse in someone being told that they are too old or too ill to be recognised as a Gypsy or Traveller. Elder people are often overlooked and that is why Derbyshire Gypsy Liaison Group undertook the elders' study *Life on and off the Hard Shoulder* (2019).

Between 2017 and 2019 I was the Gypsy and Traveller community's specialist adviser on the Women and Equalities Committee inquiry into inequalities faced by Gypsy, Roma and Traveller communities. The report, *Tackling inequalities faced by Gypsy, Roma and Traveller communities*, was published in April 2019. The Committee was concerned that, although many Gypsy and Traveller families live in settled accommodation, government policy-making was focused on unauthorised encampments, and that this focus had eclipsed a wide range of crucial issues in relation to policy and service provision. However, in my view, the important subject of culturally appropriate accommodation was not addressed in depth and within the historic context of Gypsy and Traveller culture. The Committee report did however highlight the severe racism and prejudice that Gypsy, Roma and Traveller (GRT) communities face and, whether Gypsy and Traveller people are settled or not, this is an issue that needs addressing. It also highlighted important issues such as bullying in schools and domestic violence.

Through good networks of sites, both public and private, the access to education, health and social care can be addressed, but changing hearts and minds of the settled population will take far longer.

So, we now come to the Autumn of 2019 and, unfortunately, the old prejudice against Gypsy and Traveller communities has raised its head once again. On the 5 November 2019 Priti Patel, the Home Secretary, launched a consultation on measures to criminalise trespass in England and Wales. Increased police powers would, in effect, criminalise the way of life of Gypsies and Travellers.

In response to a similar consultation by the Ministry of Housing, Communities and Local Government (MHCLG) in 2018 the National Police Chiefs' Council and the Association of Police and Crime Commissioners said: 'The lack of sufficient and appropriate accommodation for Gypsies and Travellers remains the main cause of incidents of unauthorised encampment and unauthorised development by these groups'.

Criminalisation of trespass would almost certainly breach the Human Rights Act 1998 and the Equality Act 2010. That is why there is a need for a book such as this one.

There needs to be a huge shift in society to address the inequalities that Gypsy and Traveller people face. In the absence of that shift we need to use the law to challenge these inequalities.

Roma integration should have been addressed in 2011 when the European Commission published a *Framework for National 'Roma' Integration Strategies* (NRIS) (within Europe Roma is an all-embracing umbrella term for GRT) which was adopted by all the European Union member states. The European Commission indicated that the strategy should have the four main pillars of education, employment, accommodation and health and discuss improvement on discrimination issues.

Consequently, the UK agreed to develop a NRIS. However rather than establishing a specific policy to address GRT inclusion, the UK government chose to use pre-existing social inclusion policies to promote integration and to adopt 28 measures aimed at improving outcomes for GRT across education, employment, health and accommodation as well as the criminal justice system. However, it lacked a timeline for crucial goals and resources to improve the situation that many GRT find themselves in.

In 2018 Lord Bourne, the Minister for Faith and Integration, announced that there would be a GRT Strategy, and this was confirmed by his successor in the role, Viscount Younger. We would hope that the MHCLG will work with community groups and members. There will need to be identified goals and identified resources. There needs to be private and public provision of sites delivered under the planning system in the same way conventional housing is dealt with. There are families who cannot own their own land and need a place on a rented local authority site in the same way that people need social housing,

It is urgent that we address the shortfall of sites in a constructive and meaningful way.

However, it came as no surprise that the Conservative manifesto, produced for the 12 December 2019 General Election, in the section on 'crime', states: 'We will tackle unauthorised traveller camps. We will give the police new powers to arrest and seize the property and vehicles of trespassers who set up unauthorised encampments, in order to protect our communities. We will make intentional trespass a criminal offence, and we will also give councils greater powers within the planning system.'

In light of the consultation and the General Election, we wait to see what happens next, with this book in our hands.

Dr Siobhan Spencer MBE
1 December 2019

Preface and acknowledgements

At a Legal Action Group (LAG) training day on the subject of Gypsy and Traveller Law back in September 2002, a Romani Gypsy called out from the back of the room and asked us to write a book on the subject so that she and other Gypsies and Travellers could learn more about their rights.

We decided to take up the challenge and approached LAG with a rough plan for a book. LAG were very interested in the idea and agreed that there was a real need for a book that could highlight the law and issues that had an impact on the lives of Gypsies and Travellers.

By the time the first edition was published in August 2004 there had already been several dramatic changes in the legal landscape. Following several more fundamental changes in the next three years we realised a second edition would be required and this was published in August 2007.

Since then even more dramatic changes have taken place:

- Law and policy in England and Wales have increasingly diverged. In general terms the Welsh Government have shown more sympathy to the rights of Gypsies and Travellers;
- For the first time security of tenure has been introduced on local authority Gypsy/Traveller rented sites in both countries;
- There have been sweeping changes in planning policy;
- A very controversial planning definition of the term 'Gypsies and Travellers' has been introduced in England in 2015 as opposed to the very inclusive definition in Wales.

These are to name just some of the changes. We started work in earnest on a third edition in December 2014. We have finally got there!

We would like to thank our co-authors in this endeavour who are: Sharon Baxter, Tessa Buchanan, Stephen Cottle, Owen Greenhall, Tim Jones, Mike McIlvaney, Dr Angus Murdoch and David Watkinson.

We would also like to thank Dr Siobhan Spencer MBE, one of the great campaigners for Gypsies and Travellers, for providing the foreword.

We would further like to thank all the staff at LAG and, particularly, Esther Pilger for her enthusiasm and encouragement and for believing that we would eventually get to the end. Special thanks are also due from Marc to his wife Zoe for her support and patience while he worked on editing the book.

We are grateful to a number of people for providing us with information and comments on various parts of the book: Ranjit Bains for comments on the enforcement section in the unauthorised encampments chapter, Desmond Rutledge for helping to draft the housing benefit section in the rented sites chapter, Siobhan Spencer for her assistance on the organisations list and Ella Gunn for some helpful editing work.

We must also pay tribute to the other lawyers and advisers who have specialised in the representation of Gypsies and Travellers and who have, through their case work, helped bring about many of the developments that we discuss in this book. Aside from those already mentioned in their roles as co-authors we would like to mention: Jeremy Browne, Keith Coughtrie, Zia Nabi, Parminder Sanghera and James Stark. We would further like to mention the Romani Gypsy and Traveller Team at Garden Court Chambers and the Travellers' Advice Team administrator, Emma Westwood.

We would like to pay special tribute to our wonderful colleagues in the various Gypsy and Traveller support and campaigning groups. We would especially like to mention: Derbyshire Gypsy Liaison Group; Friends, Families and Travellers; Herts GATE; Leeds GATE; London Gypsies and Travellers; National Federation of Gypsy Liaison Groups; Travelling Ahead and The Traveller Movement. We would also like to thank the All Party Parliamentary Group on Gypsies, Travellers and Roma for their great support and especially their co-chairs, Kate Green MP and Baroness Whitaker. It is also important to mention the general support given by the partners and staff at CLP and the administrative team at Garden Court Chambers. None of the cases taken by CLP and Garden Court would have ever got off the ground without the expert support of the administrative and secretarial teams at CLP and Garden Court.

Above all, our thanks go to our Gypsy and Traveller clients who, through their courage, tenacity, enthusiasm and humour, have kept us going despite the worst setbacks.

Finally, we would like to dedicate this book to Lord Eric Avebury who passed away in 2016, always a great friend and supporter, author of the Caravan Sites Act 1968 and surely the greatest ever campaigner for Gypsies and Travellers. He is sorely missed by all those who fight for the rights of Gypsies, Roma and Travellers but he continues to inspire us in the fight for equality for these groups.

The law as it relates to Gypsies and Travellers is correct as of 30 November 2019.

Marc Willers QC and Chris Johnson
30 November 2019

Contributors

Marc Willers QC is the joint head of chambers at Garden Court Chambers. He specialises in human rights, environmental, planning and discrimination law with a particular emphasis on the representation of Gypsies and Travellers. He was named Legal Aid Barrister of the Year in 2011. Marc has appeared in a number of key cases, including *Coster v UK, Clarke v Tunbridge Wells BC, Smith v First Secretary of State and Mid-Bedfordshire DC, Smith v Secretary of State for Trade and Industry and the London Development Agency, Buckland v UK* and he also represented a number of Irish Travellers in their high profile legal challenge of Basildon Borough Council's decision to evict them from their land on a site known as Dale Farm. Marc is the editor of the Council of Europe's handbook *Ensuring access to rights for Roma and Travellers: the role of the European Court of Human Rights* and he regularly writes for *Legal Action* and other legal publications and presents seminars on human rights and other issues both in the UK and abroad. Marc is also a member of the Irish Bar, a trustee of Friends, Families and Travellers and a member of the European Roma Rights Centre's board.

Chris Johnson heads up the Travellers Advice Team at Community Law Partnership and was a founding partner in 1999. He has acted in some of the leading cases involving Gypsies and Travellers including three cases in the House of Lords and one in the Supreme Court. He travels the country to represent them, as well as lecturing, training, writing and campaigning on issues affecting Gypsies' and Travellers' rights. He writes regularly for *Legal Action, Travellers Times* and other publications. Chris is a member of Greenpeace, Free Tibet Campaign and Liberty.

Sharon Baxter graduated with joint honours in law and politics at Birmingham University. She qualified as a solicitor in 1993, while working at McGrath & Co Solicitors. Having gained experience in housing, family and personal injury law, she then specialised in housing law, joining CLP in 2001. Sharon works in the Travellers Advice Team at Community Law Partnership, advising on accommodation issues including evictions, planning matters, and homelessness. Sharon was the instructing solicitor in *Buckland v UK*.

Tessa Buchanan is a barrister at Garden Court Chambers. She has particular expertise in social welfare law, including community care, housing, homelessness, and planning. Her practice is primarily publicly funded and she has significant experience in representing Romani Gypsy, Irish Traveller, and Roma clients in a wide range of matters. She is the vice-chair of the Housing Law Practitioners Association, a trustee of London Gypsies and Travellers, and co-author of *Housing Allocation and Homelessness* (fifth edition, Lexis Nexis, 2018).

Stephen Cottle is a barrister at Garden Court Chambers and is ranked in the Legal 500 for his work in both social housing and civil liberties and human rights. He particularly specialises in work involving Gypsies and Travellers. Published work includes *Using the Housing Act 2004* (Jordans), *The Housing Law Handbook* (Law Society, 2nd edn forthcoming 2020) and *Gypsy and Traveller sites: the revised planning definition's impact on assessing accommodation needs'* (Equality & Human Rights Commission, 2019). Stephen also provided a commentary for *Rewriting Children's Judgments from Academic Vision to New Practice* (Hart, 2017).

Owen Greenhall is a barrister at Garden Court Chambers. He has a mixed common law practice with a particular interest in discrimination claims brought on behalf of Gypsies and Travellers. He was junior counsel for the claimants in *The Traveller Movement & Others v Wetherspoons* and is regularly instructed in civil claims relating to discrimination in the provision of goods and services.

Tim Jones is a barrister from No 5 Chambers who specialises in town and country planning law with a particular emphasis on its human rights and equality aspects. His many Gypsy and Traveller cases include *Moore and Coates v Secretary of State, Chapman v UK, R v Hereford and Worcester County Council ex p Smith, Butler and North East Somerset DC* and *R (Marden PC) v Herefordshire Council*. He is a trustee of the National Federation of Gypsy Liaison Groups. He is also a member of the Bars of Ireland and Northern Ireland and a mediator.

Mike McIlvaney studied politics and sociology at Durham University and following graduation studied law at Leeds. Passionate about the rights of the politically and socially oppressed, he embarked on a career in social welfare law and has worked in both private practice and the voluntary sector. For the past 20 years he has specialised in housing and has taken cases to the Court of Appeal, House of Lords and Supreme Court and represented clients in some of the leading cases in this area of the law. He was a founding partner of the Community Law Partnership.

Dr Angus Murdoch is a planning consultant who has specialised in representing Gypsies and Travellers for over 25 years during which time he has taken many cases for Gypsies and Travellers from local level up to the Supreme Court, including both *South Bucks DC v Porter* and *South Bucks DC v Porter (No 2)*. Angus became a Chartered Member of the Royal Town Planning Institute in 2006 and, after 10 years working for the Community Law Partnership, set up his own planning practice, Murdoch Planning, in 2009.

David Watkinson, barrister (retired from litigation 2013), is an accredited mediator and practised for 40 years in housing and planning law (the latter chiefly on behalf of Gypsies and Travellers). His many reported cases include *Atkinson, Porter (No 1), Codona* and *Doe, Yates and Eames*. In 2006 he represented the residents of the affected Gypsy and Traveller sites at the Olympic Public Inquiry. Positions held included chair of the housing and land committee of the Civil Justice Council (advising the Lord Chancellor on law reform), vice-chair of the Housing Law Practitioners Association, and founder and joint head of Garden Court Chambers. In 2005 he received the Legal Aid Barrister of the Year Award.

Contents

Table of cases

Cotswold Grange Country Park LLP v Secretary of State for Communities and Local Government [2014] EWHC 1138 (Admin), [2014] 4 WLUK 361, [2014] JPL 981	4.28, 4.187
Cresswell v Hodgson [1951] 2 KB 92, [1951] 1 All ER 710, [1951] 1 TLR 414, [1951] 2 WLUK 59, CA	3.86
Crump v Gilmore [1969] 1 WLUK 532, 68 LGR 56, (1969) 113 SJ 998, (1969) *Times*, November 5, DC	7.43
D v United Kingdom (30240/96) [1997] 5 WLUK 64, (1997) 24 EHRR 423, 2 BHRC 273, (1998) 42 BMLR 149, (1997) *Times*, May 12, ECtHR	7.157
D (a minor) v Refugee Appeals Tribunal and another [2011] IEHC 431, HC (Ireland)	7.115
DH v Czech Republic (57325/00) [2007] 11 WLUK 289, (2008) 47 EHRR 3, 23 BHRC 526, [2008] ELR 17, ECtHR	2.129, 2.133, 2.134, 2.167–2.170, 2.174, 2.234
Dartford BC v Secretary of State for Communities and Local Government [2017] EWCA Civ 141, [2017] PTSR 737, [2017] 3 WLUK 346, [2017] 2 P & CR 9, (2017) *Times*, May 4; *Affirming* [2016] EWHC 635 (Admin), [2016] 1 WLUK 387	4.68, 4.151
Davis v Tonbridge and Malling BC [2004] EWCA Civ 194, [2004] 2 WLUK 710, (2004) 101(10) LSG 30, (2004) 148 SJLB 270, [2004] NPC 30, (2004) *Times*, March 5, (2004) *Independent*, March 5	2.117, 2.118
Dawkins v Crown Suppliers (PSA) [1993] 1 WLUK 969, [1993] ICR 517, [1993] IRLR 284, (1993) *Times*, February 4, (1993) *Independent*, February 12, (1993) *Guardian*, February 1, CA	8.47
Day v Sheffield City Council August 1988 *Legal Action* 19	3.212
de Freitas v Permanent Secretary of Ministry of Agriculture, Fisheries, Lands and Housing [1999] 1 AC 69, [1998] 3 WLR 675, [1998] 6 WLUK 553, 4 BHRC 563, (1998) 142 SJLB 219, PC (Antigua and Barbuda)	2.65
Dear v Secretary of State for Communities and Local Government [2015] EWHC 29 (Admin), [2015] 1 WLUK 292	2.101, 2.183
Delfi AS v Estonia (64569/09), 2014, ECtHR	8.172
Demetri v Westminster City Council [2000] 1 WLR 772, [1999] 11 WLUK 140, (2000) 32 HLR 470, (1999) 96(45) LSG 32, (1999) 143 SJLB 277, (1999) *Times*, November 11, CA	6.97
Demir v Turkey (34503/97) [2008] 11 WLUK 256, [2009] IRLR 766, (2009) 48 EHRR 54, ECtHR	2.235
Din (Taj) v Wandsworth LBC [1983] 1 AC 657, [1981] 3 WLR 918, [1981] 3 All ER 881, [1981] 11 WLUK 248, (1981-82) 1 HLR 73, 78 LGR 113, (1981) 125 SJ 828, (1981) *Times*, November 27, HL	6.133

Hall v Bull [2013] UKSC 73, [2013] 1 WLR 3741, [2014] 1 All ER 919, [2013] 11 WLUK 753, [2014] HRLR 4, 36 BHRC 190, [2014] Eq LR 76, (2013) 157(46) SJLB 37	8.102
Hall v Wandsworth LBC [2004] EWCA Civ 1740, [2005] 2 All ER 192, [2004] 12 WLUK 576, [2005] HLR 23, [2005] BLGR 350, (2005) 102(4) LSG 30, (2005) *Times*, January 7	6.96
Hallam v Avery; Smith v Cheltenham BC [2000] 1 WLR 966, [1999] 12 WLUK 298, [2000] ICR 583, [2000] BLGR 452, (2000) 97(1) LSG 23, (2000) 144 SJLB 32, (2000) *Times*, February 7, (1999) *Independent*, December 21, CA	8.68
Hambleton DC v Bird [1995] 3 WLUK 385, [1995] 3 PLR 8, [1996] JPL 675, [1995] EG 67 (CS), [1995] NPC 58, CA	2.114, 4.236, 4.240
Handyside v United Kingdom (A/24) [1976] 12 WLUK 53, (1979–80) 1 EHRR 737, ECtHR	8.172
Hart DC v Benford [2006] EWHC 240 (QB), [2006] 2 WLUK 507, [2006] JPL 1318, [2006] 9 EG 183 (CS), [2006] NPC 21	4.250
Hearne v National Assembly for Wales [1999] 10 WLUK 733, (1999) *Times*, November 10, (1999) *Independent*, November 11, CA	4.122
Hedges v Secretary of State for the Environment [1996] 11 WLUK 226, (1997) 73 P & CR 534, [1996] EG 191 (CS), QBD	4.136
Hewage v Grampian Health Board [2012] UKSC 37, [2012] 4 All ER 447, 2013 SC (UKSC) 54, 2013 SLT 1191, [2012] 7 WLUK 809, [2012] ICR 1054, [2012] IRLR 870, [2012] Eq LR 884, 2012 GWD 25-521, (2012) *Times*, October 29	8.121
Holt v Reading BC [2013] EWCA Civ 641, [2014] PTSR 444, [2013] 6 WLUK 173, [2013] HLR 40, [2014] L & TR 7, [2013] 25 EG 108 (CS)	3.86
Horvath and Kiss v Hungary (11146/11) [2013] 1 WLUK 579, (2013) 57 EHRR 31, [2013] Eq LR 835, [2013] ELR 102, ECtHR	2.179, 2.180, 7.114
Hotak v Southwark LBC [2015] UKSC 30, [2016] AC 811, [2015] 2 WLR 1341, [2015] 3 All ER 1053, [2015] PTSR 1189, [2015] 5 WLUK 319, [2015] HLR 23, [2015] BLGR 530, (2015) *Times*, May 25	6.30, 6.128
Hounslow LBC v Powell; Leeds City Council v Hall; Birmingham City Council v Frisby; Salford City Council v Mullen [2011] UKSC 8, [2011] 2 AC 186, [2011] 2 WLR 287, [2011] 2 All ER 129, [2011] PTSR 512, [2011] 2 WLUK 762, [2011] HRLR 18, [2011] UKHRR 548, [2011] HLR 23, [2011] BLGR 363, [2011] 1 P & CR 20, [2011] 9 EG 164 (CS), (2011) 155(8) SJLB 31, [2011] NPC 24, (2011) *Times*, March 1	2.91, 2.92, 2.93, 5.44–5.46, 5.47, 5.51, 5.52, 5.53, 5.54

South Buckinghamshire DC v Porter (No 1) [2003] UKHL 26, [2003] 2 AC 558, [2003] 2 WLR 1547, [2003] 3 All ER 1, [2003] 5 WLUK 673, [2003] HRLR 27, [2003] UKHRR 1344, [2003] BLGR 449, [2003] 2 PLR 101, [2003] JPL 1412, [2003] 23 EG 135 (CS), (2003) 100(22) LSG 32, (2003) 147 SJLB 626, [2003] NPC 70, (2003) *Times*, May 23; *Affirming* [2001] EWCA Civ 1549, [2002] 1 WLR 1359, [2002] 1 All ER 425, [2001] 10 WLUK 381, [2002] BLGR 443, [2002] 2 P & CR 16, [2002] 3 PLR 1, [2002] JPL 608, (2001) 98(46) LSG 35, (2001) *Times*, November 9	2.111–2.116, 2.117, 2.118, 4.5, 4.164, 4.168, 4.236–4.249, 4.230, 4.253, 4.257
South Buckinghamshire DC v Porter (No 2) [2004] UKHL 33, [2004] 1 WLR 1953, [2004] 4 All ER 775, [2004] 7 WLUK 44, [2005] 1 P & CR 6, [2004] 4 PLR 50, [2004] 28 EG 177 (CS), (2004) 101(31) LSG 25, (2004) 148 SJLB 825, [2004] NPC 108, (2004) *Times*, July 2, (2004) *Independent*, July 6	4.149, 4.196, 4.259
South Buckinghamshire DC v Smith [2006] EWHC 281 (QB), [2006] 2 WLUK 628, [2006] JPL 1519, [2006] NPC 22	4.258
South Cambridgeshire DC v Flynn 2006] EWHC 1320 (QB), [2006] 6 WLUK 73, [2007] BLGR 471, [2007] JPL 440, [2006] NPC 65	4.258
South Cambridgeshire DC v Gammell; Bromley LBC v Maughan [2005] EWCA Civ 1429, [2006] 1 WLR 658, [2005] 10 WLUK 916, [2006] BLGR 193, [2006] JPL 873, (2005) *Times*, November 3	4.259
South Cambridgeshire DC v Secretary of State for Communities and Local Government and Julie Brown [2008] EWCA Civ 1010	4.140, 4.150
Stevenage BC v ML (HB) [2016] UKUT 164 (AAC)	3.196
Stevens v Secretary of State for Communities and Local Government [2013] EWHC 792 (Admin), [2013] 4 WLUK 108, [2013] 2 EGLR 145, [2013] JPL 1383, [2013] ACD 97	2.101, 2.104, 2.105, 2.183, 4.176
Steward v Kingston upon Thames RLBC [2007] EWCA Civ 565, [2007] 5 WLUK 544, [2007] HLR 42, (2007) 151 SJLB 711	2.52, 6.118, 6.139
Stirrup v Secretary of State for the Environment CO/383/93 3 December 1993, Local Authority Law 1/94 2, QBD	4.95

Table of statutes

Table of statutory instruments

Table of circulars and guidance

Department of the Environment Circulars

Office of the Deputy Prime Minister Circulars

Welsh Office Circulars

Guidance

Planning Policy Guidance Notes

Planning policy papers

Reports

Table of EU and international legislation

EU conventions and treaties

EU Directives

International conventions, treaties and statutes

Abbreviations

A&E	accident and emergency
ACAS	Advisory, Conciliation and Arbitration Service
ASBCPA 2014	Anti-social Behaviour, Crime and Policing Act 2014
CAB	Citizens' Advice Bureau
CCG	clinical commissioning group
CED	Committee on the Elimination of Discrimination
CEDAW	Committee for the Elimination of Discrimination against Women
CERD	Committee on the Elimination of Racial Discrimination
CESCR	International Committee for Economic, Social and Cultural Rights
CFA 2014	Children and Families Act 2014
CJEU	Court of Justice of the European Union
CJPOA 1994	Criminal Justice and Public Order Act 1994
CLA 1977	Criminal Law Act 1977
CPAG	Child Poverty Action Group
CPI	consumer prices index
CPO	compulsory purchase order
CPR	Civil Procedure Rules
CPS	Crown Prosecution Service
CQC	Care Quality Commission
CRC	Committee on the Rights of the Child
CRE	Commission for Racial Equality
CSA 1968	Caravan Sites Act 1968
CSCDA 1960	Caravan Sites and Control of Development Act 1960
DCLG	Department for Communities and Local Government

DETR	Department of the Environment, Transport and the Regions
DfCSF	Department for Children, Schools and Families
DFG	disabled facilities grant
DHP	discretionary housing payment
DMPO 2015	Town and Country Planning (Development Management Procedure) (England) Order 2015
DoE	Department of the Environment
DPA 1998	Data Protection Act 1998
DPD	development plan document
DWP	Department for Work and Pensions
EA 1996	Education Act 1996
EASS	Equality Advisory and Support Service
ECF	exceptional case funding
ECRI	European Commission against Racism and Intolerance
EAT	Employment Appeal Tribunal
ECA 1972	European Communities Act 1972
ECHR	European Convention on Human Rights
ECRI	European Commission against Racism and Intolerance
ECtHR	European Court of Human Rights
EEA	European Economic Area
EHC	education and health care
EHRC	Equality and Human Rights Commission
EPA 1990	Environment Protection Act 1990
EqA 2006	Equality Act 2006
EqA 2010	Equality Act 2010
ERRC	European Roma Rights Centre
ESA 2008	Education and Skills Act 2008
ESO	education supervision order
EU	European Union
FCPNM	European Framework Convention for the Protection of National Minorities
FGM	female genital mutilation
FRA	EU Agency for Fundamental Rights
FT(PC)	First-tier Tribunal (Property Chamber) (England)
GPDO 2015	Town and Country Planning (General Permitted Development) (England) Order 2015
GP	general practitioner

GTAA	Gypsy and Traveller Accommodation Assessment
HA 1985	Housing Act 1985
HA 1996	Housing Act 1996
HA 2004	Housing Act 2004
HB	Housing benefit
HCEO	High Court enforcement officer
HGCRA 1996	Housing Grants, Construction and Regeneration Act 1996
HMO	house in multiple occupation
HRA 1998	Human Rights Act 1998
HRC	Human Rights Committee
HSCA 2012	Health and Social Care Act 2012
H(W)A 2014	Housing (Wales) Act 2014
HWB	Health and Wellbeing Board
IRP	independent review panel
JSNA	Joint Strategic Needs Assessment
LASPO 2012	Legal Aid, Sentencing and Punishment of Offenders Act (LASPO) 2012
LCA 1973	Land Compensation Act 1973
LDA	London Development Agency
LDS	local development scheme
LEA	local education authority
LGSCO	Local Government and Social Care Ombudsman
LHA	local housing allowance
LPA	local planning authority
MHA 1983	Mobile Homes Act 1983
MHA 2013	Mobile Homes Act 2013
MH(W)A 2013	Mobile Homes (Wales) Act 2013
MWG	Ministerial Working Group
NATT	National Association of Teachers of Travellers
NDP	neighbourhood development plan
NGO	non-governmental organisation
NHS	National Health Service
NICE	National Institute for Health and Care Excellence
NPCC	National Police Chiefs' Council
NPPF	National Planning Policy Framework
NPPG	National Planning Practice Guidance
NRIS	National Roma Integration Strategy
ODPM	Office of the Deputy Prime Minister

Ofsted	Office for Standards in Education, Children's Services and Skills
PACE	Parliamentary Assembly of the Council of Europe
PCP	provision, criterion or practice
PCPA 2004	Planning and Compulsory Purchase Act 2004
PD	practice direction
PDL	previously developed land
PDR	permitted development rights
PGTSS 2018	*Planning for Gypsy, Traveller and Showpeople Sites* (2018)
PPTS 2012	*Planning policy for traveller sites* (2012)
PPTS 2015	*Planning policy for traveller sites* (2015)
PRPSH	private registered providers of social housing
PSED	public sector equality duty
PSPO	public spaces protection orders
pw	per week
RPT	Residential Property Tribunal (Wales)
RPI	retail prices index
RSL	registered social landlord
SSCLG	Secretary of State for Communities and Local Government
SSFA 1998	School Standards and Framework Act 1998
SEN	special educational needs
SPOC	single point of contact
SSEFRA	Secretary of State for the Environment, Food and Rural Affairs
SSSI	sites of special scientific interest
TCPA 1990	Town and Country Planning Act 1990
TESS	Traveller Educational Support Services
TEU	Treaty on European Union
TFEU	Treaty on the Functioning of the European Union
TSN	temporary stop notice
UC	universal credit
UNCRC	United Nations Convention on the Rights of the Child
WAG	Welsh Assembly Government
WMS	written ministerial statement

CHAPTER 1

Introduction

Introduction

1.1 In 2003, BBC News Online reported:

> Police arrested a total of six men on suspicion of inciting racial hatred after a bonfire society torched an effigy of a caravan with a gypsy family painted on the side. The tableau, which was burnt at Firle Bonfire Society's celebrations in East Sussex, caused outrage because of the controversial display. The society denies any claims the caravan, which had PIKEY written on the side . . . was designed to be racist.[1]

1.2 The scene described above could easily have been taken from a medieval European genocide, but it was not: the caravan-torching incident took place after a group of Travellers had set up camp near the village. Fortunately, the caravan in question was not occupied by real people but was made from plywood and adorned to look like a stereotypical modern Gypsy caravan, complete with paintings of Gypsy and Traveller children on the side.

1.3 The Firle bonfire incident sparked a national debate in the media about the treatment of our Gypsy and Traveller population, and about the racism they have experienced for many hundreds of years and which continues to the present day. Following the Firle incident, the Commission for Racial Equality (CRE) launched a four-year strategy[2] aimed at tackling the discrimination suffered by Gypsies and Travellers. Quoting from an opinion poll conducted in England, the strategy stated:

> . . . more than one-third of adults who took part admitted to being personally prejudiced against Gypsies and Travellers. This was greater than the levels of prejudice reported towards lesbians and gay men, other ethnic minorities and people with disabilities.[3]

1 BBC News Online, 'Six arrests over burnt gypsy effigy', 11 November 2003.

2 *Gypsies and Travellers: a strategy for the CRE*, 2004–2007 (CRE, 2004).

3 *Gypsies and Travellers: a strategy for the CRE*, 2004–2007, p6. Reference should also be made to the severely negative comments about Gypsies and Travellers made by Michael Howard MP, then leader of the Conservative party, during the 2005 General Election campaign and the vitriolic campaign in the *Sun* newspaper at the same time under the heading 'Stamp on the Camps' – see the discussion in Clark and Greenfields, *Here to stay: the Gypsies and Travellers of Britain*, University of Hertfordshire Press, 2006, pp1–3. In 2015, Community Law Partnership represented some Irish Travellers in a case where the local authority had agreed to let the family stay on a particular unauthorised encampment but the family were forced to move due to racist abuse and stone-throwing from local residents.

1.4 Romani Gypsies and Irish Travellers are accepted as being racial groups for the purposes of the Equality Act (EqA) 2010.[4] Discrimination against them – as well as inciting racial hatred towards them – is prohibited by law in the United Kingdom. Those involved in the effigy burning purported to defend their actions by saying that their anger was not aimed at the Gypsies and Travellers themselves, but at the local authorities, whose lack of action in providing sufficient lawful sites for Gypsies and Travellers in the area inevitably led to more unsatisfactory locations being occupied. Gypsies and Travellers in their turn argue that the lack of authorised sites means that they have no option but to stop where they can, before being moved on again to some other village or town where another eviction will confront them in the near future.[5]

1.5 The Firle bonfire incident illustrates some of the issues which we will be considering in this book: the implications of the lack of lawful sites for Gypsies and Travellers; the role of the local authorities, the police and the media; and how the law operates in relation to these minority groups.

1.6 This book covers the law in England and Wales. The legal position in both countries has begun to diverge. From the perspective of Gypsies and Travellers the changes in England have been negative while those in Wales have been positive.

1.7 In England the following major changes have taken place in recent years:

- The Localism Act 2011 has curtailed the ability to apply for retrospective planning and revoked the regional strategies that had previously contained pitch targets[6]
- The enactment of the Legal Aid, Sentencing and Punishment of Offenders Act (LASPO) 2012 and subsequent legal aid changes and cuts have had serious implications on the provision of legal aid for Gypsies and Travellers[7]
- *Planning policy for traveller sites* issued in March 2012 (PPTS 2012) changed the national planning policy in England and replaced Office of the Deputy Prime Minister Circular 01/06 (hereafter 'ODPM Circular 01/06')[8]

4 See chapter 8, below, for an analysis of equality legislation.

5 See, for example, the *Gypsies and Travellers: Community, Equality and Discrimination*, pamphlet, The Traveller Movement, June 2015.

6 See para 4.41, below.

7 See para 1.59, below.

8 See para 1.59, below.

- The 2005 Temporary Stop Notice (TSN) regulations[9] were withdrawn,[10] meaning that a TSN can now be issued to prevent the stationing of caravans on land which are used for residential purposes.[11]
- *Planning policy for traveller sites* issued on 31 August 2015 (PPTS 2015) replaced PPTS 2012 and, in doing so, changed the meaning of 'Gypsies and Travellers' for planning purposes[12] so that it excludes those Gypsies and Travellers who had ceased travelling permanently for reasons of ill-health or old age.

Meanwhile, in Wales the Welsh Government has:

- introduced a national Gypsy Roma Traveller Integration Strategy in 2013;[13] this was replaced by an updated strategy in June 2018;[14]
- introduced very constructive guidance on unauthorised camping;[15]
- re-introduced the duty for local authorities to meet the assessed need for Gypsy and Traveller caravan sites.[16]

1.8 What has remained common to both England and Wales is the relentlessly negative publicity which accompanies policy and law changes relating to Gypsies and Travellers.

1.9 To give just one example, when the Secretary of State for Communities and Local Government (SSCLG) released his consultation on *Planning and travellers* on 14 September 2014, the Sunday Times headline was *Ministers hand councils tough new powers to evict gypsies* (in fact no such powers were contained in the proposals) and the photo that accompanied the article showed riot police and protesters on barricades at the Dale Farm eviction in 2011 (whereas most

9 Town and Country Planning (Temporary Stop Notice) (England) Regulations 2005 SI No 206.

10 By the Town and Country Planning (Temporary Stop Notice) (England) (Revocation) Regulations 2013 SI No 830.

11 See para 4.208, below, and note that failure to comply with a TSN can result in a fine of up to £20,000.

12 See further below at para 1.36 and para 4.103.

13 *Travelling to a Better Future' – A Gypsy and Traveller Framework for Action and Delivery Plan* (Welsh Government, November 2013).

14 *Enabling Gypsies, Roma and Travellers plan* (Welsh Government, June 2018): https://gov.wales/enabling-gypsies-roma-and-travellers-plan.

15 *Guidance on Managing Unauthorised Camping* (Welsh Government, December 2013); and see para 5.185, below.

16 See paras 3.17–3.19, below.

Gypsy and Traveller planning cases relate to one pitch sites and do not involve riot police and barricades).[17]

1.10 Before we can properly understand the contemporary treatment of Gypsies and Travellers in the United Kingdom, there is a need to place it within some kind of historical context. The remainder of this introduction tries to provide just such a context, starting with a brief examination of the vexed question of who are the Gypsies and Travellers.

Who are the Gypsies and Travellers?

Overview

1.11 The CRE (now superseded by the Equality and Human Rights Commission (EHRC)) estimated that:

> Of the 200,000 to 300,000 Travellers in England, by far the largest group are Romani Gypsies, who have been in England since the early 16th century. Romani Gypsies have been recognised as a racial group since 1988 . . . Irish Travellers, who have been travelling in England as a distinct social group since the 1800s, received legal recognition as a racial group in England and Wales in 2000 . . .[18]

It should be noted that there are two other indigenous ethnic groups of Gypsies and Travellers in the United Kingdom: the Welsh Gypsy Travellers (or Kale)[19] and Scottish Gypsy Travellers.[20] However, the following brief historical overview will concentrate on Romani

17 Dale Farm was, at the time (2011), the largest unauthorised development involving Travellers in the United Kingdom. See 'Dale Farm eviction: as it happened', *The Telegraph*, 20 October 2011: www.telegraph.co.uk/news/uknews/law-and-order/8835560/Dale-Farm-eviction-as-it-happened.html.

18 *Gypsies and Travellers: a strategy for the CRE*, 2004–2007 (CRE 2004) p3, note 2.

19 There is considerable controversy among Gypsy and Traveller academics and writers about the existence of Kale as a separate type of Traveller group. However, the report by Niner, *Accommodation needs of Gypsy-Travellers in Wales*, Welsh Assembly Government, 2006, differentiates Welsh Gypsies as a separate group from English Gypsies (see, for example, at para 1.8). See also the discussion in Kenrick and Clark, *Moving on: the Gypsies and Travellers of Britain*, University of Hertfordshire Press, 1996, pp38–39.

20 See the Scottish Government website at: www.gov.scot/Topics/People/Equality/gypsiestravellers.

Gypsies and Irish Travellers before turning to deal with the emergence of non-ethnic New Travellers in the United Kingdom.[21]

1.12 Most people have some idea of what is meant by terms such as 'Gypsies' and 'New Age Travellers'. In contemporary, anti-nomadic discourse, 'real Gypsies' occupy the top rung of a sliding scale of authenticity, while 'New Age Travellers', denied this status, are generally portrayed as pseudo-vagrants, criminals or the dispossessed underclass. While it is not denied that fundamental differences do exist between these groups (particularly in language and customs), the similarities between them – both in terms of their treatment by the state and (relatedly) their economic nomadism – are often overlooked.

Historical context[22]

1.13 The nomads who came to be known as 'Gypsies' were 'the first . . . Asian immigrants to Europe'[23] and had migrated from India around 1,000 AD, with the first of three main waves arriving in Britain four or five centuries ago (the second at the end of the 19th century and the third in the 1960s). These early Gypsies had an itinerant economy and specialised in metal working, fortune telling, craft-making and musicianship.[24] Their preference for self-employment soon earned them the antipathy of some of the most powerful groups in society at the time, as such economic independence was perceived as a rejection of the master–servant relationship inherent in the Guilds' monopoly of production, as well as 'a carnivalesque incitement to disorder'.[25]

1.14 There is some controversy around why they are called Gypsies, with many claiming that European states believed they had come from Egypt, perhaps fleeing religious persecution, and that 'Gypsy' is an adaptation of 'Egyptian':

21 'New Traveller' is the term preferred by this (non-ethnic) group of Travellers themselves, though we will refer to 'New Age Traveller' where it is relevant in the historical context. See Kenrick and Clark, *Moving On*, pp117–136.

22 For an extremely detailed history, see Cressy, *Gypsies: an English history*, Oxford University Press, 2018.

23 Acton, *Gypsy Politics and Social Change*, Routledge, Kegan Paul, 1974, p27.

24 Many Gypsy groups reflect the predominant occupation in which they are involved. For example, the Kalderas, or copperworkers, from whom the word 'cauldron' has been appropriated in English. Liegeois, *Gypsies and Travellers: socio-cultural data, socio-political data*, Council of Europe, 1987, p39.

25 Stewart, *The Puzzle of Roma Persistence*, University of Hertfordshire Press, 1997, p85.

> These long-haired tent-dwellers who appeared among villages and town dwellers, defied classification, and they were given diverse names connected with an imagined origin or an imperfectly understood identity.[26]

1.15 Their dark skin colour[27] provided a ready focus for discrimination and the 'race' dimension is clearly evident in popular mythology of the time. The subsequent stereotyping of Gypsies invoked fears of the 'Black Heathen' alongside themes of idleness, indiscipline and depravity – themes which persist to this day. Thus, the historical oppression of Gypsy people can be seen to have ethnic, racial and class bases. These three factors are not mutually exclusive in Gypsy history – on the contrary, they are mutually reinforcing. Indeed, the three overlap to the extent that it is impossible to be sure where the influence of one ends and the others begin. Any such obvious deviations from established norms were subject to the most severe social and penal sanctions at the time and Gypsy nomads were particularly vulnerable to such punishment. In this way, their economic skills (which were a fundamental part of their nomadic identity) set them at odds with the dominant ideology of work in both feudal society (as 'masterless men'[28]) and in later capitalist societies (through their continued resistance to proletarianisation).

1.16 Within a short period of time after their arrival in Britain, Gypsies became seen as lazy, dirty, parasitic deviants and subject to repressive legislation aimed at expelling and, ultimately, exterminating the Gypsy population. The first such law aimed explicitly against them was Henry VIII's Proclamation of 1530:

> Diverse and many outlandish people calling themselves Egyptians, have gone from place to place and used great and subtle means to deceive the people, bearing them in hand that they by palmistry could tell men's and women's fortunes . . . and have deceived the people of their money and have also committed many heinous felonies and robberies.[29]

1.17 Initially, the punishment for being an 'Egyptian' at this time was banishment, but the state had trouble identifying exactly who was and who was not a 'Gypsy', as a great many indigenous, dispossessed people roamed the land during the Tudor period. Then, in 1553

26 Liegeois, *Gypsies and Travellers*, p13.

27 Walvin, *There ain't no black in the Union Jack*, Routledge, 1973, makes the case that British people have 'always found blackness a peculiar and important point of difference', and this is also relevant when considering anti-nomadism.

28 Fraser, *The Gypsies*, Blackwell, 1995, p35.

29 22 Henry VIII c10 of 1530.

Queen Mary passed the Egyptians Act which decreed that the death penalty should be imposed on anyone who was a Gypsy, or anyone 'who shall become of the fellowship or company of Egyptians'. The offence remained on the statute books for over two centuries in Britain.

1.18 The anti-Gypsy ideology combined with the anti-vagrant ideology of the time, a fact clearly reflected in the language of the other draconian legislation, such as the 1554 'Order For the Avoiding of All Doubts and Ambiguities' which re-asserted the intended victims of the legislation as:

> . . . all such sturdy and false vagabonds of that sort living only upon the spoil of the simple people [including those] in any company or fellowship of vagabonds commonly called or calling themselves 'Aegyptians'.

These laws had a populist reflection in contemporary folk tales and mythology which demonstrate that, as early as the 16th century, the stereotype was firmly fixed in the sedentary imagination that Gypsies were work-shy parasites worthy only of contempt:

> The local people, disconcerted by such unclassifiable originality in dress, language, way of life and possible mode of association, accused them of witchcraft, banditry and of spreading disease. In this way there grew up the dark and fearful image of a nomad with a soul as black as his skin, damned for all time in the eyes of a frightened society.[30]

1.19 It is important to underline the fact that the persecution of Gypsy people was not restricted to Britain but was a pan-European affair. During the 16th, 17th and 18th centuries, laws were passed in every single European state to control the 'Gypsy problem' in similarly repressive ways:

> For the next 200 years . . . there is a depressing uniformity about the response of most European powers to the presence of Gypsies. They continued to be viewed as criminals simply because of their position in society and, on top of that, the special racial prejudices remained, together with religious hostility towards what was seen as their heathenish practices and sorcery. More generally, they suffered from the tide of repression that was arising everywhere against vagabondage and the 'sturdy beggar'. The authorities could not come to terms with masterless men, with no fixed domicile and useless as a workforce: in their eyes, that status was in itself an aberration, at odds with the established order, and had to be put right by coercion and pressure of the gyves.[31] Yet when the Gypsies offered legitimate services to the settled population, they

30 Liegeois, *Gypsies and Travellers*, p44.

31 'Gyves' meaning shackles or fetters (*The Chambers Dictionary*, 1994).

> were at risk from the ill-will attracted by transient traders and artisans who violated local monopolies, or from the abhorrence that occupations such as peddler or tinker or entertainer aroused among those in power.[32]

1.20 For the Gypsies who had migrated to Britain (as well as indigenous Travellers) commerce formed an important dimension of their economic survival, and while they may have strived to remain culturally independent of their sedentary neighbours, the fact that they traded goods and services with sedentary society meant that economic interdependence became (and has remained) a feature of Gypsy life. Not only did nomadic groups hawk the wares they had made (or bought) in towns and villages which they passed on the road, but they frequently made their nomadic habits coincide with traditional horse and harvest fairs and other meeting places. Here, not only were their skills in trade and craftsmanship in demand, but their musical and entertainment abilities could also earn them a living. By the 19th century, Gypsies had become familiar sights at these fairs, and many would arrange their annual travel routes so that they could attend fairs following the harvest, thus making a living from both:

> Fairs and race-meetings formed a major part of the Gypsy calendar, giving some structure to the timing and direction of their travels, and providing a meeting place for families and friends as well as allowing them to engage in the serious business of horse-dealing . . . Once the harvests were in, the movement from town to country was reversed.[33]

1.21 Once again, it can be seen how their nomadism (while fundamental to their identity) is permeated with economic dimensions, primarily in terms of the historical bases of their persecution, but also in the fact that the patterns of their nomadism in Britain evolved in relation to the availability of viable economic niches in the wider society. This is demonstrated by the fact that many Gypsies moved with and for the harvest as agricultural workers and used these routes to ply their other trades, for example, at the fairs. These sites in turn became a focus of cultural celebration for Gypsy and Traveller people themselves, thus reinforcing the economic centrality of nomadism for their identity:

> For the Gypsy and the Traveller travelling has many functions. It permits social organisation, it sanctions adaptability and flexibility and makes the practice of trading possible . . . Apart from its social function, travel has an equally important economic role. This is evident for certain

32 Fraser, *The Gypsies*, p129.

33 Fraser, *The Gypsies*, p110.

> occupations: nomadic trades observe the dates of holidays and fairs, cattle dealers those of cattle markets, agricultural workers the season for picking fruit, grapes and olives [in Europe]. Generally speaking, the essential characteristic of the occupations practised is self-employment, which in turn necessitates extensive prospecting with frequent journeying, sometimes to distant parts in search of custom, for artisan or trader, for artist or merchant. Gypsies and Travellers cling to their occupational independence, which has so far guaranteed their adaptability.[34]

Racialising Gypsy people

1.22 Well into the 19th century, the persecution of Gypsy people by the populace at large was still encouraged by many European states. For example, in Holland, 'Gypsy hunts' were organised on a regional basis, and not only was it an offence to be a Gypsy, but it was also perfectly lawful to kill one. The racial dimension in this persecution is revealed in the vocabulary of intolerance used against them. Both the Dutch and Italian languages share the simile 'as black as a Gypsy'.[35]

1.23 In the 19th century, a new stereotype, the 'real Romani' or 'genuine Gypsy', evolved, alongside contemporary concerns with racial purity. In time, the pseudo-science of racial hygiene would come to concur with ill-informed 'Gypsyologists' and posit the existence of small, racially pure groups of 'genuine Gypsies' in the midst of a population of congenitally degenerate subproletariat people who had taken to the travelling life in order to avoid work, taxes and other social responsibilities.[36] In other words, the 'Gypsy problem' had become overtly racialised:

> From now onwards alongside the stereotype dirty, dishonest, child-stealing villain we have the dark, handsome, violin-playing lover-Gypsy, a 'noble savage', camping in the woodlands and living off the Earth . . . It is allowed that there exists somewhere . . . the true Romanies . . . racially pure, clean in habits, noble in spirit. But they are never found; they are, of course, a phantom people. Parliamentary debates, in Britain and elsewhere, contain many references to these imaginary beings.[37]

1.24 The Nazi Holocaust provides the clearest example of how the articulation of this ancient hatred of nomads became translated into a

34 Liegeois, *Gypsies and Travellers*, pp52–53, note 13.

35 Kenrick and Puxon, *The destiny of Europe's Gypsies*, Chatto-Heinemann, 1972, p113.

36 Kenrick and Puxon, *The destiny of Europe's Gypsies*, p54

37 Kenrick and Puxon, *The destiny of Europe's Gypsies*, p30 and p41.

national policy of racial hygiene. Ethnic Gypsies became the target of genocidal policies under the Third Reich and half a million of them lost their lives precisely because they were Gypsies. While the methods of mass destruction employed by the Nazis may have been unprecedented,[38] the targets of their repression were not. What was unique was that Nazi ideology was able to provide an inescapable biological racism which legitimised existing prejudices.[39]

1.25 For example, the scientist in charge of 'Race Hygiene and Population Biology' at the Reich Department of Health, Dr Ritter, conducted 'research' on Gypsy genealogy, which ultimately formed part of the legitimation for the extermination policies which followed. His findings confirmed his belief that:

> Most gypsies are not gypsies at all, but rather the products of matings with the German criminal asocial subproletariat . . . More than 90 per cent of so-called 'gypsies' are of mixed-blood. It has been demonstrated that gypsies, in their racial crosses in our homeland, have mated predominantly with Yenisch [non-Gypsy Travellers] and with asocial criminal elements and that this has led to the formation of a Yenisch-gypsy lumpenproletariat which costs the state enormous sums in welfare costs . . . The gypsy question can only be considered solved when the main body of asocial and good-for-nothing gypsy individuals of mixed-blood is collected together in large labour camps and kept working there, and when the further breeding of this population of mixed-blood is stopped once and for all.[40]

1.26 Thus the ideology of Gypsy romanticism was contrasted with the savage treatment of nomads in the real world. What the myth of the 'real Romani' legitimated, both in Britain and in Europe, was the persecution of Gypsies and Travellers who did not conform to the stereotypical notions of Gypsyhood held by the dominant society. As Okely puts it, 'real Gypsies are those who best fit the stereotype of the observer'.[41] An important legacy from this period is that it remains a continuing 'sedentary obsession'[42] to attempt to distinguish these 'genuine Gypsies' from other nomads, and the state's attempts to divide nomads along these arbitrary lines continues to today. To take just one example, in a radio interview in 1999, the then Home Secretary, Jack Straw MP, sought to draw a distinction between genuine Romani Gypsies and 'travellers masquerading as

38 See Bauman, *Modernity and the Holocaust*, Polity Press, 1989.

39 See the discussion of 'hate crime' in chapter 8 para 8.170 onwards, below.

40 Cited in Muller-Hill, *Murderous Science*, Methuesen, New York, 1988, p69.

41 Okely, *The Traveller-Gypsies* (Cambridge University Press, 1983) p27.

42 Fraser, *The Gypsies*, Blackwell, 1995, p27.

law-abiding gypsies',[43] when referring to an incident involving Travellers in the West Midlands.

Irish Travellers

1.27 There is a common misconception that Irish Travellers originated as the 'dispossessed' of the 'Great Famine' in the mid-19th century whereas, in fact, there is reference to Travellers in Ireland long before Romany Gypsies arrived on the shores of Britain. O'Riain states:

> There is evidence which points to the existence from the fifth century of indigenous nomadic groups in Ireland. In the twelfth century the name Tynkler or Tynker was given to a group of nomads who for a long time had maintained a separate identity, social organisation and dialect.[44]

1.28 Irish Travellers and Romani Gypsies share the reliance on 'self-employment' and each has a distinct language (Shelta and Romani, respectively).[45]

1.29 Members of both ethnic groups also share a common experience of prejudice and discrimination. For Irish Travellers in Ireland, the prejudice increased over time and now continues unabated:

> In the case of Ireland, the radical disavowal of 'tinkers'[46] and Travellers probably occurred much later than elsewhere in western Europe. It was particularly exacerbated by the decimation of plebeian agrarian society from the late nineteenth century onwards and the growth of a bourgeois Irish nationalism and clericalism after the Famine.[47]

1.30 Paradoxically, the Irish nationalism of the 19th century and the (eventual) independence of the south of Ireland in the 20th century led not to the inclusion but to the exclusion of Irish Travellers, who were subject to the same assumptions, prejudices and mythology as beset their nomadic counterparts in Britain:

> Nomadism on the other hand, and Travelling communities within Ireland, were looked on as social anomalies, relics from a 'barbarous' past that was best forgotten because they represented all that was backward, unstable and evil about Irish society.[48]

43 'Scattergun Straw', *Guardian*, 20 August 1999.

44 O'Riain, *Solidarity with Travellers*, Roadside Books, Dublin, 2000, p8.

45 These languages have different origins. Shelta is derived from Gaelic and Romani from Sanskrit.

46 Nowadays a derogatory name for Irish Travellers.

47 MacLaughlin, *Travellers and Ireland*, p15.

48 MacLaughlin, *Travellers and Ireland*, p28.

1.31 The experience that Irish Travellers did share with the poor in Ireland was emigration. Thus, they arrived in Britain:

> Although Irish emigration to England began several centuries ago, the first reliable report of Irish Travellers dates from 1850.[49]

1.32 Once in Britain, Irish Travellers experienced the same prejudice that the Romani Gypsies had long been experiencing. One can bring the story up to date by reference to an incident that occurred in 2003:

> [T]hat year saw what most believed from the evidence was the racially motivated murder of Johnny Delaney, a teenage [Irish] Traveller, who was attacked in the vicinity of an unauthorised encampment, where members of his family lived and who he had been visiting. In court proceedings the jury were technically unable to identify a racial motive and punish the perpetrators accordingly.[50]

The end of the road for nomadism?

1.33 Stewart[51] argues that successive generations have prematurely rung the funeral knell for nomadism and have prophesied its impending destruction. We have been told that Gypsies in particular are anachronistic throwbacks whose allegedly pre-industrial employment patterns – such as fruit-picking, peg-making and horse-trading – have been made increasingly obsolete through technological and social change:

> Every age, ours as much as its predecessors, believes it will be the last to be blessed (or cursed) by the presence of Gypsies. Well-wishers and hostile commentators, romantics and cynics alike are of fixed opinion that the 'wanderers of the world' have at last been 'domesticated', their way of life finally outmoded and that the 'time of the Gypsies' has run out . . . In truth, Gypsies all over Europe have been remarkably successful in preserving their way of life, adapting to changed conditions in order to remain the same.[52]

1.34 As Kenrick and Bakewell observe:

> [For Gypsy people] work is not an end in itself but a means of earning money while staying independent. Independence requires mobility and adaptability. The Gypsies . . . have adapted their trades successfully to

49 Kenrick and Bakewell, *On the verge: the Gypsies of England*, University of Hertfordshire Press, 1990, p10.

50 Crawley, *Moving forward: the provision of accommodation for Travellers and Gypsies*, The Institute for Public Policy Research, 2004, p60.

51 Stewart, *The puzzle of Roma persistence*.

52 Stewart, *The puzzle of Roma persistence*, p82.

> growing industrialisation. [They] rarely have one single occupation but practice a combination of trades, such as scrap-collecting, tarmacking, hawking, fortune-telling and so on. These trades also require minimum equipment which enables them to stay mobile . . . Work patterns distinguish the Gypsy and Travelling people from other groups. There may be migrant workers but rarely do these remain as independent of wage labour as the Gypsies.[53]

1.35 Fraser provides a good example of some of the ways in which social change has been absorbed by Gypsies and Travellers:

> In the face of urbanisation, industrialisation and other European pressures, Gypsies showed themselves able to maintain their autonomy by exploiting opportunities created by the dominant system. They resisted temptations to go over to wage-labour, as so many others were doing. Most – even when settled – seem to have clung tenaciously to some ideal of community and independence and self-employment. In Britain, urbanisation did not prove incompatible with maintaining a degree of nomadism . . . they moved from village to town where necessary and abandoned old trades in favour of new activities more suited to the times, but without compromising their freedom, their ethnic identity or their occupational and residential flexibility . . . A less resilient culture might have succumbed completely; the Gypsies did not.[54]

Defining Gypsies in law

1.36 The relative influence of race, ethnicity and class in the history of the treatment of Gypsy and Traveller people has a contemporary reflection in the sometimes contradictory ways in which the British state has attempted to define who is and who is not a Gypsy in law. For the purposes of the Equality Act (EqA) 2010, Romani Gypsies are defined, by reference to belonging to a 'racial group' through birth or marriage and thus by ethnic criteria. However, in planning law, Gypsies (sometimes referred to as 'gipsies' in statutes and reported cases) are defined as:

> . . . persons of a nomadic habit of life, whatever their race or origin[55]

and the law is concerned with how the Gypsy concerned makes their living, rather than the circumstances of their birth.

53 Kenrick and Bakewell, *On the verge*, pp14–15.

54 Fraser, *The Gypsies*, p93.

55 For a full discussion of the definition of 'Gypsy' for planning law purposes, see chapter 4 para 4.103 onwards, below.

1.37 That definition stems from the case of *Mills v Cooper*[56] in which the high court considered the interpretation of Highways Act 1959 s127 and its prohibition on Gypsies camping on the highway. The court, convinced that parliament could not have intended to explicitly discriminate against ethnic Gypsies or Travellers, decided that the use of the term 'Gypsy' in the statute must be concerned with one's lifestyle rather than ethnicity. Similarly, 'Gypsies' were defined in the Caravan Sites and Control of Development Act (CSCDA) 1960 as 'persons of nomadic habit of life, whatever their race or origin'.[57]

Accommodation for Gypsies and Travellers

1.38 In *R v Lincolnshire CC ex p Atkinson; R v Wealden DC ex p Wales and Stratford*,[58] one of the leading cases in which Gypsies and Travellers challenged the use of eviction powers given to local authorities by the Criminal Justice and Public Order Act (CJPOA) 1994, Sedley J (as he then was) gave a useful potted history of the post-war legislative history:

> It is relevant to situate this new and in some ways draconic legislation [CJPOA 1994] in its context. For centuries the commons of England provided lawful stopping places for people whose way of life was or had become nomadic. Enough common land had survived the centuries of enclosure to make this way of life still sustainable, but by section 23 of the Caravan Sites and Control of Development Act 1960 local authorities were given the power to close the commons to travellers. This they proceeded to do with great energy, but made no use of the concomitant power given to them by section 24 of the same Act to open caravan sites to compensate for the closure of the commons. By the Caravan Sites Act 1968, therefore, Parliament legislated to make the section 24 power a duty, resting in rural areas on county councils rather than district councils (although the latter continued to possess the power to open sites). For the next quarter of a century there followed a history of non-compliance with the duties imposed by the Act of 1968, marked by a series of decisions of this court holding local authorities to be in breach of their statutory duty; but to apparently little practical effect. The default powers vested in central government, to which the court was required to defer, were rarely if ever used. The culmination of the tensions underlying the history of non-compliance was the enactment of the sections of

56 [1967] 2 All ER 100.

57 CSCDA 1960 s24(8). This analysis is continued further at para 4.103 onwards, below.

58 (1996) 8 Admin LR 529; [1997] JPL 65.

> the Act of 1994 . . . There followed, in section 80(1), the wholesale repeal of the material part, Part II, of the Caravan Sites Act 1968.[59]

1.39 The Conservative government's position on the repeal of the duty to provide sites by the CJPOA 1994 was that, in the future, Gypsy and Traveller sites would be provided solely through private endeavour by Gypsies and Travellers themselves utilising the planning system.[60] With no duty in place, public site provision effectively ground to a halt and the number of pitches available began to decline.[61] In the meantime, private site provision has failed to keep up with the demand as Gypsies and Travellers have faced enormous opposition from local residents and local authorities when trying to establish private sites for themselves.

1.40 The cumulative effect of poverty and the steady diminution of stopping places has impacted on Britain's nomadic populations in serious ways.[62] Allied with the loss of traditional sites has been a concomitant decline in the health of Gypsies and Travellers,[63] due to the extremely poor environmental conditions that often exist on unauthorised sites, most of which will be without basic services, such as water, refuse collection or sanitation.

> While it is self-evident that unsited Travellers, as a direct result of their difficulties in obtaining both preventative health care and medical treatment, experience far greater health inequalities than the majority of the settled population, it is also true that members of the community living at authorised sites, or in housing, are still over-represented in terms of preventable ill health, premature death and disability.[64]

1.41 In 2015 the EHRC published a report entitled *Is Britain Fairer*[65] and in 2016 it published another report entitled *Is England Fairer*[66] as well as a spotlight report entitled *England's most disadvantaged groups: Gypsies, Travellers and Roma.*[67] In the latter report, the EHRC identified the most up-to-date evidence and statistics on the education,

59 *Atkinson* (1996) 8 Admin LR 529 at 533–534.

60 See chapter 4 below.

61 See chapter 3 below.

62 See Le Bas, *The Stopping Places: A Journey through Gypsy Britain*, Chatto & Windus, 2018.

63 See chapter 7, below.

64 Clark & Greenfields, *Here to Stay*, University of Hertfordshire Press, 2006, p182.

65 See: www.equalityhumanrights.com/en/britain-fairer/britain-fairer-report.

66 See: www.equalityhumanrights.com/sites/default/files/is_england_fairer.pdf.

67 See: www.equalityhumanrights.com/sites/default/files/ief_gypsies_travellers_and_roma.pdf.

employment, living standards, health, and imprisonment of Gypsies, Travellers and Roma as well as the negative attitudes and hostility that they experience from the general public, police and other authorities, fuelled by political rhetoric and the media. Having done so, the EHRC concluded that little had changed since *Research report 12: Inequalities experienced by Gypsy and Traveller communities* had been published in 2009.

1.42 This brings us back to the question of defining 'Gypsies' at law. Over the years the courts have continued to emphasise the centrality of economy over ethnicity. The association in the sedentary mind between Gypsies and economic nomadism has now become so strong that such travel has become the essential element of Gypsy status in law. The implications of institutionalising the legal definition of 'Gypsy' in this way remain unresolved. This brings us to a consideration of 'New Travellers', since, arguably, it was this group which the definition was ultimately intended to exclude from provision.

New Travellers

> Many people feel that the law operates unfairly in that it was intended to support the traditional way of life of Romani peoples but has been used by several groups of hippies, drug-takers and law-breakers who drive around in old cars and vans . . .[68]

1.43 Quite in what way these 'hippies' were supposed to have used the Caravan Sites Act (CSA) 1968 (which introduced a duty on certain local authorities to provide sites) is not made clear by the authors of the above statement, but it is untenable to suggest that any significant number of them benefited from site provision under the Act.[69] Local authorities had failed to provide anywhere near adequate provision for traditional Gypsies and Travellers, let alone this new type of Traveller – who were, if anything, even more despised than traditional (ethnic) Gypsies and Travellers. Elsewhere, various arms of the state reinforced the view that the 'hippies' should be treated differently than traditional nomads:

> The situation has become more complex in recent years with the emergence of groups who do not wish to use the sites that are provided, may

68 Barclay, *Gypsy caravan sites*, House of Commons Research Note 92/30.

69 There are currently believed to be just two New Traveller local authority sites in England and none in Wales. The two sites were established after the repeal of the duty to provide sites – information from the Travellers' Advice Team at the Community Law Partnership. No official statistics are available.

travel in large numbers, may not be nomadic and for whom the 1968 Act provisions may not have been provided. These may include some of the group colloquially known as New Age Travellers.[70]

1.44 The meaning of the word 'nomadic' was at the centre of a court case in 1992 in which South Hams District Council in Devon argued that a group of New Age Travellers encamped in their area were not Gypsies and were therefore owed no duty regarding site provision.[71] The court confirmed the economic meaning of nomadism, namely that to be a statutory Gypsy one's travel must be related to how one makes a living:

> . . . the definition of 'gypsies' [in CSCDA 1960 s24(8) and CSA 1968 s16] imports the requirement that there should be some recognisable connection between the wandering or travelling and the means whereby the persons concerned make or seek their livelihood. Persons, or individuals, who move from place to place merely as the fancy may take them and without any connection between the movement and their means of livelihood fall outside these statutory definitions.[72]

1.45 The case established that 'Gypsy status'[73] could be gained and lost depending on the lifestyle of the individual Gypsy or Traveller. As such, the case failed to exclude New Travellers as a group – as many local authorities had hoped – but rather established a somewhat paradoxical situation wherein a Romani Gypsy or Irish Traveller by birth living on a static caravan site could well fall outside the definition. An additional implication is that some New Travellers clearly might qualify as statutory 'Gypsies', provided their travel had an economic purpose.

1.46 Kenrick and Puxon discern a historical pattern here:

> When the racial theories are swept aside, we find that the detractors have once more changed ground. Once again, they assert that the majority of people who call themselves gypsies are not gypsies at all. They are social misfits, the drop-outs of society who have taken up a pseudo-gypsy way of life to avoid social responsibilities, taxes and other inconveniences of modern life.[74]

1.47 As Fraser has stated:

70 Consultation Paper, *Reform of the Caravan Sites Act*, Department of the Environment (DoE), March 1992.

71 *R v South Hams DC ex p Gibb* [1994] 4 All ER 1012.

72 [1994] 4 All ER 1012 at 1012.

73 That is, qualification as a statutory Gypsy.

74 Kenrick and Puxon, *The destiny of Europe's Gypsies*, pp30–31.

> If excuse is needed for having plunged here into such legal niceties, it lies in the fact that we shall find the question of Gypsy identity has attended their passage through Europe ever since they first arrived, and these legal debates in the English courts serve very well to illustrate an important dilemma which refuses to go away in any discussion of Gypsies. Is it the way of life that is paramount in definition?[75]

1.48 While the media-hype around what became known (to everyone apart from themselves) as 'New Age Travellers' focused heavily on one particular group, the 'Peace Convoy', even by the early 1980s there were many 'alternative' Travelling groups staging festivals and fairs throughout the summer months. As well as performing as jugglers, musicians, clowns and fire-eaters, and trading things they had made or bought, many of these New Travellers also focused their nomadism around the fruit-picking and the fairs, and, like the Gypsies before them, their rejection of fixed-wage labour attracted particular prejudice. Free festivals themselves ultimately became expressly prohibited and were subject to repressive measures by the state – including a paramilitary assault against New Travellers by the police at the so-called 'Battle of the Beanfield' near Stonehenge in 1985.[76] By these actions, the economic and social basis of the New Traveller community itself became criminalised.

1.49 There are profound similarities between the function of nomadism for traditional Gypsy and Traveller people and for New Travellers.[77] The courts have recognised these similarities since the earliest days of New Traveller culture, although both central and local government have been loathe to accept this reality in practice:

> In 1986, a Yorkshire court ruled that a group known as 'The Mutants' were Gypsies within the meaning of the [1968 Caravan Sites] Act. In Avon, a New Age Traveller, Mr Rexworthy, was ruled to be a Gypsy. [Yet] the Government has stated . . . in Parliament that it does not on the whole see New Age Travellers as Gypsies, to be helped by the 1968 Act.[78]
>
> . . .
>
> The distinction being made between acceptable 'true Gypsies' and unacceptable other Travellers is akin to the 19th century concerns over the 'genuine Romani'. Like previous dividing practices, spoken tolerance for

75 Fraser, *The Gypsies*, p5.

76 See Worthington, ed, *The Battle of the Beanfield*, Enabler Publications, 2005.

77 This fact is increasingly recognised in planning appeals. Many of the New Travellers discussed in chapter 4, below, on planning law have been officially accepted as 'gipsies' due to their employment patterns.

78 Kenrick and Bakewell, *On the verge*, p50.

'real Gypsies' is always expressed in relation to another, less defined group, be it 'half-breeds', Didicois, Irish Travellers, tinkers, vagrants or New Age Travellers.[79]

Culture

1.50 It is important, when advising Gypsies and other ethnic Travellers of the law in this area, to have regard to their cultural values (a lot of which are shared). Some areas of commonality include:

- a tradition of nomadism and living in caravans;
- the dominant position of the family and living in extended family groups;
- early and close kin marriage;
- work patterns;
- rituals surrounding death and marriage;
- relationship with the dominant settled society;
- language;
- the experience of discrimination.[80]

1.51 Where relevant, reference is made to Gypsy and ethnic Traveller culture throughout this book.

Outline of the book

1.52 This book is intended to provide a comprehensive coverage of the domestic law as it relates to Gypsies and Travellers in England and Wales.

1.53 The book is structured as follows:

- Chapter 2 will address the impact of the Human Rights Act (HRA) 1998 on the domestic law relating to Gypsies and Travellers and how international laws can be used to protect and promote the rights of Gypsies and Travellers.
- The law relating to public rented site provision in England and Wales has changed quite dramatically as a result of amendments made to the Mobile Homes Act 1983 and the introduction of the Mobile Homes (Wales) Act 2013 which have resulted in residents

79 Kenrick and Bakewell, *On the verge*, p52.

80 See, for example, Clark and Greenfields, *Gypsies and Travellers*, pp28–56; McDonagh, 'Ethnicity and culture' in *Travellers: citizens of Ireland*, pp26–31.

on local authority Gypsy and Traveller sites gaining security of tenure for the first time. These issues are discussed in chapter 3.

- Planning law and policy is of particular importance to those Gypsies and Travellers attempting to set up their own sites and is dealt with in chapter 4. There have also been some dramatic changes in planning law over recent years.
- The need for adequate site provision of all sorts stems from the large numbers of Gypsies and Travellers who remain on unauthorised encampments and the law on this subject is dealt with in chapter 5.
- Over recent years the potential importance and use of homelessness legislation has come to the fore, and the law on this area is dealt with in chapter 6.
- Education and health are central concerns for Gypsies and Travellers and the law relating to these two areas is discussed in chapter 7.
- As with the HRA 1998, equality legislation has a significant impact on all the areas of law discussed and is considered in chapter 8.

1.54 Each chapter flags up potential or expected changes to the law and 'grey areas' where they exist.

1.55 The appendices contain useful matters for reference.

1.56 All references in the text to Gypsies and Travellers will be to Romani Gypsies and Irish Travellers, Scottish and Welsh Gypsy Travellers and New Travellers unless otherwise stated.

1.57 It should be noted that the Council of Europe use the term 'Roma' collectively to refer to Roma, Sinti, Kale, and other related groups in Europe, as well as ethnic minorities such as Romani Gypsies, Irish Travellers and Welsh and Scottish Gypsy Travellers. All references to 'Roma' in the text will accord with that meaning of the term.

1.58 Travelling Showpeople are discussed where relevant.[81] However, this book does not deal with houseboat dwellers or bargees, since the law relating to them is very different and outside the scope of this work, though occasional reference is made to them where a particular piece of law is also of relevance to them.[82]

81 For a discussion of Travelling Showpeople, see Kenrick and Clark, *Moving On*, pp35–37.

82 For a discussion of Water Gypsies, see Sandford, *Rokkering to the Gorjios*, University of Hertfordshire Press, 1973, pp75–78.

1.59 Despite immense and vehement opposition, the previous Conservative and Liberal Democrat Coalition Government introduced swingeing restrictions on and cuts to the legal aid system in England and Wales. Therefore, there is a discussion on legal aid at the end of several chapters.[83]

1.60 The law as it relates to Gypsies and Travellers in England and Wales is correct as at 30 November 2019.

83 For details of the campaign run by Gypsies and Travellers and their supporters against legal aid cuts, the No Mad Laws Campaign, see: www.nomadlaws.co.uk/.

CHAPTER 2

Using domestic, European and international law to protect Gypsy, Traveller and Roma rights

continued

Introduction

2.1 This chapter provides the reader with a guide to the most significant European and international human rights treaties that can be used to protect the rights of Gypsies, Travellers and Roma, and explains how the protection of 'Roma rights' has developed domestically.

2.2 It begins by examining the Council of Europe and its various treaties, the most well-known of which is the European Convention on Human Rights (ECHR). It considers the case-law of the European Court of Human Rights (ECtHR) and how this has been applied in United Kingdom (UK) domestic courts through the Human Rights Act (HRA) 1998. The chapter then goes on to consider how the Council of Europe's other treaties and their monitoring bodies, including the European Committee of Social Rights as well as the United Nations (UN) human rights mechanisms, can be used to promote the rights of Gypsies, Travellers and Roma.

2.3 At the time of writing, it is not known whether the UK will remain within the European Union (EU). In the circumstances, this chapter considers how EU equality law is currently applied in the UK.

Discrimination faced by Roma in Europe

2.4 The Council of Europe and the EU use the term 'Roma' to refer collectively to diverse communities including Roma, Sinti, Kale, and other related groups in Europe, as well as ethnic minorities that identify themselves as Romani Gypsies, Irish Travellers, and Welsh and Scottish Gypsy Travellers. In the UK, Roma is frequently used to refer to people of Romani background from Central and Eastern European countries who have moved to the UK over the past couple of decades. Gypsies and Travellers generally refers to nomadic or formally nomadic groups who are indigenous to the UK or whose ancestors have been in living in the UK for several centuries.[1]

2.5 There are an estimated 10–12 million Roma living in Europe, comprising the largest minority group in the continent.[2] Roma have been subjected to some of the worst forms of discrimination

1 See: the UK's National Roma Integration Strategy, p2, at: http://ec.europa.eu/justice/discrimination/files/roma_uk_strategy_en.pdf; and D Smith (2016) *Local engagement for Roma inclusion, Locality Study Medway (UK), 2016,* Fundamental Rights Agency, available at: http://fra.europa.eu/en/project/2015/local-engagement-roma-inclusion-leri-multi-annual-roma-programme#Medway.

2 See: http://ec.europa.eu/justice/discrimination/roma/index_en.htm.

since their arrival in Europe more than eight centuries ago. From 500 years of slavery in Wallachia and Moldavia (modern day Romania)[3] to the internment of 10,000–12,000 Gypsies in 18th century Spain simply for being Gypsies.[4] Then in the 20th century, it is estimated that between 500,000 and 1,500,000 Roma were killed during the Holocaust, which is often referred to as the Porrajmos (the Devouring).[5]

2.6 The extensive discrimination faced by Roma was formally recognised by the Council of Europe as long ago as 1969 when its Parliamentary Assembly adopted Recommendation 563 (1969) on the *Situation of Gypsies and other Travellers in Europe.*[6] Since then there has been no shortage of commitments, declarations and expressions of good intentions by member states aimed at improving the lives of Roma in Europe. However, progress has all too often been thwarted at the stage where policies are to be implemented at a national or local level and consequently there has been little real improvement.

2.7 A report by the EU Agency for Fundamental Rights (FRA) in 2009 found that many Roma experience poor housing conditions; face the highest levels of discrimination in access to housing, education, employment and health care; and that as a result, their chances in the labour market are diminished.[7] In a 2016 report on discrimination, the FRA found that 80 per cent of Roma live below the at-risk-of-poverty threshold; a third live in housing without tap water; and one in ten live in housing without electricity in the nine EU member states with the highest Roma populations.[8]

3 P Petcut, *Wallachia and Moldavia,* Council of Europe Factsheets on Roma, history, culture and language, available at: www.coe.int/t/dg4/education/roma/histoCulture_en.asp.

4 A Gomez Alfaro, *The Great 'Gypsy' Round-up in Spain,* Council of Europe Factsheets on Roma history, culture and language, available at: www.coe.int/t/dg4/education/roma/histoCulture_en.asp.

5 E Keen (2014) *Right to Remember: A Handbook for Education with Young People on the Roma Genocide* Council of Europe available at: https://rm.coe.int/CoERMPublicCommonSearchServices/DisplayDCTMContent?documentId=090000168008b633, p27. See also chapter 1 at xxx.

6 Available at: http://assembly.coe.int/nw/xml/XRef/Xref-XML2HTML-en.asp?fileid=14599&lang=en.

7 *Data in focus report: the Roma* (01, EU Minorities and Discrimination Survey, 2009), FRA, available at: http://fra.europa.eu/fraWebsite/attachments/EU-MIDIS_ROMA_EN.pdf.

8 *EU-Midas II Second European Union Minorities and Discrimination Survey: Roma Selected Findings,* FRA, available at: http://fra.europa.eu/en/publication/2016/eumidis-ii-roma-selected-findings.

2.8 Faced with high levels of discrimination in their countries of origin, many Roma from the newer member states of the EU migrate to older member states. However, another FRA report found that Roma who moved states encountered difficulties registering their residence and, as a result, they face similar difficulties in accessing healthcare, public housing and work in their new countries of residence.[9]

2.9 Meanwhile, as far right groups have gained political ground in recent years across Europe, hate speech against Roma has increased markedly with politicians using racist and stereotyping rhetoric.[10] This worrying trend was highlighted in July 2010, when members of the French Government used Roma migrants from Eastern Europe as scapegoats for a rise in criminality and civil unrest in the country. The then French President, Nicolas Sarkozy, said that Roma camps were a source of 'illicit trafficking, profoundly unfit living conditions, the exploitation of children for the purpose of begging, prostitution or crime' and announced that the government would dismantle Roma camps and repatriate migrants from Eastern Europe.[11]

2.10 It was against this backdrop that, on 20 October 2010, the Council of Europe issued *The Strasbourg Declaration on Roma,* which recognised that Roma across Europe continue to be 'socially and economically marginalised'. In doing so the member states adopted a list of priorities and steps aimed at securing non-discrimination, social inclusion, and the empowerment of Roma.[12]

2.11 In April 2011, the European Commission followed suit by publishing *An EU Framework for national Roma integration strategies up to 2020,* which sets out goals for Roma inclusion in education,

9 *The situation of Roma EU citizens moving to and settling in other EU member states,* FRA, 2009, available at: http://fra.europa.eu/fraWebsite/research/publications/publications_per_year/2009/pub_cr_roma-movement_en.htm. Similar conclusions were reached by the Council of Europe's Commissioner on Human Rights in *Human Rights of Roma and Travellers,* Council of Europe, 2012, available at: www.coe.int/t/commissioner/source/prems/prems79611_GBR_CouvHumanRightsOfRoma_WEB.pdf.

10 *Human rights of Roma and Travellers in Europe,* Commissioner for Human Rights, February 2012, pp40–45.

11 *Recent rise in national security discourse in Europe, the case of Roma,* Parliamentary Assembly of the Council of Europe, 2010, Doc 12386, available at: http://assembly.coe.int/nw/xml/XRef/Xref-DocDetails-EN.asp?FileID=12543&lang=EN.

12 The *Strasbourg Declaration* is available at: https://wcd.coe.int/ViewDoc.jsp?id=1691607.

employment, health and housing across the EU.[13] The Framework invited member states to present the European Commission with their strategy for Roma inclusion or for specific policy measures for the Roma within their wider social inclusion policies. Despite these efforts at the European Union, Gypsies, Travellers and Roma continue to suffer discrimination.

The Council of Europe

Introduction

2.12 The Council of Europe is a pan-European organisation based in Strasbourg which is made up of 47 member states, encompassing all countries in Europe (apart from Belarus) and including Russia and Turkey. The Council of Europe is a distinct international institution from the EU, albeit all 28 member states of the EU are also members of the Council of Europe. The UK's membership of the Council of Europe will not be directly affected by its exit from EU (Brexit).

2.13 The principal aims of the Council of Europe are to promote the rule of law and human rights through its treaties and monitoring bodies.[14] Its main organs are the Committee of Ministers and the Parliamentary Assembly.[15] The Committee of Ministers is the Council of Europe's decision-making body and monitors member states' compliance with their undertakings. It is comprised of the Minister of Foreign Affairs of each member state. It meets at Ministerial level once a year. The member states' permanent representatives meet once a week.[16] The Parliamentary Assembly of the Council of Europe (PACE) is made up of representatives of the national parliaments of each member state. It meets four times a year for a week long plenary session. It has a consultative role and also monitors member states' compliance with their undertakings under the various conventions and treaties that they have adopted.[17] Both the Committee of Ministers and PACE adopt resolutions which are useful sources of information

13 The UK's response is available at: http://ec.europa.eu/justice/discrimination/files/roma_uk_strategy_en.pdf.
14 See the preamble and Article 3 of the Statute of the Council of Europe.
15 Statute of the Council of Europe Article 10.
16 See: www.coe.int/en/web/tirana/committee-of-ministers.
17 See: www.coe.int/en/web/tirana/parliamentary-assembly.

and guidance on how the Council of Europe's various treaties should be interpreted.[18]

2.14 The Council of Europe has numerous conventions and monitoring bodies. This chapter will look at:

- the European Convention on Human Rights (ECHR or 'the convention');
- the European Court of Human Rights (ECtHR);
- the European Social Charter (ESC) and the European Committee of Social Rights;
- the Framework Convention for the Protection of National Minorities;
- the European Commission against Racism and Intolerance; and
- the Commissioner for Human Rights.

The European Convention on Human Rights

Overview

2.15 The Council of Europe's most well-known treaty is the European Convention for the Protection of Human Rights and Fundamental Freedoms, more commonly referred to as the European Convention on Human Rights, which was adopted by the founding members of the Council of Europe in 1950 in order to promote civil and political rights. The convention sets out legally binding obligations on contracting parties to guarantee that the rights enshrined within it are available to everyone in their jurisdiction. Some of the main rights protected by the convention and its protocols are:

- Article 2: The right to life
- Article 3: Prohibition of torture, inhuman and degrading treatment or punishment
- Article 4: Prohibition of slavery and forced labour
- Article 5: The right to liberty and security
- Article 6: The right to a fair trial
- Article 7: No punishment without law
- Article 8: The right to respect for private and family life, home and correspondence
- Article 9: Freedom of thought, conscience and religion
- Article 10: Freedom of expression
- Article 11: Freedom of assembly and association

18 Reports and resolutions can be found on the search engines of the Committee of Ministers and PACE on the Council of Europe's website: www.coe.int.

- Article 12: The right to marry
- Article 13: The right to an effective remedy
- Article 14: Prohibition of discrimination in the enjoyment of the rights set forth in the Convention
- Protocol 1:
  - Article 1: The right to peaceful enjoyment of possessions
  - Article 2: The right to education
  - Article 3: The right to free elections
- Protocol 4:
  - Article 4: Prohibition of collective expulsions of aliens[19]
- Protocol 12:
  - Article 1: General prohibition of discrimination[20]
- Protocol 13:
  - Article 1: Prohibition of the death penalty in all circumstances

2.16 The ECtHR was established in 1959 and determines applications from individuals or states alleging violations of one or more of the rights contained within the ECHR. It is based in Strasbourg.

The Human Rights Act 1998

2.17 Article 1 of the convention requires that its contracting parties secure to everyone within their jurisdiction the rights and freedoms contained within the convention. Individuals, non-governmental organisations (NGOs) and groups of individuals claiming to be a victim of a violation of one or more rights contained within the convention can make an application to the ECtHR in Strasbourg,[21] when all domestic remedies have been exhausted.[22]

2.18 Prior to 2000, it was not possible to rely upon the convention before the domestic courts in the UK, although an application could be taken to ECtHR once all domestic remedies had been exhausted. The main purpose of the Human Rights Act (HRA) 1998,[23] which entered into force on 2 October 2000, was to incorporate parts of the convention into UK law – giving UK domestic courts the duty to protect individuals' human rights – thereby making the convention

19 The UK has signed but not ratified Protocol 4.

20 The UK is not a signatory to Protocol 12.

21 ECHR Article 34.

22 ECHR Article 35.

23 See appendix A.

directly accessible to people in this country.[24] The HRA 1998 incorporates Articles 2–12 and Article 14 of the convention, Articles 1–3 of Protocol 1 and Article 1 of Protocol 13 into domestic law.[25] In 2015, the Conservative government pledged within its manifesto to repeal the HRA 1998 and replace it with a British Bill of Rights.[26] In its 2017 Manifesto, the Conservative party stated that it was not going to repeal or replace the HRA 1998 while the process of Brexit is underway but will consider the human rights legal framework once the process of Brexit has concluded.[27]

2.19 The HRA 1998 imposes duties on all of the 'public authorities' with which Gypsies and Travellers are frequently in contact, including:

- government ministers and departments;
- the Planning Inspectorate;
- local authorities;
- the police;
- education authorities;
- health authorities;
- social services departments; and
- the courts.[28]

In particular, HRA 1998 s6(1) makes it unlawful for a 'public authority' to act in a way which is incompatible with a convention right unless mandated to do so by legislation which cannot itself be read compatibly with convention rights.[29]

2.20 HRA 1998 s3(1) requires all legislation to be read and given effect in a way which is compatible with convention rights, 'so far as it is possible to do so'. HRA 1998 s2(1)(a) requires domestic courts to take into account judgments, decisions or advisory opinions of the ECtHR. HRA 1998 s4 empowers the High Court, Court of Appeal and Supreme Court to make a declaration of incompatibility in circumstances where the court is satisfied that a statutory provision is incompatible with a convention right.

24 See Rights Brought Home: The Human Rights Bill presented to Parliament in October 1997, available at: www.gov.uk/government/uploads/system/uploads/attachment_data/file/263526/rights.pdf.

25 HRA 1998 s1(1).

26 Conservative Party Manifesto 2015, p75.

27 *Forward, Together: our Plan for a Stronger Britain and Prosperous Future: Conservative Party and Unionist Party Manifesto* 2017, p37, available at: www.conservatives.com/manifesto.

28 HRA 1998 s6(3)(a), (b).

29 HRA 1998 s6(2).

2.21 Many of the powers exercised by public authorities which most directly affect Gypsies and Travellers are broad discretionary powers conferred by statutes in wide and open-ended terms (and clarified or further detailed in government guidance). Such powers must be interpreted so as to be compatible with convention rights, which means that the discretion which they give to public authorities must be exercised in a way which respects the convention rights of Gypsies and Travellers. To give an example, Town and Country Planning Act (TCPA) 1990 s187B confers very broad discretions on a local planning authority and the court to, respectively, apply for and grant injunctions to restrain breaches of planning control. HRA 1998 s3(1) requires that these discretionary powers be exercised in a way which is compatible with the convention rights of the Gypsies and Travellers concerned in any decision. Since the discretion-conferring language of TCPA 1990 s187B is in very broad terms, and nothing in it compels a planning authority or court to apply for or grant injunctions in breach of Article 8, it is clearly 'possible' for the provision to be interpreted compatibly with Article 8.

2.22 Though many of the cases in this chapter concentrate on planning permission and the enforcement of planning control, the principles that can be derived from cases decided by the ECtHR and domestic courts are of wider application.[30]

Relevant convention rights

2.23 The two convention rights which are or of the most particular relevance to Gypsies and Travellers living in the UK are those protected by Article 8 (right to respect for private and family life and home); and Article 14 (prohibition of discrimination in the enjoyment of other convention rights). However, it is worth noting that many of the cases brought to the ECtHR by Roma from across Europe have involved allegations of violations of other rights protected by the convention. Article 2 (right to life) cases have involved the use of lethal force by police[31] and deaths in police custody.[32] The ECtHR has found that there have been breaches of the procedural limb of Article 2 where states have failed to conduct effective investigations into attacks that

30 See chapter 4 for a discussion on planning law.

31 For example: *Nachova and others v Bulgaria* (2006) 42 EHRR 43; and *Guerdner and others v France 68780/10*, 17 April 2014.

32 For example: *Anguelova v Bulgaria* (2004) 38 EHRR 31; *Ognyanova and Choban v Bulgaria* (2007) 44 EHRR 7; and *Mižigárová v Slovakia*, App No 74832/01, 14 December 2010.

have led to death.[33] Likewise, Article 3 (prohibition of torture, inhuman and degrading treatment or punishment) complaints have been made about police brutality[34] as well as the national authorities' failure to conduct proper investigations into allegations of police brutality[35] or attacks by private individuals against Roma.[36]

2.24 The ECtHR has considered a number of cases concerning the treatment of Roma moving to other member states of the Council of Europe. The ECtHR found a violation of Article 3 (inhuman and degrading treatment) in *VM and others v Belgium*[37] where the Belgian authorities allowed an asylum seeking family of Roma origin from Serbia to remain in conditions of extreme poverty for four weeks. The ECtHR considered Articles 3 and 4 (prohibition of slavery and servitude) in *M and others v Italy and Bulgaria*[38] where Roma parents of Bulgarian nationality complained that their daughter had been forced to work and steal, and was sexually abused at the hands of another Roma family. Although the ECtHR declared the complaint under Article 4 to be inadmissible as there was insufficient evidence that she had been trafficked, it went on to find that there had been a violation of Article 3 under the procedural limb because the authorities had failed to properly investigate the applicants' complaint that their daughter had been sexually abused. In *Čonka v Belgium*,[39] the ECtHR held that there had been a violation of Article 4 of Protocol No 4 (prohibition of collective expulsion of aliens), where the Belgian authorities detained and then expelled a group of Slovakian nationals of Roma origin. The procedure followed was not sufficient for the ECtHR to eliminate doubt that the expulsion might have been collective.[40]

33 For example: *Fedorchenko and Lozenko v Ukraine*, App No 387/03, 20 September 2012.

34 For example: *Bekos and Koutropoulos v Greece* (2006) 43 EHRR 2; *Stoica v Romania* (2011) 52 EHRR 29; and *Lingurar v Romania*, App No 48474/14, 16 April 2019.

35 For example: *Jašar v The former Yugoslav Republic of Macedonia* App No 69908/01, 15 February 2007; and *Lingurar v Romania*, App No 48474/14, 16 April 2019.

36 For example: *Šečić v Croatia* (2009) 49 EHRR 18; and *Burlya and others v Ukraine*, App No 3289/10, 6 November 2018.

37 App No 60125/11, 7 July 2015.

38 App No 40020/03, 31 July 2012.

39 (2002) 34 EHRR 54.

40 (2002) 34 EHRR 54 at para 62. NB the UK has signed but not ratified Protocol No 4 to the convention.

2.25 Article 6 protects the right to a fair and public hearing within a reasonable time. In *Paraskeva Todorova v Bulgaria*,[41] the ECtHR held that a sentence of three years imprisonment imposed upon a Roma woman breached Article 14 (prohibition of discrimination) in conjunction with Article 6 (the right to a fair trial). The domestic sentencing court had commented on the applicant's ethnic origin, among the personal details used to identify her, and then refused to suspend the sentence on the grounds that there was 'an impression of impunity, especially among members of minority groups, who consider that a suspended sentence is not a sentence at all'.[42]

2.26 In *Oršuš and others v Croatia*,[43] a case concerning discrimination of Roma children in education, the Grand Chamber found that there had been a violation of Article 6(1) because the period of four years that it had taken the Croatian Constitutional Court to conclude domestic proceedings was excessive.[44] Reasonableness of the length of proceedings is to be assessed in light of the particular circumstances of the case taking into account the complexity of the case.[45] In *Moore and Coates v Secretary of State for Communities and Local Government*,[46] the High Court considered the decision by the secretary of state to recover planning appeals for determination by himself where they related to proposals for caravan pitches within the Green Belt. This had the effect of causing considerable delay in the hearing and determination of those appeals. The majority of appeals were by Romani Gypsies and Irish Travellers. The judge found that the delays amounted to a breach of Article 6 because the secretary of state had failed to show that the delays were necessary in these cases. The delays caused were not a proportionate response to the issues at hand.[47]

Article 8 decision-making

Overview

2.27 Article 8(1) provides that:

41 App No 37193/07, 25 March 2010.

42 App No 37193/07 para 10.

43 (2011) 52 EHRR 7.

44 (2011) 52 EHRR 7 at paras 109–110.

45 (2011) 52 EHRR 7 at para 108.

46 *Moore and Coates v Secretary of State for Communities and Local Government and Bromley LBC and Dartford BC and the Equality and Human Rights Commission* [2015] JPL 762.

47 [2015] JPL 762 at para 149.

(1) Everyone has the right to respect for his private and family life, his home and his correspondence.

2.28 It is important to note that Article 8 rights are not absolute and are qualified by Article 8(2) which provides that there shall be no interference with the exercise of those rights by a public authority except where the interference:

- is in accordance with the law;
- pursues a legitimate aim; and
- is necessary in a democratic society in the interests of national security, public safety or the economic wellbeing of the country, for the prevention of disorder or crime, for the protection of health or morals, or for the protection of the rights and freedoms of others.

2.29 The ECtHR adopts a structured approach to assessing claims that a contracting state has violated Article 8, which it has developed in a number of cases brought by Roma, including cases brought against the UK.[48]

1) Whether there has been an interference with rights protected by Article 8(1)

2.30 Cases brought by Roma engaging Article 8 rights have involved challenging the refusal of planning permission for caravan sites and eviction action taken against those living on unauthorised developments and encampments and other dwellings. All these cases concern the loss of a 'home' within the meaning of Article 8. It is also clear from the ECtHR's case-law that the question of whether a dwelling/property can be classed as a 'home' for the purposes of Article 8 is a question of fact and this does not depend on the lawfulness of the occupation under domestic law. The fact that the home was established unlawfully in the first place does not prevent it from falling within the scope of Article 8.[49]

2.31 In *Buckley v UK*[50] a case concerning the refusal to grant a Romani Gypsy retrospective planning permission for three caravans stationed

48 *Buckley v UK* (1997) 23 EHRR 101; *Chapman v UK* (2001) 33 EHRR 18; *Connors v UK* (2005) 40 EHRR 9; *Buckland v UK* (2013) 56 EHRR 16; *Connors v UK* (2005) 40 EHRR 9.

49 *Buckley* (1997) 23 EHRR 101 at paras 52–54; and *McCann v UK* (2008) 47 EHRR 40 at para 46; *Yordanova and others v Bulgaria*, App No 25446/06, judgment date 24 April 2012, at para 103; and *Winterstein and others v France*, App No 27013/07, judgment date 17 October 2013 at para 141.

50 *Buckley v UK* (1997) 23 EHRR 101.

on her land and enforcement action to remove the caravans, the ECtHR held that the case concerned the applicant's right to respect for her 'home' and considered it unnecessary to decide whether it also concerned the applicant's right to respect for her 'private life' and 'family life'.[51] By contrast, in the later case of *Chapman v UK*[52] the ECtHR held:

> [T]he applicant's occupation of her caravan is an integral part of her ethnic identity as a Gypsy, reflecting the long tradition of that minority of following a travelling lifestyle . . . Measures which affect the applicant's stationing of her caravans have therefore a wider impact than on the right to respect for home. They also affect her ability to maintain her identity as a Gypsy and to lead her private and family life in accordance with that tradition.

2.32 The ECtHR also observed that this was the case even though many Gypsies no longer live a wholly nomadic existence and increasingly settle for longer periods in one place in order to facilitate, for example, the education of their children.[53]

2.33 The ECtHR's clear finding that measures concerning Gypsies' stationing of their caravans affect not merely the right to respect for their 'home' in the narrow sense, but their ability as members of an ethnic minority to continue to live according to their traditional travelling lifestyle, is of considerable significance to the approach which should be taken by public authorities when determining whether any interference with such an important right is justified in all the circumstances: the more important the convention right, the greater the onus of justification on the public authority and therefore the greater the scrutiny that should be afforded to such justification by the courts.

2) Interference in accordance with the law

2.34 In *Chapman* it was conceded that the various measures which had been taken by the planning authorities that interfered with the applicant's Article 8 rights were 'in accordance with the law' for the purposes of Article 8.[54] The requirement that any interference with Article 8 rights be in accordance with the law means that there must

51 (1997) 23 EHRR 101 at paras 54–55.

52 (2001) 33 EHRR 18.

53 (2001) 33 EHRR 18 at para 73. See also *Connors v UK* (2005) 40 EHRR 9 at para 68; *Winterstein and others v France*, App No 27013/07, judgment date 17 October 2013 at para 142.

54 (2001) 33 EHRR 18 at para 79.

not only exist a formal legal basis for the interference (for example, a statutory discretion), but that any law which confers a broad discretion must also give sufficient indication as to the scope of that discretion. As the ECtHR stated in *Malone v UK*:

> [It] would be contrary to the rule of law for the legal discretion granted to the executive to be expressed in terms of an unfettered power. Consequently, the law must indicate the scope of any such discretion conferred on the competent authorities and the manner of its exercise with sufficient clarity, having regard to the legitimate aim of the measure in question, to give the individual adequate protection against arbitrary interference.[55]

2.35 Generally, a public authority's powers in relation to Gypsies and Travellers – for example, its powers of enforcement in relation to unauthorised developments – will satisfy both aspects of this requirement. If the authority is in any doubt as to whether a particular power which it intends to exercise satisfies this requirement, however, it should ask itself whether the provision in question satisfies the *Malone* test – that is, whether the provision indicates the scope of the discretion conferred on the authority, and the manner of its exercise, with sufficient clarity to give individuals in the position of those affected adequate protection against arbitrary interference.

3) Legitimate aim

2.36 The ECtHR has held in a number of cases that it is legitimate for authorities to seek to regain possession of land from persons who have no legal right to occupy it.[56] In *Chapman*, the government argued that the measures in question pursued the enforcement of planning controls which were in the interests of the economic well-being of the country and the preservation of the environment and public health. The ECtHR accepted the applicant's argument that the government had not put forward any detail to substantiate the aims allegedly pursued; however, it found that the measures pursued the legitimate aim of protecting the 'rights of others' through the preservation of the environment, and did not find it necessary to determine whether any other aims were involved.[57]

55 (1985) 7 EHRR 14 at para 68.

56 See, for example: *Connors v UK* (2005) 40 EHRR 9 at para 69; *McCann v UK* (2008) 47 EHRR 40 at para 48; *Yordanova v Bulgaria*, App No 25446/06, judgment date 5 June 2012 at para 111.

57 (2001) 33 EHRR 399 at paras 80–82.

2.37 Improvement of the urban environment by removing unsightly and substandard buildings and replacing them with modern dwellings meeting the relevant architectural and technical requirements was held to be a legitimate aim in the case of *Yordanova v Bulgaria*. Additionally, the ECtHR acknowledged that 'there is a legitimate public interest in taking measures to cope with hazards such as those that may stem from an unlawful settlement of makeshift houses lacking sewage and sanitary facilities'.[58]

2.38 Generally, the planning enforcement powers available to local authorities will pursue the legitimate aim of protecting the rights of others in the sense of environmental protection. However, it remains necessary for the authority to be satisfied in any particular case that the enforcement measure is genuinely pursued for such a legitimate aim, and not for some other illegitimate purpose such as merely appeasing a vociferous or politically important local population or group which is objecting to the particular development.[59]

4) Necessary in a democratic society

2.39 The next stage in the ECtHR's structured analysis involves consideration of the question whether an interference with Article 8 rights is 'necessary in a democratic society'. An interference will be considered 'necessary in a democratic society' if it answers a 'pressing social need' and, in particular, if it is *proportionate* to the legitimate aim pursued.[60]

Proportionality – general principles

2.40 The following general principles can be extracted from the judgments of the ECtHR concerning the assessment of the proportionality of an interference with Article 8 rights and particularly those which concern measures taken against Gypsies and Travellers to enforce planning control or those which involve the loss of a home.

The margin of appreciation

2.41 In principle, the national authorities enjoy a margin of appreciation 'insofar as the exercise of discretion involving a multitude of local factors is inherent in the choice and implementation of planning

58 App No 25446/06, 24 April 2012 at para 114.

59 *Yordanova v Bulgaria*, App No 25446/06, 24 April 2012 at para 115.

60 *Chapman v UK* (2001) 33 EHRR 18 at para 90; *Connors v UK* (2005) 40 EHRR 9 at para 81.

policies'.[61] The ECtHR is not well equipped to challenge judgments which have been made on detailed questions of local fact by a decision maker who has visited the site and heard the evidence. It recognises that national authorities are, in principle, better placed than an international court to evaluate local needs and conditions. Planning inspectors, for example, are much better placed to assess the impact of a particular use on the particular locality and, therefore, to assess the legitimacy of planning objections to that use. It is primarily a matter of relative institutional competence.

2.42 The scope of the margin of appreciation will be different in each case. The width of the margin of appreciation given to national authorities will vary according to the following factors:

1) the nature of the convention right in issue;
2) its importance to the individual;
3) the nature of the activities restricted; and
4) the nature of the aim pursued by the restrictions.[62]

Social and economic policies

2.43 The margin of appreciation will be wider in the application of social and economic policies. In both *Buckley*[63] and *Chapman*,[64] cases which concerned the refusal to grant retrospective planning permission for caravan sites on land owned by the applicants, the ECtHR held that the national authorities had a wide margin of appreciation, holding in *Buckley* that '[i]n so far as the exercise of discretion involving a multitude of local factors is inherent in the choice and implementation of planning policies, the national authorities in principle enjoy a wide margin of appreciation'.[65]

Key rights

2.44 The margin of appreciation will be narrower where an individual's effective enjoyment of intimate or key rights are at stake.[66] This is because Article 8:

61 *Chapman v UK* (2001) 33 EHRR 399 at para 92; and *Buckley v UK* (1997) 23 EHRR 101 at para 75.
62 *Buckley v UK* (1997) 23 EHRR 101 at para 76; and *Chapman* (2001) 33 EHRR 18 at para 91.
63 *Buckley v UK* (1997) 23 EHRR 101.
64 *Chapman v UK* (2001) 33 EHRR 18.
65 *Buckley v UK* (1997) 23 EHRR 101 at para 75.
66 *Yordanova and others v Bulgaria*, App No 25446/06, 24 April 2012 at para 118.

> . . . concerns rights of central importance to the individual's identity, self-determination, physical and moral integrity, maintenance of relationships with others and a settled and secure place in the community.[67]

Importantly, the ECtHR has emphasised that the loss of one's home is the most extreme form of interference with the right to respect for the home.[68]

> Where general social and economic policy considerations arise in the context of article 8 itself, the scope of the margin of appreciation will depend on the context of the case with particular significance attached to the extent of the intrusion into the personal sphere of the person concerned.[69]

2.45 The ECtHR drew a distinction in *Connors* between a situation involving the enforcement of planning control as in *Buckley* and *Chapman*, on the one hand, and where a family had been summarily evicted from a site that they had lawfully lived on for 14–15 years, as was the case in *Connors*. It was held that the serious interference with the Article 8 rights in *Connors* required:

> particularly weighty reasons of public interest by way of a justification and the margin of appreciation to be afforded to the national authorities must be regarded as correspondingly narrowed'[70]

The importance of procedural safeguards

2.46 It is clear from the case-law of the ECtHR that the requirement under Article 8 that the interference be 'necessary in a democratic society' raises a question of procedure as well as substance.[71] In determining whether the state has remained within its margin of appreciation when creating the regulatory framework, the ECtHR regards the procedural safeguards available to the individual as being 'especially material'.[72] In particular, it will:

67 *Connors v UK* (2005) 40 EHRR 9 at para 82.

68 *Yordanova and others v Bulgaria*, App No 25446/06, 24 April 2012 at para 118; *Buckland v UK* (2013) 56 EHRR 16 at para 65.

69 *Connors v UK* (2005) 40 EHRR 9 at para 82.

70 *Connors v UK* (2005) 40 EHRR 9 at para 82.

71 *Buckland v UK* (2013) 56 EHRR 16 at para 64.

72 *Chapman v UK* (2001) 33 EHRR 399 at para 92; and *Buckley v UK* (1997) 23 EHRR 101 at paras 76–77. See also *Connors v UK* (2005) 40 EHRR 9 and *Kay v UK* (2012) 54 EHRR 30 at para 67; and the commentary in chapter 3 at 3.22.

> ... examine whether the decision-making process leading to measures of interference was fair and such as to afford due respect to the interests safeguarded to the individual by article 8.[73]

2.47 Particular attention is paid to procedural safeguards in the decision-making process to compensate for the less intense standard of review adopted in relation to the substance of the measure which interferes with convention rights.

2.48 Whether, in a particular case, an individual has yet had the opportunity of taking a procedural step which they wish to take, such as exercising a right of appeal to the secretary of state against the refusal of planning permission, should, therefore, be carefully considered by a local planning authority when deciding whether or not to take enforcement action. Proceeding straight to enforcement, before allowing the Gypsy or Traveller an opportunity to persuade a planning inspector to grant planning permission may, therefore, be found to be precipitative.

Access to an independent tribunal

2.49 The ECtHR has held in a number of recent cases that since the loss of one's home is one of the most extreme forms of interference with the right under Article 8 to respect for one's home, any person at risk of an interference of this magnitude should in principle be entitled to have the proportionality and reasonableness of the measure determined by an independent tribunal.[74] The availability of judicial review proceedings will not necessarily be sufficient where the issues involve a dispute of facts between the parties. Judicial review is not well adapted for the resolution of sensitive factual questions, which are better left to the county court.[75] This applies regardless of whether or not the person has a legal right to occupy the property under domestic law.[76] Where the proportionality of the measure interfering with the Article 8 right to a home, has been raised by an applicant, the court should examine them in detail and provide adequate reasons.[77]

73 *Chapman v UK* (2001) 33 EHRR 399 at para 92; and *Buckley v UK* (1997) 23 EHRR 101 at paras 76–77.

74 *McCann v UK* (2008) 47 EHRR 40 at para 50; *Kay and others v UK* (2012) 54 EHRR 30 at para 68.

75 *Connors v UK* (2005) 40 EHRR 9 at para 92; and *McCann v UK* (2008) 47 EHRR 40 at para 53.

76 *Kay and others v UK* (2012) 54 EHRR 30 at para 68; *Yordanova and others v Bulgaria*, App No 25446/06, 24 April 2012 at para 118; and *Winterstein and others v France*, App No 27013/07, 17 October 2013 at para 148.

77 *Yordanova and others v Bulgaria* at para 118; *Winterstein and others v France* at para 148.

2.50 Thus in *Connors*, the ECtHR was not convinced of the necessity of a statutory scheme which permitted the summary eviction of a family without there being any burden to provide reasons liable to be examined by an independent tribunal. The eviction had not been attended by the requisite procedural safeguards as there was no proper justification for the serious interference with the right notwithstanding the margin of appreciation afforded to the national authorities.[78]

Requirement to give reasons

2.51 The ECtHR has held that where national authorities (including courts and tribunals) uphold a decision to evict an applicant without giving an explanation or fail to put forward reasons why the eviction is necessary, the ECtHR 'may draw the inference that the state's legitimate interest in being able to control it property should come second to the right to respect to a person's home'.[79]

A positive obligation to Gypsies, Travellers and Roma

2.52 The ECtHR has expressly recognised that the vulnerable position of Gypsies and Travellers as a minority means that some special consideration should be given to their needs and their different lifestyle, both in the relevant regulatory planning framework and in arriving at decisions in particular cases.[80] There is thus a positive obligation imposed on states by Article 8 to 'facilitate the Gypsy way of life'.[81]

2.53 There is an additional obligation to take into account the situation of 'outcast' communities and socially disadvantaged groups. The ECtHR has held that '[s]uch social groups, regardless of the ethnic origin of their members, may need assistance in order to be able effectively to enjoy the same rights as the majority population'. The needs of the group must be one of the relevant factors in the proportionality assessment.[82]

2.54 On the other hand, the state does not have a positive obligation to provide housing and the ECtHR has made it clear that a state's

78 (2005) 40 EHRR 9 at paras 94–95. See also *Buckland v UK* (2013) 56 EHRR 16 at para 70.

79 *Yordanova and others v Bulgaria*, App No 25446/06, 24 April 2012 at para 118.

80 *Buckley v UK* (1997) 23 EHRR 101 at paras 76, 80, 84.

81 *Chapman v UK* (2001) 33 EHRR 18 at para 96. However, note that in the homelessness case of *Steward v Royal Borough of Kingston upon Thames* [2007] EWCA Civ 565, the Court of Appeal was not convinced that the positive obligation to facilitate the Gypsy way of life could be extended to cover the lifestyle of New Travellers.

82 *Yordanova and others v Bulgaria*, App No 25446/06, 24 April 2012 at para 129.

decision as to whether it should provide housing to everyone is a political and not a judicial decision.[83] However, an obligation to secure shelter to particularly vulnerable individuals may flow from Article 8 in exceptional circumstances.[84] Thus, in the case of *Moldovan v Romania (No 2)* the court concluded that the right to respect for private and family life was violated by the state's failure to rebuild Romani family homes adequately after a mob of villagers, with police complicity, had burned them to the ground.[85]

Relevant factual matters

2.55 The most important factual matters which are taken into account by the ECtHR when applying its general principles to the concrete facts of a particular case in order to assess the proportionality of an interference are: a) whether the site was established lawfully, and b) whether alternative accommodation is available. If the home was established lawfully, this factor will weigh against requiring the individual to move on; conversely, where the establishment of a home in a particular place was unlawful, the position of the individual objecting to an enforcement measure is less strong. In *Chapman*, the ECtHR held that it would be 'slow to grant protection to those, who in conscious defiance of the prohibitions of the law, establish a home on an environmentally protected site'.[86] To do otherwise would act to the detriment of the protection of environmental rights of others in the community. The interference is more serious if no alternative accommodation is available. The more suitable the alternative accommodation is, the less serious the breach. The evaluation of the suitability of alternative accommodation will involve a consideration of, on the one hand, the particular needs of the person concerned and, on the other, the rights of the local community to environmental protection.

2.56 The case of *Yordanova v Bulgaria* provides us with an example of these principles. The ECtHR found that there had been a breach of Article 8 where the authorities served a removal order in 2005 on Roma residents who had been illegally occupying land in an area of Sofia since the 1960s, where the homes did not meet the basic requirements of the relevant safety and construction regulations. The ECtHR took into account the following factors:

83 *Chapman v UK* (2001) 33 EHRR 18 at para 99.

84 *Yordanova and others v Bulgaria*, App No 25446/06, 24 April 2012 at para 130.

85 (2007) 44 EHRR 16 at para 109.

86 *Chapman v UK* (2001) 33 EHRR 18 at para 102.

- the length of time that the applicants had been on the land without any action having been taken against them;
- the failure of the authorities to give reasons for the order other than stating that the applicants lived on the land unlawfully;
- the refusal of the domestic courts to hear arguments about proportionality and the lengthy period of time that the families had established themselves in the area;
- the failure of the authorities to consider the risk that the applicants would become homeless; and
- the refusal of the authorities to consider approaches specifically tailored towards the Roma community on the grounds that this would amount to discrimination against the majority population.[87]

2.57 The ECtHR held that the underprivileged status of the applicant group 'must be a weighty factor in considering approaches to dealing with their unlawful settlement' and found that in the circumstances the government had failed to establish that the removal was necessary in a democratic society.[88]

2.58 In *Winterstein and others v France*[89] the ECtHR held that there had been a violation of Article 8 in circumstances where the French courts had ordered the eviction of a number of Travellers who had been on a site for between five and thirty years. Although the penalty of a daily fine of €200 for remaining on the land was not enforced, a large number of people left the site and only four families were rehoused by the state. The domestic tribunals had failed to take into account the length of time that the families had been settled on the site and the de facto tolerance of their presence.

2.59 In both cases, the ECtHR concluded that cases involving the eviction of a whole community, which has been settled for a long period of time, should be treated differently to the eviction of an individual illegally occupying a property.[90] The principle of proportionality required that particular attention be paid to the fact that the families would become homeless as a consequence of the expulsion from the land. In *Winterstein* the ECtHR referred to a number of Council of Europe texts which stress the need, in cases of forced eviction of Roma, to provide them with alternative accommodation (except in the case of force majeure), due to their position as a vulnerable

87 App No 25446/06, 5 June 2012 at paras 120–134.

88 App No 25446/06, 5 June 2012 at para 133.

89 App No 27013/07, 17 October 2014.

90 *Yordanova v Bulgaria* App No 25446/06, 5 June 2012 at para 121; *Winterstein* App No 27013/07, 17 October 2014 para 150.

minority[91] and found that the authorities had not paid sufficient consideration to the needs of the families who had requested alternative accommodation.

Other Article 8 cases

2.60 Article 8 cases have not just involved the right to a private or home life in the context of accommodation. For example, in *Király and Dömötör v Hungary*[92] the ECtHR found that the Hungarian authorities had failed to protect the psychological integrity of the Roma applicants, and consequently their Article 8 right to a private life, following an openly racist anti-Roma demonstration, involving sporadic acts of violence, which went almost entirely without legal consequences for the perpetrators. In *VC v Slovakia*[93] the ECtHR found that there had been a violation of the Roma applicant's Article 8 right to a private and family life after she had been sterilised without her informed consent. It also held that the staff at the hospital had violated her physical integrity and caused her psychological harm in violation of Article 3.

Article 8 and relevant domestic decisions post-Human Rights Act 1998

2.61 The effect of the duties imposed on public authorities by the HRA 1998 has been considered in a number of cases before our domestic courts. As will be seen below, the approach taken by domestic courts in each of those cases has depended to a very great extent upon whether the court has been asked to review the proportionality of a decision taken by a public body (for example, a decision to compulsorily purchase land on which Gypsies or Travellers are encamped) or whether it has been asked to exercise its own original jurisdiction (for example, in a case where a local authority seeks a planning injunction to prevent Gypsies or Travellers from living on their land in breach of planning control).

Proportionality review of decisions of public bodies

2.62 Following the entry into force of the HRA 1998 in 2000, there were a number of decisions in which the House of Lords and the Court of Appeal explained how domestic courts should review a decision

91 App No 27013/07 para 159, referring to Recommendation (2005) 4 of the Committee of Ministers; and Resolution 1740(2010) of the Parliamentary Assembly.

92 App No 10851/13, 17 January 2017.

93 (2014) 59 EHRR 29.

taken by a public body which interferes with an individual's convention rights. It is now clear that the approach that must be adopted in such cases is more sophisticated than the traditional *Wednesbury* grounds of review.

2.63 In *R (Mahmood) v Secretary of State for the Home Department*,[94] an immigration case, Laws LJ stated that, even where the courts are in as good a position as the secretary of state to decide an issue which engages convention rights, they must not do so as if they were his or her surrogate. The statutory decision maker must be entitled to a 'margin of discretion'. In the same case Lord Phillips MR identified the following three principles:

1) Even where human rights were at stake, the role of the court was supervisory. The court would only intervene where the decision fell outside the range of responses open to a reasonable decision-maker.
2) In conducting a review of a decision affecting human rights, the court would subject the decision to most anxious scrutiny.
3) Where the decision interfered with human rights, the court would require substantial justification for the interference in order to be satisfied that the response fell within the range of responses open to a decision-maker. The more substantial the interference, the more that was required to justify it.[95]

Lord Phillips explained his first principle as follows:

> 38. . . . The court does not substitute its own decision for that of the executive. It reviews the decision of the executive to see whether it is permitted by law – in this instance the Human Rights Act 1998. In performing this exercise the court will bear in mind that, just as individual states enjoy a margin of appreciation which permits them to respond, within the law, in a manner which is not uniform, so there will often be an area of discretion permitted to the executive of a country before a response can be demonstrated to infringe the Convention.[96]

Expanding on his third principle, Lord Phillips said:

> 40. When anxiously scrutinising an executive decision that interferes with human rights, the court will ask the question, applying an objective test, whether the decision-maker could reasonably have concluded that the interference was necessary to achieve one or more of the legitimate aims recognised by the Convention. When considering the test of neces-

94 [2001] 1 WLR 840.
95 [2001] 1 WLR 840 at para 37.
96 [2001] 1 WLR 840 at para 38.

sity in the relevant context, the court must take into account the European jurisprudence in accordance with section 2 of the 1998 Act.[97]

2.64 In *R (Daly) v Secretary of State for the Home Department*,[98] a case where the House of Lords was asked to consider whether a policy relating to the search of prisoners' cells breached the Article 8 right of prisoners to respect for their correspondence, Lord Steyn clarified what had been said in *Mahmood* by Lord Phillips in the first sentence of the last passage quoted above. Lord Steyn said:

> 26. The explanation of the Master of the Rolls in the first sentence of the cited passage requires clarification. It is couched in language reminiscent of the traditional *Wednesbury* ground of review (*Associated Provincial Picture Houses Ltd v Wednesbury Corporation* [1948] 1 KB 223), and in particular the adaptation of that test in terms of heightened scrutiny in cases involving fundamental rights as formulated in *R v Ministry of Defence Ex p Smith* [1996] QB 517 554E–G per Sir Thomas Bingham MR. There is a material difference between the *Wednesbury* and *Smith* grounds of review and the approach of proportionality applicable in respect of review where convention rights are at stake.

2.65 Having provided that clarification, Lord Steyn stated that:

> 27. The contours of proportionality are familiar. In *de Freitas v Permanent Secretary of Ministry of Agriculture, Fisheries, Lands and Housing* [1999] 1 AC 69 the Privy Council adopted a three stage test. Lord Clyde observed, at p 80, that in determining whether a limitation (by an act, rule or decision) is arbitrary or excessive the court should ask itself:
>
>> Whether: (i) the legislative objective is sufficiently important to justify limiting a fundamental right; (ii) the measures designed to meet the legislative objective are rationally connected to it; and (iii) the means used to impair the right or freedom are no more than is necessary to accomplish the objective.

2.66 While Lord Steyn remarked that most cases would be decided the same way whichever approach was adopted, he made the point that the intensity of review is somewhat greater under the proportionality approach and highlighted three particular differences between them:

> 27. . . . First, the doctrine of proportionality may require the reviewing court to assess the balance which the decision maker has struck, not merely whether it is within the range of rational or reasonable decisions. Secondly, the proportionality test may go further than traditional grounds of review inasmuch as it may require attention to be directed to the relative

97 [2001] 1 WLR 840 at paras 37–40.

98 [2001] 2 AC 532.

weight accorded to interests and considerations. Thirdly, even the heightened scrutiny test developed in *R v Ministry of Defence, Ex p Smith* [1996] QB 517, 554 is not necessarily appropriate to the protection of human rights. It will be recalled that in *Smith* the Court of Appeal reluctantly felt compelled to reject a limitation on homosexuals in the army. The challenge based on article 8 of the Convention for the Protection of Human Rights and Fundamental Freedoms (the right to respect for private and family life) foundered on the threshold required even by the anxious scrutiny test. The European Court of Human Rights came to the opposite conclusion: *Smith and Grady v United Kingdom* (1999) 29 EHRR 493. The court concluded, at p543, para 138:

> The threshold at which the High Court and the Court of Appeal could find the Ministry of Defence policy irrational was placed so high that it effectively excluded any consideration by the domestic courts of the question of whether the interference with the applicants' rights answered a pressing social need or was proportionate to the national security and public order aims pursued, principles which lie at the heart of the court's analysis of complaints under article 8 of the Convention.

In other words, the intensity of the review, in similar cases, is guaranteed by the twin requirements that the limitation of the right was necessary in a democratic society, in the sense of meeting a pressing social need, and the question whether the interference was really proportionate to the legitimate aim being pursued.

28. The differences in approach between the traditional grounds of review and the proportionality approach may therefore sometimes yield different results. It is therefore important that cases involving convention rights must be analysed in the correct way. This does not mean that there has been a shift to merits review. On the contrary, as Professor Jowell [2000] PL 671, 681 has pointed out the respective roles of judges and administrators are fundamentally distinct and will remain so. To this extent the general tenor of the observations in *Mahmood* [2001] 1 WLR 840 are correct. And Laws LJ rightly emphasised in *Mahmood* at p847, para 18 'that the intensity of review in a public law case will depend on the subject matter in hand'. This is so even in cases involving Convention rights. In law context is everything.

2.67 In *R (Samaroo) v Secretary of State for the Home Department*[99] the Court of Appeal considered whether a decision to deport the claimant breached his rights protected by Article 8 of the convention. Having referred to the House of Lords decision in *Daly*, Dyson LJ concluded that the issue of proportionality:

99 [2001] EWCA Civ 1139.

> ... will usually have to be considered in two distinct stages. At the first stage, the question is: can the objective of the measure be achieved by means which are less interfering of an individual's right? ... At the second stage, it is assumed that the means employed to achieve the legitimate aim are necessary in the sense that they are the least intrusive of Convention Rights that can be devised in order to achieve the aim. The question at this stage of the consideration is: does the measure have an excessive or disproportionate effect on the interests of affected persons.[100]

2.68 However, it is important to note that the two-stage approach advocated by Dyson LJ in *Samaroo* has not been uniformly adopted in subsequent cases. In *Lough v The First Secretary of State*[101] a local authority refused planning permission to the owners of a site for a proposed development involving the demolition of existing buildings and redevelopment on the basis that the proposals conflicted with the authority's unitary development plan in that it caused harm to the amenity of local residents. The owners of the site appealed, and a planning inspector appointed by the secretary of state allowed their appeal. Members of a local unincorporated residents' association applied to the High Court to quash the grant of planning permission on the grounds that the proposed development breached their rights protected by Article 8 to respect for their private, family life and homes and by Article 1 of Protocol 1 (their right to peaceful enjoyment of their possessions). The application was dismissed by the High Court and a subsequent appeal to the Court of Appeal was rejected. When giving the lead judgment in the Court of Appeal Pill LJ said:

> 49. The concept of proportionality is inherent in the approach to decision making in planning law. The procedure stated by Dyson LJ in the *Samaroo* case [2001] UKHHR 1150, as stated, is not wholly appropriate to decision making in the present context in that it does not take account of the right, recognised in the Convention, of a landowner to make use of his land, a right which is, however, to be weighed against the rights of others affected by the use of the land and of the community in general. The first stage of the procedure stated by Dyson LJ does not require, nor was it intended to require that, before any development of land is permitted, it must be established that the objective of the development cannot be achieved in some other way or on some other site. The effect of the proposal on adjoining owners and occupants must however be considered in the context of Article 8, and a balancing of interests is necessary. The question whether the permission has 'an excessive or disproportionate

100 [2001] EWCA Civ 1139 at paras 19 and 21.

101 [2004] 1 WLR 2557.

> effect on the interests of affected persons' (Dyson LJ at paragraph 20) is, in the present context, no different from the question posed by the Inspector, a question which has routinely been posed by decision makers both before and after the enactment of the 1998 Act. Dyson LJ stated, at paragraph 18, that 'it is important to emphasise that the striking of a fair balance lies at the heart of proportionality'.
>
> 50. . . . The need to strike a balance is central to the conclusion in each case. There may be cases where the two-stage approach to decision making necessary in other fields is also appropriate to a decision as to land use, and the concept of proportionality undoubtedly is, and always has been, a useful tool in striking a balance, but the decision in the *Samaroo* case does not have the effect of imposing on planning law the straight-jacket advocated . . .

2.69 In a short concurring judgment Keene LJ added:

> 55. . . . the process outlined in *Samaroo* while appropriate where there is direct interference with Article 8 rights by a public body, cannot be applied without adaptation in a situation where the essential conflict is between two or more groups of private interests.

2.70 This approach was followed in the case of *R (SB) v The Governors of Denbigh High School*[102] where Lord Bingham said:

> 29. . . . the focus at Strasbourg is not and has never been on whether a challenged decision or action is the product of a defective decision-making process, but on whether, in the case under consideration, the applicant's Convention rights have been violated;
>
> 30. . . . it is clear that the court's approach to an issue of proportionality under the Convention must go beyond that traditionally adopted to judicial review in a domestic setting. The inadequacy of that approach was exposed in *Smith and Grady v The United Kingdom* [1999] 29 EHRR 493, para 138, and the new approach required under the 1998 Act was described by Lord Steyn in *R (Daly) v The Secretary of State for the Home Department* [2001] 2 AC 532, paragraphs 25–28, in terms which have never to my knowledge been questioned. There is no shift to a merits review, but the intensity of review is greater than was previously appropriate, and greater even than the heightened scrutiny test adopted by the Court of Appeal in *R v Ministry of Defence, Ex p Smith* [1996] QB 517. The domestic court must now make a value judgment, an evaluation, by reference to the circumstances prevailing at the relevant time . . . Proportionality must be judged objectively, by the court . . .
>
> 31. . . . what matters in any case is the practical outcome, not the process of the decision-making process that led to it.

102 [2006] 2 WLR 719.

Using Article 8 as a defence to possession claims

2.71 There have been a number of cases in recent years in which the domestic courts and the ECtHR have considered whether individuals with no right to continue to occupy premises as their homes could nevertheless, defend possession proceedings on the grounds that the loss of their home would breach their rights protected by Article 8.

2.72 In 2003 the House of Lords held in *Qazi v the Harrow LBC* that Article 8 could not be used to defeat a landlord's unqualified right to possession.[103] In that case, a husband and wife were joint tenants of property. They separated and the wife served a notice to quit, thus bringing the tenancy to an end. The husband's request for a sole tenancy was refused by the landlord, who issued possession proceedings. In his defence, the husband argued that the landlord had failed to give effect to his right under Article 8 to respect for his home life and the interference was not justified under Article 8(2). By a majority, the House of Lords concluded that the property was his home for the purpose of Article 8(1) but contractual and proprietary rights to possession could not be defeated by a defence based on Article 8.[104] In their dissenting judgments, Lords Bingham and Steyn took the view that an action taken by a public authority seeking possession of residential property could engage the operation of Article 8 but that this did not apply to landlords, who were not public authorities.[105]

2.73 In the following year, the ECtHR considered the case of *Connors v UK*,[106] which concerned an Irish Traveller who had been summarily evicted from a local authority run Traveller site. At the time, Gypsies and Travellers living on local authority run sites had only the most basic legal protection against eviction; they could be evicted if a local authority gave them just four weeks' notice to leave the site and it then obtained an eviction order from a court (there being no substantive defence to an application for such an order).[107] This contrasted with the position of caravan dwellers living on private mobile homes sites who had additional protection under the Mobile Homes Act (MHA) 1983: their licences to occupy pitches on such sites could only be terminated if the court was satisfied that there had been a breach of the terms of the licence agreement and, after the service of a notice to remedy the breach, the occupier had not

103 [2003] UKHL 43 at para 82.
104 [2003] UKHL 43 at para 83.
105 [2003] UKHL 43 at para 23.
106 (2005) 40 EHRR 9.
107 Caravan Sites Act 1968 s2.

complied with the notice within a reasonable time; and additionally, the court had to be satisfied that it would be reasonable for the agreement to be terminated.[108] It was MHA 1983 s5(1) that excluded those Gypsies and Travellers living on local authority sites from the additional protection afforded to caravan dwellers living on private mobile homes sites and caused a difference in treatment which seemed unjustified when the majority of Gypsies and Travellers no longer pursued a wholly nomadic way of life. However, cases brought in our domestic courts to challenge this difference in treatment met little success.[109]

2.74 The facts in *Connors* were that the applicant had received a warning in 1998 about the behaviour of his family members and visitors. Subsequently, in January 2000, a notice to quit was served requiring the family to vacate their plots without any written or detailed reasons. Two months later, the local authority issued summary proceedings for possession of the plots on the basis that the applicant and his daughter were in occupation without licence or consent. The applicant's application for permission to apply for judicial review of the local authority's decision to determine the licence was refused and the county court granted a possession order.

2.75 The government argued that there was a need to exempt local authority Gypsy sites from security of tenure provisions because the policy was aimed at catering for the special needs of Gypsies who lead a nomadic lifestyle. It was also a vital way of managing anti-social behaviour. The ECtHR was unimpressed by these arguments, pointing out that a substantial number of Gypsies no longer travel for any material period and that most sites are residential in character. Additionally, the mere fact that anti-social behaviour takes place on Gypsy sites does not mean that summary eviction is justified, since anti-social behaviour occurs on housing estates where the residents have security of tenure.[110] The ECtHR repeated what it had said in previous cases:

> 83 The procedural safeguards available to the individual will be especially material in determining whether the respondent state has, when fixing the regulatory framework, remained within its margin of appreciation. In particular, the Court must examine whether the decision-

108 MHA 1983 s2(1) and Sch 1 para 4.

109 *Somerset CC v Isaacs and Secretary of State for Transport, Local Government and the Regions* [2002] EWHC 1014 (Admin); and *R (Smith) v Barking and Dagenham LBC and Secretary of State for the Office of the Deputy Prime Minister* [2002] EWHC 2400 (Admin).

110 (2005) 40 EHRR 9 at paras 87–89.

> making process leading to measures of interference was fair and such as to afford due respect to the interests safeguarded to the individual by article 8.
>
> 84 The vulnerable position of gypsies as a minority means that some special consideration should be given to their needs and their different lifestyle both in the relevant regulatory framework and in reaching decisions in particular cases. To this extent, there is thus a positive obligation imposed on the Contracting States by virtue of Art.8 to facilitate the gypsy way of life.

2.76 The ECtHR found that the eviction had not been attended by the requisite procedural safeguards in circumstances where the applicant had not had the chance to defend eviction proceedings or the opportunity to argue in court that the eviction would be disproportionate.[111] Judicial review was insufficient to satisfy the procedural requirements of Article 8 because:

> . . . the local authority was not required to establish any substantive justification for evicting the applicant, and on this point judicial review could not provide any opportunity for an examination of the facts in dispute between the parties.[112]

2.77 In 2005, amendments to the Caravan Sites Act (CSA) 1968 s4 entered into force, enabling courts in England and Wales to suspend possession orders made against Gypsies and Travellers living on local authority sites for up to 12 months at a time.[113] Subsequent amendments to MHA 1983 s5(1) were brought into force in 2011, which enabled Gypsies and Travellers on local authority run sites in England to challenge the reasonableness of a decision to apply for a possession order in the domestic courts.[114]

2.78 The fact that those 2011 amendments to the MHA 1983 were not brought into force in Wales at the same time led the ECtHR to find that there had been a violation of Article 8 in the case of *Buckland v UK*,[115] which concerned a possession claim brought against a Romani Gypsy living on a local authority site in Wales. The Gypsy Council managed the local authority site and applied for a possession order of the applicant's pitch on the grounds that members of her family had allegedly caused a nuisance. The court granted possession but it

111 (2005) 40 EHRR 9, para 95.

112 (2005) 40 EHRR 9, para 92.

113 Amended by Housing Act 2004 s211(1).

114 Amended by Housing and Regeneration Act 2008 s321 and Sch 16. The amendments were brought into force in 2011.

115 (2013) 56 EHRR 16.

suspended the possession order pursuant to the powers under CSA 1968 s4. However, as the amendments to the MHA 1983 s5(1) had not taken effect in Wales, the ECtHR held that there had been a violation of Article 8 because the applicant had not been able to challenge the proportionality of making the possession order in the first place.[116]

2.79 Meanwhile, in 2006 the House of Lords reconsidered its decision in *Qazi* in the light of *Connors* in the case of *Kay v Lambeth LBC; Leeds City Council v Price.*[117] The majority took the view that *Qazi* was not incompatible with *Connors*. They held that where a county court was faced with a defence to a claim for possession by a public authority landlord which is based on Article 8, the county court is entitled to make the following assumptions: firstly, domestic law has struck the right balance between the competing interests involved between the person occupying the home and the landlord seeking possession; and secondly, the landowner, if a public authority, has acted compatibly with the convention rights of the individual occupier in deciding to enforce its proprietary rights.[118] It held that a defence which does not challenge the law under which the possession order is sought as being incompatible with Article 8, and only raises the occupier's personal circumstances, should be struck out.[119]

> [T]he only situations in which it would be open to the court to refrain from proceeding to summary judgment and making the possession order are these: (a) if a seriously arguable point is raised that the law which enables the court to make the possession order is incompatible with article 8, the county court in the exercise of its jurisdiction under the Human Rights Act 1998 should deal with the argument in one or other of two ways: (i) by giving effect to the law, so far as it is possible for it do so under section 3, in a way that is compatible with article 8, or (ii) by adjourning the proceedings to enable the compatibility issue to be dealt with in the High Court; (b) if the defendant wishes to challenge the decision of a public authority to recover possession as an improper exercise of its powers at common law on the ground that it was a decision that no reasonable person would consider justifiable, he should be permitted to do this provided again that the point is seriously arguable: *Wandsworth London Borough Council v Winder* [1985] AC 461. The common law as explained in that case is, of course, compatible with article 8. It provides an additional safeguard.[120]

116 (2013) 56 EHRR 16 at para 68.
117 [2006] UKHL 10.
118 [2006] UKHL 10 per Baroness Hale at para 182.
119 [2006] UKHL 10 per Lord Hope at paras 109–110.
120 [2006] UKHL 10 at para 110.

2.80 These propositions became known as gateway (a) and gateway (b). The minority (Lords Bingham, Nicholls and Walker) considered that occupiers should be able to plead Article 8 as a defence in possession proceedings, although such a defence would only be successful in highly exceptional cases.[121]

2.81 In 2008 the ECtHR considered the case of *McCann v UK*.[122] The applicant and his wife were joint tenants of local authority accommodation. They separated due to domestic violence and his wife was rehoused by the local authority. Upon realising that the applicant remained in the property, the local authority asked the wife to sign a notice to quit thus terminating the tenancy and extinguishing the applicant's rights to live at the property. The local authority issued possession proceedings in the county court and the applicant argued that it would be contrary to his Article 8 rights to be evicted on the basis of a notice to quit. The county court accepted that argument and dismissed the claim for possession on Article 8 grounds.

2.82 The Court of Appeal, applying *Qazi*, allowed the local authority's appeal. The applicant applied for permission to judicially review the decision to procure the notice to quit from his wife but this application was also dismissed and eventually he was evicted from the property. The applicant complained to the ECtHR. The court rejected the government's contention that *Connors* only applied to cases involving Gypsies and Travellers. It noted that the loss of one's home is one of the most extreme forms of interference with the right to respect for one's home.[123] It held, as in *Connors*, that the 'procedural safeguards' required by Article 8 for the assessment of the proportionality of the interference were not met by the possibility of applying for judicial review. Judicial review is not well adapted for the resolution of sensitive factual questions, which are better left to the county court.[124] The ECtHR agreed with the minority approach in *Kay*, stating that in the great majority of cases, an order for possession would continue to be made in summary proceedings and that it would be only in very exceptional cases that an applicant would succeed in raising an arguable Article 8 defence which would require a court to examine the issue.[125]

121 [2006] UKHL 10 at para 38.
122 (2008) 47 EHRR 40.
123 (2008) 47 EHRR 40 at para 50.
124 (2008) 47 EHRR 40 at para 53.
125 (2008) 47 EHRR 40 at para 54.

2.83 Later that year, the House of Lords reconsidered Article 8 in summary possession proceedings in the case of *Doherty v Birmingham City Council.*[126] The appellant had been living on a local authority run Travellers' site for a period of 17 years. In accordance with the legislation in force at the time, the local authority had an unqualified right to possession and it stated that it required vacant possession of the site to carry out essential maintenance work and was then going to manage the site for the provision of temporary accommodation for Travellers. The local authority claimed that genuine Travellers were deterred from the site because of the presence of the appellant and his family but no allegations of misconduct by them had been made. CSA 1968 s4 gives the court the power to suspend the execution of possession orders. However, at the time possession proceedings were brought against the appellant, CSA 1968 s4(6)(a) prevented the court from suspending the enforcement of a possession order in cases brought by a local authority.

2.84 The majority of the House of Lords refused to depart from what had been said in *Qazi* and *Kay*. However, applying *Connors*, Lord Hope found that this was an exceptional case where the legal framework that applied at the time was defective because the statute excluded the Gypsy community from its procedural safeguards. Gateway (a)(i) could not be used to assist in the case because the county court would have had to have applied the existing statute and would not have been able to interpret the CSA 1968 s4(6)(a) in a way which would have given effect to the appellant's rights. There was a possibility under gateway (a)(ii) for the House of Lords to make a declaration of incompatibility under HRA 1998 s4(1) but it was deemed that this was unnecessary because parliament had subsequently amended the offending provisions. In the light of the developments in the Strasbourg case law, the House of Lords also acknowledged that the traditional approach to judicial review would have to be expanded, particularly to allow the court to make its own assessment of the relevant facts.[127]

2.85 Subsequently, in *Kay v UK*[128] the ECtHR noted and welcomed the development in *Doherty* but concluded that at the time when the case advanced by the applicants in *Kay* were considered by the domestic courts, it was not possible to challenge a decision of the local authority to seek a possession order on the basis of the alleged dispropor-

126 [2008] UKHL 57.

127 [2008] UKHL 57 per Lord Scott [68] and per Lord Mance [138].

128 (2012) 54 EHRR 30.

tionality of that decision, in light of the personal circumstances of the person subject to possession proceedings. As a result, the applicants were dispossessed of their homes without having the possibility of that measure determined by an independent tribunal. Consequently, there had been a violation of Article 8.[129]

2.86 Shortly afterwards, the Supreme Court delivered its judgment in *Manchester City Council v Pinnock*,[130] which considered the protection afforded to persons occupying premises under a demoted tenancy. Lord Neuberger derived the following principles from the case-law of the ECtHR:

(a) Any person at risk of being dispossessed of his home at the suit of a local authority should in principle have the right to raise the question of the proportionality of the measure, and to have it determined by an independent tribunal in the light of article 8, even if his right of occupation under domestic law has come to an end: *McCann v UK* 47 EHRR 913, para 50; *Ćosić v Croatia* (App no 28261/06), para 22; *Zehentner v Austria* (App no 20082/02), para 59; *Paulić v Croatia* (App no 3572/06), para 43, and *Kay v UK* (App no 37341/06), paras 73–4.

(b) A judicial procedure which is limited to addressing the proportionality of the measure through the medium of traditional judicial review (i e, one which does not permit the court to make its own assessment of the facts in an appropriate case) is inadequate as it is not appropriate for resolving sensitive factual issues: *Connors v UK* 40 EHRR 189, para 92; *McCann v UK* 47 EHRR 913, para 53; *Kay v UK* (App no 37341/06), paras 72–73.

(c) Where the measure includes proceedings involving more than one stage, it is the proceedings as a whole which must be considered in order to see if article 8 has been complied with: *Zehentner v Austria* (App no 20082/02), para 54.

(d) If the court concludes that it would be disproportionate to evict a person from his home notwithstanding the fact that he has no domestic right to remain there, it would be unlawful to evict him so long as the conclusion obtains – for example, for a specified period, or until a specified event occurs, or a particular condition is satisfied.[131]

2.87 In relation to the proposition made by Lord Bingham in *Kay* that it would only be in 'very exceptional cases' that it would be appropriate for the court to consider a proportionality argument, Lord Neuberger held that it was both unsafe and unhelpful to invoke exceptionality as a guide.

129 (2012) 54 EHRR 30 at paras 73 and 74.

130 [2010] UKSC 45.

131 [2010] UKSC 45 at para 45.

> 52. . . . The question is always whether the eviction is a proportionate means of achieving a legitimate aim. Where a person has no right in domestic law to remain in occupation of his home, the proportionality of making an order for possession at the suit of the local authority will be supported not merely by the fact that it would serve to vindicate the authority's ownership rights. It will also, at least normally, be supported by the fact that it would enable the authority to comply with its duties in relation to the distribution and management of its housing stock, including, for example, the fair allocation of its housing, the redevelopment of the site, the refurbishing of sub-standard accommodation, the need to move people who are in accommodation that now exceeds their needs, and the need to move vulnerable people into sheltered or warden-assisted housing. Furthermore, in many cases (such as this appeal) other cogent reasons, such as the need to remove a source of nuisance to neighbours, may support the proportionality of dispossessing the occupiers.
>
> . . .
>
> 54. . . . Therefore, in virtually every case where a residential occupier has no contractual or statutory protection, and the local authority is entitled to possession as a matter of domestic law, there will be a very strong case for saying that making an order for possession would be proportionate. However, in some cases there may be factors which would tell the other way . . .

2.88 The effect of the above is that:

> 78. . . . an occupier who is the defendant in possession proceedings in the county court and who claims that it would be incompatible with his article 8 Convention rights for him to be put out of his home must be able to rely on those rights in defending those proceedings . . .

2.89 Lord Neuberger set out the following procedure that should apply:

> 61. . . . [A]s a general rule, article 8 need only be considered by the court if it is raised in the proceedings by or on behalf of the residential occupier. [I]f an article 8 point is raised, the court should initially consider it summarily, and if, as will no doubt often be the case, the court is satisfied that, even if the facts relied on are made out, the point would not succeed, it should be dismissed. Only if the court is satisfied that it could affect the order that the court might make should the point be further entertained.

2.90 The Supreme Court's observations relating to local authority landlords apply equally to other social landlords to the extent that they are public authorities under HRA 1998.[132] Whether they apply where a private landowner seeks a possession order is debatable.[133]

132 [2010] UKSC 45 at para 3.
133 [2010] UKSC 45 at paras 4 and 50.

2.91 A few months later, in *Hounslow LBC v Powell*[134] the Supreme Court considered two cases of possession proceedings where the occupiers had been granted an introductory tenancy under Housing Act 1996 s124 and one case where the occupier was in temporary accommodation provided under the homelessness legislation. It was held that the court has to consider whether the making of a possession order is proportionate if the occupier has raised it as an issue and it has crossed the high threshold of being arguable. The first thing that the court must consider is whether the property in question constitutes the person's home. For the purposes of Article 8, this 'will depend on the factual circumstances, namely, the existence of sufficient and continuous links with a specific place'.[135] The question will then be whether the making of the order of possession is a proportionate means of achieving a legitimate aim.[136] There will be no reason, in the overwhelming majority of cases, for the local authority to explain and justify its reasons for seeking a possession order. It can be assumed that it is acting in accordance with its duties in the distribution and management of its housing stock. The court need only be concerned with the occupier's personal circumstances and any factual objections s/he may raise and, in the light only of what view it takes of them, with the question of whether making the order for possession would be lawful and proportionate.[137]

2.92 In *Thurrock BC v West*[138] the Court of Appeal derived the following eight principles from the *Pinnock* and *Powell* cases:

> 22. . . . First, it is a defence to a claim by a local authority for possession of a defendant's home that the possession is not necessary in a democratic society within Article 8(2), that is to say it would be disproportionate in all the circumstances. An order for possession in such a case would be an infringement of the defendant's right under Article 8 to respect for his or her home and so unlawful within the Human Rights Act 1998 s. 6(1).
>
> 23 Secondly, the test is whether the eviction is a proportionate means of achieving a legitimate aim . . .
>
> 24 Thirdly, it is nevertheless clear that the threshold for establishing an arguable case that a local authority is acting disproportionately and so in

134 [2011] UKSC 8.
135 *Paulic v Croatia*, App No 3572/06, 22 October 2009.
136 [2011] UKSC 8 at para 33.
137 [2011] UKSC 8 at para 37.
138 [2013] HLR 5.

> breach of Article 8 where re-possession would otherwise be lawful is a high one and will be met in only a small proportion of cases . . .
>
> 25 Fourthly, the reasons why the threshold is so high lie in the public policy and public benefit inherent in the functions of the housing authority in dealing with its housing stock, a precious and limited public resource. Local authorities, like other social landlords, hold their housing stock for the benefit of the whole community and they are best equipped, certainly better equipped than the courts, to make management decisions about the way such stock should be administered . . .
>
> 26 Fifthly, that is why the fact that a local authority has a legal right to possession, aside from Article 8, and is to be assumed to be acting in accordance with its duties (in the absence of cogent evidence to the contrary), will be a strong factor in support of the proportionality of making an order for possession without the need for explanation or justification by the local authority . . .
>
> 29 Sixthly, an Article 8 defence on the grounds of lack of proportionality must be pleaded and sufficiently particularised to show that it reaches the high threshold of being seriously arguably . . .
>
> 30 Seventhly, unless there is some good reason not to do so, the Court must at the earliest opportunity summarily consider whether the Article 8 defence, as pleaded, and on the assumption that the pleaded facts relied upon are correct, reaches that threshold . . . If the pleaded defence does not reach that threshold, it must be struck out or dismissed . . . The resources of the court and of the parties should not be further expended on it.
>
> 31 Eighthly, even where an Article 8 defence is established, in a case where the defendant would otherwise have no legal right to remain in the property, it is difficult to imagine circumstances in which the defence could operate to give the defendant an unlimited and unconditional right to remain . . . That might be the effect of a simple refusal of possession without any qualification. It is particularly difficult to imagine how that could possibly be appropriate in a case where the defendant has never been a tenant or licensee of the local authority. Otherwise, the effect of the Article 8 defence would be that the Court would have assumed the local authority's function of allocating its housing stock, preferring the right of the defendant to remain, without any tenancy or contract, over all the other people entitled to rely on the local authority's statutory housing duties and without the benefit of any knowledge of who those people are and their circumstances and of other relevant matters which would properly guide the local authority in housing management decisions.

2.93 In *Jones v Canal and River Boat Trust*[139] the Court of Appeal considered whether the high threshold set in *Pinnock* and *Powell* for an Article 8

139 [2017] EWCA Civ 135.

claim to succeed, applies in cases where the public authority is not a local housing authority managing limited housing stock. The case concerned the Canal and River Boat Trust's decision to terminate a licence of a person to navigate his boat, which he used as his home, along a canal and an application for an injunction.

2.94 The Court of Appeal held that there was a difference between the two situations. In housing cases the courts are accustomed to balancing the relative weight of landlords against the tenants wishing to assert and preserve their Article 8 rights, particularly where the statutory scheme imports a requirement of reasonableness before a possession order can be made. However, while there may be cases where the county court would be able to determine in a *Pinnock*-style summary assessment that a boat dweller's rights under Article 8 cannot require an authority to accommodate his home on the waterways, where there is a dispute as to whether licence conditions have been met or where there are other issues in play, such as questions under the Equality Act (EqA) 2010, summary assessment would not be appropriate and the test is not as high.[140] Arguably, this approach should also apply to other public authorities, such as those with management responsibilities for caravan sites.

2.95 By way of contrast, in *McDonald v McDonald*[141] the Supreme Court made it clear that in the absence of any guidance to the contrary from the ECtHR, where a private sector landlord applies to the court for possession of a property, it is not open to the tenant to contend that Article 8 could justify the court refusing to grant an order for possession.

The best interests of the child

2.96 Article 3(1) of the United Nations Convention on the Rights of the Child 1989 provides that:

> In all actions concerning children, whether undertaken by public or private social welfare institutions, courts of law, administrative authorities or legislative bodies, the best interests of the child shall be a primary consideration.

2.97 In *Üner v the Netherlands* the ECtHR held that when assessing the proportionality of a decision to expel a foreign national criminal

140 [2017] EWCA Civ 135 at paras 41–49.

141 *McDonald (by her litigation friend Duncan J McDonald) v McDonald and others* [2016] UKSC 28. See also para 50 of *Pinnock*.

under Article 8(2), the authorities must assess the best interests and well-being of any children concerned.[142]

2.98 There is a statutory duty imposed by Children Act 2004 s11 (in Wales, Children Act 2004 s28) on local authorities to ensure that their functions are discharged having regard to the need to safeguard and promote the welfare of children. The current statutory guidance issued by the secretary of state pursuant to Children Act 2004 s11(4) and a number of other statutory provisions is entitled *Working together to Safeguard Children: A guide to inter-agency working to safeguard and promote the welfare of children*, which contains practical examples of the type of arrangements that are required under Children Act 2004 s11.[143]

2.99 In the seminal judgment of *ZH (Tanzania) v Secretary of State for the Home Department*,[144] the Supreme Court considered a corresponding duty imposed on the Secretary of State of the Home Department by Borders, Citizenship and Immigration Act 2009 s55. Baroness Hale stated that:

> In making the proportionality assessment under article 8, the best interests of the child must be a primary consideration. This means that they must be considered first. They can, of course, be outweighed by the cumulative effect of other considerations.[145]

2.100 Lord Mance added in *H (H) v Deputy Prosecutor of the Italian Republic, Genoa (Official Solicitor Intervening)* that 'a primary consideration' means:

> . . . that such interests must always be at the forefront of any decision-maker's mind, rather than that they need to be mentioned first in any formal chain of reasoning or that they rank higher than any other considerations. A child's best interests must themselves be evaluated. They may in some cases point only marginally in one, rather than another, direction. They may be outweighed by other considerations pointing more strongly in another direction.[146]

2.101 In *Stevens v Secretary of State for Communities and Local Government*[147] Hickinbottom J considered how the best interests of the child consid-

142 (2007) 45 EHRR 421 at para 58.
143 The most recent guidance was published in March 2015.
144 [2011] UKSC 4.
145 [2011] UKSC 4 at para 33. See also *Zoumbas v Secretary of State for the Home Department* [2013] UKSC 74.
146 [2012] UKSC 25 at para 98.
147 [2013] JPL 1383.

erations affect the approach to be taken by a planning decision-maker and derived the following propositions from the authorities:

(i) Given the scope of planning decisions and the nature of the right to respect for family and private life, planning decision-making will often engage article 8. In those circumstances, relevant article 8 rights will be a material consideration which the decision-maker must take into account;

(ii) Where the article 8 rights are those of children, they must be seen in the context of article 3 of the UNCRC, which requires a child's best interests to be a primary consideration;

(iii) This requires the decision-maker, first, to identify what the child's best interests are. In a planning context, they are likely to be consistent with those of his parent or other carer who is involved in the planning decision-making process; and, unless circumstances indicate to the contrary, the decision-maker can assume that that carer will properly represent the child's best interests, and can properly represent and evidence the potential adverse impact of any decision on that child's best interests;

(iv) Once identified, although a primary consideration, the best interests of the child are not determinative of the planning issue. Nor does respect for the best interests of a relevant child mean that the planning exercise necessarily involves merely assessing whether the public interest in ensuring planning controls is [sic] maintained outweighs the best interests of the child. Most planning cases will have too many competing rights and interests, and will be too factually complex, to allow such an exercise;

(v) However, no other consideration must be regarded as more important or given greater weight than the best interests of any child, merely by virtue of its inherent nature apart from the context of the individual case. Further, the best interests of any child must be kept at the forefront of the decision-maker's mind as he examines all material considerations and performs the exercise of planning judgment on the basis of them; and, when considering any decision he might make (and, of course, the eventual decision he does make), he needs to assess whether the adverse impact of such a decision on the interests of a child is proportionate;

(vi) Whether the decision-maker has properly performed this exercise is a question of substance, not form. However, if an inspector on an appeal sets out this reasoning with regard to any child's interests in play, even briefly, that will be helpful not only to those involved in the application but also to the court in any later challenge, in understanding how the decision-maker reached the decision that the adverse impact to the interests of the child to which the decision gives rise is proportionate. It will be particularly helpful if the reasoning shows that the inspector has brought his mind to bear on the adverse impact of the decision he has reached on the best interests of

> the child, and has concluded that impact is in all the circumstances proportionate . . .[148]

Statutory review of planning appeals

2.102 In *R (Egan) v Secretary of State for Transport, Local Government and the Regions and Hertsmere BC*[149] Sullivan J dismissed an application made under the Town and Country Planning Act (TCPA) 1990 s288 to quash a decision made by the secretary of state to dismiss the claimant's appeal against the council's refusal of planning permission for a Gypsy site in the Green Belt. When doing so Sullivan J concluded that a considerable measure of deference should be accorded to the judgment of the decision maker in respect of proportionality, given:

> . . . the fact that the court did not have particular expertise in the planning field, that the balancing exercise does involve matters of planning policy, and the court does not have the opportunity of looking at the site and hearing evidence about special circumstances first hand . . .[150]

2.103 Sullivan J rejected the proposition that the court should satisfy itself that the decision maker struck the right balance between Green Belt and other policy considerations, on the one hand, and the claimant's Article 8 rights, on the other.[151]

2.104 Nevertheless, in *Stevens v Secretary of State for Communities and Local Government*,[152] Hickinbottom J followed the approach taken in *R (Begum) v Denbigh High School Governors*[153] and accepted that:

148 [2013] JPL 1383 at para 69 and approved by the Court of Appeal in *Collins v Secretary of State for Communities and Local Government* [2013] EWCA Civ 1193 at paras 10–11. See also *R (Jayes) v Flintshire CC* [2017] EWHC 874 (Admin); *Allen v Secretary of State for Communities and Local Government* [2016] EWCA Civ 767; *Cash v Secretary of State for Communities and Local Government* [2015] EWHC 2357 (Admin); *Dear v Secretary of State for Communities and Local Government* [2015] EWHC 29 (Admin); and *Connors v Secretary of State for Communities and Local Government* [2014] EWHC 2358 (Admin).

149 [2002] EWHC 389 (Admin).

150 [2002] EWHC 389 (Admin) at para 51.

151 [2002] EWHC 389 (Admin) at para 49. See also *R (Lee) v First Secretary of State* [2003] EWHC 3235 (Admin) at paras 23–27 for another example of a court's consideration of proportionality in the context of a statutory review. In that case the secretary of state's decision refusing a Gypsy planning permission was quashed on the basis that one sentence in a paragraph dealing with human rights was not sufficient to dispose of the claimant's argument that a refusal of temporary planning permission would amount to a disproportionate interference with his and his family's rights under Article 8.

152 [2013] JPL 1383.

153 [2006] UKHL 15, [2007] 1 AC 100.

> 70 . . . where human rights are in play, it is for the court to make an objective assessment as to whether an adverse impact of a decision on those rights is proportionate. The conventional role of the court in planning cases (even if in the form of an application to quash under s.288 of the 1990 Act) is effectively one of considering procedural legal propriety, akin to judicial review; but, as Lord Bingham and Baroness Hale emphasised in SB and Miss Behavin', respectively . . . the role of the court in considering whether there has been a breach of human rights is different, the court being concerned, not with procedure, but the substantive issue of whether the individual's human rights have in fact been breached. On the basis of Miss Behavin', whether the decision-maker whose decision is challenged has conducted that proportionality exercise or not, is irrelevant. It is for the court to conduct that exercise, giving the weight to the material factors that it considers appropriate.[154]

2.105 Hickinbottom J held that the proper approach of the court when dealing with a TCPA 1990 s288 application was as follows:

- The application does not require a full merits review. It requires review on traditional judicial review grounds, together with consideration of whether the resulting decision engages [Article 8] and, insofar as it does, whether the adverse impact of the decision on the [Article 8] rights engaged is proportionate to the legitimate aims sought to be protected (including both the public interest, and the rights and interests of other individuals).
- In considering whether the decision breached relevant [Article 8] rights, the court is required to consider the merits, with appropriate scrutiny, but it should do so bearing in mind that the inspector's function, assigned to him by the statutory scheme and ultimately Parliament, is to consider the merits of all material considerations, including any [Article 8] rights that are engaged. The inspector is an expert and experienced, and acts in a quasi-judicial capacity, which each warrant a wide margin of discretion. He is acting in an area of social policy, which in itself attracts a wide margin of discretion. As a result, considerable deference ought to be attached to his conclusion.
- Proportionality is a question of substance and not form. If the inspector has clearly engaged with the [Article 8] rights in play, and considered them with care, given his wide margin of discretion, it is unlikely that the court will interfere with his conclusion on grounds of proportionality. If he has not – even if he has not referred to [Article 8] rights at all – on usual principles, the court will not quash his decision if his error is immaterial. If his error is material, then it is open to the court to find that the interference with the relevant human rights is in any event proportionate; or quash the decision.[155]

154 [2013] JPL 1383 at para 70.
155 [2013] JPL 1383 at para 87.

Direct action

2.106 In both *R (O'Brien and Casey) v Basildon DC*[156] and in *R (Smith) v South Norfolk Council*[157] the Administrative Court was asked to review the use by local authorities of their powers under TCPA 1990 s178 to take direct action to evict Gypsies and Travellers from sites which had been developed without planning permission. In each case the court rejected the claimants' case that the use of direct action in such circumstances was necessarily disproportionate and incompatible with Article 8 – though the decision to take direct action in the case of *O'Brien* was quashed on other grounds.

2.107 *R (Sheridan, McCarthy and others) v Basildon DC*[158] concerned a judicial review challenge of the decision by the District Council to exercise its powers under TCPA 1990 s178 to evict Irish Travellers from the Dale Farm site near Basildon. The claimants did not argue that enforcement action should never be taken. Instead they contended that it should be postponed until suitable alternative plots became available for those who were to be evicted.[159] It was accepted by the court that the District Council had a duty to take into account the best interests of the child as a primary consideration.[160] However, Ouseley J concluded that the prospects of the residents finding suitable alternative sites were low and, in those circumstances, declined the claimants the relief they sought.

Compulsory purchase

2.108 In *Lisa Smith and others v Secretary of State for Trade and Industry and the London Development Agency*[161] the Administrative Court dismissed a challenge to the Secretary of State's confirmation of a compulsory purchase order (CPO) which encompassed land required for the development of the London 2012 Olympic Games site. The challenge had been brought by Gypsies and Travellers who were living on authorised Gypsy/Traveller sites within the CPO lands. The claimants argued that the decision to confirm the CPO in circumstances where relocation sites had not yet been provided was disproportionate and breached their rights protected by Article 8 of the convention. They also argued that the court should adopt the two-

156 [2006] EWHC 1346 (Admin). For further discussion of this case see para 4.223 below.
157 [2006] EWHC 2772 (Admin) and see chapter 4 below.
158 [2011] EWHC 2938 (Admin).
159 [2011] EWHC 2938 (Admin) at para 96.
160 [2011] EWHC 2938 (Admin) at para 129.
161 [2007] EWHC 1013 (Admin); and see chapter 3 below.

stage *Samaroo* approach and ask itself the question whether the secretary of state's decision was the least intrusive measure that could be taken to achieve what was acknowledged to be a legitimate aim. In the event, Wyn Williams J concluded that the secretary of state's decision was proportionate.[162]

The court's jurisdiction to grant planning injunctions

2.109 A local planning authority that wishes to evict Gypsies and Travellers from an unauthorised site that they have established on their own land may apply for an injunction to restrain a breach of planning control.[163] Before the HRA 1998, the well-established approach of the judiciary when dealing with such applications for injunctive relief was to treat the court's discretion as being narrowly circumscribed by the fact that the local planning authority had already decided what constituted a breach of planning control. The judiciary in such cases regarded the planning authority as having already struck the balance between the general public interest, on the one hand, and the interests of the individuals who were to be evicted, on the other, and saw any role for the courts in considering questions such as the availability of alternative sites, or the hardship which would be caused by an injunction, as a usurpation of that policy-making function, and contrary to the will of parliament which had entrusted those powers to the local planning authorities. In other words, the courts adopted an entirely submissive approach to the decisions made by local planning authorities, subject only to a residual power to correct manifest errors or perverse decisions. That approach was exemplified by the decision of Hoffmann J at first instance in *Mole Valley DC v Smith*:

> There can be no doubt that requiring [the Gypsies] to leave the site would cause considerable hardship. This court, however, is not entrusted with a general jurisdiction to solve social problems. The striking of a balance between the requirements of planning policy and the needs of these defendants is a matter which, in my view, has been entrusted to other authorities.[164]

2.110 This was cited with approval in the Court of Appeal in the same case where Lord Donaldson said:

162 See also *R (Mahoney and Jones) v Secretary of State for Communities and Local Government* [2015] EWHC 589 (Admin).

163 See TCPA 1990 s187B; and chapter 4, paras 4.235–4.251, below.

164 Cited in the Court of Appeal's decision, (1992) 24 HLR 442 at 449.

> [I]t is not for the courts to usurp the policy decision-making functions of the Secretary of State . . . by a side-wind.

and Balcombe LJ:

> [T]he court is being asked to reverse the decisions of the authorities to whom Parliament has entrusted the relevant decision, not on grounds of illegality, but on grounds of policy.[165]

2.111 The central issue in the case of *South Buckinghamshire DC v Porter*[166] was whether that approach survived the coming into force of the HRA 1998, or whether the fact that the Article 8 rights of Gypsies and Travellers were engaged in such cases, meant that a court must now make an independent judgment in deciding whether or not to grant an injunction. *Porter* was a consolidated appeal against the decisions made in four separate cases by judges in the High Court. In each case, the judge at first instance had granted injunctions to restrain the use by Gypsies and Travellers of land for residential purposes in breach of planning control, and the question for the Court of Appeal and the House of Lords was, therefore, whether those judges had directed themselves correctly about the approach they should take in the exercise of their discretion.

2.112 The Court of Appeal[167] set out the approach which is to be applied by a court considering an application for an injunction brought under TCPA 1990 s187B in order to be consistent with the court's duty under HRA 1998 s6(1) to act compatibly with convention rights. The Court of Appeal held that the judge hearing an application for an injunction under section 187B is not entitled to reach his or her own independent view of the planning merits of the case, which he or she is required to take as having been decided within the planning process.[168] However, in deciding whether or not to grant injunctive relief, the judge must consider a variety of factors which must be weighed in the balance, including:

- questions of hardship for the defendant and his or her family, including the impact on the family's health and education;
- the availability of alternative sites;
- the planning history of the site;
- the need to enforce planning control in the general interest;

165 (1992) 24 HLR 442 at 449 at paras 32–33.

166 [2003] UKHL 26, [2003] 2 WLR 1547.

167 [2001] EWCA Civ 1549, [2002] 1 WLR 1359, [2002] 1 All ER 425 at paras 38D–42.

168 [2001] EWCA Civ 1549 at para 38.

- the degree and flagrancy of the breach of planning control;
- whether other enforcement measures had been tried in the past;
- whether there was any urgency in the situation;
- health and safety considerations;
- previous planning decisions;
- the local planning authority's decision to seek injunctive relief;
- the degree of environmental damage resulting from the breach of planning control; and
- the possibility that planning permission would be granted for the residential use of the site in the future.

2.113 The Court of Appeal also recognised that the weight to be given to these considerations in the balancing exercise may vary depending on a number of other factors. For example, the relevance of, and weight to be attached to, previous planning decisions will depend on matters such as how recent they are, the extent to which considerations of hardship and availability of alternative sites were taken into account, and the strength of the conclusions reached on land use and environmental issues.[169] Similarly, the relevance and weight of the local planning authority's decision will depend on the extent to which it can be shown to have had regard to all the material considerations and to have properly posed and approached the Article 8(2) questions as to necessity and proportionality.[170]

2.114 Having identified these various factors as being relevant to the striking of the necessary balance between the competing interests, the Court of Appeal held[171] that the approach to TCPA 1990 s187B that it had adopted in the earlier decision in *Hambleton DC v Bird*[172] – which precluded consideration by the judge of questions of hardship – was not consistent with the court's duty to act compatibly with convention rights contained in HRA 1998 s6(1). The Court of Appeal concluded that proportionality requires that the injunction not only be appropriate and necessary for the attainment of the public interest objective sought (the safeguarding of the environment), but also that it does not impose an excessive burden on the individual whose private interests (the Gypsy's private life and home and retention of his ethnic identity) were at stake. It was acknowledged by the Court of Appeal that a court's task in answering that question would not be an easy one, involving the striking of a balance between competing

169 [2001] EWCA Civ 1549 at para 38.
170 [2001] EWCA Civ 1549 at para 39.
171 [2001] EWCA Civ 1549 at para 41.
172 [1995] 3 PLR 8.

interests of a very different character. The Court of Appeal stated that the task was unavoidable under the HRA 1998, and that 'provided it is undertaken in a structured and articulated way, the appropriate conclusion should emerge'.[173]

2.115 Applying the new approach to the facts of the particular cases, the Court of Appeal held that in three of the four cases the judges below had determined the applications for an injunction by reference to the old approach which involved them in deferring excessively to the planning authorities' own views as to how the balance between the competing interests fell to be struck. In those three cases the injunction orders were quashed.

2.116 The Court of Appeal's approach in *Porter* was approved unanimously by the House of Lords.[174] The effect of these important decisions has been to require much more careful and explicit consideration of why measures taken against Gypsies and Travellers are justified.[175]

2.117 The decisions of the Court of Appeal and House of Lords in *Porter* represent an important advance on the position before the HRA 1998 came into force. However, the limitations of relying on Article 8 to mitigate the effects of the overall shortfall of suitable sites are shown by the decision of the Court of Appeal in *Davis v Tonbridge and Malling BC*.[176] The case concerned an appeal by Travelling Showpeople against an injunction granted pursuant to TCPA 1990 s187B requiring them to leave the site which they had occupied in the absence of any alternative site being available for them in the whole of South East England. The evidence that, despite comprehensive searches, there was no alternative site for the Travelling Showpeople in South East England was clear and undisputed. It was also clear on the evidence that the Travelling Showpeople would suffer 'undoubted', 'real' and 'great' hardship if the injunction was granted. The judge at first instance therefore acknowledged that the case posed 'the stark question whether the appellants should be compelled to leave the site when they have nowhere else to go'. Nevertheless, he held that granting the injunction was not a disproportionate response to the continuing unlawful use of the site.

2.118 The Court of Appeal, after considering in full the decisions of the Court of Appeal and House of Lords in *Porter* and the decision of the

173 [2001] EWCA Civ 1549 at para 42.

174 [2003] UKHL 26, [2003] 2 WLR 1547.

175 See paras 4.251 and 4.257–4.258, below, for reference to other cases where consideration of the principles derived from *Chapman v UK* and the approach taken in *Porter* have led courts to delay or postpone enforcement action.

176 [2004] EWCA Civ 194.

ECtHR in *Chapman*, upheld the judge's decision. It held that the judge had correctly distinguished between the decision on the planning merits, which was for the local planning authority, and the decision on enforcement, which was for the court itself. Although there was inevitably considerable overlap between these two stages, because the same circumstances fell to be considered at each stage,[177] in the Court of Appeal's view, the judge had exercised his own jurisdiction on the issue of enforcement, and his reasoning in reaching his conclusion that enforcement was not disproportionate could not be faulted.[178] The decision that it was not a disproportionate interference with the Article 8 rights of the Travelling Showpeople was, therefore, upheld, notwithstanding that this enforcement decision would cause them great personal hardship due to there being no alternative site available to them in the whole of South East England. It is a curious feature of this case, however, that it was not expressly argued that the underlying planning decision, refusing planning permission for the development, was in breach of Article 8.[179] This concession inevitably made it more difficult to argue that enforcement of that underlying decision was in breach of Article 8.

Reasons given by domestic courts for decisions on proportionality

2.119 In *Coates v South Buckinghamshire DC*,[180] an appeal against the grant of a planning injunction which had the effect of forcing Romani Gypsies to leave their land, the Court of Appeal commented upon the reasons that should be given by a court considering the issue of proportionality. Lord Phillips of Maltravers MR said:

> In my judgment there is only one cardinal rule. The judge's reasons should make clear to the parties why he has reached his decision. Where he has had to balance competing factors it will usually be possible to explain why he has concluded that some have outweighed others. Even where the competition is so unequal that the factors speak for themselves it is desirable to say so.[181]

2.120 Sedley LJ went further and said:

> 28. . . . I may perhaps add this to what Lord Phillips MR has said in paragraphs 6 and 7 of his judgment. The practical significance of the cardinal rule which he sets out, and with which I respectfully agree, is

177 [2004] EWCA Civ 194 at para 40.
178 [2004] EWCA Civ 194 at paras 42D–55 and 59D–65.
179 See, for example, [2004] EWCA Civ 194 at para 46.
180 [2004] EWCA Civ 1378.
181 [2004] EWCA Civ 1378 at para 7.

> well illustrated by the remainder of his judgment. Its legal importance has been plain since the seminal decision in the House of Lords in *R (Daly) v Home Secretary* [2001] 2 WLR 1622: see, in particular, Lord Bingham at paragraph 23 and Lord Steyn at paragraph 27. Proportionality is rarely a simple yes or no issue. Except in cases where the answer is obvious (for instance where no intelligible justification has been put forward, or where the need is plain and the invasion trivial) it requires a structured consideration of the questions now well established in Strasbourg jurisprudence: is the objective sufficiently important to justify limiting a basic right; is the measure sensibly directed to the objective; does it impair the right more than necessary?

2.121 Sedley LJ returned to the same theme in the case of *Machado v Secretary of State for the Home Department*[182] and said:

> 41. . . . I would add that proportionality is not an issue that can ordinarily be addressed in one sentence. It does not demand complexity, but it calls for a structured approach.

Article 14: general principles

The European Court of Human Rights' approach to Article 14 complaints

2.122 Article 14 states that:

> The enjoyment of the rights and freedoms set forth in this Convention shall be secured without discrimination on any ground such as sex, race, colour, language, religion, political or other opinion, national or social origin, association with a national minority, property, birth or other status.

2.123 'Other status' has been taken to include disability[183] and sexual orientation,[184] neither of which had been expressly included as grounds when the convention was originally drafted.

2.124 The Article 14 right has no independent existence and the discrimination must occur in the context of the enjoyment of another convention right for Article 14 to be actionable. The application of Article 14 does not necessarily presuppose a breach of another convention right. However, it has been held that there can be no room for its application unless the facts at issue fall within the ambit of one or more of the other rights protected by the convention.[185]

182 [2005] EWCA Civ 597.

183 *Glor v Switzerland*, App No 13444/04, 30 April 2009 at para 53.

184 *Salguiero da Silva Mouta v Portugal* (2001) 31 EHRR 47 at para 28.

185 *Abdulaziz, Cabales and Balkandi v UK* (1984) 6 EHRR 28 at para 71.

2.125 It was held in *Carson v UK* that:

> ... in order for an issue to arise under article 14 there must be a difference in the treatment of persons in analogous, or relatively similar, situations. Such a difference in treatment is discriminatory if it has no objective and reasonable justification; in other words, if it does not pursue a legitimate aim or if there is not a reasonable relation of proportionality between the means employed and the aim sought to be realised.[186]

2.126 In essence, Article 14 guarantees that different lifestyles should be taken into account and that persons in similar situations should be treated in a similar manner with respect to convention rights.

Similar treatment for persons in similar situations

2.127 In *Muñoz Díaz v Spain*,[187] the Spanish state refused to recognise a Roma woman's marriage, which had been solemnised in keeping with Roma customs and traditions. This meant that she was not entitled to her survivor's (widow's) pension, which she would otherwise have received if she had been married in accordance with Spanish law. The ECtHR held that there had been a violation of Article 14 in conjunction with Article 1 of Protocol 1 (the right to peaceful enjoyment of possessions). The ECtHR took the view that while belonging to a minority does not create an exemption from complying with marriage laws, it may have an effect on the manner in which those laws are applied.[188] The applicant's particular cultural and social situation had not been taken into account by the domestic authorities.[189] The refusal to recognise the applicant's entitlement to a survivor's pension constituted a difference in treatment in relation to the treatment afforded, by statute or case law, to other situations that must be considered equivalent in terms of the effects of good faith, such as a belief in good faith in the existence of a marriage that is null and void.[190]

Different treatment for persons in different situations

2.128 In *Thlimmenos v Greece*[191] the court held that a Jehovah's witness who was sent to jail for four years for refusing to wear a military uniform must be treated differently than 'ordinary' criminals with respect to laws preventing those with a criminal record from becoming public

186 (2010) 51 EHRR 13 at para 61.
187 (2010) 50 EHRR 49.
188 (2010) 50 EHRR 49 at para 61.
189 (2010) 50 EHRR 49 at para 64.
190 (2010) 50 EHRR 49 at para 65.
191 (2001) 31 EHRR 15.

accountants. While there was a legitimate reason for keeping convicted criminals from becoming public accountants, the same rationale did not apply to conscientious objectors, and their different circumstances compelled different treatment.[192] Likewise, in *Chapman v UK*[193] the Grand Chamber specifically recognised the different lifestyle of Roma and indicated that states have a positive obligation to facilitate that lifestyle and that in certain circumstances, this would require the state to treat Roma differently.[194]

Indirect discrimination

2.129 In *DH v Czech Republic*, the ECtHR accepted that a difference in treatment may take the form of disproportionately prejudicial effects of a general policy or measure which, though couched in neutral terms, discriminates against a particular group. Such a situation may amount to 'indirect discrimination' which does not necessarily require a discriminatory intent.[195]

The standard and burden of proof in discrimination cases

2.130 In Article 14 cases the standard of proof applied is 'beyond reasonable doubt'. This has led to some unsatisfactory outcomes.

2.131 In *Anguelova v Bulgaria*[196] the applicant's son, a Romani man, died while in police custody. The ECtHR found that the applicant's claim that his son was tortured because of his ethnicity raised 'serious arguments'[197] and noted that the state had not provided any other plausible explanation. Nonetheless, the court could not conclude 'beyond reasonable doubt' that the death and lack of a meaningful investigation into it were motivated by racial prejudice. This conclusion led Judge Bonello in a strong dissenting opinion to comment that:

> Kurds, coloureds, Muslims, Roma and others are again and again killed, tortured or maimed, but the court is not persuaded that their race, colour, nationality or place of origin has anything to do with it.[198]

2.132 The ECtHR's traditional approach to the burden and standard of proof was challenged in the case of *Nachova and others v Bulgaria*.[199]

192 (2001) 31 EHRR 15 at para 47.
193 *Chapman v UK* (2001) 33 EHRR 18.
194 *Chapman v UK* (2001) 33 EHRR 18 at para 96.
195 (2008) 47 EHRR 3 at para 184.
196 (2004) 38 EHRR 31.
197 (2004) 38 EHRR 31 at para 168.
198 (2004) 38 EHRR 31 at para 3 of Judge's Bonello's dissenting opinion.
199 (2006) 42 EHRR 43.

The applicants and interveners argued that the 'beyond reasonable doubt' standard of proof was simply too high a threshold to meet and they pointed to a growing trend by other courts to shift the burden of proof in discrimination cases. The Grand Chamber noted that the 'beyond reasonable doubt' standard had been adopted by the court, but that it had never been the intention of the court to borrow this approach from national legal systems that use that standard. It pointed out that the role of the court is 'not to rule on criminal guilt or civil liability but on contracting states' responsibility under the Convention'.[200] Therefore, in proceedings before the court:

> . . . there are no procedural barriers to the admissibility of evidence or pre-determined formulae for its assessment . . . proof may follow from the coexistence of sufficiently strong, clear and concordant inferences or of similar unrebutted presumptions of fact. Moreover, the level of persuasion necessary for reaching a particular conclusion and, in this connection, the distribution of the burden of proof are intrinsically linked to the specificity of the allegation made and the Convention right at stake.[201]

2.133 In *DH*, the Grand Chamber held that in certain circumstances the burden of proof shifts to the state:

> Where an applicant alleging indirect discrimination thus establishes a rebuttable presumption that the effect of a measure or practice is discriminatory, the burden then shifts to the respondent state, which must show that the difference in treatment is not discriminatory.[202]

2.134 It added that:

> . . . statistics which appear on critical examination to be reliable and significant will be sufficient to constitute the prima facie evidence the applicant is required to produce. This does not, however, mean that indirect discrimination cannot be proved without statistical evidence.[203]

Objective and reasonable justification

2.135 Freedom from discrimination under Article 14 is a qualified, rather than an absolute right.[204] However, any difference in treatment must have an objective and reasonable justification. In other words, the

200 (2006) 42 EHRR 43 at para 147.
201 (2006) 42 EHRR 43 at para 147; and see also *Salman v Turkey*, App No 21986/93, (2002) 34 EHRR 17.
202 (2008) 47 EHRR 3 at para 189.
203 (2008) 47 EHRR 3 at para 188.
204 Compare the position under EqA 2010 in domestic law (see paras 8.37–8.132).

different treatment must have a legitimate aim and be a means proportionate to achieving that goal.

2.136 In *Todorova v Bulgaria*[205] the ECtHR held that the refusal to suspend a sentence of three years' imprisonment imposed on a Roma woman breached Article 14 in conjunction with Article 6. The domestic sentencing court had commented on the applicant's ethnic origin, among the personal details used to identify her, and then refused to suspend the sentence on the grounds that there was 'an impression of impunity, especially among members of minority groups, who consider that a suspended sentence is not a sentence at all.' The ECtHR found that the applicant had been treated differently on grounds of race and that the reasons given by the sentencing court contained no objective justification for doing so.

Margin of appreciation

2.137 The ECtHR confers a considerable margin of appreciation on member states when determining what constitutes an objective and reasonable justification for discrimination. Whether the margin of appreciation is wide or narrow depends on:

1) *The nature of the right involved.* Contracting states have a certain margin of appreciation in assessing whether and to what extent difference in otherwise similar situations justify different treatment.[206] The scope of the margin will vary according to the circumstances, the subject matter and the background. Article 14 does not prevent states from treating groups differently in order to correct 'factual inequalities and in certain circumstances, the failure to do so without objective and reasonable justification may result in a breach'.[207] States are afforded a wide margin of appreciation when it comes to general measures of economic or social strategy. The national authorities are, in principle, better placed than international judges to appreciate what is in the public interest and the court will usually respect this unless it is 'manifestly without foundation'.[208]
2) *The level of interference.* If the right would be eliminated completely, there is unlikely to be an objective and reasonable justification

205 App No 37193/07, 25 March 2010.

206 *Thlimmenos v Greece* (2001) 31 EHRR 15 at para 40.

207 *Thlimmenos v Greece* (2001) 31 EHRR 15 at para 44; *Muñoz Díaz v Spain* (2010) 50 EHRR 49 at para 48.

208 *Muñoz Díaz v Spain* (2010) 50 EHRR 49 at para 49.

for the measure. For example, in *Aziz v Cyprus*[209] the applicant was a Turkish Cypriot living in the Greek part of Cyprus. He was unable to vote because the Cypriot constitution required Turkish Cypriots to be registered on the Turkish voting rolls and Greeks to be on the Greek rolls, thus completely depriving him of his right to vote.

3) *The public interest involved* in the category of discrimination. It was held in *Timishev v Russia*[210] that:

> . . . no difference in treatment which is based exclusively or to a decisive extent on a person's ethnic origin is capable of being objectively justified in a contemporary democratic society built on the principles of pluralism and respect for different cultures.[211]

The procedural obligation to investigate possible racist motives

2.138 Article 14 may give rise to a positive obligation on the state. The ECtHR confirmed in *Timishev* that such a positive obligation existed, at least in relation to the eradication of race discrimination:

> Racial discrimination is a particularly invidious kind of discrimination and, in view of its perilous consequences, requires from the authorities special vigilance and a vigorous reaction. It is for this reason that the authorities must use all available means to combat racism, thereby reinforcing democracy's vision of a society in which diversity is not perceived as a threat but as a source of enrichment.[212]

2.139 In *Nachova v Bulgaria*, it was found that the Bulgarian state had failed in its duty, under Article 14 read in conjunction with Article 2 of the convention, to take all possible steps to investigate whether or not discrimination may have played a part in the events that led to the killing of two Romani men who had been shot dead by a military police officer. The Grand Chamber endorsed the following principles that states must apply in order to fulfil their procedural obligation to investigate possible racist motives for acts of violence:

> States have a general obligation under article 2 of the convention to conduct an effective investigation in cases of deprivation of life. That obligation must be discharged without discrimination, as required by article 14 of the convention . . . [W]here there is suspicion that racial attitudes induced a violent act it is particularly important that the official investigation is pursued with vigour and impartiality, having regard to

209 (2005) 41 EHRR 11.

210 (2007) 44 EHRR 37.

211 (2007) 44 EHRR 37 at para 58.

212 (2007) 44 EHRR 37 at para 56.

> the need to reassert continuously society's condemnation of racism and ethnic hatred and to maintain the confidence of minorities in the ability of the authorities to protect them from the threat of racist violence. Compliance with the state's positive obligations under article 2 of the convention requires that the domestic legal system must demonstrate its capacity to enforce criminal law against those who unlawfully took the life of another, irrespective of the victim's racial or ethnic origin . . .
>
> . . . [W]hen investigating violent incidents and, in particular, deaths at the hands of state agents, state authorities have the additional duty to take all reasonable steps to unmask any racist motive and to establish whether or not ethnic hatred or prejudice may have played a role in the events. Failing to do so and treating racially induced violence and brutality on an equal footing with cases that have no racist overtones would be to turn a blind eye to the specific nature of acts that are particularly destructive of fundamental rights. A failure to make a distinction in the way in which situations that are essentially different are handled may constitute unjustified treatment irreconcilable with article 14 of the Convention (see, mutatis mutandis, *Thlimmenos v Greece* . . . [App No] 34369/97 . . .). In order to maintain public confidence in their law enforcement machinery, contracting states must ensure that in the investigation of incidents involving the use of force a distinction is made both in their legal systems and in practice between cases of excessive use of force and of racist killing. Admittedly, proving racial motivation will often be extremely difficult in practice. The respondent state's obligation to investigate possible racist overtones to a violent act is an obligation to use best endeavours and not absolute . . . The authorities must do what is reasonable in the circumstances to collect and secure the evidence, explore all practical means of discovering the truth and deliver fully reasoned, impartial and objective decisions, without omitting suspicious facts that may be indicative of . . . racially induced violence.[213]

2.140 The Grand Chamber added that:

> . . . the authorities' duty to investigate the existence of a possible link between racist attitudes and an act of violence is an aspect of their procedural obligations arising under article 2 of the Convention, but may also be seen as implicit in their responsibilities under article 14 of the convention taken in conjunction with article 2 to secure the enjoyment of the right to life without discrimination.[214]

2.141 More recently, in April 2019 in *Lingurar v Romania*[215] the ECtHR concluded that there had been a violation of both the substantive and

213 (2006) 42 EHRR 43 at para 160.

214 (2006) 42 EHRR 43 at para 161. See also *Stoica v Romania* (2011) 52 EHRR 29.

215 App No 48474/14, 16 April 2019.

procedural limbs of Article 3, in combination with Article 14, of the ECHR in circumstances where four Romani applicants had been beaten by police officers during a police raid on their home and the Romanian state had subsequently failed properly to investigate the incident. It is of particular note that for the first time in one of its judgments, the ECtHR used the terms 'ethnic profiling' and 'institutionalised racism', stating that:

> . . . the domestic courts did not censure what seems to be a discriminatory use of ethnic profiling by the authorities.[216]

> . . . Roma communities are often confronted with institutionalised racism and are prone to excessive use of force by the law-enforcement authorities . . .[217]

Although, the ECtHR did not go so far as to describe what was happening in Romania as 'institutional anti-Gypsyism', or use the term 'anti-Gypsyism' when condemning Romania, its judgment provides a damning account of how the law enforcement authorities in Romania treat Romani people. The ECtHR stated that:

> . . . the decisions to organise the police raid and to use force against the applicants were made on considerations based on the applicants' ethnic origin. The authorities automatically connected ethnicity to criminal behaviour, thus their ethnic profiling of the applicants was discriminatory.[218]

The court awarded each applicant €11,700 as just satisfaction for the violation of their rights.

Findings on Article 14 not always necessary

2.142 In the past the ECtHR has often shied away from making a finding that there has been a violation of Article 14, even where it has found that a policy or act was discriminatory. Thus, in *VC v Slovakia*, a case involving the sterilisation of a Roma woman without her informed consent, the ECtHR held that there had been violations of Article 3 and Article 8. Nevertheless, the ECtHR decided it was unnecessary to go on to consider whether there had been a violation of Article 14, notwithstanding materials by the Council of Europe's Human Rights Commissioner and the European Commission against Racism and Intolerance which identified shortcomings in domestic legislation on sterilisation, which were liable to particularly affect members of

216 At para 79.

217 At para 80.

218 At para 76.

the Roma community.[219] Whether, following its recent decision in *Lingurar*, the ECtHR will be quite so reticent in the future remains to be seen.

The assessment of Article 14 claims by domestic courts

2.143 In *Ghaidan v Godin-Mendoza*, one of the first domestic cases which considered Article 14, Lord Nicholls stated that:

> It goes without saying that article 14 is an important article of the Convention. Discrimination is an insidious practice. Discriminatory law undermines the rule of law because it is the antithesis of fairness. It brings the law into disrepute. It breeds resentment. It fosters an inequality of outlook which is demeaning alike to those unfairly benefited and those unfairly prejudiced.[220]

2.144 It was said by Lord Walker in *R (Carson) v Secretary of State for Work and Pensions* that:

> In the field of human rights, discrimination is regarded as particularly objectionable because it disregards fundamental notions of human dignity and equality before the law. Discrimination on the ground of sex or race demeans the victim by using a sexual or racial stereotype as a sufficient ground for unfavourable treatment, rather than treating her as an individual to be judged on her own merits.[221]

2.145 The decision of the Court of Appeal in *Wandsworth LBC v Michalak*[222] resulted in the adoption of an approach requiring four questions to be posed by a judge dealing with an Article 14 claim:

1) Do the facts fall within the ambit of one or more of the substantive convention rights?
2) If so, was there a difference in treatment in respect of that right between the complainant on the one hand and other persons put forward for comparison on the other?
3) Were the chosen comparators in an analogous situation to the complainant's situation?
4) If so, did the difference in treatment have an objective and reasonable justification: in other words, did it pursue a legitimate aim and did the differential treatment bear a reasonable relationship of proportionality to the aim sought to be achieved?

219 (2014) 59 EHRR 29 at paras 176–180.
220 [2004] 2 AC 557 at para 9.
221 [2006] 1 AC 173 at para 49.
222 [2003] 1 WLR 617 at para 20.

2.146 In *Ghaidan v Godin-Mendoza* Baroness Hale of Richmond issued a word of warning, making the point that, while the *Michalak* questions were a useful tool of analysis, there was considerable overlap between them and that a rigidly formulaic approach should be avoided.[223]

2.147 The House of Lords revisited the issue when it considered *R (Carson) v Secretary of State for Work and Pensions*[224] on appeal. Having referred to the *Michalak* questions, Lord Nicholls of Birkenhead said:

> 3. . . . I prefer to keep the formulation of the relevant issues in these cases as simple and non-technical as possible. Article 14 does not apply unless the alleged discrimination is in connection with a Convention right and on a ground stated in article 14. If this pre-requisite is satisfied, the essential question for the court is whether the alleged discrimination, that is, the difference in treatment of which complaint is made, can withstand scrutiny. Sometimes the answer to this question will be plain. There may be such an obvious, relevant difference between the claimant and those with whom he seeks to compare himself that their situations cannot be regarded as analogous. Sometimes, where the position is not so clear, a different approach is called for. Then the court's scrutiny may best be directed at considering whether the differentiation has a legitimate aim and whether the means chosen to achieve the aim is appropriate and not disproportionate in its adverse impact.

2.148 Likewise Lord Hoffmann and Lord Walker concluded that the question whether there had been a breach of Article 14 could be best answered without adopting the *Michalak* approach.[225] Lord Walker pointed out that the Strasbourg case law had made little use of comparators and had been able to reach an overall conclusion as to whether there had been unfair and unjustifiable discrimination on the grounds of some personal characteristic, without elaborate discussion on comparators.[226]

2.149 In addition, their Lordships indicated that a distinction was to be drawn between grounds of discrimination under Article 14 which prima facie appeared to offend respect due to the individual, as in the

223 [2004] 3 WLR 113 at para 134.

224 [2006] 1 AC 173.

225 [2006] 1 AC 173 at paras 33 and 64. See also *R (Johnson) v Secretary of State for the Home Department* [2014] EWHC 2386 (Admin) at paras 30–31 for a recent example of where the High Court said that it was usually convenient to use the *Michalak* approach but that a rigidly formulaic approach to the questions should be avoided.

226 [2006] 1 AC 173 at para 63.

case of sex or race, where very weighty reasons are required to justify the difference in treatment, and those which merely required some rational justification.[227]

2.150 The House of Lords revisited the *Michalak* approach in *AL (Serbia) v Secretary of State for the Home Department*.[228] Baroness Hale noted that:

> 23. . . . the classic Strasbourg statements of the law do not place any emphasis on the identification of an exact comparator. They ask whether 'differences in otherwise similar situations justify a different treatment'.
>
> . . .
>
> 25. . . . unless there are very obvious relevant differences between the two situations, it is better to concentrate on the reasons for the difference in treatment and whether they amount to an objective and reasonable justification.[229]

2.151 Generally domestic courts will afford public bodies a margin of discretion when considering whether a difference in treatment is justified, adopting the approach of the ECtHR. The scope of the margin of discretion will vary according to the circumstances, the subject matter and the background.[230] However, it has been held that a strict approach is called for in Article 14 cases involving race discrimination. Thus, for example, discrimination on certain grounds (sometimes referred to as 'suspect grounds') will require 'very weighty reasons' before it can be held to be justified.[231] These include sex, race, sexual orientation, illegitimacy and nationality. Indeed, it has been said that discrimination on grounds of ethnic

227 [2006] 1 AC 173 paras 15–17. See also *Westminster City Council and the First Secretary of State v Morris* [2005] EWCA Civ 1184 at para 82; and *R (Johnson) v Secretary of State for the Home Department* [2014] EWHC 2386 (Admin) at paras 30–31.

228 [2008] 1 WLR 1434.

229 See *R (JS) Secretary of State for Work and Pensions* [2015] 1 WLR 1449 at para 11 where Lord Reed considers the approach in *Carson v UK* (2010) 51 EHRR 13 at para 61.

230 Thus, in *Humphreys v HM Revenue and Customs Commissioners* [2012] UKSC 18, [2012] 1 WLR 1545 at para 19, Baroness Hale held that: 'the normally strict test for justification of sex discrimination in the enjoyment of Convention rights gives way to the "manifestly without reasonable foundation" test in the context of state benefits'.

231 See *R (Carson) v Secretary of State for Work and Pensions* [2005] UKHL 37, [2006] 1 AC 173, paras 15–17 and 55–58.

origin can never be justified.[232] That said, the approach will not necessarily be as strict if the complaint is about a form of indirect discrimination as opposed to active or direct discrimination.[233]

Key domestic Gypsy and Traveller Article 14 cases

2.152 Gypsies, Travellers and Roma are among the most marginalised groups in society and frequently suffer discrimination in their access to the most basic necessities of life. Although in theory Gypsies and Travellers enjoy the same entitlements to public services as the settled community, in practice they frequently experience discrimination in their access to services such as education and healthcare.[234] Some of the rights and interests which are protected by those basic services (for example, health and education) fall within the scope of other convention rights, such as the right not to be subjected to inhuman and degrading treatment (Article 3), the right to respect for family life (Article 8) and the right to education (Article 2 of Protocol 1). The Article 14 guarantee against discrimination in the enjoyment of convention rights can therefore be relied upon where discriminatory access to basic services impinges on these convention rights. However, attempts by Gypsies and Travellers to invoke Article 14 in our domestic courts have had mixed results to date.

Articles 8 and 14: Planning enforcement and the use of stop notices

2.153 Where a local authority has issued an enforcement notice to restrain a breach of planning control it may also issue a 'stop notice' under TCPA 1990 s183(4), prohibiting the carrying out of a specified activity on the land to which the enforcement notice relates.[235] In its original form TCPA 1990 s183 could not be used to prohibit individuals living in caravans or dwelling houses. However, the provision was amended by Planning and Compensation Act 1991 s9 and the

232 See *Timishev v Russia* (55762/00) (2007) 44 EHRR 37, para 58.

233 See *R (MA (Somalia)) v Secretary of State for the Home Department* [2013] EWCA Civ 966, para 15.

234 COM(2010) 133, Communication of the Commission to the Council, the European Parliament, the European Economic and Social Committee and the Committee of the Regions, *The Social and economic integration of Roma* 7 April 2010, see: http://eur-lex.europa.eu/legal-content/EN/TXT/HTML/?uri=CELEX:52010DC0133&from=EN.

235 See paras 4.206–4.207, below.

caravan use exemption was removed, though the dwelling house exemption was retained. In *R (Wilson) v First Secretary of State and Wychavon DC*[236] the appellant, a Gypsy, challenged the legislation by way of judicial review on grounds that it unlawfully discriminated against Romani Gypsies and Irish Travellers in breach of Article 14 of the convention and she also sought a declaration of incompatibility to that effect. Crane J dismissed the claim and the appellant appealed against that decision.

2.154 In his judgment, Richards LJ explained the issues that the Court of Appeal had to determine in the following way:

> The Secretary of State has very properly made a number of concessions which serve greatly to reduce the area of contention. It is not in dispute that (a) the operation of section 183 falls within the ambit of article 8, so as to engage article 14; (b) a higher proportion of gypsies and travellers than of any other relevant group would be likely to be affected by stop notices served under section 183 on caravans used for residential purposes; (c) therefore, although the exemption in section 183(4) appears on its face to be a neutral provision, its greater impact on gypsies and travellers than on the general population means that it is indirectly discriminatory in its effect in relation to a status falling within the scope of article 14; and (d) hence there is an onus on the State to give an objective justification for the rule as formulated. The point for decision is whether the Secretary of State has discharged the onus of justifying the provision.[237]

2.155 Thus, it was common ground that the secretary of state had the burden of justifying the admitted discrimination that occurred in 1991 (when the legislation was amended). In addition, it was accepted by the Court of Appeal that the standard of proof was a high one for the secretary of state to meet, and that any discretionary area of judgment will be narrow in cases such as this, which involved discrimination on particularly sensitive grounds such as gender or race.[238]

2.156 In the event, the Court of Appeal concluded that there was a clear distinction between the unauthorised stationing of a residential caravan on land and unauthorised development to which the dwelling house exemption applies and that the use of buildings as dwelling

236 [2007] EWCA Civ 52. See also the two JCHR Reports on the issue: paras 5.5–5.7 of the Eighth Report of Session 2003–04, *Scrutiny of bills: third progress report*; and paras 3.2–3.4 of the Tenth Report of Session 2003–04, *Scrutiny of bills: fourth progress report*.

237 [2007] EWCA Civ 52 at para 27.

238 [2007] EWCA Civ 52 at para 46.

houses will cause less environmental damage than the stationing of residential caravans on land. In the circumstances the Court of Appeal was satisfied that the difference in treatment was justified and the appeal was dismissed.[239]

Articles 8 and 14: offers of conventional housing

2.157 The protection of Article 14 has been invoked successfully in relation to the relevance of an offer of conventional housing to Gypsies and Travellers when making decisions about planning permission or consequential enforcement. In *Clarke v Secretary of State for Transport, Local Government and the Regions and Tunbridge Wells BC*[240] a planning inspector had found that conventional housing accommodation had been offered to the Gypsy family in question, and that they found the prospect distressing, having never lived in a conventional house. Nevertheless, the inspector went on to state that the offer of that accommodation detracted somewhat from the contention that the only alternative to the appeal site was an illegal roadside pitch. The High Court held that:

> 30. . . . in certain appropriate circumstances it can amount to a breach of articles 8 and 14 to weigh in the balance and hold against a Gypsy applying for planning permission, or indeed resisting eviction from Council or private land, that he or she has refused conventional housing accommodation as being contrary to his or her culture. Such circumstances, in my judgment, are and should be, limited, just as they are if, for example, it is to be alleged similarly to be impermissible, in relevant circumstances, to hold it against or penalise a religious or strictly observant Christian, Jew or Muslim because he or she will not, and thus cannot, work on certain days, or to hold it against, or penalise, a strictly observant Buddhist, Muslim, Jew or Sikh because he eats or will not eat certain foods, or will or will not wear certain clothing. It is not, and cannot be, a formality to establish this, and the onus is upon the person such as a Gypsy who seeks to establish it.

2.158 The onus was on the individual concerned to satisfy the planning inspector that they or their family do indeed have a genuine aversion to conventional housing, but once that has been established:

> . . . it would be contrary to articles 8 and 14 to expect such a person to accept conventional housing and to hold it against him or her that he

239 [2007] EWCA Civ 52 at paras 66–68.

240 [2001] EWHC Admin 800, [2002] JPL 552, July 2002 *Legal Action* 23.

has not accepted it, or is not prepared to accept it, even as a last resort factor.[241]

Articles 11 and 14: culture, traditional horse fairs and freedom of assembly and association

2.159 The right to freedom of assembly and association contained in Article 11 of the convention is a qualified right.

2.160 Thus, in *Vona v Hungary*[242] the ECtHR held that there had been no violation of Article 11 as the Hungarian authorities had acted proportionately in dissolving the Hungarian Guard Association after it had held rallies and demonstrations calling for the defence of 'ethnic Hungarians' against 'Gypsy-criminality'. The measure could be seen as pursuing the aims of public safety, prevention of disorder and the protection of rights of others. The ECtHR held that one value in a democratic society is the co-existence of members of society free from racial segregation, without which a democratic society is inconceivable.[243]

2.161 Article 11 was also in play in the case of *R v Tunbridge Wells BC ex p The Gypsy Council for Education, Culture, Welfare and Civil Rights and Eli Frankham.*[244] The High Court was asked to consider a case concerning the right of Gypsies to attend a traditional 'Horse Fair' that had been held in the village of Horsmonden, in Kent, for many years. A decision had been taken by the local authority to prohibit the holding of the annual Horse Fair on grounds that it would give rise to health and safety considerations.[245] It was the subject of an application for judicial review made by a respected elder of the Gypsy

241 [2001] EWHC Admin 800 at para 34. The decision was upheld on appeal by a unanimous Court of Appeal (see *Clarke v Secretary of State for Transport, Local Government and the Regions and Tunbridge Wells BC* [2002] EWCA Civ 819 at paras 5 and 15 of the judgment, where the Court of Appeal endorsed the important point that an aversion to conventional housing may be grounded in a belief or understanding which is an integral part of a cultural identity as a Gypsy or Traveller. See also *Price v Carmarthenshire County Council* [2003] EWHC 42 (Admin) and *Codona v Mid-Bedfordshire DC* [2004] EWCA Civ 925 See also the further discussion of these issues in chapters 4 and 6 at paras 4.171–4.175 and 6.106–6.113, below.

242 App No 35943/10, 9 July 2013.

243 App No 35943/10, 9 July 2013 at para 57.

244 7 September 2000 (unreported), Admin Court. An application was made to the ECtHR but the case was declared inadmissible in *Gypsy Council and others v UK*, App No 66336/01, Admissibility Decision of 14 May 2002.

245 The decision was made under the provisions of Public Order Act 1986 s14A (as amended by Criminal Justice and Public Order Act 1994 s70) and was approved by the secretary of state.

community and an organisation that works for the preservation of the Gypsy way of life. The decision was challenged on the basis that it breached Articles 8, 11 (the right to freedom of association and assembly) and 14 of the ECHR. However, the High Court accepted that the local authority had taken account of all relevant considerations and had struck the correct balance between the interests of the Romani Gypsy community and the interests of society in general. In addition, the High Court held that the decision was necessary and proportionate, given the circumstances of the case and the fact that an alternative venue had been proposed some 20 miles away from Horsmonden.

Article 14 and Article 1 of Protocol 1: protection of property

2.162 Article 1 of Protocol 1 of the ECHR provides that:

> Every natural or legal person is entitled to the peaceful enjoyment of his possessions. No one shall be deprived of his possessions except in the public interest and subject to the conditions provided for by law and by the general principles of international law.
> The preceding provisions shall not, however, in any way impair the right of a State to enforce such laws as it deems necessary to control the use of property in accordance with the general interest or to secure the payment of taxes or other contributions or penalties.

2.163 The Administrative Court has considered the relationship between Article 1 of Protocol 1 and Article 14 of the convention in two cases concerning Gypsies and Travellers: *R (Knowles) v Secretary of State for Work and Pensions*;[246] and *R (Mahoney and Jones) v Secretary of State for Communities and Local Government*.[247]

2.164 In *Knowles*, the claimants challenged the housing benefit regime that applied to residents of private caravan sites and argued that it was discriminatory and constituted a violation of their Article 1 of Protocol 1 rights in conjunction with Article 14. Residents of local authority run caravan sites were entitled to a full housing benefit rebate, whereas the amount of housing benefit on private sites was subject to a determination by a rent officer and normally set lower than the full contractual rent charged. It was argued that the housing benefit scheme as it relates to Gypsies and Travellers, who pay rent for pitches on privately owned sites, was discriminatory because no allowance had been made for the fact that the costs of providing

246 [2013] EWHC 19 (Admin).
247 [2015] EWHC 589 (Admin).

caravan sites for Gypsies and Travellers is higher than the costs of providing similar sites for those who are not members of the Gypsy and Traveller community. Hickinbottom J rejected the claim on the basis that the majority of the additional costs of running the sites were not attributable to accommodation costs so as to fall within the 'eligible rent' criteria of the housing benefit regime, and the additional costs which could be attributed to accommodation costs were not significant.[248] The state had a wide margin of discretion in the field of economic and social policy and the difference in treatment could be objectively and reasonably justified. Hickinbottom J was of the view that, even if Gypsies and Travellers on private sites had to make up the shortfall out of other resources, this did not mean that they would inevitably become homeless, in the sense that they would have to pitch up on the roadside, and there was no evidence before the court that anyone had.[249] The judge accepted that the shortfall in housing benefit would place severe pressure on their finances but said 'unfortunately, many on [housing benefit], whether living in mobile homes or bricks-and-mortar accommodation, live under similar pressure'.[250]

2.165 *R (Mahoney and Jones)* concerned the compulsory purchase of a caravan site by Crossrail. The question for the court was whether the Land Compensation Act (LCA) 1973 s33(2) discriminated against Gypsies and Travellers. Under LCA 1973 s29(1)(a), a person is entitled to compensation in the form of home loss payments where they are displaced from a dwelling due to a compulsory acquisition of an interest in land. By virtue of LCA 1973 s33(2), persons residing in a caravan on a caravan site are only entitled to a home loss payment if no suitable alternative site for stationing a caravan is made available. As the claimants had been provided with a suitable alternative site, they were not entitled to a home loss payment. They argued that this amounted to a breach of their Article 8 right to respect for their home and their right to peaceful enjoyment of their possessions under Article 1 of Protocol 1 (in the form of the home loss payments) in conjunction with Article 14 on the basis that the measure would disproportionately impact on Gypsies and Travellers. Lindblom J dismissed the case having held that the claimants were not in an analogous situation to those living in a dwelling-house:

248 [2013] EWHC 19 (Admin) at para 84.
249 [2013] EWHC 19 at para 97.
250 [2013] EWHC 19 at para 99.

> When a caravan dweller is compelled to move from a site where he has stationed his caravan he is able to take the caravan with him. It is mobile. By contrast, when a person who lives in a dwelling-house is displaced from it he leaves not only the location where he has made a home but also the house in which he has lived. It is immovable. This is a practical difference and in my view a significant difference.[251]

2.166 The court rejected an argument that the margin of appreciation should be narrow in this case because it concerned the loss of the claimants' home, property and community. Instead, it found that the state had a wide margin of discretion because the home loss payments were part of economic and social policy. The court applied a test of whether the measure was 'manifestly without reasonable foundation' and rejected the arguments that the measure was without a legitimate aim.[252]

The approach to Article 2 of Protocol 1: the right to education[253]

The European Court of Human Rights

2.167 The ECtHR has considered a number of cases in recent years in which Roma applicants have complained that their children's right to education has been violated in circumstances where they have been placed in separate schools or classrooms from other children. In the landmark case of *DH v The Czech Republic,*[254] the Grand Chamber held that there had been a violation of Article 14 read in conjunction with Article 2 of Protocol 1 in circumstances where 18 Roma children had been placed in special schools with the written consent of their parents.

2.168 Statistical evidence was provided to the court which showed that in 1999, 50.3 per cent of Roma children went to special schools in the city of Ostrava in comparison with 1.8 per cent of non-Roma children. The evidence also demonstrated that although Roma children only made up 2.26 per cent of pupils of primary school age, they made up 56 per cent of all children who had been assigned places in a special school. A Roma child in Ostrava was 27 times more likely to go to a special school than a non-Roma child.[255]

2.169 The Grand Chamber concluded that: at the very least, there was danger that the selection tests for the schools were biased and did not

251 [2015] EWHC 589 (Admin) at para 60.

252 [2015] EWHC 589 (Admin) at paras 77–84.

253 See paras 7.2–7.14.

254 App No 57325/00, judgment date 13 November 2007, (2008) 47 EHRR 3.

255 (2008) 47 EHRR 3 at para 18.

take into account the particular characteristics of Roma children;[256] the parents were not in a position to give informed consent to the children being placed in the special schools;[257] and that, in any case 'no waiver of the right not to be subjected to racial discrimination can be accepted'.[258]

2.170 In reaching its conclusion that the children had been subjected to indirect discrimination, in violation of the ECHR, the Grand Chamber recognised that choosing the best means to address learning difficulties of children lacking proficiency of the language of instruction is not easy and that it entails a difficult balancing exercise between competing interests. Nevertheless, the Grand Chamber commented upon the margin of appreciation in the following terms:

> . . . whenever discretion capable of interfering with the enjoyment of a convention right is conferred on the national authorities, the procedural safeguards available to the individual will be especially material in determining whether the respondent state has, when fixing the regulatory framework, remained within its margin of appreciation.[259]

2.171 In *Sampanis and others v Greece*[260] a number of Roma applicants complained of discrimination where the local school had failed to enrol their children for a year. Greece accepted that the children had missed the school year but maintained that there had been no breach of the convention because the applicants had only informally approached the school, as opposed to having made a formal application for places. The ECtHR rejected Greece's argument. It found that in approaching the school, the parents had explicitly expressed their wish to enrol their children. Given the vulnerability of the Roma community and the requirement to pay particular attention to their needs, the school should have facilitated their children's enrolment.

2.172 The following year, the children were admitted into the school, but at the beginning of the school year non-Roma parents protested about their admission, blockading the school and demanding that the Roma children be transferred to another building. The Roma parents then signed a statement, drafted by the teachers, to the effect that they wished their children to be transferred to another building. Shortly thereafter, the Roma children began receiving 'preparatory classes' in an annexe and the blockade was lifted.

256 (2008) 47 EHRR 3 at paras 200–201.
257 (2008) 47 EHRR 3 at para 202.
258 (2008) 47 EHRR 3 at para 204.
259 (2008) 47 EHRR 3 at para 206.
260 App No 32526/05, 5 June 2008.

2.173 Greece argued that the applicants' children had been placed in the 'preparatory classes' so that they could attain the same standard of education as other students. The ECtHR examined whether the state had shown that the difference in treatment was as a result of objective factors, unrelated to the ethnic origins of the children. It noted that the school had not adopted any clear criterion or suitable ways of testing the ability or learning difficulties of the children that could be used objectively to choose which children should be placed in 'preparatory classes' or in 'ordinary classes'. Furthermore, Greece was unable to provide any examples of Roma children being transferred to 'ordinary classes' despite the fact that the applicants' children had been attending lessons in the 'preparatory classes' for two years.[261]

2.174 The ECtHR accepted that the applicants had signed the statement indicating that they wished their children to be transferred to the annexe. Nevertheless, it reiterated the point made in *DH* that the waiver of the right not to be discriminated against was unacceptable and was incompatible with the convention.[262]

2.175 In *Oršuš and others v Croatia*[263] a number of Roma children attending mainstream primary school had been placed in separate classes, ostensibly on account of their inadequate command of the Croatian language. The Grand Chamber indicated that the temporary placement of children from ethnic minorities in separate classes on the basis of linguistic difficulties did not necessarily entail a breach of Article 14, and there may be circumstances under which it would be permissible. For example, it would be compatible with the convention where the purpose of segregation was to improve the separated children's command of the Croatian language to an adequate level, after which they would be transferred to mixed classes. However, where such measures disproportionately or exclusively affected members of a specific ethnic group, such a system would have to be accompanied by adequate safeguards to protect those children.[264]

2.176 The Grand Chamber examined the facts of the case in order to determine whether such safeguards existed. It noted that the test used to separate the children did not assess the children's command of the Croatian language. Furthermore, no programme had been established in order to address the special needs of Roma children

261 See *also Sampani v Greece*, App No 59608/09, 11 December 2012 and *Lavida and others v Greece*, App No 7973/10, 30 May 2013.

262 App No 32526/05, 5 June 2008 at para 95.

263 (2011) 52 EHRR 7.

264 (2011) 52 EHRR 7 at para 157.

lacking in language skills that had included a timeframe for addressing those needs and transferring the children back into mainstream classes.

2.177 The Grand Chamber held that the state had exceeded the margin of appreciation as there were:

> . . . no adequate safeguards in place capable of ensuring that a reasonable relationship of proportionality between the means used and the legitimate aim said to be pursued was achieved and maintained.[265]

2.178 It followed that placing the applicants' children in Roma-only classes had no objective and reasonable justification. Accordingly, there had been a violation of the applicants' rights protected by Article 14 taken together with Article 2 of Protocol 1. It should be noted that the Grand Chamber also found that there had been a violation of Article 6 of the convention due to the length of proceedings before the domestic courts. The state was also criticised for not taking positive measures to address issues such as poor school attendance and a primary school drop-out rate of 84 per cent among Roma pupils in the locality.[266]

2.179 In *Horváth and Kiss v Hungary*[267] two young men of Roma origin had been assessed as having mild mental disabilities and were placed in a school for the mentally disabled. The applicants argued that this was a misplacement and amounted to indirect discrimination. The ECtHR agreed and found a violation of Article 14 taken in conjunction with Article 2(1) of Protocol 1. It took into account the applicants' special needs as members of a disadvantaged group. Many of those students who had been diagnosed with mild disabilities could have been placed in mainstream schools. Many had been misdiagnosed as a result of socio-economic disadvantage or cultural difference. There had been a long history of misplacement of Roma children in special schools in Hungary and the authorities had failed to take into account their special needs as a disadvantaged group. The ECtHR held that:

> . . . in light of the recognised bias in past placement procedures . . . the State has specific positive obligations to avoid the perpetuation of past discrimination or discriminative practices disguised in allegedly neutral tests.[268]

265 (2011) 52 EHRR 7 at para 184.
266 (2011) 52 EHRR 7 at paras 176–177.
267 (2013) 57 EHRR 31.
268 (2013) 57 EHRR 31 at para 116.

2.180 The ECtHR concluded that the state had a positive obligation to undo a history of racial segregation in special schools.

The domestic approach to the right to education

2.181 The House of Lords and Supreme Court have considered Article 2 of Protocol 1 in two important domestic cases since 2000: *A v Head Teacher and Governors of Lord Grey School*[269] and *A v Essex CC*.[270] In the *Lord Grey School* case the House of Lords identified the test to be applied when determining whether Article 2 of Protocol 1 had been breached:

> . . . The underlying premise of the article was that all existing member states of the Council of Europe had, and all future member states would have, an established system of state education. It was intended to guarantee fair and non-discriminatory access to that system by those within the jurisdiction of the respective states. The fundamental importance of education in a modern democratic state was recognised to require no less. But the guarantee is, in comparison with most other Convention guarantees, a weak one, and deliberately so. There is no right to education of a particular kind or quality, other than that prevailing in the state. . . . The test, as always under the Convention, is a highly pragmatic one, to be applied to the specific facts of the case: have the authorities of the state acted so as to deny to a pupil effective access to such educational facilities as the state provides for such pupils?[271]

2.182 In order for this right to education to be practical and effective, the children of Gypsies and Travellers require a minimum degree of stability in order to be able to attend the same school and receive continuous education.

2.183 Though the traditional approach to planning law concentrated on land use, considerations of 'personal circumstances' may be material to the outcome of a case.[272] Thus, the educational needs of Gypsy and Traveller children can potentially influence decisions about whether or not to grant planning permission, or whether or not to enforce against unauthorised developments. The children's need to continue accessing a local school is frequently considered in the context of best interest considerations under Article 8. However, the High Court has held that the children's best interests, although a primary

269 [2006] UKHL 14.

270 [2010] UKSC 33.

271 [2006] UKHL 14 per Lord Bingham at para 24.

272 See paras 4.141–4.152.

consideration, are not determinative[273] and that there will be very few cases where best interest considerations will outweigh planning control.[274]

Protocol 12

2.184 Protocol 12 to the ECHR was adopted in 2000 and provides for a general prohibition of discrimination. Article 1 of Protocol 12 expands the protection contained in Article 14 so that:

> The enjoyment of any right set forth by law shall be secured without discrimination on any ground.

2.185 While the underlying goal of Protocol 12 (a general ban on discrimination) is potentially radical, it is difficult to predict how effective a tool it will be for the protection of Gypsies, Travellers and Roma in Europe. Protocol 12 came into effect in 2005 and, since then, the ECtHR has only had the opportunity to consider a complaint based on its alleged violation in one case concerning a Roma, namely, that of *Sejdic and Finci v Bosnia and Herzegovina*.[275] There, the Grand Chamber found that both Article 14 and Article 1 of Protocol 12 had been breached in circumstances where constitutional provisions prevented anyone other than individuals from the three 'constituent peoples' (Bosniaks, Croats or Serbs) from standing for election to the House of Peoples and the Presidency of Bosnia and Herzegovina. This measure particularly violated the rights of the Jewish and Roma applicants.

2.186 Unfortunately, the majority of member states have not yet ratified the Protocol,[276] including the Czech Republic, Greece, Hungary and the Slovak Republic, which all have sizeable Roma populations. Bulgaria, France and the UK have yet to sign, let alone ratify, the Protocol. Thus, at present, Article 14 remains the only viable tool for many of Europe's Gypsies, Travellers and Roma to challenge discrimination under the ECHR.

273 *Stevens v Secretary of State for Communities and Local Government* [2013] JPL 1383 at para 59.

274 *Stevens v Secretary of State for Communities and Local Government* [2013] JPL 1383 at para 68; and *Cash v Secretary of State for Communities and Local Government* [2015] EWHC 2357 (Admin) at para 60. See also: *Dear v Secretary of State for Communities and Local Government* [2015] EWHC 29 (Admin).

275 App Nos 27996/06 and 34836/06, 22 December 2009.

276 At the time of writing, only ten member states had ratified Protocol 12.

Taking a case to the European Court of Human Rights

2.187 Under ECHR Article 34, any person, NGO or group of individuals may make a complaint to the ECtHR where they claim that a state party to the ECHR has violated one of their rights. Applicants only have standing if they are a victim, potential victim or indirect victim of an alleged violation. However, the next-of-kin may bring a complaint as an 'indirect victim' where the primary victim has died.[277] Exceptionally, the ECtHR granted *locus standi* to an NGO on behalf of a victim in *Centre for Legal Resources on behalf of Valentin Câmpeanu v Romania*,[278] due to the serious nature of the allegations where the victim, who was an orphan and had no next-of-kin, had died.

2.188 An applicant must have exhausted all domestic remedies, and an application must be made within six months of the last domestic decision.[279]

2.189 A member state may refer another contracting state to the ECtHR for an alleged violation of the ECHR.[280]

2.190 Practitioners intending to make an application to the ECtHR should familiarise themselves with the Rules of the Court which are available on the ECtHR's website.[281]

2.191 The ECtHR is composed of Chambers, which are made up of combinations of judges. The Chambers decide upon the admissibility and merits of complaints made. If a case is declared admissible, it will be communicated to the member state against which the complaint is made. The member state will be given a time within which to respond. A Chamber may invite the parties to submit further evidence and will go on to consider the merits of the case.

2.192 After the delivery of a judgment by a Chamber, the parties have three months within which to ask for the case to be referred to the Grand Chamber, which is effectively the ECtHR's appeal court.

277 See *McCann and others v UK* (1996) 21 EHRR 97; and *Osman v UK* (2000) 29 EHRR 245.

278 App No 47848/08, 17 July 2014; 37 BHRC 423 [2015] Inquest LR 37.

279 Article 35(1). Once Protocol No 15 to the Convention enters into force, the time limit for making an application will reduce from six to four months from the date on which a final decision was taken.

280 Article 33.

281 See also *Ensuring Access to Rights for Roma and Travellers: The Role of the European Court of Human Rights* (2014), available at: https://mycloud.coe.int/index.php/s/4urNxMXgueGt4uk#pdfviewer.

The Grand Chamber will consider the case if it raises a serious question affecting the interpretation or application of the convention or its protocols, or a serious issue of general importance.[282] Where neither party has referred the matter from a Chamber to the Grand Chamber within the three month timeframe, the judgment becomes final.[283]

2.193 A Chamber can also relinquish its jurisdiction to the Grand Chamber at any time before it has rendered judgment in a case, if the case raises a serious question affecting the interpretation of the convention or protocols or where the resolution of a question before the Chamber might have a result inconsistent with a judgment previously delivered by the court.[284] A judgment becomes final after the Grand Chamber has delivered its judgment.[285]

2.194 Article 13 of the ECHR requires national authorities to provide an effective remedy to those whose rights protected by the convention have been violated. If the ECtHR finds that there has been a violation and that the domestic law only allows for partial reparation, then the ECtHR has the power to afford just satisfaction to the injured party.[286] This can take the form of damages.

2.195 The ECtHR has the power to consider applications for interim measures under rule 39 of the Rules of Court. The ECtHR will grant interim measures only if there is an imminent risk of irreparable damage. Requests for its application usually concern the right to life (Article 2), the right not to be subjected to torture or to inhuman or degrading treatment or punishment (Article 3) and, exceptionally, the right to respect for private and family life (Article 8).[287] Interim measures were granted in the case of *Yordonava v Bulgaria*, where Article 8 had been raised to prevent the eviction of a Roma community that had been living in their accommodation for a significant period of time. The measures were only lifted once the district mayor suspended the enforcement of a removal order.[288]

2.196 The ECtHR only has jurisdiction to consider applications relating to the convention. Nevertheless, it will often refer to other Council

282 ECHR Article 43.

283 ECHR Article 44.

284 See ECHR Articles 19–51.

285 Article 46.

286 ECHR Article 41.

287 *Al-Saadoon and Mufdi v UK* (2010) 51 EHRR 9 at para 160.

288 App No 25466/06, 24 April 2012.

of Europe or international instruments, or reports of the Council of Europe's other monitoring bodies in its judgments.[289]

European Social Charter

Overview

2.197 The ESC is a Council of Europe treaty that aims to protect economic and social rights. It was adopted in 1961 (ETS No 035) and revised in 1996 (CETS No 163). The UK has signed and ratified the 1961 ESC. It also signed the 1996 Revised ESC in 1997, but has taken no further steps to ratify the instrument. As such, only the original ESC applies to the UK.

2.198 The European Committee of Social Rights ('the Committee') is the body responsible for monitoring member states' compliance with the ESC in its original or revised form. Every year contracting states submit a report indicating how they have implemented the ESC or the revised ESC in law and in practice.

2.199 In contrast to the ECtHR, individuals cannot make complaints to the Committee directly about violations of their rights protected by the ESC. The Additional Protocol to the ESC providing for a System of Collective Complaints (CETS 158) creates a system whereby recognised trade unions and NGOs can submit collective complaints to the Committee. However, the UK has not yet adopted the Additional Protocol and so collective complaints that it has violated of ESC cannot be made to Committee.

2.200 The rights guaranteed by the ESC concern: housing, health; education; employment; legal and social protection; free movement of persons; and non-discrimination. As such it compliments, and is essentially the social and economic counterpart to, the ECHR.

2.201 Cases brought by NGOs on behalf of Roma before the Committee have involved allegations of violations of the following:

- the right to protection of health (Article 11 of the original and Revised ESC);[290]

289 See, for example, *Chapman v UK* (2001) 33 EHRR 18 where the ECtHR referred to the Framework Convention for the Protection of National Minorities, a Recommendation of the Parliamentary Assembly and General Policy Recommendation No 3 of the European Commission against Racism and Intolerance at paras 55–59.

290 *European Roma Rights Centre v Bulgaria*, Complaint No 46/2007, 3 December 2008.

- the right to social and medical assistance (Article 13 of the original and Revised ESC);[291]
- the right of the family to social, legal and economic protection, including the provision of family housing (Article 16 of the original and Revised ESC);[292]
- the right of children and young persons to social, legal and economic protection (Article 17 of the Revised ESC);
- the right of migrant workers and their families to protection and assistance (Article 19 of the original and Revised ESC);
- the right to protection against poverty and social exclusion (Article 30 of the Revised ESC);[293] and
- the right to housing (Article 31 of the Revised ESC).[294]

Article E and prohibition of discrimination

2.202 The only mention of discrimination in the original ESC is contained within the preamble which states that the enjoyment of social rights should be secured without discrimination on grounds of race; colour; sex; religion; political opinion; national extraction; or social origin. This is given more force by Article E of the Revised ESC, which is akin to Article 14 of the ECHR in that it prohibits discrimination in the enjoyment of one or more of the other rights guaranteed by the ESC. Article E provides that:

> The enjoyment of the rights set forth in this Charter shall be secured without discrimination on any ground such as race, colour, sex, language, religion, political or other opinion, national extraction or social origin, health, association with a national minority, birth or other status.

2.203 Article E prohibits two forms of discrimination: first, where persons or groups of people in an identical situation are treated differently; and, second, where differences are not taken into account. In *International Association Autism Europe v France*[295] the Committee held that discrimination may arise by failing to take due and positive

291 *Médecins du Monde – International v France*, Complaint No 67/2011, 11 September 2012.

292 *European Roma Rights Centre v Greece*, Complaint No 15/2003, 8 December 2004; *European Roma Rights Centre v Ireland*, Complaint No 100/2013, 1 December 2015.

293 *Médecins du Monde – International v France*, Complaint No 67/2011, 11 September 2012.

294 *European Roma Rights Centre v France*, Complaint No 51/2008, 19 October 2009.

295 Complaint No 13/2002, 4 November 2003 at para 52.

account of all relevant differences or by failing to take adequate steps to ensure that the rights and collective advantages that are open to all are genuinely accessible by and to all.

Right to protection of health

2.204 In *European Roma Rights Centre (ERRC) v Bulgaria*[296] the Committee held that Article 11 (the right to health) taken in conjunction with Article E of the Revised ESC imposed a positive duty on states to address inequalities in healthcare provision. The health status of Roma in Bulgaria was found to be inferior to that of the general population. The failure by the authorities to take positive measures to address exclusion, marginalisation and problems accessing healthcare amounted to a violation of Article 11 in conjunction with Article E.

Right to housing

2.205 Under Article 16(2) of the Revised ESC, member states commit to promoting the economic, legal and social protection of family life by such means as social and family benefits, fiscal arrangements, provision of family housing, benefits for the newly married, and other appropriate means. In *ERRC v Ireland*[297] the ERRC complained that the Irish Government had failed to provide sufficient accommodation for Travellers, particularly halting sites, group housing and transient halting sites. The failure to provide transient sites had a serious effect on nomadism, an important part of Traveller culture, and many families were living in unauthorised halting sites, in conditions that were unsafe, overcrowded and in most cases lacking in water, sanitary and electricity services.

2.206 The Committee found that there had been a breach of Article 16 due to the shortfall in sufficient accommodation for Travellers. It provided the following guidance:

> 56 The right to housing permits the exercise of many other rights – both civil and political as well as economic, social and cultural. It is also of central importance to the family. In order satisfy Article 16 states must promote the provision of an adequate supply of housing for families, take the needs of families into account in housing policies and ensure that existing housing be of an adequate standard and include essential services (such as heating and electricity). The Committee has stated that

296 Complaint No 46/2007, 3 December 2008.
297 Complaint No 100/2013, 1 December 2015.

adequate housing refers not only to a dwelling, which must not be substandard and must have essential amenities, but also to a dwelling of suitable size considering the composition of the family in residence. Furthermore the obligation to promote and provide housing extends to security from unlawful eviction . . .

57 The implementation of Article 16 as regards nomadic groups implies that adequate stopping places be provided in this respect Article 16 contains similar obligations to Article 8 of the European Convention of Human Rights (*European Roma Rights Center (ERRC) v Greece*, Complaint No 15/2003, Decision on the merits of 8 December 2004, § 25).

58 The Committee recalls that the rights recognised in the Social Charter must take a concrete and effective, rather than purely theoretical, form (*International Commission of Jurists v Portugal*, Complaint No 1/1998, Decision on the merits of 9 September 1999, §32).

59 This means that, for the situation to be compatible with the treaty, states parties must:

a. adopt the necessary legal, financial and operational means of ensuring steady progress towards achieving the goals laid down by the Charter;
b. maintain meaningful statistics on needs, resources and results;
c. undertake regular reviews of the impact of the strategies adopted;
d. establish a timetable and not defer indefinitely the deadline for achieving the objectives of each stage
e. pay close attention to the impact of the policies adopted on each of the categories of persons concerned, particularly the most vulnerable (*European Federation of National Organisations Working with the Homeless (FEANTSA) v France*, Complaint No 39/2006, Decision on the merits of 5 December 2007, § 54).

2.207 In *ERRC v Greece*[298] the ERRC argued that 100,000 Roma were living in substandard housing conditions contrary to Article 16 of the ESC. The Committee found that Greece had failed to take sufficient measures to improve the living conditions of Roma. There had been a violation of Article 16 of the ESC on the grounds that there were insufficient permanent dwellings available for Roma and a lack of temporary stopping facilities, which meant that Roma were living in conditions that did not meet the minimum standards. The Committee also found that there had been a further violation of Article 16 because Roma were often forcibly evicted without access to adequate legal remedies or alternative accommodation.

298 Complaint No 15/2003, 8 December 2004, para 51.

2.208 These criticisms were reiterated in *International Centre for the Legal Protection of Human Rights (INTERIGHTS) v Greece*[299] in which the Committee found that Greece had not done enough to remedy the situation of Roma since the ruling in *European Roma Rights Centre v Greece* in 2004, and a large number of Roma families continued to live in conditions that failed to meet minimum standards.

2.209 In *ERRC v France*[300] the Committee found that there had been a breach of Article 31(1) (the right to adequate housing) of the Revised ESC. Under French legislation, a caravan did not constitute housing because it is not necessary to obtain a building permit to live in such accommodation. As a result, those people living in caravans were ineligible for housing allowances and other housing loans available to those in other accommodation, which would have enabled them to purchase caravans. The Committee accepted the government's claim that the policy of providing housing allowances and loans was meant to apply to all without discrimination. However, the way in which the benefits were distributed failed to take into account the caravan lifestyle of settled Roma. Merely guaranteeing identical treatment as a means of protection is not enough. Article E imposes a positive obligation to take due account of the relevant differences and act accordingly. As a result, there had been a violation of Article 31(1) of the Revised ESC in conjunction with Article E.

Safeguards in cases involving evictions

Overview

2.210 Roma are often very vulnerable to forced evictions. The Committee has made a number of rulings on the minimum standards that should apply when evictions take place. Thus, the Committee has stated that the:

> . . . illegal occupation of a site or dwelling may justify the eviction of the illegal occupants. However, the criteria of illegal occupation must not be unduly wide, the eviction should take place in accordance with the applicable rules of procedure and these should be sufficiently protective of the rights of the persons concerned.[301]

299 Complaint No 49/2008, 11 December 2009.

300 Complaint No 51/2008, 19 October 2009.

301 *ERRC v Greece*, Complaint No 15/2003, 8 December 2004 at para 54; *ERRC v Bulgaria*, Complaint No 31/2005, 18 October 2006 at para 51.

2.211 National laws must also provide for proper eviction procedures, specifying when they must not be carried out (for example, at night or during the winter) requiring legal aid to be offered to those who need it to seek redress from the courts and other effective legal remedies including compensation for victims of illegal evictions.[302]

Events in France in 2010

2.212 France had been returning migrant Roma to Romania and Bulgaria in significant numbers since 2007 when the two states joined the EU. However, the return of migrant Roma appeared to gather pace in the summer of 2010 following the events that unravelled after a young Romani man was shot dead by police. The shooting provoked anger among the local Roma community. Following acts of public disorder committed by members of the Roma community, the French Government took steps to dismantle Roma camps and to repatriate hundreds of Roma to Romania and Bulgaria.[303]

2.213 In *Centre for Housing Rights and Evictions v France*[304] the Committee found that the French Government had failed to demonstrate that the forced evictions of Roma of Bulgarian and Romanian origin were carried out in conditions that respected their dignity. In fact, the evictions took place against a background of ethnic discrimination, involving the stigmatisation of Roma and the threat of expulsion from France. The Committee ruled that the French Government's decision to dismantle the camps amounted to a violation of Article 31(2) (obligation to prevent and reduce homelessness) in conjunction with Article E (non-discrimination) of the Revised ESC.

2.214 The Committee also found that there was a very close link between the evictions from the camps and the expulsions of Roma of Bulgarian and Romanian origin from France. The decision to return them was based on discriminatory provisions directly targeting Roma individuals and their families. The French Government had sought to justify

302 *ERRC v Italy*, Complaint No 27/2004, 7 December 2005 at para 41.

303 See: *Recent rise in national security discourse in Europe, the case of Roma*, the Parliamentary Assembly of the Council of Europe, Doc 12386, 5 October 2010, available at: http://assembly.coe.int/nw/xml/XRef/X2H-Xref-ViewPDF.asp?FileID=12543&Lang=EN; Sylvain Aubry, *'The Porrajmos: "the Gypsy Holocaust" and the continuing discrimination of Roma and Sinti after 1945' the Holocaust in History and Memory*, Vol 3, 2010, pp101–102; 'Orders to police on Roma expulsions from France leaked', *The Guardian*, 13 September 2010, available at: http://www.guardian.co.uk/world/2010/sep/13/sarkozy-roma-expulsion-human-rights; and 'France sends Roma Gypsies back to Romania', BBC News available at: www.bbc.co.uk/news/world-europe-11020429.

304 Complaint No 63/2010, 28 June 2011.

its actions by invoking the 'voluntary' nature of the repatriation, in which some Roma adults were given €300 to return.[305] However, the Committee rejected this argument. It found that consent to return was given against the backdrop of forced evictions, the real threat of expulsion from France and racial discrimination. The fact that some Roma adults were willing to accept €300 was found to demonstrate a 'situation of destitution or extreme uncertainty'.[306] The absence of economic freedom posed a threat to the effective enjoyment of their political freedom to come and go as they pleased. Therefore, they could not be assumed to have waived their right to freedom of movement. The Committee concluded that the actions of the French Government amounted to a breach of Article 19(8) (obligation that migrant workers and their families are not expelled unless they endanger national security or offend against public interest or morality) in conjunction with Article E of the Revised ESC.

2.215 Then, in *European Roma and Travellers Forum v France*,[307] it was argued that the wave of expulsions amounted to a violation of Article 19(8) of the Revised ESC in that it constituted unequal treatment with regard to expulsion from the French territory. It also violated the principle of freedom of movement under the EU's Citizenship Directive. The Committee assessed how the Directive had been transposed into French law and held that a decision to expel EU nationals from the French territory may take place in two instances: i) if for lack of resources, these persons are likely to become a burden on the social assistance system; and/or ii) if their presence constitutes a threat to public order. It concluded that:

> . . . Roma of Romanian and Bulgarian origin living in France are, indeed, to a large extent not economically active. According to many sources they wish to find employment but are unable to do so. For this reason they lead a hand to mouth existence, surviving with the extremely low income they receive through begging . . . It is also for this reason that they are forced to live on illegal campsites.
>
> This situation cannot, however, be regarded as likely to systematically place an excessive burden on social assistance budgets. Nor can the occasional instances of theft, aggressive begging or unlawful occupation of a public domain or private property be systematically deemed to constitute

305 Complaint No 63/2010, 28 June 2011 at para 72.
306 Complaint No 63/2010, 28 June 2011 at para 73.
307 Complaint No 64/2011, 24 January 2012.

a 'genuine, present and sufficiently serious threat affecting one of the fundamental interests of society' that could justify their expulsion.[308]

2.216 In the circumstances the Committee concluded that the French Government did not respect the principle of proportionality required by the Revised ESC. It found that the decision to expel Roma of Bulgarian and Roma origin amounted to a violation of Article 19(8) because it had not been based upon an examination of the personal circumstances of the individuals concerned. The measures were discriminatory in nature because they targeted the Roma community.

2.217 As the UK has not signed the Additional Protocol, the Committee cannot consider complaints made against it. However, each year the Committee adopts conclusions about the application of the ESC by the states that have ratified the ESC; and in its 2015 Conclusions, the Committee found that there was non-compliance with Article 16 of the original ESC in the UK was because the right of Gypsy and Traveller families to housing in England was not effectively guaranteed.[309]

The Framework Convention for the Protection of National Minorities

2.218 The UK has signed and ratified the Framework Convention for the Protection of National Minorities (CETS 157), which was adopted in 1998. Article 1 recognises that the protection of national minorities and of the rights and freedoms of persons belonging to those minorities forms an integral part of the international protection of human rights. Article 3 provides that every person belonging to a national minority has the right to choose to be treated or not to be treated as such.

2.219 In signing the convention, state parties undertook to:

- guarantee to persons belonging to national minorities the right of equality before the law;[310]
- adopt, where necessary, adequate measures in order to promote, in all areas of economic, social, political and cultural life, full and effective equality between persons belonging to the national minority and those belonging to the national majority;[311]

308 Complaint No 64/2011, 24 January 2012 at para 59–60.

309 European Committee on Social Rights, Conclusions XX-4 United Kingdom, Article 16, adopted on 4 December 2015 for the period of 1 January 2010 to 31 December 2013.

310 Article 4(1).

311 Article 4(2).

- promote the conditions necessary for persons belonging to national minorities to maintain and develop their culture and preserve elements of their identity, namely their religion, language, traditions and cultural heritage;[312]
- refrain from policies and practices aimed at assimilation of persons of national minorities against their will;[313]
- encourage a spirit of tolerance and intercultural dialogue;[314]
- ensure the right to freedom of assembly, association and expression to persons belonging to national minorities;[315]
- recognise the right of every person belonging to a national minority to manifest their religion or belief;[316]
- recognise that every person belonging to a national minority has the right to use freely and without interference his or her minority language;[317] and
- take measures in the fields of education and research to foster knowledge of the culture, history, language and religion of their national minorities and of the majority.[318]

2.220 Article 25 of the Framework Convention requires state parties to submit regular reports to the Secretary General of the Council of Europe. The Advisory Committee monitors state parties' implementation of the Framework Convention by undertaking visits and producing opinions in response to a state's report.

2.221 In its most recent opinion on the UK adopted in 2016,[319] the Advisory Committee found that the provision of temporary and permanent sites had deteriorated in England following: the enactment of the Localism Act 2011; and the government's adoption of planning policy entitled *Planning policy for traveller sites* in 2012, which gave local authorities the task of assessing the need for site provision for Gypsies and Travellers in their areas. The Advisory Committee noted that the persistent lack of pitches forced many Gypsies and Travellers to resort to unauthorised roadside encampments resulting

312 Article 5(1)
313 Article 5(2).
314 Article 6.
315 Article 7.
316 Article 8
317 Article 10(1).
318 Article 12(1).
319 Advisory Committee on the Framework Convention for the Protection of National Minorities, *Fourth Opinion on the UK*, Adopted on 25 May 2016, ACFC/OP/IV(2016)005.

in repeated eviction procedures[320] and it recommended that the most recent version of *Planning policy for traveller sites*, issued in 2015 – which excludes Gypsies and Travellers who have stopped travelling due to ill-health or old age from the planning definition of Gypsy or Traveller – ought to be revised. It also recommended that changes to the law be reversed to reinstate a duty on local authorities to provide sites when the need has been identified in order to ensure an adequate supply of pitches.

2.222 The Advisory Committee noted that Gypsies, Travellers and Roma continue to be the group suffering significantly more discrimination in all fields and, in particular, education in England.[321] It recommended that the domestic authorities effectively monitor the measures adopted to guarantee access to education and enhance educational achievements of Roma pupils to ensure they are not left behind.[322]

2.223 It also observed that there was a conflation between policies addressing Gypsies and Travellers, on the one hand, and Roma on the other.[323] Roma faced particular discrimination in access to: employment, working mainly in low paid and precarious jobs; housing, living in overcrowded private sector accommodation; and healthcare. The Advisory Committee also expressed particular concern about reports of the high number of Roma children being taken into foster care as a consequence of destitution and poor quality housing. It called on the authorities to step up efforts to tackle inequality.[324]

The European Commission against Racism and Intolerance

2.224 The European Commission against Racism and Intolerance (ECRI) is a Council of Europe body which monitors problems of racism, xenophobia, anti-Semitism, intolerance and discrimination on grounds such as 'race', national/ethnic origin, colour, citizenship, religion and language. It is made up of independent experts. It reviews legislation of member states and makes proposals over what action can be taken at a local, national and regional level. It writes reports on individual member states in five-year cycles. It also

320 At paras 60–65.
321 At para 36.
322 At para 115.
323 At para 16.
324 At paras 140, 142.

produces general policy recommendations. In 2011 it published a general policy recommendation on *Combating Anti-Gypsyism and Discrimination against Roma.*[325]

2.225 In 2016, ECRI expressed similar concerns to that of the Advisory Committee on the Framework Convention in its report on the UK.[326] It recommended that the authorities draw up, in consultation with Gypsy, Traveller and Roma groups, a detailed programme of integration strategies and measures to address the disadvantage suffered by all three of these communities in England, Wales, Scotland and Northern Ireland, including concrete targets, timeframes and resources, in all areas of daily life, such as education, employment, health care and accommodation, in particular addressing the shortage of caravan sites.[327]

The Commissioner for Human Rights

2.226 The Council of Europe's Commissioner for Human Rights is an impartial, non-judicial and independent post. The Commissioner is elected for a term of six years and the current Commissioner, Dunja Mijatović, was elected in 2018.

2.227 The Commissioner is mandated to promote respect for human rights across the Council of Europe's member states. This is done through country visits, thematic reporting and awareness-raising activities. The Commissioner does not receive individual complaints.[328]

2.228 In February 2012, a former Commissioner, Thomas Hammarberg, wrote to the UK Secretary of State for Communities and Local Government, expressing his concern about the evictions of families from the Dale Farm site in Basildon and the continued shortage of adequate permanent and transit sites for Gypsies and Travellers living in caravans. He called upon the government to ensure the end to violations of the right to adequate housing of Travellers in Basildon and that local authorities are made aware of the UK's obligations to respect the right to adequate housing of Gypsies and Travellers.[329]

325 ECRI *General Policy Recommendation No 13*, adopted on 24 June 2011.

326 ECRI *Report on the United Kingdom (Fifth Monitoring Cycle)*, adopted on 29 June 2016.

327 At para 109.

328 See: www.coe.int/t/commissioner/Activities/mandate_en.asp.

329 CommDH (2012) 14, available at: https://wcd.coe.int/ViewDoc.jsp?p=&id=1919233&Site=COE&direct=true.

United Nations human rights conventions and monitoring mechanisms

Overview

2.229 The UK has signed and ratified a number of UN human right treaties, including:

- International Convention on the Elimination of All Forms of Racial Discrimination 1965 – monitored by the Committee on the Elimination of Racial Discrimination (CERD);
- International Covenant on Civil and Political Rights 1966 – monitored by the Human Rights Committee (HRC);
- International Covenant on Economic, Social and Cultural Rights 1966 – monitored by the International Committee for Economic, Social and Cultural Rights (CESCR);
- Convention on the Elimination of All Forms of Discrimination against Women 1979 – monitored by the Committee for the Elimination of Discrimination against Women (CEDAW); and
- Convention on the Rights of the Child 1989 – monitored by the Committee on the Rights of the Child (CRC).[330]

2.230 Generally speaking, the monitoring committees assess the contracting parties' implementation of the conventions for which they responsible. States send periodic reports to the monitoring committees, which in turn comment on those reports and make recommendations in their 'concluding observations'.

2.231 The monitoring committees also issue General Comments or Recommendations, which deal with a theme, which is important to the convention in question. For example, CERD issued *General Recommendation No 27 on Discrimination against Roma* in 2000,[331] in which it called upon states to take action to improve the living conditions of Roma, the education of Roma children and to protect Roma against racial violence.

2.232 In its concluding observations on the UK in 2011, CERD criticised the government for proceeding with the eviction of the Gypsy and Traveller community at Dale Farm before identifying

330 The texts of the all the treaties can be found at: www.ohchr.org/EN/ProfessionalInterest/Pages/InternationalLaw.aspx.

331 Available at: www.unhchr.ch/tbs/doc.nsf/(Symbol)/11f3d6d130ab8e09c125694a0054932b?Opendocument.

and providing them with suitable, alternative, culturally appropriate accommodation.[332]

2.233 Individuals can make complaints known as communications to: the HRC, CERD, CRC and CEDAW, where the contracting state recognises the competence of the relevant committee to receive such communications. The UK only recognises CEDAW's competence to receive complaints by individuals and groups of individuals.[333]

The ECtHR's treatment of other European and international human rights instruments

2.234 The ECtHR regularly refers to other international human rights instruments and the work of human rights monitoring bodies. Thus in *DH v Czech Republic*, the ECtHR referred to:

- recommendations of the Council of Europe's Committee of Ministers, Parliamentary Assembly and ECRI;
- the Framework Convention for the Protection of National Minorities and an opinion of the Advisory Committee on the Czech Republic;
- a report of the Council of Europe's Commissioner for Human Rights;
- various EU instruments including the Race Equality Directive;[334]
- judgments of the Court of Justice of the European Union;
- various UN conventions, including the UN Convention on the Rights of the Child and the International Convention on the Elimination of All Forms of Racial Discrimination;
- as well as a judgment of the UK's House of Lords.

Likewise, in *VC v Slovakia*,[335] a case where the ECtHR found violations of Articles 3 and 8 where a Roma woman had been sterilised without her informed consent, the ECtHR considered the concluding observations of the CEDAW on Slovakia which had referred to its own determination in the case of *AS v Hungary*.[336] In that case the ECtHR upheld the complaint of a woman who claimed that she had been sterilised without her informed consent, finding that there had

332 CERD/C/GBR/CO18-20, 14 September 2011 at para 28.

333 The UK acceded to the Optional Protocol to the Convention on the Elimination of All Forms of Discrimination against Women in 2004.

334 Directive 2000/43/EC.

335 (2014) 59 EHRR 29.

336 Communication 4/2004, 29 August 2006, available at: www.un.org/womenwatch/daw/cedaw/protocol/decisions-views/Decision%204-2004%20-%20English.pdf.

been a number of violations of her rights protected by the Convention on Elimination of All Forms of Discrimination against Women.[337]

2.235 In *Demir v Turkey*[338] the respondent state objected to the ECtHR relying on international instruments, and particularly those which Turkey had not ratified. The Grand Chamber disagreed holding that:

> 67. . . . the Court has never considered the provisions of the Convention as the sole framework of reference for the interpretation of the rights and freedoms enshrined therein. On the contrary, it must also take into account any relevant rules and principles of international law applicable in relations between the contracting parties.
>
> 68 The Court further observes that it has always referred to the 'living' nature of the Convention, which must be interpreted in the light of present-day conditions, and that it has taken account of evolving norms of national and international law in its interpretation of Convention provisions.
>
> . . .
>
> 85 The Court, in defining the meaning of terms and notions in the text of the Convention, can and must take into account elements of international law other than the Convention, the interpretation of such elements by competent organs, and the practice of European states reflecting their common values. The consensus emerging from specialised international instruments and from the practice of contracting states may constitute a relevant consideration for the Court when it interprets the provisions of the Convention in specific cases.
>
> 86 In this context, it is not necessary for the respondent State to have ratified the entire collection of instruments that are applicable in respect of the precise subject matter of the case concerned. It will be sufficient for the Court that the relevant international instruments denote a continuous evolution in the norms and principles applied in international law or in the domestic law of the majority of Member States of the Council of Europe and show, in a precise area, that there is common ground in modern societies.

The use of unincorporated international treaties in domestic law

2.236 Once signed and ratified, an international treaty becomes a binding obligation under international law. However, this does not mean it

337 *NB v Slovakia*, App No 29510/10, 12 June 2012.
338 (2009) 48 EHRR 54.

becomes part of domestic law[339] and it has been repeatedly held that our domestic courts have no jurisdiction to interpret or apply unincorporated international treaties.[340]

2.237 Part of the ECHR has been incorporated into domestic law by virtue of parliament enacting the HRA 1998. By contrast, the European Social Charter has not been incorporated into domestic law.

2.238 In *R (SG) v Secretary of State for Work and Pensions*[341] the Supreme Court considered the status in English law of Article 3 of the UN Convention on the Rights of the Child, which provides that:

> In all actions concerning children, whether undertaken by public or private social welfare institutions, courts of law, administrative authorities or legislative bodies, the best interests of the child shall be a primary consideration.

2.239 Lord Hughes considered that an unincorporated treaty may be part of English law in one of three ways:

> 137. . . . First, if the construction (ie meaning) of UK legislation is in doubt, the court may conclude that it should be construed, if otherwise possible, on the footing that this country meant to honour its international obligations. Second, international treaty obligations may guide the development of the common law. For these two propositions see for example *R v Lyons (Isidore)* [2002] UKHL 44; [2003] 1 AC 976, para 13. . . . Thirdly, however, the UNCRC may be relevant in English law to the extent that it falls to the court to apply the European Convention on Human Rights ('ECHR') via the Human Rights Act 1998. The European Court of Human Rights has sometimes accepted that the Convention should be interpreted, in appropriate cases, in the light of generally accepted international law in the same field, including multi-lateral treaties such as the UNCRC . . .

2.240 Lord Kerr, in a dissenting judgment, considered that there should be an exception to the principle that unincorporated treaties are not part of domestic law. He held that international human rights treaties should be directly enforceable in the UK's courts on the basis that if the government commits itself to a standard of human rights protection, it should be held accountable in the courts as to its compliance

339 See Lord Carnwath in *R (SG and others) v Secretary of State for Work and Pensions* [2015] UKSC 16 at para 137.

340 See for example: *JH Raynor (Mincing Lane) Ltd v Department of Trade and Industry* [1990] 2 AC 418, 498; *R v Lyons (Isidore)* [2002] UKHL 44 at para 27; and *R (SG and others) v Secretary of State for Work and Pensions* [2015] UKSC 16 at para 90.

341 [2015] UKSC 16.

with those standards.[342] Nevertheless, as this was a dissenting judgment, for the time being, it seems that it will only be possible to effectively rely upon an unincorporated international human rights instruments if the circumstances identified by Lord Hughes arise in any given case.

The European Union

Overview

2.241 At the time of writing, the EU comprises 28 member states: Austria, Belgium, Bulgaria, Croatia, Cyprus, Czech Republic, Denmark, Estonia, Finland, France, Germany, Greece, Hungary, Ireland, Italy, Latvia, Lithuania, Luxembourg, Malta, Netherlands, Poland, Portugal, Romania, Slovakia, Slovenia, Spain, Sweden and the UK. However, on 29 March 2017 the UK notified the European Council of its intention to leave the EU, thus triggering Article 50 of the Treaty on European Union (TEU). Negotiations commenced on the terms upon which the UK would leave the EU in June 2017. At the time of writing, it is not known what shape Brexit will take but for the time being at least, EU law still applies in the UK.

Primary and secondary EU Law

2.242 The main sources of primary EU law are the TEU and the Treaty on the Functioning of the European Union (TFEU). Since the Lisbon Treaty entered into force, the EU's Charter of Fundamental Rights has had the same legal values as the TEU and TFEU.[343]

2.243 TFEU Article 288 provides for two main forms of secondary legislation:[344] regulations and directives. Regulations are the most direct form of secondary EU law – they are binding in their entirety and directly applicable in all member states. Directives are binding, as to the result to be achieved, upon each member state to which it is addressed, but it is left to the national authorities to decide on the form and method of implementing directives.

342 [2015] UKSC 16 at paras 256–257.

343 TEU Article 6(1).

344 TFEU Article 288 also provides for decisions, which are binding; and recommendations and opinions, which are not.

Supremacy of EU Law

2.244 The Court of Justice of the European Union (CJEU) has developed the doctrine of supremacy of EU law over domestic law in its jurisprudence.[345] This is reflected in the European Communities Act (ECA) 1972 s2(1) which states that:

> All such rights, powers, liabilities, obligations and restrictions from time to time created or arising by or under the Treaties, and all such remedies and procedures from time to time provided for by or under the Treaties, as in accordance with the Treaties are without further enactment to be given legal effect or used in the United Kingdom shall be recognised and available in law, and be enforced, allowed and followed accordingly; and the expression ['enforceable EU right'] and similar expressions shall be read as referring to one to which this subsection applies.

2.245 ECA 1972 s2(4) provides that EU law will prevail over any enactment passed or to be passed by parliament. In *R v Secretary of State for Transport ex p Factortame*[346] Lord Bridge of Harwich held that there was a presumption that Acts of Parliament are compatible with EU law.[347] Furthermore, an Act of Parliament may be 'disapplied' in order to give legal effect to a requirement of EU law.[348]

2.246 The European Union (Withdrawal Agreement) Bill was introduced into the House of Commons on 13 July 2017. In its original form, it provided for the repeal of the ECA 1972 on the date of the UK's withdrawal from the EU and the incorporation of direct EU legislation into domestic law (clauses 1 and 3).

EU law and human rights

2.247 All 28 EU member states are also members of the Council of Europe (which has 47 members) and are signatories to the ECHR, a fact which is recognised in the preamble to the Charter of Fundamental Rights. TEU Article 6(3) provides that the rights protected by the ECHR constitute general principles of EU law. The preamble to the TEU also confirms the member states' attachment to fundamental social rights as defined by the European Social Charter 1961.

345 *Costa v Enel* [1962] ECR 585.

346 [1989] 2 All ER 692.

347 [1990] 2 AC 85 at 141.

348 See *R v Secretary of State for Transport ex p Factortame* (No 1) [1990] 2 AC 86; C-213/89; *R v Secretary of State for Transport ex p Factortame* [1990] 3 CMLR 1; and *R v Secretary of State for Transport ex p Factortame (No 2)* [1991] 1 AC 603.

2.248 TEU Article 6(2), which was inserted by the Lisbon Treaty, provides for the EU to accede to the ECHR. Likewise, Article 17 of Protocol 14 to the ECHR makes provision for the EU to accede to the ECHR. A draft agreement on the accession of the EU to the ECHR was concluded in April 2013. However, in December 2014 the CJEU delivered an opinion in which it concluded that the draft agreement was not in accordance with EU law, leaving the EU's accession in some doubt.[349]

2.249 As a result, individuals are not yet entitled to bring cases against the EU itself before the ECtHR where it is alleged that one of the EU's institutions has breached their human rights protected by the ECHR. Instead, they must either complain to their national courts, which can then refer the case to the CJEU using the preliminary reference procedure; or complain about the EU indirectly to the ECtHR when bringing a case against a member state.

2.250 Generally speaking, when interpreting human rights protection under EU law, the CJEU will consider the rights protected by the ECHR and consider the jurisprudence of the ECtHR;[350] and it is to be noted that there is clearly effort on the part of both the CJEU and the ECtHR to promote harmony and avoid conflict between the two jurisdictions. In *Bosphorus v Ireland,* the ECtHR referred to a number of cases in which the CJEU has recognised the rights protected in the ECHR[351] and found that the protection of fundamental rights afforded by EU law was equivalent to that provided for by the ECHR.[352]

The EU Charter of Fundamental Rights

2.251 In 2000, the EU member states adopted the Charter of Fundamental Rights of the EU ('the Charter'). At that time, it amounted to a non-binding declaration of the list of human rights to which the member states ascribed. Since the Lisbon Treaty entered into force, the Charter has had the same legal value as the TEU and TFEU.[353] The

349 Opinion 2/13 of the CJEU, 18 December 2014.

350 See, for example: *R (NS) v Secretary of State for the Home Department* [2012] 2 CMLR 9 at paras 88–90 where the CJEU referred the ECtHR's judgment in *MSS v Belgium and Greece* (2011) 53 EHRR 2. See also the preamble to the Charter of Fundamental rights which refers to the case-law of the ECtHR.

351 *Bosphorus v Ireland* (2006) 42 EHRR 1 at paras 73–85.

352 *Bosphorus v Ireland* (2006) 42 EHRR 1 at para 165.

353 TEU Article 6(1).

EU institutions are bound to act in accordance with the Charter and the member states must also comply with its provisions when they are implementing EU law. Article 51(1) of the Charter states that:

> The provisions of this Charter are addressed to the institutions, bodies, offices and agencies of the Union with regard for the principle of subsidiarity and to the Member States only when they are implementing EU law. They shall therefore respect the rights, observe the principles and promote the application thereof in accordance with their respective powers and respecting the limits of the powers conferred on it in the treaties.[354]

2.252 The Charter draws together the rights that member states have already committed to elsewhere. Indeed, the preamble to the Charter states that:

> The Charter reaffirms . . . the rights as they result, in particular, from the constitutional traditions and international obligations common to the Member States . . . the European Convention for the Protection of Human Rights and Fundamental Freedoms as well as the Social Charters adopted by the Community as well as by the Council of Europe.

2.253 The list of rights protected by the Charter includes all the civil and political rights contained in the ECHR as well as economic, social and cultural rights. The following are significant:

- Article 4 prohibits torture and inhuman and degrading treatment.
- Article 5 prohibits slavery and forced labour.
- Article 7 protects the right to respect for one's private and family life, home and communications.
- Article 14 ensures the right to education including vocational and continuing training.
- Article 19 prohibits collective expulsions.
- Article 21 provides for a free-standing prohibition of discrimination on any ground such as sex; race; colour; ethnic or social origin; genetic features; language; religion or belief; political or any other opinion; membership of a national minority; property; birth; disability; age; or sexual orientation (discrimination on the grounds of nationality is prohibited, but only insofar as this measure is compatible with the treaties).

354 This was held to apply equally to the UK in *R (NS) v Secretary of State for the Home Department* [2012] 2 CMLR 9, despite an apparent opt-out in Protocol 30 to the Lisbon Treaty on the application of the Charter to Poland and the UK.

- Article 22 provides that the EU shall respect cultural, religious and linguistic diversity.
- Article 24 provides that children shall have the right to such protection and care as is necessary for their well-being and Article 24(2) states that in all actions relating to children, whether taken by public authorities or private institutions, the child's best interests must be a primary consideration.
- Article 34(3) recognises and respects the right to social and housing assistance so as to ensure a decent existence for all those who lack sufficient resources.
- Article 47 provides for the right to an effective remedy.

2.254 As a consequence, individuals now have the right to complain that EU law, or national legislation that implements EU law, breaches the Charter. Complaints relating to a member state's compliance with the Charter, when implementing EU law, can be brought before the national courts, which can then seek guidance from the CJEU on the correct interpretation through the preliminary reference procedure.[355]

Race Equality Directive

2.255 In 2000, the EU adopted Council Directive 2000/43/EC on implementing the principle of equal treatment between persons irrespective of racial or ethnic origin – the Race Equality Directive. It is the key piece of EU legislation designed to combat racial or ethnic discrimination. It emphasises that the principle of equality means that individuals should not be subject to less favourable treatment due to their racial or ethnic origins and it prohibits discrimination in the areas of employment; education; social protection, including social security and health care; and access to and the supply of goods and services, including housing. The Race Equality Directive applies to both the public and private sectors.[356]

2.256 The Race Equality Directive:

- required the creation of equality bodies for the promotion of equal treatment of all persons without discrimination on the grounds of racial or ethnic origin. The Equality and Human Rights Commission (EHRC) is the relevant body in the UK;[357]

355 TFEU Article 267.
356 Article 3(1).
357 Article 13.

- required member states to ensure that judicial and/or administrative procedures for the enforcement of obligations of the Directive were available to all persons who consider themselves wronged by a failure to apply the principle of equal treatment;[358]
- stipulated that member states should ensure that associations or other legal entities have the possibility of engaging in such procedures in support of or on behalf of individual victims;[359]
- reversed the burden of proof, requiring only that the complainant bring forward facts 'from which it may be presumed' that discrimination has occurred, thus requiring the defendant to prove that the principle of equal treatment has not been breached;[360]
- provided the following definitions:
  - 'direct discrimination' is defined as where 'one person is treated less favourably than another is, has been or would be treated in a comparable situation on grounds of racial or ethnic origin';[361]
  - 'indirect discrimination' is defined as occurring where 'an apparently neutral provision, criterion or practice would put persons of a racial or ethnic origin at a particular disadvantage compared with other persons, unless that provision, criterion or practice is objectively justified by a legitimate aim and the means of achieving that aim are appropriate and necessary'.[362]
  - 'harassment' shall be deemed to be discrimination within the meaning of paragraph 1, when an unwanted conduct related to racial or ethnic origin takes place with the purpose or effect of violating the dignity of a person and of creating an intimidating, hostile, degrading, humiliating or offensive environment. In this context, the concept of harassment may be defined in accordance with the national laws and practice of the member states.[363]

2.257 Member states are also required to introduce measures to protect individuals from victimisation, which is defined as any adverse treatment or adverse consequence as a reaction to a complaint or to

358 Article 7(1).
359 Article 7(2).
360 Article 8(1).
361 Article 2(1)(a).
362 Article 2(1)(b).
363 Article 2(2)(c).

proceedings aimed at enforcing compliance with the principle of equal treatment.[364]

2.258 The Race Equality Directive has been transposed into domestic law through the EqA 2006 and the EqA 2010, which are discussed in more detail in chapter 8.

2.259 The CJEU's judgment in *CHEZ Razpredelenie Bulgaria AD v Komisia za zashtita ot diskriminatsia*[365] shows how the Race Equality Directive and Article 21 of the EU's Charter of Fundamental Rights (non-discrimination) interact. A shopkeeper, in a district of a town in Bulgaria that was mainly inhabited by persons of Roma origin, complained that an electricity company, CHEZ, had discriminated against her on the grounds of ethnicity. The complainant was not Roma herself but most of her customers were. The company installed electricity meters for all consumers in that district on overhead pylons six to seven metres high, whereas in other districts the meters installed were placed at a height of 1.70 metres, usually in the consumer's property. As a consequence the complainant was not able to check her electricity meter to monitor her consumption and make sure that the bills sent to her were accurate.

2.260 It was not in dispute that the practice of placing meters higher up took place mainly in the 'Roma districts' of various Bulgarian towns but CHEZ contended that the practice was justified on account of a vast number of unlawful connections and of cases of damage and meter tampering. However, CHEZ did not substantiate its claims with any expert evidence. The CJEU made the following observations:

> 72. In the case in point, it should, first, be noted that . . . Directive 2000/43 gives specific expression, in its field of application, to the principle of non-discrimination on grounds of race and ethnic origin which is enshrined in Article 21 of the Charter.
>
> 73. Secondly, recital 3 in the preamble to Directive 2000/43 refers to various international agreements, including the International Convention on the Elimination of all Forms of Racial Discrimination, adopted on 21 December 1965. Under Article 1 of that convention, discrimination based on a person's ethnic origin constitutes a form of racial discrimination.
>
> 74. Thirdly . . . the EU legislature also sought to make clear (i) that discrimination based on racial or ethnic origin may undermine the achievement of the objectives of the Treaty, in particular the attainment

364 Article 9.

365 C-83/14, [2016] 1 CMLR 14 and see chapter 8 paras 8.85–8.86.

of a high level of employment and of social protection, the raising of the standard of living and quality of life, economic and social cohesion and solidarity, and may also undermine the objective of developing the European Union as an area of freedom, security and justice and (ii) that the prohibition of any discrimination of that type which the directive imposes as regards the areas covered by it is intended, in particular, to ensure the development of democratic and tolerant societies which allow the participation of all persons irrespective of racial or ethnic origin.

75. . . . the mere fact that the district at issue in the main proceedings is also lived in by inhabitants who are not of Roma origin does not rule out that such a practice was imposed in view of the Roma ethnic origin shared by most of that district's inhabitants.

76. . . . it is sufficient, in order for there to be direct discrimination within the meaning of Article 2(2) (a) of Directive 2000/43, that that (*sic*) ethnic origin determined the decision to impose the treatment, without prejudice to the exceptions, provided for in Articles 4 and 5 of the directive, relating to genuine and determining occupational requirements and to positive action by the Member States to prevent or compensate for disadvantages linked to racial or ethnic origin, exceptions which are not relevant in the present case.

77. Finally, under Article 8(1) of Directive 2000/43, when persons who consider themselves wronged because the principle of equal treatment has not been applied establish, before a court or other competent authority, facts from which it may be presumed that there has been direct or indirect discrimination, it shall be for the respondent to prove that there has been no breach of that principle.

2.261 The CJEU stated that it was for the national court to assess whether it can be presumed that there has been direct or indirect discrimination; but, in the instant case, the national court could take into account the fact that the company had established the practice only in urban districts known to have majority Roma populations.

84 The referring court must likewise take account of the compulsory, widespread and lasting nature of the practice at issue which, because, first, it has thus been extended without distinction to all the district's inhabitants irrespective of whether their individual meters have been tampered with or given rise to unlawful connections and of the identity of the perpetrators of that conduct and, secondly, it still endures nearly a quarter of a century after it was introduced, is such as to suggest that the inhabitants of that district, which is known to be lived in mainly by Bulgarian nationals of Roma origin, are, as a whole, considered to be potential perpetrators of such unlawful conduct. Such a perception may also be relevant for the overall assessment of the practice at issue (see, by analogy, judgment in Asociația Accept, C-81/12, EU:C:2013:275, paragraph 51).

> 87. . . . it cannot be denied that the treatment resulting from that practice is unfavourable for the inhabitants – for the most part of Roma origin – of the urban district concerned, having regard both to the fact that it is extremely difficult, or even impossible, for them to check their electricity meters for the purpose of monitoring their consumption and to that practice's offensive and stigmatising nature . . .

2.262 The CJEU went on to consider whether, if the national court decided that the practice amounted to indirect discrimination, it could be objectively justified. The CJEU held that where there is a difference in treatment on the grounds of racial or ethnic origin, the concept of objective justification must be interpreted strictly. Placing meters higher up in a location where numerous instances of tampering and unlawful connections had been recorded would constitute, in principle, a practice or criterion that was apparently neutral. However, the company would have to prove firstly, the existence of the unlawful conduct and secondly, in light of the fact that some 25 years had elapsed since the meters were installed, that there is a major risk that the damage and unlawful connections would continue. CHEZ could not discharge the burden by saying that the conduct and risks are 'common knowledge' as it had tried to do.

Citizenship Directive

2.263 The right of EU citizens and their family members to move and reside freely within the territory of the EU is enshrined in TFEU Article 21 and is implemented by Directive 2004/38/EC (the Citizenship Directive).[366]

2.264 The right is qualified. The Citizenship Directive provides that citizens of the EU have the right to reside in any other member state for up to three months without any conditions or formalities other than that they must possess a valid passport or identity card.[367] Most EU citizens have the right to remain for longer if they are workers or self-employed[368] or have sufficient resources not to become a burden on the host member state and are in possession of comprehensive sickness insurance.[369] Likewise students enrolled on a course of study are able to remain so long as they have comprehensive sickness insurance and enough resources not to become a burden on the

366 Also known as the Freedom of Movement Directive.

367 Article 6(1).

368 Article 7(1)(a).

369 Article 7(1)(b).

host member state.[370] Certain family members are also able to remain beyond three months if accompanying an EU citizen who falls into one of the above categories.[371] EU citizens who have resided in another member state for a continuous period of five years, in accordance with the Citizenship Directive, have the right to permanent residence.[372]

2.265 Member states are only able to restrict freedom of movement and residence on the grounds of public policy, public security or public health (Article 27(1)). Additionally, the Citizenship Directive sets out procedural safeguards. Article 27(2) provides that:

> Measures taken on grounds of public policy or public security shall comply with the principle of proportionality and shall be based exclusively on the personal conduct of the individual concerned ... The personal conduct of the individual concerned must represent a genuine, present and sufficiently serious threat affecting one of the fundamental interests of society. Justifications that are isolated from the particulars of the case or that rely on considerations of general prevention shall not be accepted.

2.266 It should be noted that the Citizenship Directive provides that an expulsion measure shall not be the automatic consequence of the EU citizen's recourse to the social assistance system of the host member state.[373]

2.267 The UK government has sought to transpose the Citizenship Directive through various statutory instruments including the Immigration (European Economic Area) Regulations 2016.[374]

2.268 In recent years, Roma from countries such as the Czech Republic, Slovakia, Bulgaria and Romania, like many other Europeans, have tried to exercise their Treaty rights to freedom of movement by moving to other member states of the EU. In 2009, the EU's FRA noted that:

> At member state level, there is no specific policy framework guiding the inclusion and integration of Roma EU citizens who have exercised their right to freedom of movement and residence ...[375]

370 Article 7(1)(c).

371 Article 7(1)(d).

372 Article 16.

373 Article 14(3).

374 SI No 1052.

375 *The situation of Roma EU citizens moving to and settling in other EU member states*, FRA, November 2009, p34, available at: http://fra.europa.eu/en/publication/2010/situation-roma-eu-citizens-moving-and-settling-other-eu-member-states.

> . . . research shows that often the incorrect application of the Freedom of Movement Directive by national authorities at different levels of administration that are not appropriately trained can be responsible for the de facto withdrawal of certain rights and entitlements, particularly in the area of social assistance.[376]

2.269 In conclusion FRA noted that:

> The case of Roma EU citizens settling in other EU Member States raises questions in terms of wider debates on anti-discrimination and integration and the meaning of EU citizenship and associated rights as a broad concept.
>
> The case of the Roma serves as a *litmus test:* the consequences for some of the most vulnerable citizens in the EU are an important indicator of the practical daily challenges faced by all citizens.
>
> The exclusion of many Roma EU citizens in the society of their Member State of origin and in their host Member State creates insurmountable barriers to formal employment and the ability to prove 'sufficient resources', which has a domino effect on their ability to register, and, as a consequence, to access key civil and political, economic and social rights. This raises profound questions about the effectiveness of inclusion policies.[377]

2.270 It is not clear, at the time of writing, what the implications of Brexit will be for freedom of movement between the UK and other EU member states and, in particular, for Roma who have come to the UK from other member states in recent years.

The Fundamental Rights Agency

2.271 The EU's FRA was established in 2007 and given the specific task of providing independent evidence-based assistance and expertise on fundamental rights to EU institutions and member states, thereby helping to ensure that the fundamental rights of people living in the EU are protected. FRA regularly publishes reports which are of relevance to the issues faced by Roma in the EU.[378]

376 *The situation of Roma EU citizens moving to and settling in other EU member states* at p32.

377 *The situation of Roma EU citizens moving to and settling in other EU member states* at pp9 and 75.

378 See, for example, footnote 365 above and more generally: http://fra.europa.eu/en/publications-and-resources and http://fra.europa.eu/en/theme/roma.

Conclusion

2.272 Cases highlighted in this chapter demonstrate the appalling discriminatory treatment that many Roma continue to experience across Europe. The human rights framework recognises the rights of Roma, and has the potential to provide them with significant protection against discrimination. However, the sad fact is that the implementation of judgments of the ECtHR by some member states has been lamentable.[379]

2.273 Gypsies, Travellers and Roma have had some success when using the HRA 1998 before UK domestic courts to protect their rights and tackle discrimination, but the incorporation of the ECHR into domestic law has been no substitute for effective legislation and policy which will address the chronic under provision of suitable caravan sites and tackle the glaring inequalities that Gypsies, Travellers and Roma face in the UK.

379 *Implementing Judgments: Making Court Victories Stick*, Kushen R, 2010 available at: www.errc.org/article/roma-rights-1-2010-implementation-of-judgments/3613Cached/0; and *Memorandum on the implementation of the judgments in the group of cases Barbu Anghelescu (no. 46430/99) concerning police brutality in Romania* at: www.errc.org/cms/upload/file/joint-submission-to-the-council-of-europe-on-implementation-of-police-brutality-judgments-in-romania-june-2%20016.pdf.

CHAPTER 3

Rented Gypsy/Traveller sites

continued

continued

Introduction

3.1 The scope of the Mobile Homes Act (MHA) 1983 has relatively recently been extended to apply to local authority rented Gypsy/Traveller sites (hereafter 'local authority sites'). This chapter seeks to explain the effects of the MHA 1983 on such sites and also on private rented and non-local authority rented Gypsy/Traveller sites. It also seeks to explain the effects of the two Mobile Homes Acts enacted in 2013 in England and in Wales. The chapter concludes by looking at other matters which affect rented Gypsy/Traveller sites.

3.2 There are important differences between i) private/non-local authority rented sites (hereafter 'private sites'), ii) local authority sites in England and iii) local authority sites in Wales. These differences will be pointed out as we go through the chapter. All the relevant legislation relating to sites in Wales has now been consolidated in the Mobile Homes (Wales) Act (MH(W)A) 2013. When considering private sites, regard should be had to the sections on implied and express terms below, as well as: in England, to the separate section dealing the MHA 2013; and in Wales, to the separate section dealing with the MH(W)A 2013 (particularly with regard to site licensing and similar issues).

3.3 'Rented Gypsy/Traveller sites' are sites owned by a local authority, another organisation (including private registered providers of social housing (PRPSHs) – formerly known as registered social landlords (RSLs)), private individuals or private organisations where the pitches on the site are rented out to Gypsies and/or Travellers. According to the Department of Communities and Local Government (DCLG) 'Traveller Caravan Count' of July 2017, of 22,792 caravans counted, 6,701 (29 per cent) were on 'socially rented sites' (this includes PRPSH).[1] According to the Welsh Government 'Gypsy Traveller Caravan Count' of July 2017, of 976 caravans counted, 407 (42 per cent) were on local authority sites.[2] There are no specific figures recorded in either England or Wales for private rented Gypsy/Traveller sites, though it is known anecdotally that there are very few such sites.

3.4 Although the Gypsy Count only records a snapshot on the particular day of the count and has been frequently criticised as amounting

1 See: www.gov.uk/government/uploads/system/uploads/attachment_data/file/659661/Traveller_caravan_count_July_2017.pdf.

2 See: http://gov.wales/statistics-and-research/gypsy-traveller-caravan-count/?lang=en.

to an underestimate,[3] it gives an idea of the significance of local authority provided sites so far as the accommodation of the Gypsy and Traveller population is concerned. The legal regime as it affects local authority sites is, therefore, an important factor in the lives of a very significant number of the Gypsy and Traveller population.

Provision of sites

3.5 The local authority sites currently in existence have been established under different legal powers or duties. Most were built prior to 1994 and since then some have been extended. It is fair to say that the vast majority of the local authority sites that are in existence today would not have been built but for the Caravan Sites Act (CSA) 1968. Under the CSA 1968, it was the duty of a county council, London borough, or (in Wales) a county borough to exercise their powers under Caravan Sites and Control of Development Act (CSCDA) 1960 s24 to 'provide adequate accommodation for gypsies residing in or resorting to their area'.[4] The CSA 1968 placed an obligation on county councils to determine what sites were to be provided and to acquire the land (subject to consultation and consideration of any objection through the planning process).[5] The district councils were obliged to exercise the other powers under CSCDA 1960 s24, and particularly the management of sites. The county councils were also expected to fix the charges made by the district councils for their provision and to pay the district councils any shortfall between their expenditure and receipts.[6] As a consequence, 'the majority of public sites in non-metropolitan districts are owned by county councils and managed by district councils'.[7]

3.6 The CSA 1968 duty was repealed by the Criminal Justice and Public Order Act (CJPOA) 1994, and now, in England, only the powers under CSCDA 1960 s24 remain.[8] Those powers are wide:

3 See Niner, *Counting Gypsies and Travellers: A Review of the Gypsy Caravan Count System* (ODPM, 2004).

4 CSA 1968 s6.

5 CSA 1968 ss7 and 8.

6 CSA 1968 s7.

7 DoE Circular 18/94, Welsh Office 76/94 (hereafter DoE Circular 18/94) Gypsy Sites Policy and Unauthorised Camping para 19.

8 See paras 3.17–3.19, below, for the current position in Wales.

> (1) A local authority shall have power within their area to provide sites where caravans may be brought, whether for holidays or some other temporary purposes or for use as permanent residences, and to manage the site or lease them to some other person.
> (2) . . . a local authority shall have power to do anything appearing to them desirable in connection with the provision of such sites . . .

3.7 The term 'local authority' in CSCDA 1960 s24 is defined as including a county council; a district council; the Common Council of the City of London; the Council of the Isles of Scilly; a London borough council; and, in Wales, a Welsh county council or county borough council.[9]

3.8 When the government repealed the CSA 1968 in 1994, it envisaged that CSCDA 1960 s24 would become the vehicle for the provision of local authority caravan sites for Gypsies and Travellers and amended CSCDA 1960 s24 by inserting a power to provide 'working spaces' for Gypsies and facilities for their normal activities.[10]

3.9 The government also envisaged that the network of existing sites would continue to be maintained after the repeal of the CSA 1968 duty. In Department of the Environment (DoE) Circular 18/94 local authorities were advised that:

> The Secretaries of State consider it appropriate that authorities should maintain their existing gypsy caravan sites, or should make suitable arrangements for their maintenance by leasing them to other persons who are willing and able to maintain them.[11]

3.10 The advice in DoE Circular 18/94 also made it clear that the government expected that additional sites would continue to be provided by local authorities:

> The Secretaries of State also expect authorities to continue to consider whether it is appropriate to provide further permanent caravan sites for gypsies in their areas.[12]

3.11 However, the repeal of the CSA 1968 duty led to an increase in site shortages and so in 2006 the government then decided to take a more positive approach to site provision and published new planning policy in Office of the Deputy Prime Minister (ODPM) Circular 01/2006 (hereafter Circular 1/06) *Planning for Gypsy and Traveller*

9 CSCDA 1960 s24(8) and s29(1).
10 CJPOA 1994 s80.
11 DoE Circular 18/94 para 21.
12 DoE Circular 18/94 para 22.

Caravan Sites. Circular 1/06 began with a recognition of the failure of the previous policies:

> A new Circular is necessary because evidence shows that the advice set out in [DoE] Circular 1/94 has failed to deliver adequate sites for gypsies and travellers in many areas of England over the last 10 years. Since the issue of Circular 1/94, and the repeal of local authorities' duty to provide gypsy and traveller sites there have been more applications for private gypsy and traveller sites, but this has not resulted in the necessary increase in provision.[13]

Welsh Assembly Government Circular 30/07, *Planning for Gypsy and Traveller caravan sites*, was very similar to Circular 01/06. This was replaced in Wales in June 2018 by Welsh Government Circular 005/2018: *Planning for Gypsy, Traveller and Showpeople Sites*.[14]

3.12 Circular 1/06 recognised the need for more public site provision:

> The Government recognises that many gypsies and travellers wish to find and buy their own sites to develop and manage. An increase in the number of approved private sites may also release pitches on local authority sites for gypsies and travellers most in need of public provision. However, there will remain a requirement for public site provision above the current levels. Such sites are needed for gypsies and travellers who are unable to buy and develop their own sites, or prefer to rent, and to provide transit sites and emergency stopping places where gypsies and travellers may legally stop in the course of travelling.[15]

3.13 Current government planning policy in England is now contained in *Planning policy for traveller sites* (PPTS), which was first issued by the government in 2012 and revised in 2015. One of the stated intentions of PPTS is:

> . . . to promote more private traveller site provision while recognising that there will always be those travellers who cannot provide their own sites.[16]

Thus, there is a renewed emphasis on private site provision.

3.14 PPTS also states that local planning authorities (LPAs) should, in producing their Local Plan; identify and update annually, a supply of specific deliverable sites sufficient to provide five years' worth of sites against their locally set targets; and identify a supply of specific,

13 ODPM Circular 01/06 para 3.
14 See chapter 4 paras 4.82–4.84, below.
15 ODPM Circular 01/06 para 13.
16 PPTS para 4.

developable sites or broad locations for growth, for years six to ten and, where possible, for years 11 to 15.[17]

3.15 It may be thought that LPAs will find it difficult to meet these targets without the expansion of local authority site provision. At the same time there is widespread concern that some LPAs may be underestimating the need for site provision that they should meet. Experience indicates that some are omitting elements of need that ought to be included. The system for checking the assessment of need by LPAs is contained in the Planning and Compulsory Purchase Act (P&CPA) 2004 ss19–23. In summary, these provisions mean that each development plan document is subject to an examination in public by an independent planning inspector appointed by the Secretary of State, who determines: i) whether the plan complies with various procedural requirements; ii) whether the plan is 'sound'; and iii) whether it is reasonable to conclude that the LPA has complied with any duty to co-operate. Where a development plan is adopted or revised, P&CPA 2004 s113 makes provision for it to be challenged on the basis of conventional public law principles. In *Gallagher Homes Ltd and another v Solihull MBC*[18] the inspector, in reliance on the figures advanced by the LPA, failed to make his own objective assessment of housing need. The claimants sought a declaration that adoption of the Local Plan was unlawful, and an order quashing various parts of the Local Plan. Their claim was successful. The court stated that:

> . . . the NPPF [National Planning Policy Framework] requires plan-makers to focus on full objectively assessed need for housing, and to meet that need unless (and only to the extent that) other policy factors within the NPPF dictate otherwise.[19]

3.16 It is difficult to see how there can ever be a sufficient supply of affordable sites and sufficient transit sites without local authorities resolving to secure their provision. With the emphasis in the Localism Act 2011 on local authorities deciding on the type of development that takes place in their respective areas, it will require strong political leadership for them to pass such a resolution. Until they do, an electorally unpopular accommodation need will remain unmet. Hence the need for national government to be more proactive, which is what is happening in Wales.

17 PPTS para 10.
18 [2014] EWHC 1283 (Admin).
19 [2014] EWHC 1283 (Admin) at para 97.

3.17 The approach to site provision in Wales has been transformed by the enactment of Part 3 of the Housing (Wales) Act (H(W)A) 2014, most of which came into force on 25 February 2015.[20]

3.18 HWA 2014 s103 came into force on 16 March 2016 and importantly introduces a duty to meet assessed needs, stating:

> If a local housing authority's approved assessment identifies needs within the authority's area with respect to the provision of sites on which mobile homes may be stationed the authority must exercise its powers in section 56 of the Mobile Homes (Wales) Act 2013 (power of authorities to provide sites for mobile homes) so far as may be necessary to meet those needs.

3.19 MH(W)A 2013 s56 states:

> A local authority may within its area provide sites where mobile homes may be brought, whether for holidays or other temporary purposes or for use as permanent residences, and may manage the sites or lease them to another person.

The Mobile Homes Act 1983 and the Mobile Homes (Wales) Act 2013

Introduction of security of tenure

3.20 Under the MHA 1983 those living in mobile homes stationed on land to which the Act applied (known as 'protected sites') enjoy security of tenure similar to that enjoyed by assured and secure tenants living in conventional housing so that, for example, even if they were in breach of their agreement they could argue it was not reasonable for their agreement to be terminated (and for a possession order to be made against them).

3.21 Up until relatively recently, Gypsies and Travellers living on local authority sites were treated very differently. They had no real protection against eviction. Local authority sites were not defined as protected sites under the MHA 1983 and residents could be summarily evicted provided they had been given four weeks' written notice and a court order had been obtained.

3.22 However, in 2004 the European Court of Human Rights (ECtHR) held in the case of *Connors v UK*[21] that the applicant's eviction from a local authority site using the summary procedure outlined above

20 Housing (Wales) Act 2014 (Commencement No 2) Order 2015 SI No 380.
21 (2005) 40 EHRR 9.

and without giving him an opportunity to present any defence constituted a violation of his rights protected by Article 8 of the European Convention on Human Rights (ECHR). The ECtHR stated:

> However, even allowing for the margin of appreciation which is to be afforded to the State in such circumstances, the Court is not persuaded that the necessity for a statutory scheme which permitted the summary eviction of the applicant and his family has been sufficiently demonstrated by the Government. The power to evict without the burden of giving reasons liable to be examined as to their merits by an independent tribunal has not been convincingly shown to respond to any specific goal or to provide any specific benefit to members of the gypsy community.[22]

3.23 In *Doherty v Birmingham City Council*[23] Mr Doherty raised a similar complaint: a possession order had been made against Mr Doherty despite him not having been able to defend the matter in the county court. Mr Doherty appealed the possession order and the case ultimately came before the House of Lords. Though it was accepted that Mr Doherty's human rights had been violated the House of Lords decided not to issue a declaration of incompatibility because the government was taking steps to change the law and give Gypsies and Travellers living on local authority sites security of tenure.

3.24 The change came in the form of Housing and Regeneration Act 2008 s318, which simply removed the exclusion of local authority Gypsy and Traveller sites from the meaning of protected sites contained in MHA 1983 s5(1). However, before bringing the provision into force in England, the government entered into a series of consultations.[24] The principle of extension of security of tenure was not in issue in this long consultation process. Instead, the consultations concerned the question whether there should be variations to the rights contained in the existing MHA 1983 with regard to such matters as assignment, succession, right to repair, jurisdiction and other issues.

3.25 As a result of this consultation exercise, certain changes were made to the MHA 1983 as it applies to local authority Gypsy and Traveller sites. The changes were then brought into force on English

22 (2005) 40 EHRR 9 at 94.

23 [2008] UKHL 57, [2008] 3 WLR 636.

24 The consultation papers, all from DCLG, consisted of: *A new approach for resolving disputes and to proceedings relating to Park Homes under the Mobile Homes Act 1983* (May 2008); *Implementing the Mobile Homes Act 1983 on local authority Gypsy and Traveller sites* (September 2008); and *Dispute resolution under the Mobile Homes Act 1983 (as amended): Summary of responses and further consultation* (May 2009).

local authority sites by five pieces of secondary legislation as of 30 April 2011.[25]

3.26 The Welsh Government were slower in bringing the provisions into force in Wales. In *Buckland v UK*,[26] the Gypsy Council, who managed a local authority site on behalf of Neath Port Talbot County Borough Council, took eviction action against Ms Buckland on grounds of nuisance plus arrears of water rates. In the county court, HHJ Bidder suspended the possession order made against Ms Buckland for 12 months upon condition that her son leave the site and that she paid off the water rates arrears. Ms Buckland appealed to the Court of Appeal which held that the power to suspend possession orders, contained in CSA 1968 s4, was sufficient to answer the problem identified by the ECtHR in *Connors v UK*. On 18 February 2008 the House of Lords refused Ms Buckland permission to appeal and in May 2008 she left the site. Ms Buckland then complained to the ECtHR and it concluded that her rights protected by Article 8 of the ECHR had been breached and awarded her 4,000 euros and her costs. When doing so the ECtHR observed that:

> As the Court has previously emphasised, the loss of one's home is the most extreme form of interference with the right to respect for the home. Any person at risk of an interference of this magnitude should in principle be able to have the proportionality of the measure determined by an independent tribunal in light of the relevant principles under Article 8 of the Convention, notwithstanding that, under domestic law, his right to occupation has come to an end.[27]

3.27 The ECtHR continued:

> However, the fact remains that the applicant was not able to argue that no possession order ought to have been made at all. The possibility of suspension for up to twelve months of the possession order is inadequate, by itself, to provide the necessary procedural guarantees under Article 8. Although further suspensions may be granted, suspension merely delays, and does not remove, the threat of eviction. The Court cannot accept that the fact that an individual may effectively be able to

25 Housing and Regeneration Act 2008 (Consequential Amendments to the Mobile Homes Act 1983) Order 2011 SI No 1004; Mobile Homes Act 1983 (Jurisdiction of Residential Property Tribunals) (England) Order 2011 SI No 1005; Mobile Homes Act 1983 (Amendment of Schedule 1 and Consequential Amendments) (England) Order 2011 SI No 1003; Housing and Regeneration Act 2008 (Commencement No 8 and Transitional, Transitory and Saving Provisions) Order 2011 SI No 1002; Mobile Homes (Written Statement) (England) Regulations 2011 SI No 1006.

26 (2013) 56 EHRR 16.

27 (2013) 56 EHRR 16 para 65.

> remain in her home in the long-term by making repeated applications to extend suspension of a possession order removes any incompatibility of the procedure with Article 8. It is further significant that in the present case the County Court judge considered the applicant's personal circumstances to be such that suspension was justified and he granted a suspension for the full period sought. In the circumstances it is not possible for the Court to predict what decision he might have reached on the granting of the possession order had he considered it open to him to refuse the grant on the basis of personal circumstances.
>
> Finally, the Court observes that an amendment to the Mobile Homes Act 1983 permits a court considering whether to make a possession order to examine the reasonableness of the termination of the licence . . . That amendment has entered into force in England but not in Wales. It would appear that, once it does so, domestic courts in Wales will be able to assess the proportionality of a proposed eviction in compliance with the procedural requirements of Article 8.[28]

3.28 Subsequently, the Welsh Government undertook a similar consultation process to that which had taken place in England.[29] The scope of the MHA 1983 was then extended to cover Welsh local authority sites by three statutory instruments.[30] However, those provisions have since been consolidated in the MH(W)A 2013.

How the Acts apply to different types of site

England

3.29 As a consequence of the amendments to the MHA 1983, there is a new structure to the legislation that applies to sites in England. The main body of the MHA 1983 is where one finds the terms, amongst others, as to written agreements and succession. Part 1 of Sch 1 (implied terms) is now split into:

- Chapter 1 – which details its application and interpretation;
- Chapter 2 – which details terms relating to sites other than local authority Gypsy and Traveller sites;[31]

28 (2013) 56 EHRR 16 at paras 68 and 69.

29 See *Implementing the Mobile Homes Act 1983 on local authority Gypsy and Traveller sites* (January 2013).

30 Mobile Homes Act 1983 (Amendment of Schedule 1 and Consequential Amendments) (Wales) Order 2013 SI No 1723; Housing and Regeneration Act 2008 (Consequential Amendments to the Mobile Homes Act 1983) (Wales) Order 2013 SI No 1722; Housing and Regeneration Act 2008 (Commencement No 3 and Transitional, Transitory and Saving Provisions) (Wales) Order 2013 SI No 1469.

31 Our reference to 'local authority Gypsy and Traveller sites' includes those run by county councils.

- Chapter three – which details terms relating to transit pitches on local authority Gypsy and Traveller sites;[32]
- Chapter four – which details terms relating to permanent pitches on local authority Gypsy and Traveller sites.[33]

Wales

3.30 As stated above, the position in Wales is now covered by the MH(W)A 2013. In Part 4 one finds the terms, amongst others, relating to written agreements and succession. MH(W)A 2013 Sch 2 Part 1 is split into:

- Chapter 1 – which details its application;
- Chapter 2 – which details terms relating to sites other than local authority Gypsy and Traveller sites;
- Chapter 3 – which details terms relating to transit pitches on local authority Gypsy and Traveller sites;[34]
- Chapter 4 – which details terms relating to permanent pitches on local authority Gypsy and Traveller sites.[35]

A mobile home on a protected site

All sites including local authority transit pitches

3.31 MHA 1983 s1(1) states:

> This Act applies to any agreement under which a person ('the occupier') is entitled–
> (a) to station a mobile home on land forming part of a protected site; and
> (b) to occupy the mobile home as his only or main residence.

MH(W)A 2013 s48 is worded slightly differently but has the same effect.[36]

32 'Transit pitch' is defined in chapter one as 'a pitch on which a person is entitled to station a mobile home under the terms of the agreement for a fixed period of up to three months'.

33 'Permanent pitch' is defined in Chapter One as 'a pitch which is not a transit pitch'.

34 'Transit pitch' is defined in MH(W)A 2013 s55(1) as 'a pitch on which a person is entitled to station a mobile home under the terms of an agreement for a fixed period of up to three months'.

35 'Permanent pitch' is defined in MH(W)A 2013 s55(1) as 'a pitch which is not a transit pitch'.

36 Both MHA 1983 and MH(W)A 2013 are in appendix A.

Mobile home

3.32 MHA 1983 s5(1) provides that the term 'mobile home' has the same meaning as the term 'caravan' under CSCDA 1960.

3.33 CSCDA 1960 s29(1) states that a caravan is:

> . . . any structure designed or adapted for human habitation which is capable of being moved from one place to another (whether by being towed, or by being transported on a motor vehicle or trailer) and any motor vehicle so designed or adapted, but does not include–
> (a) any railway rolling stock which is for the time being on rails forming part of a railway system, or
> (b) any tent.

In Wales MH(W)A 2013 s60(1) adopts a similar definition of the term 'caravan'.

Protected site

3.34 The definition of the term 'protected site' is contained in CSA 1968 s1. A protected site is any site that is required to have a licence by CSCDA 1960 and also one where the relevant planning permission or site licence is not for holiday use only, or otherwise limited such that there are times of the year when no caravan may be stationed on the land for human habitation. In order to qualify as a 'protected site' the land must have planning permission.[37]

3.35 In *Murphy v Wyatt*,[38] where a certificate of lawful use was granted for the use of land as a mobile home site under Town and Country Planning Act (TCPA) 1990 s191[39] it was held that this did not transform the land into a protected site because the licence agreement must come within the scope of the MHA 1983 from the outset.

3.36 In *Berkeley Leisure Group Ltd v Hampton*[40] the Court of Appeal considered whether all the pitches on a site that had a mixed residential and holiday use was a protected site. The pitches on which permanent residential occupation was permitted were specifically identified in the planning permission and site licence. It was held that as the permission and licence distinguished between different parts of the site as regards the permitted user, the site had to be treated as being sub-divided, and only part of it could be a protected site.

37 See *Balthasar v Mullane* (1985) 17 HLR 561, CA.

38 [2011] EWCA Civ 408.

39 See paras 4.37–4.38, below.

40 [2001] EWCA Civ 1474.

3.37 In *John Romans Park Homes v Hancock and others*[41] the Upper Tribunal decided that the First-tier Tribunal had been right to distinguish *Berkeley*. In the instant case, the planning permission and site licence did not expressly restrict permanent residential occupation to specific parts of the site, and they did not require that a mobile home situated on any particular pitch should be occupied either seasonally or permanently. Thus the Upper Tribunal concluded that the whole of the site was a protected site to which the MHA 1983 applied.

Occupation of mobile home as main residence

3.38 Additionally, the occupier must be 'entitled' to use the mobile home as his or her only or main residence. It should be noted that, if at some stage the occupier ceases to use the mobile home as his or her main residence, that can give rise to a ground for possession[42] but it will not mean that the site is no longer a protected site provided that the occupier was entitled to use the mobile home as his or her only or main residence.

3.39 The MHA 1983 and MH(W)A 2013 do not apply to mobile homes that are rented from the site owner but in our experience local authorities that own and let out mobile homes are rare and those that do may be expected not to discriminate and to simply provide occupiers of all pitches with MHA agreements.

Written statements

Overview

3.40 Written statements must be provided in relation to all agreements entered into on all local authority Gypsy and Traveller sites after 30 April 2011 in England and after 19 November 2012 in Wales and on all non-local authority sites. In the paragraphs below we outline the relevant provisions which relate to sites in England and identify where the Welsh provisions differ.

3.41 MHA 1983 s1(2) states:

> Before making an agreement to which this Act applies, the owner of the protected site ('the owner') shall give to the proposed occupier under the agreement a written statement which–
> (a) specifies the names and addresses of the parties;

41 [2018] UKUT 249 (LC).

42 See para 3.89 onwards, below.

(b) includes particulars of the land on which the proposed occupier is to be entitled to station the mobile home that are sufficient to identify that land;
(c) sets out the express terms to be contained in the agreement(including any site rules (see Section 2C));[43]
(d) sets out the terms to be implied by section 2(1) below; and
(e) complies with such other requirements as may be prescribed by regulations made by the appropriate national authority.[44]

3.42 MHA 1983 ss1(2)(d) and 2(1) refer to the implied terms contained in MHA 1983 Sch 1 Part 1 (see further below).[45]

3.43 With regard to agreements entered into after 30 April 2011 in England, the Mobile Homes (Written Statement) (England) Regulations 2011[46] contain a standard statement in the Schedule. Written statements for such agreements 'must be in the form set out in that Schedule or a form substantially to the same effect'.[47]

3.44 With regard to agreements entered into after 19 November 2012 in Wales, the Mobile Homes (Written Statement) (Wales) Regulations 2012[48] contained a standard statement in the Schedule. As with England, written statements for such agreements 'must be in the form set out in that Schedule or a form substantially to the same effect'.[49] The 2012 Regulations have now been replaced in Wales by the Mobile Homes (Written Statement) (Wales) Regulations 2014.[50]

3.45 MHA 1983 s1(3) states:

> The written statement required by subsection (2) above must be given–
> (a) not later than 28 days before the date on which any agreement for the sale of the mobile home to the proposed occupier is made, or
> (b) (if no such agreement is made before the making of the agreement to which this Act applies) not later than 28 days before the date on which the agreement to which this Act applies is made.[51]

3.46 MHA 1983 s1(4) states:

43 The reference to site rules was inserted by MHA 2013 s9(2).
44 MH(W)A 2013 s49(1) is worded slightly differently but has the same effect.
45 Similarly, MH(W)A 2013 s49(1)(d) refers to the implied terms contained in MH(W)A 2013 Sch 2 Part 1 (see further para 3.76 onwards, below).
46 SI No 1006.
47 Mobile Homes (Written Statement) (England) Regulations 2011 SI No 1006 reg 3.
48 SI No 2675.
49 Mobile Homes (Written Statement) (Wales) Regulations 2012 No 2675 reg 3.
50 SI No 1762.
51 MH(W)A 2013 s49(2) is worded differently but has the same effect.

> But if the proposed occupier consents in writing to that statement being given to him by a date ('the chosen date') which is less than 28 days before the date mentioned in subsection 3(a) or (b) above, the statement must be given to him not later than the chosen date.[52]

3.47 MHA 1983 s1(7) states:

> A statement required to be given to a person under this section may either be delivered to him personally or sent to him by post.[53]

3.48 MHA 1983 s1(5) states:

> If any express term (other than a site rule (see section 2C))–[54]
> (a) is contained in an agreement to which this Act applies, but
> (b) was not set out in a written statement given to the proposed occupier in accordance with subsections (2) to (4) above,
> the term is unenforceable by the owner or any person within section 3(1).[55]

3.49 MHA 1983 s3(1) makes it clear that an agreement is binding on 'any successor in title of the owner and any person claiming through or under the owner or any such successor', for example, a leaseholder or tenant of the owner or a successor.[56]

3.50 MHA 1983 s1(5) and MH(W)A 2013 s49(4) provide a strong incentive for the owner to make sure that he or she provides the requisite written statement because if the agreement formalities are not complied with, any further express terms that the owner might wish to rely on, will not be enforceable. It should also be noted that the occupier can still rely on any express terms even if MHA 1983 s1(2)–(4) and MH(W)A 2013 s49(1)–(3) have not been complied with.

3.51 MHA 1983 s1(6) states:

> If the owner has failed to give the occupier a written statement in accordance with subsections (2) to (4) above, the occupier may, at any time after the making of the agreement, apply to the [First-tier Tribunal (Property Chamber) [hereafter FT(PC)] in England/Residential Property Tribunal [hereafter RPT] in Wales] for an order requiring the owner–
> (a) to give him a written statement which complies with paragraphs (a) to (e) of subsection (2) . . ., and
> (b) to do so not later than such date as is specified in the order.[57]

52 MH(W)A 2013 s49(3) is worded differently but has the same effect.

53 MH(W)A 2013 s49(6) is worded differently but has the same effect.

54 Reference to site rules was added by MHA 2013 s9(3).

55 MH(W)A 2013 s49(4) is worded slightly differently but has the same effect.

56 MH(W)A 2013 s53(1) is worded slightly differently but has the same effect.

57 MH(W)A 2013 s4(5) is worded slightly differently but has the same effect.

3.52 An application can be made by the occupier if no written statement is provided or if a defective written statement is provided (eg a statement that adds in express terms that have not been agreed between the parties). The penalty for non-compliance with an order containing a penal notice would be committal under County Court Rules 1981 Order 29 (as retained in force by Civil Procedure Rules (CPR) Sch 1).

3.53 MHA 1983 s2(3) states:

> The appropriate judicial body may, on the application of either party made within the relevant period, make an order–
> (a) varying or deleting any express term of the agreement other than a site rule (see section 2C);[58]
> (b) in the case of any express term to which section 1(6) above applies other than a site rule (see section 2C),[59] provide for the term to have full effect or to have such effect subject to any variation specified in the order.[60]

3.54 The FT(PC) in England and the RPT in Wales have wide powers under these sections. MHA 1983 s2(4) states:

> On an application under this section, the [FT(PC)] shall make such provision as [the FT(PC)] considers just and equitable in the circumstances.[61]

3.55 MHA 1983 s2(3A) states, with regard to MHA 1983 s2(3):

> 'the relevant period' means the period beginning with the date on which the agreement is made and ending–
> (a) six months after that date, or
> (b) where a written statement relating to the agreement is given to the occupier after that date (whether or not in compliance with an order under section 1(6) above), six months after the date on which the statement is given . . .[62]

3.56 MHA 1983 s2(6) states:

> Subsections (2) to (4) do not apply in relation to a person occupying or proposing to occupy a transit pitch in England on a local authority gypsy and traveller site or a county council gypsy and traveller site.[63]

58 Reference to site rules was added by MHA 2013 s9(4)(a).
59 Reference to site rules was added by MHA 2013 s9(4)(b).
60 MH(W)A 2013 s50(3) is worded slightly differently but has the same effect.
61 MH(W)A 2013 s50(5) is worded slightly differently but has the same effect.
62 MH(W)A 2013 s50(4) is worded slightly differently but has the same effect.
63 MH(W)A 2013 s49(8) is worded slightly differently but has the same effect.

3.57 Thus occupiers of transit sites do not have a right to apply to the FT(PC) or the RPT with regard to any written statement.

Transitional arrangements for existing agreements

3.58 The Housing and Regeneration Act 2008 (Commencement No 8 and Transitional, Transitory and Saving Provisions) Order 2011[64] applies to agreements for the occupation of pitches on local authority Gypsy and Traveller sites which existed on 30 April 2011. The order disapplies MHA 1983 ss1(2)–(9) and 2(2)–(4) but inserts identical or very similar terms into such agreements. The order also requires that local authorities should give existing occupiers written statements containing the implied and express terms of the agreement within 28 days of 30 April 2011. Those written statements 'must be in the form set out in the Schedule to this Order or a form substantially to the same effect'.[65] Precisely the same terms apply in Wales except the relevant date is 10 July 2013 – see the Housing and Regeneration Act 2008 (Commencement No 3 and Transitional, Transitory and Saving Provisions) (Wales) Order 2013.[66]

3.59 The authors are aware of some local authorities that failed to provide written statements within the requisite time period and of others that unlawfully attempted to alter existing express terms or to add completely new express terms without agreement with the occupiers when providing written statements. On the other hand, many local authorities have simply used the form in the Schedule to the Order and imported the existing express terms (removing those that are in conflict with any implied term) into the new statement. This is perfectly lawful.

3.60 Those advising Gypsies and Travellers on the validity of express terms should compare the terms in the old (pre 30 April 2011 in England and pre 10 July 2013 Wales) agreement with those in the new agreement. Any express terms in the new agreement which were altered or added without the consent of the occupier will be unenforceable.

3.61 MHA 2013 and MH(W)A 2013 stipulate that 'site rules' on private sites are express terms of the agreement.[67]

64 SI No 1002.

65 Housing and Regeneration Act 2008 (Commencement No 8 and Transitional, Transitory and Saving Provisions) Order 2011 SI No 1002 reg 6(1).

66 SI No 1469.

67 See further para 3.157 onwards, below.

Succession

All sites

3.62 MHA 1983 s3(1) states:

> An agreement to which this Act applies shall be binding on and enure for the benefit of any successor in title of the owner and any person claiming through or under the owner or any such successor.[68]

3.63 With regard to the occupier, MHA 1983 s3 states:

> (3) Where a person entitled to the benefit of and bound by an agreement to which this Act applies dies at a time when he is occupying the mobile home as his only or main residence, the agreement shall enure for the benefit of and be binding on–
> (a) any person residing with that person ('the deceased') at that time being–
> (i) the widow or widower or surviving civil partner of the deceased;
> (ii) in default of a widow or widower or surviving civil partner so residing, any member of the deceased's family; or
> (b) in default of any such person so residing, the person entitled to the mobile home by virtue of the deceased's will or under the law relating to intestacy but subject to subsection (4) below.
> (4) An agreement to which this Act applies shall not enure for the benefit of or be binding upon a person by virtue of subsection (3)(b) above in so far as–
> (a) it would, but for this subsection, enable or require that person to occupy the mobile home; or
> (b) it includes terms implied by virtue of paragraph 5 or 9 of Part 1 of Schedule 1 of Chapter 2, or paragraph 5 of Chapter 4 to this Act.[69]

3.64 Thus the order of succession is: widow, widower or surviving civil partner; other member of the deceased's family; the person entitled to the mobile home under any will or by intestacy.

3.65 If the agreement passes by will or intestacy (MHA 1983 s3(3)(b)), the successor does not become entitled or bound to occupy the mobile home (unless the owner consents to this form of succession upon request). The owner cannot use the successor's lack of occupation as a ground for possession but nor can the successor give the mobile home and the agreement away.[70] The net effect is that the successor would have an agreement that the owner could not terminate but which the successor could realise by sale. It appears that on

68 MH(W)A 2013 s53(2) is worded slightly differently but has the same effect.

69 MH(W)A 2013 s53(3) is worded differently but has the same effect.

70 MHA 2013 s3(3)(b) and MH(W)A 2013 s53(4).

sites that come under MHA 1983 Part 1 Sch 1 Chapter 2 or under MH(W)A 2013 Sch 2 Part 1 Chapter 2, the purchaser of the mobile home and the agreement from a successor would have the benefit of the agreement without the limitations imposed by MHA 1983 s3(4). This would not be possible on local authority Gypsy and Traveller sites where there is no assignment in England and limited assignment in Wales.[71]

3.66 By way of comparison, succession for secure tenants (ie tenants of local authority houses or flats) is dealt with in Housing Act (HA) 1985 s87 which provides that there can only be one statutory succession to a surviving spouse (this includes civil partners) or a member of the deceased tenant's family (and the latter must have lived with the deceased tenant for at least 12 months previously).

3.67 MHA 1983 s5(3) states:

> A person is a member of another's family within the meaning of this Act if he is his spouse, civil partner, parent, grandparent, child, grandchild, brother, sister, uncle, aunt, nephew or niece; treating–
> (a) any relationship by marriage or civil partnership as a relationship by blood, any relationship of the half blood as a relationship of the whole blood and the step child of any person as his child; and
> (b) an illegitimate person as the legitimate child of his mother and reputed father;
> or if they live together as husband or wife or as if they were civil partners.

3.68 MH(W)A 2013 s55(3) states that:

> . . . the following are members of a person's family–
> (a) The person's spouse or civil partner or any person who lives together with the person as a partner in an enduring family relationship,
> (b) The person's parents, grandparents, children and grandchildren (including any person who is in that relationship by virtue of a marriage or civil partnership or an enduring family relationship) and any other person treated by the person as a child of the person's family, and
> (c) The person's brothers, sisters, uncles, aunts, nephews and nieces (including any person who is in that relationship by virtue of a marriage or civil partnership or an enduring family relationship).

3.69 The wording of MHA 1983 s5(3) and MH(W)A 2013 s55(3) is somewhat different. 'Cohabitees' would seem to be covered by MHA 1983 by the reference to living together 'as husband or wife or as if they were civil partners' and also covered by MH(W)A 2013 by the phrase

71 See para 3.99 onwards, below.

'enduring family relationship'. However, it would seem that 'enduring family relationship' in the Welsh legislation must have a wider meaning which will have to be decided on a case-by-case basis.

3.70 The MHA 1983 and the MH(W)A 2013 do not provide a means of choosing between competing successors, e.g. two members of the deceased's family who were living with him/her at the time of death. If they cannot elect one amongst themselves then an application would have to be made by one or both of them to the appropriate judicial body; in England to the FT(PC)and in Wales to the RPT.

3.71 The normal rule is that, in order for statutory succession to take place, the deceased must have been using the mobile home as his residence and the person claiming to succeed must have been residing at the time of death.

3.72 There is no specific exclusion for transit sites though succeeding to a severely time limited agreement may not be of much value.

Jurisdiction

All sites

3.73 The Mobile Homes Act 1983 (Jurisdiction of Residential Property Tribunals) (England) Order 2011 has transferred all disputes under the MHA 1983 except possession actions to FT(PC)s in England. MHA 1983 Sch 1 Part 1 para 5 in both Chapter 2 and Chapter 4 is amended by adding a new para 5A as follows:

> (1) This paragraph applies in relation to a protected site in England . . .
> (2) The owner is entitled to terminate the agreement forthwith if–
>   (a) on the application of the owner, a tribunal has determined that, having regard to its condition, the mobile home is having a detrimental effect on the amenity of the site; and
>   (b) then, on the application of the owner, the appropriate judicial body, having regard to the tribunal's determination and to any other circumstances, considers it reasonable for the agreement to be terminated.
> (3) Sub-paragraphs (4) and (5) apply if, on an application to the tribunal under sub-paragraph (2)(a)–
>   (a) the tribunal considers that, having regard to the present condition of the mobile home, it is having a detrimental effect on the amenity of the site, but
>   (b) it also considers that it would be reasonably practicable for particular repairs to be carried out on the mobile home that would result in the mobile home not having that detrimental effect, and
>   (c) the occupier indicates to the tribunal that the occupier intends to carry out those repairs.

(4) In such a case, the tribunal may make an interim order–
   (a) specifying the repairs that must be carried out and the time within which they must be carried out; and
   (b) adjourning the proceedings on the application for such period specified in the interim order as the tribunal considers reasonable to enable the repairs to be carried out.

(5) If the tribunal makes an interim order under sub-paragraph (4), it must not make a determination under sub-paragraph (2)(a) unless it is satisfied that the specified period has expired without the repairs having been carried out.

The position in Wales is governed by MH(W)A 2013 s54(1), (2) and (3); Sch 2 Part 1 Chapter 2 paras 5, 6 and 7; and Sch 2 Part 1 Chapter 4 paras 38, 39 and 40, which are worded slightly differently but have the same effect, subject to what is stated below.

3.74 In Wales, the jurisdiction of the court is dis-applied under MH(W)A 2013 s54(4) if 'the owner and occupier have entered into an arbitration agreement before the question [of the owner seeking to terminate the agreement] arises and the agreement applies to that question.' In such circumstances the matter will be dealt with by the RPT.

3.75 In the consultation prior to the introduction of the MHA 1983 (in amended form) on local authority Gypsy and Traveller sites, a majority of Gypsy and Traveller support groups opposed the transfer of most disputes to the FT(PC) or the RPT since legal aid is not usually available for such tribunals. In fact most such disputes (except possession actions that involve court proceedings, matters of serious disrepair and challenges to pitch fee increases), since 1 April 2013, will not be eligible for legal aid at all, whether proceedings are taken in court or at tribunal.[72]

The Mobile Homes Act 1983 and the Mobile Homes (Wales) Act 2013 – implied terms

Introduction

3.76 MHA 1983 s2(1) and MH(W)A 2013 s50(1) imply into all agreements in England and Wales the terms set out in MHA 1983 Sch 1 Part 1 and MH(W)A 2013 Sch 2 Part 1 respectively. These terms cannot be altered or removed by any express term. Under MHA 1983 s2(2) and MH(W)A 2013 s50(2) either party to an agreement in England and

72 See para 3.226 onwards, below.

Wales can apply to a FT(PC) in England or a RPT in Wales for a term to be implied covering the matters listed in MHA 1983 Sch 1 Part II and MH(W)A 2013 Sch 2 Part 2 respectively, namely:

- the sums payable by the occupier in pursuance of the agreement and the times at which they are to be paid;
- the review at yearly intervals of the sums so payable;
- the provision or improvement of services available on the protected site, and the use by the occupier of such services;
- the preservation of the amenity of the protected site.

The right to make such an application does not apply to transit pitches on local authority Gypsy and Traveller sites: MHA 1983 s2(6) and MH(W)A 2013 s50(6).

Duration of agreement

3.77 Subject to the provisions for termination by owner or occupier, an agreement will subsist except it shall not extend beyond the date when the owner's estate or interest determines or beyond the date when any planning permission expires. On transit sites, the agreement cannot subsist beyond the relevant three-month period.[73] Thus, sites that are governed by MHA 1983 Sch 1 Part 1 Chapters 2 and 4; and MH(W)A 2013 Sch 2 Part 1 Chapters 2 and 4, subject to the above, agreements can, effectively, be indeterminate. If the owner sells the site, then the new owner will take it subject to the MHA 1983 or the MH(W)A 2013.[74]

Termination by occupier

England and Wales: non-local authority sites and permanent pitches on local authority sites

3.78 MHA 1983 Sch 1 Part 1 Chapters 2 and 4, para 3 states:

> The occupier shall be entitled to terminate the agreement by notice in writing given to the owner not less than four weeks before the date on which it is to take effect.[75]

73 MHA 1983 Sch 1 Part 1 Chapters 2, 3 and 4, paras 1 and 2; and MH(W)A 2013 Sch 2 Part 1 Chapter 2 paras 2 and 3, Chapter 3 paras 26 and 27, and Chapter 4 paras 35 and 36.

74 See, in England, CSA 1968 s1 and, in Wales, MH(W)A 2013 s2.

75 MH(W)A 2013 Sch 2 Part 1 Chapter 2 para 4 and Chapter 4 para 37 are worded slightly differently but have the same effect.

3.79 Problems can arise when an occupier leaves the site without giving proper notice. He or she can accrue pitch fee arrears and this may cause further problems when he or she seeks allocation of a local authority pitch in the future.

Termination by owner – notice and harassment

England and Wales: non-local authority sites and permanent pitches on local authority sites

3.80 Under CSA 1968 s2 (which applies to sites in England) and MH(W)A 2013 s41 (Wales), any notice to terminate must be of at least four weeks duration.

3.81 It should also be noted that, under CSA 1968 s3 (England):

> (1) . . . a person shall be guilty of an offence under this section–
> (a) if, during the subsistence of a residential contract, he unlawfully deprives the occupier of his occupation on the protected site of any caravan which the occupier is entitled by the contract to station and occupy, or to occupy, as his residence thereon;
> (b) if, after the expiration or determination of a residential contract, he enforces, otherwise than by proceedings in the court, any right to exclude the occupier from the protected site or from any such caravan, or to remove or exclude any such caravan from the site;
> (c) if, whether during the subsistence or after the expiration or determination of a residential contract, with intent to cause the occupier–
> (i) to abandon the occupation of the caravan or remove it from the site, or.
> (ii) to refrain from exercising any right or pursuing any remedy in respect thereof, he does acts calculated to interfere with the peace or comfort of the occupier or persons residing with him, or persistently withdraws or withholds services or facilities reasonably required for the occupation of the caravan as a residence on the site.[76]

3.82 MHA 2013 s12 amends the CSA 1968 by adding a new s3(1AA) which provides that a site owner in England, or his or her agent, will commit an offence if he or she knowingly or recklessly provides information or makes a representation to a person which is false or misleading and is designed to make the occupier abandon his or her home or fail to exercise his or her rights or to make a prospective

76 MH(W)A 2013 s42(1)–(4) is worded slightly differently but has the same effect except as mentioned below.

purchaser abandon his or her interest. MH(W)A 2013 s42(6) is in virtually identical terms.

3.83 Whereas the CSA 1968 refers to 'persistently' withdrawing or withholding services or facilities, the MH(W)A 2013 removes the word 'persistently' suggesting that, on Welsh sites, any withdrawal or withholding of a service or facility reasonably required may be sufficient to trigger the section.

Termination by owner – reasonableness

3.84 There are, as detailed below, three criteria under which an owner can seek to terminate an agreement. In each case a possession order will only be granted if the court is satisfied that it is reasonable to do so.

3.85 Many of the grounds of possession against tenants of houses and flats contain a similar condition with regard to 'reasonableness'.[77] Cases involving tenants may, therefore, provide useful guidance on the approach that a court should adopt when determining reasonableness, although every case will turn on its particular facts.[78] There are many examples of circumstances that may be relevant:

- the financial position of the parties;
- hardship to people living with the occupier;
- the length of time the occupier has lived at the premises;
- previous warnings, previous breaches of agreement and previous possession orders;
- the landlord's reasons for wanting to obtain possession;
- the health of the occupier and his or her family and relatives;
- the age of the occupier and other household members;
- the best interests of any children, including disruption of education;
- the public interest;
- the conduct of the parties;
- remorse or denial of any defaulter;
- in rent arrears cases, whether or not the occupier is entitled to housing benefit and, if so, whether or not it has been paid.

This is not an exhaustive list.

77 See: Rent Act 1977 Sch 15; Housing Act 1985 Sch 2; Housing Act 1988 Sch 2 Part II.

78 See Luba, Gallagher, McConnell and Madge, *Defending Possession Proceedings*, Legal Action Group, 8th edn, 2016, pp118–121 and 146 (and where specific grounds for possession are dealt with elsewhere in the text).

3.86 A judge dealing with reasonableness should only consider matters that have been specifically pleaded by the landlord in support of his case.[79] The issue of reasonableness must be decided in each case in the light of its own facts.[80] The court must take into consideration the effect on the parties, firstly, if the order is made and, secondly, if it is not.[81]

Termination by owner – breach of agreement

England and Wales: non-local authority sites and permanent pitches on local authority sites

3.87 The owner is entitled to terminate the agreement forthwith if, on the application of the owner, the court:

(a) is satisfied that the occupier has breached a term of the agreement and, after service of a notice to remedy the breach, has not complied with the notice within a reasonable time; and
(b) considers it reasonable for the agreement to be terminated.[82]

3.88 If an occupier disputes service of a notice to remedy the breach then he or she will need to address the point in his or her defence or else the occupier will be taken to have admitted the allegation that the notice has been served.[83]

Termination by owner – only or main residence

England and Wales: non-local authority sites and permanent pitches on local authority sites

3.89 The owner is entitled to terminate the agreement forthwith if, on the application of the owner, the court:

(a) is satisfied that the occupier is not occupying the mobile home as his/her only or main residence; and
(b) considers it reasonable for the agreement to be terminated.[84]

79 *Laimond Properties Ltd v Raeuchle* (2011) 33 HLR 113, April 2000 *Legal Action* 31, CA.
80 *Holt v Reading BC* [2013] EWCA Civ. 641.
81 *Cresswell v Hodgson* [1951] 2 KB 92.
82 MHA 1983 Sch 1 Part 1 Chapters 2 and 4, para 4; and MH(W)A 2013 Sch 2 Part 1 Chapter 2 para 5 and Chapter 4 para 38.
83 *Loveridge v Henley* [2004] EWCA Civ 173.
84 MHA 1983 Sch 1 Part 1 Chapters 2 and 4, para 5; and MH(W)A 2013 Sch 2 Part 1 Chapter 2 para 6 and Chapter 4 para 39.

3.90 The date for assessing whether the requirement for occupation is fulfilled is the date on which the matter is heard and determined.[85]

3.91 It is important to stress that the additional criterion of 'reasonableness' means that the court could decide that the occupier was not occupying the mobile home as his or her only or main residence but nevertheless conclude, based on the explanation provided by the occupier and/or perhaps an undertaking that he or she will occupy it again as the only or main residence, that it was not reasonable to grant a possession order.

3.92 In this regard, it may be useful to take note of cases that relate to 'secure tenants' of houses and flats. In order to retain security, a secure tenant must fulfil the 'tenant condition' ie that the house or flat is his or her 'only or principal home'.[86] Temporary absences caused by, for example, holidays, stays in hospital and working away do not affect security, but a permanent absence will lead to loss of security.[87]

Termination by owner – mobile home detrimental to the amenity of the site

England and Wales: non-local authority sites and permanent pitches on local authority sites

3.93 The owner is entitled to terminate the agreement forthwith if:

(a) on the application of the owner, a [FT(PC)/RPT] has determined that, having regard to its condition, the mobile home is having a detrimental effect on the amenity of the site; and
(b) then, on the application of the owner, the court, having regard to the [FT(PC)'s/RPT's] determination and to any other circumstances, considers it reasonable for the agreement to be terminated.

The [FT(PC)/RPT] may make an interim order if–

(a) the [FT(PC)/RPT] considers that, having regard to the present condition of the mobile home, it is having a detrimental effect on the amenity of the site; but
(b) it also considers that it would be reasonably practicable for particular repairs to be carried out on the mobile home that would result in the mobile home not having that detrimental effect, and
(c) the occupier indicates to the [FT(PC)/RPT] that s/he intends to carry out those repairs.

85 *Omar Parks Ltd v Elkington* [1992] 1 WLR 1270.

86 Housing Act 1985 s81. See, for example, *Islington LBC v Boyle* [2012] HLR 18.

87 See Luba, Gallagher, McConnell and Madge, *Defending Possession Proceedings*, Legal Action Group, 8th edn, 2016, pp399–401.

In such a case, the [FT(PC)/RPT] may make an interim order–
(a) specifying the repairs that must be carried out, and the time within which they must be carried out; and
(b) adjourning the proceedings for such period as the [FT(PC)/RPT] considers reasonable to enable the repairs to be carried out.[88]

3.94 There are no reported cases on eviction as a result of a caravan or mobile home being found to have a detrimental effect on the amenity of the site. Most cases should not come to trial if the matter can be remedied. The mischief that owners may want to avoid is that an unsightly caravan will deter new investment. The main question may be to do with how much of the site is affected. That could be assessed by the nature of the visual receptors, the prominence of the mobile home and/or whether views are localised within a small area or obtained from across the entire site.

Termination by owner – suspension of possession orders

3.95 In England, CSA 1968 s4 (as amended, from 18 January 2005, by Housing Act 2004 s211) and, in Wales, MH(W)A 2013 s44 make provision for a judge to suspend possession orders for periods of up to 12 months (potentially an order can be suspended consecutively and not just on one occasion).

3.96 It is unlikely that a possession order against an occupier of a transit pitch would be suspended, apart from for a very short period.

Recovery of overpayments by occupier

England and Wales: non-local authority sites and permanent pitches on local authority sites

3.97 Where the agreement is terminated, the occupier is entitled to recover from the owner so much of any payment made by the occupier in pursuance of the agreement as is attributable to a period beginning after the termination.[89]

3.98 This issue will most likely arise when rent has been paid in advance.

88 MHA 1983 Sch 1 Part 1 Chapters 2 and 4 para 5A; and MH(W)A 2013 Sch 2 Part 1 Chapter 2 para 7(1)–(3) and Chapter 4 para 40(1)–(3).

89 MHA 1983 Sch 1 Part 1 Chapters 2 and 4, para 7; and MH(W)A 2013 Sch 2 Part 1 Chapter 2 para 8 and Chapter 4 para 43.

Assignment

3.99 Occupiers of private sites have a right to assign. By contrast occupiers of local authority Gypsy and Traveller sites in England do not have a right to assign but those in Wales do have limited rights to do so.

3.100 Prior to MHA 2013 (in England) and MH(W)A 2013 (in Wales) coming into force the consent of the owner was required before an assignment could take place and it was known that some 'rogue park owners' had abused their power to withhold consent in order to force occupiers to sell to them for a vastly reduced price.[90]

England and Wales: non-local authority sites

3.101 MHA 1983 Sch 1 Part 1 Chapter 2 paras 7A and 7B deal with sale of a mobile home on a protected site in England. Para 7A states:

> (1) This paragraph and paragraph 7B apply in relation to a protected site in England.
> (2) Where the agreement is a new agreement, the occupier is entitled to sell the mobile home and to assign the agreement to the person to whom the mobile home is sold (referred to in this paragraph as the 'new occupier') without the approval of the owner.
> (3) In this paragraph and paragraph 7B, 'new agreement' means an agreement–
> (a) which was made after the commencement of this paragraph, or
> (b) which was made before, but which has been assigned after, that commencement.[91]
> (4) The new occupier must, as soon as reasonably practicable, notify the owner of the completion of the sale and assignment of the agreement.
> (5) The new occupier is required to pay the owner a commission on the sale of the mobile home at a rate not exceeding such rate as may be prescribed by regulations made by the Secretary of State.[92]
> (6) Except to the extent mentioned in sub-paragraph (5), the owner may not require any payment to be made (whether to the owner or otherwise) in connection with the sale of the mobile home and the assignment of the agreement to the new occupier.
> (7) The Secretary of State may by regulations prescribe procedural requirements to be complied with by the owner, the occupier or the new occupier in connection with–

90 See, for example, Communities and Local Government Committee Report, *Park Homes*, June 2012.

91 Para 7A added by MHA 2013 s10(2) and brought into force on 26 May 2013.

92 This is set at ten per cent – Mobile Homes (Selling and Gifting) (England) Regulations 2013 SI No 981 reg 8.

(a) the sale of the mobile home and assignment of the agreement;
(b) the payment of commission by virtue of sub-paragraph (5).[93]

In Wales, the MH(W)A 2013 Sch 2 Part 1 Chapter 2 para 9 is worded slightly differently but has the same effect. In Wales, the Welsh Ministers as opposed to the secretary of state have power to make regulations.[94]

3.102 MHA 1983 Sch 1 Part 1 Chapter 2 para 7B and MH(W)A 2013 Sch 2 Part 1 Chapter 2 para 10 deal with assignments prior to the change in the legislation in both England and Wales in 2013.

3.103 MHA 1983 Sch 1 Part 1 Chapter 2 paras 8A and 8B deal with gift of a mobile home on a protected site in England. Para 8A states:

(1) This paragraph and paragraph 8B apply in relation to a protected site in England.
(2) Where the agreement is a new agreement (as defined by paragraph 7A(3)), provided that the occupier has supplied the owner with the relevant evidence, the occupier is entitled to give the mobile home, and to assign the agreement, to a member of the occupier's family (referred to in this paragraph as the 'new occupier') without the approval of the owner.
(3) The relevant evidence is–
    (a) evidence, or evidence of a description, prescribed in regulations made by the Secretary of State that the person to whom the occupier proposes to give the mobile home, and to assign the agreement, is a member of the occupier's family, or
    (b) any other satisfactory evidence that the person concerned is a member of the occupier's family.[95]
(4) The new occupier must, as soon as reasonably practicable, notify the owner of the receipt of the mobile home and assignment of the agreement.
(5) The owner may not require any payment to be made (whether to the owner or otherwise) in connection with the gift of the mobile home, and the assignment of the agreement, as mentioned in subparagraph (2).
(6) The Secretary of State may by regulations prescribe procedural requirements to be complied with by the owner, the occupier or the new occupier in connection with the gift of the mobile home, and assignment of the agreement, as mentioned in sub-paragraph (2).[96]

93 See Mobile Homes (Selling and Gifting) (England) Regulations 2013 SI No 981.
94 The relevant regulations in Wales are the Mobile Homes (Selling and Gifting) (Wales) Regulations 2014 SI No 1763. As in England, the rate of commission is set at ten per cent (para 8 of those regulations).
95 See Mobile Homes (Selling and Gifting) (England) Regulations 2013 SI No 981 reg 6.
96 See Mobile Homes (Selling and Gifting) (England) Regulations 2013 SI No 981.

MH(W)A 2013 Sch 2 Part 1 Chapter 2 para 12 is worded slightly differently but has the same effect.[97]

3.104 MHA 1983 Sch 1 Part 1 Chapter 2 para 8B and MH(W)A 2013 Sch 2 Part 1 Chapter 2 para 13 deal with gifts prior to the change in the legislation in both England and Wales in 2013.

England and Wales: permanent pitches on local authority sites

3.105 Assignment is not permitted on English local authority Gypsy and Traveller sites.

3.106 Assignment on Welsh local authority Gypsy and Traveller sites is dealt with in MH(W)A 2013 Sch 2 Part 1 Chapter 2 paras 41 and 42. Para 41 states:

> (1) The occupier ('A') may assign the agreement–
> (a) to a person who is a member of A's family, or
> (b) to another person ('B') if the conditions in sub-paragraph (2) are met.
> (2) The conditions are–
> (a) A must have the approval of the owner; and
> (b) B must–
> (i) be an occupier of a permanent pitch on a relevant site, and
> (ii) have the approval of the owner to the assignment of B's agreement to A or to another occupier of a permanent pitch on a relevant site.
> (3) A relevant site for the purposes of sub-paragraph (2) is a local authority Gypsy and Traveller site in the area of the local authority in which the site on which the pitch to which A's agreement relates is located.
> (4) Neither the occupier nor the owner may require any payment to be made (whether to the occupier or owner or otherwise) in connection with the assignment of the agreement under this paragraph.

3.107 This provision not only introduces a limited right to assign on Welsh local authority sites but also a limited right to exchange (limited in that it only applies within the same local authority area).

3.108 Para 42 states:

> (1) The occupier may serve on the owner a request to approve for the purposes of paragraph 41, an assignment to a person named in the request ('the proposed occupier').
> (2) Where the request relates to an assignment under paragraph 41(1)(a) the request must include satisfactory evidence that the proposed occupier is a member of the occupier's family.

97 See Mobile Homes (Selling and Gifting) (Wales) Regulations 2014. Para 6 deals with the evidence required to show that the proposed occupier is a member of the occupier's family.

(3) Where the owner receives a request under sub-paragraph (1), the owner must, within 28 days beginning with the date on which the request is received–
  (a) approve the assignment, unless it is reasonable for the owner not to do so, and
  (b) serve on the occupier notice of the owner's decision ('a decision notice').
(4) If a person ('P') receives a request under sub-paragraph (1) and P–
  (a) while not being the owner, has an estate or interest in the land, and
  (b) believes that another person is the owner.
  And that other person has not received such a request, P owes a duty to the occupier (enforceable by a claim in tort for breach of statutory duty, as well as by action for breach of an implied term) to take such steps as are reasonable to secure that the other person receives the request within the period of 28 days beginning with the date on which P receives it.
(5) If the approval is withheld, the decision notice must specify the reasons for withholding it.
(6) Where a fee lawfully due from the occupier has not been paid or any term of the agreement has been broken or not performed, the approval required for the purpose of paragraph 41 may be given subject to a condition requiring the occupier to pay the outstanding fee, remedy the breach or perform the obligation.
(7) Except as provided by sub-paragraph (6), the approval required for the purpose of paragraph 41 cannot be given subject to a condition and a condition imposed otherwise than as so provided is to be disregarded.
(8) If the owner fails to serve the notice or withholds approval to the assignment the occupier may apply to the tribunal for an order declaring that the assignment is approved for the purposes of paragraph 41 and the tribunal may make such an order if it thinks fit.
(9) If the question arises as to whether the notice required by sub-paragraph (3)(b) was served within the required period of 28 days, it is for an owner to show that the notice was so served.
(10) If the owner did not approve the assignment and the question arises whether it was reasonable for the owner not to do so, it is for the owner to show that it was reasonable.
(11) A request or notice under this paragraph–
  (a) must be in writing, and
  (b) may be served by post.
(12) Subject to sub-paragraph (13), an application to the tribunal under sub-paragraph (8) by an occupier must be made–
  (a) within the period of three months beginning with the day after the date on which the occupier receives the decision notice, or
  (b) where the occupier receives no decision notice, within the period of three months beginning with the date which is 29 days after the date upon which the occupier served the request under sub-paragraph (1).

(13) A tribunal may permit an application under sub-paragraph (8) to be made to the tribunal after the applicable period specified in sub-paragraph (12) if it is satisfied that, in all the circumstances, there are good reasons for the failure to apply before the end of that period and for any delay since then in applying for permission to make the application out of time.

3.109 By way of contrast, the assignment of secure tenancies of local authority houses and flats is governed by HA 1985 s91, which states:

(1) A secure tenancy . . . –

. . . is not capable of being assigned except in the cases mentioned in subsection (3).

. . .

(3) The exceptions are–

(a) an assignment in accordance with section 92 (assignment by way of exchange);

(b) an assignment in pursuance of an order made under–

(i) section 24 of the Matrimonial Causes Act 1973 (property adjustment orders in connection with matrimonial proceedings),

(ii) section 17(1) of the Matrimonial and Family Proceedings Act 1984 (property adjustment orders after overseas divorce, &c.),

(iii) paragraph 1 of Schedule 1 to the Children Act 1989 (orders for financial relief against parents), or

(iv) Part 2 of Schedule 5, or paragraph 9(2) or (3) of Schedule 7, to the Civil Partnership Act 2004 (property adjustment orders in connection with civil partnership proceedings or after overseas dissolution of civil partnership, etc.);

(c) an assignment to a person who would be qualified to succeed the tenant if the tenant died immediately before the assignment.

3.110 The lack of any right to exchange and/or to assign a pitch on a local authority site to a potential successor (in England) may give a Gypsy or Traveller occupier of such a site the ability to challenge the legislation on grounds of discrimination. Such a challenge might be brought by way of an application for a declaration of incompatibility.[98]

Re-siting of mobile home

England and Wales: non-local authority sites and permanent pitches on local authority sites

3.111 If an owner of a site wishes to re-site a mobile home in order to enable works to be carried out on the site then the MHA 1983 applies as follows (note that the passages in square brackets only apply to

98 See HRA 1998 s4.

permanent pitches on local authority Gypsy and Traveller sites in England):[99]

> The owner is entitled to require that the occupier's right to station the mobile home is exercisable for any period in relation to another pitch forming part of the protected site [or a pitch forming part of another protected site] ('the other pitch') if (and only if)–
> (a) on the application of the owner, [the FT(PC)] is satisfied that the other pitch is broadly comparable to the occupier's original pitch and that it is reasonable for the mobile home to be stationed on the other pitch for that period; or
> (b) the owner needs to carry out essential repair or emergency works that can only be carried out if the mobile home is moved to the other pitch for that period, and the other pitch is broadly comparable to the occupier's original pitch.

3.112 In Wales, MH(W)A 2013 Sch 2 Part 1 Chapter 2 para 14 and Chapter 4 para 44 are in very similar terms, except, with regard to private sites, that if the owner needs to carry out essential repair or emergency works, then he or she needs to make an application to the RPT who must be satisfied of the need for the works and that the other pitch is broadly comparable to the occupier's original pitch, unless 'the urgency of the need means that it is impracticable to make an application before the mobile home is re-sited' (Chapter 2 para 14(1)(b)). In a case covered by para 14(1)(b), such an application must be made immediately and, if the tribunal is not so satisfied, 'the owner must immediately secure that the mobile home is returned to the original pitch' (Chapter 2 para 14(2)).

3.113 In the case of a local authority site in Wales, a pitch forming part of another protected site is broadly comparable to the occupier's original pitch only if it provides access to health and education services required by the occupier which is, as far as reasonably practicable, broadly comparable to the access provided by the occupier's original pitch.[100]

3.114 In both England and Wales, the owner must pay all the costs and expenses incurred by the occupier in connection with the mobile home being moved to and from the other pitch.

> 'Essential repair or emergency works' means (the text below in square brackets only applies to local authority Gypsy and Traveller sites)–
> (a) repairs to the base where the mobile home is stationed;

99 MHA 1983 Sch 1 Part 1 Chapter 2 para 10 and Chapter 4 para 8.
100 MH(W)A 2013 Sch 2 Part 1 Chapter 4 para 44(2).

(b) [repairs to any outhouses and facilities provided by the owner of the pitch and to any gas, electricity, water, sewerage or other services or other amenities provided by the owner in such outhouses];
(c) works or repairs needed to comply with any relevant legal requirements; or
(d) works or repairs in connection with restoration following flood, landslide or other natural disaster.[101]

3.115 Thus it can be seen that if a local authority wishes to carry out works on a Gypsy and Traveller site in England and Wales then: the 'other pitch' can be on a different site; and 'essential repair or emergency works' can include works to outhouses (often known as 'amenity blocks') and other facilities on such a site.

Quiet enjoyment of the mobile home

3.116 The occupier of a pitch on both permanent and transit sites shall be entitled to quiet enjoyment of the mobile home together with the pitch during the continuance of the agreement, subject to re-siting of the mobile home (see above) and the owner's right of entry to the pitch (see below).[102]

3.117 The covenant for quiet enjoyment is broken by some actual disturbance in the possession of the pitch. Unlawful eviction would be an obvious example. Stopping supply of services would be another. Harassment by the owner would also be a breach of the occupier's quiet enjoyment of his or her premises.[103]

Owners' right of entry to the pitch

3.118 The owner of any site may enter the pitch without prior notice between the hours of 9am and 6pm:

a) to deliver written communications, including post and notices, to the occupier; and
b) to read any meter for gas, electricity, water, sewerage or other services supplied by the owner.

101 MHA 1983 Sch 1 Part 1 Chapter 2 para 10(3) and (4) and Chapter 4 para 8(3) and (4); MH(W)A 2013 Sch 2 Part 1 Chapter 2 para 14(4) and (5) and Chapter 4 para 44(4) and (5).

102 MHA 1983 Sch 1 Part 1 Chapter 2 para 11, Chapter 3 para 6 and Chapter 4 para 9; MH(W)A 2013 Sch 2 Part 1 Chapter 2 para 15, Chapter 3 para 31 and Chapter 4 para 45.

103 For further information see Arden, Brown and Madge-Wyld, *Quiet Enjoyment*, Legal Action Group, 8th edn, 2017.

3.119 The owner may also enter the pitch to carry out essential repair or emergency works on giving as much notice to the occupier (whether in writing or otherwise) as is reasonably practicable in the circumstances.

3.120 Unless the occupier has agreed otherwise, the owner may enter the pitch for a reason other than one specified above only if he or she has given the occupier at least 14 clear days' written notice of the date, time and reason for his or her visit.

3.121 The rights conferred above do not extend to the mobile home. Therefore, importantly, the owner has no right of access to the mobile home without the occupier's consent.[104]

The pitch fee

England and Wales: non-local authority sites and permanent pitches on local authority sites

3.122 'Pitch fee' means:

> . . . the amount which the occupier is required by the agreement to pay to the owner for the right to station the mobile home on the pitch and for use of the common areas of the protected site and their maintenance, but does not include amounts due in respect of gas, electricity, water and sewerage and other services, unless the agreement expressly provides that the pitch fee includes such amounts.

It should be noted that the provisions below with regard to pitch fees do not apply to transit sites.[105]

3.123 The pitch fee can only be changed either:

(a) with the agreement of the occupier, or
(b) if the [FT(PC)/RPT], on the application of the owner or occupier, considers it reasonable for the pitch fee to be changed and makes an order determining the amount of the new pitch fee.

The pitch fee is reviewed annually as at the review date. At least 28 clear days before the review date the owner shall serve on the occupier

104 MHA 1983 Sch 1 Part 1 Chapter 2 paras 11–15, Chapter 3 paras 7–10, and Chapter 4 paras 10–13; MH(W)A 2013 Sch 2 Part 1 Chapter 2 para 16, Chapter 3 para 32 and Chapter 4 para 46.

105 MHA 1983 Sch 1 Part 1 Chapter 2 para 29, Chapter 3 para 13, and Chapter 4 para 27. There is just one definition in MH(W)A 2013 at s62. This is worded slightly differently but has the same effect.

a written notice setting out his proposals in respect of the new pitch fee.[106]

3.124 If a local authority site owner purports to impose an increased pitch fee and the occupier believes this is being done unlawfully, the occupier would have to challenge this increase by way of judicial review.[107]

3.125 If the occupier agrees, the new fee will be payable as from the review date. If the occupier does not agree, the owner can apply to the FT(PC)/RPT. In the meantime, the occupier is obliged to keep paying the current pitch fee until the revised pitch fee is decided either by agreement or by court order. The revised pitch fee will still be payable from the review date, although the occupier will not be treated as being in arrears until the 28th day after the date when the revised pitch fee is determined. In other words the occupier has 28 days to catch up with payments. If the owner fails to serve the notice of the new pitch fee within the timescale outlined above, there is a mechanism for dealing with that situation.[108] In the case of private sites in Wales (ie sites under MH(W)A 2013 Sch 2 Part 1 Chapter 2), when the owner serves any notice of increase of pitch fee, it must be in a specified form.[109]

3.126 When determining the amount of the new pitch fee particular regard shall be had to:

(a) any sums expended by the owner since the last review date on improvements–
  (i) which are for the benefit of the occupiers of mobile homes on the protected site;
  (ii) which were the subject of consultation (see further below);
  (iii) to which a majority of the occupiers have not disagreed in writing or which, in the case of such disagreement, a [FT(PC)/RPT], on the application of the owner, has ordered should be taken into account when determining the amount of the new pitch fee.
(b) any decrease in the amenity of the protected site since the last review date; and
(c) the effect of any enactment which has come into force since the last review date.[110]

106 MHA 1983 Sch 1 Part 1 Chapter 2 paras 16 and 17, and Chapter 4 paras 14 and 15; MH(W)A 2013 Sch 2 Part 1 Chapter 2 para 17(1)–(3) and Chapter 4 para 47(1)–(3).

107 For the procedure on judicial review, see Manning, Salmon and Brown *Judicial Review Proceedings: A practioner's guide*, 3rd edition, LAG 2013.

108 MHA 1983 Sch 1 Part 1 Chapter 2 para 17, and Chapter 4 para 15. MH(W)A 2013 Sch 2 Part 1 Chapter 2 para 17(5)–(9) and Chapter 4 para 47(4)–(8).

109 MH(W)A 2013 Sch 2 Part 1 Chapter 2 para 23.

110 MHA 1983 Sch 1 Part 1 Chapter 2 para 18(1) and Chapter 4 para 16(1); MH(W)A 2013 Sch 2 Part 1 Chapter 2 para 18(1) and Chapter 4 para 48(1).

3.127 In the case of a protected site in England, when calculating what constitutes a majority of the occupiers, each mobile home is taken to have only one occupier and, in the event of there actually being more than one occupier in a mobile home, its occupier is taken to be the occupier whose name first appears on the agreement.[111] In the case of a protected site in Wales, when calculating what constitutes a majority of the occupiers, each pitch is to be taken to have only one occupier and, in the event of there being more than one occupier of a pitch, its occupier is to be taken to be whichever of them the occupiers agree or, in default of agreement, the one whose name first appears on the agreement.[112]

3.128 Additionally, when determining the new pitch fee for private sites in Wales, regard must be had to:

a) any deterioration in the condition of the site or any adjoining land which is occupied or controlled by the owner;
b) any reduction in the services which the owner supplies and any deterioration in the quality of those services;

but no regard is to be had to any costs incurred by the owner since the last review date for the purpose of complying with provisions in MH(W)A 2103 Sch 2 Part 1 which were not contained in the MHA 1983.[113]

3.129 Additionally, when determining the amount of the new pitch fee in England and Wales, any costs incurred by the owner in connection with expanding the protected site shall not be taken into account and no regard shall be had to any costs incurred by the owner in relation to the conduct of any proceedings under the MHA 1983 or under the agreement.[114]

3.130 In the case of private sites in England and Wales, when determining the amount of a new pitch fee, no regard may be had to any fee required to be paid by the owner for an application for site licence conditions to be altered or for an application for consent to transfer the site licence.[115]

3.131 In the case of private and permanent local authority sites in England, there is a presumption that the pitch fee shall increase or

111 MHA 1983 Sch 1 Part 1 Chapter 2 para 18(2) and Chapter 4 para 16(2).
112 MH(W)A 2013 Sch 2 Part 1 Chapter 2 para 18(3) and Chapter 4 para 48(2).
113 MH(W)A 2013 Sch 2 Part 1 Chapter 2 paras 18(1)(b), (c) and (2).
114 MHA 1983 Sch 1 Part 1 Chapter 2 para 19 and Chapter 4 para 17; MH(W)A 2013 Sch 2 Part 1 Chapter 2 para 19 and Chapter 4 para 49.
115 MHA 1983 Sch 1 Part 1 Chapter 2 para 19(3); and MH(W)A 2013 Sch 2 Part 1 Chapter 2 para 19(2)(a).

decrease by a percentage which is no more than any percentage increase or decrease in the retail prices index (RPI) since the last review date, unless this would be unreasonable having regard to the matters listed above.[116]

3.132 In the case of a protected site in Wales, unless it would be unreasonable having regard to the matters listed above, there is a presumption that the pitch fee will increase or decrease by a percentage which is no more than any percentage increase or decrease in the consumer prices index (CPI) calculated by reference only to–

a) the latest index, and
b) the index published for the month which was 12 months before that to which the latest index relates.[117]

3.133 For anyone advising a Gypsy or Traveller occupier of a site, the RPI in England or the CPI in Wales will, therefore, be the starting point for any assessment of the proposed new fee.

3.134 There are a number of reported cases dealing with the issue of disputed increases in pitch fees. Frequently the cases concern the question of what issues are relevant to the owner's justification for an increase.[118]

Occupier's obligations

England and Wales: non-local authority sites and permanent pitches on local authority sites

3.135 Under MHA 1983 Sch 1 Part 1 Chapter 2 para 21 and Chapter 4 para 19:

The occupier shall–

(a) pay the pitch fee to the owner;
(b) pay to the owner all sums due under the agreement in respect of gas, electricity, water, sewerage and other services supplied by the owner;
(c) keep the mobile home in a sound state of repair;
(d) maintain–
  (i) the outside of the mobile home, and
  (ii) the pitch, including all fences and outbuildings belonging to, or enjoyed with it, and the mobile home,

  in a clean and tidy condition, and

116 MHA 1983 Sch 1 Part 1 Chapter 2 para 20(1) and Chapter 4 para 18(1).

117 MH(W)A 2013 Sch 2 Part 1 Chapter 2 para 20(1) and Chapter 4 para 50(1).

118 See *Stroud v Weir Associates Ltd* (1987) 19 HLR 151; *Walker v Badcock* (1998) 30 HLR 513; *Howard v Kinvena Homes Ltd* (2000) 32 HLR 541; *Warfield Park Homes Ltd v Warfield Park Residents Association* [2006] EWCA Civ 283; and *du Plessis v Fontgary Leisure Parks Ltd* [2012] EWCA Civ 409.

(e) if requested by the owner, provide him with documentary evidence of any costs or expenses in respect of which the occupier seeks reimbursement.

MH(W)A 2013 Sch 2 Part 1 Chapter 2 para 21(1) and Chapter 4 para 51(1) are worded slightly differently, but have the same effect.

Owner's obligations

England and Wales: non-local authority sites and permanent pitches on local authority sites

3.136 The owner's obligations in terms of England are found in MHA 1983 Sch 1 Part 1 Chapter 2 paras 22 and 23, and Chapter 4 paras 20 and 21. The owner's obligations in terms of Wales are found in MH(W)A 2013 Sch 2 Part 1 Chapter 2 paras 22–25 and Chapter 4 paras 52–54.

Written details

England and Wales: non-local authority sites and permanent pitches on local authority sites

3.137 The owner must, if requested by the occupier, and on payment by the occupier of a charge of not more than £30, provide accurate written details of:

a) the size of the pitch and the base on which the mobile home is stationed; and
b) the location of the pitch and the base within the protected site.

Documentary evidence in support of pitch fee and other charges

3.138 The owner must, if requested by the occupier, provide (free of charge) documentary evidence in support and explanation of any new pitch fee, and any other charges payable by the occupier to the owner under the agreement.

Repairs

England and Wales: non-local authority sites and permanent pitches on local authority sites

3.139 The owner must:

- be responsible for repairing the base on which the mobile home is stationed and for maintaining any gas, electricity, water, sewerage or other services supplied by the owner to the pitch or the mobile home;
- [be responsible for repairing other amenities provided by the owner on the pitch including any outhouses and facilities provided];[119]
- maintain in a clean and tidy condition those parts of the protected site, including access ways, site boundary fences and trees, which are not the responsibility of any occupier of a mobile home stationed on the protected site.

3.140 When advising a Gypsy or Traveller about the repairing obligations of the owner of a protected site, it will also be important to have regard to any express terms in the written statement that may extend the obligations.

Consultation about improvements

England and Wales: non-local authority sites and permanent pitches on local authority sites

3.141 The owner must consult the occupier about improvements to the protected site in general, and in particular about those which the owner wishes to be taken into account when determining the amount of any new pitch fee.

3.142 To 'consult' the occupier means:

(a) to give the occupier at least 28 clear days' notice in writing of the proposed improvements which–
  (i) describes the proposed improvements and how they will benefit the occupier in the long and short term;
  (ii) details how the pitch fee may be affected when it is next reviewed; and
  (iii) states when and where the occupier can make representations about the proposed improvements; and
(b) to take into account any representations made by the occupier about the proposed improvements before undertaking them.[120]

119 The text in square brackets only applies to permanent pitches on local authority Gypsy and Traveller sites in England and Wales. It was added in since such sites commonly have amenity blocks which may contain a kitchen, bathroom/shower, toilet and utility room.

120 MHA 1983 Sch 1 Part 1 Chapter 2 para 24, and Chapter 4 para 22; MH(W)A 2013 Sch 2 Part 1 Chapter 2 para 22(2) and Chapter 4 para 52(2).

Consultation with qualifying residents' association

England and Wales: non-local authority sites and permanent pitches on local authority sites

3.143 The owner must consult a qualifying residents' association (see further below), if there is one, about all matters which relate to the operation and management of, or improvements to, the protected site and which may affect the occupiers either directly or indirectly.

3.144 To:

> . . . 'consult' a qualifying residents' association [or occupiers] means:
> (a) to give the association [or occupiers] at least 28 clear days' notice in writing of the matters referred to in paragraph 20(g) which–
>   (i) describes the matters and how they may affect the occupiers either directly or indirectly in the long and short term; and
>   (ii) states when and where the association [or occupiers] can make representations about the matters; and
> (b) to take into account any representations made by the association [or occupiers] before proceeding with the matters (the parts in square brackets above only apply to non-local authority sites in Wales).[121]

Doing nothing to adversely affect occupier's ability to perform obligations

England and Wales: non-local authority sites and permanent pitches on local authority sites

3.145 The owner must not do or cause to be done anything which may adversely affect the ability of the occupier to perform his or her obligations.[122] In addition, on private sites in Wales, the owner must not do or cause to be done anything which deters the occupier from making internal or external improvements to the mobile home subject to any restrictions in the agreement or any enactment.[123]

121 MHA 1983 Sch 1 Part 1 Chapter 2 para 25, and Chapter 4 para 23; MH(W)A 2013 Sch 2 Part 2 Chapter 2 para 22(3) and Chapter 4 para 52(3).

122 MHA 1983 Sch 1 Part 1 Chapter 2 para 23, and Chapter 4 para 21; MH(W)A 2013 Sch 2 Part 1 Chapter 2 para 21(2) and Chapter 4 para 51(2).

123 MH(W)A 2013 Sch 2 Part 1 Chapter 2 para 21(2)–(4).

Owner's name and address

3.146 This implied term mirrors Landlord and Tenant Act 1987 ss47 and 48 (which apply to tenants of premises in England and Wales) and applies to all sites, including transit sites.

3.147 The owner must inform the occupier and any qualifying residents' association of an address in England or Wales at which notices (including notices of proceedings) may be served upon the owner by the occupier or a qualifying residents' association. Failure to provide this information means that any amount otherwise due from the occupier in respect of the pitch fee will be treated as not due at any time before the owner does so comply. Further, any demand for payment of the pitch fee or in respect of services supplied or other charges, must contain the name and address of the owner and, if not in England and Wales, must also contain an address in England and Wales at which notices (including notices of proceedings) may be served. Once again, if this information is not supplied then the amount demanded will not be treated as being due until the owner supplies the necessary information.[124]

3.148 If advising a Gypsy or Traveller resident concerning this implied term, it is wise to advise them to set aside any pitch fee or other charges since they will be payable if and when the occupier complies with his or her obligations.

Qualifying residents' association

England and Wales: non-local authority sites and permanent pitches on local authority sites

3.149 A residents' association is a qualifying residents' association if:

(a) it represents occupiers of mobile homes on the site;
(b) at least 50% of the occupiers of the mobile homes on the site are members of the association;
(c) it is independent from the owner, who, together with any agent or employee of the owner, is excluded from membership;
(d) subject to (c) above, membership is open to all occupiers who own a mobile home on the site;
(e) it maintains a list of members which is open to public inspection together with the rules and constitution of the association;

124 MHA 1983 Sch 1 Part 1 Chapter 2 paras 26 and 27, Chapter 3 paras 11 and 12, and Chapter 4 paras 24 and 25; MH(W)A 2013 Sch 2 Part 1 Chapter 2 paras 24 and 25, Chapter 3 paras 33 and 34, and Chapter 4 paras 53 and 54.

(f) it has a chair, secretary and treasurer who are elected by and from among the members;

(g) with the exception of administrative decisions taken by the chair, secretary and treasurer acting in their official capacities, decisions are taken by voting and there is only one vote for each mobile home;

(h) the owner has acknowledged in writing to the secretary that the association is a qualifying residents' association, or, in default, the [FT(PC)/RPT] has so ordered.[125]

3.150 In England, when calculating the percentage of occupiers for the purpose of (b) above, each mobile home is taken to have only one occupier and, in the event of there being more than one occupier of a mobile home, its occupier is taken to be the occupier whose name first appears on the agreement.[126]

3.151 In Wales, when calculating the percentage of occupiers for the purpose of (b) above, where there is more than one occupier of a mobile home, the one who is to be the member of the association is whichever of them the occupiers agree will be a member or, in default of agreement, the one whose name appears first on the agreement to station the mobile home on the site.[127]

Transit pitches on local authority sites

3.152 In England, in July 2018, there were 330 transit pitches[128] and in Wales, in July 2018, there were only two transit pitches.[129] It can be seen from these figures that there is a completely inadequate supply of transit pitches in England and Wales.

3.153 The following implied terms also apply to transit pitches on local authority Gypsy and Traveller sites in England and Wales: duration of the agreement; recovery of overpayments; quiet enjoyment; owner's right of entry to the pitch; owner's name and address (see above for full details of these implied terms).

125 MHA 1983 Sch 1 Part 1 Chapter 2 para 28, and Chapter 4 para 26; MH(W)A 2013 s61(1) and (2) – there are other requirements in terms of Wales – see MH(W)A 2013 s61(3)–(8). Assistance in setting up a residents' association can be obtained from: The Traveller Movement; Friends, Families and Travellers; The National Federation of Gypsy Liaison Groups see appendix D.

126 MHA 1983 Sch 1 Part 1 Chapter 2 para 28(2), and Chapter 4 para 26(2); MHA 1983 Sch 1 Part 1 Chapter 2 para 28, Chapter 4 para 26.

127 MH(W)A 2013 s61(2).

128 See: www.gov.uk/government/statistics/traveller-caravan-count-july-2018.

129 See: https://gov.wales/docs/statistics/2018/180926-gypsy-traveller-caravan-count-july-2018-en.pdf.

3.154 In addition, there are provisions for early termination of an agreement to occupy a transit pitch by both the occupier and the owner.

3.155 The occupier may terminate the agreement before the expiry of the fixed period set out in the agreement by notice in writing to the owner. The owner may terminate the agreement before the expiry of the fixed period set out in the agreement:

(a) without being required to show any reason, by giving written notice not less than four weeks before the date on which that notice is to take effect; or
(b) forthwith, where–
  (i) the occupier has breached a term of the agreement and, after service of a notice to remedy the breach, has not complied with the notice within a reasonable time; or
  (ii) the owner considers it reasonable for the agreement to be terminated.[130]

3.156 Clearly the above provision is designed to make it easier for an owner to terminate a transit pitch agreement and to avoid litigation from occupiers of transit pitches. Nevertheless, such decisions by a local authority may potentially be susceptible to judicial review.

Mobile Homes Act 1983 and Mobile Homes (Wales) Act 2013 – express terms

3.157 Express terms cannot override or seek to exclude implied terms.[131] Examples of express terms are those that refer to: nuisance and anti-social behaviour; numbers of pets; construction of sheds, fences etc; visitors; business use of pitch; bonfires; numbers, parking and/or types of vehicles; and periods of time away travelling.

3.158 It should be noted that the provisions governing unfair terms in consumer contracts in England and Wales[132] would not apply to the terms statutorily implied by the MHA 1983 and the MH(W)A 2013.

130 MHA 1983 Sch 1 Part 1 Chapter 3 para 3; and MH(W)A 2013 Sch 2 Part 1 Chapter 3 paras 28 and 29.

131 MHA 1983 s2(1); and MH(W)A 2013 s50(1).

132 See Consumer Rights Act 2015 Part 2 ss61–76.

The effects of the Mobile Homes Act 2013 in England

3.159 The MHA 2013 applies to private sites in England.[133] The MHA 2013 implements many of the proposals contained in the DCLG consultation paper *A better deal for mobile home owners* (April 2012) and the recommendations made by the Communities and Local Government Select Committee in its report *Park Homes* (June 2012). The Committee found 'widespread malpractice' in the sector and concluded that the existing legislative framework was 'inadequate.' The MHA 2013 deals with: site licensing; the 'fit and proper person' test; site rules; assignment;[134] and pitch fees.

3.160 MHA 2013 s1 amends the CSCDA 1960 to enable local authorities to charge fees in relation to their licensing functions on 'relevant protected sites' (which excludes sites used for holiday caravans and those sites where year round occupation is prohibited).[135]

3.161 CSCDA 1960 s5A requires the local authority to inform the licence holder of the matters to which they have had regard when fixing the fee. A local authority will be able to apply to the FT(PC) for an order to recover overdue fees. Failure to comply with such an order will enable the local authority to apply for an order revoking the site licence. Fees will also be payable for:

- an application to alter the conditions attached to a licence; and
- an application for consent to transfer a site licence.

3.162 Site owners will be able to recover the cost of the annual licence fee through the pitch fee review in the first year that the licence becomes payable by the site owner. Thereafter, the fee will remain part of the pitch fee and will be uprated in line with the RPI. Significantly, the costs of any fee to apply for site licence conditions to be altered or for consent to transfer a site licence cannot be passed on to the occupiers of a site via the pitch fee.[136]

3.163 MHA 2013 s2 amends the CSCDA 1960 to give a local authority a discretion as to whether or not to grant or transfer a site licence.[137]

133 Apart from with regard to the amendment to CSA 1968 by MHA 2013 s12 – see para 3.82, above.

134 See para 3.94 onwards, above.

135 See CSCDA 1960 ss3(2A), (7), (8), 5A, 8(1A), (1B), 10(1A) and 10A. See also the Mobile Homes (Site Licensing) (England) Regulations 2014 SI No 442, which came into force on 1 April 2014.

136 See above at para 3.119.

137 CSCDA 1960 ss3(4), (5), (5A)–(5F) and 10(1B)–(1F).

3.164 MHA 2013 s3 amends CSCDA 1960 to provide that appeals against conditions attached to a site licence will be to a FT(PC). The FT(PC) will be able to attach a new condition to a site licence where it varies or cancels a condition.[138]

3.165 MHA 2013 s4 amends CSCDA 1960 to provide that, in the event of a breach of a licence condition, the local authority will be able to serve a compliance notice on the owner. The owner will have a right of appeal to a FT(PC). If the owner fails to adhere to the terms of a compliance notice without reasonable excuse they will be guilty of an offence.[139]

3.166 MHA 2013 s5 amends CSCDA 1960 to give a local authority the power to enter and carry out works on a site where the owner has been convicted of failing to comply with the steps set out in compliance notices. A local authority may take emergency action if the owner has failed to comply with a condition attached to a site licence and there is imminent risk of serious harm to the health or safety of any person who is or may be on the land. The local authority has power to reclaim expenses associated with carrying out necessary compliance works and/or emergency action.[140]

3.167 MHA 2013 s8 (which is not yet in force) amends CSCDA 1960 to give the Secretary of State new regulation making powers under which he or she will be able to prohibit the use of land as a relevant protected site in England unless the local authority is satisfied that the owner, or the person appointed to manage the site, is a 'fit and proper person'.

3.168 MHA 2013 s9[141] amends the MHA 1983 by making site rules, where they exist, an express term in the written statement. This provision applies to new agreements but also applies retrospectively to existing agreements.[142] In addition, the Mobile Homes (Site Rules) (England) Regulations 2014[143] introduce a new procedure[144] whereby site owners must consult the occupiers before changing the site rules.

138 CSCDA 1960 ss7(1), (1A), 8(2) and (4). In terms of transfer of jurisdiction to the FT(PC), see the Transfer of Tribunal Functions (Mobile Homes Act 2013 and Miscellaneous Amendments) Order 2014 SI No 1900.

139 CSCDA 1960 ss9A, 9B and 9C.

140 CSCDA 1960 ss9D, 9E and 9F.

141 Which came into force on 26 May 2013.

142 MHA 1983 ss2C–2D.

143 SI No 5.

144 With effect from 4 February 2014.

3.169 MHA 2013 s11[145] amends MHA 1983[146] (the provision applying retrospectively to existing agreements) to require site owners, when serving the notice of pitch fee increase, to also provide a document satisfying the requirements set out in MHA 1983 Sch 1 Part 1 Chapter 2 para 25A and the Mobile Home (Pitch Fees) (Prescribed Form) (England) Regulations 2013.[147]

Mobile Homes (Wales) Act 2013, site licensing, site rules and the fit and proper person test

3.170 The provisions with regard to site licensing, site rules and the 'fit and proper person' test in MH(W)A 2013 only apply to protected sites in Wales and consolidate all legislation with regard to mobile home sites in Wales. The relevant provisions are MH(W)A 2103 ss7, 9–10, 15–19, 28–37, and 52. Unless stated otherwise, these provisions do not apply to local authority Gypsy and Traveller sites in Wales. They do not apply to holiday or touring caravan sites. As with the MHA 2013, these parts of the MH(W)A 2013 are designed to deal with widespread malpractice and 'rogue site owners' on private rented sites and bring forward many of the proposals contained in the Welsh Government white paper *Homes for Wales: A White Paper for Better Lives and Communities* (May 2012).[148]

Other matters outside the scope of the Mobile Homes Acts

Allocation of pitches

3.171 There is no specific statutory regime that applies to the allocation of pitches on local authority sites and the position can be compared with that relating to the allocation of local authority houses and flats, where Housing Act 1996 Part VI applies. Nevertheless, as a public authority, a local authority will be expected to organise and manage

145 Which came into force on 26 May 2013.

146 MHA 1983 Sch 1 Part 1 Chapter 2 paras 17(2A), (6A), (11), (12), 18(1), (1A), 19(4), 20(A1), (A2) and 25A(1).

147 SI No 1505, which came into force on 26 July 2013.

148 The provisions mentioned under this heading all came into force on 1 October 2014.

this process in a reasonable and transparent fashion. This is exemplified by the case of *R (Piggott) v Bedfordshire CC*.[149]

3.172 Mrs Piggott occupied a pitch on a local authority site as a trespasser and then applied for a pitch on the site (she wanted to remain on the site as her daughter and other members of her family were living there, she was seriously ill and needed their care and support). Mrs Piggott sought to challenge the decision to take possession proceedings by way of judicial review. It was agreed that the fact that Mrs Piggott was a squatter did not prevent her from making an application (although the council had initially taken that view). Burton J held that the council should have considered three matters: 1) the needs of the applicant; 2) the needs and requirements of others (also applicants) 'who should not be prejudiced by the unauthorised jumping of the gun of the applicant'; and 3) the jumping of the gun itself to see whether it should make any difference at all or how far it should make a difference.[150] The council had failed to make a comparison of her position with that of the others on the waiting list for a pitch. Even though the council had offered Mrs Piggott a pitch on another site, it was held that she was entitled to be considered for a pitch on the site where she was camped. Mrs Piggott was subsequently offered and accepted a licence of a pitch on the site.

3.173 Most local authorities operate a waiting list system for the allocation of pitches and will have written policies in place. An adviser dealing with a query from a Gypsy or Traveller on allocations will need to have regard to these written policies. They should also have regard to the relevant government guidance. DCLG have produced guidance for English local authorities and the Welsh Government have done likewise for Welsh local authorities.[151]

3.174 In *R (McDonagh) v Hackney LBC*[152] the claimant was an Irish Traveller who had been resorting to the Hackney area since 1982 and the evidence was that the local authority's Travellers Site Manager had known her for many years. Faced with eviction from land next to one of the local authority's official sites, the claimant challenged the local authority's site allocation policy ('the policy') by way of judicial review and the case was heard by Kenneth Parker J. The policy provided that:

149 [2002] EWHC 77 (Admin).

150 [2002] EWHC 77 (Admin) at para 34.

151 DCLG, *Gypsy and Traveller Site Management: Good Practice Guide* July 2009, chapter 7; Welsh Government, *Managing Gypsy Traveller Sites in Wales: Guidance*, May 2015, chapter 4.

152 [2012] EWHC 373 (Admin).

> Everyone on the list must live in the borough. Where people are forced out of the borough through lack of anywhere to stay, they can stay on the list only as long as they are still using an address in Hackney as c/o for benefits . . . and schools etc . . .
>
> Standard registration must be renewed every year by the end of January and at this time checks will be made again and people currently on the list may be excluded if they no longer qualify . . .

3.175 In 2009 the claimant was on an unauthorised encampment in the local authority's area. Her attempt to put her name on the list failed because she did not produce the required documentation. Later that year, with the assistance of the London Gypsy and Traveller Unit, the claimant submitted the required documentation. However, the claimant did not appreciate that she would need to re-register in January 2010 and as a consequence she was removed from the waiting list. The claimant applied once again to join the waiting list in May 2011 but by then she was a long way down the list.

3.176 The judge summarised the claimant's case as follows:

> In essence, submitted Mr Jones [counsel for the claimant], given [Mrs McDonagh's] special vulnerability and public authority failure, Hackney's policy was irrational because it unfairly prejudiced travellers who were in the position of Mrs McDonagh, namely who had been driven from Hackney and who had been unable, despite demonstrable connection with Hackney, to secure and retain a place on the waiting list . . .
>
> Mr Jones accepted . . . that Hackney was entitled to have a requirement that to be admitted to the relevant waiting list an applicant needed a demonstrable connection with Hackney . . . However, he contended that the specific criteria to show that connection were arbitrary, and in certain cases unduly burdensome, especially for those who might not be able to read and write . . .[153]

3.177 The judge concluded that the policy was lawful. When doing so he relied upon the House of Lords decision in *R (Ahmad) v Newham LBC*[154] and stated:

> I accept that the specific context in Ahmad was different. Nonetheless, the case at its core involved a challenge to a policy that was designed to ration a scarce resource, in which there would be competing arrangements and potential winners and losers whatever policy was chosen . . .

153 [2012] EWHC 373 (Admin) at paras 19 and 20.

154 [2009] UKHL 14, [2009] HLR 31.

> ... For my part, I discern no irrationality in the starting point of Hackney's policy that requires a residential connection with the borough, nor in the requirement that residence must be contemporary ...[155]

3.178 Despite this judgment, it does not seem satisfactory that a Traveller who had resorted to the area since 1982 and was extremely well known to the local authority, was excluded from the waiting list simply because she was not able to comply with the local authority's procedural requirements.

3.179 In *R (VC) v North Somerset Council* CO/3801/2015[156] an Irish Traveller challenged a 'local connection' requirement contained within the local authority's housing allocations scheme, which had been extended beyond Housing Act 1996 Part VI allocations to cover Gypsy/Traveller site allocations. The effect of that requirement was that the claimant, who could not point to a local connection to North Somerset, was denied entry to the council's housing register.

3.180 The claim was brought on a number of grounds including, in particular, that the council had failed to pay due regard to statutory equality objectives (in accordance with section 149 of the Equality Act (EqA) 2010) and that the local connection requirement was, in any event, indirectly discriminatory in relation to Gypsies and Travellers and unjustifiably so. The claimant argued that many ethnic Gypsies and Travellers still lived a nomadic lifestyle (in the absence of sufficient permanent sites to meet their accommodation needs) and that, as a consequence, the local connection requirement was likely to have an adverse effect on more Gypsies and Travellers than members of the settled population. The claimant's case was supported by the Equality and Human Rights Commission (EHRC), which agreed that there was a differential impact and that it was difficult to see how a local connection requirement in an allocations scheme could ever be justified for ethnic groups whose members are nomadic. The council did not file any evidence to suggest that it had discharged its duty under EqA 2010 s149 or to support its position that any discrimination could be objectively justified.

3.181 In the event the case settled on the day before the trial of the claim and, on 2 February 2016, Collins J approved an order by which the council undertook:

a) to place the claimant on its housing register; and
b) to undertake a review of its housing allocations scheme, specifically with reference to EqA 2010 s149.

155 [2012] EWHC 373 (Admin) at paras 26 and 27.
156 Unreported.

3.182 The case of *R (TW, SW and EM) v Hillingdon LBC and EHRC (intervener)*[157] involved allocation for housing to Irish Travellers and may be of assistance to Gypsies and Travellers seeking a pitch who are refused access to a waiting list because of residence requirements.

3.183 The local authority allocated its social housing in accordance with an allocations policy dating from 2016. Under that policy, applicants for social housing were placed into Bands (A, B, C or D) according to priority for social housing which they had under the policy; with a person in Band A having a better chance of being allocated housing than a person in B, C or D.

3.184 The claimants were Irish Travellers. TW was a single parent who was placed in Band D because she had not lived in the Borough for ten years. EM was a carer for his three adult disabled children and he was informed that he did not meet the criteria to be given social housing. The claimants argued that the residence criterion indirectly discriminated against them as Irish Travellers on the ground of race. The claimants also argued that the council's decision to adopt the allocations policy failed to comply with Children Act 2004 s11 (which required it to have regard to the need to safeguard and promote the welfare of children).

3.185 Supperstone J gave the judgment in the case. With regard to the residence requirement he stated:

> Whether a residence requirement is lawful will depend on whether it can be justified. A residence requirement, especially one as long as ten years, is highly likely to have a significant and adverse impact on Irish Travellers. Irish Travellers are significantly less likely than members of other racial groups to have resided in a particular location in the UK continuously for at least ten years. However there is no evidence that the Council sought to assess the extent of the disadvantage on Irish Travellers or considered whether it was justified or what might be done to reduce it. Further, there is no evidence from the Council to show that a shorter period than ten years would undermine their stated objectives.

3.186 The Court of Appeal upheld Supperstone J's judgment on the discrimination point (while not accepting the Children Act point).[158]

Disability discrimination

3.187 Issues involving discrimination on grounds of disability will be addressed in chapter 8 which deals with the EqA 2010.[159]

157 [2018] EWHC 1791 (Admin), 13 July 2018.

158 *R (Ward and others) v Hillingdon LBC* [2019] EWCA Civ 692.

159 See para 8.94 onwards, below.

Housing benefit

Background

3.188 Housing benefit (HB) is administered and paid by the local housing authority. The statute law, regulations and case-law about housing benefit are vast and complicated. Only issues relevant to Gypsies and Travellers will be touched on here. For any further information, reference should be made to books such as those produced by the Child Poverty Action Group (CPAG) and Shelter which are updated annually.[160]

3.189 Subject to satisfying a means test, a person will be eligible to claim HB to help pay the rent if he or she is liable to make payments in respect of the dwelling which he or she occupies as his or her home.[161] The HB rules define 'dwelling' so as to include the land a caravan or mobile home, used as the home, stands on.[162] This means that Gypsies and Travellers may be eligible to claim HB both in respect of the caravan or a mobile home they live in and the site on which the caravan or mobile home stands. If the Gypsy or Traveller owns the caravan or mobile home, then they can still claim help with the site fee.

3.190 In broad terms, there are three systems for determining HB payments on Gypsy and Traveller sites:

- If a Gypsy or Traveller occupies a caravan on a site owned by the local authority, then HB is paid as rent rebate and is paid on 100 per cent of the rent charged (excluding any deductions for ineligible charges), but the amount of HB paid could be reduced by the bedroom tax and/or the benefit cap.
- If a Gypsy or Traveller occupies a caravan on a site that is privately owned, then HB is paid through the rent allowance system and the rent on which HB is claimed must in each case be referred to a rent officer at the Valuation Office Agency for a rent determination which is generally much less than 100 per cent of the rent charged. As a result, Gypsies and Travellers who live on these sites will face a shortfall in their rent which they are required to find from their own resources. They may be able to get a discretionary

160 *Welfare Benefits and Tax Credits Handbook* (Child Poverty Action Group) and *Help with Housing Costs Volume 2: Guide to Housing Benefit* (Shelter/CIH), both published annually.

161 Housing Benefit (HB Regs) 2006 SI No 213 reg 12(1)(g).

162 HB Regs 2006 reg 2(4)(b).

housing payment to help make up the difference. The amount of HB paid could also be reduced by the benefit cap.

- If a Gypsy or Traveller occupies a caravan on a site owned or administered by a housing association or county council, then HB is paid through the rent allowance system but without reference to a rent officer and HB will normally pay 100 per cent of the rent charged (excluding any deductions for ineligible charges), but the amount of HB paid could be reduced by the bedroom tax and/or the benefit cap.
- Finally, there are some Gypsy and Traveller sites that come under the definition of 'exempt accommodation' where HB is paid under the pre-January 1996 rules, when the rent restrictions rules did not involve a reference to a rent officer. The rules have been preserved[163] to meet the rents of certain non-profit making groups involved in providing specialist supported accommodation with care, support or supervision to those on Gypsy and Traveller sites at levels that reflects the higher costs of providing this type of site. 'Support' in this context has been held to mean 'the giving of advice and assistance to a claimant in coping with the practicalities of his life, and in particular his occupation of the property'.[164] HB will normally meet 100 per cent of the rent charged but the HB authority has the power to restrict the HB paid if the rent charged is unreasonably high in comparison with suitable alternative accommodation available to the claimant elsewhere, using the pre-1996 test.[165] Those living on 'exempt sites' are not subject to the benefit cap and the bedroom criteria is not part of the 1996 scheme.

3.191 From April 2008, the individual assessment by rent officers was generally replaced by local housing allowance (LHA) rates, ie flat rates set locally by the Valuation Office Agency, based upon the location and size of the dwelling. Gypsy and Traveller sites remain under the old scheme for HB but when HB is replaced by universal credit (UC), then private caravan sites will be assessed using the LHA method.

163 Housing Benefit and Council Tax Benefit (Consequential Provisions) Regulations 2006 SI No 217 Sch 3.

164 *Chorley BC v IT* [2010] AACR 2, at para 71(7).

165 *Birmingham City Council v SS and SA (Roshni intervening)* [2016] EWCA Civ 1211, [2017] AACR 8, at paras 51–54.

3.192 In *R (Knowles) v Secretary of State for Work and Pensions,*[166] it was argued that private sites should be treated in the same way as local authority sites on the basis that Gypsies and Travellers had increased accommodation costs because of their mode of living. Accordingly, the failure to treat a claim for HB made on a private site in the same way as a claim for HB made on a public site was a form of *Thlimmenos* discrimination[167] – a failure to make provision to cater for the difference.[168] The High Court, however, concluded that the evidence did not show that there was unjustifiable discrimination and noted that there was no evidence that a single Gypsy or Traveller had been made 'homeless' (in the sense of having to pitch by the roadside) because of the difference in the way HB was paid on the site in question.[169] It therefore remains possible that if a case is presented on different facts, the outcome could be different.

The benefit cap

3.193 Since 2010, the HB system has been subject to a programme of cuts and changes under the general heading of 'welfare reform'. Changes which impact on Gypsies and Travellers claiming HB include the household benefit cap and the bedroom tax. The benefit cap limits the total amount of benefit that people of working age can receive. The benefits affected include child benefit; child tax credit; income-related employment and support allowance; income support; income-based jobseeker's allowance; as well as HB and UC. If someone's total entitlement to these benefits is more than the cap, then their benefits will be reduced by the excess. Initially, the benefit cap was administered by local authorities through deductions from HB payments. In the longer term, it forms part of the UC system (see below). The benefit cap was initially introduced in 2013 at £500 per week (pw) for couples and lone parents, and at £350pw for single claimants. The level of the benefit cap was subsequently lowered in 2016 to £384.62pw and £257.69pw respectively for those living outside Greater London and £442.31pw and 296.35pw for those living in Greater London.[170] The cap will not apply for a grace period if the claimant had previously been in work for a year. A claimant will

166 [2013] EWHC 19 (Admin).

167 *Thlimmenos v Greece* (2001) 31 EHRR 411.

168 See *Burnip and others v Birmingham City Council* [2012] EWCA Civ 629, [2013] AACR 7.

169 [2013] EWHC 19 (Admin), para 97(xiv).

170 Welfare Reform and Work Act 2016 s8.

also not be affected by the benefit cap if they are in receipt of benefit because of a disability or health condition that stops them from working or they care for someone with a disability. There is an online calculator available at gov.uk which will provide an estimate of by how much a claimant's HB or UC will be reduced under the benefit cap. Claimants affected by the benefit cap can apply for a discretionary housing payment to help meet the shortfall in their HB or UC.[171]

3.194 The lawfulness of the original benefit cap was challenged in *R (SG and JS) v Secretary of State for Work and Pensions*[172] on the grounds that it amounted to indirect discrimination against women, contrary to Article 14, read with Article 1 of Protocol 1 and/or Article 8 of the ECHR, because those most likely to be affected were lone parents. On the issue of whether the difference in treatment complained of was justified, the claimants also relied on Article 3(1) of the United Nations Convention on the Rights of the Child (UNCRC). The challenge was dismissed, the Supreme Court holding by a majority of three to two that Article 3(1) of the UNCRC was not relevant and that the differential impact of the legislation was justified. The revised benefit cap has also been challenged but this time the discrimination alleged was more narrowly defined. In *R (DA and others) v Secretary of State for Work and Pensions*[173] the claimants included lone parent mothers with children under two and under five years of age who argued that they and their children should be treated differently (*Thlimmenos* discrimination) by exempting them from the cap. The claimant again argued that the court was required to assess whether, when formulating the policy, the government breached Article 3.1(1) of the UNCRC given that the victims of the alleged discrimination were lone parents of children below school age as well as those children in their own right. By a majority of 5:2 the Supreme Court concluded that the evidence showed that the government had evaluated the likely impact of the revised cap on lone parents with young children and that it had assessed their best interests as part of its overall consideration. Hence, while those households were significantly affected by the revised cap, the claimants had not been able to demonstrate that the policy was 'manifestly without reasonable foundation' – the test applicable for state benefits. The court took into account the availability of discretionary

171 Discretionary Financial Assistance Regulations 2001 SI No 1167 reg 2; *Discretionary Housing Payments Guidance Manual (March 2018) – Good Practice Guide*, Section 1 pp 25–27.

172 [2015] UKSC 16, [2015] PTSR 471.

173 [2019] UKSC 21.

housing payments (DHPs), which, it said, can be used to mitigate the hardship caused by the reduction of HB or housing costs within UC to such households on a bespoke basis.[174]

The bedroom tax

3.195 What has become known as 'the bedroom tax' (or spare room subsidy) introduced a bedroom criteria to reduce the amount of HB that can be paid to working-aged claimants by 14 per cent if they are deemed to have one spare bedroom, or by 25 per cent if they have more than one bedroom than necessary. The lawfulness of the bedroom tax was challenged on the basis that it treated persons with a disability differently to non-disabled people and this was a form of *Thlimmenos* discrimination, in breach of ECHR Article 14. The Supreme Court[175] ruled that the availability of the DHP scheme provided a reasonable foundation for the government's decision not to create a blanket exception to the rule for anyone suffering from a disability. Both the HB[176] regulations and the UC regulations[177] contain some limited exemptions under which a claimant may qualify for an additional bedroom, eg if they need an overnight carer. There is a specific exclusion for Gypsies and Travellers from the bedroom tax for 'payments in respect of the site on which a caravan or mobile home stands'.[178] In *FT v Perth and Kinross Council and Secretary of State for Work and Pensions*, the Upper Tribunal has ruled that this exemption only applies where, as a matter of fact, there is a distinct payment in respect of a site or pitch.[179] The Upper Tribunal also rejected a submission that the application of the bedroom tax to a Gypsy or Traveller claimant occupying a mobile home was a violation of the claimant's ECHR rights saying that the payment by the local authority of DHPs to cover the shortfall mitigated the adverse effect of the application of the rule.[180]

174 [2019] UKSC 21, paras 30 and 88.

175 *R (Carmichael and others) v Secretary of State for Work and Pensions, (formerly known as R (MA) v Secretary of State for Work and Pensions)* [2016] UKSC 58, [2017] AACR 9. The court did qualify this by saying the general justification provided by DHPs did not apply to cases where there was 'a transparent medical need for an additional bedroom' (para 42).

176 HB Regs 2006 SI No 213 regs 13D(3A) and B13.

177 Universal Credit Regulations (UC Regs) 2013 SI No 376 Sch 4 paras 12 and 36.

178 HB Regs 2006 SI No 213 reg A13(2)(c).

179 [2019] UKUT 43 (AAC) at para 12.

180 [2019] UKUT 43 (AAC) at para 18.

3.196 In cases where the bedroom tax does apply to a caravan or a mobile home it is important to bear in mind that there is no definition of what counts as a 'bedroom' in the HB or the UC regulations and the guidance from case-law must be followed. In *SSWP v Nelson*,[181] a three-judge panel of the Upper Tribunal held that determining whether a room is a bedroom involves a factual enquiry. The actual use to which the room has been put will not be relevant to the issue of what is a bedroom, save in exceptional circumstances, eg where a room has been converted with the consent of the landlord.[182] Even the re-designation of a room on the advice of a social worker cannot be taken into account as a relevant factor.[183] The definition of overcrowding in the Housing Act 2004[184] cannot be used to determine what a bedroom is under the HB regulations as the two statutory regimes are different (eg overcrowding law takes account of living rooms as well as bedrooms) and the meaning in one cannot be read over to the other.[185] The description given by the landlord is just the start of the factual enquiry. Where the tenant disputes whether a particular room falls to be treated as a bedroom, the HB authority or the Department for Work and Pensions (DWP) still need to consider practical considerations including size, configuration and overall dimensions, access, natural and electric lighting, ventilation and privacy.[186] For a room to function as a bedroom not only must there be space for a bed, it must also provide for clothes storage, a flat surface of some sort on which to place necessary items, as well as sufficient free space for dressing and undressing.[187]

Universal credit

3.197 Another aspect of welfare reform is the introduction of UC. When the roll-out of UC is complete, it will take the place of six current means-tested benefits and tax credits, which the UC rules describe as 'legacy benefits': child tax credit; working tax credit; income-related employment and support allowance; HB; income support; and

181 *Secretary of State for Work and Pensions v James Nelson and David Nelson and Fife Council (HB)* [2014] UKUT 525 (AAC) [2015] AACR 21.

182 *SSWP v Nelson* [2014] UKUT 0525 (AAC) at paras 27–29.

183 *Secretary of State for Work and Pensions v The City of Glasgow Council and another* [2017] Scot CS CSIH 35 at para 25.

184 *Stevenage BC v ML (HB)* [2016] UKUT 164 (AAC), at para 5.

185 *SSWP v Nelson* [2014] UKUT 0525 (AAC) at paras 53–54.

186 [2014] UKUT 0525 (AAC) at para 31.

187 [2014] UKUT 0525 (AAC) at para 33. Applied in *M v Secretary of State for Work and Pensions (UC)* [2017] UKUT 443 (AAC) at para 65.

income-based jobseeker's allowance. The roll-out of the full digital service of UC to all areas of the country was completed in December 2018. Gypsies and Travellers who are currently getting any of the six legacy benefits listed above can continue to receive those benefits. However, a change of circumstances may mean that they will be required to claim UC. The process whereby people are moved onto UC because of a change in circumstances while on legacy benefits is called 'natural migration'. However, claimants receiving the severe disability premium in a legacy benefit were prevented from moving onto UC by natural migration by the introduction of a 'gateway' on 9 January 2019 which gives them transitional protection.[188] Eventually, all existing claimants will be moved onto UC by the DWP – even if there has been no change of circumstances. This process is referred to as 'managed migration'. The government plans to start transferring around 10,000 people in 2019 as part of a pilot scheme. They plan to complete the managed migration process by December 2023. From 16 May 2019, couples where one partner is aged above pension credit age and the other is aged under pension credit age, are no longer able to make a new claim for pension credit. Instead they are required to claim UC.[189]

3.198 The rules for calculating the housing costs element within UC are complex but similar to those used in HB. The UC regulations require the claimant to be liable to make payments in respect of the accommodation he or she occupies as his or her home.[190] For Gypsies and Travellers this includes a caravan or mobile home and payments in respect of the site on which the accommodation stands.[191] The UC regulations, like HB, make provision for when a person is treated as liable to make payments[192] and when they are treated as occupying their home despite temporary absences.[193]

3.199 For Gypsies and Travellers living on private sites, the housing costs element in UC is based on the LHA.[194] For Gypsies and Travellers living on sites run by a social landlord, their UC housing

188 Universal Credit (Transitional Provisions) (SDP Gateway) Amendment Regulations 2019 SI No 10.

189 Welfare Reform Act 2012 (Commencement No 31 and Savings and Transitional Provisions and Commencement No 21 and 23 and Transitional and Transitory Provisions (Amendment)) Order 2019 SI No 376.

190 Welfare Reform Act 2012 s11(1); UC Regs 2013 SI No 376 reg 25.

191 UC Regs 2013 SI No 376 Sch 1 para 2(d).

192 UC Regs 2013 SI No 376 Sch 2.

193 UC Regs 2013 SI No 376 Sch 3.

194 UC Regs 2013 SI No 376 Sch 4 paras 20–25.

costs element will normally be 100 per cent of their actual housing costs, but this will not include service charges that are not covered by UC or charges for utilities such as water or electricity.[195] As with HB, the UC rules use a bedroom criteria[196] to determine how many bedrooms the claimant's household is deemed to need. Where Gypsies and Travellers live on a privately owned site, the rent element itself will be limited to the rooms allowed under the LHA. Where the site is owned by a social landlord, including a local authority, the UC paid for the caravan or mobile home could be subject to a reduction due to the bedroom criteria of up to 25 per cent. On both types of site, if a non-dependent – ie someone who is not a member of the family for benefit purposes[197] – is living in the claimant's household, then a deduction may need to be made unless the claimant or the non-dependent comes within one of the exemptions. Under the UC rules a flat-rate deduction is made (currently of £70.06 per month or £16.17 per week) for each non-dependent (this is called a housing cost contribution).[198] This replaces the non-dependent deductions in HB, where different rates apply according to the non-dependent's gross income.

3.200 For those living on a site that comes under the 'exempt accommodation' rules (which, since 2014, has been reclassified as a form of 'specified accommodation'[199]) housing cost cannot be met through UC and must be paid through HB instead. A Gypsy and Traveller living on an 'exempt site' can still receive UC to pay their living costs, but they are required to make a separate claim for HB to cover the cost of the rent and/or the site fee.

3.201 Aspects of the UC system that are likely to have a negative impact on Gypsies and Travellers include:

- UC is paid monthly in arrears, and it is an inherent part of the system that new claims are not put into payment for at least five weeks (an assessment period of four weeks and a further seven days before benefit is paid into the claimant's account). The lack of funds during the initial six weeks can cause or exacerbate debt problems, particularly rent arrears. The government introduced a two-week run-on for HB and a greater availability of advance

195 UC Regs 2013 SI No 376 Sch 4 paras 30–36.
196 UC Regs 2013 SI No 376 Sch 4 paras 8 and 10, the size criteria.
197 UC Regs 2013 SI No 276 Sch 4 para 9(2).
198 UC Regs 2013 SI No 376 Sch 4 para 14(1).
199 Housing Benefit and Universal Credit (Supported Accommodation) (Amendment) Regulations 2014 SI No 771.

payments (a payment on account which is recouped from future payments) to try and address these problems.

- Like other claimants, a Gypsy or Traveller claimant will be expected to make their UC claim online.[200] As part of this process, an online UC account is created for the claimant, called an online journal. The claimant is expected to use the journal to manage their claim, communicate with the DWP and check their payment statements. However, if a Gypsy or Traveller is unable to use the online claims process, even with assistance, for example, because they cannot read or write, they can apply by phone.[201] The DWP must also consider making a home visit when a claimant has been identified as being vulnerable or having complex needs due to health issues.[202]
- If a Gypsy or Traveller is accepted to be in 'gainful self-employment' under UC,[203] they will be subject to the 'minimum income floor', which sets a minimum level of assumed income from self-employment.[204] The floor is based on the appropriate national minimum wage for full-time work (ie 35 hours per week).[205] However, it does not apply during the 'start-up period' for the business, which is one year.[206]
- The child element of UC (and existing claims for tax credits) is restricted for third and subsequent children born after 6 April 2017, subject to certain exemptions. Over the next few years, more and more families and children will be affected by 'the two-child limit' – around two million children by 2020/21, and three million children by 2025. This is clearly going to have a major impact on those Gypsies and Travellers on a low income who have large families.[207] In *R (SC and CB) v Secretary of State for Work and Pensions*,[208] two single mothers with three and five children respectively, with the help of CPAG, brought a challenge against the two child-limit. They argued that the imposition of the rule was incompatible with their rights under the ECHR. The Court of Appeal dismissed the challenge, holding that the aims of the measure were legitimate

200 UC (Claims and Payments) Regs 2013 SI No 380 reg 8(1) and Sch 2.
201 UC (Claims and Payments) Regs 2013 reg 8(2).
202 See 'Home Visits' (last updated July 2017) from the House of Commons library.
203 UC Regs 2013 SI No 376 reg 64.
204 UC Regs 2013 reg 62.
205 UC Regs 2013 reg 90.
206 UC Regs 2013 regs 62(5) and 63.
207 *Unhappy Birthday! The Two-Child Limit at One Year Old*, CPAG, April 2018.
208 [2019] EWCA Civ 615.

and, given the wide area of judgment afforded to the legislature in matters of social and economic policy, the difference was justified, even when full account was taken of the best interests of the children whose interests were adversely affected by the measure. CPAG are seeking leave to appeal to the Supreme Court.

Discretionary housing payments

3.202 The DHP scheme enables local authorities to provide further financial assistance to claimants in receipt of HB or UC who require additional help with their housing costs due to a shortfall in the rent due and the amount of HB or UC they are entitled to receive.[209] Each year, the DWP allocates funds to local authorities to support the payment of DHPs. These awards are cash-limited. However, a local authority is able to supplement the DHP budget from its general funds so long as it does not exceed the overall cash limit. Legislation lays down a limit of two and a half times the DWP contribution.[210] If a local authority does not spend the entire amount allocated by the DWP, this must be returned at the end of the financial year – it cannot be carried over. The DHP funding allocated to local authorities increased dramatically between 2010 and 2017 (from £20m in 2010/11 to £166.5m in 2017/18). The *DHP Guidance Manual and DHP Good Practice Guide*[211] issued to local authorities by the DWP makes it clear that part of the purpose of DHPs is to address some of the shortfalls created by welfare reforms.[212] The DHP scheme does not confer an entitlement to DHPs. Instead, the regulations provide that the local authority has a wide discretion as to whether or not to make DHPs in a particular case and how much the DHP should be.[213] A DHP decision does not carry a right of appeal, but there is provision for an internal review.[214] If the decision to refuse a DHP is upheld on review, then the only legal remedy available to the claimant is by way of judicial review.

3.203 An example of a successful challenge to a DHP decision is *R (Hardy) v Sandwell MBC*,[215] in which the council's policy of always

209 Discretionary Financial Assistance Regulations 2001 SI No 1167 reg 2(1).

210 Discretionary Housing Payments (Grants) Order 2001 SI No 2340 art 7; DHP Guidance 1.10.

211 *Discretionary Housing Payments Guidance Manual*, published 28 August 2013, updated 21 March 2018.

212 DHP Guidance Manual para 1.2.

213 DFA Regs 2001 SI No 1167 reg 2(2).

214 DFA Regs 2001 reg 6(3).

215 [2015] EWHC 890 (Admin).

taking account of the care component of DLA when assessing DHPs was held to be unlawful as it failed to have due regard to the DHP guidance, and that this amounted to a failure by the council to exercise its discretion. Another example is *R (Halvai) v Hammersmith and Fulham LBC,*[216] in which the court held that the local authority had acted unlawfully in refusing to make a DHP to a disabled woman living in an adapted home because it failed to understand that DHPs could be a long-term solution and ignored guidance that it would be appropriate to award DHPs for an indefinite period where an individual needed further assistance with housing costs and their circumstances were unlikely to change.

3.204 During the bedroom tax litigation, the courts said the existence of the DHP scheme was key to accepting the government's justification for the discriminatory impact of the bedroom criteria on the disabled. In short, the case-law holds that DHPs should be used by local authorities to plug the discriminatory gap.[217] That being so, it is suggested that the DHP provisions and DHP guidance should be applied accordingly and the local authorities reminded of that, if necessary. Indeed, in *FT v Perth and Kinross Council and Secretary of State for Work and Pensions*, where the claimant had no choice other than to rent a three-bedroom chalet if she wanted to continue to live on the site for Gypsy Travellers, which had been her home for 30 years, the judge observed that, if the local authority were not making available a DHP to cover any shortfall created by applying the bedroom tax, it might have been in some difficulty arguing there was no violation of the claimant's ECHR rights.[218]

Fire precautions

3.205 In England, CSCDA 1960 s24(2A) states that:

> Before exercising the power to provide a site . . . the local authority shall consult the fire authority, if they are not themselves the fire authority –
> (a) as to measures to be taken for preventing and detecting the outbreak of fire on the site; and
> (b) as to the provision and maintenance of means of fighting fire on it.

In Wales, MH(W)A 2013 s11 states that:

216 [2017] EWHC 802 (Admin), (2017) 20 CCLR 517.

217 See *R (Hardy) v Sandwell MBC (Zacchaeus 2000 Trust intervening)* [2015] EWHC 890 (Admin) at 48 and 62.

218 *FT v Perth and Kinross Council and Secretary of State for Work and Pensions (HB)* [2019] UKUT 43 (AAC) at para 23.

> (1) The local authority must, in considering what conditions to impose in a site licence relating to any land, consult the fire and rescue authority as to the extent to which any model standards relating to fire precautions which have been specified . . . are appropriate to the land.
>
> (2) If–
>
> (a) no such standards have been specified, or
>
> (b) any standard that has been specified appears to the fire and rescue authority to be inappropriate to the land,
>
> the local authority must consult the fire and rescue authority as to what conditions relating to fire precautions ought to be imposed instead.

Somewhat surprisingly, local authorities in England and Wales need only consult with the fire authority and do not necessarily have to follow the advice given to them as a result of such consultation, albeit that the Welsh provisions are more extensive.

3.206 DCLG and the Welsh Government have published model standards under CSCDA 1960 s5(6)[219] making precise recommendations as to the facilities to be provided on caravan sites, for example, as to the provision of fire alarms, fire extinguishers, water supply, and the distance of caravans from each other. However, somewhat perversely, none of them apply to local authority Gypsy and Traveller caravan sites and there is no obligation on local authorities to abide by the recommendations. Nevertheless, they may and can be used as a good practice guide and are sometimes used in written statements.

3.207 The DCLG *Model Standards 2008 for Caravan Sites in England* state:

> 1. The Boundaries and Plan of the Site
>
> (i) The Boundaries of the site from any adjoining land shall be clearly marked by a man made or natural feature.
>
> (ii) No caravan or combustible structure shall be positioned within 3 metres of the boundary of the site.
>
> (a) A plan of the site shall be supplied to the Local Authority upon the application for a licence and, thereafter whenever there is a material change to the boundaries or layout of the site, or at any other time on the demand of the local authority.
>
> (b) The plan supplied must clearly illustrate the layout of the site including all relevant structures, features and facilities on it and shall be of suitable quality.

219 It should be noted that, in Wales, the power to specify model standards is now contained in MH(W)A 2013 s10.

2. Density, Spacing and Parking Between Caravans

(i) Except in the case aforementioned in sub paragraph (iii) and subject to the sub paragraph (iv), every caravan must where practicable be spaced at a distance of no less than 6 metres (the separation distance) from any other caravan which is occupied as a separate residence.

(ii) No caravan shall be stationed within 2 metres of any road or communal car park within the site or more than 50 metres from such a road within the site.

(iii) Where a caravan has retrospectively been fitted with cladding from Class 1 fire rated materials to its facing walls, then the separation distance between it and an adjacent caravan may be reduced to a minimum of 5.25 metres.

(iv) In any case mentioned in sub paragraph (i) or (iii):

(a) A porch attached to the caravan may protrude one metre into the separation distance and must not exceed the height of the caravan. Where a porch is installed only one door may be permitted at that entrance to the home, either on the porch or on the home.

(b) Eaves, drainpipes and bay windows may extend into the separation distance provided the total distance between the extremities of two facing caravans is not less than 5 metres, except where sub paragraph (iii) applies in which case the extension into the separation distance shall not exceed 4.25 metres.

(c) Any structure including steps, ramps etc (except a garage or car port) which extends more than 1 metre into the separation distance shall be of non-combustible construction. There should be a 4.5 metre clear distance between any such structure and any adjacent caravan.

(d) A garage or car port may only be permitted within the separation distance if it is of non-combustible construction.

(e) Windows in structures within the separation distances shall not face towards the caravan on either side.

(f) Fences and hedges, where allowed and forming the boundary between adjacent caravans, should be a maximum of 1 metre high.

(g) Private cars may be parked within the separation distance provided that they do not obstruct entrances to caravans or access around them and they are a minimum of 3 metres from an adjacent caravan.

(v) The density of caravans on a site shall be determined in accordance with relevant health and safety standards and fire risk assessments.

Virtually identical standards apply in Wales (but also do not apply to Gypsy and Traveller sites).[220]

220 WAG, *Model Standards 2008 for Caravan Sites in Wales.*

3.208 Strong recommendations are also contained in Welsh Government *Designing Gypsy and Traveller Sites: Guidance* (May 2015).[221] These have reference to the Regulatory Reform (Fire Safety) Order 2005[222] which applies to England and Wales. The order does not encompass individual caravans on pitches but does cover amenity blocks and the common parts of a site. A great deal of the order is similar or identical to the provisions contained in the *Model Standards 2008 for Caravan Sites in Wales.*

3.209 In *Horace Piggott v Sheffield City Council*[223] an attempt was made to sue a council for failure to provide/maintain fire-fighting equipment on its Gypsy caravan site, allegedly resulting in the destruction of the claimant's caravan and contents. HHJ Mettyear dismissed the claim finding:

1) there was no duty of care imposed by law in the circumstances of the case;
2) had there been a duty of care he would have found a breach of duty as the water pressure in the standpipes was too low for fire-fighting;
3) however, on the facts, he found that the loss would have occurred even if there had been no breach of duty – if the water pressure had been sufficient, the caravan and its contents would still have been destroyed, and so the breach of duty made no difference.

This was a case in which the council had decided to carry out major renovation works to the site and all fire-fighting equipment was removed from the site including fire-extinguishers and means of alarm, leaving only two standpipes. The judge accepted the council's contention that the purpose of measures for dealing with fire on a caravan site (for example, fire extinguishers, a telephone or alarm system) was not to protect the occupier or property of the occupier of the caravan in which the fire started but to prevent the spread of fire from one caravan to another. Accordingly, there was not the proximity sufficient to establish a duty of care, nor was it fair, just and reasonable to impose liability, although the reduction of the ability to fight fires as a result of the council's actions was foreseeable.

221 DCLG, *Designing Gypsy and Traveller Sites: Good Practice Guide* (May 2008) was withdrawn by DCLG by letter from the Chief Planning Officer on 31 August 2015.

222 SI No 1541.

223 23 January 1998, Sheffield County Court, HHJ Mettyear (unreported).

Environmental Protection Act 1990

3.210 When the conditions on a rented site fall below a certain standard, a Gypsy or Traveller occupier of a site may be able to prosecute the owner as the person responsible for a statutory nuisance under Environmental Protection Act (EPA) 1990 s82. A statutory nuisance within the meaning of EPA 1990 s79(1)(a) includes 'premises in such a state as to be prejudicial to health'. The phrase 'prejudicial to health' is further defined as 'injurious or likely to cause injury to health'.[224] The defendant in (what are commonly known as) 'section 82 proceedings' is 'the person responsible for the nuisance' defined as 'the person to whose act, default or sufferance [permission] the nuisance is attributable'.[225] The owner of the premises is the proper defendant if the person responsible cannot be found.[226] Statutory nuisance proceedings are often brought by local authorities against private owners[227] but, by EPA 1990 s82, a private individual who is 'aggrieved' (that is, affected) by the conditions can bring a prosecution. A notice specifying the problem must first be served 21 days before the proceedings can be commenced. Section 82 proceedings are dealt with by the magistrates' court. The court can convict, fine,[228] and order compensation, works and costs. Tenants or other occupiers of houses have frequently used these proceedings in respect of conditions not covered by their tenancy agreements, for example, damp caused by excessive condensation.

3.211 However, section 82 proceedings can be problematic. The burden of proof is to the criminal standard ('beyond a reasonable doubt') rather than the civil standard ('the balance of probability').[229] No public funding is available for representation although proceedings may be conducted by a lawyer paid on a conditional fee basis, that is, on the basis that the representative will only be paid if successful.[230] However, a lawyer instructed on such a basis is not entitled to charge an additional success fee in cases brought under EPA 1990. In addition, it should be remembered that the prosecutor may well be ordered to pay the defendant's costs if the case is rejected. Though public funding is available to obtain an expert's report, for example,

224 EPA 1990 s79(7).
225 EPA 1990 s82(4)(a) and s79(7) respectively.
226 EPA 1990 s82(4)(c).
227 EPA 1990 s80.
228 Up to level 5 on the standard scale.
229 *R v Newham Justices ex p Hunt* [1976] 1 WLR 420.
230 Access to Justice Act 1999 s27(1).

from an independent Environmental Health Officer, before the trial (subject to what is said below about legal aid) it will not cover the cost of the expert's attendance at court.

3.212 By way of example, a Gypsy or Traveller might use section 82 proceedings when the owner of a site has failed to deal with dampness caused by condensation in an amenity block or have failed to properly deal with rodent infestation. In the past, Gypsies and Travellers have gained advantages by using such proceedings. Thus, in *Day v Sheffield City Council*,[231] a wide ranging order was obtained, requiring a programme to deal with rat infestation, internal site lighting, hard surfacing, provision of a dustbin for each pitch and weekly refuse collection.

Site provision

3.213 In 2002 the Niner report on *The Provision and Condition of Local Authority Gypsy/Traveller Sites in England* calculated that a grand total of £123.5m was needed to bring sites up to standard over a 30-year period.[232]

3.214 The CJPOA 1994 repealed the secretary of state's power to pay grants to local authorities for the provision of sites. However, the Homes and Communities Agency in England and the Welsh Government in Wales have annual budgets for the allocation of funds for provision of new pitches and refurbishment of pitches on local authority sites.

Grants

3.215 Disabled facilities grants (DFGs) are mandatory grants administered by local authorities under the Housing Grants, Construction and Regeneration Act (HGCRA) 1996. HA 2004 s224 amended HGCRA 1996 s1 to extend DFGs to all occupiers of caravans including Gypsies and Travellers on local authority sites (who had not previously been covered).

3.216 In addition, it should be noted that social services have a general duty to assist disabled children within their area under the Children Act 1989 by 'providing a range and level of services appropriate to

231 August 1988 *Legal Action* 19.

232 *The Provision and Condition of Local Authority Gypsy/Traveller Sites in England* 2002 at p21, Table 3.

their needs'.[233] Children Act 1989 defines a disabled person as a person who is 'blind, deaf or dumb, suffers from mental disorder of any kind or is substantially and permanently handicapped by illness, injury or congenital deformity or other such disability as may be prescribed'.[234] A service may (in other words, it is for the local authority to decide) include the provision of accommodation, and assistance in kind or in cash (and may be provided for the family of the child as well).[235] It is suggested that these provisions of the Children Act 1989 could be used to improve conditions for a disabled Gypsy or Traveller child whether they live on a public or a private rented site.

Major development projects

3.217 In England, DCLG *Planning policy for Traveller sites* (PPTS)[236] states:

> Local planning authorities should work with the planning applicant and the affected traveller community to identify a site or sites suitable for relocation of the community if a major development proposal requires the permanent or temporary relocation of a traveller site. Local planning authorities are entitled to expect the applicant to identify and provide an alternative site, providing the development on the original site is authorised.[237]

3.218 In Wales, Government (WG) Circular 005/2018 *Planning for Gypsy, Traveller and Showpeople Sites* states:

> A major development or redevelopment project may require the permanent or temporary relocation of a Gypsy or Traveller site. When determining applications for such development, it may be appropriate to attach conditions or secure planning obligations requiring the developer to identify and provide an alternative site, providing the original site has a legal status. The planning authority should work with the developer and the affected Gypsy and Traveller Community to identify a site (or sites) that would be suitable for relocating this community. In proposing relocation regard will need to be paid to the social, economic and environmental needs of the Gypsy and Traveller community and the potential benefits of the relocation to the locality and the broader area. It will also be necessary to ensure that any relocation does not impact on the legal or human rights of the existing site residents.[238]

233 Children Act 1989 s1(1).

234 Children Act 1989 s17(11).

235 Children Act 1989 s17(3), (6) and (7).

236 PPTS was first issued in 2012. The latest version was issued on 31 August 2015.

237 PPTS 2015 para 21.

238 WG Circular 005/2018 paras 53–54.

3.219 The wording of an earlier English planning circular issued in 2006 (Circular 1/06)[239] had been in very similar terms with regard to major redevelopment projects as WG Circular 005/2018. Reliance was placed on the relevant paragraph of Circular 1/06 by the Gypsy and Traveller claimants in *Lisa Smith and others v The Secretary of State for Trade and Industry and the London Development Agency*.[240] The London Development Agency (LDA) was the body charged with delivering the necessary land for the London Olympics 2012. Two local authority Gypsy/Traveller sites had to be relocated because of the Olympics. In 2006 a public inquiry took place into the enormous compulsory purchase order (CPO) that the LDA sought. The two sites were included in the CPO. Following the conclusion of the Inquiry, the Planning Inspector made recommendations to the Secretary of State. With regard to the two sites, he stated:

> In my opinion, although the benefits of [the CPO] are very compelling, a small group should not be left to pay any excessive personal and social cost for those benefits to be achieved. ... Against this background, I consider that [the CPO] should not be confirmed until the Secretary of State is satisfied that suitable relocation sites will be available to meet the reasonable needs of the Gypsies and Travellers that would be displaced.[241]

Despite that recommendation the Secretary of State confirmed the CPO before alternative sites had been found for the Gypsies and Travellers. In his decision letter, the Secretary of State noted that potential relocation sites were under consideration and stated that:

> [he was] confident that the LDA are fully aware of the issues involved and . . . will make strenuous effort to deal with them so as to ensure the satisfactory relocation of the gypsies and travellers. However . . . the Secretary of State appreciates that there is a risk of failure on the relevant timescale that cannot be eliminated but having regard in particular to the clear and overwhelming importance of [the CPO] and the urgency of the timing issues . . . considers it right to confirm the Order now.[242]

One Gypsy from one site and two Irish Travellers from the other site appealed against the confirmation of the CPO.[243] They claimed that the confirmation of the Order was an unlawful interference with their rights under article 8 of the ECHR, that the Secretary of State had failed to properly take account of their right to respect for their traditional way of

239 ODPM Circular 1/06 para 57.
240 [2007] EWHC 1013 (Admin).
241 [2007] EWHC 1013 (Admin) at para 8.
242 [2007] EWHC 1013 (Admin) at para 10.
243 Appeal brought under Acquisition of Land Act 1981 s24.

life and the positive obligation on the State to facilitate that way of life,[244] and that the Secretary of State had failed to use the least intrusive means of achieving the legitimate aim.[245] Wyn Williams J dismissed the appeal, stating:

> I do not find that [the Secretary of State's] decision to confirm the order was unjustified or disproportionate. In my judgment, it was the least intrusive measure available to him. Realistically, the only way of ensuring that a substantial proportion of the Order lands (which included the sites) was under the control of the LDA by mid 2007 was to make the order. No other measure, in my judgment would have achieved that objective. Further, the need for the land to be under the control of the LDA by that date was unchallenged and, indeed, on the evidence before both the Inspector and [the Secretary of State], unchallengeable.[246]

It should be pointed out that the London Olympics was, self-evidently, an exceptional project and that it is unlikely that other development/redevelopment work will be on that scale or of that importance.

Management and design of local authority sites

3.220 Both DCLG and the Welsh Government have produced detailed sets of guidance on the management of local authority sites.[247] The Welsh Government also have detailed guidance on site design.[248] Many site managers are members of the National Association of Gypsy and Traveller Officers.[249]

3.221 However, it should be noted that the English management guidance was published before the scope of the MHA 1983 was extended to cover local authority sites and should, therefore, now be read in the context of the MHA 1983, as amended.

244 Reliance being placed in that regard on *Chapman v UK* (2001) 33 EHRR 399.

245 Reliance being placed in that regard on *R (Samaroo) v SSHD* [2001] EWCA Civ 1139; [2001] UKHRR 1150.

246 [2007] EWHC 1013 Admin at para 50. An earlier challenge to the withdrawal by the LDA of a potential relocation site which had been favoured by the Gypsies concerned was also dismissed: *R (Smith) v LDA* [2007] EWHC 636 Admin.

247 DCLG, *Gypsy and Traveller Site Management: Good Practice Guide* (July 2009); Welsh Government *Managing Gypsy and Traveller Sites in Wales: Guidance* (May 2015).

248 Welsh Government, *Designing Gypsy and Traveller Sites: Guidance* (May 2015). The English guidance on site design was withdrawn on 31 August 2015.

249 See appendix D.

Home loss payments

3.222 Land Compensation Act (LCA) 1973 s29 provides for home loss payments for 'a person . . . displaced from a dwelling on any land.'

3.223 However LCA 1973 s33 deals with 'caravan dwellers' and states:

> No home loss payment . . . shall be made to any person by virtue of this section except where no suitable alternative site for stationing a caravan is available to him on reasonable terms.

3.224 The fact that the LCA 1973 treated caravan dwellers differently was the subject of an unsuccessful judicial review.[250]

Group housing

3.225 Group housing involves the provision of bungalows for Gypsies and Travellers with space for a touring caravan so that they can continue to pursue their 'nomadic habit of life'. Group housing is extremely common in the Republic of Ireland but there are currently only two such sites in England and Wales (both in London). It appears that such an arrangement will create a secure tenancy under HA 1985 s79.[251]

Legal aid

3.226 The Legal Aid, Sentencing and Punishment of Offenders Act (LASPO) 2012 took many areas of social welfare law outside the scope of legal aid. After years of campaigning for the introduction of proper rights and obligations on local authority sites which led to the amendment of the MHA 1983, it is very disappointing that only the following matters remain in scope:

- possession actions;[252]
- matters involving risk to health or safety in a rented home (home including a 'caravan, houseboat or other vehicle');[253]
- judicial review claims, which would include a challenge to a local authority's pitch fee increase.[254]

250 *R (Mahoney and others) v SSCLG* [2015] EWHC 589 (Admin).

251 See Johnson and Watkinson, 'The legal status of group housing for Gypsies and Travellers' May 2008 *Legal Action* 40.

252 Which come under 'loss of home' – see LASPO 2012 Sch 1 Part 1 para 33.

253 LASPO 2012 Sch 1 Part 1 para 35.

254 LASPO 2012 Sch 1 Part 1 para 19. However, it should be noted that there are limitations on payments of costs in such cases – see chapter 1.

3.227 Importantly, it should be noted that legal aid is not available to Gypsies and Travellers who apply to the FT(PC)/RPT for redress when a local authority or other site owner fails properly to address disrepair issues (unless one can obtain exceptional funding under LASPO 2012 s10).[255]

3.228 Legal aid is not available for advice in relation to housing benefit. However, legal aid is available for an appeal on a point of law from a decision of the Upper Tribunal or higher court on matters relating to the provision of housing benefit and it is still available to cover the cost of seeking judicial review of decisions made by local authorities on housing benefit.

3.229 It follows that Gypsies and Travellers who live on local authority sites in England and Wales may find it difficult or impossible to enforce the important new rights that they have been granted in recent years simply because they will not be able to obtain public funding to seek legal advice. For example, there is anecdotal evidence that many local authorities have introduced unlawful written statements without proper consultation procedures and/or by imposing new express terms on occupiers. Without the availability of legal advice it is very difficult for such unlawful practices and actions to be challenged.

Conclusion

3.230 The long-awaited extension of the scope of the MHA 1983 to local authority Gypsy and Traveller sites in England and Wales has revolutionised the situation for the residents of such sites Having finally been given security of tenure, it is hoped that residents now have the confidence to raise other issues, such as an owner's poor site management or failure to comply with obligations, safe in the knowledge that they cannot be evicted from the site for no good reason. It is also hoped that residents' associations will now become more common.

3.231 That said, residents may well find it difficult or impossible to enforce many of their new rights without legal aid to cover the provision of advice and representation.

3.232 On local authority sites the lack of any proper statutory framework for allocations procedures remains problematic. However, perhaps the more important point to make is that there remains a significant shortfall in public site provision which will need to be addressed urgently if those Gypsies and Travellers who cannot afford to buy and develop their own sites are to enjoy the benefits of living in a safe and secure home.

255 See chapter 5 para 5.248, below.

CHAPTER 4

Planning law

continued

Introduction

4.1 In 1960, parliament passed the Caravan Sites and Control of Development Act (CSCDA) 1960. It was designed to regulate and control private caravan sites and provided that no occupier of land could use it as a caravan site without a site licence and that a site licence could not be obtained unless planning permission had been granted for the use of the land for such a purpose. CSCDA 1960 s23 gave local authorities the power to close common land to Gypsies and other Travellers and it was used enthusiastically by local authorities. CSCDA 1960 s24 also gave local authorities the power to provide caravan sites to compensate for the closure of the commons. However, local authorities failed to make use of this power and in the absence of lawful stopping places and sites it became increasingly difficult for the Gypsy and Traveller population to carry on their nomadic way of life.

4.2 In 1968, having recognised the problems caused by the CSCDA 1960, parliament passed the Caravans Sites Act (CSA) 1968. The Act imposed a duty on county councils and unitary authorities to provide public-sector sites for 'gipsies'. Thus, CSA 1968 s6 required local authorities 'so far as may be necessary to provide adequate accommodation for gipsies residing in or resorting to their area' and CSA 1968 s16 defined 'gipsies' as 'persons of a nomadic habit of life, whatever their race or origin'.

4.3 From 1970 to 1994, a significant number of sites for Gypsies and Travellers was established in accordance with that duty. However, the duty was widely flouted and many authorities failed to comply with their obligation to make adequate provision.[1]

> For centuries the commons of England provided lawful stopping places for people whose way of life was or had become nomadic. Enough common land had survived the centuries of enclosure to make this way of life still sustainable, but by s.23 of the Caravan Sites and Control of Development Act 1960 local authorities were given powers to close the commons to Travellers. This they proceeded to do with great energy, but made no use of the concomitant power given to them by s.24 of the same Act to open caravan sites to compensate for the closure of the commons. By the Caravan Sites Act 1968, therefore, Parliament legislated to make the s.24 power a duty . . . For the next quarter of a century there followed a history of non-compliance with the duties imposed by the Act of 1968,

1 See, for example, *R v Hereford & Worcester CC ex p Smith* [1988] COD 3.

> marked by a series of decisions of this Court holding local authorities to be in breach of their statutory duty, to apparently little practical effect . . .[2]

4.4 The Criminal Justice and Public Order Act (CJPOA) 1994 repealed CSA 1968 s6, and, at that time, the government rightly forecasted that the repeal of the statutory duty to provide sites was 'expected to lead to more applications for private gypsy sites'. It had already published planning advice on the provision of sites for Gypsies and Travellers in the form of Department of Environment (DoE) Circular 1/94 *Gypsy sites and planning*, which advised local planning authorities (LPAs) that they should assess the needs of Gypsies and Travellers within their areas and then produce a plan which identified locations suitable for sites; and that they should only rely on criteria-based policies where it was impossible to identify suitable sites within their areas.[3]

4.5 Since then, planning law has played an increasingly important role in the provision of sites where Gypsies and Travellers can place their caravans and live in them. However, statistics show that, while in general LPAs allow most planning applications for settled members of the public, they refuse most applications by Gypsies and Travellers, forcing a disadvantaged section of the population to go to the trouble and expense of appealing those refusals. As Lord Bingham said in *South Buckinghamshire DC v Porter*:[4]

> In the case of Gypsies, the problem was compounded by features peculiar to them. Their characteristic lifestyle debarred them from access to conventional sources of housing provision. Their attempts to obtain planning permission almost always met with failure: statistics quoted by the European Court of Human Rights in *Chapman v United Kingdom*[5] . . . showed that . . . 90 per cent of applications made by Gypsies had been refused whereas 80 per cent of all applications had been granted. But for many years the capacity of sites authorised for occupation by Gypsies has fallen well short of that needed to accommodate those seeking space on which to station their caravans.[6]

4.6 The advice in Circular 1/94 that LPAs assess need and cater for that need by identifying land on which Gypsy sites could be established,

2 *R v Lincolnshire CC, ex p Atkinson* (1996) 8 Admin LR 529.

3 Department of the Environment Circular 1/94, Welsh Office 2/94 (hereafter Circular 1/94), para 4.

4 *South Buckinghamshire DC v Porter (No 1)* [2003] UKHL 26, [2003] 2 AC 558.

5 *Chapman v UK* (2001) 33 EHRR 399, (2001) 10 BHRC 48, ECtHR (GC), para 66.

6 [2003] 2 AC 558 at 569–570, para 13.

was largely ignored. The vast majority of LPAs failed to assess the needs of Gypsies and Travellers within their areas, simply adopting instead criteria-based policies without providing any reason as to why it was impossible to adopt location-based policies.

4.7 In 2006, having recognised that the advice in Circular 1/94 had not been followed by LPAs, the Labour government issued new planning advice on the provision of sites for Gypsies and Travellers in England in the form of Office of the Deputy Prime Minister (ODPM) Circular 1/06 *Planning for Gypsy and Traveller caravan sites.*

4.8 In March 2012, the Coalition government replaced Circular 1/06 with *Planning policy for traveller sites* (PPTS 2012). Then, on 31 August 2015, the Conservative government published a revised version of this document (PPTS 2015).

4.9 Meanwhile, in Wales, in 2007 the Welsh Assembly Government (WAG) issued WAG Circular 30/2007, *Planning for Gypsy and Traveller caravan sites,* which included similar advice to that in Circular 1/06. Then, in June 2018 WAG Circular 30/2007 was replaced by Circular 005/2018 *Planning for Gypsy, Traveller and Showpeople Sites* (PGTSS 2018).[7]

4.10 The new advice is detailed below and this chapter aims to ensure that Gypsies and Travellers and those who represent them are aware of key points of current planning law and policy.[8]

Structure of the planning system

Legislation

4.11 Since 1947, the development of land in England and Wales has been subject to controls imposed by the Town and Country Planning Acts (TCPAs). The present law is mainly contained in the TCPA 1990 (which has been greatly amended by subsequent legislation – including the Planning and Compulsory Purchase Act (PCPA) 2004. Some sections of the TCPA 1990 make different provision for planning in England and Wales. Similar regimes exist in Scotland and Northern Ireland and a broadly similar regime exists in the Republic of Ireland.

7 Circular 005/2018 can be found at appendix B. It will be noted that unlike the UK government, the Welsh government shows Gypsies and Travellers the courtesy of using capital letters for 'Gypsy' and 'Traveller'.

8 On the same date, the Conservative government cancelled the helpful 'Designing Gypsy and Traveller Sites – Good Practice Guide'.

4.12 TCPA 1990 is divided into 14 parts, of which the most important for Gypsies and Travellers are:

- Part III – control over development, which includes the need for planning permission, consideration of applications for planning permission and appeals against refusal of planning permission;
- Part VII – enforcement, which provides for various means of enforcing against breaches of planning control; and
- Part XII – validity, which provides for High Court challenges to various decisions related to planning, including the decisions of planning inspectors on development management and enforcement appeals.

4.13 PCPA 2004 Part 3, which deals with development, is also of particular importance. There are also many statutory instruments. The more important are considered in this chapter. They deal with both substantive and procedural matters.

National planning policy

4.14 English national planning policy is contained in the National Planning Policy Framework (NPPF);[9] PPTS 2015;[10] the online National Planning Practice Guidance (NPPG);[11] and written ministerial statements (WMSs).[12] Welsh national planning policy is contained in Planning Policy Wales (edn 8, January 2016); Technical Advice Notes; and circulars, including Circular 005/2018 *Planning for Gypsy, Traveller and Showpeople Sites* (PGTSS 2018).[13]

Local planning policy

4.15 Local planning policy is contained in what is known as the development plan, which, despite its name, usually consists in England, of more than one document. London is the only part of England where there is still a regional policy which is contained in the London Plan, published in March 2015.

9 First issued in 2012 and revised and reissued in 2018.

10 Issued in August 2015.

11 See: http://planningguidance.communities.gov.uk.

12 Very occasionally a site will involve consideration of waste policy contained in National Planning Policy for Waste (October 2014).

13 Issued in June 2018.

4.16 In general the main bodies responsible for planning are unitary authorities and district councils,[14] which are responsible for producing local plans. However, National Park authorities are responsible for producing local plans for National Parks. English county councils have responsibility for minerals and waste plans, which will seldom affect Gypsies and Travellers. In England parish councils[15] and, where these do not exist, neighbourhood forums, can produce neighbourhood development plans (NDPs). All these documents form parts of the development plan.

4.17 In Wales, the unitary authority produce the development plans, except in National Parks, where the responsible body is the National Park authority.

4.18 LPAs are required to produce: a local development scheme (LDS) giving details of the development plan documents (DPDs) and other documents that it will be preparing. The secretary of state can 'direct' the LPA to make amendments. Such a direction was made against South Gloucestershire Council in respect of its failure to deal adequately with Gypsies and Travellers within its LDS. DPDs form part of the development plan.

4.19 PCPA 2004 s38(6) read with TCPA 1990 s70(2) provides that planning applications should be determined in accordance with the development plan, unless material considerations indicate otherwise. Given the importance of development plans for the determination of planning applications, it is not surprising that major economic concerns, such as housebuilders and the minerals industry, keep an eye on their preparation in order to ensure that their interests are fully borne in mind. A major cause of inequality between the planning system's provision of accommodation for house-dwellers and its provision of accommodation for Gypsies and Travellers is that, while powerful and well-financed bodies ensure that the interests of housebuilders are recognised, Gypsies' and Travellers' organisations do not have the resources to monitor all emerging development plans and to challenge the absence of adequate policies to meet the accommodation needs of Gypsies and Travellers.[16] As a result, while the amendment of Green Belt boundaries to meet the need for future

14 Sometimes called borough councils.

15 Sometimes called town councils.

16 The only case in which a Gypsy or Traveller has successfully challenged a development plan is *Butler v Bath and North East Somerset DC* [2003] EWCA Civ 1614; [2004] JPL 941. There have been many successful challenges by housebuilders and other developers.

housing has taken place on many occasions, they have never been changed to meet the future needs of Gypsies and Travellers.

4.20 Gypsies and Travellers and those advising them should consider objecting to the absence of appropriate policies in revised DPDs before they are adopted. These objections may include, for example: that the DPD makes inadequate provision for Gypsies and Travellers; that some land adjoining existing sites should be allocated for expansion; that transit sites close to trunk roads should be provided for use by Gypsies and Travellers; and that existing sites located in the Green Belt (together with some adjoining land to allow for expansion), should no longer be designated as such.

4.21 Localism Act 2011 Part 6 Chapter 3 introduced a new element into English development plans, namely, the NDP. Parish councils have a right (but not a duty) to produce these. In areas where there is no parish, a neighbourhood forum can be established to produce one. The body promoting an NDP is known as the qualifying body. NDPs do not have to cover all areas of policy. They are likely to be of particular interest to Gypsies and Travellers and those who represent them where either they contain specific Gypsy and Traveller policies or they contain policies that would impede the development of needed Gypsy and Traveller sites.

4.22 A NDP must satisfy five basic conditions:[17]

1) having regard to national policies and advice contained in guidance issued by the secretary of state, it is appropriate to make it;
2) the making of the NDP contributes to the achievement of sustainable development;
3) the making of the NDP is in general conformity with the strategic policies contained in the development plan for the area of the authority (or any part of that area);
4) the making of the NDP does not breach, and is otherwise compatible with, EU obligations;
5) the making of the NDP is not likely to have a significant effect on a European site or a European offshore marine site. A NDP must also be compatible with the rights of the European Convention on Human Rights (ECHR) contained in the Human Rights Act (HRA) 1968.

17 The first four are under TCPA 1990 Sch 4B para 8 (as modified by PCPA 2004 s38C). The fifth is prescribed by the Neighbourhood Planning (General) Regulations 2012 Sch 2.

4.23 In practice, those considering a specific Gypsy and Traveller NDP policy or a policy that would impede the development of needed sites are likely to concentrate on the first three basic conditions and on human rights. It may also be appropriate to consider under the fourth basic condition whether a NDP is compatible with the EU Race Equality Directive.[18] With regard to the third basic condition, a policy that deals with meeting a district's need for Gypsy and Traveller sites will be a strategic policy. Hence, a NDP must be in general conformity with the adopted development plan.[19]

Planning authorities

4.24 Most planning decisions are taken by the LPA for the area concerned. In most English Gypsy and Traveller cases the relevant LPA will be the district council, metropolitan borough, London borough or national park authority.[20] In Wales the LPA will be the county council, county borough council or national park authority.

Development

4.25 The meaning of 'development' is central to the system of development management and the term is defined in TCPA 1990 s55(1) as follows:

> . . . 'development', means the carrying out of building, engineering, mining or other operations in, on, over or under land, or the making of any material change in the use of any buildings or other land.

4.26 This definition is divided into two limbs:

- 'the carrying out of building, engineering, mining or other operations', known as 'operational development'; and
- the making of a material change of use.

4.27 Various operations and uses are deemed not to be development, including the use of land for the purposes of agriculture or forestry.[21] The stationing of a residential caravan on land for the purposes of

18 Directive 2000/43 on implementing the principle of equal treatment between persons irrespective of racial or ethnic origin, [2000] OJ L180/22.

19 *BDW Trading (t/a Barratt Homes) v Cheshire West and Chester BC* [2014] EWHC 1470, para 82.

20 See TCPA 1990 ss1–9 and PCPA 2004 s37.

21 TCPA 1990 s55(2).

agriculture, for example, for fruit or hop picking or to attend ewes during lambing, does not therefore constitute development.

Planning permission

4.28 Planning permission is required for the development of land, unless the operation or use is lawful.[22] TCPA 1990 s191(2) provides that:

> . . . uses and operations are lawful at any time if–
> (a) no enforcement action may then be taken in respect of them (whether because they did not involve development or require planning permission or because the time for enforcement action has expired or for any other reason); and
> (b) they do not constitute a contravention of any of the requirements of any enforcement notice then in force.

A person wishing to find out whether an existing use or operation is lawful may apply to the LPA for a certificate of lawfulness under TCPA 1990 s191 (or TCPA 1990 s192 in the case of a proposed use or operation).[23] This procedure is used both where there the limitation period for taking action for a breach of planning control has expired and where there is a dispute as to the meaning of a planning permission.[24]

Permitted development

4.29 Some matters (mainly of a minor nature) are granted planning permission by statutory instruments, known as development orders, the most important of which is the Town and Country Planning (General Permitted Development) (England) Order (GPDO) 2015. These include:

- certain minor operations, such as the erection of gates, walls and fences below specified heights;[25] and

22 TCPA 1990 s57. The Housing and Planning Act 2016 s150 introduces a new concept called 'permission in principle'. It seems that this is unlikely to affect Gypsies and Travellers, being, at least initially, mainly directed at the building on brownfield land of houses (sometimes with associated retail, community and commercial uses).

23 See para 4.38, below.

24 For an example of this procedure being used in the case of an old caravan site permission, see *Cotswold Grange Country Park v Secretary of State for Communities and Local Government* [2014] EWHC 1138 (Admin), [2014] JPL 981.

25 GPDO 2015, Sch 2, Part 2, Class A. Thus, Gypsies and Travellers will be permitted to erect gates, fences, walls or other means of enclosure up to one metre in height where they adjoin a highway used by vehicular traffic and up to two metres high elsewhere on the boundary of their land.

- certain temporary buildings and uses, such as moveable structures required in connection with building or engineering operations.[26]

4.30 In addition, and importantly, there are permitted development rights which enable land to be used for short periods of time by people camping in caravans. [27] Article 3 of the GPDO 2015 states:

> (1) Subject to the provisions of this Order and regulations 75 to 78 of the Conservation of Habitats and Species Regulations 2017 (general development orders), planning permission is hereby granted for the classes of development described as permitted development in Schedule 2.

4.31 GPDO 2015 Sch 2 Part 5 is entitled 'Caravan sites and recreational campsites'. Class A of this Part ('Use of land as caravan site') reads as follows:

> **Permitted development**
>
> A. The use of land, other than a building, as a caravan site in the circumstances referred to in paragraph A.2.
>
> *Condition*
>
> A.1 Development is permitted by Class A subject to the condition that the use is discontinued when the circumstances specified in paragraph A.2 cease to exist, and all caravans on the site are removed as soon as reasonably practicable.
>
> Interpretation of Class A
>
> A.2 The circumstances mentioned in Class A are those specified in paragraphs 2 to 10 of Schedule 1 to the 1960 Act (cases where a caravan site licence is not required), but in relation to those mentioned in paragraph 10 do not include use for winter quarters.

4.32 CSCDA 1960 Sch 1 paras 2, 3, and 10 are key. They read as follows:

> **Use by a person travelling with a caravan for one or two nights**
>
> 2 Subject to the provisions of paragraph 13 of this Schedule, a site licence shall not be required for the use of land as a caravan site by a person travelling with a caravan who brings the caravan on to the land for a period which includes not more than two nights—
>
> (a) if during that period no other caravan is stationed for the purposes of human habitation on that land or any adjoining land in the same occupation, and

26 GPDO 2015 Sch 2 Part 4 Class A.

27 See also para 5.242.

(b) if, in the period of twelve months ending with the day on which the caravan is brought on to the land, the number of days on which a caravan was stationed anywhere on that land or the said adjoining land for the purposes of human habitation did not exceed twenty-eight.

Use of holdings of five acres or more in certain circumstances

3 (1) Subject to the provisions of paragraph 13 of this Schedule, a site licence shall not be required for the use as a caravan site of land which comprises, together with any adjoining land which is in the same occupation and has not been built on, not less than five acres—

(a) if in the period of twelve months ending with the day on which the land is used as a caravan site the number of days on which a caravan was stationed anywhere on that land or on the said adjoining land for the purposes of human habitation did not exceed twenty-eight, and

(b) if in the said period of twelve months not more than three caravans were so stationed at any one time.

(2) The Minister may by order contained in a statutory instrument provide that in any such area as may be specified in the order this paragraph shall have effect subject to the modification–

(a) that for the reference in the foregoing sub-paragraph to five acres there shall be substituted a reference to such smaller acreage as may be specified in the order, or

(b) that for the condition specified in head (a) of that sub-paragraph there shall be substituted a condition that the use in question falls between such dates in any year as may be specified in the order, or subject to modification in both such respects.

(3) The Minister may make different orders under this paragraph as respects different areas, and an order under this paragraph may be varied by a subsequent order made thereunder.

(4) An order under this paragraph shall come into force on such date as may be specified in the order, being a date not less than three months after the order is made; and the Minister shall publish notice of the order in a local newspaper circulating in the locality affected by the order and in such other ways as appear to him to be expedient for the purpose of drawing the attention of the public to the order.

. . .

Travelling showmen

10 (1) Subject to the provisions of paragraph 13 of this Schedule, a site licence shall not be required for the use of land as a caravan site by a travelling showman who is a member of an organisation of travelling showmen which holds for the time being a certificate granted under this paragraph and who is, at the time, travelling for the purposes of his business or who has taken up winter quarters on the land with his

equipment for some period falling between the beginning of October in any year and the end of March in the following year.

(2) For the purposes of this paragraph the Minister may grant a certificate to any organisation recognised by him as confining its membership to bona fide travelling showmen; and a certificate so granted may be withdrawn by the Minister at any time.[28]

4.33 Clearly, the permitted development rights contained within the GDPO 2015 are subject to qualification and limitation. Thus:

- Paragraph 2 only permits encampments which consist of 1 caravan and then only for a period of 2 nights at a time, with a maximum use of the local authority land for 28 days per year.
- Paragraph 3 permits encampments of up to three caravans on local authority land which exceeds five acres in size, providing the land is not used for such encampments for more than 28 days per year.
- Paragraph 10 applies only to a Travelling Showperson who is a member of a certificated organisation of Travelling Showpeople and who is travelling for the purposes of his or her business. Moreover, the use of land for winter quarters is expressly excluded.

4.34 Nevertheless, the remains that the GPDO 2015 provides those Romani Gypsies and Irish Travellers camping on land for short periods of time, or Travelling Showpeople travelling for the purposes of their business, with certain permitted development rights: and their encampments will not breach planning control unless they exceed the scope or ambit of those rights.

4.35 All the permitted development rights are subject to conditions, which are contained in the GPDO and which must be checked before relying on them. They may be withdrawn by a direction under GPDO 2015 article 4(1) made in respect of a specified area or removed by a planning condition. However, this will not affect the legality of development that has already been carried out under the GPDO.[29]

4.36 In Wales, similar permitted development rights arise under GPDO 2015's predecessor, the Town and Country Planning (General Permitted Development) Order 1995. This has been subject to various amendments that only apply in Wales.

28 Paragraph 3 is 'Subject to the provisions of paragraph 13' of CSCDA 1960 Sch 1 which provides that the Minister may on the application of a local authority issue an order withdrawing the permitted development rights in respect of land specified within the order.

29 *R v Epping Forest DC ex p Strandmill Ltd* [1990] JPL 415.

Immunity from enforcement

4.37 TCPA 1990 s171B establishes two different limitation periods for enforcement action that can be taken by an LPA in circumstances where a breach of planning control has occurred:

> (1) Where there has been a breach of planning control consisting in the carrying out without planning permission of building, engineering, mining or other operations in, on, over or under land, no enforcement action may be taken after the end of the period of four years beginning with the date on which the operations were substantially completed.
> (2) Where there has been a breach of planning control consisting in the change of use of any building to use as a single dwelling house, no enforcement action may be taken after the end of the period of four years beginning with the date of the breach . . .
> (3) In the case of any other breach of planning control, no enforcement action may be taken after the end of ten years beginning with the date of the breach . . .

4.38 In general, a failure to take enforcement action within the appropriate period will result in the use or operation becoming lawful.[30] Those Gypsies and Travellers who can prove that they have used land for residential purposes in breach of planning control for more than ten years, without enforcement action having been taken against them, may make an application under TCPA 1990 s191 for a certificate of lawfulness. However, a magistrates' court may extend the periods concerned where an 'apparent breach, or any of the matters constituting the apparent breach, has (to any extent) been deliberately concealed' and 'the court considers it just to make the order having regard to all the circumstances'.[31]

Applications for planning permission and the power to decline

4.39 In most cases it will be necessary to apply to the LPA for planning permission for the proposed development.[32] A fee must be paid to cover the cost of such an application.[33]

30 TCPA 1990 s191(2).

31 TCPA 1990 s171BC – see also s171BA and s171BB.

32 TCPA 1990 s62.

33 Town and Country Planning (Fees for Applications, Deemed Applications, Requests and Site Visits) (England) Regulations 2012; and Town and Country Planning (Fees for Applications, Deemed Applications and Site Visits) (Wales) Regulations 2015.

4.40 In general, there is no limit to the number of times that an application for planning permission can be made. However, TCPA 1990 ss70A, 70B and 70C provide exceptions to this rule.[34]

4.41 TCPA 1990 s70A provides a LPA with the power to decline to determine an application where, within the last two years, either the secretary of state has dismissed an appeal or refused a similar application or the LPA has itself refused a similar application; and the LPA thinks that there 'there has been no significant change since the refusal or . . . dismissal'.[35] The power is discretionary.

4.42 TCPA 1990 s70B gives English LPAs the power to decline to determine an application for planning permission which is similar to an application that is already under consideration.

4.43 TCPA 1990 s70C gives English LPAs the power to decline to determine certain applications in respect of land which is subject to a pre-existing enforcement notice. It states:

> (1) A local planning authority in England may decline to determine an application for planning permission for the development of any land if granting planning permission for the development would involve granting, whether in relation to the whole or any part of the land to which a pre-existing enforcement notice relates, planning permission in respect of the whole or any part of the matters specified in the enforcement notice as constituting a breach of planning control.
>
> (2) For the purposes of the operation of this section in relation to any particular application for planning permission, a 'pre-existing enforcement notice' is an enforcement notice issued before the application was received by the local planning authority.

4.44 For the LPA to be able to exercise the power to decline to determine the application, the following must apply:

- an enforcement notice was issued before the application for planning permission was received by the LPA;
- the enforcement notice related to at least part of the land subject to the application; and
- the application seeks planning permission for a matter or matters specified in the enforcement notice as constituting a breach of planning control.

4.45 TCPA 1990 s70C is a power, not a duty, so that a LPA may determine such an application and, if it declines to do, it will be vulnerable to

34 See appendix A.

35 PCPA 2004 s43 extended this power to decline to determine applications.

judicial review on normal public-law principles (eg failing to bear in mind material factors).[36]

4.46 If the LPA does not give notice that it has exercised its TCPA 1990 s70C power within the period laid down by the Town and Country Planning (Development Management Procedure) (England) Order (DMPO) 2015 for making a decision then an applicant can appeal the LPA's non-determination under TCPA 1990 s78(2).

4.47 There is no right of appeal against an LPA's refusal to determine an application under TCPA 1990 ss70A, 70B or 70C; but the exercise of the power is susceptible to judicial review. In *R (Jeeves and Baker) v Gravesham BC*[37] the court considered a judicial review brought by Gypsies against a TCPA 1990 s70A decision. Collins J had regard to government guidance and quashed the LPA's decision. When doing so he said that the power to decline to determine a second application should only be used in narrow circumstances such as where the applicant is abusing the right to apply for planning permission by attempting to exert pressure on the authority.

4.48 Applicants who wish to make a further planning application after the refusal of planning permission by the LPA or the dismissal of an appeal against such a refusal, should consider whether they can wait until the expiry of the two-year period or whether the application can be changed significantly in a genuine attempt to meet the objections to the original proposal.

Development and the stationing of caravans on land

4.49 A common mistake in Gypsy and Traveller planning cases is to treat the placing of a caravan on land as an operational development. Although it may involve associated operational development, such as the construction of roadways, hardstanding and amenity blocks, the placing of the caravan on land is in itself, not operational development, However, the stationing of a caravan on land for residential purposes, where the planning unit has previously had a wholly non-

36 In *O'Brien v South Cambridgeshire DC and Secretary of State for Communities and Local Government* [2016] EWHC 36 (Admin) an Irish Traveller challenged a local planning authority's decision to decline to determine her planning application under TCPA 1990 s70C. In a particularly detailed judgment, Lewis J considered the underlying statutory purpose of the power, and the question of proportionate enforcement action under Article 8 of the ECHR, within the context of alleged, delayed and abusive reliance by a planning authority upon an extant enforcement notice issued in 2005.

37 [2006] EWHC 1249 (Admin), [2006] JPL 1743.

residential use (for example, on a field in agricultural use), will constitute a material change of use and thus development.[38] Usually, this will require express planning permission.[39] If the previous use of the land was for another type of caravan site, such as a site for Travelling Showpeople or a touring caravan site, it will be a question of fact and degree whether the change of its use to a site for Gypsies and Travellers is sufficient to be material.

The meaning of 'caravan'

4.50 The definition of the term 'caravan' used in TCPA 1990 is contained in CSCDA 1960 s29(1):[40]

> 'caravan' means any structure designed or adapted for human habitation which is capable of being moved from one place to another (whether by being towed, or by being transported on a motor vehicle or trailer) and any motor vehicle so designed or adapted, but does not include–
> (a) any railway rolling stock which is for the time being on rails forming part of a railway system, or
> (b) any tent.

4.51 The word 'caravan' also covers certain structures composed of not more than two sections, which are capable, when disassembled, of being moved by road. Thus, Caravan Sites Act (CSA) 1968 s13[41] states that a 'caravan' is:

> A structure designed or adapted for human habitation which–
> (a) is composed of not more than two sections separately constructed and designed to be assembled on a site by means of bolts, clamps or other devices; and
> (b) is, when assembled, physically capable of being moved by road from one place to another (whether by being towed, or by being transported on a motor vehicle or trailer), shall not be treated as not being (or as not having been) a caravan within the meaning of Part I of the Caravan Sites and Control of Development Act 1960 by reason only that it cannot lawfully be so moved on a highway when assembled.
> For the purposes of Part I of the Caravan Sites and Control of Development Act 1960, the expression 'caravan' shall not include a structure designed

38 *Restormel BC v Secretary of State for the Environment* [1982] JPL 785.

39 For circumstances where express provision is not required for the stationing of a caravan see paras 4.30–4.36, above.

40 *Wyre Forest DC v Secretary of State for the Environment* [1990] 2 AC 357. CSCDA 1960 s29(1) also defines 'caravan site'.

41 As amended in England by the Caravan Sites Act 1968 and Social Landlords (Permissible Additional Purposes) (England) Order 2006 (Definition of Caravan) (Amendment) (England) Order 2006.

or adapted for human habitation which falls within paragraphs (a) and (b) of the foregoing subsection if its dimensions when assembled exceed any of the following limits, namely–

(a) length (exclusive of any drawbar): 65.616 feet (20 metres);
(b) width: 22.309 feet (6.8 metres);
(c) overall height of living accommodation (measured internally from the floor at the lowest level to the ceiling at the highest level): 10.006 feet (3.05 metres).

4.52 Thus, whilst it may be thought that in normal English the terms 'caravan' and 'mobile home' convey different meanings, they are synonymous in planning, caravan sites and mobile homes legislation and cover almost everything that would be called a caravan, caravanette, camper-van, trailer-home, mobile home or park home.

Material considerations in Gypsy and Traveller site planning applications

Overview

4.53 PCPA 2004 s38(6) provides:

> If regard is to be had to the development plan for the purpose of any determination to be made under the planning Acts the determination must be made in accordance with the plan unless material considerations indicate otherwise.

Read with TCPA 1990 s 70(2) that provision stipulates that planning applications should be determined in accordance with the development plan unless material considerations indicate otherwise. Thus, decision-makers should at some stage in their decision-making process decide whether the development would accord with the development plan.[42] The following paragraphs consider the key 'material considerations' that affect applications for planning permission for Gypsy and Traveller caravan sites.

Relevant government policy and advice

4.54 At the outset it should be noted that the Supreme Court has held that the proper interpretation of planning policy is a matter of law, and

42 *R (Hampton Bishop PC) v Herefordshire Council* [2014] EWCA Civ 878, [2015] 1 WLR 2367 per Richards LJ, para 28.

a failure by a decision-maker to understand and apply relevant policy will amount to an error of law.[43]

4.55 Planning applications for Gypsy and Traveller sites may engage a wide variety of policy covered in England by the NPPF, PPTS 2015, NPPG and WMSs; and in Wales by Planning Policy Wales (edn 8, January 2016), Technical Advice Notes and circulars, including, most importantly, PPGTS 2018.

The National Planning Policy Framework

4.56 In March 2012 the government issued the NPPF. It was revised and re-issued in July 2018 and then again in February 2019. The NPPF must be taken into account in the preparation of local and neighbourhood plans, and is a material consideration in planning decisions. It should be read in conjunction with PPTS 2015.

4.57 The NPPF explains that the purpose of the planning system is to contribute to the achievement of sustainable development and that there are three dimensions to sustainable development: economic, social and environmental.[44] The social objective, which can wrongly be forgotten in Gypsy and Traveller cases, involves providing support to 'strong, vibrant and healthy communities, by ensuring that a sufficient number and range of homes can be provided to meet the needs of present and future generations'.

4.58 Issues of sustainability are important and should not only be considered in terms of transport mode and distances from services. In the context of Gypsy and Traveller cases such considerations should include:

a) the promotion of peaceful and integrated co-existence between the site and the local community;
b) the wider benefits of easier access to GP and other health services;
c) children attending school on a regular basis;
d) the provision of a settled base that reduces the need for long-distance travelling and possible environmental damage caused by unauthorised encampment; and
e) not locating sites in areas at high risk of flooding, including functional floodplains, given the particular vulnerability of caravans –

43 *Tesco Stores Limited v Dundee City Council* [2012] UKSC 13, [2012] JPL 1078.

44 See paras 7–9 of the NPPF.

though, in fact, most Gypsies and Travellers are highly skilled at moving caravans very quickly when there is a risk of flooding.[45]

4.59 Paragraph 10 of the NPPF states that there is 'a presumption in favour of sustainable development' 'at the heart' of the Framework is a presumption in favour of sustainable development. Importantly, para 11 continues:

> For decision-taking this means . . .
> d) where there are no relevant development plan policies, or the policies which are most important for determining the application are out-of-date, granting permission unless:
> i. the application of policies in this Framework that protect areas or assets of particular importance provides a clear reason for refusing the development proposed; or
> ii. any adverse impacts of doing so would significantly and demonstrably outweigh the benefits, when assessed against the policies in this Framework taken as a whole;[46]

4.60 Among other things this means that where specific policies restricting development do not apply and where there are no relevant development plan policies or those which do exist are out-of-date, then planning permission should be granted unless 'any adverse impacts of doing so would significantly and demonstrably outweigh the benefits'. In such circumstances, if the development would only cause a limited amount of harm, then it should have good prospects of success.

4.61 Section 5 (paras 59–79) of the NPPF is headed 'Delivering a sufficient supply of homes' and states as follows:

> 59. To support the Government's objective of significantly boosting the supply of homes, it is important that a sufficient amount and variety of land can come forward where it is needed, that the needs of groups with specific housing requirements are addressed and that land with permission is developed without unnecessary delay.
>
> 60. To determine the minimum number of homes needed, strategic policies should be informed by a local housing need assessment, conducted

45 See *Barnsley MBC v Secretary of State for Communities and Local Government* [2010] EWHC 206 (Admin) for a case where an LPA unsuccessfully argued that Romani Gypsies should continue to live on a site subject to frequent and deep, life-threatening, flooding.

46 Examples of the 'specific policies' mentioned in para 11(d)i are listed in NPPF's footnote 6. They include policies relating to internationally protected nature conservation sites, sites of special scientific interest, Green Belts, local green spaces, areas of outstanding natural beauty, national parks, designated heritage assets and areas at risk of flooding or coastal change.

> using the standard method in national planning guidance – unless exceptional circumstances justify an alternative approach which also reflects current and future demographic trends and market signals. In addition to the local housing need figure, any needs that cannot be met within neighbouring areas should also be taken into account in establishing the amount of housing to be planned for.
>
> 61. Within this context, the size, type and tenure of housing needed for different groups in the community should be assessed and reflected in planning policies (including, but not limited to, those who require affordable housing, families with children, older people, students, people with disabilities, service families, travellers, people who rent their homes and people wishing to commission or build their own homes).

4.62 Paragraph 73 of the NPPF advises LPAs that they should identify and update annually a supply of specific deliverable sites sufficient to provide a minimum of five years' worth of housing against their housing requirements set out in adopted strategic policies; and that:

> For the avoidance of doubt, a five year supply of deliverable sites for travellers – as defined in Annex 1 to Planning Policy for Traveller Sites – should be assessed separately, in line with the policy in that document.

4.63 Section 13 (paras 133–147) of the NPPF, which is headed 'Protecting Green Belt land' begins by stating that the government 'attaches great importance to Green Belts' and that the fundamental aim of Green Belt policy is to prevent urban sprawl by keeping land permanently open. Green Belt land should not be confused with the term 'greenfield', which is normally used simply to describe land that has not been developed. Green Belt land may include previously developed land, while most greenfield land is not Green Belt.

4.64 Paragraph 143 of the NPPF provides:

> Inappropriate development is, by definition, harmful to the Green Belt and should not be approved except in very special circumstances.

4.65 Paragraph 144 of the NPPF continues:

> When considering any planning application, local planning authorities should ensure that substantial weight is given to any harm to the Green Belt. 'Very special circumstances' will not exist unless the potential harm to the Green Belt by reason of inappropriateness, and any other harm resulting from the proposal, is clearly outweighed by other considerations.

4.66 Paragraph 145 of the NPPF provides that LPAs should regard the construction of new buildings as inappropriate in the Green Belt, subject to a number of exceptions, including:

> . . . limited infilling or the partial or complete redevelopment of previously developed land, whether redundant or in continuing use (excluding temporary buildings), which would:
> - not have a greater impact on the openness of the Green Belt than the existing development; or
> - not cause substantial harm to the openness of the Green Belt, where the development would re-use previously developed land and contribute to meeting an identified affordable housing need within the area of the local planning authority.

4.67 The glossary in Annex 2 of the NPPF defines previously developed land (PDL) as:

> Land which is or was occupied by a permanent structure, including the curtilage of the developed land (although it should not be assumed that the whole of the curtilage should be developed) and any associated fixed surface infrastructure. This excludes: land that is or was last occupied by agricultural or forestry buildings; land that has been developed for minerals extraction or waste disposal by landfill, where provision for restoration has been made through development management procedures; land in built-up areas such as residential gardens, parks, recreation grounds and allotments; and land that was previously developed but where the remains of the permanent structure or fixed surface structure have blended into the landscape.

4.68 In general, it is easier to obtain planning permission for development on PDL than on a greenfield site. In *Dartford BC v Secretary of State for Communities and Local Government*[47] the High Court considered an application under TCPA 1990 s288 brought by an LPA to quash a planning inspector's decision granting planning permission for a single-pitch Gypsy and Traveller site with the curtilage of PDL. The inspector had noted that the appeal site was within a rural area but had concluded that 'as the mobile home and tourer would be located within the curtilage of developed land it should be treated as previously-developed land'. Both the High Court and the Court of Appeal upheld the inspector's decision.[48] On appeal Lewison LJ helpfully said:

> 'Land in built-up areas' cannot mean land not in built-up areas . . . If a new building is a partial redevelopment of a previously developed site it is not to be regarded as inappropriate redevelopment in the Green Belt, provided that it has no greater impact on the openness of the Green Belt

47 [2016] EWHC 635 (Admin), Charles George QC sitting as a Deputy High Court Judge.

48 [2017] EWCA Civ 141, [2017] 2 P&CR 9.

than the existing development; and a new dwelling within [the curtilage of an existing permanent structure] will not be an 'isolated' home.

4.69 In Wales, the principal national policy document is entitled the Planning Policy Wales (edn 10, December 2018) and it includes the following advice:

> **Gypsies and Travellers**
> 4.2.35 Local authorities are required to assess the accommodation needs of Gypsy and Traveller families and to allocate sites to meet the identified need.[49] Where a Gypsy and Traveller Accommodation Assessment (GTAA) identifies an unmet need, a planning authority should allocate sufficient sites in their development plan to ensure that the identified pitch requirements for residential and/or transit use can be met. Planning authorities will need to demonstrate that sites are suitable for development and deliverable in the identified timescales.[50] In drawing up policies planning authorities should consult providers of social housing, representatives of Gypsies and Travellers communities and landowners in areas likely to be appropriate for site provision. The consultation should be undertaken in a manner that is consistent with the planning authority's Community Involvement Scheme.

Planning policy for traveller sites

4.70 In August 2015 the Conservative government issued a revised version of PPTS. Lang J explained the relationship between PPTS and NPPF in *Wenman v Secretary of State for Communities and Local Government*[51] in para 37 of her judgment:

> The PPTS emphasises that the NPPF is applicable in determining planning applications for Traveller sites. In my view, the PPTS is supplementary to the NPPF. Where the PPTS makes specific provision for Traveller sites, in aspects of policy which are also addressed by the NPPF, then the PPTS will take priority, thus avoiding duplication or conflict.

49 In a footnote, Planning Policy Wales reminds LPAs that the assessment of Gypsy and Traveller accommodation needs, and the duty to make provision for sites where the assessment identifies need, are statutory requirements under the Housing (Wales) Act 2014.

50 In another footnote, Planning Policy Wales refers to the fact that further detail on the process of providing Gypsy and Traveller sites through the planning system is contained in PGTSS 2018: see https://gov.wales/topics/planning/policy/circulars/welshgovcirculars/wgc 005-2018/?lang=en.

51 [2015] EWHC 925 (Admin), October 2015 *Legal Action* 29–31, para 37.

4.71 PPTS 2015 para 4 states that the government's aims in respect of Gypsy and Traveller sites are:

> a. that local planning authorities should make their own assessment of need for the purposes of planning
> b. to ensure that local planning authorities, working collaboratively, develop fair and effective strategies to meet need through the identification of land for sites
> c. to encourage local planning authorities to plan for sites over a reasonable timescale
> d. that plan-making and decision-taking should protect Green Belt from inappropriate development
> e. to promote more private traveller site provision while recognising that there will always be those travellers who cannot provide their own sites
> f. that plan-making and decision-taking should aim to reduce the number of unauthorised developments and encampments and make enforcement more effective
> g. for local planning authorities to ensure that their Local Plan includes fair, realistic and inclusive policies
> h. to increase the number of traveller sites in appropriate locations with planning permission, to address under provision and maintain an appropriate level of supply
> i. to reduce tensions between settled and traveller communities in plan-making and planning decisions
> j. to enable provision of suitable accommodation from which travellers can access education, health, welfare and employment infrastructure
> k. for local planning authorities to have due regard to the protection of local amenity and local environment.

4.72 PPTS 2015 para 10 begins:

> Local planning authorities should, in producing their Local Plan:
> a) identify and update annually, a supply of specific deliverable sites sufficient to provide 5 years' worth of sites against their locally set targets . . .

4.73 Like its predecessor, the PPTS 2015 allows for rural sites in general. However, it is more restrictive when it comes to the development of sites in the Green Belt, areas of outstanding natural beauty (AONBs) and other designated land.

4.74 Paragraph 16 of PPTS 2015 echoes the NPPF in requiring the existence of 'very special circumstances' to justify Green Belt development and states that:

> Inappropriate development is harmful to the Green Belt and should not be approved, except in very special circumstances. Traveller

> sites (temporary or permanent) in the Green Belt are inappropriate development.

However, in guidance that is stricter than that in PPTS 2012, decision-makers are advised that:

> Subject to the best interests of the child, personal circumstances and unmet need are unlikely to clearly outweigh harm to the Green Belt and any other harm so as to establish very special circumstances.

4.75 PPTS 2015 para 24 states:

> Local planning authorities should consider the following issues amongst other relevant matters when considering planning applications for traveller sites:
> a) the existing level of local provision and need for sites
> b) the availability (or lack) of alternative accommodation for the applicants
> c) other personal circumstances of the applicant
> d) that the locally specific criteria used to guide the allocation of sites in plans or which form the policy where there is no identified need for pitches/plots should be used to assess applications that may come forward on unallocated sites
> e) that they should determine applications for sites from any travellers and not just those with local connections
>
> However, as para 16 makes clear, subject to the best interests of the child, personal circumstances and unmet need are unlikely to clearly outweigh harm to the Green Belt and any other harm so as to establish very special circumstances.

4.76 The application of the advice in PPTS 2015 on the grant of planning permission for sites in the Green Belt was considered in the case of *Doncaster MBC v Secretary of State for Communities and Local Government and AB*.[52] The local authority challenged a planning inspector's decision to grant a Romani Gypsy family planning permission for a Gypsy site in the Doncaster Green Belt. The local authority argued that the Green Belt policy in PPTS 2015 had raised the bar so high that planning permission for sites in the Green Belt should only be granted in the most exceptional cases. The Judge, Gilbart J, rejected the challenge, stating that:

> In my judgment, this is a Decision Letter over which an experienced Inspector has taken a great deal of care to address all relevant issues in a fair and balanced manner. The views he reached on the merits were plainly ones he was entitled to reach, both within the bounds of the law

52 [2016] EWHC 2876 (Admin).

> and of the [NPPF] and the [PPTS]. Neither are designed, written or intended to prevent the grant of permission in proper cases for such developments in the Green Belt, and it does nothing to water down the strength of national policy. This case involved the combination of a development whose adverse effects on openness was limited, a very strong case of personal circumstances, and an admitted need for pitches, where the supply was uncertain, in the view of successive Inspector.[53]

This is an important clarification of the correct approach to Gypsy and Traveller Green Belt cases. Some local planning authorities have taken too strict an approach to the determination of Gypsy and Traveller cases since the issue of PPTS 2015 and this judgment has already been used by those representing Gypsies and Travellers to demonstrate to local planning authorities and planning inspectors that it is still right to grant permission for Gypsy and Traveller sites in the Green Belt in proper cases.

4.77 PPTS 2015 para 25 states:

> Local planning authorities should very strictly limit new traveller site development in open countryside that is away from existing settlements or outside areas allocated in the development plan. Local planning authorities should ensure that sites in rural areas respect the scale of, and do not dominate, the nearest settled community, and avoid placing an undue pressure on the local infrastructure.[54]

4.78 PPTS 2015 para 27 states:

> If a local planning authority cannot demonstrate an up–to-date 5 year supply of deliverable sites, this should be a significant material consideration in any subsequent planning decision when considering applications for the grant of temporary planning permission. The exception is where the proposal is on land designated as Green Belt; sites protected under the Birds and Habitats Directives and / or sites designated as Sites of Special Scientific Interest; Local Green Space, an Area of Outstanding Natural Beauty, or within a National Park (or the Broads).

4.79 While that advice refers specifically to the grant of temporary planning permission the fact is that it is also open to decision-makers to give the lack of an up to date five-year supply of deliverable sites weight when considering whether to grant permanent permission.

53 [2016] EWHC 2876 (Admin) para 88.

54 The 2015 revision of PPTS added the word 'very' to the text which formed PPTS 2012 para 23; but PPTS 2015 para 25 still allows for sites to be located in open countryside that is not 'away' from settlements, subject to size or outside allocated areas and recognises that there will be sites in rural areas.

4.80 The most controversial aspect of the advice in PPTS 2015 concerns the adoption of an ill-conceived and regressive revised definition of the term 'gypsies and travellers' in Annex 1:

> 1. For the purposes of this planning policy 'gypsies and travellers' means:
>
> Persons of nomadic habit of life whatever their race or origin, including such persons who on grounds only of their own or their family's or dependants' educational or health needs or old age have ceased to travel temporarily, but excluding members of an organised group of travelling showpeople or circus people travelling together as such.
>
> 2. In determining whether persons are 'gypsies and travellers' for the purposes of this planning policy, consideration should be given to the following issues amongst other relevant matters:
> a) whether they previously led a nomadic habit of life
> b) the reasons for ceasing their nomadic habit of life
> c) whether there is an intention of living a nomadic habit of life in the future, and if so, how soon and in what circumstances.

4.81 This new definition excludes those who are too old to travel for an economic purpose and those whose permanent disabilities prevent such travel, making it more difficult for the most vulnerable members of the Gypsy and Traveller community to obtain planning permission for a site on which they can live in caravans in accordance with their traditional way of life.[55]

Planning for Gypsy, Traveller and Showpeople Sites[56]

4.82 The Welsh guidance contained in PGTSS is much the same as PPTS 2015 and is to be found in appendix B. However, it should be noted that PGTSS has a much wider and fairer definition of 'Gypsies and Travellers' than PPTS 2015 and advises that the term refers to:

> (a) Persons of a nomadic habit of life, whatever their race or origin, including –

55 Quite apart from the difficulties that the application may have for individuals seeking planning permission, there is a concern that LPAs will only address the accommodation needs of Gypsies and Travellers that fall within the definition. The issue was addressed in a report entitled *Gypsy and Traveller sites: the revised planning definition's impact on assessing accommodation needs*, Cottle et al, published by the Equalities and Human Rights Commission in September 2019.

56 It is noteworthy that, unlike the UK government, the Welsh government shows Gypsies and Travellers the courtesy of using capital letters when referring to them.

(i) Persons who, on grounds only of their own or their family's or dependant's educational or health needs or old age, have ceased to travel temporarily or permanently, and
(ii) Members of an organised group of travelling show people or circus people (whether or not travelling together as such); and

(b) All other persons with a cultural tradition of nomadism or of living in a mobile home.

4.83 In addition, the advice in PGTSS para 39 on the location of sites is less restrictive than the advice in PPTS 2015:

> 39. Sites in the countryside, away from existing settlements, can be considered for Gypsy and Traveller sites if there is a lack of suitable sustainable locations within or adjacent to existing settlement boundaries. In assessing the suitability of such sites, local authorities should be realistic about the availability, or likely availability, of alternatives to the car in accessing local services. Over rigid application of national or development plan policies that seek a reduction in car borne travel in order to effectively block proposals for any Gypsy and Traveller Site in a countryside location would be inappropriate. Sites should be considered in context and in relation to the local infrastructure, population size and density to ensure they are in proportion to local settled communities.

Designated areas and site location

4.84 Much of England and Wales is designated, usually under an adopted development plan. The most significant designations of land relate to National Parks, AONB and Green Belts.

4.85 The National Parks and AONB of England and Wales together cover around 29 per cent of the combined area of two countries. In addition, about 13 per cent of England is designated as Green Belt. The overlap between National Parks and AONB, on the one hand, and Green Belts on the other, is comparatively small.

4.86 It has long been policy that inappropriate development in a Green Belt should only be allowed if 'very special circumstances' exist. This remains the case under the NPPF and PPTS 2015.[57]

4.87 Green Belt boundaries cannot be altered by an application for planning permission, but can be altered when Local Plans are made. Those making representations on behalf of Gypsies and Travellers in respect of DPDs should consider proposing alterations to Green Belt boundaries to allow for both existing and proposed Gypsy and Traveller sites. In the case of existing Gypsy or Traveller sites in a

57 See paragraphs 133–147 of the NPPF and PPTS para 16.

Green Belt, consideration should be given to excluding them, together with a modest area for future expansion (perhaps a further 50 per cent), from the Green Belt.

4.88 The reality is that most Gypsies and Travellers want to live in rural areas and will, in any event, be unable to live elsewhere. Government policy means that their prospects of gaining permission are better on land that is neither Green Belt, nor subject to a national designation such as AONB or sites of special scientific interest (SSSI).

4.89 Gypsies and Travellers would be best advised to avoid trying to establish sites on land that is situated within the Green Belt, an AONB or other area which is covered by some form of national designation in parts of the country where other land not subject to such designation can be found within a reasonable distance, but not necessarily in the same district, to meet their needs.

4.90 However, in parts of the country where all the land is Green Belt or subject to some other form of national designation, (particularly around Greater London) it is inevitable that land for Gypsy and Traveller sites will have to be found in those designated areas.

4.91 In areas where there is a substantial amount of undesignated rural land it ought, with goodwill from all concerned, to be relatively easy to locate suitable sites for Gypsies and Travellers. Unfortunately, that goodwill is often lacking.

4.92 In other areas, the fact that most land is designated will not remove the need to provide for Gypsies' and Travellers' accommodation. In such circumstances, those concerned with the provision of sites might consider three approaches.

4.93 First, there are sites that are naturally screened so that they have little or no visual impact: former military sites such as anti-aircraft emplacements and redundant utility sites, such as a former substation, may well have natural screening that has developed over the years and may be available at a price that Gypsies and Travellers could afford. Although these may in many respects be suitable for Gypsy and Traveller sites, advisers should be aware that such sites may be contaminated and should give their clients a clear warning of this possibility. They should firmly advise site investigation before purchase.[58] Some former quarries may also be suitable, although physical safety in them should be given particular consideration.

58 Gypsies and Travellers should be advised to instruct a conveyancing solicitor or a licensed conveyancer to undertake a Local Land Search with the LPA.

4.94 Second, a 'sieve map' process may be adopted to determine preferred areas. Under this process the land of greatest importance within the LPA's area is excluded first. In assessing importance, national designations such as AONB and SSSI are of greater importance than local designations or landscape character areas. Further areas may be excluded in order of importance, but the process stops before the area of land remaining is too small to permit a realistic search for sites. In an area that was mainly undesignated land, all designated land might be excluded by this method. In an area that has wholly designated land, sites would be permitted in areas carrying the designation(s) of least importance. This is an entirely appropriate method of meeting a planning need.[59]

4.95 Third, an approach based on the needs of Gypsies and Travellers can be adopted. This is likely to lead to a search for sites reasonably close to (but not immediately adjoining) settlements of sufficient size to contain basic facilities such as a primary school, doctor's surgery and shop(s), with access to a road appropriate for a lorry towing a caravan. At its best, such an approach can lead to the identification of sites where Gypsies and Travellers accommodation needs can be met in areas where they wish to live. However, if not done properly, such an approach can result in the adoption of a policy consisting of so many mandatory criteria that it is unrealistic to expect that a site could be found which complies with its requirements. The criteria used should be reasonable. Thus in *Stirrup v Secretary of State for the Environment*,[60] a district council had interpreted a county council's policy as meaning that all Gypsy and Traveller sites should have mains services readily and economically available. The High Court held that 'a requirement of mains services for a single caravan might well be *Wednesbury*[61] unreasonable'.

Development plan policies for Gypsy and Traveller sites

4.96 PCPA 2004 s38(6) read with TCPA 1990 s70(2) provides that planning applications should be determined in accordance with

59 *Buckinghamshire CC v Hall Aggregates* [1985] JPL 634.

60 (1993) 3 December, CO/383/93, Local Authority Law 1/94 2.

61 *Associated Provincial Picture Houses Ltd v Wednesbury Corporation* [1948] 1 KB 223.

the development plan, unless material considerations indicate otherwise.

4.97 Formerly, Circular 1/94 required LPAs to carry out a quantitative assessment of the need for Gypsy and Traveller sites within their areas and identify, wherever possible, locations suitable for Gypsy and Traveller sites, whether local authority or private sites, in their development plans. Where it was not possible to do so, LPAs were required to set out clear, realistic criteria for suitable locations, as a basis for site provision policies. In fact, few, if any, LPAs in England and Wales carried out a quantitative assessment of need, and almost all the LPAs adopted criteria-based policies without looking to see whether they could identify sites in their areas.

4.98 The government advice on the assessment of the need for pitch provision was revised in Circular 1/06 and then again in PPTS 2012 and PPTS 2015 which provides that LPAs should, in producing their local plan, identify and update annually a supply of specific, deliverable sites sufficient to provide 5-years' worth of sites against their locally set targets.[62]

4.99 However, few LPAs have adopted DPDs which comply with that policy requirement and until they do planning applications will continue to be assessed against existing (often inadequate) development plans. It should, however, be remembered that development plan policies that predate and are in conflict with national policy will be treated as being out of date. In such circumstances, LPAs should appreciate that, when planning inspectors determine appeals against the refusal of planning permission for a Gypsy or Traveller site, they are likely to give significantly greater weight to national policy than to, for example, an unrealistic and out-of-date, criteria-based local plan policy.

Other material considerations

4.100 LPAs are required to have regard to all considerations that are material to an application but the legislation does not provide specific guidance on what considerations might be regarded as material. It has therefore been left to the courts to determine what is capable of amounting to a material consideration. In general, the courts have avoided placing limits on what might constitute a material consideration in any given case.

62 See PPTS 2015 para 10.

4.101 In the majority of cases concerning Gypsies and Travellers, the proposed use of a piece of land as a Gypsy caravan site will conflict with some policies contained in the development plan. In such circumstances, Gypsies and Travellers will only be granted planning permission if they can show that there are material considerations that outweigh the development plan policy objections and justify the grant of planning permission. The phrase 'material considerations' is broad. As Cooke J stated in *Stringer v Minister of Housing and Local Government*:

> In principle . . . any consideration which relates to the use and development of land is capable of being a planning consideration. Whether a particular consideration falling within that broad class is material in any given case will depend on the circumstances.[63]

4.102 Considerations that may be of particular relevance to applications for planning permission made by Gypsies and Travellers include:

- Gypsy and Traveller ethnicity and status in planning terms;
- the general need for Gypsy and Traveller sites;
- the availability of suitable, affordable alternative sites;
- the applicant's need for a Gypsy or Traveller site;
- personal circumstances;
- human rights; and
- the best interests of children.

Ethnic Gypsies and Travellers and their planning status ('Gypsy status')

Ethnicity

4.103 Romani Gypsies are a separate racial group for the purposes of the EqA 2010.[64] Irish Travellers are also recognised as a separate ethnic group.[65]

63 [1971] 1 All ER 65 at 77.

64 *Commission for Racial Equality v Dutton* [1989] QB 783.

65 *O'Leary v Allied Domecq* (2000) 29 August (unreported) Central London County Court, HHJ Goldstein. For further consideration of this point, see para 8.44, below. In addition, see the Race Relations (Northern Ireland) Order 1997 article 5(3)(a), which, for the avoidance of doubt, makes express provision for 'the Irish Traveller community'. Since 2003, the EU Race Equality Directive (Directive 2000/43/EC; 2000 OJ L180/22) has protected both Romani Gypsies and Irish Travellers. For a detailed consideration of this Directive see T Jones, 'The Race Directive: Redefining Protection from Discrimination in EU Law' (2003) EHRLR 515.

4.104 The impact of their ethnicity on planning was made clear in *Moore and Coates v Secretary of State for Communities and Local Government*.[66] That case related to two separate applications made by two Romani Gypsy women who had sought planning permission to continue living with their children on their land in the Green Belt. Both were refused planning permission at first instance and their planning appeals were recovered by the secretary of state, Eric Pickles MP (that is, the secretary of state decided that he, rather than a planning inspector, would decide the appeals) in accordance with his practice laid down in two WMSs of recovering all Gypsy and Traveller Green-Belt appeals. This practice created two problems for Gypsies and Travellers: first, the secretary of state's decisions are notoriously slow to be issued when compared with the decisions made by his inspectors; secondly, decisions taken by the secretary of state were generally less favourable than inspectors to Gypsies and Travellers and never more favourable.

4.105 Ms Moore and Ms Coates alleged that the secretary of state had indirectly discriminated against them when providing a public-function, contrary to EqA 2010 s19 and s29. Secondly, they argued that he had breached the public sector equality duty (PSED) under EqA 2010 s149.[67] This states, among other things:

> (1) A public authority must, in the exercise of its functions, have due regard to the need to–
> (a) eliminate discrimination, harassment, victimisation and any other conduct that is prohibited by or under this Act;
> (b) advance equality of opportunity between persons who share a relevant protected characteristic and persons who do not share it;
> (c) foster good relations between persons who share a relevant protected characteristic and persons who do not share it . . .
>
> (3) Having due regard to the need to advance equality of opportunity between persons who share a relevant protected characteristic and persons who do not share it involves having due regard, in particular, to the need to–
> (a) remove or minimise disadvantages suffered by persons who share a relevant protected characteristic that are connected to that characteristic;
> (b) take steps to meet the needs of persons who share a relevant protected characteristic that are different from the needs of persons who do not share it . . .

66 [2015] EWHC 44 (Admin), [2015] LGR 405. This case is also considered under the human rights section of this chapter.

67 See paras 8.133–8.145 and 8.159.

> (5) Having due regard to the need to foster good relations between persons who share a relevant protected characteristic and persons who do not share it involves having due regard, in particular, to the need to–
> (a) tackle prejudice, and
> (b) promote understanding.
> (7) The relevant protected characteristics are– . . . race . . .

4.106 The alleged discrimination was indirect, rather than direct discrimination, because the secretary of state's practice of recovering all Gypsy and Traveller Green-Belt appeals had a disproportionate effect on those brought by ethnic Gypsies and Travellers. Gilbart J held:

> A policy which imposes greater delays on a racial group's planning appeals than it does on others who also wish to set up a habitation in the Green Belt is patently discriminatory, subject of course to whether the SSCLG can show it to be a proportionate means of achieving a legitimate aim.[68]

The learned judge had no doubt that the secretary of state had failed to do this stating:

> . . . the Secretary of State and his Minister have in my judgment fallen far short of showing that the recovery of all such appeals was a proportionate way of achieving his objective. . . . a notable feature of the evidence for the SSCLG is that it shows that his officials repeatedly advised against the course being followed, and recommended the course of selecting a few cases so that a clear message could be given, while drawing attention to the increasing delays being caused to interested parties. Yet there is an absence of any evidence from the SSCLG in these proceedings of why the Minister or the SSCLG thought that their preferred approach was proportionate, and why none of the alternatives being suggested to them would not meet the objectives they had identified.[69]

4.107 Gilbart J concluded that:

> . . . the application of WMS1 was in fact a practice whereby all appeals were recovered . . . the practice therefore adopted after its publication was discriminatory within the meaning of s 19.[70]

4.108 The *Moore and Coates* judgment provides a basis for relying upon EqA 2010 s19 indirect discrimination where Gypsy and Traveller caravan-dwellers are treated less favourably than the equivalent house-dwellers.

68 At para 97.
69 At para 125.
70 At para 126.

4.109 In the past there was a tendency to treat EqA 2010 s149 as a formality. It was briefly mentioned; but, in reality, it had not been considered as a factor when the decision concerned was made. A series of cases outside the field of planning[71] have made it clear that it is a duty that is much more than that. Gilbart J applied those cases to planning. He had no doubt that there was a breach of this duty:

> The fact is that this in truth not a case whether the regard the Secretary of State and his Ministers had was 'due regard.' The fact is that, on the evidence filed by the SSCLG, they had no regard at all.[72]
>
> I am therefore in no doubt that there has been a failure to comply with the PSED. It is not a case of the SSCLG and his Ministers addressing it but falling short; it is one of not addressing it all, and not doing so on either occasion when changes in policy were being considered. Even if I thought that the SSCLG and his Ministers had considered the issue, I would still have found on the evidence before me that they had not had due regard. That is because, as I have already concluded, the steps taken . . . have not been shown to be proportionate.[73]
>
> In devising and considering a policy or practice, the PSED requires actual consideration, and the Court of Appeal expects evidence of a structured attempt to focus upon the details of equality issues. I reiterate that that principle applies as much to Ministerial consideration and decisions as it does to those of other public bodies. The disadvantaging of a racial group . . . without having a legitimate aim or without having a proportionate approach to its achievement, or a failure to have due regard to issues of equality, is no more or less objectionable if it is occasioned by Ministerial decision making.[74]

4.110 These findings are having major consequences. Planning inspectors are more aware of the PSED. *Moore and Coates* has already been applied in a non-Gypsy planning case involving breach of the duty towards disabled people.[75] It should be considered in other cases where a public body treats Gypsies and Traveller caravan-dwellers less favourably than the equivalent house-dwellers. The potential effect of the PSED finding is wide. It will apply to almost all public-sector decision-makers, including the secretary of state, Ministers,

71 Including *Bracking v Secretary of State for Work and Pensions* [2013] EWCA Civ 1345; and *R (Brown) v Secretary of State for Work and Pensions* [2008] EWHC 3158 (Admin). See also paras 8.141–8.143 below.

72 At para 134.

73 Paras 135 and 136.

74 Para 138.

75 *LDRA Ltd v Secretary of State for Communities and Local Government* [2016] EWHC 950 (Admin); [2016] All ER (D) 53 (May), Lang J, 6 May 2016.

local planning authorities, inspectors and examiners.[76] It will often be particularly helpful to remember that the duty must be 'exercised in substance, with rigour, and with an open mind' and that it is not a question of 'ticking boxes'.[77] Rather there should be 'evidence of a structured attempt to focus upon the details of equality issues'.[78] Many past officer's reports would fail this test, as would some inspectors' and examiners' reports and decisions.

4.111 The case of *Mulvenna and Smith v Secretary of State for Community and Local Government* concerned Mr Pickles' decision to recover a number of other planning appeals for his own determination solely on the basis that they concerned 'Gypsy sites in the Green Belt'. Having done so, Mr Pickles rejected his planning inspector's recommendation in each case that planning permission be granted and he dismissed both appeals.

4.112 Some months after the appeals had been dismissed, in January 2015, Gilbart J gave judgment in the case of *Moore and Coates v Secretary of State for Communities and Local Government*.[79] Ms Moore and Ms Coates had challenged Mr Pickles' decision to recover their planning appeals by way of judicial review at a time before he had the opportunity to determine their appeals and argued that his recovery policy was unlawful. During the course of those proceedings, the SSCLG filed evidence from a senior civil servant, Mr Richard Watson, which made it quite clear that Mr Pickles was applying the criteria for the recovery of planning appeals brought by Gypsies and Travellers in respect of Green Belt sites in a way that had a discriminatory impact on ethnic Gypsies and Travellers, and Gilbart J quashed the decisions on that basis.

4.113 When those representing Ms Mulvenna and Mr Smith read the *Moore and Coates* judgment and the judge's references to the evidence given by Mr Watson, they understood for the first time what had been happening behind the scenes at the Department for Communities and Local Government (DCLG) and how the recovery policy had been applied in a discriminatory way by Mr Pickles and that their clients had also been the victims of discrimination.

76 The public bodies to which EqA 2010 s149 applies are listed in EqA 2010 Sch 19, while Sch 18 gives exceptions to the duty – these exceptions are unlikely to apply to matters relating to planning and race discrimination.

77 Aikens LJ, giving the judgment of the Divisional Court, in *R (Brown) v Secretary of State for Work and Pensions* [2008] EWHC 3158 (Admin), [2009] PTSR 1506.

78 Moore at para 134.

79 See paras 4.104–4.110 above.

However, their position was clearly different in that their appeal decisions had already been determined.

4.114 In the event, it was considered that there were grounds to:

- challenge the original recovery decisions in both their cases – out of time – on the basis that they could not have known of the SSCLG's discriminatory recovery practice before the disclosure of Mr Watson's evidence in the *Moore and Coates* judgment (as an aside it should be noted that Mr Watson's evidence had been privileged up to the point it was used in the trial of the *Moore and Coates* case);
- and on the basis that his subsequent determination of their appeals was null and void – applying what is known as the 'domino effect'.

4.115 At first instance, the case came before Mr Justice Cranston who decided that he would not exercise his discretion to extend time to allow Ms Mulvenna and Mr Smith to challenge the recovery decisions themselves and subsequent appeal decisions out of time. He also decided that in any event the admittedly unlawful recovery decisions did not make the subsequent appeal decisions a nullity.

4.116 The Court of Appeal reviewed Mr Justice Cranston's decision and concluded that it was lawful. In what many would consider a harsh decision, given the fact that the appellants could not possibly have known what was going on behind the scenes at the DCLG, the court decided that it was far too late to allow the appellants to challenge the recovery decisions. In addition, the court held that even if the appellants' challenges to the recovery decisions were successful, that would not undermine the appeal decisions made by Mr Pickles, because, in their view: challenges to appeal decisions could only be made by way of claims brought under TCPA 1990 s288 within six weeks of the decision made; and the jurisdiction to determine appeals always vested in the SSCLG and therefore an unlawful recovery decision made no difference.

4.117 It is important to note that the judgment in *Moore and Coates* remains intact. In addition, the authors understand that the appellants in *Mulvenna* and other cases have sought leave to appeal to the Supreme Court.

Gypsy status

4.118 In order to benefit from the positive parts of government guidance on the provision of Gypsy and Traveller sites, it is not enough for an applicant to prove that he or she is an ethnic Gypsy or Traveller – an applicant must show that he or she is entitled to what has become known as 'Gypsy status'.

4.119 From 1994 until 2006, the word 'Gypsies' was defined for the purposes of the provision of caravan sites for Gypsies and Travellers in legislation not on grounds of ethnicity but as meaning:

> . . . persons of nomadic habit of life, whatever their race or origin, but does not include members of an organised group of travelling showmen, or persons engaged in travelling circuses, travelling together as such.[80]

This issue has generated a considerable amount of litigation.

4.120 In *Greenwich LBC v Powell*,[81] Lord Bridge of Harwich stated that a person could be a statutory Gypsy if he led a nomadic way of life only seasonally.

4.121 The case of *R v Shropshire CC ex p Bungay*,[82] concerned a Gypsy family that had not travelled for some 15 years in order to care for its elderly and infirm parents. An aggrieved local resident in the area of the family's recently approved Gypsy site sought judicial review of the local authority's decision to accept that the family had retained their Gypsy status even though it had not travelled for some considerable time. Dismissing the claim, the judge held that a person could remain a Gypsy even if he or she did not travel, provided that their nomadism was held in abeyance and not abandoned.

4.122 In *Hearne v National Assembly for Wales*,[83] a traditional ethnic Gypsy was held not to be a Gypsy for the purposes of planning law as he had stated that he intended to abandon his nomadic habit of life, lived in a permanent dwelling, and was taking a course that led to permanent employment.

4.123 In *R v South Hams DC ex p Gibb*,[84] the Court of Appeal considered the statutory definition further and qualified it by holding that there should be some recognisable connection between the travelling of those claiming to be Gypsies and the means whereby they made or sought their livelihood:

> . . . the definition of 'Gypsies' . . . imports the requirement that there should be some recognisable connection between the wandering or

80 CSCDA 1960 s24(8). The same definition was formerly contained in CSA 1968 s16 and stems from the decision of the Divisional Court in *Mills v Cooper* [1967] 2 WLR 1343.

81 [1989] 1 AC 995 at 15.

82 [1991] 23 HLR 195.

83 22 October 1999, (1999) *Times*, 10 November.

84 [1995] QB 158.

> travelling and the means whereby the persons concerned make or seek their livelihood. Persons, or individuals, who move from place to place merely as the fancy may take them and without any connection between the movement and their means of livelihood fall outside these statutory definitions . . .[85]

4.124 The latter part of the Court of Appeal's interpretation of the statutory definition of 'Gypsy' involves a consideration of whether the individual concerned travels to seek or make their livelihood and this point has been considered further in a number of cases. For example, in *Maidstone BC v Secretary of State for the Environment*,[86] it was held that a Romani Gypsy who bred horses and travelled to horse fairs at Appleby, Stow-in-the-Wold and the New Forest, where he bought and sold horses, and who remained away from his permanent site for up to two months of the year, at least partly in connection with this traditional Gypsy activity, was entitled to be accorded Gypsy status.

4.125 In *Basildon DC v First Secretary of State and Cooper*,[87] the Court of Appeal accepted that a Romani woman was a statutory Gypsy, in circumstances where she travelled to traditional Gypsy fairs during the summer months and sold craft items at those events.

4.126 LPAs often go to considerable lengths to try to 'prove' that the Gypsies or Travellers seeking planning permission were not entitled to Gypsy status.

4.127 The Welsh Assembly's Equality of Opportunity Committee[88] recognised this tendency and considered that the weaknesses in the planning system are indicated by the increasing consideration of the provisions of the HRA 1998 in relation to legal action being taken by Gypsies and Travellers on planning issues. The Committee noted the:

> . . . apparent obsession with finding ways to prove that an individual is not a 'Gypsy' for the purposes of the planning system. This approach is extremely unhelpful . . . and there can be no doubt that actual mobility at any given time is a poor indicator as to whether someone should be considered a Gypsy or a Traveller.[89]

85 [1994] 4 All ER 1012 at 1021.

86 [1996] JPL 584.

87 [2004] EWCA Civ 473.

88 Review of Service Provision for Gypsies and Travellers, National Assembly for Wales, 2003.

89 Review of Service Provision for Gypsies and Travellers at p58.

4.128 In *Wrexham CBC v The National Assembly for Wales*,[90] the courts considered once more the question of whether an individual can lose her or his Gypsy status, particularly in relation to cases where old age and ill-health has led to Gypsies and Travellers not being able to travel. In *Berry*, a planning inspector had allowed a planning enforcement appeal for an ethnic Irish Traveller family in Wrexham, only to see the decision challenged in the High Court on the grounds that the elder breadwinner in the family, Mr Berry, was no longer a 'Gypsy' because he had become too ill to continue to travel for work. In his judgment, Sullivan J decided that he could not see anything in *R v South Hams DC ex p Gibb*[91] to suggest that, had the Court of Appeal been confronted with what might be described as a 'retired' Gypsy, it would have said that he had ceased to be a statutory Gypsy because he had become too ill and/or too old to travel in order to search for work. Indeed, Sullivan J stated that he believed:

> . . . such an approach would be contrary to common sense and common humanity . . . It would be inhuman pedantry to approach the policy guidance . . . upon that basis . . .[92]

4.129 Wrexham CBC appealed against the decision of Sullivan J and the Court of Appeal allowed the appeal.[93] In doing so, Auld LJ stated that the following propositions of law should be applied:

> (2) Whether applicants for planning permission are of a 'nomadic way of life' as a matter of planning law and policy is a functional test to be applied to their normal way of life at the time of the determination. Are they at that time following such a habit of life in the sense of a pattern and/or a rhythm of full time or seasonal or other periodic travelling? The fact that they may have a permanent base from which they set out on, and to which they return from, their periodic travelling may not deprive them of nomadic status. And the fact that they are temporarily confined to their permanent base for personal reasons such as sickness and/or possibly the interests of their children, may not do so either, depending on the reasons and the length of time, past and projected, of the abeyance of their travelling life. But if they have retired permanently from travelling for whatever reason, ill health, age or simply because they no longer wish to follow that way of life, they no longer have a 'nomadic way of life'. That is not to say they cannot recover it later, if their circumstances and intention change . . . But that would arise if and when they

90 [2002] EWHC 2414 (Admin).

91 [1995] QB 158.

92 [2002] EWHC 2414 (Admin) at para 20.

93 [2003] EWCA Civ 835.

made some future application for permission on the strength of that resumption of the status.

(3) Where, as here, a question is raised before a Planning Inspector as to whether applicants for planning permission are 'gypsies' for the purpose of planning law and policy, he should: (i) clearly direct himself to, and identify, the statutory and policy meaning of that word; and (ii) as a second and separate exercise, decide by reference to that meaning on the facts of the case whether the applicants fall within it . . .

(4) In making the second, factual, decision whether applicants for planning permission are gypsies, the first and most important question is whether they are – to use a neutral expression – actually living a travelling life, whether seasonal or periodic in some other way, at the time of the determination. If they are not, then it is a matter of fact and degree whether the current absence of travelling means that they have not acquired or no longer follow a nomadic habit of life.

(5) On such an issue of fact and degree, the decision-maker may find any one or more of the following circumstances relevant and, if so, of varying weight: (i) the fact that the applicants do or do not come from a traditional gypsy background and/or have or have not followed a nomadic way of life in the past – the possible relevance in either case being that respectively they may be less or more likely to give it up for very long or to abandon it entirely; (ii) the fact that the applicants do or do not have an honest and realistically realisable intention of resuming travelling and, if they do, how soon and in what circumstances; (iii) the reason or reasons for the applicants not living a travelling way of life at the time of the determination and their likely duration'.

Gypsy status and English government guidance

4.130 The decision in *Berry* left ethnic Gypsies and Travellers who had been forced to cease travelling on grounds of old age or ill-health in a particularly unfortunate position – in effect they were precluded from relying on the positive government guidance in Circular 1/94 on the provision of Gypsy and Traveller sites at the very time when they needed a settled base on which to station their caravans in accordance with their lifelong traditional way of living. The Court of Appeal's decision did not reflect the fact that the state owed a positive duty under ECHR Article 8 to facilitate the Gypsy way of life[94] and Mr Berry took his case to the European Court of Human Rights (ECtHR). However, before the ECtHR could consider it, his re-determined planning and enforcement appeals were allowed,

94 *Chapman v UK* (2001) 33 EHRR 399 at para 73.

meaning he was no longer a 'victim' for ECHR purposes. As a consequence, the court found his case to be inadmissible.

4.131 The question whether a person could retain their nomadic status, notwithstanding illness or old age, was dealt with head-on when the government published Circular 1/06, which changed the policy definition of the term 'Gypsies and Travellers'. Its paragraph 15 stated:

> For the purposes of this Circular 'gypsies and travellers' means
>
> Persons of nomadic habit of life whatever their race or origin, including such persons who on grounds only of their own or their family's or dependants' educational or health needs or old age have ceased to travel temporarily or permanently, but excluding members of an organised group of travelling show people or circus people travelling together as such.

4.132 To a substantial extent, this reversed the effect of the Court of Appeal's judgment in *Berry*; although it does not follow that all Gypsies and Travellers who wished to seek planning permission for a caravan site were able to rely upon the positive government guidance in Circular 1/06. For example, if applicants had willingly given up travelling to take up employment, then they would not be able to do so. Disputes concerning 'Gypsy status' continued to arise in planning appeals.

4.133 The original PPTS issued in 2012 by the Coalition Government retained the Circular 1/06 definition. However, the Conservative government issued a more restrictive definition in PPTS 2015:

> 1. For the purposes of this planning policy 'gypsies and travellers' means:
>
> Persons of nomadic habit of life whatever their race or origin, including such persons who on grounds only of their own or their family's or dependants' educational or health needs or old age have ceased to travel temporarily, but excluding members of an organised group of travelling showpeople or circus people travelling together as such.
>
> 2. In determining whether persons are 'gypsies and travellers' for the purposes of this planning policy, consideration should be given to the following issues amongst other relevant matters:
> a) whether they previously led a nomadic habit of life
> b) the reasons for ceasing their nomadic habit of life
> c) whether there is an intention of living a nomadic habit of life in the future, and if so, how soon and in what circumstances.

4.134 By deleting the words 'or permanently' from the planning definition the government has made it more difficult for those ethnic Gypsies and Travellers who are too old to travel for an economic purpose and those whose permanent disabilities prevent such travel to obtain planning permission for a site on which they can live in accordance with their traditional way of life. At the time of writing there is pending before the Court of Appeal a renewed application for permission to challenge an Inspector's appeal decision (based in part on her conclusion that a Romani Gypsy family did not qualify for Gypsy status because they had ceased travelling due to ill health) on the grounds that the PPTS 2015 definition breaches the PSED and the positive duty to facilitate the Gypsy way of life as given effect by Article 8 of the ECHR.[95]

Gypsy status in Wales

4.135 By way of stark contrast, the definition of *Gypsies and Travellers* used in the Welsh Circular PGTSS 2018 is that contained within Housing (Wales) Act 2014 s108:

> Gypsies and Travellers means: (a) Persons of a nomadic habit of life, whatever their race or origin, including – (i) Persons who, on grounds only of their own or their family's or dependant's educational or health needs or old age, have ceased to travel temporarily or permanently, and (ii) Members of an organised group of travelling show people or circus people (whether or not travelling together as such); and (b) All other persons with a cultural tradition of nomadism or of living in a mobile home.

The need for Gypsy and Traveller sites

4.136 The case of *Hedges v Secretary of State for the Environment*[96] is authority for the fact that the national, regional and local need for additional site provision is capable of being a material consideration in planning applications made by Gypsies and Travellers. *Hedges* is also an authority for the proposition that the personal need of a Gypsy or Traveller for a site is a material consideration that should be considered independently of the question of personal circumstances and hardship.[97] An extensive national need remains with a local need in most districts.

95 *Lisa Smith v Secretary of State for Housing Communities and Local Government* (CO/41/2019).

96 [1996] 73 P&CR 534 at 545.

97 [1996] 73 P&CR 534 at 545.

Assessment of the need for Caravan sites

4.137 In recent years need has been assessed in Gypsy and Traveller Accommodation Assessments (GTAAs). The quality and accuracy of these assessments has varied greatly. Those advising Gypsies and Travellers should not assume they are correct but rather subject them to detailed scrutiny. For example, advisers should ask whether clients who were present in the district at the time of the assessment were included in the GTAA and whether local Gypsies and Travellers and their support groups consider the assessment to be robust?

4.138 Until July 2016, local housing authorities were required by Housing Act (HA) 2004 s225 to carry out an assessment of the accommodation needs of Gypsies and Travellers as part of their broader obligation under the Housing Act (HA) 1985 s8(1). Then the law was changed so that the duty under s8(1) includes 'a duty to consider the needs of people residing in or resorting to their district with respect to the provision of – (a) sites on which caravans can be stationed'.[98] This is not limited to ethnic Gypsies and Travellers or those who fall within the definition in PPTS 2015, but extends to other caravan dwellers such as those that reside on in park homes, whose circumstances may be very different from those of Gypsies and Travellers.

4.139 In carrying out its section 8 duty, local housing authorities should:

- remember that the needs of the district are not confined to the needs of persons living in it at the time;[99]
- 'have regard to the special needs of chronically sick or disabled persons';[100] and
- 'review any information which has been brought to their notice, including in particular information brought to their notice as a result of the consideration of the housing conditions in their district under section 3 of the Housing Act 2004'.[101]

The availability of alternative sites

4.140 The approach to be adopted to the issue of alternative sites availability was considered in *Doncaster MBC v First Secretary of State and*

98 Housing and Planning Act 2016 s124 which came into force on 12 July 2016.

99 *Watson v Minister of Local Government and Planning* [1951] 2 KB 779, 783 and the words 'resorting to' in the amended section 8.

100 Chronically Sick and Disabled Persons Act 1970 s3(1).

101 Housing Act 1985 s8(2).

Angela Smith.[102] The LPA challenged the grant of planning permission for a Gypsy site in the Green Belt and, in particular, the planning inspector's view that:

> The absence of any alternative, available, affordable, acceptable and suitable land to which the site occupants could move has to be afforded considerable weight in favour of the development.

The LPA argued that the inspector had set too high a threshold when considering whether there were alternative sites that could accommodate the occupants. The judge disagreed. He noted that, in *Chapman v UK*, the ECtHR had said that the evaluation of suitable alternative accommodation for Gypsies would involve a consideration of the particular needs of the person concerned, his or her family requirements and financial resources; and he concluded that the inspector's assessment of that issue had been entirely in accord with both the decision in *Chapman* and government policy.[103]

Personal circumstances

4.141 The traditional approach in planning law to land-use factors and personal circumstances is contained in Lord Scarman's speech in *Great Portland Estates plc v Westminster CC*:

> ... the principle ... is now well settled. It was stated ... in one sentence in *East Barnet Urban District Council v British Transport Commission* ... Lord Parker CJ said ... 'what is really to be considered is the character of the use of the land, not the particular purpose of a particular occupier.' These words have rightly been recognised as extending beyond the issue of change of use: they are accepted as a statement of general principle in planning law. They apply to development plans as well as to planning control ... However, like all generalisations, Lord Parker CJ's statement has its own limitations. Personal circumstances of an occupier, personal hardship, the difficulties of businesses which are of value to the character of a community are not to be ignored in the administration of planning control. It would be inhuman pedantry to exclude from the control of our environment the human factor. The human factor is always present, of course, indirectly as the background to the consideration of the character of land use. It can, however, and sometimes should, be given direct effect as an exceptional or special circumstance. But such circumstances, when they arise, fall to be considered

102 [2007] EWHC 1034 (Admin), George Bartlett QC.

103 It should also be noted that there is no requirement in planning policy or case law for an applicant to prove that no alternative sites are available: see *South Cambridgeshire DC v SSCLG and Julie Brown* [2008] EWCA Civ 1010 para 37.

not as a general rule but as exceptions to a general rule to be met in special cases. If a planning authority is to give effect to them, a specific case has to be made and the planning authority must give reasons for accepting it.[104]

4.142 While personal circumstances carry little or no weight in the vast majority of planning cases, they are often of crucial importance when Gypsies and Travellers apply for planning permission due primarily to the chronic under-provision of authorised sites and the consequent impact this has on Gypsies and Travellers life chances. Personal circumstances are particularly relevant where the proposed site is situated within a Green Belt.

4.143 As has already been noted, there is a general presumption against inappropriate development within the Green Belt. Inappropriate development is, by definition, harmful to the Green Belt and such development should not be approved, except in 'very special circumstances'.[105] It is for the evidence to justify inappropriate development and 'very special circumstances' will not exist unless the harm by reason of inappropriateness, and any other harm, is clearly outweighed by other considerations.

4.144 Gypsy and Traveller sites are not categorised as 'appropriate development' and, in practice, a Gypsy or Traveller seeking planning permission for a site within the Green Belt will have to show that there is a pressing need for further sites, that there are no suitable sites available and/or that their personal circumstances justify the grant of planning permission.

4.145 In *Doncaster MBC v Secretary of State for the Environment, Transport and the Regions*[106] and *R (Chelmsford BC) v First Secretary of State*,[107] Sullivan J emphasised the importance of the guidance then in PPG 2[108] and, in Doncaster he also emphasised the fact that it is important that the need to establish the existence of '"very special circumstances" . . . is not watered down'.[109]

4.146 However, a combination of factors, none of them very special in their own right, can, when taken together, amount to very special

104 [1985] AC 661 at 669–670.

105 Now NPPF para 143.

106 [2002] EWHC 808 (Admin).

107 [2003] EWHC 2978 (Admin).

108 Planning Policy Guidance note 2, which was revoked when the NPPF was issued. see now NPPF paras 133–147.

109 [2002] EWHC 808 (Admin) at para 74.

circumstances. In *Basildon DC v First Secretary of State,*[110] the LPA challenged a decision taken by an inspector to grant a Gypsy family planning permission for a site in the Green Belt. The inspector had concluded that very special circumstances existed having taken account of a number of factors, including:

- the local authority's failure to assess the needs of Gypsies and Travellers within its area;
- the severe shortage of suitable alternative and available sites within the area;
- the educational needs of the children of the family; and
- the fact that the dismissal of the appeal would force the family to choose between abandoning their traditional way of life by accepting local authority housing in order to keep their children in school and a return to life on the road.

4.147 The LPA argued that very special circumstances could not merely be factors that weigh in favour of granting planning permission but that each factor relied upon had to be of such a quality that it could reasonably be called 'very special'. Sullivan J rejected this, making it clear that:

> 10. . . . There is no reason why a number of factors ordinary in themselves cannot combine to create something very special. The claimant's approach flies in the face of the approach normally adopted to the determination of planning issues: to consider all relevant factors in the round . . .
>
> 17. The short answer to the claimant's argument is that in planning, as in ordinary life, a number of ordinary factors when combined together result in something very special. Whether any particular combination amounts to very special circumstances . . . will be a matter for the planning judgment of the decision-taker.

Sullivan J distinguished the case from the *Doncaster* and *Chelmsford* cases – in both those cases only the apparently unexceptional educational needs of children living on the site had been relied upon as 'very special circumstances'.

4.148 The education of the children of Gypsies and Travellers may be of particular relevance in a planning application and if those needs are sufficiently strong (for example, because a child has special educational needs that can only be met while the child is living on a settled site), then they may be sufficient to clearly outweigh the objections to

110 [2004] EWHC 2759 (Admin).

the use of land within the Green Belt as a caravan site (on their own or in conjunction with other considerations). Similarly, health considerations are often a very important factor in planning cases and can prove to be crucial.

4.149 In *South Buckinghamshire DC v Porter (No 2)*, the House of Lords accepted that a combination of Gypsy status, the lack of alternative sites in the area and Mrs Porter's chronic ill-health amounted to very special circumstances.[111]

4.150 *First Secretary of State v Simmons*[112] was another case where the courts considered a decision-maker's conclusion on the issue of whether 'very special circumstances' existed to justify development in a Green Belt. The local planning authority issued an enforcement notice requiring Mr Simmons to discontinue the use of Green Belt land for stationing caravans on the basis that its use as a Gypsy caravan site constituted inappropriate development in the Green Belt. On appeal against the enforcement notice, the secretary of state found that there was an unmet need for sites in the locality, but did not consider that this was sufficient to amount to 'very special circumstances'. The secretary of state noted that Mr Simmons' pattern of travel took him to areas of the country that were not within the Green Belt, that there had been no real effort to find an alternative site outside the Green Belt, and that this weighed against his case.[113] The Court of Appeal upheld the secretary of state's decision. It follows that Gypsies and Travellers seeking planning permission for a site on land in an area within the Green Belt or covered by some form of national designation, would be well advised to present evidence to show that they need to live in that area, for example, because of local connections or other commitments, or that they have searched for alternative sites beyond the designated area in vain.[114] Evidence of a search having been carried out could include correspondence with local estate agents and local authorities as well as evidence of actual searches that have been undertaken.

111 [2004] UKHL 33, para 55.

112 [2005] EWCA Civ 1295. By way of an update, Mr and Mrs Simmons' obtained permanent planning permission on appeal in January 2017.

113 See also *Buckley v UK* (1996) 23 EHRR 101.

114 Though it should not be forgotten that there is no requirement in planning policy or case law for an applicant to prove that no alternative sites are available: See *South Cambridgeshire DC v SSCLG and Julie Brown* [2008] EWCA Civ 1010, para 37.

4.151 Since then, very special circumstances have been found in many appeal decisions.[115] In *Doncaster MBC v Secretary of State for Communities and Local Government*,[116] Gilbart J made it clear that:

> The new policy PPTS does not prevent a decision maker . . . from giving whatever weight they consider they should to a consideration which is material. The PPTS does not prevent it by its terms. If a decision maker could not rely on either to establish the very special circumstances required, the words in the PPTS would be surplusage. Further, a decision maker is not bound to apply a policy, provided he or she gives reasons for not doing so, as is long settled legal principle. What the PPTS does do is to say to decision makers that the policy regards it as unlikely that unmet need and personal circumstances are to be enough to overcome the hurdle posed by Green Belt policy. It does not say that either or both could not do so.[117]

4.152 Where personal circumstances tip the balance in favour of a grant of planning permission, the permission is likely to be subject to a condition making its benefit personal to the applicants and their dependants.

Intentional unauthorised development

4.153 On 31 August 2015 chief planning officers were notified that 'intentional unauthorised development' should be considered a material consideration to be weighed in the determination of planning appeals and retrospective planning applications received after that date. The government's rationale for this policy change was made clear in a WMS issued on 17 December 2015 which stated: that it was concerned about the harm that is caused where the development of land has been undertaken in advance of obtaining planning permission; that in such cases, there is no opportunity to appropriately limit or mitigate the harm that has already taken place; and that such cases can involve local planning authorities having to take expensive and time-consuming enforcement action.

115 Including *Dartford BC v Secretary of State for Communities and Local Government* [2016] EWHC 635 (Admin); *Rose Meadow Farm Ltd v South Staffordshire Council* [2015] PAD 66, para 30; *Thurrock BC v Secretary of State for Communities and Local Government* [2016] EWHC 200 (Admin); *Coates v Dartford BC*, APP/T2215/A/12/2182990; *McDonagh v South Gloucestershire Council*, APP/P0119/W/15/3065767 [2016] PAD 18; and *Barney-Smith v East Dorset DC*, APP/U1240/W/16/3147485.

116 [2016] EWHC 2876 (Admin).

117 Para 69.

Fear of crime

4.154 In *Smith v First Secretary of State*[118] the Court of Appeal quashed an inspector's decision to refuse planning permission for a Gypsy site in circumstances where he had based his decision, in part, on local residents' fears that crime would increase in the area if planning permission were granted. Rather than being based on extrapolation from past events, this fear arose from assumptions as to the characteristics of the future occupiers that was unsupported by evidence. The Court of Appeal held that 'fear' had to have a reasonable basis, and the object of that fear had to be the use of the land. A caravan site is not inherently likely to cause difficulties to neighbours. As Buxton LJ said:

> But a caravan site is not like a polluting factory or bail hostel, likely of its very nature to produce difficulties for its neighbours. Granted that the evidence of recently past events attributable to the site was sparse, or on a strict view non-existent, the fear must be that the concern as to future events was or may have been based in part on the fact that the site was to be a gypsy site. It cannot be right to view land use for that purpose as inherently creating the real concern that attaches to an institution such as a bail hostel.[119]

4.155 Where concern for the future rested not on extrapolation from past events, but at least partly on assumptions unsupported by evidence as to the characteristics of the future occupiers, then it must not be taken into account. The decision was remitted to the secretary of state for reconsideration and the families subsequently gained five years' temporary planning permission.

Human rights as a material consideration

4.156 Local authorities, planning inspectors, the secretary of state and the courts are all public bodies for the purposes of HRA 1998 s6(3) and are, therefore, subject to the duty imposed by HRA 1998 s6(1) to act compatibly with the ECHR when dealing with applications for planning permission made by Gypsies and Travellers.[120]

4.157 In 2001, the ECtHR gave its judgment in five cases brought by British Gypsies who had been refused planning permission to place

118 [2005] EWCA Civ 859; [2006] JPL 386.

119 At para 10.

120 For a detailed consideration of the HRA 1998 as it affects Gypsies and Travellers see chapter 2 above.

their caravan homes on their own land.[121] The UK government settled a sixth case, in which the ECtHR had previously found a breach of the ECHR, by a payment of £60,000 and full costs.[122]

4.158 The applicants in each case had complained of breaches of various ECHR rights, notably Article 8. This provides:

> (1) Everyone has the right to respect for his private and family life, his home and his correspondence.
>
> (2) There shall be no interference by a public authority with the exercise of this right except such as is in accordance with the law and is necessary in a democratic society in the interests of national security, public safety or the economic well-being of the country, for the prevention of disorder or crime, for the protection of health or morals, or for the protection of the rights and freedoms of others.

4.159 The lead case, *Chapman v UK*,[123] concerned a Gypsy woman who had bought land in the Three Rivers District of Hertfordshire. This district contained no provision for Gypsies and Travellers and was in a county that had a history of under-provision for Gypsies and Travellers. This had led to a High Court declaration that the local authority was in breach of the (now repealed) statutory duty to provide Gypsy caravan sites.[124] Mrs Chapman's land was, however, situated in a Green Belt.

4.160 The ECtHR first considered whether the prima facie rights contained in article 8(1) were in issue. It unanimously held that they were, not only in the case of the right to respect for home (which in the light of an earlier decision of the ECtHR in *Buckley v UK*[125] the government had conceded), but also in the case of the right to respect for private and family life. As the ECtHR said:

> ... the applicant's occupation of her caravan is an integral part of her ethnic identity as a Gypsy, reflecting the long tradition of that minority of following a travelling lifestyle. This is the case even though, under the pressure of development and diverse policies or from their own volition, many Gypsies no longer live a wholly nomadic existence and increasingly settle for long periods in one place in order to facilitate, for example,

121 *Chapman v UK* (2001) 33 EHRR 399. See also *Beard v UK* (2001) 33 EHRR 442; *Coster v UK* (2001) 33 EHRR 479; *Smith (Jane) v UK* (2001) 33 EHRR 712; and *Lee v UK* (2001) App No 25289/94.

122 *Varey v UK* App No 26662/95.

123 (2001) 33 EHRR 399, (2001) 10 BHRR 48.

124 *R v Secretary of State for the Environment ex p Lee* 54 P&CR 311; *R v Secretary of State for the Environment ex p Smith* [1988] COD 3.

125 (1996) 23 EHRR 101.

> the education of their children. Measures which affect the applicant's stationing of her caravans have therefore a wider impact than on the right to respect for home. They also affect her ability to maintain her identity as a Gypsy and to lead her private and family life in accordance with that tradition.[126]

4.161 The judges of the ECtHR disagreed on whether the interference by the state was justified as 'necessary in a democratic society'. A majority of ten of the 17 judges held that it was, while a minority dissented. There was a distinct difference between the Western European judges, a majority of whom found in the applicants' favour, and the Eastern European ones who, with the exception of the Slovak judge, found in favour of the UK government. Schiemann LJ, the ad hoc UK judge, also found in the government's favour.

4.162 The majority recognised that:

> . . . there may be said to be an emerging international consensus amongst the Contracting States of the Council of Europe recognising the special needs of minorities and an obligation to protect their security, identity and lifestyle [see in particular the Framework Convention for the Protection of Minorities[127]], not only for the purpose of safeguarding the interests of the minorities themselves but to preserve a cultural diversity of value to the whole community.[128]

However, they were 'not persuaded that the consensus is sufficiently concrete for it to derive any guidance as to the conduct or standards which Contracting States consider desirable in any particular situation'.[129] In so stating, they left open the possibility that the consensus may harden sufficiently for the ECtHR to bear it in mind in future judgments.

4.163 The majority also recognised a positive obligation on states to facilitate the Gypsy way of life:

> As intimated in the *Buckley* judgment, the vulnerable position of Gypsies as a minority means that some special consideration should be given to their needs and their different lifestyle both in the relevant regulatory planning framework and in arriving at the decisions in particular cases . . . To this extent there is thus a positive obligation imposed on the

126 *Chapman v UK* (2001) 33 EHRR 399, (2001) 10 BHRR 48, para 73.

127 Framework Convention for the Protection of National Minorities, Strasbourg, 1/2/1195, Council of Europe Doc ETS 157.

128 *Chapman v UK* (2001) 33 EHRR 399, (2001) 10 BHRR 48, para 93.

129 (2001) 33 EHRR 399, para 94.

> Contracting States by virtue of Article 8 to facilitate the Gypsy way of life . . .[130]

4.164 However, the majority relied upon the doctrine of 'margin of appreciation'[131] to find for the government, holding:

> . . . a margin of appreciation must, inevitably, be left to the national authorities, who by reason of their direct and continuous contact with the vital forces of their countries are in principle better placed than an international court to evaluate local needs and conditions.[132]

This doctrine depends on the international nature of the ECtHR. It does not apply to national courts acting under the HRA 1998.[133]

4.165 While the government succeeded, it did not escape criticism from the majority, who commented:

> . . . the issue for determination . . . is not the acceptability or not of a general situation, however deplorable, in the United Kingdom in the light of the United Kingdom's undertakings in international law, but the narrower one whether the particular circumstances of the case disclose a violation of the applicant's, Mrs Chapman's, right to respect for her home under article 8 . . .[134]

4.166 The minority delivered a strong dissenting judgment in respect of Article 8. They accepted:

> . . . that the examination of planning objections to a particular use of a site is not a role for which this Court is well-suited . . . Where town and country planning is concerned, the Court has previously noted that this involves the exercise of discretionary judgment in the implementation of policies adopted in the interest of the community . . .[135]

4.167 However, the dissenting judges took a different approach to the treatment of minorities stating:

> There is an emerging consensus amongst the member States of the Council of Europe recognising the special needs of minorities and an obligation to protect their security, identity and lifestyle, not only for the purpose of safeguarding the interests of the minorities themselves but also in order to preserve a cultural diversity of value to the whole community. This consensus includes a recognition that the protection of

130 (2001) 33 EHRR 399, para 96.

131 See paras 2.41–2.42.

132 (2001) 33 EHRR 399, para 91.

133 See the Court of Appeal decision in *South Buckinghamshire DC v Porter* [2001] EWCA Civ 1549, para 25, per Simon Brown LJ (upheld by the House of Lords).

134 (2001) 33 EHRR 399, para 100.

135 (2001) 33 EHRR 399, joint dissenting opinion, p435.

the rights of minorities, such as Gypsies, requires not only that Contracting States refrain from policies or practices which discriminate against them but that also, where necessary, they should take positive steps to improve their situation through, for example, legislation or specific programmes. We cannot therefore agree with the majority's assertion that the consensus is not sufficiently concrete or with their conclusion that the complexity of the competing interests renders the Court's role a strictly supervisory one . . .[136]

4.168 The dissenting judges bore in mind the difficulties of Gypsies, stating:

> The long-term failures of local authorities to make effective provision for Gypsies in their planning policies is evident from the history of implementation of measures concerning Gypsy sites, both public and private . . . the Government is already well aware that the legislative and policy framework does not provide in practice for the needs of the Gypsy minority and that their policy of leaving it to local authorities to make provision for Gypsies has been of limited effectiveness . . . it is in our opinion disproportionate to take steps to evict a Gypsy family from their home on their own land in circumstances where there has not been shown to be any other lawful, alternative site reasonably open to them. It would accordingly be for the authorities to adopt such measures as they consider appropriate to ensure that the planning system affords effective respect for the home, private life and family life of Gypsies such as the applicant.[137]

4.169 In addition to joining the dissenting opinion, Judge Bonello emphasised Hertfordshire County Council's proven non-compliance with the law. In a separate opinion he stated:

> A public authority owes as great an obligation to comply with the law as any individual. Its responsibility is eminently more than that of individuals belonging to vulnerable classes who are virtually forced to disregard the law in order to be able to exercise their fundamental right to a private and family life – individuals who have to contravene the law due to the operation of the prior failures of the public authorities. In the present case, both the public authorities and the individual had undoubtedly trespassed the boundaries of legality. But it was the public authority's default in observing the law that precipitated and induced the subsequent default by the individual. That failure of the authorities has brought about a situation which almost justifies the defence of necessity. Why a human rights court should look with more sympathy at the far-reaching

136 (2001) 33 EHRR 399, pp435–436.

137 (2001) 33 EHRR 399, p438. In granting leave to appeal in *South Buckinghamshire DC v Porter* [2001] EWCA Civ 1549, Sedley LJ stated that our domestic courts could refer to the minority decision in *Chapman v UK*.

> breach of law committed by the powerful, than at that forced on the weak, has not yet been properly explained.[138]

4.170 Though the applicants in *Chapman* were unsuccessful, the HRA 1998 principles derived from that case are of general application and will be relevant in almost every case where Gypsies and Travellers seek planning permission for use of land as a caravan site. Mrs Chapman subsequently gained planning permission to remain on her land. The decision in *Chapman* can be contrasted with the case of *Chichester DC v First Secretary of State*,[139] where the Court of Appeal upheld the decision of a planning inspector in circumstances where he had concluded that the refusal of planning permission would breach the article 8 rights of a Gypsy family.

Human rights and offers of conventional housing

4.171 The provisions of the HRA 1998 and the ECHR have been applied by the domestic courts to determine whether the availability of conventional housing should be taken into consideration (that is, a material consideration) when Gypsies and Travellers seek planning permission for their own caravan sites.

4.172 In *Clarke v Secretary of State for the Environment, Transport and the Regions*,[140] an inspector dismissed an appeal against the local planning authority's refusal of planning permission to site a Gypsy caravan in a special landscape area. Mr Clarke argued that the inspector had wrongly taken into account an offer by the authority of conventional housing accommodation and that this was in breach of ECHR Articles 8 and 14.[141] At first instance Burton J held:

> ... it can amount to a breach of articles 8 and 14 to weigh in the balance and hold against a Gypsy applying for planning permission, or indeed resisting eviction from ... land, that he or she has refused conventional housing accommodation as being contrary to his or her culture. Such circumstances ... are and should be, limited, just as they are if ... it is to be alleged similarly to be impermissible, in relevant circumstances, to hold it against or penalise a religious or strictly observant Christian, Jew or Muslim because he or she will not, and thus cannot work on certain

138 (2001) 33 EHRR 399, p 441.

139 [2004] EWCA Civ 1248, [2005] 1 WLR 279.

140 [2001] EWHC 800 Admin, [2002] JPL 552.

141 See para 4.158 above, for Article 8. Article 14 provides: 'The enjoyment of the rights and freedoms set forth in this Convention shall be secured without discrimination on any ground such as sex, race, colour, language, religion, political or other opinion, national or social origin, association with a national minority, property, birth or other status.'

> days, or to hold it against, or penalise, a strictly observant Buddhist, Muslim, Jew or Sikh because he eats or will not eat certain foods, or will not wear certain clothing It is not, and cannot be, a formality to establish this, and the onus is upon the person such as a Gypsy who seeks to establish it.[142]

4.173 After considering the need to establish Gypsy status, he said:

> . . . if such be established then . . . bricks and mortar, if offered, are unsuitable, just as would be the offer of a rat-infested barn.[143] It would be contrary to articles 8 and 14 to expect such a person to accept conventional housing and to hold it against him or her that he has not accepted it, or is not prepared to accept it, even as a last resort factor.[144]

4.174 The inspector's decision was quashed on the basis that he either took into account impermissible factors relating to conventional housing or made insufficient findings in respect of such factors.

4.175 The LPA's appeal was dismissed and the Court of Appeal held that the approach of Burton J was entirely in accord with the approach of the ECtHR in *Chapman*.[145] Buxton LJ held:

> What the judge seems to me to be . . . rightly directing the inspector to, is a careful examination of the objections of the Clarke family to living in conventional housing in order to determine the extent to which article 8 is truly engaged, and the nature of its engagement by the combination of their Gypsy identity and their opposition to conventional housing. Only when the inspector has made that determination in clearer terms than he adopted in his present letter will it be possible for him properly to engage in the balancing consideration that Burton J envisages . . . This was a case where a Convention right was potentially engaged and in such cases a more intense scrutiny of the facts upon which that right is asserted needs to be engaged in before the court can indulge in the balancing exercise that article 8(2) imposes on it.[146]

The best interests of children

4.176 The best interests of children are of special importance.[147] Although the claimant in *Stevens v Secretary of State for Communities and Local Government*[148] failed in her bid to quash an appeal decision in which

142 [2001] EWHC 800 (Admin), para 30.
143 See *R v South Herefordshire DC ex p Miles* 17 HLR 82, per Woolf J.
144 [2001] EWHC 800 Admin, para 34.
145 *Chapman v UK* (2001) 33 EHRR 399.
146 [2002] EWCA Civ 819, para 15.
147 See paras 2.96–2.101.
148 [2013] EWHC 792 (Admin).

a planning inspector had refused her planning permission for a Gypsy site in the Green Belt, the judgment of Hickinbottom J contains comments that are likely to be of importance in many Gypsy and Traveller cases:

> 60. . . . the interests of any relevant children cannot properly be regarded as something distinct and apart from the necessary section 70 balancing exercise: they are an integral, and important, part of that exercise . . .
>
> 69. . . . in respect of the approach of a planning decision-maker, the following propositions can be derived.
>
> i) Given the scope of planning decisions and the nature of the right to respect for family and private life, planning decision-making will often engage article 8. In those circumstances, relevant article 8 rights will be a material consideration which the decision-maker must take into account.
>
> ii) Where the article 8 rights are those of children, they must be seen in the context of article 3 of the UNCRC,[149] which requires a child's best interests to be a primary consideration.
>
> iii) This requires the decision-maker, first, to identify what the child's best interests are. In a planning context, they are likely to be consistent with those of his parent or other carer who is involved in the planning decision-making process; and, unless circumstances indicate to the contrary, the decision-maker can assume that that carer will properly represent the child's best interests, and properly represent and evidence the potential adverse impact of any decision upon that child's best interests.
>
> iv) Once identified, although a primary consideration, the best interests of the child are not determinative of the planning issue. Nor does respect for the best interests of a relevant child mean that the planning exercise necessarily involves merely assessing whether the public interest in ensuring planning controls is maintained outweighs the best interests of the child. Most planning cases will have too many competing rights and interests, and will be too factually complex, to allow such an exercise.
>
> v) However, no other consideration must be regarded as more important or given greater weight than the best interests of any child, merely by virtue of its inherent nature apart from the context of the individual case. Further, the best interests of any child must be kept at the forefront of the decision-maker's mind as he examines all material considerations and performs the exercise of planning judgment on the basis of them; and, when considering any decision he might make (and, of course, the eventual decision he does make), he needs to assess whether the adverse impact of such a decision on the interests of the child is proportionate.

149 United Nations Convention on the Rights of the Child.

vi) Whether the decision-maker has properly performed this exercise is a question of substance, not form. However, if an inspector on an appeal sets out his reasoning with regard to any child's interests in play, even briefly, that will be helpful not only to those involved in the application but also to the court in any later challenge, in understanding how the decision-maker reached the decision that the adverse impact to the interests of the child to which the decision gives rise is proportionate. It will be particularly helpful if the reasoning shows that the inspector has brought his mind to bear upon the adverse impact of the decision he has reached on the best interests of the child, and has concluded that that impact is in all the circumstances proportionate . . .'

Psychiatric evidence

4.177 Psychiatric evidence will be important in some cases. In *AZ v Secretary of State for Communities and Local Government*[150] AZ challenged a planning inspector's decision to dismiss his planning appeal on grounds that the inspector failed properly to consider the psychiatric evidence, AZ's rights under ECHR Article 8 and those of his family, and the possibility of a personal condition, temporary permission or both. The High Court upheld his application for the following reasons:

1) the inspector wrongly limited consideration of the psychiatric, psychological and medical evidence to AZ's fear of enclosed spaces;
2) an ECHR Article 8 proportionality assessment was not the same as a consideration of whether AZ's personal circumstances amounted to very special circumstances and the inspector should have undertaken a structured balancing exercise or proportionality assessment and properly considered AZ's family life; and
3) having ruled out granting permanent planning permission, the inspector should have considered: i) amending the terms of the permission to reduce the perceived harm; ii) a personal condition; iii) a time-limited condition; and iv) the appropriate length of a time-limited condition

Making an application for planning permission

4.178 An application for planning permission should include a plan showing the boundaries of the site; and the application fee. The site area should be specified in the application form, preferably in square

150 [2012] EWHC 3660 (Admin), [2013] JPL 713.

metres or hectares. Although a high degree of mathematical precision is seldom essential, guesses can cause difficulty at a later stage. Advisers may also wish to consider submitting information on the following matters:

- evidence of the applicant's PPTS 2015 Gypsy status and of Gypsy ethnicity, including details of travelling by the applicant and by family members for the purpose of work and copies (not originals in case they are lost) of family photographs;
- where applicants and their families have ceased travelling temporarily, evidence of any intention to resume travelling or of the health or educational reasons for ceasing to travel;
- details and evidence of any factors relevant to the personal circumstances of members of the family, in particular any health, educational or other welfare needs. Ill-health should be evidenced by a detailed letter or report from the relevant GP or consultant. Letters from headteachers and/or Traveller education support staff can also be of considerable benefit. If any potential occupier is registered disabled, this should be stated;
- details and evidence of attempts to find alternative sites, including, for example, letters to local estate agents and evidence of inquiries of local authorities;
- evidence of any aversion to conventional housing;
- occupational needs;
- any specific need for accommodation that would assist Romani Gypsies and Irish Travellers who keep animals, particularly horses and ponies;
- details of failure of policy;[151]
- how any harm to visual amenity can be overcome by a landscaping condition.

Conditions

4.179 TCPA 1990 s70(1)(a) enables LPAs to grant planning permissions subject to conditions. In practice, all planning permissions include some conditions. It is important to think carefully about conditions, offering ones that make planning permission more likely while

151 For recent examples of appeal decisions that bore this in mind see *McDonagh v South Gloucestershire Council* APP/P0119/W/15/3065767 [2016] PAD 18, paras 25–26; and *Barney-Smith v East Dorset DC* APP/U1240/W/16/3147485, para 46.

avoiding ones that will cause problems in the future. In Gypsy and Traveller cases these may include, among others, the following:

- a condition limiting the occupation of the site to Gypsies as defined in PPTS 2015;
- a condition making the planning permission temporary;
- a condition making the planning permission personal to certain specific individuals;[152]
- a landscaping condition; and
- a condition setting back gates and hedges or fencing in the interests of highway safety.

4.180 Conditions can be very useful, enabling permission to be granted where it would otherwise be refused. As NPPF para 54 states:

> Local planning authorities should consider whether otherwise unacceptable development could be made acceptable through the use of conditions or planning obligations . . .

4.181 Government advice on conditions is contained in NPPF para 55 and 206. The latter repeats longstanding advice, providing:

> Planning conditions should be kept to a minimum and only imposed where they are necessary, relevant to planning and to the development to be permitted, enforceable, precise and reasonable in all other respects'.

4.182 Further guidance on conditions is given in the NPPG's section on the 'Use of Planning Conditions', including:

> When used properly, conditions can enhance the quality of development and enable development proposals to proceed where it would otherwise have been necessary to refuse planning permission, by mitigating the adverse effects of the development. The objectives of planning are best served when the power to attach conditions to a planning permission is exercised in a way that is clearly seen to be fair, reasonable and practicable. It is important to ensure that conditions are tailored to tackle specific problems, rather than standardised or used to impose broad unnecessary controls.[153]

> Circumstances where a temporary permission may be appropriate include where a trial run is needed in order to assess the effect of the development on the area or where it is expected that the planning circumstances will change in a particular way at the end of that period.[154]

152 Typically the appellant and other adult residents and their dependants – as to the meaning of dependants see *Shortt v Secretary of State for Communities and Local Government* [2015] EWCA Civ 1192.

153 NPPG reference ID: 21a-001-20140306.

154 NPPG reference ID: 21a-014-20140306.

> Unless the permission otherwise provides, planning permission runs with the land and it is rarely appropriate to provide otherwise. There may be exceptional occasions where granting planning permission for development that would not normally be permitted on the site could be justified on planning grounds because of who would benefit from the permission. For example, conditions limiting benefits to a particular class of people, such as new residential accommodation in the open countryside for agricultural or forestry workers, may be justified on the grounds that an applicant has successfully demonstrated an exceptional need. A condition used to grant planning permission solely on grounds of an individual's personal circumstances will scarcely ever be justified in the case of permission for the erection of a permanent building, but might, for example, result from enforcement action which would otherwise cause individual hardship.[155]

4.183 DoE Circular 11/95 appendix A contains model conditions.[156] Advisers should consider whether to suggest such conditions when seeking planning permission or appealing against the refusal of permission. For example, if a business use of part of the site is proposed, a condition against working at night and on Sundays and bank and public holidays might be appropriate. Possible conditions are given in appendix A, such as:

> 65. No machinery shall be operated, no process shall be carried out and no deliveries taken at or despatched from the site outside the following times [ ] nor at any time on Sundays, Bank or Public Holidays.

4.184 If planning permission would not have been granted for use of land as a caravan site, but for the fact that it is to meet the needs of Gypsies and Travellers, a condition limiting occupancy to Gypsies as defined in planning policy may be appropriate. If permission is granted in an unsatisfactory location because of a need for sites that the LPA anticipates will be met within a few years, a temporary permission may be appropriate. Similarly, if the site is only justified by personal circumstances, a personal permission may be appropriate. In practice, most applicants will accept the imposition of a condition that limits occupation to Gypsies and Travellers. Applicants often give reasons why a personal or temporary permission is not necessary, but then state, in the alternative, that they would prefer the imposition of such a condition rather than suffer an outright refusal.

155 NPPG reference ID: 21a-015-20140306

156 The rest of the circular has been revoked. See: www.gov.uk/government/publications/the-use-of-conditions-in-planning-permissions-circular-11-1995.

4.185 Where a LPA refuses an application on a ground that could be overcome by a condition, this is often the basis for an application at appeal for a partial award of costs to cover the costs of fighting that ground. Where it has been necessary to employ expert witnesses to challenge such a ground, for example, in the case of a highway or flooding objection, these costs may be considerable.

4.186 Conditions limiting the grant of planning permission to a specific period are known as temporary permissions. These are common in Gypsy and Traveller cases, especially where an LPA says they will have an appropriate policy in place in a few years' time. In *Linfoot v Secretary of State for Communities and Local Government*[157] HHJ Sycamore quashed a decision of a planning inspector, who had refused an appeal against a refusal of an application for temporary planning permission for change of use for the siting of caravans. The inspector had failed to take into account the argument that there was a reasonable expectation that alternative sites would become available in the wider area. His decision focused entirely on the district's needs and on the absence of evidence that the LPA would embark on a new needs assessment. Given the findings as to the significant need at regional and county level, it followed that it was reasonable to expect that sites would become available in the wider area. He had failed to take into account, when considering temporary permission, whether planning circumstances would change in the wider area within the time for which temporary permission was sought. There was a real possibility that consideration of that matter would have made a difference. There was substantial doubt as to whether he had reached the decision having taken account of all relevant matters.

4.187 Words within the grant of a planning permission do not have the same effect as a condition. So, for example, if there is a planning permission for ten caravans on a site without a planning condition limiting the number of caravans on it, the site can be expanded up to the point where the expansion involves a material change of use. This can apply to old planning permissions granted at a time when it was not necessarily understood. Hickinbottom J clearly explained the point in a case relating to a Park Homes site:[158]

> ... the grant identifies what can be done – what is permitted – so far as use of land is concerned; whereas conditions identify what cannot be done – what is forbidden. Simply because something is expressly

157 [2012] EWHC 3514 (Admin).

158 *Cotswold Grange Country Park v Secretary of State for Communities and Local Government* [2014] EWHC 1138 (Admin); [2014] JPL 981.

permitted in the grant does not mean that everything else is prohibited. Unless what is proposed is a material change of use – for which planning permission is required, because such a change is caught in the definition of development – generally, the only things which are effectively prohibited by a grant of planning permission are those things that are the subject of a condition, a breach of condition being an enforceable breach of planning control.[159]

Appealing against a refusal of planning permission

4.188 If the LPA refuses permission, the applicant may appeal to the secretary of state[160] within six months of the date of refusal of permission. However where there is an enforcement notice in a place this period is reduced to 28 days.[161]

4.189 Most appeals are determined by an inspector appointed by from the Planning Inspectorate. Some are determined by the secretary of state or the Welsh Ministers (in reality, a civil servant acting on their behalf) after consideration of a report prepared by an inspector.[162] There are four procedures for an appeal:

1) the appeal is determined by an inspector having taken account of written representations submitted by the parties; or
2) a hearing is held and the appeal is determined by an inspector; or
3) an inquiry is held and the appeal is determined by an inspector; or
4) the appeal is determined by the secretary of state following an inquiry held by an inspector.

The four different types of appeal are governed by different procedural rules. The time limits imposed by these must be obeyed. Failure to do so may disadvantage the appellant considerably.

159 At para 15.

160 (Or Welsh Ministers) TCPA 1990 s78.

161 Town and Country Planning (General Development Procedure) (Amendment) (England) Order 2010 No 567 art 6, which came into force on 6 April 2010. This has since been consolidated and is now in the Town and Country Planning (Development Management Procedure) Order 2015 art 37(2) and (7).

162 Town and Country Planning (Determination of Appeals by Appointed Persons) (Prescribed Classes) Regulations 1997 mean that most appeals are determined by planning inspectors. In particular, regs 3 and 4 provide that appeals under TCPA 1990 s78 (appeals against planning decisions and failure to take such decisions) and s174 (appeals against enforcement notices) will be dealt with by inspectors unless the secretary of state takes the exceptional step of recovering them.

4.190 An appeal is a fresh determination of the merits of an application. As such, although the history of the matter may be of relevance, the principal matters are likely to be the factual situation and the current policy position at the date of the appeal.

4.191 Advisers assisting Gypsies and Travellers should, therefore, include in the appeal documentation the material adduced in support of the application. In addition, they should also answer the reasons given by the LPA for refusing planning permission and bring their evidence up to date (particularly where a case relies on personal circumstances and welfare needs). Where the LPA is relying upon policies that conflict with government advice (for example, an old criteria-based policy that, in practice, included a combination of criteria that is too difficult to meet), then that point should be explicitly made. The inspector should be invited to disregard any racist material such as letters from local residents containing offensive assertions against Romani Gypsies or Irish Travellers. Thorough preparation is necessary. If a point is omitted, it will not normally be possible to raise it in a subsequent challenge before the High Court.[163]

Challenging a planning appeal decision in the High Court

4.192 An appeal decision taken in respect of the refusal of a planning application may only be challenged by an application to the High Court under TCPA 1990 s288 on the ground that the appeal decision was not within the powers of, or did not comply with, the relevant requirements of the TCPA 1990. An application for permission to make such a challenge can only be made within six weeks of the date on the decision letter. This period cannot be extended under any circumstances.

4.193 The principles affecting a statutory review under TCPA 1990 s288 were conveniently summarised in *Seddon Properties v Secretary of State for the Environment*:[164]

- decision-makers must not act perversely;

163 *Smith v Secretary of State for the Environment, Transport and the Regions* [2001] EWCA Civ 1550. In that case it had not been argued at the planning inquiry that the development plan did not comply with DoE Circular 1/94.

164 42 P&CR 26–28, Forbes J – for a fuller report see [1978] 2 EGLR 148. The same principles apply to judicial review of an LPA's decision to grant planning permission.

- they must not take into account irrelevant matters or fail to take into account that which is relevant;
- they must abide by statutory procedures; and
- they must not depart from the principles of natural justice.

4.194 Case-law has made it clear that:

- questions of planning judgment are for the decision-maker, not the court;[165]
- the requirement to take into account all relevant considerations is limited to those matters which might cause the decision-maker to reach a different decision;[166] and
- the decision-maker, while required to have regard to every material consideration, need only state reasons in respect of the principal controversial issues.[167]

4.195 So, for example, a decision of the secretary of state was quashed where he had to deal with the issue of the grant of temporary planning permission and proportionality in the context of the ECHR Article 8 right but had failed to do so.[168]

4.196 Decision-makers have a duty to give adequate and intelligible reasons. The House of Lords restated this when it upheld a decision to grant a Gypsy family planning permission in *South Buckinghamshire District Council v Porter (No 2)*.[169] In that case, Lord Brown of Eaton-under-Heywood, delivering the only reasoned judgment, summarised the case-law on the adequacy of reasons in terms that it will seldom be necessary to go beyond:

> The reasons for a decision must be intelligible and they must be adequate. They must enable the reader to understand why the matter was decided as it was and what conclusions were reached on the 'principal important controversial issues', disclosing how any issue of law or fact was resolved. Reasons can be briefly stated, the degree of particularity required depending entirely on the nature of the issues falling for decision. The reasoning must not give rise to a substantial doubt as to whether the decision-maker erred in law, for example by misunderstanding some relevant policy or some other important matter or by failing to reach a

165 *City of Edinburgh v Secretary of State for Scotland* [1997] 1 WLR 1447 at 1458–1459, per Lord Clyde.

166 *Bolton MBC v Secretary of State for the Environment* 61 P&CR 343, at 352–353, CA, per Glidewell LJ.

167 *Bolton MBC v Secretary of State for the Environment* 71 P&CR 309 at 314, per Lord Lloyd of Berwick, HL.

168 *Lee v First Secretary of State* [2003] EWHC 3235.

169 [2004] UKHL 33; [2004] 1 WLR 1953, para 36.

rational decision on relevant grounds. But such adverse inference will not readily be drawn. The reasons need refer only to the main issues in the dispute, not to every material consideration. They should enable disappointed developers to assess their prospects of obtaining some alternative development permission, or, as the case may be, their unsuccessful opponents to understand how the policy or approach underlying the grant of permission may impact upon future such applications. Decision letters must be read in a straightforward manner, recognising that they are addressed to parties well aware of the issues involved and the arguments advanced. A reasons challenge will only succeed if the party aggrieved can satisfy the court that he has genuinely been substantially prejudiced by the failure to provide an adequately reasoned decision.

4.197 Procedure for these statutory challenges is governed by TCPA 1990 s288, Civil Procedure Rules 1998 Part 54 and Practice Directions 54E 8C, 54D and 54E. Claims are started in the Administrative Court Office of the High Court in Birmingham, Cardiff, Leeds, London or Manchester, but may ultimately be heard in other cities such as Bristol. Applications are made by a claim form supported by a witness statement that exhibits the appeal decision and other relevant documents, including relevant extracts from (but not the whole of) policy documents. The Claim Form should be served on the Government Legal Department on behalf of the secretary of state, the LPA as second defendant and any other party with an interest in the land. The High Court will generally consider the question of permission without a hearing. Unless the court records that the application is totally without merit, a claimant may request that a refusal decision is reconsidered at a hearing.

4.198 In applications where only one party appears on each side, costs normally follow the event. Where there are a number of defendants costs are at the discretion of the court and there are no absolute rules. Where the secretary of state succeeds in defending his or her decision, he or she will normally be entitled to the whole of his or her costs. A defendant LPA or developer will not normally be entitled their costs unless they can demonstrate that they had advanced an argument not covered by the secretary of state or that they had an interest that required separate representation.[170] In *Barnsley MBC v Secretary of*

170 *Bolton MBC v Secretary of State for the Environment* [1995] 1 WLR 1176, where on the facts both the secretary of state and the developer were entitled to costs. However, where defendants successfully resists an application at the permission stage, they may be awarded the costs of the acknowledgment of service: *Mount Cook Land Ltd v Westminster City Council* [2003] EWCA Civ 1346; [2004] 2 P&CR 22.

State for Communities and Local Government[171] his Honour Judge Roger Kaye QC (sitting as a High Court Judge) awarded both the secretary of state and a Romani Gypsy defendant costs, the judge noting, this 'was a case which closely, directly, and intimately touched the second defendant, his family, their culture and future living and health needs'.

Enforcement

Overview

4.199 If a development is carried out without the grant of the required planning permission, the LPA may:

- issue an enforcement notice (with or without a stop notice) if it considers it expedient to do so having regard to the provisions of the development plan and to any other material considerations;
- issue a temporary stop notice;
- seek a planning enforcement injunction;
- take direct action and execute the works required by an enforcement notice;
- take no action.

Government guidance on enforcement

4.200 Guidance on enforcement against those who are using land in breach of planning control is contained in NPPF para 58:

> Effective enforcement is important to maintain public confidence in the planning system. Enforcement action is discretionary, and local planning authorities should act proportionately in responding to suspected breaches of planning control . . .

4.201 It follows that disproportionate action in enforcement is contrary to government policy.

Considerations of common humanity

4.202 *R v Lincolnshire CC ex p Atkinson*[172] concerned the exercise of powers under CJPOA 1994 s77 in relation to unauthorised encampments.[173] Commenting on DoE Circular 18/94 Sedley J said:

171 [2010] EWHC 206 (Admin).
172 *R v Lincolnshire CC ex p Atkinson* [1997] JPL 65; (1996) 8 Admin LR 529.
173 See para 5.113.

> Detailed analysis of these passages and debate about what legal force, if any, an advisory circular of this kind possesses has been made unnecessary by the realistic concession of counsel for both local authorities that whether or not they were spelt out in a departmental circular the matters mentioned in the paragraphs ... would be material considerations in the public law sense that to overlook them in the exercise of a local authority's powers under sections 77 to 79 of the Act ... would be to leave a relevant matter out of account and so jeopardise the validity of any consequent step. The concession is rightly made because those considerations in the material paragraphs which are not statutory are considerations of common humanity, none of which can properly be ignored when dealing with one of the most fundamental human needs, the need for shelter with at least a modicum of security.

4.203 These considerations of common humanity must also be taken into account in reaching decisions in relation to enforcement action in respect of alleged breaches of planning control.[174]

Enforcement notices

4.204 An LPA may issue an enforcement notice where it appears to it that there has been a breach of planning control and that it is expedient to issue the notice, having regard to the provisions of the development plan and to any other material considerations.[175] As has been stated above,[176] TCPA 1990 s171B deals with time limits for the enforcement of planning control. Its effect is that:

> an enforcement notice must be issued within four years of the date of the breach of planning control where it relates to a breach consisting of–
> (i) the carrying out without planning permission of building, engineering, mining or other operations in, on, over or under land; or
> (ii) the making without planning permission of a change of use of any building to use it as a single dwelling house;
>
> in the case of any other breach of planning control, no enforcement action may be taken more than ten years after the date of the breach.

Enforcement notices should state 'the matters which appear to the local planning authority to constitute the breach of planning control' and 'specify the steps which the authority require to be taken, or the activities which the authority require to cease, in order to achieve whole or partial remediation'.[177] If an enforcement notice fails to

174 *R v Kerrier DC ex p Uzell Blythe* (1996) 71 P&CR 566, 571.
175 TCPA 1990 s172(1).
176 See paras 4.37–4.38.
177 TCPA 1990 s173(1)(a), (2) and (4).

comply with these requirements, it may be held to be a nullity and therefore of no effect.[178]

4.205 An enforcement notice must specify the date on which it is to take effect and service of the notice must take place not more than 28 days after its date of issue and not less than 28 days before the date specified in it, as the date on which it is to take effect.[179] An enforcement notice that required immediate compliance was a nullity, without legal effect and incapable of amendment.[180]

Stop notices

4.206 Where an LPA has issued an enforcement notice, TCPA 1990 s183 provides that it can also issue a stop notice requiring that an activity that contravenes planning control ceases immediately. There is no right of appeal against a stop notice though one can challenge the LPA's decision to issue such a notice by way of judicial review.

4.207 In *R (Clare Wilson) v First Secretary of State*,[181] the claimant sought a declaration that TCPA 1990 s183 was incompatible with Articles 8 and 14 of the ECHR. She pointed out that stop notices cannot be used to prohibit the use of any building as a dwelling house, but can be used in circumstances where Gypsies and Travellers use caravans for residential purposes without planning permission. She argued that this difference in treatment had an unjustifiable and disproportionate effect. At first instance, Crane J disagreed, taking the view that greater harm was likely to occur when a caravan was brought onto land than that which was likely to occur when a building was used as a dwelling house and that the difference in treatment was justified on that basis. The Court of Appeal upheld that decision and the claimant was refused permission to appeal to the House of Lords.[182]

Temporary stop notices

4.208 Since 2005 LPAs have had the additional enforcement power to issue temporary stop notices (TSNs) which can be used in certain circumstances to stop a breach of planning control with immediate

178 *Miller-Mead v Minister of Housing and Local Government* [1963] 2 QB 196.
179 TCPA 1990 s172(3).
180 *R (Lynes) v West Berkshire DC* [2002] EWHC 1828 (Admin).
181 [2005] EWHC 2970 (Admin).
182 [2007] EWCA Civ 52.

effect. The relevant provisions are contained in the TCPA 1990 ss171E–171H.

4.209 Section 171F states that:

> (1) A temporary stop notice does not prohibit–
> (a) the use of a building as a dwelling house;
> (b) the carrying out of an activity of such description or in such circumstances as is prescribed.

4.210 The Town and Country Planning (Temporary Stop Notice) (England) Regulations 2005 stated that TSNs should not be used in relation to the residential use of caravans in breach of planning control in the following circumstances:

> The circumstances are that–
> (a) the caravan is stationed on the land immediately before the issue of the temporary stop notice; and
> (b) the caravan is at that time occupied by a person as his main residence;
> unless the local planning authority consider that the risk of harm to a compelling public interest arising from the stationing of the caravan is so serious so as to outweigh any benefit, to the occupier of the caravan, in the stationing of the caravan for the period for which the temporary stop notice has effect.

4.211 However, the Town and Country Planning (Temporary Stop Notice) (England) (Revocation) Regulations 2013 revoked this provision.

4.212 The explanation given by the DCLG for the change was:

> The regulation restricts council's use of Temporary Stop Notices on unauthorised sites where a caravan is used as a main residence. This can discourage local councils from serving stop notices where it may be beneficial to do so.
>
> The revocation gives local councils greater freedom to make a decision on the basis of local circumstances and on whether serving Temporary Stop Notices in respect of caravans used as main residences is appropriate. It remains for local councils to consider the consequences of taking enforcement action and whether the action is necessary and proportionate in the circumstances.

4.213 The practical effect of the revocation in England is unclear. At first glance it would enable TSNs to be used against caravans as a main residence without impediment. However, if a LPA fails to consider the human rights and equality implications of use of a TSN, it may be vulnerable to an application for judicial review,[183] if the use of a

183 Any such application should be made very promptly as an urgent matter so that it is heard while the TSN is still in force. The Planning Court disapproves of academic applications.

TSN is disproportionate. The balancing exercise required by the Human Rights Act will inevitably involve weighing in the balance 'the risk of harm to a compelling public interest arising from the stationing of the caravan' and 'any benefit, to the occupier of the caravan'.

4.214 The Equalities Statement that accompanied the revocation of the Regulations provides helpful comments on the limitations placed on TSNs by human rights and equality legislation:

> Local authorities in exercising these powers are required to have due regard to the requirements of the European Convention of Human Rights under the Human Rights Act 1998 and Equality Act 2010. It will still be for local authorities to balance the impacts of using their enforcement powers against individuals in breach of planning control against wider impacts on the local area. [Page 2]
>
> Section 149 of the Equality Act 2010 requires authorities to consider the needs of people who share 'protected characteristics' and to have 'due regard' to the need to eliminate unlawful discrimination, promote equality of opportunity, and promote good relations between people from different groups. Romany Gypsies and Irish Travellers are recognised as having a protected characteristic under the Equality Act 2010. In accordance with section 149 of the Equality Act 2010, the government and local authorities must have due regard to the needs of these protected groups in the exercise of their functions. The government and local authorities are also under a duty through the Human Rights Act 1998 to 'facilitate the gypsy way of life' in relation to ethnic Gypsies. The revocation of the Town and Country Planning (Temporary Stop Notice) (England) Regulations 2005 is likely to impact on Romany Gypsies and Irish Travellers.
>
> In addition to section 149 of the Equality Act 2010, there are other regulations that are relevant to the implications of this proposal for Gypsies and Travellers:
>
> - Safeguards are provided by the . . . European Convention on Human Rights, in particular Article 1 of Protocol 1, Article 6, Article 8, and Article 14 . . .
> - Local authorities are still required to carry out assessments of the accommodation needs of Gypsies and Travellers, as set out in section 8 of the Housing Act 1985. The Housing Act also requires authorities to prepare a strategy demonstrating how the accommodation needs of Gypsies and Travellers will be met as part of their housing strategies.
> - Taken together, the Planning and Compulsory Purchase Act 2004 and Housing Act 1985 provide legislative protection to ensure that (a) the accommodation needs of the traveller community are assessed; and (b) that local plans must be sound, meaning inter alia that they

> present the most appropriate strategy, when considered against the reasonable alternatives, based on proportionate evidence (which must include the accommodation needs of the traveller community).
>
> However, local councils, as public authorities, are required to have due regard to the Human Rights Act 1998 and the Equality Act 2010 when discharging their functions, including enforcement action. This proposal does not change this situation. In determining whether to issue a Temporary Stop Notice in respect of a caravan being used as a main residence, local authorities will need to consider the impact on the occupants and their families. This will include considerations of the consequences of the notice, the potential for the occupants to be displaced to the roadside or other inappropriate locations as well as the ability of occupants to access local services.

4.215 Guidance on TSNs is given in the NPPG, which points out that:

> The provisions of the European Convention on Human Rights, such as Article 1 of the First Protocol, Article 8 and Article 14, are relevant

4.216 TSNs may not lawfully be used in a way that contravenes the ECHR. Before issuing a TSN, the LPA must be satisfied that there has been a breach of planning control and that 'it is expedient that the activity which amounts to the breach is stopped immediately'.[184] Section 171E(3) requires the LPA to give reasons for issuing the TSN on the face of the notice. The LPA must therefore be satisfied that immediate cessation of the activity is expedient in the circumstances and must set out its reasons for this decision on the face of the TSN.

Enforcement notice appeals

4.217 There is a right of appeal against an enforcement notice to the secretary of state or Welsh Ministers on one or more of the following seven grounds:

a) that, in respect of any breach of planning control which may be constituted by the matters stated in the notice, planning permission ought to be granted or, as the case may be, the condition or limitation concerned ought to be discharged;
b) that those matters have not occurred;
c) that those matters (if they occurred) do not constitute a breach of planning control;

184 TCPA 1990 s171E(1)(b).

d) that, at the date when the notice was issued, no enforcement action could be taken in respect of any breach of planning control which may be constituted by those matters;
e) that copies of the enforcement notice were not served as required by section 172;
f) that the steps required by the notice to be taken, or the activities required by the notice to cease, exceed what is necessary to remedy any breach of planning control which may be constituted by those matters or, as the case may be, to remedy any injury to amenity which has been caused by any such breach;
g) that any period specified in the notice in accordance with section 173(9) falls short of what should reasonably be allowed.[185]

4.218 It is common for Gypsies and Travellers who are served with an enforcement notice, requiring them to cease the use of land for residential purposes, to appeal against the notice on ground (a).[186] An appeal brought under ground (a) will be determined by a planning inspector having regard to exactly the same matters that would be taken into account on a planning appeal and it should be prepared in much the same way.

4.219 In addition, it is common for Gypsies and Travellers to appeal against such an enforcement notice on ground (g). Those advising Gypsies and Travellers should always consider whether the enforcement notice should be appealed on ground (g). If the time for compliance is too short, for example, because it will take the occupant of the site longer to find alternative accommodation, then a ground (g) appeal could be brought. If extensive works, such as the removal of hardstanding, are required and the appellant is impecunious, a ground (g) appeal will probably be appropriate.

4.220 Appeals brought under grounds (b), (c), (d) and (e) depend on the facts and the evidence available to prove the point in issue.

4.221 When deciding whether to appeal on ground (f), it is important to consider whether the enforcement notice enforces against existing rights such as fencing and gates permitted by the GPDO 2015.[187] Appellants who wish to rely on ground (f) should specify, without prejudice to their position on other grounds, the arguments in

185 TCPA 1990 s174(2) as substituted by the Planning and Compensation Act 1991 s6.

186 But see the limits on ground (a) appeals where there is an enforcement notice in place, paras 4.43–4.47, below.

187 See para 4.29, above.

relation to existing rights and indicate the variations of the notice that would be appropriate if the other grounds of appeal failed.[188]

4.222 As with all planning appeals, the timetable for enforcement appeals should be strictly observed. If it is not, the appellant may be seriously disadvantaged.

4.223 TCPA 1990 s174(2A) and (2B) limits the right of appeal against enforcement notices in England on ground (a) as follows:

> (2A) An appeal may not be brought on the ground specified in subsection (2)(a) if -
> (a) the land to which the enforcement notice relates is in England, and
> (b) the enforcement notice was issued at a time –
> (i) after the making of a related application for planning permission, but
> (ii) before the end of the period applicable under section 78(2) in the case of that application.
>
> (2B) An application for planning permission for the development of any land is, for the purposes of subsection (2A), related to an enforcement notice if granting planning permission for the development would involve granting planning permission in respect of the matters specified in the enforcement notice as constituting a breach of planning control.

4.224 Where this provision applies it is absolute and involves no discretion. It prevents appeals against an enforcement notice on ground (a), but not an appeal on other grounds will apply:

- the enforcement notice was issued after the making of a related application for planning permission, ie an application for planning permission that would involve granting permission in respect of the matters specified in the enforcement notice as constituting a breach of planning control; and
- the enforcement notice was issued before the period prescribed by the Town and Country (Development Management Procedure) (England) Order 2015 for making an appeal.

4.225 TCPA 1990 s177 deals with the grant or modification of planning permission on an appeal against an enforcement notice. In England, there is power to grant planning permission if an enforcement appeal is allowed; however, that power can only be exercised if the appeal was brought under ground (a). No such restriction applies to

188 *Taylor v Secretary of State for the Environment, Transport and the Regions* [2001] EWCA Civ 1254.

enforcement appeals which relate to land in Wales. Thus TCPA 1990 s177(1C) and (5) provide:

> (1C) If the land to which the enforcement notice relates is in England, subsection (1)(a) applies only if the statement under section 174(4) specifies the ground mentioned in section 174(2)(a).
>
> ...
>
> (5) Where an appeal against an enforcement notice is brought under section 174 and–
> (a) the land to which the enforcement notice relates is in Wales, or
> (b) that land is in England and the statement under section 174(4) specifies the ground mentioned in section 174(2)(a),
>
> the appellant shall be deemed to have made an application for planning permission in respect of the matters stated in the enforcement notice as constituting a breach of planning control.

Appeal against an enforcement notice appeal decision to the High Court

4.226 TCPA 1990 s289(1) provides for a further appeal on a point of law to the High Court against a decision on an appeal against an enforcement notice.[189] The court's permission is required.[190] Such an appeal may be brought in circumstances where there is a properly arguable case that:

- the decision was perverse;
- there was a breach of the rules of natural justice;
- there was an absence of evidence to support a finding of fact;
- the decision-maker took account of irrelevant factors or failed to bear in mind relevant factors.

4.227 Procedure is governed by TCPA 1990 s289, Civil Procedure Rules 1998 r52.20 and Practice Direction 52D. The appeal must be made within 28 days.[191] Unlike the position regarding section 288 applications, there is power to extend this time limit. Reasons must be given for an extension of time and the power to extend is not intended to be an 'easy escape route for lack of reasonable expedition'.

189 In *Jarmain v Secretary of State for the Environment, Transport and the Regions* [2001] EWHC 1140 Admin, Gibbs J held that an appeal against a decision made in respect of an enforcement notice appeal must be made pursuant to TCPA 1990 s289 and not s288.

190 Section 289(6).

191 Practice Direction 52D 26.1(1).

Prosecution for breach of an enforcement notice

4.228 Non-compliance with an enforcement notice is a criminal offence contrary to TCPA 1990 s179. It is an offence triable either way and is punishable in the magistrates' court with a fine not exceeding £20,000 and in the Crown Court with an unlimited fine. When determining the amount of any fine to be imposed the court 'shall in particular have regard to any financial benefit which has been accrued or appears likely to accrue to [the defendant] in consequence of the offence'.[192]

4.229 In such a prosecution it must be shown that the 'enforcement notice' issued by the LPA is formally valid (and has not been set aside) and that it is not possible to challenge its lawfulness.[193] Where owners of land are prosecuted for breach of an enforcement notice, they have a defence if they can show that everything that could be expected to be done to secure compliance with the notice was done. However, in *Wycombe District Council v Wells*,[194] a case involving a Gypsy who had been prosecuted for failing to comply with an enforcement notice which required him to cease using his land as a caravan site, Newman J held that the defence could not be established by demonstrating that the reason for non-compliance with the enforcement notice was that no alternative site was available. The decision in *Wells* emphasises the importance of producing full evidence in support of one's case for planning permission or on appeal against the refusal of permission or an enforcement notice. Many have suffered because they left matters until too late.

4.230 It is not open to a defendant to challenge the validity of an enforcement notice on any of the grounds upon which an appeal against the notice may be made under TPCA 1990 s174(2).[195]

Direct action

4.231 Where any steps required by an enforcement notice are not taken within the period for compliance with the notice, the LPA may enter the land and take those steps. It may then recover from the owner of the land any expenses reasonably incurred by them in doing so.[196]

192 TCPA 1990 s179(9).

193 *R v Wicks* [1998] AC 92.

194 TCPA 1990 s179(3). See also *R v Clarke* [2002] JPL 1372; and *R v Wood* [2001] EWCA Crim 1395, [2002] JPL 219.

195 TCPA 1990 s285.

196 TCPA 1990 s178.

4.232 In *R (Mitchell and Hearne) v Horsham DC*,[197] it was decided that LPAs should only resort to such action having given careful consideration to the personal circumstances of those who would be affected and having taken account of all relevant government planning policy.

4.233 In *R (O'Brien) v Basildon DC*[198] Ouseley J quashed the defendant LPA's decision to take direct action against some families because the LPA had failed to take account of the prospects of success at a forthcoming planning inquiry; and the difference between the views of the planning inspectorate and the LPA on the level of need within the district. When doing so, he said:

> The power given by section 178 . . . for residential eviction is a drastic power[199] . . . It is in my view necessary for a local planning authority in deciding whether to use section 178 to consider and weigh various factors: the degree of harm done to the interests protected by planning control; the need for a swift or urgent remedy; the need to uphold and enforce planning control embodied in an effective enforcement notice and the criminal law; the personal circumstances and impact on the individuals of removal.[200] Part of that will involve the question of whether they have somewhere else to go or whether inevitably they will have to camp on the roadside, or in some other unauthorised Green Belt location of indeterminate harm. But it is also relevant, and the more plainly so where the conclusion is that the occupants have nowhere lawful or suitable to go[201] . . . an appeal decision might be imminent with obvious good prospects of success in the light of other decisions nearby; the removal of a group of gypsies for them shortly after to be reinstated after a successful appeal would be plainly disproportionate[202] . . . I consider that for a decision to use section 178 to be lawful, consideration of the occupiers' prospects of success in a planning application or appeal and the timing of the resolution of that issue is necessary. If that is not done, a material consideration will have been ignored and action may well be disproportionate, depending on the prospects, the timing of the decision, the degree of harm, and so on.[203]

4.234 However, in 2011 the same judge rejected a high profile judicial review challenge of Basildon's decision to take direct action against

197 [2003] EWHC 234 (Admin).
198 [2006] EWHC 1346 (Admin), [2007] 1 P&CR 16.
199 Para 183.
200 Para 184.
201 Para 185.
202 Para 186.
203 Para 186.

the Irish Traveller families living on their own land without planning permission known as Dale farm.

Planning injunctions

4.235 TCPA 1990 s187B(1) provides that where an LPA considers 'it necessary or expedient for any actual or apprehended breach of planning control to be restrained by injunction, they may apply to the court for an injunction'.

4.236 The judgment of the House of Lords in *South Buckinghamshire DC v Porter (No 1)*[204] is not only the leading decision on the use of TCPA 1990 s187B against Gypsies and Travellers, but it is also helpful in other fields of planning law and practice. The judgment related to four cases. In each case, LPAs had been granted planning injunctions under section 187B which required Gypsies and Travellers, who were living in caravans on land without planning permission, to move off their land. The Gypsies and Travellers appealed to the Court of Appeal and argued that the injunctions should not have been granted on human rights grounds. The Court of Appeal unanimously allowed their appeals, holding that its earlier decision in the case of *Hambleton DC v Bird*,[205] which had greatly limited the power of a judge to refuse a section 187B injunction, was no longer good law (if it ever had been such).[206]

4.237 Simon Brown LJ giving the leading judgment in the Court of Appeal, stated that a judge:

> . . . should not grant injunctive relief unless he would be prepared if necessary to contemplate committing the defendant to prison for breach of the order, and that he would not be of this mind unless he had considered for himself all questions of hardship for the defendant and his family if required to move, necessarily including therefore, the availability of suitable alternative sites.[207]

4.238 Simon Brown LJ indicated that a judge was entitled to take account of countervailing considerations against the need to enforce planning control, for example:

- the degree and the flagrancy of the (postulated) breach;
- whether conventional enforcement measures had been tried;

204 [2003] UKHL 26; [2003] 2 AC 558.

205 [1995] 3 PLR 8.

206 *South Buckinghamshire DC v Porter; Chichester DC v Searle; Wrexham CBC v Berry; Hertsmere BC v Harty* [2001] EWCA Civ 1549; [2002] 1 All ER 425.

207 [2002] 1 WLR 1359 at 1377–1378.

- the urgency of the situation;
- health and safety considerations;
- whether the injunction was intended to remove a Gypsy or Traveller from a site or prevent him moving on to a site; and
- previous planning decisions – the relevance of which would depend upon a variety of matters including: their age; the extent to which considerations of hardship and the availability of alternative sites was taken into account; the strength of the conclusions reached on the land use and environmental issues; and whether a defendant had the opportunity to make his or her case for at least a temporary personal planning permission.

4.239 Simon Brown LJ added that:

> . . . whilst it is not for the court to question the correctness of the existing planning status of the land, the court in deciding whether or not to grant an injunction (and if so, whether and for how long to suspend it) is bound to come to some broad view as to the degree of environmental damage resulting from the breach and the urgency or otherwise of bringing it to an end. In this regard the court need not shut its mind to the possibility of the planning authority itself coming to reach a different planning judgment in the case.[208]

4.240 Finally, Simon Brown LJ stated that:

> . . . the court's discretion is absolute and injunctive relief is unlikely unless properly thought to be 'commensurate' – in today's language, proportionate . . . whatever view one takes of the correctness of the *Hambleton* approach in the period prior to the coming into force of the Human Rights Act 1998, to my mind it cannot be thought consistent with the court's duty under section 6(1) to act compatibly with Convention rights. Proportionality requires not only that the injunction be appropriate and necessary for the attainment of the public interest objective sought – here the safeguarding of the environment – but also that it does not impose an excessive burden on the individual whose private interests – here the gypsy's private life and home and the retention of his ethnic identity – are at stake.[209]

4.241 The LPAs' subsequent appeals were dismissed by the House of Lords. In doing so, their Lordships endorsed the guidance given by the Court of Appeal.[210] Having considered the arguments and previous decisions, Lord Bingham stated that the power to grant an

208 [2002] 1 WLR 1359 at 1377–1378.

209 [2002] 1 WLR 1359 at 1378.

210 *South Buckinghamshire DC v Porter and others (No 1)* [2003] UKHL 26, [2003] 2 AC 558.

injunction under TCPA 1990 s187B was a discretionary power, and that 'the court is not obliged to grant an injunction because a local authority considers it necessary or expedient for any actual or apprehended breach of planning control to be restrained by injunction' and that 'the court must decide whether in all the circumstances it is just to grant the relief sought'.[211]

4.242 Lord Bingham added:

> . . . the Secretary of State was entitled to have regard to the personal circumstances of the Gypsies . . . When application is made . . . under section 187B, the evidence will usually make clear whether, and to what extent, the local planning authority has taken account of the personal circumstances of the defendant and any hardship an injunction may cause. If it appears that these aspects have been neglected and on examination they weigh against the grant of relief, the court will be readier to refuse it. If it appears that the local planning authority has fully considered them and nonetheless resolved that it is necessary or expedient to seek relief, this will ordinarily weigh heavily in favour of granting relief, since the court must accord respect to the balance which the local planning authority has struck between public and private interests. It is, however, ultimately for the court to decide whether the remedy sought is just and proportionate in all the circumstances . . .[212]

4.243 Lord Bingham continued, explaining that:

> The court should ordinarily be slow to make an order which it would not at that time be willing, if need be, to enforce by imprisonment.[213]

He doubted that ECHR Article 8 added to domestic law, stating in respect of the *Buckley*[214] and *Chapman*[215] judgments:

> . . . when asked to grant injunctive relief under section 187B the court must consider whether, on the facts of the case, such relief is proportionate in the Convention sense, and grant relief only if it judges it to be so. Although domestic law is expressed in terms of justice and convenience rather than proportionality, this is in all essentials the task which the court is in any event required by domestic law to carry out.[216]

4.244 Lord Bingham concluded his judgment by stating that:

211 [2003] 2 WLR 1547, 1562.
212 [2003] 2 AC 558 at 580 para 31, [2003] 2 WLR 1547, 1564.
213 [2003] 2 WLR 1547,1565.
214 *Buckley v UK* (1996) 23 EHRR 101, [1997] 2 PLR 10.
215 *Chapman v UK* (2001) 33 EHRR 399, (2001) 10 BHRC 48.
216 [2003] 2 WLR 1547, 1566.

> The guidance given by the Court of Appeal in the judgment of Simon Brown LJ . . . was in my opinion judicious and accurate in all essential respects and I would endorse it.[217]

4.245 Lord Steyn agreed, adopting similar reasoning to Lord Bingham, and stated, having referred to Article 8:

> Even if it had previously been possible to ignore great or marked hardship in the exercise of discretion under section 187B – a hypothesis which I do not accept – such an approach is no longer possible.[218]

4.246 Commenting on the fact that TCPA 1990 s187B empowers an LPA to apply for an injunction, whether or not it has exercised or is proposing to exercise any of its other planning enforcement powers, Lord Clyde said:

> . . . that does not mean that the court may not take account of the facts regarding any other remedy which the authority have pursued or the fact that they have not pursued any other remedy.

The key words of his opinion are:

> . . . section 187B(2) allows and has always allowed the court in the exercise of its discretion in granting an injunction to weigh up the public interest in securing the enforcement of planning policy and planning decisions against the private interests of the individuals who are allegedly in breach of planning control. In particular . . . it is open to the court to consider questions of hardship, particularly as regards health, arising out of the effect on such individuals of a grant of an injunction.[219]

Lord Clyde also pointed out that in Gypsy and Traveller cases 'considerations of humanity may be particularly acute owing to their particular traditions and lifestyle'.[220]

4.247 Lord Hutton said:

> . . . it is not for the court to act merely as a rubber stamp to endorse the decision of the local planning authority to stop the use by the particular defendant in breach of planning control. Moreover the court is as well placed as the local planning authority to decide whether the considerations relating to the human factor outweigh purely planning considerations; the weight to be attached to the personal circumstances of a defendant in deciding whether a coercive order should be made against him is a task which is constantly performed by the courts.[221]

217 [2003] 2 WLR 1547, 1566.
218 [2003] 2 WLR 1547, 1572.
219 [2003] 2 WLR 1547, 1574 and 1576.
220 [2003] 2 WLR 1547, 1577.
221 [2003] 2 WLR 1547, 1580.

4.248 Lord Scott dealt with the criteria that govern the Court's approach to grant of section 187B injunctions applications:

> . . . the court must take into account all or any circumstances of the case that bear upon the question whether the grant would be 'just and convenient'. Of particular importance, of course, will be whether or not the local planning authority can establish not only that there is a current or apprehended breach of planning control but also that the ordinary statutory means of enforcement are not likely to be effective in preventing the breach or bringing it to an end. In a case in which the statutory procedure of enforcement notice, prosecution for non-compliance and exercise by the authority of such statutory self-help remedies as are available had not been tried and where there was no sufficient reason to assume that, if tried, they would not succeed in dealing with the breach, the local planning authority would be unlikely to succeed in persuading the court that the grant of an injunction would be just and convenient.[222]

4.249 Lord Scott also stated that the jurisdiction to grant TCPA 1990 s187B injunctions 'is one of great delicacy and to be used with caution'.[223]

4.250 Since *Porter (No 1)*, LPAs have met with varying success in applications for planning injunctions. For example, in *Hart DC v Benford*[224] the LPA's evidence was equivocal and challenged and the court concluded that the grant of an injunction would not be proportionate. In *Stratford-upon-Avon DC v Hitchman*,[225] the High Court refused an application for a planning injunction because of lack of precision.

4.251 In other cases courts have refused to grant injunctions to force Gypsies and Travellers to leave their sites;[226] or granted an injunction but allowed an extended period of time for compliance.[227]

Without notice injunctions

4.252 LPAs sometimes obtain 'without notice' TCPA 1990 s187B injunctions. An applicant who applies for an interim remedy without notice

222 [2003] 2 WLR 1547, 1584.

223 [2003] 2 AC 558, 599 para 96.

224 [2006] EWHC 240 (QB), [2006] JPL 1318.

225 [2002] Env LR 7.

226 See, for example, *South Cambridgeshire DC v Price* [2008] EWHC 1234 (Admin), *Brentwood BC v Ball* [2009] EWHC 2433 (QB); and the more recent case of *Guildford BC v Cooper* [2019] EWHC 1283 (QB) where the decision to refuse an injunction was clearly influenced by the court's consideration of the best interests of the children.

227 See, for example, *Waverley BC v Lee* [2003] EWHC 29 (QB); *Mid-Bedfordshire DC v Smith* [2003] EWHC 932 (QB).

to the respondent is under a duty to investigate the facts and to present the evidence on which they rely fairly. Mummery LJ explained the extent of the duty in *Memory Corporation v Sidhu (No 2)*:[228]

> It cannot be emphasised too strongly that at an urgent without notice hearing for a freezing order, as well as for a search order or any other form of interim injunction, there is a high duty to make full, fair and accurate disclosure of material information to the court and to draw the court's attention to significant factual, legal and procedural aspects of the case. It is the particular duty of the advocate to see that the correct legal procedures and forms are used; that a written skeleton argument and a properly drafted order are prepared by him personally and lodged with the court before the oral hearing; and that at the hearing the court's attention is drawn by him to unusual features of the evidence adduced, to the applicable law and to the formalities and procedure to be observed.

4.253 A LPA that failed to draw the court's attention to the principles laid down in *Porter (No 1)* would certainly be in breach of this well-known duty.

4.254 In *Fitzgerald v Williams* Sir Thomas Bingham MR, said (using the Latin term 'ex parte' for what is now referred to as 'without notice'):[229]

> In seeking ex parte relief an applicant must disclose to the judge any fact known to him which might affect the judge's decision whether to grant relief or what relief to grant. It is no answer for an applicant who falls down on his duty to show that his breach of duty was committed in good faith and inadvertently, or to show that the relief would have been granted even had he complied with his duty. The courts have traditionally insisted on strict compliance with this rule, as affording essential protection to an absent defendant, and as applications for ex parte relief have multiplied so the importance of complying with this duty has grown. The law does not however require a judge to whom an application for discharge is made to grant that relief on proof that there was material which should have been but had not been disclosed to the original judge. The later judge has then to exercise his own judgment whether, in all the circumstances, the interests of justice are best served by discharging, or maintaining, or varying the original order. In making this judgment he will have regard to the importance of securing compliance with the fundamental principle, but he will have regard also to the significance in the context of the particular case of the facts which had not been disclosed when they should have been.

4.255 Practice Direction 25A – Interim Injunctions para 3.3 states:

228 [2000] 1 WLR 1443, 1459–1460.
229 [1996] QB 657, 667–668.

> The evidence must set out the facts on which the applicant relies for the claim being made against the respondent, including all material facts of which the court should be made aware.

4.256 Where an LPA obtains a without notice injunction in breach of these well-known requirements, the court's attention should be drawn to its breach of duty and affected respondents should consider making an application to set aside or vary the injunction.

Suspension

4.257 In *Porter (No 1)*, Lord Scott said:

> . . . If the court thought that there was a real prospect that an appeal against an enforcement notice or a fresh application by the defendant for the requisite planning permission might succeed, the court could adjourn the injunction application until the planning situation had become clarified. But where the planning situation is clear and apparently final the court would, in my opinion, have no alternative but to consider the injunction application without regard to the merits of the planning decisions.[230]

4.258 Gypsies and Travellers defending injunctions and other enforcement action can argue that they should not be forced to leave their land until they have had the opportunity to seek at least the grant of temporary planning permission. That argument has been successful in a number of cases, including *South Bucks DC v Smith*.[231] In that case a Gypsy family had been living on their land in breach of planning control for a period of 32 years. However, they persuaded the court that there was a realistic prospect that their fresh planning application would be granted and that they should not be forced to leave the land before the application was determined. In the event they were granted temporary planning permission and the judge's decision was vindicated. However, similar arguments have failed in other cases where Gypsies and Travellers had moved on to land in knowing breach of injunctions and enforcement notices.[232]

230 *South Buckinghamshire DC v Porter (No 1)* [2003] UKHL 26; [2003] 2 AC 558, para 100.

231 [2006] EWHC 281 QB. See also by way of example, *Ashford BC v JR* [2016] EWHC 908 (QB), 22 March 2016, Hickinbottom J.

232 *South Bedfordshire DC v Price* [2006] EWCA Civ 493; *Wychavon DC v Rafferty* [2006] EWCA Civ 628; *South Cambridgeshire DC v Flynn* [2006] EWHC 1320, QB, but see Sedley LJ's dissenting judgement in *Coates v South Bucks DC* [2004] EWCA Civ 1378.

Contempt/applications to vary

4.259 In *South Cambridgeshire DC v Gammell, Bromley LBC v Maughan,*[233] the Court of Appeal explained what Gypsies and Travellers who had entered land subject to a planning injunction should do when they became aware of its terms. The Court of Appeal stated:

> . . . the correct course for a person subject to an injunction was to apply to vary or discharge it. At that stage the principles in *South Buckinghamshire v Porter* . . . as to bearing in mind personal circumstances would apply. It was not to take action in breach of it. A person in breach of the injunction should apply immediately to vary or discharge it. If he had knowledge of the injunction, he should give an explanation for his breach. The Court would then bear all the circumstances in mind, including the reason for the breach, the order and the personal circumstances.[234]

The option to take no action

4.260 Finally, it should be noted that LPAs are not obliged to take enforcement action. Rather, they are only entitled to take enforcement action where they consider it expedient.[235]

Legal representation and funding

4.261 Gypsy and Traveller planning law is a specialist area in which only a small number of solicitors firms and barristers regularly act.

4.262 Legal aid is available for Gypsies and Travellers to defend planning injunctions and to make applications and appeals under TCPA 1990 ss288 and 289 respectively if it involves the loss of the home. Legal aid is also available to make applications for judicial review.

Town planners

4.263 Planning and enforcement appeals are often complex and LPAs will have experienced and well-resourced officers to support their case and may also be represented by counsel. That being so it is important that Gypsies and Travellers consider instructing specialist chartered town planners as their agents and advocates in the appeal process. Organisations such as Friends, Families and Travellers (FFT) and

233 [2005] EWCA Civ 1429.

234 [2005] EWCA Civ 1429, para 33.

235 *R (Prokopp) v London Underground Ltd* [2003] EWCA Civ 961; [2004] 1 P&CR 31; *R v Leominster DC ex p Pothecary* [1998] JPL 335, per Schiemann LJ, 345.

the Derbyshire Gypsy Liaison Group (DGLG) can provide lists of suitably experienced planning consultants, as can the web-based *Travellers Times*.[236] Normally the expense of such instruction would be borne by the appellant, but there are limited circumstances in which individuals who qualify on hardship grounds can apply to the Legal Aid Agency for exceptional case funding (ECF) for representation by counsel at appeal. Applications for ECF can only be made by solicitors.

Expert evidence

4.264 Where complex matters relating to, for example, flood risk, highway safety or landscape impact arise, Gypsies and Travellers should also consider instructing experts in those fields to address those parts of the appeal in order to maximise the prospects of success. Once again, organisations such as FFT and DGLG can signpost Gypsies and Travellers to such experts.

Conclusion

4.265 Gypsies and Travellers are amongst the most disadvantaged racial groups in our society, with low levels of life expectancy, high vulnerability to serious illness, poor mental health, high child mortality rates and low levels of educational attainment and literacy. A key contributor to the poor socio-economic condition of Romani Gypsies and Travellers is the fact that thousands of families still have no lawful place to station their caravans and live their traditional way of life.

4.266 Meeting the accommodation needs of Gypsies and Travellers (and thereby improving the life chances of their families) should be a relatively simple task, but it will not be achieved unless and until Parliament grasps the nettle and reimposes the duty on English local authorities to provide a sufficient number of suitable permanent and transit sites.[237]

236 At: www.travellerstimes.org.uk.

237 Compare the position in Wales: see chapter 3, paras 3.17–3.19.

CHAPTER 5

Evictions from unauthorised encampments

continued

Introduction

5.1 An 'unauthorised encampment' is generally defined as 'an encampment of caravans and/or vehicles on land without the landowner's or occupier's consent and therefore constituting a trespass',[1] and is to be differentiated from an unauthorised development.[2]

5.2 Local authorities are the principal public bodies responsible for the management of unauthorised encampments. However, there are many other bodies and individuals that may be involved in the eviction of Gypsies and Travellers from unauthorised encampments, including: the police; government departments; other public authorities; and private landowners.

5.3 This chapter begins by detailing the different 'methods' that can be used to evict those living on unauthorised encampments, and explains which method is available to which body or individual and what 'substantive defences' might be deployed by those facing eviction in each case. The term 'substantive defence' is used to indicate a defence that can be raised in any court of first instance. The chapter then moves on to identify what (if any) 'public law challenges' might be available to those facing eviction, that is, challenges that could be made by way of judicial review in an attempt to prevent eviction taking place.[3] It should be emphasised at the outset that 'substantive defences' will not often be of practical use in cases where a public body uses its powers to evict Gypsies and Travellers from unauthorised encampments and that it is much more likely that the eviction will be prevented, or at least postponed if a 'public law challenge' is mounted and it can be shown that the public body's decision to seek eviction was unlawful on public law grounds.

1 That is the definition set out in Welsh Government *Guidance on Managing Unauthorised Camping 2013* para 2.

2 Refer to chapter 4.

3 Following *Doherty v Birmingham City Council and the Secretary of State for Communities and Local Government* [2006] EWCA Civ 1736, it is now clear that, where possession action is taken in the county court or the High Court, the public law challenge can be taken by way of defence in that same action– see para 5.159 et seq, below. However, see the discussion on legal aid at para 5.247. A 'public law challenge' will not be available against an individual.

Methods of eviction and substantive defences

Civil Procedure Rules Part 55 possession proceedings

Who can use them?

Anyone with sufficient interest in the land including, potentially, a licensee[4]

5.4 Civil Procedure Rules (CPR) 1998 Part 55 has taken the place of County Court Rules (CCR) Order 24 (in the county court) and Rules of the Supreme Court Order (RSC) 113 (in the High Court), both of which had previously provided the procedures for the eviction of trespassers.

5.5 CPR 55.1(b) states:

> ... 'a possession claim against trespassers' means a claim for the recovery of land which the claimant alleges is occupied only by a person or persons who entered or remained on the land without the consent of a person entitled to possession of that land but does not include a claim against a tenant or subtenant whether his tenancy has been terminated or not.

5.6 Possession claims must normally be commenced in the county court[5] but exceptionally they can be commenced in the High Court.[6] CPR 55.6 deals with service of claims against 'trespassers':

> Where, in a possession claim against trespassers, the claim has been issued against 'persons unknown' [as it usually is[7]], the claim form, particulars of claim and any witness statements must be served on those persons by–
> (a)
> (i) attaching copies of the claim form, particulars of claim and any witness statements to the main door or some other part of the land so that they are clearly visible; and
> (ii) if practicable, inserting copies of those documents in a sealed transparent envelope addressed to 'the occupiers' through the letter box;[8] or
> (b) placing stakes in the land in places where they are clearly visible and attaching to each stake copies of the claim form, particulars of claim

4 *Manchester Airport Authority v Dutton* [1999] 2 All ER 675.

5 CPR 55.3(1).

6 See para 5.10, below.

7 See CPR 55.3(4).

8 This method of service may be relevant to Gypsies or Travellers parked within the curtilage of a building (area of land attached to a dwelling-house), especially where there are also 'trespassers' residing in the building itself.

and any witness statements in a sealed transparent envelope addressed to 'the occupiers'.[9]

5.7 A CPR Part 55 claim is commenced by using claim form N5 and, in a claim against trespassers, the standard particulars of claim form, N121. Both these forms must be used.[10] The 'Jackson Report'[11] recommended that strict compliance with court orders should become the norm. It stated that fewer delays should result in lower costs and, given the increased emphasis on compliance with rules and court orders, if these forms have not been used, then the judge may well strike the claim out.[12] It is suggested that any argument that such a defect should be waived under CPR Part 3.10 should be countered by reference to CPR Part 1 ('the overriding objective') which emphasises, among other things, that a court should do justice and enforce compliance with the rules. The 'trespasser' does not have to file a defence[13] but clearly would want to do so if he or she denies being a 'trespasser' or wishes to raise one of the other 'substantive defences' listed below.

5.8 A solicitor or adviser instructed by a Gypsy or Traveller who is threatened with eviction should carefully consider whether the claimant has complied with the procedural rules and proved that he or she is entitled to possession. If there is no 'substantive defence' to a claim brought by a public body but the decision to evict is susceptible to public law challenge (see further below), then a defence will have to be filed and served as soon as feasible or a judicial review application will have to be lodged (see further below under 'legal aid').

Has title been proved?

5.9 The claimant will need to prove title to, or sufficient interest in, the land.[14] This is usually achieved by the production of a witness statement or affidavit (from a person who has authority to give such

9 This is the method of service normally employed for unauthorised encampments but it is also common for notices to be attached to vehicles on a site.

10 See CPR Practice Direction (PD) 55.1.5.

11 Lord Justice Jackson produced a report largely on costs issues in December 2009 – Ministry of Justice *Review of Civil Litigation Costs; Final Report*, known as 'the Jackson Report'. See: www.judiciary.gov.uk/publications/review-of-civil-litigation-costs/.

12 See, for example, *Durrant v Chief Constable of Avon & Somerset Constabulary* [2013] EWCA Civ 1624.

13 CPR 55.7(2).

14 CPR PD 55. para 2.6.

evidence) which will have attached to it either office copy entries from the Land Registry, conveyances, leases or other relevant official documents proving title to the land. In the absence of such proof, the defendants' adviser may wish to do a Land Registry search themselves. Alternatively, the defendants or their adviser may wish to make inquiries of local residents who may be able to cast some light on the question of ownership of, or legal interest in, a piece of land. In the case of unregistered land, the authors have known of instances where it has proved difficult for the claimant to prove title.

Should the matter have been commenced in the High Court?

5.10 If brought in the High Court, a separate certificate from the claimant (verified by a statement of truth) explaining why this has been done is required.[15] CPR PD 55A para 1.3 states:

> Circumstances which may, in an appropriate case, justify starting a claim in the High Court are if–
> (1) there are complicated disputes of fact;
> (2) there are points of law of general importance; or
> (3) the claim is against trespassers and there is a substantial risk of public disturbance or of serious harm to persons or property which properly require immediate determination.

Was sufficient notice given and has service been properly effected?

5.11 CPR Part 55.5(2) states:

> In a possession claim against trespassers the defendant must be served with the claim form, particulars of claim and any witness statements–
> (a) in the case of residential property, not less than five days; and
> (b) in the case of other land, not less than two days, before the hearing date.

Simple failure of service may not be enough, in itself, to defend the claim. The defendant may need to show some prejudice to his or her case or disadvantage as a result of the failure of service, for example, an inability to investigate the question of title in the time allowed. However, again, following the Jackson reforms, judges may take a stricter view in relation to a failure to serve.

5.12 Gypsies or Travellers who are 'trespassers' and who are occupying land within the curtilage of a residential building (for example, in the yard of a disused house) are required to be served five clear working days before the hearing date while those camping on 'other land' are

15 CPR 55.3(2).

only entitled to two clear working days' notice.[16] For example, in an action taken against Gypsies and Travellers camping on a car park where the hearing date is on:

- a Thursday, then the claim form, particulars of claim and evidence in support, should be delivered no later than on the previous Monday, provided that is a working day;
- a Monday, then the same documents should be delivered no later than on the previous Wednesday.[17]

5.13 There is provision for the court to shorten the above time limits.[18] CPR PD 55.3 para 2 states:

> Particular consideration should be given to the exercise of this power if:
> (1) the defendant, or a person for whom the defendant is responsible, has assaulted or threatened to assault:
> (a) the claimant;
> (b) a member of the claimant's staff;
> (c) another resident in the locality;
> (2) there are reasonable grounds for fearing such an assault; or
> (3) the defendant, or a person for whom the defendant is responsible, has caused serious damage or threatened to cause serious damage to the property or to the home or property of another resident in the locality.

5.14 In such a case, the claimant should make an application for the abridgement or shortening of time on form N244.[19] If the application is allowed by the court, service could be shortened to the day before the hearing. Self-evidently, an adviser or solicitor assisting a Gypsy or Traveller on an unauthorised encampment who is facing such a short deadline will have to make a very quick assessment of possible 'substantive defences' or 'public law challenges' and may be able to set aside an order for abridgement in circumstances where:

- the allegations are denied;
- responsibility for the persons who have caused or threatened to cause serious damage is denied – for example, where the Gypsy or

16 Notes to CPR Part 55, 55.5(2). CPR 2.8(4) states: 'Where the specified period is – (a) five days or less and (b) includes (i) a Saturday or Sunday; or (ii) a Bank Holiday, Christmas Day or Good Friday, that day does not count.'

17 Defendants are given at least two clear working days' notice so that they can obtain legal advice, if it is required. If the hearing date was on a Monday and service was effected on the Friday, then the defendant might be unable to obtain such advice.

18 CPR 3.1(2)(a).

19 Notes to CPR Part 55, 55.5(3).

Traveller is encamped on a site with others over whom he or she has no responsibility or control;

- any assertion that the damage caused or threatened involves 'serious damage' is denied.

The hearing

5.15 If there is no defence to the claim for possession of land occupied by trespassers, or if the court rejects any defence raised, then it has long been held that the court has no discretion and that it must order possession forthwith. This principle has become known as the 'rule in *McPhail*'[20] and it was upheld in a case involving a Traveller.[21] We believe, however, that this rule can no longer stand – see further below.[22]

5.16 In practice there will normally be a delay before the bailiff, in the case of a county court order, or the High Court enforcement officer (HCEO) in the case of a High Court order,[23] sets an eviction date. Moreover, the claimant retains a discretion as to when to apply for a warrant (or writ in the High Court) of possession (which entitles the claimant to enforce the possession order and evict the trespassers). Failure by a local authority or other public authority to take into account new welfare considerations that arise after the date of the possession order could give rise to a 'public law challenge'.[24] Though notice by the bailiff or HCEO is not required,[25] it is common practice for the bailiff or HCEO to notify the 'trespassers' of the date they have set for eviction. Nevertheless, this practice is not always followed

20 The principle was first stated by the Court of Appeal in *McPhail v Persons unknown* [1973] 3 All ER 393.

21 *Boyland & Son v Rand* [2006] EWCA Civ 1860.

22 See para 5.43, below.

23 Previously a sheriff executed High Court writs but this practice was repealed by Courts Act (CA) 2003 s99. For further discussion of this change see [2004] LS Gaz, 22 April, p31.

24 For a full discussion of 'public law challenges' see para 5.159 onwards, below.

25 The Courts Service provides a form N54 to notify those subject to possession orders of impending eviction but there is no obligation to use it. However, in *London & Quadrant Housing Association v Watson* Central London County Court 31 October 2014, May 2015 *Legal Action* 44, HHJ Saggerson allowed an appeal by the defendant against the refusal of an application for re-entry because the district judge did not take into account the importance of the N54 notice as explained in *St Brice v Southwark LBC* [2002] 1 WLR 1537.

and it is, therefore, a good idea to be proactive and to contact the bailiff or HCEO and ask whether a warrant (or writ) of possession has been issued and, if so, when they will be carrying out the eviction.[26] At the initial possession hearing, the Gypsy or Traveller could apply to be joined as a named party to the proceedings.[27] However, unless they have a defence to the proceedings, there is no point applying to be joined since it will merely open up the possibility of an order for costs. If there is any concern that the bailiff or HCEO will not give notice of the intention to enforce the possession order, it is perfectly acceptable to invite the court to direct the officer concerned to give not less than 48 hours' notice, or whatever notice is deemed appropriate to the circumstances. The district judge bench is likely to be sympathetic to such a request particularly where children and vulnerable adults are involved.

Warrants of possession and restitution

5.17 The usual High Court practice is for the claimant to apply for the writ of possession on notice to the defendant, as was held to be the requirement of RSC Ord 45 r2 and r4 (preserved by CPR Part 50) in *Fleet Mortgage Ltd v Lower Maisonette 46 Eaton Place*.[28] In the county court, no notice is required. This difference has been noted by the Court of Appeal.[29] If an additional incident of trespass occurs more than three months after the date on which the original possession order was granted, the claimant will have to apply for a warrant of restitution (writ of restitution in the High Court). Permission is required for a warrant (or writ) of possession which is sought more than three months after the date of the order and is also required for a warrant

26 CPR Part 39, 39.3 sets out the circumstances in which a party who fails to attend the hearing may apply to set aside the order. The party must: act promptly; have a good reason for not attending; and, have a reasonable prospect of success at trial. However reference should also be made to CPR Part 3.1 and the court's general powers of management. Under CPR Part 3.1(2)(m), the court may, among other things, 'take any other step or make any other order for the purpose of managing the case and furthering the overriding objective'. The case of *Hackney LBC v Findlay* [2011] EWCA Civ 8, makes it clear that both provisions can be applied in a set aside hearing and that the provisions of CPR Part 39.3, although they should generally be applied by analogy, are not an absolute requirement.

27 CPR Part 19, 19.4.

28 [1972] 1 WLR 765.

29 See *Leicester CC v Aldwinkle* [1991] HLR 40.

(or writ) of restitution regardless of when it is sought.[30] However, no notice of any of the above applications needs to be given to the defendants.[31]

5.18 CPR Part 83 provides, with regard to warrants of possession, that:

> 26(10) A warrant of possession to enforce an order for possession in a possession claim against a trespasser under Part 55 ('a warrant of possession against a trespasser') may be issued at any time after the date on which possession is ordered to be given.
>
> 26(11) No warrant of possession against a trespasser may be issued after the expiry of 3 months from the date of the order without the permission of the court.

CPR Part 88 provides, with regard to writs of possession, that:

> 13(3) The court's permission is not required for the issue of a writ of possession in a possession claim against trespassers under Part 55 unless the writ is to be issued after the expiry of three months from the date of the order.
>
> 13(4) An application for permission under paragraph (3) may be made without notice being served on any other party unless the court orders otherwise.

5.19 In *Wiltshire CC v Fraser*,[32] it was held that a warrant (or writ) of restitution may be issued to recover land from occupants who are neither parties to the original proceedings nor dispossessed by the original order, provided there is a plain and sufficient nexus (or link) between the order for possession and the need to effect further recovery of the land. In *Fraser*, a possession order against trespassers was obtained

30 CPR Part 83.13(5) deals with writs of restitution. While the rule concerns High Court enforcement, it is likely that the courts will hold that writs of restitution are available in the county court applying County Courts Act 1984 s76: 'In any case not expressly provided for by or in pursuance of this Act, the general principles of practice in the High Court may be adopted and applied to proceedings in a county court.' This is particularly so as county courts were able to issue writs of restitution prior to the CPR coming into force – see also CCR Order 1 r6 as preserved by CPR Part 51 and Sch 2. However, note that if the new incident of trespass (even if it does not involve all of the original trespassers) occurs within the three months following the order, a warrant (or writ) of possession can be sought without the need for permission.

31 For circumstances where a warrant (or writ) might be set aside, see *Leicester CC v Aldwinkle* [1991] HLR 40, CA. Though that case involved the tenancy of a dwellinghouse, the principles outlined in it (especially with regard to oppressive use of warrants) may occasionally be of use to Gypsies or Travellers faced with a warrant, for example, if there was not a sufficient nexus or link with the previously obtained possession order.

32 [1986] 1 WLR 109.

and executed in 1983. In 1985 there was a new incident of trespass and two of the trespassers were defendants in the original proceedings. This was held to be a sufficient nexus.

5.20 Simon Brown J (as he then was) stated:

> Given that the writ of restitution can be issued to recover land from occupants who were neither party to the original proceedings nor dispossessed by the earlier writ of possession, in what circumstances should this be permitted? In my judgment this will always depend upon the particular facts of the individual case . . . The writ of restitution being in aid of execution, it would be appropriate to permit its issue only in those cases where there was a plain and sufficient nexus between the original recovery of possession and the need to effect further recovery of the same land. Putting it another way, the court will be bound to ask itself: are the acts or episodes of trespass of which the owners complain during the overall period in question properly to be regarded as essentially one transaction?[33]

5.21 Therefore, where at least one defendant who was on the land in question at the time of the original order, returns to the same piece of land, the claimant will be able to obtain a warrant (or writ) of restitution. However, it is also common for a claimant to seek to obtain a warrant (or writ) in other circumstances. For example:

- where the trespassers involved in the latter incident of trespass are acquaintances of a defendant or defendants who was or were involved in the original possession action;
- where the trespassers involved in the later incident of trespass were directed to the land or told about the land by a previous defendant or defendants;
- where a registration plate on a vehicle present on the land in question at the time the original possession order was obtained is the same as the registration plate on a vehicle present at the later incident of trespass.

With regard to these examples, and ones like them, it is questionable whether a court would hold that there was 'essentially one transaction'.

5.22 Clearly, if there is no nexus or link between the original and the subsequent incidents of trespass, the claimant will not be able to obtain a warrant (or writ) of restitution and will have to seek a fresh possession order.

33 [1986] 1 WLR 109 at 113.

5.23 Government guidance on welfare enquiries, applicable to local authorities and other public authorities, will still be relevant whether or not a warrant (or writ) of restitution can be obtained, and/or some or all of the original defendants are involved in the subsequent incident of trespass, provided there is a sufficient period of time between the two incidents of trespass. The point being that even if exactly the same group of trespassers have returned to the same piece of land, there may have been a significant change in their personal circumstances that ought to be taken into account before a decision is taken to proceed with further eviction action. In the event that a local authority or other public body fails to comply with government guidance, then a public law challenge of the decision to apply for or rely on the warrant (or writ) could be taken by way of judicial review.

Article 8 as a defence

5.24 One starts from the position that a landowner has a basic right to obtain possession against people who are trespassing on his or her land. It is not necessary to discuss the political, philosophical and cultural clashes between nomadism and sedentism but clearly some of those issues colour the legal position.[34] After the introduction of the Human Rights Act (HRA) 1998 in October 2000, the question arose as to whether it would be possible for a trespasser to raise a defence under European Convention on Human Rights (ECHR) Article 8 (the right to respect for his or her private and family life, home and correspondence) before the court of first instance in eviction proceedings.

5.25 Article 8 of the ECHR provides that everyone has the right to respect for their private and family life, their home and their correspondence.[35] Attempts by those faced with possession proceedings to use Article 8 as a defence have been met with varying degrees of success in recent years. Our domestic courts began by taking a very negative approach to the proposition that Article 8 could be raised as a defence in such proceedings (see, for example, *Qazi v Harrow LBC*[36]) while the European Court of Human Rights (ECtHR) has

34 For a wider discussion of these issues see Hawes and Perez, *The Gypsy and the state: the ethnic cleansing of British society*, The Policy Press, 1996; Clark and Greenfields, *Here to stay: the Gypsies and Travellers of Britain*, University of Hertfordshire Press, 2006.

35 See para 2.96 onwards, above.

36 [2003] 4 All ER 461.

consistently taken the opposite position (see, for example *Connors v UK*[37]). However, more recently, the House of Lords' successor, the Supreme Court, has moved itself toward a position which is more in line with that of the ECtHR.

5.26 In *Doherty v Birmingham City Council*,[38] the Court of Appeal referred to the House of Lords' decision in *Kay v Lambeth LBC; Leeds City Council v Price* where Lord Hope said (para 110):[39]

> . . . I would hold that a defence which does not challenge the law under which the possession order is sought as being incompatible with Article 8 but is based only on the occupier's personal circumstances should be struck out. Where domestic law provides for personal circumstances to be taken into account, as in a case where the statutory test is whether it would be reasonable to make a possession order, then a fair opportunity must be given for the arguments in favour of the occupier to be presented. But if the requirements of the law have been established and the right to recover possession is unqualified, the only situations in which it would be open to the court to refrain from proceeding to summary judgment and making the possession order are these: (a) if a seriously arguable point is raised that the law which enables the court to make the possession order is incompatible with Article 8, the county court in the exercise of its jurisdiction under the Human Rights Act 1998 should deal with the argument in one or other of two ways: (i) by giving effect to the law, so far as it is possible for it to do so under section 3 [HRA 1998], in a way that is compatible with Article 8, or (ii) by adjourning the proceedings to enable the compatibility issue to be dealt with in the High Court; (b) if the defendant wishes to challenge the decision of a public authority to recover possession as an improper exercise of its powers at common law on the ground that it was a decision that no reasonable person would consider justifiable, he should be permitted to do this provided again that the point is seriously arguable . . .

The two possible situations in which a possession order might be challenged identified by Lord Hope have since become known as 'gateways (a) and (b)' and were approved by the House of Lords in *Doherty*. This development led to arguments that would normally have been made by way of judicial review in the High Court being raised instead by way of defence in possession proceedings in the county court.

37 (2005) 40 EHRR 9.

38 [2008] UKHL 57, [2009] 1 AC 367.

39 [2006] UKHL 10.

5.27 The judgment of the Supreme Court in the case of *Pinnock v Manchester City Council*[40] put an end to the differences between the two jurisdictional approaches.

5.28 Mr Pinnock had been a secure tenant of Manchester City Council (MCC) since 1978. A local authority tenant of a house or flat is a 'secure tenant' for the purposes of the Housing Act (HA) 1985. In most cases, a possession order can only be obtained against a secure tenant under the HA 1985 if a ground of possession is proved to the satisfaction of the court and if the court considers it reasonable to grant such a possession order.

5.29 Mr Pinnock lived with his partner, Ms Walker, and, from time to time, with all or some of their five children. Possession action was taken by MCC due to allegations of anti-social behaviour made against Ms Walker and the children.

5.30 In June 2007, the judge found a large number of the allegations to be well founded and made a demotion order. HA 1985 s82A (inserted by the Anti-social Behaviour Act 2003) provides the court with power to make a 'demotion order' and thus create a 'demoted tenancy' where the tenant has engaged, or has threatened to engage, in 'housing-related anti-social conduct' or in conduct which consists of or involves using the 'premises for unlawful purposes' and it is reasonable to make the order. A demoted tenancy lasts for a year unless the landlord brings possession proceedings within that year. The effect of a demoted tenancy is that, if proceedings are brought, the landlord is entitled to a possession order so long as compliance with the procedure set out in the HA 1985 is proved.

5.31 Within the following year MCC took additional possession action due to further allegations made against two of the adult children. A possession order was made. Mr Pinnock appealed to the Court of Appeal who dismissed his appeal. He then appealed to the Supreme Court. A panel of nine judges heard the appeal as it involved a challenge to previous House of Lords' judgments on the question whether a defendant could raise a defence under Article 8 in possession proceedings brought by a public authority.

5.32 The Supreme Court examined the House of Lords' judgments and also a number of ECtHR judgments on the same issue. Lord Neuberger gave a judgment with which the whole panel agreed.

5.33 Lord Neuberger summarised the propositions established by the ECtHR judgments (in para 45 of his judgment) as follows:

40 [2010] UKSC 45, [2011] 2 AC 104.

> (a) Any person at risk of being dispossessed of his home at the suit of a local authority should in principle have the right to raise the question of the proportionality of the measure, and to have it determined by an independent tribunal in the light of article 8, even if his right of occupation under domestic law has come to an end . . .
> (b) A judicial procedure which is limited to addressing the proportionality of the measure through the medium of traditional judicial review (i.e. one which does not permit the court to make its own assessment of the facts in an appropriate case) is inadequate as it is not appropriate for resolving sensitive factual issues . . .
> (d) If the court concludes that it would be disproportionate to evict a person from his home notwithstanding the fact that he has no domestic right to remain there, it would be unlawful to evict him so long as the conclusion remains – for example, for a specified period, or until a specified event occurs, or a particular condition is satisfied.
>
> Although it cannot be described as a point of principle, it seems that the [ECtHR] has also franked the view that it will only be in exceptional cases that article 8 proportionality would even arguably give a right to continued possession where the applicant has no right under domestic law to remain . . .

5.34 Lord Neuberger summed up the importance of the ECtHR line of judgments as follows (paras 48 and 49):

> Where . . . there is a clear and constant line of decisions whose effect is not inconsistent with some fundamental substantive or procedural aspect of our law, and whose reasoning does not appear to overlook or misunderstand some argument or point of principle, we consider that it would be wrong for this Court not to follow that line . . .
>
> Therefore, if our law is to be compatible with article 8, where a court is asked to make an order for possession of a person's home at the suit of a local authority, the court must have the power to assess the proportionality of making the order, and, in making that assessment, to resolve any relevant dispute of fact.

5.35 All this applies to public authorities. Turning to private landlords and private landowners, Lord Neuberger stated (para 50):

> [I]t is preferable for this Court to express no view on the issue until it arises and has to be determined.

5.36 As an aside, the Supreme Court has since ruled in *McDonald v McDonald*[41] that Article 8 confers no greater powers (eg dismissal or suspension of the possession order) on a court dealing with a possession claim brought by a private landlord against an assured shorthold

41 *McDonald v McDonald* [2016] UKSC 28.

tenant under the accelerated possession procedure than those set out in statute (ie a requirement that the order be made and only suspended for up to two weeks or, exceptionally, for no more than six weeks).[42] The Supreme Court's reasons were based on the contention that the parties' rights have been determined by their contractual relationship and that the competing interests of private landlords and their tenants have been properly balanced by legislation.[43]

5.37 It now seems very unlikely that an Article 8 defence by trespassers on private land could succeed. That said, it might be argued that neither of the factors which influenced the Supreme Court's decision in *McDonald* apply – ie there is no contractual relationship and no, or very little, statutory protection of the sort which led the Supreme Court to conclude that the competing interests between landlords and tenants had been properly balanced.[44]

5.38 Both Lord Bingham, giving the minority judgment in the earlier House of Lords' case of *Kay v Lambeth LBC*,[45] and the ECtHR, giving judgment in *McCann v UK*[46] had suggested that an Article 8 defence would only be relevant in 'exceptional cases'. On this point in *Pinnock*, Lord Neuberger stated (para 51):

> [I]t seems to us to be both unsafe and unhelpful to invoke exceptionality as a guide . . .

5.39 Expanding on this, at para 52 he stated:

> We would prefer to express the position slightly differently. The question is always whether the eviction is a proportionate means of achieving a legitimate aim. Where a person has no right in domestic law to remain in occupation of his home, the proportionality of making an order for possession at the suit of the local authority will be supported not merely by the fact that it would serve to vindicate the authority's ownership rights. It will also, at least normally, be supported by the fact that it would enable the authority to comply with its duties in relation to the distribution and management of its housing stock, including, for example, the fair allocation of its housing, the redevelopment of the site, the refurbishing of sub-standard accommodation, the need to move people who are in accommodation that now exceeds their needs, and the need to move vulnerable people into sheltered or warden-assisted housing.

42 Housing Act 1988 s21(4) and Housing Act 1980 s89(1).

43 *McDonald v McDonald* [2016] UKSC 28 paras 40–46.

44 See also *Malik v Fassenfelt* [2013] EWCA Civ 798.

45 [2006] 2 AC 465.

46 (2008) 47 EHRR 40.

5.40 On this point about exceptionality, Lord Neuberger concluded (at para 54) that:

> Therefore, in virtually every case where a residential occupier has no contractual or statutory protection, and the local authority is entitled to possession as a matter of domestic law, there will be a strong case for saying that making an order for possession would be proportionate. However, in some cases there may be factors which would tell the other way.

5.41 With regard to the effect on the management of day-to-day cases, Lord Neuberger stated (para 57):

> The wide implications of this obligation will have to be worked out. As in many situations, that is best left to the good sense and experience of judges sitting in the County Court.

5.42 There will inevitably be scope for argument as to whether the eviction of a Gypsy or Traveller from an unauthorised encampment involves that person's 'home' at all – it might be said that if they have not been on the land in question for very long and so have not established 'sufficient and continuous' links, then it cannot be their 'home' (see, for example, *Leeds City Council v Price*,[47] the case heard with *Kay v Lambeth LBC*). However, any such argument can be counteracted by the point being made that the caravan is the 'home' for the purposes of Article 8, and that eviction will interfere with its use and also with the right of the Gypsy or Traveller to respect for 'private and family life'[48] and his or her traditional way of life.[49]

5.43 Six general points can be drawn from the *Pinnock* judgment:

(1) It is only where a person's 'home' is under threat that Article 8 comes into play and there may be cases where it is open to argument whether the premises involved are the defendant's home.
(2) As a general rule, Article 8 needs only be considered by the court if it is raised by or on behalf of the residential occupier. It is for the Gypsy or Traveller concerned to raise Article 8 in the defence.
(3) If an Article 8 point is raised, the court should initially consider it summarily, and if the court is satisfied that, even if the facts relied on are made out, the point would not succeed, it should

47 [2006] UKHL 10.

48 See *Brighton & Hove CC v Alleyn and others*, Brighton County Court, 5 April 2011 and *R v Hillingdon LBC ex p Ward* [2001] HRLR 40.

49 See *Chapman v UK* (2001) 33 EHRR 18 at para 96.

be dismissed. Only if the court is satisfied that it could affect the order that the court might make should the point be further entertained. Most initial possession hearings in such cases are given very short periods of time to be heard (typically no more than fifteen minutes). Basically, the Supreme Court is suggesting that this will be sufficient in most instances even where the defendant raises Article 8 as a defence.

(4) If domestic law justifies an outright order for possession, the effect of Article 8 may, albeit in exceptional cases, justify (in ascending order of effect) granting an extended period for possession, suspending the order for possession on the happening of an event, or even refusing an order altogether – a point which seems to dispose of the rule in *McPhail*.[50]

(5) The conclusion that the court must have the ability to assess the Article 8 proportionality of making a possession order in respect of a person's home may require certain statutory and procedural provisions to be revisited. For example, some of the provisions of CPR Part 55, which appear to mandate a summary procedure in some types of possession claim, may present difficulties in relation to cases where Article 8 claims are raised. Strictly speaking, therefore, the Supreme Court has not formally overturned the rule in *McPhail* but it is difficult to see how that rule can survive this judgment and it should be noted that Sir Alan Ward in the Court of Appeal in *Malik v Fassenfelt*[51] stated (at para 26) said: 'I am now satisfied that *McPhail* can no longer be regarded as good law.'

(6) The Supreme Court accepted that proportionality is more likely to be a relevant issue 'in respect of occupants who are vulnerable as a result of mental illness, physical or learning disability, poor health or frailty', and that 'the issue may also require the local authority[52] to explain why they are not securing alternative accommodation in such cases'.[53]

50 [1973] 3 All ER 393. As a consequence, an occupant of an unauthorised encampment who is, for example, very unwell or is about to give birth may apply to suspend the enforcement of a possession order.

51 [2013] EWCA Civ 798.

52 Though reference is made throughout the judgment in *Pinnock* to 'local authorities' it is clear that this decision has relevance to possession proceedings taken by all public authority landlords and landowners.

53 Which could, in the case of a Gypsy or Traveller, include a pitch (whether temporary or permanent) on an alternative site.

5.44 The Supreme Court followed its judgment in *Pinnock* in the case of *Hounslow LBC v Powell; Leeds CC v Hall; Birmingham CC v Frisby*.[54] Ms Powell was a homeless person living in homeless persons' accommodation which, under the Housing Act (HA) 1996, had no security of tenure. She fell into rent arrears and the local authority sought possession. Both Mr Hall and Mr Frisby were introductory tenants.[55] Due to allegations of anti-social behaviour in both cases the local authorities sought possession. All three defendants sought to rely on Article 8 in their defence.

5.45 The main judgment of the seven member panel of the Supreme Court was given by Lord Hope:

> 35. Mr Luba QC [for all the appellants] accepted that the threshold for raising an arguable case on proportionality was a high one which would succeed in only a small proportion of cases ... Local authorities hold their housing stock, as do other social landlords, for the benefit of the whole community. It is in the interests of the community as a whole that decisions are taken as to how it should best be administered. The court is not equipped to make those decisions, which are concerned essentially with housing management. This is a factor to which great weight must always be given, and in the great majority of cases the court can and should proceed on the basis that the landlord has sound management reasons for seeking a possession order.
>
> 36. If the threshold is crossed, the next question is what legitimate aims within the scope of article 8(2) may the claimant authority rely on for the purposes of the determination of proportionality and what types of factual issues will be relevant to its determination. ... The proportionality of making the order for possession at the suit of the local authority will be supported by the fact that making the order would (a) serve to vindicate the authority's ownership rights; and (b) enable the authority to comply with its public duties in relation to the allocation and management of its housing stock.

5.46 Lord Hope continued:

> 41. ... In the ordinary case the relevant facts will be encapsulated in the two legitimate aims [as identified above] ... It is against those aims, which should always be taken for granted, that the court must weigh up any factual objections that may be raised by the defendant and what she has to say about her personal circumstances. It is only if a defence has been put forward that is seriously arguable that it will be necessary for the judge to adjourn the case for further consideration of the issues of

54 [2011] 2 AC 186, [2011] 2 All ER 129.

55 An introductory tenancy is a form of probationary tenancy for local authority tenants inserted into the Housing Act 1985 by the Housing Act 1996.

> lawfulness or proportionality. If this test is not met, the order for possession should be granted . . .
>
> 42. . . . There is no need for the court to be troubled with these issues unless and until, at the request of the tenant, it has to consider whether it should conduct a proportionality exercise.

5.47 Clearly, the Supreme Court has set a defendant a high hurdle in attempting to show that a possession order is not proportionate in a case where, on the face of the law as it stands, it might even appear that it was mandatory for the court to grant possession (as the statute appears to say in the case of introductory tenants such as Mr Hall and Mr Frisby). If that hurdle is crossed the court then has to decide whether to dismiss the possession action altogether or to suspend the possession order.

5.48 However, in an unauthorised encampment case the allocation and management of housing stock will not be a relevant consideration. In these circumstances it is argued that what has become known as the 'structured approach' to proportionality should be applied.

5.49 In *Jones v Canal & River Trust*[56] the Canal & River Trust (CRT) claimed a declaration and an injunction that entitled it to remove the appellant's boat, 'The Mrs T', from its waterways (which cover over 2,000 miles) under British Waterways Act 1983 s8 and British Waterways Act 1971 s13. The appellant lodged a defence which raised a number of points in resistance to the claim, including a defence based upon Article 8.

5.50 If a person wishes to obtain a licence to reside on a CRT waterway, the person (subject to having insurance and a boat safety certificate) will either require a 'home mooring' or will need to use his or her vessel 'bona fide for navigation': see British Waterways Act 1995 s17(3). CRT have produced guidance which attempts to interpret the phrase 'bona fide for navigation' and is commonly known as the 'continuous cruising guidance'. The appellant also sought to challenge the lawfulness of the guidance in his defence.

5.51 In 2014, CRT asked for an order dismissing summarily the appellant's Article 8 defence. CRT argued that its claim should be judged according to the same broad criteria applicable to public housing authorities who apply for possession of residential premises and are met by Article 8 defences, as considered in the cases of *Pinnock* and

56 [2017] EWCA Civ 135, [2017] HLR 25.

Powell.[57] The county court judge adopted the *Pinnock* and *Powell* approach and struck out the appellant's Article 8 defence and a High Court judge dismissed his appeal.

5.52 On appeal the appellant argued that the *Pinnock* and *Powell* approach should be confined to housing cases. The Court of Appeal agreed and McCombe LJ (giving the leading judgment) stated (paras 52–59):

> It does not seem to me that the Pinnock line of cases demonstrate a true exception to the requirement of a structured approach to the proportionality assessment. Rather, I think, the position is that in public authority housing cases the Article 8 issues are more amenable to a pre-trial summary assessment and determination in the authority's favour than in other cases in which such issues of proportionality arise. In the Pinnock-type of case, the court is capable of deciding on such a summary application whether or not the Article 8 considerations afford seriously arguable grounds for resisting the authority's claims in whole or in part . . .
>
> It is possible that in some waterways cases the court will be able similarly to take a robust approach to claims to assert the public interest considerations in the exercise of the Respondent's powers over rights arising under Article 8. . . .
>
> In the circumstances facing the learned County Court judge in this case, however, I do not consider that the overall context of the proceedings allowed the judge summarily to dismiss the Article 8 defences as he did. . . . I will shortly summarise why I have reached this conclusion here.
>
> First, while I agree that the Respondent's property rights in the canal and the public interest in the management functions exercised by the Respondent can usually be taken as read, I am not satisfied that the judge could properly dispose of the Article 8 considerations before deciding whether the licence conditions had truly been broken and that property rights and management rights under s.8 of the 1983 Act, therefore, could be invoked unquestioningly, subject only to Convention rights. Second, it was not sought to argue that the Appellant's defence under the Equality Act 2010 could be summarily determined; it survives on the pleadings. Third, the Respondent seeks extensive relief, including injunctions restraining any mooring of any duration on the K & A [Kennet & Avon] canal, restraining navigation upon any of the extensive waterways controlled by it and an order for immediate removal of the Appellant's home, viz. the boat, from the K & A canal. With regard to this

57 See also *Thurrock BC v West* [2012] EWCA Civ 1435. In those cases where the courts had to take account of the housing management functions of local housing authorities, it was held that any Article 8 defence would need to be 'exceptional' for it to be successful.

third consideration, I do not quite see how the judge could properly say, as he did in paragraph 21 of his judgment, that Article 8 was not 'cast from [the court's] mind' on questions of relief when the relevant paragraphs of the Defence had already been struck out.

I do not accept Mr Stoner's submission . . . that the extent of the relief to be granted at the end of a trial could be re-visited in the context of Article 8. That was no doubt an intentionally helpful concession, but a difficult one to maintain in the face of the extensive relief sought by his client after all Article 8 considerations had been struck out of the Defence.

Ground 3 is directed to the County Court judge's view that it would 'impose a quite significant burden' on the Respondent by requiring it to deal in every enforcement case with any possible Article 8 points raised on behalf of a defendant. The judge doubted whether it was reasonable to impose that burden on the Respondent.

. . . In my view . . . the burden of dealing with an Article 8 defence is one that will from time to time, however, have to be shouldered by the court in assessing a defendant's personal circumstances and in the balancing exercise in weighing those circumstances against the 'given' represented by the Respondent's aims in the proceedings. I have made suggestions as to areas in which summary disposal of such defences may be possible. However, I do not consider that the judge was correct in identifying the 'burden' of dealing with Article 8 defences as a reason for striking them out summarily.

5.53 Turning back to *Powell,* there was argument in that case on the possible suspension of the order. That argument centred on Housing Act 1980 s89 which states:

(1) Where a court makes an order for the possession of any land in a case not falling within the exceptions mentioned in subsection (2) [none of these exceptions apply to Gypsies and Travellers on unauthorised encampments or unauthorised developments] . . . the giving up of possession shall not be postponed . . . to a date later than fourteen days after the making of the order, unless it appears to the court that exceptional hardship would be caused by requiring possession to be given up by that date; and shall not in any event be postponed to a date later than six weeks after the making of the order.

The Supreme Court concluded that this section was compatible with the HRA 1998.

5.54 Lord Phillips did point out an unexpected potential consequence of this (para 103):

The clear limit on the judge's discretion to postpone the operation of the order may thus, in rare cases, have the consequence that the order is refused, whereas it would otherwise have been granted, subject to postponement of its operation for a greater period than section 89 permits. This is not a consequence that Parliament can have envisaged.

5.55 In *R (JL) v Secretary of State for Defence*[58] the Court of Appeal dismissed an appeal against a judge's decision that a proportionality argument could be raised at the enforcement stage of a possession order (ie after it had been made and when a writ or warrant to bailiffs to execute the order had been issued) although only in exceptional cases, otherwise it would be an abuse of court process. The Court of Appeal said that such a case might arise where 'there is a fundamental change in the occupant's personal circumstances after the making of the possession order but before its enforcement' (para 41) or, as in that case, where the state of the law at the time of the possession hearing was that the proportionality argument could not be made (para 42). Then, in *Lawal v Circle 33 Housing Trust Ltd*[59] the Court of Appeal stated that a proportionality argument could also be raised at the enforcement stage in circumstances where an Article 8 defence had been advanced before the first instance judge but she 'either declined to hear it or peremptorily dismissed it but in either case she gave no reasons for doing so' (para 89, Sir Terence Etherton LJ). In practice, such arguments can probably only be raised by judicial review proceedings challenging the decision to request the issue of the writ or warrant as no further court hearing is normally required before such issue takes place.

Strasbourg decisions on evictions and Article 8

5.56 In *Yordanova and others v Bulgaria*[60] the ECtHR found that the threatened forcible eviction of a Roma 'shanty town' by the relevant municipal authority was a breach of Article 8. Our courts must take ECtHR judgments into account when determining any question which has arisen in connection with a right protected by the ECHR and advocates representing Gypsies and Travellers should rely on the decision in *Yordanova* when arguing that any decision to evict or remove their clients from land is disproportionate in terms of ECHR Article 8.

5.57 The facts in *Yordanova* are of interest. At the end of the 1960s and in the early 1970s the applicants or their parents and grandparents

58 [2013] EWCA Civ 449, [2013] HLR 27.

59 [2014] EWCA Civ 1514.

60 ECtHR, App No 25446/06, [2012] ECHR 758.

moved to Batalova Vodenitsa (BV), a neighbourhood of Sofia. They built their homes on state land without any authorisation. Some 200 to 300 Roma now lived there. Most of the buildings were single-storey houses. There was no sewage or plumbing. The applicants' houses did not meet the basic requirements of the relevant construction and safety regulations. Under the relevant domestic law the applicants could not obtain ownership of the land they occupied. Over the years a large number of complaints about this settlement had been made by non-Roma residents of BV.

5.58 In September 2005 the Mayor of Sofia ordered the forcible removal of the Roma living in the settlement under the Municipal Property Act. In the same month, the municipal authority agreed they would offer alternative housing to the Roma residents (no offers of alternative housing had, in fact, been made since then). Attempts were made by the applicants to challenge the removal order in the Bulgarian courts but these attempts were unsuccessful. The Bulgarian courts found that the fact that the applicants had not shown a valid legal ground for occupying the land was sufficient to establish that the removal order was valid.

5.59 In June 2008 the municipal authorities, relying on the removal order, served notices on the applicants requiring them to leave their homes failing which they would be forcibly evicted. The Roma residents applied to the ECtHR for relief and the ECtHR made an interim order that the applicants should not be evicted pending receipt by the ECtHR of detailed information about any arrangements to secure alternative housing. In concluding that there had been a breach of Article 8, the ECtHR stated (at paras 133–134):

> In general, the underprivileged status of the applicants' group must be a weighty factor in considering approaches to dealing with their unlawful settlement and, if their removal is necessary, in deciding on its timing, modalities and, if possible, arrangements for alternative shelter. This has not been done in the present case . . . In sum, the Court finds that the respondent Government failed to establish that the removal order of 17 September 2005 was necessary in a democratic society for the achievement of the legitimate aims pursued.

5.60 In *Winterstein v France*[61] the ECtHR provided a very important judgment on the question of eviction of unauthorised encampments of Gypsies and Travellers in the context of Article 8.

5.61 The applicants, 25 French citizens, had been living in mobile homes in a French town for many years. The site where the applicants' mobile homes were situated was a protected natural area under

61 ECtHR, App No 27013/07, 17 October 2013, [2013] ECHR 984.

the land-use plan of the department. The authorities never sought to enforce judgments against the applicants to leave the land, even after many years, but the authorities had taken steps to relocate several families. Four of the applicants' families received social housing, two families moved to another part of the country, and the rest of the applicants remained on the same land.

5.62 The urgent applications judge dismissed the action of the municipality to evict the residents. Another (non-urgent) action was brought by the municipality before the tribunal de grande instance, which ordered the defendants to leave the land within three months from the date of the judgment and pay a 70 euro fine per person, for each day of delay. The French Court of Appeal upheld the tribunal's judgment. The applicants did not proceed with an appeal, as they were denied legal aid.

5.63 The 25 applicants and the International Movement ATD Fourth World complained to the ECtHR, claiming that the court order amounted to a violation of Article 8 taken alone and in conjunction with Article 14 (prohibition of discrimination). A Chamber of the ECtHR held unanimously that the eviction of the Travellers from the land they occupied for many years amounted to a violation of their right to private and family lives. The ECtHR stated:

> The Court would emphasise in this context that numerous international instruments, some of which have been adopted within the Council of Europe, emphasise the necessity, in the event of the forced eviction of Roma and Travellers, of providing them with alternative housing, except in cases of force majeure.

5.64 If local or other public authorities are seeking to evict Gypsies and Travellers from unauthorised encampments in the UK they must have regard to the relevant government guidance including the need to carry out welfare enquiries (see further below). They must also have regard to Article 8 and the possibility of alternative locations and, in the case of local authorities, to their homelessness duties. *Winterstein* is clearly a very important judgment in this area and should be brought to the attention of all local and public authorities who are considering the eviction of Gypsies and Travellers.

Best interests of the child[62]

5.65 In any eviction situation involving children, it is essential that their interests are taken into account as a primary consideration.[63]

62 See also para 2.96, onwards, above.

63 See the line of cases referred to in para 2.97 onwards.

5.66 Except in an extreme case, it would seem difficult for a public authority to comply with that obligation without carrying out a child impact assessment, setting out the relevant factors and considerations, evaluating them and coming to a reasoned decision. If it has not taken such steps before deciding to evict a family with children, then a request should be made to the public authority to do so.[64]

5.67 The decision in *Eastwood v Surrey CC*[65] was made by a county court judge and thus, not authoritative. However, it does provides us with a useful example of how the 'best interests of the child' can be used in the context of a defence to eviction action brought by a local authority and also provides an excellent summary of the current legal position on this issue.

5.68 Mr and Mrs Eastwood were squatting on a vacant pitch on a Surrey County Council site. The council threatened eviction action. Mrs Eastwood was pregnant and shortly before the possession proceedings were commenced she gave birth to a son. A district judge made a possession order. The Eastwoods appealed against that decision on the basis that the best interests of the child had not been taken into account. They were successful in their appeal and the matter was remitted to the district judge. When giving judgment, HHJ Raeside reviewed the relevant authorities and, having done so, applied the law to the facts:

> 21. . . . It is accepted by Mr Cottle [counsel for the Eastwoods] that the child's human rights were not engaged until his birth in September 2012. The Local Authority therefore had an obligation to consider the child's interests either at that point or (as Mr Cottle accepted) the LA could carry out an assessment of his best interests pre-birth (in anticipation of his birth). Those interests would need to be re-evaluated if anything occurred out of the ordinary following his birth (for example, any unforeseen health or social needs) . . .
>
> 27. In my view the Appellants have clearly established that the Local Authority has failed to place the child's needs in primary place in their decision making process. The report discusses the pregnancy as a 'health problem' but nowhere is there any mention of the child itself; of the child's likely needs, of the impact on the child if possession proceedings were commenced, or if an eviction order was made. One would expect to see some sort of analysis of the welfare needs of the child and its parents

64 See also *Mohamoud v Royal Borough of Kensington and Chelsea* [2015] EWCA (Civ) 780, for the proposition that local authorities do not have a positive duty to have in place procedures to consider the best interests of the child unless that issue has been raised by the defendant in an eviction case.

65 Case No 2RH00537, Surrey County Court, 12 February 2014.

balanced with the need for the LA to run a fair system of allocation of places, remembering at all times that the child's needs are the primary consideration.

28. I recognise that the authorities state that in most cases the needs of a child can be adequately represented by consideration of the needs of the parent. But the authorities go on to give clear guidance about the role that the child's best interests must have in the decision making process. Looking at the papers I do not get the impression that any thought at all was given to the needs of the child or his welfare. . . .

29. . . . In those circumstances, the possession order must be set aside with the matter to be listed urgently before [the district judge] for further directions. I anticipate that the Local Authority will give further thought and consideration to its decision, and may exercise its decision making functions anew.

Criminal Justice and Public Order Act 1994 s61

Who can use it?

The police

5.69 Criminal Justice and Public Order Act (CJPOA) 1994 s61 states:

> (1) If the senior police officer present at the scene reasonably believes that two or more persons are trespassing on land and are present there with the common purpose of residing there for any period, that reasonable steps have been taken by or on behalf of the occupier to ask them to leave and–
> (a) that any of those persons has caused damage to the land or to property on the land or used threatening, abusive or insulting words or behaviour towards the occupier, a member of his family or an employee or agent of his, or
> (b) that those persons have between them six or more vehicles on the land,
> he may direct those persons, or any of them, to leave the land and to remove any vehicles or other property they have with them on the land.

5.70 Failure to comply with such a direction to leave may result in arrest without a warrant[66] and impoundment of vehicles.[67] Section 61(4) contains the details of the 'offence':

66 The power of arrest was originally contained in CJPOA 1994 s61(5) but is now to be found in the Police and Criminal Evidence Act 1984 s24.

67 CJPOA 1994 s62.

> If a person knowing that a direction under subsection (1) above has been given which applies to him –
> (a) fails to leave the land as soon as reasonably practicable, or
> (b) having left again enters the land as a trespasser within the period of three months beginning with the day on which the direction was given,
>
> he commits an offence and is liable on summary conviction to imprisonment for a term not exceeding three months or a fine not exceeding level 4 on the standard scale, or both.

5.71 The CJPOA 1994 s61 powers are regularly used by the police in England. By way of contrast, a report by Pat Niner, *Accommodation needs of Gypsy-Travellers in Wales* (Welsh Assembly Government, April 2006) found that the Welsh police had not used section 61 powers over the previous three-year period;[68] and the Police Scotland Guidance *Gypsies/Travellers Management of Unauthorised Encampments: Standard Operating Procedure* (2014) states:

> 6.4 Although unauthorised encampment is a criminal offence, in accordance with the Scottish Government Guidelines for Managing Unauthorised Camping by Gypsies/Travellers in Scotland, there is a general presumption against prosecution of Gypsies/Travellers for setting up unauthorised encampments. Prosecution will only be considered when:–
> a) A suitable alternative stopping place has been identified and the Gypsies/Travellers have refused to re-locate within a reasonable time (it is the responsibility of the local authority to identify the stopping place. The Police have no power to do this); or
> b) Where the use of a particular site by Gypsies/Travellers, or the excessive size of the encampment, causes a severe road safety or public health hazard; or
> c) Where the same Gypsies/Travellers have been repeatedly evicted from a site by the local authority and return after a short time.[69]

5.72 There are several 'hurdles' which the police must cross before being able to properly justify a CJPOA 1994 s61 eviction.

'The senior police officer present'

5.73 CJPOA 1994 s61(3) states:

68 See paras 5.13–5.14 of the report.

69 See also Scottish Government *Guidance for Local Authorities on Managing Unauthorised Camping by Gypsy/Travellers in Scotland* (2017) available at: www.gov.scot/Publications/2017/04/6796.

> A direction under subsection (1) above, if not communicated to the persons referred to in subsection (1) by the police officer giving the direction, may be communicated to them by any constable at the scene.

5.74 Since CJPOA 1994 s61(1) makes clear that the senior police officer must be present at the scene of the trespass, it must follow (if section 61(3) is to have any meaning) that the 'senior police officer present' must be above the rank of constable, even if he or she does not personally communicate the direction to leave. It should be noted that there is no requirement for a section 61 removal direction to be in writing and commonly it is given verbally. However, some police forces have a policy of giving a written notice and it can be important to be aware of any such written policies that exist. The Office of the Deputy Prime Minister (ODPM)/Home Office *Guide to effective use of enforcement powers – Part 1: Unauthorised encampments*[70] (hereafter 'the 2006 Encampment Guidance'), with regard to the police powers of eviction, states:

> Once a decision to use police powers is made, a uniformed police officer visits the encampment and advises the occupiers that they are required to leave by a certain date and time, and provides them with a copy of the legislation. The police may determine the period of notice to the unauthorised campers to leave, and this may be hours or days. The police may also videotape their visit to the encampment in case of later challenge or dispute.[71]

The recommendation that a copy of the relevant legislation should be provided is an important one. It would now seem logical for all police forces to incorporate the relevant piece of legislation within a formal, written notice.[72] Reference should also be made to the National Police Chiefs' Council (NPCC) *Operational Advice on Unauthorised Encampments* (2018).[73]

'Two or more persons . . . with the common purpose of residing'

5.75 Very occasionally one meets with a Gypsy or Traveller travelling alone. The police cannot use their CJPOA 1994 s61 powers against such a person. Additionally, if the Gypsies or Travellers have stopped for some purpose other than 'residing' (for example, to make a hot drink or to change a flat tyre) then section 61 cannot be used. This is

70 Issued in February 2006.

71 2006 Encampment Guidance para 48.

72 It should also be noted that 'days' may be given for the Gypsies and Travellers concerned to leave.

73 See para 5.207 onwards, below.

regardless of the perceived inconvenience of the location (for example, a super- market car park). It should also be noted that, under section 61(9) – the definition section:

> . . . a person may be regarded for the purposes of this section as having a purpose of residing in a place notwithstanding that he has a home elsewhere.

Thus, Gypsies and Travellers who, for example, have a pitch on an official site but are in the process of travelling for seasonal work, might be caught by section 61 if they stop on land without permission despite the existence of their 'home' elsewhere. It should also be noted that, unlike the local authority powers of eviction under CJPOA 1994 s77,[74] the Gypsies or Travellers do not have to be in vehicles. Thus Gypsies and Travellers in tents or benders, for example, can be served with a direction even if they do not have a vehicle.[75]

'Trespassing on land'

5.76 Trespass has its ordinary meaning. By CJPOA 1994 s61(9):

> 'land' does not include–
> (a) buildings other than–
> (i) agricultural buildings within the meaning of, in England and Wales, paragraphs 3 to 8 of Schedule 5 to the Local Government Finance Act 1988 . . .
> (ii) scheduled monuments within the meaning of the Ancient Monuments and Archaeological Areas Act 1979;
> (b) land forming part of–
> (i) a highway unless it falls within the classifications in section 54 of the Wildlife and Countryside Act 1981 (footpath, bridleway or byway open to all traffic or road used as a public path) or is a cycle track under the Highways Act 1980 or the Cycle Tracks Act 1984 . . .

5.77 Therefore, the police will not be able to serve a removal direction under CJPOA 1994 s61 on Gypsies and Travellers who are camping on the highway (subject to the exceptions detailed above). It is quite common for Gypsies or Travellers to be encamped at the end of dead-end roads, in cul-de-sacs, on lay-bys or on highway verges.[76] Section 61 cannot be used to evict them from such a site.

74 See para 5.113 onwards, below.

75 Providing CJPOA 1994 s61(1)(a) is satisfied. A 'bender' is a dome-shaped, tent-like structure, constructed by fixing tarpaulin over wooden rods or poles.

76 See also, Criminal Law Act 1977 s6 regarding use of violence to secure entry to premises (which can include the curtilage of a building).

5.78 In passing, it should be noted that squatting in a residential building is now a criminal offence under the Legal Aid, Sentencing and Punishment Act (LASPO) 2012 s144:

> (1) A person commits an offence if–
> (a) the person is in a residential building as a trespasser having entered it as a trespasser,
> (b) the person knows or ought to know that he or she is a trespasser, and
> (c) the person is living in the building or intends to live there for any period.
> (2) The offence is not committed by a person holding over after the end of a lease or licence (even if the person leaves and re-enters the building).
> (3) For the purposes of this section–
> (a) 'building' includes any structure or part of a structure (including a temporary or moveable structure), and
> (b) a building is 'residential' if it is designed or adapted, before the time of entry, for use as a place to live.

It should also be noted that 'building' does not include the land ancillary to the building (eg the garden or the yard) and, thus, Gypsies and Travellers stopping on such land are not committing an offence.

'Reasonable steps . . . by or on behalf of the occupier to ask them to leave'

5.79 The leading case on this issue is *R (Fuller) v Chief Constable of the Dorset Constabulary and Secretary of State for the Home Department.*[77] This case involved an unauthorised encampment on a former rubbish tip owned by Weymouth BC. After a period of 'toleration', and following an incident at the site concerning a confrontation between two police officers and certain Travellers, the police and the local authority simultaneously served removal directions which expired at the same time. This action was quashed by the High Court. Giving judgment, Stanley Burnton J gave a useful summary of the effect of CJPOA 1994 s61:

> In construing section 61 of the 1994 Act on the basis of common law principles, it is necessary to bear in mind that because it creates a criminal offence it is to be narrowly construed. Indeed, it creates a draconian procedure. I accept the claimants' point that Travellers are likely to comply with a direction under section 61 through fear of arrest and the forcible removal and detention of their vehicles although they may have

77 [2002] 3 All ER 57.

> an arguable justification for remaining on the land. Section 61 must, I think, be all the more narrowly construed for that reason.
>
> The claimants submitted . . . that section 61(1) assumes that the steps taken by the occupier to ask the trespassers to leave have been ineffective: i.e. they have refused to leave. Whereas section 61(1)(a) applies to persons who have already been guilty of criminal or other misconduct, section 61(1)(b) applies to persons who may have been perfectly well-behaved. It seems to me that Parliament was unlikely to have intended to bring the criminal law to bear on such trespassers who had not refused to leave when asked. On this basis, section 61(1) is to be read as impliedly requiring that the trespassers have not complied with the occupier's request that they leave as a condition of the making of a direction by the police under the section.[78]

In other words, the occupier must give notice to leave before there can be any question of the police serving a section 61 removal direction. Thus, for example, a private landowner might give 48 hours' notice for the Gypsies or Travellers to leave. If they have not left at the end of that 48-hour period, then the police can decide to use section 61. However, what is the position if the landowner or occupier is a local authority or other public authority?

5.80 In order to answer this question it is necessary to consider the extent to which local authorities and other public authorities must take account of welfare or humanitarian considerations before evicting trespassers from their land.[79] If a local authority (or other public authority) has failed to take account of humanitarian considerations before deciding to evict Gypsies or Travellers residing on their land without permission, then it is arguable that their failure to do so may, in itself, mean that reasonable steps have not yet been taken by the occupier. In the *Fuller* case, Stanley Burnton J stated:

> In my judgment, a local authority must consider the Convention rights of trespassers and their human needs generally when deciding whether or not to enforce its right to possession of that land.[80]

It must be clear, therefore, that a local authority must make enquiries into welfare issues before it can come to a decision on eviction.[81]

78 [2002] 3 All ER 57 at 69.

79 See 'public law challenges' at para 5.159 onwards, below.

80 *Fuller* [2002] 3 All ER 57 at 74.

81 Other public authorities will also be required to take account of welfare inquiries.

Has one of the additional three criteria been met?

5.81 A removal direction cannot be issued unless the senior police officer present at the scene reasonably believes that the trespassers:

- have caused damage to land or property on the land;
- have used threatening, abusive or insulting words or behaviour; or
- have six or more vehicles between them on the land.

'Damage to land or property on land'

5.82 In terms of 'damage to land', CJPOA 1994 s61(9) defines 'property' as:

> (a) in England and Wales, property within the meaning of section 10(1) of the Criminal Damage Act 1971 . . .

Criminal Damage Act 1971 s10(1) defines 'property' as:

> . . . property of a tangible nature, whether real or personal, including money and – including wild creatures . . . not including mushrooms growing wild on any land or flowers, fruit or foliage of a plant growing wild on any land.

Additionally, CJPOA 1994 s61(9), states that 'damage':

> . . . includes the deposit of any substance capable of polluting the land.

Thus, fly-tipping is probably within the definition. However, it is unclear precisely what might be encompassed by the phrase 'damage to land'. In a nineteenth-century case, *Gayford v Chouler*, a farmer was awarded compensation from someone who walked across his hay meadow thus damaging the crop.[82] It might be hoped that a modern court would consider 'damage to land' to mean something more significant than squashed grass. Some possibilities might include:

- the breaking of a lock to a gate;
- damage to a height barrier;
- cutting wood for fires.

However, without any extensive definition within CJPOA 1994 and with a dearth of case-law on this issue, it is very difficult to predict what might be encompassed by the phrase.

82 *Gayford v Chouler* [1898] 1 QB 316.

'Threatening, abusive or insulting words or behaviour'

5.83 Any 'threatening, abusive or insulting words or behaviour' must be directed to 'the occupier, a member of his family or an employee or agent of his'. 'Occupier', under CJPOA 1994 s61(9), means:

> . . . in England and Wales, the person entitled to possession of the land by virtue of an estate or interest held by him. . . .

The rest of this criterion has its ordinary meaning and will turn on the evidence presented and the answers the Gypsies or Travellers have to any allegations that are made. It will be important for police officers to make sure that they treat Gypsies and Travellers fairly and that they do not jump to the conclusion that the evidence of the occupier or his or her agent should be preferred to that of the trespassers unless there are reasonable grounds for reaching such a conclusion.

'Six or more vehicles'

5.84 The definition of 'vehicle' is extremely wide. CJPOA 1994 s61(9) states:

> 'vehicle' includes–
> (a) any vehicle, whether or not it is in a fit state for use on roads, and includes any chassis or body, with or without wheels, appearing to have formed part of such a vehicle, and any load carried by, and anything attached to, such a vehicle; and
> (b) a caravan as defined in section 29(1) of the Caravan Sites and Control of Development Act 1960.

Thus, a caravan and its towing vehicle will constitute two vehicles. Three caravans and three towing vehicles will make the requisite six. Taking the ordinary meaning of the word 'vehicle' it can be implied that it is 'constructed'. Thus a motor-bike, barrel-top wagon or even a bicycle or derelict car may be covered by the term, but clearly the horse that pulls the wagon will not. A 'caravan' is defined, under Caravan Sites and Control of Development Act (CSCDA) 1960 s29(1), as:

> . . . any structure designed or adapted for human habitation which is capable of being moved from one place to another (whether by being towed, or by being transported on a motor vehicle or trailer) and any motor vehicle so designed or adapted, but does not include–
> (a) any railway rolling stock which is for the time being on rails forming part of a railway system, or
> (b) any tent . . .

Thus, the term 'caravan' not only includes caravans as such but also camper vans, motor vehicles designed or adapted for human habitation (such as buses, lorries or removal vans) and mobile homes. Some Gypsies and Travellers have been known to park five or less vehicles on the land in question and to park the rest of their vehicles off the land, for example, on a nearby road, so as to avoid falling foul of section 61.

The statutory defence

5.85 The statutory defence to CJPOA 1994 s61 evictions is contained in section 61(6):

> In proceedings for an offence under this section it is a defence for the accused to show–
> (a) that he was not trespassing on the land, or
> (b) that he had a reasonable excuse for failing to leave the land as soon as reasonably practicable or, as the case may be, for again entering the land as a trespasser.

If Gypsies or Travellers can show that they have permission from the occupier of land to remain there, they are clearly not trespassers and the section cannot be used.

5.86 In the case of *Krumpa v DPP*,[83] the Divisional Court considered the meaning of the phrase 'reasonably practicable'[84] and concluded that the question whether something was 'reasonably practicable' should be considered objectively and was not a matter that could be determined solely by the police officer's view of what was reasonable. However, in *Fuller*,[85] Stanley Burnton J adopted a very narrow interpretation of the phrase in the context of removal directions and stated that:

> If the trespassers have failed to comply with the occupier's request, there is no reason for a direction not to take immediate effect.[86]

5.87 It is not uncommon for the police to use video evidence when dealing with an unauthorised encampment. Clearly, if the police were to take more intrusive video evidence (for example, by filming the interior of

83 [1989] Crim LR 295.

84 In the context of the Public Order Act 1986 which first introduced the police powers of eviction against Gypsies, Travellers and other trespassers.

85 [2002] 3 All ER 57 at 70.

86 Nevertheless, as mentioned at para 5.74, above, para 48 of the 2006 Encampment Guidance contemplates the police giving notice which may last 'days'.

vehicles, as has been known to happen in the past) then they may commit an unjustified interference with the rights of the trespassers to respect for their private and family life and their homes (as protected by ECHR Article 8).[87]

Obtaining a court order

5.88 Gypsies or Travellers who fail to comply with a valid removal direction under CJPOA 1994 s61 or who return to the land within the specified three-month period can face arrest and impoundment of their vehicles (that is, their homes) without the need for any court order to be obtained. If arrest or impoundment has occurred, or if the Gypsies or Travellers remain on the land in defiance of the removal direction, the police will have to seek a further order from a magistrates court. When the matter comes to court, the Gypsies or Travellers will have the opportunity of putting forward an argument that the police have failed to comply with the statutory requirements or to rely upon the statutory defence referred to above. However, in practice the very threat of arrest and/or impoundment before the matter comes to court is likely to force Gypsies and Travellers to vacate an unauthorised encampment even where they or their advisers believe that there has been a failure to comply with the statutory requirements or that the statutory defence can be advanced.

5.89 Alternatively, the use of CJPOA 1994 s61 powers may be challenged by way of judicial review if the police have acted unlawfully, for example, by:

- failing to take into account a relevant matter;
- acting unreasonably in failing to properly address a defence raised by the trespassers; or
- acting 'disproportionately' in terms of ECHR Article 8.

In practice, such a 'public law challenge' will need to be lodged very swiftly.[88]

87 See *Campbell v MGN Limited* [2004] UKHL 22. For further discussion of ECHR Article 8, see chapter 2 above. See also the Regulation of Investigatory Powers Act 2000.

88 For further discussion of Article 8 and 'proportionality', see chapter 2 above.

CJPOA 1994 s62A

Who can use it?

The police

5.90 The Anti-Social Behaviour Act 2003 inserted section 62A into CJPOA 1994.[89] Section 62A exists alongside CJPOA 1994 s61. In other words, the police can use either power, provided, of course, the necessary criteria are met. Section 62A, which is entitled 'Power to remove trespassers: alternative site available', states as follows:

> (1) If the senior police officer present at a scene reasonably believes that the conditions in subsection (2) are satisfied in relation to a person and land, he may direct the person–
> (a) to leave the land;
> (b) to remove any vehicle and other property he has with him on the land.
>
> (2) The conditions are–
> (a) that the person and one or more others ('the trespassers') are trespassing on land;
> (b) that the trespassers have between them at least one vehicle on the land;
> (c) that the trespassers are present on the land with the common purpose of residing there for any period,
> (d) if it appears to the officer that the person has one or more caravans in his possession or under his control on the land, that there is a suitable pitch on a relevant caravan site for that caravan or each of those caravans;
> (e) that the occupier of the land or a person acting on his behalf has asked the police to remove the trespassers from the land.
>
> (3) A direction under subsection (1) may be communicated to the person to whom it applies by any constable at the scene.
>
> (4) Subsection (5) applies if–
> (a) a police officer proposes to give a direction under subsection (1) in relation to a person and land, and
> (b) it appears to him that the person has one or more caravans in his possession or under his control on the land.
>
> (5) The officer must consult every local authority within whose area the land is situated as to whether there is a suitable pitch for the caravan or each of the caravans on a relevant caravan site which is situated in the local authority's area.

89 The Traveller Law Reform Coalition, when making submissions during the passage of the Anti-Social Behaviour Bill, pointed out that it was extremely insulting to Gypsies and Travellers to include unauthorised encampments per se within the scope of a measure designed to tackle anti-social behaviour.

5.91 Though the provisions in section 62A are very similar to those in section 61 there are some important differences and these will be emphasised, where they occur, below.

'The senior police officer present'

5.92 It seems that a police constable could give such a direction though there will have to be a more senior officer present.[90]

'Trespassers'

5.93 CJPOA 1994 s62A(2)(a) refers to 'the person and one or more others'. The presence of 'and' seems to indicate, as is the case with section 61, that a single Gypsy or Traveller encamped on his or her own cannot be caught by this section.[91]

'Land'

5.94 CJPOA 1994 s62E(2) states that:

> 'Land' does not include buildings other than–
> (a) agricultural buildings within the meaning of paragraphs 3 to 8 of Schedule 5 to the Local Government Finance Act 1988, or
> (b) scheduled monuments within the meaning of the Ancient Monuments and Archaeological Areas Act 1979.

'Common purpose of residing there'

5.95 If the Gypsies or Travellers are simply stopping on the way to somewhere else, for example, so that they can have a meal, then the section would not apply.[92]

'Caravans'

5.96 CJPOA 1994 s62A refers to identifying a suitable pitch for a 'caravan'. The definition section[93] gives the word 'caravan' the same meaning as that given to it in the CSCDA 1960.[94] If the Gypsies or Travellers are residing in benders or tents the section does not apply. This differs from section 61, which can be used against Gypsies or

90 See the discussion at paras 5.73–5.74, above, which applies equally here.
91 See paras 5.76–5.78, above.
92 See para 5.75, above.
93 CJPOA 1994 s62A(6).
94 For the definition of 'caravan', see para 5.84, above.

Travellers residing solely in benders or tents.[95] However, it is nowadays rare to come across Gypsies or Travellers residing in benders or tents, so there will be few cases where this issue arises in practice.

'Suitable pitch'

5.97 The inclusion of the word 'suitable' is important. No case-law exists at present to help in the definition of 'suitable pitch'. The ODPM *Guidance on Managing Unauthorised Camping* (February 2004, hereafter the '2004 Encampment Guidance')[96] states:

> The meaning of suitable pitch is not defined in the legislation. Of course, it is for the courts to interpret legislation, but the Secretary of State considers that a *suitable pitch* is one that provides basic amenities including water, toilets and waste disposal facilities. Other factors include the potential for community tension and issues of public order/anti-social behaviour need to be considered especially where the trespasser intends to remain on the site for the three month period. This could include an authorised transit site or stopping place. There should be a reasonable expectation that the pitch will be available for peaceful occupation for at least three months, except where the trespasser is expecting to move on before that time.

Additionally, the 2004 Encampment Guidance states that:

> A suitable pitch will only be available if there are currently no waiting lists for that site.

5.98 It seems unlikely that the police will be able to use CJPOA 1994 s62A to evict Gypsies and Travellers until local authorities provide sufficient sites for them. According to a report on the Guardian website in 2011, there were only 287 transit pitches in the whole of England.[97] However, there was no indication in the report of how many of those transit pitches had sufficient amenities for them to be deemed 'suitable'.

5.99 A pitch may not be suitable for a number of reasons. For example, it may be on a site occupied by people that are in dispute with the

95 See para 5.75 above.

96 The guidance on sections 62A–62E was released as an add-on to the 2004 Encampment Guidance on 7 March 2005. The Welsh Government *Guidance on Managing Unauthorised Camping 2013* (hereafter 'the 2013 Welsh Guidance') at para 63 is in very similar terms though there are subtle differences. For the full text of the 2013 Guidance see appendix C.

97 See at: www.theguardian.com/news/datablog/2011/jun/29/gypsy-sites-england-local-authority.

Gypsies and Travellers that the police wish to evict. The 2004 Encampment Guidance states:

> There must be close working between site managers and local authority and police officers dealing with unauthorised camping over allocations of pitches on sites. Site managers may be aware of issues around Gypsy/Traveller group and family compatibility, which must be taken into account when allocating pitches on residential sites.[98]

There is no equivalent section in the Welsh Government *Guidance on Managing Unauthorised Camping 2013* (hereafter 'the 2013 Welsh Guidance').

5.100 However, it can be argued that, whether in England or in Wales, the question of 'compatibility' of groups or families will be relevant to the issue of whether the pitch offered is 'suitable'. Another important factor relevant to the issue of suitability is the location of the pitch and its distance from schools, work and healthcare provision. Local authorities will also have to have regard to their allocations policy for any particular site to which it is suggested that a Gypsy or Traveller should be directed and ensure that that is also being followed.

5.101 The pitch must be on a 'relevant caravan site' which is defined as:

> . . . a caravan site which is–
> (a) situated in the area of a local authority within whose area the land is situated, and
> (b) managed by a relevant site manager.[99]

Therefore, if a Gypsy or Traveller is encamped in the area of a district council, the site could be anywhere within the relevant county council area. 'Relevant site manager' is defined as:

> (a) a local authority within whose area the land is situated;
> (b) a registered social landlord.[100]

5.102 Therefore the site must either be managed by the local authority or by a registered social landlord, such as a housing association. If the site is managed by some other organisation, even if it is owned by the local authority in question, it will not be a 'relevant caravan site'. This is an important point for advisers or solicitors to be aware of.

5.103 It may also be the case that suitable pitches can only be identified for some of the Gypsies or Travellers parked on an unauthorised

98 2004 Encampment Guidance at para 4.8.

99 CJPOA 1994 s62A(6).

100 CJPOA 1994 s62A(6). A housing association would be an example of a registered social landlord. To be a registered social landlord the body in question must be registered as such under Housing Act 1996 Part 1 Chapter 1.

encampment and it is possible for the section to be applied to only a part of the group of Gypsies or Travellers in question. However, if the group is an extended family[101] or if certain members of the group require special support from others within the group, it is suggested that those factors will also have to be taken into account in assessing the suitability of a pitch or pitches. In this regard the 2013 Welsh Guidance specifically states:

> [E]fforts should be made to find suitable pitches that would enable the unauthorised campers to remain together. If the size of the encampment is such that this is not possible, then efforts should be made to ensure that any dependent [sic] members of the encampment are not separated from necessary support.[102]

'Occupier'

5.104 CJPOA 1994 s61 provides that the occupier must take 'reasonable steps'.[103] Under section 62A the occupier (or someone acting on his behalf) merely has to ask the police to remove the trespassers and he or she does not have to give any notice to the Gypsies or Travellers or make any request for them to leave. However, if the occupier is a local authority or other public authority, it seems that it will still have to take account of welfare considerations before making a request to the police to use section 62A.[104]

'Communicated to the person'

5.105 As with CJPOA 1994 s61, there is no need for written notice to be given, though reference should be made to the NPCC guidance.[105] It appears that a Gypsy or Traveller, who is away from the land or otherwise not present when a direction to leave is communicated, may not be subject to the direction.

'Consult every local authority'

5.106 In England, this could involve not only a district council but also the relevant county council. No doubt local authorities and the police will

101 As is very common among Irish Travellers: see, for example, McDonagh *Nomadism' in Travellers: Citizens of Ireland*, The Parish of the Travelling People, Dublin, 2000, pp33–46.

102 2013 Guidance para 64.

103 See paras 5.79–5.80, above.

104 See further the discussion at para 5.162 onwards, below.

105 See also paras 5.74, above, and 5.207 onwards, below.

need to have in place policies for liaison and sharing of information. Additionally, this implies that the pitch offered could be on a county council site. If the latter site was a considerable distance away from the encampment, that factor raises the question of whether the pitch was 'suitable'.[106] Where the county council area is extremely large, it might be doubted, in relation to distance from schools or healthcare, whether anywhere in the area would automatically be 'suitable'.

Offences

5.107 A person commits an offence if he or she knows that a direction under CJPOA 1994 s62A(1) has been given which applies to him or her and the person:

(a) fails to leave the relevant land as soon as reasonably practicable;[107] or
(b) enters any land in the area of the relevant local authority as a trespasser before the end of the relevant period with the intention of residing there.[108]

The 'relevant period' is three months from the day on which the direction is given.[109] Importantly, it should be noted that this applies to all land in the relevant local authority area. However, the word 'relevant' qualifies 'local authority' in this context (contrast the position of an officer consulting the local authority or local authorities in the context of 'suitable pitch'). 'Relevant local authority' means:

(a) if the relevant land is situated in the area of more than one local authority (but is not in the Isles of Scilly), the district council or county borough council within whose area the relevant land is situated;
(b) . . . the Council of the Isles of Scilly;

in any other case, the local authority within whose area the relevant land is situated.[110]

Thus failure to comply with a direction under section 62A could result in an effective three-month ban from that local authority area (and not some wider county council area). However, if the Gypsies or Travellers, who have received a direction, stop on land in the area

106 See para 5.97 onwards, above.
107 For a discussion of the meaning of 'reasonably practicable' see para 5.86, above.
108 CJPOA 1994 s62B(1).
109 CJPOA 1994 s62B(2).
110 CJPOA 1994 s62E(6).

with the permission of the occupier, then they will not commit an offence.

5.108 If a Gypsy or Traveller is evicted by the police using CJPOA 1994 s61 and it is felt that eviction was unlawful, the only resort may be a police complaint. However, if a Gypsy or Traveller is evicted by the police using CJPOA 1994 s62A and it is felt that the eviction was unlawful, there would still be justification in lodging a court challenge (by way of judicial review) due to the effective three-month ban.

5.109 A person guilty of an offence is liable on summary conviction to imprisonment for a term not exceeding three months or a fine or both.[111] A constable may arrest a person committing an offence under this section.[112] A constable may also seize and remove any vehicles.[113]

Statutory defence

5.110 CJPOA 1994 s62B(5) states:

> In proceedings for an offence under this section it is a defence for the accused to show–
> (a) that he was not trespassing on the land in respect of which he is alleged to have committed the offence, or
> (b) that he had a reasonable excuse–
>   (i) for failing to leave the relevant land as soon as reasonably practicable, or
>   (ii) for entering the land in the area of the relevant local authority as a trespasser with the intention of residing there, or
> (c) that, at the time the direction was given, he was under the age of 18 years and was residing with his parent or guardian.

There is no case-law on the definition of 'reasonable excuse' in this context but it can be surmised that this might include mechanical breakdown or illness.[114] The exclusion of Gypsies or Travellers aged under 18 simply protects them from prosecution but will not normally (presuming they are travelling with adults) protect them from eviction. Again, as with CJPOA 1994 s61, it is likely that the section will normally be effective without the need to take the matter to court, since the threat of eviction and impoundment of their

111 The fine should not exceed level 4 on the standard scale: CJPOA 1994 s62B(3).
112 See footnote 67, above.
113 CJPOA 1994 s62C.
114 By analogy with CJPOA 1994 s77 – see further at para 5.113 onwards, below.

homes will usually be sufficient to persuade the Gypsies or Travellers to move.

5.111 As with CJPOA 1994 s61, if Gypsies or Travellers had been arrested[115] or have had their vehicles impounded[116] for failing to comply with a direction to leave under section 62A, or if they have not yet left the land (or have returned to other land in the area) in defiance of such a direction, the police would have to obtain a further order from the magistrates' court.[117]

5.112 Gypsy and Traveller support groups have voiced serious concerns about the use of CJPOA 1994 s62A.[118] The short deadlines that the police can give to Gypsies and Travellers mean that in practice it may be unlikely that a court will hear a public law challenge before eviction takes place. However, the fact that the eviction has been carried out will not render a public law challenge academic, because the Gypsies or Travellers may wish to challenge the use of section 62A in order to avoid committing an offence if they return to the area or remain in the area within three months of the day when the direction was given.

CJPOA 1994 s77

Who can use it?

Local authorities

5.113 CJPOA 1994 s77 states:

> (1) If it appears to a local authority that persons are for the time being residing in a vehicle or vehicles within that authority's area–
> (a) on any land forming part of a highway;
> (b) on any other unoccupied land; or
> (c) on any occupied land without the consent of the occupier,
> the authority may give a direction that those persons and any others with them are to leave the land and remove the vehicle or vehicles and any other property they have with them on the land.

The offence is defined by CJPOA 1994 s77(3) as follows:

> If a person knowing that a direction under subsection (1) above has been given which applies to him–

115 See footnote 67, above.

116 Under CJPOA 1994 s62C.

117 See also the discussion at para 5.88 onwards, above.

118 See also the conclusion at para 5.251, below.

(a) fails, as soon as practicable, to leave the land or remove from the land any vehicle or other property which is the subject of the direction, or
(b) having removed any such vehicle or property again enters the land with a vehicle within the period of three months beginning with the day on which the direction was given,

he commits an offence and is liable on summary conviction to a fine not exceeding level 3 on the standard scale.

5.114 This is a very wide-ranging power. There is a specific statutory defence that is discussed at para 5.127 and statutory requirements that must be met before the power can be exercised.

'Land'

5.115 'Land' for these purposes has a very wide meaning. CJPOA 1994 s77(6) states that:

> 'land' means land in the open air.

'Consent of the occupier'

5.116 Virtually all land, regardless of whether or not it is owned by the local authority, is potentially covered by CJPOA 1994 s77. The section cannot be used where the Gypsies or Travellers have the consent of the occupier to be there. However, as can be seen below,[119] local authorities can utilise planning enforcement powers in those circumstances. An attempt to argue that an encampment on land where there was no known owner or occupier was not covered by the section because the Gypsies themselves were the (adverse) occupiers, was unsuccessful at permission stage in the High Court.[120]

'Vehicle or vehicles'

5.117 In contrast to CJPOA 1994 s61, the Gypsies or Travellers must be residing in a vehicle or vehicles. Gypsies or Travellers who are not residing in vehicles (for example, because they are living instead in

119 At para 5.158, below.

120 *R (Caroline Stephenson) v East Derbyshire Magistrates' Court and Amber Valley BC* [2003] EWHC 903 (Admin), Sullivan J. In certain (rare) cases, where a Gypsy or Traveller has been residing on land that he or she did not own for 12 years or more without permission, he or she may be able to claim adverse possession of that land. However, the law on adverse possession is complex and has changed dramatically since the bringing into force of the Land Registration Act 2002. See Jourdan and Radley-Gardner, *Adverse Possession*, Butterworths, 2011 and supplement.

benders or tents) will not be covered by the section, unless they are with others residing in vehicles on the land.

'Written notice'

5.118 With regard to service of the required written notice of a removal direction under CJPOA 1994 s77, section 79 states:

> (2) Where it is impracticable to serve a relevant document on a person named in it, the document shall be treated as duly served on him if a copy of it is fixed in a prominent place to the vehicle concerned; and where a relevant document is directed to the unnamed occupants of vehicles, it shall be treated as duly served on those occupants if a copy of it is fixed in a prominent place to every vehicle on the land in question at the time when service is thus effected.
>
> (3) A local authority shall take such steps as may be reasonably practicable to secure that a copy of any relevant document is displayed on the land in question (otherwise than by being fixed to a vehicle) in a manner designed to ensure that it is likely to be seen by any person camping on the land.

If a written notice is not placed on the vehicle(s) of a Gypsy or Traveller, that may constitute a defence. The catch-all phrase in section 77(1), 'any others with them', means that Gypsies or Travellers living on the land in tents or benders will be subject to the removal direction if they are with others who are residing in vehicles on the land. In those circumstances, section 79(3) makes similar provision to that which covers CPR Part 55 proceedings for display of notices on stakes or by other prominent methods.

'As soon as practicable'

5.119 It should be noted that, in contrast to CJPOA 1994 s61(4)(a), the word 'reasonably' has been omitted from CJPOA 1994 s77(3)[121] and Gypsies and Travellers can be prosecuted if they fail to leave the land 'as soon as practicable' after a removal direction has been given. What is 'practicable' in any given case will depend upon the facts but it is likely that a magistrates' court would convict a Gypsy or Traveller who had failed to comply with a short deadline in all but exceptional cases.

121 See also para 5.86, above.

'Again enters the land . . . within the period of three months'

5.120 The question whether a Gypsy or Traveller has returned to the land within three months of the original removal direction will be a simple matter of fact. In a case where Gypsies had ignored a removal direction and remained on the land for more than three months before being prosecuted under CJPOA 1994 s79 it was unsuccessfully argued that a removal direction could only be effective for a period of three months and that there was no power to prosecute a person after that period of time had expired.[122]

Statutory defence

5.121 The statutory defence is contained within CJPOA 1994 s77(5) and can be relied on, like the other potential defences, if and when the matter comes before the magistrates' court. It states:

> In proceedings for an offence under this section it is a defence for the accused to show that his failure to leave or to remove the vehicle or other property as soon as practicable or his re-entry with a vehicle was due to illness, mechanical breakdown or other immediate emergency.

This is a fairly self-explanatory defence though there is currently no case-law to help us with the breadth (or otherwise) of the phrase 'other immediate emergency'. However, the practicalities of raising this statutory defence or arguing that any other statutory requirement has not been met (and thus turning up at court and risking a removal order and a fine) are dealt with in the conclusion to this chapter.[123]

Obtaining a court order

5.122 Under CJPOA 1994 s78:

> (1) A magistrates' court may, on a complaint made by a local authority, if satisfied that persons and vehicles in which they are residing are present on land within that authority's area in contravention of a direction given under section 77, make an order requiring the removal of any vehicle or other property which is so present on the land and any person residing in it.
> (2) An order under this section may authorise the local authority to take such steps as are reasonably necessary to ensure that the order is

122 *R (Caroline Stephenson) v East Derbyshire Magistrates' Court and Amber Valley BC* [2003] EWHC 903 (Admin).

123 At para 5.251, below.

complied with and, in particular, may authorise the local authority, by its officers and servants–

(a) to enter upon the land specified in the order; and

(b) to take, in relation to any vehicle or property to be removed in pursuance of the order, such steps for securing entry and rendering it suitable for removal, as may be so specified.

(3) The local authority shall not enter upon any occupied land unless they have given to the owner or occupier at least 24 hours' notice of their intention to do so, or unless after reasonable enquiries they are unable to ascertain their names and addresses.

5.123 Normally, therefore, such a removal order will ensure that the Gypsies or Travellers who are subject to the order will have at least 24 hours after the order is obtained within which to leave the land. This will not be the case, however, if the local authority is both the owner and the occupier of the land, or if the local authority cannot reasonably ascertain the identity of the owner or occupier. It has been the normal practice of local authorities, since this power of eviction was brought into force, to only seek a removal order and not to seek a conviction for the potential criminal offence under CJPOA s77(3).[124]

Highways Act 1980

Who can use it?

Local authorities and the police

5.124 A 'highway' is a way over which there exists a public right of passage, that is a right for all, at all seasons of the year, freely and at their will, to pass and re-pass without let or hindrance.[125] It should also be noted that a highway will include any footpaths or cycle tracks as well as the carriageway, and also any verge enjoyed by the public as part of the highway.[126]

5.125 Where a highway is created through the acquisition of land over which it passes, either by agreement or through the exercise of compulsory purchase powers, the highway authority is the owner both of the surface of the highway and the subsoil. However, where a highway is created by dedication (that is, with the permission of the landowner without releasing his or her rights over the land), the

124 See para 1.38, above.

125 *Ex p Lewis* (1888) 21 QBD 191 at 197, per Wills J.

126 See *DPP v Jones* [1999] 2 WLR 625.

subsoil[127] beneath the highway remains in the ownership of the 'dedicating landowner'.[128] Moreover, in the case of those highways which are not maintainable at public expense, both the surface of the highway and the subsoil remain within the ownership of the dedicating landowner.[129] Where the dedicating landowner retains ownership of the surface of the highway and/or the subsoil, he or she will be able to take possession action (for example, CPR Part 55 proceedings) against any trespassers on the highway.

5.126 If a person, without lawful authority or excuse, in any way wilfully obstructs the free passage along a highway, he or she is guilty of an offence.[130]

5.127 A lawful excuse will be established if it can be shown that the person causing the obstruction honestly but mistakenly believed, on reasonable grounds, that the facts were such as would make the conduct lawful.[131] However, there is no need to prove that a person intended to cause an obstruction – if an obstruction is caused and the person responsible for the obstruction acted of their own free will, that is sufficient.[132] Thus, for example, a person responsible for the obstruction will probably have a defence if his or her car has broken down and is thus causing an obstruction. Indeed, where the obstruction is of a temporary nature (as in the latter example), it will only be an offence if it is shown that the obstruction arose from unreasonable use of the highway.[133]

5.128 The case of *DPP v Jones*[134] raises an interesting question with regard to the use of highways legislation to 'move on' Gypsies or Travellers. The case did not involve action for breach of the highways

127 The surface of the road was defined by Denning LJ, in *Tithe Redemption Commission v Runcorn UDC* [1954] 2 WLR 518, as: 'the top spit, or perhaps . . . the top two spits, of the road' (at 530).

128 See *Truckell v Stock* (1957) 1 WLR 161; *Rolls v St George the Martyr, Southwark, Vestry* (1880) 14 Ch D 785.

129 See *Encyclopaedia of Highway Law and Practice*, Sweet & Maxwell, Volume 1 General Introduction para 1–003.

130 Highways Act 1980 s137(1). A person guilty of an offence is liable to a fine not exceeding level 3 on the standard scale.

131 *Cambridgeshire and Isle of Ely CC v Rust* [1972] 2 QB 426, [1972] 3 All ER 232.

132 *Arrowsmith v Jenkins* [1963] 2 QB 561.

133 *Nagy v Weston* [1965] 1 WLR 280, [1965] 1 All ER 78.

134 [1999] 2 WLR 625.

legislation but for 'trespassory assembly'.[135] The defendants took part in a peaceful, non-obstructive assembly on a highway. They were campaigning for the right to hold a festival at Stonehenge and were on the roadside verge, adjacent to the perimeter fence of the monument at Stonehenge. The House of Lords allowed the defendants' appeal against the Divisional Court finding that this amounted to a 'trespassory assembly'. The House of Lords held that the public had the right to use the highway for such reasonable and usual activities, including peaceful assembly, consistent with the primary right to use it for passage and repassage; it being a matter of fact and degree for the court in each case to decide whether the user was reasonable and not inconsistent with that primary right. Lord Irvine of Lairg stated:

> It is neither desirable in theory nor acceptable in practice for commonplace activities on the public highway not to count as breaches of the criminal law of wilful obstruction of the highway, yet to count as trespasses . . . and therefore form the basis for a finding of trespassory assembly for the purposes of the Act of 1986. A system of law sanctioning these discordant outcomes would not command respect.[136]

5.129 Gypsies or Travellers do not usually face actions on the basis of 'trespassory assemblies' but they do frequently stop for short periods on the verges of highways (which are considered to be part of the highway). Indeed, Gypsies and Travellers have been stopping in such locations, for short periods, for hundreds of years in the UK and their use of the verges for such a purpose could be described as a 'commonplace activity'. Nevertheless, it is common for Gypsies and Travellers on the verges of a carriageway to be moved on for allegedly obstructing the highway and the 'commonplace activity' argument has not yet been tested in court.

135 A 'trespassory assembly' is defined by Public Order Act 1986 s14A, as inserted by CJPOA 1994 s70, as: 'an assembly . . . intended to be held in any district at a place on land to which the public has no right of access or only a limited right of access [which] is likely to be held without the permission of the occupier of the land or to conduct itself in such a way as to exceed the limits of any permission of his or the limits of the public's rights of access and . . . may result – (i) in serious disruption to the life of the community, or (ii) where the land, or a building or monument on it, is of historical, architectural, archaeological or scientific importance, in significant damage to the land, building or monument . . .'

136 [1999] 2 AC 240 at 258B; [1999] 2 WLR 625 at 633F.

5.130 It is also an offence for any person in charge of a vehicle to cause or permit it, or a trailer (which could include a caravan) drawn by it, to remain at rest on any road in such position, condition or circumstances as to be likely to cause danger to other road users.[137]

5.131 On certain highways the keeper of any horses, cattle, sheep, goats or swine found straying on or lying on or at the side of the highway is guilty of an offence.[138]

5.132 Highways Act 1980 s149 gives highway authorities the power of impoundment:

> (1) If anything is so deposited on a highway as to constitute a nuisance, the highway authority for the highway may by notice require the person who deposited it there to remove it forthwith [and can apply to magistrates for a removal and disposal order].
> (2) If the highway authority for any highway have reasonable grounds for considering–
> (a) that anything unlawfully deposited on the highway constitutes a danger (including a danger caused by obstructing the view) to users of the highway, and
> (b) that the thing in question ought to be removed without the delay involved in giving notice or obtaining a removal and disposal order . . .
>
> the authority may remove the thing forthwith.

5.133 The 'thing unlawfully deposited' can include vehicles and caravans. If sufficient danger is caused by them being deposited on the highway then impoundment could occur. Otherwise, impoundment would not be possible without a court order.

5.134 In a case where a Gypsy or Traveller is prosecuted under any of the above statutory provisions he or she will be able to defend the proceedings successfully if the prosecuting authority are unable to satisfy the magistrates' court that all the elements of the alleged offence have been proved.

137 Road Traffic Act 1988 s22. A person guilty of an offence is liable to a fine not exceeding level 3 on the standard scale and also discretionary disqualification.

138 Highways Act 1980 s155(1). A person guilty of an offence is liable to a fine not exceeding level 3 on the standard scale. The animal in question can also be removed to the common pound.

Bye-laws

Who can use them?

Local authorities and certain other public authorities

5.135 A bye-law is an ordinance affecting the public and laid down by an authority which has been given statutory powers to do so.[139] If validly made, a bye-law has the force of law within its sphere of operation. Bye-laws made by local authorities must be confirmed by some central authority before they can have lawful effect.[140]

5.136 A local authority can either be given power to deal with specific matters or may make bye-laws for the good rule and government of the whole or any part of the area they cover, as well as for the prevention and suppression of nuisances.[141]

5.137 Bye-laws may not be made if they duplicate the provisions of other enactments.[142]

5.138 A copy of a bye-law or part of a bye-law must be provided to any person on request on payment of such sum as the authority may determine.[143]

5.139 A bye-law requires four elements for it to be valid:

a) it must be intra vires (that is, within the power of the authority making it);
b) it must not be 'repugnant' to the general law;
c) it must be certain;
d) it must be reasonable.

A bye-law must be intra vires. A local authority cannot take upon itself powers by means of a bye-law beyond the powers conferred on it by statute.[144]

5.140 A bye-law must not be repugnant to the general law. Therefore, a bye-law must not make something unlawful which the general law does not make unlawful.[145]

139 *Kruse v Johnson* [1898] 2 QB 91.
140 Local Government Act 1972 s236(3).
141 This applies to the council of a district, the council of a principal area in Wales, the council of a London borough and the Council of the Isles of Scilly: Local Government Act 1972 s235(1) as amended by the Local Government (Wales) Act 1994 s66(5), Sch 15 para 49.
142 See, for example, *Galer v Morrissey* [1955] 1 All ER 380.
143 Local Government Act 1972 s236(6) – currently the sum must not exceed 10p for every hundred words contained in the copy.
144 See, for example, *R v Wood* (1855) 5 E&B 49.
145 See, for example, *Powell v May* [1946] KB 330.

5.141 A bye-law must be certain. To be certain, a bye-law must contain a clear statement of the course of action required (or that should be avoided) and must contain sufficient information to allow people to know what is expected of them.[146]

5.142 A bye-law must be reasonable. To be reasonable, a bye-law must not be manifestly unjust, capricious, inequitable or partial in its operation, or involve oppressive interference with the rights of those subject to it. For example, in one case bye-laws imposing on landlords a duty to clean certain houses were held unreasonable where they applied to a landlord who had not reserved a right of entry to the property in question.[147]

5.143 A local authority may not waive the requirements of its bye-laws unless it has reserved the right to do so. Bye-laws made by local authorities should be interpreted benevolently and upheld if possible.[148]

5.144 The production of a printed copy of a bye-law made by a local authority which is endorsed with a certificate signed by the proper officer of the authority is prima facie evidence of the bye-law, provided the certificate states that:

a) it was made by the local authority;
b) the copy is a true copy;
c) on a specified date the bye-law was confirmed.

5.145 Bye-laws may be enforced by the imposition of fines, the removal of offenders from the place to which the bye-law relates or by injunction.

5.146 Other public authorities may be empowered to make bye-laws. For example, the Forestry Commission may make bye-laws:

- for the preservation of trees, timber and the Commissioners' property;
- for prohibiting or regulating any act or thing tending to injure or disfigure Forestry Commission land or amenities; and
- for regulating the reasonable use of the land by the public for the purposes of exercise or recreation.[149]

146 See, for example, *Percy v Hall* [1997] QB 924.

147 *Arlidge v The Metropolitan Borough of Islington* [1909] 2 KB 127.

148 *Kruse v Johnson* (1989) 2 QB 91 at 99, per Lord Russell of Killowen CJ.

149 Forestry Act 1967 s46(1). The Forestry Commission bye-laws currently in force are Forestry Commission Bye-laws 1982 SI No 648.

5.147 All of the principles with regard to validity and scope mentioned above also apply to bye-laws produced by other public authorities.[150]

5.148 If a local or other public authority prosecutes a Gypsy or Traveller for allegedly breaching a bye-law, then there may be a defence on grounds that the bye-law is invalid.[151]

Common law powers

Who can use them?

Anyone entitled to possession of the land, for example, landowner, tenant, licensee

5.149 If a trespasser peaceably enters or is on land, the person who is in, or is entitled to, possession may require him or her to leave, and, if the trespasser refuses to leave, may remove that person from the land, using no more force than is reasonably necessary.[152] The request to leave could, potentially, be a request to leave forthwith.

5.150 Such powers are available to all landowners. But an attempt to use these powers by a local or other public authority could give rise to a public law challenge by way of judicial review.[153]

5.151 However, if a trespasser enters land with force and violence, the person in possession may remove that person without a previous request to depart.[154] Once again, in the case of local or other public authorities, a potential public law challenge is not precluded, though the fact of the use of force or violence by the trespasser may assist the authority to argue that its decision to evict is 'proportionate' or 'reasonable'.

5.152 The use of more force than is 'reasonably necessary' to remove a person could result in an action for trespass to the person or property and a compensation claim for any damage caused. The person(s) carrying out the eviction or the person in possession could also be charged with having committed a criminal offence, such as assault or criminal damage, if the trespasser is injured or property is damaged during the course of the eviction.

5.153 The 2004 Encampment Guidance states:

150 *Boddington v British Transport Police* [1999] 2 AC 143.

151 *Boddington v British Transport Police* [1999] 2 AC 143.

152 Halsbury, Laws of England, Lexis Nexis, 5th edn., 2015, Vol 97 para 588.

153 See para 5.159 onwards, below.

154 See, for example, *Polkinghorne v Wright* [1845] 8 QB 197.

> The Government believes that local authorities should always follow a route which requires a court order. As local authorities and public bodies, authorities must have regard to considerations of common humanity or other statutory duties, and must ensure that the human rights of unauthorised campers are safeguarded.[155]

This would seem to preclude the use of common law powers by local and other public authorities in England. There is no equivalent section in the 2013 Welsh Guidance but it is suggested that reference could still be made to the 2004 Encampment Guidance in Welsh cases.

5.154 The 2004 Encampment Guidance also contains recommendations for other landowners using common law powers of eviction:

> Good practice guidelines for common law evictions would seek to ensure that no more than necessary 'reasonable force' is used and might include:
> - Police should always be notified of an eviction and called in to stand by to prevent a breach of the peace.
> - If police advise that it is inappropriate to carry out an eviction, it should always be delayed until an agreed time.[156]

5.155 If the person using common law powers is subsequently prosecuted for wrongful use of those powers, then a failure to follow the above guidance may be used in evidence against them.

5.156 It is also noted that Lord Denning stated that these powers were 'not to be recommended' to landowners due to the 'possible disturbance' which might be caused.[157]

5.157 Gypsies or Travellers who are residing on an unauthorised encampment which is within the 'curtilage' of a building may be able to rely on Criminal Law Act (CLA) 1977 s6. Section 6 makes it a summary offence[158] for a person without lawful authority to use or threaten violence for the purpose of securing entry to premises, in which, to his or her knowledge, someone is present who is opposed to the entry.[159] Squatters in buildings or on land ancillary to buildings will often post notices (sometimes called 'section 6 notices') on the outside of the building in order to draw attention to their presence within the building and to the fact that they are opposed to forceful entry. However, if entry can be gained without the use of violence (for example, by simply climbing over a wall or fence), then the offence

155 2004 Encampment Guidance at para 6.5.

156 2004 Encampment Guidance at para 6.16.

157 *McPhail v Persons Unknown* [1973] 3 All ER 393 at 396.

158 Punishable with six months' imprisonment or a fine or both.

159 CLA 1977 s6 does not apply to a 'displaced residential occupier' or to a 'protected intending occupier' – see CLA 1977 s7.

will not have been committed. 'Premises' includes land 'ancillary to a building'.[160] 'Premises' also includes 'any movable structure, vehicle or vessel designed or adapted for use for residential purposes'.[161] Therefore, CLA 1977 s6 will apply to violent entry upon a caravan, mobile home or houseboat.[162]

Planning enforcement

Who can use it?

Local authorities

5.158 The Town and Country Planning Act (TCPA) 1990 enables local authorities to take enforcement action against unauthorised developments by the use of enforcement notices, stop notices or injunctions.[163] Very often, the Gypsies or Travellers on such encampments may also be trying to obtain planning permission for the residential use of their land. Alternatively, the Gypsies or Travellers may be residing in their caravans on land with the consent of the owner but without the requisite planning permission. In such circumstances a local authority may threaten the owner and/or the Gypsies and Travellers with enforcement action.[164]

Public law challenges

Local authorities

Failure to provide sites

5.159 Before the duty to provide caravan sites was repealed by the CJPOA 1994[165] it was possible to apply for judicial review of a local authority's

160 CLA 1977 s12(1)(a).

161 CLA 1977 s12(2).

162 For advice on the law relating to 'squatting', contact the Advisory Service for Squatters – see appendix C below – which also produces a Squatters' Handbook.

163 The exercise of the power to issue enforcement and stop notices can be susceptible to a public law challenge by way of judicial review. By way of example see the case of *R v Kerrier DC ex p Uzell Blythe* [1996] JPL 837, where Latham J (as he then was) applied the principles of the *R v Lincolnshire CC ex p Atkinson; R v Wealden DC ex p Wales and Stratford* (1995) 8 Admin LR 529 ('*Atkinson*') to a situation involving planning enforcement powers.

164 For a full discussion of planning enforcement action affecting Gypsies and Travellers, see chapter 4 above.

165 For further discussion, see chapter 1 above.

decision to evict an unauthorised encampment; challenging the decision on grounds that the local authority in question had failed to provide sufficient (or any) sites.[166]

5.160 However, as a result of a recent legislative change it should be possible once again in Wales to argue that an eviction should not take place if the local authority have not complied with their duty to meet the assessed need for Gypsy and Traveller sites.

5.161 Part 3 of the Housing (Wales) Act (H(W)A) 2014[167] deals with Gypsies and Travellers.[168] H(W)A 2014 s103 introduces a duty to meet assessed needs, stating:

> (1) If a local housing authority's approved assessment identifies needs within the authority's area with respect to the provision of sites on which mobile homes may be stationed the authority must exercise its powers in section 56 of the Mobile Homes (Wales) Act 2013 (power of authorities to provide sites for mobile homes) so far as may be necessary to meet those needs.

And the Mobile Homes (Wales) Act 2013 s56 states:

> A local authority may within its area provide sites where mobile homes may be brought, whether for holidays or other temporary purposes or for use as permanent residences, and may manage the sites or lease them to another person.

Compliance with guidance on managing unauthorised encampments

5.162 In *R v Lincolnshire CC ex p Atkinson; R v Wealden DC ex p Wales and Stratford* ('*Atkinson*'),[169] Sedley J (as he then was) made it clear that when considering the eviction of unauthorised encampments local authorities ought to comply with Department of the Environment (DoE) Circular 18/94:[170]

166 See, for example, *West Glamorgan CC v Rafferty; R v Secretary of State for Wales ex p Gilhaney* [1987] 1 WLR 457.

167 H(W)A 2014 ss101–110.

168 H(W)A 2014 Part 3 (excluding ss103 and 104) came into force in February 2015, including the duty upon local authorities to undertake new Gypsy and Traveller Accommodation Assessments (GTAAs). The H(W)A 2014 s103 duty to meet assessed need came into force on 16 March 2016; see the Housing (Wales) Act 2014 (Commencement No 6) Order 2016 SI No 266.

169 (1996) 8 Admin LR 529.

170 *Gypsy sites policy and unauthorised camping*, issued 23 November 1994 and amended 26 July 2000. The Welsh Office Circular 76/94 is identical to the DoE Circular.

> Detailed analysis of [passages from the Circular] and debate about what legal force, if any, an advisory circular of this kind possesses has been made unnecessary by the realistic concession of counsel for both local authorities that whether or not they were spelt out in a departmental circular the matters mentioned . . . would be material considerations in the public law sense that to overlook them in the exercise of a local authority's powers under sections 77 to 79 of the Act of 1994 would be to leave relevant matters out of account and so jeopardise the validity of any consequent step. The concession is rightly made because those considerations in the material paragraphs which are not statutory are considerations of common humanity, none of which can be properly ignored when dealing with one of the most fundamental human needs, the need for shelter with at least a modicum of security.[171]

5.163 The *Atkinson* case made it clear that a public law challenge may lie if a local or other public authority fail to comply with or have proper regard to government guidance on the management of unauthorised encampments. It should be noted that there are important differences between much of the English and Welsh government guidance and as a consequence we have addressed the position in England and Wales separately below, unless otherwise stated.

5.164 Nowadays, it is very common for local authorities and police forces to have their own written policies on the management of unauthorised encampments (sometimes in the form of joint protocols) and it is important for advisers and representatives to check whether those policies have been followed in any given case. The failure to follow such a policy or protocol may also give rise to a public law challenge.

English guidance

5.165 The guidance in DoE Circular 18/94 (which is replicated in Welsh Office Circular 76/94) is a vital tool for those advising on this area of the law. Paragraph 6 states that:

> While it is a matter for local discretion to decide whether it is appropriate to evict an unauthorised gypsy encampment, the Secretary of State believes that local authorities should consider using their powers to do so wherever the gypsies concerned are causing a level of nuisance which cannot be effectively controlled. They also consider that it would usually be legitimate for a local authority to exercise these powers wherever gypsies who are camped unlawfully refuse to move onto an authorised local authority site. Where there are no such sites, and the authority reaches the view that an unauthorised gypsy encampment is not causing

171 (1995) 8 Admin LR 529 at 535.

> a level of nuisance which cannot be effectively controlled, it should consider providing basic services, such as toilets, a refuse skip and a supply of drinking water at that site.

5.166 The *Atkinson* case made it clear that local authorities must have regard to humanitarian considerations (and this is emphasised later in the Circular, as we will see below). Paragraph 6 places emphasis on the question of 'nuisance'. It follows that, if the unauthorised encampment is situated on a disused piece of land and not causing any problems, the local authority may wish to consider 'toleration' of the encampment. Eviction may lead to the group of Gypsies or Travellers moving to a less appropriate, more high-profile site. 'Toleration' might certainly be appropriate where the local authority cannot suggest an authorised permanent site, transit site or emergency stopping place that the Gypsies or Travellers could go to. On the other hand, if the encampment is situated on the town hall car park, there would need to be the most extreme welfare circumstances before a court might expect the local authority to hold back from eviction.

5.167 Paragraph 9 of Circular 18/94 states that:

> [Local authorities] should use [their] powers in a humane and compassionate way, taking account of the rights and needs of the gypsies concerned, the owners of the land in question, and the wider community whose lives may be affected by the situation.

5.168 Local authorities are also reminded of their obligations under Children Act 1989 Pt III (regarding the welfare of 'children in need'); Housing Act 1985 Pt III (now Housing Act 1996 Pt VII in England and Housing (Wales) Act 2014 Pt 2 in Wales, covering duties to homeless people), as well as those concerning the provision of education for school-age children.[172] Local authorities should also bear in mind possible assistance from local health and/or welfare services.[173]

5.169 DoE Circular 18/94 is intended to give local authorities guidance on the use of CJPOA 1994 s77. Local authorities need to carry out some form of inquiry process in order to gather the necessary information on the welfare of those camping on an unauthorised site and then adopt a suitable method by which to analyse and consider such information. They also need to demonstrate that the decision-maker has proper delegated authority, as a lack of delegated authority may

172 DoE Circular 18/94 paras 10 and 11.

173 DoE Circular 18/94 para 13.

render a decision unlawful.[174] Thus, advisers assisting Gypsies or Travellers who are facing eviction from an unauthorised encampment by a local authority, should consider requesting details of who made the decision to evict, and whether that person or those persons had properly delegated powers to do so.

5.170 Following the *Atkinson* case, some local authorities sought to test whether the general thrust of DoE Circular 18/94 would apply to other methods of eviction and there followed a line of somewhat conflicting High Court judgments.[175] However, the position was clarified in October 1998 by the publication of the then Department of the Environment, Transport and the Regions (DETR)/Home Office *Good practice guide, managing unauthorised camping.*[176] The *Good practice guide* was the result of research commissioned by the government from the University of Birmingham. The *Good practice guidance* made clear that local authorities should take into account welfare issues regardless of the method of eviction being contemplated.

5.171 The *Good practice guidance* was superseded by the ODPM *Guidance on managing unauthorised camping* ('the 2004 Encampment

174 See *R (L) v Manchester CC* [2001] EWHC 707 Admin; [2002] 1 FLR 43, a case in which Munby J quashed a policy concerning the remuneration for long-term foster carers because the preparation of the policy had not been lawfully delegated to the officers that had devised it.

175 *R v Kerrier DC ex p Uzell Blythe* [1996] JPL 837; *R v Brighton and Hove Council ex p Marmont* (1998) 30 HLR 1046; *R v Hillingdon LBC ex p McDonagh* (1999) 31 HLR 531; and *R v Leeds CC ex p Maloney* [1999] HLR 552. Broadly speaking, the judgments in *Uzell Blythe* and *Maloney* stated that Circular 18/94 (or, at least, the spirit of it) should apply to enforcement/eviction action other than just evictions under CJPOA 1994 s77, and the judgments in *Marmont* and *McDonagh* stated the contrary view, though it was at least accepted in those cases that there must be some reference to 'humanitarian considerations'.

176 This Guidance was amended in 2000. The fact that welfare inquiries should be carried out regardless of the type of eviction action was effectively confirmed in *R (Ward) v Hillingdon LBC* [2001] LGR 457, where Stanley Burnton J at 460, stated:

> [A] local authority considering exercising its powers to evict travellers . . . from an unauthorised encampment must not act in an uninformed, precipitate and inconsiderate manner. It must make adequate inquiries to elicit relevant information, including the number, age, health and needs of the travellers concerned, and make its decision having properly taken that information into account. The guidance expressly envisages that there will be circumstances in which a local authority may properly decide not to evict travellers from an unauthorised encampment.

Guidance')[177] and has since been supplemented by further guidance for England from the ODPM/Home Office, namely the *Guide to effective use of enforcement powers – Part 1: Unauthorised encampments*[178] ('the 2006 Encampment Guidance').[179] Thus, in England, those dealing with Gypsy and Traveller encampments and those advising Gypsies and Travellers on such encampments must have reference to all three codes of guidance: DoE Circular 18/94; the 2004 Encampment Guidance; and the 2006 Encampment Guidance.

5.172 The 2004 Encampment Guidance states that it uses the phrase 'Gypsies and Travellers' as a generic term to denote the whole population of those groups, families and individuals who subscribe to Gypsy/Traveller culture and/or lifestyle; and that the phrase encompasses ethnic Gypsies and Travellers and those who fall within the legal definition of a 'Gypsy' (set out in CSCDA 1960 s24 as amended by CJPOA 1994 s80).[180]

5.173 The 2004 Encampment Guidance stresses the importance for local authorities of the information-gathering process and the importance of strategies for the management of unauthorised encampments being put in place. It will be important, therefore, for advisers to obtain copies of the relevant strategies on unauthorised camping from local authorities and police authorities in order to check that they have been followed. The lack of a clear and coherent written strategy in itself may be a factor in a potential public law challenge.

5.174 The 2004 Encampment Guidance makes clear the government's emphasis on the need for site provision. Para 4.2 states that:

> Site provision is an essential element in any strategy. In a context where the number of Gypsy caravans exceeds the number of authorised places where they can stop – which is the case in England – provision of suitable accommodation for Gypsies and Travellers must be seen as a vital part of an approach to dealing with unauthorised camping. Population increase and family growth among Gypsies and Travellers must also be considered.

5.175 The 2004 Encampment Guidance, at para 4.3, continues:

177 The ODPM Guidance also resulted from further research by the University of Birmingham headed (as with the previous guidance) by Pat Niner of the Centre for Urban and Regional Studies. The Guidance came into effect on 27 February 2004. See appendix C below.

178 Issued in February 2006.

179 The 2006 Encampment Guidance was, in fact, withdrawn by the government on 31 August 2015 but, following the threat of a challenge by a Gypsy woman, was reinstated on 2 October 2015.

180 2004 Encampment Guidance Box 1 p6.

> All local authorities should review the provision of sites for Gypsies and Travellers.

5.176 The 2004 Encampment Guidance emphasises the importance of welfare inquiries and the need for public bodies to take account of considerations of common humanity.[181] This point is also highlighted in the 2006 Encampment Guidance. For example, para 77 states that:

> Local authorities should ensure that, in accordance with their wider obligations, and to ensure that they comply with Human Rights legislation, proper welfare enquiries are carried out to determine whether there are pressing needs presented by the unauthorised campers and that, where necessary, the appropriate agencies are involved as soon as possible.

5.177 The 2004 Encampment Guidance also makes it clear that the location of an encampment will be an important consideration. For example, para 5.4 states that:

> Unauthorised encampments are almost always, by definition, unlawful. However, while there are insufficient authorised sites, it is recognised that some unauthorised camping will continue. There are locations, however, where encampment will not be acceptable under any circumstances. Each encampment location must be considered on its merits against criteria such as health and safety considerations for the unauthorised campers, traffic hazard, public health risks, serious environmental damage, genuine nuisance to neighbours and proximity to other sensitive land-uses.

In the 2006 Encampment Guidance examples are given of locations that cause serious disruption and may need to be moved, for example, school grounds during term time, urban parks and business parks.[182]

5.178 It will be important for local authorities to keep written records of the inquiry process and, for this purpose, pro formas might be used.[183] At para 5.17 of the 2004 Encampment Guidance it is stated that:

> Reasonable attempts should be made to get information from unauthorised campers not present at the time of a visit. Other members of the group may sometimes be able to provide information. A letter or self-completion form may be left with clear instructions for its return (at no cost to the unauthorised camper). All such actions should be clearly recorded, and if there is still no response, this should be noted.

181 2004 Encampment Guidance paras 5.7–5.10.

182 2006 Encampment Guidance para 59.

183 2004 Encampment Guidance para 5.14.

Usually, Gypsies and Travellers will not be notified in advance of the time of a visit. More than one visit may therefore be required. Reliance on pro formas or self-completion forms may also be dependent on questions of literacy. Additionally, Gypsies and Travellers may be reluctant to give their names for fear that they will be named in court proceedings and may face court costs. Advisers assisting Gypsies and Travellers could encourage local authorities (and other public authorities) to confirm to the Gypsies and Travellers concerned that no such adverse consequences will arise if they give their names. Alternatively, the Gypsies and Travellers should be urged to provide relevant information, even if it is provided anonymously.

5.179 It is important, however, that the inquiry process is more than just a paper exercise. A proper decision-making process is required. Paragraph 5.20 of the 2004 Encampment Guidance states that:

> Any welfare needs of unauthorised campers are a material consideration for local authorities when deciding whether to start eviction proceedings or to allow the encampment to remain longer. Welfare needs do not give an open-ended 'right' for unauthorised campers to stay as long as they want in an area. For example, the presence of a pregnant woman or school age children does not, per se, mean that an encampment must remain indefinitely. To defer an eviction which is justified on other grounds, the need must be more immediate and/or of a fixed term.

5.180 The 2004 Encampment Guidance gives some specific examples of situations where good practice suggests that eviction should be delayed:

- advanced pregnancy – a period shortly before and after birth in normal circumstances, longer on medical advice if there are complications;
- ill health – indicators might include a hospital appointment booked; in-patient treatment of a close family member; period during which a condition can be diagnosed, stabilised and a course of treatment started;
- educational needs – children in school if within four weeks of the end of term or if access to special education has been gained.[184]

5.181 If the local authority decides to 'tolerate' an encampment for the time being, it must take a 'management' role.[185] The 2004 Encampment Guidance makes it clear that the same standards of behaviour should

184 2004 Encampment Guidance Box 18 p31.

185 See 2004 Encampment Guidance, chapter 7 'Managing unauthorised encampments'.

be expected of the occupants of an unauthorised encampment as might be expected of the settled community.[186] Examples of unacceptable behaviour are given such as over-large encampments; aggressive or threatening behaviour; failure to control dogs; persistent and disturbing noise; littering/fly-tipping; damage to property; or criminal activity.[187]

5.182 The 2006 Encampment Guidance explains that enforcement action will be more effective if an alternative site, even if only temporary in nature, can be identified for Gypsies and Travellers who do not have or cannot locate authorised stopping places. For example, para 61 of the 2006 Encampment Guidance states that:

> [A]ction will be more effective if there is an alternative site to which Gypsies and Travellers can be directed, either pitches on an authorised transit site, or a location which is deemed to be a more 'acceptable' unauthorised site.

5.183 Similarly, para 72 of the 2006 Encampment Guidance states that:

> Enforcement action will be quicker and more effective, and a wider range of powers can be used, where appropriate authorised provision is made for Gypsies and Travellers within the area. . . . Adequate provision will have wide benefits in the management of unauthorised camping as:
> - There will be less unauthorised camping in the first place;
> - The police will not be restricted in the use of ss 62A–E CJPOA if suitable pitches are available;
> - Legal challenges are less likely to occur or succeed;
> - The courts are more likely to grant possession orders to local authorities who show they are acting responsibly in carrying out their wider duties and who deal with each incident of unauthorised camping on its merits.

5.184 There is also an important emphasis in the 2006 Encampment Guidance on local authorities considering whether an encampment can be 'tolerated' in combination with consideration of alternative locations. Thus, under the heading 'Avoiding unnecessary enforcement action', paragraph 83 states that:

> Before taking action, landowners should consider whether enforcement is absolutely necessary. It may be that in certain circumstances, alternatives to eviction action are appropriate, for example:
> - Where unauthorised campers have chosen an unobtrusive location in which to camp it may be preferable to agree a departure date with them;

186 2004 Encampment Guidance para 7.1.
187 2004 Encampment Guidance para 7.3.

- Where unauthorised campers have chosen to stop in an unacceptable location, but where the local authority has also identified a location in the vicinity which would be much less damaging or obtrusive, unauthorised campers could be encouraged to move to this location.

Welsh guidance

5.185 In December 2013 the Welsh Assembly *Guidance on Managing Unauthorised Camping* 2005 was replaced by the Welsh Government *Guidance on Managing Unauthorised Camping 2013* (the '2013 Welsh Guidance').[188] Those advising Gypsies and Travellers in Wales will need to aware of its contents but also remember that the guidance contained in the Welsh Office Circular 76/94 *Gypsy Sites Policy and Unauthorised Camping* (which is identical to DoE Circular 18/94[189]) still remains in place.

Application

5.186 The 2013 Welsh Guidance applies to unauthorised encampments established by 'Gypsies and Travellers', a term which it defines as including:

> 5. . . . Persons with a cultural tradition of nomadism or of living in a caravan; and all other persons of a nomadic habit of life, whatever their race or origin, including –
> (i) such persons who, on grounds only of their own or their family's or dependant's educational or health needs or old age, have ceased to travel temporarily or permanently; and
> (ii) members of an organised group of travelling show people or circus people (whether or not travelling together as such).

5.187 The 2013 Welsh Guidance definition covers Romani Gypsies (including Welsh and Scottish Gypsy-Travellers), Irish Travellers, Travelling Showpeople and other Travellers who have a nomadic habit of life.

5.188 The 2013 Welsh Guidance makes it clear that there is a link between unauthorised camping and site provision and this is an important theme that runs throughout the Guidance:

> 25. The Welsh Government does not condone unauthorised encampments by Gypsies and Travellers. However, without sufficient and appropriate site provision, effective and justifiable enforcement against unauthorised encampments cannot be achieved. . . . Delivering more authorised sites coupled with effective site management will remove the

188 See appendix C.

189 See para 5.165 onwards, above.

reason for unauthorised encampments. It is vital that local authorities have protocols in place to deal appropriately and proportionately with unauthorised encampments.

31. Local authorities should recognise that it may be more cost effective to provide a site, even if that is a temporary tolerated site, than to enforce against unauthorised encampments in an area with no site provision and where there are a high number of unauthorised encampments . . . Developing and providing authorised, permanent sites would provide revenue for local authorities as occupants would be required to pay a pitch fee and Council Tax.

5.189 The 2013 Welsh Guidance places emphasis on the importance of temporary or tolerated stopping places:

35. Local authorities can consider providing temporary stopping places, which are intended to serve a particular short-term purpose and are not considered to be the permanent solution. Tolerated encampments are similar to temporary stopping places, though the latter have been set aside explicitly for the purpose of occupation and should provide basic amenities for occupiers, including waste disposal, water supply and sanitation. Temporary stopping places can also be proactively provided to relocate encampments from inappropriate locations.

5.190 In contrast to the advice issued to public authorities in England, the 2013 Welsh Guidance states that Welsh authorities need to consider carefully whether there are any alternative sites that can be found which might accommodate the Gypsies and Travellers occupying an unauthorised encampment:

41. Effectively, if an unauthorised encampment arises and there are no alternative authorised pitches in the area, local authorities have three clear paths relating to how they can resolve the encampment. Each option should be carefully considered:

Path 1 – To seek and obtain possession of the occupied site (eviction proceedings).

Path 2 – To 'tolerate' the Gypsy or Traveller occupiers, if only for a short time, until an alternative site can be found or the occupiers move on voluntarily.

Path 3 – To find an alternative site, if only on a temporary basis, and offer the Gypsy or Traveller occupiers the chance to move onto it.

Welfare enquiries

5.191 The 2013 Welsh Guidance stresses the need for adequate and meaningful welfare enquiries to be carried out before any decision is taken and introduces the concept of a single point of contact (SPOC):

> 45. The initial encampment visit by the lead local authority officer (preferably the Single Point of Contact for unauthorised camping, which is discussed later in this document) should establish any immediate concerns with the condition of the encampment or behaviour and the intentions of the occupiers. If little annoyance or impact on local residents is identified, it should not be assumed that possession action will be taken against the encampment. . . .
>
> 47. The determination of whether eviction action should be taken should be made after consideration of whether the interference with Gypsy or Traveller family life and home is justified and proportionate. . . .
>
> 48. If there is no substantial risk to public safety and no inappropriate behaviour, and no alternative authorised pitches available, the impact and benefit of evicting the occupiers should be considered carefully.
>
> 49. Tolerated encampments can be pragmatic and cost-effective in terms of finding a long-term solution to unauthorised camping in the area. . . .Toleration can also be a useful tool where local authorities have not provided enough Gypsy and Traveller accommodation in their area.
>
> 50. Proactively identifying temporary stopping places can also provide a pragmatic and cost-effective solution, which enables the local authority to relocate an encampment from an inappropriate location whilst recognising the need to provide support to the occupiers.

SPOC, initial encampment visit and full welfare assessment

5.192 With regard to the role of the SPOC, the 2013 Welsh Guidance states that (p22):

> . . . it is recommended that a lead officer is identified to undertake the following roles:
> 1. Liaise with occupiers and other affected parties.
> 2. Undertake or coordinate the necessary assessments and involvement of relevant officers to ensure needs are addressed.
> 3. Communicate the evidence and provide recommendations to senior officials who will ultimately decide what action to take.
> 4. Ensure that all stakeholders are made aware of the proposed action and disruption to all is minimised.
> 5. Be sufficiently trained to provide culturally appropriate support and to understand how various actions and circumstances may impact upon the human rights of occupiers (particularly children and vulnerable others).

5.193 The 2013 Welsh Guidance advises public authorities when a full 'Welfare Assessment' is required, how it should be conducted and what information should be gathered, and explains how that information is then assessed:

99. The Welsh Government would recommend a full Welfare Assessment be undertaken if:

- There are any obvious signs of welfare requirements, such as pregnant women, sick or disabled residents, frail elderly residents or children under 5.
- The likely duration of the encampment is over 3 days.
- There are immediate risks to the occupiers or residents such as contaminated land or traffic issues.
- There are school-age children present, within four weeks of the end of term.
- If there are obvious issues that are affecting the landowner's business or quality of life, making urgent possession action likely.

100. A full Welfare Assessment may not be required if:

- the expected duration of the encampment is 3 days or less;
- the occupiers intend to move on directly following a family event;
- the occupiers are in transit to another destination (such as to meet family or to a harbour) and are only stopping overnight.

. . .

103. Even when the encampment is likely to be 3 days or less, exceptionally the decision may be made not to allow the campers to remain. . . .

. . .

110. It is recommended that the full Welfare Assessment is undertaken no later than 3 working days after the encampment has been reported. The purpose of the assessment is to understand the needs of the encampment occupiers and to ensure that the local authority provides for any vulnerable members of the group.

111. It is recommended that the SPOC / lead officer undertakes the Welfare Assessment, gathering crucial information about the encampment . . .

A 'Code of Conduct' template is contained at Annex 1 of the 2013 Welsh Guidance.

Provision of services

5.194 The 2013 Welsh Guidance highlights the provision of services to those living on unauthorised encampments:

117. . . .When unauthorised encampments are evicted there can be considerable clean-up costs incurred by local authorities. However, providing refuse collection, toilets, and water to occupiers can drastically reduce clean-up costs after an encampment has been moved on. Welfare Assessments can help local authorities to check which of these services might be required by the occupiers and also to discover if the occupiers would be prepared and able to pay for the services. If the occupiers are willing to pay for the services used, local residents could be informed of

this so as to dispel the perception that encampment occupiers do not pay for services.

Cost-benefit analysis, assessment of locations, availability of alternative locations and the best interests of the children

5.195 All these vital issues are addressed in paras 120–136 of the 2013 Welsh Guidance and those paragraphs are essential reading for anyone advising Gypsies and Travellers who are living on unauthorised encampments in Wales.[190]

5.196 The importance of communicating the reasons for decisions to all relevant parties including local residents and relevant professionals is stressed in Section 6 of the 2013 Welsh Guidance.[191]

5.197 Finally, it is worth noting that Section 7 of the 2013 Welsh Guidance advises all local and public authorities (including the police) that they should have detailed written strategies with regard to unauthorised encampments. The lack of a clear and coherent written strategy in itself may be a factor in a potential public law challenge.

Toleration or provision of alternative sites

5.198 Both the English and Welsh Government guidance suggests that local authorities should consider the toleration of an unauthorised site or the provision of an alternative site before a decision is taken to evict Gypsies and Travellers. The approach local authorities should take was considered in *R (Casey and others) v Crawley BC and the ODPM*.[192] The case involved a group of Irish Travellers who were living on two unauthorised encampments, both on the same local authority's land. It was accepted that the sites of the encampments were not ideal locations. Burton J concluded that the welfare inquiries that had been carried out were sufficient to comply with the 2004 Encampment Guidance. He also took account of the fact that the local authority had been trying to identify a location for an authorised site and, in all the circumstances, he concluded that the decision to evict was not unlawful. Very importantly, Burton J framed three options that were available to the defendant local authority:

- i) Seek and obtain possession of the sites [Option 1].
- ii) Tolerate the claimants, if only for a short time, until an alternative could be found [Option 2].

190 See appendix C.

191 See p34.

192 [2006] EWHC 301 (Admin).

iii) Find an alternative site, if only on a temporary basis, and offer the [claimants] a move to it [Option 3].[193]

Burton J continued:

> If, in a given situation, reactively the Council can find for travellers on an unauthorised site another temporary toleration site where lawfully, and notwithstanding the lack of planning permission, they can be temporarily sited, that would be a suitable administrative decision and exercise of Option 3: but there is no need for them to have a pro-actively identified pool [of such sites] ready, even if that were feasible.[194]

5.199 If a Gypsy or Traveller is camped on land owned by a local authority and makes a homeless application to that local authority[195] then it can be argued that he or she should be allowed to remain there while the homelessness application is processed, providing that the encampment is not causing any nuisance or obstruction.

The police

5.200 It should be noted that there has been two failed attempts to argue that the police powers of eviction are incompatible with the HRA 1998.[196]

5.201 The police must take account of welfare considerations. Thus, Home Office Circular 45/94 states in relation to the police use of its powers under CJPOA 1994 s61 that:

> The decision whether or not to issue a direction to leave is an operational one for the police alone to take in the light of all the circumstances of the particular case. But in making this decision, the senior officer at the scene may wish to take account of the personal circumstances of the trespassers; for example, the presence of elderly persons, invalids, pregnant women, children and other persons whose well-being may be jeopardised by a precipitate move.

193 [2006] EWHC 301 (Admin) at para 50.

194 [2006] EWHC 301 (Admin) at para 55(ii). It should be noted that the approach explained by Burton J in *Casey* was adopted in the 2013 Welsh Guidance.

195 In reliance upon the case of *R (Price) v Carmarthenshire CC* [2003] EWHC 42 (Admin); March 2003 *Legal Action* 30. For full discussion of this case, see chapter 6 para 6.106 onwards, below.

196 *R (Fullers and others) v Chief Constable of the Dorset Constabulary and the Secretary of State for the Home Department* [2002] 3 All ER 57; *R (McCarthy) v Chief Constable of the Sussex Constabulary and the Secretary of State for the Home Department* [2007] EWHC 1520 (Admin).

5.202 The 2004 Encampment Guidance makes reference to the case of *R v Metropolitan Police ex p Small*,[197] and summarises the case-law position thus:

> Case law (Small) has established that, while police officers do not have to undertake welfare enquiries as such, they must be aware of humanitarian considerations in reaching their decisions and must ensure that all decisions are proportionate. A decision may be taken to explicitly exclude individuals or families with serious welfare needs from a section 61 direction to leave.[198]

This is further emphasised in the 2006 Encampment Guidance which states at para 63 that:

> If the anti-social behaviour is focused amongst particular individuals in the group, or if a member of the group is ill, it may be appropriate to take action to evict some people but not others.

It is difficult to see how the police officers present can take account of humanitarian considerations without first making some form of inquiry. However, if such an inquiry is undertaken and the police take account of any information regarding welfare concerns provided before deciding whether to issue a removal direction then it will be difficult to argue that the police have failed to comply with their duty.

5.203 The 2004 Encampment Guidance suggests that local authorities should respond positively to requests from the police and other public authorities for assistance in making welfare enquiries.[199]

5.204 Para 6.8 of the 2004 Encampment Guidance provides some examples of factors which might prompt police eviction:

- unacceptable behaviour by unauthorised campers at the encampment, including individual criminal activity, which cannot be controlled by means other than eviction;
- significant disruption to the life of the surrounding community;
- serious breaches of the peace or disorder caused by the encampment.

The same paragraph continues:

> Police forces/commands should not adopt blanket policies or presumptions either for or against the use of [CJPOA 1994] section 61.

5.205 The 2006 Encampment Guidance also contains very important guidance for the police. Para 46 states that:

197 Unreported leave application in the (as it then was) Crown Office List before Collins J, 27 August 1998.

198 2004 Encampment Guidance para 6.9.

199 2004 Encampment Guidance para 5.10.

A senior police officer then considers whether it is appropriate to use the power, based on various factors:

- Whether there are other activities on the encampment, such as serious breaches of the peace, disorder, criminal activity or anti-social behaviour which would necessitate police involvement under their wider powers;
- Given the impact of the unauthorised encampment on the environment and the local settled community, is it reasonable and proportionate to use police powers;
- Is action by the police legally sustainable;
- Are sufficient resources available.

5.206 With regard to the police, the 2013 Welsh Guidance states:

> 86. Police officers should not be used as a standard way of dealing with unauthorised encampments, but the involvement of police officers should not presume an eviction. The police, as with other public authorities, also have responsibility to assess the situation and the impact of the encampment before making an informed decision which minimises the impact on the safety or health of any party involved.
> 87. Where possible it is recommended that police officers visit the unauthorised encampment with a local authority officer, the landowner or an officer from another relevant agency.

Thus, it can be seen that both the 2004 Encampment Guidance and the 2013 Welsh Guidance advises that the police powers of eviction should only be utilised in more extreme or pressing circumstances.

5.207 If the local authority in whose area the unauthorised encampment occurs is not involved in its management then it is difficult to see how the police can ensure that they take account of 'humanitarian considerations' without carrying out some kind of inquiry process themselves. Indeed, some police forces have specific policies that recommend just such a procedure be followed. In this regard reference should also be made to the important NPCC *Operational Advice on Unauthorised Encampments* (2018)[200] ('the NPCC Advice ') which covers both England, Wales and Northern Ireland.

5.208 At p3, para 7 of the NPCC Advice states:

> Decisions to evict or not must, of course, be balanced (as directed by legislation and Government guidance), and be compliant with the terms of the Human Rights Act 1998, demonstrating legality, necessity, and proportionality, as well as principles of common humanity.

200 This replaces the Association of Chief Police Officers' *Guidance on Unauthorised Encampments* though the NPCC Advice largely replicates the earlier guidance. See appendix C.

5.209 There is an important recognition of the position on the ground at p4, para 9 of the NPCC Advice:

> In managing unauthorised encampments officers must be sensitive to the fact that there is a lack of pitches on authorised sites across the country, making it difficult or even impossible for people to avoid setting up unauthorised pitches.

5.210 Page 5, para 4 of the NPCC Advice makes it clear that the police themselves should take account of welfare considerations:

> Initial contact should be made with the people on the site, and an assessment made of the impact of its location, as well as the behaviour displayed by the occupants. The occupants should be spoken to in order to establish their identities and location of last site, and to ascertain their views on desired duration of stay as well as any pressing welfare needs.

5.211 A model 'Code of Conduct' that might be handed out is available at Appendix A and an 'initial site assessment form' is available at appendix B of the NPCC Advice.

5.212 Very importantly p5, para 7 indicates that eviction using police powers should only take place when justified:

> Officers should assess whether the location of the encampment, behaviour of residents or needs of the landowner justifies an eviction using police powers).

5.213 Page 6, para 11 states that:

> Assessment visits should only log details of vehicles and people where there are grounds to suspect those individuals of anti-social behaviour or criminal activity.

5.214 An 'eviction rationale record' is available at appendix C of the NPCC Advice.

5.215 Page 7, para 2 states that:

> The allegation of a crime or identification of an individual suspect at an encampment should not be grounds alone for consideration of a full group eviction.[201]

5.216 Page 7, para 3 states that:

> Where occupants at unauthorised encampments are victims of crime or anti-social behaviour, they must be given access to services in the usual way. If there is a perception that the incident is racially motivated then the matter should be dealt with in line with Hate Crime policy.

201 See also 2006 Encampment Guidance at para 63.

5.217 Joint agency protocols are recommended at p8, para 1 and it is stressed at p8, para 3 that the:

> The lead role for decision making should rest with the local authority and the use of police powers should not normally be considered as a first response.

5.218 Significantly, paras 5.1 and 5.2 re-emphasise the point that police powers should only be used where absolutely necessary in the circumstances.

5.219 Police must apply the principle of proportionality when using eviction powers. Thus, p9, para 3 states that:

> In all cases, as stated above, relevant Human Rights processes must be applied to all decisions made i.e. that the elements of s61 are satisfied, and that it is necessary and proportionate to use the powers.

5.220 In any event, it will also be important for advisers to have a copy of the relevant police authority's policy on unauthorised encampments. A flagrant failure by the police to follow written policies may also enable a public law challenge to be made.

Government departments and other public authorities

5.221 When local authorities manage unauthorised encampments they are acting as 'public authorities' for the purposes of the HRA 1998. What other bodies or organisations might come within the definition of 'public authority' in this context?

5.222 A 'public authority', for the purposes of HRA 1998 s6, can either be a 'core public authority' which exercises functions that are broadly governmental or a 'hybrid public authority', some of whose functions are of a public nature.[202] It is not possible to give a definitive list of organisations that will be seen as 'public authorities' in the context of an eviction of an unauthorised encampment. In some cases it will be clear. For example, the Forestry Commission is a non-ministerial government department which answers to the Secretary of State for the Environment, Food and Rural Affairs (SSEFRA) and given its public function is clearly a 'core public authority'. By contrast, a

202 See *Poplar Housing and Regeneration Community Association Ltd v Donaghue* [2002] QB 48, [2001] 3 WLR 183, [2002] QB 48, [2001] 4 All ER 604; *Aston Cantlow and Wilmcote with Billesley Parochial Church Council v Wallbank* [2003] UKHL 37, [2003] 3 WLR 283, [2004] 1 AC 546; *YL v Birmingham CC* [2007] UKHL 27, [2008] 1 AC 95; and *R (Weaver) v London & Quadrant Housing Trust* [2009] EWCA Civ 587, [2010] 1 WLR 363.

housing association which manages Gypsy/Traveller sites for a local authority may have both public and private functions but may be considered to be acting as a 'public authority' when managing unauthorised encampments. Whether other organisations or bodies are considered to be acting as a public authority when managing unauthorised encampments on their land will depend on the particular circumstances, for example: the powers they are using; whether those powers are statutory or otherwise; the source of their finances; and the nature of their dealings with a particular encampment.

5.223 Paragraph 8 of DoE Circular 18/94 states that:

> Where gypsies are unlawfully encamped on government-owned land, it is for the local authority, with the agreement of the land-owning department, to take any necessary steps to ensure that the encampment does not constitute a hazard to public health. It will continue to be the policy of the Secretary of State that government departments should act in conformity with the advice that unauthorised encampments should not normally be allowed to continue where they are causing a level of nuisance which cannot be effectively controlled, particularly where local authority authorised sites are available. The National Assembly for Wales will act in the same way.

5.224 The 2004 Encampment Guidance is more detailed and states that:

> 5.7 . . . The police and other public bodies who might be involved in dealing with unauthorised encampments do not have comparable duties [to local authorities] but must still, as public servants, show common humanity to those they meet.
>
> 5.8 The Human Rights Act (HRA) applies to all public bodies including local authorities (including town and parish councils), police, public bodies and the courts. With regard to eviction, the issue that must be determined is whether the interference with Gypsy/Traveller family life and home is justified and proportionate. Any particular welfare needs experienced by unauthorised campers are material in reaching a balanced and proportionate decision. The human rights of members of the settled community are also material if any authority fails to act to curb nuisance from an encampment.
>
> 5.9 Case-law is still developing with regard to the sorts of welfare enquiries, which the courts consider necessary to properly taken decisions in relation to actions against unauthorised encampments. Cases are testing the requirements under different powers, and the requirements placed on different agencies (authorities, police, and other public landowners). Very generally, court decisions to date suggest:
>
> - All public authorities need to be able to demonstrate that they have taken into consideration any welfare needs of unauthorised campers prior to making a decision to evict.

> - The courts recognise that the police and other public bodies have different resources and welfare duties from local authorities. Generally the extent and detail of appropriate enquiries is less for police and non-local authority 'public authorities' . . .
>
> 5.10 Because local authorities have appropriate skills and resources to enable them to make (or to co-ordinate) welfare enquiries, it is considered good practice for local authorities to respond positively to requests for assistance in making enquiries from the police or other public bodies.

5.225 The 2013 Welsh Guidance is directed at all the public authorities that own land in Wales and advises them as follows:

> 80. Where an unauthorised encampment occurs on Welsh Government land the same guidelines and statutory responsibilities outlined in this guidance apply.
>
> **Public authorities**
>
> 81. Local authorities and other public authorities (including National Parks) as land owners have a responsibility to their local community, including Gypsy and Traveller communities. Where an unauthorised encampment occurs on public authority land, it is recommended that officials within the authority appoint a Single Point of Contact (SPOC) or other lead officer, who would undertake the appropriate assessments. . ., coordinate other relevant authorities and provide advice to senior officials who will determine the appropriate action to take . . .
>
> 83. As local authorities have appropriate skills and resources to enable them to make (or co-ordinate) welfare assessments, it is considered good practice for local authorities to respond positively to requests for assistance in undertaking these assessments from the police or other public authorities.

5.226 There was a series of cases involving the Forestry Commission's management of unauthorised encampments on its land which culminated in *R (Kanssen) v SSEFRA*.[203] It was then the practice of the Forestry Commission, when it became aware of an unauthorised encampment, to write to the local authority to inform it of the existence of the encampment and to suggest that it carried out welfare enquiries. The standard letter used invited the local authority to inform the Forestry Commission if it wished to make any submissions regarding the management of the encampment arising from

203 [2005] EWHC 1024 (Admin).

the welfare enquiries.[204] The problem with this practice was that it was wholly dependent upon the local authority responding positively to the Forestry Commission's invitation and often resulted in no welfare enquiries being undertaken.

5.227 In *Kanssen* Owen J made it clear that the Forestry Commission must take account of any 'humanitarian considerations' that are brought to its attention but concluded that the Forestry Commission's practice of writing to the relevant local authorities was sufficient to comply with its obligations under common law and under government guidance. Owen J also concluded that the Forestry Commission does not have power under the Forestry Act 1967 and the Countryside Act 1968 to provide sites for Gypsies and Travellers.[205]

5.228 Interestingly, the Forestry Commission subsequently revised its own guidance on how its officers deal with unauthorised encampments and now advises that they should carry out welfare enquiries themselves.[206]

5.229 In the light of the decision in *Kanssen* it will be important for advisers of Gypsies or Travellers who are faced with eviction from land owned or managed by a public authority to bring welfare issues to its attention. The public authority will then need to consider those welfare issues before deciding whether to evict the encampment or whether to continue with any eviction process that has already commenced. It would also seem to be incumbent on local authorities and other public authority landowners in the area to develop joint strategies for dealing with unauthorised encampments and for local authorities to take a proactive approach to welfare enquiries when informed that an encampment is on land owned or managed by a public authority.

Other matters

Width of possession orders and injunctions

5.230 It had been the practice of certain large landowners when applying for an order to evict Gypsies or Travellers from an unauthorised

204 This approach was effectively approved in the case of *R v MAFF ex p Callaghan and others* (2000) 32 HLR 8.

205 Mr Kanssen was subsequently refused permission to appeal to the Court of Appeal: see *R (Kanssen) v SSEFRA* [2005] EWCA Civ 1453.

206 Forestry Commission, *Estate Management Guidance Notes: Unauthorised Traveller Encampments on FC Land* (2008).

encampment on their land to seek a possession order which not only covered the land on which the encampment was situated but also covered other land in their ownership in the surrounding area. The practice was endorsed by the White Book, which provides judges and legal practitioners advice on the CPR in the following terms:

> Where a claimant, such as the Forestry Commission, owns a number of parcels of land in a particular area which are susceptible to unlawful occupation and is seeking possession in respect of one such parcel which is unlawfully occupied but apprehends that if the order is made the unlawful occupiers will move to one or more of the other parcels and seeks to include them in the possession order such other areas must be clearly defined . . . The court can then include in the possession order those parcels to which on the evidence and the law the claimants are found to be entitled.[207]

5.231 However, the practice was questioned in the case of *Meier and others v Secretary of State for the Environment, Food and Rural Affairs*.[208] The SSEFRA (acting on behalf of the Forestry Commission) had sought a possession order in respect of an unauthorised encampment by a group of Travellers on land at Hethfelton Woods in Dorset. At the same time, the SSEFRA sought a wider possession order covering a large number of other woods in that part of Dorset to which it was suggested the Travellers might decamp and an injunction covering all those pieces of woodland.

5.232 In the County Court, Recorder Norman granted the possession order in respect of Hethfelton Woods but refused to grant the wider order or the injunction. The SSEFRA appealed and the Court of Appeal allowed the appeal and granted both the wider possession order and the injunction. Two of the Travellers, Ms Horie and Ms Rand, then appealed to the House of Lords (which, by the time the judgment was handed down, had been superseded by the Supreme Court).

5.233 In the event, the Supreme Court concluded that the CPR do not permit the grant of a wider possession order and overturned the Court of Appeal's judgment on that point and when doing so it also held that the earlier Court of Appeal judgment in *Drury v SSEFRA*[209] was wrong on that point. Put simply, the Supreme Court concluded

207 Civil Procedure ('the White Book') 2003, Vol 1, p1748. Reference is also made to the previous Forestry Commission practice of seeking orders covering a 20-mile radius around the encampment.

208 [2009] UKSC 11.

209 [2004] EWCA Civ 200.

that a landowner could not, as a matter of logic, obtain a wide possession order which covered land that was still in his or her possession. Lord Rodger stated (at para 9):

> [T]he Forestry Commission were at all relevant times in undisturbed possession of the parcels of land . . . That being so, an action for the recovery of possession of those parcels of land is quite inappropriate.

5.234 However, the Supreme Court expressed the view that the remedy of a quia timet injunction (ie, an injunction to restrain wrongful acts which are threatened or imminent but have not yet commenced) could be sought in circumstances where there was a risk that a Gypsy or Traveller would move from one unauthorised encampment on land owned by a public body to another parcel of land also in that public body's ownership. The Supreme Court, therefore, upheld the Court of Appeal's grant of the injunction.

5.235 Lord Neuberger went further and indicated that, in his view, the failure by the Forestry Commission to follow government guidance on unauthorised encampments with regard to the other parcels of land, should not preclude the injunction being granted. He stated (at para 87):

> I do not see how [reference to the guidance] could have justified an attack on the lawfulness of the Secretary of State seeking an injunction to restrain the defendants from setting up such unauthorised camps . . . I incline to the view that the existence and provisions of the 2004 Guidance could be taken into account by the Court when considering whether to grant an injunction and when fashioning the terms of any injunction.

5.236 In the case of *Bromley LBC v Persons unknown and London Gypsies and Travellers*[210] the London Borough of Bromley sought a final injunction against 'persons unknown prohibiting unauthorised occupation and/or deposition of waste' on 171 parcels of land owned or managed by them. The application for an injunction was clearly targeted wholly or mainly at Gypsies and Travellers. This was in a context where over 30 local authorities throughout England had already obtained such injunctions.

5.237 Bromley had obtained an interim injunction on 15 August 2018. London Gypsies and Travellers (a registered charity) were given permission to intervene in the case, so that the Gypsy and Traveller community could be represented at the final hearing which was heard by Leigh-Ann Mulcahy QC (sitting as a Deputy Judge of the High Court) on 15 May 2019.

210 [2019] EWHC 1675 (QB), 17 May 2019.

5.238 The judge delivered her judgment on 17 May 2019. After analysing relevant case-law, she set out the key issues (para 58):

> . . . the real issue for me to determine is whether the order sought is proportionate to the legitimate aim sought to be achieved. . . . I must also consider whether the terms of the injunction correspond to the threatened unlawful conduct and are not so wide that they prohibit lawful conduct, whether they are sufficiently clear and precise to enable persons potentially affected to know what they must not do, and whether the injunction has clear geographical and temporal limits.

5.239 The question of transit site provision was addressed (para 62):

> Here there is no transit site and there is no proposal for a transit site. Further, it would seem that Bromley is not supporting the provision of a transit site in Bromley . . .

The judge continued (para 63):

> Mr Smyth's answer [to the lack of transit site provision] . . . was that the Gypsy and Traveller community can occupy private land or they can go elsewhere outside the Borough. I do not regard transferring the undoubted problems the local authority has experienced to private landowners, who would themselves be entitled to seek possession orders evicting such occupants from their land, as a solution. The 'going elsewhere' option . . . transfers the difficulties to another borough, who will then in turn invoke and seek to rely on the grant of the previous injunction to seek theirs on a 'me too' approach. The problem . . . is now the cumulative effect of all these injunctions which are reaching significant numbers and continue to be applied for by new local authorities as the problem gets transferred into their area, which means there is now more force in the argument that this is a relevant factor to be considered in deciding whether to grant the relief sought.

5.240 The judge addressed Bromley's failure to undertake any equality impact assessment (para 65):

> . . . in the claim before me there is no evidence that any proper equality impact assessment(s) were carried out, whether in form or indeed in substance. There appears to have been no engagement with Gypsy and Traveller families. I have already addressed the fact that there is no evidence of any intention to provide a transit site. I am simply told that consideration was given to the fact that the Gypsy and Traveller community would be unable to live temporarily in Bromley and that it was recognised that this would cause inconvenience and difficulty, but that the stronger argument was in favour of protecting public space.

5.241 The judge also addressed the need for welfare assessments (para 67):

> It is also not clear on the evidence how any infringements of the injunction would be dealt with in future in relation to the conduct of welfare assessments as occurs at present in relation to the existing statutory scheme of enforcement pursuant to Government guidance. From the one recent incident, it does not appear. . .that any welfare assessment was carried out. It may be that none was needed, but this is again a factor that required and requires proper consideration bearing in mind the injunction is effectively replacing the existing system of statutory enforcement powers and the government guidance relating to them with a court-imposed prohibitory injunction, which is subject to the sanction of committal for breach or contempt.

Having done so, the judge held that Bromley's decision to apply for an injunction to prohibit unauthorised camping on land it owned and managed was disproportionate (para 68):

> In my view, the decision to apply for an injunction was not made having had regard to all the material considerations and did not properly pose and approach the article 8(2) questions as to necessity and proportionality or indeed the need to have regard to the best interests of children (and there are clearly children who are going to be affected by the policy that is being adopted).

5.242 The judge then noted that there are permitted development rights (PDR) under the TCPA 1990 and the Town and Country Planning (General Permitted Development Order) (England) 2015,[211] which stipulate that encampments by caravans for short periods in certain circumstances on land will not breach planning control; a point which seemed to undermine one of Bromley's main arguments (para 71):

> Whilst [PDR] cannot be exercised if the landowner does not permit their exercise, the issue arises as to when a trespass is committed. Is it at the point when a person enters the land for the purpose of exercising those rights or when that person is told the landowner does not permit that exercise and they then fail to leave? This point was raised by the intervenor but, in my view, was not satisfactorily answered by [Bromley]. . . . It is another point it seems to me the claimant needed to consider in order to ensure that the order sought was limited to unlawful conduct and was not proscribing lawful conduct.

5.243 In conclusion, the judge decided that the application for an injunction to prohibit unauthorised camping on LBB's land should be dismissed but that there was no reason not to grant an injunction prohibiting fly tipping and the disposal of waste on Bromley's land. Bromley have now appealed to the Court of Appeal.

211 See para 4.29 onwards, above.

Public spaces protection orders

5.244 The Anti-social Behaviour, Crime and Policing Act (ASBCPA) 2014 Chapter 2 introduced public spaces protection orders (PSPOs). Under ASBCPA 2014 s1:

> (1) A local authority may make a public spaces protection order if satisfied on reasonable grounds that two conditions are met.
> (2) The first condition is that–
> (a) activities carried on in a public place within the authority's area have had a detrimental effect on the quality of life of those in the locality, or
> (b) it is likely that activities will be carried on in a public place within that area and that they will have such an effect.
> (3) The second condition is that the effect, or likely effect, of the activities–
> (a) is, or is likely to be, of a persistent or continuing nature,
> (b) is, or is likely to be, such as to make the activities unreasonable, and
> (c) justifies the restrictions imposed by the notice.

5.245 At the time of writing, the authors are aware of one local authority that has made a PSPO to ban unauthorised camping on certain areas of land. It is considered that any such ban may be susceptible to challenge on grounds that it violates rights protected by Articles 8 and 14 of the ECHR and/or on grounds that it breaches the Equality Act 2010.

5.246 ASBCPA 2014 s66 provides an appeal mechanism by which the making of a PSPO may be challenged in the High Court. It is important to note that there is a strict six-week time limit in which to bring such an appeal which runs from the date on which the PSPO is made.[212] It is also important to note that a challenge by way of judicial review is specifically precluded.[213]

Legal aid

5.247 Legal Aid, Sentencing and Punishment of Offenders Act (LASPO) 2012 Sch 1 Part 1 lists those areas of law that remain within scope for legal aid. The list includes cases which could result in the 'loss of home' but it should be noted that legal aid cover is no longer provided to trespassers:

212 ASBCPA 2014 s66(3).
213 ASBCPA 2014 s66(7).

(9) In this paragraph 'home', in relation to an individual, means the house, caravan, houseboat or other vehicle or structure that is the individual's only or main residence, subject to sub-paragraph (10).

(10) References in this paragraph to an individual's home do not include a vehicle or structure occupied by the individual if–

(a) there are no grounds on which it can be argued that the individual is occupying the vehicle or structure otherwise than as a trespasser, and

(b) there are no grounds on which it can be argued that the individual's occupation of the vehicle or structure began otherwise than as a trespasser.

(11) In sub-paragraphs (9) and (10), the references to a caravan, houseboat or other vehicle include the land on which it is located or to which it is moored.

(12) For the purposes of sub-paragraph (10) individuals occupying, or beginning occupation, of a vehicle or structure as a trespasser include individuals who do so by virtue of–

(a) title derived from a trespasser, or

(b) a licence or consent given by a trespasser or a person deriving title from a trespasser.

(13) For the purposes of sub-paragraph (10) an individual who is occupying a vehicle or structure as a trespasser does not cease to be a trespasser by virtue of being allowed time to leave the vehicle or structure.

5.248 It follows that a Gypsy or Traveller facing a possession action brought under CPR Part 55 will not be eligible for legal aid to defend the action where he or she entered the land as a trespasser and where he or she has remained a trespasser since that date.[214]

5.249 However, in a debate during the passage of the LASPO bill on 12 March 2012, the government spokesperson, Lord Wallace, made the point that:

> . . . there is no legal bar on seeking a judicial review of a public authority's decision to bring possession proceedings.[215] and if there are grounds for challenging by way of judicial review the decision by a public authority to issue possession proceedings then legal aid may be available to bring such a challenge.[216]

214 Unless exceptional funding under LASPO 2012 s10 can be obtained.

215 Hansard Lords Debates, 12 March 2012 col 110.

216 See para 5.159 onwards, above.

Conclusion

5.250 The shortage of permanent and temporary site provision makes it very difficult for many Gypsies and Travellers to access healthcare and education provision enjoyed by other members of our society.

5.251 The government made the point in para 4.2 of the 2004 Encampment Guidance that unauthorised camping would only be tackled if provision of suitable accommodation was made:

> In a context where the number of Gypsy caravans exceeds the number of authorised places where they can stop – which is the case in England – provision of suitable accommodation for Gypsies and Travellers must be seen as a vital part of an approach to dealing with unauthorised camping.

Regrettably, that point has been persistently ignored by our government and the inequalities suffered faced by Gypsies and Travellers without a lawful site remain as stark as ever.[217]

217 See chapters 7 and 8 for a full discussion of the inequalities faced by Gypsies and Travellers.

CHAPTER 6

Homelessness as it relates to Gypsies and Travellers

continued

Introduction

6.1 This chapter aims to highlight aspects of the homelessness legislation in England and Wales which are of specific interest to and importance for Gypsies and Travellers. Some broad idea of the general law in this area is required, and the first part of this chapter aims to provide that.[1]

Homelessness legislation

Introduction

6.2 The relevant statutory provisions for England are to be found in a) Housing Act (HA) 1996 Part VII, as amended by the Homelessness Act 2002; and b) the Localism Act 2011.[2]

6.3 The relevant statutory provisions for Wales are to be found in the Housing (Wales) Act (H(W)A) 2014 Chapter 2.

6.4 The HA 1996 and the H(W)A 2014 place an obligation on local housing authorities to secure that suitable accommodation is available for a person who is:

- homeless;
- eligible for assistance (or, in Wales, eligible for help);
- in priority need of accommodation; and
- who did not become homeless intentionally.[3]

There are also other obligations imposed by HA 1996 and H(W)A 2014 which will be discussed further below.

1 For a full coverage of homelessness, see Arden, Bates and Vanhegan, *Homelessness and allocations*, Legal Action Group, 11th edn, 2018; and Luba, Davies, Johnston and Buchanan, *Housing allocations and homelessness: law and practice*, Lexis Nexis, 5th edn, 2018.

2 For Scotland, the relevant statute is the Housing (Scotland) Act 1987 as amended by the Housing (Scotland) Act 2001 and the Homelessness etc (Scotland) Act 2003. There is a widening gap between the situation in England and Wales and that in Scotland. The 2003 Act provides for the eventual abolition of categories of priority need and also provides for continuing duties towards intentionally homeless applicants. For Northern Ireland reference should be made to the Housing (Northern Ireland) Order 1988 as amended by the Housing (Northern Ireland) Order 2003.

3 In Wales, where applicable, see para 6.32 below.

6.5 Certain categories of person are ineligible for assistance[4] (although they may still benefit from the general 'advice and information' duty):[5]

- 'persons from abroad', which means persons who are subject to immigration control under the Asylum and Immigration Act 1996, unless they are re-qualified by regulations;[6]
- those asylum-seekers, or dependants of asylum-seekers, who are not excluded as 'persons from abroad', but who will still be ineligible for assistance if they have accommodation in the United Kingdom (UK), however temporary, which is available for their occupation;[7]

6.6 This obviously may be of relevance to Roma from Eastern Europe. If an applicant is not within these categories or is within the first category ('persons from abroad') but is 're-included' by regulation, he or she will be 'eligible for assistance'.

The Homelessness Reduction Act 2017

6.7 The Homelessness Reduction Act 2017 only applies to England.[8] It received royal assent on 27 April 2017. The government introduced a new Homelessness Code of Guidance (February 2018) and the Homelessness Reduction Act 2017 was brought into force in April 2018. The aim is stated to be to help applicants to find accommodation at an early stage. However this will rely on extensive use of the private rented sector. The Homelessness Reduction Act 2017 amends HA 1996 Part 7 and statutory references at paras 6.8–6.14 below are to the amended HA 1996.

6.8 The duty at HA 1996 s179 to provide advisory services is strengthened and is targeted at particularly vulnerable groups.

6.9 Under HA 1996 s189A, where the applicant is eligible for assistance and is homeless or threatened with homelessness, the local

4 The question of 'eligibility' can be a complex one and is beyond the scope of this book. For a full discussion of this issue see footnote 1, above.

5 HA 1996 s179; and H(W)A 2014 s60.

6 HA 1996 s185(1), (2); and H(W)A 2014 s61 Sch 2 para 1.

7 For England, see the Allocation of Housing and Homelessness (Eligibility) (England) Regulations 2006 SI No 1294. For Wales, see the Allocation of Housing and Homelessness (Eligibility) (Wales) Regulations 2014 SI No 2603 (W.257).

8 Although Homelessness Reduction Act 2017 s13 states that the Act extends to England and Wales, the legislation amended is, in fact, applicable to England only.

housing authority must assess the applicant's case including the cause of homelessness, the applicant's housing needs and what support the applicant may require including financial support (including the needs of and support required by the applicant's household). The authority and the applicant should then seek to agree what steps each will take to secure that accommodation becomes available – a written 'personalised plan'. If they cannot agree, the authority should record what advice it gave to the applicant. A copy of the plan or the advice must be given to the applicant.

6.10 Under HA 1996 s175(4), an applicant will be threatened with homelessness if it is likely that he or she will become homeless within 56 days rather than the previous 28 days. Under HA 1996 s175(5), an applicant will be deemed to be threatened with homelessness if a valid notice under HA 1988 s21 (regarding an assured shorthold tenancy) has been served expiring within 56 days. Under HA 1996 s195(2), where an authority is satisfied that an applicant is threatened with homelessness, they must take reasonable steps to help to secure that accommodation does not cease to be available. The duty lasts for 56 days (or longer if the HA 1988 s21 notice is still in force). This duty ends when the applicant has accepted or refused suitable alternative accommodation. If accommodation has not been secured, the new 'relief' duty arises. Under HA 1996 s202(1), the applicant can request a review of any decision as to whether the duty is owed, as to the steps the authority will take and as to whether the duty has ended.

6.11 Under HA 1996 s189B(1) and (2), where a local housing authority are satisfied that an eligible applicant is homeless, a new interim (or 'relief') duty arises, requiring the authority to take reasonable steps to help the applicant to secure that suitable accommodation becomes available for at least six months or such longer period not exceeding 12 months. Under HA 1996 s189B(4), where the authority are satisfied that the applicant has a priority need and is not intentionally homeless, the relief duty will come to an end (and the duty to provide interim accommodation will then arise[9]). Under HA 1996 s189B(7), the relief duty lasts for 56 days and will end before then if the applicant accepts or refuses an offer of suitable accommodation. Under HA 1996 s202(1), the applicant can request a review of any decision as to whether the duty is owed, as to the steps the authority will take and as to whether the duty has ended.

9 See below at para 6.45 below.

6.12 Under HA 1996 s188, where a local housing authority has reason to believe that an applicant may be homeless, may be eligible for assistance and may have a priority need, the duty to secure interim accommodation arises and continues during the relief duty under HA 1996 s189B(2). Under HA 1996 s188(1ZA), where the authority decides that the applicant does not have a priority need, the duty to provide interim accommodation ceases either when the authority decides that the relief duty is not owed or when the relief duty comes to an end. The Homelessness (Review Procedure etc) Regulations 2018 specifies the types of public authorities and includes hospitals and prisons.

6.13 Under HA 1996 s193B, the new 'prevention' duty under HA 1996 s195(2) and the new 'relief' duty under HA 1996 s189B(2) come to an end if an applicant has deliberately and unreasonably refused to take any step. Under HA 1996 s193B(4) and (5), the applicant must first receive a warning notice specifying the steps in the personalised plan that he or she has failed to take, warning of the consequences of not complying and giving a reasonable period within which to comply. Under HA 1996 s193B(3), the applicant can request a review if a notice is then served. Under HA 1996 s193C, an applicant who has a priority need and who has not become homeless intentionally will continue to be accommodated.

6.14 Under HA 1996 s213B, a public authority which considers that a person is or may be homeless or threatened with homelessness must ask that person to agree to the public authority notifying a local housing authority and must send the notification if the person agrees. The types of public authority will be specified in regulations, but are likely to include hospitals and prisons.

Homelessness

6.15 HA 1996 s175(2)(b) and H(W)A 2014 s55(2)(b) will be the most relevant provisions for Gypsies and Travellers, though HA 1996 s175(3) and H(W)A 2014 s55(3) may also be relevant for those Gypsies and Travellers that have left conventional housing.[10]

England

6.16 HA 1996 s175 defines 'homelessness' as follows:

10 'Conventional housing', in this context, means bricks and mortar accommodation.

(1) A person is homeless if he has no accommodation available for his occupation, in the United Kingdom or elsewhere, which he–
   (a) is entitled to occupy by virtue of an interest in it or by virtue of an order of a court,
   (b) has an express or implied licence to occupy, or
   (c) occupies as a residence by virtue of any enactment or rule of law giving him the right to remain in occupation or restricting the right of another person to recover possession.

(2) A person is also homeless if he has accommodation but–
   (a) he cannot secure entry to it, or
   (b) it consists of a moveable structure, vehicle or vessel designed or adapted for human habitation and there is no place where he is entitled or permitted both to place it and to reside in it.

(3) A person shall not be treated as having accommodation unless it is accommodation which it would be reasonable for him to continue to occupy.

(4) A person is threatened with homelessness if it is likely that he will become homeless within 56 days.[11]

Wales

6.17 H(W)A 2014 s55 is in virtually identical terms.

'Accommodation available for occupation'

England

6.18 'Accommodation available for occupation' is defined by HA 1996 s176 thus:

Accommodation shall be regarded as available for a person's occupation only if it is available for occupation by him together with–

   (a) any other person who normally resides with him as a member of his family, or
   (b) any other person who might reasonably be expected to reside with him.[12]

Wales

6.19 H(W)A 2014 s56 is in virtually identical terms except that it begins 'Accommodation may only' instead of 'shall'. No difference in meaning appears to be intended.

11 For the effect of Homelessness Reduction Act 2017, see para 6.7 onwards, above.

12 The question of extended Gypsy and Traveller families is discussed at paras 6.124–6.126, below.

'Reasonable to continue to occupy'

England

6.20 The phrase 'reasonable to continue to occupy' is defined with specific reference to cases involving violence in England by HA 1996 s177 as follows:

> (1) It is not reasonable for a person to continue to occupy accommodation if it is probable that this will lead to domestic violence or other violence against him, or against–
> (a) a person who normally resides with him as a member of his family, or
> (b) any other person who might reasonably be expected to reside with him . . .
>
> (2) In determining whether it would be, or would have been, reasonable for a person to continue to occupy accommodation, regard may be had to the general circumstances prevailing in relation to housing in the district of the local housing authority to whom he has applied for accommodation or for assistance in obtaining accommodation.

Wales

6.21 In Wales, 'reasonable to continue to occupy' is defined by H(W)A 2014 s57 as:

> (1) It is not reasonable for a person to continue to occupy accommodation if it is probable that it will lead to the person, or a member of the person's household, being subjected to abuse.
>
> (2) In this section 'member of a person's household' means–
> (a) a person who normally resides with him or her as member of his or her family, or
> (b) any other person who might reasonably be expected to reside with that person.
>
> (3) In determining whether it would be, or would have been, reasonable for a person to continue to occupy accommodation, a local housing authority–
> (a) may have regard to the general circumstances prevailing in relation to housing in the area of the local housing authority to whom the person has applied for help in securing accommodation;
> (b) must have regard to whether or not the accommodation is affordable for that person.
>
> (4) The Welsh Ministers may by order specify–
> (a) other circumstances in which it is to be regarded as reasonable or not reasonable for a person to continue to occupy accommodation . . .

6.22 Therefore the relevant term in Wales is 'abuse' and not just 'violence'. 'Abuse' is defined by H(W)A 2014 s58 as:

(1) 'Abuse' means physical violence, threatening or intimidating behaviour and any other form of abuse which, directly or indirectly, may give rise to the risk of harm; and abuse is 'domestic abuse' where the victim is associated with the abuser.

(2) A person is associated with another person if–

(a) they are or have been married to each other;

(b) they are or have been civil partners of each other;

(c) they live or have lived together in an enduring family relationship (whether they are of different sexes or the same sex);

(d) they live or have lived in the same household;

(e) they are relatives;

(f) they have agreed to marry one another (whether or not that agreement has been terminated);

(g) they have entered into a civil partnership agreement between them (whether or not that agreement has been terminated);

(h) they have or have had an intimate personal relationship with each other which is or was of significant duration;

(i) in relation to a child, each of them is a parent of the child or has, or has had, parental responsibility for the child.

(3) If a child has been adopted or falls within subsection (4), two persons are also associated with each other for the purposes this Chapter if–

(a) one is a natural parent of the child or a parent of such a natural parent, and

(b) the other is–

(i) the child, or

(ii) a person who has become a parent of the child by virtue of an adoption order, who has applied for an adoption order or with whom the child has at any time been placed for adoption.

(4) A child falls within this section if–

(a) an adoption agency, within the meaning of section 2 of the Adoption and Children Act 2002, is authorised to place the child for adoption under section 19 of that Act (placing children with parental consent) or the child has become the subject of an order under section 21 of that Act (placement orders), or

(b) the child is freed for adoption by virtue of an order made–

(i) in England and Wales, under section 18 of the Adoption Act 1976,

(ii) in Northern Ireland, under Article 17(1) or 18(1) of the Adoption (Northern Ireland) Order 1987, or

(c) the child is the subject of a Scottish permanence order which includes granting authority to adopt.

(5) In this section–

- 'adoption order' ('*gorchymyn mabwysiadu*') means an adoption order within the meaning of section 72(1) of the Adoption Act 1976 or section 46(1) of the Adoption and Children Act 2002;

- 'civil partnership agreement' ('*cytundeb partneriaeth sifil*') has the meaning given by section 73 of the Civil Partnership Act 2004;
- 'parental responsibility' ('*cyfrifoldeb rhiant*') has the meaning given by section 3 of the Children Act 1989;
- 'relative' ('*perthynas*'), in relation to a person, means that person's parent, grandparent, child, grandchild, brother, half-brother, sister, half-sister, uncle, aunt, nephew, niece (including any person who is or has been in that relationship by virtue of a marriage or civil partnership or an enduring family relationship).

'Associated person'

England and Wales

6.23 'Associated person' is defined similarly in HA 1996 s178 to the definition in H(W)A 2014 s58 save that s2(c) and (h) do not appear.

6.24 However the difference between England and Wales in relation to 'violence' or 'abuse' is not as great as it appears. Case-law has held that violence under HA 1996 s177 includes not only physical violence (actual or threatened) but other threatening or intimidating behaviour or abuse that was sufficiently serious to give rise to a risk of harm including psychological harm.[13]

6.25 It is also important to note that considerations of violence (or abuse in Wales) and the general housing circumstances of the area are not exhaustive of the matters to be taken into account when determining whether it is reasonable to continue to occupy accommodation or not. Case-law shows it can be unreasonable to continue to occupy if the applicant suffers social isolation, the rent is unaffordable, the premises are in serious disrepair or the dwelling is overcrowded 'in common parlance'.[14]

Priority need

'Priority need for accommodation'

England

6.26 In England, HA 1996 s189 deals with 'priority need for accommodation':

> (1) The following have a priority need for accommodation–

13 *Yemshaw v Hounslow LBC* [2011] UKSC 3, [2011] 1 WLR 433, [2012] HLR 16; *Waltham Forest LBC V Hussain* [2015] EWCA 14.

14 *R v Hammersmith & Fulham LBC ex p Duro-Rama* (1983) 9 HLR 71; *R v Swansea CC ex p Hearn* (1990) 23 HLR 372. *Farah v Hillingdon LBC* [2014] EWCA Civ 359, *R v Westminster CC ex p Alouat* [1989] 21 HLR 477, and reference should also be made to the English Code of Guidance para 8.28 and the Welsh Code para 13.27(iii).

(a) a pregnant woman or a person with whom she resides or might reasonably be expected to reside;
(b) a person with whom dependent children reside or might reasonably be expected to reside;
(c) a person who is vulnerable as a result of old age, mental illness or handicap or physical disability or other special reason, or with whom such a person resides or might reasonably be expected to reside;
(d) a person who is homeless or threatened with homelessness as a result of an emergency such as flood, fire or other disaster.

(2) The Secretary of State may by order–
(a) specify further descriptions of persons as having a priority need for accommodation, and
(b) amend or repeal any part of subsection (1).[15]

Wales

6.27 In Wales, H(W)A 2014 s70 deals with 'priority need for accommodation':

(1) The following persons have a priority need for accommodation for the purposes of this Chapter–
(a) a pregnant woman or a person with whom she resides or might reasonably be expected to reside;
(b) a person with whom a dependent child resides or might reasonably be expected to reside;
(c) a person–
(i) who is vulnerable as a result of some special reason (for example: old age, physical or mental illness or physical or mental disability), or
(ii) with whom a person who falls within sub-paragraph (i) resides or might reasonably be expected to reside;
(d) a person–
(i) who is homeless or threatened with homelessness as a result of an emergency such as flood, fire or other disaster, or
(ii) with whom a person who falls within sub-paragraph (i) resides or might reasonably be expected to reside;
(e) a person–
(i) who is homeless as a result of being subject to domestic abuse, or
(ii) with whom a person who falls within sub-paragraph (i) resides (other than the abuser) or might reasonably be expected to reside;
(f) a person–

15 For a discussion of extended Gypsy and Traveller families, see paras 6.124–6.126, below. 'Other special reason' is a category that may have specific relevance to single homeless Gypsies and Travellers, as discussed at para 6.127, below.

(i) who is aged 16 or 17 when the person applies to a local housing authority for accommodation or help in obtaining or retaining accommodation, or
(ii) with whom a person who falls within sub-paragraph (i) resides or might reasonably be expected to reside;

(g) a person–
(i) who has attained the age of 18, when the person applies to a local housing authority for accommodation or help in obtaining or retaining accommodation, but not the age of 21, who is at particular risk of sexual or financial exploitation, or
(ii) with whom a person who falls within sub-paragraph (i) resides (other than an exploiter or potential exploiter) or might reasonably be expected to reside;

(h) a person–
(i) who has attained the age of 18, when the person applies to a local housing authority for accommodation or help in obtaining or retaining accommodation, but not the age of 21, who was looked after, accommodated or fostered at any time while under the age of 18, or
(ii) with whom a person who falls within sub-paragraph (i) resides or might reasonably be expected to reside;

(i) a person–
(i) who has served in the regular armed forces of the Crown who has been homeless since leaving those forces, or
(ii) with whom a person who falls within sub-paragraph (i) resides or might reasonably be expected to reside;

(j) a person who has a local connection with the area of the local housing authority and who is vulnerable as a result of one of the following reasons–
(i) having served a custodial sentence within the meaning of section 76 of the Powers of Criminal Courts (Sentencing) Act 2000,
(ii) having been remanded in or committed to custody by an order of a court, or
(iii) having been remanded to youth detention accommodation under section 91(4) of the Legal Aid, Sentencing and Punishment of Offenders Act 2012,

or a person with whom such a person resides or might reasonably be expected to reside.

'Vulnerability'

England

6.28 In England, the section 189(2)(a) power (see para 6.26, above) has been used to specify:[16]

16 Homelessness (Priority Need for Accommodation) (England) Order 2002 SI No 2051.

(i) all 16- and 17-year olds, provided they are not a relevant child (as defined by the Children Act 1989), or a child to whom the local authority owes a duty to provide accommodation under Children Act 1989 s20;

(ii) any person who is aged 18 to 20, other than a relevant student,[17] who at any time after reaching the age of 16 but while still under 18 was, but is no longer, looked after, accommodated or fostered;

(iii) those who are vulnerable because they have previously been looked after, accommodated or fostered;

(iv) those who are vulnerable as a result of service in Her Majesty's regular armed forces;

(v) those who are vulnerable as a result of having served a custodial sentence, having been committed for contempt of court or having been remanded in custody;

(vi) those who are vulnerable because they have had to cease to occupy accommodation because of violence or threats of violence which are likely to be carried out.

Wales

6.29 In Wales, 'vulnerability' is further defined in H(W)A 2014 s71:

> (1) A person is vulnerable as a result of a reason mentioned in paragraph (c) or (j) of section 70(1) if, having regard to all the circumstances of the person's case–
> (a) the person would be less able to fend for himself or herself (as a result of that reason) if the person were to become street homeless than would an ordinary homeless person who becomes street homeless, and
> (b) this would lead to the person suffering more harm than would be suffered by the ordinary homeless person;
> this subsection applies regardless of whether or not the person whose case is being considered is, or is likely to become, street homeless.
> (2) In subsection (1), 'street homeless' ('digartref ac ar y stryd'), in relation to a person, means that the person has no accommodation available for the person's occupation in the United Kingdom or elsewhere, which the person–
> (a) is entitled to occupy by virtue of an interest in it or by virtue of an order of a court,
> (b) has an express or implied licence to occupy, or
> (c) occupies as a residence by virtue of any enactment or rule of law giving the person the right to remain in occupation or restricting the right of another person to recover possession;
> and sections 55 and 56 do not apply to this definition.

17 As defined by Children Act 1989 s24B(3).

6.30 In England, the concept of 'street homeless' is not part of the test of 'vulnerability'. The leading case on the issue in England is now *Hotak and others v Southwark LBC and others.*[18] The main features are that in England, as a result of *Hotak*, the question now is whether the applicant will suffer more harm than an ordinary person if that person is made homeless, rather than an ordinary actually homeless person. On this point the test in England is now more easily met than that in Wales. Further, despite the insertion of the phrase 'significantly more' in *Hotak*, as a result of a later decision by the Court of Appeal, it now appears that there is no real difference between the English and the Welsh tests as to the degree of harm. The Court of Appeal interpreted 'significant' to mean no more than 'noticeable',[19] while the Welsh test requires 'more' harm.[20]

Intentional homelessness

England and Wales

6.31 The phrase 'intentional homelessness' is defined in HA 1996 s191 as:

> (1) A person becomes homeless intentionally if he deliberately does or fails to do anything in consequence of which he ceases to occupy accommodation which is available for his occupation and which it would have been reasonable for him to continue to occupy.
> (2) For the purposes of subsection (1) an act or omission in good faith on the part of a person who was unaware of any relevant fact shall not be treated as deliberate.
> (3) A person shall be treated as becoming homeless intentionally if–
> (a) he enters into an arrangement under which he is required to cease to occupy accommodation which it would have been reasonable for him to continue to occupy, and
> (b) the purpose of the arrangement is to enable him to become entitled to assistance under this Part,
> and there is no other good reason why he is homeless.

6.32 H(W)A 2014 s77 is in virtually identical terms except that H(W)A 2014 s77 (3) reads 'may not be treated as deliberate' instead of 'shall' in the equivalent HA 1996s 191(2).Moreover, a Welsh local authority

18 [2015] UKSC 30, [2015] 2 WLR 13412

19 *Panayiotou v Waltham Forest LBC* [2017] EWCA Civ 1624 at para 64.

20 See also the English Homelessness Code of Guidance for Local Authorities 2018 paras 8.13–8.15; and the Welsh Code of Guidance to Local Authorities on the Allocation of Accommodation and Homelessness 2016 paras 16.71–16.78.

is not obliged to consider whether an applicant is intentionally homeless. By H(W)A 2014 s78 it is only required to do so if the Welsh Ministers have specified a category or categories of applicant for whom intentional homelessness is a relevant matter for consideration and the authority itself has published notice of its decision to have regard to intentionality and which of the categories it will consider.[21] The Welsh Ministers have specified (in effect) the priority need categories, ie those to whom a full (not temporary) duty may be owed.[22]

Threatened with homelessness intentionally

England

6.33 In England, there is a similar definition to cover the situation of becoming threatened with homelessness intentionally.[23]

Wales

6.34 There is no such definition in H(W)A 2014.

Local connection

6.35 If a person, or a person who might reasonably be expected to reside with him or her, does not have a local connection with the district of the authority he or she is applying to and either of them *does* have a local connection with the district of another authority, then the authority can refer the duty to accommodate to the other authority which can be an authority in England or Wales.

England

6.36 In England, a person has a local connection with the district of a local housing authority if he or she has a connection with it because:

- he or she is, or was, normally resident there of his or her own choice;
- he or she is employed there;
- of family associations; or
- of special circumstances.[24]

21 See also the Welsh Code of Guidance para 17.1.

22 Homelessness (Intentionality) (Specified Categories) Wales Regulations 2015 SI No 1123, in force from 1 December 2014.

23 HA 1996 s196.

24 HA 1996 s199(1).

6.37 In England, a person in the regular armed forces will not be considered as either employed in the district or as resident in the district.[25]

6.38 Additionally, in England a person is not resident in a district if he or she is detained under the authority of an Act of Parliament, for example, a prisoner or a patient in a mental hospital.[26] The secretary of state may specify other circumstances when someone will not be treated as either resident or employed in a district, but this power has not been used to date.[27]

Wales

6.39 In Wales, 'local connection' is defined by H(W)A 2014 s81 in similar terms as in England and the Welsh Ministers have similar powers of specification.

Preliminary duties

Inquiries

England[28]

6.40 In England, where a local authority has reason to believe that an applicant may be homeless or threatened with homelessness, it shall make such inquiries as are necessary to see whether:

- the person is eligible for assistance; and
- if so, what duty, if any, might be owed to him or her.[29]

Wales

6.41 The equivalent duty on Welsh authorities (H(W)A 2014 s62) is differently phrased and spelt out in more detail. It is a duty to carry out an assessment not to make inquiries (although, by implication, there must be inquiries before there can be an assessment). The Welsh Code of Guidance emphasises that the applicant must be given the opportunity to explain the circumstances that have led to his or her

25 HA 1996 s199(2) and (3)(a).

26 HA 1996 s199(3)(b).

27 HA 1996 s199(5). The particular position of Gypsies and Travellers who may be moving around several districts or forced by frequent evictions to move around several districts, will be discussed at para 6.141, below.

28 For the effects of Homelessness Reduction Act 2017, see from para 6.5 onwards above.

29 HA 1996 s184(1).

homelessness.[30] What factors are to be assessed are set out and include, for example, ' the circumstances that have caused the applicant to be homeless' (H(W)A 2014 s62(5)(a)). The first step is to assess whether or not the applicant is eligible for help. The circumstances when a local authority must review its assessment are set out. Also a local authority is not required to carry out an assessment if the applicant has been previously assessed and there has been no material change in the person's circumstances since there is no new information (H(W)A 2014 s 62(2)).This enacts the tests set out in *R v Harrow LBC ex p Fahia*[31] and *Gardiner v Haringey LBC*.[32]

Notification of decision

England and Wales

6.42 On completion of its inquiries or assessment, the local authority must notify the applicant of its decision in writing and, if it is against the interests of the applicant, must also notify him or her of the reasons for that decision.[33] The notification should also tell the applicant about his or her right to request a review of the decision (within 21 days).[34] Paragraph 3.18 of the English Homelessness Code of Guidance[35] states that:

> Wherever possible, it is recommended that housing authorities aim to complete their enquiries and notify the applicant of their decision within 33 working days of accepting a duty to make enquiries under s184. In many cases it should be possible for authorities to complete the inquiries significantly earlier.

Paragraph 10.52 of the Welsh Code of Guidance states that:

> . . . wherever possible Local Housing Authorities [should] aim to complete each stage of the assessment and notify the applicant of their decision in 10 working days.

6.43 The local authority may also make inquiries into whether the applicant has a local connection with the district of another local housing authority in England, Wales or Scotland.[36] If the local authority

30 Welsh Code of Guidance paras 10.22 and 10.23.
31 [1988] 30 HLR 1124.
32 [2009] EWHC 2699 (Admin).
33 HA 1996 s184(3), (6); H(W)A 2014 s63 is in similar terms.
34 HA 1996 s184(5); H(W)A 2014 s85 is in similar terms.
35 See further at para 6.92, below.
36 HA 1996 s184(2); H(W)A 2014 s80(2) is in virtually identical terms.

decides to make a local connection referral to another authority,[37] it shall still notify the applicant of this decision and of the reasons for it.[38]

6.44 The notice required to be given to the applicant, if not received by him or her, shall be treated as having been given to him or her if it is made available at the authority's office for a reasonable period for collection by him or her.[39] In other words, the burden is on the applicant who does not receive the decision to go to the local authority's office and ask for it.

Duty to secure that accommodation is available for occupation pending a decision

England

6.45 Inquiries might take some time to complete. Meanwhile, in England, if the local housing authority has reason to believe that the applicant may be homeless, eligible for assistance and has a priority need, it has a duty to secure that accommodation is available for his or her occupation pending a decision as to what duty, if any, is owed to him or her.[40] In England, the local housing authority's duty to house pending inquiries also arises – even if there is no apparent priority need – if the authority has reason to believe that the application is a second application, following a previous application in the preceding two years which resulted in an assured shorthold tenancy which has come to an end, provided that the applicant is still eligible, and did not become homeless intentionally.[41]

Wales

6.46 In Wales, the above duty pending assessment arises provided the local housing authority has reason to believe that the applicant may be homeless and eligible for assistance and has a priority need.[42]

6.47 In Wales the same duty applies if an applicant's case has been referred from a local housing authority in England and the Welsh local housing authority is satisfied that the applicant is homeless and

37 See further at paras 6.35 onwards, above.

38 HA 1996 s184(4); H(W)A 2014 ss82 and 84 are in similar terms.

39 HA 1996 s184(6); H(W)A 2014 s63(4) is in virtually identical terms.

40 HA 1996 s188(1); and see paras 6.147 onwards, below, for a more detailed discussion on the interim accommodation duty and its relevance to homeless applications made by Gypsies and Travellers. For the effects of Homelessness Reduction Act 2017, see para 6.7, above.

41 HA 1996 s188(1A), inserted by Localism Act 2011 s149.

42 H(W)A 2014 s68(2).

eligible for help so that the duty to help to secure accommodation has arisen.[43] The means by which a Welsh local authority can secure or help to secure suitable accommodation in respect of any power or duty are set out in some detail in H(W)A 2014 s64 and s65 partly in similar terms to HA 1996 s210 and partly by means of mediation, payments, guarantees, debt management support and other means as well as by provision of accommodation. These provisions are described together in chapter 12 of the Welsh Code of Guidance as the 'duty to prevent'.

6.48 Moreover, in Wales, under H(W)A 2014 s82:

> (1) Where a local housing authority notifies an applicant in accordance with section 84 that it intends to notify or has notified another local housing authority in Wales or England of its opinion that the conditions are met for the referral of the applicant's case to that other authority–
> (a) it ceases to be subject to any duty under section 68 (interim duty to secure accommodation for homeless applicants in priority need), and
> (b) it is not subject to any duty under section 73 (duty to help to secure accommodation for homeless applicants).

England and Wales

6.49 In England and Wales, the duty is placed on the authority to whom the applicant applies, regardless of any question about local connection.[44]

6.50 The accommodation available must be available for occupation by the applicant, together with any other person who normally resides with him or her as a family member or any other person who might reasonably be expected to reside with him or her.[45] The duty to provide interim accommodation will end once an applicant has been notified of the local authority's decision. However, if the applicant requests a review of the decision then the local authority has the power to provide interim accommodation pending that review.[46]

Principal duties

6.51 The principal duties that may be owed to an applicant by a local housing authority can be divided into limited duties and full duties.

43 H(W)A 2014 ss68(3) and 73.

44 HA 1996 s188(2); H(W)A 2014 s68(4).

45 HA 1996 s176; H(W)A 2014 s56(1) is in virtually identical terms.

46 HA 1996 s188(3); H(W)A 2014 s69(11).

Limited duties

Applicant is in priority need but intentionally homeless

England

6.52 In England, if the authority is satisfied that the applicant is homeless and in priority need but that he or she is intentionally homeless, it shall secure that accommodation is available for his or her occupation for such period as it considers will give the applicant a reasonable opportunity of securing accommodation for his or her occupation, and provide him or her with appropriate advice and assistance to try and locate such accommodation.[47] Such advice and assistance should include information about the likely availability in the authority's district of types of accommodation appropriate to the applicant's housing needs.[48] This advice and assistance should be provided after the applicant's housing needs have been assessed.[49]

6.53 In the case of Gypsies and Travellers, such information should presumably include details of local authority or private Gypsy/Traveller sites in the district.

Wales

6.54 In Wales, H(W)A 2014 s75 applies. This section refers back to the duty under H(W)A 2014 s73 to help to secure accommodation for an applicant who is homeless and eligible for help and which has come to an end 56 days after notification that the duty has ended under H(W)A 2014 s63 or come to an end within 56 days because reasonable steps have been taken to help to secure accommodation. Even if the local authority is satisfied that the applicant became homeless intentionally then, in the restricted circumstances set out in H(W)A 2014 s75(1) and (3), it still comes under a duty to secure that accommodation is available for the applicant if he or she does not have suitable accommodation available for a period of at least six months starting with the date of notification. This, of course, assumes the local authority has enabled itself to consider intentional homelessness at all.

6.55 Additionally a local housing authority in Wales can, effectively, decide not to take account of intentional homelessness.[50]

47 HA 1996 s190(2).

48 HA 1996 s190(5), inserted by Homelessness Act 2002 Sch 1 para 10.

49 HA 1996 s190(4), inserted by Homelessness Act 2002 Sch 1 para 10.

50 See H(W)A 2014 s75 and the Homelessness (Intentionality) (Specified Categories) (Wales) Regulations 2015 SI No 1265.

'Secure'

England

6.56 In England, if the authority provides its own accommodation in order to comply with the above duty, it will not be secure unless and until the authority notifies the applicant otherwise under the allocation provisions.[51] If the authority fulfils its duty by arranging for accommodation with a private landlord, a tenancy granted in this way cannot be an assured tenancy before the end of the period of 12 months beginning with the date when the applicant was notified of the local authority's decision or the date of notification of the decision on review or appeal, unless during that period the landlord notifies the applicant otherwise.[52]

6.57 There is a similar provision in Wales but that applies only in relation to the duties to secure accommodation pending decision, review or appeal.[53]

6.58 In England, if the authority, being satisfied that an applicant is eligible for assistance:

- is not satisfied that the applicant has a priority need; or
- is so satisfied but also concludes that he or she became threatened with homelessness intentionally,

it shall secure that he or she is provided (whether by the authority or by someone else) with advice and assistance in any attempts he or she may make to secure that accommodation does not cease to be available to him or her.[54] This advice and assistance should be provided after the applicant's housing needs have been assessed.[55] If homelessness does then occur, and the applicant is in priority need but intentionally homeless, a period of temporary accommodation[56] will then be available.

51 HA 1985 Sch 1 para 4, substituted by HA 1996 Sch 17 para 3. The allocation provisions under HA 1996 Pt VI are outside the scope of this book – see further in Arden, Bates and Vanhegan, *Homelessness and allocations* and Luba, Davies, Johnston and Buchanan, *Housing allocations and homelessness*. No doubt, in terms of Gypsy and Traveller sites under local authority control, there will usually be specific allocation policies that the local authority operates – see also chapter 3, above.

52 HA 1996 s209.

53 H(W)A 2014 ss92 and 68, 82, 85(5).

54 HA 1996 s195(5). For the effects of the Homelessness Reduction Act 2017, see at para 6.8 above.

55 HA 1996 s195(6), inserted by Homelessness Act 2002 Sch 1 para 14.

56 See paras 6.52–6.53, above.

Wales

6.59 In Wales, H(W)A 2014 s66 applies in these circumstances:

> (1) A local housing authority must help to secure that suitable accommodation does not cease to be available for occupation by an applicant if the authority is satisfied that the applicant is–
> (a) threatened with homelessness, and
> (b) eligible for help.

6.60 Under H(W)A 2014 s67 and s79 that duty comes to an end in defined circumstances, including that the applicant ceases to be threatened with homelessness and suitable accommodation is likely to be available for at least six months or such accommodation has been accepted or refused. Other circumstances are that the local authority is no longer satisfied the applicant is eligible for help or that the applicant has unreasonably failed to co-operate with the authority.

Applicant not intentionally homeless, but not in priority need

England

6.61 In England, if the authority is satisfied that the applicant did not become homeless intentionally but is also satisfied that he or she is not in priority need, it may nevertheless secure that accommodation is available for occupation by the applicant.[57] If satisfied that the applicant is not in priority need but that he or she is threatened with homelessness, though not intentionally, the authority may take reasonable steps to secure that accommodation does not cease to be available.[58]

Wales

6.62 H(W)A 2014 s66 covers the latter case but also provides that the duty is mandatory by inserting 'must' for 'may'.

Applicant has priority need and is threatened with homelessness, but not intentionally

England

6.63 Similarly, in England, if the authority is satisfied that the applicant has a priority need and is threatened with homelessness, but not intentionally, it shall take reasonable steps to ensure that accommodation does not cease to be available for his or her occupation.[59]

57 HA 1996 s192(3).
58 HA 1996 s195(9), inserted by Homelessness Act 2002 s5(2).
59 HA 1996 s195(2).

However, this duty cannot affect the right of the authority to obtain possession of its own accommodation.[60]

Wales

6.64 H(W)A 2014 s66 also covers the above case.

Full duties

Applicant is homeless, in priority need and not intentionally homeless

England and Wales

6.65 Where a local authority is satisfied that an applicant is homeless, in priority need and not intentionally homeless, it shall secure that accommodation is available for occupation by the applicant.[61] In Wales, the duty is in similar terms[62] with the addition that it is specified that the duty is owed if the applicant has suitable accommodation available for occupation but it is not likely to be available for occupation for a period of at least six months from notification under H(W)A 2014 s63. In England, an authority also owes a full duty, even if there is no priority need, if the application is a renewed application, following a previous application which resulted in an assured shorthold tenancy in the preceding two years, provided that the applicant is still eligible and did not become homeless intentionally.[63] The accommodation must also be available for any other family member who normally resides with him or her, or anyone else who might reasonably be expected to reside with him or her.[64]

6.66 A local housing authority may discharge this duty as follows:

- by securing that suitable accommodation provided by the authority is available;
- by securing that the applicant obtains suitable accommodation from some other person (which may include another local authority or a housing association); or
- by giving the applicant such advice and assistance as will secure that suitable accommodation is available from some other person.[65]

60 HA 1996 s195(3).
61 HA 1996 s193(1), (2).
62 H(W)A 2014 s75(1), (2).
63 HA 1996 s195A(1), inserted by Localism Act 2011 s149.
64 HA 1996 s176; H(W)A 2014 s56 is in virtually identical terms.
65 HA 1996 s206(1); H(W)A 2014 s64 is in similar terms.

6.67 In deciding whether accommodation is 'suitable' for a person, the local housing authority shall have regard to certain provisions of the HA 1985 and the Housing Act (HA) 2004 which relate to hazardous housing, slum clearance, overcrowding and houses in multiple occupation (HMOs).[66]

6.68 In England, the secretary of state can add to the definition of what is 'suitable' and has done so, particularly with regard to affordability of the accommodation.[67]

6.69 The Welsh Ministers can also add to the definition of what is 'suitable' and have also done so.[68]

In-area placement

6.70 In England, so far as reasonably practicable, the authority shall ensure that accommodation is available for the occupation of the applicant in its district.[69] If an applicant is placed in another area, the authority must give notice to the local housing authority with responsibility for that area; any such notice must contain certain specified details[70] and must be given in writing within two weeks of the accommodation being made available.[71]

6.71 Very similar provisions apply in Wales.[72]

'Secure'

6.72 In England, where a local authority provides its own accommodation in discharge of the duty, it is not secure.[73]

6.73 Nor do the Welsh provisions commit to providing secure accommodation.[74]

66 HA 1996 s210(1); H(W)A 2014 s59(1) is in similar terms.

67 HA 1996 s210(2). See the Homelessness (Suitability of Accommodation) Order 1996 SI No 3204; the Homelessness (Suitability of Accommodation) (England) Order 2003 SI No 3326. For a full discussion of 'suitable accommodation' as it relates to Gypsies and Travellers, see paras 6.147 onwards, below.

68 H(W)A 2014 s59(3); and the Homelessness (Suitability of Accommodation) (Wales) Order 2015 SI No 1268.

69 HA 1996 s208(1).

70 HA 1996 s208(2) and (3).

71 HA 1996 s208(4).

72 H(W)A 2014 s91.

73 HA 1985 Sch 1 para 4.

74 H(W)A 2014 s64.

Bringing full duty to an end

England

6.74 The 'full duty' owed to the applicant can be brought to an end if:

- the applicant, having been informed by the authority of the possible consequences of refusal and his or her right to request a review, refuses an offer of accommodation which the authority is satisfied is suitable for him or her and the authority then notifies him or her that it considers that it has discharged its duty;
- the applicant ceases to be eligible for assistance;
- the applicant becomes homeless intentionally from the accommodation made available for his or her accommodation;
- the applicant accepts an offer under HA 1996 Pt VI (the allocation provisions);
- the applicant accepts an offer of an assured (not an assured shorthold) tenancy from a private landlord;
- the applicant otherwise voluntarily ceases to occupy as his or her only or principal home the accommodation made available for his or her occupation;
- the applicant, having been informed of the possible consequences of refusal and his or her right to request a review of the suitability of the accommodation, refuses a final offer (which, in England, is defined as an offer 'made in writing' stating 'that it is a final offer for the purposes of [HA 1996 s193(7)]'[75]) and the authority is satisfied that the offer is suitable and that it is reasonable for the applicant to accept the offer;
- the applicant, in certain circumstances, accepts the offer of an assured shorthold tenancy from a private landlord.[76]

Wales

6.75 Similar provisions apply in Wales.[77] Differences include that in England the circumstances in which a duty can be discharged by an offer from a private landlord includes simply an offer of a fixed term tenancy. In Wales the fixed term must be for a period of at least six months.

75 HA 1996 s193(7A).

76 HA 1996 s193(5)–(8). For fuller details see Arden, Bates and Vanhegan, *Homelessness and allocations* and Luba, Davies, Johnston and Buchanan, *Housing allocations and homelessness*.

77 H(W)A 2014 ss74 and 76.

Local connection

England and Wales

6.76 In England, the local connection provisions allow one local housing authority to transfer the responsibility of ensuring that accommodation becomes available to another authority where:

- the applicant was placed in accommodation in that area by another local housing authority in the first place;[78] or
- neither the applicant nor any person who might reasonably be expected to reside with him or her has a local connection with the district of the authority they are applying to, and the applicant or a person who might reasonably be expected to reside with him or her has a local connection with the district of another authority, and neither the applicant nor a person who might reasonably be expected to reside with him or her will run the risk of domestic violence in that other area.[79]

6.77 In Wales, the provisions are very similar except that there is reference to 'domestic abuse' instead of 'domestic violence'.[80]

6.78 In England, the provisions also apply if the application is made to an authority within the period of two years beginning with the date on which the applicant accepted an offer from the authority under HA 1996 s193(7AC) (private rented sector offer), and neither the applicant nor any person who might reasonably be expected to reside with the applicant will run the risk of domestic violence in the area of the local authority.[81]

6.79 The definition of what amounts to 'local connection' is supplemented by the Local Authority Agreement, which is discussed in further detail at paras 6.141 onwards, below. The applicant can request a review of a local authority's decision that she or he has a local connection.[82] There is an arbitration system put in place to deal with disagreements between local authorities.[83] The arbitration decision itself can be subject to review and appeal.[84]

78 HA 1996 s198(4). See para 6.70, above.

79 HA 1996 s198(2).

80 H(W)A 2014 s80.

81 HA 1996 s198(2ZA), inserted by Localism Act 2011 s149.

82 HA 1996 s200(2); H(W)A 2014 s85(1)(c). Accommodation pending decisions on review is dealt with by HA 1996 s 200(5); H(W)A 2014 s82(6).

83 HA 1996 s198(5); H(W)A 2014 s80(5).

84 HA 1996 s202(1)(d), (e).

6.80 The arbitration system is set out in the Homelessness (Decisions on Referral) Order 1998,[85] which covers both England and Wales.[86]

Protection of property

England

6.81 In England, where a local authority is or has been under a duty under HA 1996 s188, s190, s193, s195 or s200,[87] it may also be under a duty to take reasonable steps to prevent the loss of an applicant's property, or prevent or mitigate damage to it.[88]

Wales

6.82 In Wales, where a local authority is or has been under a duty under H(W)A 2014 s66, s68, s75 or s82,[89] the above duty arises.[90] However, in Wales, where a local housing authority has become subject to the duty under the above sections, it continues to be subject to that duty even if the duty in respect of the applicant as described in those sections comes to an end.[91]

England and Wales

6.83 An applicant's property includes the personal property of any person reasonably expected to reside with him or her.[92]

6.84 The duty arises where the local authority has reason to believe that there is a danger of loss of, or damage to, any personal property of an applicant by reason of his or her inability to protect it or deal with it, and no other suitable arrangements have been or are being made.[93]

6.85 In other circumstances, the local authority has a power to protect property.[94] The local authority, when agreeing to protect property under these provisions, can impose reasonable charges and conditions as to the disposal of property.[95] These provisions are not

85 SI No 1578.
86 The Welsh Code of Guidance paras 18.26–18.28 refers.
87 See para 6.40, above.
88 HA 1996 s211(2).
89 See para 6.40.
90 H(W)A 2014 s93.
91 H(W)A 2014 s93(3).
92 HA 1996 s211(5); H(W)A 2014 s93(6).
93 HA 1996 s211(1); H(W)A 2014 s93(1).
94 HA 1996 s211(3); H(W)A 2014 s93(5).
95 HA 1996 s211(4); H(W)A 2014 s93(4).

reviewable but could be subject to public law challenge by way of judicial review.[96]

6.86 These provisions might be most relevant to Gypsies and Travellers who have decided to seek conventional housing. For example, such applicants may require storage for their caravans pending the provision of suitable accommodation.

Homelessness strategies

England

6.87 The Homelessness Act 2002 imposed a new duty on local authorities to carry out a homelessness review and to formulate and publish a homelessness strategy based on the results of that review.[97]

6.88 A homelessness review means a review by a local authority of:

a) the levels, and likely future levels, of homelessness in its district;
b) the activities which are carried out for any purpose mentioned in para 6.52, below, (or which contribute to their achievement); and
c) the resources available to the housing authority, the social services authority for their district, other public authorities, voluntary organisations and other persons for such activities.[98]

The purposes of the review are:

a) preventing homelessness in the district of the authority;
b) securing that accommodation is or will be available for people in the district who are or may become homeless;
c) providing support for people in the district:
   - who are or may become homeless; or
   - who have been homeless and need support to prevent them becoming homeless again.[99]

6.89 A homelessness strategy is a strategy formulated by a local housing authority to deal with those matters mentioned in para 6.88, above.[100]

96 For a fuller discussion of judicial review, see Manning, Salmon and Brown, *Judicial Review Proceedings: a practitioner's guide* (3rd edition), LAG 2013.
97 Homelessness Act 2002 s1(1) and (3).
98 Homelessness Act 2002 s2(1).
99 Homelessness Act 2002 s3(1).
100 Homelessness Act 2002 s3(1).

Wales

6.90 H(W)A 2014 ss50–52 have introduced very similar provisions regarding homelessness strategies and reviews in Wales. Welsh local authorities must adopt a homelessness strategy in 2018 and a new homelessness strategy in every fourth year after 2018.[101]

England and Wales

6.91 A local housing authority must take into account the homelessness strategy when exercising its functions.[102] It is suggested that, with regard to homeless Gypsies and Travellers, the strategy should include an assessment of available land in the local authority area and the possibility of assistance from other public authorities, neighbouring local authorities or (where relevant) the county council.[103]

Code of guidance

England

6.92 In the exercise of their functions under the homelessness provisions of HA 1996, local authorities are bound to have regard to such guidance as may from time to time be given by the secretary of state.[104] The secretary of state has issued a code of guidance.[105]

Wales

6.93 In the exercise of its functions relating to homelessness, a council of a county or county borough must have regard to guidance given by the Welsh Ministers.[106] The Welsh Ministers have issued a code of guidance.[107]

101 H(W)A 2014 s50(2).

102 Homelessness Act 2002 s1(5); H(W)A 2014 s50(4).

103 See further at para 6.177, below.

104 HA 1996 s182.

105 English Homelessness Code of Guidance for Local Authorities. The latest code was issued by the then Department for Communities and Local Government (DCLG) on 2 September 2006.

106 H(W)A 2014 s98(1).

107 Code of guidance to local authorities on allocation of accommodation and homelessness, 2015.

Reviews and appeals

England

6.94 In England, applicants have a statutory right to request an internal review[108] of any of the following decisions regarding:

- eligibility for assistance;
- what duty is owed to an applicant found to be homeless or threatened with homelessness;
- referral to another authority under the local connection provisions;
- whether the conditions for local connection referral are met;
- what duty is owed following a local connection referral; or
- any decision about the suitability of accommodation offered in discharge of duty.

Wales

6.95 In Wales, the provisions are very similar[109] except that, where an applicant is owed a duty to be provided with accommodation because he or she is homeless and eligible for assistance[110] and, after a period of 56 days has elapsed, the local authority is satisfied that reasonable steps have been taken to help to secure that suitable accommodation is available for occupation by the applicant,[111] an applicant has the right to request a review of whether or not reasonable steps were taken.[112]

England and Wales

6.96 The review procedure includes provisions (supplemented by case-law) that, if there is a deficiency or irregularity in the original decision or in the manner in which it was made, but the reviewer is minded to make a decision against the applicant's interests, the reviewer must give notice to the applicant of such, with reasons, and that the applicant may make representations orally, in writing or both at the applicant's choice.[113] Case-law has established that 'deficiency or irregularity' are wider terms than 'error of law'. They cover 'some-

108 HA 1996 s202. For the effects of Homelessness Reduction Act 2017, see above at paras 6.7 onwards.

109 H(W)A 2014 s85.

110 H(W)A 2014 s73.

111 H(W)A 2014 s74(2), (3).

112 H(W)A 2014 s85(2).

113 Homelessness (Review Procedures) Regulations 2018 SI No 223 reg 7(2); Homelessness (Review Procedure) (Wales) Regulations 2015 SI No 1266 reg 5(2).

thing lacking' in the original decision which affected its fairness, eg the failure to address a significant issue or addressing it inadequately.[114] The codes now incorporate this case-law.[115] A failure to properly address any issue by the original decision maker engages the provision even if all other issues are properly addressed. The introduction of new facts during the review process will render the original decision deficient even if these new facts had been present and could have been raised when the original decision was made. This regulation has been found to be beneficial to Gypsies and Travellers in practice. A failure to comply with it by the reviewer can be a ground of appeal to the county court.

6.97 The right to a review does not include the right to a review of an earlier decision made following a review.[116] If the local authority in question has a procedure involving a further 'review' stage, it is important that the Gypsy or Traveller (or their adviser or solicitor) obtain confirmation that the previous decision no longer stands, otherwise, it will be necessary to appeal to the county court within the necessary time limit from the original review decision.[117]

6.98 Pending the outcome of the review, the local authority has a discretion to provide accommodation for the applicant.[118]

6.99 There is a right to request a review of the suitability of such accommodation if offered (whether accepted or not.)[119]

6.100 An appeal can be made to the county court if the applicant either:

- is dissatisfied with the outcome of the review; or
- has not been notified of the outcome within the time limit prescribed.[120]

6.101 Appeal lies only on a point of law, whether arising from the original decision (if the local authority has failed to conclude the review within the time prescribed) or from the decision on review.[121]

6.102 The applicant must file the appeal within 21 days of notification of the review decision or of the date when he or she should have been

114 *Hall v Wandsworth LBC* [2005] HLR 23; *Makisi v Birmingham CC* [2011] HLR 27; *Mitu v Camden LBC* [2011] EWCA Civ 1249.

115 English Code of Guidance paras 19.12–19.14; Welsh Code of Guidance para 20.13.

116 HA 1996 s202(2); H(W)A 2014 s85(4).

117 *Demetri v Westminster CC* [2000] 1 WLR 772.

118 HA 1996 s188(3); H(W)A 2014 s69(11).

119 HA 1996 s202(1A); H(W)A 2014 s85(3).

120 HA 1996 s204(1); H(W)A 2014 s88(1).

121 HA 1996 s204(1); H(W)A 2014 s88(1).

notified. The court has power to extend time, but only for good reason.[122]

6.103 Pending an appeal, the local authority has a discretion to provide accommodation for the applicant.[123] If the authority refuses or fails to do so, the applicant may also appeal that decision to the county court.[124]

6.104 The procedures to be adopted on review and on appeal to the county court are detailed in Arden, Bates and Vanhegan, *Homelessness and Allocations*, LAG, 11th edition 2018.

Criminal offences

England and Wales

6.105 It is a criminal offence knowingly or recklessly to make a statement which is false in a material particular, or knowingly to withhold information which an authority has reasonably required in connection with the exercise of its functions under the homelessness legislation, with intent to induce an authority to believe that the person making the statement or withholding the information, or any other person, is entitled to accommodation or assistance.[125]

Effect of the homelessness legislation on Gypsies and Travellers

R (Price) v Carmarthenshire CC[126]

6.106 Mrs Price and her family are Irish Travellers and were homeless in terms of the legislation because they were living on an unauthorised encampment and did not have an authorised pitch for their caravans.[127] The family had been resorting to Carmarthenshire for several years and applied to the local authority for homeless persons accommodation. In 2001 Mrs Price had made an inquiry about conventional (that is, bricks and mortar) accommodation. When she made her subsequent homeless application to the local authority, Mrs Price

122 HA 1996 s204(1); H(W)A 2014 s88(1).
123 HA 1996 s204(4); H(W)A 2014 s88(5).
124 HA 1996 s204A; H(W)A 2014 s89.
125 HA 1996 s214(1); H(W)A 2014 s97(1).
126 [2003] EWHC 42 (Admin); March 2003 *Legal Action* 30.
127 HA 1996 s175(2)(b); H(W)A 2014 s55(2)(b) – see para 6.16, above.

explained that she had made her earlier inquiry purely because of pressure from a local authority officer and that she had had no intention of moving into conventional housing.

6.107 In the planning case of *Clarke v Secretary of State for the Environment Transport and the Regions*,[128] the High Court (later upheld by the Court of Appeal) had overturned the decision of a planning inspector who had refused planning permission to Mr Clarke, a Romani Gypsy, in circumstances where the inspector had taken into account a previous offer of settled accommodation that had been made to him by the local authority. Burton J, at first instance, stated that, if an 'aversion to conventional housing' were established then 'bricks and mortar, if offered, are unsuitable, just as would be the offer of a rat-infested barn'.[129]

6.108 In Mrs Price's case, the local authority had regard to the *Clarke* decision, but concluded from the facts of Mrs Price's case (including the fact that her mother, who had previously travelled, now lived in a bungalow due to ill-health, and her sister, who travelled with her, had previously lived in settled accommodation for a short period of time) that she did not have a 'cultural aversion to conventional housing'. It offered her a house which she refused. It then sought to evict her from the piece of its own land where it had, until then, been 'tolerating' her encampment. Mrs Price sought judicial review of the local authority's decision.

6.109 In the High Court, Newman J quashed the decision to evict, stating:

> In order to meet the requirements and accord respect, something more than 'taking account' of an applicant's gypsy culture is required. As the court in Chapman[130] stated, respect includes the positive obligation to act so as to facilitate the gypsy way of life, without being under a duty to guarantee it to an applicant in any particular case.[131]

6.110 Newman J also found that, in seeking to respect her Gypsy way of life, the local authority's approach was flawed because it had given too much weight to the fact that she had seemingly been prepared to give it up to live in conventional housing in 2001 and had used this as sufficient reason for disregarding her Gypsy way of life altogether when considering her wishes. Equally he found that, had the local

128 *Clarke v Secretary of State for the Environment, Transport and the Regions and Tunbridge Wells BC* [2001] EWHC 800 Admin; [2002] JPL 552; July 2002 *Legal Action* 23. For full discussion of this case see para 4.172, above.

129 [2001] EWHC 800 Admin at para 34.

130 *Chapman v UK* (2001) 33 EHRR 399; and see chapter 2, above.

131 *R (Price) v Carmarthenshire CC* [2003] EWHC 42 (Admin) at para 19.

authority reached the conclusion that her cultural commitment to traditional life was so powerful as to present great difficulty in her living in conventional housing, the local authority was not bound by duty to find her a pitch, but her cultural commitment would have been a significant factor in considering how far the authority should go to facilitate her traditional way of life.

6.111 Following on from the *Price* case, the government in its next version of the English Homelessness Code of Guidance for Local Authorities,[132] amended the section that deals with homeless Gypsies and Travellers. The current 2018 version of the Guidance has replicated that new section:

> Where a duty to secure accommodation [for a Gypsy or Traveller] arises but an appropriate site is not immediately available, the housing authority may need to provide an alternative temporary solution until a suitable site or some other suitable option, becomes available. Some Gypsies and Travellers may have a cultural aversion to the prospect of 'bricks and mortar' accommodation. In such cases, the authority should seek to provide an alternative solution.[133]

The reference in the previous English Code to homeless Gypsies and Travellers had been criticised in the *Price* case.

6.112 No similar passage appears in the Welsh Code of Guidance. The only reference to this issue is: 'Authorities should be aware of cultural factors in addressing suitability of accommodation (*R (Price) v Carmarthenshire County Council*)'.[134]

6.113 There is no reason why house boat dwellers might not be able to avail themselves of the court's decision in the *Price* case.

When is a Gypsy or Traveller regarded as being homeless?

6.114 A Gypsy or Traveller is homeless if there is no place where he or she is entitled or permitted to place his or her caravan or vehicle.[135] In this context, what do the words 'entitled' or 'permitted' mean?

6.115 In *R v Chiltern DC ex p Roberts et al*,[136] the applicants were Travelling Showpeople who had lost their winter accommodation.

132 Issued by DCLG on 2 September 2006.

133 Para 16.44.

134 Welsh Code of Guidance para 19.11.

135 HA 1996 s175(2)(b); H(W)A 2014 s55(2)(b).

136 (1990) 23 HLR 387, QBD.

They were travelling in connection with their work during the summer months when they made their application. When travelling from fair to fair, they were permitted to stay on land provided by the organisers of the fairs. They were held not to be 'homeless' since, at the time of the applications, they were 'permitted' to stop in various places.

6.116 In *Smith v Wokingham DC*,[137] the applicants were parked in a caravan on land belonging to the county council. Though they had no express permission or licence, they had lived at this encampment for two-and-a-half years. The county court judge decided that this amounted to 'permission' and, accordingly, that they were not homeless.

6.117 In *R (O'Donoghue) v Brighton and Hove CC*,[138] the applicant had been allowed to place her caravans on a piece of land owned by the local authority for a 'tolerated' period of 30 days. Once that period had ended, she made a homelessness application to the authority. The authority decided that she was not homeless and, therefore, that it did not, at that stage, owe her any duty to provide interim accommodation. No eviction action had yet been commenced by the local authority. In refusing permission to proceed with a judicial review application concerning the failure to provide interim accommodation, Jackson J held that the applicant had effectively been given implicit permission to remain before eviction action was commenced and that the judicial review application was premature. When refusing permission to appeal that decision, the Court of Appeal agreed that the application for judicial review was premature because no eviction action had been taken but accepted that it was arguable that the applicant no longer had permission to remain on the land and that she was homeless at the time that she made her application.

6.118 *Steward v Royal Borough of Kingston-upon-Thames*[139] was a case taken by a homeless New Traveller who challenged a finding that she had made herself intentionally homeless when she had left conventional housing some years previously.[140] Reliance was placed upon the *O'Donoghue* decision, since Ms Steward had managed to remain on a number of unauthorised sites for long periods of time (in one case for over a year) before any eviction action was commenced. Ms Steward argued: that her encampment on those sites had been 'permitted'; that each occasion on which she was evicted from those

137 April 1980 *LAG Bulletin* 92, CC.

138 [2003] EWCA Civ 459.

139 [2007] EWCA Civ 565, [2007] HLR 42.

140 See para 6.132, below.

sites amounted to a new incidence of homelessness; and that the investigation of any potential intentionality should relate to that new incident. In rejecting that argument, the Court of Appeal gave the word 'permitted' a restricted meaning. For an encampment to be 'permitted', there would need to be some positive indication from the landowner that the Gypsies or Travellers could remain for the time being (rather than simply inaction or failure to commence eviction action), albeit that such indication might fall short of amounting to a licence. Buxton LJ accepted the finding of the judge at first instance who had stated:

> I accept the submissions of counsel [for the local authority], that unlawful occupation of disused sites as [a] trespasser, from which he could have been evicted at any time if the landowner chose, is far removed from settled accommodation.[141]

Making a homeless application

6.119 A homeless Gypsy or Traveller has to make a homelessness application to a local authority before any of these matters can be considered.

6.120 Gypsies and Travellers can encounter considerable problems when first trying to make an application. Some authorities may try to put them on the ordinary housing register or may say that they are not homeless because they have their caravan or caravans. They might be turned away because they are told that the authority only has conventional housing. This is unlawful. A local authority that has reason to believe that an applicant may be homeless or threatened with homelessness must investigate the matter further and must accept and process an application from that applicant.[142] In *R (Aweys and others) v Birmingham CC*, Collins J stated:

> It is apparent that the threshold for the duty of Councils to act under s184 is a low one . . . since it arises if they have reason to believe the applicant may be homeless or threatened with homelessness. In the vast majority of cases, the making of the application will mean that it is difficult if not impossible for the Council not to believe that the applicant may be homeless or threatened with homelessness. Furthermore, no particular form of application is prescribed. This is not surprising since the provisions are dealing with people who are likely to be vulnerable and who cannot be expected to have obtained legal advice or to have an acquaintance with the statutory provisions. If it is apparent from what is said by an applicant (for there is no requirement that an application be in

141 [2007] EWCA Civ 565 at para 11.

142 HA 1996 s184(1) and H(W)A 2014 s62(1) – and see paras 6.40–6.41, above.

writing) or from anything in writing that he may be homeless or threatened with homelessness, the duty is triggered.[143]

6.121 Many Gypsies and Travellers are illiterate or have limited literacy skills. As a consequence, they may encounter difficulties when making homelessness applications. It is important to remember that an application under the homelessness legislation does not have to be made in any particular form (as Collins J explained in *Aweys*). In the earlier case of *Roberts*,[144] a letter from the applicants' solicitors, giving appropriate particulars in a schedule, was held to amount to an application. Though *Aweys* makes it clear that applications can be made orally, it is advisable that they are made in writing so as to ensure that there is a record of the application having been made and the details of the application. It is suggested that a written application could include some or all of the following information:

- details and dates of birth of the applicant and his or her family (if any);
- previous accommodation over, say, the last five years[145] – in many cases, the applicant will have been moving frequently from one unauthorised encampment to another and it is suggested that a general history of encampments, concentrating in particular on the districts or areas in which he or she had been residing, would be sufficient;
- details of health problems if 'priority need' is in question;
- details of schools, colleges and employment (to ensure that the local authority focuses on the provision of suitable accommodation within a reasonable distance of such educational establishments and/or areas in which work is undertaken);
- details of local connections, including reference to other family members in the area (to address the issue of 'local connection');
- if the applicant has previously occupied conventional housing, then the local authority should be told why that accommodation was vacated (to address the question whether the applicant is intentionally homeless).[146]

6.122 Though a local authority may insist, as part of its own homelessness procedures, on an interview and/or the completion of an application

143 [2007] EWHC 52 (Admin) at para 8, 2007 [HLR] 27.

144 *R v Chiltern DC ex p Roberts et al* (1990) 23 HLR 387, QBD, and see para 6.115, above.

145 See the discussion of 'local connection' at para 6.141 onwards below.

146 See para 6.132 onwards, below.

form, the important point here is that a letter written by the applicant's advisers will clearly be sufficient to ensure that the local authority investigates whether the applicant is eligible for assistance and whether it owes any duty to him or her. Additionally, application forms that are used typically do not cater for the needs of Gypsies and Travellers. For example, there may be no optional box for indicating that the applicant requires an authorised site or pitch for their caravan or vehicle. It may be wise for a solicitor or adviser to assist their client in filling in such a form to ensure that no misunderstandings arise. The local authority to whom the application is made could be asked to send any application form to the adviser or solicitor so that they can assist their client in completing it.

6.123 If a local authority insists on a formal interview taking place where a Gypsy or Traveller has made a homeless application then it may be wise, if possible, for someone (for example, from a local Gypsy or Traveller support group) to accompany the applicant to the interview to ensure, once again, that the local authority processes the application correctly. Those advising Gypsies and Travellers have met with many instances where, for example, applicants have simply been turned away by local authorities without a formal application having been accepted or where it transpires that the local authority has processed the application on the basis that it is for conventional, 'bricks and mortar' accommodation when the applicants specifically requested a site for their caravans. Practical support for the applicant can, therefore, be very important.

6.124 Some Gypsy and Traveller families travel around as an extended family group. This is especially so with Irish Travellers.[147] If an extended family group has always travelled together, it could be argued that one application should be taken from the whole group rather than a series of applications from each 'household'. This argument is based on HA 1996 s176 (H(W)A 2014 s56 is in virtually identical terms):

> Accommodation shall be regarded as available for a person's occupation only if it is available for occupation by him together with–
> (a) *any other person who normally resides with him as a member of his family or*
> (b) *any other person who might reasonably be expected to reside with him* . . . [emphasis added].

147 See, for example, McDonagh, '*Nomadism*' in *Travellers: citizens of Ireland*, The Parish of the Travelling People, Dublin, 2000, pp33–46.

6.125 The Welsh Code of Guidance does not refer specifically to 'extended families' although at para 8.7 it states:

> The phrase 'member of the family' although not defined will include those with close blood or marital relationships . . . and where such a person is an established member of the household . . . that accommodation must provide for him or her as well.

The English Code of Guidance is in virtually identical terms (para 6.7).

6.126 There is, as yet, no case-law on this particular point except that, in the context of a decision as to which family members of an extended family were to be accommodated in discharge of duty as persons who 'might reasonably be expected to reside with' the applicant, Simon Brown J in *R v Lambeth LBC ex p Ly* stated:

> [I]t is a question of fact to be decided by the local authority. Moreover, in determining this question of fact, it seems to me that many different considerations may well come into play. Certainly it will be pertinent always to consider the true nature and ambit of the family unit concerned and questions of blood relationship, dependency and so forth within the family; dependency, that is, both emotional and financial.[148]

Priority need[149]

6.127 In the case of *Myhill and Faith v Wealden DC*,[150] the applicants, who were single men, argued that they were 'vulnerable' for some 'other special reason' for the purposes of HA 1996 s189(1)(c) on the basis that:

- as Travellers they were statistically far more likely to be homeless than the general population – the government statistics presented to the court, which were not challenged by the local authority, indicated that whereas 1.2 per cent of settled households were homeless, 18 per cent (at that time) of Gypsies and Travellers were homeless;
- Gypsies and Travellers were much less likely to be able to find accommodation due to the acknowledged lack of sites;

148 (1986) 19 HLR 51 at 55.

149 See paras 6.26 onwards, above, for the details of the categories of 'priority need'.

150 [2004] EWCA Civ 224; April 2004 *Legal Action* 34; 23 November 2003, Tunbridge Wells County Court.

- while on unauthorised encampments, Gypsies and Travellers faced possible criminal prosecution under the Criminal Justice and Public Order Act 1994.

6.128 The county court judge rejected these arguments. He relied on the following quote from the judgment of Hobhouse LJ in one of the leading cases on 'priority need', *R v Camden LBC ex p Pereira*:

> The Council must ask itself whether the applicant is, when homeless, less able to fend for himself than an ordinary homeless person so that injury or detriment to him will result when a less vulnerable person would be able to cope without harmful effects . . .[151]

6.129 In refusing permission to appeal to the Court of Appeal, Buxton LJ stated:

> The focus [in the above quote] is quite clearly on the ability of the individual to deal with the condition of homelessness, rather than on the question to which the statistics and oral arguments in this case go, of how likely it is that the persons when they become homeless will remain such.[152]

6.130 A person who is homeless or threatened with homelessness as a result of an emergency, such as flood, fire or other disaster, is also in 'priority need'.[153] In the case of *Scott-Higgs v Brighton and Hove CC*,[154] the single applicant had been residing in his caravan on an unauthorised encampment. The local authority obtained a possession order against him but had not yet enforced the order when, after going out one day, the applicant returned to find his caravan had disappeared (it was never established what happened to the caravan). He applied as a homeless person to the local authority for accommodation. He claimed that the loss of his caravan should mean that he was in priority need. The local authority found him not to be in priority need. The judge at first instance upheld this decision. On appeal, the Court of Appeal stated that the loss of one's caravan in such circumstances could come within the definition of 'flood, fire or other disaster', but that his homelessness was not as a result of this event. He was already homeless since he did not have an authorised place to pitch his

151 (1999) 31 HLR 317 at 330. But see now the new test on 'vulnerability', in terms of England, in *Hotak and others v LB Southwark and others* [2015] UKSC 3, [2015] HLR 23, [2015] 2 WLR 1341 – see further para 6.30, above. In Wales, 'vulnerable' is defined in H(W)A 2014 s71 – see further para 6.29, above.

152 *Myhill and Faith v Wealden DC* [2004] EWCA Civ 224 at para 5.

153 HA 1996 s189(1)(d); H(W)A 2014 s70(1)(D).

154 [2003] 3 All ER 753, CA.

caravan. He could not, therefore, be said to be in priority need. It should be noted that, if Mr Scott-Higgs had been on an authorised encampment (for example, a licensee on a local authority site) and his caravan had disappeared, then he would have been in priority need. In other words, in such a situation, the loss of the caravan would have caused his homelessness.

6.131 In the absence of any duty to provide sites,[155] there remains a huge problem for homeless Gypsies and Travellers who (especially in the light of the *Myhill and Faith* case) are not considered to be in priority need.

Intentional homelessness

6.132 A local authority will only conclude that a person is intentionally homeless if he or she has deliberately done or failed to do something in consequence of which he or she has ceased to occupy accommodation which is available for his or her occupation and which it would have been reasonable for him or her to continue to occupy.[156] Thus, it is clear that there must be a causal link between a person's deliberate act or omission and the loss of accommodation; a person can only be considered to be intentionally homeless if his or her deliberate act or omission caused the homelessness.

6.133 There have been a number of cases where the courts have had to consider whether the causal link or 'chain of causation' has been broken by an intervening event. For example, in *Din v Wandsworth LBC*,[157] the House of Lords held that the chain of causation will be broken in circumstances where a person has lived in 'settled accommodation'[158] for a period of time.

6.134 In *R v Harrow LBC ex p Fahia*,[159] the applicant had been found intentionally homeless and was placed in a guest-house where she remained for over a year. She was evicted from the guest house when her housing benefit was cut (through no fault of her own) and she could no longer afford the rent. The local authority did not accept

155 Repealed by the Criminal Justice and Public Order Act 1994. But see H(W)A 2014 s103 – see paras 3.6 and 3.17–3.19 above.

156 See para 6.31 onwards above, HA 1996 s191(1) and H(W)A 2014 s77.

157 [1983] 1 AC 657. See also *Saba Haile v Waltham Forest LBC* [2015] UKSC 34.

158 The question of what constitutes 'settled accommodation' has been considered by the courts in a number of cases. For further discussion see Arden, Bates and Vanhegan, *Homelessness and allocations* and Luba, Davies, Johnston and Buchanan *Housing allocations and homelessness*.

159 [1998] 1 WLR 1396, [1998] 30 HLR 1124 (HL), 1997 29 HLR 974 (CA).

that the period of time in the guest house amounted to 'settled accommodation'. However, the Court of Appeal allowed the homeless applicant's appeal. It held that events other than securing settled accommodation could break the chain of causation and ordered that the local authority reconsider whether the change in the applicant's entitlement to housing benefit amounted to such an event.

6.135 Similarly, in *R v Basingstoke and Deane DC ex p Bassett*,[160] the fact that the applicant had spent a period of time staying with her sister-in-law (an arrangement which it was accepted the applicant was entitled to believe would continue but ceased when her sister-in-law separated from her husband and left the accommodation) was held to break the chain of causation.

6.136 By way of contrast, in *R v Hackney LBC ex p Ajayi*,[161] the applicant had left accommodation in Nigeria to come to London. After staying with various friends for short periods, she moved in with another friend in January 1996, just as she discovered that she was pregnant. When the baby was born, her friend asked her to leave. It was held that the chain of causation had not been broken and that the decision that she was 'intentionally homeless' because of leaving the accommodation in Nigeria, was correct.

6.137 These cases indicate that it will very much be a matter of fact and degree, based on the circumstances of an individual case, as to whether the chain of causation has been broken. In Wales the local housing authority is required by statute to assess whether there has been a material change in circumstances and whether there is new information materially affecting an assessment where an applicant has been previously assessed.[162]

6.138 It is not uncommon for homeless Gypsies and Travellers to have previously lived in 'bricks and mortar' accommodation for a period of time and the vast majority of New Travellers will, at one time or another, have lived in conventional housing.[163] When considering whether a Gypsy or Traveller is intentionally homeless, a local authority will pay particular attention to any periods that he or she spent living in bricks and mortar to see whether the applicant ceased to

160 (1983) 10 HLR 125, QBD.

161 (1997) 30 HLR 473, QBD.

162 H(W)A 2014 s 62(2).

163 The casework of the Travellers' Advice Team at the Community Law Partnership demonstrates that there are now adult New Travellers who were born on the road and have never lived in conventional housing – there are no official statistics available.

occupy the accommodation as a result of a deliberate act or omission or whether he or she left such accommodation in circumstances where it was reasonable for him or her to continue to occupy it.

6.139 In *Steward v Royal Borough of Kingston-upon-Thames*,[164] Ms Steward had left conventional housing some years previously to move onto the road. On applying as homeless to the local authority, she was found to be intentionally homeless. The Court of Appeal held that Ms Steward's encampment on a number of unauthorised sites for lengthy periods of time without eviction action did not break the 'chain of causation'. However, the chain might be broken, in other circumstances, if it could be said that an encampment was 'permitted', for example, if a local authority or landowner gives a Gypsy or Traveller a positive indication that he or she will be able to stay on an unauthorised site for a lengthy period of time.

6.140 Where a Gypsy or Traveller has been found intentionally homeless because he or she left conventional housing, the solicitor or adviser assisting them on a review or appeal will have to examine the past history of accommodation carefully and avoid taking matters at face value. For example:

- if a Gypsy or Traveller leaves conventional housing because it transpires that he or she has a psychological aversion to 'bricks and mortar', it may not be possible to say that he or she left the accommodation and became homeless as a result of a deliberate act or omission and it can be argued that it was not reasonable for him or her to continue to occupy the accommodation – in such a case expert evidence from a psychiatrist or other relevant professionals should be obtained;
- if a New Traveller only ever lived in insecure accommodation (such as a 'squat') it may be argued that the accommodation did not amount to settled accommodation;
- a previous eviction from conventional housing may not have been the fault of the Gypsy or Traveller applicant, for example, it may have been because of housing benefit department errors which led to rent arrears in circumstances where the Gypsy or Traveller applicant did not realise that the problem could have been resolved without the need for eviction to take place.

164 [2007] EWCA Civ 565. See also para 6.118, above.

Local connection

6.141 The statutory provisions relating to 'local connection'[165] are further explained in the guidance known as the Local Authority Agreement.[166] The guidance states that:

- 'Normal residence' in an area should be residence for at least six months in the area during the previous 12 months, or for not less than three years during the previous five-year period.
- Regarding employment in an area, it is recommended that confirmation should be obtained from the applicant's employer and it should be established that the employment is not of a casual nature.
- 'Family associations' normally arise when an applicant or member of the household has parents, adult children or brothers or sisters who have been resident in the area for at least five years at the date of the application and the applicant indicates a wish to be near them. Only in exceptional circumstances would the residence of relatives other than those listed above be taken to establish a local connection. The residence of children in another area from that of their parents cannot be taken to be residence of their own choice and therefore does not constitute a local connection. However, a referral should not be made to another local authority on the grounds of family association if the applicant objects.
- There may be special circumstances which the local authority considers give rise to a local connection in the area. The fact that an applicant seeks to return to an area where he or she was brought up or lived in the past may be grounds for finding a local connection.

6.142 The Local Authority Agreement also lists certain exceptions to the above categories:

- time spent in the service of the regular armed forces;
- time spent in detention under the authority of an Act of parliament (for example, prisons, mental hospitals);

165 See paras 6.35 onwards, above.

166 *Guidelines for Local Authorities and Referees* agreed by Association of London Government, Convention of Scottish Local Authorities, Local Government Association and the Welsh Local Government Association. This is also the guidance referred to in para 18.7 of the Welsh Allocation and Homelessness Code of Guidance.

- time spent as a result of an earlier homeless application, in accommodation secured by another local authority under the homelessness legislation within the last five years;
- time spent in hospital;
- time spent in an institution in which households are accepted only for a limited period (for example, refuges and rehabilitation centres).

It should be stressed that if a homeless applicant has a local connection with the area of the local authority to which he or she applies, then a referral to another local authority will not be possible even if the applicant also has a local connection with that other authority's area.

6.143 The Local Authority Agreement is not a statute but is strong guidance and cannot be ignored. Nevertheless, it is suggested that the guidance should not be applied too rigidly by local authorities in the case of homeless Gypsies and Travellers and that their particular circumstances and the difficulties they face should also be taken into account. By way of example, it is perhaps worth looking at the guidance on 'normal residence' and 'family associations':

- According to the guidance, a Gypsy or Traveller would have to have spent at least six months in the area during the last 12 months to have a local connection, but it is suggested that a local authority should not apply the guidance too rigidly in the case of Gypsies or Travellers who have been frequently forced to move from one unauthorised encampment to another, particularly when eviction action taken by the local authority itself forced them to spend a period of time in a neighbouring local authority's area.
- The extended family is an essential part of Irish Traveller culture[167] and the list of relatives in the guidance, by which an applicant can establish a local connection with an area, may be too narrow in the case of an Irish Traveller. For example, it has been held to be too narrow in a case concerning a former asylum-seeker.[168]

6.144 In a county court case, an Irish Traveller, Ms Connors, with five children, two of whom are disabled owing to a lung condition and hearing impairments, had travelled all her life except for a short period in which she lived in a house. In June 2014 she had to leave a

167 See, for example, McDonagh, 'Nomadism' in *Travellers: citizens of Ireland*, pp33–46.

168 *Ozbek v Ipswich BC* [2006] EWCA Civ 534, [2006] HLR 41.

Traveller site in Stroud and relocated to the Forest of Dean District Council ('FoD') area. She moved her caravan onto a former Traveller site and commenced occupation. Her sister, who helped her with managing the children, lived just five minutes away. FoD commenced possession proceedings and Ms Connors made a homeless application. In August 2014, FoD decided that Ms Connors was owed a full re-housing duty but that she did not have a local connection with the FoD area because she was not normally resident or employed or had any enduring family relationships with others in the area, and also that there were no special circumstances to take into account. Accordingly, her local connection was with Stroud DC and they sought to refer her back there. That decision was upheld in a homeless review in December 2014. An appeal was subsequently issued.

6.145 The appeal raised seven grounds of appeal including that FoD had erred in law in failing to take account of or have any regard to Ms Connors' protected characteristic under the Equality Act (EqA) 2010, namely being a member of an ethnic group of Irish Travellers capable of being discriminated against on the grounds of her membership of that group. In particular, that FoD had failed to properly consider:

a) how long a Traveller's relatives should be required to be normally resident in an area before establishing a connection by family association, as by the very nature of their way of life residence for five years is much less likely to be established than if they were not a Traveller; and
b) in failing to have regard to the same matters when deciding to exercise its discretion to refer and, in doing so, failing to comply with its public sector equality duty under EqA 2010 s149.

It was submitted that the travelling way of life means by its very nature that Irish Travellers are less likely to remain in particular areas for long periods, and that this should be taken into account in considering whether an Irish Traveller is normally resident in that area or has a local connection by reason of family associations. Irish Travellers might well have areas to which they resort much more often than others, and the likelihood that due to their way of life they may stay in one area for shorter periods should be taken into account in deciding whether they have a local connection. This is underlined by EqA 2010 s149, which requires, in relation to every decision taken by a public authority, proper consideration of their protected characteristic and whether it should be taken into account in the decision-making process. The respondent council only considered this question in relation to what accommodation could be provided, and this was plainly inadequate.

6.146 The appeal was allowed on six of the seven grounds, including the EqA ground. Recorder Blunt QC found that, while the FoD had been mindful of the fact that Ms Connors is an Irish Traveller with protected characteristics:

> . . . they only took account of those characteristics when referring to attempts to find an alternative traveller's pitch, as well as in relation to the suitability of conventional housing. However, it is plain that no account was taken of them in relation to the question of whether or not the Appellant has a local connection with the Respondents' district by reason of the length of her residence or her sister's residence there: this is because the Review Panel effectively treated any periods of residence short of those set out in the guidelines . . . as being irrelevant. The Review Panel . . . were obliged to take account of the Appellant's and her sister's 'protected characteristic'. Again, therefore, I consider this ground of appeal to be made out.[169]

Suitable interim accommodation[170]

6.147 It can be seen above that if a local authority has reason to believe that an applicant may be homeless, eligible for assistance and in priority need, it has a duty to secure that accommodation is available pending its final decision.[171] If, having conducted inquiries, the local authority decides that a full duty is not owed to the applicant,[172] then the local authority has a power to ensure that accommodation is available pending any review of that decision requested by the applicant.[173] If the original decision is upheld on review, the local authority, once again, then has a power to secure that accommodation is available pending a county court appeal.[174]

6.148 Interim accommodation must be suitable.[175] When deciding what is suitable, a local authority must have regard to the slum clearance, overcrowding and 'houses in multiple occupation' provisions of the HA 1985. The case-law and statutory instruments to date have almost entirely related to the provision of conventional housing.

169 *Connors v Forest of Dean DC*, November 2015 *Legal Action* 30, para 62.
170 See para 6.45, above.
171 HA 1996 s188(1); H(W)A 2014 s68(1), (2).
172 HA 1996 s184; H(W)A 2014 s69(1), (2).
173 HA 1996 s188(3); H(W)A 2014 s69(11).
174 HA 1996 s204(4); H(W)A 2014 s89(4).
175 HA 1996 s210; H(W)A 2014 s68(1).

6.149 *Codona v Mid-Bedfordshire DC*[176] involved the offer of B&B accommodation to a homeless Gypsy and her extended family. Leanne Codona rejected the offer on the basis of her 'cultural aversion to conventional housing', which was accepted as being of the strongest form. The Court of Appeal approved the decision in *R (Price) v Carmarthenshire CC*.[177] However, the Court of Appeal also held that the offer of B&B accommodation was not 'unsuitable' despite the fact that the local authority had simply investigated three authorised Gypsy/Traveller sites in the area (none of which had any vacancies) before making the offer of B&B.

6.150 The Court of Appeal in *Codona* approved the following relevant considerations when assessing a Gypsy's or Traveller's application for accommodation:

- whether the applicant and, if relevant, his or her family, live in a caravan or caravans;
- whether they are Romani or subscribe to a Gypsy culture;
- whether they are nomadic for a substantial part of the year;
- whether the nomadism is linked to their livelihood;[178]
- whether they subscribe to the relevant features of the Gypsy life in question, such as an aversion to conventional housing.[179]

6.151 The Court of Appeal stressed the minimum line of suitability as established in cases involving settled people.[180] However, Auld LJ concluded:

> [T]his was a case in which the Council was required as a matter of relative urgency to find accommodation for an extended family occupying some six or seven caravans, who were insisting, because of their aversion to conventional housing, on being provided an alternative site for all of their caravans on which they could continue to live together. Despite careful enquiries by the Council it could find no such site. Nor could it provide at short notice long-term conventional bricks and mortar housing for the extended family. It was driven, therefore, as a short-term measure, to offer short-term accommodation of a bed and breakfast nature. In doing so, it was clearly acting as a matter of last resort and

176 [2005] HLR 1.

177 [2003] EWHC 42 (Admin); March 2003 *Legal Action* 30; and see paras 6.106 onwards, above.

178 Though it should be remembered that this nomadism can have ceased temporarily (or also permanently in Wales). See further paras 4.103 onwards, above.

179 [2005] HLR 1 at 17.

180 For example, *R v Newham LBC ex p Ojuri (No 3)* (1998) 31 HLR 452.

> with the clear understanding . . . that the duration of their stay in such accommodation was to be kept as short as possible.[181]

6.152 It is important to notice the stress the Court of Appeal placed on the issues of 'urgency' and 'last resort'. If the homeless Gypsy or Traveller has somewhere to stay in the meantime or if a 'temporary', 'tolerated' site (perhaps on the local authority's own land) can be identified in the interim, then there may be no need to act so swiftly and more time can be taken over the process of locating a suitable pitch or site. Elsewhere in the judgment the Court of Appeal seems to suggest that evidence of psychiatric as opposed to psychological harm might be required to show aversion to conventional housing. There seems little justification for such a preference since psychiatric and psychological harm in this context would appear to be two sides of the same coin.

6.153 Upon dismissal of her appeal (and upon the House of Lords refusing her permission to appeal further), Leanne Codona made an application to the European Court of Human Rights (ECtHR). The ECtHR found her application to be inadmissible.[182] The ECtHR stated:

> The Court recalls that article 8 does not in terms recognise the right to be provided with a home . . . let alone a specific home or category of home . . .
>
> . . . It recalls that the scope of any positive obligation to house the homeless is limited . . . It therefore considers that that obligation must be even more limited as regards an obligation to house a homeless person in a specific class of accommodation chosen by that person and where the person has previously been living on land in breach of planning regulations . . . Against this, the Court recalls that there is a positive obligation imposed on the Contracting States by virtue of article 8 to facilitate the gypsy way of life (see *Chapman* at 96). It notes that the domestic courts in the instant case found that the applicant had a 'cultural aversion' to living in bricks and mortar accommodation and is prepared to accept that this aversion can be identified as forming part of the applicant's gypsy way of life. Following *Chapman* the Court does not rule out that, in principle, article 8 could impose a positive obligation on the authorities to provide accommodation for a homeless gypsy which is such that it facilitates their 'gypsy way of life'. However, it considers that this obligation could only arise where the authorities had such accommodation at their disposal and were making a choice between offering such accommodation or accommodation which was not 'suitable' for the cultural

181 [2005] HLR 1 at 20.

182 App No 485/05, 7 February 2006; September 2006 *Legal Action* 21.

> needs of a gypsy. In the instant case, however, it appears to be common ground that there were, in fact, no sites available upon which the applicant could lawfully place her caravan. In the premises, the Court cannot conclude that the authorities were then under a positive obligation to create such a site for the applicant (and her extended family) . . . Finally, the Court does not consider that the apparent change in the policy of the respondent State[183] regarding the provision of caravan sites relied upon by the applicant is in fact of relevance to the present case. Although it welcomes any steps taken to increase the number of caravan sites, it must consider the situation by reference to facts as they stand . . .

6.154 Accommodation outside the local authority's area may be suitable depending on the circumstances of the case. In deciding the question of suitability, the local authority must consider the individual needs of the applicant and his or her family, including those relating to work, education and health.[184] The local authority must have regard to the need to safeguard and promote the welfare of the children in the household. It is also an obligation to offer accommodation as close as possible to where they were previously living.[185] It will be important, therefore, that the homeless Gypsy or Traveller supplies the local authority with all relevant information with regard to work in the area, schools attended and whether this involves special educational needs, registration with a local general practitioner or attendance at a local hospital, the need for support from relatives or friends in the area and any other relevant matters.

6.155 The report by Niner, *Local authority Gypsy/Traveller sites in England*,[186] indicated that, on the 324 local authority Gypsy sites recorded by the January 2002 Gypsy Count, there were only 307 transit pitches. Given the severe shortfall in suitable pitches, it is suggested that in cases where a homeless Gypsy or Traveller is camping on local authority land and the encampment is not causing any undue nuisance, then it would be reasonable for the local authority to permit him or her to remain on the land while his or her homelessness application is processed. Alternatively, the local authority could seek to identify temporary sites, perhaps on disused or underused land[187]

183 Namely the introduction of HA 2004 s225 and the then new ODPM Circular 01/06.

184 See, for example, *R v Newham LBC ex p Sacupima* [2001] HLR 2, CA, [2001] HLR 1, QBD. See also *R (Cafun) v Bromley LBC* 17 October 2000, QBD (unreported), [2000] All ER (D) 1425, January 2001 *Legal Action* 27.

185 *Nzolomeso v City of Westminster* [2015] UKSC 22.

186 ODPM, 2003.

187 This could include other public authority land or even private land.

where facilities could be provided.[188] Indeed, a local authority's decision to proceed with the eviction from its own land of a homeless Gypsy or Traveller when the local authority had failed to comply with the duty to secure that accommodation is available pending their final decision could well result in a public law challenge by way of judicial review.[189]

The full duty to accommodate

6.156 It now appears clear that a local authority which has decided that it has a full duty to accommodate a homeless applicant under HA 1996 s193(2) or H(W)A 2014 s75(3)[190] must comply with the duty immediately.[191]

6.157 Where a local authority is satisfied that a homeless Gypsy or Traveller has a sufficient degree of 'cultural aversion to conventional housing' such that it should use its best endeavours to seek a suitable pitch or site, it will be incumbent on that authority to show that it has taken all reasonable steps to do so.

6.158 The Court of Appeal returned to this subject in *Lee v Rhondda Cynon Taf BC*.[192] The Gypsy appellant appealed against the suitability of an offer of a house largely on the grounds that she had a cultural aversion to bricks and mortar accommodation. Giving the leading judgment, Longmore LJ stated:

> Mr Knafler [for the appellant] submits that [the consideration by the local authority of the appellant's position as a Gypsy] was not lawful and adequate because RCT [Rhondda Cynon Taf] did not consider whether they should acquire an alternative site. That however seems to me to be, in the context of a homelessness application, wrong . . . Homelessness applications are expected to be determined within a short timeframe, ideally at least within 33 days of an acceptance of a requisite duty. If a new site is to be acquired for stationing a caravan for residential purposes, that will usually mean a new use which will typically require planning permission. That will require determination by the local authority planning committee, especially if it means a departure from the local development plan, which it may well, and any decision so made is liable

188 By way of example, a tap could be installed for water, refuse collection services set up and portaloos provided.

189 As, indeed, occurred in the *Price* case itself.

190 See para 6.65 above.

191 See Collins J in *R (Aweys and others) v Birmingham CC* [2007] EWHC 52 (Admin) at para 24.

192 [2008] EWCA Civ 1013, [2008] All ER (D) 436 (July), [2008] November *Legal Action* 20.

> to be appealed. After all that, land would have to be bought if it is not already owned by the local authority itself. All this is, in my judgment, inconsistent with the manner in which homelessness applications are expected to be dealt with by the housing department, and especially since they are expected to be dealt with a degree of promptness. As, moreover, the recorder himself observed that is really inconsistent with the law as laid down by *Price* and *Codona*, to the effect that bricks and mortar accommodation is at any rate capable of being suitable accommodation even for a Gypsy.
>
> All that is not to say that there might not be unusual circumstances in which a local housing authority might be expected to do more than consider availability and sites within their own area. If, for example, there was a question of an applicant being at risk of suffering psychiatric harm, it might well be that the local authority should take that consideration into account, specifically in deciding what, or what further, enquiries they should make. In the present case, however, there is no risk of any such psychiatric harm . . .[193]

6.159 The point arose again in the case of *Thompson v Mendip DC*.[194] Miss Thompson was a New Traveller who had been travelling for over 20 years. She could not find an authorised stopping place for herself. Faced with yet another eviction action, she made a homeless application to Mendip District Council. The council accepted that it had a duty to ensure that Miss Thompson obtained accommodation and it offered her a bungalow. She refused this offer on the basis that she had an aversion to bricks and mortar. A psychiatric report was obtained which stated:

> A large part of her aversion to conventional accommodation relates to her psychiatric history . . . I cannot imagine her living in a crowded urban environment, surrounded by many other people in buildings, as such a setting would make her very anxious and worsen her depression, as well as conflicting with her cultural values . . . Overall, I am satisfied that Miss Thompson is suffering from a depressive illness. I would rate this in the mild to moderate range of severity . . . In my opinion it is likely beyond reasonable doubt that Miss Thompson would become more depressed if she were evicted from the current site. It is likely she would suffer a similar effect if she moved into conventional accommodation, especially if it were in a built up area as opposed to being able to park her caravan on an official site.

193 [2008] EWCA Civ 1013, [2008] All ER (D) 436 (July), [2008] November *Legal Action* 20, paras 16 and 17.

194 Taunton County Court, 3 December 2010, HHJ Bromilow.

6.160 A council review upheld the offer of the bungalow as this 'was the only type of accommodation which could be offered at this time due to there currently being no suitable alternative to facilitate Miss Thompson's cultural lifestyle'. Miss Thompson appealed to the county court and HHJ Bromilow allowed the appeal. He stated:

> Given the unchallenged medical evidence, the decision to offer this appellant bricks and mortar accommodation must be regarded as unreasonable. . .I consider the offer of accommodation made to this appellant does fall below the minimum level when considering her circumstances, which must include her mental health.

6.161 David Watkinson, counsel for Miss Thompson, had also argued that the decision-maker had failed to take into account the availability of alternative sites. HHJ Bromilow also accepted this submission, stating:

> [I]t is plain that the existence of sites with potential to accommodate the appellant, whether or not in the ownership of the respondent, was either not known to the decision maker, ignored by him, or if reasonable enquiries had been taken would have been known to him for his consideration.

HHJ Bromilow also addressed the earlier decision of the CA in *Codona*, in which it had been held that the offer of bricks and mortar as temporary accommodation to Ms Codona amounted to suitable accommodation. The judge concluded that the decision in *Codona* was 'limited to circumstances of urgency' which did not apply in Miss Thompson's case.

6.162 Following the threat of eviction at Dale Farm,[195] a large number of the Travellers made homeless applications. *Sheridan and others v Basildon BC*[196] involved the first of these cases to reach the Court of Appeal, following the rejection of offers of bricks and mortar accommodation made to the Travellers. It was argued in all the three cases that were heard by the Court of Appeal that the offers were unsuitable.

6.163 In the case of Mrs Flynn, this was 'put largely on cultural grounds' (para 7) but there was no psychiatric evidence. Psychiatric evidence was produced for Mr and Mrs Sheridan (who, though still married, lived separately).

6.164 In the case of Mr Sheridan, Patten LJ (giving the leading judgment of the Court of Appeal) stated:

195 See para 1.9.

196 [2012] EWCA Civ 335, [2012] HLR 29.

> Although he referred to not wanting to live in bricks and mortar, he did not suggest in terms that this would have a serious impact on his mental health in itself. The recurring theme in all his reported complaints is that, without the close support of his wife and family, he would be unable to manage his medication and his life would collapse.[197]

6.165 With regard to Mrs Sheridan, the psychiatrist, Dr Slater, stated:

> I believe that if Mrs Sheridan and the children were forced to move into any bricks and mortar accommodation, she would experience significant depression and anxiety, even if the house was of high quality. Her sense of dislocation would relate to losing her familiar location, a heightened sense of isolation from her culture and the loss of the ready access to support she currently enjoys . . . It is possible that her distress about what she would see as an impossible situation might drive her to deliberately harm herself, although I believe that any such act would not be with the intention of killing herself.[198]

6.166 The Travellers also relied on a report from a planning consultant, Alison Heine, who examined the failure of Basildon BC to provide sufficient pitches and who also suggested ten possible locations for sites.

6.167 Patten LJ referred to the two leading Court of Appeal cases on this subject: *Codona v Mid-Bedfordshire DC* and *Lee v Rhondda Cynon Taf CBC*. Patten LJ also stressed that there is a line which denotes a minimum standard (sometimes known as the *Wednesbury* line):

> If the only accommodation available falls below this line then a lack of resources or inability to provide more suitable accommodation is no answer.[199]

6.168 Patten LJ rejected the Travellers' arguments based upon the local authority's failure to provide sufficient pitches and to look for alternative sites:

> It seems to me to be completely unrealistic to expect a housing officer on a s202 review to conduct a general inquiry into strategic questions about the preparation of a homelessness strategy and the adequacy of site provision.[200]

In any event, Mrs Heine's report had been considered by the local authority.

6.169 On the question of 'cultural aversion', Patten LJ concluded:

197 [2012] EWCA Civ 335, [2012] HLR 29 at para 10.
198 [2012] EWCA Civ 335, [2012] HLR 29 at para 15.
199 [2012] EWCA Civ 335, [2012] HLR 29 at para 32.
200 [2012] EWCA Civ 335, [2012] HLR 29 at para 56.

> A cultural aversion to bricks and mortar is not enough to make the offer of such accommodation Wednesbury unreasonable even if (as in Mrs Sheridan's case) it may risk bouts of depression. It is reasonable for those to be treated if they occur in just the same way as she has sought and obtained treatment for depression in the past. . . . The answer to the s204 appeals of both Mr and Mrs Sheridan is that the risk of depression . . . is the consequence not of the offers of accommodation which have been made but of the applicants' removal from Dale Farm.[201]

6.170 This seems a rather surprising conclusion, particularly in relation to Mrs Sheridan, for two reasons:

a) the Court of Appeal seem to be saying that the fact that harm may occur may still not make the offer unsuitable because of the availability of care from the NHS once that harm occurs;
b) the Court of Appeal got their facts wrong – the psychiatric evidence in Mrs Sheridan's case was that she would be caused psychiatric harm *if* she had to live in bricks and mortar accommodation and not just because she would have to leave Dale Farm.

6.171 Nevertheless, it is now apparent that it will be very difficult to challenge an offer of bricks and mortar accommodation unless there is a psychiatric report that contains clear evidence that there will be psychiatric harm caused if the Gypsy or Traveller in question is forced to move into such accommodation. Advisers for Gypsies and Travellers will need to ask psychiatrists very targeted questions when asking for a report to be prepared, for example:

- Regardless of other factors, will my client suffer psychiatric harm if he or she had to live in bricks and mortar accommodation?
- If so, why do you reach this conclusion?
- If psychiatric harm will be caused, how severe would this harm be?

6.172 In *Slattery v Basildon BC*,[202] Ms Slattery was another of the Irish Travellers who were evicted from the Dale Farm site. Thereafter she moved to a different part of the site where she continued to occupy the land in question unlawfully. She applied as a homeless person and was offered bricks and mortar accommodation which she refused.

6.173 The Court of Appeal (Briggs LJ giving the leading judgment) referred back to the previous[203] Court of Appeal Judgment in *Sheridan*

201 [2012] EWCA Civ 335, [2012] HLR 29 at paras 49 and 50.
202 [2014] EWCA Civ 30, 22 January 2014.
203 [2012] EWCA Civ 335.

and others v Basildon BC. They noted that, on the particular facts of Mr and Mrs Sheridan's cases, the court had concluded that the risk of psychiatric harm was mainly the consequence of the eviction from Dale Farm, together with their seeking and being offered separate accommodation (since they no longer lived together) rather than a consequence of the offer of bricks and mortar accommodation as opposed to caravan pitches.

6.174 Ms Slattery's appeal firstly to the High Court and then to the Court of Appeal was supported by a psychiatric report. Referring to this report, Briggs LJ stated:

> . . . it is striking that Dr Slater's opinion predicted consequences flowing from the eviction, and associated loss of community support as more serious than those specifically attributable to a move into bricks and mortar accommodation. In his view the former risked the obstacle to recovery caused by hospitalisation, whereas her aversion to bricks and mortar might lead her to be unable to occupy a house, or lead her to return to live with another Traveller. More generally, those passages in Dr Slater's report, read in the context of the report as a whole, clearly identified her eviction and consequential separation from the support of the Traveller community at Dale Farm as the most serious threats to her psychiatric wellbeing.[204]

6.175 Briggs LJ concluded:

> In this case, although Judge Maloney's summary of the thrust of Dr Slater's report might be said to be more precise than that of the review panel, I consider that they both reasonably (and indeed correctly) extract the gist of it, namely that the ongoing threat to Ms Slattery's mental well-being had more to do with eviction, and the consequential loss of the valuable support of her Traveller community, than to the aversion which would flow from being accommodated in bricks and mortar housing, rather than a mobile home or a caravan.[205]

6.176 It might be argued that the *Sheridan* and *Slattery* cases should be seen in the very particular context of the Dale Farm eviction. However many Gypsy and Traveller advisers point out that it is extremely unlikely that a homeless non-Gypsy or Traveller would be offered a caravan on a pitch as suitable accommodation. Many such advisers feel that the issue needs to be addressed by the Supreme Court at some stage since the leading Court of Appeal judgments to date seem to have put almost impassable obstacles in the way of homeless Gypsies or Travellers who are seeking authorised pitches.

204 [2014] EWCA Civ 30 at para 17.
205 [2014] EWCA Civ 30 at para 26.

6.177 Local authorities are no longer obliged to keep registers of disused or underused land. However, the National Land Use Database[206] may be of great assistance to a local authority, combined with its own knowledge of land in its area. Additionally, the Gypsy or Traveller applicant may have good local knowledge of the area and may be able to provide the local authority with examples of pieces of land that might be suitable. It is also suggested that it will not be sufficient for the local authority simply to have regard to any vacant pitches on authorised sites in the area. If there are vacant pitches on a site, the local authority may also have to have regard to the allocations policy for that particular site before offering a pitch to a homeless applicant.[207]

6.178 The *ODPM Guidance on managing unauthorised camping*[208] states:

> There must be close working between site managers and local authority ... dealing with unauthorised camping over allocations of pitches on sites. Site managers may be aware of issues around Gypsy/Traveller group and family compatibility, which must be taken into account when allocating pitches on residential sites.[209]

In other words, the question of 'compatibility' of groups or families will also be relevant to the issue of suitability. Another relevant matter may be the location of the accommodation and its distance from schools, employment and healthcare facilities.

6.179 Obviously, New Travellers who are homeless can also make homeless applications. When it comes to the duty to accommodate, it should be remembered that the central issue is 'suitability'. Therefore, in the case of New Travellers, they may not be able to show a 'cultural aversion to conventional housing', but it should be sufficient if they can show an 'aversion to conventional housing'. It is accepted that it may be more difficult for a New Traveller to show such an aversion. Nevertheless, it should be remembered that many New Travellers have spent many years travelling and some were born on the road.

6.180 The vast majority of homeless Gypsies or Travellers will have their own caravan or living vehicle but will not have an authorised pitch where they can place it. If a Gypsy or Traveller no longer has his

206 A partnership project between MHCLG, English Partnerships and Ordnance Survey.

207 See further the discussion on 'allocation' at paras 3.171 onwards, above.

208 *Guidance on managing unauthorised camping*, ODPM, February 2004.

209 *Guidance on managing unauthorised camping* at para 4.8. This Guidance applies to England only. The equivalent Welsh *Guidance on Managing Unauthorised Camping* (2013) does not contain a similar passage.

or her caravan or living vehicle,[210] it is arguable that the duty to secure that accommodation becomes available might include the provision of a suitable caravan or vehicle.[211]

6.181 Those advising homeless Gypsies or Travellers who are owed the duty to secure accommodation, may have to consider obtaining expert reports on the question of 'aversion to housing' (for example, from a psychiatrist or other medical practitioner) and/or from a planning consultant or land surveyor on the question of available land in an area. Those providing reports on the availability of land will have to have regard to the relevant development plans and government guidance.[212]

Legal aid

6.182 'Homelessness' remains in scope for legal aid.[213]

Conclusion

6.183 While local authorities work towards the provision of a five-year deliverable supply of sites in England[214] or implement the duty to meet assessed need in Wales,[215] it would seem both humane and cost effective for local authorities to identify locations within their areas where homeless Gypsies and Travellers could camp on a temporary basis.[216]

210 See, for example, the *Scott-Higgs* case for an example at para 6.130, above.

211 This argument was raised in *Price* but was not referred to in the judgment.

212 For detailed discussion of these and other planning issues, see chapter 4, above.

213 Legal Aid, Sentencing and Punishment of Offenders Act (LASPO) 2012 Sch 1 Part 1 para 34.

214 See para 4.72, above.

215 See paras 3.17–3.19, above.

216 And see also the model of 'negotiated stopping' developed by Leeds Gypsy and Traveller Exchange: http://leedsgate.co.uk/negotiated-stopping/whats-not-evaluation-negotiated-stopping-released.

CHAPTER 7

Education and healthcare

continued

Introduction

7.1 This chapter is designed to provide the reader with an overview of the law in England[1] relating to education and healthcare insofar as it may affect the lives of Gypsies and Travellers and their children.

Education

The right to education

7.2 The right to an education is enshrined in Article 26 of the Universal Declaration of Human Rights; Articles 28 and 29 of the United Nations Convention on the Rights of the Child; and Articles 13 and 14 of the International Covenant on Economic, Social and Cultural Rights. Common to all of these provisions are the following principles:

- that primary or elementary education should be compulsory and free to all; and
- that education should be directed to the full development of the child's personality and to the strengthening of respect for human rights and fundamental freedoms.

7.3 In addition, Article 12 of the European Framework Convention for the Protection of National Minorities (FCPNM) requires states to 'promote equal opportunities for access to education at all levels for persons belonging to national minorities'.

7.4 The right to education is also protected by Article 2 of Protocol 1 to the European Convention on Human Rights (ECHR),[2] which states that:

> No person shall be denied the right to education. In the exercise of any functions which it assumes in relation to education and to teaching, the State shall respect the right of parents to ensure such education and teaching in conformity with their own religious and philosophical convictions.

1 Readers seeking an overview of education and healthcare law in Wales may wish to consult LawWales, an online collaboration between the Welsh Government and Westlaw UK which provides explanatory narrative and commentary regarding all areas of law devolved to Wales.

2 See chapter 2 paras 2.167–2.183.

7.5 Article 2 of Protocol 1 has been incorporated into UK law by the Human Rights Act (HRA) 1998, subject to the following reservation:

> ... in view of certain provisions of the Education Acts in the United Kingdom, the principle affirmed in the second sentence of Article 2 is accepted by the United Kingdom only so far as it is compatible with the provision of efficient instruction and training, and the avoidance of unreasonable public expenditure.

7.6 This reflects the wording of Education Act (EA) 1996 s9, which confirms the 'general principle' that:

> ... pupils are to be educated in accordance with the wishes of their parents, so far as that is compatible with the provision of efficient instruction and training and the avoidance of unreasonable public expenditure.

7.7 Case-law on the right to education enshrined by Article 2 of Protocol 1 has established the following principles:

- It does not require states to establish, or to subsidise, education of any particular type or at any particular level.[3]
- It does guarantee to individuals the right to access such educational establishments as exist;[4] the guarantee applies to primary, secondary, and higher levels of education;[5] however, it does not necessarily entail a right of access to a particular institution.[6]
- The right to education must be effective and meaningful.[7]
- The right to education includes a right to obtain official recognition of the studies completed.[8]
- The right encompasses a right to an 'effective' education, however, this does not mean the 'most effective' education possible but that the education must reach a minimum standard.[9]
- The right to education is not absolute; it can be subject to limitations, provided that such limitations do not injure the substance of the right;[10] the limitations must be foreseeable for those

3 *Belgian Linguistics Case* (1979–80) 1 EHRR 252.
4 *Belgian Linguistics Case* (1979–80) 1 EHRR 252; *Ali v UK* [2011] ECHR App No 40385/06.
5 *Velyo Velev v Bulgaria* [2014] ELR 424.
6 *Ali v UK* [2011] ECHR, App No 40385/06.
7 *Belgian Linguistics Case* (1979–80) 1 EHRR 252.
8 *Belgian Linguistics Case* (1979–80) 1 EHRR 252; *Ali v UK* [2011] ECHR App No 40385.
9 *R (Holub) v Secretary of State for the Home Department* [2001] 1 WLR 1359.
10 *Ali v UK* [2011] ECHR 40385/06.

concerned, in pursuit of a legitimate aim, and proportionate to that aim.[11]

7.8 A number of duties imposed on, inter alia, the secretary of state, local education authorities, and parents give effect to the right to education.

7.9 The secretary of state must promote the education of the people of England.[12]

7.10 Local education authorities have a statutory duty to ensure that there are sufficient schools available in their area for providing primary and secondary education to children of compulsory school age which is appropriate to the ages, abilities, aptitudes, and needs of the pupils. The local authority must in particular have regard to the need for securing that special educational provision is made for pupils who have special educational needs.[13] Local authorities must also make arrangements for the provision of suitable education, at school or otherwise, for children of compulsory school age who, by reason of illness, exclusion from school, or otherwise, may not for any period receive suitable education unless such arrangements are made for them.[14]

7.11 The parents of children who are of compulsory school age (five to 16[15]) are under a duty to 'cause' that child to receive sufficient full-time education suitable to his or her age, ability, aptitude and any special educational needs.[16]

7.12 The wishes and beliefs of the parents are of central (though not decisive) importance in determining where and how a child is educated. Article 2 of Protocol 1 requires that states 'respect the right' of parents to have their children educated 'in conformity with their own religious and philosophical convictions'. 'Respect' means more than simply 'acknowledge' or 'take into account'. However, the state has a margin of appreciation as to how it reconciles the exercise of its functions in relation to education with respect for parents' rights.[17]

7.13 Further, as stated above, EA 1996 s9 requires local education authorities to have regard to the 'general principle' that pupils are to be educated 'in accordance with the wishes of their parents, so far as

11 *Sahin v Turkey* [2007] 44 EHRR 5; *Ali v UK* [2011] ECHR App No 40385/06.
12 EA 1996 s10.
13 EA 1996 s14.
14 EA 1996 s19.
15 EA 1996 s8.
16 EA 1996 s7.
17 *Lautsi v Italy* (2012) 54 EHRR 3.

this is compatible with the provision of efficient instruction and training and the avoidance of unreasonable expenditure'. Local authorities must give parents the opportunity to express a preference as to which school they wish their child to attend and must then comply with parental preference unless to do so would be prejudicial to efficient education or the efficient use of resources.[18] These duties are owed to all children residing in the area of a local authority, whether permanently or temporarily, and must therefore apply to Gypsy and Traveller children residing with their families on an unauthorised site on a temporary basis.

7.14 Since June 2013, children who are above compulsory school age are obliged to be participating in full-time education or training, an apprenticeship, or be in full-time occupation with part-time education or training.[19] Local authorities are under a duty to promote the fulfilment of this obligation.[20]

The structure of the educational system in England

7.15 There are five stages of education in England:

1) Early years – This concerns education for three- and four-year-olds.
2) Primary – This comprises nursery (under five); infant or Key Stage 1 (five to seven or eight); and junior or Key Stage 2 (up to 11 or 12). It is generally provided in primary schools, although in some areas it is partly covered by middle schools.
3) Secondary – This concerns education for children from 11 or 12 up to 16. It is generally provided by secondary schools, although in some areas it is partly covered by middle schools.
4) Further education – This covers all non-advanced courses taken after the period of compulsory education and includes A-levels.
5) Higher education – This comprises education which is of a standard higher than A-level; it includes undergraduate and postgraduate courses.

7.16 All children aged between five and 16 are entitled to a free place at a state school. There are a number of different types of state school, for example:

18 School Standards and Framework Act (SSFA) 1998 s86.
19 Education and Skills Act (ESA) 2008 s2.
20 ESA 2008 s10.

- Local education authority maintained schools – These are funded by the local authority; they include community schools, some special schools, voluntary controlled schools (often religious or faith schools), voluntary aided schools (also often religious or faith schools) and foundation and trust schools; a comprehensive school is a maintained school which is not selective; these schools must follow the National Curriculum.
- Academies – These are funded by the government and are independently managed and operate outside the control of the local authority; pupils attending academies do not have to follow the National Curriculum; free schools are a type of academy.
- Grammar schools – These can be run by the local authority, a foundation body, or a trust; they select all or most of their pupils on the basis of academic ability.
- Faith schools – These can be voluntary aided schools, voluntary controlled schools, or academies which are associated with a particular religion.

7.17 Independent schools are funded by fees or charitable trust funds and do not have to follow the National Curriculum.

Gypsies, Travellers, and education

7.18 It is widely accepted that Gypsy and Traveller pupils face great difficulties in the education system. This is demonstrated by the following statistics:[21]

- In 2016, 13 per cent of Gypsy and Roma children and 19 per cent of Irish Traveller children reached the expected standard in reading, writing, and arithmetic at Key Stage 2, compared to 53 per cent of all pupils.[22]
- In 2016, 10.3 per cent of Gypsy and Roma children and 21.3 per cent of Irish Traveller achieved 5 GCSEs at A* to C in English and Maths, compared to 63 per cent of all pupils;[23]
- In 2016, 26 pre cent of Gypsy and Roma pupils and 36 per cent of Irish Traveller pupils achieved a 'good level of development' at the

21 A recent report has warned that figures on educational attainment amongst Gypsy, Roma and Traveller children should be treated with caution: LKMco, *The underrepresentation of Gypsy, Roma and Traveller pupils in higher education* (July 2017), p8.

22 DfE, *National curriculum assessments: key stage 2, 2016 (revised)* (June 2017).

23 DfE, *Revised GCSE and equivalent results in England: 2015 to 2016* (July 2017).

early years foundation stage, compared to 69 per cent of pupils nationally.[24]
- In 2014, three to four per cent of Gypsy, Roma, and Travellers aged 18–30 accessed higher education, compared to 43 per cent nationally.[25]

7.19 These difficulties are due to a combination of factors which together make it more difficult for Gypsy and Traveller children to attend school, or to achieve their potential when attending school:

- Gypsy and Traveller pupils experience and/or anticipate racist harassment and bullying; and schools' responses to bullying are often inadequate, which can lead to self-exclusion.
- There can be a lack of validation of Gypsy and Traveller culture in schools; Gypsy and Traveller parents fear that the education of their children in schools may lead to cultural assimilation; the curriculum can lack, or be perceived as lacking, relevance to the Gypsy and Traveller way of life.
- Parents who have low levels of literacy and who gained limited benefits from their own education may have low aspirations for their children's academic achievement; schools often fail to promote Gypsy and Traveller children's participation in education; teachers may have low expectations of their Gypsy and Traveller pupils, or may even behave in a racist manner themselves;[26] the pressure of national targets may make some schools less willing to admit Gypsy and Traveller children.
- Schools may fail to pass on records when children move.
- Repeated eviction and enforced mobility leads to interrupted learning.
- Gypsy and Traveller pupils usually attend schools with lower than average rates of achievement: a 2009 report found that 40 per cent of Gypsy and Traveller pupils with only Key Stage 2 SAT results (indicating an already disrupted education) attended schools in the lowest quintile (fifth) of attainment. It was noted that such schools were more likely to have vacancies and therefore children from newly arrived or less assertive families were more likely to

24 LKMco, *The underrepresentation of Gypsy, Roma and Traveller pupils in higher education* (July 2017), p7.

25 LKMco, *The underrepresentation of Gypsy, Roma and Traveller pupils in higher education* (July 2017), p8.

26 A survey by the Traveller Movement found that the most common experience of discrimination in school related to the conduct of teachers: The Traveller Movement, *The last acceptable form of racism?* (September 2017), pp11–12.

be given places in them.[27] A further barrier to educational attainment is financial deprivation;[28] in a report published in 2014 it was noted that, of all pupils registered as Gypsy, Roma or Irish Traveller, 43.2 per cent were eligible for free school meals in primary schools; 45.3 per cent were eligible in secondary schools; and 57.5 per cent were eligible in special schools.[29]

7.20 Formerly, most local authorities provided specialist Traveller Educational Support Services (TESS) to help Gypsy and Traveller pupils and parents to access education and to provide practical advice and support to schools admitting them. Unfortunately, many of those services have been disbanded or have seen their staffing levels drastically reduced due to funding cuts.[30]

7.21 The National Association of Teachers of Travellers (NATT) can provide information regarding local Traveller Education Support Services, as well as information about books and other educational resources designed specifically for Gypsy and Traveller children.[31]

Admission to school

7.22 Securing a place for their child at the school of their choice is an issue of immense importance for most parents.

7.23 The Secretary of State for Education is obliged to issue a Code for school admissions.[32] The current School Admissions Code came into force on 19 December 2014. When determining their admission arrangements and making decisions on applications, admission authorities, governing bodies and local authorities must act in accordance with this Code.[33] Academies will also be obliged to

27 Department for Education (DfE), *Improving the outcomes for Gypsy, Roma and Traveller pupils: final report* (2010).

28 See Traveller Movement, *Child poverty in the Gypsy and Traveller communities* (January, 2014).

29 Traveller Movement, *Child poverty in the Gypsy and Traveller communities* (January 2014) para 2.3. See also section 4 of the *Race Disparity Audit* issued by the Cabinet Office in October 2017 (revised March 2018) at https://assets.publishing.service.gov.uk/government/uploads/attachment_data/file/686071/Revised_RDA_report_March_2018.pdf/

30 Freedom of Information requests showed that nearly half of 127 local authorities had either abolished their TESS or drastically cut staffing levels: www.independent.co.uk/news/uk/politics/cuts-threaten-traveller-childrens-schooling-2330282.html.

31 NATT can be contacted by visiting their website at: www.natt.org.uk.

32 SSFA 1998 s84(1).

33 SSFA 1998 s84(3).

comply with the Code by virtue of the terms of their funding arrangements.[34]

7.24 Admission arrangements, and the criteria used to determine the allocation of school places, must be fair, clear, and objective.[35] They must also comply with the HRA 1998 and the Equality Act (EqA) 2010. This means that they must not discriminate, directly or directly, on the ground of race. In addition, each local authority must have a Fair Access Protocol to help place children who have not managed to find a school place during the normal admissions round.[36] This is aimed at assisting the most vulnerable children and the Protocol must include Gypsy, Roma and Traveller children.[37]

7.25 However, despite these apparent safeguards, some of the admissions criteria described in the Code as being among the 'most common' may work to the disadvantage of Gypsy and Traveller children. For example, giving preference to children who have (or have had) siblings at the school or who have attended feeder schools could operate unfairly against children from Gypsy and Traveller families who have recently moved into the area. Similarly, a criterion based on ease of access by public transport could also put Gypsy and Traveller children at a disadvantage, given the remote location of many Gypsy and Traveller sites.

7.26 In a case that went to the Irish Supreme Court,[38] an Irish Traveller sought to challenge an admissions policy which gave preference to children whose fathers had attended the school (referred to as 'the Parental Rule'). It was argued that this was indirectly discriminatory[39] because for generations Irish Travellers, and in particular male Irish Travellers, had not participated in secondary level education. This 'background of grave educational deprivation' meant that Irish Traveller children would be less able to meet the Parental Rule as it was 'based on the disadvantages suffered or advantages enjoyed by earlier generation'.[40] This was exemplified by the appellant, John Stokes, whose father had not participated in secondary education.

34 School Admissions Code 2014, para 4.

35 School Admissions Code 2014, para 14.

36 School Admissions Code, para 3.9.

37 School Admissions Code, para 3.15.

38 *Mary Stokes (on behalf of her son John Stokes) v Christian Brothers High School Clonmel Tipperary* [2015] IESC 13.

39 Indirect discrimination was defined in the Equal Status Act 2000 s3 as 'where an apparently neutral provision' put a person with a particular characteristic 'at a particular disadvantage compared with other persons'.

40 *Mary Stokes (on behalf of her son John Stokes) v Christian Brothers High School Clonmel Tipperary* [2011] No. 15 CAT para 22.

7.27 The appellant succeeded in the Equality Tribunal, but lost in the Circuit Court and then again in the High Court. The High Court judge considered the meaning of the word 'particular' and found that no indirect discrimination existed because:

> ... the disadvantage relates to persons in addition to travellers and is not peculiar or restricted to travellers, and does not distinguish them among others of the kind (i.e. applicants for admission).

Irish Travellers were not put at any particular disadvantage because:

> ... there are others in the same position as they are ... everyone who is not the son of a past pupil is at a disadvantage by virtue of the rule.[41]

7.28 In the Supreme Court, a majority of the judges found that McCarthy J had erred in his approach to the meaning of indirect discrimination. In cases of indirect discrimination, they held, the provision would be 'by definition, apparently neutral'. The question was whether, 'at the level of the category rather than at the level of the individual' members of a protected category were disadvantaged. The fact that 'persons generally' who did not have a father who had attended the school were adversely affected was irrelevant because children whose parents did not go to secondary school were not a protected category, unlike Travellers.[42] The correct question was: 'Has it been shown that a member of the Travelling community is at a disadvantage compared with a non-Traveller as a result of the measure under challenge?'.[43] However, the appeal was still dismissed. There was 'simply no evidence or material on which any realistic assessment' of this question could have been made. This did not mean that there was no disadvantage, simply that the evidence to allow such a conclusion had not been provided.[44]

7.29 Parents wishing to challenge admission arrangements should make an objection to the Schools Adjudicator.[45] Any such objection must be made by 15 May each year following the determination of the admission arrangements for that year.[46] A decision of the adjudic-

41 *Mary Stokes (on behalf of her son John Stokes) v Christian Brothers High School Clonmel Tipperary* [2011] No. 15 CAT.

42 *Mary Stokes (on behalf of her son John Stokes) v Christian Brothers High School Clonmel Tipperary* [2015] IESC 13, para 8.

43 *Mary Stokes (on behalf of her son John Stokes) v Christian Brothers High School Clonmel Tipperary* [2015] IESC 13, judgment of Clarke J, para 11.

44 *Mary Stokes (on behalf of her son John Stokes) v Christian Brothers High School Clonmel Tipperary* [2015] IESC 13, para 11.

45 SSFA 1998 s88H.

46 School Admissions (Admission Arrangements and Co-ordination of Admission Arrangements) Regulations 2012 SI No 8.

ator will be binding, though it may be challenged by way of judicial review.

7.30 It seems that parents can also challenge admission arrangements during the course of an appeal against a decision to offer their child a place at a particular school, given that the School Admissions Appeals Code states that the appeal panel must consider:

> . . . whether the admission arrangements (including the area's co-ordinated admission arrangements) complied with the mandatory requirements of the School Admissions Code and Part 3 of the School Standards and Framework Act 1998.[47]

However, the courts have repeatedly taken a conservative approach to the role of the appeal panel in considering the legality of such arrangements. In *R (Buckinghamshire CC) v School Admissions Independent Appeal Panel for Buckinghamshire*,[48] Baker J held that the words 'mandatory requirements' in para 3.2 of the Code limited what could be looked at by the panel.

7.31 It may also be possible to bring a judicial review challenge without making an objection to the adjudicator, but where such an objection could have been made the High Court may find that this was an adequate alternative remedy. The safest course must therefore be to make an objection to the adjudicator.

7.32 As referred to above, parents who wish to challenge a decision made in their child's case, as opposed to the admission arrangements in general, have the right to appeal to an independent appeals panel.[49] Appeals in respect of maintained schools and academies are governed by the School Admission Appeals Code.[50] This emphasises that appeal panels 'perform a judicial function and must be transparent, accessible, independent and impartial, and operate according to principles of natural justice'.[51] The Code provides that admission authorities must set a timetable for organising and hearing appeals under which appellants have at least 20 school days from the date of notification of the decision to prepare and lodge their appeal and appeals are heard within 40 school days of that deadline.[52]

7.33 For all appeals (except for infant class size appeals) the panel must follow a two-stage process.

47 School Admission Appeals Code (February 2012) para 3.2.

48 [2009] EWHC 1679 (Admin).

49 SSFA 1998 s94.

50 DfE, *School Admission Appeals Code* (February 2012).

51 DfE, *School Admission Appeals Code* (February 2012), para 1.2.

52 DfE, *School Admission Appeals Code* (February 2012). paras 2.1–2.3.

7.34 The first stage examines the decision to refuse admission. The panel must first consider whether the admission arrangements complied with the mandatory requirements of the School Admissions Code and Part 3 of the SSFA 1998 and whether the arrangements were correctly and impartially applied in this case. It must then consider whether the admission of additional children would prejudice the provision of efficient education or the efficient use of resources. It must uphold the appeal at this first stage where it finds that:

- the admission arrangements did not comply with the relevant law or were not correctly and impartially applied; and the child would have been offered a place if they had complied or been correctly and impartially applied; or
- the admission of additional children would not prejudice the provision of efficient education or efficient use of resources (unless the panel is hearing multiple appeals and to uphold all appeals would seriously prejudice the provision of efficient education or efficient use of resources, in which case the panel must proceed to the second stage).

The panel must also proceed to the second stage where it finds that:

- the admission arrangements did comply with admissions law and were correctly and impartially applied; or
- that even if they did not comply, or were not properly applied, the child would not have been offered a place; and
- that the admission of additional children would prejudice the provision of efficient education or efficient use of resources.

7.35 At the second stage, the panel must balance the prejudice to the school against the appellant's case for the child to be admitted. If the panel considers that the appellant's case outweighs the prejudice to the school, it must uphold the appeal. In multiple cases, the panel must not compare the individual cases unless it finds that there are more cases in which the prejudice to the school is outweighed than the school can admit; in that instance it must compare the cases and uphold the strongest of those cases.

7.36 The rules regarding infant class size appeals (where admission has been refused on the grounds that it would breach the infant class size limit and this cannot be avoided without prejudicing the provision of efficient education or efficient use of resources) are different, as regulations limit the size of an infant class to 30 pupils per teacher.[53] These

53 School Admissions (Infant Class Sizes) (England) Regulations 2012 SI No 10.

rules are set out at section 4 of the School Admissions Appeals Code. In brief, an appeal may only be upheld at the first stage where:

- the admission of additional children would not breach the infant class size limit; or
- the admission arrangements did not comply with admissions law or were not correctly and impartially applied and the child would have been offered a place if they did/were; or
- the decision to refuse admission was not a decision which a reasonable authority would have made.

7.37 Where there are multiple appeals which would have succeeded at the first stage, the panel must proceed to the second stage and compare each case before deciding which, if any, to uphold. An appellant who is dissatisfied with the decision made by the independent appeal panel may seek judicial review of the decision on a point of law. They may also complain to the Local Government and Social Care Ombudsman (LGSCO) about maladministration on the part of the appeal panel, but the ombudsman is not able to overturn the decision.

Attendance at school

7.38 For the reasons given above, attendance by Gypsy and Traveller pupils has been historically low. A 2003 report by the Office for Standards in Education, Children's Services and Skills (Ofsted) found that the average attendance rate for Traveller pupils was around 75 per cent, which was the worst attendance profile of any ethnic minority group and well below the national average. Gypsy and Traveller pupils have significantly higher levels of absence from schools than pupils from other ethnic groups.[54] There is a particular issue in respect of attendance at secondary school. One report found that just over half of the Gypsy and Traveller pupils identified in Year 6 in 2003 were still attending school in Year 11 in 2008.[55] In 2003, Ofsted estimated that 12,000 Gypsy, Roma, and Traveller children might not be registered at secondary schools in England and Wales.[56] Even when Gypsy and Traveller pupils do transfer to secondary school, many do not continue to attend beyond the age of 14. A 2010 report found that only 38.3 per cent of Irish Travellers reached statutory

54 DfE, *Improving the outcomes for Gypsy, Roma and Traveller pupils: final report* (2010).

55 DfE, *Improving the outcomes for Gypsy, Roma and Traveller pupils: final report* (2010).

56 Ofsted publications centre, *Provision and support for Traveller pupils*, (2003).

leaving age.[57] The problems with attendance apply not only to mobile Gypsies and Travellers but also to those who are housed or settled.[58]

7.39 The above-mentioned 2010 report by the Department for Education (DfE) found that strategies used by schools to encourage attendance and transition included:

- having an identified key individual in school to build relationships with pupils and families;
- increasing the monitoring and analysis of attendance;
- taking a more flexible approach to the curriculum;
- engaging parents with the school in addressing attendance issues;
- building an inclusive ethos; and
- liaising with the feeder school.[59]

A case study published in 2014 looked at schools which were succeeding in improving the attainment and attendance of Gypsy, Roma and Traveller pupils. Factors identified as contributing to this included fostering strong community relations, having high expectations of attendance, working with families and increasing parental engagement, promoting an inclusive ethos and supporting the transition to secondary school.[60]

7.40 EA 1996 s7 provides that:

> The parent of every child of compulsory school age shall cause him to receive efficient full-time education suitable
> (a) to his age, ability and aptitude, and
> (b) to any special educational needs he may have,
>
> either by regular attendance at school or otherwise.

7.41 A child is of compulsory school age from the first of the 31 March, 31 August, or 31 December, following his or her fifth birthday until the last Friday in June of the school year in which he or she reaches the age of 16.[61]

57 DfE, *Improving the outcomes for Gypsy, Roma and Traveller pupils: final report* (2010).

58 DfE, *Improving the outcomes for Gypsy, Roma and Traveller pupils: final report* (2010).

59 DfE, *Improving the outcomes for Gypsy, Roma and Traveller pupils: final report* (2010).

60 See: www.gov.uk/government/case-studies/gypsy-roma-and-traveller-pupils-supporting-access-to-education.

61 Education (Start of Compulsory School Age) Order 1998 SI No 1607; and EA 1996 s8.

7.42 In *R v Secretary of State for Education and Science ex p Talmud Torah Madizikei Hedass School Trust*[62] it was held that education is 'suitable' if it primarily equips a child for life in the community of which he or she is a member, as long as it does not foreclose the child's option later to adopt some other form of life if he or she wishes to do so.

7.43 If a child is registered at a school, but fails to attend that school regularly, then the parent is guilty of an offence under EA 1996 s444(1). An offence under section 444(1) is punishable with a fine. Subject to the defences set out below, this offence is one of strict liability and parents cannot defend a prosecution by claiming that they had no knowledge of their child's non-attendance or by claiming that they had done all they reasonably could have done to ensure that their child attended school.[63] An argument that the absence of a requirement for proof of any knowledge or fault on the part of the parent is a breach of ECHR Article 6(2) has been rejected by the High Court.[64]

7.44 If a child is registered at a school and fails to attend regularly, and the parent knows that the child is failing to attend regularly and fails to cause the child to attend, then the parent is guilty of a more serious offence under EA 1996 s444(1A). An offence under this section is punishable with a larger fine, imprisonment not exceeding three months, or both. Parents will have a defence if they prove that they had a reasonable justification for failing to cause the child to attend regularly.[65]

7.45 No offence will be committed under either EA 1996 s444(1) or (1A) if the parent proves that:

- the pupil was prevented from attending by reason of illness or any unavoidable cause – the unavoidable cause must relate to the child, not the parent, and must be in the nature of an emergency;[66]
- the pupil's absence was authorised by the school or, in the case of alternative provision, by a person authorised to grant leave;

62 *The Times*, 12 April 1985.

63 *Islington LBC v D* [2011] EWHC 990 (Admin); *Bath and North East Somerset DC v Warman* [1999] ELR 881; and *Crump v Gilmore* [1968] LGR 56.

64 *Barnfather v Islington LBC and the Secretary of State for Education and Skills* [2003] ELR 263.

65 EA 1996 s444(1B).

66 *Islington LBC v D* [2011] EWHC 990 (Admin).

- the absence was on a day exclusively set apart for religious observance by the religious body to which the parent belongs;
- the local authority is under a duty to provide transport to school and has failed to do so;
- in certain circumstances, the school is not within walking distance and the local authority has not made suitable arrangements for boarding accommodation to be provided or for the child to be registered at a school nearer to his or her home.

7.46 Of particular significance for Gypsy and Traveller parents, no offence will be committed where the parent proves that:

- the child has no fixed abode;
- the parent is engaged in a trade or business of a nature that requires him or her to travel from place to place;
- the child has attended school as a registered pupil as regularly as the nature of that business permits; and
- if the child has attained the age of six, that he or she has attended school for at least 200 half-day sessions during the period of 12 months ending with the date on which proceedings were instituted.[67]

7.47 This defence has been criticised on the basis that that it may deny Gypsy and Traveller children equality of access to education. As far back as 1985, a Committee of Inquiry into the Education of Children from Ethnic Minority Groups expressed its fear that:

> . . . the specific provision . . . although presumably intended originally to protect travelling parents from unreasonable prosecution for failing to send their children to school, may in practice serve to deprive travellers' children of equality of access to education; LEAs [local education authorities] may see this provision in the Act as offering a convenient excuse for not enforcing school attendance for travellers' children, rather than, as we would wish, striving to achieve full time attendance by all school age children in their areas.[68]

7.48 Almost 20 years later, a ministerial working group looking at tackling inequalities experienced by Gypsies and Travellers noted the government's belief that:

67 EA 1996 s444(6).

68 Committee of Inquiry into the Education of Children from Ethnic Minority Groups, *Education for All* (The Swann Report), HMSO, 1985.

> . . . this concession has come to be seen by some schools – and by Gypsy and Traveller families themselves – as giving tacit consent for mobile pupils to benefit only from a significantly shortened school year.

It made a commitment to 'look again' at this defence and to consult on whether or not it should be repealed.[69] However, no action has been taken to date.

7.49 As an alternative to prosecution under section 444(1), the local authority may issue a penalty notice under EA 1996 s444A, although there is no requirement for them do so before prosecuting.

7.50 However, there is a legal requirement for a local authority, prior to prosecution, to consider applying to the court for an education supervision order (ESO). This order may be made where the court is satisfied that the child concerned is of compulsory school age and is not being properly educated, ie that the child is not receiving efficient full-time education suitable to his or her age, ability and aptitude and any special educational needs (SEN) the child may have.[70] An ESO makes the authority responsible for advising, supporting, and giving directions to the child and his or her parents so as to ensure that the child is properly educated. While an ESO is in place, a parent's duties under EA 1996 ss7 and 444 are superseded by their duty to comply with any directions made under the ESO.[71] An ESO will last for one year and may be extended for no more than three years.[72] A persistent failure to comply with a reasonable direction given under an ESO is an offence punishable by a fine.[73]

7.51 To protect the continuity of learning for Gypsy and Traveller children, the concept of 'dual registration' has been introduced. If parents inform their 'base' school or the TESS that the family will be travelling and intend to return by a given time, the school may keep the child's place for them and record their absence as authorised. The child can then register at other schools while the family is travelling. Gypsy and Traveller parents can also take advantage of 'school-based distance learning' whereby teachers and the TESS work together to provide pupils with a package of curriculum-based material to be taken away and studied by them while the family are travelling.[74]

69 DCLG, *Progress report by the ministerial working group on tackling inequalities experienced by Gypsies and Travellers* (2012), para 11.

70 Children Act 1989 s36.

71 Children Act 1989 Sch 3 para 13.

72 Children Act 1989 Sch 3 para 15.

73 Children Act 1989 Sch 3 para 18.

74 See the Education (Pupil Registration) (England) Regulations 2006 SI No 1751.

7.52 16- and 17-year-olds are, since 2013, under a duty to participate in appropriate full-time education or training, or to be in full-time occupation and participating in 'sufficient' relevant training or education.[75] Local authorities are under a duty to promote the fulfilment of this duty.[76] Education and Skills Act (ESA) 2008 s46 contains provisions whereby an attendance notice may be served on a young person who is not complying with the duty to participate in education or training but these provisions are not yet in force.

Transport to school

7.53 Under EA 1996 s508B(1), local authorities in England are under an obligation in respect of certain 'eligible' children to make:

> . . . such travel arrangements as they consider necessary in order to secure that suitable home to school travel arrangements, for the purpose of facilitating the child's attendance at the relevant educational establishment in relation to him, are made and provided free of charge in relation to the child.

7.54 EA 1996 Sch 35B sets out which children are 'eligible'. They are, in summary:

- children of compulsory school age who are attending a school which is not within walking distance, where the authority have not made arrangements for them to board at the school or attend a nearer school;[77]
- children of compulsory school age who have SEN, a disability, or a mobility problem because of which they cannot reasonably be expected to walk to school;
- children of compulsory school age who cannot reasonably be expected to walk to school because the route they could reasonably be expected to take is unsafe;
- children who are entitled to free school meals or whose parents are in receipt of maximum working tax credit where:
  - the child is aged eight to ten (inclusive) and the nearest suitable school is more than two miles away;

75 ESA 2008 ss1, 2.

76 ESA 2008 s10.

77 Walking distance is defined by EA 1996 s444(5) as being two miles for a child under the age of eight, and three miles for a child aged eight or above.

- the child is aged 11 or above, he or she attends a school more than two but not more than six miles away, and there are not three or more suitable nearer schools;
- the child is aged 11 or above, he or she attends a school more than two but not more than 15 miles away, and the school is the nearest suitable school based on a preference due to the parent's religion or belief.

7.55 EA 1996 s508B(4) defines 'travel arrangements' as:

> . . . travel arrangements of any description, including the direct provision of transport and, if arranged with the consent of the child's parent, an escort, the payment of travelling expenses, or the payment of a travel allowance.

7.56 Under EA 1996 Sch 35C, a local authority may make a school travel scheme for their area. EA 1996 s508E(3) makes clear that, if such a scheme is in force, the authority will not have any functions under EA 1996 ss508B or 508C. However, by virtue of EA 1996 Sch 35C, local authorities must include in their schemes very similar obligations towards eligible children as those contained in EA 1996 s508B. Under Sch 35C para 10(1), a school travel scheme may not come into force unless approved by the secretary of state.

7.57 As alluded to above, parents will have a defence to the charge of failing to send their child to school under EA 1996 s444 if the local authority had a duty to make travel arrangements in respect of the child and have failed to do so.[78]

7.58 It may be that, pursuant to the dual registration provisions, Gypsy and Traveller pupils are registered at more than one school. In their cases, the relevant educational establishment for the purposes of arranging travel is whichever of the schools they are attending at the relevant time.[79]

7.59 EA 1996 s508A places a duty on local authorities in England to promote the use of sustainable modes of travel to meet the school travel needs of their area. 'Sustainable modes of travel' are defined as modes of travel which the authority consider may improve the physical well-being of those who use them and/or the environmental well-being of the area.

78 See *R v Devon CC ex p George* [1988] 3 All ER 1002; and EA 1996 s444 as amended by Education and Inspections Act 2006 s82.

79 School Travel (Pupils with Dual Registration) (England) Regulations 2007 SI No 1367.

7.60 Guidance promulgated by the Department for Education, *Home to school travel and transport guidance: Statutory guidance for local authorities* (July 2014),[80] states that the maximum each way journey length should be no longer than 45 minutes for a child of primary school age and 75 minutes for a child of secondary school age.

7.61 Local authorities also have discretionary powers under EA 1996 s508C to make school travel arrangements in respect of children who are not entitled to free transport. This may be by way of providing transport free of charge; providing transport for which a charge is levied; or paying reasonable travel expenses. Local authorities also have a discretion under EA 1996 s509A to provide a child who is receiving early years education otherwise than at a school with travel assistance where they are satisfied that, without such assistance, the child may be unable to attend.

7.62 The *Home to school travel and transport guidance* (July 2014) states that local authorities should have complaints and appeals procedures for parents to follow if they wish to complain about the service provided or to appeal a decision about the eligibility of their child for travel support. These procedures should be published alongside the local authority's travel policy statement. Annex 2 of the guidance sets out a recommended review/appeals process. This provides for an initial review by a senior officer of the local authority followed by a review by an independent appeal panel. If a parent considers that their appeal has not been dealt with in accordance with the procedure, or there have been other irregularities in its handling, they may refer the matter to the LGSCO. If an appellant considers the decision of the independent appeals panel to be flawed on public law grounds then they may seek judicial review.

7.63 Local authorities have different duties in respect of persons of sixth-form age. Under EA 1996 s509AA, a local authority must prepare and publish an annual transport policy specifying the arrangements for the provision of transport or otherwise that the authority considers it necessary to make for facilitating the attendance of persons of sixth-form age receiving education or training. The DfE's guidance, *Post-16 transport to education and training: Statutory guidance for local authorities* (October 2017), emphasises that the overall intention of this duty is to ensure that:

80 Available at https://assets.publishing.service.gov.uk/government/uploads/attachment_data/file/575323/Home_to_school_travel_and_transport_guidance.pdf.

- learners of sixth-form age are able to access the education and training of their choice; and
- if support for access is needed, it will be assessed and provided where necessary.[81]

7.64 The guidance provides that the transport policy is intended to inform young people and their parents about what transport arrangements and support are available:[82] it should therefore be clear and provide enough detail to enable young people to make informed choices.[83] The guidance also states that local authorities must have particular regard to the needs of those 'who could not access education or training provision if no training were made', 'the most vulnerable or socially excluded' and those who 'are vulnerable to becoming not in education, employment or training'.[84] Gypsy and Traveller pupils are likely to fall within these groups.

7.65 Pursuant to EA 1996 s509AB(2), the transport policy must specify arrangements for persons receiving full-time education or training at establishments other than local authority maintained schools which are 'no less favourable than the arrangements specified for pupils of the same age attending such schools'.

7.66 The *Post-16 transport to education and training guidance* also makes clear that, while local authorities do not have a statutory obligation to provide free or subsidised transport:

> . . . when making their assessment of what is required, local authorities must act reasonably, taking into account all relevant matters, such as the needs of their population, the local transport infrastructure and the resources available.[85]

7.67 The transport policy must include the procedure for making a complaint. Complaints should first be made to the local authority. If not resolved to the satisfaction of a young person or their parent, they may then complain to the LGSCO or the secretary of state.[86] The

81 DfE, *Post-16 transport to education and training: Statutory guidance for local authorities* (October 2017), para 5.

82 DfE, *Post-16 transport to education and training: Statutory guidance for local authorities* (October 2017), para 13.

83 DfE, *Post-16 transport to education and training: Statutory guidance for local authorities* (October 2017), para 14.

84 DfE, *Post-16 transport to education and training: Statutory guidance for local authorities* (October 2017), para 16.1

85 DfE, *Post-16 transport to education and training: Statutory guidance for local authorities* (October 2017), para 3.

86 DfE, *Post-16 transport to education and training: Statutory guidance for local authorities* (October 2017), para 27.

secretary of state may direct a local authority to make transport arrangements or provide reasonable travelling expenses where particular transport arrangement or financial assistance are not covered by the transport policy statement.[87] The secretary of state also has powers to give directions to a local authority where they are behaving unreasonably or have failed to discharge a duty.[88]

Special educational needs

7.68 Gypsy and Traveller pupils are reported to have the highest level of SEN of all ethnic minority groups.[89] Irish Traveller pupils are 2.7 times more likely than other white British pupils to be diagnosed as having SEN, and Gypsy and Roma pupils 2.6 times more likely.[90] The DfE has suggested that this may be due to interrupted schooling; families lacking information or experiencing problems accessing appropriate health care; or schools failing to respond appropriately to cultural difference.[91]

7.69 The law relating to SEN underwent significant changes with the passing of the Children and Families Act (CFA) 2014. The old regime, contained within the EA 1996, will continue to apply for children who already had statements of SEN when the new provisions came into force on 1 September 2014. However, by 1 April 2018 all children with statements must have transitioned to the new regime.[92]

7.70 A child has 'special educational needs' for the purposes of the CFA 2014 if she or he has a 'learning difficulty or disability which calls for special educational provision to be made for him or her'.[93] A child has a learning difficulty or disability if he or she:

- is of compulsory school age or a young person[94] and has a significantly greater difficulty in learning than the majority of others of the same age;

87 EA 1996 s509AA(9).
88 EA 1996 ss496 and 497.
89 DfE, *Improving the outcomes for Gypsy, Roma and Traveller pupils: final report* (2010).
90 EHRC, *Inequalities experienced by Gypsy and Traveller communities: A review* (2009).
91 DfE, *Improving the outcomes for Gypsy, Roma and Traveller pupils: final report* (2010).
92 Children and Families Act 2014 (Transitional and Saving Provisions) (No 2) Order 2014 SI No 2270.
93 CFA 2014 s20(1).
94 Defined in CFA 2014 s83 as a person over compulsory school age but under 25.

- is of compulsory school age or a young person and has a disability which prevents or hinders him or her from making use of facilities of a kind generally provided for others of the same age in mainstream schools or mainstream post-16 institutions;[95] or
- is under compulsory school age but is likely to fall within one of the above categories when of compulsory school age (or would be likely to if no special educational provision were made).[96]

7.71 'Special educational provision', for a child aged two or more or a young person, is defined as 'educational or training provision that is additional to, or different from, that made generally available for others of the same age' in mainstream institutions.[97] For a child under two, it means educational provision 'of any kind'.[98]

7.72 A parent who is concerned that his or her child may have SEN can ask the local authority to assess those needs. Local authorities are under a number of duties to identify and assess, or consider assessing, the needs of children who have, or may have, SEN:

- Authorities must exercise their functions with a view to identifying all the children and young people in their area who have, or may have, SEN and/or a disability.[99]
- An education and health care (EHC) needs assessment (an assessment of the child's educational, health care, and social needs)[100] may be requested by a child's parent, a young person themselves, or a person acting on behalf of a school or post-16 institution;[101] upon receiving such a request the local authority must determine 'whether it may be necessary for special educational provision to be made for the child or young person in accordance with an EHC plan';[102] and if it concludes not, it must notify the parent or young person of the reasons why.[103]
- In addition, if no EHC plan is maintained for a child or young person, he or she has not been assessed during the previous six months, and the local authority determines that it may be neces-

95 CFA 2014 s20(2).
96 CFA 2014 s20(3).
97 CFA 2014 s21(1).
98 CFA 2014 s21(2).
99 CFA 2014 s22.
100 CFA 2014 s36(2).
101 CFA 2014 s36(1).
102 CFA 2014 s36(3).
103 CFA 2014 s36(5).

sary for special educational provision to be made for him or her[104] then (after notifying the child's parent or young person and having regard to their views[105]) if it is of the opinion that the child or young person may have SEN and that it may be necessary for special educational provision to be made, it must secure an EHC needs assessment.[106]

7.73 After an EHC needs assessment has been carried out, the local authority must notify the parent or young person of the outcome, whether it proposes to prepare an EHC plan, and the reasons for its decision.[107] The local authority must prepare and maintain an EHC plan where, 'in the light of an EHC needs assessment, it is necessary for special educational provision to be made' for the child or young person.[108] The authority must consult the parent or young person about the plan and give them the opportunity to make representations on a draft. An EHC plan is defined as a plan specifying:

- the child's or young person's SEN;
- the outcomes sought for him or her;
- the special educational provision required by him or her;
- any health care provision reasonably required by the learning difficulties and disabilities which result in the child or young person having SEN;
- any social care provision which must be made for him or her under Chronically Sick and Disabled Persons Act 1980 s2; and
- any other social care provision reasonably required by the learning difficulties and disabilities which result in the SEN.[109]

7.74 The local authority is under a duty to secure the special educational provision specified in the EHC plan for the child or young person.[110] Any health care provision specified must be arranged by the responsible commissioning body.[111]

7.75 There can sometimes be a dispute between the parents and the local authority or other bodies over which school the child should attend. If the parents request that a particular school be named in their

104 CFA 2014 s36(6).
105 CFA 2014 s36(7)–(8).
106 CFA 2014 s36(8).
107 CFA 2014 s36(9).
108 CFA 2014 s37(1).
109 CFA 2014 s37(2).
110 CFA 2014 s42(2).
111 CFA 2014 s42(3).

child's EHC plan, the local authority must name that school unless the school is unsuitable for the age, ability, aptitude or SEN of the child, or the attendance of the child would be incompatible with the provision of efficient education for others or the efficient use of resources.[112] If the school would be unsuitable, or the child's attendance incompatible, or if no request for a particular school is made, then the local authority must name a school or type of school which they think would be appropriate.[113] The authority must provide for the child to be educated in mainstream schooling unless that is incompatible with the wishes of the child's parent or the young person or it is incompatible with the provision of efficient education for others and there are no reasonable steps that could be taken to prevent that incompatibility.[114] The school specified must admit the child or young person.[115]

7.76 An authority must review an EHC plan every 12 months and must reassess a child's educational, health care and social care needs if requested by the parent, young person or school (unless it has carried out an assessment or re-assessment within the last six months, or 'it is not necessary' to undertake a further assessment[116]).[117] An authority may only cease to maintain an EHC plan if it is no longer responsible for the child or young person or it determines that the plan is no longer necessary.[118]

7.77 A child's parent or a young person may appeal to the First-tier Tribunal against any of the following matters:

- a decision not to undertake an EHC needs assessment;
- a decision, following an EHC needs assessment, that it is not necessary for special educational provision to be made in accordance with an EHC plan;
- where an EHC plan is maintained:
  - the SEN specified in the plan;
  - the special educational provision specified in the plan;
  - the school or type of school specified in the plan;
  - the fact that no school is named in the plan; and
- a decision to cease to maintain a plan.[119]

112 CFA 2014 s39(1), (3), (4).
113 CFA 2014 ss37(5) and 40(1)–(2).
114 CFA 2014 s33(2)–(3).
115 CFA 2014 s43.
116 Special Educational Needs and Disability Regulations 2014 SI No 1530 reg 24.
117 CFA 2014 s44.
118 CFA 2014 s45.
119 CFA 2014 s51.

7.78 Parties to an appeal are encouraged to attempt mediation and, except where the decision concerns the school specified (or not) in the plan, the parent or young person seeking to appeal must first obtain a certificate showing that they have been informed about and either refused or attended mediation.[120]

7.79 One of the aims of the new legislation was to achieve greater participation by children, young people, and their parents in decision-making at both an individual and a strategic level. Pursuant to this, when exercising their functions in relation to special educational needs, local authorities must have regard to:

- the views, wishes and feelings of the child, young person, or parent;
- the importance of them participating as fully as possible in any decision;
- the importance of them being provided with the information and support necessary to participate in those decisions; and
- the need to support them in order to help the child or young person achieve the best possible outcomes.[121]

7.80 Local authorities must also publish information about the education, health, care, training and educational travel provision it expects to be available for children and young people in its area, or for whom they are responsible, who have SEN or a disability. This is known as the 'local offer'.[122] In addition, authorities must arrange for children, young people, and parents to be provided with advice and information about matters relating to SEN.[123]

7.81 Of particular relevance to mobile Gypsy and Traveller children with SEN are the duties on local authorities to co-operate with each other. If a local authority requests the co-operation of another local authority, then that authority must comply with the request unless they consider that doing so would be incompatible with their duties or otherwise have an adverse effect on the exercise of their functions.[124] Further, where a child or young person with an EHC plan moves into the area of another local authority, the old authority must transfer the plan on the day of the move or within 15 working days. The EHC plan must be treated as if it had been made by the new

120 CFA 2014 s55.
121 CFA 2014 s19.
122 CFA 2014 s30.
123 CFA 2014 s32.
124 CFA 2014 s31.

authority, and the new authority must within 6 weeks of the transfer inform the parent or young person that the plan has been transferred, whether it proposes to undertake a new assessment, and whether it proposes to review the plan.[125]

Exclusion from school

Background

7.82 Gypsy and Traveller pupils suffer from disproportionality high levels of school exclusion. In 2015/16 the rates of permanent and fixed-term exclusions were highest for Gypsy, Traveller and Roma pupils amongst all ethnic groups[126] and a 2012 report highlighted the fact that on average Gypsy, Traveller and Roma pupils were four times more likely to be excluded from school than those from the whole school population.[127] This disparity is recognised in the statutory guidance on exclusions entitled *Exclusion from maintained schools, academies and pupil referral units in England* (September 2017), which notes that Gypsy, Roma and Irish Traveller pupils are among the ethnic groups with the highest rates of exclusion. The guidance states that head teachers should consider what extra support might be needed to identify and address the needs of such pupils, such as drawing on the support of TESS or other professionals 'to help build trust when engaging with families from Traveller communities'.[128]

7.83 EA 2002 s51A states that:

1) The head teacher of a maintained school in England may exclude a pupil from the school for a fixed period or permanently.
2) The teacher in charge of a pupil referral unit in England may exclude a pupil from the unit for a fixed period or permanently.

125 Special Educational Needs and Disability Regulations 2014 SI No 1530 reg 15.

126 DfE, *Permanent and Fixed Period Exclusions in England: 2015 to 2016*, July 2017. The report warned that, as this population is relatively small, the figures should be treated with caution.

127 See the Office of the Children's Commissioner's report, *They never give up on you* (2012); and the Traveller Movement report, *Never giving up on them: School exclusions of Gypsy, Traveller and Roma pupils in England* (2016). Note also that at p71 of the Office for the Children's Commissioner's report it was said that the research showed that appeals against the exclusion of Gypsy, Traveller and Roma pupils had been 100 per cent successful.

128 DfE, *Exclusion from maintained schools, academies and pupil referral units in England* (September 2017), p11.

Procedure

Overview

7.84 The procedure for excluding pupils is governed by the EA 2002, the School Discipline (Pupil Exclusions and Reviews) Regulations 2012,[129] and the aforementioned statutory guidance. The following must have regard to this guidance when carrying out their functions relating to exclusions:

- head teachers;
- governing boards;
- local authorities;
- academy trusts;
- independent review panel members;
- independent review panel clerks; and
- SEN experts.

7.85 There are three principal stages to an exclusion.

Stage 1: The head teacher's decision to exclude

7.86 An exclusion may be for a fixed term or terms, not exceeding 45 school days in a single academic year,[130] or it may be permanent. Informal or unofficial exclusions are unlawful.[131]

7.87 A decision to exclude a pupil permanently is a last resort, and should only be taken:

> . . . in response to a serious breach or persistent breaches of the school's behaviour policy; and where allowing the pupil to remain in school would seriously harm the education or welfare of the pupil or others in the school.[132]

7.88 It would appear that there is no power to exclude a pupil on a precautionary basis. EA 2002 s51A(10) defines 'exclude' as meaning only 'exclude on disciplinary grounds'. In the case of *An application by JR17 for judicial review (Northern Ireland)*[133] the Supreme Court held that, where the relevant scheme contained only a power to exclude

129 SI 2012 No 1033.

130 School Discipline (Pupil Exclusions and Reviews) Regulations 2012 SI No 1033 reg 4.

131 DfE, *Exclusion from maintained schools, academies and pupil referral units in England* (September 2017), p10.

132 DfE, *Exclusion from maintained schools, academies and pupil referral units in England* (September 2017), p6.

133 [2010] UKSC 27.

on disciplinary and not precautionary, grounds, a precautionary exclusion would be unlawful: there was no common law or general managerial power to exclude a pupil as a precaution.

7.89 The decision to exclude must be 'lawful, reasonable, and fair'.[134] When establishing the facts in relation to an exclusion decision, the head teacher should apply the civil standard of proof, ie the balance of probabilities[135] – although the more serious the allegation, the more cogent the proof that will be required.[136] The guidance states that 'where practical, head teachers should give pupils an opportunity to present their case before taking the decision to exclude'.[137] In fact, head teachers may have to do more than give pupils such an opportunity only 'where practical': in the case of *An Application by JR17* the 'right accorded . . . to a pupil to put his or her version of events before a decision to suspend is made' was said to be 'fundamental'.[138] In that case, the failure to give the pupil a chance to respond to the allegations against him was one of the grounds on which the exclusion was found to be unlawful.

7.90 Whenever a head teacher excludes a pupil, he or she must, without delay, notify the parents of:

- the period of exclusion;
- the reasons for the exclusion;
- the parents' right to make representations about the exclusion to the governing body;
- how the representations should be made;
- and, where there is a legal requirement for the governing body to consider the exclusion, the parents' right to attend the meeting, be represented, and to bring a friend.[139]

The head teacher should also draw the parents' attention to relevant sources of free and impartial information and local services, includ-

134 DfE, *Exclusion from maintained schools, academies and pupil referral units in England* (September 2017), p6.

135 DfE, *Exclusion from maintained schools, academies and pupil referral units in England* (September 2017), p9.

136 *Re B (Children) (Sexual Abuse: Standard of Proof)* [2008] UKHL 35.

137 DfE, *Exclusion from maintained schools, academies and pupil referral units in England* (September 2017), p10.

138 *An application by JR17 for Judicial Review (Northern Ireland)* [2010] UKSC 27, para 50.

139 DfE, *Exclusion from maintained schools, academies and pupil referral units in England* (September 2017), p12.

ing the TESS.[140] This information should be provided in a way which is clear and easily understood:[141] where the parents have limited literacy, this may require the information to be provided orally as well as in writing. The head teacher must also, without delay, inform the governing board and local authority of:

- a permanent exclusion;
- an exclusion which would result in the pupil being excluded for more than five school days in a term; or
- an exclusion which would result in the pupil missing a public examination or national curriculum test.[142]

7.91 Where a pupil is permanently excluded or excluded for a fixed term of more than five school days (or for fixed-period exclusions on five consecutive school days), the governing body (or local authority in relation to a pupil excluded from a pupil referral unit) must arrange suitable education for any pupil of compulsory school age. This alternative provision must begin no later than the sixth day of the exclusion.[143]

Stage 2: Review of the head teacher's exclusion decision

7.92 The governing board must meet to consider the reinstatement of a pupil within 15 school days of receiving notice of an exclusion which: is permanent; is a fixed-term exclusion which would bring the pupil's total number of school days of exclusion to more than 15 in a term; or would result in a pupil missing a public examination or national curriculum test.[144] Where a pupil has been excluded for more than five but less than 15 school days in a term, and the parents have made representations, the governing board must within 50 school days consider whether the pupil should be reinstated.[145] Where a pupil has been excluded for five or fewer school days in a term, parents

140 DfE, *Exclusion from maintained schools, academies and pupil referral units in England* (September 2017), p14.

141 DfE, *Exclusion from maintained schools, academies and pupil referral units in England* (September 2017), p14.

142 DfE, *Exclusion from maintained schools, academies and pupil referral units in England* (September 2017), p15.

143 DfE, *Exclusion from maintained schools, academies and pupil referral units in England* (September 2017), p16.

144 DfE, *Exclusion from maintained schools, academies and pupil referral units in England* (September 2017), p18.

145 DfE, *Exclusion from maintained schools, academies and pupil referral units in England* (September 2017), p18.

may make representations which must be considered, but there is no right to a meeting.[146]

7.93 Where legally required to consider an exclusion, the governing board must consider the interests and circumstances of the excluded pupil, including the circumstances in which the pupil was excluded, and must have regard to the interests of other pupils and people working at the school.[147] The governing board must consider any representations made by parents, the head teacher or a representative from the local authority.[148] The governing board should apply the civil standard of proof.[149] When deciding whether or not a pupil should be reinstated, the governing board should consider whether the decision to exclude was lawful, reasonable and procedurally fair and must itself act in accordance with the rules of natural justice.[150] In *R v Governors of W School and West Sussex CC ex p K*,[151] the court held that the decision of the governing body to exclude K should be quashed on the basis that it had been unfair and procedurally flawed in circumstances where K had been handicapped in the presentation of his defence, the 'evidence' included the verbal opinions of an anonymous police officer, and only lip-service had been paid to the standard of proof.

7.94 The governing board can either uphold an exclusion or direct the reinstatement of the pupil.[152] The governing board must notify the parents, head teacher and local authority of their decision and the reasons for it without delay.[153] If the pupil is to be permanently excluded, the governing board must provide notification of certain other matters, including in particular the parents' right to ask for the decision to be reviewed by an independent review panel (IRP).[154]

146 DfE, *Exclusion from maintained schools, academies and pupil referral units in England* (September 2017), p19.

147 DfE, *Exclusion from maintained schools, academies and pupil referral units in England* (September 2017), p20.

148 DfE, *Exclusion from maintained schools, academies and pupil referral units in England* (September 2017), p20.

149 DfE, *Exclusion from maintained schools, academies and pupil referral units in England* (September 2017), p20.

150 DfE, *Exclusion from maintained schools, academies and pupil referral units in England* (September 2017), p21.

151 [2001] ELR 311.

152 DfE, *Exclusion from maintained schools, academies and pupil referral units in England* (September 2017), p21.

153 DfE, *Exclusion from maintained schools, academies and pupil referral units in England* (September 2017), p22.

154 DfE, *Exclusion from maintained schools, academies and pupil referral units in England* (September 2017), p22.

Stage 3: Further review by an independent review panel

7.95 An application for a review by the IRP must be made within 15 school days of notice being given to the parents by the governing board of their decision to uphold a permanent exclusion or within 15 school days of the final determination of a claim of discrimination under the EqA 2010 in relation to the exclusion.[155] The review must then begin within another 15 school days thereafter (although it can subsequently be adjourned).[156] The IRP must be comprised of representatives from the categories of school governors, head teachers and lay members.[157] The IRP's role is to reconsider the governing board's decision not to reinstate the pupil. In so doing they must consider the interests and circumstances of the pupil, including the circumstances of their exclusion, and the interests of other pupils and people working at the school.[158] The IRP must apply the civil standard of proof.[159] The IRP can take account of new evidence, but when considering whether or not the original decision was flawed it can only take account of evidence that was available to the governing board when the decision was made or would have been available had the governing board acted reasonably.[160]

7.96 All parents have the right to request that a SEN expert be present at the IRP hearing, whether or not the pupil is recognised to have SEN.[161] The role of the SEN expert is to provide impartial advice about how SEN could be relevant to the exclusion.[162]

7.97 The IRP can:

- uphold the exclusion decision;
- recommend that the governing board reconsiders its decision; or

155 DfE, *Exclusion from maintained schools, academies and pupil referral units in England* (September 2017), p27.

156 DfE, *Exclusion from maintained schools, academies and pupil referral units in England* (September 2017), pp27–28.

157 DfE, *Exclusion from maintained schools, academies and pupil referral units in England* (September 2017), pp28–29.

158 DfE, *Exclusion from maintained schools, academies and pupil referral units in England* (September 2017), p35.

159 DfE, *Exclusion from maintained schools, academies and pupil referral units in England* (September 2017), p35.

160 DfE, *Exclusion from maintained schools, academies and pupil referral units in England* (September 2017), pp35–36.

161 DfE, *Exclusion from maintained schools, academies and pupil referral units in England* (September 2017), p33.

162 DfE, *Exclusion from maintained schools, academies and pupil referral units in England* (September 2017), p39.

- if it considers that the decision of the governing body was flawed on judicial review principles, quash the decision and direct that the matter is reconsidered; when making this direction, the IRP has the power to order that, if the governing board does not offer to reinstate the pupil within ten school days, the school must pay £4,000 (or suffer an equivalent readjustment in its budget).[163]

7.98 It had been held that the hearings of independent appeal panels (the panels which preceded IRPs) do not engage Article 6 of the ECHR (which guarantees the right to a fair trial in the determination of civil rights and obligations and criminal charges) as there was no private right to an education.[164] However, a report by the Office for the Children's Commissioner in March 2012 expressed concern that the lack of any power for IRPs to insist on a reinstatement meant that there were insufficient safeguards against the school acting unreasonably or unlawfully.[165] The report recommended that IRPs should be given the power to reinstate excluded pupils. Despite this, the government has since confirmed that it has no plans to implement this recommendation.

Challenges

7.99 A challenge to the decision of the IRP lies by way of judicial review.

7.100 Schools are public authorities and must comply with the HRA 1998 and the EqA 2010. The latter means that they must not directly or indirectly discriminate against, harass or victimise pupils because of their:

- age;
- disability;
- gender reassignment;
- marriage or civil partnership;
- pregnancy or maternity;
- race;
- religion or belief;
- sex; or
- sexual orientation.

163 DfE, *Exclusion from maintained schools, academies and pupil referral units in England* (September 2017), pp35–36.

164 *R (B) v Head Teacher and Governing Body of Alperton Community School* [2001] EWHC 229 (Admin).

165 See the Office of the Children's Commissioner's report, *They never give up on you* (2012).

They must comply with the public sector equality duty (PSED),[166] which requires them to:

- have due regard to the need to eliminate discrimination, harassment, victimisation and any other conduct prohibited by the EqA 2010;
- advance equality of opportunity between persons who share a relevant protected characteristic and persons who do not; and
- foster good relations between persons who share a relevant protected characteristic and persons who do not.

7.101 If it is alleged that the exclusion process is tainted by discrimination, then the injured party may bring a claim before the First-tier Tribunal (in cases of alleged disability discrimination) or a county court.

7.102 An unlawful exclusion will not necessarily constitute a breach of a pupil's rights under Article 2 of Protocol 1 of the ECHR. In *Ali v UK*[167] the European Court of Human Rights (ECtHR) held that Article 2 did not necessarily entail a right of access to a particular institution, and it did not require schools to offer alternative education 'covering the full national curriculum' to pupils who had been temporarily excluded. The Supreme Court went further in *An Application by JR17*, finding that there was no breach of Article 2 as the state provided educational facilities for pupils who were suspended, the applicant had not been denied access to these facilities and that the fact that 'the standard or quality of the education provided may have been low is not material'.[168] We would argue that it is difficult to understand why the standard of the alternative education is not relevant, even though the threshold for what is required may in some cases be low.

Threatened with exclusion

7.103 If the child of a Gypsy or Traveller is threatened with exclusion, then for initial assistance he or she should contact the local TESS, if there is one, or the NATT. However, it may also be necessary to seek specialist independent legal advice.

Suitable education

7.104 A child who has been excluded from school should still receive a suitable education and EA 1996 s19(1) provides that:

166 See also para 7.110 below and, more generally, chapter 8 paras 8.133–8.159.

167 (2011) 54 EHRR 12.

168 *An application by JR17 for judicial review (Northern Ireland)* [2010] UKSC 27, para 65.

> Each local authority shall make arrangements for the provision of suitable education at school or otherwise than at school for those children of compulsory school age who, by reason of illness, exclusion from school or otherwise, may not for any period receive suitable education unless such arrangements are made for them.

7.105 Where a Gypsy or Traveller parent has concerns regarding the provision of education to an excluded child, he or she may wish to challenge the school or the local authority by bringing a claim for judicial review and/or damages.

Discrimination[169]

7.106 Romani Gypsies, Irish Travellers and Scottish Gypsy Travellers have all been recognised as distinct racial groups under the EqA 2010 or its predecessor legislation.[170] Welsh Gypsy Travellers (or Kale) have also been recognised as part of a minority group[171] and it is likely that they would be recognised by the courts as a distinct group in their own right although there is as yet no case-law to that effect.

7.107 EqA 2010 Part 6 outlaws racial discrimination, victimisation, and harassment in education. Discrimination may be direct or indirect. In particular, schools and institutions of further and higher education are prohibited from discriminating against or victimising a person:

- in the arrangements they make for deciding who is offered admission;
- as to the terms on which they offer to admit the person;
- by not admitting the person as a pupil/student;
- in the way they provide the pupil/student with education or afford them access to a benefit, facility or service;
- by not providing the pupil/student with education; by not affording him or her access to a benefit, facility or service; by excluding him or her; or by subjecting him or her to any other detriment.

169 See chapter 8 for more detailed consideration of this topic.

170 *Moore and Coates v Secretary of State for Communities and Local Government* [2015] EWHC 44 (Admin) para 58; and the 2008 Scottish Employment Tribunal case of *MacLennan v Gypsy Traveller Education and Information Project* 23 June 2008, unreported (case no S/132721/07): see EHRC, *Gypsy Travellers in Scotland: A resource for the media*, updated June 2013.

171 *Commission for Racial Equality v Dutton* [1989] 2 WLR 17 at 801.

7.108 These obligations apply to:

- schools maintained by local authorities;
- independent educational institutions;
- alternative provision Academies that are not independent educational institutions;
- special schools;
- universities;
- 16 to 19 Academies; and
- other institutions within the further and/or higher education sector.[172]

7.109 EqA 2010 s29 provides that a person concerned with the provision of a service to the public or who is exercising a public function must not discriminate, harass or victimise a person in the course of so doing. There are limits to this prohibition in respect of age-related, sex, and religious or belief-related discrimination but not in respect of racial discrimination.

7.110 EqA 2010 s149 also imposes on public bodies, including the governing bodies of educational establishments, a statutory duty known as the public sector equality duty (PSED):

> (1) A public authority must, in the exercise of its functions, have due regard to the need to–
> (a) eliminate discrimination, harassment, victimisation and any other conduct that is prohibited by or under this Act;
> (b) advance equality of opportunity between persons who share a relevant protected characteristic and persons who do not share it;
> (c) foster good relations between persons who share a relevant protected characteristic and persons who do not share it.
>
> (2) A person who is not a public authority but who exercises public functions must, in the exercise of those functions, have due regard to the matters mentioned in subsection (1).
>
> (3) Having due regard to the need to advance equality of opportunity between persons who share a relevant protected characteristic and persons who do not share it involves having due regard, in particular, to the need to–
> (a) remove or minimise disadvantages suffered by persons who share a relevant protected characteristic that are connected to that characteristic;
> (b) take steps to meet the needs of persons who share a relevant protected characteristic that are different from the needs of persons who do not share it;

172 EqA 2010 ss85 and 91.

(c) encourage persons who share a relevant protected characteristic to participate in public life or in any other activity in which participation by such persons is disproportionately low.

. . .

(5) Having due regard to the need to foster good relations between persons who share a relevant protected characteristic and persons who do not share it involves having due regard, in particular, to the need to–
(a) tackle prejudice, and
(b) promote understanding.

(6) Compliance with the duties in this section may involve treating some persons more favourably than others; but that is not to be taken as permitting conduct that would otherwise be prohibited by or under this Act.

7.111 If an ethnic Gypsy or Traveller parent believes that his or her child has been the subject of racial discrimination, then legal advice should be sought. County courts have jurisdiction to determine a claim regarding a contravention of EqA 2010 Part 6 (though, if the case relates to disability discrimination, the matter should be brought to the First-tier Tribunal (Special Educational Needs and Disability)).[173] The claim must be brought within six months of the date of the act to which it relates.[174] If the claim is made out, then a county court has the power to grant any remedy which could have been granted by the High Court in proceedings in tort or on a claim for judicial review.[175]

7.112 It can be difficult to gather evidence of the discrimination suffered by Gypsy and Traveller pupils due to their reluctance to identify as such: a 2010 report found that almost 70 per cent of Gypsy and Traveller pupils ascribed themselves differently at some point over a period of six years, and approximately 50 per cent of pupils changed their ascribed ethnicity on transferring from primary to secondary school.[176]

7.113 A number of cases involving discrimination against Roma in education have come before the ECtHR in recent years. In *Oršuš v Croatia*[177] the court found that there had been a violation of Article 14 where Roma pupils had been educated in Roma-only classes with a Roma-only curriculum. The government had sought to defend the

173 EA 2010 s114.

174 EA 2010 s118.

175 EA 2010 s119.

176 DfE, *Improving the outcomes for Gypsy, Roma and Traveller pupils: final report* (2010).

177 (2011) 52 EHRR 7.

system on the grounds that the separate classes were necessary due to the Roma pupils' insufficient command of the Croatian language. The court held that, while Article 14 did not prevent domestic authorities from treating groups differently in order to correct factual inequalities between them (and sometimes they were required to do so), very weighty reasons would be needed to justify a difference of treatment based exclusively on ethnic origin. The court held that:

> . . . the vulnerable position of Roma/Gypsies means that special consideration should be given to their needs and their different lifestyle both in the relevant regulatory framework and in reaching decisions in particular cases.[178]

7.114 In *Horváth and Kiss v Hungary*[179] the court considered complaints from two young men of Roma origin who claimed that they had been wrongly placed in a school for the mentally disabled due to their ethnic origin and that there was, generally, an over-representation of Roma pupils amongst children with a disability placed in special schools. The court found that there had been a 'systematic misdiagnosis of mental disability'; that 'the misplacement of Roma children in special schools has a long history across Europe' and that the main causes of misdiagnosis were Roma's socio-economic disadvantages and cultural differences,[180] and held that there had been a violation of Article 2 of Protocol 1 read in conjunction with Article 14 of the ECHR.

7.115 In 2012, the Irish High Court quashed a decision to deport a Roma child to Serbia where, it was held the likely denial of access to even a basic education would violate his human rights and amount to persecution[181]

Bullying

7.116 Gypsy, Roma and Traveller children are especially vulnerable in a school setting and can be subjected to bullying.[182] One report found that nearly 90 per cent of children from a Gypsy, Roma or Traveller

178 (2011) 52 EHRR 7 at para 48.

179 (2013) 57 EHRR 31.

180 (2013) 57 EHRR 31 paras 110–116.

181 *D (a minor) v Refugee Appeals Tribunal another* [2011] IEHC 431.

182 EHRC, *England's most disadvantaged groups: Gypsies, Travellers and Roma*, March 2016.

background had experienced racial abuse.[183] Bullying has been repeatedly recognised as one of the barriers to education for these pupils: a report by the Equality and Human Rights Commission (EHRC) in 2009 found that 'racist harassment and bullying', together with 'the inadequacy of many schools' responses' was 'the most prominent theme' in analyses of the low levels of educational participation and attainment.[184]

7.117 Maintained schools must have measures to encourage good behaviour and respect for others on the part of pupils and, in particular, to prevent all forms of bullying among pupils.[185] These measures must be publicised in a written document and must be made generally known within the school and to parents.[186] Independent schools must draw up and implement an effective anti-bullying strategy.[187]

7.118 Guidance given by the DfE, *Preventing and tackling bullying: Advice for headteachers, staff and governing bodies* (July 2017), emphasises that bullying is often motivated by prejudice against particular groups and reminds schools of their obligations under the EqA 2010. It recommends that schools 'openly discuss differences between people that could motivate bullying' and 'teach children that using any prejudice based language is unacceptable'.[188] If a school failed to respond to bullying against a Gypsy or Irish Traveller pupil at all, or failed to respond as effectively as when such behaviour was targeted against pupils from other ethnic groups, then it could be guilty of discrimination. A failure to draw up anti-bullying measures addressing racist bullying may also be a breach of the PSED.[189]

7.119 Schools have a duty to take such care of their pupils as a careful parent would in similar circumstances. This includes a duty to take positive steps to protect their well-being.[190] A school may be liable in

183 P Lane et al, Anglia Ruskin University, *Gypsy, Traveller and Roma: Experts by Experience* (October 2014), p3.

184 EHRC, *Inequalities experienced by Gypsy and Traveller communities: A review*, 2009.

185 EIA 2006 s89(1)(b).

186 EIA 2006 s89(6).

187 Education (Independent School Standards) Regulations 2014 SI No 3283 reg 10.

188 DfE, *Preventing and tackling bullying: Advice for headteachers, staff and governing bodies* (2017), pp5, 8, 11.

189 By analogy, the Explanatory Notes to the EqA 2010 state: 'The duty could lead a school to review its anti-bullying strategy to ensure that it addresses the issue of homophobic bullying, with the aim of fostering good relations, and in particular tackling prejudice against gay and lesbian people.'

190 *Gower v Bromley LBC* [1999] ELR 356 at 359.

negligence if it fails to take steps to protect a pupil from bullying. In determining what a reasonable school might be expected to do, relevant factors will include the extent to which it was foreseeable that failure to take steps would result in harm to the victim; the extent of the risk; the magnitude of the harm; and the practicability and likely effectiveness of any possible steps.[191]

Education otherwise than at school

7.120 Parents have the right to educate their child at home, provided that the child receives 'efficient full-time education suitable (a) to his age, ability and aptitude and (b) to any special educational needs he may have'.[192] This is known as 'elective home education'. Parents are not required to register or seek approval from the local authority in order to educate their child at home. The National Curriculum need not be followed and formal testing is not required.

7.121 Local authorities are under a duty to make arrangements enabling them to establish, insofar as it is possible for them to do so, the identities of children in their area who are not registered at a school and who are not receiving suitable education at home.[193] However, they have no powers to insist on seeing and questioning children in order to establish whether they are receiving a suitable education. Parents are not obliged to respond to informal requests for information about the education being provided, although they may be well-advised to do so to avoid more formal action being taken.

7.122 If it appears to a local authority that a child is not receiving suitable education, the authority 'shall serve a notice in writing on the parent requiring him to satisfy them within the period specified in the notice that the child is receiving such education'.[194] If a parent on whom a notice has been served fails to satisfy the local authority within the period specified in the notice, which shall not be less than 15 days,[195] that the child is receiving suitable education, and in the opinion of the authority 'it is expedient that the child should attend school', then the authority shall serve a school attendance order on the parent. This requires the parent to register the child at a named

191 *Bradford-Smart v West Sussex County Council* [2002] EWCA Civ 7 at para 35.
192 EA 1996 s7.
193 EA 1996 s436A.
194 EA 1996 s437(1).
195 EA 1996 s437(2).

school.[196] If a parent on whom a school attendance order has been served fails to comply with the requirements of the order they are guilty of an offence under EA 1996 s443, unless they prove that the child is receiving a suitable education otherwise than at school. A parent convicted of an offence under EA 1996 s443 can be punished with a fine. The guidance issued by the Department for Children, Schools and Families (DfCSF), *Ensuring children's right to education* (2008), makes clear that before serving an Order, the local authority 'should make every effort to engage the parent and help them get their children onto a school roll'.[197]

7.123 Separate guidance issued by the DfCSF, *Elective home education: guidelines for local authorities* (November 2007), reminds local authorities that they should:

> . . . have an understanding of and be sensitive to, the distinct ethos and needs of Gypsy, Roma and Traveller communities. It is important that these families who are electively home educating are treated in the same way as any other families. Home education should not necessarily be regarded as less appropriate than in other communities.[198]

7.124 The right to educate one's child at home is clearly in keeping with Article 9 (the right to freedom of thought, conscience and religion) and Article 10 (the right to freedom of expression) of the ECHR, but it must be balanced against the right of the child to receive an effective education. Families educating their children at home often receive very little support from the local authority. Questionnaires completed by or on behalf of 20 local authorities in 2004 showed that 25 per cent of the local authorities did not have a written Elective Home Education policy and only two provided educational materials. The arrangements for providing home education were found to be poorly supported and monitored. Nearly half of the authorities, and 94 per cent of the TESS surveyed, reported concerns over whether the Gypsy, Roma and Traveller children were receiving a full-time and appropriate education.[199]

7.125 For many Gypsy and Traveller families, the decision to educate a child at home is caused by dissatisfaction with the school system.

196 EA 1996 s437(3).

197 DfCS, *Ensuring Children's Right to Education* (2008), p.3.

198 DfCSF, *Elective Home Education: Guidelines for Local Authorities* (November 2007), para 5.11.

199 Department for Education and Skills (DfES), *The situation regarding the current policy, provision and practice in Elective Home Education for Gypsy, Roma and Traveller children* (2004).

The responses from local authorities to the 2004 questionnaires revealed that nearly 3,000 children in 20 local authorities were registered for Elective Home Education (of which two-thirds were secondary level) and it was estimated that between 16 per cent and 35 per cent of these were Gypsy, Roma or Traveller children. The reasons for choosing home education were said to include fear of racist bullying, fear of cultural erosion and perceived lack of relevance of the secondary school curriculum.

Education of children under school age

7.126 As recognised by the guidance issued by the DfE, *Early education and childcare: Statutory guidance for local authorities* (March 2017), high quality education at an early stage has lasting benefits for children.[200] Local authorities in England are under a general duty to improve the well-being of young children[201] in their area and to reduce inequalities between young children in their area.[202] So far as is reasonably practicable, they must secure sufficient childcare to meet the needs of parents who work or are in education or training which could reasonably be expected to lead to work.[203] They must also take steps to identify parents or prospective parents in their area who would otherwise be unlikely to take advantage of early childhood services and to encourage them to take advantage of those services.[204] The statutory guidance emphasises that local authority must meet their duties under the EqA 2010 when securing early education places.[205]

7.127 Local authorities are under a duty to secure the following free educational provision for young children:

- 570 hours per year over at least 38 weeks of the year for 'eligible' two-year-olds. This includes the most vulnerable children such as children from financially deprived backgrounds, children in care, or children with SEN.[206]

200 DfE, *Early education and childcare: Statutory guidance for local authorities* (March 2017), p7.

201 A child is a 'young child' in the period from his birth up to the 1 September following his or her fifth birthday: Childcare Act 2006 s19.

202 Childcare Act 2006 s1.

203 Childcare Act 2006 s6.

204 Childcare Act 2006 s3(3).

205 DfE, *Early education and childcare: Statutory guidance for local authorities* (March 2017), p13.

206 Childcare Act 2006 s7 and the Local Authority (Duty to Secure Early Years Provision Free of Charge) Regulations 2014 SI No 2147 regs 1, 3, 4.

- 570 hours per year over at least 38 weeks of the year for three- and four-year-olds.
- An additional 570 hours per year for three- and four-year-olds of working parents.[207]

7.128 Despite this, Gypsy and Traveller children often lack adequate play opportunities and access to early years provision due to factors such as: a lack of safe play areas on roadside sites; the location of public sites in dangerous environments such as close to major roads or in remote areas; and constant evictions.[208]

7.129 It was recognised that Sure Start centres played a positive role in reaching out to Gypsies and Travellers in respect of early years provision.[209] However, in recent years these have faced significant funding cuts with many closures.

Improving the educational outcomes of Gypsy and Traveller children

7.130 The EHRC in its 2009 review[210] identified a number of factors which could be helpful in addressing inequality. These included:

- a strong and coherent race equality policy that specifically includes Gypsies and Travellers;
- a school culture based on equality policies and a positive approach to valuing diversity;
- dedicated liaison staff;
- raising teachers' expectations of their Gypsy and Traveller pupils;
- flexibility of response to Gypsy and Traveller pupils' needs and flexibility of curriculum;
- continuity of learning; and
- distance learning packs.

7.131 A report produced by the DfE in 2010 looked at strategies employed by schools to address Gypsy and Traveller attainment. These included:

- tracking performance data, and analysing this by ethnicity;

207 Childcare Act 2016 s1; and the Childcare (Early Years Provision Free of Charge) (Extended Entitlement) Regulations 2016 SI No 1257.

208 EHRC, *Inequalities experienced by Gypsy and Traveller communities: A review* (2009).

209 DfES, *Aiming high: raising the achievement of Gypsy Traveller pupils* (2003).

210 EHRC, *Inequalities experienced by Gypsy and Traveller communities: A review* (2009).

- an emphasis on staff valuing and celebrating Gypsy and Traveller culture;
- the use of positive role models from the Gypsy and Traveller community;
- taking a flexible and creative approach to personalising the curriculum to keep pupils engaged;
- identifying key individuals to liaise with families;
- the provision of mentoring support; and
- focusing on 'soft' outcomes such as enjoyment, health, and well-being, in addition to quantifiable results.

7.132 A 2014 review of 'UK Progress on the European Union Framework for National Roma Integration Strategies',[211] which looked at Gypsy and Traveller experiences as well as Roma, made four specific recommendations:

1) All schools should have clear policies on preventing bullying, and the DfE and local authorities should ensure that specific anti-bullying policies are used effectively.
2) Gypsy, Roma, and Traveller pupils should be included as a specific group receiving Pupil Premium payments.
3) Central funding for Gypsy, Roma and Traveller History Month should be re-established[212] and the history of these groups should be included in the broader curriculum.
4) Schools and education services should monitor the progress of all Gypsy, Roma and Traveller children. TESS should be funded and supported.[213]

TESS had, as this recommendation indicates, formerly played a very significant role in promoting education for Gypsies and Travellers through outreach work, advocacy, facilitation of access, curriculum development, in-school support and other services. The EHRC report of 2009 hailed TESS as being 'of crucial importance' and emphasised that 'it is essential that they are adequately and securely funded'.[214] Unfortunately, despite this strong recommendation, such services have been subject to cuts and many have been disbanded.

211 Published by Anglia Ruskin University with support from the Joseph Rowntree Foundation.

212 This was also recommended by the Traveller Movement in its September 2017 report, *The last acceptable form of racism?*

213 P Lane et al, Anglia Ruskin University, *Gypsy, Traveller and Roma: Experts by Experience* (October 2014), p48.

214 EHRC, *Inequalities experienced by Gypsy and Traveller communities: A review* (2009).

7.133 In April 2019 the Traveller Movement published *A Good Practice Guide for improving outcomes for Gypsy, Roma and Traveller Children in education*[215] which makes a number of important recommendations that would lead to an improvement in their educational attainment.

7.134 In the same month, the Women and Equalities Committee published its report entitled *Tackling inequalities faced by Gypsy, Roma and Traveller communities.*[216] In essence, the report concluded that Gypsy, Roma and Traveller communities have been 'comprehensively failed' by policy-makers.

7.135 The report found that Gypsy, Roma and Traveller people have the worst outcomes of any ethnic group across a huge range of areas, including education. The Committee stated that it was intolerable that any child should not be receiving a suitable education. Many parents, schools and local authorities are letting down Gypsy and Traveller children. The Committee said that the first priority for the government, local authorities and Ofsted must be to ensure that the legal right to an education is not denied to any child, including Gypsy, Roma and Traveller children. Home education should be a positive, informed choice, not a reaction to either a poor school environment or family expectations. In addition, the Committee stated that schools should, as part of their responsibilities under the PSED, be challenging race and gender stereotypes wherever they encounter them and that Ofsted should ensure that inspectors are actively inspecting schools for gender and racial stereotyping.

Legal aid

7.136 Legal aid is available, subject to means and merits tests, for the following educational law matters:[217]

- *SEN* – Legal aid is available for appeals to the First-tier Tribunal for Special Educational Needs and Disability. This could include challenges against the content of EHC plans or against a refusal to issue such a plan. However, funding is only available for a solicitor to help prepare the case. It will not cover representation in front of the tribunal, although it is available for a subsequent chal-

215 See: https://travellermovement.org.uk/phocadownload/TTM%20Good%20Practice%20Guide%20Education_web.pdf.

216 See: https://publications.parliament.uk/pa/cm201719/cmselect/cmwomeq/360/full-report.html.

217 Legal Aid, Sentencing and Punishment of Offenders Act 2012 Sch 1.

lenge on a point of law from the First-tier Tribunal to the Upper Tribunal.

- *Judicial review* – Legal aid is available for applications to bring a judicial review of a public authority's act, decision or omission.
- *Discrimination* – Legal aid is available to challenge contraventions of the EqA 2010. This could include cases where a child has been discrimination by their school or local education authority.

Healthcare

The right to healthcare[218]

7.137 It is a fundamental principle of the National Health Service (NHS) that everyone who is ordinarily resident in the UK is entitled to healthcare which is free at the point of need.[219]

7.138 To be 'ordinarily resident' in the UK, a person must be in the UK lawfully, voluntarily and 'for settled purposes as part of the regular order of their life for the time being'.[220] Since 6 April 2015, if the person is a non-European Economic Area (EEA) national who is subject to immigration control, he or she must have indefinite leave to remain in order to be ordinarily resident.[221]

7.139 For people who are not ordinarily resident in the UK, the position is complicated and the following is intended only as a summary. In brief, some healthcare is always free to everyone regardless of residence (except where the overseas visitor travelled to the UK for the purpose of receiving the treatment in question), including:

- care and treatment provided by a general practitioner (GP);
- accident and emergency (A&E) services, but not including any services provided after the person has been admitted as an inpatient, or at an outpatient appointment;
- services provided otherwise than at, or by staff employed to work at, or under the direction of, a hospital;
- family planning services;

218 Information about health services for overseas visitors to Wales is available at: www.wales.nhs.uk/nhswalesaboutus/budgetcharges/overseasvisitors.

219 National Health Service (NHS) Act 2006 s175. This principle does not extend to all types of treatment: for example, there may be charges for dental treatment, prescriptions, and eye care treatment.

220 *R v Barnet LBC ex p Shah* [1983] 2 AC 309.

221 Immigration Act 2014 s39.

- services provided for the diagnosis and treatment of specified infectious diseases;
- diagnosis and treatment of sexually transmitted infections; and
- treatment required for a physical or mental condition caused by torture, female genital mutilation (FGM) or domestic or sexual violence.[222]

7.140 Further, the following categories of overseas visitors will be exempt from charges:

- refugees, asylum-seekers, and individuals receiving support under certain provisions of the Immigration and Asylum Act 1999 or the Care Act 2014;
- children looked after by a local authority;
- victims or suspected victims of modern slavery or human trafficking;
- those receiving compulsory treatment under a court order, or who are in prison, immigration detention, or mental health detention;
- those who have paid the health surcharge, are exempt from paying, have had the requirement to pay waived, or are covered by transitional arrangements;[223]
- those with an enforceable EU right to free healthcare;
- UK Government employees and war pensioners; and
- those covered by reciprocal healthcare agreements, other international obligations, and employees on UK-registered ships.[224]

The structure of the NHS

7.141 As of 1 April 2013, the structure of the NHS in England underwent a radical overhaul by virtue of the Health and Social Care Act (HSCA) 2012.

7.142 The Department of Health is responsible for health and social care policy and legislation.

7.143 Clinical commissioning groups (CCGs) plan and commission healthcare services for their local area. Membership includes GPs,

222 National Health Service (Charges to Overseas Visitors) Regulations 2015 SI No 238 reg 9.

223 The health surcharge was introduced under the Immigration (Health Charge) Order 2015 SI No 792 and is payable from 6 April 2015 by non-EEA nationals who apply for a visa to enter or remain in the UK for a period of more than six months.

224 National Health Service (Charges to Overseas Visitors) Regulations 2015 SI No 238 Part 4.

nurses, lay representatives and hospital doctors. The services they commission include urgent and emergency care; maternity and newborn services; elective hospital care; community health services; mental health; and learning disability services.

7.144 CCGs are supported by:

- Commissioning Support Units, which provide technical and practical support;
- Clinical Senates, which provide independent, strategic advice to inform decision-making; and
- Strategic Clinical Networks, which focus on priority service areas such as cardiovascular health, mental health, maternity, young people and cancer.

7.145 Another commissioning group is NHS England. This is responsible for commissioning specialist care, military healthcare, offender healthcare and primary care. It also regulates, and allocates resources to, the CCGs. This regulatory role includes conducting a performance assessment each financial year to monitor how CCGs have discharged their functions and, in particular, their duties to improve the quality of services and reduce inequalities and expenditure.

7.146 The services commissioned by these bodies are then delivered by a range of organisations. These include:

- GPs, dentists, optometrists, pharmacists, walk-in centres and the NHS 111 service, which provide primary care services;
- acute trusts, which provide secondary care and more specialised services;
- ambulance trusts, which are responsible for emergency care including the NHS 999 service and, in some areas, non-emergency hospital transport and the NHS 111 service;
- mental health trusts; and
- foundation and non-foundation community health trusts, which provide services such as district nurses, health visitors and school nurses.

7.147 Public health, which concerns issues such as disease outbreak prevention, health promotion, major incident response, and research and development, is the responsibility of Public Health England.

7.148 Health and Wellbeing Boards aim to promote the co-operation of leaders in the health and social care system in order to improve care across the different services and reduce health inequalities. Their membership includes locally elected representatives, CCG representatives, Healthwatch England[225] representatives, and the Directors of Adult Social Services and Children's Services.

7.149 Performance within the NHS is monitored and regulated by a variety of organisations. These include: Monitor; the Trust Development Authority; the National Quality Board; the Care Quality Commission (CQC); Healthwatch England; and professional regulatory bodies such as the General Medical Council and the Nursing and Midwifery Council.

Gypsy and Traveller health

7.150 A number of studies have identified higher rates of morbidity and mortality among the Gypsy and Traveller population:

- 66 per cent of Gypsies and Travellers in a recent study reported having bad, very bad or poor health.[226]
- Gypsies and Travellers report the highest levels of perinatal infant mortality of all ethnic minorities in Britain.[227]
- 42 per cent of Gypsies and Travellers have a long-term illness, compared to 18 per cent of the general population.[228]
- Gypsies and Travellers are three times more likely to have a chronic cough or bronchitis, even after smoking is taken into account.[229]
- 22 per cent of Gypsies and Travellers reported suffering from asthma and 34 per cent reported chest pain (compared to five per cent and 22 per cent respectively, of the general population).[230]

225 Healthwatch England was created by HSCA 2012 s181. Healthwatch England is described on its website as 'the independent national champion for people who use health and social care services': www.healthwatch.co.uk/about-us (accessed 28 November 2017).

226 Inclusion Health and the Traveller Movement, *Impact of insecure accommodation and the living environment on Gypsies' and Travellers' health*, 2016.

227 Friends, Families and Travellers, *Annual Report 2010–2011*.

228 G Parry, *The Health status of Gypsies and Travellers in England*, Journal of Epidemiology and Community Health 61:3, pp198–204, as cited in Royal College of General Practitioners and Inclusion Health, *Improving access to health care for Gypsies and Travellers, homeless people and sex workers* (September 2013).

229 G Parry et al (2004), *The Health Status of Gypsies and Travellers in England*, University of Sheffield.

230 G Parry et al (2004), *The Health Status of Gypsies and Travellers in England*, University of Sheffield.

- Gypsies and Travellers are nearly three times more likely than the average to be anxious and over twice as likely to be depressed.[231]
- Health outcomes among Gypsies and Travellers living in bricks and mortar are considerably worse than those living in caravans[232] due to their increased isolation from their community networks and experiences of discrimination from settled neighbours.[233]
- The life expectancy of Gypsies and Travellers has been estimated to be between ten and 12 years less than the general population.[234]
- Irish Travellers are three times more likely to die by suicide than the general population.[235]
- Gypsies and Travellers suffer from poorer health at a younger age – the majority of respondents to a recent study reported their health to be bad or very bad by the time they were in their mid to late thirties.[236]

7.151 There is also evidence that Roma people suffer from similar health inequalities to those identified among Gypsy and Traveller people. This includes a high prevalence of diabetes, cardiovascular disease, premature myocardial infarction, obesity, asthma and mental health issues such as stress, anxiety and depression.[237]

7.152 The health outcomes for Gypsies and Travellers are worse even when compared with socio-economically matched comparators.[238] Gypsies and Travellers experience a range of challenges making access to healthcare difficult:

231 G Parry et al (2004), *The Health Status of Gypsies and Travellers in England*, University of Sheffield.

232 G Parry et al (2004), *The Health Status of Gypsies and Travellers in England*, University of Sheffield.

233 Friends, Families and Travellers, *Inclusion of Gypsy Traveller health needs in Joint Strategic Needs Assessments: A review* (February 2015).

234 P Lane et al, Anglia Ruskin University, *Gypsy, Traveller and Roma: Experts by Experience* (October 2014), p5.

235 M Rose-Walker (2008), *Suicide among the Irish Traveller Community 2000–2006*, Wicklow County Council.

236 Inclusion Health and the Traveller Movement, *Impact of insecure accommodation and the living environment on Gypsies' and Travellers' health*, 2016.

237 EHRC, *England's most disadvantaged groups: Gypsies, Travellers and Roma*, March 2016.

238 National Inclusion Health Board, *Hidden Needs: Identifying Key Vulnerable Groups in Data Collections: Vulnerable Migrants, Gypsies and Travellers, Homeless People, and Sex Workers*, 2014, p27.

- poor living conditions;[239]
- difficulty in registering with a GP, due in particular to some GP practices' (unlawful) insistence on the patient providing proof of identity and proof of a permanent address;[240]
- poor literacy and, for recent migrant Roma communities, poor English, which makes navigating the health system difficult;[241]
- experiencing, or anticipating, racism and discrimination from healthcare providers;[242] and
- a lack of awareness and understanding from health professionals about the beliefs and culture of Gypsy and Traveller communities.[243]

7.153 These difficulties result in an increased reliance on A&E and walk-in centres, which could lead to problems with follow-up care and continuity of care.[244] Gypsies and Travellers are admitted more often to secondary care services and are re-admitted more frequently.[245]

7.154 Research by Friends, Families and Travellers and Northumbria University found that Gypsy and Traveller engagement with health services was improved where the service was provided by outreach workers who had experience of working with Gypsy and Traveller

239 P Lane et al, Anglia Ruskin University, *Gypsy, Traveller and Roma: Experts by Experience* (October 2014), p41.

240 DCLG, *Progress report by the ministerial working group on tackling inequalities experienced by Gypsies and Travellers* (2012). In March 2017 the NHS published a leaflet aimed at Gypsy, Roma, and Traveller communities entitled *How to register with a doctor (GP)*. This stated that 'There is no regulatory requirement to prove identity, address, immigration status or an NHS number in order to register as a patient and no contractual requirement for GPs to request this'. NHS Guidelines are clear that 'If a patient cannot produce any supportive documentation but states that they reside within the practice boundary then practices should accept the registration': NHS England, *Patient Registration: Standard Operating Principles for Primary Medical Care (General Practice)* (November 2015).

241 DCLG, *Progress report by the ministerial working group on tackling inequalities experienced by Gypsies and Travellers* (2012).

242 Royal College of General Practitioners and Inclusion Health, *Improving access to health care for Gypsies and Travellers, homeless people and sex workers* (September 2013) and The Traveller Movement, *The last acceptable form of racism?* (September 2017), p15.

243 DCLG, *Progress report by the ministerial working group on tackling inequalities experienced by Gypsies and Travellers* (2012).

244 DCLG, *Progress report by the ministerial working group on tackling inequalities experienced by Gypsies and Travellers* (2012).

245 Royal College of General Practitioners and Inclusion Health, *Improving access to health care for Gypsies and Travellers, homeless people and sex workers* (September 2013).

communities.[246] However, the creation of specialist services can sometimes lead to a 'siloing' of provision resulting in poorer services and a lack of wider accountability.[247]

7.155 In its report[248] published in April 2019 the Women and Equalities Committee noted that Gypsy, Roma and Traveller people have some of the worst health outcomes of any group; and experience difficulties accessing healthcare services due to discrimination or language and literacy barriers and the fact that service-providers were not considering Gypsy, Roma and Traveller people properly when they design their services. Thus, it was recommended that the EHRC should conduct a formal inquiry under EqA 2006 s16 into how Joint Strategic Needs Assessments are including Gypsy, Roma and Traveller health needs.

Health equality and human rights

7.156 The NHS and its constituent organisations are public bodies and as a consequence they have a duty to comply with the provisions of the ECHR.[249]

7.157 The ECHR does not give individuals an express right to medical treatment. However, it is clear that there could be circumstances where the failure to provide such treatment or the withdrawal of services could amount to a breach of Article 2 (the right to life) and/or Article 3 (the prohibition of inhuman and degrading treatment) of the ECHR.[250] Likewise, negligent treatment could also engage Articles 2 and 3. Moreover, when a person is seeking healthcare it is highly likely that Article 8 (the right to respect for one's private and family life) of the ECHR will also be engaged.[251]

7.158 Further, Article 14 prohibits discrimination on the grounds of (among other things) race; national or social origin; or association with a national minority.[252] It is not a free-standing right but relates

246 Friends, Families and Travellers, *The National Gypsy and Traveller Health Inclusion Project 2012–15.*

247 Friends, Families and Travellers, *The National Gypsy and Traveller Health Inclusion Project 2012–15.*

248 See: https://publications.parliament.uk/pa/cm201719/cmselect/cmwomeq/360/full-report.html.

249 HRA 1998 s6.

250 See, for example, *D v UK* (1997) 24 EHRR 423.

251 See chapter 2 paras 2.27–2.29 and 2.60.

252 See Article 14 in appendix A.

to 'the enjoyment of' the other rights and freedoms set out in the Convention.[253]

7.159 Discrimination is also prohibited under the EqA 2010.[254] A public authority must not directly[255] or indirectly[256] discriminate against a person in respect of a protected characteristic, which includes race.[257] By way of example, refusing to allow a person to register as a patient if they do not have a permanent address may well constitute indirect discrimination against a nomadic Gypsy or Traveller.

7.160 Further, NHS bodies must also comply with the PSED set out at EqA 2010 s149.[258]

7.161 The purpose of the PSED is 'to integrate consideration of equality and good relations into the day-to-day business of public authorities'.[259] The public authority must 'consider how a function can affect different groups in different ways'.[260] The PSED applies not just to policy development and high-level decision-making but also to decisions taken in individual cases.[261]

7.162 The PSED also imposes a number of specific duties on certain public authorities.[262] The organisations subject to the duties include the CQC; Health Education England; Monitor; NHS Blood and Transplant; the NHS Business Services Authority; an NHS foundation trust; CCGs; the NHS Commissioning Board; the National Institute for Health and Care Excellence (NICE); the Health Research Authority; the Health and Social Care Information Centre; and Special Health Authorities. A body subject to the specific duties is required to:

- publish information annually to demonstrate its compliance with the general duty; and

253 See chapter 2 paras 2.122–2.124.

254 See chapter 8 paras 8.50–8.107.

255 EqA 2010 s13.

256 EqA 2010 s19.

257 EqA 2010 s4.

258 See chapter 7 paras 7.100 and 7.106, and chapter 8 paras 8.133–8.159.

259 EHRC, *The Essential Guide to the Public Sector Equality Duty: England (and Non-Devolved Public Authorities in Scotland and Wales)*, July 2014, p8.

260 EHRC, *The Essential Guide to the Public Sector Equality Duty: England (and Non-Devolved Public Authorities in Scotland and Wales)*, July 2014 p8.

261 *Pieretti v Enfield LBC* [2010] EWCA Civ 1104 at 26; EHRC, *The Essential Guide to the Public Sector Equality Duty: England (and Non-Devolved Public Authorities in Scotland and Wales)*, July 2014, p12.

262 Equality Act 2010 (Specific Duties) Regulations 2011 SI No 2260.

- publish specific and measurable objectives every four years that it thinks it should achieve in order to further the aims of the general duty.

7.163 Further, the HSCA 2012 amended the NHSA 2006 to impose a new duty on the secretary of state to have regard to the need to reduce inequalities between the people of England with respect to the benefits that they can obtain from the health service,[263] and upon NHS England[264] and CCGs[265] to have regard to the need to reduce inequalities when exercising their functions.

7.164 Significantly for Gypsies and Travellers, Health and Wellbeing Boards must produce a Joint Strategic Needs Assessment (JSNA) to identify and address local inequalities.[266] This should provide an accurate picture of the demographics and health and social needs of vulnerable groups within their local area and should describe how existing services meet those needs and whether there are any gaps in provision. Having identified those needs, local authorities should then establish a Joint Health and Wellbeing Strategy to determine how those needs will be met and then commission new services to fill any gaps in provision identified by the JSNA.[267] It is clearly vital that the needs of Gypsies and Travellers are included in JSNAs, but one report found that only two out of 33 London boroughs included a chapter on Gypsy and Traveller health needs.[268] Another report noted that the vast majority of Gypsies and Travellers remain living close to their birth place but that many local authorities and local communities still fail to recognise them as having a legitimate right to live and raise their families in the area and concluded that the failure to recognise them as part of the community had a negative effect on planning and accommodation decisions.[269]

263 NHS Act 2006 s1C.

264 NHS Act 2006 s13G.

265 NHS Act 2006 s14T.

266 See Local Government and Public Involvement in Health Act 2007 s116; and HSCA 2012 s196.

267 Royal College of General Practitioners and Inclusion Health, *Improving access to health care for Gypsies and Travellers, homeless people and sex workers* (September 2013).

268 Friends, Families and Travellers, *Inclusion of Gypsy Traveller health needs in Joint Strategic Needs Assessments: A review* (February 2015).

269 Inclusion Health and the Traveller Movement, *Impact of insecure accommodation and the living environment on Gypsies' and Travellers' health*, 2016; and see also the recommendation of the Women and Equalities Committee's report at para 7.154 above.

Community care

7.165 The structure of community care law was fundamentally changed with the passing of the Care Act 2014. Previously, adult social care law had a number of different legislative sources, such as the National Health Service and Community Care Act 1990, the National Assistance Act 1948 and the Chronically Sick and Disabled Persons Act 1971. The Care Act 2014 aimed to consolidate the law in this area into one statute and in addition to enact several significant reforms. Most of Part 1 of the Care Act 2014, which contains the new legal framework for adult social care, came into force on 1 April 2015.

7.166 One notable exception to this consolidating process is found in Mental Health Act 1983 s117, which imposes the duty to provide after-care services to former mental health patients. This has been amended by the Care Act 2014, but remains as a freestanding duty under the Mental Health Act 1983.

7.167 Local authorities are under a general duty, when exercising a function under Care Act 2014 Part 1 in the case of an individual, to promote that individual's well-being,[270] which is said to mean:

- physical and mental health and emotional well-being;
- personal dignity;
- protection from abuse and neglect;
- control by the individual over their daily life;
- participation in work, education, training or recreation;
- social and economic well-being;
- relationships;
- suitability of accommodation; and
- the individual's contribution to society.[271]

In exercising their functions, local authorities must have regard to a number of matters, including the starting assumption that the individual is best-placed to judge their own well-being and the importance of involving the individual as fully as possible in decision-making.[272] These principles establish expectations for how local authorities should exercise their functions but do not require the local authority to take any particular action.[273]

270 Care Act 2014 s1(1).

271 Care Act 2014 s1(2).

272 Care Act 2014 s1(3).

273 DoH, *Care and Support Statutory Guidance: Issued under the Care Act 2014* (updated August 2017), para 1.17.

7.168 Local authorities are also under a general duty to take steps to prevent or delay the development of needs for care and support or to reduce existing needs for care and support[274] and to establish and maintain a service for providing people in its area with information and advice relating to care and support for adults and support for carers.[275]

7.169 Where it appears to a local authority that an adult may have needs for care and support, the authority must carry out a needs assessment of whether or not the adult does have needs and, if so, what those needs are.[276] The threshold to trigger the duty to assess is low and, if met, the local authority cannot refuse to carry out a needs assessment because it thinks the level of need may be low, or that the adult may have significant financial resources.[277] The Care and Support (Assessment) Regulations 2014[278] stipulate how assessments should be conducted. The needs assessment may involve, or be followed by, a financial assessment.[279]

7.170 If the needs assessment process identifies needs[280] for care and support, then the authority must proceed to determine whether any of those needs meet the eligibility criteria.[281] These criteria are set out in the Care and Support (Eligibility Criteria) Regulations 2015.[282] An adult's needs will meet the eligibility criteria if:

- they arise from or are related to a physical or mental impairment or illness;
- as a result of those needs the adult is unable to achieve two or more 'specified outcomes'; and
- as a consequence there is, or is likely to be, a significant impact on the adult's well-being.[283]

The 'specified outcomes' include matters such as:

- managing and maintaining nutrition;

274 Care Act 2014 s2(1).

275 Care Act 2014 s4.

276 Care Act 2014 s9(1).

277 Care Act 2014 s9(3).

278 SI No 2827.

279 Care Act 2014 s17.

280 'Need' means 'something more than merely 'want' but falls far short of 'cannot survive without': *R (Davey) v Oxfordshire CC (EHRC intervening)* [2017] EWHC 254 (Admin) at para 57.

281 Care Act 2014 s13(1).

282 SI No 313.

283 Care and Support (Eligibility Criteria) Regulations 2015 SI No 313 reg 2(1).

- managing toilet needs;
- maintaining personal hygiene;
- maintaining a habitable home environment;
- accessing and engaging in work, training, education or volunteering; or
- carrying out responsibilities for a child.[284]

The local authority must give the adult a written record of their decision, including reasons, on whether or not any of the needs meet the eligibility criteria.[285]

7.171 The local authority will be under an individually enforceable duty to meet any needs which meet the eligibility criteria if the adult is ordinarily resident in their area, or (of particular relevance to Gypsies and Travellers) present in their area but of no settled residence, and if the financial criteria[286] are met.[287]

7.172 'Ordinary residence' was defined in *Barnet LBC ex p Shah* as:

> . . . a man's abode in a particular place or country which he has adopted voluntarily and for settled purposes as part of the regular order of his life for the time being, whether of short or of long duration.[288]

An adult can be ordinarily resident in an area even if their accommodation there is of a temporary nature.[289]

7.173 Any dispute about the area in which the adult is ordinarily resident will be resolved by the secretary of state or a person appointed by him or her.[290] The dispute must not be allowed to disrupt or delay the provision of care to an adult.[291]

7.174 Where the adult's resources are above the financial limit, the local authority may charge them for the costs of providing care and support.[292] The authority also has a power to meet an adult's needs

284 Care and Support (Eligibility Criteria) Regulations 2015 SI No 313 reg 2(2).

285 Care Act 2014 s13(2).

286 Care Act 2014 ss14–18; and the Care and Support (Charging and Assessment of Resources) Regulations 2014 SI No 2672.

287 Care Act 2014 s18.

288 [1982] 2 AC 309 at p343. The situation of adults who lack capacity was considered in *R (Cornwall Council) v Secretary of State for Health* [2015] UKSC 46.

289 *Mohamed v Hammersmith and Fulham LBC* [2001] UKHL 57 at para 18.

290 Care Act 2014 s40.

291 Care and Support (Disputes Between Local Authorities) Regulations 2014 SI No 2829 reg 2.

292 Care Act 2014 ss14–17.

where they do not meet the eligibility criteria, or when the adult is not ordinarily resident in their area.[293]

7.175 Where the local authority is under a duty, or has decided, to meet certain needs then it must prepare a care and support plan which specifies how those needs are going to be met.[294]

7.176 Care Act 2014 s8 gives examples of the way in which needs may be met. These include: accommodation in a care home; care and support at home or in the community; counselling and other types of social work; the provision of goods and facilities; and the provision of information, advice and advocacy.[295]

7.177 A local authority providing care and support to a Gypsy or Traveller must do so in a way which is compliant with their duties under the EqA 2010 and with the HRA 1998. This may mean providing support on a mobile basis or providing accommodation in culturally-appropriate accommodation.

7.178 The provisions relating to adults receiving care who move to or between different local authorities will be of particular relevance to Gypsies and Travellers. Where an adult who is receiving care has a 'genuine' intention to move to the area of a different local authority, the original local authority must provide the new local authority with a copy of the care plan and the most recent needs assessment. The new local authority must carry out a new needs assessment and in doing so must have regard to the original care plan. If the new needs assessment reaches a different conclusion on the adult's needs, a written explanation must be provided.[296] If the new needs assessment has not been completed on the day of the intended move, then the new authority must continue to meet the adult's needs which the original authority has been meeting.[297] If the person receiving care is only temporarily in the area of a different local authority then the area of ordinary residence will not change and this local authority remains responsible for meeting their needs.[298] Where a person splits their time equally between two areas, the question is to which of the two areas the person has the stronger link.[299]

293 Care Act 2014 s19.

294 Care Act 2014 ss25–26.

295 Care Act 2014 s8.

296 Care Act 2014 s37.

297 Care Act 2014 s38.

298 *Care and Support Statutory Guidance: Issued under the Care Act 2014* (updated August 2017), paras 19.71–19.73 and Annex H.

299 *Care and Support Statutory Guidance: Issued under the Care Act 2014* (updated August 2017), para 19.73.

7.179 In cases concerning children, the relevant powers and duties are found in the Children Act 1989. A child will be eligible for support under this Act if they are 'in need' as defined by Children Act 1989 s17(10):

> For the purposes of this Part, a child shall be taken to be in need if:
> (a) he is unlikely to achieve or maintain, or to have the opportunity of achieving or maintaining, a reasonable standard of health or development without the provision for him of services by a local authority under this Part;
> (b) his health or development is likely to be significantly impaired, or further impaired, without the provision for him of such services; or
> (c) he is disabled.

7.180 The terms 'disability', 'development' and 'health' are defined in Children Act 1989 s17:

> (11) For the purposes of this Part, a child is disabled if he is blind, deaf or dumb or suffers from mental disorder of any kind or is substantially and permanently handicapped by illness, injury or congenital deformity or such other disability as may be prescribed; and in this Part–
> 'development' means physical, intellectual, emotional, social or behavioural development; and
> 'health' means physical or mental health.

7.181 Local authorities owe a general duty to children in need as set out at Children Act 1989 s17:

> (1) It shall be the general duty of every local authority (in addition to the other duties imposed on them by this Part)–
> (a) to safeguard and promote the welfare of children within their area who are in need; and
> (b) so far as is consistent with that duty, to promote the upbringing of such children by their families, by providing a range and level of services appropriate to those children's needs.

7.182 Local authorities have a duty to assess children within their area who are or may be in need, as confirmed by the House of Lords in *R (G) v Barnet LBC; R (W) v Lambeth LBC; R (A) v Lambeth LBC*:[300]

> The first step towards safeguarding and promoting the welfare of a child in need by providing services for him and his family is to identify the child's needs for those services. It is implicit in section 17(1) that a local authority will take reasonable steps to assess, for the purposes of the Act, the needs of any child in its area who appears to be in need. Failure to carry out this duty may attract a mandatory order in an appropriate case,

300 [2003] UKHL 57 at 32.

as occurred in *R (AB and SB) v Nottinghamshire County Council* (2001) 4 CCLR 295. Richards J ordered a local authority to carry out a full assessment of a child's needs in accordance with the guidance given by the Secretary of State in 'Framework for the Assessment of Children in Need and their Families (March 2000).

7.183 The duty to assess is triggered by the physical presence of a child in need in a local authority's area and it follows that more than one local authority may be subject to the duty to assess.[301]

7.184 The local authority has a power, but not a duty, to meet the assessed needs.[302] However, the power must be exercised in such a way as to promote the purposes of the statute and any decision not to provide the services 'will no doubt, and not least because a child is involved, be subjected to strict and, it may be, sceptical scrutiny'.[303]

7.185 A case of particular relevance to Gypsies and Travellers is that of *R (J) v Worcestershire CC*.[304] This concerned a child with Down's syndrome, J, whose family were seventh generation fairground travellers and part of the Gypsy community. They spent the winter in the area of the defendant local authority but between February and November would travel, passing through the areas of approximately 16 different authorities. The defendant local authority assessed J as being a child in need but concluded that it had no power to provide services once he had left their area.

7.186 Holman J upheld the judicial review challenge to this decision. The judge began his judgment with the following memorable paragraph:

> Everyone loves a funfair. They are part of the tapestry of our national life. But there would be no funfairs without the travelling families who own the rides and amusements, erect them, man them, and then take them on to the next site or pitch. This case concerns one such family, but all counsel agree and submit that the issue which arises is one of widespread and general importance to all local authorities and many travelling or itinerant families.[305]

301 *R (Stewart) v Wandsworth LBC* [2002] 1 FLR 469.

302 *R (G) v Barnet LBC; R (W) v Lambeth LBC; R (A) v Lambeth LBC* [2003] UKHL 57.

303 *R (VC) v Newcastle City Council* [2012] PTSR 546.

304 [2014] EWCA Civ 1518.

305 *R (J) v Worcestershire CC* [2013] EWHC 3845 (Admin) at para 1.

7.187 Holman J stated later that:

> It must be a hard life and a hard working one, but it is a good life and an honourable one, which brings fun and joy to many people. And it is the life of the family's culture and choosing.[306]

7.188 Holman J concluded that:

> . . . under section 17(1) of the Children Act 1989, pursuant to assessments of the claimant's needs made at times when he is actually present within their area, the Worcestershire County Council do have the *power*, for so long as he remains a child who is a child in need, to provide a range and level of services appropriate to his needs both inside and outside their area, and at times when the claimant is not physically within their area (but is within England and Wales).[307]

7.189 The council's appeal against this decision was dismissed by the Court of Appeal, which held that:

> . . . a purposive construction of section 17 leads to only one result, namely that a local authority has the power to provide services for a child in need who they have assessed regardless of the circumstances which have led to that child being no longer physically present in the area of that local authority.[308]

Environmental health

7.190 Another matter of great concern to Gypsies, Travellers and healthcare practitioners alike is the clear link between the poor living environment and poor health of many Gypsies and Travellers. In 2013, a report by the Royal College of General Practitioners and Inclusion Health identified poor living conditions and environmental factors as the single most influential contributing factor to the poor health status of Gypsies and Travellers.[309] The effect of the living environment and accommodation insecurity on Gypsies' and Travellers' health was considered further in a study produced by Inclusion Health and the Traveller Movement in 2016. The study found that 'the conditions in which members of this group are born, grow, live, work and age contribute significantly to their poor physical and mental health'. In respect of mental health, it was noted that the majority of the respondents to the study who suffered from anxiety

306 *R (J) v Worcestershire CC* [2013] EWHC 3845 (Admin) at para 9.

307 *R (J) v Worcestershire CC* [2013] EWHC 3845 (Admin) at para 55.

308 *R (J) v Worcestershire CC* [2014] EWCA Civ 1518 at para 34.

309 *Improving access to health care for Gypsies and Travellers, homeless people and sex workers* (September 2013).

and depression either lived in conditions where they felt very insecure due to their planning status, the threat of eviction, and/or poor site conditions, or lived reluctantly in bricks and mortar.[310]

7.191 Gypsies and Travellers on unauthorised sites in particular have the poorest access to health care and often greater health needs. Unauthorised sites are likely to be situated in an unhealthy environment on contaminated land or by the roadside. A JSNA review completed in respect of the Brighton and Hove area found that Travellers in the city were four times more likely than the national average to be on an unauthorised site and that the lack of sanitation facilities, waste disposal, clean drinking, and/or electricity had a negative impact on health.[311]

7.192 Frequent evictions also take their toll on health. A JSNA produced in Devon stated that:

> . . . the threat of and the continuing cycle of evictions associated with homelessness among caravan dwellings across Devon and United Kingdom is unacceptable. The cumulative impact of such evictions particularly on children's development whilst under researched is likely to be severe for some children as well as for adults.[312]

Further, those living on unauthorised sites are more likely to experience discrimination and hate crime, leading to anxiety and depression.[313]

7.193 One particular problem for those Gypsies and Travellers without an authorised site results from the lack of access to fresh water. A variety of health problems can result from the lack of water and poor sanitation including skin diseases, gastro-enteritis, hepatitis and other infections. In particular, Gypsies and Travellers on unauthorised sites are more likely to suffer from bowel and bladder problems.[314]

7.194 While there is no statutory duty on local authorities to provide water to those living on unauthorised encampments, Department of Environment (DoE) Circular 18/94,[315] (Welsh Office Circular 76/94),

310 Inclusion Health and the Traveller Movement, *Impact of insecure accommodation and the living environment on Gypsies' and Travellers' health*, 2016.

311 Friends, Families and Travellers, *Inclusion of Gypsy Traveller health needs in Joint Strategic Needs Assessments: A review* (February 2015).

312 Friends, Families and Travellers, *Inclusion of Gypsy Traveller health needs in Joint Strategic Needs Assessments: A review* (February 2015).

313 Inclusion Health and the Traveller Movement, *Impact of insecure accommodation and the living environment on Gypsies' and Travellers' health*, 2016.

314 Friends, Families and Travellers, *The National Gypsy and Traveller Health Inclusion Project 2012–15.*

315 See appendix B.

Gypsy sites policy and unauthorised camping, advises local authorities to consider tolerating the presence of Gypsies and Travellers on temporary or unofficial sites and to examine ways of minimising the level of nuisance on such sites. Local authorities should be encouraged to comply with the advice in DoE Circular 18/94 by providing basic services such as toilets, a refuse skip and a supply of drinking water to those camped on unauthorised sites.[316]

7.195 Alternatively, it may be possible to persuade a local authority to provide water in circumstances where there are children in need living on the site.

7.196 It is not only those living on the roadside that suffer health problems associated with their environment. Gypsies and Travellers living on permanent sites may, paradoxically, experience even worse conditions and resultant health complaints. Permanent sites are often found in isolated and environmentally poor areas (by, or sometimes under, major roads or railways, and often near rubbish dumps, on former industrial sites or close to sewage plants) where health problems can stem from poor air quality, poor drainage and the contamination of land.[317] Common environmental issues experienced by Gypsies and Travellers on both authorised and unauthorised sites include busy roads; noise pollution; poor air quality; proximity to industrial sites; vermin; overcrowding and fire hazards; and poor quality paving or hardstanding.[318]

7.197 Where an authorised caravan site run by a private individual or body is in such a state that it is prejudicial to health or a nuisance, then a resident Gypsy or Traveller is entitled to make a complaint to the local authority. If the local authority is satisfied that a statutory nuisance exists, is likely to occur or is likely to recur in its area, then it has a duty to serve an abatement notice[319] on the 'person' responsible.

316 In a report from the Chartered Institute of Environmental Health, *Travellers and Gypsies: an alternative strategy*, 1995, it was stated that: 'Emergency and temporary unofficial encampments can threaten public health. Local authorities must mitigate against this by providing basic sanitation, wholesome water and by removing refuse.' See also the ODPM *Guidance on managing unauthorised camping*, February 2004 and the ODPM *Guide to effective use of enforcement powers. Part 1: Unauthorised encampments*, 2006. See further chapter 5.

317 See also chapters 3 and 8.

318 Inclusion Health and the Traveller Movement, *Impact of insecure accommodation and the living environment on Gypsies' and Travellers' health*, 2016.

319 Environmental Protection Act (EPA) 1990 s80. See chapter 3, above, for a full discussion of this issue and explanation of the various terms.

Contravention of, or failure to comply with, an abatement notice without reasonable excuse is a criminal offence.[320]

7.198 In a case where a local authority caravan site is in such a state that it is prejudicial to health or a nuisance, then a resident Gypsy or Traveller is entitled to make a complaint to the magistrates' court and request that the statutory nuisance be brought to an end.[321] Failure to comply with such an order is a criminal offence. A resident on a local authority site may also be able to challenge poor site management and maintenance under the Mobile Homes Act (MHA) 1983.[322]

7.199 One factor affecting both authorised and unauthorised sites is fuel poverty. A project by the London Gypsy and Traveller Unit (now known as London Gypsies and Travellers) found that every household surveyed spent more than ten per cent of their income on heating and was therefore in 'some degree of fuel poverty'. The survey also revealed a high incidence of respiratory problems and that 'most households had difficulty keeping warm'.[323] The problem is exacerbated for older Gypsies and Travellers by the difficulties of claiming the winter fuel allowance without a permanent address.[324]

Medical records, privacy and the ECHR

7.200 An individual has a right to access their medical records under the Data Protection Act (DPA) 1998 s7. This includes the right: to be told whether any personal data are being held about them; to be given a description of the data; the purpose for which they are held and the recipients to whom they may be disclosed; and to have communicated to them in an intelligible form the content of that data and their source.[325] Data includes any recorded information held by a public authority[326] and specifically includes health records.[327]

7.201 An individual can always make an informal request to see, or obtain copies of, their medical records. However, in order to exercise their statutory right to access, they must make a written application.[328]

320 EPA 1990 s80(4).

321 EPA 1990 s82.

322 See chapter 3.

323 London Gypsy Traveller Unit, *Health through warmth community project.*

324 Friends, Families and Travellers, *Inclusion of Gypsy Traveller health needs in Joint Strategic Needs Assessments: A review* (February 2015).

325 DPA 1998 s7(1).

326 DPA 1998 s1(1).

327 DPA 1998 ss1(1) and 68(1).

328 DPA 1998 s7(2)(a).

7.202 The data controller may require payment of a fee for providing the information.[329] The maximum fee payable is prescribed by regulations and is currently £10 or, where a hard copy is sought (and the request does not relate exclusively to data which are processed automatically), £50.[330]

7.203 If the data controller reasonably requires further information in order to satisfy himself or herself of the identity of the person making the request and to locate the information sought, and has informed the applicant of that requirement, then the data controller is not obliged to comply with the request unless he or she is supplied with that information.[331]

7.204 Where a valid request has been made, the data controller must comply with it promptly and in any event within 40 days.[332]

7.205 There are, however, a number of exceptions to the duty to provide disclosure under the DPA 1998. For example, disclosure need not be provided of material that would be likely to prejudice criminal investigations,[333] national security[334] or where the disclosure would be likely to cause serious harm to the physical or mental health of the data subject or another person.[335] Further, where a data controller cannot comply with a request without disclosing information relating to another identifiable individual, he or she is not obliged to give disclosure unless the other individual has consented to the disclosure or it is reasonable to comply without their consent.[336] However, this does not excuse a data controller from providing as much of the information as can be communicated without disclosing the identity of the other individual.[337]

7.206 If a data controller does not comply with the request, the applicant may apply to the county court or High Court for an order compelling the data controller to comply with the request.[338]

7.207 Where a person seeks disclosure of the medical records of someone who is deceased, the application is made under the Access

329 DPA 1998 s7(2)(b).

330 Data Protection (Subject Access) (Fees and Miscellaneous Provisions) Regulations 2000 SI No 191.

331 DPA 1998 s7(3).

332 DPA 1998 s7(8), (10).

333 DPA 1998 s29.

334 DPA 1998 s28.

335 Data Protection (Subject Access Modification) (Health) Order 2000 SI No 413.

336 DPA 1998 s7(4).

337 DPA 1998 s7(5).

338 DPA 1998 ss7(9) and 15.

to Health Records Act 1990. The application can only be made by the deceased person's personal representative or by someone who may have a claim arising out of the deceased person's death.[339]

7.208 The protection of medical data and records falls within Article 8 of the ECHR. It was stated by the ECtHR in *Z v Finland*[340] that:

> . . . the protection of personal data, not least medical data, is of fundamental importance to a person's enjoyment of his or her right to respect for private and family life as guaranteed by Article 8 of the Convention. Respecting the confidentiality of health data is a vital principle in the legal systems of all the Contracting Parties to the Convention. It is crucial not only to respect the sense of privacy of a patient but also to preserve his or her confidence in the medical profession and in the health services in general.

7.209 The ECtHR also held that any state measures compelling the disclosure of medical information without the patient's consent would 'call for the most careful scrutiny'.[341]

7.210 Disclosure of confidential medical files without a patient's consent may well constitute both a breach of the patient's Article 8 rights and a breach of the DPA 1998 which is actionable under HRA 1998 s6 or DPA 1998 s13. Likewise, any decision taken by a public body to restrict the disclosure of an individual's medical reports will engage Article 8 and it should be possible to challenge such a decision by way of judicial review where it can be said that the restriction is unreasonable or disproportionate.[342]

Legal aid

7.211 Legal aid is available subject to means and merits tests, for a variety of healthcare law matters, including:[343]

- Community care services – Legal aid is available in respect of community care matters, such as challenges under Care Act 2014 Part 1 and Children Act 1989 s17.
- Judicial review – Legal aid is available for applications to bring a judicial review of a public authority's act, decision or omission.
- Discrimination – Legal aid is available to challenge contraventions of the EqA 2010.

339 Access to Health Records Act 1990 s3(1).

340 (1998) 25 EHRR 371 at para 95.

341 (1998) 25 EHRR 371 at para 96.

342 See, for example, *Gaskin v UK* (1989) 12 EHRR 36.

343 Legal Aid, Sentencing and Punishment of Offenders Act 2012 Sch 1.

- Human rights – Legal aid is available in respect of a claim in tort or for damages alleging a significant breach of ECHR rights by a public authority.
- Environmental protection – Legal aid is available to seek injunctions to stop nuisance arising from certain prescribed types of pollution.
- Mental health – Legal aid is available for matters relating to the Mental Health Act 1983 and the Mental Capacity Act 2005.

Conclusion

7.212 In 2016, the EHRC published a report entitled *England's most disadvantaged groups: Gypsies, Travellers and Roma* in which it was noted that:

> Some people in our society are being left further behind because they face particular barriers in accessing important public services and are locked out of opportunities.[344]

Proper access to education and healthcare is central to enabling Gypsies, Travellers and Roma to achieve their full potential. Further work is needed to ensure that members of this vulnerable minority are not denied the rights enjoyed by others in our society.

344 EHRC, *England's most disadvantaged groups: Gypsies, Travellers and Roma*, March 2016.

CHAPTER 8

Using domestic legislation to tackle race discrimination

continued

Introduction

8.1 This chapter will explain how domestic equality legislation can be used to tackle race discrimination suffered by Gypsies, Travellers and Roma. It should be read in conjunction with chapter 2 which highlights the key provisions of the European Convention on Human Rights (ECHR), the European Union's Charter of Fundamental Rights and other international treaties and conventions which can also be used to protect and promote the rights of Gypsies, Travellers and Roma.

Prejudice and discrimination suffered by Gypsies, Travellers and Roma

8.2 On 27 January 2017, the 72nd anniversary of the day Soviet troops liberated the Nazi death camp at Auschwitz-Birkenau was commemorated. The Nazis murdered six million Jews in the Holocaust. Yet there was little mention of the hundreds of thousands of Roma and Sinti people that were also murdered by the Nazis during World War II, in what has become known as the Porrajmos (the 'Devouring').[1]

8.3 How were the Nazis able to commit these terrible crimes with impunity? The Nazi propaganda machine played a very significant role by reinforcing age old prejudices. Roma and Sinti were made scapegoats, blamed for the ills of society, dehumanised and characterised or stereotyped as anti-social thieves and vagabonds. The propaganda campaign worked – the settled population were conditioned to believe what they were being told (by what would now clearly be understood as 'hate speech'[2]) and there was little opposition when Roma and Sinti were rounded up before being transported to camps from which they would never return.

8.4 More than 70 years later, the horror of the Nazi concentration camps is hard to imagine, but the widespread prejudice that Roma

1 Though Sinti people do not refer to themselves as Roma; they share many of the some customs and beliefs as Roma.

2 The Council of Europe's Committee of Minsters' Recommendation 97(20) defined the term in the following way:

> [T]he term 'hate speech' shall be understood as covering all forms of expression which spread, incite, promote or justify racial hatred, xenophobia, anti-Semitism or other forms of hatred based on intolerance, including: intolerance expressed by aggressive nationalism and ethnocentrism, discrimination and hostility against minorities, migrants and people of immigrant origin.

face in Europe (known as 'anti-Gypsyism' or 'Romaphobia') has not abated and is an unwelcome fact of their daily lives. Politicians throughout Europe continue to use hate speech against Roma. This in turn creates a climate in which racist violence is thought acceptable by offenders and, tragically, in recent years, Roma have been the victims of violent racist attacks and murder. For example, in 2012 a Slovakian policeman shot dead three Roma and severely injured two more in a killing spree which he said was motivated by a desire to 'solve the Roma problem'. In 2013, four men with links to nationalist organisations were jailed in Hungary for nine separate attacks on Roma and the murder of six people. Meanwhile, Roma continue to be forcibly evicted from their homes without the provision of suitable alternative accommodation, their children continue to suffer segregation in schools and they tend to live on the margins of society.

8.5 Here in the United Kingdom (UK), Romani Gypsies, Travellers and Roma migrants are among the most discriminated ethnic groups, routinely targeted by those using hate speech both online[3] and in other media platforms.

8.6 While Gypsies and Travellers have been living in the UK for hundreds of years, they remain one of the most disadvantaged racial groups in our society – with low levels of life expectancy; high vulnerability to serious illness; poor mental health; high child mortality rates; and low levels of educational attainment and literacy. A key contributor to the poor socio-economic status of Gypsies and Travellers is that thousands of families still have no lawful place to station their caravans and live their traditional way of life. Meeting the accommodation needs of Gypsies and Travellers should be a relatively simple task, but in the face of widespread prejudice among the settled population, there has been little political will to introduce legislation to achieve that goal. Meanwhile, those Gypsies and Travellers without lawful sites continue to face eviction and a forced nomadic life in which children cannot attend school and healthcare needs are not properly addressed.

8.7 Romani Gypsies, Irish Travellers and Scottish and Welsh Gypsy Travellers are all entitled to protection from discrimination under our equality legislation. However, although this legislation has been in force for decades and has developed considerably to protect against increasingly subtle forms of discrimination, Gypsies and Travellers

3 By way of example, a recent survey showed that Romani Gypsies and Travellers were the number one targets of hate speech on twitter – see: www.wired.co.uk/news/archive/2014–06/18/hatebrain-stats-uk.

still experience discrimination of the most overt kind. By way of example, 'No blacks, no Irish, no dogs' signs disappeared long ago, but 'No Travellers' signs, used intentionally to exclude Gypsies and Travellers, are still widespread.

8.8 In 2004, Trevor Phillips, the then Chair of the Commission for Racial Equality (CRE), compared the prejudice experienced by Gypsies and Travellers living in the UK to that of black people living in the American Deep South in the 1950s; and in 2005, Sarah Spencer, a CRE Commissioner, drew further attention to their plight in an article entitled 'Gypsies and Travellers: Britain's forgotten minority':[4]

> The European Convention on Human Rights ... was a key pillar of Europe's response to the Nazi holocaust in which half a million Gypsies were among those who lost their lives. The Convention is now helping to protect the rights of this community in the United Kingdom ...
>
> The majority of the 15,000 caravans that are homes to Gypsy and Traveller families in England are on sites provides by local authorities, or which are privately owned with planning permission for this use. But the location and condition of these sites would not be tolerated for any other section of society. 26 per cent are situated next to, or under, motorways, 13 per cent next to runways. 12 per cent are next to rubbish tips, and 4 per cent adjacent to sewage farms. Tucked away out of sight, far from shops and schools, they can frequently lack public transport to reach jobs and essential services. In 1997, 90 per cent of planning applications from Gypsies and Travellers were rejected, compared to a success rate of 80 per cent for all other applications ... 18 per cent of Gypsies and Travellers were homeless in 2003 compared to 0.6 per cent of the population ... Lacking sites on which to live, some pitch on land belonging to others; or on their own land but lacking permission for caravan use. There follows a cycle of confrontation and eviction, reluctant travel to a new area, new encampment, confrontation and eviction. Children cannot settle in school. Employment and health care are disrupted. Overt discrimination remains a common experience ... There is a constant struggle to secure the bare necessities, exacerbated by the inability of many adults to read and write, by the reluctance of local officials to visit sites, and by the isolation of these communities from the support of local residents ... But we know that these are communities experiencing severe disadvantage. Infant mortality is twice the national average and life expectancy at least 10 years less than that of others in their generation.

4 [2005] EHRLR 335.

Reports and strategies on tackling inequalities and improving integration

Common Ground

8.9 In an attempt to improve the situation, in 2005 the CRE conducted a major research project into how local authorities in England and Wales were promoting equality of opportunity and good race relations in their work relating to site provision for Romani Gypsies and Irish Travellers. The findings of that research were published in the report, *Common Ground: Equality, Good Race Relations and Sites for Gypsies and Irish Travellers*.[5]

8.10 The inquiry included:

- the analysis of the answers to a detailed three-part questionnaire which had been sent to all 410 local authorities in England and Wales, and which resulted in a response rate of 58 per cent;
- a detailed on-site analysis in nine local authority areas, comprising document analysis, interviews with local authority staff and councillors, relevant police, education and health officials, local Gypsies and Irish Travellers and local residents;
- a public call for evidence, resulting in the consideration of 403 responses from police forces, health authorities, Traveller education support services, Gypsies and Travellers and other interested parties.

8.11 The report identified areas of good practice in every area. A few local authorities showed strong leadership on the issue of Gypsy and Traveller sites: some had taken steps to encourage relationships of trust to develop between those living on Gypsy and Traveller sites and local residents; some resourced and managed sites well; and there was evidence of local authorities assisting Gypsies and Travellers to identify land to buy to establish their own sites.

8.12 However, overall, the inquiry gave cause for concern. The report showed that Gypsies and Travellers passed through almost every local authority in England and Wales (91 per cent), and that in over a tenth of local authorities they were the largest ethnic minority group. Despite those facts, the vast majority of local authorities had done little to address the inequalities faced by Gypsies and Travellers.

8.13 One of the most important points of concern which the report identified was the significant community tension relating to the

5 See: www.compas.ox.ac.uk/media/ER–2005-Gypsies_Irish_Travellers_Equality_CRE.pdf.

establishment of Gypsy and Traveller sites; this issue was acknowledged by the majority of local authorities (67 per cent), but few had taken steps to promote good race relations or taken any other action to investigate and address the root causes of the community tension.

8.14 The vast majority of local authorities that reported community tension said that unauthorised encampments were a cause (94 per cent), while almost half also pointed to planning applications and enforcement as another cause (46 per cent). While the CRE's findings on this point were not surprising, it is disturbing to note that only a tenth of local authorities had identified unauthorised encampments as an issue relevant to race equality and race relations in their statutory race equality schemes. While recognising that tensions centre on problems resulting from the lack of authorised Gyspy and Traveller sites, only a small proportion had adequately assessed site needs (34 per cent), and fewer still had developed concrete plans to provide sites, or taken steps to facilitate private provision. This community tension tended to generate considerable public resistance to providing any more public and private sites, thereby creating a vicious circle.

8.15 The report also identified organisational problems in relation to Gypsy and Traveller sites. It showed a notable lack of council leadership on the issue of Gypsy and Traveller sites at either councillor or officer level, and weak organisational arrangements. Frequently, there was found to be a lack of joined-up working between different departments with responsibility for Gypsy and Traveller sites, leading to counterproductive effects. Often, those with specific responsibility for working with those on Gypsy and Traveller sites were insufficiently senior to have an impact and were separated from mainstream functions. There was an overall lack of coherent policy framework in relation to Gypsy and Traveller sites, not helped by a failure to collect sufficient data and to conduct meaningful consultation before policies were formulated.

8.16 The inquiry was not a formal investigation and the report's conclusions had no legal implications. Nevertheless, the CRE made 56 recommendations for change which were designed to help achieve the goal of replacing:

> . . . the vicious circle of unmet need and public hostility . . . with a sustainable approach to planning, providing and managing Gypsy sites in England and Wales.

The recommendations were aimed at the government, local authorities, police forces and other key organisations with a role to play in the provision and management of Gypsy and Traveller sites and were drafted in an attempt to help public bodies comply with their race equality duty in relation to Gypsies and Travellers.

8.17 After its formation the CRE's successor, the Equality and Human Rights Commission (EHRC) reviewed the position of Gypsies and Travellers in our society and its findings in *Common Ground* and in 2009 it published two further reports: *Inequalities experienced by Gypsy and Traveller communities: A review*;[6] and *Gypsies and Travellers; simple solutions for living together.*[7]

8.18 The aim of the *Inequalities* report was to draw together the evidence from across a wide range of Gypsies' and Travellers' experiences in order to set out clearly the full extent of the inequalities and discrimination they face in our society.

8.19 In the executive summary of the *Inequalities* report, its authors stated that:

> Racism towards most ethnic minority groups is now hidden, less frequently expressed in public, and widely seen as unacceptable. However, that towards Gypsies and Travellers is still common, frequently overt and seen as justified. Abusive media coverage and overtly racist statements from local and national politicians add to the ignorance and prejudice of many members of the settled population, while those in authority frequently fail to challenge them. Complaints abound from members of the communities included in this review: of services being not welcoming or refused; of employment offers being withdrawn; and of people being harassed in or dismissed from employment. While Gypsies and Travellers have experienced such hostility for centuries, what is remarkable – and shameful – is that this continues in the present day, despite a wealth of legislation to promote equality and human rights and protect against discrimination.

8.20 The authors of the *Inequalities* report noted that the lack of suitable, secure accommodation underpins many of the inequalities that Gypsy and Traveller communities experience:

> Many Gypsies and Travellers are caught between an insufficient supply of suitable accommodation on the one hand, and the insecurity of unauthorised encampments and developments on the other: they then face a cycle of evictions, typically linked to violent and threatening behaviour from private bailiff companies. Roadside stopping places, with no facilities and continued instability and trauma, become part of the way of life.

6 See: www.equalityhumanrights.com/sites/default/files/documents/research/12inequalities_experienced_by_gypsy_and_traveller_communities_a_review.pdf.

7 See: www.equalityhumanrights.com/en/gypsies-and-travellers-simple-solutions-living-together.

Health deteriorates, while severe disruptions occur to access to education for children, healthcare services and employment opportunities. In order to avoid the eviction cycle or to access vital services, many families reluctantly accept the alternative of local authority housing. They are however, typically housed on the most deprived estates, sharing the wider environmental disadvantages of their neighbours and exposed to more direct and immediate hostility focused on their ethnicity or lifestyle. This also involves dislocation from their families, communities, culture and support systems, leading to further cycles of disadvantage.

8.21 The authors of the *Inequalities* report also highlighted a number of other key areas of concern from among the severe, wide-ranging and mutually reinforcing inequalities and problems faced by Gypsies and Travellers, including the fact that:

- they tend to die earlier than the rest of the population;
- they experience worse health, yet are less likely to receive effective, continuous healthcare;
- their children's educational achievements are worse, and declining still further (contrary to the national trend);
- their children's participation in secondary education is extremely low; and discrimination and abusive behaviour on the part of school staff and other students are frequently cited as reasons for children and young people leaving education at an early age;
- there is a lack of access to pre-school, out-of-school and leisure services for children and young people;
- there is an unquantified but substantial negative psychological impact on children who experience repeated brutal evictions, family tensions associated with insecure lifestyles, and an unending stream of overt and extreme hostility from the wider population;
- employment rates are low, and poverty high;[8]
- there is an increasing problem of substance abuse among unemployed and disaffected young people;
- there are high suicide rates among the Gypsy and Traveller communities;
- within the criminal justice system, because of a combination of unfair treatment at different stages and other inequalities affecting the communities, there is a process of accelerated criminalisation at a young age, leading rapidly to custody;

8 Issues which were subsequently addressed by Andrew Ryder and Dr Margaret Greenfields in the Irish Traveller Movement in Britain report entitled *Roads to Success: Routes to Economic and Social Inclusion for Gypsies and Travellers* (2010) – see: www.travellermovement.org.uk/wp-content/uploads/2014/01/Roads-to-Success-Economic-and-Social-Inclusion-for-Gypsies-and-Travellers-report-.pdf.

- policy initiatives and political systems that are designed to promote inclusion and equality frequently exclude Gypsies and Travellers;
- there is a lack of access to culturally appropriate support services for people in the most vulnerable situations, such as women experiencing domestic violence;
- Gypsies' and Travellers' culture and identity receive little or no recognition, with consequent and considerable damage to their self-esteem.

8.22 The authors of the *Inequalities* report recorded the fact that many members of the Gypsy and Traveller communities were striving to address their problems and stand up for their rights and that Gypsy and Traveller organisations were responsible for a number of initiatives designed to tackle inequalities. In addition, it was noted that some local authorities had worked together with Gypsy and Traveller communities to produce 'myth-busting' information in order to provide the general public with more accurate information about the lifestyles and needs of the communities, and to combat ignorance and hostility.

8.23 However, the authors of the *Inequalities* report considered the problems to be immense and recommended that public bodies and private organisations with which Gypsies and Travellers have contact take urgent action to ensure that Gypsies and Travellers have access to the same services and can exercise the same rights as the rest of the population.

8.24 The EHRC report *Gypsies and Travellers; simple solutions for living together* focused on caravan site provision, and highlighted examples of good practice by local authorities and the business case for making adequate provision. The report made it clear that political will and leadership at a national and local level is essential if progress is to be made on this issue. The report noted that media coverage of Gypsy and Traveller issues often focuses on environmental damage and community tensions caused by unauthorised encampments, and suggested that with proper provision in place, the issue would drop down the agenda, opening up opportunities for more positive representations of the Gypsy and Traveller communities. The report also noted that Gypsy and Traveller groups are very diverse, and often have different needs and agendas; and that even well intentioned local authorities often struggle to consult and include Gypsies and Travellers in their policy-making and service provision. As a consequence, local authorities were advised to provide training for their staff and learn from examples of best practice around the country.

National Roma integration strategies

8.25 In April 2011, the European Commission published *An EU Framework for National Roma Integration Strategies up to 2020* (the 'Framework for National Roma Integration Strategies').[9] It emphasised the need for national strategies to address the four EU Roma integration goals of inclusion in education, employment, health and housing across the EU. The Framework states that it is 'crucial . . . to ensure that national, regional and local policies focus on Roma in a clear and specific way, and address the needs of Roma with explicit measures to prevent and compensate for disadvantages they face'. To this end, EU member states were asked to submit by the end of 2011 National Roma Integration Strategies (NRISs), which specify how they will contribute to the achievement of the Framework goals. The Framework states that NRISs are required to set 'achievable national goals for Roma integration' and to identify disadvantaged regions where communities are most deprived. It was expected that sufficient funding would be allocated from national budgets which could be complemented by EU funding, with 26.5 billion euros available to support social inclusion. Importantly, the NRISs were to be designed 'in close cooperation and continuous dialogue' with Roma non-governmental organisations (NGOs) and other stakeholders.

8.26 The government's Ministerial Working Group (MWG) on preventing and tackling inequalities experienced by Gypsies and Travellers was given the task of addressing the Framework's requirements. Rather than produce a NRIS, the government provided the Commission with a collection of documents which it considered satisfied the requirements of the Framework. In relation to England, the government provided the EU with the *Progress report by the ministerial working group on tackling inequalities experienced by Gypsies and Travellers*[10] which contained 28 'proposed commitments' across a range of departments and its general integration strategy for minority communities, entitled *Creating the conditions for integration*. The

9 In the Framework the term 'Roma' is used, as it is by the Council of Europe and the EU, collectively to include Roma, Sinti, Kale and other related groups in Europe, as well as ethnic minorities that identify themselves as Romani Gypsies, Irish Travellers and Welsh and Scottish Gypsy Travellers.

10 See: www.gov.uk/government/uploads/system/uploads/attachment_data/file/6287/2124046.pdf.

government's submissions with regard to the position in Scotland and Northern Ireland consisted of a summary of a range of policies, without an overarching framework; while the government's submission with regard to Wales was based upon the Welsh government's own framework *'Travelling to a Better Future': A Gypsy and Traveller Framework for Action and Delivery Plan.*[11]

8.27 In an address to the European Platform for Roma inclusion on 22 March 2012, Viviane Reding, the Vice-President of the European Commission, made a preliminary assessment of the NRISs submitted by member states. Ms Reding emphasised the 'general need to apply a comprehensive approach' with 'strong coordination and monitoring' and indicated 'that there is still a lot of room for improvement'; she also placed particular emphasis on the needs of women and children.

8.28 The European Commission subsequently published a Communication reviewing the NRISs submitted by member states.[12] The Communication tends to focus on the positives, rather than the negatives and highlights examples of best practice. However, a careful reading shows the UK's response to the Framework is lacking in key areas: in healthcare, for example, the UK fails to satisfy any of the four basic measures required by the Framework; while in relation to employment, the UK is assessed as endorsing the general goal of the Framework, but only satisfying one out of the seven specific measures the Framework requires. Perhaps a point of even greater concern, not identified by the EU in its Communication, was the fact that the UK's response said nothing about the integration of non-indigenous Roma, despite the fact that the size of that community in the UK may well exceed 300,000 people.[13]

8.29 In its Communication, the EU Commission also criticises all those member states, including the UK, that have failed to allocate

11 See: http://learning.gov.wales/docs/learningwales/publications/121115gypsytravelleren.pdf.

12 National Roma Integration Strategies: a first step in the implementation of the EU Framework (2012) at: http://ec.europa.eu/justice/discrimination/files/roma_nat_integration_strat_en.pdf.

13 See also *Civil Society Monitoring on the Implementation of the National Roma Integration Strategy in the United Kingdom in 2012 and 2013* (Ryder and Cemlyn, 2014) – www.birmingham.ac.uk/Documents/college-social-sciences/social-policy/iris/2014/UK-civil-society-monitoring-report-en–1.pdf; and *Experts by experience: Gypsy, Traveller and Roma: Reviewing UK Progress on the European Union Framework for National Roma Integration Strategies* (Lane, Spencer and Jones, 2014) – www.birmingham.ac.uk/Documents/college-social-sciences/social-policy/iris/2014/Experts-by-Experience—JRTF-Report-Oct–2014.pdf.

sufficient funds to their NRISs and recommended that member states should show a clear commitment to securing their financing up to 2020. Whether the UK will abide by this recommendation remains to be seen.

8.30 In 2013, Raquel Rolnik, the United Nations Special Rapporteur on adequate housing, issued her report on the UK,[14] in which she noted that:

> 69. The lack of appropriate and culturally adequate residential and transit accommodation is often at the root of the stigma and discrimination faced by Gypsies and Travellers in the United Kingdom, underpinning a range of other problems, from access to education or work to appropriate health care or inclusion in community life.[15] There are concerns about the quality and location of sites, such as those under motorways or next to sewage works. Many Gypsies and Travellers are caught between an insufficient supply of suitable accommodation on the one hand, and the insecurity of unauthorized encampments and developments on the other. They face a cycle of evictions, linked to violent and threatening behaviour. In order to avoid evictions or to gain access to services, many households reluctantly accept housing in buildings, which is culturally inadequate. They are, however, often housed in the most deprived estates and exposed to more direct and immediate hostility focused on their ethnicity or lifestyle.[16]

And she recommended that the government:

> Strengthen efforts to address stigma and discrimination for the Gypsy and Traveller communities in relation to the wider spectrum of rights, starting with the recognition that cultural adequacy in housing is a pillar for inclusion, and that legislation and policy are not enough to overcome local obstacles; and
>
> . . .
>
> Promote and protect the right to adequate housing without discrimination on any grounds; in particular, refrain from establishing mechanisms that can result in indirect discrimination against migrants or Roma in access to adequate housing.

14 *Report of the Special Rapporteur on adequate housing as a component of the right to an adequate standard of living, and on the right to non-discrimination in this context* at: www.ohchr.org/EN/HRBodies/HRC/. . ./A_HRC_25_54_Add.2_ENG.DOC.

15 EHRC, submission to the Committee on the Elimination of Racial Discrimination on the eighteenth to twentieth periodic reports of the United Kingdom (2011), pp60–70.

16 EHRC, submission to the Committee on the Elimination of Racial Discrimination on the eighteenth to twentieth periodic reports of the United Kingdom (2011), pp60–70.

8.31 In 2015, the EHRC published a report entitled *Is Britain Fairer*[17] and in 2016 it published *Is England Fairer*[18] and a spotlight report entitled *England's most disadvantaged groups: Gypsies, Travellers and Roma.*[19] In the latter report, the EHRC identified the most up-to-date evidence and statistics on the education, employment, living standards, health and imprisonment of Gypsies, Travellers and Roma,[20] as well the negative attitudes and hostility that they experience from the general public, police and other authorities, fuelled by political rhetoric and the media. Having done so, the EHRC concluded that little had changed since the *Inequalities* report had been published in 2009.[21]

The Equality and Human Rights Commission

8.32 The Equality Act (EqA) 2006 established the EHRC. The new Commission took over the responsibilities previously fulfilled by the CRE, the Disability Rights Commission and, in October 2007, the Equal Opportunities Commission. In addition, the EHRC was given powers and duties as a national human rights institution.

8.33 EqA 2006 s3 provides that:

> The [EHRC] shall exercise its functions ... with a view to encouraging and supporting the development of a society in which–
> (a) people's ability to achieve their potential is not limited by prejudice or discrimination,
> (b) there is respect for and protection of each individual's human rights,
> (c) there is respect for the dignity and worth of each individual,
> (d) each individual has an equal opportunity to participate in society, and
> (e) there is mutual respect between groups based on understanding and valuing of diversity and on shared respect for equality and human rights.

17 See: www.equalityhumanrights.com/en/britain-fairer/britain-fairer-report.

18 See: www.equalityhumanrights.com/sites/default/files/is_england_fairer.pdf.

19 See: www.equalityhumanrights.com/sites/default/files/ief_gypsies_travellers_and_roma.pdf.

20 See *Overlooked and Overrepresented: Gypsy, Traveller and Roma children in the youth justice system* (Traveller Movement, 2016) – http://travellermovement.org.uk/wp-content/uploads/Overlooked-and-Overrepresented-Gypsy-Traveller-and-Roma-children-in-the-youth-justice-system.pdf. See also *Voices Unheard – A Study of Irish Travellers in Prison* (Mac Gabhann, 2011) – www.irishchaplaincy.org.uk/Publisher/File.aspx?ID=81554.

21 See also the Women and Equalities Committee's report entitled *Tackling inequalities faced by Gypsy, Roma and Traveller communities* (2019) – https://publications.parliament.uk/pa/cm201719/cmselect/cmwomeq/360/full-report.html.

8.34 The EHRC has a duty to use its powers to:

- promote and encourage good practice and an awareness of rights about equality;
- promote understanding of diversity and human rights and work towards the elimination of unlawful discrimination and harassment;[22]
- monitor the effectiveness of the equality and human rights enactments;[23] and
- identify changes that have taken place in society or are expected to occur which are relevant to its duties under EqA 2006 ss8 and 9 and the results that our society should aim to achieve for the purpose of encouraging and supporting the development of a society which the EHRC seeks to promote.[24]

8.35 The EHRC has the power to issue statutory guidance on public functions and associations. Courts and tribunals considering the obligations and duties imposed by equality legislation are obliged to consider any part of the statutory guidance which appear to be relevant to proceedings before them.[25] So far three codes of practice have been issued: on equal pay; employment; and services, public functions and associations. In the light of the government's decision not to lay further codes before parliament, additional draft codes of practice have been published as 'technical guidance'. These draft codes include information on: the public sector equality duty (PSED); schools and further and higher education; age discrimination in services; and public functions and associations.

8.36 The EHRC's general enforcement powers are outlined later in this chapter.

Race discrimination: the domestic legal framework

8.37 On 1 October 2010, the Equality Act (EqA) 2010 came into force. It consolidated many separate pieces of equality legislation already on our statute books,[26] including the Race Relations Act (RRA) 1976,

22 EqA 2006 ss8 and 9.
23 EqA 2006 s11.
24 EqA 2006 s12.
25 EqA 2006 s15(4).
26 Including legislation which transposed EU equality law, such as the Race Equality Directive 2000/43/EC, into domestic law – see chapter 2 para 2.255–2.258.

and brought in a number of new provisions which are intended to clarify and strengthen equality law in Great Britain.[27]

8.38 The EqA 2010 provided a generalised and harmonised approach to anti-discrimination legislation. Central to the operation of the Act is the concept of 'protected characteristics', that is:

- age;
- disability;
- gender reassignment;
- marriage and civil partnership;
- pregnancy and maternity;
- race;
- religion or belief;
- sex; and
- sexual orientation.[28]

The EqA 2010 is designed to address discrimination on the grounds of these protected characteristics.[29]

8.39 EqA 2010 ss5–12 set out further particulars of each protected characteristic. In relation to race, section 9 states:

> **Race**
> (1) Race includes–
> (a) colour;
> (b) nationality;
> (c) ethnic or national origins.
> (2) In relation to the protected characteristic of race–
> (a) a reference to a person who has a particular protected characteristic is a reference to a person of a particular racial group;
> (b) a reference to persons who share a protected characteristic is a reference to persons of the same racial group.
> (3) A racial group is a group of persons defined by reference to race; and a reference to a person's racial group is a reference to a racial group into which the person falls.
> (4) The fact that a racial group comprises two or more distinct racial groups does not prevent it from constituting a particular racial group.

27 It should be noted that the EqA 2006 remains in force, albeit as amended by the EqA 2010 and the Enterprise and Regulatory Reform Act 2013. It should also be noted that the provisions of the EqA 2010 do not generally apply to Northern Ireland.

28 EqA 2010 s4.

29 EqA 2010 s14 made provision for prohibiting discrimination on the basis of a combination of two protected characteristics; however, the section has not been brought into force.

8.40 This chapter focuses on the provisions relating to race (and ethnicity) rather than upon the other protected characteristics. It is important to note that EqA 2010 s9 allows a racial group to consist of two or more distinct racial subgroups. A racial group may also be defined by reference to more than one racial characteristic under the Act (for example, Black Britons.)[30]

Racial groups – protection for Gypsies and Travellers

8.41 The EqA 2010 protects all racial groups from discrimination. The criteria for determining whether a group constitutes an ethnic group are set out in the House of Lords judgment in the case of *Mandla (Sewa Singh) v Dowell Lee.*[31] The Lords held that to constitute an 'ethnic group' under the then in force RRA 1976, a group had to regard itself, and be regarded by others, as a distinct community by virtue of certain characteristics. Two essential factors are:

- a long, shared history, of which the group is conscious as distinguishing it from other groups, and the memory of which it keeps alive;
- a cultural tradition of its own, including family and social customs and manners, often but not necessarily associated with religious observance.

8.42 Other relevant considerations which are likely to indicate, but are not essential to define a distinct ethnic group include:

- a common geographical origin or descent from a small number of common ancestors;
- a common language, not necessarily peculiar to that group;
- a common literature peculiar to the group;
- a common religion different from that of neighbouring groups or from the general
- community surrounding it;
- being a minority or being an oppressed or a dominant group within a larger community.

30 Explanatory Notes to the EqA 2010 para 50.
31 [1983] 2 AC 548.

8.43 Romani Gypsies and Irish Travellers have been held to be separate 'ethnic' groups for the purpose of the EqA 2010. In *CRE v Dutton*[32] the Court of Appeal found that Romani Gypsies were a minority with a long, shared history, a common geographical origin and a cultural tradition of their own and were hence an ethnic group for the purposes of the RRA 1976 (they would similarly satisfy the criteria under the EqA 2010).

8.44 In *O'Leary v Allied Domecq*[33] HHJ Goldstein, sitting with two assessors, reached a similar decision in respect of Irish Travellers in a discrimination claim brought in the county court. The decision in *O'Leary* is not binding on higher courts. However, the ethnic status of Irish Travellers has now been accepted by the courts on a number of occasions[34] and it is extremely unlikely that their ethnic status would be open to challenge again in the UK. This position is reinforced by the fact that in Northern Ireland, Irish Travellers are explicitly protected from discrimination under the Race Relations (Northern Ireland) Order 1997, article 5. As HHJ Goldstein said in *O'Leary:*

> . . . if indeed it be the case, as the defence argue, that Irish travellers do not bring themselves within the definition of an ethnic social group under the Act, then we have a very strange anomaly that Irish travellers are protected in Ireland but not protected in England as a result of legislation by a British government.[35]

8.45 Scottish Gypsy Travellers were first recognised by the courts as a separate ethnic group in an unreported Scottish employment tribunal case in 2008[36] and their ethnicity has been accepted by the Scottish government.[37]

32 [1989] 2 WLR 17.

33 *P O'Leary and others v Allied Domecq and others* (2000) 29 August, unreported, Central London County Court, HHJ Goldstein.

34 For recent examples see: *Traveller Movement and others v JD Wetherspoon plc* (2015) 18 May, unreported, Central London County Court, HHJ Hand QC; and *Moore and Coates v Secretary of State for Communities and Local Government* [2015] EWHC 44 (Admin) at 58.

35 *P O'Leary and others v Allied Domecq and others* at p26 of the judgment.

36 *MacClellan v Gypsy Traveller Education Information Project* (2008) 23 June, unreported (case no S/132721/07). See *Gypsy Travellers in Scotland: A resource for the media* published by the EHRC in spring 2013 at: www.amnesty.org.uk/sites/default/files/ehrc_gypsy_travellers_in_scotland_media_resource_june_2013.pdf. See also Mr MacClellan's petition to the Scottish parliament which outlines the historical discrimination suffered by Gypsy Travellers in Scotland at: http://archive.scottish.parliament.uk/business/petitions/pdfs/PE1363.pdf.

37 See the Scottish government website at: www.gov.scot/Topics/People/Equality/gypsiestravellers.

8.46 The distinct racial identity of Welsh Gypsy Travellers has yet to be considered by the courts although there was some recognition of Welsh Gypsy Travellers' ethnicity in the observations made by Nicholls LJ in *Dutton*.[38]

8.47 New Travellers and other occupational Travellers do not come within the definition of a racial group. In *O'Leary*,[39] HHJ Goldstein made it clear that the court's decision would not enable all Travellers to claim ethnic status, and that it should not be seen as 'opening the floodgates to endless applications from amorphous groups seeking to take advantage of this decision'.[40] Furthermore, it was made clear by Stocker LJ in *Dutton*[41] that a strong case would need to be made by New Travellers and other occupational Travellers to fit within the definition of a 'racial group' and 'the fact alone that a group may comply with all or most of the relevant criteria does not establish that such a group is of ethnic origin'.[42]

Ethnicity, nomadism and the meaning of the words 'Gypsy' and 'Traveller'

8.48 Romani Gypsies and other ethnic Travellers are protected from discrimination by the EqA 2010 whether or not they pursue a nomadic way of life. It is their ethnic identity rather than any specific practices which makes them eligible for protection.

8.49 It is important to remember that the meaning of the words 'Gypsy' and 'Traveller' in government planning guidance relating to the provision of caravan sites is not based on ethnicity but rather on 'a nomadic habit of life'.[43] It follows that a person can have Romani Gypsy or Traveller ethnicity and hence, in principle, be able to rely on

38 [1989] 2 WLR 17 at 27.

39 *P O'Leary and others v Allied Domecq and others* at p39 of the judgment.

40 Those Travellers that are not recognised members of an ethnic group can still use ECHR Article 14 to challenge discrimination in respect of any of the other rights that they enjoy under the convention.

41 [1989] 2 WLR 17 at 34.

42 See, for example, *Dawkins v Department of the Environment* [1993] IRLR 284 where the EAT held that Rastafarians were not an ethnic group because, although they share a common religion and meet some of the other criteria, it was considered that they do not have a sufficiently long shared history and that there was not enough to distinguish them from the rest of the African Caribbean community.

43 See chapters 1 and 4 and annex 1 of DCLG *Planning policy for traveller sites*, found in appendix B.

the anti-discrimination provisions of the EqA 2010, but at the same time be excluded from the positive advice on the provision of accommodation for Gypsies and Travellers in government planning guidance (for example, if he or she has permanently abandoned a nomadic way of life).[44] Conversely, a person with a nomadic habit of life who is not an ethnic Traveller would, in principle, be able to rely on the planning guidance provisions, but would not fall within the protected characteristic of race under the EqA 2010.

Direct discrimination

Definition

8.50 EqA 2010 s13(1) defines direct discrimination in the following terms:

> A person (A) discriminates against another (B) if, because of a protected characteristic, A treats B less favourably than A treats or would treat others.

8.51 While succinctly formulated, each of the elements of the definition of direct discrimination in EqA 2010 s13(1) deserves analysis.

'Less favourable treatment'

8.52 In *Jones v Tower Boot Co Ltd*,[45] the Court of Appeal explicitly endorsed a purposive approach to the interpretation of anti-discrimination legislation. The court approved the following comment of Templeman LJ in *Savjani v Inland Revenue Commissioners* regarding the RRA 1976:

> . . . the Act was brought in to remedy a very great evil. It is expressed in very wide terms, and I should be slow to find that the effect of something which is humiliatingly discriminatory in racial matters falls outside the ambit of the Act.[46]

8.53 In accordance with this purposive construction, the case law supports a generous interpretation of the term 'less favourable treatment':

i) 'less favourable treatment' is wide enough to cover 'any disadvantage';[47]

44 See chapter 4.
45 [1997] ICR 254.
46 [1981] QB 458 at 466–467.
47 *Jeremiah v Ministry of Defence*, [1980] QB 87 at 99, [1980] ICR 13.

ii) 'less favourable treatment' and 'detriment' are measured principally from the perspective of the victim;[48]

iii) words or acts of discouragement can be less favourable treatment;[49] and

iv) deprivation of choice will be less favourable treatment.[50]

8.54 Similarly, references in the EqA 2010 to an 'act' (however expressed) include an 'omission to act' whether that be a deliberate omission, a refusal to act, or a failure to act.[51] Any of these omissions may therefore constitute 'less favourable treatment'.

8.55 Segregation on racial grounds will automatically constitute less favourable treatment.[52]

8.56 An example of the wide definition of 'less favourable treatment' is provided in the case of *Chief Constable of West Yorkshire Police v Khan*[53] where refusing to provide a reference, even though it was known it would be a bad reference, was held to be less favourable treatment.

'Others'

8.57 The definition of direct discrimination through 'less favourable' treatment intrinsically requires a comparison to be made between the treatment of the complainant and how the alleged discriminator 'treats or would treat others'. The inclusion of the words 'or would treat' in EqA 2010 s13(1) shows that there need not be another actual person who was less favourably treated for direct discrimination to take place. A claim may be brought on the basis of a *hypothetical* comparator: a hypothetical person of a different racial group in a similar situation to the complainant.

8.58 When making a comparison between cases for the purposes of EqA 2010 s13 it is clearly important to consider the right kind of comparator, whether hypothetical or real. In simple cases of race discrimination, it is often easy to identify the relevant comparator: a person of a different racial group to the complainant who is in the same situation. Some variation in the circumstances is permissible

48 *Shamoon v Chief Constable of the Royal Ulster Constabulary* [2003] UKHL 11 at 105.

49 *Simon v Brimham Associates* [1987] ICR 596 at 600.

50 *Gill v El Vino Co* [1983] QB 425 at 430.

51 EqA 2010 s212(2) and (3).

52 EqA 2010 s13(5).

53 [2001] UKHL 48.

when making the comparison, but there must be no 'material difference' between the circumstances.[54] A factor which did not influence the decision complained of is not likely to be material.[55] Importantly, a difference in circumstance which is itself based on discriminatory criteria *will* constitute a material difference ruling out the choice of comparator. This issue arose in a claim for sex discrimination challenging a council's policy of providing free swimming for pensioners, given the different retirement ages for women and men of 60 and 65 respectively. The defendant sought to argue that the correct comparator for a man of 61 (who would not be given free swimming), was a woman of non-pensionable age (who would similarly not be given free swimming) rather than a woman of 61 (who would be). It was held that this was an incorrect choice of comparator because the criteria of 'pensionable age' was itself based on discriminatory circumstances.[56] The role of comparators in discrimination claims is examined in further depth below.

'Because of'

8.59 The term 'because of' implies a broad range of protection[57] and includes claims based on 'association' – that is, where a person is treated less favourably because of his or her association with someone who has the protected characteristic.[58] It also covers claims based on 'perception': that is, where a person faces a detriment because they are wrongly thought to have the protected characteristic.[59] In addition it covers claims based on a 'refusal to comply with instruction':

54 EqA 2010 s23.

55 *Shamoon v Chief Constable of the Royal Ulster Constabulary* [2003] ICR 337, para 9.

56 *James v Eastleigh BC* [1990] 2 AC 751, [1990] IRLR 288.

57 The 'because of' formulation in EqA 2010 s13(1) replaced the previously used 'on racial grounds' formulation in RRA 1976 s1(1)(a). According to the Explanatory Notes: 'This change in wording does not change the legal meaning of the definition, but rather is designed to make it more accessible to the ordinary user of the Act' (para 61).

58 See the Explanatory Notes to the EqA 2010 at para 59; *EBR Attridge Law LLP v Coleman* UKEAT/0071/09, 30 October 2009; *Traveller Movement and others v JD Wetherspoon plc* (2015) 18 May, unreported, Central London County Court, HHJ Hand QC; and paras 8.9–8.71, below.

59 For example, if an employer rejects a job application from a white person, who he or she wrongly thinks is black because the applicant had an African-sounding name, then this would be direct discrimination (see Explanatory Notes at para 63).

that is, where a person suffers detrimental treatment because they refuse to comply with a discriminatory instruction or practice.[60]

8.60 The law adopts an objective approach in identifying the factual grounds for differential treatment. This is often expressed as using a 'but for' test, that is: but for the protected characteristic would the complainant have been treated the same way?[61] Where the factual criteria which influenced the alleged discriminator are clear, there is little need to explore the mental processes of the discriminator in order to ascertain why he or she acted as he or she did. Where the factual criteria are not clear, then it is necessary to consider what factors the discriminator did in fact rely upon. However, this does not render the test any less objective since it is the facts that operated in the mind of the discriminator that are relevant and not his or her subjective motivation.[62]

8.61 Two consequences flow from this objective approach. First, where the differential treatment is based on a criterion that is inextricably linked to or bound up with a protected characteristic then this will be differential treatment 'because of' the protected characteristic. Second, 'benign motivation' cannot justify direct discrimination. Both of these features are exemplified in the case of *R (E) v Governing Body of JFS*[63] which concerned entry criteria to a Jewish school that were based on a potential pupil's matrilineal descent from a Jewish woman. The majority of the Supreme Court held that notwithstanding that the purpose of the school was to make entry subject to religious criteria (which would be an exception to direct discrimination) the matrilineal test was a test of ethnic origin.[64] Similarly, since there is no statutory basis on which direct discrimination can be justified (save in the case of age[65]), the benign motives of the school to apply otherwise permissible religious selection criteria did not prevent a finding of direct discrimination.[66] Good intentions are simply irrelev-

60 In *Showboat Entertainment Centre Ltd v Owens* [1984] ICR 65 direct discrimination against an employee on racial grounds occurred when an employee was dismissed for disobeying his employer's unlawful instruction not to admit black customers to an entertainment centre. See also Explanatory notes at para 63. Instructions to discriminate are themselves unlawful under EqA 2010 s111.

61 *James v Eastleigh BC* [1990] IRLR 288 at para 10; and *R (E) v Governing Body of JFS* [2010] 2 AC 728 at para 16.

62 See *R (E) v Governing Body of JFS* [2010] 2 AC 728 at para 23.

63 [2010] 2 AC 728.

64 [2010] 2 AC 728 per Lord Philips at para 45.

65 See EqA 2010 s13(2).

66 [2010] 2 AC 728 per Baroness Hale at para 54 and 71.

ant to the question whether differential treatment is 'because of' a protected characteristic.

8.62 The law recognises that persons will often have more than one reason for acting as they do and a direct discrimination claim does not require that a protected characteristic be the only basis for differential treatment. What is required is that the protected characteristic has a 'significant influence on the outcome'.[67] Similarly, the law recognises that subconscious bias may form the basis of direct discrimination and there is no need for an alleged discriminator to be aware that he is acting in a discriminatory manner or because of a protected characteristic.[68] However, an alleged discriminator who simply acts unreasonably, but not because of a protected characteristic, will not commit direct discrimination.[69] As discrimination rarely takes place openly and may not even be conscious it will often have to be proved as a matter of inference.

Comparators

8.63 The role that comparators play in discrimination cases is worthy of some scrutiny. As set out above, the concept of 'less favourable treatment' is defined by comparison to some 'other'. Similarly, when deciding if the difference in treatment is 'because of' a protected characteristic it is often useful to compare the position of the complainant with that of others. The 'less favourable treatment' question and the 'why' question are distinct; however, since answering both involves making comparisons this can introduce confusion in the choice of comparator.

8.64 In *Shamoon v Chief Constable of the RUC*[70] Lord Nicholls commented that when the two-questions are 'intertwined', 'the less favourable treatment issue cannot be resolved without, at the same time, deciding the reason why issue'.[71] In such circumstances, Lord Nicholls preferred concentrating simply on the question: 'why was the complainant treated as he or she was?' With the use of a single 'compendious question'[72] one is able to 'avoid arid and confusing

67 *Nagajaran v London Regional Transport* [2000] 1 AC 501.

68 *Nagajaran v London Regional Transport* [2000] 1 AC 501.

69 *Glasgow City Council v Zafar* [1997] 1 WLR 1659.

70 [2003] UKHL 11.

71 [2003] UKHL 11 at para 8.

72 See *R (Carson) v Secretary of State for Work and Pensions* [2003] EWCA Civ 797 at para 61 in the context of an Article 14 claim.

disputes about the identification of the appropriate comparator'.[73] However, adopting a single-question approach must not be used as a means to bring in justification for direct discrimination since motive is irrelevant to such claims.

8.65 A second distinction which may be drawn in the role of comparators is the distinction between their essential role in the definition of discrimination as opposed to their evidential use in presenting a claim. It is an essential element of 'less favourable treatment' that a claimant suffered a detriment in comparison to a comparator. In a given case, no actual comparator may be in sufficiently similar circumstances to qualify as a comparator for the statutory test of 'less favourable treatment' and the claimant may then rely on a hypothetical comparator. However, actual comparators 'have a quite separate evidential role'.[74] The treatment of an actual comparator may be used as *evidence* from which an inference may be drawn that discriminatory treatment has occurred. The strength of the evidence will depend on the similarities and differences between the actual comparator and the complainant.

Stereotypes

8.66 Cases of direct discrimination will often involve the stereotyping of particular groups with assumptions made about a person's likely behaviour and attributes. The case of *R (European Roma Rights Centre) v Prague Immigration Officer*[75] involved a challenge to the screening operation conducted by UK immigration officers at Prague Airport. The object of the screening operation was to stop asylum-seekers travelling to the UK at a time when it was well known that almost all Czech asylum-seekers were Roma (since they had historically been subject to poor treatment). The House of Lords found that when conducting this operation, UK immigration officers: treated Roma with greater scepticism than non-Roma; questioned Roma for longer and more intensively; and were more likely to refuse leave to enter to Roma than non-Roma. Baroness Hale ruled that 'the operation was inherently and systematically discriminatory and unlaw-

73 *Shamoon v Chief Constable of the RUC* [2003] UKHL 11 at para 11.

74 See Lord Scott in *Shamoon v Chief Constable of the RUC* [2003] UKHL 11 at para 109.

75 [2005] 2 AC 1.

ful'.[76] The House of Lords also approved the following comments from the dissenting judgment of LJ Laws in the Court of Appeal:

> The mistake that might arise in relation to stereotyping would be a supposition that the stereotype is only vicious if it is *untrue*. But that cannot be right. If it were, it would imply that direct discrimination can be justified; whereas it is entirely plain that the legislature has advisedly chosen to allow justification of indirect, but not direct, discrimination. . . . the reality is that the officer treated the Roma less favourably because Roma are (for very well understood reasons) more likely to wish to seek asylum and thus, more likely to put forward a false claim to enter as a visitor. The officer has applied a stereotype; though one which may very likely be true. That is not permissible.[77]

8.67 The case of *Smith and Smith v Cheltenham BC and others*[78] provides a clear example of direct discrimination against a Gypsy. The claimant, a Gypsy woman, had hired the Pittville Pump Rooms from the council for a reception for her daughter's wedding, and paid a deposit on the booking. Further wedding arrangements were then made, including catering and the printing of invitations. As a result of several allegations of disorder in recent years, and rumours about the forthcoming wedding, the police became concerned that the wedding celebrations might involve public disorder and liaised with the council, including the manager of the venue, to voice these concerns. The council then attached conditions to the hire of the venue, including a requirement that entry should be by ticket only, and that a further deposit should be paid. The claimant and her daughter were very upset and booked an alternative venue (where the event took place without incident). They subsequently brought an action against the council for breach of contract and discrimination in the provision of goods and services under the then in force RRA 1976[79] and against individual police officers for knowingly aiding the council to discriminate.[80]

8.68 HHJ Rutherford found in their favour and awarded damages against the council. He stated:

76 [2005] 2 AC 1 at para 97.

77 Comments by LJ Laws at para 108 and 109 in *R (European Roma Rights Centre) v Immigration Officer at Prague Airport* [2003] EWCA Civ 666 approved by Baroness Hale at para 81 and 82 in *R (European Roma Rights Centre) v Prague Immigration Officer* [2005] 2 AC 1.

78 (1999) 7 June, unreported, Bristol County Court, HHJ Rutherford.

79 RRA 1976 ss20 and 21.

80 RRA 1976 s33, which prohibited a person from knowingly aiding another to do an act in breach of the RRA 1976.

> I find that there is no foundation for the assertions of the police that the Gypsy problems of 1997 were linked to the Smith family. The truth is that as soon as the word 'Gypsy' appears assumptions are made that large numbers will descend and cause trouble.

However, the judge concluded that the police had not acted unlawfully because they had not knowingly aided the council in discriminating against the claimant and her daughter and were not involved in the council's decision.[81]

8.69 The case of *Traveller Movement and others v JD Wetherspoon plc*[82] provides us with a more recent example. On 17 November 2011 the Traveller Movement[83] held its annual conference at the Resource Centre on Holloway Road in London. At the end of the conference, the delegates were invited to carry on their discussions at the Coronet Pub next door. A number of people, including a solicitor, a priest, a police inspector and a number of Irish Travellers and Romani Gypsies took up that invitation only to be refused entry to the pub by doormen employed by JD Wetherspoon on grounds that they had attended the Traveller Movement's conference.

8.70 Having been refused entry, 18 delegates and the Traveller Movement brought a race discrimination claim against JD Wetherspoon. HHJ Hand QC heard the case and concluded that JD Wetherspoon's staff had directly discriminated against the Traveller Movement itself and eight of the claimants by refusing them entry to the pub. When giving judgment HHJ Hand QC said:

> In my judgment the whole of the thinking of [Wetherspoon's pub manager], in so far as it can be inferred from the evidential material, was suffused with the stereotypical assumption that Irish Travellers and English Gypsies cause disorder wherever they go. In my judgment this is a racial stereotyping of those with that ethnic origin. It can be reduced to this crude proposition; whenever Irish Travellers and English Gypsies go to public houses violent disorder is inevitable because that is how they behave.

8.71 HHJ Hand QC's decision is important for a number of reasons. First, it sends out a strong signal to service providers that they will be punished if they discriminate against Gypsies and Travellers. Second,

81 The Court of Appeal upheld the decision of HHJ Rutherford: see *Hallam and Smith v Avery and Lambert* [2001] 1 WLR 655.

82 (2015) 18 May, unreported, Central London County Court, HHJ Hand QC. See a copy of the judgment at http://howe.co.uk/wp-content/uploads/2015/05/Judgement.pdf.

83 Formerly known as the Irish Traveller Movement in Britain.

it represents a classic example of a case in which the EqA 2010 has been successfully used by people who have been subjected to discrimination because of their association with members of an ethnic group. Third, it was one of the first cases in which a court has concluded that a registered charity is entitled to protection under the EqA 2010.[84]

Indirect discrimination

8.72 Indirect discrimination occurs in the circumstances set out in EqA 2010 s19:

> (1) A person (A) discriminates against another (B) if A applies to B a provision, criterion or practice which is discriminatory in relation to a relevant protected characteristic of B's.
>
> (2) For the purposes of subsection (1), a provision, criterion or practice is discriminatory in relation to a relevant protected characteristic of B's if–
>
> (a) A applies, or would apply, it to persons with whom B does not share the characteristic,
>
> (b) it puts, or would put, persons with whom B shares the characteristic at a particular disadvantage when compared with persons with whom B does not share it
>
> (c) it puts, or would put, B at that disadvantage, and
>
> (d) A cannot show it to be a proportionate means of achieving a legitimate aim.

8.73 In general terms, indirect discrimination is concerned with policies that are on their face neutral between protected groups but which have a disproportionate negative impact on a particular class. Classic examples include fixed working hours (which may disproportionately disadvantage women who are more likely to have childcare commitments) or requirements for job applicants to have particular national educational qualifications (which may disproportionately disadvantage non-British job applicants).

8.74 In the context of Gypsies and Travellers, requirements on access to services for customers that are harder to satisfy for those who do not live in bricks and mortar accommodation are potential sources of

84 On the basis that the Traveller Movement, which is a registered charity and a company limited by guarantee, was a 'legal person' for the purposes of the EqA 2010 and therefore entitled to protection under the Act. This principle was followed in the EAT in the case of *EAD Solicitors LLP v Garry Abrams Ltd* [2015] BCC 882.

indirect discrimination. For example, a hotel's requirement that a potential customer has a fixed address before it will accept a room reservation might well disproportionately disadvantage Gypsies and Travellers who live on unauthorised sites.

8.75 One significant difference between direct and indirect discrimination is that the latter, unlike the former, can be justified if it is a proportionate means of achieving a legitimate aim. The range of objectives that might be regarded as a legitimate aim is not defined. The aim need not have been consciously or explicitly articulated by the alleged discriminator at the time of the act complained of, but it must nonetheless be the genuine objective.[85]

8.76 As with the notion of 'less favourable treatment', the purposive interpretation of the EqA 2010 favours interpreting the phrase 'provision, criterion or practice' (PCP) in EqA 2010 s19 with a 'broad scope'.[86] It includes formal policies and contractual terms as well as informal practices and decisions. The terms 'provision', 'criterion' and 'practice' are not to be read discretely and technical matters of classification are to be avoided – 'what matters is not the precise label, but whether A is so conducting his affairs so as to effect discrimination against B'.[87]

8.77 The definition of indirect discrimination is based on the notion of a disparate impact which disadvantages a protected group. As with direct discrimination, the notion of comparison is central to the definition, though the comparison is now to be made with the relevant pool of persons to whom the provision is applied.

8.78 Where a PCP is 'essentially' or 'intrinsically' liable to affect a protected group and risks putting members of that group at a disadvantage, then it will be held to be indirectly discriminatory.[88] Where the PCP is not 'intrinsically' discriminatory, then a statistically disparate impact will suffice. Alternatively, the reference to 'applies or would apply' and 'puts or would put' in EqA 2010 s19(2) makes it clear that, as with direct discrimination, hypothetical comparisons may be made.

85 *Seldon v Clarkson Wright & Jakes and others* [2012] UKSC 16.

86 *Rutherford v Secretary of State for Trade and Industry (No 2)* [2006] UKHL 19.

87 *Moore and Coates v Secretary of State for Communities and Local Government* [2015] EWHC 44 (Admin).

88 For example, making deductions from benefits for dependent children when those children stay with grandparents overseas but not making similar deductions when children stay with grandparents in the UK will inherently disadvantage migrant workers, see *Secretary of State for Work and Pensions v Bobezes* [2005] EWCA Civ 111. See also *O'Flynn v Adjudication Officer* [1996] ECR 2417.

8.79 In *Commission for Racial Equality v Dutton*[89] the Court of Appeal concluded that a 'no traveller' sign displayed in a pub amounted to indirect, rather than direct, discrimination. On the facts of the case, the sign was to be interpreted as referring to a wider nomadic group and not just to ethnic Gypsies or Irish Travellers. It therefore did not directly discriminate against ethnic Gypsies and Travellers. However, as Nicholls LJ stated:

> Clearly the proportion of gypsies who will satisfy the 'No Travellers' condition is considerably smaller than the proportion of non-gypsies . . . a far higher proportion of gypsies are leading a nomadic way of life than the rest of the population in general or, more narrowly, than the rest of the population who might wish to resort to the Cat and Mutton [public house].[90]

8.80 The case of *Moore and Coates v Secretary of State for Communities and Local Government, Bromley LBC and Dartford BC and Equality and Human Rights Commission*[91] provides an excellent example of circumstances in which Gypsies and Travellers have suffered indirect discrimination as a result of an executive decision. In 2013 Mr Eric Pickles MP, the secretary of state, decided to recover all planning and enforcement notice appeals involving Traveller sites in the Green Belt for his own determination due to concerns that planning inspectors were not giving sufficient weight to the need to protect the Green Belt. Planning appeals that were recovered by the secretary of state then took much longer to determine than those left to planning inspectors. The policy applied to all Traveller sites whether relating to ethnic or non-ethnic Travellers. However, those representing Gypsies and Travellers questioned why Mr Pickles had singled out such sites for special scrutiny and in 2014 two Romani Gypsy women, Charmaine Moore and Sarah Coates challenged Mr Pickles' decision to recover their planning appeals by way of judicial review.

8.81 Gilbart J held that the Secretary of State's decision to recover all the appeals relating to Traveller sites was unlawful because it indirectly discriminated against Gypsies and Travellers. There was some dispute between the parties as to the appropriate pool of comparators. Gilbart J ruled that the correct pool was 'persons wishing to seek planning permission for a habitation in the Green Belt' because:

89 [1989] 2 WLR 17.

90 [1989] 2 WLR 17 at 29.

91 [2015] EWHC 44 (Admin).

> I take very seriously Baroness Hale's observations . . . that one should avoid placing technical obstacles in the way of establishing that indirect discrimination has occurred. . . . In the real world, what has happened here is that in the case of the Green Belt there is a marked and obvious difference between those on the one hand who seek to live there (or allow others to do so), and to that end seek planning permission on appeal to construct a house, or indeed several houses, within it, or who seek to convert a building or buildings to residential use, and on the other, those who seek to live there as well but are gypsies or travellers, many of whom are likely to be ethnic gypsies or travellers.[92]

8.82 In considering whether the disparate impact could be justified, the judge held that the need to ensure that planning policy was properly applied could, in principle, be a legitimate aim.[93] However, the means adopted were not proportionate to this aim. It was not necessary to recover all Traveller site planning appeals in order to ensure that planning policy was followed; a representative group of appeals could have been recovered for determination for that purpose. That alternative approach would have affected a far smaller number of persons and therefore have had less impact on Gypsies and Travellers:[94]

> . . . a notable feature of the evidence for the SSCLG is that it shows that his officials repeatedly advised against the course being followed, and recommended the course of selecting a few cases so that a clear message could be given, while drawing attention to the increasing delays being caused to interested parties. Yet there is an absence of any evidence from the SSCLG in these proceedings of why the Minister or the SSCLG thought that their preferred approach was proportionate, and why none of the alternatives being suggested to them would not meet the objectives they had identified . . . It was left to [counsel for the SSCLG] without evidence but with forensic bravery, to assert that the Minister had good reason to do so.[95]

8.83 The judge noted that the secretary of state's written policies referred only to 'considering appeals relating to traveller sites for recovery' and did not stipulate that all such appeals would be recovered. On its face, the written policy could be taken to be proportionate. However, the application of the policy was in fact a practice whereby all appeals were recovered. That practice was disproportionate and hence constituted indirect discrimination.[96]

92 [2015] EWHC 44 (Admin) at para 96.
93 [2015] EWHC 44 (Admin) at para 120.
94 [2015] EWHC 44 (Admin) at para 124.
95 [2015] EWHC 44 (Admin) at para 125.
96 [2015] EWHC 44 (Admin) at para 126.

8.84 The case of *R (Gullu) v Hillingdon LBC; R (Ward) v Hillingdon LBC*[97] provides us with another example of how Gypsies and Travellers can be the victims of indirect discrimination when seeking local authority housing. Hillingdon's housing allocation policy prioritised people who had been resident in the local area for ten years and the Court of Appeal held: that it indirectly discriminated against both refugees and Irish Travellers, who would be less likely to be prioritised than others; and that the local authority had not shown any justification for that discrimination.[98]

8.85 In the case of *CHEZ Razpredelenie Bulgaria AD v Komisia za zashtita ot diskriminatsia*[99] the Court of Justice of the European Union (CJEU) held that a claimant could complain of indirect discrimination by association. The case concerned a policy of a Bulgarian electricity supplier to install electricity meters for all customers in predominantly Roma districts at a height of between six and seven metres from the ground. This compared to a normal height of 1.7 metres. The aim of the policy was to prevent unlawful connections being made to the electricity supply. However, the consequence of the policy was that customers were unable to readily check their own meter to monitor consumption and ensure that bills were accurate. The measure also had a stigmatising effect. The claim was brought by a resident in an area subject to the policy who did not identify herself as Roma. Under Article 2(2)(b) of Directive 2000/43 ('the Race Equality Directive'),[100] indirect discrimination occurs when a practice 'would put persons of a racial or ethnic origin at a particular disadvantage'. The CJEU ruled that the principle of prohibiting indirect discrimination was designed to benefit all persons who suffered a detriment and not simply those who were themselves a member of the ethnic group concerned and that indirect discrimination by association could occur in circumstances 'where a collective measure affects persons who have a certain ethnic origin or those who, without possessing that origin, suffer, together with the former, the less favourable treatment or particular disadvantage resulting from that measure'.[101]

8.86 The *CHEZ* case raises concerns about the compatibility of our domestic law with the Race Equality Directive. EqA 2010 s19 defines

97 [2019] EWCA Civ 692.

98 See chapter 6 generally for the law on the provision of housing.

99 C-83/14 [2016] 1 CMLR 14; and see chapter 2 paras 2.259–2.262.

100 See paras 2.259–2.262.

101 C-83/14 [2016] 1 CMLR 14 at para 60.

indirect discrimination in domestic law as occurring when a person A applies a provision, criterion or practice 'which is discriminatory in relation to a relevant protected characteristic of B's'. On its face, the wording of EqA 2010 s19 requires that those who suffer indirect discrimination must themselves possess the relevant protected characteristic and does not allow for claims to be brought by association.[102] How our domestic courts respond to the CJEU's judgment in the *CHEZ* case remains to be seen.

Harassment

8.87 EqA 2010 s26(1) defines harassment as follows:

> A person (A) harasses another (B) if–
> (a) A engages in unwanted conduct related to a protected characteristic, and
> (b) the conduct has the purpose or effect of–
> (i) violating B's dignity, or
> (ii) creating an intimidating, hostile, degrading, humiliating or offensive environment for B.

8.88 It is axiomatic that harassment must be unwanted conduct. However, a victim of harassment need not make any objections known before the conduct qualifies as harassment. As with discrimination, conduct will include both acts and a failure to act.[103] Conduct may be said to 'create' an intimidating, hostile, degrading, humiliating or offensive environment when it 'causes the environment to begin to be as it is'.[104] Creation of such an environment may take place over time. Sometimes one person will create the environment in part, but another will make it worse, in which case it is created by the actions of both.[105]

8.89 It follows from the definition in EqA 2010 s26(1)(b) that harassment may take two forms: first, when the purpose of the conduct is to violate the victim's dignity (or create an intimidating, hostile,

102 By comparison, claims of direct discrimination can be brought by association; the differential treatment must simply be 'because of' a protected characteristic in general and not necessarily the protected characteristic possessed by the victim. See para 8.59, above.

103 EqA 2010 s212(2).

104 *Conteh v Parking Partners Ltd* [2011] ICR 341.

105 *Conteh v Parking Partners Ltd* [2011] ICR 341 at para 28. The extent to which each party has contributed to the environment may be relevant to damages but not to liability.

degrading, humiliating or offensive environment); and second, when the effect of the conduct is to have such consequences. It is only in the second form of harassment that the court is required to take into account the factors referred in EqA 2010 s26(4), namely:

> In deciding whether conduct has the effect referred to in subsection (1)(b), each of the following must be taken into account–
> (a) the perception of B;
> (b) the other circumstances of the case;
> (c) whether it is reasonable for the conduct to have that effect.

8.90 Nevertheless, the purpose or intent behind conduct remains relevant even if the second effect-based harassment is alleged to have occurred, since the intention behind the conduct will go to an assessment of whether it is reasonable for the conduct to have such effect: for example, 'a humorous remark between friends may have a very different effect than exactly the same words spoken vindictively by a hostile speaker'.[106]

8.91 Harassment on the basis of race under EqA 2010 s26 is unlawful in all contexts covered by the EqA 2010.[107] In relation to employment, EqA 2010 s40 originally provided further protection against an employer that failed to prevent employees experiencing harassment from third parties such as customers or clients.[108] However, those provisions have since been repealed.[109] The extent to which such third party harassment claims may nonetheless be brought under EqA 2010 s26 and the degree to which this is required by the EU Race Equality Directive remains to be seen.

Victimisation

8.92 EqA 2010 s27 provides protection, not from discriminatory treatment, but from being subject to adverse treatment as a consequence of having made a complaint about discrimination:

> (1) A person (A) victimises another person (B) if A subjects B to a detriment because–

106 *Grant v HM Land Registry and EHRC* [2011] EWCA Civ 769.

107 The coverage in relation to some of the other protected characteristics is more limited.

108 An employer will be liable for acts of harassment by employees under standard principles of vicarious liability as enacted in EqA 2010 s109.

109 As of 1 October 2013, by virtue of the Enterprise and Regulatory Reform Act 2013 s65 and SI 2013 No 2227.

(a) B does a protected act, or
(b) A believes that B has done, or may do, a protected act.

(2) Each of the following is a protected act–
(a) bringing proceedings under this Act;
(b) giving evidence or information in connection with proceedings under this Act;
(c) doing any other thing for the purposes of or in connection with this Act;
(d) making an allegation (whether or not express) that A or another person has contravened this Act.

(3) Giving false evidence or information, or making a false allegation, is not a protected act if the evidence or information is given, or the allegation is made, in bad faith.

(4) This section applies only where the person subjected to a detriment is an individual.

(5) The reference to contravening this Act includes a reference to committing a breach of an equality clause or rule.

8.93 Victimisation therefore occurs when a person is treated less favourably than another because they have brought or are believed to have brought legal proceedings under EqA 2010; or because they have given evidence or information on behalf of someone else's complaint under EqA 2010; or because they have complained of racial discrimination. The detrimental treatment does not need to be intentional.[110] Protection against victimisation remains even if the underlying claim does not succeed. The protection is, however, lost when the original allegation of discrimination is made in bad faith.

Scope of the Equality Act 2010

8.94 The scope of the EqA 2010 is wide but not unlimited. Although a broad range of conduct is covered, it remains the case that the provisions of the Act only apply in specified areas and there are variations in coverage between the different protected characteristics. However, race is one of the protected characteristics given greatest protection under the EqA 2010.

110 See *Nagarajan v London Regional Transport* [2000] 1 AC 501.

Employment

8.95 Protection from discrimination in the employment sphere is widely drawn. It is unlawful for an employer to discriminate against an employee:

- as to the terms of employment;
- in the way access is afforded to opportunities for promotion, transfer, training or any other benefit or service;
- by dismissing the employee from employment,[111] or
- by subjecting the employee to any other detriment.[112]

Similarly, an employer must not discriminate against an applicant for employment: in the application procedures; as to the terms on which employment is offered; or by withholding a job offer.[113] Victimisation and harassment against employees and applicants for employment is also unlawful.[114]

8.96 The concept of 'employment' is itself given a wide interpretation and is defined as: 'employment under a contract of employment, a contract of apprenticeship or a contract personally to do work'[115] and agency workers are protected. Discrimination, harassment and victimisation[116] of former employees is also unlawful where the conduct arises out of and is closely connected to the employment relationship.[117] This includes a refusal to provide a reference because of the race of the former employee. One limitation on the scope of the EqA 2010 in the workplace is that volunteers, who do not have any written or implied contract of employment, are not protected under the employment provisions of the EqA 2010.[118]

111 'Dismissal' from employment includes a refusal to renew or extend a fixed term contract: see EqA 2010 ss39(7) and 40.

112 EqA 2010 s39(2).

113 EqA 2010 s39(1).

114 EqA 2010 s39(3), (4).

115 EqA 2010 s83(2).

116 Discrimination and harassment of ex-employees are explicitly outlawed by EqA 2010 s108. In *Rowstock v Jessemey* [2014] EWCA Civ 185 the Court of Appeal held that the failure to prohibit victimisation of ex-employees was a drafting error (para 36). In order to give effect to EU law, and on domestic principles of construction, prohibition of post-employment victimisation must be taken as implied by EqA 2010 s108.

117 EqA 2010 s108.

118 As confirmed by the Supreme Court in *X v Mid Sussex Citizens Advice Bureau and another* [2012] UKSC 59.

Education

8.97 The 'responsible body' of a school is prohibited from discriminating against pupils and prospective pupils:

- by admitting them on different terms to other pupils;
- by rejecting their application;
- by withholding benefits, facilities or services or offering such benefits on differential terms;
- by excluding them; or
- by subjecting them to any other detriment.[119]

Harassment and victimisation are also prohibited.[120] Pupils are protected from victimisation arising from acts done by their parents unless the child has acted in bad faith.[121] However, discrimination, harassment and victimisation are not prohibited if they relate to anything done in connection with the content of the curriculum.[122] For schools maintained by the local authority, the responsible body is the local authority or the school's governing body.[123] For independent schools and academies, the responsible body is the proprietor.[124] Further and higher education institutions are subject to similar prohibitions on discrimination, harassment and victimisation as those which apply to schools.

Goods, facilities or services

8.98 It is unlawful for a service provider to discriminate against anyone requiring the provision of goods, facilities or services.[125] A service provider includes anyone who is concerned in the provision of goods, facilities or services to the public or a section of the public.[126] Payment is not required and therefore charities, voluntary groups and public bodies who provide services to a section of the public fall within this

119 EqA 2010 s85(1), (2).

120 EqA2010 s85(3), (4), (5).

121 Under EqA 2010 s86(3) where the child has acted in good faith but a false complaint in bad faith has been presented by the parent the child is still protected from victimisation.

122 EqA 2010 s89(2).

123 EqA 2010 s85(9)(a).

124 EqA 2010 s85(9)(b).

125 EqA 2010 s29(1).

126 EqA 2010 s29(1).

provision.[127] Discrimination covers both direct and indirect discrimination and includes:

- a refusal to provide the services;
- providing a lesser standard of services; or
- not providing the services in the same manner or on the same terms as they are usually provided.[128]

Discrimination on racial grounds is prohibited against anyone who requires the services; this includes those who are given the services and those who unsuccessfully seek the services.[129]

8.99 Similarly, a service provider must not harass a person who requires the services on racial grounds or victimise them in the provision of the services because they have made a complaint about discrimination or harassment. Unlawful discrimination and harassment can also take place after any relationship of service provision has ended if the objectionable conduct arises out of and is closely connected to that provision.[130]

8.100 EqA 2010 s29(1) could be used, for example, where an electricity or water company refuses to provide services for ethnic Gypsies or Travellers living on a site, or provides substandard services on racial grounds. *Smith and Smith v Cheltenham BC*[131] is an example of the successful use of the equivalent provisions in the RRA 1976. More recently, *Traveller Movement and others v JD Wetherspoon plc*[132] is an example of a case concerning direct discrimination in the provision of services, namely a refusal to allow entry to a public house. Owing to the unfortunate persistence of racial stereotypes concerning Gypsies and Travellers, the 'night time economy' is one area in which discrimination against these ethnic groups continues to take place. The refusal of service in pubs, restaurants, nightclubs and taxis on grounds that are blatantly, and sometimes overtly, racist is shocking.

127 EqA 2010 s29(1). Whilst public functions are distinct from services, EqA 2010 s29 applies to services provided 'in the exercise of public functions' (EqA 2010 s31(3)).

128 EqA 2010 ss29(2) and 31(7).

129 EqA 2010 s31(6).

130 EqA 2010 s108(1).

131 (1999) 7 June, unreported, Bristol County Court, HHJ Rutherford; and see paras 8.67–8.68 above.

132 (2015) 18 May, unreported, Central London County Court, HHJ Hand QC.

Public functions

8.101 It is unlawful for any person exercising a public function to do anything that constitutes discrimination, harassment or victimisation.[133] It follows that, for example, the discriminatory use of 'stop and search' or arrest powers by the police would be unlawful.[134] Persons exercising public functions include police officers, the Crown Prosecution Service (CPS),[135] regulatory bodies, local authorities and government departments as well as other private and voluntary organisations acting on behalf of public bodies. Further protection against discriminatory acts by public authorities is provided for by the public sector equality duty (PSED).[136]

Housing

8.102 It is unlawful for someone to discriminate against another when disposing of premises, for example, when selling or subletting premises.[137] It is also unlawful for someone who manages occupied premises to discriminate in the way they:

- give or withhold benefits or facilities to the occupier;
- evict the occupier (or take steps to secure eviction); or
- subject the occupier to any other detriment.[138]

Harassment and victimisation of occupiers and those applying for premises is similarly unlawful.[139] These provisions apply to site provision and management. So, for example, a Romani Gypsy or ethnic Traveller could bring a claim that a site owner had discrimin-

133 See EqA 2010 s29(6). In this section, a 'public function' is a function of a public nature for the purposes of the HRA 1998 (EqA 2010 s31(4)). Where a public authority provides a service, protection from discrimination is provided under the services provisions.

134 See *ZH v Commissioner of Police of the Metropolis* [2013] EWCA Civ 69.

135 While decisions to prosecute are not covered by the EqA 2010, matters incidental to the investigation, such as ignoring or minimising a victim's complaint about criminal offences, are covered (*Alder v Chief Constable of Humberside Police and others* [2006] EWCA Civ 1741).

136 EqA 2010 s149; and see paras 8.133–8.159 below.

137 EqA 2010 s33(1).

138 EqA 2010 s35(1).

139 EqA 2010 ss33(3)–(4) and 35(2)–(3).

ated against him when allocating pitches.[140] There is an exemption for short-stay accommodation such as hotels, bed-and-breakfasts and hostels which are covered under the 'services' provisions.[141] Other statutory exceptions to the protection provided by the EqA 2010 in relation to the disposal of premises by owner-occupiers or the management of 'small premises' in which the landlord or a relative of the landlord resides do not apply to discrimination based on race.[142]

Discrimination by other bodies

8.103 Trade unions, employers' associations and professional and trade associations have a dual role as employers and providers of services specifically covered by the EqA 2010. They are also responsible for making sure that their representatives and members do not discriminate unlawfully, on racial grounds:

- in the way they admit members; or
- in the way they treat them, as colleagues, supervisors or subordinates.[143]

8.104 The EqA 2010 also applies to membership clubs. It is unlawful for clubs and associations to discriminate or harass on racial grounds in membership and the provision of benefits, facilities or services to members or by subjecting a member to any other detriment.[144] Specific protection is also provided to guests of club members.[145] Victimisation for bringing a complaint of discriminatory treatment is also prohibited. These provisions only apply to clubs and associations of 25 or more members and where admission is regulated by a constitution.[146] There are also specific exemptions for 'single characteristic' clubs where membership is restricted to those who share a protected characteristic: Irish clubs are hence lawful.[147] However, while the restriction can be on the basis of race it cannot be on the

140 Where premises are allocated by a local authority exercising public functions then protection against discrimination will fall under the services and public functions provisions of the EqA 2010.

141 See *Hall v Bull* [2013] UKSC 73; and *Black v Wilkinson* [2013] EWCA Civ 820.

142 EqA 2010 Sch 5.

143 EqA 2010 s57.

144 EqA 2010 s101.

145 EqA 2010 s102.

146 EqA 2010 s107(2).

147 EqA 2010 Sch 16.

basis of colour.[148] Clubs that are genuinely open to all members of the public will be covered by the sections relating to the provision of services.

8.105 The EqA 2010 does not apply to the content of racist newspaper articles or to racist broadcasts. However, where it is considered that an article or broadcast amounts to an 'incitement to racial hatred' then the police may prosecute the person(s) responsible for breaching provisions of the Public Order Act 1986.[149] Any member of the public can refer such material to the police. Although the EHRC has no legal powers to deal with such cases, it may refer matters to the police directly.[150] A complaint about the content of broadcast media can be made to Ofcom[151] and complaints about newspapers and magazines may be made to the Independent Press Standards Organisation.[152]

'No Traveller' signs and other discriminatory advertisements

8.106 Where a discriminatory advertisement genuinely discourages a job applicant or a potential service user from applying for a job or using a service because of their race, then a claim may be brought under the anti-discrimination provisions relating to employment or provision of services. However, such claims cannot be brought by those who are not intending to apply for the job or use the service.[153]

8.107 The EHRC may bring enforcement action against those that post 'No Traveller' signs and other discriminatory advertisements.[154] The

148 See EqA 2010 Sch 16 para 4. Thus a 'whites only' club would be unlawful.

149 See also paras 8.170–8.179 below on hate speech.

150 In October 2003, the CRE referred the burning of an effigy of a Gypsy caravan in Firle, Sussex to the police (see chapter 1 at paras 1.1–1.3, above). The police subsequently launched an investigation and a number of people were arrested – though no one was ever prosecuted in relation to the incident.

151 See: www.ofcom.org.uk/tv-radio-and-on-demand/how-to-report-a-complaint.

152 See: www.ipso.co.uk/make-a-complaint/.

153 If a court or tribunal found that a person was not genuinely interested in applying for a job but pretended to be for the purpose of bringing a discrimination claim, then the claimant would face costs if the claim was unsuccessful (*Keane v Investigo and others* [2009] UKEAT/0389/09/SM).

154 Enforcement action by the EHRC may be taken either under EqA 2010 s111 on the basis that the advertisement induces or causes others to commit discrimination. Alternatively, EqA 2006 s24A(3) empowers the EHRC to take action in relation to persons making arrangements which would, if applied to a relevant individual, amount to discrimination under EqA 2010.

EHRC's practice is to ask the respondent to remove the sign and to seek a formal agreement that the act will not be repeated. Where necessary, proceedings may be brought under the EqA 2006.[155] Options available to the EHRC include issuing an 'Unlawful Act Notice' which sets out the act complained of and the remedial action needed, and states that if compliance does not occur then a criminal offence may be committed.[156] Similarly the EHRC may apply to a court for an injunction requiring a person to remove a discriminatory advertisement or sign.[157]

Pursuing a complaint of discrimination

8.108 If a Gypsy or Traveller considers that he or she has been the victim of direct or indirect discrimination, or has been victimised or harassed on grounds of race (or indeed, any of the other protected characteristics covered by the EqA 2010), then advice should be sought on whether the circumstances amount to unlawful discrimination and an action may be brought under the EqA 2010.

8.109 A complainant can seek assistance from a Citizens' Advice Bureau (CAB), a local Race Equality Council (which is an independent voluntary organisation), the Equality Advisory and Support Service (EASS), a solicitor or other suitable advice agency. Information is also available from the EHRC.

8.110 Legal aid is available for discrimination claims.[158] In addition, EqA 2006 s28 covers the provision of legal assistance by the EHRC and provides that:

> (1) The Commission may assist an individual who is or may become a party to legal proceedings if–
> (a) the proceedings relate or may relate (wholly or partly) to a provision of the Equality Act 2010, and
> (b) the individual alleges that he has been the victim of behaviour contrary to a provision of that Act.

EqA 2006 s28(4) makes it clear that assistance can include the provision of legal advice, legal representation and the facilities for the settlement of a dispute. The EHRC publishes a Strategic Litigation

155 This is similar to the action in *CRE v Dutton* [1989] 2 WLR 17.

156 EqA 2006 ss21 and 22.

157 EqA 2006 s24.

158 See Legal Aid, Sentencing and Punishment of Offenders Act 2012 Sch 1 para 43.

Policy on its website[159] which sets out the factors that will be considered when deciding whether to provide assistance in a case. In broad terms, the EHRC looks to assist in cases which may set a legal precedent or address widespread or systematic discrimination issues.

8.111 Cases involving race discrimination in employment are heard in employment tribunals. Other race discrimination cases are heard in the county court (in England and Wales).[160] In many cases it is advisable to settle a case before it gets to a full hearing, if the terms are acceptable to both parties or are the same or better than what would be granted by a court or tribunal. In practice, a significant proportion of cases are settled on agreed terms. A settlement may take the form of an agreement to pay a sum of money or an apology which may also contain an undertaking to work with the EHRC to bring the respondent into compliance with the EqA 2010.

8.112 In employment cases, the Advisory, Conciliation and Arbitration Service (ACAS) must be informed of the intention to bring a complaint and the Early Conciliation Service will be offered to help the parties reach a settlement. ACAS is an independent body set up to act as a go-between in disputes. If notification of the intention to bring a claim is not made to ACAS, then the employment tribunal will reject the complaint. There is no obligation to accept ACAS's advice, but, if a settlement is reached through ACAS, it is legally binding and will bring any claim to an end. Conciliation services can be offered up to the tribunal hearing. ACAS cannot assist with settling county or sheriff court cases.

Time limits for making a complaint

8.113 There are short time limits for bringing a discrimination claim. Time runs from the date on which the discriminatory act occurred or ceased to occur. There are separate time limits for county court and tribunal proceedings. Generally, a complaint made to the employment tribunal must be lodged within three months (that is, no later than three months less one day) of the act of discrimination complained of.[161] Exceptionally, and only in very limited circum-

159 See: www.equalityhumanrights.com.

160 Sheriff court in Scotland.

161 EqA 2010 s123(1)(a). Under EqA 2010 s140B, instituting the ACAS Early Conciliation process will stop the clock on the limitation period until either party indicates that they no longer wish to participate in settlement or one month has passed (further extendable by 14 days if ACAS views that settlement is nearing completion).

stances, the court or tribunal will consider a late complaint or claim when it is 'just and equitable' to do so.[162]

8.114 Complaints brought in the county court (or sheriff's courts in Scotland) must be brought within six months (that is, no later than six months less one day) of the act of discrimination about which complaint is made.[163] The court does have a residual discretion to extend the time for bringing a claim when it is 'just and equitable' to do so.[164] However, it is not possible for parties to a claim to agree to extend the time limit without the approval of the court.

8.115 In the case of a county court claim made under the EqA 2010 against a university, the six-month time limit may be extended to nine months if the matter is first referred to a student complaints scheme within the initial six-month period.[165] There is no longer a similar provision to extend the limitation period for general discrimination complaints by referring the matter to the EHRC.[166]

Reverse burden of proof

8.116 The courts have long recognised the difficulties in proving discrimination claims because discrimination rarely takes place in the open and is even more rarely admitted.[167] EqA 2010 s136 provides for a reversal of the standard burden of proof. Once a claimant proves facts from which a court or tribunal could make a finding of discrimination, EqA 2010 s136 shifts the burden of proof to the defendant to prove that the reason for differential treatment was not discriminatory and states that:

> (1) This section applies to any proceedings relating to a contravention of this Act.
> (2) If there are facts from which the court could decide, in the absence of any other explanation, that a person (A) contravened the provision concerned, the court must hold that the contravention occurred.
> (3) But subsection (2) does not apply if A shows that A did not contravene the provision.

162 EqA 2010 s123(1)(b).
163 EqA 2010 s118(1)(a).
164 EqA 2010 s118(1)(b).
165 EqA 2010 s118(2).
166 Enterprise and Regulatory Reform Act 2013 s64(13)(b).
167 *Blundell v St Andrew's Catholic Primary School Governors* [2007] ICR 1451 at para 34.

8.117 Guidance on the implementation of reverse burden of proof provisions was provided by the Court of Appeal in *Igen Ltd v Wong*.[168] The burden of proof provisions require a court or tribunal to adopt a two-stage process. The first stage requires the claimant to establish facts from which the court or tribunal could conclude that the defendant has committed the unlawful act of discrimination. The second stage only comes into effect if those facts have been proven, and requires the defendant to prove that he or she did not commit, or is to be treated as if he or she did not commit, the unlawful act.[169] Although two stages are referred to, this applies to the court or tribunal's reasoning process once all the evidence has been heard, rather than to any formal division of the evidence.[170]

8.118 The first stage requires the claimant to establish facts from which a reasonable court or tribunal could properly conclude that discrimination occurred.[171] This includes evidence of differential treatment and a difference in status and may require more. The court or tribunal does not need to be satisfied at this stage that the facts 'would' lead it to the conclusion that discrimination occurred, only that a reasonable tribunal could properly draw this conclusion.[172] Once the burden of proof has shifted then, since the facts necessary to provide a non-discriminatory explanation would normally be known to the defendant, the court or tribunal 'would normally expect cogent evidence to discharge that burden of proof'.[173]

8.119 Factors which *must not* be taken into account when considering whether the burden of proof has shifted include any exculpatory explanation put forward by the defendant. However, the fact that inconsistent explanations are put forward may be considered in support of the claimant, since in such a case it is 'the fact of the inconsistency that is being included and not the explanations themselves'.[174] Similarly, the court or tribunal may take account of the fact that there are several instances of differential treatment with the same alleged perpetrator.[175]

168 [2005] EWCA Civ 142.

169 [2005] EWCA Civ 142 at para 17.

170 [2005] EWCA Civ 142 at para 19.

171 *Madrassy v Nomura International Plc* [2007] EWCA Civ 33 at para 57.

172 *Igen Ltd v Wong* [2005] EWCA Civ 142 at paras 14 and 76.

173 *Igen Ltd v Wong* [2005] EWCA Civ 142 at paras 14 and 76.

174 *Veolia Environmental Services UK v Gumbs* (Appeal No UKEAT/0487/12/BA) at para 57.

175 *Veolia Environmental Services UK v Gumbs* (Appeal No UKEAT/0487/12/BA) at para 64.

8.120 Factors that *may* be taken into account when deciding if the burden of proof shifts include evidence from the defendant that the differential treatment did not occur, was not less favourable treatment, or that the comparators are not truly like the claimant.

8.121 Lord Hope in the Supreme Court case of *Hewage v Grampian Health Board*[176] appeared to constrain the role of the burden of proof provisions to cases 'where there is room for doubt'. In cases where the court or tribunal can make positive findings one way or the other, he considered that the provisions 'have nothing to offer'.[177] Clearly, where a court is satisfied that conduct occurred which is 'axiomatically discriminatory and inexplicable in non-discriminatory terms', such as the use of racist abuse, there is no need to consider the shift in the burden of proof.[178]

8.122 One further tool that can be of considerable assistance to claimants in discrimination claims is the questionnaire procedure.[179] A claimant may put a list of questions to the defendant on matters relevant to the claim. The procedure can be used to obtain documents relevant to the claim, data on current practice and any relevant policies or training. The procedure may also be used to obtain an initial explanation from the defendant as to the reason for any detrimental treatment. Questions may, and often will, be asked prior to issuing a claim. There is no obligation on the defendant to respond to the questions put; however, the court or tribunal dealing with the claim may draw inferences from a failure to answer or from the giving of evasive or equivocal answers.[180] The effective use of the questionnaire procedure requires careful consideration of the questions asked.

176 [2012] ICR 1054.

177 [2012] ICR 1054 at para 32.

178 *Veolia Environmental Services UK v Gumbs* (Appeal No UKEAT/0487/12/BA) at paras 52 and 53.

179 EqA 2010 s138. The statutorily specified procedure for submitting questions was repealed by Enterprise and Regulatory Reform Act 2013 s66. However, the provisions for submitting informal questions remain. Guidance on the informal procedure is produced by ACAS – www.acas.org.uk/media/pdf/m/p/Asking-and-responding-to-questions-of-discrimination-in-the-workplace.pdf.

180 EqA 2010 s138(4) sets out the circumstances in which adverse inferences may be drawn. A period of eight weeks from service of the questions before an inference may be drawn as to the failure to respond.

Remedies

8.123 In employment cases, if a complaint is upheld, then the employment tribunal can order that compensation, or damages, be paid to the applicant. The amount may include a sum for lost earnings and benefits and a sum for injury to feelings. There is no ceiling to the amount a tribunal can award, although it will normally follow guidelines and precedents from previous cases.[181] If the case is successful, the tribunal can also recommend that the employer take certain steps to enable the complainant to work without further discrimination.

8.124 If the case is not successful, the applicant will not automatically be ordered to pay the other side's legal costs, but the tribunal may make an applicant pay if it thinks he or she acted unreasonably, frivolously or vexatiously in pursuing the case. An appeal against the tribunal's decision can be made to the Employment Appeal Tribunal, but only on a point of law. An appeal must be lodged within 42 days.

8.125 In the county court[182] if the case is successful, the court can order that damages be paid by the defendant to the claimant and, if necessary, the court can also grant an injunction to prevent a recurrence of the discriminatory act.[183] The amount of damages awarded may include a sum to compensate the claimant for any losses and a sum for injury to feelings.[184] There is no ceiling to the level of damages that a court can award, but awards tend to be lower than those made by tribunals. If the case is withdrawn before trial or is ultimately unsuccessful, then the claimant will normally be ordered to pay the defendant's legal costs.

8.126 Damages will be awarded for any financial losses flowing from a discriminatory act, for example the loss of a job or promotion. It will be for the claimant to establish the losses incurred. Where, in a discrimination claim, differential treatment has been materially influenced by a protected characteristic, but the same outcome would have occurred in any event, damages will be limited. For example, if a person succeeds in an unlawful dismissal claim due to discrimination but the employer can show that the claimant may have lost their

181 See *Vento v Chief Constable of West Yorkshire (No 2)* [2003] ICR 318.
182 Sheriff court in Scotland.
183 EqA 2010 s119(2).
184 EqA 2010 s119(4).

job in any event due to wider redundancies, then damages may be reduced.[185]

8.127 If discriminatory treatment results in physical or psychiatric injury (in the form of a recognised medical condition), then an award will be made for compensation. Again, it is for the claimant to establish that the injury suffered was due to the discriminatory treatment and expert medical evidence is likely to be required. Guidelines on the level of awards for personal injury claims is published by the Judicial College.[186]

8.128 Damages are also awarded for injury to feelings (this is separate to any award for psychiatric harm). The leading case on the level of awards remains *Vento v Chief Constable of West Yorkshire Police (No 2)*[187] in which the Court of Appeal stated:

> 65 Employment tribunals and those who practise in them might find it helpful if this court were to identify three broad bands of compensation for injury to feelings, as distinct from compensation for psychiatric or similar personal injury. (i) The top band should normally be between £15,000 and £25,000. Sums in this range should be awarded in the most serious cases, such as where there has been a lengthy campaign of discriminatory harassment on the ground of sex or race. This case falls within that band. Only in the most exceptional case should an award of compensation for injury to feelings exceed £25,000. (ii) The middle band of between £5,000 and £15,000 should be used for serious cases, which do not merit an award in the highest band. (iii) Awards of between £500 and £5,000 are appropriate for less serious cases, such as where the act of discrimination is an isolated or one off occurrence. In general, awards of less than £500 are to be avoided altogether, as they risk being regarded as so low as not to be a proper recognition of injury to feelings.
>
> 66 There is, of course, within each band considerable flexibility, allowing tribunals to fix what is considered to be fair, reasonable and just compensation in the particular circumstances of the case.
>
> 67 The decision whether or not to award aggravated damages and, if so, in what amount must depend on the particular circumstances of the discrimination and on the way in which the complaint of discrimination has been handled.
>
> 68 Common sense requires that regard should also be had to the overall magnitude of the sum total of the awards of compensation for non-pecuniary loss made under the various headings of injury to feelings,

185 *Chagger v Abbey National plc* [2009] EWCA Civ 1202.

186 The 14th edn of the Judicial College Guidelines for the assessment of General Damages in Personal Injury cases was published on 14 September 2017.

187 [2002] EWCA Civ 1871.

psychiatric damage and aggravated damage. In particular, double recovery should be avoided by taking appropriate account of the overlap between the individual heads of damage. The extent of overlap will depend on the facts of each particular case.

8.129 On 4 September 2017, the President of the Employment Tribunals announced the results of a consultation into the *Vento* guidelines in EAT claims.[188] The President set out bands which are given in the table below:

Band	Nature of act	Vento Award	Updated (2017) with 10% uplift
Top band	Lengthy campaign of discriminatory harassment	£15,000–£25,000	£25,200–£42,000
Middle band	Serious cases	£5,000–£15,000	£8,400–£25,000
Lower band	Act of discrimination isolated or one-off occurrence	£500–£5,000	£800–£8,400

8.130 In *Kemeh v Ministry of Defence*[189] the Court of Appeal approved the approach of the Employment Appeal Tribunal in placing a single racial slur with aggravating features at the top of the lower band identified in *Vento*.

8.131 Guidance on damages for single-incident discrimination claims in the provision of services can be found in the county court case of *Traveller Movement & Others v JD Wetherspoon plc*.[190] The trial judge laid down a clear benchmark of £3,000 for a one-off refusal of service on grounds of race where the incident is not accompanied by racial slurs or other aggravating features.

8.132 Factors which may be taken into account in deciding the level of award for a discrimination claim includes:

- Was the incident of discrimination one-off or repeated over a period of time? If repeated over time what was the length of time and was there any earlier challenge to the treatment?

188 This followed the decision in *Simmons v Castle* [2012] EWCA Civ 1039, [2013] 1 WLR 1239 that tortious damages for pain, suffering and loss of amenity should be increased by ten per cent and the extension of this decision to discrimination claims in the employment tribunal in *De Souza v Vinci Construction (UK) Ltd* [2017] EWCA Civ 879.

189 [2014] EWCA Civ 91.

190 (2015) 18 May, unreported, Central London County Court, HHJ Hand QC.

- Were racial slurs used?
- Was any refusal of service communicated directly to the person affected or passed via an intermediary.
- Did the incident(s) occur in public?
- How significant was the impact of the act(s) of discrimination on the claimant?
- Was any form of apology offered?

The public sector equality duty

Meaning of the duty

8.133 The PSED is set out in EqA 2010 s149. It reads:

> (1) A public authority must, in the exercise of its functions, have due regard to the need to–
> (a) eliminate discrimination, harassment, victimisation and any other conduct that is prohibited by or under this Act;
> (b) advance equality of opportunity between persons who share a relevant protected characteristic and persons who do not share it;
> (c) foster good relations between persons who share a relevant protected characteristic and persons who do not share it;
> (2) A person who is not a public authority but who exercises public functions must, in the exercise of those functions, have due regard to the matters mentioned in subsection (1) . . .

8.134 The importance of the PSED was recognised by Gilbart J in the case of *Moore and Coates v SSCLG* when he stated that:

> . . . Equality duties are an integral and important part of the mechanisms for ensuring the fulfilment of the aims of anti-discrimination legislation, and have been so for many years . . .[191]

8.135 The EHRC guidance on the PSED states:

> The broad purpose of the general equality duty is to integrate consideration of equality and good relations into the day-to-day business of public authorities. It is an integral part of the mechanisms for fulfilling the requirements of the Equality Act 2010. If a public authority does not consider how a function can affect different groups in different ways, the function may not meet its own objectives. . . . This can contribute to greater inequality and poor outcomes.[192]

191 [2015] EWHC 44 (Admin) at para 130.
192 EHRC, *The Essential Guide to the Public Sector Equality Duty* (July 2014, p7).

Scope of the duty

8.136 The PSED applies to all listed public authorities[193] and other bodies that exercise public functions.[194] It applies to local authorities; police; schools; higher and further educational institutions; health bodies; and central government. When applied to a private body exercising a public function, the PSED only applies to the exercise of those public functions.[195]

8.137 The general equality duty under the PSED is to have 'due regard' to the three objectives set out in EqA 2010 s149(1)(a)–(c) in the exercise of public functions. All bodies subject to the PSED must comply with this core duty. The EHRC has not issued a statutory Code of Practice in relation to the PSED due to the government's reluctance to support such a code. However, the EHRC has issued guidance on the operation of the PSED both generally and in particular areas.

8.138 EqA 2010 s149(3) and (5) provide further explanation of the PSED as follows:

> (3) Having due regard to the need to advance equality of opportunity between persons who share a relevant protected characteristic and persons who do not share it involves having due regard, in particular, to the need to–
> (a) remove or minimise disadvantages suffered by persons who share a relevant protected characteristic that are connected to that characteristic;
> (b) take steps to meet the needs of persons who share a relevant protected characteristic that are different from the needs of persons who do not share it;
> (c) encourage persons who share a relevant protected characteristic to participate in public life or in any other activity in which participation by such persons is disproportionately low.
>
> . . .
>
> (5) Having due regard to the need to foster good relations between persons who share a relevant protected characteristic and persons who do not share it involves having due regard, in particular, to the need to–
> (a) tackle prejudice, and
> (b) promote understanding.

193 As set out in EqA 2010 Sch 19.

194 EqA 2010 s149(2).

195 EqA 2010 s149(2).

8.139 Compliance with the PSED may involve treating some persons more favourably than others unless such action would otherwise constitute discrimination.[196]

8.140 The PSED applies both to policy formation and general practice as well as to the treatment of individual cases.[197] Its effects will typically be seen in engagement and consultation exercises and equality impact assessments.

8.141 In *Bracking v Secretary of State for Work and Pensions*[198] McCombe LJ summarised the principles to be derived from the authorities on EqA 2010 s149, as follows:

> (1) Equality duties are an integral and important part of the mechanisms for ensuring the fulfilment of the aims of anti-discrimination legislation.[199]
> (2) An important evidential element in the demonstration of the discharge of the duty is the recording of the steps taken by the decision maker in seeking to meet the statutory requirements.[200]
> (3) The relevant duty is upon the Minister or other decision maker personally. What matters is what he or she took into account and what he or she knew. Thus, the Minister or decision maker cannot be taken to know what his or her officials know or what may have been in the minds of officials in proffering their advice.[201]
> (4) A Minister must assess the risk and extent of any adverse impact and the ways in which such risk may be eliminated before the adoption of a proposed policy and not merely as a 'rearguard action', following a concluded decision.[202]
> (5) Applying these principles requires that:[203]
> i) The public authority decision maker must be aware of the duty to have 'due regard' to the relevant matters;
> ii) The duty must be fulfilled before and at the time when a particular policy is being considered;
> iii) The duty must be 'exercised in substance, with rigour, and with an open mind'. It is not a question of 'ticking boxes'; while there

196 EqA 2010 s149(6).

197 *Pieretti v Enfield LBC* [2010] EWCA Civ 1104.

198 [2013] EWCA Civ 1345, para 26.

199 *R (Elias) v Secretary of State for Defence* [2006] EWCA Civ 1293 at para 274.

200 *R (BAPIO Action Ltd) v Secretary of State for the Home Department* [2006] EWCA Civ 1293.

201 *R (National Association of Health Stores) v Secretary of State for Health* [2005] EWCA Civ 154 per Sedley LJ at paras 26–27.

202 *R (Kaur & Shah) v Ealing LBC* [2008] EWHC 2062 (Admin) per Moses LJ, sitting as a Judge of the Administrative Court, at paras 23–24.

203 *R (Brown) v Secretary of State for Work and Pensions* [2008] EWHC 3158 (Admin).

is no duty to make express reference to the regard paid to the relevant duty, reference to it and to the relevant criteria reduces the scope for argument;

iv) The duty is non-delegable; and

v) Is a continuing one.

vi) It is good practice for a decision maker to keep records demonstrating consideration of the duty.

(6) Having general regard to issues of equality is not the same as having specific regard, by way of conscious approach to the statutory criteria.[204]

(7) Officials reporting to or advising Ministers/other public authority decision makers, on matters material to the discharge of the duty, must not merely tell the Minister/decision maker what he/she wants to hear but they have to be 'rigorous in both enquiring and reporting to them'.[205]

(8) It is for the Court to decide for itself if due regard has been had, but providing this is done it is for the decision maker to decide what weight to give to the equality implications of the decision.[206]

(9) The duty of due regard under the statute requires public authorities to be properly informed before taking a decision. If the relevant material is not available, there will be a duty to acquire it and this will frequently mean that some further consideration with appropriate groups is required.[207]

(10) The duty to have due regard concerns the impact of the proposal on all persons with the protected characteristic and also, specifically, upon any particular class of persons with a protected characteristic who might most obviously be adversely affected by the proposal.[208]

8.142 Having 'due regard' means having 'proportionate regard' which is appropriate in the circumstances.[209] The number of persons affected and degree of impact are therefore relevant:

204 *R (Meany) v Harlow DC* [2009] EWHC 559 (Admin) per Davis J at para 84, approved in *R (Bailey) v Brent LBC* [2011] EWCA Civ 1586 at paras 74–75.

205 *R (Domb) v Hammersmith & Fulham LBC* [2009] EWCA Civ 941 (per Sedley LJ at para 79).

206 *R (Hurley & Moore) v Secretary of State for Business, Innovation and Skills* [2012] EWHC 201 (Admin) per Elias LJ at paras 77–78.

207 *R (Hurley & Moore) v Secretary of State for Business, Innovation and Skills* per Elias LJ at para 89.

208 *Bracking v Secretary of State for Work and Pensions* [2013] EWCA Civ 1345 per McCombe LJ at para 40.

209 *R (Baker) v Secretary of State for Communities and Local Government* [2008] EWCA Civ 141.

> ... in a case where large numbers of vulnerable people, many of whom fall within one or more of the protected groups ..., are affected, the due regard necessary is very high.[210]

8.143 As to the need for decision makers to be able provide evidence that due regard was had to the PSED, McCombe LJ stated:

> ... it seems to me that the 2010 Act imposes a heavy burden upon public authorities in discharging the PSED and in ensuring that there is evidence available, if necessary, to demonstrate that discharge. It seems to have been the intention of Parliament that these considerations of equality of opportunity (where they arise) are now to be placed at the centre of formulation of policy by all public authorities, side by side with all other pressing circumstances of whatever magnitude.

And:

> In the absence of evidence of a 'structured attempt to focus upon the details of equality issues' (per my Lord, Elias LJ in *Hurley & Moore*) a decision maker is likely to be in difficulties if his or her subsequent decision is challenged.[211]

8.144 There is a further power for a minister to impose specific duties on listed public authorities.[212] The current regulations require listed public authorities to publish annual information relating to persons with protected characteristics (for example, racial groups) who are either employed by the body or affected by its policies or practices.[213] Every four years listed authorities must publish one or more objectives it considers it should in order to comply with any of the things set out in EqA 2010 s149(1).[214] The objectives must be specific and measurable.[215]

210 *R (Hajrula) v London Councils* [2011] EWHC 448 (Admin) at para 69. The case concerned a challenge to the defendant's decision to cut funding paid to the Roma Support Group.

211 *Bracking v Secretary of State for Work and Pensions* [2013] EWCA Civ at paras 60–61.

212 The power is set out in EqA 2010 s153 and may only be applied to those public authorities listed in EqA 2010 Sch 19.

213 Equality Act 2010 (Specific Duties) Regulations 2011 SI No 2260 reg 2. There is an exception from the employee requirement for public authorities with fewer than 150 employees. There are additional duties for Welsh authorities (including engagement and procurement duties) and Scottish authorities (including a duty to mainstream equality, the publication of gender pay gap information and procurement duties).

214 Equality Act 2010 (Specific Duties) Regulations 2011 SI No 2260 reg 3(1).

215 Equality Act 2010 (Specific Duties) Regulations 2011 SI No 2260 reg 3(3).

8.145 Compliance with the PSED may be secured by way of judicial review in the High Court by a person who is directly affected or has sufficient interest, such as the EHRC itself.[216] A failure to comply with the PSED does not give a freestanding right to bring a civil claim for damages in the county court.[217] However, a failure to comply with the PSED may be used as evidence to support a discrimination claim in appropriate circumstances.

How can the public sector equality duty be used in practice?

8.146 In essence, the PSED requires public bodies to be proactive about equality. Rather than wait for cases of discrimination to be brought against them, public bodies are advised to:

- collect data on all areas of their employment, service delivery and other functions;
- analyse the results;
- establish whether there is an adverse impact on certain racial groups; and
- where this adverse impact cannot be justified within the wider policy aim, to make changes to mitigate this impact.

For example, if a local authority was collecting data on user satisfaction of particular relevant services and analysing this by reference to racial groups, it may discover that a particular group was dissatisfied with the services offered, or under-represented as users of particular services in comparison with local census data. The authority would need to look further into the reasons for this situation and make necessary changes if the reason could not be justified.

8.147 The PSED could bring major benefits for Gypsies and Travellers. If implemented effectively, it would mean that all listed public bodies were actively monitoring their policies for adverse impact on all racial groups, including those policies generally affecting Gypsies and Travellers. If they found that Gypsies and Travellers were adversely affected, and if this could not be justified within the wider goals of their policies, then they should change the policy. They should also be actively assessing the impact of any new or proposed policies and consulting Gypsies and Travellers on those policies. Consultation responses and impact assessments should be publicly

216 EqA 2006 s30.
217 EqA 2010 s156.

available to Gypsies and Travellers. Public authority staff should also be trained on the PSED and any relevant parts of the additional duties.

8.148 The section below highlights what should be expected of various public authorities in relation to Gypsies and Travellers. It should be noted that the suggestions set out below are not all statutory requirements, but suggested good practice in order to ensure compliance with the PSED.

Ethnic monitoring

8.149 The effective implementation of the PSED relies on monitoring and the collection of disaggregated data, the analysis of results, the identification of disproportionalities and the making of changes where they cannot be justified. The 2011 census was the first to include a dedicated tick box that allowed respondents to self-identify as 'Gypsy or Irish Traveller'. Public authorities, including police forces, should be encouraged to collect more detailed local data and to ensure that, where data is lacking, detailed consultation is used to ascertain the impact of policies. For consultation to be meaningful, it has to be carried out in a way that actively engages the consultees in an appropriate way.

Local authorities

8.150 Where there are Gypsies and Travellers in a local authority's area, or where Gypsies and Travellers periodically enter its area, a local authority should:

- assess the impact of its policies and functions on Gypsies and Travellers, for example, in areas such as planning, planning enforcement, site provision, site management, eviction and homelessness;
- consult on and assess the impact of new policies and monitor existing policies that are likely to have a particular impact on Gypsies and Travellers; and
- consider how they can foster good relations between Gypsies and Travellers and the rest of the community, particularly in the context of planning enforcement and eviction.

Local authorities will need to consider relevant functions, whether they are providing them directly or securing services from external suppliers through contractual arrangements. If a local authority engages an external supplier to provide services on its behalf then it will still be responsible for meeting the PSED, even though the supplier has no direct positive legal obligation to do so. This means that local authorities need to build equality considerations into the procurement process to the extent necessary to ensure compliance with the duty. Of relevance to Gypsies and Travellers may be the appointment of site managers, the engagement of companies providing electricity and facilities to sites and the use of a private company employed to carry out planning enforcement or eviction.

Police

8.151 Policies adopted by the police for dealing with the management of unauthorised encampments and eviction will impact particularly on Gypsies and Travellers, and each police force or authority will need to establish whether their policies have, or could have, an unjustifiably adverse impact on Gypsies and Travellers.

8.152 They will also need to examine more general policies to assess the impact that they have on Gypsies and Travellers. For example, if monitoring showed that Gypsies and Travellers were overrepresented in records showing the ethnic status of those refused bail at the police station, then the police force would need to conduct a thorough examination of its policies on the grant of bail to see if there was any justification for the statistics. If there was no such justification, then the police force would be obliged to make necessary changes to its policies in order to mitigate the adverse impact of those policies on Gypsies and Travellers.

8.153 The police will also need to ensure that they comply with their duty to promote good relations between Gypsies and Travellers and the rest of the community, particularly in the event of evictions or enforcement, where there may be issues of public order. It follows that the police will also need to take appropriate action when dealing with complaints of incitement to racial hatred against Gypsies and Travellers.

Schools

8.154 Schools (and local education authorities) should also consider how their policies, in particular those on exclusion and admission and those relating to attainment, affect Gypsy and Traveller pupils and whether changes could be made to promote equal opportunities for Gypsies and Travellers.

8.155 Schools should also consider how to foster good race relations in the school environment, for example, by developing aspects of the curriculum which celebrate Gypsy and Traveller culture, or through strong leadership, particularly where there may be unauthorised encampments in the local area, and hostility to such encampments. Schools need to ensure that they have adequate policies in place on racism and bullying and that complaints made by Gypsy and Traveller pupils are taken seriously.

Health bodies

8.156 Health bodies should consider how they are promoting equal opportunities for Gypsies and Travellers, how their staff are trained to be aware of the particular issues facing Gypsies and Travellers and how their general policies could impact on Gypsies and Travellers. If, for example, they established that there were disproportionately low levels of registration or take-up of preventative healthcare by Gypsies and Travellers in comparison with other racial groups, changes should be considered to improve the access and uptake of healthcare by Gypsies and Travellers.

Central government and devolved administrations

8.157 With their responsibilities for creating law and policy, and providing a leadership role for other public authorities, central government departments, the Scottish parliament and Scottish government and the Welsh government and the National Assembly for Wales all have a vital role to play through their PSED.

8.158 Government departments and devolved administrations have an obligation to fulfil their PSED in respect of their internal work, and the policies and strategies they produce. Policies and green and white papers, are all within the scope of the EqA 2010, and arrangements should be made to consult on and assess the impact of those policies that are relevant to equality. Government departments also have an important leadership role to play in assisting the bodies in their sector to comply with the PSED.

Planning

8.159 The case of *Moore and Coates v SSCLG*[218] provides an example of the use of the PSED to secure tangible results for Gypsies and Travellers

218 [2015] EWHC 44 (Admin).

in the planning sphere. The claimants challenged the Secretary of State's practice of recovering all planning and enforcement notice appeals involving Traveller sites in the Green Belt for his determination, ostensibly in order to ensure that the policy protection for the Green Belt laid down in *Planning policy for traveller sites*[219] (PPTS) was properly applied. When challenged by way of judicial review, Gilbart J found that the Minister was in breach of the PSED by failing to have due regard to the general duties, stating in trenchant terms:

> 131. Was 'due regard' had in this case? I remind myself of what McCombe LJ said in *Bracking* . . . The duty to have due regard concerns the impact of the proposal on all persons with the protected characteristic and also, specifically, upon any particular class of persons within a protected category who might most obviously be adversely affected by the proposal.
>
> 132. I do not accept [the Secretary of State's] submission that the consideration of equality at the time of PPTS in 2012 meant that there was no need for the matter to be addressed when considering whether to alter the practice of recovery in 2013–4. Gypsies and travellers were affected by a policy dealing with how the issues in their applications and appeals were to be considered (the PPTS) but they would also be affected by a policy which affected the way in which the procedure for determination of their appeals was to be conducted, and especially so as the effect was, as is common ground, to cause very considerable delays in determination. Indeed the fact that the PPTS and its Equality Assessment rightly recognised the particular disadvantages suffered by their ethnic group, was a very good reason for the SSCLG and his Ministers to recognise that care had to be taken if their position as compared to other appellants was not to be worsened.
>
> 133. But it must also be observed that there is no evidence that the reason put forward by Mr Warren [counsel for the SSCLG] was actually a reason which was ever in the mind of the SSCLG or Ministers at all. The Court has read all of the redacted Ministerial submissions. Despite the very clear guidance of the Court of Appeal, oft repeated, no one in the Department seems to have thought that Ministers or officials should even consider the tests which the law required them to address before embarking on the practice or policy. Apart from the single warning which was given by officials in March 2013 there is no mention of the issue or of the questions which statute said had to be addressed. Mr Warren says that the EHRC does not suggest that a formal Equality Impact Assessment had to be carried out in order for 'due regard' to be had. But even assuming that that is right, that does not mean that there was no requirement for an assessment or consideration of *any* kind.

219 See chapter 4 and appendix B.

> 134. The fact is that this in truth [is] not a case whether the regard the Secretary of State and his Ministers had was 'due regard.' The fact is that, on the evidence filed by the SSCLG, they had no regard at all. As the authorities cited above make clear, evidence is required that due regard was actually had. The Court is unable to assume that due regard was had simply because Counsel for the SSCLG asserts that it was, however engagingly. The Court of Appeal could not have been plainer in the several authorities recited earlier that the duty requires actual consideration, and that it expects evidence of a structured attempt to focus upon the details of equality issues. That applies as much to Ministerial consideration and decisions as it does to those of other public bodies. That omission is notable, given the care taken at the time of the PPTS by the SSCLG and his Department to address the issues in question.
>
> 135. I am therefore in no doubt that there has been a failure to comply with the PSED. It is not a case of the SSCLG and his Ministers addressing it but falling short; it is one of not addressing it [at] all, and not doing so on either occasion when changes in policy were being considered.
>
> 136. Even if I thought that the SSCLG and his Ministers had considered the issue, I would still have found on the evidence before me that they had not had due regard. That is because, as I have already concluded, the steps taken to achieve a legitimate end (giving the clear steer) have not been shown to be proportionate.
>
> 137. In the case of both Mrs Moore and Ms Coates, only one reason was given for the recovery of their respective appeals, which was the fact the appeals related to travellers pitches in the Green Belt. No other reason was given in writing, nor appears in Mr Watson's evidence, which suggests that either possessed any other feature, or raised any other issue, requiring recovery by the SSCLG. I conclude therefore that their appeals' recoveries were each vitiated by the breach of this duty and by the indirect discrimination towards the ethnic group of which they are members.

The Equality and Human Rights Commission's general powers

8.160 The EHRC has several general powers to ensure compliance with discrimination and human rights law.

The EHRC's power to issue a compliance notice

8.161 EqA 2006 s31 gives the EHRC the power to assess the extent to which, or the manner in which, a public body has complied with the

PSED under the EqA 2010. Where the EHRC has carried out an assessment and considers that a public body has failed to comply with a duty under the EqA 2010 then the EHRC may serve a 'compliance notice' on the body requiring it to comply with the duty and to inform the EHRC within 28 days of the steps that it has taken, or is taking, to comply with the duty.[220]

8.162 Where the EHRC considers that a public body has failed to comply with a requirement of a compliance notice, then: in a case where it is considered that a breach of EqA 2010 s149 has occurred, the EHRC has the power to apply to the High Court (or in Scotland, the Court of Session) for an order requiring the body to comply; and, in respect of a breach of 'specific duties', it may apply to the county court (or in Scotland, the sheriff's court) for such an order.[221]

Inquiries

8.163 EqA 2006 s16 gives the EHRC the power to conduct an 'inquiry' into any matter relating to the duties that it has under EqA 2006 ss8 and 9 to promote equality, diversity and human rights.[222] If, in the course of an inquiry, the EHRC suspects that a person or body (whether public or private) may have committed an unlawful act, then the EHRC may commence an 'investigation' into that matter, using its powers under EqA 2006 s20. However, the EHRC is required, so far as is possible, to exclude consideration of an unlawful act from its inquiry and should not make any reference to the commission of an unlawful act by a specified person or body in its report of an inquiry.[223]

Investigations

8.164 EqA 2006 s20(1)(a) gives the EHRC the power to investigate whether or not a person or body (whether public or private) has committed an unlawful act. The EHRC may only conduct such an exercise if it suspects that the person concerned has committed such an act. The EHRC's investigative powers replace those formerly vested in the CRE to conduct 'belief investigations' into discriminatory practices, which could only be undertaken where there was a reasonable belief

220 EqA 2006 s32(2).
221 EqA 2006 s32(8) and (9).
222 See para 8.34 above.
223 EqA 2006 s16(2) and (3).

that discrimination had occurred or was occurring and the complaint was made by or about a specific named body or bodies.

8.165 In 1980, the CRE conducted four named formal investigations into suspected unlawful discrimination against a Gypsy. These investigations examined allegations that certain residents of the village of Brymbo (near Wrexham) had unlawfully sought to influence Wrexham Maelor Borough Council to withhold council housing from an applicant because he was a Gypsy: two of the investigations examined the conduct of local residents; one, the conduct of a councillor; and the other, the conduct of the local community council.

8.166 One of the residents had organised a petition which was submitted to the council asking them not to house the Gypsy family in question. The petition stated 'we do not approve of the gypsies coming to live in Brymbo' and further that 'should our objections be ignored we are prepared to take whatever action is appropriate to further our objections'. The resident in question was further quoted in the local newspaper as saying 'the gypsies will move in here over our dead bodies'. Another named subject of the investigation made similar comments to a TV reporter. Brymbo Community Council had written to the council following a committee meeting expressing their 'profound dismay at the intentions of Wrexham Maelor Borough Council's Housing Department, to house another family of itinerants in the Brymbo area'. These actions were deemed to be in breach of RRA 1976 s31, which prohibited the use of pressure to discriminate and, of the four subjects of the investigation, three were issued with non-discrimination notices. The CRE concluded that the councillor was not guilty of discrimination.

Unlawful act notices

8.167 If the EHRC has conducted an investigation and is satisfied that the person or body has committed an unlawful act then it may issue an 'unlawful act notice'.[224] The notice must specify the unlawful act and the provision of the equality enactments by virtue of which the act is unlawful. In addition, the unlawful act notice may require the person or body to prepare an action plan for the purpose of avoiding repetition or continuation of the unlawful act and may recommend action

224 See EqA 2006 s21(1), but note that a person or body issued with an unlawful act notice may appeal to the appropriate court or tribunal against the notice and, on appeal, the notice may be affirmed, annulled or varied (EqA 2006 s21(6)).

to be taken for that purpose.[225] Alternatively, the EHRC may enter into an agreement with a person or body such that an undertaking is given not to commit an unlawful act of a specified kind.[226] The EHRC may apply for an order requiring a party to such an agreement to comply with an undertaking given pursuant to the agreement.[227]

Injunctions

8.168 EqA 2006 s24 gives the EHRC the power to apply to the county court for an injunction[228] to restrain a person or body that it thinks is likely to commit an act which is contrary to equality legislation and is therefore unlawful.

The EHRC's power to institute or intervene in legal proceedings

8.169 EqA 2006 s30 gives the EHRC the capacity to institute or intervene in legal proceedings whether for judicial review or otherwise, if it appears to the EHRC that the proceedings are relevant to a matter in connection with which it has a function.[229]

Hate speech and the media

Background

8.170 Negative media coverage of Gypsies and Travellers in the UK is rife and has drawn criticism from a number of international bodies and organisations.[230] By way of example, in its 2010 Report on the UK,

225 EqA 2006 s21(4) and note that there are specific provisions relating to action plans in EqA 2006 s22.

226 EqA 2006 s23.

227 EqA 2006 s24(2) and (3).

228 Application should be made to a sheriff for an interdict in Scotland.

229 See by way of example, the intervention made by the EHRC in *Moore and Coates v SSCLG* [2015] EWHC 44 (Admin).

230 See UN Human Rights Council Eighth Session, 2008, Report of the Working Group on the Universal Periodic Review United Kingdom of Great Britain and Northern Ireland, p15, para 15 – http://lib.ohchr.org/HRBodies/UPR/Documents/Session1/GB/A_HRC_8_25_United_Kingdom_E.pdf; and UN CERD, September 2011, Concluding Observations, Seventy Ninth Session, United Kingdom of Great Britain and Northern Ireland, p6, para 27, p2, para 11 –www2.ohchr.org/english/bodies/cerd/docs/CERD.C.GBR.CO.18–20.pdf.

the European Commission against Racism and Intolerance (ECRI)[231] stated that it was concerned to note that:

> ... Gypsies and Travellers are regularly presented in a negative light in the mainstream media, and in particular in the tabloid press, where they are frequently portrayed, for example, as being by definition associated with ... sponging off British society, making bogus claims for protection and being troublemakers. ECRI is concerned not only at the racist and xenophobic messages themselves that are thus propagated by the media, but also by the fact that civil society actors have in some cases observed direct links between minority groups targeted by the media and minority groups targeted in violent attacks.[232]

Right to freedom of expression and hate speech

8.171 As a society we place great value in the right to free speech, or freedom of expression. That right is protected by Article 10 of the ECHR.

8.172 The right to freedom of expression necessarily covers expression that may 'offend, shock or disturb the State or any sector of the population'.[233] Moreover, it should not be forgotten that democracy is not without its rough edges and that tough talk is part of the cut and thrust of public debate and discourse. However, Article 10 does not protect hate speech, whether it is expressed by politicians, journalists or individuals.

8.173 The case of *Feret v Belgium*[234] amply demonstrates the point. The European Court of Human Rights (ECtHR) dismissed a complaint brought by the chairman of the Front National political party that his Article 10 rights had been violated when he was convicted for publicly inciting hatred, following complaints relating to the distribution of election campaign leaflets. The ECtHR observed that the leaflets

231 See: www.coe.int/t/dghl/monitoring/ecri/country-by-country/united_kingdom/GBR-CbC-IV–2010–004-ENG.pdf.

232 See also Rachel Morris, Cardiff Law School, Gypsies and Travellers; Press regulation and Racism, Communications Law, 2000 Vol 5, No 6 p213 – www.media-diversity.org/en/additional-files/documents/Z%20Current%20MDI%20Resources/Gypsies,%20Travellers%20and%20the%20media%20-%20press%20regulation%20and%20racism%20in%20the%20UK.pdf; and the EHRC guidance *Gypsy Travellers in Scotland – a resource for the media*. The guidance was last updated in April 2016 and can be downloaded from the EHRC website at: www.equalityhumanrights.com/en/scottish-news/scottish-news/gypsy-travellers-scotland-resource-media.

233 See *Handyside v UK* (1976) 1 EHRR 737 at para 49; and also *Delfi As v Estonia* (2014) (App No 64569/09).

234 (2009) App No 15615/07.

presented immigrant communities as criminally-minded and keen to exploit the benefits they derived from living in Belgium and that they also sought to make fun of the immigrants concerned, with the inevitable risk of arousing, particularly among less knowledgeable members of the public, feelings of distrust, rejection or even hatred towards foreigners. Although the ECtHR recognised that freedom of expression is especially important for elected representatives of the people, it reiterated that it was crucial for politicians, when expressing themselves in public, to avoid comments that might foster intolerance.

8.174 The internet can provide those who wish to disseminate hate speech with the chance to spread words of hate with unprecedented effectiveness. Some online comments may be read by thousands, whilst others will be completely overlooked; whether a comment goes 'viral' is likely to depend upon the nature of the comment, the form of expression used, the platform chosen (eg a personal website, blog, forum, online news comment threads, Facebook, Twitter or YouTube) and its audience.

Inciting racial hatred

8.175 In the UK, those using hate speech (in whatever form[235]) may commit the criminal offence of inciting racial hatred. Whether they do so will depend upon whether the words used are 'threatening, abusive or insulting' and they intend to 'stir up racial hatred'[236] or, 'having regard to all the circumstances racial hatred is likely to be stirred up thereby'.[237]

8.176 In addition, those who publish hate speech may also commit a criminal offence.[238] However, publishers will not be guilty of an offence if they can show that they were 'not aware of the content of the material and did not suspect, and had no reason to suspect, that it was threatening, abusive or insulting.'[239]

235 This can include such things as making a speech, displaying a racist election poster, publishing written material, performing a play or broadcasting something in the media.

236 Racial hatred is defined in Public Order Act (POA) 1986 s17 as 'hatred against a group of persons . . . defined by reference to colour, race, nationality (including citizenship) or ethnic or national origins'.

237 See POA 1986 s18.

238 See POA 1986 s19.

239 See POA 1986 s19(2).

Decisions to prosecute

8.177 The CPS explains the way in which it deals with racist crime in a policy document entitled *Prosecution Policy on Racist and Religious Crime.*[240] It should be noted that prosecutions for incitement to racial hatred cannot be brought without the permission of the Attorney-General and that a decision to prosecute will only be taken if there is enough evidence to provide a realistic prospect of conviction and if it is considered that a prosecution is needed in the public interest. Significantly, the *Policy* states that:

> If the case passes the evidential stage and it is a case of racial or religious hate crime, or it is motivated by discrimination against the victim's ethnic or national origin, or religion or belief, it is more likely that a prosecution is required in the public interest[241]

8.178 In an associated *Public Statement on Prosecuting Racist and Religious Hate Crime*, the CPS also state:

> Hate crimes often have a disproportionate impact on the victim because they are being targeted for a personal characteristic. We recognise that hate crime not only impacts the individual victim but also the wider community. Hate incidents as one-offs or a related series of events can send reverberations through communities, just as they can reinforce established patterns of prejudice and discrimination. This is why it is so important for hate crime to be prosecuted effectively.[242]

8.179 In addition, the CPS has issued *Guidelines for prosecutors on assessing the public interest in cases affecting the media*[243] which make clear that the media should not be afforded special status under the criminal law. The Guidelines explain that the CPS should consider whether the public interest served by the publication outweighs the overall criminality and gives examples of conduct which is capable of serving the public interest, such as the disclosure of the fact that a criminal offence has been committed or the fact that a miscarriage of justice has occurred.[244] However, in the absence of such circumstances there

240 See: www.cps.gov.uk/legal/p_to_r/racist_and_religious_crime/#a01 last updated 21 August 2017.

241 See: www.cps.gov.uk/legal/p_to_r/racist_and_religious_crime/#a01.

242 See: www.cps.gov.uk/publications/docs/racist-religious-hate-crime-statement–2017.pdf (published August 2017).

243 See: www.cps.gov.uk/legal/d_to_g/guidance_for_prosecutors_on_assessing_the_public_interest_in_cases_affecting_the_media_/ published 13 September 2012.

244 See para 31 of the Guidelines.

can be no excuse for the reporting of hate speech and a prosecution should be brought.

Conclusion

8.180 While race equality legislation in the UK has developed considerably over the last 40 years, it has had relatively little impact on the discrimination that Gypsies and Travellers experience within our community. However, as can be seen from the cases of *Moore and Coates v SSCLG* and *Traveller Movement and Others v JD Wetherspoon plc,* there is no doubt that existing equality legislation can be used to bring significant improvements to the lives of Gypsies and Travellers. It is up to Gypsies and Travellers and those advising them to stand up to the discrimination they face and to challenge it in the courts whenever they can. In that way real progress can be made for future generations.

8.181 Likewise, it is vitally important that those affected by hate speech report it to the police and that the authorities properly investigate such complaints. There is a clear and compelling public interest in prosecuting perpetrators and, if the CPS and the Attorney-General use their powers effectively, then we may yet tackle what has become known as the last bastion of socially acceptable racism in the UK.

APPENDICES

APPENDIX A

Extracts from legislation[1]

CARAVAN SITES ACT 1968 SS2–4

Minimum length of notice

2 In any case where a residential contract is determinable by notice given by either party to the other, a notice so given shall be of no effect unless it is given not less than four weeks before the date on which it is to take effect.

Protection of occupiers against eviction and harassment, false information etc

3(1) Subject to the provisions of this section, a person shall be guilty of an offence under this section–

- (a) if, during the subsistence of a residential contract, he unlawfully deprives the occupier of his occupation on the protected site of any caravan which the occupier is entitled by the contract to station and occupy, or to occupy, as his residence thereon;
- (b) if, after the expiration or determination of a residential contract, he enforces, otherwise than by proceedings in the court, any right to exclude the occupier from the protected site or from any such caravan, or to remove or exclude any such caravan from the site;
- (c) if, whether during the subsistence or after the expiration or determination of a residential contract, the person–
  - (i) does anything likely to interfere with the peace or comfort of the occupier or persons residing with the occupier; or
  - (ii) persistently withdraws or withholds services or facilities reasonably required for the occupation of the caravan as a residence on the site, and (in either case) knows, or has reasonable cause to believe, that that conduct is likely to cause the occupier to abandon the occupation of the caravan or remove it from the site or to refrain from exercising any right or pursuing any remedy in relation to the caravan.

1 © Crown copyright. Reproduced as amended up to date to 1 December 2019.

(1A) Subject to the provisions of this section, the owner of a protected site or his agent shall be guilty of an offence under this section if, whether during the subsistence or after the expiration or determination of a residential contract–

(a) he does acts likely to interfere with the peace or comfort of the occupier or persons residing with him, or

(b) he withdraws or withholds or, if the site concerned is in Wales, persistently withdraws or withholds services or facilities reasonably required for the occupation of the caravan as a residence on the site, and (in either case) he knows, or has reasonable cause to believe, that that conduct is likely to cause the occupier to do any of the things mentioned in subsection (1)(c)(i) or (ii) of this section.

(1AA) The owner of a protected site or the owner's agent is guilty of an offence under this section if, during the subsistence of a residential contract, the owner or (as the case may be) agent–

(a) knowingly or recklessly provides information or makes a representation which is false or misleading in a material respect to any person, and

(b) knows, or has reasonable cause to believe, that doing so is likely to cause–

(i) the occupier to do any of the things mentioned in subsection (1)(c)(i) or

(ii), or a person who is considering whether to purchase or occupy the caravan to which the residential contract relates to decide not to do so.

(1B) References in subsections (1A) and (1AA) of this section to the owner of a protected site include references to a person with an estate or interest in the site which is superior to that of the owner.

(2) References in this section to the occupier include references to the person who was the occupier under a residential contract which has expired or been determined and, in the case of the death of the occupier (whether during the subsistence or after the expiration or determination of the contract), to any person then residing with the occupier being–

(a) the widow, widower or surviving civil partner of the occupier; or

(b) in default of a widow, widower or surviving civil partner so residing, any member of the occupier's family.

(3) A person guilty of an offence under this section shall, without prejudice to any liability or remedy to which he may be subject in civil proceedings, liable on summary conviction–

(a) in the case of a first offence, to a fine not exceeding the statutory maximum;

(b) in the case of a second or subsequent offence, to a fine not exceeding the statutory maximum or to imprisonment for a term not exceeding 6 months, or to both.

(4) In proceedings for an offence under paragraph (a) or (b) of subsection (1) of this section it shall be a defence to prove that the accused believed, and had reasonable cause to believe, that the occupier of the caravan had ceased to reside on the site.

(4A) In proceedings for an offence under subsection (1)(c) of this section it shall be a defence to prove that the accused had reasonable grounds for doing the acts or withdrawing or withholding the services or facilities in question.

(5) Nothing in this section applies to the exercise by any person of a right to take possession of a caravan of which he is the owner, other than a right conferred by or arising on the expiration or determination of a residential contract, or to anything done pursuant to the order of any court.

Provision for suspension of eviction orders

4(1) If in proceedings by the owner of a protected site the court makes an order for enforcing in relation thereto any such right as is mentioned in paragraph (b) of subsection (1) of section 3 of this Act, the court may (without prejudice to any power apart from this section to postpone the operation or suspend the execution of an order, and subject to the following provisions of this section) suspend the enforcement of the order for such period not exceeding twelve months from the date of the order as the court thinks reasonable.

(2) Where the court by virtue of this section suspends the enforcement of an order, it may impose such terms and conditions, including conditions as to the payment of rent or other periodical payments or of arrears of such rent or payments, as the court thinks reasonable.

(3) The court may from time to time, on the application of either party, extend, reduce or terminate the period of suspension ordered by virtue of this section, or vary any terms or conditions imposed thereunder, but shall not extend the period of suspension for more than twelve months at a time.

(4) In considering whether or how to exercise its powers under this section, the court shall have regard to all the circumstances, and in particular to the questions–

(a) whether the occupier of the caravan has failed, whether before or after the expiration or determination of the relevant residential contract, to observe any terms or conditions of that contract, any conditions of the site licence, or any reasonable rules made by the owner for the management and conduct of the site or the maintenance of caravans thereon;

(b) whether the occupier has unreasonably refused an offer by the owner to renew the residential contract or make another such contract for a reasonable period and on reasonable terms;

(c) whether the occupier has failed to make reasonable efforts to obtain elsewhere other suitable accommodation for his caravan (or, as the case may be, another suitable caravan and accommodation for it).

(5) Where the court makes such an order as is mentioned in subsection (1) of this section but suspends the enforcement of that order by virtue of this section, the court shall make no order for costs unless it appears to the court, having regard to the conduct of the owner or of the occupier, that there are special reasons for making such an order.

(6) The court shall not suspend the enforcement of an order by virtue of this section if–

(a) no site licence under Part 1 of the Caravan Sites and Control of Development Act 1960 (c 62) is in force in respect of the site; and

(b) paragraph 11 of Schedule 1 to that Act does not apply;

and where a site licence in respect of the site is expressed to expire at the end of a specified period, the period for which enforcement may be suspended by virtue of this section shall not extend beyond the expiration of the licence.

MOBILE HOMES ACT 1983

Particulars of agreements

1(1) This Act applies to any agreement under which a person ('the occupier') is entitled–

(a) to station a mobile home on land forming part of a protected site; and

(b) to occupy the mobile home as his only or main residence.

(2) Before making an agreement to which this Act applies, the owner of the protected site ('the owner') shall give to the proposed occupier under the agreement a written statement which–

(a) specifies the names and addresses of the parties;

(b) includes particulars of the land on which the proposed occupier is to be entitled to station the mobile home that are sufficient to identify that land;

(c) sets out the express terms to be contained in the agreement (including any site rules (see section 2C));

(d) sets out the terms to be implied by section 2(1) below; and

(e) complies with such other requirements as may be prescribed by regulations made by the Secretary of State.

(3) The written statement required by subsection (2) above must be given–

(a) not later than 28 days before the date on which any agreement for the sale of the mobile home to the proposed occupier is made, or

(b) (if no such agreement is made before the making of the agreement to which this Act applies) not later than 28 days before the date on which the agreement to which this Act applies is made.

(4) But if the proposed occupier consents in writing to that statement being given to him by a date ('the chosen date') which is less than 28 days before the date mentioned in subsection (3)(a) or (b) above, the statement must be given to him not later than the chosen date.

(5) If any express term other than a site rule (se section 2C)–

(a) is contained in an agreement to which this Act applies, but

(b) was not set out in a written statement given to the proposed occupier in accordance with subsections (2) to (4) above, the term is unenforceable by the owner or any person within section 3(1) below.

This is subject to any order made by the appropriate judicial body under section 2(3) below.

(6) If the owner has failed to give the occupier a written statement in accordance with subsections (2) to (4) above, the occupier may, at any time after the making of the agreement, apply to the appropriate judicial body for an order requiring the owner–

(a) to give him a written statement which complies with paragraphs (a) to (e) of subsection (2) (read with any modifications necessary to reflect the fact that the agreement has been made), and

(b) to do so not later than such date as is specified in the order.

(7) A statement required to be given to a person under this section may be either delivered to him personally or sent to him by post.

(8) Any reference in this section to the making of an agreement to which this Act applies includes a reference to any variation of an agreement by virtue of which the agreement becomes one to which this Act applies.

(8A) Subsections (3), (4) and (6) do not apply in relation to a person occupying or proposing to occupy a transit pitch on a local authority gypsy and traveller site or a county council gypsy and traveller site and in such cases, the reference in subsection (5) to subsections (2) to (4) is to be treated as a reference to subsection (2).

(8B) In subsection (8A) 'county council gypsy and traveller site', 'local authority gypsy and traveller site' and 'transit pitch' all have the same meanings as in paragraph 1(4) of Chapter 1 of Part 1 of Schedule 1 to this Act.

(9) Regulations under this section–
- (a) shall be made by statutory instrument;
- (b) shall be subject to annulment in pursuance of a resolution of either House of Parliament; and
- (c) may make different provision with respect to different cases or descriptions of case, including different provision for different areas.

Terms of agreements

2(1) In any agreement to which this Act applies there shall be implied the applicable terms set out in Part I of Schedule 1 to this Act; and this subsection shall have effect notwithstanding any express term of the agreement.

(2) The appropriate judicial body may, on the application of either party made within the relevant period, order that there shall be implied in the agreement terms concerning the matters mentioned in Part II of Schedule 1 to this Act.

(3) The appropriate judicial body may, on the application of either party made within the relevant period, make an order–
- (a) varying or deleting any express term of the agreement other than a site rule (see section 2C);
- (b) in the case of any express term to which section 1(6) above applies other than a site rule (see section (2C), provide for the term to have full effect or to have such effect subject to any variation specified in the order.

(3A) In subsections (2) and (3) above 'the relevant period' means the period beginning with the date on which the agreement is made and ending–
- (a) six months after that date, or
- (b) where a written statement relating to the agreement is given to the occupier after that date (whether or not in compliance with an order under section 1(6) above), six months after the date on which the statement is given;

and section 1(8) above applies for the purposes of this subsection as it applies for the purposes of section 1.

(4) On an application under this section, the appropriate judicial body shall make such provision as the court considers just and equitable in the circumstances.

(5) The supplementary provisions in Part 3 of Schedule 1 to this Act have effect for the purposes of paragraphs 8 and 9 of Part 1 of that Schedule.

(6) Subsections (2) to (4) do not apply in relation to a person occupying or proposing to occupy a transit pitch on a local authority gypsy and traveller site or a county council gypsy and traveller site.

(7) In subsection (6) 'county council gypsy and traveller site', 'local authority gypsy and traveller site' and 'transit pitch' all have the same meanings as in paragraph 1(4) of Chapter 1 of Part 1 of Schedule 1 to this Act.

Power to amend implied terms

2A(1) The Secretary of State may by order make such amendments of Part 1 or 2 of Schedule 1 to this Act as the Secretary of State considers appropriate.

(2) An order under this section–

(a) shall be made by statutory instrument;

(b) may make different provision with respect to different cases or descriptions of case, including different provision for different areas;

(c) may contain such incidental, supplementary, consequential, transitional or saving provisions as the authority making the order considers appropriate.

(3) Without prejudice to the generality of subsections (1) and (2), an order under this section may–

(a) make provision for or in connection with the determination by the court of such questions, or the making by the court of such orders, as are specified in the order;

(b) make such amendments of any provision of this Act as the authority making the order considers appropriate in consequence of any amendment made by the order in Part 1 or 2 of Schedule 1.

(4) The first order made under this section in relation to England or Wales respectively may provide for all or any of its provisions to apply in relation to agreements to which this Act applies that were made at any time before the day on which the order comes into force (as well as in relation to such agreements made on or after that day).

(5) No order may be made under this section unless the Secretary of State has consulted–

(a) such organisations as appear to Secretary of State to be representative of interests substantially affected by the order; and

(b) such other persons as Secretary of State considers appropriate.

(6) No order may be made under this section unless a draft of the order has been laid before, and approved by a resolution of, each House of Parliament.

Power to amend implied terms: Scotland

2B(1) The Scottish Ministers may by order make such amendments of Part 1 or 2 of Schedule 1 to this Act as they consider appropriate.

(2) An order under this section–

(a) shall be made by statutory instrument;

(b) may make different provision with respect to different cases or descriptions of case;

(c) may contain such incidental, supplementary, consequential, transitional or saving provisions as the Scottish Ministers consider appropriate.

(3) Without prejudice to the generality of subsections (1) and (2), an order under this section may–

(a) make provision for or in connection with the determination by the court of such questions, or the making by the court of such orders, as are specified in the order;

(b) make such amendments of any provision of this Act as the Scottish Ministers consider appropriate in consequence of any amendment made by the order in Part 1 or 2 of Schedule 1.

(4) The first order made under this section may provide for all or any of its provisions to apply in relation to agreements to which this Act applies that were made at any time before the day on which the order comes into force (as well as in relation to such agreements made on or after that day).

(5) No order may be made under this section unless the Scottish Ministers have consulted–

(a) such organisations as appear to them to be representative of interests substantially affected by the order; and

(b) such other persons as they consider appropriate.

(6) No order may be made under this section unless a draft of the order has been laid before, and approved by a resolution of, the Scottish Parliament.

Site rules

2C(1) In the case of a protected site, other than a gypsy and traveller site, for which there are site rules, each of the rules is to be an express term of each agreement to which this Act applies that relates to a pitch on the site (including an agreement made before commencement or one made before the making of the rules).

(2) The 'site rules' for a protected site are rules made by the owner in accordance with such procedure as may be prescribed which relate to–

(a) the management and conduct of the site, or

(b) such other matters as may be prescribed.

(3) Any rules made by the owner before commencement which relate to a matter mentioned in subsection (2) cease to have effect at the end of such period beginning with commencement as may be prescribed.

(4) Site rules come into force at the end of such period beginning with the first consultation day as may be prescribed, if a copy of the rules is deposited with the local authority before the end of that period.

(5) Where a site rule is varied, the rule as varied comes into force at the end of such period beginning with the first consultation day as may be prescribed, if–

(a) the rule is varied in accordance with such procedure as may be prescribed, and

(b) a copy of the rule as varied is deposited with the local authority before the end of that period.

(6) Where a site rule is deleted, the deletion comes into force at the end of such period beginning with the first consultation day as may be prescribed, if–

(a) the rule is deleted in accordance with such procedure as may be prescribed, and

(b) notice of the deletion is deposited with the local authority before the end of that period.

(7) Regulations may provide that a site rule may not be made, varied or deleted unless a proposal to make, vary or delete the rule is notified to the occupiers of the site in question in accordance with the regulations.

(8) Regulations may provide that site rules, or rules such as are mentioned in subsection (3), are of no effect in so far as they make provision in relation to prescribed matters.

(9) Regulations may make provision as to the resolution of disputes–

(a) relating to a proposal to make, vary or delete a site rule;

(b) as to whether the making, variation or deletion of a site rule was in accordance with the applicable prescribed procedure;

(c) as to whether a deposit required to be made by virtue of subsection (4), (5) or (6) was made before the end of the relevant period.

(10) Provision under subsection (9) may confer functions on a tribunal.

(11) Regulations may–

(a) require a local authority to establish and keep up to date a register of site rules in respect of protected sites in its area;

(b) require a local authority to publish the up-to-date register;

(c) provide that any deposit required to be made by virtue of subsection (4), (5) or (6) must be accompanied by a fee of such amount as the local authority may determine.

Section 2C: supplementary provision

2D(1) This section applies for the purposes of section 2C.

(2) 'Commencement' means the commencement of that section.

(3) 'First consultation day' means the day on which a proposal made under regulations under subsection (7) of that section is notified to the occupiers of the site in accordance with the regulations.

(4) A reference to the local authority is a reference to the local authority in whose area the protected site in question is situated.

(5) A reference to a gypsy and traveller site is a reference to a county council gypsy and traveller site or a local authority gypsy and traveller site (each of which has the meaning given by paragraph 1(4) of Chapter 1 of Part 1 of Schedule 1).

(6) 'Prescribed' means prescribed in regulations; and the power to make regulations is exercisable by the Secretary of State.

(7) The regulations must be made by statutory instrument and may–

(a) make different provision for different cases or descriptions of case, including different provision for different areas;

(b) contain incidental, supplementary, transitional or saving provisions.

(8) The regulations are subject to annulment in pursuance of a resolution of either House of Parliament.

Successors in title

3(1) An agreement to which this Act applies shall be binding on and enure for the benefit of any successor in title of the owner and any person claiming through or under the owner or any such successor.

(2) Where an agreement to which this Act applies is lawfully assigned to any person, the agreement shall enure for the benefit of and be binding on that person.

(3) Where a person entitled to the benefit of and bound by an agreement to which this Act applies dies at a time when he is occupying the mobile home as his only or main residence, the agreement shall enure for the benefit of and be binding on–

(a) any person residing with that person ('the deceased') at that time being–

(i) the widow, widower or surviving civil partner of the deceased; or

(ii) in default of a widow, widower or surviving civil partner so residing, any member of the deceased's fairly; or

(b) in default of any such person so residing, the person entitled to the mobile home by virtue of the deceased's will or under the law relating to intestacy but subject to subsection (4) below.

(4) An agreement to which this Act applies shall not enure for the benefit of or be binding on a person by virtue of subsection (3)(b) above in so far as–

(a) it would, but for this subsection, enable or require that person to occupy the mobile home; or

(b) it includes terms implied by virtue of paragraph 5, 8A, 8B or 9 of Chapter 2 or paragraph 5 of Chapter 4 of Part I of Schedule 1 to this Act.

Jurisdiction of a tribunal or the court

4(1) In relation to a protected site, a tribunal has jurisdiction–
(a) to determine any question arising under this Act or any agreement to which it applies; and
(b) to entertain any proceedings brought under this Act or any such agreement, subject to subsections (2) to (6).

(2) Subsection (1) applies in relation to a question irrespective of anything contained in an arbitration agreement which has been entered into before that question arose.

(3) In relation to a protected site, the court has jurisdiction–
(a) to determine any question arising by virtue of paragraph 4, 5 or 5A(2)(b) of Chapter 2, or paragraph 4, 5 or 6(1)(b) of Chapter 4, of Part 1 of Schedule 1 (termination by owner) under this Act or any agreement to which it applies; and
(b) to entertain any proceedings so arising brought under this Act or any such agreement, subject to subsections (4) to (6).

(4) Subsection (5) applies if the owner and occupier have entered into an arbitration agreement before the question mentioned in subsection (3)(a) arises and the agreement applies to that question.

(5) A tribunal has jurisdiction to determine the question and entertain any proceedings arising instead of the court.

(6) Subsection (5) applies irrespective of anything contained in the arbitration agreement mentioned in subsection (4).

(7) [Repealed.]

Interpretation

5(1) In this Act, unless the context otherwise requires–

'the appropriate judicial body' means whichever of the court or a tribunal has jurisdiction under section 4;

'arbitration agreement' means an agreement in writing to submit to arbitration any question arising under this Act or any agreement to which it applies;

'the court' means–
(a) in relation to England, the county court or, where the parties have entered into an arbitration agreement that applies to the question to be determined, the arbitrator;
(b) in relation to Scotland, the sheriff having jurisdiction where the protected site is situated or, where the parties have so agreed, the arbiter;

'local authority' has the same meaning as in Part I of the Caravan Sites and Control of Development Act 1960;

'mobile home' has the same meaning as 'caravan' has in that Part of that Act;

'owner', in relation to a protected site, means the person who, by virtue of an estate or interest held by him, is entitled to possession of the site or would be so entitled but for the rights of any persons to station mobile homes on land forming part of the site;

planning permission' means permission under Part III of the Town and Country Planning Act 1990 or Part III of the Town and Country Planning (Scotland) Act 1997;
protected site' has the same meaning as in Part I of the Caravan Sites Act 1968;
'a tribunal'means, where the parties have entered into an arbitration agreement that applies to the question to be determined and that question arose before the agreement was made, the arbitrator; or, in other cases–

(a) in relation to England, the First-tier Tribunal or, where determined by or under Tribunal Procedure Rules, the Upper; and
(b) in relation to Wales, a residential property tribunal.

(2) In relation to an agreement to which this Act applies–

(a) any reference in this Act to the owner includes a reference to any person who is bound by and entitled to the benefit of the agreement by virtue of subsection (1) of section 3 above; and
(b) subject to subsection (4) of that section, any reference in this Act to the occupier includes a reference to any person who is entitled to the benefit of and bound by the agreement by virtue of subsection (2) or (3) of that section.

(3) A person is a member of another's family within the meaning of this Act if he is his spouse, civil partner, parent, grandparent, child, grandchild, brother, sister, uncle, aunt, nephew or niece; treating–

(a) any relationship by marriage or civil partnership as a relationship by blood, any relationship of the half blood as a relationship of the whole blood and the stepchild of any person as his child; and
(b) an illegitimate person as the legitimate child of his mother and reputed father;

or if they live together as husband and wife or as if they were civil partners.

(4) In relation to land in Scotland, any reference in this Act to an 'estate or interest' shall be construed as a reference to a right in, or to, the land.

Short title, repeals, commencement and extent

6(1) This Act may be cited as the Mobile Homes Act 1983.

(2) The enactments mentioned in Schedule 2 to this Act are hereby repealed to the extent specified in the third column of that Schedule.

(3) This Act shall come into force on the expiry of the period of one week beginning with the day on which it is passed.

(4) This Act does not extend to Northern Ireland.

SCHEDULE 1: AGREEMENTS UNDER ACT

PART I: TERMS IMPLIED BY ACT

Duration of agreement

1(1) The implied terms set out in Chapter 2 apply to all agreements which relate to a pitch except an agreement which relates to a pitch on a local authority gypsy and traveller site or a county council gypsy and traveller site.

(2) The implied terms set out in Chapter 3 apply to an agreement which relates to a transit pitch on a local authority gypsy and traveller site or a county council gypsy and traveller site.

(3) The implied terms set out in Chapter 4 apply to an agreement which relates to a permanent pitch on a local authority gypsy and traveller site or a county council gypsy and traveller site.

(4) In this Part of this Schedule–

'caravan site' has the same meaning as in Part 1 of the Caravan Sites and Control of Development Act 1960,

'county council gypsy and traveller site' means any land which–

(a) is occupied by a county council as a caravan site providing accommodation for gypsies and travellers, and

(b) is a protected site,

'gypsies and travellers' means persons of nomadic habit of life, whatever their race or origin, but does not include members of an organised group of travelling showpeople, or persons engaged in travelling circuses, travelling together as such,

'local authority gypsy and traveller site' means any land which–

(a) is occupied by a local authority as a caravan site providing accommodation for gypsies and travellers, and

(b) is a protected site,

'permanent pitch' means a pitch which is not a transit pitch,

'pitch' means the land, forming part of a protected site and including any garden area, on which an occupier is entitled to station a mobile home under the terms of the agreement, and

'transit pitch' means a pitch on which a person is entitled to station a mobile home under the terms of the agreement for a fixed period of up to 3 months.

Chapter 2: Agreements Relating to Pitches Except Pitches on Local Authority Gypsy and Traveller Sites and County Council Gypsy and Traveller Sites

Duration of Agreement

1 Subject to paragraph 2 below, the right to station the mobile home on land forming part of the protected site shall subsist until the agreement is determined under paragraph 3, 4, 5 or 5A below.

1A(1) The right to station the mobile home under in paragraph 1 is not affected by–

(a) the expiry of a Part 1A site licence in accordance with section 32J(1)(b)(ii) of the 1960 Act,

(b) the refusal to issue or renew a Part 1A site licence under section 32D of the 1960 Act,

(c) the revocation of a Part 1A site licence under section 32L of the 1960 Act, or

(d) the expiry of a site licence in accordance with section 83(2) of the Housing (Scotland) Act 2014 (asp 14).

(2) Sub-paragraph (1) applies in relation to agreements that were made at any time before the day on which that sub-paragraph comes into force (as well as in relation to agreements made on or after that day).

(3) In this paragraph–

'the 1960 Act' means the Caravan Sites and Control of Development Act 1960 (c 62), and

'Part 1A site licence' has the same meaning as in section 32Z6 of the 1960 Act.

2(1) If the owner's estate or interest is insufficient to enable him to grant the right for an indefinite period, the period for which the right subsists shall not extend beyond the date when the owner's estate or interest determines.

(2) If planning permission for the use of the protected site as a site for mobile homes has been granted in terms such that it will expire at the end of a specified period, the period for which the right subsists shall not extend beyond the date when the planning permission expires.

(3) If before the end of a period determined by this paragraph there is a change in circumstances which allows a longer period, account shall be taken of that change.

Termination by occupier

3 The occupier shall be entitled to terminate the agreement by notice in writing given to the owner not less than four weeks before the date on which it is to take effect.

4 The owner shall be entitled to terminate the agreement at a date to be determined by the court if, on the application of the owner, the appropriate judicial body–

(a) is satisfied that the occupier has breached a term of the agreement and, after service of a notice to remedy the breach, has not complied with the notice within a reasonable time; and

(b) considers it reasonable for the agreement to be terminated.

5 The owner shall be entitled to terminate the agreement at a date to be determined by the court if, on the application of the owner, the appropriate judicial body–

(a) is satisfied that the occupier is not occupying the mobile home as his only or main residence; and

(b) considers it reasonable for the agreement to be terminated].

5A(1) [Repealed.]

(2) The owner is entitled to terminate the agreement forthwith if–

(a) on the application of the owner, a tribunal has determined that, having regard to its condition, the mobile home is having a detrimental effect on the amenity of the site; and

(b) then, on the application of the owner, the appropriate judicial body, having regard to the tribunal's determination and to any other circumstances, considers it reasonable for the agreement to be terminated.

(3) Sub-paragraphs (4) and (5) apply if, on an application to the tribunal under sub-paragraph (2)(a)–

(a) the tribunal considers that, having regard to the present condition of the mobile home, it is having a detrimental effect on the amenity of the site, but

(b) it also considers that it would be reasonably practicable for particular repairs to be carried out on the mobile home that would result in the mobile home not having that detrimental effect, and

(c) the occupier indicates to the tribunal that the occupier intends to carry out those repairs.

(4) In such a case, the tribunal may make an interim order–

(a) specifying the repairs that must be carried out and the time within which they must be carried out; and

(b) adjourning the proceedings on the application for such period specified in the interim order as the tribunal considers reasonable to enable the repairs to be carried out.

(5) If the tribunal makes an interim order under sub-paragraph (4), it must not make a determination under sub-paragraph (2)(a) unless it is satisfied that the specified period has expired without the repairs having been carried out.

6 [Repealed.]

Repayment of sums paid by occupier on termination of agreement

7 Where the agreement is terminated as mentioned in paragraph 3, 4, 5 or 6, the owner must, within 2 months of the date of the termination, repay to the occupier so much of any payment made by the occupier in pursuance of the agreement as is attributable to a period beginning after the date of termination.

Sale of mobile home

7A(1) [Repealed.]

(2) Where the agreement is a new agreement, the occupier is entitled to sell the mobile home and to assign the agreement to the person to whom the mobile home is sold (referred to in this paragraph as the 'new occupier') without the approval of the owner.

(3) In this paragraph and paragraph 7B, 'new agreement' means an agreement–

(a) which was made after the commencement of this paragraph, or
(b) which was made before, but which has been assigned after, that commencement.

(4) The new occupier must, as soon as reasonably practicable, notify the owner of the completion of the sale and assignment of the agreement.

(5) The new occupier is required to pay the owner a commission on the sale of the mobile home at a rate not exceeding such rate as may be prescribed by regulations made by the Secretary of State.

(6) Except to the extent mentioned in sub-paragraph (5), the owner may not require any payment to be made (whether to the owner or otherwise) in connection with the sale of the mobile home and the assignment of the agreement to the new occupier.

(7) The Secretary of State may by regulations prescribe procedural requirements to be complied with by the owner, the occupier or the new occupier in connection with–
(a) the sale of the mobile home and assignment of the agreement;
(b) the payment of commission by virtue of sub-paragraph (5).

7B(1) Where the agreement is not a new agreement, the occupier is entitled to sell the mobile home and assign the agreement without the approval of the owner if–
(a) the occupier serves on the owner a notice (a 'notice of proposed sale') that the occupier proposes to sell the mobile home, and assign the agreement, to the person named in the notice (the 'proposed occupier'), and
(b) the first or second condition is satisfied.

(2) The first condition is that, within the period of 21 days beginning with the date on which the owner received the notice of proposed sale ('the 21-day period'), the occupier does not receive a notice from the owner that the owner has applied to a tribunal for an order preventing the occupier from selling the mobile home, and assigning the agreement, to the proposed occupier (a 'refusal order').

(3) The second condition is that–
(a) within the 21-day period–
(i) the owner applies to a tribunal for a refusal order, and
(ii) the occupier receives a notice of the application from the owner, and
(b) the tribunal rejects the application.

(4) If the owner applies to a tribunal for a refusal order within the 21-day period but the occupier does not receive notice of the application from the owner within that period–
(a) the application is to be treated as not having been made, and
(b) the first condition is accordingly to be treated as satisfied.

(5) A notice of proposed sale must include such information as may be prescribed in regulations made by the Secretary of State.

(6) A notice of proposed sale or notice of an application for a refusal order–

(a) must be in writing, and

(b) may be served by post.

(7) An application for a refusal order may be made only on one or more of the grounds prescribed in regulations made by the Secretary of State; and a notice of an application for a refusal order must specify the ground or grounds on which the application is made.

(8) The person to whom the mobile home is sold ('the new occupier') is required to pay the owner a commission on the sale of the mobile home at a rate not exceeding such rate as may be prescribed by regulations made by the Secretary of State.

(9) Except to the extent mentioned in sub-paragraph (8), the owner may not require any payment to be made (whether to the owner or otherwise) in connection with the sale of the mobile home and the assignment of the agreement.

(10) The Secretary of State may by regulations prescribe procedural requirements to be complied with by the owner, the occupier, a proposed occupier or the new occupier in connection with–

(a) the sale of the mobile home and assignment of the agreement;

(b) the payment of commission by virtue of sub-paragraph (8).

7C(1) Regulations under paragraph 7A or 7B must be made by statutory instrument and may–

(a) make different provision for different cases or descriptions of case, including different provision for different areas or for sales at different prices;

(b) contain incidental, supplementary, transitional or saving provisions.

(2) Regulations under paragraph 7A or 7B are subject to annulment in pursuance of a resolution of either House of Parliament.

8 [Repealed.]

Gift of mobile home

8A(1) [Repealed.]

(2) Where the agreement is a new agreement (as defined by paragraph 7A(3)), provided that the occupier has supplied the owner with the relevant evidence, the occupier is entitled to give the mobile home, and to assign the agreement, to a member of the occupier's family (referred to in this paragraph as the 'new occupier') without the approval of the owner.

(3) The relevant evidence is–

(a) evidence, or evidence of a description, prescribed in regulations made by the Secretary of State that the person to whom the occupier proposes to give the mobile home, and to assign the agreement, is a member of the occupier's family, or

(b) any other satisfactory evidence that the person concerned is a member of the occupier's family.

(4) The new occupier must, as soon as reasonably practicable, notify the owner of the receipt of the mobile home and assignment of the agreement.

(5) The owner may not require any payment to be made (whether to the owner or otherwise) in connection with the gift of the mobile home, and the assignment of the agreement, as mentioned in sub-paragraph (2).

(6) The Secretary of State may by regulations prescribe procedural requirements to be complied with by the owner, the occupier or the new occupier in connection with the gift of the mobile home, and assignment of the agreement, as mentioned in sub-paragraph (2).

8B(1) Where the agreement is not a new agreement (as defined by paragraph 7A(3)), the occupier is entitled to give the mobile home, and assign the agreement, to a member of the occupier's family (referred to in this paragraph as the 'proposed occupier') without the approval of the owner if–

- (a) the occupier serves on the owner a notice (a 'notice of proposed gift') that the occupier proposes to give the mobile home to the proposed occupier, and
- (b) the first or second condition is satisfied.

(2) The first condition is that, within the period of 21 days beginning with the date on which the owner received the notice of proposed gift ('the 21-day period'), the occupier does not receive a notice from the owner that the owner has applied to a tribunal for an order preventing the occupier from giving the mobile home, and assigning the agreement, to the proposed occupier (a 'refusal order').

(3) The second condition is that–

- (a) within the 21-day period–
  - (i) the owner applies to a tribunal for a refusal order, and
  - (ii) the occupier receives a notice of the application from the owner, and
- (b) the tribunal rejects the application.

(4) If the owner applies to a tribunal for a refusal order within the 21-day period but the occupier does not receive notice of the application from the owner within that period–

- (a) the application is to be treated as not having been made, and
- (b) the first condition is accordingly to be treated as satisfied.

(5) A notice of proposed gift must include–

- (a) the relevant evidence (as defined by paragraph 8A(3)), and
- (b) such other information as may be prescribed in regulations made by the Secretary of State.

(6) A notice of proposed gift or notice of an application for a refusal order–

- (a) must be in writing, and
- (b) may be served by post.

(7) An application for a refusal order may be made only on one or more of the grounds prescribed in regulations made by the Secretary of State; and a notice of an application for a refusal order must specify the ground or grounds on which the application is made.

(8) The owner may not require any payment to be made (whether to the owner or otherwise) in connection with the gift of the mobile home, and the assignment of the agreement, as mentioned in sub-paragraph (1).

(9) The Secretary of State may by regulations prescribe procedural requirements to be complied with by the owner, the occupier, a proposed occupier or the person to whom the mobile home is given in connection with the gift of the mobile home, and assignment of the agreement, as mentioned in sub-paragraph (1).

8C(1) Regulations under paragraph 8A or 8B must be made by statutory instrument and may–

(a) make different provision for different cases or descriptions of case, including different provision for different areas;

(b) contain incidental, supplementary, transitional or saving provisions.

(2) Regulations under paragraph 8A or 8B are subject to annulment in pursuance of a resolution of either House of Parliament.

9(1) This paragraph applies to an agreement which relates to a pitch other than a pitch on–

(a) a local authority gypsy and traveller site; or

(b) a registered social landlord gypsy and traveller site.

(2) Subject to sub-paragraph (5), the occupier is entitled to gift the mobile home, and to assign the agreement, to a member of the occupier's family (the 'new occupier') without the approval of the owner.

(3) The occupier must, if requested by the owner, give the owner such evidence as the owner, acting reasonably, may require to confirm that the new occupier is a member of the occupier's family.

(4) The new occupier must, as soon as practicable, notify the owner of the new occupier's acceptance of the gift of the mobile home and assignation of the agreement.

(5) Neither the gift nor the assignation are to have any effect until the owner has received the evidence mentioned in sub-paragraph (3) and the notification required in sub-paragraph (4).

(6) The owner may not require any payment to be made (whether to the owner or otherwise) in connection with the gift of the mobile home, and the assignation of the agreement.

Re-siting of mobile home

10(1) The owner shall be entitled to require that the occupier's right to station the mobile home is exercisable for any period in relation to another pitch forming part of the protected site ('the other pitch') if (and only if)–

(a) on the application of the owner, the appropriate judicial body is satisfied that the other pitch is broadly comparable to the occupier's original pitch and that it is reasonable for the mobile home to be stationed on the other pitch for that period; or

(b) the owner needs to carry out essential repair or emergency works that can only be carried out if the mobile home is moved to the other pitch for that period, and the other pitch is broadly comparable to the occupier's original pitch.

(2) If the owner requires the occupier to station the mobile home on the other pitch so that he can replace, or carry out repairs to, the base on which the mobile home is stationed, he must if the occupier so requires, or the [appropriate judicial body] on the application of the occupier so orders, secure that the mobile home is returned to the original pitch on the completion of the replacement or repairs.

(3) The owner shall pay all the costs and expenses incurred by the occupier in connection with his mobile home being moved to and from the other pitch.

(4) In this paragraph and in paragraph 13 below, 'essential repair or emergency works' means–

(a) repairs to the base on which the mobile home is stationed;

(b) works or repairs needed to comply with any relevant legal requirements; or

(c) works or repairs in connection with restoration following flood, landslide or other natural disaster.

Quiet enjoyment of the mobile home

11 The occupier shall be entitled to quiet enjoyment of the mobile home together with the pitch during the continuance of the agreement, subject to paragraphs 10, 12, 13 and 14.

Owner's right of entry to the pitch

12 The owner may enter the pitch without prior notice between the hours of 9 am and 6 pm

(a) to deliver written communications, including post and notices, to the occupier; and

(b) to read any meter for gas, electricity, water, sewerage or other services supplied by the owner.

13 The owner may enter the pitch to carry out essential repair or emergency works on giving as much notice to the occupier (whether in writing or otherwise) as is reasonably practicable in the circumstances.

14 Unless the occupier has agreed otherwise, the owner may enter the pitch for a reason other than one specified in paragraph 12 or 13 only if he has given the occupier at least 14 clear days' written notice of the date, time and reason for his visit.

15 The rights conferred by paragraphs 12 to 14 above do not extend to the mobile home.

The pitch fee

16 The pitch fee can only be changed in accordance with paragraph 17, either–

(a) with the agreement of the occupier, or

(b) if the appropriate judicial body, on the application of the owner or the occupier, considers it reasonable for the pitch fee to be changed and makes an order determining the amount of the new pitch fee.

17(1) The pitch fee shall be reviewed annually as at the review date.

(2) At least 28 clear days before the review date the owner shall serve on the occupier a written notice setting out his proposals in respect of the new pitch fee.

(2A) A notice under sub-paragraph (2) which proposes an increase in the pitch fee is of no effect unless it is accompanied by a document which complies with paragraph 25A.

(3) If the occupier agrees to the proposed new pitch fee, it shall be payable as from the review date.

(4) If the occupier does not agree to the proposed new pitch fee–

(a) the occupier] may apply to the appropriate judicial body for an order under paragraph 16(b) determining the amount of the new pitch fee;

(b) the occupier shall continue to pay the current pitch fee to the owner until such time as the new pitch fee is agreed by the occupier or an order determining the amount of the new pitch fee is made by the appropriate judicial body under paragraph 16(b); and

(c) the new pitch fee shall be payable as from the review date but the occupier shall not be treated as being in arrears until the 28th day after the date on which the new pitch fee is agreed or, as the case may be, the 28th day after the date of the appropriate judicial body's order determining the amount of the new pitch fee.

(5) An application under sub-paragraph (4)(a) may be made at any time after the end of the period of 28 days beginning with the review date but no later than three months after the review date.

(6) Sub-paragraphs (7) to (10) apply if the owner–

(a) has not served the notice required by sub-paragraph (2) by the time by which it was required to be served, but

(b) at any time thereafter serves on the occupier a written notice setting out his proposals in respect of a new pitch fee.

(6A) A notice under sub-paragraph (6)(b) which proposes an increase in the pitch fee is of no effect unless it is accompanied by a document which complies with paragraph 25A.

(7) If (at any time) the occupier agrees to the proposed pitch fee, it shall be payable as from the 28th day after the date on which the owner serves the notice under sub-paragraph (6)(b).

(8) If the occupier has not agreed to the proposed pitch fee–

(a) the owner or the occupier may apply to the appropriate judicial body for an order under paragraph 16(b) determining the amount of the new pitch fee;

(b) the occupier shall continue to pay the current pitch fee to the owner until such time as the new pitch fee is agreed by the occupier or an order determining the amount of the new pitch fee is made by the appropriate judicial body under paragraph 16(b); and

(c) if the appropriate judicial body makes such an order, the new pitch fee shall be payable as from the 28th day after the date on which the owner serves the notice under sub-paragraph (6)(b).

(9) An application under sub-paragraph (8) may be made at any time after the end of the period of 56 days beginning with date on which the owner serves the notice under sub-paragraph (6)(b) but no later than four months after the date on which the owner serves that notice.

(9A) A tribunal may permit an application under sub-paragraph (4)(a) or (8)(a) to be made to it outside the time limit specified in sub-paragraph (5) (in the case of an application under sub-paragraph (4)(a)) or in sub-paragraph (9) (in the case of an application under sub-paragraph (8)(a)) if it is satisfied that, in all the circumstances, there are good reasons for the failure to apply within the applicable time limit and for any delay since then in applying for permission to make the application out of time.

(10) The occupier shall not be treated as being in arrears–

(a) where sub-paragraph (7) applies, until the 28th day after the date on which the new pitch fee is agreed; or

(b) where sub-paragraph (8)(b) applies, until the 28th day after the date on which the new pitch fee is agreed or, as the case may be, the 28th day after the date of the appropriate judicial body's order determining the amount of the new pitch fee.

(11) Sub-paragraph (12) applies if a tribunal, on the application of the occupier of a pitch, is satisfied that–

(a) a notice under sub-paragraph (2) or (6)(b) was of no effect as a result of sub-paragraph (2A) or (6A), but

(b) the occupier nonetheless paid the owner the pitch fee proposed in the notice.

(12) The tribunal may order the owner to pay the occupier, within the period of 21 days beginning with the date of the order, the difference between–

(a) the amount which the occupier was required to pay the owner for the period in question, and

(b) the amount which the occupier has paid the owner for that period.

18(1) When determining the amount of the new pitch fee particular regard shall be had to–

(a) any sums expended by the owner since the last review date on improvements–

(i) which are for the benefit of the occupiers of mobile homes on the protected site;

(ii) which were the subject of consultation in accordance with paragraph 22(e) and (f) below; and

(iii) to which a majority of the occupiers have not disagreed in writing or which, in the case of such disagreement, the appropriate judicial body, on the application of the owner, has ordered should be taken into account when determining the amount of the new pitch fee;

(aa) any deterioration in the condition, and any decrease in the amenity, of the site or any adjoining land which is occupied or controlled by the owner since the date on which this paragraph came into force (in so far as regard has not previously been had to that deterioration or decrease for the purposes of this sub-paragraph);

(ab) any reduction in the services that the owner supplies to the site, pitch or mobile home, and any deterioration in the quality of those services, since the date on which this paragraph came into force (in so far as regard has not previously been had to that reduction or deterioration for the purposes of this sub-paragraph);

(b) [Repealed.]

(ba) any direct effect on the costs payable by the owner in relation to the maintenance or management of the site of an enactment which has come into force since the last review date; and]

(c) [Repealed.]

(1A) But. . . no regard shall be had, when determining the amount of the new pitch fee, to any costs incurred by the owner since the last review date for the purpose of compliance with the amendments made to this Act by the Mobile Homes Act 2013.

(2) When calculating what constitutes a majority of the occupiers for the purposes of sub-paragraph (1)(b)(iii) each mobile home is to be taken to have only one occupier and, in the event of there being more than one occupier of a mobile home, its occupier is to be taken to be the occupier whose name first appears on the agreement.

(3) In a case where the pitch fee has not been previously reviewed, references in this paragraph to the last review date are to be read as references to the date when the agreement commenced.

19(1) When determining the amount of the new pitch fee, any costs incurred by the owner in connection with expanding the protected site shall not be taken into account.

(2) When determining the amount of the new pitch fee, no regard may be had to any costs incurred by the owner in relation to the conduct of proceedings under this Act or the agreement.

(3) When determining the amount of the new pitch fee, no regard may be had to any fee required to be paid by the owner by virtue of–

(a) section 8(1B) of the Caravan Sites and Control of Development Act 1960 (fee for application for site licence conditions to be altered);

(b) section 10(1A) of that Act (fee for application for consent to transfer site licence).

(4) When determining the amount of the new pitch fee, no regard may be had to any costs incurred by the owner in connection with–

(a) any action taken by a local authority under sections 9A to 9I of the Caravan Sites and Control of Development Act 1960 (breach of licence condition, emergency action etc);

(b) the owner being convicted of an offence under section 9B of that Act (failure to comply with compliance notice).

20(A1) Unless this would be unreasonable having regard to paragraph 18(1), there is a presumption that the pitch fee shall increase or decrease by a percentage which is no more than any percentage increase or decrease in the retail prices index calculated by reference only to–

(a) the latest index, and

(b) the index published for the month which was 12 months before that to which the latest index relates.

(A2) In sub-paragraph (A1), 'the latest index'–

(a) in a case where the owner serves a notice under paragraph 17(2), means the last index published before the day on which that notice is served;

(b) in a case where the owner serves a notice under paragraph 17(6), means the last index published before the day by which the owner was required to serve a notice under paragraph 17(2).

Occupier's obligations

21 The occupier shall–

(a) pay the pitch fee to the owner;

(b) pay to the owner all sums due under the agreement in respect of gas, electricity, water, sewerage or other services supplied by the owner;

(c) keep the mobile home in a sound state of repair;

(d) maintain–

(i) the outside of the mobile home, and

(ii) the pitch, including all fences and outbuildings belonging to, or enjoyed with, it and the mobile home, in a clean and tidy condition; and

(e) if requested by the owner, provide him with documentary evidence of any costs or expenses in respect of which the occupier seeks reimbursement.

Owner's obligations

22 The owner shall–

(a) if requested by the occupier, and on payment by the occupier of a charge of not more than £30, provide accurate written details of–

(i) the size of the pitch and the base on which the mobile home is stationed; and

(ii) the location of the pitch and the base within the protected site;

and such details must include measurements between identifiable fixed points on the protected site and the pitch and the base;

(b) if requested by the occupier, provide (free of charge) documentary evidence in support and explanation of–

(i) any new pitch fee;

(ii) any charges for gas, electricity, water, sewerage or other services payable by the occupier to the owner under the agreement; and

(iii) any other charges, costs or expenses payable by the occupier to the owner under the agreement;

(c) be responsible for repairing the base on which the mobile home is stationed and for maintaining any gas, electricity, water, sewerage or other services supplied by the owner to the pitch or to the mobile home;

(d) maintain in a clean and tidy condition those parts of the protected site, including access ways, site boundary fences and trees, which are not the responsibility of any occupier of a mobile home stationed on the protected site;

(e) consult the occupier about improvements to the protected site in general, and in particular about those which the owner wishes to be taken into account when determining the amount of any new pitch fee; and

(f) consult a qualifying residents' association, if there is one, about all matters which relate to the operation and management of, or improvements to, the protected site and may affect the occupiers either directly or indirectly.

23 The owner shall not do or cause to be done anything which may adversely affect the ability of the occupier to perform his obligations under paragraph 21(c) and (d) above.

24 For the purposes of paragraph 22(e) above, to 'consult' the occupier means–

(a) to give the occupier at least 28 clear days' notice in writing of the proposed improvements which–

(i) describes the proposed improvements and how they will benefit the occupier in the long and short term;

(ii) details how the pitch fee may be affected when it is next reviewed; and

(iii) states when and where the occupier can make representations about the proposed improvements; and

(b) to take into account any representations made by the occupier about the proposed improvements, in accordance with paragraph (a)(iii), before undertaking them.

25 For the purposes of paragraph 22(f) above, to 'consult' a qualifying residents' association means–

(a) to give the association at least 28 clear days' notice in writing of the matters referred to in paragraph 22(f) which–

(i) describes the matters and how they may affect the occupiers either directly or indirectly in the long and short term; and
(ii) states when and where the association can make representations about the matters; and
(b) to take into account any representations made by the association, in accordance with paragraph (a)(ii), before proceeding with the matters.

25A(1) The document referred to in paragraph 17(2A) and (6A) must–
(a) be in such form as the Secretary of State may by regulations prescribe,
(b) specify any percentage increase or decrease in the retail prices index calculated in accordance with paragraph 20(A1),
(c) explain the effect of paragraph 17,
(d) specify the matters to which the amount proposed for the new pitch fee is attributable,
(e) refer to the occupier's obligations in paragraph 21(c) to (e) and the owner's obligations in paragraph 22(c) and (d), and
(f) refer to the owner's obligations in paragraph 22(e) and (f) (as glossed by paragraphs 24 and 25).

(2) Regulations under this paragraph must be made by statutory instrument.

(3) The first regulations to be made under this paragraph are subject to annulment in pursuance of a resolution of either House of Parliament.

(4) But regulations made under any other provision of this Act which are subject to annulment in pursuance of a resolution of either House of Parliament may also contain regulations made under this paragraph.

Owner's name and address

26(1) The owner shall by notice inform the occupier and any qualifying residents' association of the address in England or Wales at which notices (including notices of proceedings) may be served on him by the occupier or a qualifying residents' association.

(2) If the owner fails to comply with sub-paragraph (1), then (subject to sub-paragraph (5) below) any amount otherwise due from the occupier to the owner in respect of the pitch fee shall be treated for all purposes as not being due from the occupier to the owner at any time before the owner does so comply.

(3) Where in accordance with the agreement the owner gives any written notice to the occupier or (as the case may be) a qualifying residents' association, the notice must contain the following information–
(a) the name and address of the owner; and
(b) if that address is not in England or Wales, an address in England or Wales at which notices (including notices of proceedings) may be served on the owner.

(4) Subject to sub-paragraph (5) below, where–

(a) the occupier or a qualifying residents' association receives such a notice, but

(b) it does not contain the information required to be contained in it by virtue of sub-paragraph (3) above, the notice shall be treated as not having been given until such time as the owner gives the information to the occupier or (as the case may be) the association in respect of the notice.

(5) An amount or notice within sub-paragraph (2) or (4) (as the case may be) shall not be treated as mentioned in relation to any time when, by virtue of an order of any court or tribunal, there is in force an appointment of a receiver or manager whose functions include receiving from the occupier the pitch fee, payments for services supplied or other charges.

(6) Nothing in sub-paragraphs (3) to (5) applies to any notice containing a demand to which paragraph 27(1) below applies.

27(1) Where the owner makes any demand for payment by the occupier of the pitch fee, or in respect of services supplied or other charges, the demand must contain–

(a) the name and address of the owner; and

(b) if that address is not in England or Wales, an address in England or Wales at which notices (including notices of proceedings) may be served on the owner.

(2) Subject to sub-paragraph (3) below, where–

(a) the occupier receives such a demand, but

(b) it does not contain the information required to be contained in it by virtue of sub-paragraph (1), the amount demanded shall be treated for all purposes as not being due from the occupier to the owner at any time before the owner gives that information to the occupier in respect of the demand.

(3) The amount demanded shall not be so treated in relation to any time when, by virtue of an order of any court or tribunal, there is in force an appointment of a receiver or manager whose functions include receiving from the occupier the pitch fee, payments for services supplied or other charges.

Qualifying residents' association

28(1) A residents' association is a qualifying residents' association in relation to a protected site if–

(a) it is an association representing the occupiers of mobile homes on that site;

(b) at least 50 per cent of the occupiers of the mobile homes on that site are members of the association;

(c) it is independent from the owner, who together with any agent or employee of his is excluded from membership;

(d) subject to paragraph (c) above, membership is open to all occupiers who own a mobile home on that site;

(e) it maintains a list of members which is open to public inspection together with the rules and constitution of the residents' association;

(f) it has a chairman, secretary and treasurer who are elected by and from among the members;

(g) with the exception of administrative decisions taken by the chairman, secretary and treasurer acting in their official capacities, decisions are taken by voting and there is only one vote for each mobile home; and

(h) the owner has acknowledged in writing to the secretary that the association is a qualifying residents' association, or, in default of this, the [appropriate judicial body] has so ordered.

(2) When calculating the percentage of occupiers for the purpose of sub-paragraph (1)(b) above, each mobile home shall be taken to have only one occupier and, in the event of there being more than one occupier of a mobile home, its occupier is to be taken to be the occupier whose name first appears on the agreement.

Interpretation

29 In this Chapter–

'pitch fee' means the amount which the occupier is required by the agreement to pay to the owner for the right to station the mobile home on the pitch and for use of the common areas of the protected site and their maintenance, but does not include amounts due in respect of gas, electricity, water and sewerage or other services, unless the agreement expressly provides that the pitch fee includes such amounts;

'retail prices index' means the general index (for all items) published by the Statistics Board or, if that index is not published for a relevant month, any substituted index or index figures published by the Board;

'review date' means the date specified in the written statement as the date on which the pitch fee will be reviewed in each year, or if no such date is specified, each anniversary of the date the agreement commenced; and

'written statement' means the written statement that the owner of the protected site is required to give to the occupier by section 1(2) of this Act.

Chapter 3: Agreements Relating to Transit Pitches on a Local Authority Gypsy and Traveller Site or a County Council Gypsy and Traveller Site

Duration of agreement

1 Subject to paragraph 2, the right to station the mobile home on the transit pitch subsists until the fixed period set out in the agreement expires or termination of the agreement under paragraph 3 or 4, whichever is sooner.

2(1) If the owner's estate or interest is insufficient to enable the owner to grant the right for the fixed period set out in the agreement, the period for which the right subsists does not extend beyond the date when the owner's estate or interest determines.

(2) If planning permission for the use of the protected site as a site for mobile homes has been granted in such terms that it will expire at the end of a specified period, the period for which the right subsists does not extend beyond the date when the planning permission expires.

(3) If planning permission for the use of the protected site as a site for mobile homes has been granted in terms such that it requires the owner to limit the duration of stay for mobile homes on the site, the period for which the right subsists does not extend beyond that duration.

Early termination by occupier

3 The occupier may terminate the agreement before the expiry of the fixed period set out in the agreement by giving written notice to the owner.

Early termination by owner

4 The owner may terminate the agreement before the expiry of the fixed period set out in the agreement–

(a) without being required to show any reason, by giving written notice not less than four weeks before the date on which that notice is to take effect, or

(b) forthwith, where–

(i) the occupier has breached a term of the agreement and, after service of a notice to remedy the breach, has not complied with the notice within a reasonable time, and

(ii) the owner considers it reasonable for the agreement to be terminated.

Recovery of overpayments by occupier

5 Where the agreement is terminated as mentioned in paragraph 3 or 4, the occupier is entitled to recover from the owner so much of any payment made by the occupier in pursuance of the agreement as is attributable to a period beginning after the termination.

Quiet enjoyment of the mobile home

6 The occupier is entitled to quiet enjoyment of the mobile home together with the pitch during the continuance of the agreement, subject to paragraphs 7, 8 and 9.

Owner's right of entry to the pitch

7 The owner may enter the pitch without prior notice between the hours of 9am and 6pm–

(a) to deliver written communications, including post and notices, to the occupier; and

(b) to read any meter for gas, electricity, water, sewerage or other services supplied by the owner.

8(1) The owner may enter the pitch to carry out essential repair or emergency works on giving as much notice to the occupier (whether in writing or otherwise) as is reasonably practicable in the circumstances.

(2) In this paragraph, 'essential repair or emergency works' means–

(a) repairs to the base on which the mobile home is stationed;

(b) repairs to any outhouses and facilities provided by the owner on the pitch and to any gas, electricity, water, sewerage or other services or other amenities provided by the owner in such outhouses;

(c) works or repairs needed to comply with any relevant legal requirements; or

(d) works or repairs in connection with restoration following flood, landslide or other natural disaster.

9 Unless the occupier has agreed otherwise, the owner may enter the pitch for a reason other than one specified in paragraph 7 or 8 only if the owner has given the occupier at least 14 clear days' written notice of the date, time and reason for the owner's visit.

10 The rights conferred by paragraphs 7 to 9 do not extend to the mobile home.

Owner's name and address

11(1) The owner must by notice inform the occupier of the address in England or Wales at which notices (including notices of proceedings) may be served on the owner by the occupier.

(2) If the owner fails to comply with sub-paragraph (1), then any amount otherwise due from the occupier to the owner in respect of the pitch fee is to be treated for all purposes as not being due from the occupier to the owner at any time before the owner does so comply.

(3) Where in accordance with the agreement the owner gives any written notice to the occupier the notice must contain the name and address of the owner.

(4) Where–

(a) the occupier receives such a notice, but

(b) it does not contain the information required to be contained in it by virtue of sub-paragraph (3),

the notice is to be treated as not having been given until such time as the owner gives the information to the occupier in respect of the notice.

(5) Nothing in sub-paragraphs (3) and (4) applies to any notice containing a demand to which paragraph 12(1) applies.

12(1) Where the owner makes any demand for payment by the occupier of the pitch fee, or in respect of services supplied or other charges, the demand must contain the name and address of the owner.

(2) Where–

(a) the occupier receives such a demand, but

(b) it does not contain the information required to be contained in it by virtue of sub-paragraph (1),

the amount demanded is to be treated for all purposes as not being due from the occupier to the owner at any time before the owner gives that information to the occupier in respect of the demand.

Interpretation

13 In this Chapter, 'pitch fee' means the amount which the occupier is required by the agreement to pay to the owner for the right to station the mobile home on the pitch and for use of the common areas of the protected site and their maintenance, but does not include amounts due in respect of gas, electricity, water, sewerage or other services, unless the agreement expressly provides that the pitch fee includes such amounts.

Chapter 4: Agreements Relating to Permanent Pitches on a Local Authority Gypsy and Traveller Site or a County Council Gypsy and Traveller Site

Duration of agreement

1 Subject to paragraph 2, the right to station the mobile home on land forming part of the protected site subsists until the agreement is determined under paragraph 3, 4, 5 or 6.

2(1) If the owner's estate or interest is insufficient to enable the owner to grant the right for an indefinite period, the period for which the right subsists does not extend beyond the date when the owner's estate or interest determines.

(2) If planning permission for the use of the protected site as a site for mobile homes has been granted in terms such that it will expire at the end of a specified period, the period for which the right subsists does not extend beyond the date when the planning permission expires.

(3) If before the end of a period determined by this paragraph there is a change in circumstances which allows a longer period, account is to be taken of that change.

Termination by occupier

3 The occupier is entitled to terminate the agreement by notice in writing given to the owner not less than four weeks before the date on which it is to take effect.

Termination by owner

4 The owner is entitled to terminate the agreement forthwith if, on the application of the owner, the appropriate judicial body–

(a) is satisfied that the occupier has breached a term of the agreement and, after service of a notice to remedy the breach, has not complied with the notice within a reasonable time; and

(b) considers it reasonable for the agreement to be terminated.

5 The owner is entitled to terminate the agreement forthwith if, on the application of the owner, the appropriate judicial body–

(a) is satisfied that the occupier is not occupying the mobile home as the occupier's only or main residence; and

(b) considers it reasonable for the agreement to be terminated.

6(1) The owner is entitled to terminate the agreement forthwith if–

(a) on the application of the owner, a tribunal has determined that, having regard to its condition, the mobile home is having a detrimental effect on the amenity of the site, and

(b) then, on the application of the owner, the appropriate judicial body, having regard to the tribunal's determination and to any other circumstances, considers it reasonable for the agreement to be terminated.

(2) Sub-paragraphs (3) and (4) apply if, on an application to the tribunal under sub-paragraph (1)(a)–

(a) the tribunal considers that, having regard to the present condition of the mobile home, it is having a detrimental effect on the amenity of the site, but

(b) it also considers that it would be reasonably practicable for particular repairs to be carried out on the mobile home that would result in the mobile home not having that detrimental effect, and

(c) the occupier indicates to the tribunal that the occupier intends to carry out those repairs.

(3) In such a case the tribunal may make an interim order–

(a) specifying the repairs that must be carried out and the time within which they must be carried out, and

(b) adjourning the proceedings on the application for such period specified in the interim order as the tribunal considers reasonable to enable the repairs to be carried out.

(4) If the tribunal makes an interim order under sub-paragraph (3), it must not make a determination under sub-paragraph (1)(a) unless it is satisfied that the specified period has expired without the repairs having been carried out.

6A [Repealed.]

6B [Repealed.]

Recovery of overpayments by occupier

7 Where the agreement is terminated as mentioned in paragraph 3, 4, 5 or 6, the occupier is entitled to recover from the owner so much of any payment made by the occupier in pursuance of the agreement as is attributable to a period beginning after the termination.

Re-siting of mobile home

8(1) The owner is entitled to require that the occupier's right to station the mobile home is exercisable for any period in relation to another pitch forming part of the protected site or a pitch forming part of another protected site ('the other pitch') if (and only if)–

(a) on the application of the owner, a tribunal is satisfied that the other pitch is broadly comparable to the occupier's original pitch and that it is reasonable for the mobile home to be stationed on the other pitch for that period; or

(b) the owner needs to carry out essential repair or emergency works that can only be carried out if the mobile home is moved to the other pitch for that period, and the other pitch is broadly comparable to the occupier's original pitch.

(1A) [Repealed.]

(2) If the owner requires the occupier to station the mobile home on the other pitch so that the owner can replace, or carry out repairs to, the base on which the mobile home is stationed, the owner must if the occupier so requires, or *the court* [a tribunal] on the application of the occupier so orders, secure that the mobile home is returned to the original pitch on the completion of the replacement or repairs.

(3) The owner must pay all the costs and expenses incurred by the occupier in connection with the mobile home being moved to and from the other pitch.

(4) In this paragraph and in paragraph 11, 'essential repair or emergency works' means–

(a) repairs to the base on which the mobile home is stationed;

(b) repairs to any outhouses and facilities provided by the owner on the pitch and to any gas, electricity, water, sewerage or other services or other amenities provided by the owner in such outhouses;

(c) works or repairs needed to comply with any relevant legal requirements; or

(d) works or repairs in connection with restoration following flood, landslide or other natural disaster.

Quiet enjoyment of the mobile home

9 The occupier is entitled to quiet enjoyment of the mobile home together with the pitch during the continuance of the agreement, subject to paragraphs 8, 10, 11 and 12.

Owner's right of entry to the pitch

10 The owner may enter the pitch without prior notice between the hours of 9am and 6pm–

(a) to deliver written communications, including post and notices, to the occupier; and

(b) to read any meter for gas, electricity, water, sewerage or other services supplied by the owner.

11 The owner may enter the pitch to carry out essential repair or emergency works on giving as much notice to the occupier (whether in writing or otherwise) as is reasonably practicable in the circumstances.

12 Unless the occupier has agreed otherwise, the owner may enter the pitch for a reason other than one specified in paragraph 10 or 11 only if the owner has given the occupier at least 14 clear days' written notice of the date, time and reason for the owner's visit.

13 The rights conferred by paragraphs 10 to 12 do not extend to the mobile home.

The pitch fee

14 The pitch fee can only be changed in accordance with paragraph 15, either–

(a) with the agreement of the occupier, or

(b) if *the court* [a tribunal], on the application of the owner or the occupier, considers it reasonable for the pitch fee to be changed and makes an order determining the amount of the new pitch fee.

15(1) The pitch fee will be reviewed annually as at the review date.

(2) At least 28 clear days before the review date the owner must serve on the occupier a written notice setting out the owner's proposals in respect of the new pitch fee.

(3) If the occupier agrees to the proposed new pitch fee, it is payable as from the review date.

(4) If the occupier does not agree to the proposed new pitch fee–

(a) the owner may apply to *the court* [a tribunal] for an order under paragraph 14(b) determining the amount of the new pitch fee;

(b) the occupier must continue to pay the current pitch fee to the owner until such time as the new pitch fee is agreed by the occupier or an order determining the amount of the new pitch fee is made by *the court* [a tribunal] under paragraph 14(b); and

(c) the new pitch fee is payable as from the review date but the occupier is not to be treated as being in arrears until the 28th day after the date on which the new pitch fee is agreed or, as the case may be, the 28th day after the date of *the court* [a tribunal] order determining the amount of the new pitch fee.

(5) An application under sub-paragraph (4)(a) may be made at any time after the end of the period of 28 days beginning with the review date but no later than three months after the review date.

(6) Sub-paragraphs (7) to (11) apply if the owner–

(a) has not served the notice required by sub-paragraph (2) by the time by which it was required to be served, but

(b) at any time thereafter serves on the occupier a written notice setting out the owner's proposals in respect of a new pitch fee.

(7) If (at any time) the occupier agrees to the proposed pitch fee, it is payable as from the 28th day after the date on which the owner serves the notice under sub-paragraph (6)(b).

(8) If the occupier has not agreed to the proposed pitch fee–

(a) the owner may apply to *the court* [a tribunal] for an order under paragraph 14(b) determining the amount of the new pitch fee;

(b) the occupier must continue to pay the current pitch fee to the owner until such time as the new pitch fee is agreed by the occupier or an order determining the amount of the new pitch fee is made by a tribunal under paragraph 14(b); and

(c) if a tribunal makes such an order, the new pitch fee is payable as from the 28th day after the date on which the owner serves the notice under sub-paragraph (6)(b).

(9) An application under sub-paragraph (8) may be made at any time after the end of the period of 56 days beginning with the date on which the owner serves the notice under sub-paragraph (6)(b) but no later than four months after the date on which the owner serves that notice.

(10) A tribunal may permit an application under sub-paragraph (4)(a) or (8)(a) to be made to it outside the time limit specified in sub-paragraph (5) (in the case of an application under sub-paragraph (4)(a)) or in sub-paragraph (9) (in the case of an application under sub-paragraph (8)(a)) if it is satisfied that, in all the circumstances, there are good reasons for the failure to apply within the applicable time limit and for any delay since then in applying for permission to make the application out of time.

(11) The occupier is not to be treated as being in arrears–

(a) where sub-paragraph (7) applies, until the 28th day after the date on which the new pitch fee is agreed; or

(b) where sub-paragraph (8)(b) applies, until the 28th day after the date on which the new pitch fee is agreed or, as the case may be, the 28th day after the date of a tribunal order determining the amount of the new pitch fee.

16(1) When determining the amount of the new pitch fee particular regard must be had to–

(a) any sums expended by the owner since the last review date on improvements–

(i) which are for the benefit of the occupiers of mobile homes on the protected site;

(ii) which were the subject of consultation in accordance with paragraph 20(f) and (g); and

(iii) to which a majority of the occupiers have not disagreed in writing or which, in the case of such disagreement, a tribunal, on the application of the owner, has ordered should be taken into account when determining the amount of the new pitch fee;

(b) any decrease in the amenity of the protected site since the last review date; and

(c) the effect of any enactment which has come into force since the last review date.

(2) When calculating what constitutes a majority of the occupiers for the purposes of sub-paragraph (1)(a)(iii) each mobile home is to be taken to have only one occupier and, in the event of there being more than one occupier of a mobile home, its occupier is to be taken to be the occupier whose name first appears on the agreement.

(2A) [Repealed.]

(3) In a case where the pitch fee has not been previously reviewed, references in this paragraph to the last review date are to be read as references to the date when the agreement commenced.

17 When determining the amount of the new pitch fee no regard may be had to–

(a) any costs incurred by the owner in connection with expanding the protected site, or

(b) any costs incurred by the owner in relation to the conduct of proceedings under this Act or the agreement.

18(1) There is a presumption that the pitch fee will increase or decrease by a percentage which is no more than any percentage increase or decrease in the retail prices index since the last review date, unless this would be unreasonable having regard to paragraph 16(1).

(1A) [Repealed.]

(1B) [Repealed.]

(2) Paragraph 16(3) applies for the purposes of this paragraph as it applies for the purposes of paragraph 16.

Occupier's obligations

19 The occupier must–

(a) pay the pitch fee to the owner;

(b) pay to the owner all sums due under the agreement in respect of gas, electricity, water, sewerage or other services supplied by the owner;

(c) keep the mobile home in a sound state of repair;

(d) maintain–

(i) the outside of the mobile home, and

(ii) the pitch, including all fences and outbuildings belonging to, or enjoyed with, it and the mobile home, in a clean and tidy condition; and

(e) if requested by the owner, provide the owner with documentary evidence of any costs or expenses in respect of which the occupier seeks reimbursement.

Owner's obligations

20 The owner must–

(a) if requested by the occupier, and on payment by the occupier of a charge of not more than £30, provide accurate written details of–

(i) the size of the pitch and the base on which the mobile home is stationed; and

(ii) the location of the pitch and the base within the protected site;

and such details must include measurements between identifiable fixed points on the protected site and the pitch and the base;

(b) if requested by the occupier, provide (free of charge) documentary evidence in support and explanation of–

(i) any new pitch fee;

(ii) any charges for gas, electricity, water, sewerage or other services payable by the occupier to the owner under the agreement; and

(iii) any other charges, costs or expenses payable by the occupier to the owner under the agreement;

(c) be responsible for repairing the base on which the mobile home is stationed and for maintaining any gas, electricity, water, sewerage or other services supplied by the owner to the pitch or to the mobile home;

(d) be responsible for repairing other amenities provided by the owner on the pitch including any outhouses and facilities provided;

(e) maintain in a clean and tidy condition those parts of the protected site, including access ways, site boundary fences and trees, which are not the responsibility of any occupier of a mobile home stationed on the protected site;

(f) consult the occupier about improvements to the protected site in general, and in particular about those which the owner wishes to be taken into account when determining the amount of any new pitch fee; and

(g) consult a qualifying residents' association, if there is one, about all matters which relate to the operation and management of, or improvements to, the protected site and may affect the occupiers either directly or indirectly.

21 The owner must not do or cause to be done anything which may adversely affect the ability of the occupier to perform the occupier's obligations under paragraph 19(c) and (d).

22 For the purposes of paragraph 20(f), to 'consult' the occupier means–

(a) to give the occupier at least 28 clear days' notice in writing of the proposed improvements which–

(i) describes the proposed improvements and how they will benefit the occupier in the long and short term;

(ii) details how the pitch fee may be affected when it is next reviewed; and

(iii) states when and where the occupier can make representations about the proposed improvements; and

(b) to take into account any representations made by the occupier about the proposed improvements, in accordance with paragraph (a)(iii), before undertaking them.

23 For the purposes of paragraph 20(g), to 'consult' a qualifying residents' association means–

(a) to give the association at least 28 clear days' notice in writing of the matters referred to in paragraph 20(g) which–

(i) describes the matters and how they may affect the occupiers either directly or indirectly in the long and short term; and

(ii) states when and where the association can make representations about the matters;

(aa) no regard may be had to any costs paid, or to be paid, by the owner in connection with expenses recovered by a local authority under–

(i) section 32Z2(2) of the Caravan Sites and Control of Development Act 1960;

(ii) subsection (1)(a) or (c) of section 32Z3 of that Act; or

(iii) section 32Z4 of that Act;

(ab) no regard may be had to any costs paid, or to be paid, by the owner in connection with the owner being convicted of an offence under Part 1A of the Caravan Sites and Control of Development Act 1960; and

(b) to take into account any representations made by the association, in accordance with paragraph (a)(ii), before proceeding with the matters.

Owner's name and address

24(1) The owner must by notice inform the occupier and any qualifying residents' association of the address in England or Wales at which notices (including notices of proceedings) may be served on the owner by the occupier or a qualifying residents' association.

(2) If the owner fails to comply with sub-paragraph (1), then any amount otherwise due from the occupier to the owner in respect of the pitch fee is to be treated for all purposes as not being due from the occupier to the owner at any time before the owner does so comply.

(3) Where in accordance with the agreement the owner gives any written notice to the occupier or (as the case may be) a qualifying residents' association, the notice must contain the name and address of the owner.

(4) Where–

(a) the occupier or a qualifying residents' association receives such a notice, but

(b) it does not contain the information required to be contained in it by virtue of sub-paragraph (3), the notice is to be treated as not having been given until such time as the owner gives the information to the occupier or (as the case may be) the association in respect of the notice.

(5) Nothing in sub-paragraphs (3) and (4) applies to any notice containing a demand to which paragraph 25(1) applies.

25(1) Where the owner makes any demand for payment by the occupier of the pitch fee, or in respect of services supplied or other charges, the demand must contain the name and address of the owner.

(2) Where–

(a) the occupier receives such a demand, but

(b) it does not contain the information required to be contained in it by virtue of sub-paragraph (1),

the amount demanded is to be treated for all purposes as not being due from the occupier to the owner at any time before the owner gives that information to the occupier in respect of the demand.

Qualifying residents' association

26(1) A residents' association is a qualifying residents' association in relation to a protected site if–

(a) it is an association representing the occupiers of mobile homes on that site;

(b) at least 50 per cent of the occupiers of the mobile homes on that site are members of the association;

(c) it is independent from the owner, who together with any agent or employee of the owner is excluded from membership;

(d) subject to paragraph (c), membership is open to all occupiers who own a mobile home on that site;

(e) it maintains a list of members which is open to public inspection together with the rules and constitution of the residents' association;

(f) it has a chair, secretary and treasurer who are elected by and from among the members;

(g) with the exception of administrative decisions taken by the chair, secretary and treasurer acting in their official capacities, decisions are taken by voting and there is only one vote for each mobile home; and

(h) the owner has acknowledged in writing to the secretary that the association is a qualifying residents' association, or, in default of this, *the court* [a tribunal] has so ordered.

(2) When calculating the percentage of occupiers for the purpose of sub-paragraph (1)(b), each mobile home is to be taken to have only one occupier and, in the event of there being more than one occupier of a mobile home, its occupier is to be taken to be the occupier whose name first appears on the agreement.

(2A) [Repealed.]

Interpretation

27 In this Chapter–

'pitch fee' means the amount which the occupier is required by the agreement to pay to the owner for the right to station the mobile home on the pitch and for use of the common areas of the protected site and their maintenance, but does not include amounts due in respect of gas, electricity, water, sewerage or other services, unless the agreement expressly provides that the pitch fee includes such amounts;

'retail prices index' means the general index (for all items) published by the Statistics Board or, if that index is not published for a relevant month, any substituted index or index figures published by the Board;

'review date' means the date specified in the written statement as the date on which the pitch fee will be reviewed in each year, or if no such date is specified, each anniversary of the date the agreement commenced; and

'written statement' means the written statement that the owner of the protected site is required to give to the occupier by section 1(2) of this Act.]

PART II MATTERS CONCERNING WHICH TERMS MAY BE IMPLIED BY [APPROPRIATE JUDICIAL BODY]

1 [Repealed.]

2 The sums payable by the occupier in pursuance of the agreement and the times at which they are to be paid.

3 The review at yearly intervals of the sums so payable.

4 The provision or improvement of services available on the protected site, and the use by the occupier of such services.

5 The preservation of the amenity of the protected site.

6 [Repealed.]

7 [Repealed.]

PART III [REPEALED.]

TOWN AND COUNTRY PLANNING ACT 1990 (EXTRACTS)

Meaning of 'development' and 'new development'

55(1) Subject to the following provisions of this section, in this Act, except where the context otherwise requires, 'development,' means the carrying out of building, engineering, mining or other operations in, on, over or under land, or the making of any material change in the use of any buildings or other land.

(1A) For the purposes of this Act 'building operations' includes–
- (a) demolition of buildings;
- (b) rebuilding;
- (c) structural alterations of or additions to buildings; and
- (d) other operations normally undertaken by a person carrying on business as a builder.

(2) The following operations or uses of land shall not be taken for the purposes of this Act to involve development of the land–
- (a) the carrying out for the maintenance, improvement or other alteration of any building of works which–
  - (i) affect only the interior of the building, or
  - (ii) do not materially affect the external appearance of the building, and are not works for making good war damage or works begun after 5th December 1968 for the alteration of a building by providing additional space in it underground;
- (b) the carrying out on land within the boundaries of a road by a highway authority of any works required for the maintenance or improvement of the road but, in the case of any such works which are not exclusively for the maintenance of the road, not including any works which may have significant adverse effects on the environment;
- (c) the carrying out by a local authority or statutory undertakers of any works for the purpose of inspecting, repairing or renewing any sewers, mains, pipes, cables or other apparatus, including the breaking open of any street or other land for that purpose;
- (d) the use of any buildings or other land within the curtilage of a dwellinghouse for any purpose incidental to the enjoyment of the dwellinghouse as such;
- (e) the use of any land for the purposes of agriculture or forestry (including afforestation) and the use for any of those purposes of any building occupied together with land so used;
- (f) in the case of buildings or other land which are used for a purpose of any class specified in an order made by the Secretary of State under this section, the use of the buildings or other land or, subject to the provisions of the order, of any part of the buildings or the other land, for any other purpose of the same class;

(g) the demolition of any description of building specified in a direction given by the Secretary of State to local planning authorities generally or to a particular local planning authority.

(2A) The Secretary of State may in a development order specify any circumstances or description of circumstances in which subsection (2) does not apply to operations mentioned in paragraph (a) of that subsection which have the effect of increasing the gross floor space of the building by such amount or percentage amount as is so specified.

(2B) The development order may make different provision for different purposes.

(3) For the avoidance of doubt it is hereby declared that for the purposes of this section–

(a) the use as two or more separate dwellinghouses of any building previously used as a single dwellinghouse involves a material change in the use of the building and of each part of it which is so used;

(b) the deposit of refuse or waste materials on land involves a material change in its use, notwithstanding that the land is comprised in a site already used for that purpose, if–

(i) the superficial area of the deposit is extended, or

(ii) the height of the deposit is extended and exceeds the level of the land adjoining the site.

(4) For the purposes of this Act mining operations include–

(a) the removal of material of any description–

(i) from a mineral working deposit;

(ii) from a deposit of pulverised fuel ash or other furnace ash or clinker; or

(iii) from a deposit of iron, steel or other metallic slags; and

(b) the extraction of minerals from a disused railway embankment.

(4A) Where the placing or assembly of any tank in any part of any inland waters for the purpose of fish farming there would not, apart from this subsection, involve development of the land below, this Act shall have effect as if the tank resulted from carrying out engineering operations over that land; and in this subsection–

'fish farming' means the breeding, rearing or keeping of fish or shellfish (which includes any kind of crustacean and mollusc);

'inland waters' means waters which do not form part of the sea or of any creek, bay or estuary or of any river as far as the tide flows; and

'tank' includes any cage and any other structure for use in fish farming.

(5) Without prejudice to any regulations made under the provisions of this Act relating to the control of advertisements, the use for the display of advertisements of any external part of a building which is not normally used for that purpose shall be treated for the purposes of this section as involving a material change in the use of that part of the building.

(6) [Repealed.]

Applications for planning permission or permission in principle

62(1) A development order may make provision as to applications for planning permission or permission in principle made to a local planning authority.

(2) Provision referred to in subsection (1) includes provision as to–
(a) the form and manner in which the application must be made;
(b) particulars of such matters as are to be included in the application;
(c) documents or other materials as are to accompany the application.

(2A) In subsections (1) and (2) references to applications for planning permission include references to–
(a) applications for consent, agreement or approval as mentioned in section 61DB(2), and
(b) applications for approval under section 61L(2).

(3) The local planning authority may require that an application for planning permission must include–
(a) such particulars as they think necessary;
(b) such evidence in support of anything in or relating to the application as they think necessary.

(4) But a requirement under subsection (3) must not be inconsistent with provision made under subsection (1).

(4A) Also, a requirement under subsection (3) in respect of an application–
(a) must be reasonable having regard, in particular, to the nature and scale of the proposed development; and
(b) may require particulars of, or evidence about, a matter only if it is reasonable.

(5) A development order must require that an application for planning permission of such description as is specified in the order must be accompanied by such of the following as is so specified–
(a) a statement about the design principles and concepts that have been applied to the development;
(b) a statement about how issues relating to access to the development have been dealt with.

(6) The form and content of a statement mentioned in subsection (5) is such as is required by the development order.

(7) In subsection (8) 'a relevant application' means the application for planning permission or permission in principle in a case where a person–
(a) has been required by section 61W(1) to carry out consultation on a proposed application for planning permission or permission in principle, and
(b) is going ahead with making an application for planning permission or permission in principle (whether or not in the same terms as the proposed application).

(8) A development order must require that a relevant application be accompanied by particulars of–
(a) how the person complied with section 61W(1),
(b) any responses to the consultation that were received by the person, and

(c) the account taken of those responses.

(9) In subsection (10), a 'relevant Welsh application' means an application for planning permission, in a case where a person–

(a) has been required by section 61Z to carry out consultation on a proposed application for planning permission for the development of land, and

(b) is going ahead with making an application for planning permission for the development (whether or not in the same terms as the proposed application).

(10) A development order must require a relevant Welsh application to be accompanied by a report (the 'pre-application consultation report') giving particulars of–

(a) how the applicant complied with section 61Z;

(b) any responses to the consultation received from persons consulted under section 61Z(3) or (4);

(c) the account taken of those responses.

(11) A development order may make provision about the form and content of the pre-application consultation report.

Determination of applications: general considerations

70(1) Where an application is made to a local planning authority for planning permission–

(a) subject to section 62D(5) and sections 91 and 92, they may grant planning permission, either unconditionally or subject to such conditions as they think fit; or

(b) they may refuse planning permission.

(1A) Where an application is made to a local planning authority for permission in principle–

(a) they may grant permission in principle; or

(b) they may refuse permission in principle.

(2) In dealing with an application for planning permission or permission in principle the authority shall have regard to–

(a) the provisions of the development plan, so far as material to the application,

(aza) a post examination draft neighbourhood development plan, so far as material to the application,

(aa) any considerations relating to the use of the Welsh language, so far as material to the application,

(b) any local finance considerations, so far as material to the application, and

(c) any other material considerations.

(2ZZA) The authority must determine an application for technical details consent in accordance with the relevant permission in principle.

This is subject to subsection (2ZZC).

(2ZZB) An application for technical details consent is an application for planning permission that–

(a) relates to land in respect of which permission in principle is in force,

(b) proposes development all of which falls within the terms of the permission in principle, and

(c) particularises all matters necessary to enable planning permission to be granted without any reservations of the kind referred to in section 92.

(2ZZC) Subsection (2ZZA) does not apply where–

(a) the permission in principle has been in force for longer than a prescribed period, and

(b) there has been a material change of circumstances since the permission came into force.

'Prescribed' means prescribed for the purposes of this subsection in a development order.

(2ZA) Subsection (2)(aa) applies only in relation to Wales.

(2A) [Subsections (1A), (2)(b) and (2ZZA) to (2ZZC) do not] apply in relation to Wales

(3) Subsection (1) has effect subject to section 65 and to the following provisions of this Act, to sections 66, 67, 72 and 73 of the Planning (Listed Buildings and Conservation Areas) Act 1990 and to section 15 of the Health Services Act 1976.[1]

(3) Subsection (1) has effect subject to the following–

(a) section 65 and the following provisions of this Act;

(b) section 15 of the Health Services Act 1976;

(c) sections 66, 67, 72 and 73 of the Planning (Listed Buildings and Conservation Areas) Act 1990;

(d) regulations under section 5 of the Housing and Planning Act 2016 (starter homes requirements).[2]

(3A) See also section 100ZA, which makes provision about restrictions on the power to impose conditions under subsection (1)(a) on a grant of planning permission in relation to land in England.[3]

(3B) For the purposes of subsection (2)(aza) (but subject to subsections (3D) and (3E)) a draft neighbourhood development plan is a post examination draft neighbourhood development plan' if–

(a) a local planning authority have made a decision under paragraph 12(4) of Schedule 4B with the effect that a referendum or referendums are to be held on the draft plan under that Schedule,

(b) the Secretary of State has directed under paragraph 13B(2)(a) of that Schedule that a referendum or referendums are to be held on the draft plan under that Schedule,

1 Substituted by words in italics below by the Housing and Planning Act 2016 s5(8). Not yet in force.

2 Inserted by the Housing and Planning Act 2016 s5(8). Not yet in force.

3 Inserted by the Neighbourhood Planning Act 2017 s14(4), Sch 3 paras 1, 2. Not yet in force.

(c) an examiner has recommended under paragraph 13(2)(a) of Schedule A2 to the Planning and Compulsory Purchase Act 2004 (examination of modified plan) that a local planning authority should make the draft plan, or
(d) an examiner has recommended under paragraph 13(2)(b) of that Schedule that a local planning authority should make the draft plan with modifications.

(3C) In the application of subsection (2)(aza) in relation to a post examination draft neighbourhood development plan within subsection (3B)(d), the local planning authority must take the plan into account as it would be if modified in accordance with the recommendations.

(3D) A draft neighbourhood development plan within subsection (3B)(a) or (b) ceases to be a post examination draft neighbourhood development plan for the purposes of subsection (2)(aza) if–
(a) section 38A(4)(a) (duty to make plan) or (6) (cases in which duty does not apply) of the Planning and Compulsory Purchase Act 2004 applies in relation to the plan,
(b) section 38A(5) (power to make plan) of that Act applies in relation to the plan and the plan is made by the local planning authority,
(c) section 38A(5) of that Act applies in relation to the plan and the local planning authority decide not to make the plan,
(d) a single referendum is held on the plan and half or fewer of those voting in the referendum vote in favour of the plan, or
(e) two referendums are held on the plan and half or fewer of those voting in each of the referendums vote in favour of the plan.

(3E) A draft neighbourhood development plan within subsection (3B)(c) or (d) ceases to be a post examination draft neighbourhood development plan for the purposes of subsection (2)(aza) if–
(a) the local planning authority make the draft plan (with or without modifications), or
(b) the local planning authority decide not to make the draft plan.

(3F) The references in subsection (3B) to Schedule 4B are to that Schedule as applied to neighbourhood development plans by section 38A(3) of the Planning and Compulsory Purchase Act 2004.

(4) In this section–
'local finance consideration' means–
(a) a grant or other financial assistance that has been, or will or could be, provided to a relevant authority by a Minister of the Crown, or
(b) sums that a relevant authority has received, or will or could receive, in payment of Community Infrastructure Levy;
'Minister of the Crown' has the same meaning as in the Ministers of the Crown Act 1975;
'relevant authority' means–
(a) a district council;
(b) a county council in England;
(c) the Mayor of London;
(d) the council of a London borough;

(e) a Mayoral development corporation;
(f) an urban development corporation;
(g) a housing action trust;
(h) the Council of the Isles of Scilly;
(i) the Broads Authority;
(j) a National Park authority in England;
(k) the Homes and Communities Agency; or
(l) a joint committee established under section 29 of the Planning and Compulsory Purchase Act 2004.

Power to decline to determine subsequent application[4]

70A(1) A local planning authority may decline to determine a relevant application if–

(a) any of the conditions in subsections (2) to (4) is satisfied, and
(b) the authority think there has been no significant change in the relevant considerations since the relevant event.

(2) The condition is that in the period of two years ending with the date on which the application mentioned in subsection (1) is received the Secretary of State has refused a similar application made to the Secretary of State under section 62A or referred to him under section 76A or 77.

(3) The condition is that in that period the Secretary of State has dismissed an appeal–

(a) against the refusal of a similar application, or
(b) under section 78(2) in respect of a similar application.

(4) The condition is that–

(a) in that period the local planning authority have refused more than one similar application, and
(b) there has been no appeal to the Secretary of State against any such refusal or if there has been such an appeal, it has been withdrawn.[5]

(4A) A local planning authority in England may also decline to determine a relevant application if–

(a) the condition in subsection (4B) is satisfied, and
(b) the authority think there has been no significant change in the relevant considerations since the relevant event.

(4B) The condition is that–

(a) in the period of two years ending with the date on which the application mentioned in subsection (4A) is received the Secretary of State has refused a similar application,
(b) the similar application was an application deemed to have been made by section 177(5), and

4 Check status of s70A in relation to Wales.

5 Please check s70A(4)(b) in relation to Wales. Not in force in Wales as at 1 December 2019.

(c) the land to which the application mentioned in subsection (4A) and the similar application relate is in England.

(5) A relevant application is–

(a) an application for planning permission for the development of any land;

(aa) an application for permission in principle for the development of any land;

(b) an application for approval in pursuance of section 60(1A), (2), (2A) or (2B).

(6) The relevant considerations are–

(a) the development plan so far as material to the application;

(b) any other material considerations.

(7) The relevant event is–

(a) for the purposes of subsections (2), (4) and (4B) the refusal of the similar application;

(b) for the purposes of subsection (3) the dismissal of the appeal.

(8) Subject to subsection (9), an application is similar to another application if (and only if) the local planning authority think that the development and the land to which the applications relate are the same or substantially the same.

(9) An application within subsection (5)(a) or (b) is not similar to an earlier application within subsection (5)(aa).

Power to decline to determine overlapping application

70B(1) A local planning authority may decline to determine an application for planning permission, or permission in principle,] for the development of any land which is–

(a) made on the same day as a similar application, or[6]

(b) made at a time when any of the conditions in subsections (2) to (4) applies in relation to a similar application.

(2) The condition is that a similar application is under consideration by the local planning authority and the determination period for that application has not expired.

(3) The condition is that a similar application is under consideration by the Secretary of State in pursuance of section 62A, 76A or 77 or on an appeal under section 78 and the Secretary of State has not issued his decision.

(4) The condition is that a similar application–

(a) has been granted by the local planning authority,

(b) has been refused by them, or

(c) has not been determined by them within the determination period, and the time within which an appeal could be made to the Secretary of State under section 78 has not expired.

(4A) A local planning authority in England may also decline to determine an application for planning permission, or permission in principle,

6 Check status of s70B(1)(a) in relation to Wales.

for the development of any land in England which is made at a time when the condition in subsection (4B) applies in relation to a similar application.

(4B) The condition is that–

(a) a similar application is under consideration by the Secretary of State,

(b) the similar application is an application deemed to have been made by section 177(5), and

(c) the Secretary of State has not issued his decision.

(5) An application is similar to another application if (and only if) the local planning authority think that the development and the land to which the applications relate are the same or substantially the same.

(6) The determination period is–

(a) the period prescribed by the development order for the determination of the application, or

(b) such longer period as the applicant and the authority have agreed for the determination of the application.

(7) If a local planning authority exercise their power under subsection (1)(a) to decline to determine an application made on the same day as a similar application, they may not also exercise that power to decline to determine the similar application.[7]

Power to decline to determine retrospective application

70C(1) A local planning authority may decline to determine an application for planning permission [or permission in principle] for the development of any land if granting planning permission for the development would involve granting, whether in relation to the whole or any part of the land to which a pre-existing enforcement notice relates, planning permission in respect of the whole or any part of the matters specified in the enforcement notice as constituting a breach of planning control.

(2) For the purposes of the operation of this section in relation to any particular application for planning permission or permission in principle, a 'pre-existing enforcement notice' is an enforcement notice issued before the application was received by the local planning authority.

Right to appeal against planning decisions and failure to take such decisions

78(1) Where a local planning authority–

(a) refuse an application for planning permission or grant it subject to conditions;

(aa) refuse an application for a permission in principle;

7 Check status of s70B(7) in relation to Wales.

(b) refuse an application for any consent, agreement or approval of that authority required by a condition imposed on a grant of planning permission or grant it subject to conditions; or
(c) refuse an application for any approval of that authority required under a development order, a Mayoral development order or a neighbourhood development order or grant it subject to conditions,

the applicant may by notice appeal to the Secretary of State.

(2) A person who has made such an application to the local planning authority may also appeal to the Secretary of State if the local planning authority have done none of the following–
(a) given notice to the applicant of their decision on the application;
(aa) given notice to the applicant that they have exercised their power under section 70A or 70B[8] or 70C to decline to determine the application;
(b) given notice to him that the application has been referred to the Secretary of State in accordance with directions given under section 77,

within such period as may be prescribed by the development order or within such extended period as may at any time be agreed upon in writing between the applicant and the authority.

(3) Any appeal under this section shall be made by notice served within such time and in such manner as may be prescribed by a development order.

(4) The time prescribed for the service of such a notice must not be less than–
(a) 28 days from the date of notification of the decision; or
(b) in the case of an appeal under subsection (2), 28 days from the end of the period prescribed as mentioned in subsection (2) or, as the case may be, the extended period mentioned in that subsection.

(4A) A notice of appeal under this section must be accompanied by such information s may be prescribed by a development order.

(4AA) An appeal under this section may not be brought or continued against the refusal of an application for planning permission if–
(a) the land to which the application relates is in Wales,
(b) granting the application would involve granting planning permission in respect of matters specified in an enforcement notice as constituting a breach of planning control, and
(c) on the determination of an appeal against that notice under section 174, planning permission for those matters was not granted under section 177.

(4AB) An appeal under this section may not be brought or continued against the grant of an application for planning permission subject to a condition, if—

8 Check s70B in relation to Wales.

(a) the land to which the application relates is in Wales,

(b) an appeal against an enforcement notice has been brought under section 174 on the ground that the condition ought to be discharged, and

(c) on the determination of that appeal, the condition was not discharged under section 177.

(4B) [Repealed.]

(4BA) Once notice of an appeal under this section to the Welsh Ministers has been served, the application to which it relates may not be varied, except in such circumstances as may be prescribed by a development order.

(4BB) A development order which makes provision under subsection (4BA) must provide for an application which is varied to be subject to such further consultation as the Welsh Ministers consider appropriate.

(4C) [Repealed.]

(4D) [Repealed.]

(5) For the purposes of the application of 79(1) and (3), 253(2)(c), 266(1)(b), 288(10)(b), 319A(7)(b) and 319B(7)(b) in relation to an appeal under subsection (2), it shall be assumed that the authority decided to refuse the application in question.

PART VII: ENFORCEMENT

INTRODUCTORY

General interpretation of Chapter II

171(1) Subject to the following provisions of this section, in this Chapter–

'the affected area', in relation to an agricultural unit, means so much of that unit as, on the date of service, consists of land falling within any paragraph of Schedule 13;

'agricultural' has the same meaning as in section 109 of the Agriculture Act 1947 and references to the farming of land include references to the carrying on in relation to the land of agricultural activities;

'agricultural unit' means land which is occupied as a unit for agricultural purposes, including any dwellinghouse or other building occupied by the same person for the purpose of farming the land;

'annual value' means–

(a) in the case of a hereditament which is shown in a local non-domestic rating list and none of which consists of domestic property or property exempt from local non-domestic rating, the value shown in that list as the rateable value of that hereditament on the date of service;

(b) in the case of a hereditament which is shown in a local non-domestic rating list and which includes domestic property or property exempt from local domestic rating, the sum of–

(i) the value shown in that list as the rateable value of that hereditament on the date of service; and
(ii) the value attributable to the non-rateable part of that hereditament in accordance with subsections (2) and (3);

(c) in the case of any other hereditament, the value attributable to that hereditament in accordance with subsections (2) and (3);

'blight notice' has the meaning given in section 149(5);
'the claimant' has the meaning given in section 150(4);
'hereditament' means a relevant hereditament within the meaning of section 64(4)(a) to (c) of the Local Government Finance Act 1988;
'national policy statement' has the meaning given by section 5(2) of the Planning Act 2008;
'special enactment' means a local enactment, or a provision contained in an Act other than a local or private Act, which is a local enactment or provision authorising the compulsory acquisition of land specifically identified in it; and in this definition 'local enactment' means a local or private Act, or an order confirmed by Parliament or brought into operation in accordance with special parliamentary procedure.

(2) The value attributable to a hereditament, or the non-rateable part of it, in respect of domestic property shall be the value certified by the relevant valuation officer as being 5 per cent. of the compensation which would be payable in respect of the value of that property if it were purchased compulsorily under statute with vacant possession and the compensation payable were calculated in accordance with Part II of the Land Compensation Act 1961 by reference to the relevant date.

(3) The value attributable to a hereditament, or the non-rateable part of it, in respect of property exempt from local non-domestic rating shall be the value certified by the relevant valuation officer as being the value which would have been shown as the rateable value of that property on the date of service if it were a relevant non-domestic hereditament consisting entirely of non-domestic property, none of which was exempt from local non-domestic rating.

(4) Land which (apart from this subsection) would comprise separate hereditaments solely by reason of being divided by a boundary between rating areas shall be treated for the purposes of the definition of 'hereditament' in subsection (1) as if it were not so divided.

(5) In this section–

'date of service' has the same meaning as in section 168;
'relevant valuation officer' means the valuation officer who would have determined the rateable value in respect of the hereditament for the purposes of Part III of the Local Government Finance Act 1988 if the hereditament had fulfilled the conditions set out in section 42(1)(b) to (d) of that Act;
'relevant date' is the date by reference to which that determination would have been made;

and expressions used in the definition of 'annual value' in subsection (1) or in subsection (2) or (3) which are also used in Part III of that Act have the same meaning as in that Part.

Expressions used in connection with enforcement

171A(1) For the purposes of this Act–

(a) carrying out development without the required planning permission; or

(b) failing to comply with any condition or limitation subject to which planning permission has been granted,

constitutes a breach of planning control.

(2) For the purposes of this Act–

(a) the issue of an enforcement notice (defined in section 172); or

(aa) the issue of an enforcement warning notice (defined in section 173ZA); or

(b) the service of a breach of condition notice (defined in section 187A),

constitutes taking enforcement action.

(3) In this Part 'planning permission' includes permission under Part III of the 1947 Act, of the 1962 Act or of the 1971 Act.

Time limits

171B(1) Where there has been a breach of planning control consisting in the carrying out without planning permission of building, engineering, mining or other operations in, on, over or under land, no enforcement action may be taken after the end of the period of four years beginning with the date on which the operations were substantially completed.

(2) Where there has been a breach of planning control consisting in the change of use of any building to use as a single dwellinghouse, no enforcement action may be taken after the end of the period of four years beginning with the date of the breach.

(2A) There is no restriction on when enforcement action may be taken in relation to a breach of planning control in respect of relevant demolition (within the meaning of section 196D).

(3) In the case of any other breach of planning control, no enforcement action may be taken after the end of the period of ten years beginning with the date of the breach.

(4) The preceding subsections do not prevent–

(a) the service of a breach of condition notice in respect of any breach of planning control if an enforcement notice in respect of the breach is in effect; or

(b) taking further enforcement action in respect of any breach of planning control if, during the period of four years ending with that action being taken, the local planning authority have taken or purported to take enforcement action in respect of that breach.

Time limits in cases involving concealment

171BA(1) Where it appears to the local planning authority that there may have been a breach of planning control in respect of any land in England, the authority may apply to a magistrates' court for an order under this subsection (a 'planning enforcement order') in relation to that apparent breach of planning control.

(2) If a magistrates' court makes a planning enforcement order in relation to an apparent breach of planning control, the local planning authority may take enforcement action in respect of–

(a) the apparent breach, or

(b) any of the matters constituting the apparent breach, at any time in the enforcement year.

(3) 'The enforcement year' for a planning enforcement order is the year that begins at the end of 22 days beginning with the day on which the court's decision to make the order is given, but this is subject to subsection (4).

(4) If an application under section 111(1) of the Magistrates' Courts Act 1980 (statement of case for opinion of High Court) is made in respect of a planning enforcement order, the enforcement year for the order is the year beginning with the day on which the proceedings arising from that application are finally determined or withdrawn.

(5) Subsection (2)–

(a) applies whether or not the time limits under section 171B have expired, and

(b) does not prevent the taking of enforcement action after the end of the enforcement year but within those time limits.

Planning enforcement orders: procedure

171BB(1) An application for a planning enforcement order in relation to an apparent breach of planning control may be made within the 6 months beginning with the date on which evidence of the apparent breach of planning control sufficient in the opinion of the local planning authority to justify the application came to the authority's knowledge.

(2) For the purposes of subsection (1), a certificate–

(a) signed on behalf of the local planning authority, and

(b) stating the date on which evidence sufficient in the authority's opinion to justify the application came to the authority's knowledge, is conclusive evidence of that fact.

(3) A certificate stating that matter and purporting to be so signed is to be deemed to be so signed unless the contrary is proved.

(4) Where the local planning authority apply to a magistrates' court for a planning enforcement order in relation to an apparent breach of planning control in respect of any land, the authority must serve a copy of the application–

(a) on the owner and on the occupier of the land, and

(b) on any other person having an interest in the land that is an interest which, in the opinion of the authority, would be materially affected by the taking of enforcement action in respect of the apparent breach.

(5) The persons entitled to appear before, and be heard by, the court hearing an application for a planning enforcement order in relation to an apparent breach of planning control in respect of any land include–

(a) the applicant,

(b) any person on whom a copy of the application was served under subsection (4), and

(c) any other person having an interest in the land that is an interest which, in the opinion of the court, would be materially affected by the taking of enforcement action in respect of the apparent breach.

(6) In this section 'planning enforcement order' means an order under section 171BA(1).

Making a planning enforcement order

171BC (1) A magistrates' court may make a planning enforcement order in relation to an apparent breach of planning control only if–

(a) the court is satisfied, on the balance of probabilities, that the apparent breach, or any of the matters constituting the apparent breach, has (to any extent) been deliberately concealed by any person or persons, and

(b) the court considers it just to make the order having regard to all the circumstances.

(2) A planning enforcement order must–

(a) identify the apparent breach of planning control to which it relates, and

(b) state the date on which the court's decision to make the order was given.

(3) In this section 'planning enforcement order' means an order under section 171BA(1).

PLANNING CONTRAVENTION NOTICES

Power to require information about activities on land

171C(1) Where it appears to the local planning authority that there may have been a breach of planning control in respect of any land, they may serve notice to that effect (referred to in this Act as a 'planning contravention notice') on any person who–

(a) is the owner or occupier of the land or has any other interest in it; or

(b) is carrying out operations on the land or is using it for any purpose.

(2) A planning contravention notice may require the person on whom it is served to give such information as to–

(a) any operations being carried out on the land, any use of the land and any other activities being carried out on the land; and
(b) any matter relating to the conditions or limitations subject to which any planning permission in respect of the land has been granted, as may be specified in the notice.

(3) Without prejudice to the generality of subsection (2), the notice may require the person on whom it is served, so far as he is able–
(a) to state whether or not the land is being used for any purpose specified in the notice or any operations or activities specified in the notice are being or have been carried out on the land;
(b) to state when any use, operations or activities began;
(c) to give the name and [postal] address of any person known to him to use or have used the land for any purpose or to be carrying out, or have carried out, any operations or activities on the land;
(d) to give any information he holds as to any planning permission for any use or operations or any reason for planning permission not being required for any use or operations;
(e) to state the nature of his interest (if any) in the land and the name and [postal] address of any other person known to him to have an interest in the land.

(4) A planning contravention notice may give notice of a time and place at which–
(a) any offer which the person on whom the notice is served may wish to make to apply for planning permission, to refrain from carrying out any operations or activities or to undertake remedial works; and
(b) any representations which he may wish to make about the notice, will be considered by the authority, and the authority shall give him an opportunity to make in person any such offer or representations at that time and place.

(5) A planning contravention notice must inform the person on whom it is served–
(a) of the likely consequences of his failing to respond to the notice and, in particular, that enforcement action may be taken; and
(b) of the effect of section 186(5)(b).

(6) Any requirement of a planning contravention notice shall be complied with by giving information in writing to the local planning authority.

(7) The service of a planning contravention notice does not affect any other power exercisable in respect of any breach of planning control.

(8) In this section references to operations or activities on land include operations or activities in, under or over the land.

Penalties for non-compliance with planning contravention notice

171D(1) If, at any time after the end of the period of twenty-one days beginning with the day on which a planning contravention notice has been served on any person, he has not complied with any requirement of the notice, he shall be guilty of an offence.

(2) An offence under subsection (1) may be charged by reference to any day or longer period of time and a person may be convicted of a second or subsequent offence under that subsection by reference to any period of time following the preceding conviction for such an offence.

(3) It shall be a defence for a person charged with an offence under subsection (1) to prove that he had a reasonable excuse for failing to comply with the requirement.

(4) A person guilty of an offence under subsection (1) shall be liable on summary conviction to a fine not exceeding level 3 on the standard scale.

(5) If any person–

(a) makes any statement purporting to comply with a requirement of a planning contravention notice which he knows to be false or misleading in a material particular; or

(b) recklessly makes such a statement which is false or misleading in a material particular, he shall be guilty of an offence.

(6) A person guilty of an offence under subsection (5) shall be liable on summary conviction to a fine not exceeding level 5 on the standard scale.

TEMPORARY STOP NOTICES

Temporary stop notice

171E(1) This section applies if the local planning authority think–

(a) that there has been a breach of planning control in relation to any land, and

(b) that it is expedient that the activity (or any part of the activity) which amounts to the breach is stopped immediately.

(2) The authority may issue a temporary stop notice.

(3) The notice must be in writing and must–

(a) specify the activity which the authority think amounts to the breach;

(b) prohibit the carrying on of the activity (or of so much of the activity as is specified in the notice);

(c) set out the authority's reasons for issuing the notice.

(4) A temporary stop notice may be served on any of the following–

(a) the person who the authority think is carrying on the activity;

(b) a person who the authority think is an occupier of the land;

(c) a person who the authority think has an interest in the land.

(5) The authority must display on the land–

(a) a copy of the notice;

(b) a statement of the effect of the notice and of section 171G.

(6) A temporary stop notice has effect from the time a copy of it is first displayed in pursuance of subsection (5).

(7) A temporary stop notice ceases to have effect–
 (a) at the end of the period of 28 days starting on the day the copy notice is so displayed,
 (b) at the end of such shorter period starting on that day as is specified in the notice, or
 (c) if it is withdrawn by the local planning authority.

Temporary stop notice: restrictions

171F(1) A temporary stop notice does not prohibit–
 (a) the use of a building as a dwelling house;
 (b) the carrying out of an activity of such description or in such circumstances as is prescribed.

(2) A temporary stop notice does not prohibit the carrying out of any activity which has been carried out (whether or not continuously) for a period of four years ending with the day on which the copy of the notice is first displayed as mentioned in section 171E(6).

(3) Subsection (2) does not prevent a temporary stop notice prohibiting–
 (a) activity consisting of or incidental to building, engineering, mining or other operations, or
 (b) the deposit of refuse or waste materials.

(4) For the purposes of subsection (2) any period during which the activity is authorised by planning permission must be ignored.

(5) A second or subsequent temporary stop notice must not be issued in respect of the same activity unless the local planning authority has first taken some other enforcement action in relation to the breach of planning control which is constituted by the activity.

(6) In subsection (5) enforcement action includes obtaining the grant of an injunction under section 187B.

Temporary stop notice: offences

171G(1) A person commits an offence if he contravenes a temporary stop notice–
 (a) which has been served on him, or
 (b) a copy of which has been displayed in accordance with section 171E(5).

(2) Contravention of a temporary stop notice includes causing or permitting the contravention of the notice.

(3) An offence under this section may be charged by reference to a day or a longer period of time.

(4) A person may be convicted of more than one such offence in relation to the same temporary stop notice by reference to different days or periods of time.

(5) A person does not commit an offence under this section if he proves–
 (a) that the temporary stop notice was not served on him, and

(b) that he did not know, and could not reasonably have been expected to know, of its existence.

(6) A person convicted of an offence under this section is liable on summary conviction, or on conviction on indictment, to a fine.

(7) In determining the amount of the fine the court must have regard in particular to any financial benefit which has accrued or has appeared to accrue to the person convicted in consequence of the offence.

Temporary stop notice: compensation

171H(1) This section applies if and only if a temporary stop notice is issued and at least one of the following paragraphs applies–

(a) the activity which is specified in the notice is authorised by planning permission or a development order or local development order;

(b) a certificate in respect of the activity is issued under section 191 or granted under that section by virtue of section 195;

(c) the authority withdraws the notice.

(2) Subsection (1)(a) does not apply if the planning permission is granted on or after the date on which a copy of the notice is first displayed as mentioned in section 171E(6).

(3) Subsection (1)(c) does not apply if the notice is withdrawn following the grant of planning permission as mentioned in subsection (2).

(4) A person who at the time the notice is served has an interest in the land to which the notice relates is entitled to be compensated by the local planning authority in respect of any loss or damage directly attributable to the prohibition effected by the notice.

(5) Subsections (3) to (7) of section 186 apply to compensation payable under this section as they apply to compensation payable under that section; and for that purpose references in those subsections to a stop notice must be taken to be references to a temporary stop notice.

Issue of enforcement notice

172(1) The local planning authority may issue a notice (in this Act referred to as an 'enforcement notice') where it appears to them–

(a) that there has been a breach of planning control; and

(b) that it is expedient to issue the notice, having regard to the provisions of the development plan and to any other material considerations.

(2) A copy of an enforcement notice shall be served–

(a) on the owner and on the occupier of the land to which it relates; and

(b) on any other person having an interest in the land, being an interest which, in the opinion of the authority, is materially affected by the notice.

(3) The service of the notice shall take place–

(a) not more than twenty-eight days after its date of issue; and

(b) not less than twent-eight days before the date specified in it as the date on which it is to take effect.

. . .

Appeal against enforcement notice

174(1) A person having an interest in the land to which an enforcement notice relates or a relevant occupier may appeal to the Secretary of State against the notice, whether or not a copy of it has been served on him.

(2) An appeal may be brought on any of the following grounds–

(a) that, in respect of any breach of planning control which may be constituted by the matters stated in the notice, planning permission ought to be granted or, as the case may be, the condition or limitation concerned ought to be discharged;

(b) that those matters have not occurred;

(c) that those matters (if they occurred) do not constitute a breach of planning control;

(d) that, at the date when the notice was issued, no enforcement action could be taken in respect of any breach of planning control which may be constituted by those matters;

(e) that copies of the enforcement notice were not served as required by section 172;

(f) that the steps required by the notice to be taken, or the activities required by the notice to cease, exceed what is necessary to remedy any breach of planning control which may be constituted by those matters or, as the case may be, to remedy any injury to amenity which has been caused by any such breach;

(g) that any period specified in the notice in accordance with section 173(9) falls short of what should reasonably be allowed.

(2A) An appeal may not be brought on the ground specified in subsection (2)(a) if–

(a) the land to which the enforcement notice relates is in England, and

(b) the enforcement notice was issued at a time–

(i) after the making of a related application for planning permission, but

(ii) before the end of the period applicable under section 78(2) in the case of that application.

(2B) An application for planning permission for the development of any land is, for the purposes of subsection (2A), related to an enforcement notice if granting planning permission for the development would involve granting planning permission in respect of the matters specified in the enforcement notice as constituting a breach of planning control.

(2C) Where any breach of planning control constituted by the matters stated in the notice relates to relevant demolition (within the meaning of section 196D), an appeal may also be brought on the grounds that–

(a) the relevant demolition was urgently necessary in the interests of safety or health;

(b) it was not practicable to secure safety or health by works of repair or works for affording temporary support or shelter; and

(c) the relevant demolition was the minimum measure necessary.

(2D) An appeal against an enforcement notice may not be brought on the ground that planning permission ought to be granted in respect of a breach of planning control constituted by a matter stated in the notice, as specified in subsection (2)(a), if–

(a) the land to which the enforcement notice relates is in Wales, and

(b) the enforcement notice was issued after a decision to refuse planning permission for a related development was upheld on an appeal under section 78 (and for this purpose development is "related" if granting planning permission for it would involve granting planning permission in respect of the matter concerned).

(2E) An appeal may not be brought on the ground that a condition or limitation ought to be discharged, as specified in subsection (2)(a), if—

(a) the land to which the enforcement notice relates is in Wales, and

(b) the enforcement notice was issued after a decision to grant planning permission subject to the condition or limitation was upheld on an appeal under section 78.

(2F) For the purposes of subsections (2D) and (2E), references to a decision that has been upheld on an appeal include references to a decision in respect of which–

(a) the Welsh Ministers have, under section 79(6), declined to determine an appeal or to proceed with the determination of an appeal;

(b) an appeal has been dismissed under section 79(6A).]

(3) An appeal under this section shall be made–

(a) by giving written notice of the appeal to the Secretary of State before the date specified in the enforcement notice as the date on which it is to take effect; or

(b) by sending such notice to him in a properly addressed and pre-paid letter posted to him at such time that, in the ordinary course of post, it would be delivered to him before that date; or

(c) by sending such notice to him using electronic communications at such time that, in the ordinary course of transmission, it would be delivered to him before that date.

(4) A person who gives notice under subsection (3) shall submit to the Secretary of State, either when giving the notice or within the prescribed time, a statement in writing–

(a) specifying the grounds on which he is appealing against the enforcement notice; and

(b) giving such further information as may be prescribed.

(5) If, where more than one ground is specified in that statement, the appellant does not give information required under subsection (4)(b)

in relation to each of those grounds within the prescribed time, the Secretary of State may determine the appeal without considering any ground as to which the appellant has failed to give such information within that time.

(6) In this section 'relevant occupier' means a person who–
  (a) on the date on which the enforcement notice is issued occupies the land to which the notice relates by virtue of a licence; and
  (b) continues so to occupy the land when the appeal is brought.

. . .

Grant or modification of planning permission on appeals against enforcement notices

177(1) On the determination of an appeal under section 174, the Secretary of State may–
  (a) grant planning permission in respect of the matters stated in the enforcement notice as constituting a breach of planning control, whether in relation to the whole or any part of those matters or in relation to the whole or any part of the land to which the notice relates;
  (b) discharge any condition or limitation subject to which planning permission was granted;
  (c) determine whether, on the date on which the appeal was made, any existing use of the land was lawful, any operations which had been carried out in, on, over or under the land were lawful or any matter constituting a failure to comply with any condition or limitation subject to which planning permission was granted was lawful and, if so, issue a certificate under section 191.

(1A) The provisions of sections 191 to 194 mentioned in subsection (1B) shall apply for the purposes of subsection (1)(c) as they apply for the purposes of section 191, but as if–
  (a) any reference to an application for a certificate were a reference to the appeal and any reference to the date of such an application were a reference to the date on which the appeal is made; and
  (b) references to the local planning authority were references to the Secretary of State.

(1B) Those provisions are: sections 191(5) to (7), 193(4) (so far as it relates to the form of the certificate), (6) and (7) and 194.

(1C) Subsection (1)(a) applies only if the statement under section 174(4) specifies the ground mentioned in section 174(2)(a).

(2) In considering whether to grant planning permission under subsection (1), the Secretary of State shall have regard to the provisions of the development plan, so far as material to the subject matter of the enforcement notice, and to any other material considerations.

(3) The planning permission that may be granted under subsection (1) is any planning permission that might be granted on an application under Part III.

(4) Where under subsection (1) the Secretary of State discharges a condition or limitation, he may substitute another condition or limitation for it, whether more or less onerous.

(4A) Section 100ZA (which makes provision about restrictions on the power to impose conditions or limitations on a grant of planning permission in relation to land in England) applies in relation to conditions substituted under subsection (4) as it applies in relation to conditions imposed on a grant of planning permission to develop land which is granted on an application made under Part 3.

(5) Where–

(a) an appeal against an enforcement notice is brought under section 174, and

(b) the statement under section 174(4) specifies the ground mentioned in section 174(2)(a),

the appellant shall be deemed to have made an application for planning permission in respect of the matters stated in the enforcement notice as constituting a breach of planning control.

(5A) Where–

(a) the statement under subsection (4) of section 174 specifies the ground mentioned in subsection (2)(a) of that section;

(b) any fee is payable under regulations made by virtue of section 303 in respect of the application deemed to be made by virtue of the appeal; and

(c) the Secretary of State gives notice in writing to the appellant specifying the period within which the fee must be paid,

then, if that fee is not paid within that period, the appeal, so far as brought on that ground, and the application shall lapse at the end of that period.]

(6) Any planning permission granted under subsection (1) on an appeal shall be treated as granted on the application deemed to have been made by the appellant.

(7) In relation to a grant of planning permission or a determination under subsection (1) the Secretary of State's decision shall be final.

(8) For the purposes of section 69 the Secretary of State's decision shall be treated as having been given by him in dealing with an application for planning permission made to the local planning authority.

Execution and cost of works required by enforcement notice

178(1) Where any steps required by an enforcement notice to be taken are not taken within the period for compliance with the notice, the local planning authority may–

(a) enter the land and take the steps; and

(b) recover from the person who is then the owner of the land any expenses reasonably incurred by them in doing so.

(2) Where a copy of an enforcement notice has been served in respect of any breach of planning control–

(a) any expenses incurred by the owner or occupier of any land for the purpose of complying with the notice, and
(b) any sums paid by the owner of any land under subsection (1) in respect of expenses incurred by the local planning authority in taking steps required by such a notice to be taken,

shall be deemed to be incurred or paid for the use and at the request of the person by whom the breach of planning control was committed.

(3) Regulations made under this Act may provide that–
(a) section 276 of the Public Health Act 1936, (power of local authorities to sell materials removed in executing works under that Act subject to accounting for the proceeds of sale);
(b) section 289 of that Act (power to require the occupier of any premises to permit works to be executed by the owner of the premises); and
(c) section 294 of that Act (limit on liability of persons holding premises as agents or trustees in respect of the expenses recoverable under that Act),

shall apply, subject to such adaptations and modifications as may be specified in the regulations, in relation to any steps required to be taken by an enforcement notice.

(4) Regulations under subsection (3) applying section 289 of the Public Health Act 1936 may include adaptations and modifications for the purpose of giving the owner of land to which an enforcement notice relates the right, as against all other persons interested in the land, to comply with the requirements of the enforcement notice.

(5) Regulations under subsection (3) may also provide for the charging on the land of any expenses recoverable by a local planning authority under subsection (1).

(6) Any person who wilfully obstructs a person acting in the exercise of powers under subsection (1) shall be guilty of an offence and liable on summary conviction to a fine not exceeding level 3 on the standard scale.

Offence where enforcement notice not complied with

179(1) Where, at any time after the end of the period for compliance with an enforcement notice, any step required by the notice to be taken has not been taken or any activity required by the notice to cease is being carried on, the person who is then the owner of the land is in breach of the notice.

(2) Where the owner of the land is in breach of an enforcement notice he shall be guilty of an offence.

(3) In proceedings against any person for an offence under subsection (2), it shall be a defence for him to show that he did everything he could be expected to do to secure compliance with the notice.

(4) A person who has control of or an interest in the land to which an enforcement notice relates (other than the owner) must not carry on

any activity which is required by the notice to cease or cause or permit such an activity to be carried on.

(5) A person who, at any time after the end of the period for compliance with the notice, contravenes subsection (4) shall be guilty of an offence.

(6) An offence under subsection (2) or (5) may be charged by reference to any day or longer period of time and a person may be convicted of a second or subsequent offence under the subsection in question by reference to any period of time following the preceding conviction for such an offence.

(7) Where–

(a) a person charged with an offence under this section has not been served with a copy of the enforcement notice; and

(b) the notice is not contained in the appropriate register kept under section 188,

it shall be a defence for him to show that he was not aware of the existence of the notice.

(8) A person guilty of an offence under this section shall be liable on summary conviction, or on conviction on indictment, to a fine.

(9) In determining the amount of any fine to be imposed on a person convicted of an offence under this section, the court shall in particular have regard to any financial benefit which has accrued or appears likely to accrue to him in consequence of the offence.

STOP NOTICES

Stop notices

183(1) Where the local planning authority consider it expedient that any relevant activity should cease before the expiry of the period for compliance with an enforcement notice, they may, when they serve the copy of the enforcement notice or afterwards, serve a notice (in this Act referred to as a 'stop notice') prohibiting the carrying out of that activity on the land to which the enforcement notice relates, or any part of that land specified in the stop notice.

(2) In this section and sections 184 and 186 'relevant activity' means any activity specified in the enforcement notice as an activity which the local planning authority require to cease and any activity carried out as part of that activity or associated with that activity.

(3) A stop notice may not be served where the enforcement notice has taken effect.

(4) A stop notice shall not prohibit the use of any building as a dwellinghouse.

(5) A stop notice shall not prohibit the carrying out of any activity if the activity has been carried out (whether continuously or not) for a period of more than four years ending with the service of the notice; and for the purposes of this subsection no account is to be taken of any period during which the activity was authorised by planning permission.

(5A) Subsection (5) does not prevent a stop notice prohibiting any activity consisting of, or incidental to, building, engineering, mining or other operations or the deposit of refuse or waste materials.

(6) A stop notice may be served by the local planning authority on any person who appears to them to have an interest in the land or to be engaged in any activity prohibited by the notice.

(7) The local planning authority may at any time withdraw a stop notice (without prejudice to their power to serve another) by serving notice to that effect on persons served with the stop notice.

. . .

Injunctions restraining breaches of planning control

187B(1) Where a local planning authority consider it necessary or expedient for any actual or apprehended breach of planning control to be restrained by injunction, they may apply to the court for an injunction, whether or not they have exercised or are proposing to exercise any of their other powers under this Part.

(2) On an application under subsection (1) the court may grant such an injunction as the court thinks appropriate for the purpose of restraining the breach.

(3) Rules of court may provide for such an injunction to be issued against a person whose identity is unknown.

(4) In this section 'the court' means the High Court or the county court.

CERTIFICATE OF LAWFUL USE OR DEVELOPMENT

Certificate of lawfulness of existing use or development

191(1) If any person wishes to ascertain whether–

(a) any existing use of buildings or other land is lawful;

(b) any operations which have been carried out in, on, over or under land are lawful; or

(c) any other matter constituting a failure to comply with any condition or limitation subject to which planning permission has been granted is lawful,

he may make an application for the purpose to the local planning authority specifying the land and describing the use, operations or other matter.

(2) For the purposes of this Act uses and operations are lawful at any time if–

(a) no enforcement action may then be taken in respect of them (whether because they did not involve development or require planning permission or because the time for enforcement action has expired or for any other reason); and

(b) they do not constitute a contravention of any of the requirements of any enforcement notice then in force.

(3) For the purposes of this Act any matter constituting a failure to comply with any condition or limitation subject to which planning permission has been granted is lawful at any time if–

(a) the time for taking enforcement action in respect of the failure has then expired; and

(b) it does not constitute a contravention of any of the requirements of any enforcement notice or breach of condition notice then in force.

(3A) In determining for the purposes of this section whether the time for taking enforcement action in respect of a matter has expired, that time is to be taken not to have expired if–

(a) the time for applying for an order under section 171BA(1) (a 'planning enforcement order') in relation to the matter has not expired,

(b) an application has been made for a planning enforcement order in relation to the matter and the application has neither been decided nor been withdrawn, or

(c) a planning enforcement order has been made in relation to the matter, the order has not been rescinded and the enforcement year for the order (whether or not it has begun) has not expired.

(4) If, on an application under this section, the local planning authority are provided with information satisfying them of the lawfulness at the time of the application of the use, operations or other matter described in the application, or that description as modified by the local planning authority or a description substituted by them, they shall issue a certificate to that effect; and in any other case they shall refuse the application.

(5) A certificate under this section shall–

(a) specify the land to which it relates;

(b) describe the use, operations or other matter in question (in the case of any use falling within one of the classes specified in an order under section 55(2)(f), identifying it by reference to that class);

(c) give the reasons for determining the use, operations or other matter to be lawful; and

(d) specify the date of the application for the certificate.

(6) The lawfulness of any use, operations or other matter for which a certificate is in force under this section shall be conclusively presumed.

(7) A certificate under this section in respect of any use shall also have effect, for the purposes of the following enactments, as if it were a grant of planning permission–

(a) section 3(3) of the Caravan Sites and Control of Development Act 1960 or section 7(1) of the Mobile Homes (Wales) Act 2013;

(b) section 5(2) of the Control of Pollution Act 1974; and

(c) section 36(2)(a) of the Environmental Protection Act 1990.

Certificate of lawfulness of proposed use or development

192(1) If any person wishes to ascertain whether–
(a) any proposed use of buildings or other land; or
(b) any operations proposed to be carried out in, on, over or under land,
would be lawful, he may make an application for the purpose to the local planning authority specifying the land and describing the use or operations in question.

(2) If, on an application under this section, the local planning authority are provided with information satisfying them that the use or operations described in the application would be lawful if instituted or begun at the time of the application, they shall issue a certificate to that effect; and in any other case they shall refuse the application.

(3) A certificate under this section shall–
(a) specify the land to which it relates;
(b) describe the use or operations in question (in the case of any use falling within one of the classes specified in an order under section 55(2)(f), identifying it by reference to that class);
(c) give the reasons for determining the use or operations to be lawful; and
(d) specify the date of the application for the certificate.

(4) The lawfulness of any use or operations for which a certificate is in force under this section shall be conclusively presumed unless there is a material change, before the use is instituted or the operations are begun, in any of the matters relevant to determining such lawfulness.

. . .

Validity of enforcement notices and similar notices

285(1) The validity of an enforcement notice shall not, except by way of an appeal under Part VII, be questioned in any proceedings whatsoever on any of the grounds on which such an appeal may be brought.

(2) Subsection (1) shall not apply to proceedings brought under section 179 against a person who–
(a) has held an interest in the land since before the enforcement notice was issued under that Part;
(b) did not have a copy of the enforcement notice served on him under that Part; and
(c) satisfies the court–
(i) that he did not know and could not reasonably have been expected to know that the enforcement notice had been issued; and
(ii) that his interests have been substantially prejudiced by the failure to serve him with a copy of it.

(3) Subject to subsection (4), the validity of a notice which has been served under section 215 on the owner and occupier of the land shall not, except by way of an appeal under Chapter II of Part VIII, be

questioned in any proceedings whatsoever on either of the grounds specified in section 217(1)(a) or (b).

(4) Subsection (3) shall not prevent the validity of such a notice being questioned on either of those grounds in proceedings brought under section 216 against a person on whom the notice was not served, but who has held an interest in the land since before the notice was served on the owner an occupier of the land, if he did not appeal against the notice under that Chapter.

(5), (6) [Repealed.]

Proceedings for questioning the validity of other orders, decisions and directions

288(1) If any person–

(a) is aggrieved by any order to which this section applies and wishes to question the validity of that order on the grounds–

(i) that the order is not within the powers of this Act, or

(ii) that any of the relevant requirements have not been complied with in relation to that order; or

(b) is aggrieved by any action on the part of the Secretary of State or the Welsh Ministers to which this section applies and wishes to question the validity of that action on the grounds–

(i) that the action is not within the powers of this Act, or

(ii) that any of the relevant requirements have not been complied with in relation to that action,

he may make an application to the High Court under this section.

(1A) If a person is aggrieved by a relevant costs order made in connection with an order or action to which this section applies and wishes to question its validity, the person may make an application to the High Court under this section (whether or not as part of an application made by virtue of subsection (1)) on the grounds–

(a) that the relevant costs order is not within the powers of this Act, or

(b) that any of the relevant requirements have not been complied with in relation to the order.

(2) Without prejudice to subsection (1) or (1A), if the authority directly concerned with any order to which this section applies, or with any action on the part of the Secretary of State or the Welsh Ministers to which this section applies, or with any relevant costs order, wish to question the validity of that order or action on any of the grounds mentioned in subsection (1) or (1A) (as the case may be), the authority may make an application to the High Court under this section.

(3) [Repealed.]

(4) This section applies to any such order as is mentioned in subsection (2) of section 284 and to any such action on the part of the Secretary of State or the Welsh Ministers as is mentioned in subsection (3) of that section.

(4A) An application under this section may not be made without the leave of the High Court.

(4B) An application for leave for the purposes of subsection (4A) must be made before the end of the period of six weeks beginning with the day after–

(a) in the case of an application relating to an order under section 97 that takes effect under section 99 without confirmation, the date on which the order takes effect;

(b) in the case of an application relating to any other order to which this section applies, the date on which the order is confirmed;

(c) in the case of an application relating to an action to which this section applies, the date on which the action is taken;

(d) in the case of an application relating to a relevant costs order, the date on which the order is made.

(4C) When considering whether to grant leave for the purposes of subsection (4A), the High Court may, subject to subsection (6), make an interim order suspending the operation of any order or action the validity of which the person or authority concerned wishes to question, until the final determination of–

(a) the question of whether leave should be granted, or

(b) where leave is granted, the proceedings on any application under this section made with such leave.

(5) On any application under this section the High Court–

(a) may, subject to subsection (6), by interim order suspend the operation of the order or action, the validity of which is questioned by the application, until the final determination of the proceedings;

(b) if satisfied that the order or action in question is not within the powers of this Act, or that the interests of the applicant have been substantially prejudiced by a failure to comply with any of the relevant requirements in relation to it, may quash that order or action.

(6) The High Court may not suspend a tree preservation order under subsection (4C) or (5)(a).

(7) In relation to a tree preservation order, or to an order made in pursuance of section 221(5), the powers conferred on the High Court by subsection (4C) or (5) shall be exercisable by way of quashing or (where applicable) suspending the operation of the order either in whole or in part, as the court may determine.

(8) References in this section to the confirmation of an order include the confirmation of an order subject to modifications as well as the confirmation of an order in the form in which it was made.

(9) In this section–

'relevant costs order' has the same meaning as in section 284;

'the relevant requirements'–

(a) in relation to any order or action to which this section applies, means any requirements of this Act or of the Tribunals and Inquiries Act 1992, or of any order, regulations or rules made under either of those Acts, which are applicable to that order or action;

(b) in relation to a relevant costs order, means any requirements of this Act, of the Local Government Act 1972 or of the Tribunals and Inquiries Act 1992, or of any order, regulations or rules made under any of those Acts, which are applicable to the relevant costs order.

(10) Any reference in this section to the authority directly concerned with any order or action to which this section applies–

(a) in relation to any such decision as is mentioned in section 284(3)(f), is a reference to the council on whom the notice in question was served and, in a case where the Secretary of State has modified or the Welsh Ministers have modified such a notice, wholly or in part, by substituting another local authority or statutory undertakers for that council, includes a reference to that local authority or those statutory undertakers;

(b) in any other case, is a reference to the authority who made the order in question or made the decision or served the notice to which the proceedings in question relate, or who referred the matter to the Secretary of State or the Welsh Ministers, or, where the order or notice in question was made or served by the Secretary of State or the Welsh Ministers, the authority named in the order or notice.[9]

(11) References in this Act to an application under this section do not include an application for leave for the purposes of subsection (4A).

Appeals to High Court relating to enforcement notices and notices under sections 207 and 215

289(1) Where the Secretary of State gives a decision in proceedings on an appeal under Part VII against an enforcement notice the appellant or the local planning authority or any other person having an interest in the land to which the notice relates may, according as rules of court may provide, either appeal to the High Court against the decision on a point of law or require the Secretary of State to state and sign a case for the opinion of the High Court.

(2) Where the Secretary of State gives a decision in proceedings on an appeal under Part VIII against a notice under section 207, the appellant or the local planning authority or any person (other than the appellant) on whom the notice was served may, according as rules of court may provide, either appeal to the High Court against the decision on a point of law or require the Secretary of State to state and sign a case for the opinion of the High Court.

(3) At any stage of the proceedings on any such appeal as is mentioned in subsection (1), the Secretary of State may state any question of law arising in the course of the proceedings in the form of a special case for the decision of the High Court.

9 Check status of s288(10) in relation to Wales.

(4) A decision of the High Court on a case stated by virtue of subsection (3) shall be deemed to be a judgment of the court within the meaning of section 16 of the Senior Courts Act 1981 (jurisdiction of the Court of Appeal to hear and determine appeals from any judgment of the High Court).

(4A) In proceedings brought by virtue of this section in respect of an enforcement notice, the High Court or, as the case may be, the Court of Appeal may, on such terms if any as the Court thinks fit (which may include terms requiring the local planning authority to give an undertaking as to damages or any other matter), order that the notice shall have effect, or have effect to such extent as may be specified in the order, pending the final determination of those proceedings and any re-hearing and determination by the Secretary of State.

(4B) Where proceedings are brought by virtue of this section in respect of any notice under section 207 or 215, the notice shall be of no effect pending the final determination of those proceedings and any re-hearing and determination by the Secretary of State.

(5) In relation to any proceedings in the High Court or the Court of Appeal brought by virtue of this section the power to make rules of court shall include power to make rules–

- (a) prescribing the powers of the High Court or the Court of Appeal with respect to the remitting of the matter with the opinion or direction of the court for re-hearing and determination by the Secretary of State or the Welsh Ministers; and
- (b) providing for the Secretary of State or the Welsh Ministers, either generally or in such circumstances as may be prescribed by the rules, to be treated as a party to any such proceedings and to be entitled to appear and to be heard accordingly.

(5A) Rules of court may also provide for the High Court or, as the case may be, the Court of Appeal to give directions as to the exercise, until such proceedings in respect of an enforcement notice are finally concluded and any re-hearing and determination by the Secretary of State has taken place, of any other powers in respect of the matters to which such a notice relates.

(6) No proceedings in the High Court shall be brought by virtue of this section except with the leave of that Court and no appeal to the Court of Appeal shall be so brought except with the leave of the Court of Appeal or of the High Court.

(7) In this section 'decision' includes a direction or order, and references to the giving of a decision shall be construed accordingly.

CRIMINAL JUSTICE AND PUBLIC ORDER ACT 1994 SS 61, 62A–E, 77, 78

PART V: PUBLIC ORDER: COLLECTIVE TRESPASS OR NUISANCE ON LAND

Power to remove trespassers on land

61(1) If the senior police officer present at the scene reasonably believes that two or more persons are trespassing on land and are present there with the common purpose of residing there for any period, that reasonable steps have been taken by or on behalf of the occupier to ask them to leave and–

(a) that any of those persons has caused damage to the land or to property on the land or used threatening, abusive or insulting words or behaviour towards the occupier, a member of his family or an employee or agent of his, or

(b) that those persons have between them six or more vehicles on the land,

he may direct those persons, or any of them, to leave the land and to remove any vehicles or other property they have with them on the land.

(2) Where the persons in question are reasonably believed by the senior police officer to be persons who were not originally trespassers but have become trespassers on the land, the officer must reasonably believe that the other conditions specified in subsection (1) are satisfied after those persons became trespassers before he can exercise the power conferred by that subsection.

(3) A direction under subsection (1) above, if not communicated to the persons referred to in subsection (1) by the police officer giving the direction, may be communicated to them by any constable at the scene.

(4) If a person knowing that a direction under subsection (1) above has been given which applies to him–

(a) fails to leave the land as soon as reasonably practicable, or

(b) having left again enters the land as a trespasser within the period of three months beginning with the day on which the direction was given,

he commits an offence and is liable on summary conviction to imprisonment for a term not exceeding *51 weeks*[1] or a fine not exceeding level 4 on the standard scale, or both.

(4A) Where, as respects Scotland, the reason why these persons have become trespassers is that they have ceased to be entitled to exercise access rights by virtue of–

(a) their having formed the common purpose mentioned in subsection (1) above; or

1 Words in italics not yet in force. See Criminal Justice Act 2003.

(b) one or more of the conditions specified in paragraphs (a) and (b) of that subsection having been satisfied,

the circumstances constituting that reason shall be treated, for the purposes of subsection (4) above, as having also occurred after these persons became trespassers.

(4B) In subsection (4A) above 'access rights' has the meaning given by the Land Reform (Scotland) Act 2003.

(5) [Repealed.]

(6) In proceedings for an offence under this section it is a defence for the accused to show–

(a) that he was not trespassing on the land, or

(b) that he had a reasonable excuse for failing to leave the land as soon as reasonably practicable or, as the case may be, for again entering the land as a trespasser.

(7) In its application in England and Wales to common land this section has effect as if in the preceding subsections of it–

(a) references to trespassing or trespassers were references to acts and persons doing acts which constitute either a trespass as against the occupier or an infringement of the commoners' rights; and

(b) references to 'the occupier' included the commoners or any of them or, in the case of common land to which the public has access, the local authority as well as any commoner.

(8) Subsection (7) above does not–

(a) require action by more than one occupier; or

(b) constitute persons trespassers as against any commoner or the local authority if they are permitted to be there by the other occupier.

(9) In this section–

'common land' means–

(a) land registered as common land in a register of common land kept under Part 1 of the Commons Act 2006; and

(b) land to which Part 1 of that Act does not apply and which is subject to rights of common as defined in that Act;[2]

'commoner' means a person with rights of common as so defined;[3]

'land' does not include–

(a) buildings other than–

(i) agricultural buildings within the meaning of, in England and Wales, paragraphs 3 to 8 of Schedule 5 to the Local Government Finance Act 1988 or, in Scotland, section 7(2) of the Valuation and Rating (Scotland) Act 1956, or

(ii) scheduled monuments within the meaning of the Ancient Monuments and Archaeological Areas Act 1979;

2 Check status of s61(9)(b) in relation to Wales.

3 Check status of s61(9)(b) in relation to Wales.

(b) land forming part of–
  (i) a highway unless it is a footpath, bridleway or byway open to all traffic within the meaning of Part III of the Wildlife and Countryside Act 1981, is a restricted byway within the meaning of Part II of the Countryside and Rights of Way Act 2000] or is a cycle track under the Highways Act 1980 or the Cycle Tracks Act 1984; or
  (ii) a road within the meaning of the Roads (Scotland) Act 1984 unless it falls within the definitions in section 151(2)(a)(ii) or (b) (footpaths and cycle tracks) of that Act or is a bridleway within the meaning of section 47 of the Countryside (Scotland) Act 1967;

'the local authority', in relation to common land, means any local authority which has powers in relation to the land under section 9 of the Commons Act 2006;[4]

'occupier' (and in subsection (8) 'the other occupier') means–
(a) in England and Wales, the person entitled to possession of the land by virtue of an estate or interest held by him; and
(b) in Scotland, the person lawfully entitled to natural possession of the land;

'property', in relation to damage to property on land, means–
(a) in England and Wales, property within the meaning of section 10(1) of the Criminal Damage Act 1971; and
(b) in Scotland, either–
  (i) heritable property other than land; or
  (ii) corporeal moveable property,

and 'damage' includes the deposit of any substance capable of polluting the land;

'trespass' means, in the application of this section–
(a) in England and Wales, subject to the extensions effected by subsection (7) above, trespass as against the occupier of the land;
(b) in Scotland, entering, or as the case may be remaining on, land without lawful authority and without the occupier's consent; and

'trespassing' and 'trespasser' shall be construed accordingly;

'vehicle' includes–
(a) any vehicle, whether or not it is in a fit state for use on roads, and includes any chassis or body, with or without wheels, appearing to have formed part of such a vehicle, and any load carried by, and anything attached to, such a vehicle; and
(b) a caravan as defined in section 29(1) of the Caravan Sites and Control of Development Act 1960;

and a person may be regarded for the purposes of this section as having a purpose of residing in a place notwithstanding that he has a home elsewhere.

. . .

4 Check status of s61(9)(b) in relation to Wales.

Power to remove trespassers: alternative site available

62A(1) If the senior police officer present at a scene reasonably believes that the conditions in subsection (2) are satisfied in relation to a person and land, he may direct the person–

(a) to leave the land;

(b) to remove any vehicle and other property he has with him on the land.

(2) The conditions are–

(a) that the person and one or more others ('the trespassers') are trespassing on the land;

(b) that the trespassers have between them at least one vehicle on the land;

(c) that the trespassers are present on the land with the common purpose of residing there for any period;

(d) if it appears to the officer that the person has one or more caravans in his possession or under his control on the land, that there is a suitable pitch on a relevant caravan site for that caravan or each of those caravans;

(e) that the occupier of the land or a person acting on his behalf has asked the police to remove the trespassers from the land.

(3) A direction under subsection (1) may be communicated to the person to whom it applies by any constable at the scene.

(4) Subsection (5) applies if–

(a) a police officer proposes to give a direction under subsection (1) in relation to a person and land, and

(b) it appears to him that the person has one or more caravans in his possession or under his control on the land.

(5) The officer must consult every local authority within whose area the land is situated as to whether there is a suitable pitch for the caravan or each of the caravans on a relevant caravan site which is situated in the local authority's area.

(6) In this section–

'caravan' and 'caravan site' have the same meanings as in Part 1 of the Caravan Sites and Control of Development Act 1960;

'relevant caravan site' means a caravan site which is–

(a) situated in the area of a local authority within whose area the land is situated, and

(b) managed by a relevant site manager;

'relevant site manager' means–

(a) a local authority within whose area the land is situated;

(aa) a private registered provider of social housing;

(b) a registered social landlord;

'registered social landlord' means a body registered as a social landlord under Chapter 1 of Part 1 of the Housing Act 1996.

(7) The Secretary of State may by order amend the definition of 'relevant site manager' in subsection (6) by adding a person or description of person.

(8) An order under subsection (7) must be made by statutory instrument and is subject to annulment in pursuance of a resolution of either House of Parliament.

Failure to comply with direction under section 62A: offences

62B(1) A person commits an offence if he knows that a direction under section 62A(1) has been given which applies to him and

(a) he fails to leave the relevant land as soon as reasonably practicable, or

(b) he enters any land in the area of the relevant local authority as a trespasser before the end of the relevant period with the intention of residing there.

(2) The relevant period is the period of 3 months starting with the day on which the direction is given.

(3) A person guilty of an offence under this section is liable on summary conviction to imprisonment for a term not exceeding *51 weeks*[5] or a fine not exceeding level 4 on the standard scale or both.

(4) [Repealed.]

(5) In proceedings for an offence under this section it is a defence for the accused to show–

(a) that he was not trespassing on the land in respect of which he is alleged to have committed the offence, or

(b) that he had a reasonable excuse–

(i) for failing to leave the relevant land as soon as reasonably practicable, or

(ii) for entering land in the area of the relevant local authority as a trespasser with the intention of residing there, or

(c) that, at the time the direction was given, he was under the age of 18 years and was residing with his parent or guardian.

Failure to comply with direction under section 62A: seizure

62C(1) This section applies if a direction has been given under section 62A(1) and a constable reasonably suspects that a person to whom the direction applies has, without reasonable excuse–

(a) failed to remove any vehicle on the relevant land which appears to the constable to belong to him or to be in his possession or under his control; or

(b) entered any land in the area of the relevant local authority as a trespasser with a vehicle before the end of the relevant period with the intention of residing there.

(2) The relevant period is the period of 3 months starting with the day on which the direction is given.

(3) The constable may seize and remove the vehicle.

5 Words in italics not yet in force. See Criminal Justice Act 2003.

Common land: modifications

62D(1) In their application to common land sections 62A to 62C have effect with these modifications.

(2) References to trespassing and trespassers have effect as if they were references to acts, and persons doing acts, which constitute–

(a) a trespass as against the occupier, or

(b) an infringement of the commoners' rights.

(3) References to the occupier–

(a) in the case of land to which the public has access, include the local authority and any commoner;

(b) in any other case, include the commoners or any of them.

(4) Subsection (1) does not–

(a) require action by more than one occupier, or

(b) constitute persons trespassers as against any commoner or the local authority if they are permitted to be there by the other occupier.

(5) In this section 'common land', 'commoner' and 'the local authority' have the meanings given by section 61.

Sections 62A to 62D: interpretation

62E(1) Subsections (2) to (8) apply for the interpretation of sections 62A to 62D and this section.

(2) 'Land' does not include buildings other than–

(a) agricultural buildings within the meaning of paragraphs 3 to 8 of Schedule 5 to the Local Government Finance Act 1988, or

(b) scheduled monuments within the meaning of the Ancient Monuments and Archaeological Areas Act 1979.

(3) 'Local authority' means–

(a) in Greater London, a London borough or the Common Council of the City of London;

(b) in England outside Greater London, a county council, a district council or the Council of the Isles of Scilly;

(c) in Wales, a county council or a county borough council.

(4) 'Occupier', 'trespass', 'trespassing' and 'trespasser' have the meanings given by section 61 in relation to England and Wales.

(5) 'The relevant land' means the land in respect of which a direction under section 62A(1) is given.

(6) 'The relevant local authority' means–

(a) if the relevant land is situated in the area of more than one local authority (but is not in the Isles of Scilly), the district council or county borough council within whose area the relevant land is situated;

(b) if the relevant land is situated in the Isles of Scilly, the Council of the Isles of Scilly;

(c) in any other case, the local authority within whose area the relevant land is situated.

(7) 'Vehicle' has the meaning given by section 61.

(8) A person may be regarded as having a purpose of residing in a place even if he has a home elsewhere.

. . .

Power of local authority to direct unauthorised campers to leave land

77(1) If it appears to a local authority that persons are for the time being residing in a vehicle or vehicles within that authority's area

(a) on any land forming part of a highway;

(b) on any other unoccupied land; or

(c) on any occupied land without the consent of the occupier,

the authority may give a direction that those persons and any others with them are to leave the land and remove the vehicle or vehicles and any other property they have with them on the land.

(2) Notice of a direction under subsection (1) must be served on the persons to whom the direction applies, but it shall be sufficient for this purpose for the direction to specify the land and (except where the direction applies to only one person) to be addressed to all occupants of the vehicles on the land, without naming them.

(3) If a person knowing that a direction under subsection (1) above has been given which applies to him–

(a) fails, as soon as practicable, to leave the land or remove from the land any vehicle or other property which is the subject of the direction, or

(b) having removed any such vehicle or property again enters the land with a vehicle within the period of three months beginning with the day on which the direction was given,

he commits an offence and is liable on summary conviction to a fine not exceeding level 3 on the standard scale.

(4) A direction under subsection (1) operates to require persons who re'enter the land within the said period with vehicles or other property to leave and remove the vehicles or other property as it operates in relation to the persons and vehicles or other property on the land when the direction was given.

(5) In proceedings for an offence under this section it is a defence for the accused to show that his failure to leave or to remove the vehicle or other property as soon as practicable or his re'entry with a vehicle was due to illness, mechanical breakdown or other immediate emergency.

(6) In this section–

'land' means land in the open air;

'local authority' means–

(a) in Greater London, a London borough or the Common Council of the City of London;

(b) in England outside Greater London, a county council, a district council or the Council of the Isles of Scilly;

(c) in Wales, a county council or a county borough council;

'occupier' means the person entitled to possession of the land by virtue of an estate or interest held by him;

'vehicle' includes–

(a) any vehicle, whether or not it is in a fit state for use on roads, and includes any body, with or without wheels, appearing to have formed part of such a vehicle, and any load carried by, and anything attached to, such a vehicle; and

(b) a caravan as defined in section 29(1) of the Caravan Sites and Control of Development Act 1960;

and a person may be regarded for the purposes of this section as residing on any land notwithstanding that he has a home elsewhere.

(7) Until 1st April 1996, in this section 'local authority' means, in Wales, a county council or a district council.

Orders for removal of persons and their vehicles unlawfully on land

78(1) A magistrates' court may, on a complaint made by a local authority, if satisfied that persons and vehicles in which they are residing are present on land within that authority's area in contravention of a direction given under section 77, make an order requiring the removal of any vehicle or other property which is so present on the land and any person residing in it.

(2) An order under this section may authorise the local authority to take such steps as are reasonably necessary to ensure that the order is complied with and, in particular, may authorise the authority, by its officers and servants–

(a) to enter upon the land specified in the order; and

(b) to take, in relation to any vehicle or property to be removed in pursuance of the order, such steps for securing entry and rendering it suitable for removal as may be so specified.

(3) The local authority shall not enter upon any occupied land unless they have given to the owner and occupier at least 24 hours notice of their intention to do so, or unless after reasonable inquiries they are unable to ascertain their names and addresses.

(4) A person who wilfully obstructs any person in the exercise of any power conferred on him by an order under this section commits an offence and is liable on summary conviction to a fine not exceeding level 3 on the standard scale.

(5) Where a complaint is made under this section, a summons issued by the court requiring the person or persons to whom it is directed to appear before the court to answer to the complaint may be directed–

(a) to the occupant of a particular vehicle on the land in question; or

(b) to all occupants of vehicles on the land in question, without naming him or them.

(6) Section 55(2) of the Magistrates' Courts Act 1980 (warrant for arrest of defendant failing to appear) does not apply to proceedings on a complaint made under this section.

(7) Section 77(6) of this Act applies also for the interpretation of this section.

HUMAN RIGHTS ACT 1998

INTRODUCTION

The Convention Rights

1(1) In this Act 'the Convention rights' means the rights and fundamental freedoms set out in–
(a) Articles 2 to 12 and 14 of the Convention,
(b) Articles 1 to 3 of the First Protocol, and
(c) Article 1 of the Thirteenth Protocol,
as read with Articles 16 to 18 of the Convention.

(2) Those Articles are to have effect for the purposes of this Act subject to any designated derogation or reservation (as to which see sections 14 and 15).

(3) The Articles are set out in Schedule 1.

(4) The Secretary of State may by order make such amendments to this Act as he considers appropriate to reflect the effect, in relation to the United Kingdom, of a protocol.

(5) In subsection (4) 'protocol' means a protocol to the Convention–
(a) which the United Kingdom has ratified; or
(b) which the United Kingdom has signed with a view to ratification.

(6) No amendment may be made by an order under subsection (4) so as to come into force before the protocol concerned is in force in relation to the United Kingdom.

Interpretation of Convention rights

2(1) A court or tribunal determining a question which has arisen in connection with a Convention right must take into account any–
(a) judgment, decision, declaration or advisory opinion of the European Court of Human Rights,
(b) opinion of the Commission given in a report adopted under Article 31 of the Convention,
(c) decision of the Commission in connection with Article 26 or 27(2) of the Convention, or
(d) decision of the Committee of Ministers taken under Article 46 of the Convention,
whenever made or given, so far as, in the opinion of the court or tribunal, it is relevant to the proceedings in which that question has arisen.

(2) Evidence of any judgment, decision, declaration or opinion of which account may have to be taken under this section is to be given in proceedings before any court or tribunal in such manner as may be provided by rules.

(3) In this section 'rules' means rules of court or, in the case of proceedings before a tribunal, rules made for the purposes of this section–

(a) by the Lord Chancellor or the Secretary of State, in relation to any proceedings outside Scotland;
(b) by the Secretary of State, in relation to proceedings in Scotland; or
(c) by a Northern Ireland department, in relation to proceedings before a tribunal in Northern Ireland–
  (i) which deals with transferred matters; and
  (ii) for which no rules made under paragraph (a) are in force.

LEGISLATION

Interpretation of legislation

3(1) So far as it is possible to do so, primary legislation and subordinate legislation must be read and given effect in a way which is compatible with the Convention rights.

(2) This section–
(a) applies to primary legislation and subordinate legislation whenever enacted;
(b) does not affect the validity, continuing operation or enforcement of any incompatible primary legislation; and
(c) does not affect the validity, continuing operation or enforcement of any incompatible subordinate legislation if (disregarding any possibility of revocation) primary legislation prevents removal of the incompatibility.

Declaration of incompatibility

4(1) Subsection (2) applies in any proceedings in which a court determines whether a provision of primary legislation is compatible with a Convention right.

(2) If the court is satisfied that the provision is incompatible with a Convention right, it may make a declaration of that incompatibility.

(3) Subsection (4) applies in any proceedings in which a court determines whether a provision of subordinate legislation, made in the exercise of a power conferred by primary legislation, is compatible with a Convention right.

(4) If the court is satisfied–
(a) that the provision is incompatible with a Convention right, and
(b) that (disregarding any possibility of revocation) the primary legislation concerned prevents removal of the incompatibility,

it may make a declaration of that incompatibility.

(5) In this section 'court' means–
(a) the House of Lords;
(b) the Judicial Committee of the Privy Council;
(c) the Courts'Martial Appeal Court;
(d) in Scotland, the High Court of Justiciary sitting otherwise than as a trial court or the Court of Session;
(e) in England and Wales or Northern Ireland, the High Court or the Court of Appeal.

(f) the Court of Protection, in any matter being dealt with by the President of the Family Division, the Chancellor of the High Court or a puisne judge of the High Court

(6) A declaration under this section ('a declaration of incompatibility')–

(a) does not affect the validity, continuing operation or enforcement of the provision in respect of which it is given; and

(b) is not binding on the parties to the proceedings in which it is made.

Right of Crown to intervene

5(1) Where a court is considering whether to make a declaration of incompatibility, the Crown is entitled to notice in accordance with rules of court.

(2) In any case to which subsection (1) applies–

(a) a Minister of the Crown (or a person nominated by him),

(b) a member of the Scottish Executive,

(c) a Northern Ireland Minister,

(d) a Northern Ireland department,

is entitled, on giving notice in accordance with rules of court, to be joined as a party to the proceedings.

(3) Notice under subsection (2) may be given at any time during the proceedings.

(4) A person who has been made a party to criminal proceedings (other than in Scotland) as the result of a notice under subsection (2) may, with leave, appeal to the Supreme Court against any declaration of incompatibility made in the proceedings.

(5) In subsection (4)–

'criminal proceedings' includes all proceedings before the Courts'Martial Appeal Court; and

'leave' means leave granted by the court making the declaration of incompatibility or by the Supreme Court.

PUBLIC AUTHORITIES

Acts of public authorities

6(1) It is unlawful for a public authority to act in a way which is incompatible with a Convention right.

(2) Subsection (1) does not apply to an act if–

(a) as the result of one or more provisions of primary legislation, the authority could not have acted differently; or

(b) in the case of one or more provisions of, or made under, primary legislation which cannot be read or given effect in a way which is compatible with the Convention rights, the authority was acting so as to give effect to or enforce those provisions.

(3) In this section 'public authority' includes–

(a) a court or tribunal, and

(b) any person certain of whose functions are functions of a public nature,

but does not include either House of Parliament or a person exercising functions in connection with proceedings in Parliament.

(4) [Repealed.]

(5) In relation to a particular act, a person is not a public authority by virtue only of subsection (3)(b) if the nature of the act is private.

(6) 'An act' includes a failure to act but does not include a failure to–

(a) introduce in, or lay before, Parliament a proposal for legislation; or

(b) make any primary legislation or remedial order.

Proceedings

7(1) A person who claims that a public authority has acted (or proposes to act) in a way which is made unlawful by section 6(1) may–

(a) bring proceedings against the authority under this Act in the appropriate court or tribunal, or

(b) rely on the Convention right or rights concerned in any legal proceedings,

but only if he is (or would be) a victim of the unlawful act.

(2) In subsection (1)(a) 'appropriate court or tribunal' means such court or tribunal as may be determined in accordance with rules; and proceedings against an authority include a counterclaim or similar proceeding.

(3) If the proceedings are brought on an application for judicial review, the applicant is to be taken to have a sufficient interest in relation to the unlawful act only if he is, or would be, a victim of that act.

(4) If the proceedings are made by way of a petition for judicial review in Scotland, the applicant shall be taken to have title and interest to sue in relation to the unlawful act only if he is, or would be, a victim of that act.

(5) Proceedings under subsection (1)(a) must be brought before the end of–

(a) the period of one year beginning with the date on which the act complained of took place; or

(b) such longer period as the court or tribunal considers equitable having regard to all the circumstances,

but that is subject to any rule imposing a stricter time limit in relation to the procedure in question.

(6) In subsection (1)(b) 'legal proceedings' includes–

(a) proceedings brought by or at the instigation of a public authority; and

(b) an appeal against the decision of a court or tribunal.

(7) For the purposes of this section, a person is a victim of an unlawful act only if he would be a victim for the purposes of Article 34 of the Convention if proceedings were brought in the European Court of Human Rights in respect of that act.

(8) Nothing in this Act creates a criminal offence.

(9) In this section 'rules' means–
(a) in relation to proceedings before a court or tribunal outside Scotland, rules made by the Lord Chancellor or the Secretary of State for the purposes of this section or rules of court,
(b) in relation to proceedings before a court or tribunal in Scotland, rules made by the Secretary of State for those purposes,
(c) in relation to proceedings before a tribunal in Northern Ireland–
(i) which deals with transferred matters; and
(ii) for which no rules made under paragraph (a) are in force,
rules made by a Northern Ireland department for those purposes,
and includes provision made by order under section 1 of the Courts and Legal Services Act 1990.

(10) In making rules, regard must be had to section 9.

(11) The Minister who has power to make rules in relation to a particular tribunal may, to the extent he considers it necessary to ensure that the tribunal can provide an appropriate remedy in relation to an act (or proposed act) of a public authority which is (or would be) unlawful as a result of section 6(1), by order add to–
(a) the relief or remedies which the tribunal may grant; or
(b) the grounds on which it may grant any of them.

(12) An order made under subsection (11) may contain such incidental, supplemental, consequential or transitional provision as the Minister making it considers appropriate.

(13) 'The Minister' includes the Northern Ireland department concerned.

Judicial remedies

8(1) In relation to any act (or proposed act) of a public authority which the court finds is (or would be) unlawful, it may grant such relief or remedy, or make such order, within its powers as it considers just and appropriate.

(2) But damages may be awarded only by a court which has power to award damages, or to order the payment of compensation, in civil proceedings.

(3) No award of damages is to be made unless, taking account of all the circumstances of the case, including–
(a) any other relief or remedy granted, or order made, in relation to the act in question (by that or any other court), and
(b) the consequences of any decision (of that or any other court) in respect of that act,
the court is satisfied that the award is necessary to afford just satisfaction to the person in whose favour it is made.

(4) In determining–
(a) whether to award damages, or
(b) the amount of an award,
the court must take into account the principles applied by the European Court of Human Rights in relation to the award of compensation under Article 41 of the Convention.

(5) A public authority against which damages are awarded is to be treated–

(a) in Scotland, for the purposes of section 3 of the Law Reform (Miscellaneous Provisions) (Scotland) Act 1940 as if the award were made in an action of damages in which the authority has been found liable in respect of loss or damage to the person to whom the award is made;

(b) for the purposes of the Civil Liability (Contribution) Act 1978 as liable in respect of damage suffered by the person to whom the award is made.

(6) In this section–

'court' includes a tribunal;

'damages' means damages for an unlawful act of a public authority; and

'unlawful' means unlawful under section 6(1).

Judicial acts

9(1) Proceedings under section 7(1)(a) in respect of a judicial act may be brought only–

(a) by exercising a right of appeal;

(b) on an application (in Scotland a petition) for judicial review; or

(c) in such other forum as may be prescribed by rules.

(2) That does not affect any rule of law which prevents a court from being the subject of judicial review.

(3) In proceedings under this Act in respect of a judicial act done in good faith, damages may not be awarded otherwise than to compensate a person to the extent required by Article 5(5) of the Convention.

(4) An award of damages permitted by subsection (3) is to be made against the Crown; but no award may be made unless the appropriate person, if not a party to the proceedings, is joined.

(5) In this section–

'appropriate person' means the Minister responsible for the court concerned, or a person or government department nominated by him;

'court' includes a tribunal;

'judge' includes a member of a tribunal, a justice of the peace (or, in Northern Ireland, a lay magistrate) and a clerk or other officer entitled to exercise the jurisdiction of a court;

'judicial act' means a judicial act of a court and includes an act done on the instructions, or on behalf, of a judge; and

'rules' has the same meaning as in section 7(9).

REMEDIAL ACTION

Power to take remedial action

10(1) This section applies if–

(a) a provision of legislation has been declared under section 4 to be incompatible with a Convention right and, if an appeal lies–

(i) all persons who may appeal have stated in writing that they do not intend to do so;
(ii) the time for bringing an appeal has expired and no appeal has been brought within that time; or
(iii) an appeal brought within that time has been determined or abandoned; or

(b) it appears to a Minister of the Crown or Her Majesty in Council that, having regard to a finding of the European Court of Human Rights made after the coming into force of this section in proceedings against the United Kingdom, a provision of legislation is incompatible with an obligation of the United Kingdom arising from the Convention.

(2) If a Minister of the Crown considers that there are compelling reasons for proceeding under this section, he may by order make such amendments to the legislation as he considers necessary to remove the incompatibility.

(3) If, in the case of subordinate legislation, a Minister of the Crown considers–

(a) that it is necessary to amend the primary legislation under which the subordinate legislation in question was made, in order to enable the incompatibility to be removed, and
(b) that there are compelling reasons for proceeding under this section,

he may by order make such amendments to the primary legislation as he considers necessary.

(4) This section also applies where the provision in question is in subordinate legislation and has been quashed, or declared invalid, by reason of incompatibility with a Convention right and the Minister proposes to proceed under paragraph 2(b) of Schedule 2.

(5) If the legislation is an Order in Council, the power conferred by subsection (2) or (3) is exercisable by Her Majesty in Council.

(6) In this section 'legislation' does not include a Measure of the Church Assembly or of the General Synod of the Church of England.

(7) Schedule 2 makes further provision about remedial orders.

OTHER RIGHTS AND PROCEEDINGS

Safeguard for existing human rights

11 A person's reliance on a Convention right does not restrict–

(a) any other right or freedom conferred on him by or under any law having effect in any part of the United Kingdom; or
(b) his right to make any claim or bring any proceedings which he could make or bring apart from sections 7 to 9.

Freedom of expression

12(1) This section applies if a court is considering whether to grant any relief which, if granted, might affect the exercise of the Convention right to freedom of expression.

(2) If the person against whom the application for relief is made ('the respondent') is neither present nor represented, no such relief is to be granted unless the court is satisfied–

(a) that the applicant has taken all practicable steps to notify the respondent; or

(b) that there are compelling reasons why the respondent should not be notified.

(3) No such relief is to be granted so as to restrain publication before trial unless the court is satisfied that the applicant is likely to establish that publication should not be allowed.

(4) The court must have particular regard to the importance of the Convention right to freedom of expression and, where the proceedings relate to material which the respondent claims, or which appears to the court, to be journalistic, literary or artistic material (or to conduct connected with such material), to–

(a) the extent to which–

(i) the material has, or is about to, become available to the public; or

(ii) it is, or would be, in the public interest for the material to be published;

(b) any relevant privacy code.

(5) In this section–

'court' includes a tribunal; and

'relief' includes any remedy or order (other than in criminal proceedings).

Freedom of thought, conscience and religion

13(1) If a court's determination of any question arising under this Act might affect the exercise by a religious organisation (itself or its members collectively) of the Convention right to freedom of thought, conscience and religion, it must have particular regard to the importance of that right.

(2) In this section 'court' includes a tribunal.

DEROGATIONS AND RESERVATIONS

Derogations

14(1) In this Act 'designated derogation' means–

any derogation by the United Kingdom from an Article of the Convention, or of any protocol to the Convention, which is designated for the purposes of this Act in an order made by the Secretary of State.

(2) [Repealed.]

(3) If a designated derogation is amended or replaced it ceases to be a designated derogation.

(4) But subsection (3) does not prevent the Secretary of State from exercising his power under subsection (1) to make a fresh designation order in respect of the Article concerned.

(5) The Secretary of State must by order make such amendments to Schedule 3 as he considers appropriate to reflect–

(a) any designation order; or

(b) the effect of subsection (3).

(6) A designation order may be made in anticipation of the making by the United Kingdom of a proposed derogation.

Reservations

15(1) In this Act 'designated reservation' means–

(a) the United Kingdom's reservation to Article 2 of the First Protocol to the Convention; and

(b) any other reservation by the United Kingdom to an Article of the Convention, or of any protocol to the Convention, which is designated for the purposes of this Act in an order made by the Secretary of State.

(2) The text of the reservation referred to in subsection (1)(a) is set out in Part II of Schedule 3.

(3) If a designated reservation is withdrawn wholly or in part it ceases to be a designated reservation.

(4) But subsection (3) does not prevent the Secretary of State from exercising his power under subsection (1)(b) to make a fresh designation order in respect of the Article concerned.

(5) The Secretary of State must by order make such amendments to this Act as he considers appropriate to reflect–

(a) any designation order; or

(b) the effect of subsection (3).

Period for which designated derogations have effect

16(1) If it has not already been withdrawn by the United Kingdom, a designated derogation ceases to have effect for the purposes of this Act–
at the end of the period of five years beginning with the date on which the order designating it was made.

(2) At any time before the period–

(a) fixed by subsection (1), or

(b) extended by an order under this subsection,

comes to an end, the Secretary of State may by order extend it by a further period of five years.

(3) An order under section 14(1) ceases to have effect at the end of the period for consideration, unless a resolution has been passed by each House approving the order.

(4) Subsection (3) does not affect–

(a) anything done in reliance on the order; or

(b) the power to make a fresh order under section 14(1).

(5) In subsection (3) 'period for consideration' means the period of forty days beginning with the day on which the order was made.

(6) In calculating the period for consideration, no account is to be taken of any time during which–

(a) Parliament is dissolved or prorogued; or

(b) both Houses are adjourned for more than four days.

(7) If a designated derogation is withdrawn by the United Kingdom, the Secretary of State must by order make such amendments to this Act as he considers are required to reflect that withdrawal.

Periodic review of designated reservations

17(1) The appropriate Minister must review the designated reservation referred to in section 15(1)(a)–

(a) before the end of the period of five years beginning with the date on which section 1(2) came into force; and

(b) if that designation is still in force, before the end of the period of five years beginning with the date on which the last report relating to it was laid under subsection (3).

(2) The appropriate Minister must review each of the other designated reservations (if any)–

(a) before the end of the period of five years beginning with the date on which the order designating the reservation first came into force; and

(b) if the designation is still in force, before the end of the period of five years beginning with the date on which the last report relating to it was laid under subsection (3).

(3) The Minister conducting a review under this section must prepare a report on the result of the review and lay a copy of it before each House of Parliament.

Appointment to European Court of Human Rights

18(1) In this section 'judicial office' means the office of–

(a) Lord Justice of Appeal, Justice of the High Court or Circuit judge, in England and Wales;

(b) judge of the Court of Session or sheriff, in Scotland;

(c) Lord Justice of Appeal, judge of the High Court or county court judge, in Northern Ireland.

(2) The holder of a judicial office may become a judge of the European Court of Human Rights ('the Court') without being required to relinquish his office.

(3) But he is not required to perform the duties of his judicial office while he is a judge of the Court.

(4) In respect of any period during which he is a judge of the Court–

(a) a Lord Justice of Appeal or Justice of the High Court is not to count as a judge of the relevant court for the purposes of section 2(1) or 4(1) of the Senior Courts Act 1981 (maximum number of judges) nor as a judge of the Senior Courts for the purposes of section 12(1) to (6) of that Act (salaries, etc);

(b) a judge of the Court of Session is not to count as a judge of that court for the purposes of section 1(1) of the Court of Session Act 1988 (maximum number of judges) or of section 9(1)(c) of the Administration of Justice Act 1973 ('the 1973 Act') (salaries, etc);

(c) a Lord Justice of Appeal or judge of the High Court in Northern Ireland is not to count as a judge of the relevant court for the purposes of section 2(1) or 3(1) of the Judicature (Northern Ireland) Act 1978 (maximum number of judges) nor as a judge of the Court of Judicature of Northern Ireland for the purposes of section 9(1)(d) of the 1973 Act (salaries, etc);

(d) a Circuit judge is not to count as such for the purposes of section 18 of the Courts Act 1971 (salaries, etc);

(e) a sheriff is not to count as such for the purposes of section 14 of the Sheriff Courts (Scotland) Act 1907 (salaries, etc);

(f) a county court judge of Northern Ireland is not to count as such for the purposes of section 106 of the County Courts Act Northern Ireland) 1959 (salaries, etc).

(5) If a sheriff principal is appointed a judge of the Court, section 11(1) of the Sheriff Courts (Scotland) Act 1971 (temporary appointment of sheriff principal) applies, while he holds that appointment, as if his office is vacant.

(6) Schedule 4 makes provision about judicial pensions in relation to the holder of a judicial office who serves as a judge of the Court.

(7) The Lord Chancellor or the Secretary of State may by order make such transitional provision (including, in particular, provision for a temporary increase in the maximum number of judges) as he considers appropriate in relation to any holder of a judicial office who has completed his service as a judge of the Court.

(7A) The following paragraphs apply to the making of an order under subsection (7) in relation to any holder of a judicial office listed in subsection (1)(a)–

(a) before deciding what transitional provision it is appropriate to make, the person making the order must consult the Lord Chief Justice of England and Wales;

(b) before making the order, that person must consult the Lord Chief Justice of England and Wales.

(7B) The following paragraphs apply to the making of an order under subsection (7) in relation to any holder of a judicial office listed in subsection (1)(c)–

(a) before deciding what transitional provision it is appropriate to make, the person making the order must consult the Lord Chief Justice of Northern Ireland;

(b) before making the order, that person must consult the Lord Chief Justice of Northern Ireland.

(7C) The Lord Chief Justice of England and Wales may nominate a judicial office holder (within the meaning of section 109(4) of the Constitutional Reform Act 2005) to exercise his functions under this section.

(7D) The Lord Chief Justice of Northern Ireland may nominate any of the following to exercise his functions under this section–
(a) the holder of one of the offices listed in Schedule 1 to the Justice (Northern Ireland) Act 2002;
(b) a Lord Justice of Appeal (as defined in section 88 of that Act).

PARLIAMENTARY PROCEDURE

Statements of compatibility

19(1) A Minister of the Crown in charge of a Bill in either House of Parliament must, before Second Reading of the Bill–
(a) make a statement to the effect that in his view the provisions of the Bill are compatible with the Convention rights ('a statement of compatibility'); or
(b) make a statement to the effect that although he is unable to make a statement of compatibility the government nevertheless wishes the House to proceed with the Bill.

(2) The statement must be in writing and be published in such manner as the Minister making it considers appropriate.

SUPPLEMENTAL

Orders, etc, under this Act

20(1) Any power of a Minister of the Crown to make an order under this Act is exercisable by statutory instrument.

(2) The power of the Lord Chancellor or the Secretary of State to make rules (other than rules of court) under section 2(3) or 7(9) is exercisable by statutory instrument.

(3) Any statutory instrument made under section 14, 15 or 16(7) must be laid before Parliament.

(4) No order may be made by the Lord Chancellor or the Secretary of State under section 1(4), 7(11) or 16(2) unless a draft of the order has been laid before, and approved by, each House of Parliament.

(5) Any statutory instrument made under section 18(7) or Schedule 4, or to which subsection (2) applies, shall be subject to annulment in pursuance of a resolution of either House of Parliament.

(6) The power of a Northern Ireland department to make–
(a) rules under section 2(3)(c) or 7(9)(c), or
(b) an order under section 7(11),
is exercisable by statutory rule for the purposes of the Statutory Rules (Northern Ireland) Order 1979.

(7) Any rules made under section 2(3)(c) or 7(9)(c) shall be subject to negative resolution; and section 41(6) of the Interpretation Act

Northern Ireland) 1954 (meaning of 'subject to negative resolution') shall apply as if the power to make the rules were conferred by an Act of the Northern Ireland Assembly.

(8) No order may be made by a Northern Ireland department under section 7(11) unless a draft of the order has been laid before, and approved by, the Northern Ireland Assembly.

Interpretation, etc

21(1) In this Act–

'amend' includes repeal and apply (with or without modifications);

'the appropriate Minister' means the Minister of the Crown having charge of the appropriate authorised government department (within the meaning of the Crown Proceedings Act 1947);

'the Commission' means the European Commission of Human Rights;

'the Convention' means the Convention for the Protection of Human Rights and Fundamental Freedoms, agreed by the Council of Europe at Rome on 4th November 1950 as it has effect for the time being in relation to the United Kingdom;

'declaration of incompatibility' means a declaration under section 4;

'Minister of the Crown' has the same meaning as in the Ministers of the Crown Act 1975;

'Northern Ireland Minister' includes the First Minister and the deputy First Minister in Northern Ireland;

'primary legislation' means any–

(a) public general Act;
(b) local and personal Act;
(c) private Act;
(d) Measure of the Church Assembly;
(e) Measure of the General Synod of the Church of England;
(f) Order in Council–
    (i) made in exercise of Her Majesty's Royal Prerogative;
    (ii) made under section 38(1)(a) of the Northern Ireland Constitution Act 1973 or the corresponding provision of the Northern Ireland Act 1998; or
    (iii) amending an Act of a kind mentioned in paragraph (a), (b) or (c);

    and includes an order or other instrument made under primary legislation (otherwise than by the Welsh Ministers, the First Minister for Wales, the Counsel General to the Welsh Assembly Government, a member of the Scottish Executive, a Northern Ireland Minister or a Northern Ireland department) to the extent to which it operates to bring one or more provisions of that legislation into force or amends any primary legislation;

'the First Protocol' means the protocol to the Convention agreed at Paris on 20th March 1952;

'the Sixth Protocol' means the protocol to the Convention agreed at Strasbourg on 28th April 1983;

'the Eleventh Protocol' means the protocol to the Convention (restructuring the control machinery established by the Convention) agreed at Strasbourg on 11th May 1994;

'the Thirteenth Protocol' means the protocol to the Convention (concerning the abolition of the death penalty in all circumstances) agreed at Vilnius on 3rd May 2002;

'remedial order' means an order under section 10;

'subordinate legislation' means any–

(a) Order in Council other than one–
  (i) made in exercise of Her Majesty's Royal Prerogative;
  (ii) made under section 38(1)(a) of the Northern Ireland Constitution Act 1973 or the corresponding provision of the Northern Ireland Act 1998; or
  (iii) amending an Act of a kind mentioned in the definition of primary legislation;

(b) Act of the Scottish Parliament;

(ba) Measure of the Mational Assembly for Wales;

(bb) Act of the National Assembly for Wales;

(c) Act of the Parliament of Northern Ireland;

(d) Measure of the Assembly established under section 1 of the Northern Ireland Assembly Act 1973;

(e) Act of the Northern Ireland Assembly;

(f) order, rules, regulations, scheme, warrant, byelaw or other instrument made under primary legislation (except to the extent to which it operates to bring one or more provisions of that legislation into force or amends any primary legislation);

(g) order, rules, regulations, scheme, warrant, byelaw or other instrument made under legislation mentioned in paragraph (b), (c), (d) or (e) or made under an Order in Council applying only to Northern Ireland;

(h) order, rules, regulations, scheme, warrant, byelaw or other instrument made by a member of the Scottish Executive, a Northern Ireland Minister or a Northern Ireland department in exercise of prerogative or other executive functions of Her Majesty which are exercisable by such a person on behalf of Her Majesty;

'transferred matters' has the same meaning as in the Northern Ireland Act 1998; and

'tribunal' means any tribunal in which legal proceedings may be brought.

(2) The references in paragraphs (b) and (c) of section 2(1) to Articles are to Articles of the Convention as they had effect immediately before the coming into force of the Eleventh Protocol.

(3) The reference in paragraph (d) of section 2(1) to Article 46 includes a reference to Articles 32 and 54 of the Convention as they had effect immediately before the coming into force of the Eleventh Protocol.

(4) The references in section 2(1) to a report or decision of the Commission or a decision of the Committee of Ministers include references to a report or decision made as provided by paragraphs 3, 4 and 6 of Article 5 of the Eleventh Protocol (transitional provisions).

(5) [Repealed.]

Short title, commencement, application and extent

22(1) This Act may be cited as the Human Rights Act 1998.

(2) Sections 18, 20 and 21(5) and this section come into force on the passing of this Act.

(3) The other provisions of this Act come into force on such day as the Secretary of State may by order appoint; and different days may be appointed for different purposes.

(4) Paragraph (b) of subsection (1) of section 7 applies to proceedings brought by or at the instigation of a public authority whenever the act in question took place; but otherwise that subsection does not apply to an act taking place before the coming into force of that section.

(5) This Act binds the Crown.

(6) This Act extends to Northern Ireland.

(7) [Repealed.]

SCHEDULE 1: THE ARTICLES

PART I: THE CONVENTION: RIGHTS AND FREEDOMS

Article 2: Right to life

1 Everyone's right to life shall be protected by law. No one shall be deprived of his life intentionally save in the execution of a sentence of a court following his conviction of a crime for which this penalty is provided by law.

2 Deprivation of life shall not be regarded as inflicted in contravention of this Article when it results from the use of force which is no more than absolutely necessary:

(a) in defence of any person from unlawful violence;

(b) in order to effect a lawful arrest or to prevent the escape of a person lawfully detained;

(c) in action lawfully taken for the purpose of quelling a riot or insurrection.

Article 3: Prohibition of torture

No one shall be subjected to torture or to inhuman or degrading treatment or punishment.

Article 4: Prohibition of slavery and forced labour

1 No one shall be held in slavery or servitude.

2 No one shall be required to perform forced or compulsory labour.

3 For the purpose of this Article the term 'forced or compulsory labour' shall not include:

(a) any work required to be done in the ordinary course of detention imposed according to the provisions of Article 5 of this Convention or during conditional release from such detention;

(b) any service of a military character or, in case of conscientious objectors in countries where they are recognised, service exacted instead of compulsory military service;

(c) any service exacted in case of an emergency or calamity threatening the life or well'being of the community;

(d) any work or service which forms part of normal civic obligations.

Article 5: Right to liberty and security

1 Everyone has the right to liberty and security of person. No one shall be deprived of his liberty save in the following cases and in accordance with a procedure prescribed by law:

(a) the lawful detention of a person after conviction by a competent court;

(b) the lawful arrest or detention of a person for non'compliance with the lawful order of a court or in order to secure the fulfilment of any obligation prescribed by law;

(c) the lawful arrest or detention of a person effected for the purpose of bringing him before the competent legal authority on reasonable suspicion of having committed an offence or when it is reasonably considered necessary to prevent his committing an offence or fleeing after having done so;

(d) the detention of a minor by lawful order for the purpose of educational supervision or his lawful detention for the purpose of bringing him before the competent legal authority;

(e) the lawful detention of persons for the prevention of the spreading of infectious diseases, of persons of unsound mind, alcoholics or drug addicts or vagrants;

(f) the lawful arrest or detention of a person to prevent his effecting an unauthorised entry into the country or of a person against whom action is being taken with a view to deportation or extradition.

2 Everyone who is arrested shall be informed promptly, in a language which he understands, of the reasons for his arrest and of any charge against him.

3 Everyone arrested or detained in accordance with the provisions of paragraph 1(c) of this Article shall be brought promptly before a judge or other officer authorised by law to exercise judicial power and shall be entitled to trial within a reasonable time or to release pending trial. Release may be conditioned by guarantees to appear for trial.

4 Everyone who is deprived of his liberty by arrest or detention shall be entitled to take proceedings by which the lawfulness of his detention

shall be decided speedily by a court and his release ordered if the detention is not lawful.

5 Everyone who has been the victim of arrest or detention in contravention of the provisions of this Article shall have an enforceable right to compensation.

Article 6: Right to a fair trial

1 In the determination of his civil rights and obligations or of any criminal charge against him, everyone is entitled to a fair and public hearing within a reasonable time by an independent and impartial tribunal established by law. Judgment shall be pronounced publicly but the press and public may be excluded from all or part of the trial in the interest of morals, public order or national security in a democratic society, where the interests of juveniles or the protection of the private life of the parties so require, or to the extent strictly necessary in the opinion of the court in special circumstances where publicity would prejudice the interests of justice.

2 Everyone charged with a criminal offence shall be presumed innocent until proved guilty according to law.

3 Everyone charged with a criminal offence has the following minimum rights:

(a) to be informed promptly, in a language which he understands and in detail, of the nature and cause of the accusation against him;

(b) to have adequate time and facilities for the preparation of his defence;

(c) to defend himself in person or through legal assistance of his own choosing or, if he has not sufficient means to pay for legal assistance, to be given it free when the interests of justice so require;

(d) to examine or have examined witnesses against him and to obtain the attendance and examination of witnesses on his behalf under the same conditions as witnesses against him;

(e) to have the free assistance of an interpreter if he cannot understand or speak the language used in court.

Article 7: No punishment without law

1 No one shall be held guilty of any criminal offence on account of any act or omission which did not constitute a criminal offence under national or international law at the time when it was committed. Nor shall a heavier penalty be imposed than the one that was applicable at the time the criminal offence was committed.

2 This Article shall not prejudice the trial and punishment of any person for any act or omission which, at the time when it was committed, was criminal according to the general principles of law recognised by civilised nations.

Article 8: Right to respect for private and family life

1 Everyone has the right to respect for his private and family life, his home and his correspondence.

2 There shall be no interference by a public authority with the exercise of this right except such as is in accordance with the law and is necessary in a democratic society in the interests of national security, public safety or the economic well-being of the country, for the prevention of disorder or crime, for the protection of health or morals, or for the protection of the rights and freedoms of others.

Article 9: Freedom of thought, conscience and religion

1 Everyone has the right to freedom of thought, conscience and religion; this right includes freedom to change his religion or belief and freedom, either alone or in community with others and in public or private, to manifest his religion or belief, in worship, teaching, practice and observance.

2 Freedom to manifest one's religion or beliefs shall be subject only to such limitations as are prescribed by law and are necessary in a democratic society in the interests of public safety, for the protection of public order, health or morals, or for the protection of the rights and freedoms of others.

Article 10: Freedom of expression

1 Everyone has the right to freedom of expression. This right shall include freedom to hold opinions and to receive and impart information and ideas without interference by public authority and regardless of frontiers. This Article shall not prevent States from requiring the licensing of broadcasting, television or cinema enterprises.

2 The exercise of these freedoms, since it carries with it duties and responsibilities, may be subject to such formalities, conditions, restrictions or penalties as are prescribed by law and are necessary in a democratic society, in the interests of national security, territorial integrity or public safety, for the prevention of disorder or crime, for the protection of health or morals, for the protection of the reputation or rights of others, for preventing the disclosure of information received in confidence, or for maintaining the authority and impartiality of the judiciary.

Article 11: Freedom of assembly and association

1 Everyone has the right to freedom of peaceful assembly and to freedom of association with others, including the right to form and to join trade unions for the protection of his interests.

2 No restrictions shall be placed on the exercise of these rights other than such as are prescribed by law and are necessary in a democratic society in the interests of national security or public safety, for the prevention of disorder or crime, for the protection of health or morals or for the protection of the rights and freedoms of others. This Article shall not prevent the imposition of lawful restrictions on the exercise of these rights by members of the armed forces, of the police or of the administration of the State.

Article 12: Right to marry

Men and women of marriageable age have the right to marry and to found a family, according to the national laws governing the exercise of this right.

Article 14: Prohibition of discrimination

The enjoyment of the rights and freedoms set forth in this Convention shall be secured without discrimination on any ground such as sex, race, colour, language, religion, political or other opinion, national or social origin, association with a national minority, property, birth or other status.

Article 16: Restrictions on political activity of aliens

Nothing in Articles 10, 11 and 14 shall be regarded as preventing the High Contracting Parties from imposing restrictions on the political activity of aliens.

Article 17: Prohibition of abuse of rights

Nothing in this Convention may be interpreted as implying for any State, group or person any right to engage in any activity or perform any act aimed at the destruction of any of the rights and freedoms set forth herein or at their limitation to a greater extent than is provided for in the Convention.

Article 18: Limitation on use of restrictions on rights

The restrictions permitted under this Convention to the said rights and freedoms shall not be applied for any purpose other than those for which they have been prescribed.

PART II: THE FIRST PROTOCOL

Article 1: Protection of property

Every natural or legal person is entitled to the peaceful enjoyment of his possessions. No one shall be deprived of his possessions except in the public interest and subject to the conditions provided for by law and by the general principles of international law.

The preceding provisions shall not, however, in any way impair the right of a State to enforce such laws as it deems necessary to control the use of property in accordance with the general interest or to secure the payment of taxes or other contributions or penalties.

Article 2: Right to education

No person shall be denied the right to education. In the exercise of any functions which it assumes in relation to education and to teaching, the State shall respect the right of parents to ensure such education and teaching in conformity with their own religious and philosophical convictions.

Article 3: Right to free elections

The High Contracting Parties undertake to hold free elections at reasonable intervals by secret ballot, under conditions which will ensure the free expression of the opinion of the people in the choice of the legislature.

PART III: ARTICLE 1 OF THE THIRTEENTH PROTOCOL

Article 1: Abolition of the death penalty

The death penalty shall be abolished. No one shall be condemned to such penalty or executed.

SCHEDULE 2: REMEDIAL ORDERS

Orders

1(1) A remedial order may–

(a) contain such incidental, supplemental, consequential or transitional provision as the person making it considers appropriate;

(b) be made so as to have effect from a date earlier than that on which it is made;

(c) make provision for the delegation of specific functions;

(d) make different provision for different cases.

(2) The power conferred by sub-paragraph (1)(a) includes–

(a) power to amend primary legislation (including primary legislation other than that which contains the incompatible provision); and

(b) power to amend or revoke subordinate legislation (including subordinate legislation other than that which contains the incompatible provision).

(3) A remedial order may be made so as to have the same extent as the legislation which it affects.

(4) No person is to be guilty of an offence solely as a result of the retrospective effect of a remedial order.

Procedure

2 No remedial order may be made unless–

(a) a draft of the order has been approved by a resolution of each House of Parliament made after the end of the period of 60 days beginning with the day on which the draft was laid; or

(b) it is declared in the order that it appears to the person making it that, because of the urgency of the matter, it is necessary to make the order without a draft being so approved.

Orders laid in draft

3(1) No draft may be laid under paragraph 2(a) unless–

(a) the person proposing to make the order has laid before Parliament a document which contains a draft of the proposed order and the required information; and
(b) the period of 60 days, beginning with the day on which the document required by this sub-paragraph was laid, has ended.

(2) If representations have been made during that period, the draft laid under paragraph 2(a) must be accompanied by a statement containing–
(a) a summary of the representations; and
(b) if, as a result of the representations, the proposed order has been changed, details of the changes.

Urgent cases

4(1) If a remedial order ('the original order') is made without being approved in draft, the person making it must lay it before Parliament, accompanied by the required information, after it is made.

(2) If representations have been made during the period of 60 days beginning with the day on which the original order was made, the person making it must (after the end of that period) lay before Parliament a statement containing–
(a) a summary of the representations; and
(b) if, as a result of the representations, he considers it appropriate to make changes to the original order, details of the changes.

(3) If sub-paragraph (2)(b) applies, the person making the statement must–
(a) make a further remedial order replacing the original order; and
(b) lay the replacement order before Parliament.

(4) If, at the end of the period of 120 days beginning with the day on which the original order was made, a resolution has not been passed by each House approving the original or replacement order, the order ceases to have effect (but without that affecting anything previously done under either order or the power to make a fresh remedial order).

Definitions

5 In this Schedule–

'representations' means representations about a remedial order (or proposed remedial order) made to the person making (or proposing to make) it and includes any relevant Parliamentary report or resolution; and

'required information' means–
(a) an explanation of the incompatibility which the order (or proposed order) seeks to remove, including particulars of the relevant declaration, finding or order; and
(b) a statement of the reasons for proceeding under section 10 and for making an order in those terms.

Calculating periods

6 In calculating any period for the purposes of this Schedule, no account is to be taken of any time during which–

(a) Parliament is dissolved or prorogued; or
(b) both Houses are adjourned for more than four days.

7(1) This paragraph applies in relation to–
(a) any remedial order made, and any draft of such an order proposed to be made–
(i) by the Scottish Ministers; or
(ii) within devolved competence (within the meaning of the Scotland Act 1998) by Her Majesty in Council; and
(b) any document or statement to be laid in connection with such an order (or proposed order).

(2) This Schedule has effect in relation to any such order (or proposed order), document or statement subject to the following modifications.

(3) Any reference to Parliament, each House of Parliament or both Houses of Parliament shall be construed as a reference to the Scottish Parliament.

(4) Paragraph 6 does not apply and instead, in calculating any period for the purposes of this Schedule, no account is to be taken of any time during which the Scottish Parliament is dissolved or is in recess for more than four days.

SCHEDULE 3: RESERVATION

PART I

[Repealed.]

PART II: RESERVATION

At the time of signing the present (First) Protocol, I declare that, in view of certain provisions of the Education Acts in the United Kingdom, the principle affirmed in the second sentence of Article 2 is accepted by the United Kingdom only so far as it is compatible with the provision of efficient instruction and training, and the avoidance of unreasonable public expenditure.

Dated 20 March 1952. Made by the United Kingdom Permanent Representative to the Council of Europe.

SCHEDULE 4: JUDICIAL PENSIONS

Duty to make orders about pensions

1(1) The appropriate Minister must by order make provision with respect to pensions payable to or in respect of any holder of a judicial office who serves as an ECHR judge.

(2) A pensions order must include such provision as the Minister making it considers is necessary to secure that–

(a) an ECHR judge who was, immediately before his appointment as an ECHR judge, a member of a judicial pension scheme is entitled to remain as a member of that scheme;
(b) the terms on which he remains a member of the scheme are those which would have been applicable had he not been appointed as an ECHR judge; and
(c) entitlement to benefits payable in accordance with the scheme continues to be determined as if, while serving as an ECHR judge, his salary was that which would (but for section 18(4)) have been payable to him in respect of his continuing service as the holder of his judicial office.

Contributions

2 A pensions order may, in particular, make provision–
(a) for any contributions which are payable by a person who remains a member of a scheme as a result of the order, and which would otherwise be payable by deduction from his salary, to be made otherwise than by deduction from his salary as an ECHR judge; and
(b) for such contributions to be collected in such manner as may be determined by the administrators of the scheme.

Amendments of other enactments

3 A pensions order may amend any provision of, or made under, a pensions Act in such manner and to such extent as the Minister making the order considers necessary or expedient to ensure the proper administration of any scheme to which it relates.

Definitions

4 In this Schedule–

'appropriate Minister' means–
(a) in relation to any judicial office whose jurisdiction is exercisable exclusively in relation to Scotland, the Secretary of State; and
(b) otherwise, the Lord Chancellor;

'ECHR judge' means the holder of a judicial office who is serving as a judge of the Court;

'judicial pension scheme' means a scheme established by and in accordance with a pensions Act;

'pensions Act' means–
(a) the County Courts Act Northern Ireland) 1959;
(b) the Sheriffs' Pensions (Scotland) Act 1961;
(c) the Judicial Pensions Act 1981; or
(d) the Judicial Pensions and Retirement Act 1993;
(e) the Public Service Pensions Act 2013; and

'pensions order' means an order made under paragraph 1.

MOBILE HOMES (WALES) ACT 2013 SS1–3, 40–57, SCH 2

Part 1 Introduction

Overview of Act

1(1) This Act makes provision about mobile home sites in Wales.

(2) In this Act–

(a) Part 2 makes provision for and in connection with the licensing of regulated sites etc,

(b) Part 3 makes provision for protection from eviction from protected sites,

(c) Part 4 makes provision about the terms of agreements for stationing mobile homes on protected sites,

(d) Part 5 makes provision under which local authorities may provide sites for mobile homes and may prohibit the stationing of mobile homes on commons, and

(e) Part 6 makes supplementary and general provision.

Mobile home sites subject to Act

2(1) In this Act 'regulated site' means any land in Wales on which a mobile home is stationed for the purposes of human habitation (including any land in Wales used in conjunction with that land), other than–

(a) a site which Schedule 1 provides is not to be a regulated site, or

(b) a holiday site.

(2) In this Act 'protected site' means land which is–

(a) a regulated site, or

(b) a site that would be a regulated site but for paragraph 11 of Schedule 1.

(3) In subsection (1) 'holiday site' means a site in respect of which the relevant planning permission or the site licence for the site under the Caravan Sites and Control of Development Act 1960–

(a) is expressed to be granted for holiday use only, or

(b) requires that there are times of the year when no mobile home may be stationed on the site for human habitation.

(4) For the purpose of determining whether or not a site is a holiday site, any provision of the relevant planning permission or of the site licence which permits the stationing of a mobile home on the land for human habitation all year round is to be ignored if the mobile home is authorised to be occupied by–

(a) the person who is the owner of the site, or

(b) a person employed by that person but who does not occupy the mobile home under an agreement to which Part 4 applies.

(5) In this Act 'local authority Gypsy and Traveller site' means land owned by a local authority for the stationing of mobile homes providing accommodation for Gypsies and Travellers.

Owners of sites

3 In this Act 'owner', in relation to any land, means the person who, by virtue of an estate or interest in the land–

(a) is entitled to possession of the land, or

(b) would be entitled to possession of the land but for the rights of any other person under any licence or contract granted in respect of the land (including a licence or contract to station or occupy a mobile home there),

but see also sections 39(2), 42(7) and 55(2)(a).

. . .

Part 3: Protection from Eviction

Application of Part

40 This Part applies in relation to any licence or contract (whenever made) under which a person is entitled–

(a) to station a mobile home on a protected site and occupy it as the person's residence, or

(b) if the mobile home is stationed on the protected site by another, to occupy it as the person's residence.

Minimum length of notice

41 In any case where a residential contract is determinable by notice given by either party to the other, a notice is of no effect unless it is given not less than 4 weeks before the date on which it is to take effect.

Protection of occupiers against eviction and harassment, false information etc

42(1) A person to whom any of subsections (2) to (6) applies commits an offence.

(2) This subsection applies to a person if, during the subsistence of a residential contract, the person unlawfully deprives the occupier of the mobile home of occupation on the protected site of any mobile home which the occupier is entitled by the contract to station and occupy, or to occupy, as the occupier's residence on the protected site.

(3) This subsection applies to a person if, after the expiry or determination of a residential contract, the person enforces, otherwise than by proceedings in the court, any right to exclude the occupier of the mobile home from the protected site or from any such mobile home, or to remove or exclude any such mobile home from the protected site.

(4) This subsection applies to a person if (whether during the subsistence, or after the expiry or determination, of a residential contract) with intent to cause the occupier of the mobile home–

(a) to abandon the occupation of the mobile home or remove it from the site, or

(b) to refrain from exercising any right or pursuing any remedy in respect of that, the person does acts likely to interfere with the peace or comfort of the occupier or persons residing with the occupier, or withdraws or withholds services or facilities reasonably required for the occupation of the mobile home as a residence on the site.

(5) This subsection applies to a person if the person is, or is the agent of, the owner of the protected site and (whether during the subsistence or after the expiration or determination of a residential contract)–

(a) the person does acts likely to interfere with the peace or comfort of the occupier of the mobile home or persons residing with the occupier, or

(b) withdraws or withholds services or facilities reasonably required for the occupation of the mobile home as a residence on the site,

and (in either case) the person knows, or has reasonable cause to believe, that that conduct is likely to cause the occupier to do any of the things mentioned in subsection (4)(a) or (b).

(6) This subsection applies to a person if the person is, or is the agent of, the owner of a protected site and, during the subsistence of a residential contract, the person–

(a) knowingly or recklessly provides information or makes a representation which is false or misleading in a material respect to any person, and

(b) knows, or has reasonable cause to believe, that doing so is likely to cause–

(i) the occupier to do any of the things mentioned in subsection (4)(a) or (b), or

(ii) a person who is considering whether to purchase or occupy the mobile home to which the residential contract relates to decide not to do so.

(7) In subsections (5) and (6) references to the owner of a protected site include references to a person with an estate or interest in the site which is superior to that of the owner.

(8) In this section references to the occupier of the mobile home include references to the person who was the occupier of the mobile home under a residential contract which has expired or been determined and, in the case of the death of the occupier (whether during the subsistence or after the expiry or determination of the contract), to any person then residing with the occupier.

(9) Nothing in this section applies to the exercise by the owner of a mobile home of a right to take possession of the mobile home, other than a right conferred by or arising on the expiry or determination of a residential contract, or to anything done pursuant to the order of any court.

43 Offences under section 42: supplementary

(1) In proceedings for an offence of contravening section 42(2) or (3) it is a defence to prove that the accused believed, and had reasonable cause

to believe, that the occupier of the mobile home had ceased to reside on the site.

(2) In proceedings for an offence of contravening section 42(5) it is a defence to prove that the accused had reasonable grounds for doing the acts or withdrawing or withholding the services or facilities in question.

(3) A person guilty of an offence under section 42 is liable–
- (a) on summary conviction, to a fine or to imprisonment for a term not exceeding 12 months, or to both, or
- (b) on conviction on indictment, to a fine or to imprisonment for a term not exceeding 2 years, or to both.

44 Provision for suspension of eviction orders

(1) If in proceedings by the owner of a protected site the court makes an order for enforcing in relation to the site any such right as is mentioned in section 42(3), the court may (without prejudice to any power apart from this section to postpone the operation or suspend the execution of an order) suspend the enforcement of the order for such period not exceeding 12 months from the date of the order as the court thinks reasonable.

(2) Where the court by virtue of this section suspends the enforcement of an order, it may impose such terms and conditions, including conditions as to the payment of rent or other periodical payments or of arrears of such rent or payments, as the court thinks reasonable.

(3) The court may from time to time, on the application of either party, extend, reduce or terminate the period of suspension ordered, or vary any terms or conditions imposed, but may not extend the period of suspension for more than 12 months at a time.

(4) In considering whether or how to exercise its powers under this section, the court must have regard to all the circumstances which include (but are not limited to) the questions–
- (a) whether the occupier of the mobile home has failed, whether before or after the expiry or determination of the relevant residential contract, to observe any terms or conditions of that contract, any conditions of the site licence, or any reasonable rules made by the owner of the protected site for the management and conduct of the site or the maintenance of mobile homes on it,
- (b) whether the occupier of the mobile home has unreasonably refused an offer by the owner to renew the residential contract or make another residential contract for a reasonable period and on reasonable terms, and
- (c) whether the occupier of the mobile home has failed to make reasonable efforts to obtain elsewhere other suitable accommodation for the mobile home or another suitable mobile home and accommodation for it.

(5) Where the court makes an order such as is mentioned in subsection (1) but suspends the enforcement of the order, the court may not

make any order for costs unless it appears to the court, having regard to the conduct of the owner of the protected site or of the occupier of the mobile home, that the circumstances of the case are exceptional.

(6) The court may not suspend the enforcement of an order by virtue of this section if–

(a) no site licence is in force in respect of the site, and

(b) the site is not owned by a local authority;

and where a site licence in respect of the site is expressed to expire at the end of a specified period, the period for which enforcement may be suspended by virtue of this section does not extend beyond the expiry of the site licence.

Supplementary

45(1) The power of the court under section 44 to suspend the enforcement of an order extends to any order made but not executed before the commencement of this Part.

(2) Nothing in this Part affects the operation of section 13 of the Compulsory Purchase Act 1965.

(3) The Protection from Eviction Act 1977 does not apply to any premises consisting of a mobile home stationed on a protected site.

Offences

46 Proceedings for an offence under this Part may be instituted by any local authority.

Interpretation

47(1) In this Part–

'occupier' ('*meddiannydd*') in relation to a mobile home and a protected site, means the person entitled as mentioned in section 40 in relation to a mobile home and the protected site;

'residential contract' ('*contract preswyl*') means a licence or contract within that section.

(2) In this Part 'the court' means the county court.

Part 4: Mobile Home Agreements

Agreements to which Part applies

48(1) This Part applies to any agreement under which a person is entitled–

(a) to station a mobile home on a protected site, and

(b) to occupy the mobile home as the person's only or main residence.

(2) In this Part 'occupier', in relation to a mobile home and a protected site, means the person entitled as mentioned in subsection (1) in relation to a mobile home and the protected site (but see also section 55(2)(b)).

Particulars of agreements

49(1) Before making an agreement to which this Part applies, the owner of the protected site must give to the proposed occupier under the agreement a written statement which–

(a) specifies the names and addresses of the parties,

(b) includes particulars of the land on which the proposed occupier is to be entitled to station the mobile home that are sufficient to identify that land,

(c) sets out the express terms to be contained in the agreement (including any site rules),

(d) sets out the terms to be implied by section 50(1), and

(e) complies with such other requirements as may be prescribed by regulations made by the Welsh Ministers.

(2) The written statement required by subsection (1) must be given–

(a) no later than 28 days before the date on which any agreement for the sale of the mobile home to the proposed occupier is made, or

(b) (if no such agreement is made before the making of the agreement to which this Part applies) no later than 28 days before the date on which the agreement to which this Part applies is made.

(3) But if the proposed occupier consents in writing to that statement being given by a date ('the chosen date') which is less than 28 days before the date mentioned in subsection (2)(a) or (b), the statement must be given to the proposed occupier not later than the chosen date.

(4) If any express term other than a site rule–

(a) is contained in an agreement to which this Part applies, but

(b) was not set out in a written statement given to the proposed occupier in accordance with subsections (1) to (3),

the term is unenforceable by the owner or any person within section 53(1); but this is subject to any order made by the appropriate judicial body under section 50(3).

(5) If the owner has failed to give the occupier a written statement in accordance with subsections (1) to (3) the occupier may, at any time after the making of the agreement, apply to the appropriate judicial body for an order requiring the owner–

(a) to give the occupier a written statement which complies with paragraphs (a) to (e) of subsection (1) (read with any modifications necessary to reflect the fact that the agreement has been made), and

(b) to do so not later than such date as is specified in the order.

(6) A statement required to be given to a person under this section may be either delivered to the person personally or sent to the person by post.

(7) Any reference in this section to the making of an agreement to which this Part applies includes a reference to any variation of an agreement by virtue of which the agreement becomes one to which this Part applies.

(8) Subsections (2), (3) and (5) do not apply in relation to a person occupying or proposing to occupy a transit pitch on a local authority Gypsy and Traveller site; and in such a case the reference in subsection (4) to subsections (1) to (3) is to be treated as a reference to subsection (1).

Terms of agreements

50(1) The applicable terms set out in Part 1 of Schedule 2 are implied in any agreement to which this Part applies; and this subsection has effect despite any express term of the agreement.

(2) The appropriate judicial body may, on the application of either party made within the relevant period, order that terms concerning the matters mentioned in Part 2 of Schedule 2 are to be implied in the agreement.

(3) The appropriate judicial body may, on the application of either party made within the relevant period, make an order–

(a) varying or deleting any express term of the agreement other than a site rule,

(b) in the case of any express term to which section 49(4) applies other than a site rule, providing for the term to have full effect or to have such effect subject to any variation specified in the order.

(4) In subsections (2) and (3) 'the relevant period' means the period beginning with the date on which the agreement is made and ending–

(a) 6 months after that date, or

(b) where a written statement relating to the agreement is given to the occupier after that date (whether or not in compliance with an order under section 49(5)), 6 months after the date on which the statement is given;

and subsection (7) of section 49 applies for the purposes of this subsection as it applies for the purposes of that section.

(5) On an application under this section, the appropriate judicial body must make such provision as it considers just and equitable in the circumstances.

(6) Subsections (2) to (4) do not apply in relation to a person occupying or proposing to occupy a transit pitch on a local authority Gypsy and Traveller site.

Power to amend implied terms

51(1) The Welsh Ministers may by order make such amendments of Schedule 2, apart from paragraph 11, as they consider appropriate.

(2) Without prejudice to the generality of subsection (1), an order under this section may–

(a) make provision for or in connection with the determination by the court or a tribunal of such questions, or the making by the court or a tribunal of such orders, as are specified in the order, or

(b) make such amendments of any other provision of this Part as the Welsh Ministers consider appropriate in consequence of any amendment made in Schedule 2 by the order.

Site rules

52(1) In the case of a protected site, other than a local authority Gypsy and Traveller site, for which there are site rules, each of the rules is to be an express term of each agreement to which this Part applies that relates to a pitch on the site (including an agreement made before commencement or one made before the making of the rules).

(2) The 'site rules' for a protected site are rules made by the owner, in accordance with such procedure as may be prescribed by regulations made by the Welsh Ministers, which relate to–

(a) the management and conduct of the site, or

(b) such other matters as may be prescribed by regulations made by the Welsh Ministers.

(3) Any rules made by the owner before the coming into force of this section which relate to a matter mentioned in subsection (2) cease to have effect at the end of such period beginning with the day on which this section comes into force as may be prescribed by regulations made by the Welsh Ministers.

(4) Site rules come into force at the end of such period beginning with the first consultation day as may be prescribed by regulations made by the Welsh Ministers, if before the end of that period a copy of the rules is deposited with the local authority in whose area the protected site is situated.

(5) Where a site rule is varied, the rule as varied comes into force at the end of such period beginning with the first consultation day as may be prescribed by regulations made by the Welsh Ministers, if–

(a) the rule is varied in accordance with the procedure prescribed by regulations made by the Welsh Ministers, and

(b) a copy of the rule as varied is before the end of that period deposited with the local authority in whose area the protected site is situated.

(6) Where a site rule is deleted, the deletion comes into force at the end of such period beginning with the first consultation day as may be prescribed by regulations made by the Welsh Ministers, if–

(a) the rule is deleted in accordance with such procedure as may be prescribed by regulations made by the Welsh Ministers, and

(b) notice of the deletion is deposited before the end of that period deposited with the local authority in whose area the protected site is situated.

(7) The Welsh Ministers may by regulations provide that a site rule may not be made, varied or deleted unless a proposal to make, vary or delete the rule is notified to the occupiers of mobile homes on the site in question in accordance with the regulations.

(8) The Welsh Ministers may by regulations provide that site rules, or rules such as are mentioned in subsection (3), are of no effect in so far as they make provision in relation to matters prescribed by the regulations.

(9) The Welsh Ministers may by regulations make provision as to the resolution of disputes–

(a) relating to a proposal to make, vary or delete a site rule,

(b) as to whether the making, variation or deletion of a site rule was in accordance with the applicable procedure prescribed by the regulations,

(c) as to whether a deposit required to be made by virtue of subsection (4), (5) or (6) was made before the end of the relevant period.

(10) Provision under subsection (9) may confer functions on a tribunal.

(11) The Welsh Ministers may by regulations–

(a) require a local authority to establish and keep up to date a register of site rules in respect of protected sites in its area,

(b) require a local authority to publish the up'to'date register,

(c) provide that any deposit required to be made by virtue of subsection (4), (5) or (6) must be accompanied by a fee of such amount as the local authority may determine.

(12) In this section 'first consultation day' means the day on which a proposal made under regulations under subsection (7) is notified to the occupiers of mobile homes on the site in accordance with the regulations.

Successors in title

53(1) An agreement to which this Part applies is binding on, and has effect for the benefit of, any successor in title of the owner and any person claiming through or under the owner or any such successor.

(2) Where an agreement to which this Part applies is lawfully assigned to any person, the agreement has effect for the benefit of, and is binding on, that person.

(3) Where a person entitled to the benefit of and bound by an agreement to which this Part applies dies, the agreement has effect for the benefit of, and is binding on–

(a) any person residing in the mobile home as that person's only or main residence at that time, being–

(i) the widow, widower or surviving civil partner of the deceased or the surviving partner of an enduring family relationship of the deceased, or

(ii) in default of a person within sub-paragraph (i) residing in the mobile home as that person's only or main residence at that time, any member of the deceased's family, or

(b) in default of any such person residing in the mobile home as that person's only or main residence at that time, the person entitled to the mobile home by virtue of the deceased's will or under the law relating to intestacy, but subject to subsection (4).

(4) An agreement to which this Part applies does not have effect for the benefit of, and is not binding on, a person by virtue of subsection (3)(b) in so far as–

(a) it would, but for this subsection, enable or require that person to occupy the mobile home, or
(b) it includes terms implied by virtue of paragraph 6, 12, 13, 39 or 41 of Schedule 2.

Jurisdiction of a tribunal or the court

54 (1) A tribunal has jurisdiction–
(a) to determine any question arising under this Part or any agreement to which it applies, and
(b) to entertain any proceedings brought under this Part or any such agreement,
subject to subsections (2) to (6).
(2) Subsection (1) applies in relation to a question irrespective of anything contained in an arbitration agreement which has been entered into before that question arose.
(3) The court has jurisdiction–
(a) to determine any question arising by virtue of paragraph 5, 6, 7(1)(b), 38, 39 or 40(1)(b) of Schedule 2 under this Part or any agreement to which it applies, and
(b) to entertain any proceedings arising by virtue of any of those provisions brought under this Part or any such agreement,
subject to subsections (4) to (6).
(4) Subsection (5) applies if the owner and occupier have entered into an arbitration agreement before the question mentioned in subsection (3)(a) arises and the agreement applies to that question.
(5) A tribunal has jurisdiction to determine the question and entertain any proceedings arising instead of the court.
(6) Subsection (5) applies irrespective of anything contained in the arbitration agreement mentioned in subsection (4).

Interpretation

55(1) In this Part–
'the appropriate judicial body' ('*corff barnwrol priodol*') means whichever of the court or a tribunal has jurisdiction under section 54;
'arbitration agreement' ('*cytundeb cymrodeddu*') means an agreement in writing to submit to arbitration any question arising under this Part or any agreement to which it applies;
'the court' ('*y llys*') means the county court for the district in which the protected site is situated or, where the parties have entered into an arbitration agreement that applies to the question to be determined, the arbitrator;
'occupier' ('*meddiannydd*') has the meaning given by section 48(2) (but see also subsection (2)(b));
'permanent pitch' ('*llain barhaol*') means a pitch which is not a transit pitch;
'pitch' ('*llain*') means the land, forming part of a protected site and including any garden area, on which an occupier is entitled to station a mobile home under the terms of an agreement;

'transit pitch' (*'llain dramwy'*) means a pitch on which a person is entitled to station a mobile home under the terms of an agreement for a fixed period of up to 3 months;

'tribunal' (*'tribiwnlys'*) means a residential property tribunal or, where the parties have entered into an arbitration agreement that applies to the question to be determined and that question arose before the agreement was made, the arbitrator;

'site rules' (*'rheolau safle'*) has the meaning given by section 52(2).

(2) In relation to an agreement to which this Part applies–

(a) any reference in this Part to the owner includes a reference to any person who is bound by and entitled to the benefit of the agreement by virtue of subsection (1) of section 53, and

(b) subject to subsection (4) of that section, any reference in this Part to the occupier includes a reference to any person who is entitled to the benefit of and bound by the agreement by virtue of subsection (2) or (3) of that section.

(3) For the purposes of this Part the following are members of a person's family–

(a) the person's spouse or civil partner or any person who lives together with the person as a partner in an enduring family relationship,

(b) the person's parents, grandparents, children and grandchildren (including any person who is in that relationship by virtue of a marriage or civil partnership or an enduring family relationship) and any other person treated by the person as a child of the person's family, and

(c) the person's brothers, sisters, uncles, aunts, nephews and nieces (including any person who is in that relationship by virtue of a marriage or civil partnership or an enduring family relationship).

Part 5: Powers of Local Authorities

Power to provide sites for mobile homes

56 (1) A local authority may within its area provide sites where mobile homes may be brought, whether for holidays or other temporary purposes or for use as permanent residences, and may manage the sites or lease them to another person.

(2) A local authority has power to do anything appearing to it desirable in connection with the provision of such sites and the things which it has power to do include (but are not limited to)–

(a) acquiring land which is in use as a mobile home site or which has been laid out as a mobile home site,

(b) providing for the use of those occupying mobile home sites any services for their health or convenience, and

(c) providing, in or in connection with sites for the accommodation of Gypsies and Travellers, working space and facilities for the carrying on of activities normally carried on by them.

(3) In exercising its powers under this section a local authority must have regard to any standards specified by the Welsh Ministers under section 10.

(4) Before exercising the power under subsection (1) to provide a site the local authority must consult the fire and rescue authority–

(a) as to measures to be taken for preventing and detecting the outbreak of fire on the site, and

(b) as to the provision and maintenance of means of fighting fire on it.

(5) A local authority must make in respect of sites managed by it, and of any services or facilities provided or made available under this section, such reasonable charges as it may determine.

(6) A local authority may make available the services and facilities provided under this section for persons whether or not they normally reside in its area.

(7) A local authority may, where it appears to it that–

(a) a mobile home site or an additional mobile home site in needed in its area, or

(b) that land which is in use as a mobile home site should in the interests of the users of mobile homes be taken over by the local authority,

acquire land, or any interest in land, compulsorily.

(8) The power conferred by subsection (7) is exercisable in any particular case only if the local authority is authorised by the Welsh Ministers to exercise it.

(9) The Acquisition of Land Act 1981 has effect in relation to the acquisition of land, or an interest in land, under subsection (7).

(10) A local authority does not have power under this section to provide mobile homes.

Power to prohibit mobile homes on commons

57(1) This section applies to any land in Wales which is or forms part of a common and is not–

(a) land to which section 193 of the Law of Property Act 1925 (rights of public over certain commons and waste lands) applies,

(b) land subject to a scheme under Part 1 of the Commons Act 1899 (schemes for the regulation and management of certain commons), or

(c) land as respects which a site licence is for the time being in force.

(2) A local authority may make with respect to land to which this section applies and which is in its area an order prohibiting, either absolutely or except in such circumstances as may be specified in the order, the stationing of mobile homes on the land for the purposes of human habitation.

(3) A person who stations a mobile home on any land in contravention of an order under subsection (2) for the time being in force with respect to the land commits an offence.

(4) A person guilty of an offence under subsection (3) is liable on summary conviction to a fine not exceeding level 1 on the standard scale.

(5) A local authority must take all reasonable steps to secure that copies of any order under subsection (2) which is for the time being in force with respect to any land in its area are displayed on the land so as to give persons entering the land warning of the existence of the order.

(6) A local authority has the right to place on the land the notices that it considers necessary for the performance of its duty under subsection (5).

(7) An order made by a local authority under subsection (2) may be revoked at any time by a subsequent order made under that subsection by the local authority or may be varied so as to exclude any land from the operation of the order or so as to introduce any exception, or further exception, from the prohibition imposed by the order.

(8) Where the whole or part of any land to which an order under subsection (2) is in force ceases to be land to which this section applies, the order ceases to have effect with respect to the land or that part of it.

(9) Where an order ceases to have effect with respect to part only of any land, the local authority must cause any copy of the order which is displayed on that part of the land with respect to which the order remains in force to be amended accordingly.

(10) Schedule 3 makes further provision with respect to orders under subsection (2).

(11) In this section 'common' includes any land subject to be enclosed under the Inclosure Acts 1845 to 1882 and any town or village green.

. . .

SCHEDULE 2 TERMS OF MOBILE HOME AGREEMENTS

(introduced by section 50)

Part 1 Terms Implied by Act

CHAPTER 1: Application

1(1) The implied terms set out in Chapter 2 apply to all agreements except an agreement which relates to a pitch on a local authority Gypsy and Traveller site.

(2) The implied terms set out in Chapter 3 apply to an agreement which relates to a transit pitch on a local authority Gypsy and Traveller site.

(3) The implied terms set out in Chapter 4 apply to an agreement which relates to a permanent pitch on a local authority Gypsy and Traveller site.

(4) In this Part–

'consumer prices index' ('*mynegai prisiau defyddwyr*') means the general index of consumer prices (for all items) published by the Statistics Board or, if that index is not published for a relevant month, any substituted index or index figures published by the Board;

'review date' ('*dyddiad yr adolygiad*'), in relation to an agreement, means the date specified in the written statement as the date on which the pitch fee will be reviewed in each year or, if no such date is specified, each anniversary of the date the agreement commenced;

'written statement' ('*datganiad ysgrifenedig*') means the written statement that the owner of the protected site is required to give to the occupier of the mobile home by section 49(1).

CHAPTER 2: Agreements Relating to Pitches Except Those on Local Authority Gypsy and Traveller Sites

Duration of agreement

2 Subject to paragraph 3, the right to station the mobile home on land forming part of the protected site subsists until the agreement is determined under paragraph 4, 5, 6 or 7.

3(1) If the owner's estate or interest is insufficient to enable the owner to grant the right for an indefinite period, the period for which the right subsists does not extend beyond the date when the owner's estate or interest determines.

(2) If planning permission for the use of the protected site as a site for mobile homes has been granted in terms such that it will expire at the end of a specified period, the period for which the right subsists does not extend beyond the date when the planning permission expires.

(3) If before the end of a period determined by this paragraph there is a change in circumstances which allows a longer period, account is to be taken of that change.

Termination

4 The occupier is entitled to terminate the agreement by notice in writing given to the owner not less than 4 weeks before the date on which it is to take effect.

5 The owner is entitled to terminate the agreement immediately if, on the application of the owner, the appropriate judicial body–

(a) is satisfied that the occupier has breached a term of the agreement and, after service of a notice to remedy the breach, has not complied with the notice within a reasonable time, and

(b) considers it reasonable for the agreement to be terminated.

6 The owner is entitled to terminate the agreement immediately if, on the application of the owner, the appropriate judicial body–

(a) is satisfied that the occupier is not occupying the mobile home as the occupier's only or main residence, and

(b) considers it reasonable for the agreement to be terminated.

7(1) The owner is entitled to terminate the agreement immediately if–

(a) on the application of the owner, a tribunal has determined that, having regard to its condition, the mobile home is having a detrimental effect on the amenity of the site, and
(b) then, on the application of the owner, the appropriate judicial body, having regard to the tribunal's determination and to any other circumstances, considers it reasonable for the agreement to be terminated.

(2) Sub-paragraphs (3) and (4) apply if, on an application to the tribunal under sub-paragraph (1)(a)–
(a) the tribunal considers that, having regard to the present condition of the mobile home, it is having a detrimental effect on the amenity of the site, but
(b) it also considers that it would be reasonably practicable for particular repairs to be carried out on the mobile home that would result in the mobile home not having that detrimental effect, and
(c) the occupier indicates to the tribunal that the occupier intends to carry out those repairs.

(3) In such a case, the tribunal may make an interim order–
(a) specifying the repairs that must be carried out and the time within which they must be carried out, and
(b) adjourning the proceedings on the application for such period specified in the interim order as the tribunal considers reasonable to enable the repairs to be carried out.

(4) If the tribunal makes an interim order under sub-paragraph (3), it must not make a determination under sub-paragraph (1)(a) unless it is satisfied that the specified period has expired without the repairs having been carried out.

Recovery of overpayments by occupier

8 Where the agreement is terminated as mentioned in paragraph 4, 5, 6 or 7, the occupier is entitled to recover from the owner so much of any payment made by the occupier in pursuance of the agreement as is attributable to a period beginning after the termination.

Sale of mobile home

9(1) Where the agreement is a new agreement, the occupier is entitled to sell the mobile home and to assign the agreement to the person to whom the mobile home is sold (the 'new occupier') without the approval of the owner.

(2) In this paragraph and paragraphs 10, 12 and 13, 'new agreement' means an agreement–
(a) which was made after the commencement of this paragraph, or
(b) which was made before, but which has been assigned after, that commencement.

(3) The new occupier must, as soon as reasonably practicable, notify the owner of the completion of the sale and assignment of the agreement.

(4) The new occupier is required to pay the owner a commission on the sale of the mobile home at a rate not exceeding such rate as may be prescribed by regulations made by the Welsh Ministers.

(5) Except to the extent mentioned in sub-paragraph (4), the owner may not require any payment to be made (whether to the owner or otherwise) in connection with the sale of the mobile home and the assignment of the agreement to the new occupier.

(6) The Welsh Ministers may by regulations prescribe procedural requirements to be complied with by the owner, the occupier or the new occupier in connection with–

(a) the sale of the mobile home and assignment of the agreement, or

(b) the payment of commission by virtue of sub-paragraph (4).

10(1) Where the agreement is not a new agreement, the occupier is entitled to sell the mobile home and assign the agreement without the approval of the owner if–

(a) the occupier serves on the owner a notice (a 'notice of proposed sale') that the occupier proposes to sell the mobile home, and assign the agreement, to the person named in the notice (the 'proposed occupier'), and

(b) the first or second condition is satisfied.

(2) The first condition is that, within the period of 21 days beginning with the date on which the owner received the notice of proposed sale ('the 21-day period'), the occupier does not receive a notice from the owner that the owner has applied to a tribunal for an order preventing the occupier from selling the mobile home, and assigning the agreement, to the proposed occupier (a 'refusal order').

(3) The second condition is that–

(a) within the 21-day period–

(i) the owner applies to a tribunal for a refusal order, and

(ii) the occupier receives a notice of the application from the owner, and

(b) the tribunal rejects the application.

(4) If the owner applies to a tribunal for a refusal order within the 21-day period but the occupier does not receive notice of the application from the owner within that period–

(a) the application is to be treated as not having been made, and

(b) the first condition is accordingly to be treated as satisfied.

(5) A notice of proposed sale must include such information as may be prescribed in regulations made by the Welsh Ministers.

(6) A notice of proposed sale or notice of an application for a refusal order–

(a) must be in writing, and

(b) may be served by post.

(7) An application for a refusal order may be made only on one or more of the grounds prescribed in regulations made by the Welsh Ministers; and a notice of an application for a refusal order must specify the ground or grounds on which the application is made.

(8) The person to whom the mobile home is sold ('the new occupier') is required to pay the owner a commission on the sale of the mobile home at a rate not exceeding such rate as may be prescribed by regulations made by the Welsh Ministers.

(9) Except to the extent mentioned in sub-paragraph (8), the owner may not require any payment to be made (whether to the owner or otherwise) in connection with the sale of the mobile home and the assignment of the agreement.

(10) The Welsh Ministers may by regulations prescribe procedural requirements to be complied with by the owner, the occupier, a proposed occupier or the new occupier in connection with–

(a) the sale of the mobile home and assignment of the agreement, and

(b) the payment of commission by virtue of sub-paragraph (8).

11(1) This paragraph applies where the occupier proposes to sell the mobile home, and assign the agreement, pursuant to paragraph 9 or 10.

(2) The occupier must, not later than 28 days before the completion of the sale of the mobile home and assignment of the agreement, provide the proposed occupier with–

(a) such documents, or documents of such description, as may be prescribed in regulations made by the Welsh Ministers, and

(b) such other information as may be prescribed in the regulations, in the form prescribed in them.

(3) But if the proposed occupier consents in writing to the documents and other information concerned being provided by a date ('the chosen date') which is less than 28 days before the completion of the sale and assignment of the agreement, the occupier must provide the documents and other information to the proposed occupier not later than the chosen date.

(4) The documents and other information which may be prescribed in regulations under sub-paragraph (2) include (but are not limited to)–

(a) a copy of the agreement,

(b) a copy of the site rules (if any) for the protected site on which the mobile home is stationed,

(c) details of the pitch fee payable under the agreement,

(d) a forwarding address for the occupier,

(e) in a case within paragraph 9, information about the requirement imposed by virtue of sub-paragraph (3) of that paragraph,

(f) details of the commission which would be payable by the proposed occupier by virtue of paragraph 9(4) or 10(8),

(g) information about such requirements as are prescribed in regulations under paragraph 9(6) or 10(10).

(5) Documents or other information required to be provided under this paragraph may be delivered to the prospective purchaser personally or sent by post.

(6) A claim that a person has broken the duty under sub-paragraph (2) or (3) may be made the subject of civil proceedings in the same manner as any other claim in tort for breach of statutory duty.

Gift of mobile home

12(1) Where the agreement is a new agreement, provided that the occupier has supplied the owner with the relevant evidence, the occupier is entitled to give the mobile home, and to assign the agreement, to a member of the occupier's family (the 'new occupier') without the approval of the owner.

(2) The relevant evidence is–

(a) evidence, or evidence of a description, prescribed in regulations made by the Welsh Ministers that the person to whom the occupier proposes to give the mobile home, and to assign the agreement, is a member of the occupier's family, or

(b) any other satisfactory evidence that the person concerned is a member of the occupier's family.

(3) The new occupier must, as soon as reasonably practicable, notify the owner of the receipt of the mobile home and assignment of the agreement.

(4) The owner may not require any payment to be made (whether to the owner or otherwise) in connection with the gift of the mobile home, and the assignment of the agreement, as mentioned in sub-paragraph (1).

(5) The Welsh Ministers may by regulations prescribe procedural requirements to be complied with by the owner, the occupier or the new occupier in connection with the gift of the mobile home, and assignment of the agreement, as mentioned in sub-paragraph (1).

13(1) Where the agreement is not a new agreement, the occupier is entitled to give the mobile home, and assign the agreement, to a member of the occupier's family (the 'proposed occupier') without the approval of the owner if–

(a) the occupier serves on the owner a notice (a 'notice of proposed gift') that the occupier proposes to give the mobile home to the proposed occupier, and

(b) the first or second condition is satisfied.

(2) The first condition is that, within the period of 21 days beginning with the date on which the owner received the notice of proposed gift ('the 21-day period'), the occupier does not receive a notice from the owner that the owner has applied to a tribunal for an order preventing the occupier from giving the mobile home, and assigning the agreement, to the proposed occupier (a 'refusal order').

(3) The second condition is that–

(a) within the 21-day period–

(i) the owner applies to a tribunal for a refusal order, and

(ii) the occupier receives a notice of the application from the owner, and

(b) the tribunal rejects the application.

(4) If the owner applies to a tribunal for a refusal order within the 21-day period but the occupier does not receive notice of the application from the owner within that period–

(a) the application is to be treated as not having been made, and

(b) the first condition is accordingly to be treated as satisfied.

(5) A notice of proposed gift must include–

(a) the relevant evidence under paragraph 12(2), and

(b) such other information as may be prescribed in regulations made by the Welsh Ministers.

(6) A notice of proposed gift or notice of an application for a refusal order–

(a) must be in writing, and

(b) may be served by post.

(7) An application for a refusal order may be made only on one or more of the grounds prescribed in regulations made by the Welsh Ministers; and a notice of an application for a refusal order must specify the ground or grounds on which the application is made.

(8) The owner may not require any payment to be made (whether to the owner or otherwise) in connection with the gift of the mobile home, and the assignment of the agreement, as mentioned in sub-paragraph (1).

(9) The Welsh Ministers may by regulations prescribe procedural requirements to be complied with by the owner, the occupier, a proposed occupier or the person to whom the mobile home is given in connection with the gift of the mobile home, and assignment of the agreement, as mentioned in sub-paragraph (1).

Re-siting of mobile home

14(1) The owner is entitled to require that the occupier's right to station the mobile home is exercisable for any period in relation to another pitch forming part of the protected site ('the other pitch') if–

(a) on the application of the owner, a tribunal is satisfied that the other pitch is broadly comparable to the occupier's original pitch and that it is reasonable for the mobile home to be stationed on the other pitch for that period, or

(b) the owner needs to carry out essential repair or emergency works that can only be carried out if the mobile home is moved to the other pitch for that period, and either–

(i) on an application by the owner a tribunal is satisfied of that need and that the other pitch is broadly comparable to the occupier's original pitch, or

(ii) the urgency of the need means that it is impracticable to make an application before the mobile home is re'sited.

(2) In a case where sub-paragraph (ii) of paragraph (b) of sub-paragraph (1) applies, the owner must immediately make an application to a tribunal and if the tribunal is not satisfied as mentioned in sub-paragraph (i) of that paragraph the owner must immediately secure that the mobile home is returned to the original pitch.

(3) If the owner requires the occupier to station the mobile home on the other pitch so that the owner can replace, or carry out repairs to, the base on which the mobile home is stationed, the owner must, if the occupier requires the owner to do so or a tribunal on the application of the occupier orders the owner to do so, secure that the mobile home is returned to the original pitch on the completion of the replacement or repairs.

(4) The owner must pay all the costs and expenses incurred by the occupier in connection with the mobile home being moved to and from the other pitch.

(5) In this paragraph and paragraph 16 'essential repair or emergency works' means–

(a) repairs to the base on which the mobile home is stationed,
(b) works or repairs needed to comply with any relevant legal requirements, or
(c) works or repairs in connection with restoration following flood, landslide or other natural disaster.

Quiet enjoyment of the mobile home

15 The occupier is entitled to quiet enjoyment of the mobile home together with the pitch during the continuance of the agreement, subject to paragraphs 14 and 16.

Owner's right of entry to the pitch

16(1) The owner may enter the pitch without prior notice between the hours of 9 am and 6 pm–

(a) to deliver written communications, including post and notices, to the occupier, and
(b) to read any meter for gas, electricity, water, sewerage or other services supplied by the owner.

(2) The owner may enter the pitch to carry out essential repair or emergency works on giving as much notice to the occupier (whether in writing or otherwise) as is reasonably practicable in the circumstances.

(3) Unless the occupier has agreed otherwise, the owner may enter the pitch for a reason other than one specified in sub-paragraph (1) or (2) only if the owner has given the occupier at least 14 clear days' written notice of the date, time and reason for the visit.

(4) The rights conferred by this paragraph do not extend to the mobile home.

The pitch fee

17(1) The pitch fee can only be changed in accordance with this paragraph, either–

(a) with the agreement of the occupier, or
(b) if a tribunal, on the application of the owner or the occupier, considers it reasonable for the pitch fee to be changed and makes an order determining the amount of the new pitch fee.

(2) The pitch fee must be reviewed annually as at the review date.

(3) At least 28 clear days before the review date the owner must serve on the occupier a written notice setting out proposals in respect of the new pitch fee.

(4) A notice under sub-paragraph (3) which proposes an increase in the pitch fee is of no effect unless it is accompanied by a document which complies with paragraph 23.

(5) If the occupier agrees to the proposed new pitch fee, it is payable as from the review date.

(6) If the occupier does not agree to the proposed new pitch fee–

(a) the owner or the occupier may apply to a tribunal for an order under sub-paragraph (1)(b) determining the amount of the new pitch fee,

(b) the occupier must continue to pay the current pitch fee to the owner until such time as the new pitch fee is agreed by the occupier or an order determining the amount of the new pitch fee is made by the tribunal under sub-paragraph (1)(b), and

(c) the new pitch fee is payable as from the review date but the occupier is not to be regarded as being in arrears until the 28th day after the date on which the new pitch fee is agreed or, as the case may be, the 28th day after the date of the tribunal's order determining the amount of the new pitch fee.

(7) An application under sub-paragraph (6)(a) may be made at any time after the end of the period of 28 days beginning with the review date but no later than 3 months after the review date.

(8) Sub-paragraphs (9) to (12) apply if the owner–

(a) has not served the notice required by sub-paragraph (3) by the time by which it was required to be served, but

(b) at any time afterwards serves on the occupier a written notice setting out proposals in respect of a new pitch fee.

(9) A notice under sub-paragraph (8)(b) which proposes an increase in the pitch fee is of no effect unless it is accompanied by a document which complies with paragraph 23.

(10) If (at any time) the occupier agrees to the proposed pitch fee, it is payable as from the 28th day after the date on which the owner serves the notice under sub-paragraph (8)(b).

(11) If the occupier has not agreed to the proposed pitch fee–

(a) the owner or the occupier may apply to a tribunal for an order under sub-paragraph (1)(b) determining the amount of the new pitch fee,

(b) the occupier must continue to pay the current pitch fee to the owner until such time as the new pitch fee is agreed by the occupier or an order determining the amount of the new pitch fee is made by a tribunal under sub-paragraph (1)(b), and

(c) if the tribunal makes such an order, the new pitch fee is payable as from the 28th day after the date on which the owner serves the notice under sub-paragraph (8)(b).

(12) An application under sub-paragraph (11) may be made at any time after the end of the period of 56 days beginning with date on which the owner serves the notice under sub-paragraph (8)(b) but no later than 4 months after the date on which the owner serves that notice.

(13) A tribunal may permit an application under sub-paragraph (6)(a) or (11)(a) to be made to it outside the time limit specified in sub-paragraph (7) (in the case of an application under sub-paragraph (6)(a)) or in sub-paragraph (12) (in the case of an application under sub-paragraph (11)(a)) if it is satisfied that, in all the circumstances, there are good reasons for the failure to apply within the applicable time limit and for any delay since then in applying for permission to make the application out of time.

(14) The occupier is not to be treated as being in arrears–

(a) where sub-paragraph (10) applies, until the 28th day after the date on which the new pitch fee is agreed, or

(b) where sub-paragraph (11)(b) applies, until the 28th day after the date on which the new pitch fee is agreed or, as the case may be, the 28th day after the date of the tribunal's order determining the amount of the new pitch fee.

(15) Sub-paragraph (16) applies if a tribunal, on the application of the occupier, is satisfied that–

(a) a notice under sub-paragraph (3) or (8)(b) was of no effect as a result of sub-paragraph (4) or (9), but

(b) the occupier nonetheless paid the owner the pitch fee proposed in the notice.

(16) The tribunal may order the owner to pay the occupier, within the period of 21 days beginning with the date of the order, the difference between–

(a) the amount which the occupier was required to pay the owner for the period in question, and

(b) the amount which the occupier has paid the owner for that period.

18(1) When determining the amount of the new pitch fee particular regard is to be had to–

(a) any sums expended by the owner since the last review date on improvements–

(i) which are for the benefit of the occupiers of mobile homes on the protected site,

(ii) which were the subject of consultation in accordance with paragraph 22(1)(e) and (f), and

(iii) to which a majority of the occupiers have not disagreed in writing or which, in the case of such disagreement, a tribunal, on the application of the owner, has ordered should be taken into account when determining the amount of the new pitch fee,

(b) any deterioration in the condition, and any decrease in the amenity, of the site or any adjoining land which is occupied or controlled by the owner since the date on which this sub-paragraph came into force (in so far as regard has not previously been had to that deterioration or decrease for the purposes of this sub-paragraph),

(c) any reduction in the services that the owner supplies to the site, pitch or mobile home, and any deterioration in the quality of those services, since the date on which this sub-paragraph came into force (in so far as regard has not previously been had to that reduction or deterioration for the purposes of this sub-paragraph), and

(d) any direct effect on the costs payable by the owner in relation to the maintenance or management of the site of an enactment which has come into force since the last review date.

(2) But no regard is to be had, when determining the amount of the new pitch fee, to any costs incurred by the owner since the last review date for the purpose of complying with provisions contained in this Part which were not contained in the Mobile Homes Act 1983 in its application in relation to Wales before the coming into force of this Part.

(3) When calculating what constitutes a majority of the occupiers for the purposes of sub-paragraph (1)(a)(iii) each mobile home is to be taken to have only 1 occupier and, in the event of there being more than 1 occupier of a mobile home, its occupier is to be taken to be whichever of them the occupiers agree or, in default of agreement, the one whose name appears first on the agreement.

(4) In a case where the pitch fee has not been previously reviewed, references in this paragraph to the last review date are to be read as references to the date when the agreement commenced.

19(1) When determining the amount of the new pitch fee, any costs incurred by the owner in connection with expanding the protected site are not to be taken into account.

(2) When determining the amount of the new pitch fee, no regard may be had to–

(a) any costs incurred by the owner in relation to the conduct of proceedings under this Part or the agreement,

(b) any fee required to be paid by the owner by virtue of section 6 or 13, or

(c) any costs incurred by the owner in connection with–

(i) any action taken by a local authority under sections 15 to 25, or

(ii) the owner being convicted of an offence under section 18.

20(1) Unless it would be unreasonable having regard to paragraph 18(1), there is a presumption that the pitch fee is to increase or decrease by a percentage which is no more than any percentage increase or decrease in the consumer prices index calculated by reference only to–

(a) the latest index, and

(b) the index published for the month which was 12 months before that to which the latest index relates.

(2) In sub-paragraph (1) 'the latest index'–

(a) in a case where the owner serves a notice under paragraph 17(3), means the last index published before the day on which that notice is served, and
(b) in a case where the owner serves a notice under paragraph 17(8)(b) means the last index published before the day by which the owner was required to serve a notice under paragraph 17(3).

Occupier's obligations and owner's corresponding obligations

21(1) The occupier must–
(a) pay the pitch fee to the owner,
(b) pay to the owner all sums due under the agreement in respect of gas, electricity, water, sewerage or other services supplied by the owner,
(c) keep the mobile home in a sound state of repair,
(d) maintain–
(i) the outside of the mobile home, and
(ii) the pitch, including all fences and outbuildings belonging to, or enjoyed with, it and the mobile home,
in a clean and tidy condition, and
(e) if requested by the owner, provide the owner with documentary evidence of any costs or expenses in respect of which the occupier seeks reimbursement.

(2) The owner must not do or cause to be done anything–
(a) which may adversely affect the ability of the occupier to perform the obligation under sub-paragraph (1)(c) or which may deter the occupier from making internal improvements to the mobile home or interfere with the occupier's ability to do so, or
(b) which may adversely affect the ability of the occupier to perform the obligations under sub-paragraph (1)(d) or which may deter the occupier from making external improvements to the mobile home or interfere with the occupier's ability to do so.

(3) Sub-paragraph (2) does not authorise the occupier to carry out works to the mobile home which are prohibited by the terms of the agreement or by or under any enactment.

(4) Where the terms of the agreement permit works to the mobile home to be carried out only with the permission of the owner, that permission must not be unreasonably withheld.

Owner's other obligations

22(1) The owner must–
(a) if requested by the occupier, and on payment by the occupier of a charge of not more than £30, provide accurate written details of–
(i) the size of the pitch and the base on which the mobile home is stationed, and
(ii) the location of the pitch and the base within the protected site,

and the details must include measurements between identifiable fixed points on the protected site and the pitch and the base,

(b) if requested by the occupier, provide (free of charge) documentary evidence in support and explanation of–
   (i) any new pitch fee,
   (ii) any charges for gas, electricity, water, sewerage or other services payable by the occupier to the owner under the agreement, and
   (iii) any other charges, costs or expenses payable by the occupier to the owner under the agreement,

(c) be responsible for repairing the base on which the mobile home is stationed and for maintaining any gas, electricity, water, sewerage or other services supplied by the owner to the pitch or to the mobile home,

(d) maintain in a clean and tidy condition those parts of the protected site, including access ways, site boundary fences and trees, which are not the responsibility of any occupier of a mobile home stationed on the protected site,

(e) consult the occupier about improvements to the protected site in general, and in particular about those which the owner wishes to be taken into account when determining the amount of any new pitch fee, and

(f) consult a qualifying residents' association (if there is one) or (otherwise) occupiers of mobile homes stationed on the protected site, about all matters which relate to the operation and management of, improvements to, or any proposed change of use of, the protected site and may affect the occupiers either directly or indirectly.

(2) For the purposes of sub-paragraph (1)(e), to 'consult' the occupier means–

(a) to give the occupier at least 28 clear days' notice in writing of the proposed improvements which–
   (i) describes the proposed improvements and how they will benefit the occupier in the long and short term,
   (ii) details how the pitch fee may be affected when it is next reviewed, and
   (iii) states when and where the occupier can make representations about the proposed improvements, and

(b) to take into account any representations made by the occupier about the proposed improvements, in accordance with paragraph (a)(iii), before undertaking them.

(3) For the purposes of sub-paragraph (1)(f), to 'consult' a qualifying residents' association or occupiers means–

(a) to give the association or occupiers at least 28 clear days' notice in writing of the matters referred to in sub-paragraph (1)(f) which–
   (i) describes the matters and how they may affect the occupiers either directly or indirectly in the long and short term, and

(ii) states when and where the association or occupiers can make representations about the matters, and

(b) to take into account any representations made by the association or occupiers, in accordance with paragraph (a)(ii), before proceeding with the matters.

23 The document referred to in paragraph 17(4) and (9) must–

(a) be in such form as the Welsh Ministers may by regulations prescribe,

(b) specify any percentage increase or decrease in the consumer prices index calculated in accordance with paragraph 20,

(c) explain the effect of paragraph 17,

(d) specify the matters to which the amount proposed for the new pitch fee is attributable,

(e) refer to the occupier's obligations in paragraph 21(1)(c) to (e) and the owner's obligations in paragraph 22(1)(c) and (d), and

(f) refer to the owner's obligations in paragraph 22(1)(e) and (f) (as glossed by paragraph 22(2) and (3)).

Owner's name and address

24(1) The owner must by notice inform the occupier and any qualifying residents' association of the address in England or Wales at which notices (including notices of proceedings) may be served on the owner by the occupier or a qualifying residents' association.

(2) If the owner fails to comply with sub-paragraph (1), then (subject to sub-paragraph (5)) any amount otherwise due from the occupier to the owner in respect of the pitch fee is to be treated for all purposes as not being due from the occupier to the owner at any time before the owner complies with sub-paragraph (1).

(3) Where in accordance with the agreement the owner gives any written notice to the occupier or a qualifying residents' association, the notice must contain the following information–

(a) the name and address of the owner, and

(b) if that address is not in England or Wales, an address in England or Wales at which notices (including notices of proceedings) may be served on the owner.

(4) Subject to sub-paragraph (5), where–

(a) the occupier or a qualifying residents' association receives such a notice, but

(b) it does not contain the information required to be contained in it by virtue of sub-paragraph (3),

the notice is to be treated as not having been given until such time as the owner gives the information to the occupier or qualifying residents' association in respect of the notice.

(5) An amount or notice within sub-paragraph (2) or (4) is not to be treated as mentioned in relation to any time when, by virtue of an order of any court or tribunal, there is in force an appointment of a receiver or manager whose functions include receiving from the

occupier the pitch fee, payments for services supplied or other charges.

(6) Nothing in sub-paragraphs (3) to (5) applies to any notice containing a demand to which paragraph 25(1) applies.

25(1) Where the owner makes any demand for payment by the occupier of the pitch fee, or in respect of services supplied or other charges, the demand must contain–

(a) the name and address of the owner, and

(b) if that address is not in England or Wales, an address in England or Wales at which notices (including notices of proceedings) may be served on the owner.

(2) Subject to sub-paragraph (3), where–

(a) the occupier receives such a demand, but

(b) it does not contain the information required to be contained in it by virtue of sub-paragraph (1),

the amount demanded is to be treated for all purposes as not being due from the occupier to the owner at any time before the owner gives that information to the occupier in respect of the demand.

(3) The amount demanded is not to be treated as not being due in relation to any time when, by virtue of an order of any court or tribunal, there is in force an appointment of a receiver or manager whose functions include receiving from the occupier the pitch fee, payments for services supplied or other charges.

CHAPTER 3: Agreements Relating to Transit Pitches on Local Authority Gypsy and Traveller Sites

Duration of agreement

26 Subject to paragraph 27 the right to station the mobile home on the transit pitch subsists until–

(a) the fixed period set out in the agreement expires, or

(b) termination of the agreement under paragraph 28 or 29,

whichever is sooner.

27(1) If the owner's estate or interest is insufficient to enable the owner to grant the right for the fixed period set out in the agreement, the period for which the right subsists does not extend beyond the date when the owner's estate or interest determines.

(2) If planning permission for the use of the protected site as a site for mobile homes has been granted in terms such that it will expire at the end of a specified period, the period for which the right subsists does not extend beyond the date when the planning permission expires.

(3) If planning permission for the use of the protected site as a site for mobile homes has been granted in terms such that it requires the owner to limit the duration of stay for mobile homes on the site, the period for which the right subsists does not extend beyond that duration.

Termination

28 The occupier is entitled to terminate the agreement before the expiry of the fixed period set out in the agreement by notice in writing given to the owner.

29 The owner is entitled to terminate the agreement before the expiry of the fixed period set out in the agreement–

(a) without being required to show any reason, by giving written notice not less than 4 weeks before the date on which that notice is to take effect, or

(b) immediately, where–

(i) the occupier has breached a term of the agreement and, after service of a notice to remedy the breach, has not complied with the notice within a reasonable time, and

(ii) the owner considers it reasonable for the agreement to be terminated.

Recovery of overpayments by occupier

30 Where the agreement is terminated as mentioned in paragraph 28 or 29, the occupier is entitled to recover from the owner so much of any payment made by the occupier in pursuance of the agreement as is attributable to a period beginning after the termination.

Quiet enjoyment of the mobile home

31 The occupier is entitled to quiet enjoyment of the mobile home together with the pitch during the continuance of the agreement, subject to paragraph 32.

Owner's right of entry to the pitch

32(1) The owner may enter the pitch without prior notice between the hours of 9 am and 6 pm–

(a) to deliver written communications, including post and notices, to the occupier, and

(b) to read any meter for gas, electricity, water, sewerage or other services supplied by the owner.

(2) The owner may enter the pitch to carry out essential repair or emergency works on giving as much notice to the occupier (whether in writing or otherwise) as is reasonably practicable in the circumstances.

(3) In this paragraph 'essential repair or emergency works' means–

(a) repairs to the base on which the mobile home is stationed,

(b) repairs to any outhouses and facilities provided by the owner on the pitch and to any gas, electricity, water, sewerage or other services or other amenities provided by the owner in such outhouses,

(c) works or repairs needed to comply with any relevant legal requirements, or

(d) works or repairs in connection with restoration following flood, landslide or other natural disaster.

(4) Unless the occupier has agreed otherwise, the owner may enter the pitch for a reason other than one specified in sub-paragraph (3) or (2) only if the owner has given the occupier at least 14 clear days' written notice of the date, time and reason for the visit.

(5) The rights conferred by this paragraph do not extend to the mobile home.

Owner's name and address

33(1) The owner must by notice inform the occupier of the address in England or Wales at which notices (including notices of proceedings) may be served on the owner by the occupier.

(2) If the owner fails to comply with sub-paragraph (1), then any amount otherwise due from the occupier to the owner in respect of the pitch fee is to be treated for all purposes as not being due from the occupier to the owner at any time before the owner complies with sub-paragraph (1).

(3) Where in accordance with the agreement the owner gives any written notice to the occupier the notice must contain the name and address of the owner.

(4) Where–

(a) the occupier receives such a notice, but

(b) it does not contain the information required to be contained in it by virtue of sub-paragraph (3),

the notice is to be treated as not having been given until such time as the owner gives the information to the occupier in respect of the notice.

(5) Nothing in sub-paragraphs (3) and (4) applies to any notice containing a demand to which paragraph 34(1) applies.

34(1) Where the owner makes any demand for payment by the occupier of the pitch fee, or in respect of services supplied or other charges, the demand must contain the name and address of the owner.

(2) Where–

(a) the occupier receives such a demand, but

(b) it does not contain the information required to be contained in it by virtue of sub-paragraph (1),

the amount demanded is to be treated for all purposes as not being due from the occupier to the owner at any time before the owner gives that information to the occupier in respect of the demand.

CHAPTER 4: Agreements Relating to Permanent Pitches on Local Authority Gypsy and Traveller Sites

Duration of agreement

35 Subject to paragraph 36, the right to station the mobile home on land forming part of the protected site subsists until the agreement is determined under paragraph 37, 38, 39 or 40.

36(1) If the owner's estate or interest is insufficient to enable the owner to grant the right for an indefinite period, the period for which the right subsists does not extend beyond the date when the owner's estate or interest determines.

(2) If planning permission for the use of the protected site as a site for mobile homes has been granted in terms such that it will expire at the end of a specified period, the period for which the right subsists does not extend beyond the date when the planning permission expires.

(3) If before the end of a period determined by this paragraph there is a change in circumstances which allows a longer period, account is to be taken of that change.

Termination

37 The occupier is entitled to terminate the agreement by notice in writing given to the owner not less than 4 weeks before the date on which it is to take effect.

38 The owner is entitled to terminate the agreement immediately if, on the application of the owner, the appropriate judicial body–

(a) is satisfied that the occupier has breached a term of the agreement and, after service of a notice to remedy the breach, has not complied with the notice within a reasonable time, and

(b) considers it reasonable for the agreement to be terminated.

39 The owner is entitled to terminate the agreement immediately if, on the application of the owner, the appropriate judicial body–

(a) is satisfied that the occupier is not occupying the mobile home as the occupier's only or main residence, and

(b) considers it reasonable for the agreement to be terminated.

40(1) The owner is entitled to terminate the agreement immediately if–

(a) on the application of the owner, a tribunal has determined that, having regard to its condition, the mobile home is having a detrimental effect on the amenity of the site, and

(b) then, on the application of the owner, the appropriate judicial body, having regard to the tribunal's determination and to any other circumstances, considers it reasonable for the agreement to be terminated.

(2) Sub-paragraphs (3) and (4) apply if, on an application to the tribunal under sub-paragraph (1)(a)–

(a) the tribunal considers that, having regard to the present condition of the mobile home, it is having a detrimental effect on the amenity of the site, but

(b) it also considers that it would be reasonably practicable for particular repairs to be carried out on the mobile home that would result in the mobile home not having that detrimental effect, and

(c) the occupier indicates to the tribunal that the occupier intends to carry out those repairs.

(3) In such a case, the tribunal may make an interim order–

(a) specifying the repairs that must be carried out and the time within which they must be carried out, and

(b) adjourning the proceedings on the application for such period specified in the interim order as the tribunal considers reasonable to enable the repairs to be carried out.

(4) If the tribunal makes an interim order under sub-paragraph (3), it must not make a determination under sub-paragraph (1)(a) unless it is satisfied that the specified period has expired without the repairs having been carried out.

Assignment of agreement

41(1) The occupier ('A') may assign the agreement–

(a) to a person who is a member of A's family, or

(b) to another person ('B') if the conditions in sub-paragraph (2) are met.

(2) The conditions are that–

(a) A must have the approval of the owner, and

(b) B must–

(i) be an occupier of a permanent pitch on a relevant site, and

(ii) have the approval of the owner to the assignment of B's agreement to A or to another occupier of a permanent pitch on a relevant site.

(3) A relevant site for the purposes of sub-paragraph (2) is a local authority Gypsy and Traveller site in the area of the local authority in which the site on which the pitch to which A's agreement relates is located.

(4) Neither the occupier nor the owner may require any payment to be made (whether to the occupier or owner or otherwise) in connection with the assignment of the agreement under this paragraph.

42(1) The occupier may serve on the owner a request to approve for the purposes of paragraph 41, an assignment to a person named in the request ('the proposed occupier').

(2) Where the request relates to an assignment under paragraph 41(1)(a) the request must include satisfactory evidence that the proposed occupier is a member of the occupier's family.

(3) Where the owner receives a request under sub-paragraph (1), the owner must, within 28 days beginning with the date on which the request is received–

(a) approve the assignment, unless it is reasonable for the owner not to do so, and

(b) serve on the occupier notice of the owner's decision ('a decision notice').

(4) If a person ('P') receives a request under sub-paragraph (1) and P–

(a) while not being the owner, has an estate or interest in the land, and

(b) believes that another person is the owner,

and that other person has not received such a request, P owes a duty to the occupier (enforceable by a claim in tort for breach of statutory duty, as well as by action for breach of an implied term) to take such steps as are reasonable to secure that the other person receives the request within the period of 28 days beginning with the date on which P receives it.

(5) If the approval is withheld, the decision notice must specify the reasons for withholding it.

(6) Where a fee lawfully due from the occupier has not been paid or any term of the agreement has been broken or not performed, the approval required for the purpose of paragraph 41 may be given subject to a condition requiring the occupier to pay the outstanding fee, remedy the breach or perform the obligation.

(7) Except as provided by sub-paragraph (6), the approval required for the purpose of paragraph 41 cannot be given subject to a condition and a condition imposed otherwise than as so provided is to be disregarded.

(8) If the owner fails to serve the notice or withholds approval to the assignment the occupier may apply to the tribunal for an order declaring that the assignment is approved for the purposes of paragraph 41 and the tribunal may make such an order if it thinks fit.

(9) If the question arises as to whether the notice required by sub-paragraph (3)(b) was served within the required period of 28 days, it is for an owner to show that the notice was so served.

(10) If the owner did not approve the assignment and the question arises whether it was reasonable for the owner not to do so, it is for the owner to show that it was reasonable.

(11) A request or notice under this paragraph–
- (a) must be in writing, and
- (b) may be served by post.

(12) Subject to sub-paragraph (13), an application to the tribunal under sub-paragraph (8) by an occupier must be made–
- (a) within the period of 3 months beginning with the day after the date on which the occupier receives the decision notice, or
- (b) where the occupier receives no decision notice, within the period of 3 months beginning with the date which is 29 days after the date upon which the occupier served the request under sub-paragraph (1).

(13) A tribunal may permit an application under sub-paragraph (8) to be made to the tribunal after the applicable period specified in sub-paragraph (12) if it is satisfied that, in all the circumstances, there are good reasons for the failure to apply before the end of that period and for any delay since then in applying for permission to make the application out of time.

Recovery of overpayments by occupier

43 Where the agreement is terminated as mentioned in paragraph 37, 38, 39 or 40, the occupier is entitled to recover from the owner so much of any payment made by the occupier in pursuance of the agreement as is attributable to a period beginning after the termination.

Re-siting of mobile home

44(1) The owner is entitled to require that the occupier's right to station the mobile home is exercisable for any period in relation to another pitch forming part of the protected site or a pitch forming part of another protected site ('the other pitch') if–

(a) on the application of the owner, a tribunal is satisfied that the other pitch is broadly comparable to the occupier's original pitch and that it is reasonable for the mobile home to be stationed on the other pitch for that period, or

(b) the owner needs to carry out essential repair or emergency works that can only be carried out if the mobile home is moved to the other pitch for that period, and the other pitch is broadly comparable to the occupier's original pitch.

(2) A pitch forming part of another protected site is, for the purposes of sub-paragraph (1)(a), broadly comparable to the occupier's original pitch only if it provides access to health and education services required by the occupier which is, as far as reasonably practicable, broadly comparable to the access provided by the occupier's original pitch.

(3) If the owner requires the occupier to station the mobile home on the other pitch so that the owner can replace, or carry out repairs to, the base on which the mobile home is stationed, the owner must, if the occupier requires the owner to do so or a tribunal on the application of the occupier orders the owner to do so, secure that the mobile home is returned to the original pitch on the completion of the replacement or repairs.

(4) The owner must pay all the costs and expenses incurred by the occupier in connection with the mobile home being moved to and from the other pitch.

(5) In this paragraph and in paragraph 46 'essential repair or emergency works' means–

(a) repairs to the base on which the mobile home is stationed,

(b) repairs to any outhouses and facilities provided by the owner on the pitch and to any gas, electricity, water, sewerage or other services or other amenities provided by the owner in such outhouses,

(c) works or repairs needed to comply with any relevant legal requirements, or

(d) works or repairs in connection with restoration following flood, landslide or other natural disaster.

Quiet enjoyment of the mobile home

45 The occupier is entitled to quiet enjoyment of the mobile home together with the pitch during the continuance of the agreement, subject to paragraphs 44 and 46.

Owner's right of entry to the pitch

46(1) The owner may enter the pitch without prior notice between the hours of 9 am and

6 pm–

(a) to deliver written communications, including post and notices, to the occupier, and

(b) to read any meter for gas, electricity, water, sewerage or other services supplied by the owner.

(2) The owner may enter the pitch to carry out essential repair or emergency works on giving as much notice to the occupier (whether in writing or otherwise) as is reasonably practicable in the circumstances.

(3) Unless the occupier has agreed otherwise, the owner may enter the pitch for a reason other than one specified in sub-paragraph (1) or (2) only if the owner has given the occupier at least 14 clear days' written notice of the date, time and reason for the owner's visit.

(4) The rights conferred by this paragraph do not extend to the mobile home.

The pitch fee

47(1) The pitch fee can only be changed in accordance with this paragraph, either–

(a) with the agreement of the occupier, or

(b) if a tribunal, on the application of the owner or the occupier, considers it reasonable for the pitch fee to be changed and makes an order determining the amount of the new pitch fee.

(2) The pitch fee must be reviewed annually as at the review date.

(3) At least 28 clear days before the review date the owner must serve on the occupier a written notice setting out the owner's proposals in respect of the new pitch fee.

(4) If the occupier agrees to the proposed new pitch fee, it is payable as from the review date.

(5) If the occupier does not agree to the proposed new pitch fee–

(a) the owner may apply to a tribunal for an order under sub-paragraph (1)(b) determining the amount of the new pitch fee,

(b) the occupier must continue to pay the current pitch fee to the owner until such time as the new pitch fee is agreed by the occupier or an order determining the amount of the new pitch fee is made by a tribunal under sub-paragraph (1)(b), and

(c) the new pitch fee is payable as from the review date but the occupier is not to be regarded as being in arrears until the 28th day after the date on which the new pitch fee is agreed or, as the case may be, the 28th day after the date of the order of the tribunal determining the amount of the new pitch fee.

(6) An application under sub-paragraph (5)(a) may be made at any time after the end of the period of 28 days beginning with the review date but no later than 3 months after the review date.

(7) Sub-paragraphs (8) to (12) apply if the owner–
  (a) has not served the notice required by sub-paragraph (3) by the time by which it was required to be served, but
  (b) at any time afterwards serves on the occupier a written notice setting out the owner's proposals in respect of a new pitch fee.

(8) If (at any time) the occupier agrees to the proposed pitch fee, it is payable as from the 28th day after the date on which the owner serves the notice under sub-paragraph (7)(b).

(9) If the occupier has not agreed to the proposed pitch fee–
  (a) the owner may apply to a tribunal for an order under sub-paragraph (1)(b) determining the amount of the new pitch fee,
  (b) the occupier must continue to pay the current pitch fee to the owner until such time as the new pitch fee is agreed by the occupier or an order determining the amount of the new pitch fee is made by a tribunal under sub-paragraph (1)(b), and
  (c) if a tribunal makes such an order, the new pitch fee is payable as from the 28th day after the date on which the owner serves the notice under sub-paragraph (7)(b).

(10) An application under sub-paragraph (9) may be made at any time after the end of the period of 56 days beginning with the date on which the owner serves the notice under sub-paragraph (7)(b) but no later than 4 months after the date on which the owner serves that notice.

(11) A tribunal may permit an application under sub-paragraph (5)(a) or (9)(a) to be made to it outside the time limit specified in sub-paragraph (6) (in the case of an application under sub-paragraph (5)(a)) or in sub-paragraph (10) (in the case of an application under sub-paragraph (9)(a)) if it is satisfied that, in all the circumstances, there are good reasons for the failure to apply within the applicable time limit and for any delay since then in applying for permission to make the application out of time.

(12) The occupier is not to be treated as being in arrears–
  (a) where sub-paragraph (8) applies, until the 28th day after the date on which the new pitch fee is agreed, or
  (b) where sub-paragraph (9)(b) applies, until the 28th day after the date on which the new pitch fee is agreed or, as the case may be, the 28th day after the date of a tribunal order determining the amount of the new pitch fee.

48(1) When determining the amount of the new pitch fee particular regard is to be had to–
  (a) any sums expended by the owner since the last review date on improvements–
    (i) which are for the benefit of the occupiers of mobile homes on the protected site,

(ii) which were the subject of consultation in accordance with paragraph 52(1)(f) and (g), and

(iii) to which a majority of the occupiers have not disagreed in writing or which, in the case of such disagreement, a tribunal, on the application of the owner, has ordered should be taken into account when determining the amount of the new pitch fee,

(b) any decrease in the amenity of the protected site since the last review date, and

(c) the effect of any enactment which has come into force since the last review date.

(2) When calculating what constitutes a majority of the occupiers for the purposes of sub-paragraph (1)(a)(iii) each mobile home is to be taken to have only 1 occupier and, in the event of there being more than 1 occupier of a mobile home, its occupier is to be taken to be whichever the occupiers agree or, in default of agreement, the occupier whose name first appears on the agreement.

(3) In a case where the pitch fee has not been previously reviewed, references in this paragraph to the last review date are to be read as references to the date when the agreement commenced.

49 When determining the amount of the new pitch fee no regard may be had to–

(a) any costs incurred by the owner in connection with expanding the protected site, or

(b) any costs incurred by the owner in relation to the conduct of proceedings under this Part or the agreement.

50(1) Unless it would be unreasonable having regard to paragraph 48(1), there is a presumption that the pitch fee will increase or decrease by a percentage which is no more than any percentage increase or decrease in the consumer prices index calculated by reference only to–

(a) the latest index, and

(b) the index published for the month which was 12 months before that to which the latest index relates.

(2) In sub-paragraph (1) 'the latest index' means–

(a) in the case where the owner serves a notice under paragraph 47(3), the latest index published before the day on which that notice is served, and

(b) in the case where the owner serves a notice under paragraph 47(7)(b), the latest index published before the day by which the owner was required to serve a notice under paragraph 47(3).

Occupier's obligations and owner's corresponding obligations

51(1) The occupier must–

(a) pay the pitch fee to the owner,

(b) pay to the owner all sums due under the agreement in respect of gas, electricity, water, sewerage or other services supplied by the owner,

(c) keep the mobile home in a sound state of repair,
(d) maintain–
(i) the outside of the mobile home, and
(ii) the pitch, including all fences and outbuildings belonging to, or enjoyed with, it and the mobile home,

in a clean and tidy condition, and
(e) if requested by the owner, provide the owner with documentary evidence of any costs or expenses in respect of which the occupier seeks reimbursement.

(2) The owner must not do or cause to be done anything which may adversely affect the ability of the occupier to perform the occupier's obligations under sub-paragraph (1)(c) and (d).

Owner's other obligations

52(1) The owner must–
(a) if requested by the occupier, and on payment by the occupier of a charge of not more than £30, provide accurate written details of–
(i) the size of the pitch and the base on which the mobile home is stationed, and
(ii) the location of the pitch and the base within the protected site,

and such details must include measurements between identifiable fixed points on the protected site and the pitch and the base,
(b) if requested by the occupier, provide (free of charge) documentary evidence in support and explanation of–
(i) any new pitch fee,
(ii) any charges for gas, electricity, water, sewerage or other services payable by the occupier to the owner under the agreement, and
(iii) any other charges, costs or expenses payable by the occupier to the owner under the agreement,
(c) be responsible for repairing the base on which the mobile home is stationed and for maintaining any gas, electricity, water, sewerage or other services supplied by the owner to the pitch or to the mobile home,
(d) be responsible for repairing other amenities provided by the owner on the pitch including any outhouses and facilities provided,
(e) maintain in a clean and tidy condition those parts of the protected site, including access ways, site boundary fences and trees, which are not the responsibility of any occupier of a mobile home stationed on the protected site,
(f) consult the occupier about improvements to the protected site in general, and in particular about those which the owner wishes to be taken into account when determining the amount of any new pitch fee, and
(g) consult a qualifying residents' association (if there is one) about all matters which relate to the operation and management of, or

improvements to, the protected site and may affect the occupiers either directly or indirectly.

(2) For the purposes of sub-paragraph (1)(f), to 'consult' the occupier means–

(a) to give the occupier at least 28 clear days' notice in writing of the proposed improvements which–

(i) describes the proposed improvements and how they will benefit the occupier in the long and short term,

(ii) details how the pitch fee may be affected when it is next reviewed, and

(iii) states when and where the occupier can make representations about the proposed improvements, and

(b) to take into account any representations made by the occupier about the proposed improvements, in accordance with paragraph (a)(iii), before undertaking them.

(3) For the purposes of sub-paragraph (1)(g), to 'consult' a qualifying residents' association means–

(a) to give the association at least 28 clear days' notice in writing of the matters referred to in sub-paragraph (1)(g) which–

(i) describes the matters and how they may affect the occupiers either directly or indirectly in the long and short term, and

(ii) states when and where the association can make representations about the matters, and

(b) to take into account any representations made by the association, in accordance with paragraph (a)(ii), before proceeding with the matters.

Owner's name and address

53(1) The owner must by notice inform the occupier and any qualifying residents' association of the address in England or Wales at which notices (including notices of proceedings) may be served on the owner by the occupier or a qualifying residents' association.

(2) If the owner fails to comply with sub-paragraph (1), then any amount otherwise due from the occupier to the owner in respect of the pitch fee is to be treated for all purposes as not being due from the occupier to the owner at any time before the owner does comply with that sub-paragraph.

(3) Where in accordance with the agreement the owner gives any written notice to the occupier or (as the case may be) a qualifying residents' association, the notice must contain the name and address of the owner.

(4) Where–

(a) the occupier or a qualifying residents' association receives such a notice, but

(b) it does not contain the information required to be contained in it by virtue of sub-paragraph (3),

the notice is to be treated as not having been given until such time as the owner gives the information to the occupier or (as the case may be) the association in respect of the notice.

(5) Nothing in sub-paragraphs (3) and (4) applies to any notice containing a demand to which paragraph 54(1) applies.

54(1) Where the owner makes any demand for payment by the occupier of the pitch fee, or in respect of services supplied or other charges, the demand must contain the name and address of the owner.

(2) Where–

(a) the occupier receives such a demand, but

(b) it does not contain the information required to be contained in it by virtue of sub-paragraph (1), the amount demanded is to be treated for all purposes as not being due from the occupier to the owner at any time before the owner gives that information to the occupier in respect of the demand.

Part 2: Matters Concerning which Terms may be Implied by the Appropriate Judicial Body

55 The sums payable by the occupier in pursuance of the agreement and the times at which they are to be paid.

56 The review at yearly intervals of the sums payable by the occupier in pursuance of the agreement.

57 The provision or improvement of services available on the protected site, and the use by the occupier of such services.

58 The preservation of the amenity of the protected site.

HOUSING (WALES) ACT 2014 SS101–108

Part 3: Gypsies and Travellers

Meeting Accommodation Needs

Assessment of accommodation needs

101(1) A local housing authority must, in each review period, carry out an assessment of the accommodation needs of Gypsies and Travellers residing in or resorting to its area.

(2) In carrying out an assessment under subsection (1) a local housing authority must consult such persons as it considers appropriate.

(3) In subsection (1), 'review period' means–

(a) the period of 1 year beginning with the coming into force of this section, and

(b) each subsequent period of 5 years.

(4) The Welsh Ministers may amend subsection (3)(b) by order.

Report following assessment

102(1) After carrying out an assessment a local housing authority must prepare a report which–

(a) details how the assessment was carried out;

(b) contains a summary of–

(i) the consultation it carried out in connection with the assessment, and

(ii) the responses (if any) it received to that consultation;

(c) details the accommodation needs identified by the assessment.

(2) A local housing authority must submit the report to the Welsh Ministers for approval of the authority's assessment.

(3) The Welsh Ministers may–

(a) approve the assessment as submitted;

(b) approve the assessment with modifications;

(c) reject the assessment.

(4) If the Welsh Ministers reject the assessment, the local housing authority must–

(a) revise and resubmit its assessment for approval by the Welsh Ministers under subsection (3), or

(b) conduct another assessment (in which case section 101(2) and this section apply again, as if the assessment were carried out under section 101(1)).

(5) A local housing authority must publish an assessment approved by the Welsh Ministers under this section.

Duty to meet assessed needs

103(1) If a local housing authority's approved assessment identifies needs within the authority's area with respect to the provision of sites on which mobile homes may be stationed the authority must exercise its powers in section 56 of the Mobile Homes (Wales) Act 2013 (power of authorities to provide sites for mobile homes) so far as may be necessary to meet those needs.

(2) But subsection (1) does not require a local housing authority to provide, in or in connection with sites for the stationing of mobile homes, working space and facilities for the carrying on of activities normally carried out by Gypsies and Travellers.

(3) The reference in subsection (1) to an authority's approved assessment is a reference to the authority's most recent assessment of accommodation needs approved by the Welsh Ministers under section 102(3).

Failure to comply with duty under section 103

104(1) If the Welsh Ministers are satisfied that a local housing authority has failed to comply with the duty imposed by section 103 they may direct the authority to exercise its powers under section 56 of the Mobile Homes (Wales) Act 2013 so far as may be necessary to meet the needs identified in the authority's approved assessment.

(2) Before giving a direction the Welsh Ministers must consult the local housing authority to which the direction would relate.

(3) A local housing authority must comply with a direction given to it.

(4) A direction given under this section–

(a) must be in writing;

(b) may be varied or revoked by a subsequent direction;

(c) is enforceable by mandatory order on application by, or on behalf of, the Welsh Ministers.

Provision of information upon request

105(1) A local housing authority must provide the Welsh Ministers with such information (and at such times) as they may require in connection with the exercise of their functions under this Part.

(2) The Welsh Ministers may exercise their powers under this section generally or in relation to a particular case.

Guidance

106(1) In exercising its functions under this Part, a local housing authority must have regard to any guidance given by the Welsh Ministers.

(2) The Welsh Ministers may–

(a) give guidance either generally or to specified descriptions of authorities;

(b) revise the guidance by giving further guidance under this section;

(c) withdraw the guidance by giving further guidance under this section or by notice.

(3) The Welsh Ministers must publish any guidance or notice under this section.

Duties in relation to housing strategies

107(1) This section applies where a local housing authority is required under section 87 of the Local Government Act 2003 to have a strategy in respect of meeting the accommodation needs of Gypsies and Travellers residing in or resorting to its area.

(2) The local housing authority must–

(a) have regard to any guidance given by the Welsh Ministers in preparing its strategy;

(b) take the strategy into account in exercising its functions (including functions exercisable other than as a local housing authority).

General

108 Interpretation

In this Part–

'accommodation needs' ('*anghenion llety*') includes, but is not limited to, needs with respect to the provision of sites on which mobile homes may be stationed;

'Gypsies and Travellers' ('*Sipsiwn a Theithwyr*') means–

(a) persons of a nomadic habit of life, whatever their race or origin, including–

(i) persons who, on grounds only of their own or their family's or dependant's educational or health needs or old age, have ceased to travel temporarily or permanently, and

(ii) members of an organised group of travelling show people or circus people (whether or not travelling together as such), and

(b) all other persons with a cultural tradition of nomadism or of living in a mobile home;

'mobile home' ('*cartref symudol*') has the meaning given by section 60 of the Mobile Homes (Wales) Act 2013.

APPENDIX B

Circulars

GYPSY SITES POLICY AND UNAUTHORISED CAMPING (DOE CIRCULAR 18/94)

Introduction

1 This Circular offers guidance on the provisions in sections 77 to 80 of the Criminal Justice and Public Order Act 1994 ('the 1994 Act') which affect gypsies and unauthorised campers. The Act received Royal Assent on 3 November 1994, and sections 77 to 80 came into force on the same day.

Definition of 'gipsies'

2 Section 24 of the Caravan Sites and Control of Development Act 1960 ('the 1960 Act'), as amended by section 80 of the 1994 Act, provides that 'gipsies':

> 'means persons of nomadic habit of life, whatever their race or origin, but does not include members of an organised group of travelling showmen, or of persons engaged in travelling circuses, travelling together as such'.

3 The courts have recently clarified the definition of the word 'gipsies' in section 16 of the Caravan Sites Act 1968 ('the 1968 Act'), which was repealed by section 80 of the 1994 Act. In *R v South Hams District Council, ex parte Gibb* and two other applications – *The Times,* 8 June 1994; *The Independent,* 15 June 1994 – the Court of Appeal held that 'gipsies' meant persons who wandered or travelled for the purpose of making or seeking their livelihood, and did not include persons who moved from place to place without any connection between their movement and their means of livelihood. All references to 'gypsies' in this Circular are references to 'gipsies' in this sense.

Powers to control unauthorised camping

4 Section 77 of the 1994 Act empowers a local authority[1] to direct persons residing unlawfully in vehicles within the area of that local authority on highway land, other unoccupied land or occupied land

1 In England, a county council, a district council, a London borough council, the Common Council of the City of London and the Council of the Isles of Scilly; and in Wales, a county council or district council until 1 April 1996 (and a county council or county borough council thereafter).

without the consent of the occupier to leave the land and remove their vehicles and any other property they have with them on the land. It is an offence for a person, knowing that such a direction has been given to him, to fail to comply with it as soon as practicable. It is also an offence for a person so directed to re-enter the land concerned with a vehicle within three months of the date of the direction. In any proceedings brought for an offence, it is a defence for an accused person to show that his failure to comply with a direction or his re-entry of land was due to mechanical breakdown, illness or other immediate emergency. If a person who has been directed to leave does so as soon as practicable, and does not re-enter the land within three months of the date of the direction, no offence is committed.

5 Section 78 of the 1994 Act provides that a magistrates' court may, on a complaint by a local authority, make an order requiring the removal from land of any vehicle and property and any person residing in it, and authorising an authority to enter the land and remove the vehicle and property. It is an offence for a person wilfully to obstruct any person authorised to carry out the order. This power is modelled closely on the power that was available to authorities for areas designated under the 1968 Act, although it should be noted that sections 77 and 78 apply to any unauthorised camper, not just to gypsies.

Policy towards unauthorised encampments of gypsies

6 Whilst it is a matter for local discretion to decide whether it is appropriate to evict an unauthorised Gypsy encampment, the Secretary of State believes that local authorities should consider using their powers to do so wherever the Gypsies concerned are causing a level of nuisance which cannot be effectively controlled. They also consider that it would usually be legitimate for a local authority to exercise these powers wherever Gypsies who are camped unlawfully refuse to move onto an authorised local authority site. Where there are no such sites, and the authority reaches the view than an unauthorised Gypsy encampment is not causing a level of nuisance which cannot be effectively controlled, it should consider providing basic services, such as toilets, a refuse skip and a supply of drinking water at the site.

7 Local authorities should also try to identify possible emergency stopping places, as close as possible to the transit routes used by Gypsies, where Gypsy families would be allowed to camp for short periods. Authorities should consider providing basic services on these temporary sites.

8 Where Gypsies are unlawfully camped on Government-owned land, it is for the local authority, with the agreement of the land-owning Department, to take any necessary steps to ensure that the encampment does not constitute a hazard to public health. It will continue to be the policy of the Secretary of State that Government Department should act in conformity with the advice that unauthorised encampments should not normally be allowed to continue where they are causing a level of nuisance which cannot be effectively controlled. The National Assembly for Wales will act in the same way.

9 The Secretary of State continues to consider that local authorities should not use their powers to evict Gypsies needlessly. He considers that local should use their powers in a humane and compassionate way, taking account of the rights and needs of the Gypsies concerned, the owners of land in question, and the wider community whose lives may be affected by the situation.[2]

Local authorities' obligations under other legislation

10 Social services departments and local housing authorities are reminded of their obligations under Part III of the Children Act 1989 (Local Authority Support for Children and Families); and Part III of the Housing Act 1985 (Housing the Homeless). The Secretaries of State expect authorities to take careful account of these obligations when taking decisions about the future maintenance of authorised gypsy caravan sites and the eviction of persons from unauthorised sites.

11 Local education authorities should bear in mind their statutory duty to make appropriate educational provision available for all school-age children in their area, whether resident temporarily or permanently. As noted in paragraph 33 of Circular 11/88 and paragraph 9 of Circular 11/92 from the Department for Education (formerly the Department of Education and Science) and paragraph 6 of the annex (revised annually) to Welsh Office Circular 52/90, this duty embraces traveller children. Local education authorities should take careful account of the effects of an eviction on the education of children already enrolled, or in the process of being enrolled, at a school. Where an authority decides to proceed with an eviction, and any families concerned move elsewhere in the same area, alternative educational arrangements must be made in accordance with the requirements of the law appropriate to the children's ages, abilities and aptitudes.

12 The Secretaries of State also expect local authorities who decide to proceed with evictions to liaise with other local authorities who may have statutory responsibilities to discharge in respect of those persons who are being evicted.

13 Local authorities should also bear in mind that families camped unlawfully on land may need or may be receiving assistance from local health or welfare services. When they have decided to proceed with an eviction, they should liaise with the relevant statutory agencies, particularly where pregnant women or newly-born children are involved, to ensure that those agencies are not prevented from fulfilling their obligations towards these persons.

Repeal of Part II of the Caravan Sites Act 1968

14 Section 80(1) of the 1994 Act repeals:

2 Paras 6–9 above were inserted by an unnumbered DETR circular dated 26 June 2000.

(a) the duty of local authorities to provide and manage sites (sections 6 and 7 of the 1968 Act);
(b) the requirement for a county council to consult the relevant district council before adopting a proposal to acquire or appropriate land for such a site (section 8);
(c) the Secretary of State's powers to direct a local authority to provide a site (section 9) and to designate the area of a local authority (section 12); and
(d) the powers for a designated authority to deal with unauthorised camping (sections 10 and 11).

15 Section 80(2) of the 1994 Act amends section 24 of the 1960 Act so as to allow a local authority to provide working space on gypsy caravan sites. Section 80(4) of the 1994 Act ensures that the repeal of the definition of the word 'gipsies' in section 16 of the 1968 Act does not affect the interpretation of that word in the definition of a 'protected site' in section 5(1) of the Mobile Homes Act 1983, or in any document embodying planning permission granted under the Town and Country Planning Act 1990 before 3 November 1994.

16 Section 80(3) of the 1994 Act makes transitional arrangements for those cases where the Secretary of State has issued a direction under section 8(3)(a) of the 1968 Act to a local authority to abandon a proposal for a gypsy caravan site, or under section 8(3)(c) of the 1968 Act to make an application to him for planning permission.

17 Directions under section 8(3)(a) of the 1968 Act will remain valid; directions under section 8(3)(b) and (c) of the 1968 Act will cease to have effect. However, where a local authority has made an application for planning permission to the Secretary of State before 3 November 1994, they may elect either to withdraw that application or to request the Secretary of State to determine it. In the latter case, the application would be treated as having been referred to the Secretary of State under section 77 of the Town and Country Planning Act 1990. Local authorities with outstanding directions under section 8(3)(c) of the 1968 Act, may, therefore, wish to notify their decision to the relevant Government Office for their region, or to the Welsh Office.

18 Section 80(5) of the 1994 Act repeals the power of the Secretaries of State for the Environment and for Wales to pay grant to local authorities in respect of capital expenditure for gypsy caravan sites under section 70 of the Local Government, Planning and Land Act 1980, except for the purposes of applications for grant received by the Secretaries of State before 3 November 1994. The repeal of section 70 does not apply to Scotland.

Future management of local authority gypsy caravan sites

19 Section 7 of the 1968 Act made provision for a sharing of functions between county councils and non-metropolitan district councils: county councils were required to acquire or appropriate land, set charges for the use of sites and contribute towards the costs incurred by district councils in managing the sites. District councils were required to provide and

manage the site. The majority of public sites in non-metropolitan districts are owned by county councils and managed by district councils.

20 The Secretaries of State consider that the repeal of section 7 of the 1968 Act removes from district councils the delegation to manage sites on land owned by county councils. County councils become responsible for managing these sites by virtue of section 24 of the 1960 Act. Nonetheless, the Secretaries of State consider that authorities have adequate powers to make suitable arrangements for the maintenance and management of sites depending on local circumstances. In particular, section 101 of the Local Government Act 1972 empowers a local authority to arrange for the discharge of its functions by another local authority. Such an arrangement would enable a district council to continue to manage a site and the county council to contribute towards their expenses.

21 The Secretaries of State consider it important that authorities should maintain their existing gypsy caravan sites, or should make suitable arrangements for their maintenance by leasing them to other persons who are willing and able to maintain them.

22 The Secretaries of State also expect authorities to continue to consider whether it is appropriate to provide further permanent caravan sites for gypsies in their areas. Section 24 of the 1960 Act enables county councils, district councils and London borough councils to establish and manage sites or to lease them to another person and, as amended by section 80(2) of the 1994 Act, to provide working space on gypsy caravan sites.

'Gypsy sites and planning'

23 Local authorities are reminded of the advice in Department of the Environment (DoE) Circular 1/94 (Welsh Office (WO) Circular 2/94), 'Gypsy Sites and Planning', dealing with the planning aspects of sites for gypsy caravans.

Bi-annual counts of gypsy caravans

24 The Department of the Environment and the Welsh Office intend to continue to ask local authorities to provide data for the compilation of the biannual counts of gypsy caravans in England and Wales on the same basis as at present.

Cancellations

25 DoE Circular 28/77 (WO Circular 51/77), DoE Circular 57/78 (WO Circular 97/78), and paragraphs 19 to 23 and Annex 2 of DoE Circular 8/81 (WO Circular 13/81) are now cancelled. DoE Circular 11/79 (WO Circular 11/79) is also cancelled, apart from Annex A which lists the capital costs of gypsy caravan site provision which are eligible for grant.

Financial and manpower implications

26 This Circular advises local authorities of the repeal of their duty to provide gypsy caravan sites and of the introduction of new discretionary powers to control unauthorised camping. Its contents are

considered unlikely to have any net manpower or resource implications for local authorities.

Contact points

27 Any enquiries on the contents of this Circular may be referred to the following contact points:

in England
R J Netto
Homelessness Policy Division
Department of the Environment, Room N13/08
2 Marsham Street, London SW1P 3EB.
Telephone: 0171 276 4708; or

Ms L Patrick
Homelessness Policy Division
Department of the Environment
Room N13/10, 2 Marsham Street
London SW1P 3EB.
Telephone: 0171 276 3244.

in Wales
Mrs R Douglas
Planning Division, Welsh Office
Room GO40, Cathays Park
Cardiff CF1 3NQ.
Telephone: 0222 823476.

The Chief Executive
County Councils in England and Wales
District Councils in England and Wales
London Borough Councils
Council of the Isles of Scilly
The Town Clerk, City of London

PLANNING POLICY FOR TRAVELLER SITES, DCLG 2015[3]

INTRODUCTION

1. This document sets out the Government's planning policy for traveller[4] sites. It should be read in conjunction with the National Planning Policy Framework. Guidance on the Framework can be found at: http://planningguidance.planningportal.gov.uk/
2. Planning law requires that applications for planning permission must be determined in accordance with the development plan, unless material considerations indicate otherwise.[5] This policy must be taken into account in the preparation of development plans, and is a material consideration in planning decisions. Local planning authorities preparing plans for and taking decisions on traveller sites should also have regard to the policies in the National Planning Policy Framework so far as relevant
3. The Government's overarching aim is to ensure fair and equal treatment for travellers, in a way that facilitates the traditional and nomadic way of life of travellers while respecting the interests of the settled community.
4. To help achieve this, Government's aims in respect of traveller sites are:
   a. that local planning authorities should make their own assessment of need for the purposes of planning
   b. to ensure that local planning authorities, working collaboratively, develop fair and effective strategies to meet need through the identification of land for sites
   c. to encourage local planning authorities to plan for sites over a reasonable timescale
   d. that plan-making and decision-taking should protect Green Belt from inappropriate development
   e. to promote more private traveller site provision while recognising that there will always be those travellers who cannot provide their own sites
   f. that plan-making and decision-taking should aim to reduce the number of unauthorised developments and encampments and make enforcement more effective

3 © Crown Copyright 2015.

4 See Annex 1 for the definition of traveller for the purposes of this statement.

5 Sections 19(2)(a) and 38(6) of the Planning and Compulsory Purchase Act 2004 and section 70(2) of the Town and Country Planning Act 1990. In relation to neighbourhood plans, under section 38B and C and paragraph 8(2) of new Schedule 4B to the 2004 Act (inserted by the Localism Act 2011 section 116 and Schedules 9 and 10) the independent examiner will consider whether having regard to national policy is appropriate to make the plan.

g. for local planning authorities to ensure that their Local Plan includes fair, realistic and inclusive policies
h. to increase the number of traveller sites in appropriate locations with planning permission, to address under provision and maintain an appropriate level of supply
i. to reduce tensions between settled and traveller communities in plan-making and planning decisions
j. to enable provision of suitable accommodation from which travellers can access education, health, welfare and employment infrastructure
k. for local planning authorities to have due regard to the protection of local amenity and local environment

5. To benefit those engaged in planning for traveller sites, specific planning policies for traveller sites are clearly set out in this separate document. The Government intends to review this policy when fair and representative practical results of its implementation are clear.

6. The Government still intends to review in the future whether Planning Policy for Traveller Sites should be incorporated within the wider National Planning Policy Framework. This will be considered as part of any wider review of the Framework.

USING EVIDENCE

Policy A: Using evidence to plan positively and manage development

7. In assembling the evidence base necessary to support their planning approach, local planning authorities should:
a) pay particular attention to early and effective community engagement with both settled and traveller communities (including discussing travellers' accommodation needs with travellers themselves, their representative bodies and local support groups)
b) cooperate with travellers, their representative bodies and local support groups; other local authorities and relevant interest groups to prepare and maintain an up- to-date understanding of the likely permanent and transit accommodation needs of their areas over the lifespan of their development plan, working collaboratively with neighbouring local planning authorities
c) use a robust evidence base to establish accommodation needs to inform the preparation of local plans and make planning decisions.

PLAN-MAKING

Policy B: Planning for traveller sites

8. Local Plans must be prepared with the objective of contributing to the achievement of sustainable development. To this end, they should be consistent with the policies in the National Planning Policy Framework, including the presumption in favour of sustainable development and the application of specific policies in the Framework, and this planning policy for traveller sites.

9. Local planning authorities should set pitch targets for gypsies and travellers as defined in Annex 1 and plot targets for travelling showpeople as defined in Annex 1 which address the likely permanent and transit site accommodation needs of travellers in their area, working collaboratively with neighbouring local planning authorities.[6]

10. Local planning authorities should, in producing their Local Plan:
   a) identify and update annually, a supply of specific deliverable sites sufficient to provide 5 years' worth of sites against their locally set targets[7]
   b) identify a supply of specific, developable sites, or broad locations for growth, for years 6 to 10 and, where possible, for years 11–15[8]
   c) consider production of joint development plans that set targets on a cross-authority basis, to provide more flexibility in identifying sites, particularly if a local planning authority has special or strict planning constraints across its area (local planning authorities have a duty to cooperate on planning issues that cross administrative boundaries)
   d) relate the number of pitches or plots to the circumstances of the specific size and location of the site and the surrounding population's size and density
   e) protect local amenity and environment.

11. Criteria should be set to guide land supply allocations where there is identified need. Where there is no identified need, criteria-based policies should be included to provide a basis for decisions in case applications nevertheless come forward. Criteria based policies should be fair and should facilitate the traditional and nomadic life of travellers while respecting the interests of the settled community.

12. In exceptional cases, where a local planning authority is burdened by a large-scale unauthorised site that has significantly increased their need, and their area is subject to strict and special planning constraints, then there is no assumption that the local planning authority is required to plan to meet their traveller site needs in full.

6 See Annex 1 for definitions of 'pitch' and 'plot'.

7 To be considered deliverable, sites should be available now, offer a suitable location for development, and be achievable with a realistic prospect that development will be delivered on the site within five years. Sites with planning permission should be considered deliverable until permission expires, unless there is clear evidence that schemes will not be implemented within 5 years, for example they will not be viable, there is no longer a demand for the type of units or sites have long term phasing plans

8 To be considered developable, sites should be in a suitable location for traveller site development and there should be a reasonable prospect that the site is available and could be viably developed at the point envisaged

13. Local planning authorities should ensure that traveller sites are sustainable economically, socially and environmentally. Local planning authorities should, therefore, ensure that their policies:
    a) promote peaceful and integrated co-existence between the site and the local community
    b) promote, in collaboration with commissioners of health services, access to appropriate health services
    c) ensure that children can attend school on a regular basis
    d) provide a settled base that reduces both the need for long-distance travelling and possible environmental damage caused by unauthorised encampment
    e) provide for proper consideration of the effect of local environmental quality (such as noise and air quality) on the health and well-being of any travellers that may locate there or on others as a result of new development
    f) avoid placing undue pressure on local infrastructure and services
    g) do not locate sites in areas at high risk of flooding, including functional floodplains, given the particular vulnerability of caravans
    h) reflect the extent to which traditional lifestyles (whereby some travellers live and work from the same location thereby omitting many travel to work journeys) can contribute to sustainability.

Policy C: Sites in rural areas and the countryside

14. When assessing the suitability of sites in rural or semi-rural settings, local planning authorities should ensure that the scale of such sites does not dominate the nearest settled community.

Policy D: Rural exception sites

15. If there is a lack of affordable land to meet local traveller needs, local planning authorities in rural areas, where viable and practical, should consider allocating and releasing sites solely for affordable traveller sites. This may include using a rural exception site policy for traveller sites that should also be used to manage applications. A rural exception site policy enables small sites to be used, specifically for affordable traveller sites, in small rural communities, that would not normally be used for traveller sites.[9] Rural exception sites should only be used for affordable traveller sites in perpetuity. A rural exception site policy should seek to address the needs of the local community by accommodating households who are either current residents or have an existing family or employment connection, whilst also ensuring that rural areas continue to develop as sustainable, mixed, inclusive communities

Policy E: Traveller sites in Green Belt

16. Inappropriate development is harmful to the Green Belt and should not be approved, except in very special circumstances. Traveller sites

9 Small rural settlements have been designated for enfranchisement and right to acquire purposes (under Section 17 of the *Housing Act 1996*) by SI 1997 Nos 620–25 inclusive and SI 1999 No 1307.

(temporary or permanent) in the Green Belt are inappropriate development. Subject to the best interests of the child, personal circumstances and unmet need are unlikely to clearly outweigh harm to the Green Belt and any other harm so as to establish very special circumstances.

17. Green Belt boundaries should be altered only in exceptional circumstances. If a local planning authority wishes to make an exceptional, limited alteration to the defined Green Belt boundary (which might be to accommodate a site inset within the Green Belt) to meet a specific, identified need for a traveller site, it should do so only through the plan- making process and not in response to a planning application. If land is removed from the Green Belt in this way, it should be specifically allocated in the development plan as a traveller site only.

Policy F: Mixed planning use traveller sites

18. Local planning authorities should consider, wherever possible, including traveller sites suitable for mixed residential and business uses, having regard to the safety and amenity of the occupants and neighbouring residents. Local planning authorities should consider the scope for identifying separate sites for residential and for business purposes in close proximity to one another if mixed sites are not practical.

19. Local planning authorities should have regard to the need that travelling showpeople have for mixed-use yards to allow residential accommodation and space for storage of equipment.

20. Local planning authorities should not permit mixed use on rural exception sites.

Policy G: Major development projects

21. Local planning authorities should work with the planning applicant and the affected traveller community to identify a site or sites suitable for relocation of the community if a major development proposal requires the permanent or temporary relocation of a traveller site. Local planning authorities are entitled to expect the applicant to identify and provide an alternative site, providing the development on the original site is authorised.

DECISION-TAKING

Policy H: Determining planning applications for traveller sites

22. Planning law requires that applications for planning permission must be determined in accordance with the development plan,[10] unless material considerations indicate otherwise.[11]

10 Section 38(1) of the Planning and Compulsory Purchase Act 2004: this includes adopted or approved development plan documents i.e. the Local Plan and neighbourhood plans which have been made in relation to the area (and the London Plan).

11 Section 38(6) of the Planning and Compulsory Purchase Act 2004 and section 70(2) of the Town and Country Planning Act 1990.

23. Applications should be assessed and determined in accordance with the presumption in favour of sustainable development and the application of specific policies in the National Planning Policy Framework and this planning policy for traveller sites.

24. Local planning authorities should consider the following issues amongst other relevant matters when considering planning applications for traveller sites:
    a) the existing level of local provision and need for sites
    b) the availability (or lack) of alternative accommodation for the applicants
    c) other personal circumstances of the applicant
    d) that the locally specific criteria used to guide the allocation of sites in plans or which form the policy where there is no identified need for pitches/plots should be used to assess applications that may come forward on unallocated sites
    e) that they should determine applications for sites from any travellers and not just those with local connections

    However, as paragraph 16 makes clear, subject to the best interests of the child, personal circumstances and unmet need are unlikely to clearly outweigh harm to the Green Belt and any other harm so as to establish very special circumstances.

25. Local planning authorities should very strictly limit new traveller site development in open countryside that is away from existing settlements or outside areas allocated in the development plan. Local planning authorities should ensure that sites in rural areas respect the scale of, and do not dominate, the nearest settled community, and avoid placing an undue pressure on the local infrastructure.

26. When considering applications, local planning authorities should attach weight to the following matters:
    a) effective use of previously developed (brownfield), untidy or derelict land
    b) sites being well planned or soft landscaped in such a way as to positively enhance the environment and increase its openness
    c) promoting opportunities for healthy lifestyles, such as ensuring adequate landscaping and play areas for children
    d) not enclosing a site with so much hard landscaping, high walls or fences, that the impression may be given that the site and its occupants are deliberately isolated from the rest of the community

27. If a local planning authority cannot demonstrate an up–to-date 5 year supply of deliverable sites, this should be a significant material consideration in any subsequent planning decision when considering applications for the grant of temporary planning permission.[12] The

12 There is no presumption that a temporary grant of planning permission should be granted permanently. For further guidance please see: http://planningguidance.planningportal.gov.uk/blog/guidance/use-of-planning-conditions/what-approach-should-be-taken-to-imposing-conditions/ (paragraph14)

exception is where the proposal is on land designated as Green Belt; sites protected under the Birds and Habitats Directives and / or sites designated as Sites of Special Scientific Interest; Local Green Space, an Area of Outstanding Natural Beauty, or within a National Park (or the Broads).

28. Local planning authorities should consider how they could overcome planning objections to particular proposals using planning conditions or planning obligations including:
   a) limiting which parts of a site may be used for any business operations, in order to minimise the visual impact and limit the effect of noise
   b) specifying the number of days the site can be occupied by more than the allowed number of caravans (which permits visitors and allows attendance at family or community events)
   c) limiting the maximum number of days for which caravans might be permitted to stay on a transit site.

Policy I: Implementation

29. The policies in this revised Planning Policy for Traveller Sites apply from the day of publication. This replaces the version published in March 2012.

30. The implementation policies set out in the National Planning Policy Framework will apply also to plan-making and decision-taking for traveller sites. In applying those implementation provisions to traveller sites, references in those provisions to policies in the National Planning Policy Framework should, where relevant, be read to include policies in this planning policy for traveller sites.

ANNEX 1: GLOSSARY

1. For the purposes of this planning policy 'gypsies and travellers' means:

   Persons of nomadic habit of life whatever their race or origin, including such persons who on grounds only of their own or their family's or dependants' educational or health needs or old age have ceased to travel temporarily, but excluding members of an organised group of travelling showpeople or circus people travelling together as such.

2. In determining whether persons are 'gypsies and travellers' for the purposes of this planning policy, consideration should be given to the following issues amongst other relevant matters:
   a) whether they previously led a nomadic habit of life
   b) the reasons for ceasing their nomadic habit of life
   c) whether there is an intention of living a nomadic habit of life in the future, and if so, how soon and in what circumstances.

3. For the purposes of this planning policy, 'travelling showpeople' means:

> *Members of a group organised for the purposes of holding fairs, circuses or shows (whether or not travelling together as such). This includes such persons who on the grounds of their own or their family's or dependants' more localised pattern of trading, educational or health needs or old age have ceased to travel temporarily, but excludes Gypsies and Travellers as defined above.*

4. For the purposes of this planning policy, 'travellers' means 'gypsies and travellers' and 'travelling showpeople' as defined above.
5. For the purposes of this planning policy, 'pitch' means a pitch on a 'gypsy and traveller' site and 'plot' means a pitch on a 'travelling showpeople' site (often called a 'yard'). This terminology differentiates between residential pitches for 'gypsies and travellers' and mixed-use plots for 'travelling showpeople', which may / will need to incorporate space or to be split to allow for the storage of equipment.

CIRCULAR 005/2018: PLANNING FOR GYPSY, TRAVELLER AND SHOWPEOPLE SITES, JUNE 2018[13]

PLANNING FOR GYPSY, TRAVELLER AND SHOWPEOPLE SITES

INTRODUCTION

1. This circular provides updated guidance on the planning aspects of identifying sustainable sites for Gypsies and Travellers. It also outlines how planning authorities and Gypsies and Travellers can work together to achieve this aim. It supersedes advice contained in Circular 30/2007 '*Planning for gypsy and traveller caravan sites*', Circular 78/91 *'Travelling Showpeople'* and Circular 76/94 *'Gypsy Sites Policy and Unauthorised Camping'* which are hereby cancelled.

DEFINITION

2. The definition of 'Gypsies and Travellers' for the purposes of this Circular is contained within section 108 of the Housing (Wales) Act 2014. Gypsies and Travellers means:
   (a) Persons of a nomadic habit of life, whatever their race or origin, including –
      (i) Persons who, on grounds only of their own or their family's or dependant's educational or health needs or old age, have ceased to travel temporarily or permanently, and
      (ii) Members of an organised group of travelling show people or circus people (whether or not travelling together as such); and
   (b) All other persons with a cultural tradition of nomadism or of living in a mobile home.
3. The intention of the above definition is to ensure that ethnic Romani Gypsies and Irish Travellers are included, as well as those from any ethnic group who follow a nomadic habit of life. Members of these communities do not necessarily need to demonstrate a continued nomadic habit of life to be considered to be Gypsies or Travellers.
4. The definition also includes Travelling Showpeople. New Travellers could also be captured by the definition if they can demonstrate a cultural tradition of nomadism or of living in mobile homes.
5. Travelling Showpeople are self-employed business people who travel the country holding fairs, chiefly during the summer months. Although their work is of a peripatetic nature, Travelling Showpeople nevertheless require permanent sites for activities such as the storage and maintenance of their equipment and for residential purposes. Such sites are often called yards or Winter quarters by Showpeople themselves. Nevertheless, these sites must be available for occupation all year round.
6. Most Showpeople are members of the Showmen's Guild of Great Britain and are required by the Guild to follow a code of practice on the use of their sites. Membership of the Guild provides Showpeople

13 © Crown Copyright 2018, Welsh Government (WG 35300).

with exemption from the site licencing requirements of the Mobile Homes (Wales) Act 2013 when they are travelling for the purposes of business, or where they occupy Winter quarters on the land with equipment for some period between the beginning of October in any year and the end of March the following year. However, they only enjoy permitted development rights under Part 5 of Schedule 2 of the Town and Country Planning (General Permitted Development) Order 1995 when travelling for the purpose of their business. They are, therefore, required to seek planning permission to establish all other sites.

GYPSIES AND TRAVELLERS – A CONTEXT

7. The Well-being of Future Generations (Wales) Act 2015 sets a framework for local authorities across Wales to ensure the 'sustainable development principle' (meeting the needs of the present without compromising the ability of future generations to meet their own needs) is met. Section 4 of the Act puts in place a number of well-being goals which authorities are to seek to achieve in order to meet this principle. These goals include achieving 'a Wales of cohesive communities', containing attractive, viable, safe and well-connected communities, and 'a Wales of vibrant culture and thriving Welsh language', containing a society that promotes and protects culture, heritage and the Welsh language.

8. Housing is a fundamental issue that affects the lives of people across Wales, including our Gypsy and Traveller communities. The Welsh Government seeks to ensure a wide choice of accommodation is available to meet the needs of all members of the community. It is reflective of the Government's commitment to ensure equality of opportunity for all sections of the community and in this instance, Gypsies and Travellers should have equal access to culturally appropriate accommodation as all other members of the community.

9. The Welsh Government is committed to working with local authorities to deliver new Gypsy and Traveller sites. This commitment is addressed through the availability of Sites Capital Grant funding for the development of new sites.[14] Changes to legislation through the Housing (Wales) Act 2014 and the Mobile Homes (Wales) Act 2013 have also supported this objective.

10.

11. The provision of Gypsy and Traveller sites is one of several key issues that need to be addressed through the plan making process. Where a lack of appropriate sites and insufficient provision exists within local authority areas, this has a significant detrimental impact on the lives of Gypsies and Travellers. Delivering appropriate Gypsy and Traveller

14 Further information on where the use of Sites Capital Grant funding may be applicable can be found in the Designing Gypsy and Traveller Sites in Wales document (refer to Annex A for further information) and elsewhere on the Gypsies and Travellers section of the Welsh Government website: http://gov.wales/gypsytravellers

site accommodation will have a beneficial impact on the communities' ability to access other essential services. Delivery of appropriate site accommodation for Gypsy and Traveller communities could also have a beneficial impact on the settled community by reducing the number of legal challenges and costs incurred in challenging unauthorised encampments.

12. The definition of a Gypsy and Traveller site for the purposes of this Circular does not include a dwelling (i.e. housing that falls within Use Class C3 under the Town and Country Planning [Use Classes] Order 1987[as amended]). Those Gypsies and Travellers who wish to live in bricks and mortar accommodation will have their needs met through provision of appropriate housing. The mechanism within the planning system for local authorities[15] to ensure a sufficient supply of land for housing is set out in Planning Policy Wales (PPW).

13. Some Gypsies and Travellers may wish to find and buy their own sites to develop and manage. An increase in the number of approved private sites may also release pitches on local authority sites for Gypsies and Travellers most in need of public provision. However, there will remain a requirement for public site provision above the current levels. Such sites are needed for Gypsies and Travellers who are unable to buy and develop their own sites, or prefer to rent, and to provide transit sites and temporary stopping places where Gypsies and Travellers may legally stop in the course of travelling.

14. Delivering more Gypsy and Traveller sites, whether public or private, is an issue for local authorities to address, as they have to find local solutions for local needs. The Welsh Government has developed a suite of supporting information encompassing grants and guidance documents[16] which will aid local authorities to meet their responsibilities in relation to accommodation provision for Gypsy and Travellers.

DUTY TO PROVIDE SITES

15. The Housing (Wales) Act 2014 places a legal duty upon local authorities to ensure that the accommodation needs of Gypsies and Travellers are properly assessed and that the identified need for pitches is met. Local authorities are required to exercise their powers under section 56 of the Mobile Homes (Wales) Act 2013, as far as necessary, to ensure Gypsy and Traveller sites are provided for the unmet need. This does not necessarily mean that additional local authority owned sites will be required but where they are needed the local authority is responsible for ensuring they are provided.

15 Please note the local authority does not carry out the planning function for land falling within the area of the Brecon Beacons, Pembrokeshire Coast or Snowdonia National Parks within Wales. The planning authority for these areas lies within the remit of the relevant National Park Authority rather than a local authority.

16 References to Welsh Government guidance documents on Gypsies and Travellers can be found at Annex A.

16. In order to be able to properly assess the accommodation needs of Gypsies and Travellers, section 101 of the Housing (Wales) Act 2014 introduces a requirement for local authorities to carry out an assessment of the accommodation needs of Gypsies and Travellers residing in or resorting to its area. Such assessments are to be carried out at least every 5 years after adoption of the initial assessment in 2016. They must be subject to consultation with Gypsies and Travellers and be submitted to the Welsh Ministers for approval, along with a report detailing how the assessment was carried out. Detailed Welsh Government guidance has been published which local authorities must have regard to in preparing such assessments, titled: 'Undertaking Gypsy and Traveller Accommodation Assessments (GTAAs) guidance'.

17. PPW states that local authorities are required to assess the accommodation needs of Gypsy families and have policies for the provision of Gypsy sites in their development plans. The findings of the GTAA will be a key consideration in the plan making, monitoring and review process for an authority's development plan. The GTAA will form part of the development plan evidence base that will be subject to public scrutiny through the plan preparation process and public examination. It will be a matter for the Inspector appointed to examine the development plan to consider the weight to attach to any emerging GTAA and how it relates to the plan before them.

18. This planning circular outlines the importance of:
   - involving Gypsies and Travellers proactively in the GTAA and planning process via Community Involvement Schemes in development plan preparation and ensuring communication is direct and accessible;
   - considering potential site sustainability, including access to suitable community facilities for occupiers;
   - guidance for Gypsies and Travellers making planning applications;
   - how local authorities working together regionally to prepare GTAAs may be of benefit in identifying accommodation needs and suitable site provision during the planning process;
   - planning authorities identifying suitable locations in development plans for permanent and transit sites that meet the needs of Gypsies and Travellers;
   - including a criteria-based policy in development plans that will provide a clear and fair rationale for the determining of Gypsy and Traveller site planning applications; and
   - local authorities' responsibilities under Equality and Human Rights legislation and case law.

19. By utilising this Circular and the two Welsh Government guidance documents detailed below, local authorities should be equipped with the tools to undertake the accommodation assessment and to meet the identified pitch needs.

- Undertaking Gypsy and Traveller Accommodation Assessments Guidance;[17] and
- Designing Gypsy and Traveller Sites in Wales.[18]

20. An overview of the planning process to be followed by local authorities when making provision for Gypsy and Traveller caravan sites is set out in Diagram 1 [not reproduced here].

PROVIDING THE EVIDENCE BASE

21. The assessment of Gypsy and Traveller accommodation needs, and the duty to make provision for sites where the assessment identifies need, became statutory requirements under the Housing (Wales) Act 2014. The Welsh Government publication *"Undertaking Gypsy and Traveller Accommodation Assessments Guidance"*[19] sets out the proposed process of assessing these needs and how to undertake a Gypsy and Traveller Accommodation Assessment (GTAA).

22. An important part of completing GTAAs, which will also support planning for sites, is keeping accurate records of authorised and unauthorised sites in the local authority area. Local authorities should routinely update the All Wales Caravan Count system when sites occur to ensure data is as robust as possible.

23. The GTAAs provide the key source of information enabling local authorities to assess the level of additional Gypsy and Traveller accommodation provision that is required when preparing their development plans. Assessments undertaken on a regional basis could provide benefits in terms of consistency in approach across local authorities to identifying need for Gypsy and Traveller sites and associated cost savings (see paragraphs 26 to 28 for further information on regional working).

24. The results of the GTAA make it possible for local authorities to identify the number of Gypsy and Traveller households which require additional pitches immediately, within 5 years, and over the development plan period. This will include:
    - the types of accommodation required to meet the need (i.e. residential or transit sites, specific sites for Travelling Showpeople or Romani Gypsies/Irish Travellers etc);
    - the number of households already residing in the Local Authority in unsuitable accommodation (i.e. overcrowded, living in conventional housing with an aversion to bricks and mortar etc);
    - the level of households on unauthorised developments or on authorised sites with temporary permission, which is likely to increase the unmet need if planning permission is not granted;
    - the likely rate of household formation; and

17 See Annex A for further information.

18 See Annex A for further information.

19 See Annex A for further information.

- the number of households with a realistic opportunity to move to preferred type of accommodation, which may free up spare pitches or bricks and mortar capacity.

25. Local authorities will also need to have regard to their other statutory duties, including those in respect of homelessness under Part 2 of the Housing (Wales) Act 2014 and to their obligations under the Equality Act 2010.

26. The Housing (Wales) Act 2014 requires Local Authorities to undertake a GTAA at least every 5 years. However Local Authorities have the flexibility to undertake GTAAs more frequently if a material change in the level of need in the area has been identified.[20] Where such circumstances arise, local authorities should address this change in need through provision of appropriate sites. This could result in the review of an authority's development plan in order to address any shortfalls in site provision through the planning process.

REGIONAL WORKING

27. Local authorities should consider whether there is benefit from working collaboratively in order to prepare a GTAA that covers a region.[21] This could be appropriate due to mobility between areas where neighbouring local authorities are aware that their Gypsy and Traveller populations regularly move across administrative boundaries. A regional GTAA could help to deliver a better understanding of travelling patterns and accommodation needs across local authorities. This could result in a common approach and consistency across the area in identifying need and allocating suitable Gypsy and Traveller sites in development plans. Specifically, a regional assessment could provide evidence to assist local authorities in managing unauthorised encampments, as they will be able to demonstrate that they have considered accommodation needs for transit provision on a regional basis. Cross boundary discussions between local authorities on individual GTAAs could also assist in identifying where transit needs could be met. Working in regional partnerships may also result in cost savings and improve the data available to assess need.

28. A regional GTAA provides the evidence base on accommodation needs to inform development plan preparation. It is essential the data arising from jointly conducted assessments remains capable of disaggregation to the local authority level. This will ensure each partner

20 See Annex A for details of Welsh Government guidance containing information on how local authorities are to undertake a Gypsy and Traveller Accommodation Assessment. This guidance contains advice on the circumstances where local authorities are to review and update their Assessments at Chapter 6.

21 See Annex A for details of Welsh Government guidance containing information on how local authorities are to undertake a Gypsy and Traveller Accommodation Assessment. This guidance also contains information on how local authorities can work together regionally to prepare such Assessments.

retains ownership of their evidence base and can produce information that is specific to the situation within each individual local authority. The data must be disaggregated to a local authority level as legislation under the Housing (Wales) Act 2014 prescribes that individual local authorities are responsible for meeting their identified Gypsy Traveller accommodation needs. Therefore, there should not be any trade off of permanent residential sites between partner authorities during preparation of their respective development plans.

29. In addition to the preparation of GTAAs, there are the tools in place to support regional working in the planning system. Regional working in this regard could include preparation of Strategic Development Plans and Joint Local Development Plans that span local authority boundaries where there are larger than local issues to consider. It is considered possible for this regional working to support the identification of Gypsy and Traveller sites. As for collaboration on GTAAs, any regional working undertaken through the planning system which leads to the identification of Gypsy Traveller site provision must be disaggregated back to individual local authority assessments of need. There should not be any trade off of permanent sites between partner authorities during this process, due to the reasons given in the previous paragraph.

DEVELOPMENT PLANS

Involving the Gypsy and Traveller Community

30. At an early stage in the preparation of development plans, planning authorities must discuss Gypsies and Travellers' accommodation needs directly with Gypsies and Travellers themselves, their representative bodies and local support groups. It should be recognised that Gypsies and Travellers are not a single community and have different values and attitudes with differing preferences for sites.

31. A list of relevant contacts is provided in Annex A but a local knowledge base should be developed by the local authority and the voluntary sector, about the different communities within and travelling through the area. For example some planning authorities use the results of regular consultation presented by site management officers, Gypsy and Travellers contact officers and multi agency forums.

32. Planning authorities should ensure they proactively include Gypsies and Travellers in the development plan preparation process to ensure that their views are taken into account. This will help avoid tensions and conflicts that could arise if unauthorised development or encampments take place.[22]

33. Section 63 of the Planning and Compulsory Purchase Act 2004 requires planning authorities to prepare their development plan in

22 Further guidance on consulting with stakeholders regarding Gypsy Traveller site proposals can be found in the Welsh Government's Designing Gypsy and Traveller Sites document (refer to Annex A for further information)

accordance with a Community Involvement Scheme (CIS), in which they will set out their policy on engaging with their community in preparing the development plan. Planning authorities should put in place arrangements so that communication with Gypsies and Travellers is direct and accessible to ensure conflict and tensions are minimised. Face to face consultation is likely to be the most effective means of gathering the views of these communities.

34. It should be recognised that Gypsy and Traveller communities are not organised in such a way that it is easy to identify who might represent the interest of any particular community, so developing local knowledge and trust is important. Identifying and understanding the needs of groups who find it difficult, for a number of reasons, to engage with planning processes is essential. One such difficulty is a lack of resources. As with all other sections of the community, planning authorities should consider what funding sources are available for such groups. One potential source of assistance that could help Gypsy and Traveller communities to participate more effectively in the planning system is Planning Aid Wales (contact details are included at Annex D of this circular).

35. Each CIS as part of the Delivery Agreement for the development plan will need to be agreed with the Welsh Government. It is up to each planning authority to decide whether to include consultation and involvement of Gypsy and Traveller communities as part of the submitted CIS, depending on the issues arising in their local area. If a planning authority fails to demonstrate efforts to engage with any Gypsy and Traveller communities where it should have, that authority would be at risk of failing to comply with procedural tests that must be adhered to for a development plan to be adopted.

Identifying Gypsy and Traveller Sites

36. Where a GTAA identifies an unmet need, planning authorities should allocate sufficient sites in development plans to ensure that the identified pitch requirements for residential and / or transit use can be met. Planning authorities will need to demonstrate that sites are suitable and deliverable in the identified timescales. With such policies in place there will be more certainty for all concerned when planning applications are determined.

37. When identifying sites the planning authority should work with the Gypsy and Traveller community. This should include encouraging Gypsies and Travellers and private landowners to put forward candidate sites as part of the development plan preparation process (Development Plan Manual[23]).

38. Issues of site sustainability are important for the health and well being of Gypsy and Travellers not only in respect of environmental issues but also for the maintenance and support of family and social

23 See paragraph 5.3.4. Edition 2. August 2015. Welsh Government. http://gov.wales/topics/planning/policy/policy-and-guidance-on-development-plans/ldpmanual/?lang=en

networks. Consideration may include the following matters as listed below. This list is not exhaustive and regard should also be had to other national planning policy requirements set out in Planning Policy Wales and Technical Advice Notes:

- opportunities for growth within family units;
- the promotion of peaceful and integrated co-existence between the site and the local community;
- access to health and education services;
- access to utilities including water, waste water disposal and waste collection services;
- access by walking and cycling, public transport and private motor vehicles (including emergency vehicles);
- suitable nearby or on-site safe play areas[24];
- contribution to a network of transit sites which reduce the need for long-distance travelling or unauthorised encampments;
- not locating sites in zone C2 risk of flooding and only considering sites for location within zone C1 risk of flooding in line with guidance contained in TAN 15[25], given the particular vulnerability of caravans; and
- regard for areas designated as being of international, national and local importance for biodiversity and landscape – see paragraphs 56–57 below.

39. In deciding where to provide for Gypsy and Traveller sites, planning authorities must first consider sustainable locations within or adjacent to existing settlement boundaries with access to local services e.g., education settings, health services and shops.

40. Sites in the countryside, away from existing settlements, can be considered for Gypsy and Traveller sites if there is a lack of suitable sustainable locations within or adjacent to existing settlement boundaries. In assessing the suitability of such sites, local authorities should be realistic about the availability, or likely availability, of alternatives to the car in accessing local services. Over rigid application of national or development plan policies that seek a reduction in car borne travel in order to effectively block proposals for any Gypsy and Traveller Site in a countryside location would be inappropriate. Sites should be considered in context and in relation to the local infrastructure, population size and density to ensure they are in proportion to local settled communities.

24 The Welsh Government's guidance Designing Gypsy and Traveller Sites in Wales, as referenced in Annex A and throughout this Circular, provides detailed information on how Gypsy and Traveller sites are to be designed and facilities that should be provided on sites. This guidance should be read in conjunction with this Circular when determining the sustainability of potential sites for Gypsies and Travellers.

25 Technical Advice Note 15: Development and Flood Risk. July 2004. Welsh Assembly Government.

41. All sites considered as options for a site allocation in a development plan must have their social, environmental and economic impacts assessed in accordance with the requirements of sustainability appraisal. (Section 3 of the Development Plan Manual[26] introduces the process of sustainability appraisal; section 5 explains the process with regard to Evidence Gathering and Objectives; and section 6 explains the process in the context of Strategic Options and Preferred Strategy). When considering sites for allocation in development plans planning authorities will also need to have regard to the following Welsh Government guidance documents:
    - Designing Gypsy and Traveller Sites in Wales[27];
    - Managing Gypsy and Traveller Sites in Wales Guidance[28]; and
    - Undertaking Gypsy and Traveller Accommodation Assessments Guidance.[16]
42. Sites, whether public or private, should be identified having regard to highways considerations. In setting their policies, planning authorities should have regard to the potential for noise and other disturbance from the movement of vehicles to and from the site, the stationing of vehicles on the site, and on-site business activities. However, projected vehicle movements for Gypsy and Traveller sites should be assessed on an individual basis for each site. Proposals should not be rejected if they would give rise to only modest additional daily vehicle movements and/or the impact on minor roads would not be significant.
43. Permanent residential pitches should be for residential purposes only and potentially hazardous activity on pitches should not be encouraged. Hazardous activities on sites not designated for work purposes can lead to health and safety, pollution and environmental concerns. However, local authorities may wish to consider the provision of designated working space in a separate part of the site, where there is a demonstrable reason why specific on-site facilities need to be provided. For example, Showpeople sites are likely to require separate facilities for the storage and maintenance of fairground rides.
44. There may also be situations where Gypsies and Travellers need to store equipment used in their work or require grazing land and the planning authority will have to decide if the provision of such space is possible and ensure adequate separation from residential areas.
45. Where Gypsies and Travellers require additional space for work related activities they should be encouraged to pursue private leasing agreements for nearby space and/or facilities. Local authorities that have commercial land for rent, for example garages, could make these lists available to site residents wishing to pursue this option and

26 http://gov.wales/topics/planning/policy/policy-and-guidance-on-development-plans/ldpmanual/?lang=en

27 See Annex A for further information.

28 Refer to Chapter 5. Further information on this document can be found at Annex A.

should work proactively with Gypsies and Travellers to find suitable alternative facilities.

46. Further guidance on how sites are to be designed for specific groups of Gypsies and Travellers, including Travelling Showpeople, can be found in the Welsh Government's guidance: Designing Gypsy and Traveller Sites in Wales.[29]

47. Where a local authority experiences unauthorised encampments[30] due to Gypsies and Travellers 'passing through' an area and the authority has an inadequate supply of transit pitches, temporary stopping places could be identified for short-term occupation. Temporary stopping places help to reduce unauthorised encampments preventing social, economic or environmental issues whilst facilitating the traditional Gypsy and Traveller way of life. Temporary stopping places must make provision for waste disposal, water supply and sanitation at a minimum.[31] However, temporary stopping places are only a short term, rather than a long term, solution. They are not planning designations and should not be addressed through land use allocation policies in development plans.[32] Where there is clear, identified need to address in relation to Gypsies and Travellers passing through an area, sustainable transit sites would be required. The Mobile Homes (Wales) Act 2013 sets out the requirement for maximum length of three months occupancy for these sites. Further, it also allows occupiers of transit pitches the right to four weeks notice if the local authority intends to end their occupation early for any reason.

48. There are a number of ways in which planning authorities can identify specific sites and make land available:

- Local authorities have discretion to dispose of land for less than best consideration where it will help to secure the promotion or improvement of the economic, social or environmental well-being of the area.[33]
- Authorities should also consider making full use of any registers of unused and under-used land owned by public bodies as an aid to identifying suitable locations. Vacant or under-used local authority land may be appropriate.

29 See Annex A for further information.

30 See Annex A for further information.

31 Further information on temporary stopping places can be found at Chapter 7 of the Designing Gypsy Sites in Wales document, details on which can be found at Annex A.

32 Further information on transit sites can be found at Chapter 6 of the Designing Gypsy and Traveller Sites in Wales document, details on which can be found at Annex A.

33 As set out in National Assembly for Wales Circular 41/03, "Local Government Act 1972: General Disposal Consent (Wales) 2003, Disposal of land in Wales by Authorities for less than Best Consideration".

- Authorities should also consider whether it might be appropriate to exercise their compulsory purchase powers to acquire an appropriate site.
- Co-operation between neighbouring local authorities can provide more flexibility in identifying transit sites.

48. A planning authority which, exceptionally, is unable to meet all assessed future needs through specific site locations should give in the development plan a reasoned explanation why that has not been possible supported by relevant evidence. It must explain what criteria will be used to ensure adequate provision and state the detailed measures it will take to ensure that adequate provision is made during the plan period.

Criteria based policies

49. Criteria based policies will be required in the development plan in order to guide determination of planning applications. Such criteria based policies should adhere to sustainability requirements, having regard to site considerations set out under paragraph 37 and other national planning policy requirements set out in Planning Policy Wales and Technical Advice Notes. Criteria based policies must be fair, reasonable, realistic and effective in delivering sites. Planning policies that rule out or place undue constraints on the development of Gypsy and Traveller sites should not be included in development plans.

50. Annex B contains guidance on good practice criteria. The Welsh Government has the power to intervene in the plan-making process where it considers that the constraints being proposed by planning authorities are too great or have been inadequately justified.

Monitoring Development Plan Gypsy and Traveller site policies

51. The Planning and Compulsory Purchase Act 2004, requires the planning authority to produce an annual monitoring report (AMR). The AMR is the main mechanism for reviewing the relevance and success of the development plan and identifying any changes necessary. One of the main purposes of the AMR is to consider whether objectives set out in the development plan are being achieved. It requires that, where a policy specified in the development plan is not being implemented; the annual monitoring report must identify that policy. The AMR should clearly set out:
   - the reasons why that policy is not being implemented;
   - the steps (if any) that the planning authority intend to take to secure that the policy is implemented; and
   - whether the planning authority intends to prepare a revision of the development plan to replace or amend that policy.

52. Further guidance is contained in the Development Plan Manual.[34]

34 Refer to Section 9. http://gov.wales/topics/planning/policy/policy-and-guidance-on-development-plans/ldpmanual/?lang=en

MAJOR DEVELOPMENT PROJECTS

53. A major development or redevelopment project may require the permanent or temporary relocation of a Gypsy or Traveller site. When determining applications for such development, it may be appropriate to attach conditions or secure planning obligations requiring the developer to identify and provide an alternative site, providing the original site is authorised. The planning authority should work with the developer and the affected Gypsy and Traveller community to identify a site (or sites) that would be suitable for relocating the community.

54. In proposing relocation regard will need to be paid to the social, economic and environmental needs of the Gypsy and Traveller community and the potential benefits of the relocation to the locality and the broader area. It will also be necessary to ensure that any relocation does not impact on the legal or human rights of the existing site residents.

DESIGNATED AREAS

55. National planning policy on Green Belts and Green Wedges is set out in PPW.[35] There is a general presumption against inappropriate development within Green Belts or green wedges. New Gypsy and Traveller sites in the Green Belt or green wedges are likely to be inappropriate development. National planning policy on Green Belts or green wedges applies equally to applications for planning permission for Gypsy and Traveller sites and other residential uses. Alternatives should be explored before Green Belt or green wedge locations are considered. Pressure for development of sites on Green Belt or green wedge land can usually be avoided if the planning authority allocates sufficient sites elsewhere in its area, to meet identified need.

56. PPW contains national planning policy guidance on development in areas with nationally recognised designations – in respect of the statutory landscape designations,[36] development control[37] and statutory nature conservation designations.[38] Any statutory duties associated with a designation must be complied with. That guidance is applicable to planning applications for any residential development within those areas, including for Gypsy and Traveller sites.

57. PPW offers further guidance on local landscape and local nature conservation designations.[39] Planning applications for Gypsy and Traveller sites should be considered in accordance with national planning policy guidance for those designations.

35 Refer to Section 4.8 of PPW.

36 Refer to Paragraph 5.3.3 of PPW.

37 Refer to Paragraph 5.3.6 of PPW.

38 Refer to Paragraph 5.3.8 of PPW.

39 Refer to Paragraphs 5.3.2 and 5.3.11 of PPW.

PLANNING APPLICATIONS

58. Section 38 of the Planning and Compulsory Purchase Act 2004 provide that determinations of applications for planning permission shall be made in accordance with the development plan unless material considerations indicate otherwise. Other considerations for Gypsy and Traveller site applications will usually include the impact on the surrounding area, the existing level of provision and need for sites which is evidenced as part of the Gypsy and Traveller Accommodation Assessment for the area.

59. PPW makes it clear personal permissions are exceptions and would rarely outweigh more general planning considerations. The availability (or lack of) alternative accommodation for the applicants and their specific personal circumstances can be material considerations, provided a condition is attached to the permission making it personal to the occupiers. Personal permissions are only relevant to situations where uses or operational development must cease and be removed once the occupiers move or their material circumstances otherwise change.

60. Guidance on temporary permissions is set out in Circular 016/2014 and should only be issued in specific circumstances. Detailed evidence of need for Gypsy and Traveller sites is identified by each local authority as part of their Gypsy and Traveller Accommodation Assessment, which should inform site provision within development plans. Providing for this need would therefore warrant permanent permissions to be granted for Gypsy and Traveller sites and it should be rare to grant temporary permissions.

61. In considering specific provisions for sites, regard should be had to the Welsh Government's guidance documents on Gypsies and Travellers – in particular, the Designing Gypsy and Traveller Sites in Wales document when considering site size, layout and facilities.[40] Standards for private sites can be found in the Model standards 2008 for Caravan Sites in Wales document.[41] Permission to develop Gypsy and Travellers sites outside of settlement boundaries could be granted subject to sustainability criteria set out in national planning policy if there are no realistic, suitable sites available within or adjacent to settlement boundaries to accommodate Gypsies and Travellers (as defined under section 108 of the Housing (Wales) Act 2014).

62. To encourage private site provision, planning authorities should offer advice and practical help with planning procedures to Gypsies and Travellers who wish to acquire their own land for development. Gypsies and Travellers should always consult planning authorities on planning matters before buying land on which they intend to establish any caravan site, for which planning permission will almost always be required (more guidance on both of these aspects is contained in Annexes C and D).

40 See Annex A for further information.

41 See Annex A for further information.

63. Pre-application discussions are particularly important to avoid misunderstanding and subsequent problems over planning permission. Constructive and positive engagement on all sides will promote trust and may help to avoid breaches of planning control. The aim should be as far as possible to help Gypsies and Travellers to provide for themselves, to allow them to secure the kind of sites they need, but in locations that are appropriate in planning policy terms. This will help to avoid breaches of planning control, and enable firm enforcement against such breaches. In particular, questions of road access, the availability of services, potential conflict with statutory undertakers or agricultural interests, and any significant environmental impacts should be resolved at the earliest opportunity. In line with guidance in TAN 15,[42] planning authorities should consult Natural Resources Wales about flood risk.

64. Any facts that may be relevant should be established and considered before determining planning applications. Gypsies and Travellers should co-operate by responding to requests for information relevant to their applications.

65. Planning authorities should not refuse applications because the applicant has no local connection. But they are entitled to refuse applications in locations that do not comply with planning policies, especially where the authority has complied with this guidance and proceeded properly to ensure needs identified by accommodation assessments are being met.

66. Planning authorities should consider how they could overcome planning objections to particular proposals using planning conditions or planning obligations, including:

a.) Limiting which parts of a site may be used for any hazardous activity, in order to minimise the visual impact and limit the effect of noise

b.) Specifying the number of days the site can be occupied by more than the allowed number of caravans (which permits visitors and allows attendance at family or community events).

67. In appropriate circumstances planning authorities may impose conditions to limit the proportion of a Travelling Showpeople site which may be covered by fairground equipment, and the hours during which such equipment may be tested, in order to safeguard local amenity. However, planning authorities should avoid imposing conditions prohibiting either residential use or the maintenance of equipment (or unduly restricting the hours during which this activity can be carried out), as such conditions would effectively nullify the benefit of any permission for a permanent Travelling Showpeople's site.

68. Conditions and obligations should only be used where they would make development of a site acceptable. They should not be used to defer matters that can be resolved during determination of a planning application. Annex B provides further sources of information on the

42 Technical Advice Note 15: Development and Flood Risk. July 2004. Welsh Assembly Government.

use of conditions and obligations in planning permissions for Gypsy and Traveller sites.

69. In considering whether to enforce against land being used as a Gypsy and Traveller site or to refuse planning permission for such use, planning authorities should assess what effect, if any, the absence of existing site provision would have on the ability to take, and defend, such actions successfully in any subsequent appeal. Planning authorities should have regard to the duty in Section 103 of the Housing (Wales) Act 2014 – requiring an authority to exercise its powers to meet any needs for site provision that are identified through its Gypsy and Traveller Accommodation Assessment – in deciding on an appropriate course of action to take.

ENFORCEMENT

70. It is important that planning policies and controls are respected by all sections of the community and that, where it is expedient to do so, effective enforcement action is taken by the planning authority. Planning authorities should work collaboratively with other authority departments using the full range of statutory and non-statutory measures to deal holistically with the issues raised by unauthorised encampments.

71. An unauthorised encampment is an encampment of caravans and/or vehicles on land without the landowner's or occupier's consent and therefore constituting trespass. Unauthorised development refers to a camp or group of caravans and vehicles on land which may or may not belong to the occupier but which does not have the necessary planning permission.[43]

72. When considering enforcement action against unauthorised development, the Town and Country Planning Act 1990, provides several tools to enable planning authorities to take enforcement action, including:

- Enforcement notice (s.172);
- Breach of condition notice (s.187A);
- Stop notice (s.183);
- Temporary stop notice (s.171E); and
- Injunctions (s.187B).

73. Planning authorities should be guided by the advice in the Development Management Manual.[44] Further advice on the enforcement powers available to planning authorities and their use can be found in:

43 Further guidance for planning authorities on unauthorised development can be found in the Development Management Manual. http://gov.wales/topics/planning/policy/development-management-manual/development-management-manual-without-annexes/?lang=en

44 http://gov.wales/topics/planning/policy/development-management-manual/?lang=en

- Enforcing Planning Control: Legislative Provision and Procedural Requirements[45]; and
- Managing Unauthorised Camping guidance.[46]

Temporary Stop Notices

74. Sections 171 E to 171H of the Town and Country Planning Act 1990 makes provision for temporary stop notices. The ability to serve a temporary stop notice maybe used to immediately stop further development of land as a Gypsy and Traveller site to prevent its further intensification for a period of 28 days. During this time the planning authority is able to decide which course of enforcement action, using the other tools available to them under the Town and Country Planning Act 1990, is most appropriate to tackle the breach of planning control.

75. There is no right of appeal against a temporary stop notice and so before one is issued, the planning authority should consider, as with all enforcement action, their duties under the Human Rights Act 1998, the Equality Act 2010 and also the Housing (Wales) Act 2014. Where a local authority has an identified unmet need for Gypsy and Traveller accommodation, this should form a material consideration in their decision whether or not to serve a temporary stop notice against an unauthorised site.

APPEALS

76. There will be occasions when planning authorities refuse planning permission for Gypsy and Traveller sites. A Planning Inspector will determine any subsequent appeal in accordance with the development plan and all other material considerations which should already have been addressed at the application stage. These will include the GTAA available, existing and planned provision of, and need for sites in the planning authority's area, the accuracy of the data used to assess need, the methodology employed in the needs assessment and how up-to-date it is, information on pitch availability on public and private sites, personal circumstances and alternative accommodation options.

HUMAN RIGHTS AND EQUALITY OF OPPORTUNITY

77. The provisions of the Human Rights Act 1998 which incorporates the European Convention on Human Rights into domestic law should be considered as an integral part of local authorities' decision-making – including its approach to the question of what are material considerations in planning cases. Planning authorities should consider the consequences of refusing or granting planning permission, or taking enforcement action, on the rights of the individuals concerned, both Gypsies and Travellers and local residents, and whether it is necessary

45 Welsh Office Circular 24/97

46 Published by Welsh Government. Dated 2013. See Annex A for further information

and proportionate in the circumstances. If there is any doubt about the application of provisions of the Convention in particular cases, legal advice should be sought. The obligation on public authorities to act compatibly with Convention rights does not give Gypsies and Travellers a right to establish sites in contravention of planning control.

78. Section 149 of the Equality Act 2010 prohibits racial discrimination by planning authorities in carrying out their planning functions. In addition, the majority of public authorities, including local authorities, have a general duty under the 2010 Act to actively seek to eliminate unlawful discrimination and to advance equality of opportunity and foster good race relations in all they do. The development plan Community Involvement Scheme is particularly important in this regard.

79. When policies are changed or new ones introduced, authorities should assess and consult on their likely impact, and where an adverse impact is identified which cannot be justified, changes should be made. It is particularly important that authorities consider all the racial groups served by the authority in order to assess the impact of their policies on these groups. Romani Gypsies and Irish Travellers have been recognised by the Courts as being distinct ethnic groups, covered by the 2010 Act. Under the general duty mentioned above, there is a requirement that local authorities seek to promote good race relations between Gypsies and Travellers and the settled community. This is important in the context of Gypsy and Traveller site planning.

MONITORING PLANNING APPLICATIONS

80. Planning authorities should monitor and critically analyse the decisions on applications for sites for Gypsies and Travellers. Authorities should use the results of such analysis to inform policy development. In this regard, planning authorities are advised to maintain an ongoing list of all planning applications they receive for the development of Gypsy and Traveller sites. They could use this list to monitor the outcomes of planning applications against accommodation need identified in their Gypsy and Traveller Accommodation Assessment. The compiling of such data could also provide a useful evidence base to inform Gypsy and Traveller site provision during development plan preparation, monitoring and review.

ANNEX A

References and List of Organisations of interest to Gypsies and Travellers

REFERENCES

Undertaking Gypsy and Traveller Accommodation Assessments Guidance, Welsh Government, May 2015 http://gov.wales/docs/dsjlg/publications/equality/150223-gypsy-traveller-accommodation-assessmentsv2-en.pdf

Guidance on Managing Unauthorised Camping, Welsh Government, December 2013 http://gov.wales/docs/dsjlg/publications/equality/131220-guidance-managing-unauthorised-camping-2013-en.pdf

Royal Town Planning Institute (February 2007) Good Practice Note 4 Series: Planning for Gypsies and Travellers. http://rtpi.org.uk/knowledge/publications/planning-for-gypsies-and-travellers/

Designing Gypsy and Traveller Sites Guidance, Welsh Government, May 2015 http://gov.wales/docs/dsjlg/publications/equality/150528-designing gypsy and traveller-sites-en.pdf

Managing Gypsy and Traveller Sites in Wales Guidance, Welsh Government, May 2015 http://gov.wales/docs/dsjlg/publications/equality/150528-managing-gypsy-and-traveller-sites-en.pdf

Planning Your Community: A guide to Local Development Plans (Welsh Assembly Government Booklet July 2006) http://gov.wales/topics/planning/policy/policy-and-guidance-on-development-plans/ldpguide/?lang=en

Model standards 2008 for Caravan Sites in Wales (Welsh Assembly Government document, July 2008) http://gov.wales/topics/housing-and-regeneration/publications/model-standards-2008-for-caravan-sites-in-Wales/?lang=en

ORGANISATIONS

Welsh Government

Equality & Prosperity Division
Education and Public Services Group
Welsh Government
Merthyr Tydfil
CF48 1UZ

Equalityandprosperitymailbox@gov.wales

Wales-based organisations:

Travelling Ahead Advice and Advocacy Service
Tros Gynnal Plant
Goldtops House
8a Pentonville
Newport
NP20 5HB
01633 509 544
Freephone Advice Line: 0808 802 0025
travellingahead@trosgynnalplant.org.uk
www.travellingahead.com

Gypsies and Travellers Wales
Trowbridge Community Centre
Caernarvon Way

Trowbridge
Cardiff
CF3 1RU
029 2021 4411
info@gtwales.org.uk mailto:admincgtp@btconnect.com

Gwent Gypsy and Traveller Service (serving the Newport, Torfaen and Blaenau Gwent areas)
07773 250 015
01633 833 540
gtreferrals@gwalia.com

Romani Cultural and Arts Company
Temple Court
13a Cathedral Road
Cardiff
CF11 9HA
isaacblake@romaniarts.co.uk
http://www.romaniarts.co.uk

The Bridges Project
Merthyr Tydfil
01685 353959
Lb2@smt.org.uk

The Showmen's Guild of Great Britain ***(Travelling Showpeople only)***
South Wales –
7 Rhigos Gardens Cardiff
CF24 4LS
07949 289 075
Sgwales1@gmail.com

North Wales –
11 St. Mary's Place
Bury
Lancashire
BL9 0DZ
01617 629 502
leesashowmensguild@yahoo.com
http://www.showmensguild.co.uk

The Travellers School Charity ***(New Travellers only)***
Ty Loveden House
26 Bridge Street
Aberystwyth
Ceredigion
SY23 1QB
07786 466 107
info@travellersschool.org.uk
http://www.travellersschool.org.uk

Planning Aid Wales
First Floor
174 Whitchurch Road
Cardiff
CF14 3NB
02920 625000
http://www.planningaidwales.org.uk

Equality and Human Rights Commission Wales
Block 1
Spur D
Government Buildings
St Agnes Road
Cardiff
CF14 4YY
02920 447710
Wales@equalityhumanrights.com

Other UK community support organisations:

The Traveller Movement
The Resource Centre
356 Holloway Road
London
N7 6PA
020 7607 2002
info@travellermovement.org.uk
http://www.travellermovement.org.uk

Friends, Families and Travellers
Community Base
113 Queens Road
Brighton
BN1 3XG
01273 234777
Fft@gypsy-traveller.org
www.gypsy-traveller.org

The National Federation of Gypsy Liaison Groups
c/o Derbyshire Gypsy Liaison Group
1-3 Ladygrove Mill
Lady Grove Road
Two Dales
Matlock
DE4 2FG
01629 732744
natglg@outlook.com
http://www.nationalgypsytravellerfederation.org

The Gypsy Council(for Education, Culture, Welfare and Civil Rights)
8 Hall Road
Aveley
Romford
Essex
RM15 4HD
07963 565 952
info@gypsy-association.com
http://www.gypsy-association.com

ANNEX B

Good Practice – Criteria

1. Gypsies and Travellers have the same rights and responsibilities within the planning system as every other citizen. Plan policies and criteria for the establishment of Gypsy and Traveller caravan sites should be fair, reasonable, realistic and effective, and written in a positive manner that offer some certainty that where the criteria (not necessarily all of them) are met planning permission will be granted.
2. Ambiguous plan policies stating that permission 'may be granted' or that the authority 'will take account of' factors should be avoided as they increase uncertainty. Alternative wording might include 'planning permission will be granted "provided that the following criteria/requirements are [clearly] satisfied. . . . .".
3. The list of criteria adopted by a planning authority should not be excessive as the more criteria there are, and the more restrictive they are, the greater the likelihood of authorities refusing planning permission. A more positive approach should be taken to making adequate provision for Gypsies and Travellers in appropriate locations – particularly by those planning authorities whose present policies have failed to meet current needs. The process by which criteria are adopted in development plans will be subject to close scrutiny.
4. For all kinds of site, consideration must be given to vehicular access from the public highway, as well as provision for parking, turning and servicing on site, and road safety for occupants and visitors. Landscaping and planting with appropriate trees and shrubs can help sites blend into their surroundings, give structure and privacy, and maintain visual amenity. Enclosing a site with too much hard landscaping, high walls or fences can not only give the impression of deliberately isolating the site and its occupants from the rest of the community but could also be visually intrusive – both situations should be avoided.
5. Sites should be considered in context and in relation to the local infrastructure, population size and density to ensure they are in proportion to local settled communities. Further guidance on the size of sites and their design can be found in the Welsh Government's Designing Gypsy and Traveller Sites Guidance, as referenced in Annex A of this document.

Criteria which are unacceptable

6. It has not been uncommon for criteria to be so restrictive and extensive that in practice it is impossible or virtually impossible for an application to comply with them all. The following criteria have been taken from local authority plans and represent examples of criteria that are considered generally **unacceptable**:

'Each unit of accommodation on the site shall have been brought onto the site by the occupier(s) for the time being who shall remove the accommodation from the site when ceasing to use it for residential purposes'.

This criterion does not accommodate the nomadic and traditional lifestyle whereby many Gypsies and Travellers have one caravan to live in, and one that is more mobile that they use when travelling.

A requirement that the accommodation is brought onto site by the occupier does not allow provision to be made for other family members who may not themselves, perhaps for reasons of ill health, physically move their own accommodation onto the site.

'There shall be no more than [x] caravans' (on any site)

Setting a maximum number as a blanket policy through a development plan policy is arbitrary.

Any maximum number of caravans to be sited on any particular site should be identified through a planning condition after having regard to the circumstances of the individual planning application which would include specific size of site, surrounding population size and density and the requirements of the applicant.

"Applications from Gypsies and Travellers with no local connection will not normally be allowed"

Gypsies and Travellers are often nomadic and so will not always have local connections. Planning authorities have to determine applications for development from anyone who submits them.

As the business in which Gypsies and Travellers have traditionally engaged decline, the new trades and businesses they take up often necessitate new locations and settled salaried employment.

It is not appropriate to require applicants to have a local connection to successfully achieve planning consent.

"The site does not impact on any area with natural/wildlife interest"

All development by its very nature will have some impact on wildlife. The criteria should be more tightly, but reasonably, defined.

"The site shall not encroach into the countryside"

This is unrealistic. Such policies have been used to thwart site provision.

> ***"Sites will only be permitted where there is a clearly identified unmet need in the Gypsy and Traveller Accommodation Assessment"***
>
> This would be unacceptable as it would act against freedom of movement for Gypsies and Travellers who wish to develop their own sites. Such restrictions would not be placed on non-Gypsies and Travellers who move to a new area and seek to build a house.

Also see the following providing information about suggested conditions in Gypsy Traveller site permissions:

- Circular 016/2014, The Use of Planning Conditions for Development Management, Welsh Government
- Link to model conditions published by the Planning Inspectorate: http://gov.wales/topics/planning/appeals/model-conditions/?lang=en

Refer to Welsh Office Circular 13/97, Planning Obligations for information about the use of planning obligations in planning permissions.

ANNEX C

Guidance to Planning Authorities in dealing with planning applications from Gypsies and Travellers

1. Gypsies and Travellers have the same rights and responsibilities within the planning system as all other applicants for planning permission. In dealing with applications and enquiries from Gypsies and Travellers planning officers and planning department staff should act in a professional manner and treat enquiries from Gypsies and Travellers even-handedly. Planning Aid Wales (contact details at Annex A) is a source of free independent advice and information that Gypsy and Travellers may wish to use.
2. It is particularly important if unauthorised development is to be avoided for planning authorities to establish a level of trust and co-operation with the local Gypsy and Traveller community. Entrenched positions on both sides are likely to lead to tensions, conflict and delay.
3. Planning authorities may wish to consider designating a named person to deal with all such enquiries/applications or have a named person with whom the applicants can maintain contact. Staff responsible for dealing with Gypsy and Traveller applications should be given specific training.
4. Planning authorities need to provide early, clear pre-application advice and may wish to consider producing leaflets explaining the planning system, and consider using other media – such as video/dvd and audio communication – where this would better meet the needs of the Gypsy and Traveller community. Similarly early explanation of fees for statutory pre-application services should be provided and the range of discretionary pre-application services, which may be provided

with or without an accompanying fee.[47] At any pre-application meeting planning authorities should give an informal indication of the chances of getting permission, highlight any possible difficulties and whether these may be overcome and explain the planning process to applicants who are unfamiliar with it.

5. Planning authorities need to make Gypsies and Travellers aware of standards they can expect from the authority, standards expected from them and their rights to complain, including to the authority's monitoring officer and the Public Services Ombudsman.

6. Planning departments may need to consult other departments and agencies with an interest, particularly housing, social services and education departments, health and highways authorities. Other important sources of advice are Gypsy Liaison Officers (or their equivalents) usually, but not always, based in local authorities where such Officers are made available.

ANNEX D

Guidance for Gypsies and Travellers making planning applications

Introduction

1. Members of the Gypsy and Traveller communities have the same rights and responsibilities within the planning system as members of other communities. Planning permission is normally required for any changes of use of land. As with development submitted by anyone the only times permission would not be required are:
   i. if the land has already been granted planning permission for a particular type of land use and development of this type would be taking place on the land; or
   ii. the use of the land has been established over a period of time without valid planning enforcement action having been taken by the planning authority. This time period is 4 years for building or other similar physical works which do not represent a change of land use, or 10 years where the development has represented a change of land use. Siting caravans on land is a use of the land in planning terms.

Pre-application procedure

2. When looking for a site Gypsies and Travellers should find out whether
   i. there are any existing sites in the locality (with planning permission) available to rent or buy;

47 Further information on fees payable to planning authorities in respect of pre-application services is set out in the Development Management Manual. http://gov.wales/topics/planning/policy/development-management-manual/development-management-manual-without-annexes/?lang=en

ii. if not, whether the planning authority can identify any sites that may be or could become available.

3. If the outcome of the queries outlined above is negative and you are looking to develop a new site, it is probable that you will need to apply for planning permission. When the planning authority considers your application they will first look to see what their development plan says about the site you have chosen.

4. Consequently, **before committing to a site and applying for planning permission you should take the following steps.** This is to ensure there are no obvious constraints which would prevent you from developing the site and committing to unnecessary expenditure:-

i. contact the planning authority[48] in order to identify the development plan policies relevant to Gypsy and Traveller caravan site use and establish whether the site you are interested in is in a Green Belt, green wedge or other area of special protection. Development in such areas is subject to stricter control and the likelihood of getting planning permission usually is much lower than if the site were not within an area enjoying this special protection. Planning authorities are able to charge a fee for any information provided on a site and proposal before a planning application is submitted. When you contact the planning authority, they can advise on any fees that may be payable.

ii. Prepare information indicating
- the area of your search for a site
- whether there are particular reasons for selecting the site you have e.g. family circumstances, work or other requirements
- whether there are other sites available and, if so, why you consider them to be unsuitable
- the number of caravans proposed for the site.

iii. prepare an assessment of the suitability of the site and the use to be made of it in relation to:
- access for vehicles and pedestrians
- closeness to main road network
- ground conditions and levels of land
- how close it is to schools and other facilities
- existence of landscaping or whether the site could be screened by additional planting
- current and previous land uses for the site and compatibility with neighbouring uses.
- connections to essential services such as water and electricity

iv. You should also consider undertaking a search of the local land charges registers (held by the local authority) to establish whether

48 This will be the Planning Department of the local authority unless the land falls within the area of the Brecon Beacons, Pembrokeshire Coast or Snowdonia National Parks – if the land is located within a National Park, you should contact the National Park Authority.

there are any restrictions (such as injunctions) on the use of the land.

5. When you have completed all this you should seek a meeting with officers of the planning authority to discuss your proposals and the information provided. They will give you their professional opinion on the case prepared and may be able to suggest ways in which it could be made more acceptable to the planning authority. They will not, however, be able to give any guarantees or undertaking that planning permission will be granted. That decision will in most cases be made by the Planning Committee.

Making the planning application

6. You should make your planning application and wait for permission *before* you go on the site. Entering a site without planning permission is likely to be a breach of planning control and may be subject to enforcement action.

7. When making your application for a Gypsy and Traveller caravan site you should provide as much detail as possible at the outset including site layout, landscaping, access, and number of caravans.

What happens next?

8. Planning authorities will normally decide applications within eight weeks of their being submitted. If the planning authority requests further information from you on the application during this time, you should co-operate by responding to any such requests accordingly. If your planning permission is granted, you must comply with any conditions that accompany the permission. Your planning authority can advise on this process if you require any assistance. If you are refused planning permission, or the planning authority fail to determine the application within the 8 week period (or such longer period as you may have agreed with them), it is open to you to appeal to the Welsh Ministers. Any appeal must be submitted within 6 months of the date of the refusal of planning permission or of the date on when the application should have been decided (the end of the 8 weeks period or any longer period you might have agreed).

Details on how to submit an appeal and how the appeals process works is available on the Planning Appeals section of the Welsh Government website: http://gov.wales/topics/planning/appeals/?lang=en, or from:

The Planning Inspectorate Wales
Crown Buildings
Cathays Park
Cardiff
CF10 3NQ

Telephone: 029 2082 3866
Fax: 029 2082 5150
Email: wales@pins.gsi.gov.uk

9. Gypsies and Travellers should be aware of **Planning Aid Wales**, a voluntary service grant funded by the Welsh Government offering free, independent and professional advice and support on town planning matters to community groups and individuals who cannot afford to employ a planning consultant:

Planning Aid Wales
First Floor
174 Whitchurch Road
Heath
Cardiff
CF14 3NB

Telephone: 029 2062 5000
Email: Complete an online enquiry form at the website address listed below.
Website: www.planningaidwales.org.uk

APPENDIX C

Guidance

GUIDANCE ON MANAGING UNAUTHORISED CAMPING (ODPM/HOME OFFICE 2004)

1. Introduction

Background to the Guidance

1.1 *Managing Unauthorised Camping: A Good Practice Guide* was first issued by DETR and the Home Office in 1998 and has influenced the approaches adopted by local authorities, police and others. There have been a number of developments since 1998, which together have led to a need to re-examine and revise this guidance.

1.2 Relevant developments since the issue of the previous guidance in 1998 include:

- Amendments to DETR Circular 18/94 and to Chapter 5 of the *Good Practice Guide* were issued in July 2000. The amendments dealt with advice about 'toleration' of encampments and made clear that there will always be some circumstances where an unauthorised encampment cannot to be allowed to remain and where prompt action is required.
- The Association of Chief Police Officers (ACPO) issued guidance to its members on Collective Trespass or Nuisance on Land (including unauthorised camping) in 1996, 1999 and again in August 2000 in parallel with the DETR/Home Office *Guide*.
- In 2001 the results of research monitoring the impact of the DETR/Home Office *Good Practice Guide* were published. The report, by Edinburgh College of Art/Heriot-Watt University in conjunction with the Universities of Bristol and Cardiff, concludes that the *Guide* has been fairly influential in how local authorities and police forces tackle unauthorised camping. The research also highlights some perceived inadequacies and gaps in the guidance which this new Guidance aims to address. (See Annex C for a summary of the main findings.)
- The Human Rights Act 1998 (HRA) came into force in October 2000, incorporating the European Convention on Human Rights into British law.
- The Act means that all eviction and enforcement decisions made by public authorities must be 'proportionate'. Potential challenge under the HRA means that all decision-making must be fully recorded and evidenced to withstand scrutiny (see 5.7-5.9 and Annex D).
- The Race Relations (Amendment) Act 2000 has extended responsibilities given by the Race Relations Act 1976. Public authorities - including local authorities and the police - have a general duty to eliminate unlawful discrimination, promote equality of opportunity and good race relations in carrying out their functions. The 2000 Act also gives public bodies specific duties. Both Gypsies and Irish Travellers are now recognised as ethnic minorities against whom discrimination is unlawful. (See Annex D for more details.) In October 2003, the Commission for Racial Equality published a consultation draft entitled *Gypsies and Traveller - A Strategy 2003-2006* which sets out the Commissions own proposed role. It will be finalised during early 2004.
- A new £17 million Gypsy Sites Refurbishment Grant (GSRG) challenge fund was established with funding made available for three years from 2001/2. GSRG meets 75% of approved refurbishment costs for local authority Gypsy sites, with the aim of raising standards and helping to keep existing sites available for use - in part to help reduce the disruption of unauthorised camping. In its third year (2002/3) GSRG was extended to provide 100% funding for provision of transit and stopping place sites on a pilot basis. A further sum of £16 million has been announced for two further years of GSRG support (2004-6) for both site refurbishment and transit site and stopping place provision.
- The *National Policing Plan 2003-2006* identifies that the primary objective for the police service for the Plan's three-year duration is to deliver improved police performance and greater public reassurance with particular regard to four priorities including tackling anti-social behaviour and disorder.

- In March 2003, the Government published a White Paper *Respect and Responsibility*, which sets out the stand to be taken against anti-social behaviour. Communities, public services and authorities will be empowered to tackle anti-social behaviour. In return everyone is expected to play their part in setting and enforcing proper standards of behaviour. This guidance should be read in the context of that agenda.
- The Anti-social Behaviour Act 2003 includes measures to tackle anti-social behaviour, littering and fly-tipping. Part 7 introduces a new police power to evict unauthorised campers (see 6.12-6.13).

1.3 The Guidance has been produced against this developing background:

- In July 2002, the Office of the Deputy Prime Minister (ODPM) and the Home Office issued a joint press release outlining the Government's new approach to tackling unauthorised camping and signalling its intention to introduce stronger police powers to move on unauthorised encampments provided there was adequate site provision; these enhanced powers have now been provided in Part 7 of the Anti-social Behaviour Act 2003.
- In December 2002, the Government set out, and consulted upon, its broad policy towards unauthorised camping in a *Draft Framework Guide on Managing Unauthorised Gypsy/Traveller Encampments*. Central to the approach is the view that the use of stronger enforcement powers and adequate site provision must be linked.
- *Managing Unauthorised Camping Operational Guidance* was issued as a consultation paper by ODPM and the Home Office in April 2003 (closing date 23 May 2003). The consultation paper was sent to 1,500 organisations and a total of 87 responses were received from a wide range of organisations and individuals.
- Following consultation on the *Draft Framework Guide* and the *Operational Guidance*, it was decided that it would be clearer and less confusing to combine the two documents. The current Guidance therefore reflects the Government's broad policy towards unauthorised camping and incorporates comments received through consultation on both documents.
- As noted above, Part 7 of the Anti-social Behaviour Act 2003 introduces a new police power to evict unauthorised campers. ODPM and the Home Office will consult on guidance on the operation of these new powers in early 2004. Once finalised, it is intended that this will be incorporated into Chapter 6 of the current *Guidance on Managing Unauthorised Encampments* in the section on 'Powers Available to the Police'.

Aims of this Guidance

1.4 This Guidance takes account of all the changes outlined above. Its overall objective is to assist local authorities, police and others to tackle unauthorised camping to minimise the disruption it can cause. In doing this, it aims:

- To help strike an appropriate balance between the needs and legitimate expectations of members of the settled community, local businesses and other landowners, and Gypsies and Travellers.
- To set out recommended courses of action which all local authorities and police forces should follow to provide an effective response to unauthorised camping in their areas.
- To encourage a more consistent approach across the country, building on current good practice and sharing experience.
- To be practical yet creative in the face of a difficult reality.
- To show how to engage the settled and Gypsy/Traveller communities in order to achieve 'buy in' to the strategy, which is vital to ensure effective delivery.

Guidance on Managing Unauthorised Camping

1.5 The Guidance is primarily aimed at local authorities and police who share responsibility for managing unauthorised camping, but will also be relevant to all bodies likely to be involved in partnership approaches. While the Guidance is advisory, local authorities and police are strongly advised to bear it mind when devising and implementing their approaches, and are reminded that the courts may consider it as a material consideration in eviction or other enforcement decisions.

Use of Terms

1.6 Certain terms, conventions and abbreviations are used throughout the Guidance, and these are summarised in Box 1. A distinction is made between 'unauthorised camping' (a form of trespass) and 'unauthorised development' (a form of development of land without planning consent). This distinction is important because it affects the enforcement powers, which can be used. While paragraphs 6.20 to 6.24 refer specifically to planning enforcement powers available for dealing with 'unauthorised developments'; most of this Guidance deals with managing 'unauthorised encampments'.

Box 1 : Terms and abbreviations used in the Guidance

Gypsies and Travellers: used as a generic term to denote the whole population of those groups, families and individuals who subscribe to Gypsy/Traveller culture and/or lifestyle. The term encompasses ethnic Gypsies and Travellers and those who fall within the legal definition of a 'Gypsy' (s24 of the Caravan Sites and Control of Development Act 1960 as amended by s80 of the Criminal Justice and Public order Act 1994).

Unauthorised campers: people living on unauthorised encampments.

Unauthorised encampments: term restricted to encampments of caravans and/or other vehicles on land without the landowner or occupier's consent and constituting trespass.

Unauthorised development: Gypsy sites are among the types of development, which require planning permission. This term is used where such development is carried out on land with the agreement of the landowner, but without the appropriate planning permission.

Unauthorised sites: term used in Chapter 2 when describing findings from the Gypsy caravan count which include both unauthorised encampments and unauthorised development.

Sites or Gypsy/Traveller sites: term generally restricted to authorised sites with relevant planning consents (includes sites owned by local authorities and private owners).

Occupier of land: term used in its legal sense as 'the person entitled to possession of the land by virtue of an estate or interest held by him'. This might include a landowner, tenant or licensee but **not** unauthorised campers temporarily in 'occupation' of the land without any legal estate or interest.

ABCs : Acceptable Behaviour Contracts

ACPO : Association of Chief Police Officers

ASB : anti-social behaviour

ASBOs : Anti-Social Behaviour Orders

CJPOA : Criminal Justice and Public Order Act 1994

GSRG : Gypsy Sites Refurbishment Grant

HRA : Human Rights Act 1998

LPA : Local Planning Authority

ODPM : Office of the Deputy Prime Minister

PPG : Planning Policy Guidance Note

RSL : registered social landlord

TCPA : Town and Country Planning Act 1990

1.7 In the course of consultation on this Guidance a number of policy documents and leaflets were submitted as examples of current practice. Some of these are referred to in boxes at various points throughout the Guidance. Rather than reproducing submitted items in full or in part, the titles and author organisations are referred to and can be contacted by those who are interested. No more than five examples have been included under any heading. Chapter 9 provides useful references to other material referred to in this Guidance together with details of how they might be accessed.

2. Context

2.1 Gypsies and Travellers are a part of British life, and have been so for many centuries. They make up a very small minority within the wider population. Some Gypsies and Travellers live in caravans or other vehicles and follow a lifestyle, which is nomadic or semi-nomadic, in that it involves travel during at least part of the year.

2.2 At present there are more Gypsy/Traveller caravans in circulation than there are 'authorised' legal places for them to stop. At any one time there are around 3,500 Gypsy/Traveller caravans on unauthorised sites in England. Hardly any of these could be accommodated on existing authorised sites specifically provided for Gypsies and Travellers.

2.3 Unauthorised encampments vary enormously

- in size : from a couple of vehicles to groups with over 100 caravans
- in location : from the hidden away and unobtrusive to neighbours, to the highly visible and intrusive
- in behaviour of unauthorised campers : from those where no-one on the encampment causes any nuisance to others, to those where many cause nuisance
- in impact on the land : from groups who leave a camping area tidier than they found it, to those who leave the land damaged and with mountains of fly-tipped trade waste and domestic refuse

Numbers and Scale

2.4 Local authorities carry out the twice-yearly Gypsy caravan count for ODPM. It gives an indication of the numbers of Gypsy caravans on authorised (public and private) and unauthorised sites on set dates in January and July. While the counts may not be completely accurate - not least because of the technical problems of counting all Gypsy caravans over a large area - they provide local authorities with useful information about the accommodation needs of Gypsies who reside in or resort to their areas on the count dates. They also provide authorities; the Planning Inspectorate and the Secretary of State with some of the background information required when planning matters (development plans, planning applications, appeals and enforcement actions) are being considered.

2.5 The count has been carried out for over twenty years. Over this period the total number of Gypsy caravans has increased by some 70% while the number on unauthorised sites has decreased by between 500 to 1,000 from 4,600 (as counted in July 1979) thanks to the growth of private and public authorised site provision as well as movement of Gypsies and Travellers into housing.

2.6 In July 2003, about 14,700 Gypsy caravans were counted, of which 3,979 were on unauthorised sites. This latter figure can be split between 2,315 caravans on unauthorised encampments and 1,664 on Gypsy-owned land, which are likely to represent unauthorised developments. July counts consistently reveal higher numbers of Gypsy caravans on unauthorised sites. Over the past few years, on average, there have been about 800 more Gypsy caravans on unauthorised sites across England in July than in January, reflecting a seasonal element in travelling patterns.

2.7 Geographically, the counts consistently show highest numbers of Gypsy caravans on unauthorised sites in Eastern, Southeast and Southwest regions. Some local authorities, for example South Gloucestershire and some districts in Cambridgeshire and Norfolk, consistently have large numbers on unauthorised sites. Very generally, the patterns reflect traditional areas of resort for Gypsies and Travellers and - importantly - work opportunities for Gypsies and Travellers involved in various contracting (eg aspects of the building trade, garden and tree work), trading (eg carpets and furniture) and seasonal agricultural work.

2.8 There are three main Gypsy/Traveller groupings in England: traditional English (Romany) Gypsies, traditional Irish Travellers, and New Travellers. The first two groupings are accepted as ethnic minorities for the purposes of race relations legislation. There are smaller numbers of Welsh Gypsies and Scottish Travellers. The different groupings have different economic, social, cultural and lifestyle characteristics. While there are many examples of peaceful co-existence of Gypsy/Traveller groups, mixing can sometimes lead to friction.

Recent Research

2.9 Research for ODPM on the provision and condition of local authority Gypsy/Traveller sites in England was carried out by the Centre for Urban and Regional Studies at the University of Birmingham. A summary report was published in October 2002, and the full report in July 2003. The research made the following points.

- There is some evidence of a trend towards greater 'settlement' among some Gypsy/Traveller groups. However, other individuals and families have no desire to 'settle' and will continue to travel actively. Other more 'settled' Gypsies and Travellers - or their children - may take up active travelling when personal or family circumstances allow it. Some Gypsies and Travellers will continue to travel for the foreseeable future.
- In order to accommodate the desire for nomadism, between 2,000 and 2,500 additional authorised transit/mobility pitches were estimated to be needed before 2007. At present there are only about 500 transit pitches provided on authorised local authority and private sites.
- The research also estimated a requirement for up to 2,500 further pitches on residential sites for Gypsies and Travellers, which could be provided either by local authorities or Gypsies and Travellers themselves.
- Gypsies and Travellers, police and local authority personnel acknowledged to the researchers the existence of a minority of 'problem families' among the Travelling community who - whether on sites or on the roadside - are associated with criminal and anti-social behaviour, damage to property and fly-tipping. 'Problem families' cause problems for the majority law-abiding Gypsies and Travellers who also fear that this very visible minority disproportionately affects settled community images and stereotypes of the Travelling community as a whole.

2.10 The general context and recent research suggest:

- While unauthorised camping is much more significant in some areas, almost any local authority is at risk of encampment and should be prepared to deal with encampment.
- Unauthorised encampments vary widely. Local authorities, police and others dealing with unauthorised camping therefore need to be prepared to react to individual circumstances.
- Getting to know local travelling patterns and groups is critical to building a sound strategy. Getting to know individuals and building trust at a personal level with regular Gypsy and Traveller visitors can prevent problems developing.
- The nature of travelling and unauthorised encampment means it cannot be sensibly seen as a purely local phenomenon. An eviction in one area may have the effect of merely pushing the encampment over a local boundary for another authority to deal with. Local authorities and police forces should work together across boundaries to assess needs and determine strategies in response to unauthorised camping over the wider area. At a minimum, authorities should work together at county level, ideally at regional or sub-regional level.
- Good preparation and planning can minimise the disruption of unauthorised encampments. For this, sound intelligence and good networking is essential between local authorities and police forces in an area to keep everyone informed of Gypsy/Traveller groups and their movements. At the least, neighbouring authorities and other agencies that offer services for Gypsies and Travellers should always be informed when a large encampment is to be evicted.

3. Developing a Strategy for Unauthorised Camping

3.1 It is often impossible to predict just where and when an unauthorised encampment will occur. However, a purely reactive response to encampments as they arise is likely to be both inefficient and ineffective. Local authorities, police forces and other bodies need to be clear how they will respond to an encampment, who will take the lead, who else will be involved and under what circumstances.

3.2 To be effective this information should be clearly set out in an unauthorised encampments strategy and protocol. The strategy must be developed through consultation with all key stakeholders if it is to be effective; and it must seek to balance the rights and responsibilities of the travelling and settled communities.

Objectives of an Unauthorised Camping Strategy

3.3 The key objectives in a strategy for unauthorised encampments should include:

- Being able to plan ahead to minimise problems and to avoid the need to deal with everything on a crisis basis.
- Ensuring that the needs and legitimate expectations of all parties - Gypsies and Travellers, landowners and the settled community - are considered.
- Setting a framework within which clear, consistent and appropriate decisions can be made on unauthorised encampments to minimise disruption.
- Linking the approach to unauthorised camping firmly to other strategies and policies affecting Gypsies and Travellers (site provision, planning, health, education, housing etc).
- Directly involving all those with an interest in the process of developing the strategy so as to achieve maximum 'buy-in' and ownership.
- Reaching - as far as is possible - agreement so that all relevant parties will sign up to the strategy and its implementation.
- Clarifying roles and responsibilities so all parties to the strategy know who will do what in different circumstances, within the realistic limits of what is possible and allowing some flexibility for individual stakeholders.
- Ensuring that policies and approaches reflect the human rights of both the settled and travelling communities, and are compliant with race relations legislation including new requirements actively to promote equality of opportunity and good race relations.
- Ensuring the prevention of anti-social behaviour and effective enforcement against perpetrators.

3.4 Each local strategy will have its own objectives. Possible objectives are illustrated in Box 2.

Box 2 : Objectives of a Local Policy on Gypsy and Traveller Issues

The objectives of the policy are:

- To balance the rights and needs of resident communities with those of Gypsies and Travellers.
- To manage unauthorised encampments in an efficient and effective way taking account of the potential level of nuisance for local residents and the rights and responsibilities of Gypsies and Travellers.
- To work with partners in other authorities, the voluntary sector and the Police to address issues of social exclusion amongst Gypsy and Traveller communities.

Formulating the Strategy

Taking the Lead

3.5 It is appropriate that local authorities take the lead in formulating the strategy, and have responsibility for overseeing and monitoring its implementation, and for ensuring that the process is driven forward and does not become bogged down in inter-organisational wrangles and unacceptable delays. In areas of two-tier local government there should be clear agreement whether the county or district council will take the lead; both are clearly key players. Greater consistency and a wider perspective may be achieved where county councils take the lead.

3.6 The process of producing a strategy involves a number of key stages (see Box 3), which must be planned out and timetabled at the start. A named officer of the local authority should undertake this essential task, with the task fully recognised in his/her job description. It would be appropriate for the lead officer to be familiar with Gypsy and Traveller communities and their needs, and able to call on other experienced officers with skills suited to each stage of strategy development.

Box 3 : Key Stages in Developing a Strategy

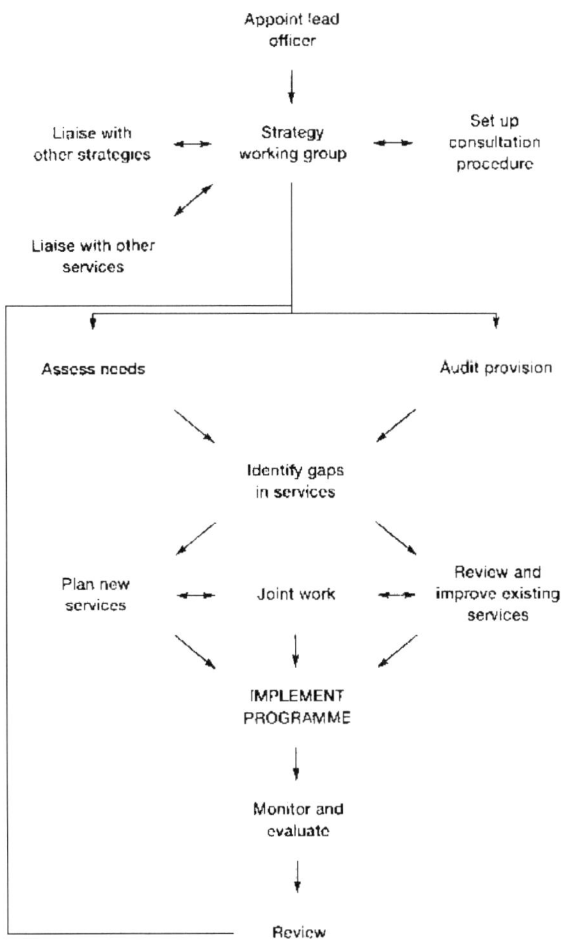

Who Should be Involved?

3.7 While local authorities take the lead, it is essential that many others are involved in the process and are willing to sign up to the strategy when it is agreed and published. Generating commitment among participants is an important part of the strategy building process.

3.8 Annex E shows the stakeholders - including Gypsies and Travellers - who might be involved in the strategy process and the ways in which they might be engaged. Key players should be closely involved, perhaps within a working party or steering group charged with moving the strategy process forward. Focus groups or consultative meetings could be used to engage other stakeholders. A designated local authority officer should be given overall responsibility for seeing the process through; he or she must have sufficient seniority to negotiate commitment from partners.

Box 4 : Consultation and Involvement in Developing a Strategy

Dorset County Council consulted widely on a Gypsy and Traveller Issues Report. Following this consultation a County Council Member Policy and Scrutiny Review Panel was formed which met nine times and heard evidence from a wide range of people including district council officers, county council officers concerned with education and children, police, groups representing Traveller views and a solicitor. One meeting was a site visit to residential site, an unauthorised encampment and to meet a farmer and residents neighbouring another unauthorised encampment.

West Sussex County Council adopted its strategy for Gypsies and Travellers in West Sussex following extensive consultation with interested parties and stakeholders. Bodies consulted included: district, town and parish councils, other local authorities, the police, business interests, landowners and farmers, residents' associations, organisations representing Gypsies, and members of the public.

Elements to be Included in the Strategy

3.9 There are ten essential elements to be thought through in any strategy for dealing with unauthorised camping:

- The legislative background for the strategy (this is summarised in Annex D which also deals more fully with human rights and race equality issues).
- Local information and data on which the strategy is based (see 3.10 and 3.11).
- Arrangements and protocols for sharing information (see 3.12).
- The approach to be taken on site provision (see Chapter 4).
- The policy to be followed when unauthorised encampments arise, setting out clearly the alternative courses of action to be taken and the circumstances which determine that action (see Chapter 5).
- Working arrangements and protocols for the involvement of different agencies (see 3.13-3.21).
- Resources for the strategy and constraints within which partners operate (see 3.22-3.24).
- Arrangements for communicating the strategy widely (see 3.25-3.28).
- Arrangements for monitoring the strategy and ensuring that it remains appropriate and is effective in practice, and meets race equality objectives (see 3.29-3.30).
- Involvement of other parts of the local authority, for example planning, education and social services, to ensure that there is a coherent authority-wide holistic approach to Gypsies/Travellers. In two-tier authorities this will involve both county and district councils (see 3.31).

Local Information for the Strategy

3.10 The starting point for a local strategy must be sound information on the characteristics and cultures of Gypsies and Travellers who reside in and resort to the area. Such information might include numbers, family structures, economic activity, travelling patterns, accommodation needs, health and education needs. Information on Gypsy/Traveller culture is relevant in helping to develop an effective strategy, which will actually work.

3.11 Gypsy caravan counts provide a starting point. Other potential sources of information include monitoring of unauthorised encampments, planning applications and education records. Box 5 provides examples of Gypsy/Traveller needs assessments, which have used information from a range of sources.

Box 5 : Examples of assessments of Gypsy/Traveller accommodation needs

Assessments of accommodation needs have been made by:

LB Southwark

Derbyshire (through the Derbyshire Gypsy Liaison Group)

Wychavon

Sevenoaks District Council (through the PPG 3 housing needs assessment process)

In addition to information from the caravan count and other secondary sources, these also drew on experience of local professionals and research with local Gypsies and Travellers through interviews and discussions. Detailed references are in Chapter 9.

Fenland District Council has undertaken a one-year information gathering exercise, which has involved Gypsies and Travellers on all local authority and private sites and on the roadside. This identified travelling routes and reasons for coming to the District and highlighted Gypsy/Traveller expectations on health and welfare and led to wider understanding of needs.

Sharing Information

3.12 Sharing information at county and sub-regional level can help particularly when looking at travelling patterns and considering site provision. Where information is shared between partner agencies working together, protocols may be developed to deal with issues of professional confidentiality and data protection. Arrangements will already have been made for sharing information in relation to crime and disorder matters between partners in Crime and Disorder Partnerships.

Working Arrangements and Protocols - Towards Implementation

3.13 A strategy needs to spell out working arrangements. The local authority should be the lead agency in managing unauthorised camping in its area, and the strategic working arrangements should reflect this. The lead authority might, by agreement, be either the county or the district council in two-tier areas. There will be circumstances - which should be spelled out clearly - when other agencies will take the lead, for example the police may lead in the use of Criminal Justice and Public Order Act (CJPOA) s61 where urgent action is needed.

3.14 Named officers should be identified in each local authority and police basic command unit with clear responsibility for dealing with unauthorised camping. These officers need to be at a level, which enables them to take on the ground operational and enforcement decisions. It is important that all key stakeholders - including Gypsies and Travellers, elected members, members of the public and other local authority/police officers - know who these officers are. The information could be made available through the local authority web pages and in leaflets provided to the settled and travelling communities.

3.15 The responsible officer in a local authority should establish procedures for reporting to and informing elected members about encampments. It is particularly important that local members (and parish councils in areas where they exist) are kept closely in touch with action affecting encampments in their wards. They can provide a valuable channel for communication between local authority officers and members of the public as a supplement to direct contacts. It is important that elected members are fully aware of the legislative background, local strategies and policies on managing unauthorised encampments including, for example, their race relations responsibilities.

3.16 Other organisations, departments and sections likely to be involved in dealing with unauthorised encampments and in providing services to Gypsies and Travellers should be identified. These are likely to include Traveller Education Services, social services, environmental health, housing and health services. It may be appropriate to include the RSPCA where unauthorised campers are known to have horses, dogs or other animals. Where trading activities are a cause for concern, trading standards officers, Inland Revenue and Customs and Excise officers might also be included. Lists should be compiled of named contact officers in each stakeholder body with full contact details including telephone, fax and e-mail addresses; these lists must be kept up-to-date as people change jobs or responsibilities.

3.17 Responsibilities within the strategy for dealing with unauthorised camping must be recognised within the job descriptions and workloads of all these officers. While calls on their time will be variable and responsive to the number and nature of encampments arising, it is important to think through cover arrangements for their release from other duties when needed. Over time it should be possible to build up an estimate of the likely demands on their time.

3.18 Regular liaison meetings involving officers in all stakeholder organisations encourage good personal and working relationships to develop. People respond more easily to requests from people they know and trust. Liaison meetings provide an opportunity to discuss current issues and concerns and to review on-the-ground working arrangements in the light of experience.

Box 6 : Examples of Liaison Groups

Bedfordshire County Council set up a multi-agency forum in January 2002, which has commissioned independent research on Traveller community needs.

Kent Unauthorised Encampments Monitoring and Liaison Groups, between them, include representatives of all three tiers of local government, the police, health and Gypsy organisations.

Wiltshire County Council has set up a Gypsy and Traveller Officers' Liaison Group comprising officers from all departments actively involved in managing unauthorised camping; The Group's membership may be widened in the future to include police, health services, district council housing officers and certain voluntary agencies. The County Council has also established a Residents' Consultation Group for residents of its semi-permanent Gypsy sites in the county.

3.19 In some areas working relationships have been further cemented by joint training events where officers from different organisations, with different perspectives and professional interests learn together. Training should be balanced in coverage and include human rights, equalities and race relations. In some places Gypsies and Travellers have been directly involved in providing training to local authority and police personnel.

Box 7 : Examples of Joint Training
Derbyshire Gypsy Liaison Group has been extensively involved in training with the police. In conjunction with **Derbyshire Constabulary** they have produced inter-agency interactive training exercises and facilitation notes on unauthorised encampments.
Fenland District Council runs training for all members of their local strategic partnership, Primary Care Trust, police, fire and rescue and voluntary organisations. This aims to explain the culture and traditions of Gypsy people. A freelance Gypsy journalist is central to the training and explains how public bodies can better work with the media over Gypsy issues.
West Sussex County Council has reached agreement at county level with **Sussex Police** on the way training should be approached. The County Council is encouraging relevant local authority staff in each district to get together with district police commanders to agree local implementation plans.

3.20 In many areas across the country working arrangements between relevant bodies have been formalised into protocols or service level agreements. These set out the respective responsibilities of signatories, lines of command and communication, and may include performance targets.

- Protocols commonly involve local authorities (county and district councils in two-tier local government areas) and police.
- Protocols or service level agreements may also be relevant between lead local authority departments and education, health and welfare departments involved in making welfare enquiries at encampments. Such agreements set out the means of communication to be followed and provide targets for response times.

Box 8 : Examples of Protocols between Local Authorities and Police
Derbyshire: Good practice guide for unauthorised encampments: Joint protocol between Derbyshire County Council, Derbyshire Gypsy Liaison Group, Derbyshire Constabulary and the NHS.
Devon: Joint Policy and Practice Guidelines relating to people of nomadic lifestyle residing in or resorting to Devon: Devon County Council and Devon & Cornwall Constabulary.
Essex: A joint protocol for managing unauthorised encampments in Harlow: Essex County Council, Harlow District Council and Essex Police.
Kent: Kent protocol on the management of unauthorised encampments: Kent County Council, district and unitary councils, Kent County Constabulary.
Leicestershire: The Code of Practice for Travellers in Leicestershire, Leicester and Rutland: county council, district and unitary councils and Leicestershire Constabulary.
Wiltshire: Wiltshire County Council and Wiltshire Constabulary are currently developing a protocol for managing unauthorised camping incidents. This builds upon a successful Inter-Departmental protocol already in place within the County Council, which includes, amongst other sensitive issues, a Disclosure Statement, which addresses data protection and information sharing constraints.

3.21 In a few areas (for example Milton Keynes) arrangements for joint working between the local authority and police are still closer in a jointly staffed 'unit'. Advocates refer to the consistency of approach possible through true joint working; it avoids unnecessary duplication of effort; it means that there is less possibility of people being referred backwards and forwards between organisations. In such a structure it is important that reporting lines and accountability arrangements are carefully thought through.

Box 9 : Joint Working
Northamptonshire: A Countywide Traveller Unit has been established jointly funded by district councils, the county council, police and primary care trust, with a contribution from the Northamptonshire Chamber. Police and health workers are seconded to the Unit.

Resources

3.22 The Government believes that spending to achieve the pro-active approach towards site provision and managing unauthorised camping as set out here represents better value for money than the current position. Spending now on site provision should reduce the costs of dealing with unauthorised camping.

3.23 Local authorities and police should seek to apply Best Value principles to their strategy for dealing with unauthorised camping. Box 10 sets out some of the actions, which might be helpful in an area with extensive and/or frequent unauthorised encampments.

Box 10 : An Application of Best Value Principle to Dealing with Unauthorised Camping

Best Value principles suggest that local authorities and the police should:

- Identify what they are spending at present on dealing with unauthorised camping. Few organisations keep accurate records, which accurately identify all the costs involved in unauthorised camping, for example responding to complaints from the public.
- Estimate the costs borne by others, including local businesses and landowners. It may not be possible always to arrive at a monetary value, but attempting it ensures that wider implications of actions are clearer.
- Consider the indirect costs of unauthorised encampments in terms of, for example, additional costs to health and education services and others involved in fostering the greater social inclusion of Gypsies and Travellers.
- Compare these with the possible costs and benefits of taking a more pro-active approach to site provision and managing unauthorised camping on a partnership basis.

3.24 At present not all authorities have a budget for dealing with unauthorised camping, and staffing responsibilities are sometimes vague. Good practice suggests that all authorities should have a formal budget, based on past experience and best intelligence on future needs.

Communicating the Strategy

3.25 The strategy for unauthorised camping should be published and widely disseminated to local businesses, landowners, local residents, and Gypsies and Travellers. Objectives in publishing and publicising the strategy include:

- Making clear what can be achieved and over what time scales so as to mould realistic expectations among both the settled and Gypsy/Traveller communities.
- Making clear who is responsible for what elements of the strategy and its implementation. For example, it is appropriate that all members of the public should contact the police directly over matters involving crime associated with unauthorised encampments and that Gypsies and Travellers are encouraged to do so. The local authority might be the appropriate point of contact for other issues. This means listing names, telephone numbers and addresses.

3.26 A number of local authorities already provide information leaflets and/or have material on their web-sites dealing with unauthorised camping. Use of web-sites to provide information on local policy accords well with the Government's local e-government strategy.

Box 11 : Example of Information Leaflet on Unauthorised Camping
In **Bedfordshire**, the county council, district councils, Bedfordshire Police and the Bedford & Luton Community NHS Trust have jointly produced a leaflet *Travellers and the Law*. **Kent Unauthorised Encampments Working Group** has produced a leaflet *Unauthorised Encampment : a document to answer your frequently asked questions*. **Suffolk County Council** has produced a leaflet Unlawful Traveller Encampments in Suffolk, which is largely based on questions and answers. **Telford Borough Council** has leaflets primarily intended to provide information to members of the public and landowners; these are also available on its web-site.

3.27 A 'communications strategy' is itself an important element in the strategy towards unauthorised encampments. A positive and co-ordinated approach to managing communication is an important element of a comprehensive strategy. Many bodies are likely to be involved in dealing with unauthorised encampments and other Gypsy/Traveller matters. A key aim of this strategy is to assure the travelling and settled community that effective action is being taken where necessary.

3.28 Deciding a co-ordinated approach to media briefings will reduce confusion and the possibility of conflicting accounts. The Commission for Racial Equality has issued Guidance to journalists on *Travellers, Gypsies and the media* which local authorities may find useful in encouraging a positive, or at least neutral, local press coverage for local encampments and other Gypsy/Traveller issues.

Monitoring the Strategy

3.29 It is important to monitor the strategy as it is implemented and review the need for change in the light of that monitoring.

- Monitoring arrangements need to be planned and resourced from the beginning. It would be appropriate for the local authority, as lead agency, to take responsibility, perhaps reporting back to a steering group including representatives of other key agencies.
- Obviously monitoring should identify progress towards meeting the objectives of the strategy. Protocols and other arrangements for partnership working are other obvious areas to be monitored and reviewed. In all cases, monitoring should identify areas, which have worked well and less well in order to learn from the process in recasting the strategy and/or its implementation.
- Above all, monitoring is required to ensure that the strategy leads to action on the ground. The strategy should not be merely a paper exercise.

3.30 Sound information is essential to monitoring. The Government sees great merit in encouraging local authorities, along with their police partners, to develop improved standard records of unauthorised encampments. As a minimum, information should be collected and monitored on the location of encampments, the number of caravans/vehicles involved and the duration of each encampment. Standardisation of information would allow aggregated data to be assembled across a county or region and would facilitate the exchange of data about unauthorised encampments between different areas. A review of the national Gypsy counts system has been undertaken and an amended system is to be introduced shortly.

A Holistic Approach

3.31 Unauthorised camping does not exist in a vacuum. Developing a strategic approach towards managing unauthorised camping provides an opportunity for local authorities and others to consider policies towards Gypsies and Travellers in a holistic manner, if they have not already done so. Relevant policy areas are land use planning (including development planning, planning control and enforcement), housing and homelessness, environmental health, health and education. Many general strategic approaches to dealing with local issues, crime and social exclusion are also very relevant and might refer to Gypsies and Travellers. Under-pinning all such work is policy on diversity, equality and human rights - not just towards Gypsies and Travellers, but towards the whole population of a local authority area.

Box 12 : Example of Contents of a Policy on Gypsy and Traveller Issues

The Dorset County Council Gypsy and Traveller Policy 2003 is comprehensive in coverage. Its sections are:

1. Introduction
2. Objectives
3. Travelling patterns in Dorset
4. Policies on site Provision and the management of unauthorised encampments
5. Site protection
6. Land use planning
7. Housing
8. Education, health and welfare
9. Making decisions on unauthorised encampments
10. Provision of services for encampments
11. Keeping people informed
12. Strategic background and joint working arrangements
13. Staff and other resource issues

Box 13 : Strategies and Partnerships Relevant to Gypsies and Travellers
■ Local strategic partnerships and community strategies ■ Community Cohesion Policies ■ Supporting People ■ Homelessness Strategies ■ Children and Young People's Partnerships ■ Sure Start and Early Years ■ Connexions ■ Primary Care Group Trust commissioning plans ■ Crime and Disorder Reduction Strategies ■ Race Equality Schemes ■ Anti-poverty strategies ■ Local Agenda 21 strategies In **Devon** there are examples of holistic working: ■ *Travellers Making Connexions : A good practice guide for multi-agency work*, Connexions Cornwall & Devon and Devon County Council ■ The Health Forum Social Inclusion Task Group has identified Travellers in Devon as a group where inequalities in health exist alongside other service provision issues. A Traveller Forum has been formed with a wide membership including Travellers. A report is being finalised addressing *Travellers Wellbeing*.

4. Site Provision and Unauthorised Camping

4.1 Local authorities do not have a duty to provide sites for Gypsies. They do, however, have the power to do so (under s24 of the Caravan Sites and Control of Development Act 1960). Circulars 1/94 and 18/94 both encourage authorities to consider the need for site provision. Local Planning Authorities essentially control the creation of new public and private authorised sites through development plan policies and development control.

A Range of Accommodation

4.2 Site provision is an essential element in any strategy. In a context where the number of Gypsy caravans exceeds the number of authorised places where they can stop - which is the case in England - provision of suitable accommodation for Gypsies and Travellers must be seen as a vital part of an approach to dealing with unauthorised camping. Population increase and family growth among Gypsies and Travellers must also be considered.

4.3 All local authorities should review the provision of sites for Gypsies and Travellers. Site provision can be provided publicly or privately and take a variety of forms:

- Residential sites provide long-term settled accommodation. Most current local authority site provision is residential. Many private sites also provide long-term accommodation for individual families on an owner-occupier basis or commercially.
- Transit sites are also provided both by local authorities and private owners, though much less frequently. Transit sites, with varying levels of amenities, provide for Gypsies and Travellers who want to stay for a period of up to about three months in an area.
- Less formal stopping places are also rare. These would be identified areas of land to which Gypsies and Travellers could be directed when they come to an area, and where they could stop for a short time - perhaps up to a month.
- Emergency stopping places would be locations where families have stopped which are judged suitable for a short stay. Facilities might be temporarily provided at such locations.

4.4 All local authorities experiencing unauthorised encampments should provide either transit sites or stopping places to cater for Gypsies and Travellers moving within or passing through their area. This might be done on a collaborative basis between neighbouring authorities. Some provision could be made by private individuals at no cost to the local authority.

4.5 Gypsies and Travellers should be involved in site planning and design to ensure that sites are well used and are safe and appropriate to the cultures and lifestyles of Gypsy and Traveller families, including children.

Site Provision and Land Use Planning

4.6 The Government's policy on Gypsy sites and planning is set out in DoE Circular 1/94 and it provides for a flexible approach. The Circular puts Gypsies on the same footing in planning law as everyone else whilst recognising their special circumstances. It is designed to ensure that applications for Gypsy caravan sites are treated in the same way as any other form of development. It places emphasis on assessing the need for Gypsy site provision (also stressed in *Planning Policy Guidance (PPG) 3: Housing*, para 13). Local authorities should identify suitable locations for Gypsy sites in their development plans wherever possible (re-iterated in *PPG 12: Development Plans*, para 4.14). Failing this they should identify clear and realistic criteria for suitable locations as a basis for their site provision policies. Local authorities should encourage Gypsies to consult with them on planning matters before buying land on which they intend to camp and for which planning permission would be required.

4.7 Instances of unauthorised camping may be reduced if local planning authorities follow the advice in DoE Circular 1/94 which encourages them to identify suitable sites in their local plans wherever possible for Gypsies to buy and to settle (see 4.6).

- Sites on traditional routes are likely to be well used and sustainable. It may be easier to gain acceptance for sites in areas where Gypsies and Travellers traditionally stop and are a known part of the local community.
- Sites, which are screened from view, may be deemed suitable by Gypsies and Travellers as well as by the settled community.
- Granting temporary planning permissions for sites in a planned sequence might make provision more acceptable to the settled community. This is particularly appropriate for stopping places where little fixed infrastructure may be involved. Temporary sites could be provided in advance of longer-term development proposals.

Authorised Sites and Managing Unauthorised Camping

4.8 If authorised sites are to contribute effectively to reducing the disruption caused by some unauthorised camping, site management and management of unauthorised camping must be integrated. At the least:

- Local authority and police officers dealing with unauthorised encampments should have information about vacancies on local authority sites within their area, and ideally in neighbouring areas. Ideally, local authority officers should also be prepared to assist unauthorised campers without local accommodation to find places on privately-owned sites and in permanent housing if this is requested.
- There must be close working between site managers and local authority and police officers dealing with unauthorised camping over allocations of pitches on sites. Site managers may be aware of issues around Gypsy/Traveller group and family compatibility, which must be taken into account when allocating pitches on residential sites.
- More specifically, where police are seeking to use the new powers under s62A of the Criminal Justice and Public Order Act 1994 (inserted by the Anti-social Behaviour Act 2003), a police officer must consult the local authorities in whose area the encamped land lies about the availability of suitable pitches on relevant sites. ODPM and the Home Office will be consulting in detailed guidance on the use of these powers, which will then be incorporated into a revised version of this Guidance.
- Transit sites and stopping places must be managed to prevent Gypsies and Travellers staying longer than the maximum permitted stay. Site turnover must be maintained if such sites are to continue to cater for Gypsies and Travellers with a nomadic lifestyle. Reluctance to move from transit sites and stopping places may indicate a need for further residential site provision.

Site Protection

4.9 Protection of land, which is vulnerable to unauthorised encampment, is a valid part of a strategy, but should not be the sole strategy. Some authorities have undertaken protection works on their own land and/or have advised private landowners how best to secure their land.

- Site protection work is not cheap. A risk assessment should be carried out before investing, including consideration of risks of encampment, nuisance arising from encampment on that land, and cost of effectively protecting the site.

- Site protection and continuing development of open land can have the effect of forcing Gypsies and Travellers to camp in prominent and still more unsuitable places including farmland and other private land, prompting complaints from the landowner. Site protection must only be considered alongside the creation of permanent sites, transit sites and stopping places to ensure that there are places for Gypsies and Travellers to stop without causing disruption.

5. Making Decisions on Unauthorised Encampments

5.1 This chapter deals with some of the considerations to be borne in mind by local authorities, police and others when making decisions about how to deal with unauthorised encampments as they occur. Its aim is to help:

- To make clear, consistent and appropriate decisions on unauthorised encampments.
- To ensure that a balance is struck between the needs of all parties.
- To ensure that decisions taken will withstand challenge.

5.2 Sections below cover the policy statement; carrying out welfare enquiries; and reaching decisions.

A Policy Statement

5.3 It is important that the local authority produces a policy statement, which includes:

- A statement of which travelling people the policy relates to. Many policies relate to **all** travelling groups including non-traditional Travellers since the issues raised by encampments are similar and the education, welfare and homelessness duties owed are identical.
- Identification of the action to be considered in respect of land not owned by the local authority (see 6.17).
- The responsibilities of different authorities and agencies. The statement should set out which authority will act in specified circumstances where county and district councils, and sometimes other agencies including national ones, share responsibilities (for example on highways), and the circumstances in which the police might take the lead.
- The alternative courses of action to be taken. This should set out clearly the circumstances in which eviction processes would be instigated and the circumstances in which an encampment might remain for a period under regular review.
- The characteristics of encampment sites, which would normally trigger rapid eviction proceedings (see 5.4-5.6).
- The standards of behaviour expected from unauthorised campers on encampments (see 7.3).
- The circumstances in which an authority might provide rubbish storage and collection services, water supply or toilets to an encampment (see 7.15).

Box 14 : Examples of Policy Statements and Procedures Guides
Adur District Council: Policy and guidance: Travellers and unauthorised encampments.
Dorset County Council*:* Dealing with unauthorised camping: procedure.
Leicestershire County Council : Policy and Administration Procedure statement in relation to unauthorised encampments by Gypsies and Travellers
Suffolk County Council : Unlawful Traveller encampments in Suffolk : a strategy
Wiltshire County Council: Policy statement in relation to unauthorised Gypsy and Traveller encampments.

Unacceptable Encampment Locations

5.4 Unauthorised encampments are almost always, by definition, unlawful. However, while there are insufficient authorised sites, it is recognised that some unauthorised camping will continue. There are locations, however, where encampment will not be acceptable under any circumstances. Each encampment location must be considered on its merits against criteria such as health and safety considerations for the unauthorised campers, traffic hazard, public health risks, serious environmental damage, genuine nuisance to neighbours and proximity to other sensitive land-uses. The list in Box 15 of sites where an unauthorised encampment would not normally be acceptable is illustrative only and is not intended to be exhaustive.

Box 15 : Some Examples of Types of Site where Unauthorised Camping would Normally be Unacceptable

- A Site of Special Scientific Interest (SSSI) where an encampment endangers a sensitive environment or wildlife
- School car park or playing fields (especially in term time)
- An urban park
- Car parks, including hospital, supermarket or leisure facility car parks
- An industrial estate
- Recreation ground and public playing fields
- A site where pollution from vehicles or dumping could damage ground water or water courses
- A derelict area with toxic waste or other serious ground pollution
- A village green or other open area within a residential area
- The verge of a busy road where fast traffic is a danger to unauthorised campers' children

5.5 Wherever possible, local authorities and/or police should seek to prevent Gypsies and Travellers from establishing an encampment in an unacceptable location. Where this proves impossible, they should attempt to encourage the unauthorised campers to move to an authorised site where available. Identification of possible 'acceptable' sites could assist local authorities and the police in the management of unauthorised encampments in circumstances where there are no available pitches on authorised sites. If the unauthorised campers refuse to move from an unacceptable location, eviction processes (including appropriate welfare enquiries) should be commenced.

5.6 To be effective, such an approach requires a very swift response from the local authority and/or police. Ideally, initial contact should be made within 24 hours of the encampment being established.

Welfare Enquiries

Requirements to Make Welfare Enquiries

5.7 Local authorities may have obligations towards unauthorised campers under other legislation (mainly regarding children, homelessness and education). Authorities should liaise with other local authorities; health and welfare services who might have responsibilities towards the families of unauthorised campers. Some form of effective welfare enquiry is necessary to identify whether needs exist which might trigger these duties or necessitate the involvement of other sectors, including the voluntary sector, to help resolve issues. The police and other public bodies who might be involved in dealing with unauthorised encampments do not have comparable duties but must still, as public servants, show common humanity to those they meet.

5.8 The Human Rights Act (HRA) applies to all public authorities including local authorities (including town and parish councils), police, public bodies and the courts. With regard to eviction, the issue that must be determined is whether the interference with Gypsy/Traveller family life and home is justified and proportionate. Any particular welfare needs experienced by unauthorised campers are material in reaching a balanced and proportionate decision. The human rights of members of the settled community are also material if an authority fails to act to curb nuisance from an encampment.

5.9 Case law is still developing with regard to the sorts of welfare enquiries, which the courts consider necessary to properly taken decisions in relation to actions against unauthorised encampments. Cases are testing the requirements under different powers, and the requirements placed on different agencies (authorities, police, and other public landowners). Very generally, court decisions to date suggest:

- All public authorities need to be able to demonstrate that they have taken into consideration any welfare needs of unauthorised campers prior to making a decision to evict.
- The courts recognise that the police and other public bodies have different resources and welfare duties from local authorities. Generally the extent and detail of appropriate enquiries is less for police and non-local authority 'public authorities'.
- In the case of local authorities, the onus of making welfare enquiries appears to be greater when using Criminal Justice and Public Order Act 1994 s77, where the use of the section can result in criminal sanctions, than when using landowners' civil powers against trespass. Local authorities should, however, make thorough welfare enquiries whatever powers they intend to use.

5.10 Because local authorities have appropriate skills and resources to enable them to make (or to co-ordinate) welfare enquiries, it is considered good practice for local authorities to respond positively to requests for assistance in making enquiries from the police or other public bodies.

Procedures for Making Enquiries

5.11 Speed of response is key to managing unauthorised encampments so as to minimise disruption. There should be a recognised system, which ensures that all reports of new encampments reach the lead officer as quickly as possible. Passing on information rapidly should be part of protocols and joint working arrangements between agencies/departments (see 3.20). Staff on local authority switchboards and at call centres should know how to handle calls from the public and to whom they should be referred. Police call handlers require similar briefing and information that might take the form of frequently asked questions (FAQs) based on mutually agreed policies.

5.12 Ideally, an initial visit should be made to a new encampment within 24 hours of the authority becoming aware of it unless the location is very unobtrusive or remote. An encampment should always be visited very rapidly if initial reports indicate exceptional problems. The initial visit is the first step in making decisions about, and effectively managing, unauthorised encampments. It has several functions:

- To check the accuracy of initial reports/complaints of an encampment, and to gather basic information on its location and size. This information enables issues such as land ownership to be checked.
- Where an encampment location is likely to prove unacceptable (see 5.4 5.5), officers at the initial visit might try to encourage the unauthorised campers to move to an authorised site where a place is available, or to a less immediately unacceptable location chosen by the unauthorised campers themselves.
- To collect basic information from the unauthorised campers about the families and vehicles involved, and about past and intended future movement, anticipated length of stay and reasons for stay.

- To collect initial information from unauthorised campers on any perceived welfare, health or educational needs. Such information is the starting point for liaison with other relevant departments. Where school-age children are present, the Traveller Education Service should be notified. Similarly social services or health authorities should be notified where there seem to be social, welfare or health needs to be further assessed and met.
- The initial visit should note the state of the encampment - how well it is kept, any damage, rubbish accumulation and so on. This will provide baseline information from which subsequent changes can be monitored. Photographs can provide a useful record of potential health and safety issues; people should not be photographed without their express consent.
- Officers at an initial visit can also note any features of the encampment or its location that is likely to be particularly problematic or which might affect future decisions.
- The initial visit is also an opportunity for giving information to unauthorised campers about:
    - the standard of behaviour expected of them. Where a Code of Expected Behaviour has been developed (see 7.3 et seq), copies should be provided and, where necessary in the event of any reading difficulties, be clearly explained to avoid misunderstanding;
    - what is going to happen next, what procedures the authority or police are likely to follow and what this means for the unauthorised campers; and
    - names and addresses of local services and sources of advice likely to be useful to the unauthorised campers. Information ideally should include locations of housing providers, health, education and social services, and waste disposal facilities.

Box 16 : Examples of Information Leaflets Provided to Gypsies and Travellers
Information leaflets for Gypsies and Travellers normally set out the main policy approach adopted by the local authority, a code of expected behaviour and useful contact addresses for services and advice.
Devon County Council: On the Road - Guidelines for people of a nomadic lifestyle
Dorset County Council: Notice to Travellers
Essex County Council: Guidance notes for Gypsy/Travellers in Essex
Suffolk County Council: Notice to Travellers on unauthorised camp sites

5.13 Welfare enquiries should always be carried out as swiftly as possible where the initial visit indicates that the unauthorised campers may have serious unmet health or welfare needs or where it seems likely that the encampment will lead to serious disruption or nuisance.

5.14 It is vital that all information given and received during visits and enquiries is clearly recorded. This is helpful to the local authority, especially if different officers are involved at a later date. It will also form the basis of an audit trail for subsequent decisions in case of challenge. Pro formas have been developed by many authorities (see Box 17) to collect and record this initial information. Some authorities and police forces have developed scoring matrices as an aid to assessing risk and decision making.

Box 17 : Example of a Pro-Forma used to Record Data on Encampments
Adur District Council: Welfare checks for Travellers
Coventry City Council: Traveller enquiry form, and Form for guidance of authorising officer
Devon County Council: Unauthorised occupation notification, and Personal circumstances questionnaire
Devon & Cornwall Constabulary: Checklist and record of action taken by officers attending alleged trespass on land
Leicestershire County Council: Unauthorised occupation Social Assessment Report

5.15 Information gathered in the course of visits and enquiries is subject to data protection legislation. Authorities should make clear the purposes for which information is being collected and give assurances about how it will be used and to whom it might be passed. Chapter 9 provides reference to the web-site of the Information Commissioner for guidance on data protection issues.

5.16 Local authorities have no powers to insist that information be given. Some information may be confidential and require the unauthorised camper to give consent to follow up, for example, medical records. A sensitive approach is necessary, and authorities should always bear in mind issues of confidentiality and data protection. Where information is refused, the fact that questions were asked and not answered should be clearly recorded to avoid any subsequent claim for failure to take some relevant consideration into account. If unauthorised campers give reasons for not responding, these should also be noted. Unauthorised campers should be informed of any possible consequences of not providing information when requested. If they want to provide information through another person they trust, they should be able to do so provided that arrangements can be made quickly.

5.17 Reasonable attempts should be made to get information from unauthorised campers not present at the time of a visit. Other members of the group may sometimes be able to provide information. A letter or self-completion form may be left with clear instructions for its return (at no cost to the unauthorised camper). All such actions should be clearly recorded, and if there is still no response, this should be noted.

5.18 When visiting and managing unauthorised encampments, local authorities and police should adopt the same legal and careful health and safety procedures and practices as they apply to any other activity they are engaged in.

Reaching Decisions

5.19 Decisions about what action to take in connection with an unauthorised encampment must be made in the light of information gathered. Decisions must always be:

- 'Lawful' - that is in line with local policy and procedures, taking into account relevant considerations and not taking into account the irrelevant.
- 'Reasonable' in the legal sense of not being perverse or irrational in the light of the evidence available.
- 'Balanced' in that they take account of the rights and needs of both the settled community and Gypsies and Travellers.
- 'Proportionate' - what is proportionate will vary according to the precise circumstances of each encampment, including the nature of the location and the behaviour and needs of the unauthorised campers.

Making Decisions

5.20 Any welfare needs of unauthorised campers are a material consideration for local authorities when deciding whether to start eviction proceedings or to allow the encampment to remain longer. Welfare needs do not give an open-ended 'right' for unauthorised campers to stay as long as they want in an area. For example, the presence of a pregnant woman or school age children does not, per se, mean that an encampment must remain indefinitely. To defer an eviction which is justified on other grounds, the need must be more immediate and/or of a fixed term. Box 18 gives some examples of welfare needs to be considered by local authorities, although the list is not intended to be exhaustive and all cases must be judged on their individual merits. Good practice suggests that eviction should be delayed while such acute welfare needs exist and are being met; during this period the encampment should be pro-actively managed (see Chapter 7).

Box 18 : Some Examples of Welfare Needs to be Considered in Eviction Decisions
Advanced pregnancy: a period shortly before and after birth in normal circumstances; longer on medical advice if there are complications. **Ill health**: indicators might include a hospital appointment booked; in-patient treatment of a close family member; period during which a condition can be diagnosed, stabilised and a course of treatment started. **Educational needs**: children in school if within 4 weeks of the end of term or if access to special education has been gained.

5.21 In some circumstances it may be appropriate to exclude a single person or family with welfare need from eviction action taken against the larger group. However, this must always be sensitively handled to ensure that an individual is not isolated and unsupported, leading to still greater need. In practice, groups may prefer to move on together. It is important that the appropriate authority follows up identified welfare needs whether or not the encampment is moved on.

Arrangements for Making Decisions

5.22 Responsibility for taking decisions must be clearly identified within the authority's (and/or police) policies and procedures, whether delegated to officers or retained by elected members.

5.23 Some authorities have established special procedures for reaching decisions, for example:

- Structures which ensure that decisions are taken by officers who have not been directly involved in site visits or contact with unauthorised campers. It is argued that this increases the consistency, logic and objectivity of decisions. Since all evidence is presented to the 'authorising officer' in writing such a procedure ensures that there is a clear record of the decision and the issues considered.

- Some authorities have arrangements for joint site visits and/or case conferences for reaching decisions on 'difficult' cases. Such procedures ensure that all parties are represented and have the opportunity to influence the decision. Case conferences could include representatives of the unauthorised campers and the local settled community, although there would need to be clear 'rules' for making decisions in the absence of consensus.

5.24 It is important that decisions to pro-actively manage encampments for a period are kept under review. Circumstances can change quickly, for example if newcomers join the encampment and swell its size unacceptably or if behaviour deteriorates.

Recording Decisions

5.25 All decisions (including any decision to allow an encampment to remain for a period) must be fully recorded and documented. Any damage and nuisance should be charted in writing; a photographic or video record might also be taken in support. Records should also be kept of all complaints received about the encampment, with comments as to their validity. Information passed to unauthorised campers should be recorded, along with offers of assistance made - for example help with a housing application, offer of a pitch on an authorised site - and the response. Similarly it would be good practice to record the fact that an encampment was unproblematic and did **not** cause nuisance or damage. Any complaints received, including any from Gypsy/Traveller unauthorised campers, should be recorded.

5.26 Records can provide valuable information on the number and nature of unauthorised encampments in an area and which sites are particularly prone to encampment. This information is useful in assessing the need for further site provision, site protection priorities and in setting budgets and appropriate staffing levels. It provides material on which a risk-based response to encampments could be developed drawing on past experience relating to the site or the group/family involved. Standard minimum information, to be collected in all areas, as suggested in paragraph 3.30, would facilitate information sharing and better planning.

6. Resorting to Eviction

6.1 This chapter covers the eviction process itself. Once a decision to evict an unauthorised encampment has been properly taken, the aims should be:

- To act quickly and efficiently.
- To use powers most appropriate to the circumstances.
- To reduce scope for challenge through the courts by ensuring that policies and procedures are properly followed so as to reduce cost and delay.

6.2 The first three sections relate to eviction powers available to local authorities, police and other landowners. The final section in the chapter (6.20-6.24) deals with local planning authority powers to enforce against unauthorised development (ie Gypsies and Travellers 'developing' land as a caravan site without planning consent).

Powers Available to Local Authorities

6.3 Many encampments are dealt with through negotiation. Where this fails, local authorities have two main sets of powers to tackle unauthorised encampments:

- A landowner (including a local authority) can obtain a possession order in the civil courts requiring the removal of trespassers from property, including land. Under the Civil Procedures Rules Part 55 the claim must be issued in the County Court in whose jurisdiction the property or land is situated. Exceptionally the claim may be issued in the High Court if there is substantial risk of public disturbance or of serious harm to persons or property which properly require immediate determination.
- The Criminal Justice and Public Order Act 1994 (CJPOA) gives local authorities in England and Wales powers to make directions to leave land being used by itinerant groups (s77). It is an offence to fail to comply with such a direction. In proceedings for an offence under this section, it is a defence for the accused to show that his failure to leave or to remove the vehicle or other property as soon as practicable, or his re-entry with a vehicle, was due to illness, mechanical breakdown or other immediate emergency. If the direction to leave is not complied with, the local authority can apply to magistrates' court for an order requiring the removal of vehicles and any occupants from the land (s78).

6.4 Box 19 summarises some of the main features of the two sets of powers, highlighting differences and similarities.

Box 19 : Some Features of Civil and Criminal Justice and Public Order Act Powers for Local Authorities

Civil Powers	CJPOA ss77 and 78
Only on land in LA ownership	On private as well as LA land where encampment is without the consent of the occupier of the land
Possession orders are effective against anyone on the land, not necessarily those resident when the notice was first served	Only effective against people directed to leave. All newcomers must be served with directions to leave

Civil orders can cover wide geographical areas where a real threat of further encampment can be demonstrated	It is an offence for unauthorised campers to return within three months to land they have been directed to leave; only applies to the same individuals
There is no defence to an action for trespass (other than showing non-trespass)	It is a defence for the accused to show that his failure to leave or to remove the vehicle or other property as soon as practicable, or his re-entry with a vehicle, was due to illness, mechanical breakdown or other immediate emergency
No criminalising effect	Can have the effect of criminalising Gypsy/Traveller unauthorised campers who fail to move when directed to leave, a factor taken seriously by the courts. In practice, authorities normally proceed against the unauthorised campers by way of complaint for an order requiring them to remove their vehicles from the land, and not for the criminal offence of contravening a direction to leave the land.
County court bailiffs can be used; their services must be paid for and may lead to delay in enforcement. . It is recommended that the police attend such evictions in order to prevent a breach of the peace	Responsibility for eviction lies with the local authority. Officers or agents of the local authority may use reasonable force to evict. It is recommended that the police attend such evictions in order to prevent a breach of the peace
Often seen as safe and relatively straightforward	Potentially quicker than civil powers, but greater risk of being effectively contested

Local authorities have responsibilities to make welfare enquiries when reaching eviction decisions, to take into account considerations of common humanity, and to honour the other statutory duties they may have towards the unauthorised campers
Unauthorised campers can attend and be represented at the court hearing
Decisions can be similarly challenged by means of judicial review on the grounds that they have been reached improperly

6.5 Other legal measures may be available to local authorities:

- The Government believes that local authorities should always follow a route which requires a court order. As local authorities and public bodies, authorities must have regard to considerations of common humanity or other statutory duties, and must ensure that the human rights of unauthorised campers are safeguarded.
- Local highways authorities have powers to evict unauthorised campers from highway land in certain circumstances under the Highways Acts. Section 143 of the Highways Act 1980 requires unauthorised campers to be given 28 days notice to leave, and its use may be unsuitable where rapid eviction is called for.
- Local bylaws may have provisions for evicting unauthorised campers from car parks, parks or other public areas.

Powers Available to the Police

6.6 Powers are available to the police under the Criminal Justice and Public Order Act 1994 ss61-62E.

Criminal Justice and Public Order Act 1994 Section 61

6.7 Under s61 of the CJPOA, the police have discretionary powers to direct trespassers to leave land. The senior police officer present can direct trespassers to leave if reasonable steps have been taken by or on behalf of the landowner/occupier to ask them to leave and there are two or more people intending to reside on the land. Any one of three further conditions must be met:

- if any of those persons has caused damage to the land or to property on the land; or
- used threatening, abusive or insulting words or behaviour towards the occupier, a member of his family or an employee or agent of his; or
- those persons have between them six or more vehicles on the land.

Section 61 cannot be used on land on the highway (with limited specific exclusions listed by s61 (9)(b)). It is an offence to fail to leave the land as soon as reasonably practicable or to enter the land again as a trespasser within three months of the date the direction was given.

6.8 The current ACPO guidance notes that there can be no blanket policies, but refers to some of the circumstances in which it might be appropriate to use s61 against an encampment.

- The statutory conditions must obviously be met (see 6.7). Case law (*Fuller*) has determined that any notice period given to unauthorised campers must have expired before s61 can be used. In other words, the unauthorised campers must clearly have failed to respond to requests from or on behalf of the legal occupier of the land to leave before the police can act. Some police forces have streamlined this process by drawing up standard documents which, when signed by the owner/occupier of the land, give the police authority to act as their agents in dealing with the encampment.
- The fact that a landowner initially allows an encampment to remain does not preclude subsequent police action so long as it is clear that reasonable steps have since been taken by the landowner/occupier to get the unauthorised campers to move, and that they have failed to do so.
- The fact that a local authority has started to make welfare enquiries cannot be taken as an indication that the encampment is being allowed to remain since this is an essential precondition for eviction action.
- The decision to use s61 is an operational one. Its early use should always be considered where it is likely to be a proportionate response, and especially where there is evidence of:
    - unacceptable behaviour by unauthorised campers at the encampment, including individual criminal activity, which cannot be controlled by means other than eviction;
    - significant disruption to the life of the surrounding community;
    - serious breaches of the peace or disorder caused by the encampment.
- Where triggers such as the above are experienced, good practice suggests that police should be prepared to act as long as the statutory conditions are met. Police forces/commands should not adopt blanket policies or presumptions either for or against the use of s61.

6.9 Home Office Circular 45/1994 says 'The decision whether or not to issue a direction to leave is an operational one for the police alone to take in the light of all of the circumstances of the particular case. But in making his decision the senior officer at the scene may wish to take account of the personal circumstances of the trespassers; for example, the presence of elderly persons, invalids, pregnant women, children and other persons whose well-being may be jeopardised by a precipitate move.' Case law (*Small*) has established that, while police officers do not have to undertake welfare enquiries as such, they must be aware of humanitarian considerations in reaching their decisions and must ensure that all decisions are proportionate. A decision may be taken to explicitly exclude individuals or families with serious welfare needs from a s61 direction to leave.

6.10 Above all, s61 should be used within the framework of a jointly agreed strategy for managing unauthorised camping (see Chapter 3). Local authorities, police and other stakeholders should agree the sorts of circumstances in which s61 might be considered appropriate. It is also important that s61 should be used consistently within a local area.

Box 20 : Example of a Local Agreement for the Use of Section 61
The joint protocol on unauthorised encampments within the Borough of Northampton between **Northampton Borough Council** and **Northamptonshire Police** includes a local agreement for the use of s61. It specifies exceptional circumstances in which the police may be requested by the Council or choose themselves to consider using their powers under s61.

6.11 Regular exchange of monitoring information on unauthorised encampments between police and local authority personnel is important. In particular, each party should keep the other informed about decisions taken and progress.

Criminal Justice and Public Order Act 1994 Section 62A to 62E

6.12 Sections 67 to 71 of the Anti-social Behaviour Act 2003 insert sections 62A to 62E into the Criminal Justice and Public Order Act 1994 (CJPOA). The legislation provides the police with a power to direct trespassers to leave land and to remove any vehicles and other property from the land, where there is a suitable pitch available on a caravan site elsewhere in the local authority area. Where a direction has been given to a person, it is an offence for that person to enter any land in the local authority as a trespasser within three months of the direction being given.

6.13 This power will be enacted on 27 February 2004 and ODPM and the Home Office are consulting separately on draft guidance for its implementation in practice. Once guidance on the use of s62 is finalised, it will be incorporated into this Guidance.

Powers Available to Other Landowners

6.14 Several government bodies are major landowners and their land may be subject to unauthorised encampment - examples include the Forestry Commission and the Highways Agency. Public bodies should ask local authorities to assist with welfare enquires and local authorities should be prepared to help with these.

6.15 Private landowners may obtain a possession order through the civil courts requiring the removal of trespassers from their land, using Civil Procedures Rules Part 55 in the county court. Private landowners have no welfare responsibilities towards Gypsies and Travellers and would not be expected to take unauthorised campers' needs into account when deciding to evict.

6.16 Some private landowners seek to avoid the expense and costs of going to court by using common law rights to recover land from trespassers using 'reasonable force' as necessary. Such action is lawful, and some firms of bailiffs have carried out many evictions effectively and without trouble. Good practice guidelines for common law evictions would seek to ensure that no more than necessary 'reasonable force' is used and might include:

- Police should always be notified of an eviction and called in to stand by to prevent a breach of the peace.
- If police advise that it is inappropriate to carry out an eviction, it should always be delayed until an agreed time.

6.17 There is a role for local authorities and police in managing unauthorised camping on private land.

- As a minimum, local authorities should inform private landowners about their rights to recover land from trespassers, through the courts or using common law powers; authorities should not offer legal advice to landowners but rather refer them to Citizens' Advice Bureaux or solicitors. Authorities should remind landowners about the importance of using reputable bailiffs and only 'reasonable force'.
- Within the overall strategy for managing unauthorised camping, the local authority might consider acting more directly against encampments when requested by a private landowner, particularly if the police are not prepared to use s61 to evict the encampment.
- Police should take action if any criminal offences are perpetrated during eviction action by bailiffs or private firms.

Some Procedural Points

6.18 This guidance is not concerned with detailed procedures involved in court actions for eviction. Some pointers to good practice for local authorities were noted in *Managing Unauthorised Camping: A Good Practice Guide* issued in 1998 and are still valid:

- Both main sets of powers for taking eviction action involve their own detailed procedures for serving notices, entering cases into court, providing statements (civil powers) or witnesses (CJPOA) for evidence and so on. There is advantage in drawing up a detailed procedures guide as a checklist that everything is done properly and no necessary action missed. Losing an eviction action through an avoidable mistake is a waste of resources, and threatens the credibility of the authority.
- In drawing up detailed procedures, the close involvement of a legal officer is essential. Day-to-day liaison for legal advice while dealing with a specific encampment is also desirable to avoid omissions and to ensure the most effective case for eviction is built.
- Most authorities will probably use in-house legal expertise for preparation and court work. In some circumstances it may be desirable to use an external solicitor, which can be cost-effective where a local solicitor has special expertise.
- Good relations should be built with court officials to ensure a speedy service and to ensure that particularly urgent cases can be given priority when needed. The leaflet *Getting the best out of the court system: Claims for possession* issued by DTLR, the Court Service and the Welsh Assembly stresses the importance of establishing links with local courts. It is, of course, essential to establish what paperwork the courts will require and to ensure that it is always provided. It is also desirable to develop fast-track in-house processes to fit around court workings.
- It is important to be able to show that directions have been properly served if cases are to succeed at court. This normally means either personal service on the occupiers of each vehicle and/or attaching a copy of the direction to each caravan as well as posting the direction on the site. A verbal explanation of the direction should be given wherever possible as a supplement to the written documents to cater for possible reading difficulties.
- It is usual to proceed against unnamed persons occupying the land. This is specifically allowed in the CJPOA and may be the only practical course where unauthorised campers are unwilling to give their names. Getting comprehensive information on vehicles is important for identification purposes.
- Most authorities will probably think it appropriate to use council personnel to serve notices and so on. Where external bailiffs or other agents are employed, the authority must be satisfied that their behaviour is at all times lawful and in accord with human rights and race relations requirements.

- Serving directions, and site visits in general, can raise issues of personal safety for officers involved. Sensible precautions should be taken to avoid confrontation and personal danger. In certain circumstances, a police presence may be appropriate while notices are served.
- Local authorities have discretion to set notice periods beyond the legal minimum. For example, the direction to leave served under the CJPOA can require unauthorised campers to leave in 24 hours, 48 hours or a longer period. Decisions about the length of notice given should be taken in the light of the circumstances of each encampment, with a view to being more generous where problems are not extreme.

Preparing for Eviction

6.19 Eviction proceedings should not be commenced unless the authority is able to go the whole way to forced eviction if necessary.

- Every effort should be made to avoid forced eviction.
- Many encampments include children, who will find forced eviction especially stressful and frightening. All authority and other personnel involved in an eviction should remember this and seek to ensure that their actions have the least possible harmful effect on children.
- Authorities should think, in general terms at least, about options for forced eviction. Plans should be formulated on such matters as which personnel would be involved and which towing contractors would be used. An in-principle agreement should be reached with the police about where towed vehicles would be put.
- Other services should be alerted prior to a forced eviction. This should include warning social services (who may need to provide temporary care for children in the rare cases where parents are arrested and held in custody), Traveller Education Services and homelessness officers, and could also involve finding accommodation for horses and dogs.
- Many authorities do not employ council staff in forced evictions. Where bailiffs or other agencies and contractors are employed, a code of expected behaviour should be drawn up. This code must recognise that private bodies have a local authority's human rights and race relations responsibilities while acting as their agent.
- A senior local authority officer should always attend forced evictions to ensure that all agents follow codes of behaviour. The officer should attempt to encourage the unauthorised campers to move voluntarily wherever possible.
- Police should be involved at a very early stage in planning a forced eviction. They will be able to advise on personal safety issues. In addition, forced evictions could have implications for traffic management and the like.
- Elected members and other local stakeholders should be notified in advance of forced eviction. It is also appropriate routinely to inform neighbouring local authorities and police areas since the displaced unauthorised campers may look for other encampment sites locally.
- The respective roles of the local authority, police and other agencies in forced eviction should be clearly established in the local strategy for managing unauthorised camping. Since this is an area where good practice is hard to establish, it is particularly important that all agencies should monitor and evaluate local instances of eviction and learn from that experience.

Enforcing against Unauthorised Development

6.20 Where Gypsies and Travellers (or anyone else) buy land and develop it as a caravan site without planning consent, any enforcement must be through the planning system; the powers described above against trespass cannot be used.

6.21 A breach of planning control is not in itself an offence; enforcement is a matter for the discretion of the local planning authority. Decisions to enforce must be made on planning grounds. Some key factors may include whether the breach of control unacceptably affects public amenity, highway safety, the Green Belt, public landscape, or the existing use of land or buildings meriting protection in the public interest. The action taken should be proportionate to the breach.

6.22 The current enforcement regime provides a mix of powers with which to deal with breaches of planning control in a controlled but flexible manner. The main powers are summarised in Box 21.

Box 21 : Main Planning Enforcement Powers to be used against Unauthorised Development
The discretionary powers available to local planning authorities (LPAs) were set out in the Planning and Compensation Act 1991 which amended the Town and Country Planning Act 1990 (TCPA 1990). Section references below refer to the TCPA 1990 as amended. **Planning contravention notice (s171C)**: This may be used where it appears that there may have been a breach of planning control and the LPA requires information about the activities on the land or to find out more about the nature of the recipient's interest in the land. **Enforcement notice (s172)**: This requires steps to be taken to remedy the specified breach within a given period. There is a right of appeal to the Secretary of State against an enforcement notice. If the notice is upheld, failure to comply is an offence with a maximum penalty on conviction of £20,000 (unlimited in the Crown Court). **Stop notice (ss183-184)**: This has the effect of immediately stopping any activity which contravenes planning control; an enforcement notice must also be served. There is no right of appeal to a stop notice, but compensation may be payable if an appeal against the associated enforcement notice is allowed on legal grounds. If a stop notice is contravened the resulting offence can be prosecuted in the Magistrates' Court with a maximum penalty on conviction of £20,000 (unlimited in the Crown Court). **Breach of condition notice (s187A):** Where there is a failure to comply with any condition or limitation imposed on a grant of planning permission this procedure provides a fast-track enforcement option to secure compliance with no statutory right of appeal to the Secretary of State. **Injunctions (s187b)**: The LPA is able to seek an injunction in the High Court or County Court to restrain any actual or expected breach of planning control. It is not necessary to serve an enforcement notice prior to applying for an injunction. **Direct action (s178)**: Where any steps required by an enforcement notice are not taken within the compliance period, the LPA may enter the land and take the required steps and recover reasonable costs incurred in doing so. The whole enforcement process must have been completed before direct action is possible. **Compulsory purchase (s226 (1)(b))**: With the authorisation of the Secretary of State, an LPA may compulsorily acquire any land in their area 'for a purpose which it is necessary to achieve in the interests of the proper planning of an area in which the land is situated'. There is scope for objection and a public local inquiry. This has been successfully used against unauthorised development in order to restore land to its lawful use for agriculture.

6.23 Case law has determined that all enforcement measures must be proportionate in the context of the Human Rights Act, and in particular the Gypsy/Traveller's rights under Article 8. Guidance on using planning enforcement powers is available in Circular 10/97, Planning Policy Guidance 18: *Enforcing Planning Control* and *Enforcing Planning Control: Good Practice Guide for Local Planning Authorities*.

6.24 The planning enforcement system in England is currently being reviewed. One of the issues being considered is whether local authority enforcement powers are effective or whether more are needed to tackle breaches of planning control. Revised guidance to local authorities is also being considered. An announcement about the review is expected in 2004.

7. Managing Unauthorised Encampments

7.1 Although unauthorised camping is unlawful, it is likely to continue while there are insufficient spaces to accommodate Gypsies and Travellers on authorised sites. While more places are being provided it is vital that local authorities, with their police and other partners, pro-actively manage encampments to minimise the disruption caused. The principles involved are:

- To enforce the same standards of behaviour by unauthorised campers as are expected of the settled community.
- To respond rapidly to any deterioration of behaviour and growing disruption from an encampment.
- To facilitate access to services for Gypsy/Travellers on encampments.
- To keep all parties informed of decisions and actions.

7.2 The chapter also covers the special issue of dealing with mass gatherings by Gypsies and Travellers (7.30-7.37).

Behaviour at Encampments

7.3 Many local authorities (see Box 22) have drawn up Codes for Gypsy/Traveller unauthorised campers, detailing both locational and behaviour expectations. 'Acceptable behaviour' codes might include some or all of the following items:

- Small scale encampments, which can be accommodated with less disruption.
- No aggressive and threatening behaviour towards local authority and/or police officers or members of the public.
- Dogs and other animals to be kept under control.
- No persistent noise which disturbs others, especially at night, for example from work on the camp, vehicles, generators, dogs or music.
- Keeping the encampment site clean and tidy, avoiding littering and/or fly tipping on or near the site.
- No damage either to the site encamped or the surrounding area or nearby property.
- No criminal activity on the part of unauthorised campers.

Box 22 : Examples of Codes of Expected Behaviour
The code for Travellers in **Essex** Guidance notes for Travellers in **Leicestershire, Leicester City *and* Rutland**

7.4 In drawing up a Code of Expected Behaviour, local authorities should consult Gypsies and Travellers, local businesses and other landowners and other members of the settled community. The objective should be to reach consensus on behaviour standards which it is appropriate to require, and which are sensitive to cultural differences between the Travelling and settled communities.

7.5 As noted above, a basic principle in establishing a Code of Expected Behaviour is applying the same standards as would be applied to members of the settled community. In this context it is important to consider 'individual' and 'group' behaviour and responsibilities. In the settled community, a whole street or estate would not be evicted because of the criminal or anti-social behaviour of one person or household. Wherever possible, police and local authorities should seek to enforce appropriately against a troublemaker rather than automatically evicting an encampment as a whole.

7.6 It is also important to identify and take action against unacceptable behaviour towards encampments by members of the settled community. Harassment of, and violence against, Gypsy/Traveller unauthorised campers are quite unacceptable. Local authorities and police, as public bodies, have responsibilities under the Race Relations (Amendment) Act 2000 to promote good race relations.

7.7 Tackling unacceptable behaviour of whatever sort requires - as outlined in Chapter 5 - rapid response, regular monitoring and determination to take appropriate enforcement action as necessary.

Dealing with Crime and Anti-Social Behaviour

7.8 Some encampments are associated with criminal and anti-social behaviour. The Government is clear that criminal and anti-social behaviour is not acceptable from unauthorised campers, just as it is not acceptable from members of the settled community. The White Paper *Respect and Responsibility* sets out the stand to be taken against anti-social behaviour. Measures provided (see 7.11-7.12 and Box 23) empower communities, public services and authorities to tackle anti-social behaviour. In return the Government expects everyone to play their part in setting and enforcing proper standards of behaviour. This Guidance should be read in the context of that agenda.

7.9 Dealing with any criminal behaviour on the part of unauthorised campers is properly the responsibility of the police. Other enforcement agencies may be involved depending on the nature of the crime, including Trading Standards Officers, Inland Revenue and Customs and Excise enforcement officers where there are indications of fraudulent trading, tax or excise evasion. A co-ordinated approach to enforcement is the key.

7.10 No group should be above the law. Where action is justified, there should be no blanket presumption against enforcing against members of the Travelling community on grounds of expediency. Where law enforcement agencies demonstrate a commitment to taking action where appropriate and are clearly determined to tackle crime, it is probable that some Gypsy/Traveller unauthorised campers will avoid that locality and some may amend their behaviour. A pro-active approach taken in one area may increase unauthorised camping in an adjoining area where a less active approach is taken. Consistency of approach is desirable.

7.11 Anti-social behaviour (see Box 23) can also arise at some unauthorised encampments. Both police and local authorities have a role here. Under the Police Reform Act 2002, the Government introduced improved measures for tackling anti-social behaviour including allowing Anti-Social Behaviour Orders (ASBOs) to be made following conviction for a criminal offence as well as on application to the civil magistrate's court, and allowing ASBOs to prohibit specified acts of anti-social behaviour across any geographical area up to and including the whole of England and Wales. This should help counter displacement of anti-social behaviour. Orders can also be made in the county court where the defendant is the principal party in related proceedings such as possession proceedings or eviction notices where the persons to be evicted from the area are named individuals. These changes were accompanied by Home Office guidance published in November. The white paper *Respect and Responsibility* strengthens the changes described above and outlines new measures which are to be introduced. The Anti-Social Behaviour Act 2003 will introduce further relevant changes to ASBOs, allowing Housing Action Trusts and county councils to apply for ASBOs, enabling persons to be joined to county court proceedings to seek an order against them and empowering local authorities to prosecute ASBO breaches.

7.12 It is important that local authorities and police seriously consider the possibility of using ASBOs against unauthorised campers and/or negotiating Acceptable Behaviour Contracts (see Box 23). The use of either measure would represent an opportunity to discuss behaviour with unauthorised campers, defining with and for them what is and is not acceptable.

Box 23 : Tackling Anti-Social Behaviour

The Crime and Disorder Act 1998 introduced Anti-Social Behaviour Orders (ASBOs) to tackle persistent anti-social behaviour (ASB). The scope of the orders was extended by the Police Reform Act 2002, which was accompanied by Home Office guidance on ASBOs and ABCs. Further improvements to the functioning of ASBOs were made in the Anti-Social Behaviour Act 2003.

ASB: is defined in the Crime and Disorder Act 1998 s1 as behaving in *'a manner that caused or was likely to cause harassment, alarm or distress to one or more persons not of the same household'*

ASBOs: are available to local authorities, police (including the British Transport Police) and Registered Social Landlords (RSLs') by application at a magistrates' court or on conviction in criminal proceedings. Orders are available in the county court where the person is the Defendant in related proceedings. Interim orders can also be obtained. From early 2004 Housing Action Trusts and county councils will also be able to apply for ASBOs, and persons will be able to be joined to county court proceedings where their anti-social behaviour is relevant to the principal proceedings for the purpose of seeking an order against them. To obtain an ASBO it is necessary to show that the person(s) concerned have acted in an anti-social manner and an order is necessary to protect others from further anti-social acts by the individual(s). The rules of evidence are civil but a standard of proof equivalent to the criminal standard (beyond reasonable doubt) should be applied. The order must be negative, prohibiting the individual(s) from specified actions (which can include a general prohibition of acting in an anti-social manner) in specified areas which can be any defined part of or the whole of England and Wales. Breach of an ASBO is a criminal offence and has to be proved to the criminal standard of evidence beyond reasonable doubt. Conviction for breach carries the normal maximum sentence in the Magistrates' Court (6 months in prison, a fine or both) and five years and/or a fine in the Crown Court.

Acceptable Behaviour Contracts: have been developed, initially by Islington Council, as an informal way of dealing with low-level ASB and nipping it in the bud. They can be used with adults and young people and are tenure-neutral although they have been used mainly against teenagers in social rented housing. The perpetrator is interviewed by a council officer in the presence of parents and police, and is asked to sign a 'contract' agreeing not to engage in specified anti-social acts. The ABC principles might be adapted for use in relation to Gypsies/Travellers and unauthorised encampments. An ABC is not legally binding but it can be cited in proceedings such as for an ASBO at a later date.

Other measures: are available which can be used against specific forms of ASB, including:

- Environmental Protection Act 1990 where a problem is judged prejudicial to health or a statutory nuisance - normally enforced by the local authority environmental health department
- Noise Act 1996 - normally enforced by the local authority environmental health department
- Protection from Harassment Act 1997 - if ASB or unauthorised camper behaviour constitutes harassment, police could prosecute under this Act, or the person to whom harassment has occurred may claim damages and an injunction
- Public Order Act 1986
- Criminal Damage Act 1971

7.13 Measures to tackle crime and ASB must be set within a strategic framework. Dealing with any criminal and anti-social behaviour associated with unauthorised encampments should be considered by local Crime and Disorder Reduction Partnerships as part of their mandatory strategies (see Box 24).

Box 24 : Crime and Disorder Prevention Partnerships
The Crime and Disorder Act 1998 requires the police and local authorities - together with police authorities, health authorities and probation committees - to work together, in partnership with other agencies, to develop and implement a strategy for reducing crime and disorder in each district and unitary local authority area. County councils are to be involved in all strategies within their area. The Act also requires local authorities to have regard to crime and disorder when considering all other matters. Police and local authorities (and other partners) must follow a three year cycle: ■ Conduct and publish an audit of local crime and disorder problems, taking into account the views of those who live and work in the area ■ Determine priorities for action ■ Devise and publish a strategy which tackles these priority problems, including objectives and targets ■ Monitor progress, fine tuning the strategy as required

Dealing with Waste and Fly-tipping

7.14 Accumulations of rubbish and waste - including human waste, domestic and trade refuse - represent one of the most common problems associated with unauthorised encampments. Accumulations can be visually unpleasant, smelly, hazardous and costly to clear up. Preventing a build up of waste and/or removing it is a central element in a policy of pro-active management of encampments.

Preventing Waste

7.15 Local authorities have an important role in preventing accumulation of waste by ensuring that unauthorised campers keep encampments clean and tidy:

- Many authorities provide supplies of plastic sacks and arrange regular collection of bagged refuse. This can work well with unauthorised campers who want to conform to a Code of Expected Behaviour, and will reduce the costs of cleaning up after the encampment has left. Regular removal of domestic refuse should deter tipping by members of the settled community.

- Some groups of Gypsies and Travellers are willing to use skips for domestic waste. Again, provision and removal may be cost-effective if the alternative is a build-up of refuse acting as a magnet for other fly tipping by members of the settled community. Local authorities should check that skips would be used before providing them. It is good practice to seek to recover costs from the unauthorised campers.

- One of the common complaints about unauthorised encampments is of people urinating and defecating in public. Public defecation is a difficult and sensitive issue. The practice is a nuisance and a health hazard. However, Gypsies and Travellers have strict cultural codes about hygiene and consider it unclean to use toilet facilities in a caravan or to share facilities. When managing encampments local authorities should liaise with unauthorised campers. They should make plain that public defecation is not acceptable behaviour, and discuss what form of toilet provision the local authority can assist with to prevent it and any arrangements for payment for the service.

7.16 Regular monitoring visits to encampments should reinforce messages about keeping the site clean and tidy. Unauthorised campers need to realise that, under a pro-active approach to managing unauthorised encampments, failure to keep the site clean and tidy in breach of a Code of Expected Behaviour is likely to lead to rapid eviction. Some local authorities, which have adopted such an approach and shown a determination to encourage acceptable behaviour, have found that behaviour of unauthorised campers has improved; in some instances groups which previously left encampment sites in very poor condition are now much tidier. This is extremely cost-effective in reducing the need to spend large sums on cleaning up.

Enforcement Action

7.17 Dealing with illicit waste disposal and fly tipping is difficult - whether the culprits are Gypsy/Traveller unauthorised campers or members of the settled community. Local authorities, police and the Environment Agency all have roles to play and co-ordinated action is necessary. Gypsy/Traveller unauthorised campers should be clearly informed that everyone who produces, treats, carries or disposes of controlled waste has a 'duty of care' under s34 of the Environment Protection Act 1990. Licensed carriers should take trade waste to appropriately licensed facilities in accordance with this duty of care. Information leaflets provided to unauthorised campers should identify nearby licensed waste facilities.

7.18 Enforcement measures are available (see Box 25). Collecting sufficient evidence for successful prosecution requires - as with the measures for countering crime and ASB outlined above - determination and partnership working from the agencies involved. The case study in Box 26 shows that action can succeed.

Box 25 : Measures for Enforcing against Pollution, Littering and Fly-tipping

Water Resources Act 1991 (as amended by the Environment Act 1995) gives the Environment Agency powers to prosecute those found illegally depositing waste into controlled waters and causing a pollution offence.

Environmental Protection Act 1990 makes fly-tipping a criminal offence with a maximum penalty of a £20,000 fine and/or imprisonment up to 6 months (unlimited fine or imprisonment of up to 5 years if convicted at a Crown Court). The Government has asked the Environment Agency to vigorously prosecute any person found to be illegally disposing of waste, where they have evidence. The waste collection authority and the Environment Agency may remove fly-tipped waste and recover costs from those responsible for causing the offence. The Environment Agency has set up an emergency telephone hotline (0800 807060) for members of the public to notify them of fly tipping (and water pollution incidents). The National Fly-Tipping Prevention Group includes a number of national organisations.

Environment Protection Act 1990 (Part III) gives local authorities powers to act against statutory nuisances (prejudicial to health or a nuisance). Local authorities can serve an abatement notice, which can be appealed. Failure to comply with an abatement notice is an offence.

Anti-social Behaviour Act 2003 extends the range of powers available to local authorities for dealing with fly tipping, for instance, by giving them powers to stop, search and seize vehicles suspected of being used for fly tipping and to investigate incidents.

Box 26 : A Case Study of Action against Fly-tipping

Officers from the Environment Agency met officers of Leicestershire Constabulary in December 2002 to discuss a strategy for dealing with illegal tipping by Travellers near the M50/M1 interchange. On 13 January 2003, the police contacted the Environment Agency to confirm that their officers had witnessed the deposit of around 3 tonnes of soil amongst other waste on the site. The offender was unable to satisfactorily respond to accusations of illegal tipping lodged by the police and they were able to arrest him under Police and Criminal Evidence Act 1984 powers. An Agency officer assisted the police in the interview process and provided the police with specimen charges.

The offender was subsequently bailed to appear at a later date to answer the charges lodged against him. He appeared at Loughborough Magistrates' Court and pleaded guilty to one charge of depositing waste without the benefit of a waste management licence, contrary to s33 (1)(a) of the Environmental Protection Act 1990. He was fined £250 and ordered to pay £65 costs.

7.19 Regular site monitoring is essential if evidence is to be gathered for successful enforcement. Environmental health authorities, police and the Environment Agency need to work closely together. Surveillance to identify individuals responsible for fly tipping is likely to be resource-intensive. Covert surveillance is now governed by the Regulation of Investigatory Powers Act 2000; the Home Office has issued guidance on the use of CCTV in relation to both the Human Rights and Data Protection Acts.

Rapid Clear-up

7.20 Whilst the measures outlined above may help reduce the accumulation of rubbish, cleaning up will still be needed after some encampments.

- Sites should be cleared as soon as possible after they are vacated.
- Where appropriate, responsibilities must be agreed between county and district councils for site clearance so that there is no delay due to uncertainty or dispute. Joint arrangements - including some apportionment of costs - must be set out in a joint agreement or protocol specifying speed of response.
- Some refuse left may need special care in collection and disposal, including hazardous industrial waste, excreta and drug-related waste. Contractors should be warned accordingly.

Recording Information

7.21 The state of the site on departure and the clean-up cost are relevant factors to record in the encampment log. A group's previous behaviour may well inform the approach adopted if they visit the area again. If the sharing of standard information becomes more common, poor behaviour in one area may in future also inform the approach adopted in another area.

Facilitating Access to Services

7.22 It is an important objective of a pro-active approach to managing encampments that Gypsy/Traveller unauthorised campers are enabled to access health, welfare and education services during the period of their stay. It is in everyone's interests that Gypsy/Traveller children are encouraged and enabled to complete their education. Arranging access to services will be easier when unauthorised campers conform to a Code of Expected Behaviour and may be permitted to stay longer. Local authorities should facilitate access to services and act as main contact point for specialist service providers. Information from the welfare enquiries will indicate what services are required.

A Robust Approach to Eviction

7.23 A pro-active approach to managing unauthorised camping involves keeping encampments under review. Police and local authorities should be prepared to review eviction decisions as circumstances change since the balance of interests will change as well. While a decision to evict might not have been 'proportionate' initially, experience of disruption to the settled community, crime or anti-social behaviour may justify eviction at a later date. The fact that an encampment has been permitted to remain for a period does not preclude eviction proceedings - whether by the local authority or police using s61 - being started at a later date provided proper procedures are followed.

Keeping People Informed

7.24 As noted in Chapter 3, communications and publicity arrangements are an important element in any strategy for managing unauthorised camping. It is important that other agencies/departments, Gypsies and Travellers, elected members and members of the settled community are kept informed about what is happening and what can be expected to happen with encampments.

7.25 An agreed communications strategy between partner organisations in an area should determine which agency will lead on providing information. Normally this should be the local authority in its role as lead agency in dealing with unauthorised camping. Communications with the press and members of the public should be co-ordinated and consistent to avoid confusion. One aim of a communications strategy should be to increase understanding and tolerance between the settled and travelling communities in line with duties to promote good race relations placed on local authorities and police by the Race Relations (Amendment) Act 2000.

7.26 Gypsy/Traveller unauthorised campers should always be clearly informed about what is expected of them and what is going to happen. Information should normally be by word of mouth as well as written to avoid communication problems because of any reading difficulties. Contact and communication should be at least weekly.

7.27 Any encampment is likely to be of concern to local residents and businesses. Elected members should be regularly briefed on encampments in their wards; they can pass information on to their constituents. In addition, the local authority should provide information to local residents, and especially to complainants, using resources of the internet and e-mail where appropriate.

7.28 Special arrangements may be appropriate for large and/or high profile encampments. In addition to the measures described above, these might include:

- Regular press briefings.
- Well-publicised advice lines for Gypsies and Travellers and other members of the public to ring for information.
- A special leaflet or newsletter to be distributed locally explaining background, events and plans for dealing with the encampment.
- Links to regularly updated information through the council's web-site. Police and other agencies likely to be approached for information should include hyperlink connections to information on local authority web pages.

7.29 Such measures will obviously be costly in staff time. However, in the case of a major encampment local authorities and police will have to deal with complaints and queries anyway, and planning will make this easier. Being pro-active in this way should reduce scope for rumour and misinformation, and confusion. It could provide opportunities to manage the message to avoid unnecessarily negative coverage and reduce inter-community tension. It could also be helpful in gathering evidence for fly-tipping or other ASB which could be used in enforcement action.

Dealing with Mass Gatherings

7.30 Gatherings, which bring families together for a short period of time for weddings, funerals or traditional fairs and other events, are an important element of Gypsy/Traveller culture. These traditional gatherings must always be handled sensitively and with respect.

7.31 In the past few years a number of other mass gatherings of Gypsies and Travellers have occurred, when several hundred vehicles and people have met up and camped for a period, as at Great Yarmouth (December 1999) and Bournemouth (December 2001)

7.32 Mass gatherings are not spontaneous events but are to some extent planned by those taking part. The Government believes that it is not acceptable for large numbers of Gypsies and Travellers (or anyone else) to turn up in an area and cause severe disruption. The Government also recognises that there are large gatherings which are part of the Gypsy and Traveller tradition such as Appleby Fair in Cumbria.

7.33 The responsibility for managing lawful gathering should lie with the Gypsies and Travellers themselves. Gypsies and Travellers, ideally, should provide advance notice of a mass gathering, and should themselves make arrangements for water, refuse and hygiene services. At the very least, Gypsy/Traveller 'leaders' at a gathering should be prepared to negotiate with local authority and police officers and to act in a co-operative manner so as to minimise disruption.

7.34 Local authorities and police can make advance plans for dealing with such mass gatherings (including those where 'leaders' do not co-operate fully):

- It would be appropriate to include handling a major gathering and encampment of Gypsies and Travellers within the local emergency plan and local Crime and Disorder Plans.
- In emergency plans, local authorities should think ahead about how they might prepare emergency accommodation, negotiate with farmers for the use of their fields, identify supplies of portable toilets, water supply, waste disposal etc. The authority's Chief Emergency Planning Officer might become involved in preparing and co-ordinating plans.
- Close joint working between local authority personnel and police is key to managing mass gatherings. Dealing with hundreds of people and vehicles is likely to be beyond the resources of a single authority or police area. Local authorities and police have come together for joint planning at regional level in some parts of the country following recent experiences in order to be able to rapidly mobilise resources on a sufficient scale.
- Joint planning should extend to sharing information and intelligence aimed at anticipating the size and location of gatherings.

7.35 Section 14A of the Public Order Act 1986 provides for the prevention of 'trespassory assemblies', and s14 provides for the imposition of conditions on all assemblies. Section 14C of the Public Order Act 1986 creates a power for police to turn people away from trespassory assemblies when a banning order is in force. Box 27 gives more details. Acting to ban a mass gathering under these powers clearly requires close co-operation and agreement between the local police and local authority. This can only be contemplated when advance intelligence of the gathering is available sufficiently long in advance to allow the various procedures to be followed and approvals to be sought. Enforcing such a ban - if agreed by the Secretary of State - will obviously have major staffing implications.

Box 27 : Preventing Trespassory Assemblies

Public Order Act 1986 s14A

A public assembly is a gathering of 20 or more people on land in the open air. A Chief Police Officer may take steps to prohibit such an assembly, provided that:

- The assembly must be on land to which the public has no right of access or limited right of access **AND**
- The assembly is likely to be held without the permission of the owner/occupier of the land or to conduct itself in a way as to exceed the limits of any permission or limits the public's right of access **AND**
- May result in serious disruption to life of the community.

If these conditions are fulfilled the Chief Officer may apply to the District Council for an order preventing trespassory assemblies for a specific period. This order may only be granted with the permission of the Secretary of State for the Home Department. The order may ban assemblies for up to 4 days within a radius of 5 miles. The order may be renewed.

It is an offence to organise such an assembly knowing that it as been prohibited, or to take part knowing it has been prohibited.

Public Order Act 1986 s14C

Creates a power for police to turn people away who are travelling towards trespassory assemblies. It is operative within the area covered by the banning order. A person who fails to comply is liable to arrest.

Public Order Act 1986 s14

A senior police officer is able to impose conditions on public assemblies. The officer may impose conditions if s/he reasonably believe that the assembly may result in:

- Serious public disorder **OR**
- Serious damage to property **OR**
- Serious disruption to the life of the community.

These conditions, which must be in writing, may be in regard to location, duration and maximum numbers attending. It is an offence to knowingly organise a public assembly in breach of the conditions, or to take part knowingly. These offences carry a statutory power of arrest.

7.36 When an illegal mass gathering is anticipated and likely to go ahead, emergency plans may need to be implemented. All relevant bodies, especially local authorities and police, should be on alert. Security (24 hour) may be appropriate to protect especially vulnerable and sensitive pieces of land.

7.37 Should a mass gathering take place, enforcement action as detailed in Chapter 6 should be considered.

Box 28 : An Aide Memoire on Mass Incursions

Drawing on recent experiences of mass gatherings, the National Crime and Operations Faculty, Uniform Operational Support at Bramshill put together:

Mass Incursions : An Aide Memoire

8. Evaluation of the Guidance

8.1 The Office of the Deputy Prime Minister and the Home Office are committed to evaluating the impact of this Operational Guidance to check:

- the extent to which local authorities and the police have adopted the Guidance; and
- its effectiveness in bringing about improvements on the ground.

8.2 In the light of evaluation - and changing circumstances - further Guidance may be issued in future as appropriate. ODPM and the Home Office will be pleased to receive comments on the Operational Guidance and suggestions for ways in which it might be improved.

9. Useful References and Contacts

Various pieces of guidance have been referred to in this Operational Guidance. These are listed below, together with other useful references ordered in the relevant Chapters of the Guidance. Useful contacts are listed at the end. ALL INTERNET ADDRESSES ARE VALID AT DECEMBER 2003.

Chapter 1

Department of Environment, Transport and the Regions/Home Office (1998) Managing *Unauthorised Camping: A Good Practice Guide*, DETR; Revised Chapter 5 issued July 2000

Cowan, D, Donson, F, Higate, P, Lomax, D & Third, H (2001) *The Management of Unauthorised Camping: Monitoring the Good Practice Guide*, Research Paper 77, Edinburgh College of Art/Heriot-Watt University

Commission for Racial Equality (2003) *Gypsies and Travellers - A Strategy 2003-2006 Consultation Draft*, CRE (http://www.cre.gov.uk/downloads/docs/GandT_strat.doc)

Gypsy Sites Refurbishment Grant (GSRG) 2004/05: Bidding Guidance (http://www.odpm.gov.uk/stellent/groups/odpm_housing/documents/page/odpm_house_025116.hcsp)

Home Office (2002) *National Policing Plan 2003-2006 (http://www.policereform.gov.uk/natpoliceplan/*)

Home Office (2003) *Respect and Responsibility (http://www.official-documents.co.uk/document/cm57/5778/5778.pdf*)

Chapter 2

Counts of Gypsy caravans are published on the ODPM website at (http://www.odpm.gov.uk/stellent/groups/odpm_housing/documents/page/odpm_house_602529.xls)

Niner, P (2002) *The Provision and Condition of Local Authority Gypsy/Traveller Sites in England*, ODPM (http://www.odpm.gov.uk/stellent/groups/odpm_housing/documents/page/odpm_house_602542.hcsp)

Niner, P (2003) *Local Authority Gypsy/Traveller Sites in England*, ODPM (http://www.odpm.gov.uk/stellent/groups/odpm_housing/documents/page/odpm_house_023012.pdf)

Chapter 3

Derbyshire Gypsy Liaison Group (1998) *Moving Base*, DGLG

Hopkinson, G, Ingram, M & Wishart, B (undated) *Where's the Real Choice? What are the accommodation needs of Travellers in Wychavon?* Evesham & Pershore Housing Association

Southwark Housing (2000) *Needs of the Traveller Community in Southwark*, LB Southwark

Morris, R & Clements, L (2002) *At what cost? The economics of Gypsy and Traveller encampments*, The Policy Press

Local e-Government Strategy (http://www.localegov.gov.uk/Nimoi/sites/ODMP/resources/20021127 Final NS with cover.pdf)

Commission for Racial Equality (2000) *Guidance for Journalists: Travellers, Gypsies and the Media*, CRE (http://www.cre.gov.uk/media/guidetj.html)

DETR (2001) *Local strategic partnerships - Government guidance* (http://www.neighbourhood.gov.uk/formatteddoc.asp?id=95)

LGA (2002) *Guidance on Community Cohesion (http://www.homeoffice.gov.uk/docs/cc_guidance.pdf)*

DETR (2001) *Supporting People: policy into practice*, see http://www.spkweb.org.uk

Children and Young People's Strategic Partnerships (within Local Strategic Partnerships)

Sure Start, see http://www.surestart.gov.uk

Connexions, see http://www.connexions.gov.uk

Home Office (1999) Guidance on Statutory Crime and Disorder Partnerships, see http://www.homeoffice.gov.uk/docs/partcont.html

Race Equality Schemes, see http://www.cre.gov.uk/duty/duty_schemes.html

Department of Transport, Local Government and the Regions (2002) *Homelessness Strategies: A Good Practice Handbook*, DTLR (http://www.odpm.gov.uk/stellent/groups/odpm_homelessness/documents/pdf/odpm_home_pdf_601517.pdf)

Chapter 4

DoE Circular 1/94: *Gypsy Sites and Planning*, January 1994 (see Annex B)

Planning Policy Guidance 3 *Housing*, ODPM (http://www.odpm.gov.uk/stellent/groups/odpm_planning/documents/pdf/odpm_plan_pdf_606933.pdf)

Planning Policy Guidance 12 Development *Plans*, ODPM (http://www.odpm.gov.uk/stellent/groups/odpm_planning/documents/pdf/odpm_plan_pdf_606929.pdf)

Chapter 5

Web-site of the Information Commissioner's - http://www.informationcommissioner.gov.uk

Chapter 6

Fuller v Chief Constable of Dorset, [2001] EWHC Admin 1057

Home Office Circular 45/1994

R v The Commissioner of the Metropolis ex parte Small (not reported)

Department of Environment, Transport and the Regions/Home Office (1998) *Managing Unauthorised Camping: A Good Practice Guide*, DETR; Revised Chapter 5 issued July 2000

DTLR, the Court Service and the Welsh Assembly: *Getting the best out of the court system: Claims for possession (http://www.courtservice.gov.uk/cms/media/best_court_system.pdf)*

Planning Policy Guidance 18 *Enforcing Planning Control* 1991 (http://www.odpm.gov.uk/stellent/groups/odpm_planning/documents/page/odpm_plan_606903.pdf)

DoE Circular 10/97 *Enforcing Planning Control: Legislative provisions and Procedural Requirements (http://www.odpm.gov.uk/stellent/groups/odpm_planning/documents/pdf/odpm_plan_pdf_606834.pdf)*

DoE *Enforcing Planning Control: Good Practice for Local Planning Authorities*, 1997

Chapter 7

Home Office (2003) *Respect and Responsibility (http://www.official-documents.co.uk/document/cm57/5778/5778.pdf)*

Home Office (2002) *A Guide to Anti-Social Behaviour Orders and Acceptable Behaviour Contracts (http://www.crimereduction.gov.uk/asbos9.pdf)*

Environment Protection Act 1990 s34, *Waste Management: The Duty of Care: A Code of Practice (http://www.defra.gov.uk/environment/waste/management/doc/pdf/waste_man_duty_code.pdf)*

Fly Tipping Stakeholders Forum, *Fly Tipping Guidance (http://www.environment-agency.gov.uk/commondata/105385/flytip.PDF)*

Home Office (2001) CCTV*: Implications for Public Space Surveillance in the Light of the Data Protection Act 1998* see http:// www.crimereduction.gov.uk/cctv7.htm

Home Office (2001) *CCTV and the Human Rights Act*, see http:// www.crimereduction.gov.uk/cctv13.htm

Mass Incursions: An Aide Memoire Contact: National Crime and Operations Faculty, Uniformed Operational Support, Bramshill (01256 602777)

Useful Contacts

Gypsy/Traveller bodies and support groups

Advisory Council for the Education of Romany and Other Travellers (ACERT)

Moot House, The Stow, Harlow, Essex CM20 3AG

01279 418666

Gypsy Council

(President: Hughie Smith) Spring Lanes Caravan Park, Bickerton, Nr Wetherby, North Yorks LS22 5ND

01937 842782

Gypsy Council for Education, Culture, Welfare and Civil Rights

(Chairman: Charles Smith)

8 Hall Road, Aveley, Romford, Essex RM15 4HD

01708 868986

Irish Traveller Movement in Britain

The Old Library Building, Willesden Green Library Centre, 95 High Road, Willesden, London NW10 2ST

020 8459 7638

London Gypsy and Traveller Unit

6 Westgate Street, London E8 3RN

020 8533 2002

Derbyshire Gypsy Liaison Group

Ernest Bailey Community Centre, New Street, Matlock, Derbyshire DE4 3FE

01629 583300

Friends, Families and Travellers

Community Base, 113 Queens Road, Brighton, East Sussex BN1 3XG

01273 234777

Community Law Partnership

Ruskin Chambers, 191 Corporation Street, Birmingham, West Midlands B4 6RP

0121 685 8595

Travellers' Times

The Rural Media Company, Sullivan House, 72080 Widemarsh Street, Hereford HR4 9HG

01432 344039

Central Government

ODPM

Gypsy and Traveller Branch , Eland House, Bressenden Place, London SW1E 5DU

020 7944 4400

Home Office

Crime Reduction and Community Safety Group, 50 Queen Annes Gate, London SW1H 9AT

0800 000 1585

Department for Education and Skills

Ethnic Minority Achievement Unit, Sanctuary Building, Great Smith Street, London SW1P 3BT

0870 000 2288

Department of Health

Primary Care Access, Quarry House, Quarry Hill, Leeds LS2 7UE

020 7210 4850

Other bodies

Commission for Racial Equality

St Dunstan's House, 201-211 Borough High Street, London SE1 1GZ

020 7939 0000

Local Government Association

Local Government House, Smith Square, London SW1P 3HZ

020 7644 3000

National Association of Gypsy and Traveller Officers

c/o George Summers, Estates Practice Department, Hampshire County Council, The Castle, Winchester, Hampshire SO23 9DS

01962 847315

National Association of Health Workers with Travellers

(Chair : Sarah Rhodes) Travellers Health Project, Central Health Clinic, Tower Hill, Bristol BS2 0JD

0117 922 7570

National Association of Teachers of Travellers

c/o Lucy Beckett, Advisory Service for the Education of Travellers, Room L25, Cricket Road Centre, Cricket Road, Oxford OX4 3DW

01865 428089

Annex A: DoE Circular 18/94

A: DoE Circular 18/94: Gypsy Sites Policy and Unauthorised Camping + Revision of Advice on 'Toleration' issued 26 July 2000

Annex B: DoE Circular 1/94

B: DoE Circular 1/94: Gypsy Sites and Planning

Annex C: Summary Points from Research Monitoring the Good Practice Guide on Managing Unauthorised Camping

In 2001 the results of research monitoring the impact of the DETR/Home Office Good Practice Guide were published[1]. The research was carried out by Edinburgh College of Art/Heriot-Watt University in conjunction with the Universities of Bristol and Cardiff. It involved a telephone survey of 263 local authorities which explored the pattern of unauthorised camping. Some of the main findings relating to unauthorised camping are:

Unauthorised camping is a widespread phenomenon - 92% of responding local authorities had experience of it in the twelve months before the survey.

The average number of reported incidents of unauthorised camping in the past year was 22, although this varied widely and almost half of authorities reported ten incidents or fewer. A separate incident could be the same Gypsy/Traveller group moving onto different sites in the area. The speed with which an encampment is moved on is one factor in the number of separate incidents experienced.

The average number of different locations in an authority area subject to unauthorised camping in the last year was 13, again with wide variation.

Unauthorised camps involving 20 caravans and more were far less common than camps involving a dozen caravans or fewer. Only 8% of responding local authorities had experienced an encampment of 50 or more caravans in the past year.

Local authority respondents said that most encampments were small scale and relatively unproblematic while a minority were extremely high profile and associated with crime, damage, dumping and other anti-social behaviour.

Irish Travellers were most often reported as having camped on unauthorised sites in the past year (70% of authorities), followed by Gypsy Travellers (58%) and New Travellers (23%).

The most common sites for unauthorised encampments were vacant or derelict land, industrial estates, car parks and roadsides or verges. Other types of sites, for example, parks and recreation areas, green lanes and bye-ways, farm land and wooded areas were used less often.

The three main factors influencing unauthorised camping were seasonal travelling, work opportunities and visiting other Gypsies and Travellers in the area.

Local authorities' experiences of changes over the past five years were mixed, with no clear trends emerging in terms of frequency of unauthorised camping, number of locations used, use of authorised sites or number of caravans in the groups.

---

[1] Cowan, D, Donson, F, Higate, P, Lomax, D & Third, H (2001) *The Management of Unauthorised Camping: Monitoring the Good Practice Guide*, Research Paper 77, Edinburgh College of Art/Heriot-Watt University

Annex D: A Summary of the Legislative Framework

This annex summarises the main legislative framework relevant to a strategy for managing unauthorised camping. Most of the provisions are described in greater detail in the text of the Guidance. Exceptionally, human rights and race relations responsibilities which are referred at various points in the text are set out in more detail below.

Site Provision

- The Caravan Sites and Control of Development Act 1960 s24 gives local authorities discretionary powers to provide caravan sites.
- While there is no duty on local authorities to provide Gypsy sites, DoE Circular 18/94 makes clear that authorities should maintain their existing Gypsy caravan sites, and should continue to consider whether it is appropriate to provide further permanent caravan sites for Gypsies in their areas.
- Government is currently reviewing policy on Gypsy site provision. Gypsy Sites Refurbishment Grant makes limited funding available for provision of transit and emergency stopping places.
- Private site provision is governed by planning legislation. DoE Circular 1/94 sets out the Government's policy on Gypsy site provision and urges local planning authorities to consider, and to look favourably, at applications for Gypsy sites in development planning and development control.

Dealing with Unauthorised Encampments

- There is no specific legislative duty placed on local authorities to deal with unauthorised encampments by Gypsies and Travellers.
- Local authorities can take action as landowners through civil actions against trespass using Civil Procedure Rules Part 55, heard in a County Court.
- Local authorities have powers given by the Criminal Justice and Public Order 1994 ss77 and 78 (see Chapter 6). These require cases to be brought in the Magistrates' Court.
- Common law rights to recover land from trespassers are also available to local authorities over land they occupy. Authorities are, however, advised not to use such powers unless there is exceptional justification for doing so and, for example, the police are unable to use their powers under s61 of the CJPOA (see 6.5 above).
- DoE Circular 18/94 provides guidance to local authorities on the exercise of s77 powers, and reminds them of their other duties towards Travellers in terms of education, children and homelessness legislation.
- Case law (starting with the judgement of Sedley J in *R v Wealden District Council ex parte Wales*) has developed and clarified the courts' expectations of the welfare enquiries and decision-making processes local authorities should adopt in making evictions under 1994 Act and other powers.
- Where Travellers camp on land which they own or on other private land with the consent of the landowner, district councils may take planning enforcement action, or prosecute for running a caravan site without a site licence.
- The Police have parallel powers granted by s61 of the CJPOA (see Chapter 6). Action under s61 is normally much quicker than under s77, and the welfare considerations less onerous although there are certain conditions in the legislation which have to be fulfilled before eviction can take place.

- The Anti-social Behaviour Act 2003 added new ss61A and 62A into the CJPOA which give police enhanced eviction powers in circumstances where there are suitable pitches on relevant Gypsy sites to accommodate the caravans affected. These sections come into force on 27 February 2004 and guidance as to their operation will be issued.

Other Enforcement Measures

- District authorities have powers to deal with statutory nuisance (which could include, for example, rubbish accumulation at unauthorised encampments) and noise (see Chapter 7 of this Guide).
- The Crime and Disorder Act 1998 places a duty on chief police officers and local authorities to work together to develop and implement a strategy for reducing crime and disorder. Section 17 imposes a duty on all local authorities (and others) to *'without prejudice to any other obligation imposed upon it . . . exercise its functions with due regard to . . . the need to do all it reasonably can to prevent crime and disorder in its area'.*

Service Provision for Gypsies and Travellers

- Gypsies and Travellers are entitled to access health, housing, education and welfare services as citizens in the same way as members of the settled community.
- There is specific recognition of the needs of Traveller children in accessing education, with a Traveller Grant payable under s488 of the Education Act 1996.

Human Rights

The Human Rights Act 1998 incorporates the European Convention on Human Rights into British law. Several Convention rights are relevant in dealing with unauthorised camping. The main relevant rights are:

Article 8: Right to respect for private and family life

1. Everyone has the right to respect for his private and family life, his home and his correspondence.
2. There shall be no interference by a public authority with the exercise of this right except such as is in accordance with the law and is necessary in a democratic society in the interests of national security, public safety or the economic well-being of the country, for the prevention of disorder or crime, for the protection of health or morals, or for the protection of the rights and freedoms of others.

Case law has established that, while neither eviction action against trespassers nor planning enforcement is incompatible with HRA, either could potentially breach Article 8 rights if not properly used. Authorities, and other public bodies covered by the HRA, must be able to demonstrate that all eviction and enforcement decisions are 'proportionate' in weighing individual harm (in the loss of 'home' for the Gypsy or Traveller) against the wider public interest. Potential challenge under the HRA means that all decision-making must be fully recorded and evidenced to withstand scrutiny.

First Protocol, Article 1: Protection of property

Every natural and legal person is entitled to the peaceful enjoyment of his possessions. No-one shall be deprived of his possessions except in the public interest and subject to the conditions provided for by law and by the general principles of international law.

The preceding provisions shall not, however, in any way impair the right of a State to enforce such laws as it deems necessary to control the use of property in accordance with the general interest or to secure the payment of taxes or other contributions or penalties.

This Article might be seen as protecting the settled community's right to quiet enjoyment of their possessions, which might be threatened by nuisance, noise or anti-social behaviour from a problematic unauthorised encampment. This should be one of the considerations to be borne in mind by local authorities and police when considering eviction action. To date there is no relevant case law.

First Protocol, Article 2: Right to education

> No person shall be denied the right to education. In the exercise of any functions which it assumes in relation to education and to teaching, the State shall respect the right of parents to ensure such education and teaching in conformity with their own religious and philosophical convictions.

Education of Gypsy/Traveller children is frequently raised in cases dealing with eviction proceedings, and particularly with planning enforcement actions against unauthorised development. In such cases the question resolves itself to one of the balance between the individual harm to Gypsy/Traveller childrens' educational needs and the public interest harm in allowing unauthorised development to persist. To date there is no specific case law on arguments relying on this Article in this context.

Article 14: Prohibition of discrimination

> The enjoyment of the rights and freedoms set forth in this Convention shall be secured without discrimination on any ground such as sex, race, colour, language, religion, political or other opinion, national or social origin, association with a national minority, property birth or other status.

While Article 14 rights are potentially engaged in any action concerning Gypsies and Travellers (as ethnic groups and national minorities), the Article can only be successfully argued if another Article is found to be breached. Where a claim under any Article is rejected, it follows that any claim under Article 14 also falls.

Race Relations and Equalities

The Race Relations Act 1976 as amended by the Race Relations (Amendment) Act 2000 gives public authorities - including ODPM, the Home Office, local authorities and the police - a general duty to eliminate unlawful discrimination, and to promote equality of opportunity and good race relations in carrying out their functions. It also gives listed public bodies specific duties including one to create and publish a Race Equality Scheme which details how they will meet the general duty. In developing new policies or strategies public authorities must assess their impact on different racial groups, and they must consult. If the impact is negative and disproportionate to the aim of the policy, it must be changed. Once implemented, policies must be monitored for their effect on different racial groups. Authorities must publish the results of monitoring and consultation.

Both Gypsies and Irish Travellers are recognised as ethnic minorities. Policies for managing unauthorised camping are likely to affect Gypsies and Travellers significantly. The RRA means that local authorities and police must assess the impact of proposed policies on Gypsies and Irish Travellers and must consult on them. If the policies are likely to have a disproportionately negative impact on Gypsies and Irish Travellers, authorities must ensure that this impact is not disproportionate to the aims and importance of the policies. If it is, it is important to take measures to reduce this adverse impact or consider other ways to achieve the aims, which would mitigate its negative effect.

Since eviction of unauthorised campers and enforcement against unauthorised development are likely to have a large effect on the public, and in particular on the Gypsy/Traveller population, they are functions highly relevant to the RRA general duty and should be prioritised in Race Equality Schemes. When evicting and enforcing, authorities need to ensure that they act in a way which meets the three elements of the general duty and so as to have the minimum negative impact on the Gypsies and Travellers involved.

Guidance on Managing Unauthorised Camping

Local authorities and police must always be able to show that they have properly considered the race and equalities implications of their policies and actions in relation to unauthorised encampments and unauthorised development by Gypsies and Irish Travellers. They must be able to demonstrate that their polices and actions are proportionate bearing in mind all the circumstances of the case.

Annex E: Interests to be involved in the Development of a Strategy for Unauthorised Camping

Organisation/party	Main topics of interest	Possible means of involvement
Local authorities **NB** In two-tier areas both county and district councils will be involved	Planning and information; race relations; site provision and land use planning; site protection; housing and homelessness; Traveller education; social services; refuse collection; unauthorised camping; communication and public relations	Lead development of Strategy development; key personnel involved in working groups or committees; others in ad hoc groupings and/or written consultation
Local politicians, councillors and MPs	All aspects including unauthorised encampment	Leadership and engendering support for the Strategy
Local Health Authority	Gypsy/Traveller health in all forms of accommodation and on unauthorised encampments; welfare assessments	Nominated officer to be consulted as Strategy develops; continuing involvement in implementation
Neighbouring local authorities	All aspects to inform own Strategies	Joint planning and shared working could be efficient and lead to a sub-regional approach
Police	Planning and information; race equality; dealing with crime, anti-social behaviour and threats to public order from unauthorised encampments; communication and public relations	Key player in developing the Strategy; continuing role in its implementation
Gypsies and Travellers	All aspects including needs assessment; service delivery; advice on site provision and unauthorised camping	Through national, regional or local representative bodies; consultation with local Gypsies and Travellers on their needs and aspirations. Written material, conferences and individual personal contact
Gypsy/Traveller support groups and advisors	Potentially all aspects including unauthorised encampment	Local contact, conferences, consultation through written media

Guidance on Managing Unauthorised Camping

Parish and town councils	Site provision and land use planning; site protection; unauthorised camping; and communications and public relations	Consultation on perceived issues, priorities and ideas; consultation on draft and final Strategy. Written material and conferences
Settled community	Especially site planning and land use planning; site protection; and unauthorised camping	Consultation on perceived issues, priorities and ideas; consultation on draft and final Strategy. Written material and feedback arrangements. Citizen jury?
Private landowners	Unauthorised camping	Consult on perceived problems and constraints and to agree respective roles in acting on unauthorised encampments
Crime & Disorder Reduction Partnership, Local Strategic Partnerships	Dependent on nature of partnership	Exchange information and consultation to ensure consistency and shared priorities
Highways Agency	Unauthorised camping	Consult to agree respective roles in acting on unauthorised encampments
Environment Agency	Fly tipping and pollution associated with unauthorised encampments	Consult to agree respective roles in acting on unauthorised encampments
Forestry Commission	Major land owner in some areas which may be affected by unauthorised camping	Consult to agree respective roles in acting on unauthorised encampments
English Nature	Unauthorised camping as it affects Sites of Special Scientific Interest	Consult to identify key areas and agree respective roles in acting on unauthorised encampments
National Trust	Major land owner in some areas which may be affected by unauthorised camping	Consult to agree respective roles in acting on unauthorised encampments
Ministry of Defence	Major land owner in some areas which may be affected by unauthorised camping	Consult to agree respective roles in acting on unauthorised encampments
Local press and other media	All aspects of the Strategy; especially site provision and unauthorised camping	Regular media briefings and invitations to all public events to ensure full appreciation of the issues and to encourage balanced coverage

GUIDE TO EFFECTIVE USE OF ENFORCEMENT POWERS

PART 1: UNAUTHORISED ENCAMPMENTS (ODPM, 2006)

Introduction

1 Some parts of the country experience regular unauthorised encampments, which can cause disruption and conflict locally, and can be expensive and time-consuming to clear. The Government's policies on Gypsy and Traveller accommodation and enforcement are set within a framework of rights and responsibilities in which everyone's rights must be equally respected but where, at the same time, equal standards of behaviour are expected from all. Creating and sustaining strong communities is at the heart of the Government's Respect agenda and will have benefits for the settled and Gypsy and Traveller communities alike.

2 Unauthorised camping is a problem which requires a range of solutions. The Government has already introduced new housing and planning policies to ensure that in the future the accommodation needs of Gypsies and Travellers will be properly understood and properly addressed, part of which is a new obligation on local authorities to identify suitable locations in their areas that can be used for the establishment of new public and private Gypsy and Traveller sites. In the meantime the Government is working with the Gypsy and Traveller community to find pragmatic local solutions to accommodation shortages while the longer-term policies take effect.

3 But part of the solution also lies in swift and effective enforcement. Where problematic encampments are allowed to remain, or repeatedly return, community hostility and conflict will be inflamed, and a sustainable long-term solution will become much harder to achieve. Effective enforcement will promote confidence in the ability of local agencies to manage Gypsy and Traveller issues properly, and forms an essential backdrop to the provision of more authorised sites. Local people need to know that they and their local environment can be and will be protected.

4 Strong powers are available to the police, local authorities and other landowners to deal with unauthorised encampments. This document provides a detailed step-by-step practical guide to the use of these powers.

5 It also sets out advice on:

- Choosing the most appropriate power.
- Speeding up the process.
- Keeping costs down.
- The eviction process.
- Preventing further unauthorised camping.

6 This document is intended for elected officials and others in the community who have an interest in how unauthorised camping by Gypsies and Travellers is managed in their area, and provides information to local authority officers and other landowners on options for dealing with such incidents.

7 This guidance explains the ways in which enforcement action can be made quicker, cheaper and more effective. Local authorities should also be aware that the wider policy they adopt towards Gypsy and Traveller issues will also make a great deal of difference. Enforcement action can be taken more swiftly, and can be more effective, where appropriate authorised provision for Gypsies and Travellers is in place within a local authority's area.

8 The use of joint protocols between the local authority, the police and any other relevant agencies is also highly effective in establishing how individual cases will be dealt with, and making sure that all parties are clear about their responsibilities and how they will work together.

9 Local authorities have an obligation to carry out welfare assessments on unauthorised campers to identify any welfare issues that need to be addressed, before taking enforcement action against them. Where police are taking enforcement action, it is good practice for them to liaise with the local authority over any welfare issues. It is also good practice for local authority officers to be present at any eviction from public land, to ensure that any welfare issues that arise at that time can be dealt with appropriately.

10 The Government is also establishing a new Task Group which draws together central and local Government, the police and other agencies to address the wide variations in the use of enforcement powers and to champion best practice. The group will act as expert advisers to the Office of the Deputy Prime Minister (ODPM) and the Home Office, who are working together to consider potential new measures to further strengthen enforcement, alongside the provision of more authorised sites.

11 Information on the Government's wider policies concerning Gypsies and Travellers, *Local authorities and Gypsies and Travellers – guide to responsibilities and powers,* can be found on the ODPM website at the following address: www.odpm.gov.uk/gypsysites

12 The information contained in this document should be read in conjunction with the joint ODPM/Home Office document, *Guidance on Managing Unauthorised Camping* and its supplementary document on Section 62A-E police powers. This gives more detailed advice on a range of matters, including toleration, joint working protocols and obligations on local authorities and other public agencies in respect of welfare enquiries.

13 Further documents will follow in this series which will provide guidance on dealing with unauthorised developments of land without planning permission, and anti-social behaviour, including fly-tipping.

Unauthorised encampment – the powers in summary

Common law powers

- can only be used by the landowner;
- are used to regain possession of land;
- does not require the involvement of the courts;
- enforced by the landowner and/or private bailiffs where necessary;
- does not provide any sanctions offence for the return of trespassers onto land.

Part 55 Civil Procedure Rules

- can only be used by the landowner;
- are used to regain possession of land;
- require civil court procedure;
- possession is enforced by county court bailiffs, where necessary;
- do not provide any sanctions for the return of trespassers onto land.

Sections 77-78 of the Criminal Justice and Public Order Act 1994

- can only be used by a local authority;
- can be used on any land within the local authority's area, irrespective of ownership;
- are used to remove identified individuals from land;
- only require the involvement of the courts when unauthorised campers do not leave when directed to do so;
- possession is enforced by local authority officers or private bailiffs employed by the local authority;
- the return of unauthorised campers and/or their vehicles to the location within three months carries criminal sanctions.

Sections 61-62 of the Criminal Justice and Public Order Act 1994

- can only be used by the police;
- can be used on any land except the highway;
- are used to remove identified individuals and/or their vehicles from land;
- there must be two or more persons trespassing on the land before the power can be used;
- do not require the involvement of the courts;
- possession is enforced by the police;
- the return of unauthorised campers to the location within three months carries criminal sanctions.

Section 62A-E of the Criminal Justice and Public Order Act 1994

- can only be used where an alternative site is available;
- can only be used by the police;
- can be used on any land;

- is used to remove identified individuals and/or their vehicles from the land;
- does not require the involvement of the courts;
- possession is enforced by the police;
- the return of unauthorised campers to the local authority area within three months carries criminal sanctions.

Unauthorised encampment – the powers in detail

Common law powers

14 All landowners can use their common law rights to recover land (ie, the tort of trespass against property). This allows the person in possession of land to evict an individual from their land, seek damages for their trespass on their land, and/or seek an injunction to prevent the trespass from occurring again.

15 Case law has established that a trespasser who enters land peaceably is entitled to a request to leave the land before being forcibly removed, while a trespasser who has entered land with force and violence may be removed without a previous request to depart.

16 If the trespasser does not leave the land the possessor of the land may use no more force than is reasonably necessary to evict him or her. Private bailiffs may be used to carry out the eviction. The issue of what is 'reasonable force' is a question of fact to be decided in beach individual case, however it must be an honestly held belief that in the particular circumstances the force that is used is reasonable, rather than excessive. Use of excessive force could give rise to a claim against the landowner by the trespassers.

17 Whenever a landowner is considering the use of common law rights he/she should notify the police of his/her intentions so that police officers can be present to prevent any breach of the peace.

18 If the police advise that, in the particular circumstances, it is inappropriate to attempt an eviction, action should always be delayed until such time as the police believe that it is safe to continue.

19 Parliament provides strong statutory powers to local authorities to enable them to deal with incidents of unauthorised camping under Section 77 of the Criminal Justice and Public Order Act 1994. The civil courts also offer an avenue to deal with unauthorised camping under Civil Procedures Rules Part 55.

Part 55 Civil Procedure Rules

20 Part 55 of Civil Procedure Rules allow any landowner to regain possession of his/her land. Where the land is leased, the terms of the lease will determine who has this power – longlessees and many short-lessees will be responsible for evictions, where they are 'person entitled to occupation of the land'. Someone with only the right, or permission, to use the land (ie, who does not have a controlling interest in it, for instance someone with the right to graze livestock) would not generally be able to recover possession of the land in this way if it is trespassed upon.

21 The first step is for the landowner to ask the trespassers to leave the land. If they refuse to do so, or ask to be allowed to remain for what the landowner considers to be an unacceptable time period, the landowner can then begin action against the unauthorised campers through the County Court.

22 If the objective is to achieve eviction as rapidly as possible, the landowner should alert the County Court to the need for expediting the case as soon as they are aware of the encampment's arrival.

23 The landowner completes the relevant documentation, including any evidence in relation to the encampment (photographs, witness statements and so on) and presents this to the court manager in the County Court. A date for a hearing is then agreed.

24 The Court then provides the landowner with the claim form to serve on the defendants (the papers can be issued to 'persons unknown' if it is not possible to ascertain the identities of the unauthorised campers). Service of the claim form can then be made by the landowner or his appointed representative (process servers can be employed to carry this out) either by handing the claim to the unauthorised campers directly, or by posting the claim in a prominent position on the land if this is not possible.

25 At the hearing, the facts of the case are set out before the judge. The landowner should provide documentation which satisfies the judge that the landowner has a legitimate interest in the land. The judge will be concerned to establish that the unauthorised campers have been dealt with appropriately before granting an eviction order but, thus satisfied, may grant the order immediately. In some cases, for instance, where the defendants have attended the hearing to defend the claim, the hearing may be adjourned to allow more time for more evidence to be gathered.

26 If the defendant fails to leave the land by the date of the hearing and the judge has agreed to grant possession to the landowner, a warrant will be issued immediately. Bailiffs (who will be court-appointed in most circumstances) will then visit the encampment and notify the defendant(s) of the eviction date and time and provide them with the eviction notice. Once again, this may be handed directly to the unauthorised campers or posted prominently on the land.

27 On the date of the eviction (which must be at least twenty four hours from the time at which the notice of eviction was served) the landowner or his appointed representative will accompany the bailiff to witness the eviction. The police should be alerted so that they can provide appropriate advice and be on hand to ensure that there are no breaches of the peace. After the eviction has taken place the land owner will then sign the warrant of possession to acknowledge that he has regained possession of the land (if court bailiffs are not available to carry out the eviction, private bailiffs may be employed in this capacity).

28 It should be noted that, where the landowner is a local authority or other public body, the necessary welfare assessments should be carried out alongside the court procedures and should be completed before any eviction is carried out.

29 Further details of the court procedures and forms can be found on line at: http://www.dca.gov.uk/civil/procedures_fin/index.htm

Sections 77-78 of the Criminal Justice and Public Order Act 1994

30 Section 77 of the CJPOA gives local authorities the power to direct individuals to remove their vehicles and belongings and to leave highway land, or any land occupied without the consent of the landowner, whether owned by the local authority itself or by any other public or private landowner.

31 Before commencing any action to evict an unauthorised encampment, local authorities have an obligation to carry out welfare assessments of the unauthorised campers. This may necessitate the involvement of local NHS bodies, where health issues are apparent.

32 Local authorities may then draw up a Direction which instructs the unauthorised campers to leave on a particular date and time. This document is approved and signed by an authorised signatory of the local authority (usually a solicitor or legal executive employed by the authority). It also identifies either individuals or vehicles on the unauthorised encampment.

33 The Direction is then served on the unauthorised campers by a local authority officer (the document must be given directly to one of the named unauthorised campers or affixed prominently to one of the vehicles).

34 If the campers have failed to move and/or remove any vehicles and other property by the date specified in the Direction, or return to the same location within three months of the date of the Direction, they are then committing a criminal offence and may be arrested by the police. If a prosecution is successful they may then be given a custodial sentence of up to three months, or be liable to a fine of up to £1,000.

35 In practice however, it can be more effective for local authorities to pursue unauthorised campers who have contravened a direction under Section 77 by using their powers under Section 78 of the CJPOA. This allows local authorities to advise the Magistrates' Court of the contravention and, if the court is satisfied, then they may grant an Order for Removal of Persons and Vehicles.

36 In the first instance, the Listing Clerk at the Magistrates' Court should be contacted in order to obtain a date for a court hearing, which is required before the Order can be issued. Depending on the location of the encampment, the local authority may ask the court to expedite the process so that the unauthorised campers can be moved quickly.

37 The appropriate local authority officer then attends the Application Court to make an application for a summons, which can be issued immediately. This summons requires the person(s) in charge of the caravan(s) to appear before a court hearing to answer the complaint.

38 The summons is then served on the unauthorised campers by the appropriate local authority officer or by a process server contracted to perform this service for the local authority.

39 A hearing in the Magistrates' Court is set for later in the day on which the summons is served, or on the following working day. A solicitor must appear at the hearing on behalf of the local authority. Good practice indicates that, where possible, the same solicitor should be used in all court proceedings relating to unauthorised camping by Gypsies and Travellers so that they have a good working knowledge of the legislation. The solicitor should be provided with all of the necessary court documents as well as any relevant background information (the findings of welfare enquiries for example). The solicitor will request that the magistrate grants an Order for Removal of Vehicles and Persons.

40 If the unauthorised campers attend the hearing and contest the eviction, the case may be adjourned in order to allow time to hear all the evidence. However, if the magistrate is satisfied that the correct procedures have been followed, the Order will be granted immediately in normal circumstances.

41 Once granted, the Order should be served on the unauthorised campers as soon as possible by a local authority officer or process server, as above.

42 Twenty-four hours must be allowed to elapse between serving the Order and any action to remove the unauthorised campers. At any point thereafter, the local authority (or private bailiffs employed on their behalf) may remove the unauthorised campers and their vehicles from the land. As with any eviction, police should be present to ensure that no breach of the peace takes place.

Sections 61-62 of the Criminal Justice and Public Order Act 1994

43 If the landowner or his agent has asked the unauthorised cam pers to leave the land by a particular date and time, and they have failed to do so, and any of the three following conditions have also been met:

- the unauthorised campers have caused damage to the land or property on the land;
- they have used threatening, abusive or insulting words or behaviour to the occupier, a member of his family or his employee or agent;
- there are six or more vehicles on the land.

44 The police can use Section 61 of the CJPOA to direct unauthorised campers to leave the site. They can do this without reference to the courts.

45 The initial step is for the landowner to make a formal request to the police that they use their powers under the CJPOA.

46 A senior police officer then considers whether it is appropriate to use the power, based on various factors:

- whether there are there other activities on the encampment, such as serious breaches of the peace, disorder, criminal activity or anti-social behaviour which would necessitate police involvement under their wider powers;

- given the impact of the unauthorised encampment on the environment and the local settled community, is it reasonable and proportionate to use police powers;
- is action by the police legally sustainable;
- are sufficient resources available.

47 Although case law (*R v The Commissioner of the Metropolitan Police ex p Small*) has established that police officers are not under any obligation to undertake welfare enquiries with unauthorised campers, they must be aware of humanitarian considerations when considering action to remove an encampment. The joint ODPM/Home Office document 'Guidance on managing unauthorised camping' recommends that local authorities should be involved in the process.

48 Once a decision to use police powers is made, a uniformed police officer visits the encampment and advises the occupiers that they are required to leave by a certain date and time, and provides them with a copy of the legislation. The police may determine the period of notice to the unauthorised campers to leave, and this may be hours or days. The police may also videotape their visit to the encampment in case of later challenge or dispute.

49 If the unauthorised campers fail to leave by the date and time specified by the police officer, or return to that location within three months of the direction, they are then committing an offence and liable on summary conviction to imprisonment for a term not exceeding three months or a fine not exceeding £2,500. Further, if a direction issued under Section 61 is contravened, a police officer may then seize and remove the vehicles under Section 62 of the CJPOA. Vehicles would be impounded in an appropriate police facility with a fee payable for their return.

Section 62A-E of the Criminal Justice and Public Order Act 1994

50 Section 62A of the CJPOA allows the police to direct trespassers to remove themselves and their vehicles and property from land where a suitable pitch on a relevant caravan site is available within the same local authority area (or within the county in two-tier local authority areas).

51 A suitable pitch on a relevant caravan site is one which is situated in the same local authority area as the land on which the trespass has occurred, and which is managed by a local authority, registered social landlord, or other person or body as specified by order by the Secretary of State. In two tier authority areas, where a district council is situated within a wider county council area, the relevant caravan site may be anywhere within the county council area.

52 The power may be used where the following conditions are met:

- at least two persons are trespassing;
- the trespassers have between them at least one vehicle on the land;
- the trespassers are present on the land with the common purpose of residing there for any period;

- it appears to the officer that the person has one or more caravans in his possession or under his control on the land, and that there is a suitable pitch on a relevant caravan site for that caravan or each of those caravans;
- the occupier of the land (ie, the freehold owner or lessee), or a person acting on the occupier's behalf has asked the police to remove the trespassers from the land.

53 If the unauthorised campers do not leave when directed to do so under **Section 62A**, or if they return to the district within three months after being directed, they are committing an offence, and the police may then use their powers under **Section 62B** of the CJPOA to arrest and detain them. If the campers are subsequently convicted of an offence under the Act, they may then be subject to a custodial sentence of not more than three months, or a fine not exceeding level 4 on the standard scale (currently, a maximum of £2,500).

54 The police may also use their powers under **Section 62C** of the CJPOA to seize and remove the vehicles and property from the land. Vehicles would be impounded in an appropriate police facility with a fee payable for their return.

55 Local authorities will need to confirm that appropriate alternative pitches are available in the area before the police use their powers (note the duty to consult local authorities within the area under Section 62A (5)) and, as with Section 61 of the CJPOA, it is good practice for local authorities to be involved in the process to ensure that any welfare needs are identified.

56 Specific guidance on the use of ss.62A-E powers was issued in March 2005, and is available on the ODPM website at: www.odpm.gov.uk/gyp-sysites.

Choosing the most appropriate power

57 The powers set out above all have different characteristics, and accordingly will be appropriate for different circumstances. The questions set out below will help agencies to determine the most appropriate power to use in different circumstances. In addition to the information that is provided here on relevant powers, it is important for the relevant enforcement provisions to be considered carefully in each situation to ensure that all requirements can be met. Local authorities and police forces should also agree protocols so that an overall policy and clear lines of responsibility are in place before the need for action arises.

58 The questions set out below will help agencies to determine the most appropriate power to use in different circumstances.

How important is speed?

59 It is unlawful for Gypsies and Travellers to camp on land they do not own without the landowner's permission. There are locations where immediate action to remove them should be taken because the presence of the encampment is seriously disrupting the ability of the

settled community to make use of facilities or to conduct their business, for instance:

- on school grounds during term time;
- on urban parks;
- on business or retail parks.

60 Similarly, swift action should be taken where the encampment is located on contaminated land or where the encampment is very close to a busy highway, potentially endangering the health and safety of the campers and others, or on land of a particularly sensitive nature, a Site of Special Scientific Interest (SSSI) for example.

61 In the above circumstances, Section 61 of the CJPOA is likely to be the most appropriate power, provided that the conditions for its use are met. The police can act immediately without reference to the courts, and can direct travellers to leave the site within a matter of hours. Clearly, this course of action will be more effective if there is an alternative site to which Gypsies and Travellers can be directed, either pitches on an authorised transit site, or a location which is deemed to be a more 'acceptable' unauthorised site.

Are there problems on the encampment such as anti-social behaviour, public disorder and so on?

62 In these circumstances it will be appropriate for the police to deal with these issues directly using their wider powers, and for them to disperse the encampment using s61 or s62A.

Is it desirable to evict some but not all the trespassers?

63 If the anti-social behaviour is focused amongst particular individuals in the group, or if a member of the group is ill, it may be appropriate to take action to evict some people but not others. In this case it may be most effective to use the powers under ss77-78 CJPOA, which focus on named individuals or vehicles, or to use the police powers.

Is the group of unauthorised campers stable, or are different vehicles arriving and departing?

64 Where the occupants of an unauthorised encampment change frequently, it may be more effective to use Civil Procedures Rules Part 55, which relate to the land itself, rather than the powers under the CJPOA, which require the individuals or vehicles on the encampment to be identified. Where these change, a new direction will have to be drawn up.

Do the unauthorised campers present welfare issues?

65 Local authority officers should conduct thorough welfare enquiries when a new encampment of Gypsies and Travellers arrives in the area. Where pressing needs for particular services are identified as part of the local authority's enquires, relevant departments or external agencies should be contacted in order to meet these needs as appropriate (health services, social services, housing departments and so on).

66 If necessary, removal of the encampment could be delayed while urgent welfare needs are addressed (unless, as above, the site on which the unauthorised campers are using is particularly sensitive or hazardous, in which case the unauthorised campers should be asked to relocate to a more appropriate location in the vicinity). Further, it may be possible to negotiate a date for the encampment to leave if, for instance, the Gypsies and Travellers have camped in the vicinity for a specific purpose; in order to attend an outpatient's appointment at the local hospital for example.

Is enforcement necessary?

67 If the Gypsies and Travellers are cooperative, only wish to stay for a short time and the encampment is not in a sensitive location, it may only be necessary to monitor the situation pending their departure. It may also be appropriate to provide the unauthorised campers with some means of disposing of rubbish and waste in order to minimise clear-up costs when they have left.

Is the decision to evict likely to be challenged?

68 In this case it may be appropriate to use Part 55 Civil Procedure Rules so that a judge can affirm the decision to evict based on the available evidence.

Are there suitable pitches available on relevant sites in the local authority area to which the unauthorised campers might go?

69 If this is the case, s62A of the CJPOA can be used.

Do particular groups repeatedly return to the area?

70 In this case it may be appropriate for the police to use their powers under section 62A, where there are suitable pitches available in the area. Section 62A can prevent campers returning to anywhere in the local authority area for a period of three months.

71 Where groups return to a specific location, ss6–62 and 77-78 can be used to prevent them returning to that location for a period of three months. It may also be appropriate to explore further options such as injunctions or Anti-Social Behaviour Orders.

Speeding up the process

Making authorised provision

72 Enforcement action will be quicker and more effective, and a wider range of powers can be used, where appropriate authorised provision is made for Gypsies and Travellers within the area. The Housing Act 2004 requires local authorities to undertake accommodation needs assessment for Gypsies and Travellers who reside in or resort to their areas, and then to set out a strategy to meet those needs. Adequate provision will have wide benefits in the management of unauthorised camping as:

- there will be less unauthorised camping in the first place;
- the police will not be restricted in the use of ss62A-E CJPOA if suitable pitches are available;

- legal challenges are less likely to occur or succeed;
- the courts are more likely to grant possession orders to local authorities who show they are acting responsibly in carrying out their wider duties and who deal with each incident of unauthorised camping on its merits.

Being prepared

73 Arrangements should be reached in advance, both within local authorities and the police themselves, but also between the parties, about how cases of unauthorised camping will be dealt with.

74 Local authorities should ensure that reports of unauthorised camping can be acted upon swiftly. They should nominate a named officer who has the appropriate level of authority to make operational decisions on the ground, and cover arrangements should be put in place for those instances where this officer is unavailable.

75 Procedures should be agreed with each agency that will be involved in the eviction process (including the police and those departments and agencies that may be called upon for assistance as a consequence of welfare enquiries). Good working relations, and clear lines of responsibility, particularly between the local authority and the police, can do a great deal to speed the processes up. Some areas that use police powers effectively have units staffed by both local authority employees and police officers.

Avoiding legal challenge

76 Considerable delays can occur if the unauthorised campers mount a legal challenge to the eviction. In some cases, this may be as part of a court process. However, a challenge can also be mounted to any public body via judicial review on the grounds that its decision-making was flawed. However, this risk can be minimised.

77 Local authorities should ensure that, in accordance with their wider obligations, and to ensure that they comply with Human Rights legislation, proper welfare enquiries are carried out to determine whether there are pressing needs presented by the unauthorised campers and that, where necessary, the appropriate agencies are involved as soon as possible.

78 Local authorities should also ensure that they follow proper procedures in dealing with an unauthorised encampment, and that their actions are fully documented. Comprehensive advice is set out in, *Managing Unauthorised Camping*, jointly issued by ODPM and Home Office, and available on the ODPM website at: www.odpm.gov.uk/gypsysites.

79 Local authorities should also prepare carefully for court appearances, making sure that evidence/court papers etc are in order, and that all legal requirements (such as serving notices) have been met.

Working with the courts

80 Local authorities should maintain regular contact with their local court service and discuss with them in advance any issues that are expected to arise. It may also be helpful for local authority officers to join the

Court User Group, which is a forum for discussing new legislation, and provides opportunities to raise issues such as court practice.

81 When unauthorised camping takes place and it is deemed that court action is appropriate, the court should be advised of any intention to file an application immediately (without waiting until all the paperwork is complete), so that the date for a hearing can be expedited.

Keeping costs down

82 Speeding up the enforcement process will in itself help to keep costs down, so the points set out in the previous section will be relevant here as well. In addition, the following points should be considered.

Avoiding unnecessary enforcement action

83 Before taking action, landowners should consider whether enforcement is absolutely necessary. It may be that in certain circumstances, alternatives to eviction action are appropriate, for example:

- where unauthorised campers have chosen an unobtrusive location in which to camp it may be preferable to agree a departure date with them;
- where unauthorised campers have chosen to stop in an unacceptable location, but where the local authority has also identified a location in the vicinity which would be much less damaging or obtrusive, unauthorised campers could be encouraged to move to this location.

84 If eviction is deemed necessary, in many cases the trespassers will leave after being served with an initial notice under Part 55 or a direction under the CJPOA powers, and no further enforcement action will be needed.

Avoiding unnecessary clean-up costs

85 Waste clearance from sites that have been used as unauthorised encampments should be undertaken rapidly in order to minimise the amount of fly-tipping that may take place after the encampment has gone. Where they can be identified, fly-tippers can also be fined for depositing waste illegally.

Avoiding unnecessary legal costs

86 Expertise and legal advice relating to unauthorised camping may be available from the district or county council, and landowners, parish councils and so on are advised to ensure that they have consulted with these bodies before taking further action. Good practice guidance and general advice on the management of unauthorised camping is also available from the ODPM, although the Department is not able to offer definitive legal advice on specific cases.

87 Local authorities should consider which parts of the enforcement process may be appropriately carried out by their own staff, as this is likely to be cheaper than contracting the work out to others. However, the local authority will wish to satisfy itself that their staff has the necessary expertise, and that their safety can be assured.

The eviction process

88 Where an eviction is being carried out by a local authority, its appointed representatives or the police, a local authority officer should always attend, as the local authority may have obligations to offer assistance to those who have been evicted, due to their wider social responsibilities. This may include temporarily caring for children where parents or guardians have been arrested and held in custody, or offering alternative accommodation to those Gypsies and Travellers who are identified as being homeless and in priority need.

89 Local authorities should also ensure that the appropriate departments, such as housing, social services, education and NHS bodies are made aware of the eviction and are in a position to be able to respond swiftly to any requests for assistance. If unauthorised campers have pets or livestock it may also be appropriate to involve the relevant bodies, the RSPCA for instance, in finding appropriate accommodation for them.

90 If an eviction is being carried out by a local authority or bailiffs, the police should be advised at an early stage so that they can advise and assist in relation to the issue of personal safety in order to minimise the possibility of physical harm. Police should also be on hand when an eviction is taking place in order to ensure that breaches of the peace do not occur. If the police recommend that the eviction should not proceed for any reason, action should be delayed until an agreed time.

91 If private bailiffs are to be used to evict unauthorised campers, stringent vetting should take place to ensure that those employed in this capacity are appropriately qualified to do so. The bailiffs should also indemnify the landowner against any potential liability (in terms of further costs incurred due to possible legal action) in respect of their activities to evict the unauthorised campers.

92 Wherever possible, the forthcoming eviction should be discussed with those on the encampment, and they should be notified of the date and time for the eviction. This will give those on the encampment time to prepare to leave, and will help to ensure that the eviction runs as safely and smoothly as possible.

93 However, there may be circumstances in which this is not appropriate – for example where those on the encampment have announced their intention of violently resisting the eviction. In this case it will be essential that the eviction is thoroughly planned, with the full involvement of the police at an early stage, and that every care is taken to ensure the safety of everyone involved.

Preventing further unauthorised camping

Following up on enforcement action

94 Where a particular group of Gypsies and Travellers repeatedly camp in a specific location, and the police or the local authority have used their powers under the CJPOA to remove them, it is important that the criminal sanctions set out in the legislation are pursued if the

unauthorised campers return within three months of being directed to leave.

Other legal action

95 Other legal remedies such as injunctions and Anti-Social Behaviour Orders (ASBOs) may be used to prevent Gypsies and Travellers from returning to an area where they have caused problems in the past. Local authorities may be able to obtain these remedies at the same time as taking court action for possession or eviction. Guidance on their use can be found at: www.together.gov.uk.

96 If injunctions or ASBOs are obtained to prevent unauthorised camping by particular groups, it is important that breaches are followed up with the appropriate legal sanctions, such as fines or imprisonment.

Provision of appropriate sites

97 The most effective method of combating unauthorised camping is to provide sites in accessible locations for those Gypsies and Travellers who pass through the area. This may not be limited to official residential and transit sites; it might also include particular locations which have been identified in the district where Gypsies and Travellers can stop for limited and agreed short periods of time, without having any adverse impact on the settled community.

Site protection measures

98 Site protection measures could also be considered in locations which are particularly vulnerable to unauthorised camping, for instance by creating earth bunds, or embankments, around the site, or by introducing height restrictions to entrances.

Additional sources of information

Part 55 Possession Claims – Department for Constitutional Affairs guidance, available on the internet at: ww.dca.gov.uk/civil/procrules_fin/contents/parts/part55.htm#4223902

Guidance on Managing Unauthorised Camping – ODPM/Home Office joint guidance, available on the internet at: ww.odpm.gov.uk/stellent/groups/odpm_housing/documents/page/odpm_house_027535.hcsp

Additional Guidance on Sections 62A-E CJPOA: www.odpm.gov.uk/stellent/groups/odpm_housing/documents/page/odpm_house_035805.hcsp

Information on the Government's Policies relating to Gypsies and Travellers: www.odpm.gov.uk/gypsysites

Information on HM Courts Service: www.hmcourts-service.gov.uk/cms/aboutus.htm

Information on tackling anti-social behaviour in the community: www.together.gov.uk

Information on fly-tipping: www.defra.gov.uk/environment/localenv/flytipping/index.htm

Glossary of terms

Breach of the Peace – a disturbance of public peace or order. Traditionally, one of the roles of the police is to 'keep the peace'. Breach of the peace is a common law offence.

Common Law – law determined as a result of decisions made by the courts as distinct from law laid down by statute.

Civil Offence – civil law governs the relationships and transactions between citizens set out in statute and common law. The majority of civil actions are heard in the 218 county courts, where cases are presided over by a district judge.

Criminal Offence – criminal law mostly involves the rules laid down by the state concerning the conduct of citizens. Most minor criminal cases, called summary offences, are heard in local Magistrates' Courts either by a panel of lay magistrates assisted by a legally-trained clerk, or by a legally-trained district judge sitting alone. The most serious offences, called indictable-only offences, are passed on by the Magistrates' Courts to the Crown Court to be heard, usually by a judge and jury. Only Crown Court judges have the power to pass sentences above a certain level of severity, and so some cases may be transferred from Magistrates' Courts for sentencing once a verdict has been reached. There are 78 Crown Court centres throughout England and Wales.

County Court – the court which deals with the majority of civil actions. Cases are presided over by a district judge.

County Court bailiff – they are employees of the County Court, and enforce County Court Judgements, such as warrants of execution for debts. They also have a role in evictions of unauthorised campers under Civil Procedures Rules Part 55.

Fly-Tipping – the illegal and unauthorised dumping of waste.

Human Rights Act – an Act passed in 1998, and brought into force in October 2000, which requires all public authorities making decisions that affect individuals to consider whether those decisions are reasonable and proportionate, bearing in mind all the circumstances.

Injunction – an order made by a Civil Court (County or High Court) which usually prohibits a somebody from doing something, based on the fact they have done it before, usually seriously and/or often. If an injunction is breached, the person can be fined or imprisoned for a contempt of the court by not according with the terms of the injunction.

Magistrates' Court – the lowest kind of criminal court in England and Wales and other common law jurisdictions. A Magistrate's Court is presided over by two or more Justices of the Peace (magistrates), or by a stipendiary magistrate, and dispenses summary justice, under powers usually limited by statute. The court will also determine committals to the Crown Court.

Private Bailiff (or Enforcement Agent) – someone who is responsible for the enforcement of court orders. Private landowners can also use them where there is no court order. Employed in the private sector. Private bailiffs can also be used to evict unauthorised campers following court proceedings under Civil Procedures Rules Part 55 where court bailiffs are not available.

Process Server – a privately employed individual who personally delivers a process (a writ compelling attendance in court) or court papers to a defendant (process servers are normally employees of private investigation companies).

Protocol – an agreement of an approach, usually between various different public bodies.

Site of Special Scientific Interest – this is a planning policy definition, and it is the name given to specific pieces of land which should not be disturbed or developed. They may be the home of, or an area resorted to by, a rare or protected animal or bird, the site may include a rare type of vegetation, or the land may contain a special geological feature or something else unique. By definition, they must not have houses, caravan sites or other development on them.

Statutory Powers – powers given by an Act of Parliament, as distinct from powers under common law.

Title (to land) – the evidence of someone's ownership of a piece of land, based on tracing the history of it, and showing legal transfer of ownership to them.

Tort – a civil wrong committed by one person against another (eg, trespassing on their land).

Unauthorised development – development of a site on land owned by Gypsies and Travellers, but for which they do not have planning permission.

Unauthorised encampment – trespassing by Gypsies and Travellers on land which they do not own (eg, playing fields, farmers' fields or other private land).

Welfare Assessments – action carried out by local authority officers with unauthorised campers to identify and address any issues that require the involvement of other local authority departments and agencies in terms of immediate health, education etc needs.

APPENDIX – PRIMARY LEGISLATION

CRIMINAL JUSTICE AND PUBLIC ORDER ACT 1994 PART V

[Not reproduced. See above in appendix B for relevant sections of CJPOA 1994.]

WELSH GOVERNMENT GUIDANCE ON UNAUTHORISED CAMPING 2013[1]

Which part of this guidance applies to the encampment I wish to resolve?

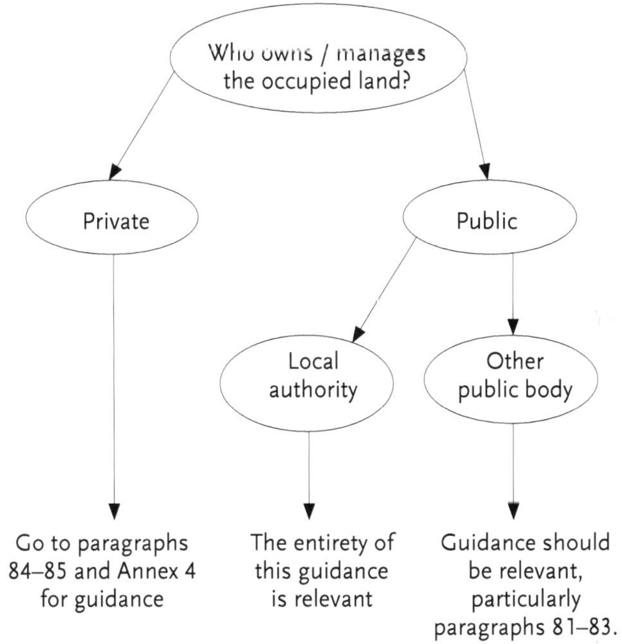

The process of responding to unauthorised camping may alter dependent upon who owns the occupied land. Public authorities have additional responsibilities which do not apply to private landowners. For more guidance on this matter, please go to the relevant page number suggested above.

A summary of potential legal powers available to all landowners is available at **Annex 4**.

Welsh Government Guidance on Managing Unauthorised Camping

Section 1 – Introduction

1. Unauthorised encampments can be the source of community tensions and require sensitive handling as public authorities attempt to find a balance between the rights of campers and local residents.

1 © Welsh Government, 2013.

2. An unauthorised encampment is an encampment of caravans and/or vehicles on land without the landowner's or occupier's consent and therefore constituting trespass.

3. Unauthorised camping does not relate to cases where land has been bought and occupied, without the appropriate planning permission. That is known as unauthorised development. These types of development will not be included in this Guidance.

4. An unauthorised encampment and its unauthorised campers, can be any group of individuals or vehicles trespassing on land. However this Guidance is aimed at addressing the specific issues around the unauthorised encampments of Gypsies and Travellers.

5. 'Gypsies and Travellers' is a generic term used to define a number of people who subscribe to the Gypsy or Traveller way of life, as well as to certain cultural and moral beliefs. This Guidance uses the following definition of Gypsies and Travellers:

   Persons with a cultural tradition of nomadism or of living in a caravan; and all other persons of a nomadic habit of life, whatever their race or origin, including –

   (i) such persons who, on grounds only of their own or their family's or dependant's educational or health needs or old age, have ceased to travel temporarily or permanently; and

   (ii) members of an organised group of travelling show people or circus people (whether or not travelling together as such)[2]

   Therefore, this Guidance may include:

   - Romani Gypsies.
   - Irish Travellers.
   - Scottish or Welsh Gypsy / Travellers.
   - European Roma.[3]
     - 'New' Travellers.
     - Show-people.

6. All of these groups are associated with the travelling way of life and can share some common beliefs and practices, but each group will have distinctive languages, traditions and ethnicity.

7. The Equality Act 2010 prohibits discrimination on the grounds of race which includes colour, nationality and ethnic or national origins. Case law has established that both Romany Gypsies and Irish Travellers are recognised racial groups for the purposes of the Race Relations Act 1976. These groups continue to be recognised racial groups for the purposes of the Equality Act 2010.

2 Housing (Assessment of Accommodation Needs) (Meaning of Gypsies and Travellers) (Wales) Regulations 2007.

3 The term "Roma" used by the Welsh Government refers to Roma, Sinti, Kale and related groups in Europe, including the Eastern groups (Dom and Lom).

The Picture in Wales

8. Gypsies and Travellers are indigenous to Wales. In 2006, the Welsh Government commissioned a report called, *"Accommodation Needs of Gypsy-Travellers in Wales"* (Niner, 2006), which estimated there were around 2,000 Gypsies and Travellers resident in Wales. However in 2009 a desk-based exercise conducted by the Welsh Government estimated that there were 4,000 Gypsies and Traveller living in Wales either on permanent sites, in transit or living in 'bricks and mortar' accommodation.

9. The Census 2011 included a new ethnic category for 'Gypsy or Irish Traveller' but the data suggested a total of just 2,785 Gypsies and Irish Travellers in Wales. Given that we know about this reluctance to disclose ethnicity, and having undertaken an informal exercise by Welsh Government officials to ask if the census 2011 had been completed by those living on sites, we recognise that this number may be an under- estimate.

10. Due to the nature of a transitory population and the reluctance to disclose ethnicity, it is difficult to obtain more accurate figures. However, it is clear that there are more Gypsies and Travellers and caravans than there are permanent sites or authorised places to stop. At the time of publication, there were no authorised Temporary Stopping Places or Transit Sites in Wales. The distinction between these types of site can be found in the glossary at the end of this guidance.

11. Figures from the Welsh Government Caravan Count suggest that the proportion of Gypsy and Traveller caravans stationed on unauthorised encampments varies between 14–23% of the total. In July 2013, the proportion was estimated as 17%, accounting for 169 caravans in total.

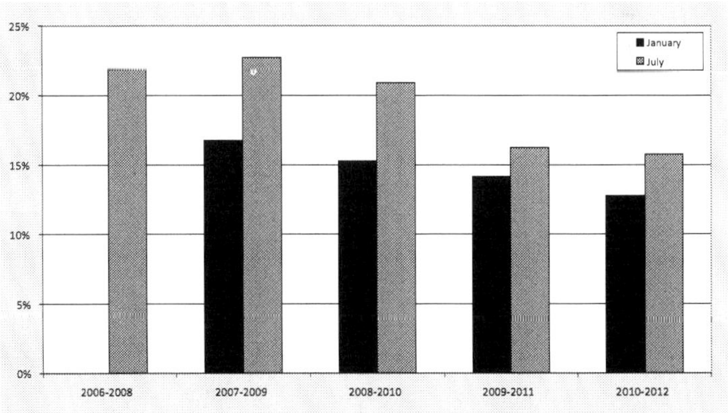

12. The Caravan Count figures are likely to underestimate the true amount of caravans on unauthorised encampments as not all encampments will be known to the local authority undertaking the survey. A report into the English Caravan Count system (Niner, *Counting*

Gypsies and Travellers: A Review of the Gypsy Caravan Count System, for the Office of the Deputy Prime Minister, 2004), highlighted reasons why this data isn't always an accurate reflection of the Gypsy and Traveller population.

13. In Wales unauthorised encampments tend to occur along the main transport routes which traditionally provided opportunities for work as well as access to the main ports for Ireland. The main routes are found along the M4 corridor as the main route from east to west in the south of Wales, the A470 as the main route from north to south Wales and along the A55 as the link from east to west in the north of Wales. However, encampments are found throughout Wales, often nowhere near these busy routes.

14. As a reflection of these routes some local authorities in Wales are more at risk of unauthorised encampments than others. However all local authorities are likely to experience some unauthorised encampments and should have policies and procedures in place to ensure that they are dealt with in a way that is effective, safe and humane to all parties involved. To facilitate this, the Welsh Government has developed this Guidance to assist local authorities to develop their own policies.

15. Gypsies and Travellers will often travel to visit cultural shows or fairs. The most high-profile Welsh show is the Royal Welsh Show in Llanelwedd, Powys. Historically, a large unauthorised encampment of Romani Gypsies and Irish Travellers will gather for the duration of the show. In recent years, Powys County Council has provided temporary planning permission for the encampment.

16. The Welsh Government committed to revising its Managing Unauthorised Camping Guidance within the UK's first Gypsy and Traveller strategy, *Travelling to a Better Future: A Gypsy and Traveller Framework for Action and Delivery Plan*. The Welsh Government also committed to create a generic protocol which local authorities could adapt to their specific area.

17. The Guidance aligns with the Welsh Government's *Strategic Equality Plan* by ensuring that Gypsy and Traveller communities are provided with the information and support they need to exercise their rights. The Welsh Government is committed to equality of opportunity for all, to allow people from different backgrounds to live harmoniously together.

Who is this Guidance for?

18. This Guidance is aimed at anyone regularly dealing with unauthorised encampments of Gypsies and Travellers, primarily local authorities in Wales.

19. However the Guidance may also be of use by other land owners including other public authorities, such as National Park Authorities or Health Boards, as well as those attending unauthorised sites and assisting local authorities in their duties, for example health visitors, Traveller Education Services (TES) and police forces.

20. The Association of Chief Police Officers (ACPO) has issued its own *"Guidance on Unauthorised Encampments"* (June 2011), which is designed specifically for members of the police visiting unauthorised sites. In conjunction with that guidance, Police may wish to consider this document when dealing with instances of unauthorised camping.

21. Though this Guidance is not aimed primarily at Gypsies and Travellers who may need to temporarily reside on an unauthorised encampment, some community members may find it to be a useful introduction to their rights and responsibilities in such a situation.

22. For the purposes of this Guidance the land owner will generally be referred to as the local authority. The Welsh Government recognises that unauthorised encampments do not occur exclusively on local authority owned land but different rules apply to private land owners. These rules will be explored briefly later in the document.

Aims of the Guidance

23. The Guidance aims to:

- Provide all parties involved in unauthorised encampments clear guidance on roles, responsibilities and rights.
- Ensure a fair and consistent approach to dealing with unauthorised encampments which complies with legislation to a standard that meets the needs of all involved.
- Set out recommended courses of action i.e. a step-by-step guide of what to do if you are dealing with an unauthorised encampment.
- Share current good practice examples.
- Provide templates for undertaking crucial welfare assessments, which local authorities across Wales can utilise.

Section 2 – Understanding Unauthorised Encampments and possible remedies

Why do unauthorised encampments occur?

24. Unauthorised encampments vary in purpose and may occur for a number of reasons. The primary reason for unauthorised encampments is the lack of authorised sites and stopping places. Nomadic Gypsies and Travellers have suffered from a systematic closure of traditional stopping places through bye-laws, strengthening of laws relating to the use of common land for camping, and landowners blocking off historical resting points. Meanwhile, demand for authorised pitches has outstripped supply to such an extent that Wales now has a severe shortage of Gypsy and Traveller sites.

25. The Welsh Government does not condone unauthorised encampments by Gypsies and Travellers. However, without sufficient and appropriate site provision, effective and justifiable enforcement against unauthorised encampments cannot be achieved. Addressing the issue of unauthorised encampment must be considered in the context of the current availability of adequate site provision. Delivering more authorised sites coupled with effective site management will remove the

reason for unauthorised encampments. It is vital that local authorities have protocols in place to deal appropriately and proportionately with unauthorised encampments. As the necessary sites and stopping places are developed these protocols will need to be invoked less and less, thereby reducing the administrative and financial implications of dealing effectively with the unauthorised encampments.

26. It is likely that each unauthorised encampment will differ from the next. They may vary in terms of:

- **Size**: typically encampments will consist of just a few caravans but can increase significantly in relation to major funerals or weddings or traditional cultural fairs.
- **Location**: from concealed grassland areas to protected land or highly visible areas e.g. on the road side. Increasingly, encampments are occurring on industrial or business parks.
- **Behaviour**: as with the settled population some encampments may cause a nuisance to the local community while others may not.
- **Impact on the land**: some groups may leave an area unspoilt and tidy while others may damage the land and leave waste behind.

27. Gypsies and Travellers may be on unauthorised encampments for a variety of reasons. These might include (though this is not an exhaustive list):

- The occupiers have no authorised pitch on which to station their caravan.
- Newly married couples may have left their parents' pitches but have no legal pitch of their own.
- To attend a family event locally such as a wedding or funeral.
- Attempts to adjust to living in 'bricks and mortar' may have failed.
- To rest overnight whilst travelling to another location, for example to a permanent site or a port.
- Health reasons, for example if a member of the group requires urgent medical care, a visit to a GP for medication or if a pregnant woman has reached her due date.
- To find work.
- To allow school-age children to attend school and receive an education.
- To provide a respite from travelling for an elderly or sick member of the group.
- Poor site management may have led to the group leaving their authorised pitch.

28. Longer term encampments will generally occur for education or healthcare reasons, or simply because there is no legal alternative pitch available.

29. Shorter term encampments can occur for a wider range of circumstances and may only last for the duration of wedding celebrations or for an extended period of hospital treatment.

30. Both types of unauthorised encampment will have consequences for the local area in terms of the provision of services, enforcement action, and access to the occupied land.

31. Local authorities should recognise that it may be more cost effective to provide a site, even if that is a temporary tolerated site, than to enforce against unauthorised encampments in an area with no site provision and where there are a high number of unauthorised encampments. Such sites could reduce community tensions, remove the potential of damaged public land, and ensure that clear-up costs are reduced. Developing and providing authorised, permanent sites would provide revenue forlocal authorities as occupants would be required to pay a pitch fee and Council Tax.

32. An authorised site is a site where Gypsies and Travellers are permitted to stay with the permission of the land owner and normally enter into a contract with the land owner and pay a rental for the pitch they stay on. These sites also require the appropriate planning permission. There are two types of pitches on authorised sites: permanent residential pitches and transit pitches.

33. A transit pitch is another name used for a pitch on an authorised site where Gypsies and Travellers may stay for a short period of time of up to 3 months (see the Mobile Homes Act 1983 Schedule 1 Part 1 Chapter 3).

34. Currently there is only one transit pitch located on permanent sites in Wales and no designated transit sites (Welsh Government Caravan Count data, July 2013). Local authorities have confirmed that mixing permanent and transit provision on one site has not often been achieved successfully due to tensions that can arise between residents on different types of pitch.

35. Local authorities can consider providing temporary stopping places, which are intended to serve a particular short-term purpose and are not considered to be the permanent solution. Tolerated encampments are similar to temporary stopping places, though the latter have been set aside explicitly for the purpose of occupation and should provide basic amenities for occupiers, including waste disposal, water supply and sanitation. Temporary stopping places can also be proactively provided to relocate encampments from inappropriate locations. The difference between these and transit sites is explained in the glossary.

36. The Welsh Government accepts that some unauthorised encampments can cause problems of anti–social behaviour and can raise community tensions. Part of the solution to this is the provision of adequate sites within the local authority area though some encampments are always likely to occur. Providing adequate sites should allow local authorities to relocate inappropriate encampments to more appropriate locations.

37. Local authorities must undertake a Gypsy & Traveller Accommodation Needs Assessment (Commonly referred to as the GTAA), as required by a combination of section 8 of the Housing Act 1985 and section 225 of the Housing Act 2004. This assessment is to identify the housing needs in a local authority area. Where the assessment identifies a lack of provision for Gypsies and Travellers a local authority may wish to consider identifying locations for new sites, providing for the identified needs and, where possible, Welsh Government encourage them to make full use of Welsh Government grants to develop new sites and expand or improve existing sites.

38. In 2011, the Welsh Government estimated a need for 350 extra pitches on Gypsy and Traveller sites in Wales. As there are currently only 366 pitches on local authority Gypsy and Traveller sites, this figure represents a severe shortage of culturally appropriate accommodation for these communities. The Welsh Government outlined its intention in the White Paper, "*Homes for Wales: A White Paper for Better Lives and Communities*", to introduce a statutory duty on local authorities to provide Gypsy and Traveller sites, where there is identified need. The Housing (Wales) Bill, introduced in the National Assembly for Wales in November 2013 makes provision for this duty.

39. The expectation is that new authorised sites should lead to a significant reduction in unauthorised encampments.

40. The Welsh Government Gypsy and Traveller Sites Grant will provide £1.5m in 2013–14 and offers up to 100% of the costs of site build costs orrefurbishment. The guidance can be found on the Welsh Government website.[4]

Approaches to Resolving Unauthorised Encampments

41. Effectively, if an unauthorised encampment arises and there are no alternative authorised pitches in the area, local authorities have three clear paths relating to how they can resolve the encampment. **Each** option should be carefully considered:

- **Path 1** – To seek and obtain possession of the occupied site (eviction proceedings).
- **Path 2** – To 'tolerate' the Gypsy or Traveller occupiers, if only for a short time, until an alternative site can be found or the occupiers move on voluntarily.
- **Path 3** – To find an alternative site, if only on a temporary basis, and offer the Gypsy or Traveller occupiers the chance to move onto it.

42. Deciding which path to take is about finding a critical balance between considering the welfare and human rights of Gypsies and Travellers, whilst safeguarding the human rights of landowners, occupiers and the public, and protecting them from health and safety hazards or public nuisance. Each encampment should be dealt with on a case-by-case basis.

43. It is recommended that local authorities undertake an initial visit to the encampment before deciding which option is the most appropriate. This will enable the gathering of key information about why the encampment has occurred, if there are any urgent welfare concerns and how long the occupiers plan to stay. There is an initial assessment pro-forma available as **Annex 2** of this document.

4 http://wales.gov.uk/topics/housingandcommunity/grants/gypsytravellergrant1213/?lang=en

44. Encampments will often be first identified by local residents and businesses who are concerned about the potential impact on them. Concerns will range from anti-social behaviour, fly-tipping, expanding camps, permanent occupation, or harm to house prices or business interests. Many of these concerns prove to be unfounded but some encampments have certainly had a direct and substantial impact on the lives of local residents. Therefore, the public may have expectations that encampments may be cleared as quickly as possible after the local authority has been notified.

45. The initial encampment visit by the lead local authority officer (preferably the Single Point of Contact for unauthorised camping, which is discussed later in this document) should establish any immediate concerns with the condition of the encampment or behaviour and the intentions of the occupiers. If little annoyance or impact on local residents is identified, it should not be assumed that possession action will be taken against the encampment.

46. Some form of effective welfare enquiry is necessary to identify whether needs exist and the local authority should liaise with other services that might have responsibilities towards the campers' families. These checks should be done as quickly as possible, ideally within 24 hours of the local authority becoming aware of the encampment.

47. The determination of whether eviction action should be taken should be made after consideration of whether the interference with Gypsy or Traveller family life and home is justified and proportionate. Any particular welfare needs experienced by unauthorised campers are material in reaching a balanced and proportionate decision. The human rights of members of the settled community are also material if an authority fails to act to curb nuisance from an encampment.

48. If there is no substantial risk to public safety and no inappropriate behaviour, and no alternative authorised pitches available, the impact and benefit of evicting the occupiers should be considered carefully.

49. <u>Tolerated encampments</u> can be pragmatic and cost-effective in terms of finding a long-term solution to unauthorised camping in the area. Evicting the occupiers will often lead to extensive costs to the local authority and police force. Furthermore, if the occupiers had settled in the area due to a lack of alternative pitches, it is likely that they will settle on another unauthorised camp within the area in the near future. This would then be accompanied by even greater costs incurred by the local authority and police force. Toleration can also be a useful tool where local authorities have not provided enough Gypsy and Traveller accommodation in their area.

50. Proactively identifying temporary stopping places can also provide a pragmatic and cost-effective solution, which enables the local authority to relocate an encampment from an inappropriate location whilst recognising the need to provide support to the occupiers.

51. Gypsies and Travellers living in caravans with nowhere to legally station them are likely to be legally homeless under section 175 of the Housing Act 1996. The circumstances of every individual will

inform what duties a local authority is subject to under the Housing Act 1996 in respect of those individuals. local authorities may wish to consider, in certain circumstances, whether it would be appropriate to tolerate the encampment until the outcome of any homelessness application is known, unless the encampment is an immediate threat to public safety or community cohesion. Welsh Government circular 30/2007 – Planning for Gypsy and Traveller caravan sites – states that,

> *"a temporary permission may be justified where it is expected that the planning circumstances will change in a particular way at the end of the period of the temporary permission. In cases where there is:*
>
> - *unmet need and;*
> - *no available alternative Gypsy and Traveller site provision in an area and; a reasonable expectation that new sites are likely to become available at the end of that period in the area which will meet that need; local planning authorities should give consideration to granting a temporary permission".*

Section 3 – Legislation

52. There is a range of legislation that is applicable with regard to unauthorised encampments. Some of this is detailed below. It is important to remember that legislation and protection by law, applies to both the land owner and also to Gypsy and Traveller communities.

Housing Act 2004

53. In December 2007, section 225 of the Housing Act 2004 was brought into force in relation to Wales. This section places a duty on local housing authorities to carry out an assessment of the accommodation needs of Gypsies and Travellers (GTAA) residing in or resorting to their district when undertaking a review of housing needs in their district under section 8 of the Housing Act 1985. The assessments will allow proper consideration to be given to the accommodation needs of Gypsies and Travellers and result in any provision being properly researched and therefore needs-based.

54. The GTAA must inform the development of a local authority Housing Strategy where that local authority has been directed by the Welsh Ministers under section 87 of the Local Government Act 2003 to prepare a strategy in respect of meeting such accommodation needs.

55. Section 225(5)(a) of the Housing Act 2004 states that the meaning of "Gypsies and Travellers" has the meaning given by regulations made by the appropriate national authority. The Welsh Ministers prescribed the definition for the purposes of section 225 of the Housing Act as:

> *Persons with a cultural tradition of nomadism or of living in a caravan; and all other persons of a nomadic habit of life, whatever their race or origin, including –*

(i) such persons who, on grounds only of their own or their family's or dependant's educational or health needs or old age, have ceased to travel temporarily or permanently; and

(ii) members of an organised group of travelling show people or circus people (whether or not travelling together as such).[5].

56. This definition clearly shows that Gypsies and Travellers who have settled in bricks and mortar housing, for any of the reasons stated, still need to be included in the GTAA. This is important as many of these people will have moved into houses as there was no legal alternative and a large proportion will fail to adjust to their new homes effectively, sometimes becoming homeless again within a short period of time. Many unauthorised encampments will occur directly because of this reason. Therefore, it is in local authorities' interests to ensure their GTAA is completed thoroughly, including surveying those who they may have believed were happy living in conventional housing.

57. Many Gypsies and Travellers have a recognised cultural aversion to living in houses but currently local authorities only currently have to provide bricks and mortar accommodation. The cultural aversion to conventional housing has been established in case law[6] and has been evidenced by various psychiatric assessments of Gypsies and Travellers. Many Gypsies and Travellers have lived their entire lives in trailers, surrounded by family and used to regular travel. Transition to housing can cause significant emotional and mental stress, as families adjust to a more sedentary lifestyle and not surrounded by their support networks. This isolation, and often prejudice from new neighbours, has led to substance abuse and mental illness amongst some. Other families have resorted to only sleeping on the ground floor and references to feeling "claustrophobic" in conventional housing are common. Many Gypsies and Travellers are simply unable to even contemplate moving into conventional housing. As a result, many families are made re-homeless due to their inability to cope with the transition within a short period of time.

Criminal Justice and Public Order Act 1994

58. Sections 61 and 62 of the Criminal Justice and Public Order Act 1994 confer powers on the police to remove any trespasser and vehicle from land. Exercise of the power is conditional on a number of factors and in any event only where the senior police officer present at the scene reasonably believes that two or more persons are trespassing on land with the common purpose of residing there for any period. Reasonable steps must also be taken by or on behalf of the

5 See Housing (Assessment of Accommodation Needs) (Meaning of Gypsies and Travellers) (Wales) Regulations 2007 (S.I. 2007/3235).

6 The phrase 'cultural aversion to conventional housing' first appeared in *Clarke v Secretary of State for the Environment, Transport and the Regions* [2001] EWHC 800 (Admin).

occupier[7] to ask them to leave. [A landowner who is a local authority or another public authority, may wish to consider this guidance in exercising their functions as it may show reasonable steps have been taken if possession action is taken.]

59. There are further conditions which must exist before the police may exercise the powers in section 61 and 62. These include:

- Any of the trespassers have caused damage to land or property (this includes to gain entry to the site);
- Any of the trespassers have used threatening, abusive or insulting words or behaviour towards the occupier of the land, their family, or an agent acting on their behalf, or;
- The trespassers have between them six or more vehicles (including caravans).

60. Subject to the above, the senior police officer present at the scene may direct the unauthorised campers to vacate the site as soon as is reasonably practicable. The ACPO Guidance sets out that the police should consider becoming involved, including the use of their powers under sections 61 and 62 where:

- ○ Local amenities are deprived to communities or significant impact on the environment.
- ○ There is a local disruption to the economy.
- ○ There is other significant disruption to the local community or environment.
- ○ There is a danger to life; and
- ○ There is a need to take preventative action.

61. It is also an offence for any trespasser who has left the land as a result of this order to return within three months of the direction being given.

62. Sections 62A – E provide further powers for the police in relation to trespassers. The police may direct a person to leave land and remove any vehicle and other property from the land if certain conditions are satisfied. The conditions are:

- There must be at least two persons trespassing on the land.
- The two persons between them have at least one vehicle on the land.
- The trespassers are on the land with the common purpose of residing there for any period.
- It appears to the police officer at the scene that the person has one or more caravans in his possession or under his control on the land and that there is a suitable pitch on a relevant caravan site for that caravan or each of those caravans; and
- The occupier of the land, or a person acting on their behalf, must also have asked the police to remove the trespassers from the land.

7 The reference to occupier is a reference to the person entitled to possession of the land in question.

63. In this guidance, a relevant caravan site is one which is situated in the same local authority area as the land on which the trespass has occurred, and which is managed by the local authority. The meaning of suitable pitch is not defined in this legislation. It is for the courts to interpret legislation, but the Welsh Government considers that a suitable pitch is one that provides basic amenities including water, toilets and waste disposal facilities. This could include a transit site or temporary stopping place, or permanent residential site. There should be a reasonable expectation that the pitch will be available for peaceful occupation for at least three months, except where the trespasser is expecting to move on before that time. In determining if a suitable pitch is available, the police officer must consult the local authority within whose area the land is situated. Normally, a suitable pitch will only be available if there are currently no waiting lists for that site.

64. In advising on whether a suitable pitch is available, the local authority should take account of the results of welfare enquiries undertaken at theencampment, which may give rise to human rights issues. In particular, efforts should be made to find suitable pitches that would enable the unauthorised campers to remain together. If the size of the encampment is such that this is not possible, then efforts should be made to ensure that any dependent members of the encampment are not separated from necessary support. For example, parents and dependent children, or adults supporting elderly or infirm relatives, should not be separated.

65. Section 77 of the Criminal Justice and Public Order Act 1994 gives local authorities the power to direct persons to leave land and remove any vehicles or property. Failure to comply with a direction is an offence and punishable by a fine. In addition, if a direction is not complied with the local authority may obtain an order from the magistrates' court under section 78 of the Act. The order may require the removal of any person on the land together with vehicles and may authorise the local authority to take such steps that are reasonably necessary to ensure that the order is complied with.

Highways Act 1980

66. Section 143 of the Highways Act 1980 gives a power to a highway authority to remove, on one month's notice, any structures set up on a highway. The definition of structure includes a caravan or vehicle and a court order is not necessary to use this section.

Civil Procedure Rules 1998

67. A possession order can be obtained in the civil courts requiring the removal of any trespassers from property under Part 55 of the Civil Procedure Rules. This remedy is also available to private landowners.

European Convention on Human Rights /Human Rights Act 1998

68. The Human Rights Act 1998 (HRA) came into force in October 2000, incorporating the European Convention on Human Rights into British law. Broadly speaking, the European Convention on Human Rights requires that all decisions made by public authorities must be compliant

with the rights conferred by the European Convention on Human Rights. Public law requires that decisions of public bodies are reasonable and proportionate having regard to all the circumstances. A public authority must determine if any interference with a Gypsy or Traveller's home and private and family life is justified and proportionate. It is recommended that all decision- making is fully recorded and evidenced. This is in order to ensure that all decisions are supported by the relevant information and evidence and in the event of the decision being revisited or reviewed, the relevant information would be readily available to the local authority. If any decision is the subject of any legal challenge the information would also assist the local authority to present their rationale for the decision so as to assist the court to determine any challenge.

69. Article 8 of the European Convention on Human Rights is of major importance in connection with the home of a Gypsy or Traveller. Article 8 states that:

"(1) Everyone has the right to respect for his private and family life, his home and his correspondence.

(2) There shall be no interference by a public authority with the exercise of this right except such as is in accordance with the law and is necessary in a democratic society in the interest of national security, public safety or the economic well-being of the country, for the protection of health or morals, or for the protection of the rights and freedoms of others".

70. "Home" can include a caravan even if it is unlawfully or illegally parked. Therefore Article 8 may apply to those persons on unauthorised encampments as well as tenants of authorised sites.

71. The European Court of Human Rights has established that Article 8 imposes a positive obligation on the United Kingdom to "facilitate the Gypsy way of life" (*Chapman v UK* (2001) 33 EHRR 399 refers). However, this is to be balanced against what is proportionate and does not prohibit a local authority taking steps to address instances of unauthorised camping.

72. Article 14 concerns prohibition of discrimination and should be read in conjunction with Article 8:

> "The enjoyment of the rights and freedoms set forth in this Convention shall be secured without discrimination on any ground such as sex, race, colour, language, religion, political or other opinion, national or social origin, association with a national minority, property, birth or other status."

Equality Act 2010

73. Section 149 requires public authorities, including local authorities and the Police, must, in the exercise of their functions, have due regard to the need to eliminate unlawful discrimination; advance equality of opportunity; and foster good relations. Both Romani Gypsies and Irish Travellers are recognised as ethnic minorities which is a protected characteristic under the Act.

72. For the purposes of the Equality Act, this ethnic minority status is not dependent on a requirement to travel.

Environmental Protection Act 1990

75. Local authorities have powers under this Act to address issues of waste, statutory nuisance and litter in its area. Local authorities may therefore wish to consider the use of such powers in appropriate circumstances.

Town and Country Planning Act 1990

76. The results of the Gypsy and Traveller Accommodation Needs Assessment are expected to provide key evidence to inform the preparation by individual local planning authorities (LPAs) of policies for caravan sites for Gypsies and Travellers in their Local Development Plan (LDP). Welsh Assembly Government Circular 30/2007, "*Planning for Gypsy and Traveller Caravan Sites*", provides the main source of national planning guidance for LPAs in respect of Gypsy and Traveller sites. Key guidance includes:

a) where there is unmet need for Gypsy and Traveller accommodation, sufficient sites should be allocated by the LPA in their LDP;
b) the LPA should work with the Gypsy and Traveller community, encouraging them to put forward candidate sites;
c) co-operation between neighbouring authorities can provide more flexibility in identifying sites;
d) fair, reasonable and realistic criteria based policies should also be included in LDPs, to cater for future or unexpected demand.

77. Where Gypsies or Travellers (or anyone else) buy land and develop it as a caravan site without planning consent, any enforcement must be through the planning system; the powers described earlier (and in **Annex 4**) against trespass cannot be used. Enforcement is a matter for the discretion of the local planning authority. Decisions to enforce must be made on planning grounds. Case law has determined that all enforcement measures must be proportionate in the context of the European Convention on Human Rights, and in particular the Gypsy or Traveller's rights under Article 8. LPAs should assess what effect, if any, the absence of existing site provision would have on the ability to take, and defend, such actions successfully in any subsequent appeal.

78. Guidance on using planning enforcement powers is available in Welsh Office Circular 24/97 and Technical Advice Note 9: *Enforcement of Planning Control*. The current enforcement regime provides a mix of powers with which to deal with breaches of planning control in a controlled but flexible manner including the issue of enforcement and stop notices.

Section 4 – Roles and Responsibilities

The Welsh Government

79. If you experience an unauthorised encampment this document sets out Welsh Government guidance about good practice. However, the Welsh Government does not have an enforcement role in regards to unauthorised Gypsy and Traveller encampments and cannot intervene on behalf of a land owner or a member of the public.

80. Where an unauthorised encampment occurs on Welsh Government land the same guidelines and statutory responsibilities outlined in this guidance apply.

Public Authorities:

81. Local authorities and other public authorities (including National Parks) as land owners have a responsibility to their local community, including Gypsy and Traveller communities. Where an unauthorised encampment occurs on public authority land, it is recommended that officials within the authority appoint a Single Point of Contact (SPOC) or other lead officer, who would undertake the appropriate assessments (which are detailed further on), coordinate other relevant authorities and provide advice to senior officials who will determine the appropriate action to take.

82. It is recommended that the SPOC will have a role that is involved with direct management of, or liaison with, unauthorised encampments in the local area. To work most effectively, the role should have 24 hour emergency fallback cover to ensure that any developments associated with the unauthorised encampment are dealt with properly and consistently at any time of the day.

83. As local authorities have appropriate skills and resources to enable them to make (or co-ordinate) welfare assessments, it is considered good practice for local authorities to respond positively to requests for assistance in undertaking these assessments from the police or other public authorities.

Other Land Owners:

84. Private land owners experiencing unauthorised Gypsy and Traveller encampments on their land are not bound by the same statutory responsibilities as public authorities, but should in the first instance contact their local authority to determine if a Gypsy and Traveller Liaison Officer (or equivalent) is in place to mediate. Alternatively, the POC / lead officer or the local police force may be able to assist.

85. Private land owners will need to seek their own legal advice when attempting to resolve unauthorised encampments on their land.

Police Forces:

86. Police officers should not be used as a standard way of dealing with unauthorised encampments, but the involvement of police officers should not presume an eviction. The police, as with other public authorities, also have responsibility to assess the situation and the impact of the encampment before making an informed decision which minimises the impact on the safety or health of any party involved.

87. Where possible it is recommended that police officers visit the unauthorised encampment with a local authority officer, the landowner or an officer from another relevant agency. Police visits can be perceived as confrontational and the presence of police officers may inflame a situation, so police personnel should be kept to a minimum while ensuring the safety of officers. The level of personnel should be determined by the attending police force in conjunction with the ACPO Guidance.

Section 5 – Step-by-Step Guide to Resolving Unauthorised Encampments

This section of the Guidance is intended for local authorities to use when addressing an unauthorised encampment that has occurred in their area. Encampments should be assessed on a case-by-case basis but this section should provide the tools for authorities to develop their approach.

***Step 1* – Encampment Reported**

88. Usually, the first knowledge of an unauthorised encampment will come from reports by local residents or businesses in the vicinity of a newly- formed encampment.

89. Local authorities must ensure that they have an effective means of responding to encampments as they occur. It is recommended that local authorities appoint a Single Point of Contact (SPOC) to deal with unauthorised encampments in their area and all staff should be made aware of their existence and contact details. It is especially important that complaints officers and switchboard operators have these details.

90. The SPOC does not necessarily need to be the same officer for every encampment. The value of having a single contact in relation to all developments related to a particular encampment is that the local authority should be able to respond swiftly to any change in circumstances. Nevertheless, the SPOC will not be the only officer involved in the response and should not be isolated in this regard. Senior leadership is required to ensure that all relevant officers can be coordinated and decisions are made on how to resolve the encampment at a senior level.

Good Practice

The role of the Single Point of Contact (SPOC)

Each local authority should develop its own protocol for responding to unauthorised camping, which will establish the procedure and personnel necessary. However, it is recommended that a lead officer is identified to undertake the following roles:

1. Liaise with occupiers and other affected parties.
2. Undertake or coordinate the necessary assessments and involvement of relevant officers to ensure needs are addressed.
3. Communicate the evidence and provide recommendations to senior officials who will ultimately decide what action to take.
4. Ensure that all stakeholders are made aware of the proposed action and disruption to all is minimised.

Be sufficiently trained to provide culturally appropriate support and to understand how various actions and circumstances may impact upon the human rights of occupiers (particularly children and vulnerable others).

91. Regardless of who notified the local authority about the existence of the encampment, managing the expectations of local communities and businesses should be considered. The publication and dissemination of information about myths and facts, or question and answer booklets may help the local authority as it responds to the encampment.

92. In the first instance the local authority should try and obtain as much information from the informant as possible, whilst taking account of the fact that the informant may wish to remain anonymous. For example, useful information may include:

- The location of the encampment.
- How long the encampment has been established.
- The number of people and vehicles present.
- If contact has been made between the informant and occupiers.
- Details of any nuisance of anti-social behaviour reported by the informant.
- Contact details for the informant if they wish to be informed of developments relating to the encampment.

***Step 2* – Initial Encampment Visit**

93. Once the informant's report of the encampment is logged, it is recommended that the SPOC or lead officer aims to conduct an Initial Encampment Visit within 24 hours, as far as this is reasonably practicable. Completing this first visit within that time period will reassure local residents or businesses that their concerns are being considered and can ensure that any immediate health and safety or welfare concerns affecting the encampment occupiers can be dealt with promptly. If the local authority becomes aware of the encampment without complaints being received, there may be less need for the SPOC to respond so quickly unless they become aware of possible welfare issues that need investigation.

94. The SPOC should be deployed to undertake an Initial Encampment Assessment (a universal template is available at **Annex 2**). This assessment is to determine whether the encampment poses any immediate threat to the residents of the encampment or the local community. This visit should also determine the intended duration of the stay and whether a full Welfare Assessment is required.

95. The purpose of the Initial Encampment Visit is to:

- Check the accuracy of the initial report.
- Determine the safety of the encampment.
- Collect basic information such as the number of occupiers and vehicles, the intended length of stay, any potential problems and the state of the land and the encampment.
- Collect initial welfare information and determine whether a full Welfare Assessment is required.
- Determine whether the involvement of additional agencies is required, such as Traveller Education Services or Health Visitors.

- Determine whether any services will be provided on the site.
- Willingness and ability of occupiers to pay for services provided;.
- Inform the occupiers of the expected standard of behaviour and consider negotiating a Code of Conduct.
- Inform the occupiers what will happen next.
- Provide the occupiers with key local contact details, including healthcare and education professionals and the SPOC / lead officer.

96. The local authority SPOC or other lead officer should be given sufficient training to help them to gather all the relevant information from encampment occupiers and local residents. This would include cultural awareness training and some basic knowledge of important indicators of welfare concerns, such as training on the United Nations Convention on the Rights of the Child. It is recommended that the local authority offers the informant an opportunity to meet with the SPOC shortly after the initial encampment assessment, as this will show that concerns are being dealt with.

97. If the SPOC is not usually the lead officer for incidents of unauthorised camping they should know who is and act quickly to ensure the information is passed on.

98. The local authority should adopt a protocol for attending encampments. It is recommended that Police personnel are kept to a minimum or that Police are not involved at all during the initial encampment assessment as this can lead to tensions.

99. The Welsh Government would recommend a full Welfare Assessment be undertaken if:

- There are any obvious signs of welfare requirements, such as pregnant women, sick or disabled residents, frail elderly residents or children under 5.
- The likely duration of the encampment is over 3 days.
- There are immediate risks to the occupiers or residents such as contaminated land or traffic issues.
- There are school-age children present, within four weeks of the end of term.
- If there are obvious issues that are affecting the landowner's business or quality of life, making urgent possession action likely.

100. A full Welfare Assessment may not be required if:

- the expected duration of the encampment is 3 days or less;
- the occupiers intend to move on directly following a family event;
- the occupiers are in transit to another destination (such as to meet family or to a harbour) and are only stopping overnight.

101. In these circumstances a decision may be made to allow the encampment to remain on a short-term basis. However, this agreement should be monitored and if the encampment exceeds the expected stay, the initial assessment and the issue of a full Welfare Assessment should be revisited.

102. Where the decision is made not to undertake a full Welfare Assessment, officers should satisfy themselves that due process has been followed, satisfy themselves that they do not consider there to be a danger to either the residents of the encampment or the local community and ensure that the appropriate action has been taken.

103. Even when the encampment is likely to be 3 days or less, exceptionally the decision may be made not to allow the campers to remain. Reasons for this are detailed below.

104. During the initial encampment visit, the local authority may wish to negotiate an agreed Code of Conduct. A generic template is available at **Annex 1**. Local authorities should consult encampment occupiers and affected local businesses, landowners and neighbours when finalising the Code. The objective should be to reach consensus on expected standards and responsibilities, which are sensitive to cultural differences between travelling and settled communities.

105. When providing occupiers with useful information and contacts, or when negotiating the Code of Conduct, it will be necessary to consider the need for accessible materials.

Good Practice

Leeds City Council & Leeds GATE – Negotiated Stopping

In January 2011, Leeds City Council published the findings of the Neighbourhoods and Environment scrutiny panel, which recommended a pilot 'Negotiated Stopping' scheme. The scheme reviewed possible land for temporary stopping places using the following criteria:

- That the land was a 'defensible space' in that land available was restricted and any encampment therefore would be restricted in size.
- That there was some 'buy-in' to the project among local business owners, the police and elected members.
- The location was safe for the families and that they were prepared to stay there.

The initial agreement lasted 3 months and the authority provided waste disposal and toilets for each family. Leeds Gypsy and Traveller Exchange (GATE) provided liaison support between occupiers and the local authority.

A second location was found soon after and local elected members have expressed that they are content for the scheme to be extended. Leeds City Council estimates that it has saved in excess of £100,000 so far through reduced eviction and cleanup costs associated with unauthorised camping.

106. Many Gypsies and Traveller have limited literacy so it is important that local authorities ensure that occupiers are able to read the Code of Conduct and other materials provided. If literacy is a problem, the local authority should ensure that occupiers are made aware of the contents of the supplied documents.

***Step 3* – Completing the Welfare Assessment**

107. A local authority is subject to a number of duties, including those contained in education, children and housing legislation. These duties apply equally in respect of Gypsy and Traveller communities and therefore local authorities should conduct an effective Welfare Assessment to ensure compliance with their legal duties.

108. All public authorities are bound to act reasonably and proportionately in exercising their functions. As local authorities have appropriate skills and resources to enable them to make (or co-ordinate) welfare assessments, it is considered good practice for local authorities to respond positively to requests for assistance in undertaking these assessments from the police or other public authorities.

109. Welfare Assessments have invariably differed in content across Wales. In order to provide consistency and to assist authorities who have previously not had a protocol in place for dealing with unauthorised encampments, we have devised a universal template for Welfare Assessments contained at **Annex 3**. The Welsh Government recommends that all local authorities utilise this template.

110. It is recommended that the full Welfare Assessment is undertaken **no later than 3 working days** after the encampment has been reported. The purpose of the assessment is to understand the needs of the encampment occupiers and to ensure that the local authority provides for any vulnerable members of the group.

111. It is recommended that the SPOC / lead officer undertakes the Welfare Assessment, gathering crucial information about the encampment including:

- How many occupiers and vehicles (including caravans) are present.
- How many of the occupiers are children.
- How many of the occupiers are elderly.
- If any occupiers are disabled.
- If there are any health issues /medical conditions affecting the occupiers e.g. hospitalised relatives, pregnant women, post-natal mothers and babies, those recovering from serious illness or injury etc.
- If there are school examinations impending.
- What local authority services are considered appropriate e.g. refuse collection, portable toilets, water etc.
- Reasons for and intended duration of stay.

112. When undertaking the Welfare Assessment, it is recommended that the SPOC is capable, or accompanied by another colleague who is capable, of assessing the needs of the encampment occupiers. Local authorities should be aware that for cultural reasons some female occupiers will not participate in this process if they are approached by male visitors. It would be good practice for a mixed gender team to undertake the Welfare Assessment, where possible.

113. It should also be recognised that the quality and quantity of information gathered during the Initial Encampment Assessment and Welfare Assessment will depend, to some extent, on the relationship the occupiers have with those asking the question. Cultural-awareness training and some time spent listening to the reasons for the encampment can often go a long way towards producing better results. It may also be advantageous to ensure that officers undertaking the welfare assessments are not the same officers who conduct enforcement proceedings.

114. These Welfare Assessments will provide the necessary information for the SPOC to liaise with relevant colleagues in the education and housing departments of the local authority or with Police and Health professionals. Some camp occupiers may be reluctant to provide full information so those undertaking the assessment should ensure that occupiers are made aware of how the information may help them if there are welfare concerns present.

115. Information gathered in the course of visits and enquiries is subject to data protection legislation. Photographs of individuals can also be considered as personal information, if those individuals are identifiable. Authorities should make clear the purpose for which information is being collected and give assurances about how it will be used and to whom it might be passed. These Welfare Assessments must be kept for audit purposes and may be required if any legal challenge is taken in response to any possession proceedings.

116. Local authorities have no power to insist that information be given to it as part of the Welfare Assessment. Where information is not disclosed, the fact that questions were asked and not answered should be clearly recorded to avoid any subsequent claim of failure to take some relevant consideration into account. If occupiers give reasons for not responding, these should also be noted. Occupiers should be informed of any possible consequences of not providing information when requested. If they want to provide information through another person they trust, they should be able to do so provided that arrangements can be made quickly.

117. When unauthorised encampments are evicted there can be considerable clean-up costs incurred by local authorities. However, providing refuse collection, toilets, and water to occupiers can drastically reduce clean-up costs after an encampment has been moved on. Welfare Assessments can help local authorities to check which of these services might be required by the occupiers and also to discover if the occupiers would be prepared and able to pay for the services. If the occupiers are willing to pay for the services used, local residents could be informed of this so as to dispel the perception that encampment occupiers do not pay for services.

118. Local authorities should seek to assess the circumstances of each family to ensure that the decision-making process about how to resolve the encampment is informed by the full facts.

> **Good Practice**
>
> **Wrexham County Borough Council & Betsi Cadwaladr University Health Board – Welfare assessments**
>
> In Wrexham, the local authority and local health board work have an established agreement for Betsi Cadwaladr university health board to attend unauthorised encampments to undertake welfare assessments when required.
>
> This system allows welfare needs to be properly assessed by professionals who are not involved in eviction procedures. This may lead to increased participation on the part of the occupiers.

***Step 4* – The cost-benefit analysis and resolving the issue**

119. Unauthorised encampments are, by definition, unlawful. However it is recognised by the Welsh Government that until the issue of site provision is properly addressed unauthorised encampments will continue to occur.

120. Each encampment location must be considered on its merits against criteria such as health and safety considerations for the unauthorised campers, traffic hazard, public health risks, serious environmental damage, genuine nuisance to neighbours and proximity to other sensitive land-uses.

121. When assessing the campers' circumstances it is particularly important that local authorities consider how the encampment impacts on children and how eviction actions will also impact on those children. This process should help local authorities to assess what action would be in the best interests of child occupants, which should be a key factor in deciding how to proceed.

122. Local authorities may consider that some encampments will be allowed to remain either on a long-term or short-term basis.

123. This decision will be determined by factors including:

- The Initial Encampment Visit Assessment.
- The Welfare Assessment.
- Local circumstances.
- General considerations such as health and safety hazards, traffic issues, public health risks and other land users.

124. There will be locations where the encampment may not be considered acceptable, because they fall into one of the categories listed below:

- National Nature Reserves, Special Areas of Conservation and Special Protection Areas and sites of Special Scientific Interest.
- School car park or playing fields.
- Car parks for other key facilities, such as hospitals.
- An urban park.
- Public playing fields.
- A site where pollution or waste from vehicles could damage ground, water or water courses.
- An area with toxic waste or other serious land contamination.
- The verge of a busy road which poses a danger to the occupiers of the encampment.
- Sites where there is potential for significant harm or disturbance to protected species known to be present at, or in close proximity to, the site.

125. The circumstances of other locations may also be material considerations for local authorities when determining whether an occupation can be acceptable. This may include flood risk on the site or that the occupation is in sensitive location of a National Park or Area of Outstanding Natural Beauty. Natural Resources Wales (NRW) can advise local authorities on consideration of these issues.

126. The local authority and relevant partner agencies will need to decide whether the individual circumstances of the encampment, for example the risks to public safety or the impact on the local community, outweigh other factors such as the welfare and human rights considerations of the encampment occupiers.

127. If the Initial Encampment Assessment identifies serious safety and welfare concerns, a local authority may wish to consider taking immediate action to either rectify the safety concerns, temporarily relocate the encampment, or evict the occupiers altogether. All possession actions will require welfare assessments to be undertaken. Relocating an encampment will be far easier if the local authority has established temporary stopping places to be utilised.

128. The Initial Encampment Assessment may also identify urgent welfare concerns, which may suggest the need of immediate medical or social care responses from the local health board or local authority. In this scenario, a local authority may consider that the encampment should be tolerated, if only for a short period of time.

129. Many encampments may fall between these two immediate concerns. The full Welfare Assessment will provide the necessary information about the occupiers to understand the reasons for the encampment and to balance the impact on the local community against the likely impact of eviction on the occupiers.

130. This cost-benefit analysis must consider the European Convention on Human Rights and whether the local authority has fulfilled its duties towards Gypsy and Traveller communities, contained in the Housing Act 2004, by undertaking thorough GTAA. Such factors may be taken into account by a court if any subsequent possession proceedings are brought. More information on this legislation can be found between paragraphs 53–57 (Housing Act) and 68–72 (European Convention on Human Rights/Human Rights Act).

131. When assessing unauthorised encampments with children and young people under 18 years of age, it is important to recognise that these children may be statutorily homeless and, as such, may be considered as 'Children in Need'. The Children Act 1989, section 20(1)(c) states that:

> *"Every local authority shall provide accommodation for any child in need within their area who appears to them to require accommodation as a result of . . . the person who has been caring for him being prevented (whether or not permanently, and for whatever reason) from providing him with suitable accommodation or care."*

132. Furthermore, section 17(1) of the Children's Act 1989 states that it is, *"the general duty of every local authority –*

(a) to safeguard and promote the welfare of children within their area who are in need; and .

(b) so far as is consistent with that duty, to promote the upbringing of such children by their families, by providing a range and level of services appropriate to those children's needs."

133. Conducting robust welfare assessments can help public authorities to ensure that they have fully considered the needs of these children and can safeguard against potential harm.

134. The Rights of Children and Young Persons (Wales) Measure 2011 enshrines the United Nations Convention on the Rights of the Child in Welsh law. Currently the Welsh Ministers must have due regard to Part 1 of the Convention in making any decision as to any provision to be included in an enactment, the formulation of new policy or a review or change of any existing policy. From May 2014 this will be expanded to the requirement to have due regard in exercising any of their functions.

135. Local health and education professionals have anecdotally reported upon the benefits of tolerating encampments, if only for a short period of time, as children are able to benefit from education and healthcare. That is not to say all encampments should be tolerated, as some can certainly be unsafe and potentially damaging to children's welfare. Nevertheless, it is crucial that local authorities fully consider the impact of potential eviction proceedings on the welfare of children, disabled or ill occupiers when undertaking their decision-making procedure.

136. There are also financial costs to consider. Local authorities who provide sites, rather than simply take quick enforcement action against unauthorised encampments, will often save money in the long-term. Adopting the following approaches to unauthorised encampments can be cost-effective:

- Providing authorised legal pitches and sites for Gypsies and Travellers if there is identified need in the area. Authorised pitches allow for local authorities to charge rent, rates and council tax to residents.

- Local authorities could avoid unnecessary enforcement costs if the encampment is likely to last three days or less.
- Providing services such as refuse collection, toilets, and fresh water can reduce clean-up costs.
- Encouraging the occupiers to pay for the services that the encampment uses can recoup a significant amount of the local authority's expenditure. Occupiers may be minded to do this if it will ease community tensions and allow them to remain at an encampment for a reasonable period of time.
- Identifying alternative temporary stopping places within the locality where unauthorised encampments could be relocated and tolerated for a short time.

137. In most circumstances, local authorities will have three paths from which to choose when resolving the issue of an unauthorised encampment and it is important that they carefully consider **each** option (see *R(Casey) v Crawley BC*):

- **Path 1** – To seek and obtain possession of the occupied site (eviction proceedings).
- **Path 2** – To tolerate the Gypsy or Traveller occupiers, if only for a short time, until an alternative site can be found.
- **Path 3** – To find an alternative site, if only on a temporary basis, and offer the Gypsy or Traveller occupiers the chance to move onto it.

138. If **Path 1** is chosen: It may be sensible to liaise with the Police about the intention to evict the occupiers. ACPO Guidance explains the Police procedure for dealing with encampments.

139. Public authorities following this path need to be satisfied that they can demonstrate that possession action is a justified and proportionate interference with the rights of the occupants, as enshrined in the European Convention on Human Rights. Proper welfare assessments should help in this regard.

140. If possession action is to be taken against the unauthorised encampment, occupiers will be served with the appropriate documentation relating to the power under which they are being removed. This may be the Criminal Justice and Public Order Act 1994 or Civil Procedures Rules Part 55. For more information, refer to paragraphs 58–65 and 67 under Section 3 – Legislation and the 'Summary of Powers' document at **Annex 4**.

141. If **Path 2** is chosen: cost-benefit analysis has shown that maintaining the encampment is the best short-term solution for all. All parties should be informed of the decision and encouraged to agree to a voluntary negotiated Code of Conduct. This Code formally explains what is expected of occupiers and, if the Code is violated, provides documentary evidence that occupiers have broken the agreement.

The local authority should search for an alternative site if the occupiers plan to stay in the area.

142. The Code of Conduct template at **Annex 1** is intended as a generic example of a negotiated code between the local authority and the encampment occupiers. The specific requirements of each encampment may require an amended version of this template. The Code may outline the provision of services, including any arrangements for water supply, refuse and sanitation. This example suggests that the local authority will provide this access, as anecdotal evidence suggests that clean-up costs are much reduced as a consequence of this provision. As the Code is voluntary, it is not enforceable but it may provide evidence of the character of the occupation during planning enforcement process or possession proceedings.

143. Though it is acceptable to request payment for services that the local authority has opted to provide to occupiers, it should be recognised that some occupiers may not be able to afford to pay. The local authority should consider whether access to these services can be provided despite costs not being met by occupiers. This is especially relevant where children, elderly, disabled, pregnant or sick individuals are present on the encampment. If authorities are not providing waste disposal facilities to an encampment, they should also consider whether occupants can utilise the local Civic Amenity Site with the vehicles they possess. Information about this service should be provided, where appropriate.

144. If **Path 3** is chosen the local authority's cost-benefit analysis has identified the current encampment as unsafe or inappropriate but the need for culturally-appropriate accommodation in its area is recognised. The occupiers may have submitted a homelessness application, which will need to be processed by the local authority. For this path to be followed alternative stopping places should be identified and the encampment moved, if only on a temporary basis.

145. Local authorities should have included a 'criteria-based' Gypsy and Traveller sites policy in their local development plan, which would allow the authority to identify appropriate sites in their area when the need arises. This should assist the local authority to find temporary stopping places in the short-term and permanent residential sites or transit sites in future.

146. When making decisions about encampments, local authorities will need to ensure that they follow the process outlined in their protocol and produce decisions that are reasonable, balanced, and proportionate. The local authority unauthorised camping protocol should establish the process and personnel required to make the decision on which path to take in relation to encampments on a case-by-case basis.

147. Whichever path is chosen, the local authority and relevant agencies should document all of their assessments and decision-making processes, including welfare assessments and the assessment of

which path to pursue. All stakeholders, including local residents, the occupiers, and agencies involved, should be informed of the decision.

148. If tolerated, the local authority may wish to revisit the decision about provision of services to the encampment. The encampment should be monitored to ensure that the negotiated Code of Conduct is not broken and to ensure that problems do not develop in the local community.

149. There is no formal limit on the duration of tolerated encampments. However, local authorities should make provision of sites where there is identified need for sites. The presence of a long-term tolerated encampment would suggest the need for a permanent site in the area, which local authorities should seek to provide.

Section 6 – Communicating Decisions

150. Regardless of which decision the Local authority takes, it is crucial that all affected parties are properly informed. It is good practice for the SPOC / lead officer to communicate the decision directly to occupiers and local residents / businesses. Written briefings could be posted to local residents and businesses explaining the reasons for the decision and how it relates to current legislation, policies and the local situation.

151. Due to low levels of literacy within Gypsy and Traveller communities, it is good practice to ensure that occupiers are able to read and comprehend the documents that they have been served with. This applies equally to accessible possession orders or a negotiated Code of Conduct. The SPOC / lead officer should direct occupiers to Gypsy and Traveller Liaison Officers, if one is employed by the local authority. In areas without this role, local Gypsy or Traveller advocacy groups, local Citizens Advice Bureaux or Regional Equality Councils may be able to help. If in any doubt, the SPOC / lead officer should be able to direct occupiers to useful support staff.

152. Key points of contact between Gypsy and Traveller communities and local services need to be made aware of any possession actions and potential knock-on effects on their service users. It is recommended that Traveller Education Services, Health Visitors and any support group involved, in particular, are informed so that they are able to support the families effectively.

153. If the decision is to evict the occupiers, the local authority may also wish to notify neighbouring local authorities to alert them to the possibility of unauthorised encampments in their area.

154. It is important that local authorities inform the landowner, if it is another public body, of its decision to take possession action or not.

155. Local authorities should consider publishing their reasoning for any actions taken in response to unauthorised camping. This document would make the case for the decision that has been reached by balancing the legal obligations of public authorities to both occupiers and local residents or businesses. By publishing this reasoning, local authorities can avoid accusations from either side that their decision was biased in some way. Transparent communication of the reasons why an encampment has been tolerated or evicted may lead to greater public understanding of what considerations need to be addressed and may possibly reduce community tension.

156. Liaising with the police and other appropriate bodies on a multi-agency media strategy may be sensible where an encampment has received considerable news coverage.

Section 7 – Local Strategies

157. The Welsh Government recommends that all local and public authorities adopt their own protocol for dealing with unauthorised encampments.

158. By having this in place, it can help to ensure a fair and consistent approach to the issues of unauthorised encampment.

Developing a Strategy

159. It is usually impossible to predict just where and when an unauthorised encampment will occur. However, a purely reactive response to encampments as they arise is both inefficient and ineffective. Local authorities, police forces and other bodies need to agree and be clear how they will respond to an encampment in a specific area, who will take the lead in what circumstances, and who else will be involved.

160. To be effective, this information should be clearly set out in an unauthorised encampments strategy and protocol. It is recommended that the strategy is developed through consultation with all key stakeholders to ensure that it is agreed and effective; and it should seek to balance the rights, responsibilities and legitimate expectations of the travelling and settled communities.

Objectives of an Unauthorised Camping Strategy

161. The key objectives in a strategy for unauthorised encampments might include:

a. Eliminating or at least minimising problems and avoiding the need to respond on a crisis basis by advance planning.
b. Ensuring that the needs, legitimate expectations and human rights of all parties – Gypsies and Travellers, landowners and the settled community – are considered.
c. Setting a framework within which clear, consistent and appropriate decisions can be made in a transparent manner, to comply with the law.
d. Linking the approach to unauthorised camping firmly to other strategies and policies affecting Gypsies and Travellers (site provision, planning, health, education, housing etc).
e. Involving all those with an interest in the process of developing the strategy.
f. Clarifying roles and responsibilities, including establishing who will co-ordinate responses and who will make the key decisions.

g. Ensuring the prevention and detection of anti-social behaviour and crime, and effective enforcement against perpetrators.

Each local strategy will have its own objectives.

Formulating the Strategy

Taking the Lead

162. Local authorities should take the lead in formulating the strategy, being responsible for overseeing and monitoring its implementation, and for ensuring that the process is driven forward.

163. The process of producing a strategy involves a number of key stages and these might include:

- Appoint a lead officer or Single Point of Contact (SPOC).
- Set up a strategy working group, with adequate support/resources and ensuring key players are involved and ensuring liaison with other services.
- Set up consultation procedures/mechanisms.
- Ensure consistency with other strategies.
- Review information from evidence gathering stage on the assessment of needs, existing provision and gaps in services/provision.
- Plan new services/improve existing ones, through joint working.
- Implement the programme.
- Monitor/evaluate/review.

Who should be Involved?

164. While local authorities take the lead, it is essential that many others are involved in the process and are willing to sign up to the strategy when it is agreed and published. Generating commitment among participants is an important part of the strategy building process.

165. Gaining participation from the local Health Board, Police force, Gypsies and Travellers themselves as well as advocacy groups who support them, Community Cohesion Co-ordinators, Community Safety officers, and local Councillors responsible for Gypsy and Traveller encampments, will strengthen the local authority's capacity to respond effectively to the situation and ensure that the services of other participations are accessible by occupiers and the settled community. Other organisations, such as Natural Resources Wales, or private landowners could be involved in this multi-agency way of working when the circumstances are appropriate.

166. Local authorities should also consider working on a regional basis to ensure that their approach to unauthorised camping and site provision is consistent.

> **Good Practice**
>
> **North Wales Gypsy & Traveller Coordination Group**
>
> The Group was established after the conclusion of the North Wales Gypsy- Traveller Accommodation Needs Assessment. The group aims to take responsibility for coordination and oversight of the planning, monitoring and evaluation of activities focused on the Gypsy and Traveller community across the six counties and the Snowdonia National Park Authority. To date the group have discussed a unified needs assessment process; approaches to Gypsy and Traveller policies within Local Development Plans; and establishing a rolling needs assessment.

Elements to be Included in the Strategy

There are a number of elements that could be included in the local strategy, many of which are laid out in this document.

1. The legislative background.
2. Local information on which the strategy is based, for example, the Gypsy and Traveller Accommodation Needs Assessments (GTAA), the Bi-Annual Caravan Count data, local figures for unauthorised encampments (including police figures) and any recurring encampment information etc.
3. Local information on the current level and locations of authorised sites.
4. The approach to be taken when informed of an unauthorised encampment, including the appointment of a lead officer or Single Point of Contact (SPOC).
5. Protocol for the sharing of information with other agencies and for contacting / involving / informing other relevant agencies.
6. The approach to be taken when entering an unauthorised encampment, setting out the roles and statutory responsibilities of all involved, the assessments to be undertaken and possible courses of action.
7. Arrangements for eviction.
8. Protocol for informing neighbouring authorities of families being "moved on".
9. Resources, constraints, and possible risks to being able to implement the strategy. This should also identify any training required for officers dealing with unauthorised encampments.
10. Monitoring and review period for the strategy.

Section 8 – Evaluation of the Guidance

The Welsh Government is committed to evaluating the impact of this Guidance to check:

- the extent to which local authorities have adopted the guidance; and

- its effectiveness in bringing about improvements on the ground.

In the light of the evaluation – and changing circumstances – further guidance may be issued in future as appropriate.

The Welsh Government will informally evaluate progress against these objectives on an on-going basis. A formal review will take place in 2017.

The Welsh Government's Fairer Futures Division will be pleased to receive comments on the guidance and suggestions for ways in which it might be improved.

The address is:

Fairer Futures Division
Local Government and Communities Department Welsh Government
Rhydycar Office
Merthyr Tydfil, CF48 1UZ

Annex 1

Negotiated Code of Conduct for Tolerated Stopping

You and your family (insert name..........................) have been permitted to remain on this land as a tolerated but unauthorised Gypsy or Traveller Encampment for a period of ....
Until ....
This is because.......................................

By staying on this land you are agreeing to this negotiated Code of Conduct which explains the standard of behaviour which is expected of you and your family.

You are expected to treat the land you have occupied and the surrounding neighbours with respect. You must also respect the rights and freedom of those who also wish or need to use the land.

- You have been permitted to park your caravan and vehicles on a particular area of land. You must not camp on any land other than that which you have been given permission to remain on.
- Camping on other publicly used land, such as parks, school fields, car parks or play areas, may lead to immediate eviction action.
- You must not force entry onto any other part of the land or buildings on the land.
- Be careful not to cause any damage to the land itself or property on it including fencing or boundary walls, fixtures or fittings. This includes any flood defences or defences to prevent trespassing. Particular care should be taken not to cause damage to parks, woodlands, school fields, or play areas.
- Vehicles should not be driven on footpaths or highways not designed for road vehicles. Doing this could put others at risk and is unlawful.
- Vehicles and caravans should also be parked in a way that does not block access for other people who want to pass or to public facilities.
- Dumping, tipping rubbish or placing waste materials or trade waste such as rubble or tree cuttings on this land may lead to eviction proceedings. Please use bins that are provided for domestic waste or dispose of trade waste at the local Civic Amenity Site (local tip).
- Burning of commercial or domestic waste is not allowed on this site. Open fires will only be permitted where basic fire safety is observed and agreed with the local authority / fire service.
- You must not dispose of or deposit any human waste on this site. You will be issued with a portable toilet.

- You will be provided with access to water supply.
- Abuse, harassment or intimidation of any person using this land lawfully will not be tolerated.
- The local authority asks that those who are willing and able to pay for received services (portable toilet, water supply, bins) notify the local authority and pay. Services may be withdrawn if they are being used inappropriately.
- You must ensure the welfare of other occupiers and animals, as far as reasonably practicable.

Annex 2

Initial Encampment Assessment

Date of Assessment	
Time of Assessment	
Assessor/s	

		Response	Comments/ Follow Up
1.	**Location of Encampment**		
2.	**Landowner Identified**		
3.	**Landowner Complaint Made**		
4.	**Number of Occupants** How many Men? How many Women? How many Children (under 18)?		
5.	**Number of Vehicles** How many Cars and Vans?		
	Any other vehicles?		
6.	**Number of Caravans**		
7.	**Number of Animals and general welfare conditions**		
8.	**Damage to Land Evident**	**Existing state of land:** **Any damage caused by gaining entry:**	
9.	**Litter or Waste Present**		

		Response	Comments/ Follow Up
10.	**Immediate Welfare Issues Identified** May include: pregnancy, elderly people, sickness, disability, receiving urgent, planned or a course of medical treatment, children close to exam period		
11.	**Impact of encampment to public, neighbours or Landowner**		
12.	**Environmental impact? (Is this a Site of Special Scientific Interest, in a flood risk area, contaminated land, protected species known, risk of polluted watercourses? Consult Natural Resources Wales)**		

Survey of Occupants			
13.	**Have you stayed in this area before?**		
	Where?		
	When?		
	Any problems encountered?		
14.	**Reasons for this stay?** There may be multiple reasons, including: Passing through, Local to the area, Work in the area, No authorised pitch, Family event, Visiting/ Holiday, Illness, Hospital Visit, Other.		
	Date of arrival?		

	How long are you expecting to stay here?		
	Are you expecting more people to arrive?		
	How many?		
	When?		
15.	Do you have permanent accommodation (pitch or bricks and mortar) anywhere else?		
	Do you want permanent accommodation (pitch or bricks and mortar) in the area? Do you want to discuss your options with a housing advice officer?		
	Are you seeking a transit pitch in the area?		
16.	Are you willing and able to pay for services on this encampment? (provide estimated cost; services should not be withheld purely due to lack of payment)	Toilets: Water: Refuse: Other:	
17.	Are there school age children on site? Are they accessing school?		
	Initial Assessment		
18.	**Are there urgent concerns that may necessitate possession action?** May include: obstruction, health and safety concerns e.g. dangerous place to stop, damage to land, threats or violence		
	Agreement that information collected is correct		
	Signature of occupier		**Date:**
	Signature of lead officer		**Date:**

Annex 3

Welfare Assessment

Date of Assessment	
Time of Assessment	
Location of Encampment	
Initial Encampment Assessment Completed?	Date
Names and Positions of Assessors At least TWO assessors required	1. 2. 3.

		Response	Comments/ Follow Up
1.	**Location of Encampment/ Address**		
	Map or Grid References		
	When was the last encampment on this land? (if known)		
	Were services provided to the site?		
	If so what services?		
	May include:		
	Water, Refuse/Skips, Toilets		
	Were services paid for?		
	(only applicable if these are the same occupants)		
2.	**Date informed of encampment**		
	How was the report made? By Who?		
	How was access gained by assessors?		

	Condition of Site Compare to condition at time of Initial Encampment Assessment		
3.	**Group Origin (if known)**		
	Romani Gypsies, Roma, Irish Travellers etc.		
	Number of Family Groups It may be that the encampment is one extended family		
	Number of Adult Occupants	Male: Female:	
	Number of Child Occupants	0 5: 6–10: 11–15: 16–17:	
4.	**Number of Caravans**	Static: Tourer size: Motor Homes: Other (describe):	
	Number of other vehicles	Cars: Vans: Lorries: Other:	
	Number and Type of Animals Please note whether these are tethered and any welfare concerns		
5.	**Reason for encampment?**		
	Expected duration of stay?		
6.	**Services provided at encampment?**	Toilets: Water: Refuse: Other:	

Welfare Issues			
7.	**Are any women pregnant?**	Yes/ No	
	Name		
	DOB		
	Due Date		
	Concerns		
	Doctor/ Practice		
	Receiving Urgent, Local Medical Treatment		
	Is the resident in good health generally? A health professional may be required to give an accurate assessment in regards to being 'moved on'.		
	Overall assessment of condition. Health professionals may need to be consulted with regard to 'moving on'.		
	Name		
	DOB		
	Due Date		
	Concerns		
	Doctor/ Practice		
	Receiving Urgent, Local Medical Treatment		
	Is the resident in good health generally? A health professional may be required to give an accurate assessment with regard to being 'moved on'.		
	Overall assessment of condition.		

	Health professionals may need to be consulted with regard to 'moving on'.		
8.	**Does anyone within the group require regular medical treatment/ examinations?**	Yes/ No	
	Name		
	DOB		
	Are they receiving treatment now? Please note the resident does not have to disclose information on their condition unless they choose to do so. However, this may impact on the decision whether or not to tolerate the encampment on a short-term basis.		
	Is that one of the reasons for the encampment? Explain if possible		
	Overall assessment of condition. Health professionals may need to be consulted with regard to 'moving on'.		
	Name		
	DOB		
	Are they receiving treatment now? Please note the resident does not have to disclose information on their condition unless they choose to do so. However, this may impact on the decision whether or not to tolerate the encampment on a short-term basis.		

	Is that one of the reasons for the encampment? Explain if possible		
	Overall assessment of condition. Health professionals may need to be consulted with regard to 'moving on'.		
9.	**Have any of the group received or are they currently in receipt of urgent medical treatment?** **Do any of the group require urgent medical treatment which has not yet been sought?**	Yes/ No	
	Name		
	DOB		
	Treatment received/ required Please include length of stay if being treated as an 'in patient' and whether or not the patient is still in hospital.		
	Hospital/ surgery		
	Is a doctor or health visitor required to visit the encampment?		
	Ongoing treatment or long term care required?		
	Overall assessment of condition. Health professionals may need to be consulted with regard to 'moving on'.		

	Name		
	DOB		
	Treatment received/ required Please include length of stay if being treated as an 'in patient' and whether or not the patient is still in hospital.		
	Hospital/ surgery attended		
	Is a doctor or health visitor required to visit the encampment?		
	On going treatment or long term care required?		
	Overall assessment of condition. Health professionals may need to be consulted with regard to 'moving on'.		
10.	**Are there any disabled or elderly persons that are unable to move on currently?**		
	Health professionals may need to be consulted.		
11.	**Number of children attending local schools?**		
	Number of children within 4 weeks of examinations?		
	Would you like the Traveller Education Service to visit?		
		Other Issues	
12.	**Did occupiers refuse to provide information?**		
	If yes, what reasons were provided?		

13.	**Have there been significant changes to the encampment since the Initial Encampment Visit? (Please explain)**		
Agreement that information collected is correct			
	Signature of occupier		**Date:**
	Signature of lead officer		**Date:**

Annex 4

Summary of Powers

Below is a list of potential legal avenues for resolving unauthorised camping. Please be aware that other powers may exist. Landowners should seek their own legal advice when utilising these powers.

The Method of Eviction	Who can use it?	What Court?
Civil Procedure Rules (CPR) Part 55	Anyone with a sufficient interest in the land including a licensee	Usually County Court, exceptionally in the High Court
Criminal Justice and Public Order Act (CJPOA) 1994 Section 61	The Police	Magistrates' Court
CJPOA 1994 Section 62A-E	The Police	Magistrates' Court
CJPOA 1994 Section 77	Local authority	Magistrates' Court
Highways Act 1980 Section 149	Highways Authority	Magistrates' Court
Bye-laws	Local authority and certain other public authorities	Magistrates' Court
Common law powers	Anyone entitled to possession of the land including a licensee	No need for Court "approval"
Planning Enforcement Powers	Local authority	Depends on type of enforcement action

Glossary

Words used in this document and what they mean:

Association of Chief Police Officers (ACPO): This is a group made up of high level police officers who help the police force make decisions and decide what they should be doing about certain issues. They also produced guidance on unauthorised encampments.

Authorised: This is something that is allowed. An authorised site has been given permission for Gypsies and Travellers to live on by the local authority. It can include publicly provided sites or privately owned sites with the necessary planning permission.

Guidance: This document is 'guidance'. This means it gives people advice on a subject but is not law.

Gypsies and Travellers: This is a term used to define lots of groups who are part of the Gypsy or Traveller way of life. Different groups can include:

- Romani Gypsies.
- Irish Travellers.
- Scottish or Welsh Gypsy/Travellers.
- European Roma.[8]
- 'New' Travellers.
- Show-people.
- Occupational Travellers.

Protocol: This is an agreed plan for how services will deal with an issue.

Public Authority: As well as councils, there are other groups like the National Parks or Natural Resources Wales who look after large areas of land for the public. Sometimes they have to evict families who have stopped in their area.

Temporary Stopping Place: These are intended to be temporary in nature to assist local authorities where a need for Gypsy and Traveller site accommodation is accepted but none is currently available. Temporary stopping places can be provided to relocate inappropriately located encampments whilst alternative sites are progressed. Unlike transit sites, these are not intended only for transient communities and should not be a permanent solution. Temporary stopping places must make provision for waste disposal, water supply and sanitation at a minimum. The Mobile Homes Act 1983 does not apply on these places as occupiers would not be legally entitled to a place on this site. These sites are also known as Emergency Stopping Places.

Tolerated encampments: This is land that Gypsies and Travellers do not have permission to stay on for good but where the local authority may decide to allow them to stay for a set period. This might be because this is a better option for everyone than the cost or impact of evicting the encampment.

Transit Site: Transit sites must be permanently designated as such

8 The term "Roma" used by the Welsh Government refers to Roma, Sinti, Kale and related groups in Europe, including the Eastern groups (Dom and Lom).

and cannot be occupied by residents for longer than 3 months at a time. This is to ensure that pitches can be used for the intended purpose of facilitating the Gypsy and Traveller nomadic way of life. Transit pitches can exist on permanent residential sites but this practice has led to negative impacts on the site in the past. Specific terms under the Mobile Homes Act 1983 apply on these sites.

Traveller Education Service (TES): These are teachers who work closely with Gypsy and Traveller children to make sure they can get an education.

Unauthorised Development: This is a camp or group of caravans and vehicles on land that belongs to the occupier but which doesn't have the necessary planning permission. This guidance does not apply to unauthorised developments. Guidance on using planning enforcement powers is available in Welsh Office Circular 24/97 and Technical Advice Note 9: *Enforcement of Planning Control.*

Unauthorised Encampment: This is a camp or group of caravans and vehicles on land which does not belong to the occupier and does not have the necessary planning permission.

Unauthorised Campers: These are the people who are living on an Unauthorised Encampment.

NATIONAL POLICE CHIEFS' COUNCIL: OPERATIONAL ADVICE ON UNAUTHORISED ENCAMPMENTS (2018)[9]

Introduction

1. This document is guidance covering the options to be considered in dealing with any people who trespass on land owned by another with an intention to reside.
2. The Equality Act 2010 makes it unlawful to treat someone less favourably because of a range of protected characteristics, including race, nationality or ethnic or national origins. The following of a nomadic lifestyle is lawful, indeed it is a culture that is recognised and protected through legislation. Romany Gypsies and Irish Travellers have been granted protection under the previous Race Relations Acts. The Public Sector Equality Duty applies to the police and places a duty on constabularies to have due regard to the need to eliminate unlawful racial discrimination and promote equality of opportunity and good relations between persons of different racial groups.
3. There is no legal right to trespass, however trespass is a civil rather than a criminal offence. The co-ordinated use of powers available under the Criminal Justice and Public Order Act 1994 allows for a proportionate response to encampments based on the behaviour of the trespassers.
4. The establishment of an unauthorised encampment can raise many concerns with the landowner and neighbouring members of the settled community. Some of these concerns are unfounded, and may be based on ignorance and prejudice; however there still remains a significant number of encampments that cause high levels of anti-social behaviour and disproportionate disruption to the community into which they move.
5. This document explains the framework within which our staff should act, recognising the requirement to balance the needs of a range of interested parties. The decision to use police powers remains at the discretion of the senior officer present. His / her decision, however, should be made in accordance with this guidance, and the grounds for any action / inaction fully recorded. Any decision to evict must be made in conjunction with the relevant on duty senior officer.
6. It is essential that the police response takes account of the issues of behaviour, whether criminal, anti-social or nuisance, in combination with the impact on the landowner and settled community rather than simply because encampments are present at a specific location. Police powers to evict people from unauthorised encampments do exist, as provided for by Sections 61 and 62 A-E, Criminal Justice & Public Order Act 1994. These powers will be used where behaviour or conduct is considered to be inappropriate, or where the impact of an encampment on others is deemed unacceptable. This position is consistent with all other areas of enforcement within the community.

9 © National Police Chief's Council, 2018.

Guidelines on the exercise of police powers concerning unauthorised encampments are given later in this document.

7. Decisions to evict or not must, of course, be balanced (as directed by legislation and Government guidance), and be compliant with the terms of the Human Rights Act 1998, demonstrating legality, necessity, and proportionality, as well as principles of common humanity. The grounds for each decision must be fully recorded by the decision maker and kept for audit processes or legal challenge for seven years.
8. The scope of this guidance does not cover the situation whereby individuals purchase land and occupy it, with or without planning permission. Such an incident would be an unauthorised development and the local / borough council would lead in this situation.
9. In managing unauthorised encampments officers must be sensitive to the fact that there is a lack of pitches on authorised sites across the country, making it difficult or even impossible for people to avoid setting up unauthorised pitches.

Operational tactics

1. All police decisions and actions must be made in compliance with the provisions of the Human Rights Act 1998. Any action should only be such as is necessary for public safety, the prevention of crime or disorder, the protection of health, or for the protection of the rights and freedom of others.
2. All police actions should be conducted in a manner compatible with the operational principles of safety, lawfulness, necessity, proportionality and common humanity. Actions should be completed in a manner that is the least intrusive to achieve the purpose. It is necessary to achieve a balance in the protection of the rights and freedom of all persons concerned with a specified unauthorised encampment.
3. Where appropriate, it is recommended that the police visit newly established encampments, and that a local supervisory officer be informed. Visits should, wherever possible be done together with the landowner, Local Authority, and other relevant agencies. PCSOs should only be deployed to encampments as part of the local neighbourhood policing team response, not in relation to confrontational situations with the occupants of unauthorised camps when they are being initially set up.
4. Initial contact should be made with the people on the site, and an assessment made of the impact of its location, as well as the behaviour displayed by the occupants. The occupants should be spoken to in order to establish their identities and location of last site, and to ascertain their views on desired duration of stay as well as any pressing welfare needs.
5. Officers should identify any offences disclosed or apparent e.g. criminal damage caused to gain entry to land, obstruction of any footpaths or other highways, any other anti-social behaviour.
6. Officers should discuss with those present what constitutes unacceptable conduct. They may consider it appropriate to give them a copy of the recommended Code of Conduct, attached at appendix A.

7. Officers should assess whether the location of the encampment, behaviour of residents or needs of the landowner justifies an eviction using police powers.
8. Liaison should be maintained with the landowner, those most affected by the establishment of the encampment and our partner agencies to assess the need for Police intervention. In accordance with guidance issued by the Ministry of Housing, Communities & Local Government (MHCLG) in England (or the Welsh Assembly Government (WAG) in Wales) the Local Authority, as lead agency for unauthorised encampments, should take an active role in engaging with the site residents and will in particular take the lead with sites established on their land, which do not require immediate Police action. Periodic visits by police officers to the site can also be beneficial to get to know site residents and also to pick up on any community tensions that may give rise to more serious incidents. These visits will be enhanced if completed along with designated Local Authority staff members. The absence of such visits will not prohibit the future use of police powers, but may help in justifying the use of these powers if this proves necessary. These visits will also provide an audit trail to support decision-making.
9. It is suggested that attending officers should complete an initial site assessment. A suggested form for this is attached at Appendix B; to be used by the senior officer present to determine the potential need to evict using police powers. This will usually only be the case where criminality, anti-social behaviour, or environmental damage is present.
10. The decision whether or not to utilise police eviction powers should be periodically reviewed to establish if circumstances have changed that will require the use of a police eviction to protect the rights of others. All information concerning the site and the site occupants should be shared with all involved agencies (subject to the provisions of the Data Protection Act), to ensure that a balanced common approach is adopted in fairness to all.
11. Assessment visits should only log details of vehicles and people where there are grounds to suspect those individuals of anti-social behaviour or criminal activity.
12. Where appropriate, vehicle and / or any person details should be checked on the Police National Computer (PNC) for 'markers' (which if present should be acted upon as appropriate). Any criminal intelligence should be submitted in the normal format using intelligence systems.
13. A separate log should be created for each unauthorised encampment notified to the Police. Any calls from the public relating to the encampment, or directly attributable to its occupants, should be recorded within the log, including any complaint calls.
14. Forces should ensure that there is a clear audit trail of decision making which sets out the rationale for all decisions made. A suggested Eviction Rationale Record is attached at Appendix C. Where separate Command and Control logs are created for specific incidents,

which relate to the encampment, these should be 'incident-matched' to the main log once concluded. At the conclusion of the occupation of the encampment the log should be endorsed suitably with the outcome, including any eviction powers used, and the general behaviour and conduct of the residents.

15. All officers and police staff are responsible for ensuring that all crimes they become aware of in the course of their duty are identified for crime recording. The principles of the Home Office Counting Rules and the National Crime Recording Standards should be used by officers and staff in their assessment of all potential crimes arising from unauthorised encampment situations.

Complaints

1. Police may receive complaints relating to the behaviour of occupants at unauthorised encampments, or from the occupants relating to other people. The initial police response to such calls should, of course, be the same as for any other incident, and graded on its priority. If attendance to see a complainant is appropriate, or to investigate a report, then an appropriately staffed police resource should attend to investigate.
2. The allegation of a crime or identification of an individual suspect at an encampment should not be grounds alone for consideration of a full group eviction. However, if the grounds exist that require the use of S61 or S62 of the Criminal Justice & Public Order Act 1994, there is power to evict that individual and his / her vehicles. Indeed, this approach complies fully with Human Rights legislation and underlines the aim of dealing effectively with issues of anti-social behaviour. The factors must be weighed accordingly, and a decision taken on the necessary and proportionate action required, and so action that may be considered will include the giving of advice, arrests, eviction or a combination of all.
3. Where occupants at unauthorised encampments are victims of crime or anti-social behaviour, they must be given access to services in the usual way. If there is a perception that the incident is racially motivated then the matter should be dealt with in line with Hate Crime policy.

Working with other agencies

1. Forces should consider working with local authorities to agree Joint Agency Protocols for the management of unauthorised encampments. Forces should also consider establishing a liaison officer to work with local authorities on the implementation of joint protocols. This should be progressed within local Community Safety Partnership (CSP) forums in England and Wales or through other relevant local strategic frameworks.
2. Following on from the above, forces and local authorities should also consider working with other major landowners in their areas to agree similar protocols for the management of unauthorised encampments.

Other major landowners may include Housing Associations, the National Trust or local farmers.

3. The lead role for decision making should rest with the local authority and the use of police powers should not normally be considered as a first response.
4. On occasions other agencies may request police officers to accompany them to an encampment to assist them for a lawful purpose. Such assistance is a matter for local discretion. Officers must take care to ensure that they do not become agents for the other parties, and on such occasions maintain neutrality from the other's purpose, but to provide reassurance to all involved that the peace will be maintained.
5. Where there are no authorised sites, and the authority reaches the view that the unauthorised encampment is not causing a level of nuisance which cannot be effectively controlled, it should consider providing services, such as toilets, a refuse skip and a supply of drinking water at that site.

Use of police powers

1. The lead role in the management of Unauthorised Encampments will be with Local Authorities. Forces should consider becoming involved in bringing about the prompt and lawful removal of unauthorised encampments, including the use of police powers under Section 61 or 62 of the Criminal Justice & Public Order Act 1994 where:

i) Local amenities are deprived to communities or significant impact on the environment.

This could include, for example, forming an encampment on any part of a recreation ground, public park, school field, village green, or depriving the public use of car parks. The fact that other sections of the community are being deprived of the amenities must be evident before action is taken.

ii) There is local disruption to the economy.

Local disruption to the economy would include forming an encampment on a shopping centre car park, or in an industrial estate, if it disrupts workers or customers, or agricultural land, if this results in the loss of use of the land for its normal purpose.

iii) There is other significant disruption to the local community or environment.

This might include where other behaviour, which is directly related to those present at an encampment, is so significant that a prompt eviction by police becomes necessary, rather than by other means.

iv) There is a danger to life.

An example of this might be an encampment adjacent to a motorway, where there could be a danger of children or animals straying onto the carriageway.

v) There is a need to take preventative action.

This might include where a group of trespassers have persistently displayed anti-social behaviour at previous sites and it is reasonably believed that such behaviour will be displayed at this newly established site. This reasoning will take on greater emphasis if the land occupied is privately owned, as the landowner will be responsible for the cleansing and repair of their property.

2. The mere presence of an encampment without any aggravating factors should not normally create an expectation that police will use eviction powers. This should be communicated to the public, landowners, local authorities, and other agencies. If a decision is made to use police powers to evict then the rationale for the decision should be clearly set out and recorded. As stated above, a suggested eviction rationale record is set out at Appendix C.
3. In all cases, as stated above, relevant Human Rights processes must be applied to all decisions made i.e. that the elements of S61 are satisfied, and that it is necessary and proportionate to use the powers.
4. Section 61 Criminal Justice & Public Order Act 1994 relies upon reasonable steps being taken, by or on behalf of the landowner, to ask trespassers to leave in every case before police powers can be used. A flow chart setting out the police powers to evict under section 61 of the Criminal Justice and Public Order Act 1994 is set out at Appendix D.
5. Section 62A of the Criminal Justice & Public Order Act 1994 creates a power for a senior police officer to direct a person to leave land and remove any vehicle or other property with him / her on that land if the senior police officer present at a scene reasonably believes that the conditions below are satisfied. The conditions are-
    - that the person and one or more others (the trespassers) are trespassing on the land;
    - that the trespassers have between them at least one vehicle on the land;
    - that the trespassers are present on the land with the common purpose of residing there for any period;
    - if it appears to the officer that the person has one or more caravans in their possession or under their control on the land, that there is a **suitable pitch** on a **relevant caravan site** for that caravan or each of those caravans;
    - that the occupier of the land or a person acting on his behalf has asked the police to remove the trespassers from the land.
6. The conditions in this section are fewer than under Section 61 and concentrate more on the simple fact of trespassing for the purpose of residence. **The crucial section here refers to the need to prove that suitable alternative sites for caravans exist.**

7. The availability of suitable pitches at authorised sites or transit facilities will be an essential consideration before powers under Section 62 A-E can be used and liaison between police forces and their local authorities will be necessary to ascertain such availability or otherwise.
8. A flow chart setting out the police powers to evict under section 62 of the Criminal Justice and Public Order Act 1994 is set out at Appendix E.
9. The six recommendations for the Police, published in 'Common Ground' by the then Commission for Racial Equality (now the Equality and Human Rights Commission) Inquiry, a summary of which is set out below, should be incorporated into all police actions concerning Gypsies, Irish Travellers and unauthorised encampments.

"Police forces should:

- Include Gypsies and Travellers in mainstream neighbourhood policing strategies, to promote race equality and good race relations.
- Target individual Gypsies and Travellers suspected of anti-social behaviour and crime on public, private and unauthorised sites, and not whole communities, and work with people from these groups and local authorities to develop preventive measures.
- Treat Gypsies and Travellers, both when they are victims and suspects, as members of the local community, and in ways that strengthen their trust and confidence in the force.
- Provide training for all relevant officers on Gypsies' and Travellers' service needs, so that officers are able to do their jobs more effectively, and promote good relations between all groups in the community they serve.
- Review formal and informal procedures for policing unauthorised encampments, to identify and eliminate potentially discriminatory practices, and ensure that the procedures promote race equality and good race relations.
- Review the way guidance is put into practice, to make sure organisations and individuals take a consistent approach, resources are used effectively and strategically, all procedures are formalised, and training needs are identified."

APPENDIX A: UNAUTHORISED ENCAMPMENTS

Code of Conduct

To ensure those members of both the settled and travelling communities can live together in a peaceful and unprejudiced way we expect you to comply with this Code of Conduct. We expect you to treat the land you have occupied with respect, and that you respect the rights and freedoms of other people who also wish to use the area.

Behaviour that may result in your eviction from a site includes the following:

- Camping upon any land designated as a public amenity, such as parks, recreation areas, school fields and similar locations (not an exhaustive list).
- Interfering with the rights and freedoms of other members of the public, including interrupting the operation of legitimate businesses.
- Forcing entry to land, by causing damage to any fixtures, fittings or landscaping (including planted areas). This includes digging away of earthwork defences, which have been placed at landowner's expense to prevent trespass.
- Causing any other damage to the land itself, or property on it. Particular care should be taken not to cause damage to those features provided as public amenities.
- Driving vehicles along any footpath, or other highway not specifically designed for road vehicles. This practice is not only unlawful but is also highly dangerous.
- Parking vehicles or caravans on any road, footpath or other highway that causes an obstruction to other people wanting to pass by. This includes parking immediately next to footpaths.
- Dumping or tipping rubbish, waste materials or trade waste such as tree cuttings, rubble, etc. It is your responsibility to keep the site clean and tidy. Council Traveller Liaison Officers can direct you to Civic Amenity Sites (Council tips) where you will be able to pay to dispose of trade waste.
- Use of the area as a toilet. You must not deposit or leave human waste openly in public areas.
- Abuse, intimidation or harassment of any person who is lawfully using the area.
- Excessive noise or other forms of anti-social behaviour.
- Animals that are not kept under control or that attack persons lawfully on the land, or nearby.
- Interference with electrical, water or gas supplies. Any person(s) found abstracting electricity, or wasting quantities of water may be subject of criminal proceedings.

These codes are the same standards of behaviour that are expected of the settled community. The police are committed to ensuring that all policing issues that affect you are balanced; however behaviour that is deemed unacceptable within society will not be tolerated.

Forces should consider how best to deliver the above information and ensure that those people to whom it is given fully understand the content.

Appendix B

INITIAL SITE ASSESSMENT FORM

DATE:	TIME:
SITE NUMBER:	(BCU ID / No. / Year)
LOCATION: URN: (BCU ID/	(This should include numbers of vehicles and people without individual detail)
LANDOWNER:	
WELFARE ISSUES:	Any welfare issues that require reporting to relevant agencies.
	(Are there any issues that would prevent eviction of all or some of the occupants? Were these issues present before this site was occupied?)
TRAVELLERS SPOKEN TO:	☐ YES CODE OF CONDUCT ISSUED ☐ YES ☐ NO ☐ NO
ETHNIC STATUS:	Romany Gypsy / Irish Traveller New Age Traveller / Non-Traveller
ANY DAMAGE PRESENT:	(Damage to gain entry & that caused whilst in situ. Also damage that had occurred prior to occupation)
LITTER or WASTE PRESENT:	

ANIMALS PRESENT:	(Numbers tied-up/untied. Have group been advised to tie up animals? What is the risk to the public?)
WHAT IS THE IMPACT TO THE PUBLIC / LANDOWNER?	Unacceptable / Significant / Minimal *(Give reasons)*
ANY OTHER INFORMATION	

OFFICER NAME:

....

Appendix C: Eviction Rationale Record

1. Location: **Date first to notice of** **Police:** **Land Owner:** **Encampment Reference No:**	
2. General Information / Summary:	
Where/what/when/why/how was the encampment established, who owns the land, how are they and others affected? Any previous history of the site and / or occupants?	
3. Factors relating to the unauthorised encampment:	
Record the number of caravans and vehicles present here, together with the factors that have been taken into account regarding the need to evict, such as anti-social behaviour and impact on other communities.	

4. Mitigating Factors relating to the camp (including welfare issues):	
Have welfare enquiries been carried out? Y / N	**(if Y attach welfare enquiry record)**
If possible, the Local Authority Traveller Liaison Officer or local Health Visitor should attend to complete health and welfare assessments. Although the s61 legislation does not prevent eviction action by the Police where no formal welfare enquires have been completed, such enquiries should be made wherever practicable. In any event, police should complete welfare enquiries at the time of service of the s61 eviction order, with any issues noted on the eviction form.	
5 Eviction decision:	
POLICE POWERS USED: OBSTRUCTION OF THE HIGHWAY ☐ SECTION 61 CJPOA 1994 ☐ DAMAGE ☐ THREATS ETC ☐ 6 VEHICLES OR MORE ☐	
A record of the grounds for the decision, including any action taken to resolve either aggravating factors or welfare issues that may have arisen. A summary of the impact on the human rights of all parties involved should be included, highlighting the legitimacy, proportionality and necessity of the eviction action.	
What date are notices to be served?:	
When should the Travellers leave by: Time: Date:	
Signed: Date:	**PRINT RANK/NO./SURNAME**

Appendix D: POLICE EVICTION POWERS

SECTION 61 CRIMINAL JUSTICE & PUBLIC ORDER ACT 1994 FLOW CHART AND GUIDANCE NOTES

IF:-

I believe that two or more of you have entered the land as trespassers, that you have a common purpose of residing on the land

- Who is the landowner?
- Are there 2 or more people?
- Have they entered the land as trespassers?
- Are caravans or other 'living' vehicles present?

↓

and that reasonable steps have been taken by or on behalf of the person entitled to possession of the land to ask you to leave

What reasonable steps has the landowner taken to ask the trespassers to leave? e.g.

- Verbal request: (supported by written statement)
- Are there witnesses to the request?
- Have notices been served requesting them to leave – who served them, and how. Were they displayed prominently?
- Do the Police have a copy of any notice served?

↓

I FURTHER BELIEVE THAT:

↓

One or more of you has caused damage to the land or property on the land

Damage can be ANY damage e.g.

- Padlock to gate
- Digging away earth mounding (cost money to have put in place or to repair)
- Could be litter in worst cases or engine oil contamination etc.

OR

↓

One or more of you has used threatening, abusive or insulting words or behaviour towards the occupier, a member of his family or an employee or agent of his.

- Equivalent to Section 5 Public Order Act
- Only applies to landowner or agent – NOT all members of public
- Will the victim provide a written statement?

OR

↓

You have between you six or more vehicles (including caravans) on the land

- Vehicles includes motor vehicles and caravans
- Where S61 applies, consider this Guidance.

THEN S61 MAY BE APPLIED. IF IT IS,

- S61 Notices must be served and copies kept (carbon)
- Details of people and vehicles must be recorded
- A 'reasonable' time (in the circumstances) must be given for them to leave the land
- Trespassers welfare issues must be taken into account

FAILURE TO COMPLY

- Power of arrest – any person who fails to comply without reasonable excuse to leave the land
- Power to seize any vehicle not removed

HUMAN RIGHTS TESTS

Is the eviction proposed:

- Legal – are the elements of Section 61 present?
- Necessary – is it necessary to evict the group?
  – Would other policing methods suffice e.g. high profile patrols, or individual arrests for other offences?
- Proportionate – is the decision balanced?
  Have the needs of the landowner or settled community been balanced with the needs of the trespassers?
  Do all the trespassers need to be evicted or can specific individuals be identified?
- Accountable – is the rationale behind the decision recorded and available?

DECISION MAKING GUIDANCE

- It is recommended that decisions to evict be made by an Officer not below the rank of Inspector.
- All decisions, whether to evict or not to evict, will be recorded, including with rationale.

Appendix E

POLICE EVICTION POWERS

SECTION 62 CRIMINAL JUSTICE & PUBLIC ORDER ACT 1994
FLOW CHART AND GUIDANCE NOTES

Encampment Arrives

- Incident created Council contacted to arrange joint visit with Police
- Initial assessment (check list)
  √ Welfare
  √ Family names
  √ Vehicles
- Group informed about available Transit Site and s62a-e

VACANT PITCHES

The group are asked to vacate and move to the transit site where they will sign up to a licence agreement and pay rent as well as being linked into appropriate services by the local authority, e.g. health and education

- Group refuse to go to the transit site
- Police initiate s62a-e and 'direct' the group to a 'suitable' pitch

OR

- to leave the borough and not return for 3 months

This is a question of available police resources and there may be times when the encampment will remain until suitable resources are available.

NO VACANT PITCHES

The encampment will be dealt with as any other encampment

APPENDIX D

Useful organisations

Advisory Council for the Education of Romany and other Travellers
The Membership Secretary, c/o Little Kiln, Pottery Road,
Bovey Tracey, Devon TQ13 9DS
tel: 0208 374 1286
email: info@acert.org.uk
website: www.acert.org.uk

Advisory Service for Squatters
Angel Alley, 84b Whitechapel High Street, London E1 7QX
tel: 020 3216 0099
email: advice@squatter.org.uk
website: www.squatter.org.uk

Association of Independent Showmen
Equalities and Cultural Rights
tel: 07803 783269 (Equalities and Cultural Rights) / 07956 994199 (planning)
email: maiks@talktalk.net

Equality and Human Rights Commission
Fleetbank House, 2-6 Salisbury Square, London EC4Y 8JX
tel: 0808 800 0082
textphone: 0808 800 0084
website: www.equalityhumanrights.com

European Roma Rights Centre
Rue Charles Martel 6-8, 1000 Brussels, Belgium
email: office@errc.org

Friends, Families and Travellers
Community Base, 113 Queens Road, Brighton BN1 3XG
tel: 01273 234777
email: fft@gypsy-traveller.org
website: www.gypsy-traveller.org

Liberty
Liberty House, 26-30 Strutton Ground, London, SW1P 2HR
tel: 020 7378 3663
website: www.libertyhumanrights.org.uk

National Bargee Traveller Association
30 Silver St, Reading RG1 2ST
tel: 0118 321 4128
email: secretariat@bargee-traveller.org.uk

National Federation of Gypsy Liaison Groups
13 Ladygrove Mill, Ladygrove Road, Two Dales, Matlock, Derbyshire DE4 2FG
tel: 01629 732744
email: info@nationalgypsytravellerfederation.org
website: www.nationalgypsytravellerfederation.org

The Travellers Advice Team
Community Law Partnership, solicitors, 4th Floor Ruskin Chambers, 1919 Corporation St, Birmingham B4 6RP
tel: 0121 685 8677 (Mon to Fri 9am–1pm)
email: communitylaw@communitylawpartnership.co.uk
website: www.communitylawpartnership.co.uk

The Traveller Movement
The Resource Centre, 356 Holloway Road, London N7 6PA
tel: 020 7607 2002
email: info@travellermovement.org.uk
website: www.travellermovement.org.uk

Travelling Ahead
Goldstops House, Pentonville, Newport NP20 5HB
tel: 02920 803267 /mobile: 07788 412760
email: travellingahead@trosgynnalplant.org.uk
website: www.travellingahead.org.uk

LOCAL ORGANISATIONS

Brentwood Gypsy Support Group
email: thosacton@yahoo.co.uk

Derbyshire Gypsy Liaison Group
1–3 Ladygrove Mill, Ladygrove Road, Two Dales, Matlock, Derbyshire, DE4 2FG
Tel: 01629 732744

Gypsies and Travellers Wales
Trowbridge Community Centre, 91 Caernarvon Way, Trowbridge CF3 1TN
tel: 02920 214411
email: admincgtp@btconnect.com

Herefordshire Travellers Support Group
Trefoil, Brinsop Common, Hereford, HR4 7AS
tel: 01432 760350
email: paebkam@aol.com

Herts GATE Gypsy and Traveller Empowerment
Vale House, 43 Cowbridge Street, Hertford, SG14 1PN
tel: 01920 412620
email: contact@gypsytravellerempowermentherts.org.uk
website: www.gypsytravellerempowermentherts.org.uk

Irish Community Care
151 Dale Street, Liverpool, L2 2AH
tel: 0151 237 3987
email: admin@iccm.org.uk

Kushti Bok
tel: 01202 474174
email: info.kushtibok@gmail.com

Leeds Gypsy and Traveller Exchange
Ground Floor, Crown Point House, 169 Cross Green Lane, Leeds LS9 0BD
tel: 0113 240 2444. Mob: 07974 574889.
email: info@leedsgate.co.uk

Lincolnshire Gypsy Liaison Group
Mercury House, Foxby Lane, Gainsborough, Lincolnshire, DN21 1DY
tel: 01427 619521.

London Gypsies and Travellers (formerly London Gypsy and Traveller Unit)
Mildmay Community Centre, Woodville Rd, Mayville Estate, London N16 8NA
tel: 020 8533 2002
email: info@londongandt.org.uk
website: http://www.londongypsiesandtravellers.org.uk

One Voice for Travellers Limited
PO Box 9635, Sudbury, Suffolk, CO10 8WW
tel: 07790 801422 / mobile 07790 803176
email: info@onevoice4travellers.org.uk

Ormiston Norfolk Travellers Initiative
Earlham Rd, Norwich NR4 7NU
tel: 07825 688403.
website: www.ormiston.org

Romani Cultural and Arts Co
Temple Court,13A Cathedral Road, Cardiff, CF11 9HA
tel: 02920 786439.
website: www.romaniarts.co.uk

Southwark Traveller Action Group
The Peckham Settlement, Goldsmith Road, Peckham, London, SE15 5TF
tel: 020 7639 1823
email: stag@peckhamsettlement.org.uk
website: www.peckhamsettlement.org.uk

Sussex Gypsies and Travellers (formerly Sussex Travellers Action Group)
tel: 07941 460866
email: Info@sussextag.org.uk
website: www.sussextag.org.uk/

Travellers Space
1 Champions Yard, Causewayhead, Penzance, Cornwall, TR18 2TA
tel: 01736 366940
email: travellerspace@yahoo.co.uk
website: www.travellerspace-cornwall.org

York Travellers Trust
20 Falsgrave, Clifton, York, YO30 7AZ
tel: 01904 630526
Fax: 01904 675444
email: travellerstrustyork@yahoo.co.uk
website: www.yorktravellerstrust.org.uk

APPENDIX E

Bibliography

BOOKS ON GYPSY AND TRAVELLER ISSUES

Acton, *Gypsy politics and social change,* Routledge, Kegan Paul, 1974

Clark and Greenfields, *Here to stay: the Gypsies and Travellers of Britain,* University of Hertfordshire Press, 2006

Coxhead, *The last bastion of racism? Gypsies, Travellers and policing,* Trentham, 2007

Cressy, *Gypsies: an English History,* Oxford University Press, 2018

Evans, *Stopping places: a Gypsy history of South London and Kent,* University of Hertfordshire Press, 2004

Fraser, *The Gypsies,* Blackwell, 1995

Hawes, *Gypsies, Travellers and the Health Service,* Policy Press, 1997

Hawes and Perez, *The Gypsy and the state: the ethnic cleansing of British society,* The Polity Press, 1996

Hyman, *Sites for Travellers: a study in five London boroughs,* London Race and Housing Research Unit, 1989

Kenrick, *Gypsies: from the Ganges to the Thames,* University of Hertfordshire Press, 2004

Kenrick and Bakewell, *On the verge: the Gypsies of England,* University of Hertfordshire Press, 1990

Kenrick and Clark, *Moving on: the Gypsies and Travellers of Britain,* University of Hertfordshire Press, 1996

Kenrick and Puxon, *The destiny of Europe's Gypsies,* Chatto-Heinemann, 1972

Le Bas, *The Stopping Places: a journey through Great Britain,* Chatto & Windus, 2018

Leigeois, *Gypsies and Travellers: socio-cultural data, socio-political data,* Council of Europe, 1987

MacLaughlin, *Travellers and Ireland: whose country, whose history?,* Cork University Press, 1995

Morris and Clements, *Gaining ground: law reform for Gypsies and Travellers,* University of Hertfordshire Press, 1999

Morris and Clements, *At what cost? The economics of Gypsy and Traveller encampments,* The Policy Press, 2002

Okely, *The Traveller-Gypsies,* Cambridge University Press, 1983

Ò Riain, *Solidarity with Travellers*, Roadside Books, Dublin, 2000
Ryder, *Sites of Resistance: Gypsies, Roma and Travellers in school, community and the academy*, UCL Institute of Education Press, 2017
Sandford, *Rokkering to the Gorjios*, University of Hertfordshire Press, 1973
Sheehan, ed, *Travellers: citizens of Ireland*, Parish of the Travelling People, Dublin, 2000
Smith, *Romany Nevi-Wesh*, Nova Foresta Publishing, 2004
Stewart, *The puzzle of Roma persistence*, University of Hertfordshire Press, 1997
Vesey-Fitzgerald, *Gypsies of Britain*, Readers Union, 1973
Worthington, ed, *The battle of the Beanfield*, Enabler Publications, 2005

LEGAL TEXTBOOKS

Arden, Bates and Vanhegan, *Homelessness and allocations*, 11th edn, Legal Action Group, 2018
Arden et al, *Encyclopedia of housing law and practice*, Sweet & Maxwell / Thomson Reuters
Baker, Carter and Hunter, *Housing and human rights law*, Legal Action Group, 2001
Encyclopaedia of planning law and practice, Thomson Reuters
Carr, Cottle, Baldwin and King, *The Housing Act 2004: a practical guide*, New Law Series, 2004
Child Poverty Action Group, *Welfare benefits and tax credits handbook*, CPAG, 2019/20
Clements, *Community care and the law*, 7th edn, Legal Action Group, 2019
Jourdan, *Adverse possession*, Bloomsbury Professional, 2011 (supplement 2017)
Jowell and Cooper, eds, *Understanding Human Rights Act principles*, Hart Publishing, 2001
Luba, Davies, Buchanan and Johnston, *Housing allocations and homelessness: law and practice*, fifth edn, Lexis Nexis, 2018
Manning, *Judicial review proceedings: a practitioner's guide*, 3rd edn, Legal Action Group, 2013
Willers, Caruso et al, *Ensuring access to Rights for Roma and Travellers. The Role of the European Court of Human Rights*, Council of Europe, 2014

OTHER BOOKS

Baumann, *Modernity and the Holocaust*, Polity Press, 1989

Lentin and McVeigh, *Racism and anti-racism in Ireland,* Beyond the Pale, 2002
Muller-Hill, *Murderous science,* Methuesen, New York, 1988
Walvin, *There ain't no black in the Union Jack,* Routledge, 1973

REPORTS

General reports

Commission for Racial Equality, *Common Ground Equality, good race relations and sites for Gypsies and Irish Travellers,* CRE, 2006
Commission for Racial Equality, *Gypsies and Travellers: a strategy for the CRE, 2004–2007,* 2004
Cottle et al, *Gypsy and Traveller Sites: The revised planning definition's impact on assessing accommodation need,* EHRC, 2019
Equality of Opportunity Committee, National Assembly for Wales, *Review of service provision for Gypsies and Travellers,* 2003
Institute for Public Policy Research, *Moving forward: the provision of accommodation for Travellers and Gypsies,* 2004
Lane, Spencer and Jones, *Experts by experience: Gypsy, Traveller & Roma,* Anglia Ruskin University, 2014
Minority Rights Group, *Roma/Gypsies: a European minority,* 1995
Niner, *Preparing regional spatial strategy reviews on Gypsies and Travellers by regional planning bodies,* CLG, 2007
Niner, *Accommodation needs of Gypsy-Travellers in Wales,* Welsh Assembly Government, 2006
Niner, *Counting Gypsies and Travellers: a review of the Gypsy caravan count system,* ODPM, 2004
Niner, *Local authority Gypsy/Traveller sites in England,* ODPM, 2003
Niner, *The provision and condition of local authority Gypsy/Traveller sites in England,* ODPM, 2002
Power, *Room to roam: England's Irish Travellers,* The Community Fund, 2004
Stonewall, *Profiles of prejudice,* 2003

Reports on education

Committee of Inquiry into the Education of Children from Ethnic Minority Groups, *Education for all,* 1985
DfES, *Aiming high: raising the achievement of Gypsy and Traveller pupils,* 2003
Ofsted, *Managing support for the attainment of pupils from minority ethnic groups,* 2001
Ofsted, *Raising the attainment of minority ethnic pupils,* 1999
Ofsted, *The education of Travelling children: a survey of educational provision for Travelling children,* 1996

Reports on health

Chartered Institute of Environmental Health, *Travellers and Gypsies: an alternative strategy*, 1995

Council of Europe, *Breaking the barriers: Romani women and access to public health*, 2003

Derbyshire Gypsy Liaison Group, *A better road*, 2003

Van Cleemput et al, *The health status of Gypsies and Travellers in England*, University of Sheffield, 2004

Index